Travel Guide

New York
New Jersey
2003

Ex_xonMobil Travel Publications

ACKNOWLEDGMENTS

We gratefully acknowledge the help of our representatives for their efficient and perceptive inspection of the lodging and dining establishments listed; the establishments' proprietors for their cooperation in showing their facilities and providing information about them; the many users of previous editions of the Mobil Travel Guides who have taken the time to share their experiences; and for their time and information, the thousands of chambers of commerce, convention and visitors bureaus, city, state, and provincial tourism offices, and government agencies who assisted in our research.

PHOTO CREDITS

Al Bello/Allsport USA/Getty Images: 45; **Todd Brininger/Lucy-Desi Museum:** 107; **Walter Choroszewski Photography:** 360, 372, 376, 414, 425; **Grace Davies Photography:** 334; **Dick Dietrich Photography:** 56; **Victor Englebert Photography:** 98, 364, 383, 395, 422; **FPG/Getty Images:** Peter Gridley: 21, 78, 122; Shinichi Kanno: 281; Richard Laird: 1, 257, 266; Michael Nelson: 225; Richard Nowitz: 366; Toyohiro Yamada: 270; **Henryk T. Kaiser/Transparencies, Inc.:** 74; **Brian McGilloway/Robert Holmes Photography:** 256; **National Baseball Hall of Fame and Museum, Cooperstown, N.Y.:** 61; **New York Stock Photo:** Peter Bennett: 258, 269, 272; Tony Perrottet: 264; **Jack Olson Photography:** 101; **James P. Rowan Photography:** 32, 43, 46, 211; **Bonnie Sue Photography:** 198; **SuperStock:** 19, 39, 72, 92, 118, 138, 221, 231, 252, 254, 259, 260, 263, 265, 267, 268, 271, 273, 288, 290, 297, 302, 313, 317, 321, 327, 328, 330, 332, 333, 338, 354, 356, 363, 412, 417, 423; Alan Briere: 172; D. Forbert: 33, 169; Rochelle Hecker: 271; **Michael Ventura/Folio, Inc.:** 156.

Maps © MapQuest 2002, www.mapquest.com

Printed by Publications International, Ltd.
7373 North Cicero Avenue
Lincolnwood, Illinois 60712

info@mobiltravelguide.com

The information contained herein is derived from a variety of third-party sources. Although every effort has been made to verify the information obtained from such sources, the publisher assumes no responsibility for inconsistencies or inaccuracies in the data or liability for any damages of any type arising from errors or omissions.

Neither the editors nor the publisher assumes responsibility for the services provided by any business listed in this guide or for any loss, damage, or disruption in your travel for any reason.

ISBN 0-7627-2616-4

Manufactured in China.

10 9 8 7 6 5 4 3 2 1

CONTENTS

New York and New Jersey

Maps

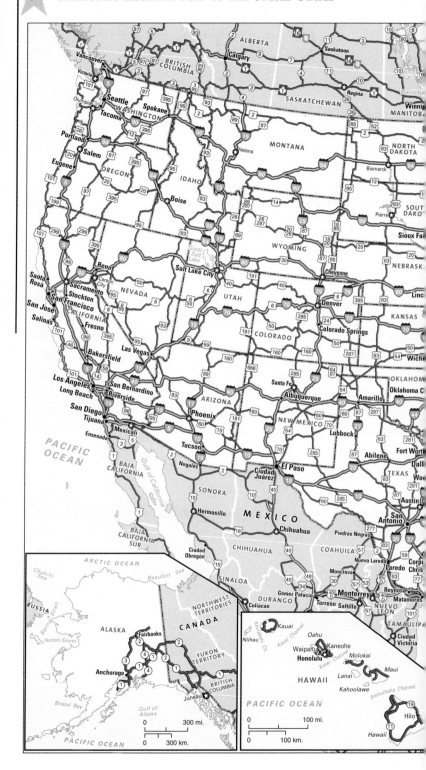

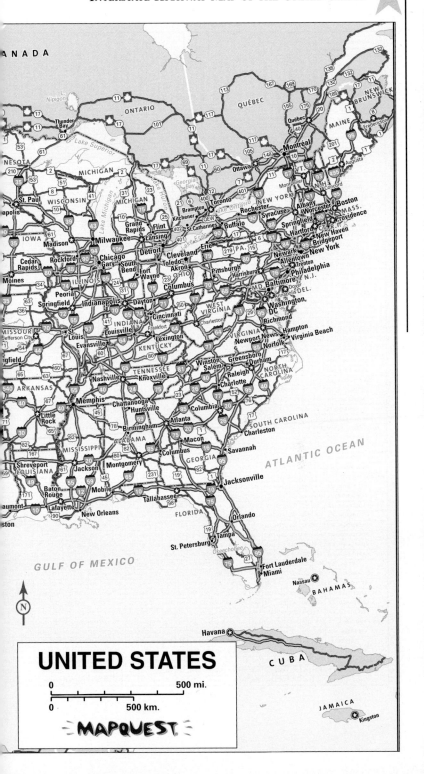

UNITED STATES

0 — 500 mi.

0 — 500 km.

MAPQUEST

Distances in chart are in miles. To convert miles to kilometers, multiply the distance in miles by 1.609

Example:
New York, NY to Boston, MA = 215 miles or 346 kilometers (215 x 1.609)

	ALBUQUERQUE, NM	ATLANTA, GA	BALTIMORE, MD	BILLINGS, MT	BIRMINGHAM, AL	BISMARCK, ND	BOISE, ID	BOSTON, MA	BUFFALO, NY	BURLINGTON, VT	CHARLESTON, SC	CHARLESTON, WV	CHARLOTTE, NC	CHEYENNE, WY	CHICAGO, IL	CINCINNATI, OH	CLEVELAND, OH	DALLAS, TX	DENVER, CO	DES MOINES, IA	DETROIT, MI	EL PASO, TX	HOUSTON, TX	INDIANAPOLIS, IN	JACKSON, MS	KANSAS CITY, MO
ALBUQUERQUE, NM		1490	1902	991	1274	1333	966	2240	1808	2178	1793	1568	1649	538	1352	1409	1619	754	438	1091	1608	263	994	1298	1157	89
ATLANTA, GA	1490		679	1889	150	1559	2218	1100	910	1158	317	503	238	1482	717	476	726	792	1403	967	735	1437	800	531	386	
BALTIMORE, MD	1902	679		1959	795	1551	2401	422	370	481	583	352	441	1665	708	521	377	1399	1690	1031	532	2045	1470	600	1032	10
BILLINGS, MT	991	1889	1959		1839	413	626	2254	1796	2181	2157	1755	2012	455	1246	1552	1597	1433	554	1007	1534	1255	1673	1432	1836	10
BIRMINGHAM, AL	1274	150	795	1839		1509	2170	1215	909	1241	466	578	389	1434	667	475	725	647	1356	919	734	1292	678	481	241	
BISMARCK, ND	1333	1559	1551	413	1509		1039	1846	1388	1773	1749	1347	1604	594	838	1144	1189	1342	693	675	1126	1597	1582	1024	1548	80
BOISE, ID	966	2218	2401	626	2170	1039		2697	2239	2624	2520	2182	2375	737	1708	1969	2040	1711	833	1369	1977	1206	1952	1852	2115	13
BOSTON, MA	2240	1100	422	2254	1215	1846	2697		462	214	1003	741	861	1961	1003	862	654	1819	2004	1326	741	2465	1890	940	1453	14
BUFFALO, NY	1808	910	370	1796	909	1388	2239	462		375	899	431	695	1502	545	442	197	1393	1546	868	277	2039	1513	508	1134	99
BURLINGTON, VT	2178	1158	481	2181	1241	1773	2624	214	375		1061	782	919	1887	930	817	567	1763	1931	1253	652	2409	1916	878	1479	13
CHARLESTON, SC	1793	317	583	2157	466	1749	2520	1003	899	1061		468	204	1783	907	622	724	1109	1705	1204	879	1754	1110	721	703	11
CHARLESTON, WV	1568	503	352	1755	578	1347	2182	741	431	782	468		265	1445	506	209	255	1072	1360	842	410	1718	1192	320	816	76
CHARLOTTE, NC	1649	238	441	2012	389	1604	2375	861	695	919	204	265		1637	761	476	520	1031	1559	1057	675	1677	1041	575	625	95
CHEYENNE, WY	538	1482	1665	455	1434	594	737	1961	1502	1887	1783	1445	1637		972	1233	1304	979	100	633	1241	801	1220	1115	1382	64
CHICAGO, IL	1352	717	708	1246	667	838	1708	1003	545	930	907	506	761	972		302	346	916	1015	337	283	1543	1108	184	750	53
CINCINNATI, OH	1409	476	521	1552	475	1144	1969	862	442	817	622	209	476	1233	302		253	958	1200	599	261	1605	1079	116	700	59
CLEVELAND, OH	1619	726	377	1597	725	1189	2040	654	197	567	724	255	520	1304	346	253		1208	1347	669	171	1854	1328	319	950	80
DALLAS, TX	754	792	1399	1433	647	1342	1711	1819	1393	1763	1109	1072	1031	979	916	958	1208		887	752	1218	647	241	913	406	55
DENVER, CO	438	1403	1690	554	1356	693	833	2004	1546	1931	1705	1360	1559	100	1015	1200	1347	887		676	1284	701	1127	1088	1290	60
DES MOINES, IA	1091	967	1031	1007	919	675	1369	1326	868	1253	1204	802	1057	633	337	599	669	752	676		606	1283	992	481	931	19
DETROIT, MI	1608	735	532	1534	734	1126	1977	741	277	652	879	410	675	1241	283	261	171	1217	1284	606		1799	1338	318	960	79
EL PASO, TX	263	1437	2045	1255	1292	1597	1206	2465	2039	2409	1754	1718	1677	801	1543	1605	1854	647	701	1283	1799		758	1489	1051	108
HOUSTON, TX	994	800	1470	1673	678	1582	1952	1890	1513	1916	1110	1192	1041	1220	1108	1079	1328	241	1127	992	1338	758		1033	445	79
INDIANAPOLIS, IN	1298	531	600	1432	481	1024	1852	940	508	878	721	320	575	1115	184	116	319	913	1088	481	318	1489	1033		675	48
JACKSON, MS	1157	386	1032	1836	241	1548	2115	1453	1134	1479	703	816	625	1382	750	700	950	406	1290	931	960	1051	445	675		74
KANSAS CITY, MO	894	801	1087	1088	753	801	1376	1427	995	1366	1102	764	956	640	532	597	806	554	603	194	795	1085	795	485	747	
LAS VEGAS, NV	578	2067	2445	965	1852	1378	760	2757	2299	2684	2371	2122	2225	843	1768	1955	2100	1331	756	1429	2037	717	1474	1843	1735	135
LITTLE ROCK, AR	900	528	1072	1530	381	1183	1808	1493	1066	1437	900	745	754	1076	662	632	882	327	984	567	891	974	447	587	256	38
LOS ANGELES, CA	806	2237	2705	1239	2092	1702	1033	3046	2572	2957	2554	2374	2453	1116	2042	2215	2374	1446	1029	1703	2310	801	1558	2104	1851	163
LOUISVILLE, KY	1320	419	602	1547	369	1139	1933	964	545	915	610	251	464	1197	299	106	356	852	1118	595	366	1499	972	112	594	516
MEMPHIS, TN	1111	389	933	1625	241	1337	1954	1353	927	1297	760	606	614	1217	539	493	742	466	1110	586	664	1217	576	464	215	536
MIAMI, FL	2155	661	1109	2554	812	2224	2883	1529	1425	1587	580	994	730	2147	1382	1141	1250	1367	2069	1632	1401	1959	1201	1196	915	146
MILWAUKEE, WI	1426	813	805	1175	763	767	1748	1100	642	1027	1003	601	857	1012	89	398	443	1010	1055	378	380	1617	1193	279	835	573
MINNEAPOLIS, MN	1339	1129	1121	839	1079	431	1465	1437	1053	1439	1173	918	1173	881	409	774	760	999	924	246	697	1530	1240	596	715	441
MONTRÉAL, QC	2172	1241	564	2093	1289	1685	2535	313	397	92	1145	822	1045	1803	1799	841	815	588	1772	1843	1165	564	2363	1892	872	1514
NASHVILLE, TN	1248	242	716	1648	194	1315	1976	1136	716	1086	543	395	397	1240	474	281	531	681	1162	725	541	1328	801	287	423	559
NEW ORLEANS, LA	1276	473	1142	1965	351	1734	2234	1563	1254	1588	783	926	713	1563	935	820	1070	525	1409	1117	1079	1116	360	826	185	932
NEW YORK, NY	2015	869	192	2049	985	1641	2491	215	400	299	773	515	631	1755	797	636	466	1589	1991	1200	615	2221	1622	2235	1660	1204
OKLAHOMA CITY, OK	546	944	1354	1227	729	1156	1694	1262	1632	1248	1022	1102	773	807	863	1073	209	681	546	1062	737	449	752	612	348
OMAHA, NE	973	989	1168	904	941	616	1234	1463	1005	1390	1290	952	1144	497	474	736	806	669	541	136	743	1236	910	618	935	188
ORLANDO, FL	1841	440	904	2333	591	2003	2662	1324	1221	1383	379	790	525	1926	1161	920	1045	1146	1847	1411	1180	1738	980	975	694	1245
PHILADELPHIA, PA	1954	782	104	2019	897	1611	2462	321	414	371	685	454	543	1725	768	576	437	1501	1744	1091	592	2147	1572	655	1135	1141
PHOENIX, AZ	466	1868	2366	1199	1723	1662	993	2706	2274	2644	2184	2035	2107	1004	1819	1876	2085	1077	904	1558	2074	432	1188	1764	1482	1360
PITTSBURGH, PA	1670	676	246	1719	763	1311	2161	567	217	438	685	223	425	1271	468	291	136	1246	1400	721	292	1893	1366	317	998	857
PORTLAND, ME	2338	1197	520	2352	1313	1944	2795	107	560	233	1101	839	959	2059	1101	960	751	1917	2102	1424	838	2563	1988	1038	1550	1525
PORTLAND, OR	1395	2647	2830	889	2599	1301	432	3126	2667	3052	2948	2610	2802	1166	2137	2398	2469	2140	1261	1798	2405	1767	2381	2280	2544	1805
RAPID CITY, SD	841	1511	1626	379	1463	167	824	1422	1678	305	913	1219	1264	1077	604	834	233	2032	1561	541	1183	1458	710
RENO, NV	1020	2440	2623	960	2392	1372	430	2919	2460	2845	2741	2403	2595	959	1930	2191	2262	1933	1054	1591	2198	1315	2072	2073	2337	1598
RICHMOND, VA	1876	527	152	2053	678	1645	2496	572	485	630	428	322	289	1760	802	530	471	1309	1688	1126	627	1955	1330	641	914	1085
ST. LOUIS, MO	1051	549	841	1341	501	1053	1699	1179	850	512	704	892	294	350	560	635	855	436	549	1242	863	239	505	252
SALT LAKE CITY, UT	624	1916	2100	548	1868	960	342	2395	1936	2322	2218	1880	2072	436	1406	1667	1738	1410	531	1067	1675	864	1501	1675	1813	1074
SAN ANTONIO, TX	818	1000	1671	1500	878	1599	1761	2092	1665	2036	1310	1344	1241	1046	1270	1231	1481	271	946	1009	1490	556	200	1186	644	812
SAN DIEGO, CA	825	2166	2724	1302	2021	1765	1096	3065	2632	3020	2483	2393	2405	1179	2105	2234	2437	1375	1092	1766	2373	730	1487	2122	1780	1695
SAN FRANCISCO, CA	1111	2618	2840	1176	2472	1749	644	3150	2677	3062	2934	2620	2759	1346	2146	2407	2478	1827	1271	1807	2415	1181	1938	2290	2232	1814
SEATTLE, WA	1463	2705	2775	816	2657	1229	500	3070	2612	2997	2973	2571	2827	1234	2062	2368	2413	2208	1329	1822	2350	1944	2449	2249	2612	1872
TAMPA, FL	1949	455	960	2348	606	2018	2677	1380	1276	1438	434	845	581	1941	1176	935	1101	1161	1862	1426	1194	1753	995	990	709	1259
TORONTO, ON	1841	958	565	1762	958	1354	2204	570	106	436	1006	537	802	1468	510	484	303	1441	1512	834	233	2032	1561	541	1103	1028
VANCOUVER, BC	1597	2838	2908	949	2791	1362	633	3204	2745	3130	3106	2701	2960	1368	2196	2501	2547	2342	1463	1956	2483	2087	2583	2383	2746	2007
WASHINGTON, DC	1896	636	38	1993	758	1545	2395	458	384	517	539	346	397	1659	701	517	370	1362	1686	1025	526	2008	1433	596	996	1083
WICHITA, KS	707	989	1276	1067	838	934	1346	1616	1184	1554	1291	953	1145	613	728	785	995	367	521	390	984	898	608	674	771	192

LOS ANGELES, CA	LOUISVILLE, KY	MEMPHIS, TN	MIAMI, FL	MILWAUKEE, WI	MINNEAPOLIS, MN	MONTRÉAL, QC	NASHVILLE, TN	NEW ORLEANS, LA	NEW YORK, NY	OKLAHOMA CITY, OK	OMAHA, NE	ORLANDO, FL	PHILADELPHIA, PA	PHOENIX, AZ	PITTSBURGH, PA	PORTLAND, ME	PORTLAND, OR	RAPID CITY, SD	RENO, NV	RICHMOND, VA	SALT LAKE CITY, UT	SAN ANTONIO, TX	SAN DIEGO, CA	SAN FRANCISCO, CA	SEATTLE, WA	ST. LOUIS, MO	TAMPA, FL	TORONTO, ON	VANCOUVER, BC	WASHINGTON, DC	WICHITA, KS
1320	1033	2155	1426	1339	2172	1248	1276	2015	546	973	1934	1954	466	2338	1395	841	1020	1876	1051	624	818	825	1111	1463	1949	1841	1597	1896	707		
419	389	661	813	1129	1241	242	473	869	944	989	440	782	1868	676	1197	2647	1511	2440	527	549	1916	1000	2166	2618	2705	455	958	2838	636	989	
602	933	1109	805	1121	564	716	1142	192	1354	1168	904	104	2366	246	520	2830	1626	2623	152	841	2100	1671	2724	2840	2775	960	565	2908	38	1276	
1547	1625	2554	1175	839	2093	1648	1955	2049	1227	904	2333	2019	1199	1799	2352	889	379	960	2053	1341	548	1500	1302	1176	816	2348	1762	949	1953	1067	
369	241	812	763	1079	1289	194	351	985	729	941	591	897	1723	763	1313	2599	1463	2392	678	501	1868	878	2192	2472	2657	606	958	2791	758	838	
1139	1337	2224	767	431	1685	1315	1734	1641	1136	616	2003	1611	1662	1311	1944	1301	320	1372	1645	1053	960	1599	1765	1749	1229	2018	1354	1362	1545	934	
1933	1954	2883	1748	1465	2535	1976	2234	2491	1506	1234	2662	2462	993	2161	2795	432	930	430	2496	1628	342	1761	1096	646	500	2677	2204	633	2395	1346	
1197	1217	2147	1012	881	1799	1240	1502	1755	773	497	1926	1725	404	1425	2059	1166	305	959	1760	892	436	1046	1179	1135	1368	1659	613				
299	539	1382	89	409	841	474	935	797	807	474	1101	768	1819	467	1101	2137	913	1930	802	294	1406	1270	2105	2146	2062	1176	510	2196	701	728	
106	493	1141	398	714	815	281	820	636	863	736	920	576	1876	292	940	2398	1219	2191	530	350	1667	1231	2234	2407	2368	935	484	2501	517	785	
356	742	1250	443	760	588	531	1070	466	1073	806	1045	437	2085	136	751	2469	1264	2262	471	560	1738	1481	2437	2478	2413	1101	303	2547	370	995	
852	466	1367	1010	999	1772	1246	1591	209	669	1146	1017	1246	1917	1240	1079	2948	1824	2741	428	850	2118	1374	3016	2934	2973	434	1006	3136	599	1367	
1118	1116	2069	1055	924	1843	1162	1409	1799	681	541	1847	1744	904	1460	2102	1261	404	1054	1688	855	531	946	1092	1171	1329	1862	1512	1463	1686	521	
595	720	1632	378	246	1165	725	1117	1121	546	136	1411	1091	1558	791	1424	1798	629	1591	1126	436	1067	1009	1766	1807	1822	1426	834	1956	1025	390	
266	752	1401	380	697	564	541	1062	743	1180	922	2001	208	627	549	1605	1490	2373	2415	2350	1194	243	2483	526	984							
1499	1112	1959	1617	1530	2363	1118	2235	737	1236	1738	2147	432	1893	2563	1767	1015	1315	1955	1242	864	556	730	1181	1944	1753	2032	2087	2008	898		
972	586	1201	1193	1240	1892	801	360	1660	449	910	980	1572	1188	1366	1988	2381	1318	2072	1330	863	1650	200	1487	1938	2449	995	1561	2583	1433	608	
464	1196	279	792	886	872	287	826	715	712	618	975	694	1135	1482	988	1550	2544	1458	2337	914	505	1813	644	1780	2312	2612	709	1183	2746	996	771
594	211	915	835	1151	1514	423	185	1223	612	935	694	1135	1482	988	1550	2544	1458	2337	914	505	1813	644	1780	2312	2612	709	1183	2746	996	771	
516	536	1466	573	441	1359	559	932	1202	348	188	1245	1141	1360	857	1525	1805	710	1598	1085	252	1074	812	1695	1814	1872	1259	1028	2007	1083	192	
1874	1611	2733	1408	1677	2596	1826	1854	2552	1214	1294	2512	2500	285	2255	2855	1035	442	2444	1610	417	1272	337	575	1256	2526	2651	2946	1036	464		
526	940	1306	215	175	1694	983	1326	1175	1367	920	2237	1093	2030	981	416	1507	600	1703	2012	2305	984	1115	2439	1036	464						
2126	1839	2759	2082	1951	2869	2054	1917	2820	1352	1567	2538	2760	369	2476	3144	971	1309	519	2682	1856	691	1356	124	385	1148	2553	2538	1291	2702	1513	
386	1084	394	711	920	175	714	739	774	704	863	678	1786	394	1062	2362	1215	2155	572	264	1631	1135	2144	2372	2364	878	589	2497	596	705		
386	1051	624	940	1306	215	396	1123	487	724	830	1035	1500	781	1451	2382	1215	2155	572	264	1859	1159	2494	2599	2534	1019	321	2648	349	597		
1084	1051	1478	1794	1671	907	874	1299	1609	1654	232	1211	2390	1167	1627	3312	2176	3105	954	1234	2581	1401	2688	3140	3370	274	1532	3504	1065	1655		
394	624	1478	337	939	569	1020	894	880	514	1257	865	1892	564	1198	2063	842	1970	899	367	1446	1343	2145	2186	1991	1272	607	2124	799	769		
1951	311	387	1255	886	1337	1211	793	883	1573	1181	1805	881	1515	1727	606	1839	1216	621	1315	1257	2043	2931	2972	2907	522	330	3041	600	637		
920	1306	1671	939	1255	1094	1632	383	1625	1300	1466	454	2637	607	282	2963	1758	2756	174	1112	2232	2043	2931	2972	2907	522	330	3041	600	637		
175	215	907	569	886	1094	539	906	703	747	686	818	1715	569	1234	2405	1269	2198	626	307	1675	954	2056	2360	2463	701	764	2597	679	748		
739	1123	1299	894	1211	383	906	1332	1469	1258	1094	91	2481	361	313	2920	1716	2713	342	956	2189	1861	2839	2929	2864	1150	507	2998	228	1391		
774	487	1609	880	793	1625	703	731	1469	463	1388	1408	1012	1174	1792	1934	871	1727	1331	505	1204	466	1370	1657	2002	1403	1295	2136	1350	161		
704	724	1654	514	383	1367	747	1121	1258	463	1433	1228	1440	928	1561	1643	545	1263	440	932	927	1630	1672	1739	1448	971	1853	1162	307			
678	1035	1211	865	1181	454	818	1245	91	1408	1228	1006	2420	306	419	2890	1686	2683	254	895	2160	1774	2779	2900	2835	1062	522	2968	140	1330		
1786	1500	2390	1892	1805	2637	1715	1548	2481	1012	1440	2169	2420	216	2304	2804	1335	1308	883	2343	1517	651	987	358	750	1513	2184	2307	1655	2362	1173		
394	780	1167	564	881	607	508	1108	367	1124	848	1101	313	1792	1561	1422	419	2804	690		3223	2019	3016	670	1279	2493	2189	3162	3233	3168	1478	668
1062	1451	1627	1198	1515	282	1234	1660	313	1792	1561	1422	419	2804	690		3223	2019	3016	670	1279	2493	2189	3162	3233	3168	1478	668	3301	556	1714	
2362	2382	3312	2063	1727	2963	2405	2663	2920	1934	1662	3091	2890	1335	2590	3223		1268	578	2925	2057	771	2321	1093	638	170	3106	2633	313	2824	1775	
1215	1247	2176	842	969	1888	1116	1463	1716	871	525	1955	1686	1308	1386	2019	1268		1151	1720	963	628	135	1363	1386	1195	1970	1243	1620	712		
2155	2175	3105	1970	1839	2756	2198	2431	2713	727	1455	2884	2683	883	2383	3016	578	1151		2718	1850	524	1870	642	217	755	2899	2426	898	2617	1568	
572	843	954	899	1216	714	626	1002	342	1331	1263	750	254	2343	341	670	2925	1720	2718		834	2194	1530	2684	2934	2869	805	660	3003	108	1274	
1631	1652	2581	1446	1315	2232	1675	1923	2189	1204	932	2360	2160	651	1859	2493	771	628	524	2194	1326		1419	754	740	839	2375	1902	973	2094	1044	
1125	739	1401	1343	1257	2043	954	560	1861	466	927	1180	1774	987	1519	2189	2322	1335	1870	1530	968	1419		1285	1737	2275	1195	1714	2410	1635	624	
124	1841	2688	2145	2014	2931	2056	1846	2839	1370	1640	2467	2719	754	2494	3162	1093	1372	642	2684	1875	754	1285		508	1271	2681	1601	1414	2720	1531	
2372	2144	3140	2186	2055	2972	2360	2298	2929	1657	1672	2918	2900	750	2599	3233	638	1368	217	2934	2066	740	1737	508		808	2933	2643	958	2834	1784	
2364	2440	3370	1991	1654	2907	2463	2739	2864	2002	1719	3149	2835	1513	2534	3168	170	1195	755	2869	2125	839	2275	1271	816		3164	2577	140	2769	1843	
878	845	274	1272	1588	522	701	668	1150	1403	1448	82	1062	2184	1019	1478	3106	1970	2899	805	1008	2375	1195	2681	2933	3164		1383	3297	916	1448	
896	1065	799	1115	600	679	1106	228	1350	1162	860	140	2362	240	556	2824	1620	2617	108	837	2094	1635	2720	2834	2769	916	563	2902			1272	
705	597	1655	769	637	1547	748	890	1391	161	307	1434	1330	1173	1046	1714	1775	712	1568	1274	441	1044	624	1531	1784	1843	1448	1217	1977	1272		

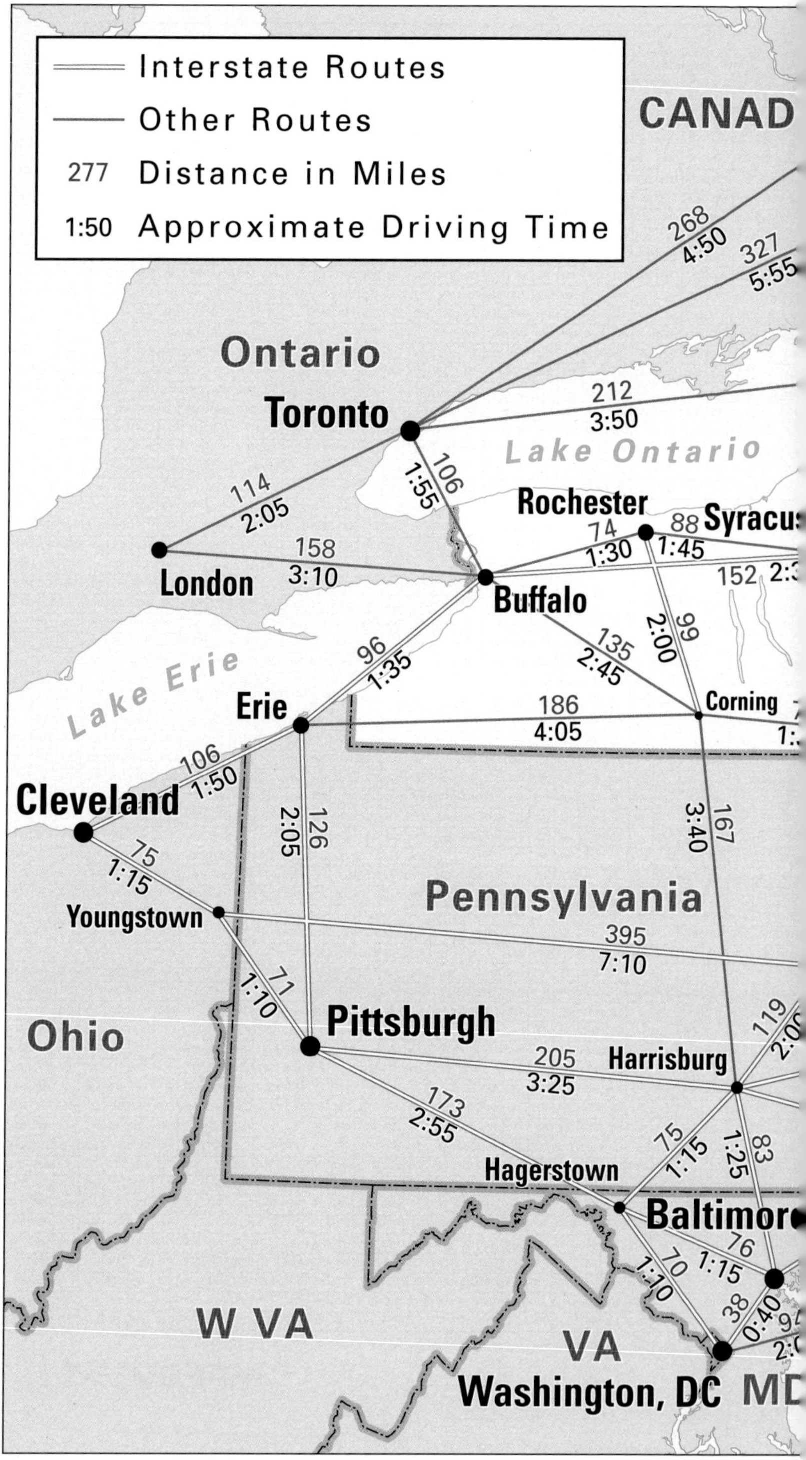

Interstate Routes

Other Routes

277 Distance in Miles

1:50 Approximate Driving Time

CANAD

268
4:50

327
5:55

Ontario

Toronto

212
3:50

Lake Ontario

Rochester

Syracu

74
1:30

88
1:45

152 2:3

106
1:55

114
2:05

158
3:10

London

Buffalo

99
2:00

135
2:45

96
1:35

Lake Erie

Corning

Erie

186
4:05

106
1:50

126
2:05

Cleveland

167
3:40

75
1:15

Youngstown

Pennsylvania

395
7:10

71
1:10

Ohio

Pittsburgh

119
2:0

205
3:25

Harrisburg

173
2:55

75
1:15

83
1:25

Hagerstown

Baltimor

76
1:15

70
1:10

38
0:40

9

2:0

W VA

VA

Washington, DC MD

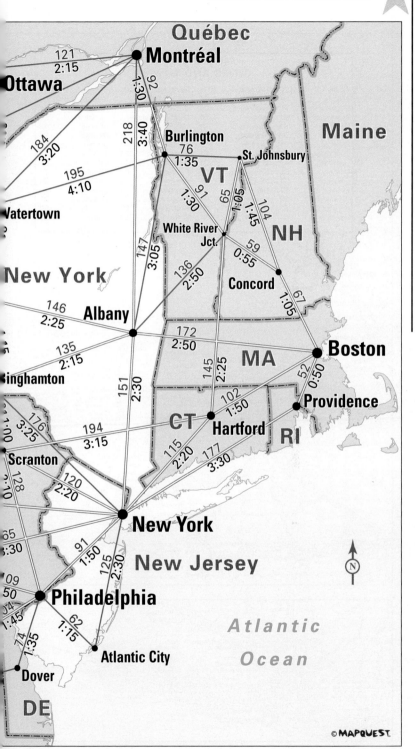

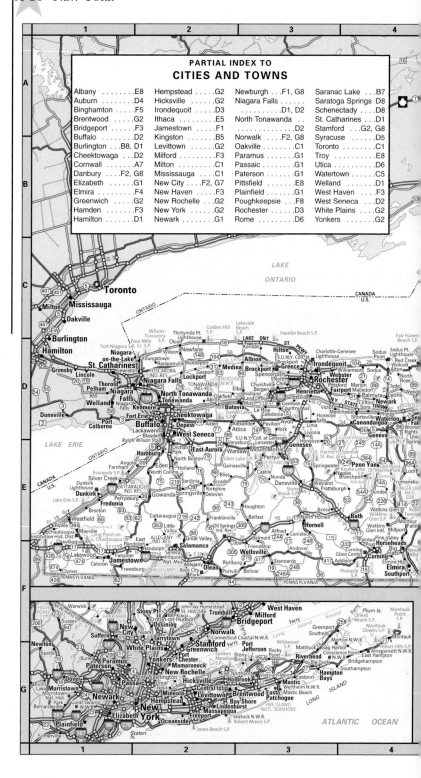

PARTIAL INDEX TO
CITIES AND TOWNS

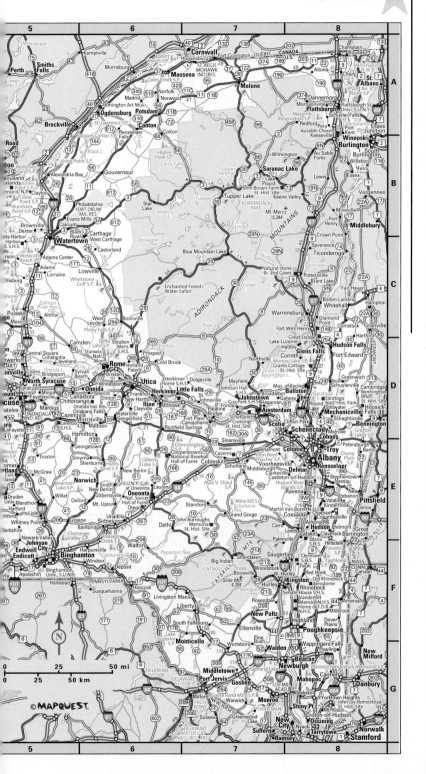

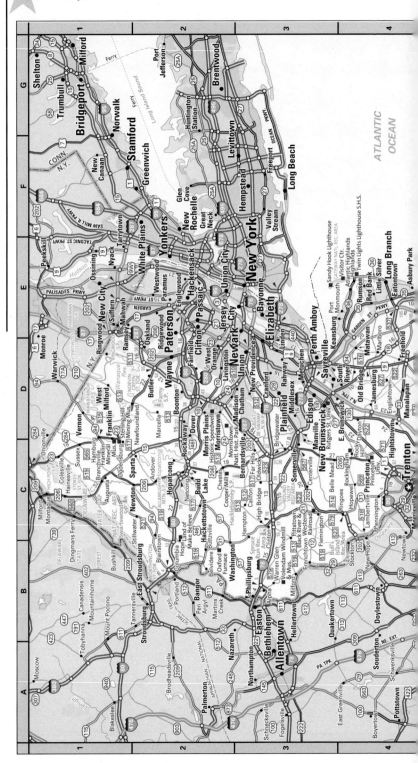

PARTIAL INDEX TO CITIES AND TOWNS

20 mi

20 km

© MAPQUEST

MAP LEGEND

TRANSPORTATION

CONTROLLED-ACCESS HIGHWAYS

Free

Toll; Toll Booth

Under Construction

Interchange and Exit Number

Ramp
Downtown maps only

OTHER HIGHWAYS

Primary Highway

Secondary Highway

Multilane Divided Highway
Primary and secondary highways only

Other Paved Road

Unpaved Road
Check conditions locally

HIGHWAY MARKERS

Interstate Route

US Route

State or Provincial Route

County or Other Route

Business Route

Trans-Canada Highway

Canadian Provincial Autoroute

Mexican Federal Route

OTHER SYMBOLS

Distances Along Major Highways
Miles in US; kilometers in Canada and Mexico

Tunnel; Pass

One-Way Street

Airport

Railroad
Downtown maps only

Auto Ferry; Passenger Ferry

RECREATION AND FEATURES OF INTEREST

National Park

National Forest; National Grassland

Other Large Park or Recreation Area

Military Lands

Indian Reservation

Small State Park with and without Camping

Public Campsite

Trail

Point of Interest

Golf Course
Professional tournament location

Hospital
City maps only

Ski Area

CITIES AND TOWNS

National Capital; State or Provincial Capital

County Seat
State maps only

Cities, Towns, and Populated Places
Type size indicates relative importance

Urban Area
State and province maps only

Large Incorporated Cities

OTHER MAP FEATURES

JEFFERSON   County Boundary and Name

Time Zone Boundary

+ *Mt. Olympus*   Mountain Peak; Elevation
7,965   Feet in US, meters in Canada and Mexico

Perennial; Intermittent River

Perennial; Intermittent or Dry Water Body

Dam

Swamp

It pays for all kinds of fuel.

***Speedpass*: today's way to pay.** Don't go on the road without *Speedpass*. You can pay for gas at the pump or just about anything inside our store. It's fast, free, and links to a check card or major credit card you already have. To join the millions who use *Speedpass*, call **1-87-SPEEDPASS** or visit speedpass.com.

We're drivers too.

With the right gas, a kid could go pretty far.

Next time you stop at an Exxon or Mobil station, consider a new destination: college. ExxonMobil is working with Upromise to help you save for a child's education. How do you start saving? Just join at upromise.com and register your credit cards. It's FREE to join. Then when you buy Exxon or Mobil gas with a credit card registered with Upromise, one cent per gallon will be contributed to your Upromise account*. This account helps you pay for the college education of any child you choose. Contributions from other Upromise participants, like GM, AT&T and Toys"R"Us, are also added to this account.** One more thing: be sure to register the credit card you linked to your *Speedpass*. That way, *Speedpass* gasoline purchases can also contribute to your account. To get your FREE *Speedpass*, go to speedpass.com or call toll free 1-87-SPEEDPASS. Upromise is an easy way to help you save for a child's education. How do we know? We're drivers too.

Join Upromise for FREE at upromise.com
For your FREE *Speedpass*, call 1-87-SPEEDPASS
or visit speedpass.com.
You must have Internet access and a valid email address to join Upromise.
*No contributions are made for diesel fuel purchases.
** Specific terms and conditions apply for each company's contributions.
Visit upromise.com for details.
Available at Exxon and Mobil stations that accept *Speedpass*.
©2002 Exxon Mobil Corporation. All rights reserved.

We're drivers too.

WELCOME

Dear Traveler,

Since its inception in 1958, Mobil Travel Guide has served as a trusted aid to auto travelers in search of value in lodging, dining, and destinations. Now in its 45th year, Mobil Travel Guide is the hallmark of our ExxonMobil family of travel publications, and we're proud to offer an array of products and services from our Mobil, Exxon, and Esso brands in North America to facilitate life on the road.

Whether business or pleasure venues, our nationwide network of independent, professional evaluators offers their expertise on thousands of travel options, allowing you to plan a quick family getaway, a full-service business meeting, or an unforgettable Five-Star celebration.

Your feedback is important to us as we strive to improve our product offerings and better meet today's travel needs. Whether you travel once a week or once a year, please take the time to complete the customer feedback form at the back of this book. Or, contact us at www.mobiltravelguide.com. We hope to hear from you soon.

Best wishes for safe and enjoyable travels.

Lee R Raymond

Lee R. Raymond
Chairman
Exxon Mobil Corporation

A WORD TO OUR READERS

In this day and age the travel industry is ever-changing, and having accurate, reliable travel information is indispensable. Travelers are back on the roads in enormous numbers. They are going on day trips, long weekends, extended family vacations, and business trips. They are traveling across the country- stopping at National Parks, major cities, small towns, monuments, and landmarks. And for 45 years, the Mobil Travel Guide has been providing this invaluable service to the traveling consumer and is committed to continuing this service well into the future.

You, the traveler, deserve the best food and accommodations available in every city, town, or village you visit. But finding suitable accommodations can be problematic. You could try to meet and ask local residents about appropriate places to stay and eat, but that time-consuming option comes with no guarantee of getting the best advice.

The Mobil Travel Guide One- to Five-Star rating system is the oldest and most respected lodging and restaurant inspection and rating program in North America. This trusted, well-established tool directs you to satisfying places to eat and stay, as well as to interesting events and attractions in thousands of locations. Mobil Corporation (now known as Exxon Mobil Corporation, following a 1999 merger) began producing the Mobil Travel Guides in 1958, following the introduction of the US Highway system in 1956. The first edition covered only 5 southwestern states. Since then, the Mobil Travel Guide has become the premier travel guide in North America, covering the 48 contiguous states and major cities in Canadian provinces. Now, ExxonMobil presents the latest edition of our annual Travel Guides series.

For the past 45 years, Mobil Travel Guide has been inspecting and rating lodging and restaurants throughout the United States and Canada. Each restaurant, motel, hotel, inn, resort, guest ranch, etc., is inspected and must meet the basic requirements of cleanliness and service to be included in the Mobil Travel Guide. Highly trained quality assurance team members travel across the country generating exhaustive inspections reports. Mobil Travel Guide management's careful scrutiny of findings detailed in the inspection reports, incognito inspections, where we dine in the restaurant and stay overnight at the lodging to gauge the level of service of the hotel and restaurant, review of our extensive files of reader comments and letters are all used in the final ratings determinations. All of this information is used to arrive at fair, accurate, and useful assessments of lodgings and restaurants. Based upon these elements, Mobil Travel Guide determines those establishments eligible for listing. Only facilities meeting Mobil Travel Guide standards of cleanliness, maintenance and stable management are listed in the Guide. Deteriorating, poorly managed establishments are deleted. A listing in the Mobil Travel Guide constitutes a positive quality recommendation; every rating is an accolade; a recognition of achievement. Once an establishment is chosen for a listing, Mobil's respected and world-famous one- to five-star rating system highlights their distinguishing characteristics.

Although the ten-book set allows us to include many more hotels, restaurants, and attractions than in past years, space limitations still make it impossible for us to include every hotel, motel, and restaurant in America. Instead, our database consists of a generous, representative sampling, with information about places that are above-average in their type. In essence, you can confidently patronize any of the restaurants, places of lodging, and attractions contained in the *Mobil Travel Guide* series.

What do we mean by "representative sampling"? You'll find that the *Mobil Travel Guide* books include information about a great variety of establishments. Perhaps you favor rustic lodgings and restaurants, or perhaps you're most comfortable with elegance and high style. Money may be no object or, like most of us, you may be on a budget. Some travelers place a high premium on 24-hour room service or special menu items. Others look for quiet seclusion. Whatever your travel needs and desires, they will be reflected in the *Mobil Travel Guide* listings.

Allow us to emphasize that we have charged no establishment for inclusion in our guides. We have no relationship with any of the businesses and attractions we list and act only as a consumer advocate. In essence, we do the investigative legwork so you won't have to.

Look over the "How to Use This Book" section that follows. You'll discover just how simple it is to quickly and easily gather all the information you need—before your trip or while on the road. For terrific tips on saving money, travel safety, and other ways to get the most out of your travels, be sure to read our special section, "Making the Most of Your Trip."

Keep in mind that the hospitality business is ever-changing. Restaurants and places of lodging—particularly small chains or stand-alone establishments—can change management or even go out of business with surprising quickness. Although we have made every effort to double-check information during our annual updates, we nevertheless recommend that you call ahead to be sure a place you have selected is open and still offers all the features you want. Phone numbers are provided, and, when available, we also list fax and Web site information.

We hope that all your travel experiences are easy and relaxing. If any aspects of your accommodations or dining motivate you to comment, please drop us a line. We depend a great deal on our readers' remarks, so you can be assured that we will read and assimilate your comments into our research. General comments about our books are also welcome. You can write us at Mobil Travel Guides,

1460 Renaissance Drive, Suite 401, Park Ridge, IL 60068, or send email to info@mobiltravelguide.com.

Take your *Mobil Travel Guide* books along on every trip. You'll be pleased by their convenience, ease of use, and breadth of dependable coverage.

Happy travels in the new millennium!

EDITORIAL CONTRIBUTORS AND CONSULTANTS FOR DRIVING TOURS, WALKING TOURS, ATTRACTIONS, EVENTS, AND PHOTOGRAPHY:

Christiane Bird is a New York native and author of *New York City Handbook* and *New York Handbook*. She is a former travel writer for the *New York Daily News* and her travel features appear in several national publications including the *New York Post, USAir Magazine, Newsday,* and *Americana.* Ms. Bird is also the author of *Neither East Nor West: One Woman's Journey Through the Islamic Republic of Iran* and *The Jazz and Blues Lover's Guide to the U.S.*

New Jersey-based **Mitch Kaplan** began as a ski writer, looking for a way to feed his snow-sliding habit. He now covers all aspects of travel, and his work has appeared in *Family Circle, Skiing, Snow Country, Continental Airlines Magazine, Westways, Endless Vacation,* and other periodicals. He is the author of the *Unofficial Guide to the Mid-Atlantic with Kids, The Golf Book of Lists, 535 Wonderful Things to Do This Weekend,* and *52 New Jersey Weekends.*

Irvina Lew is a Long Island author and freelance travel writer who has been writing about The Hamptons for almost 20 years. Ms. Lew is a member of ASJA (American Society of Journalists and Authors), and of SATW (Society of American Travel Writers). Her most recent book is *Romantic Weekends in and around New York,* and she contributed to *Fodor's Healthy Escapes* and *Bradman's Guide USA* (Manhattan). Her articles appear in *Art & Antiques, Bride's, Physicians' Travel & Meeting Guide, Sante, The Record,* and *Wine Enthusiast* and have been published in *Conde Nast Traveler, National Geographic Traveler, Newsday,* and the *New York Times.*

HOW TO USE THIS BOOK

The *Mobil Travel Guides* are designed for ease of use. Each state has its own chapter. The chapter begins with a general introduction, which provides both a general geographical and historical orientation to the state; it also covers basic statewide tourist information, from state recreation areas to seatbelt laws. The remainder of each chapter is devoted to the travel destinations within the state—cities and towns, state and national parks, and tourist areas—which, like the states, are arranged alphabetically.

The following is an explanation of the wealth of information you'll find regarding those travel destinations—information on the area, on things to see and do there, and on where to stay and eat.

Maps and Map Coordinates

Next to some destinations are a set of map coordinates. These are referenced to the appropriate state map in the front of this book. In addition, we have provided maps of selected larger cities.

Destination Information

Because many travel destinations are close to other cities and towns where visitors might find additional attractions, accommodations, and restaurants, cross-references to those places are included whenever possible. Also listed are addresses and phone numbers for travel information resources—usually the local chamber of commerce or office of tourism—as well as pertinent vital statistics and a brief introduction to the area.

What to See and Do

Almost 20,000 museums, art galleries, amusement parks, universities, historic sites and houses, plantations, churches, state parks, ski areas, and other attractions are described in the *Mobil Travel Guides*. A white star on a red background ★ signals that the attraction is one of the best in the state. Because municipal parks, public tennis courts, swimming pools, and small educational institutions are common to most towns, they are generally not represented within the city.

Following the attraction's description, you'll find the months and days it's open, address/location and phone number, and admission costs (see the inside front cover for an explanation of the cost symbols). Note that directions are given from the center of the town under which the attraction is listed, which may not necessarily be the town in which the attraction is located. Zip codes are listed only if they differ from those given for the town.

Driving and Walking Tours

The driving tours are usually day trips—though they can be longer—that make for interesting side trips. This is a way to get off the beaten track and visit an area often overlooked. These trips frequently cover areas of natural beauty or historical significance. The walking tours focus on a particularly interesting area of a city or town. Again, these can be a break from more everyday tourist attractions. The tours often include places to stop for a meal or snack.

Special Events

Special events can either be annual events that last only a short time, such as festivals and fairs, or longer, seasonal events such as horse racing, summer theater and concerts, and professional sports. Special event listings might also include an infrequently occurring occasion that marks a certain date or event, such as a centennial or other commemorative celebration.

Major Cities

Additional information on airports and ground transportation, and suburbs may be included for large cities.

Lodging and Restaurant Listings

ORGANIZATION

For both lodgings and restaurants, when a property is in a town that does not have its own heading, the listing appears under the town nearest its location with the address and town immediately after the establishment name. In large cities, lodgings located within five miles of major commercial airports are listed under a separate "Airport" heading, following the city listings.

LODGING CLASSIFICATIONS

Each property is classified by type according to the characteristics below. Because the following features and services are found at most motels and hotels, they are not shown in those listings:

- Year-round operation with a single rate structure unless otherwise quoted
- European plan (meals not included in room rate)
- Bathroom with tub and/or shower in each room
- Air-conditioned/heated, often with individual room control
- Cots
- Daily maid service
- In-room phones
- Elevators

Motels/Motor Lodges. Accommodations are in low-rise structures with rooms easily accessible to parking (which is usually free). Properties have outdoor room entry and small, functional lobbies. Service is often limited, and dining may not be offered in lower-rated motels and lodges. Shops and businesses are found only in higher-rated properties, as are bellhops, room service, and restaurants serving three meals daily.

Hotels. To be categorized as a hotel, an establishment must have most of the following facilities and services: multiple floors, a restaurant and/or coffee shop, elevators, room service, bellhops, a spacious lobby, and recreational facilities. In addition, the following features and services not shown in listings are also found:

- Valet service (one-day laundry/cleaning service)
- Room service during hours restaurant is open
- Bellhops
- Some oversize beds

Resorts. These specialize in stays of three days or more and usually offer American plan and/or housekeeping accommodations. Their emphasis is on recreational facilities, and a social director is often available. Food services are of primary importance, and guests must be able to eat three meals a day on the premises, either in restaurants or by having access to an on-site grocery store and preparing their own meals.

All Suites. All Suites' guest rooms consist of two rooms, one bedroom and one living room. Higher rated properties offer facilities and services comparable to regular hotels.

B&Bs/Small Inns. Frequently thought of as a small hotel, a bed-and-breakfast or an inn is a place of homelike comfort and warm hospitality. It is often a structure of historic significance, with an equally interesting setting. Meals are a special occasion, and refreshments are frequently served in late afternoon. Rooms are usually individually decorated, often with antiques or furnishings representative of the locale. Phones, bathrooms, or TVs may not be available in every room.

Guest Ranches. Like resorts, guest ranches specialize in stays of three days or more. Guest ranches also offer meal plans and extensive outdoor activities. Horseback riding is usually a feature; there are stables and trails on the ranch property, and trail rides and daily instruction are part of the program. Many guest ranches are working ranches, ranging from casual to rustic, and guests are encouraged to participate in ranch life. Eating is often family style and may also include cookouts. Western saddles are assumed; phone ahead to inquire about English saddle availability.

Extended Stay. These hotels specialize in stays of three days or more and usually offer weekly room rates. Service is often limited and dining might not be offered at lower-rated extended-stay hotels.

Villas/Condos. Similar to Cottage Colonies, these establishments are usually found in recreational areas. They are often separate houses, often luxuriously furnished, and rarely offer restaurants and only a small variety of services on the premises.

Conference Centers. Conference Centers are hotels with extended meeting space facilities designed to house multiday conferences and seminars. Amenities are often geared toward groups staying for longer than one night and often include restaurants and fitness facilities. Larger Conference Center Hotels are often referred to as Convention Center Hotels.

Casinos. Casino Hotels incorporate areas that offer games of chance like Blackjack, Poker, Slot machines, etc. and are only found in states that legalize gambling. Casino Hotels offer a wide range of services and amenities, comparable to regular hotels.

Cottage Colonies. These are housekeeping cottages and cabins that are usually found in recreational areas. Any dining or recreational facilities are noted in our listing.

DINING CLASSIFICATIONS

Restaurants. Most dining establishments fall into this category. All have a full kitchen and offer table service and a complete menu. Parking on or near the premises, in a lot or garage, is assumed. When a property offers valet or other special parking features, or when only street parking is available, it is noted in the listing.

Unrated Dining Spots. These places, listed after Restaurants in many cities, are chosen for their unique atmosphere, specialized menu, or local flavor. They include delis, ice-cream parlors, cafeterias, tearooms, and pizzerias. Because they may not have a full kitchen or table service, they are not given a *Mobil Travel Guides* rating. Often they offer extraordinary value and quick service.

QUALITY RATINGS

The *Mobil Travel Guides* have been rating lodgings and restaurants on a national basis since the first edition was published in 1958. For years the guide was the only source of such ratings, and it remains among the few guidebooks to rate restaurants across the country.

All listed establishments were inspected by experienced field representatives or evaluated by a senior staff member. Ratings are based upon their detailed inspection reports of the individual properties, on written evaluations of staff members who stay and dine anonymously, and on an extensive review of comments from our readers.

You'll find a key to the rating categories, ★ through ★★★★★, on the inside front cover. All establishments in the book are recommended. Even a ★ clean, convenient, limited service, usually providing a basic, informal experience. Rating categories reflect both the features the property offers and its quality in relation to similar establishments.

For example, lodging ratings take into account the number and quality of facilities and services, the luxury of appointments, and the attitude and professionalism of staff and management. A ★ establishment provides a comfortable night's lodging. A ★★ property offers more than a facility that rates one star, and the decor is well planned and integrated. Establishments that rate ★★★ are well-appointed, with full services and amenities; the lodging experience is truly excellent, and the range of facilities is extensive. Properties that have been given ★★★★ not only offer many services but also have their own style and personality; they are luxurious, creatively decorated, and superbly maintained. The ★★★★★ properties are among the best in North America, superb in every respect and entirely memorable, year in and year out.

Restaurant evaluations reflect the quality of the food and the ingredients, preparation, presentation, service levels, as well as the property's decor and ambience. A restaurant that has fairly simple goals for menu and decor but that achieves those goals superbly might receive the same number of stars as a restaurant with somewhat loftier ambitions, but the execution of which falls short of the mark. In general, ★ indicates a restaurant that's a good choice in its area, usually fairly simple and perhaps catering to a clientele of locals and families; ★★ denotes restaurants that are more highly recommended in their area; ★★★ restaurants are of national caliber, with professional and attentive service and a skilled chef in the kitchen; ★★★★ reflect superb dining choices, where remarkable food is served in equally remarkable surroundings; and ★★★★★ represent that rare group of the best restaurants in the country, where in addition to near perfection in every detail, there's that special something extra that makes for an unforgettable dining experience.

A list of the four-star and five-star establishments in each region is located just before the state listings.

Each rating is reviewed annually and each establishment must work to maintain its rating (or improve it). Every effort is made to assure that ratings are fair and accurate; the designated ratings are published purely as an aid to travelers. In general, properties that are very new or have recently undergone major management changes are considered difficult to assess fairly and are often listed without ratings.

LODGINGS

Each listing gives the name, address, directions (when there is no street address), neighborhood and/or directions from downtown (in major cities), phone number (local and 800), fax number, number and type of rooms available, room rates, and seasons open (if not year-round). Also included are details on recreational and dining facilities on the property or nearby, the presence of a luxury level, and credit card information. A key to the symbols at the end of each listing is on the inside front cover. (Note that Exxon or Mobil Corporation credit cards cannot be used for payment of meals and room charges.)

All prices quoted in the *Mobil Travel Guide* publications are expected to be in effect at the time of publication and during the entire year; however, prices cannot be guaranteed. In some localities there may be short-term price variations because of special events or holidays. Whenever possible, these price charges are noted. Certain resorts have complicated rate structures that vary with the time of year; always confirm listed rates when you make your plans.

RESTAURANTS

Each listing gives the name, address, directions (when there is no street address), neighborhood and/or directions from downtown (in major cities), phone number, hours and days of operation (if not open daily year-round), reservation policy, cuisine (if other than American), price range for each meal served, children's menu (if offered), specialties, and credit card information. In addition, special features such as chef ownership, ambience, and entertainment are noted. By carefully reading the detailed restaurant information and comparing prices, you can easily determine whether the restaurant is formal and elegant or informal and comfortable for families.

TERMS AND ABBREVIATIONS IN LISTINGS

The following terms and abbreviations are used throughout the listings:

A la carte entrees With a price, refers to the cost of entrees/main dishes that are not accompanied by side dishes.

AP American plan (lodging plus all meals).

Bar Liquor, wine, and beer are served in a bar or cocktail lounge and usually with meals unless otherwise indicated (e.g., "wine, beer").

Business center The property has a designated area accessible to all guests with business services.

Business servs avail The property can perform/arrange at least two of the following services for a guest: audiovisual equipment rental, binding, computer rental, faxing, messenger services, modem availability, notary service, obtaining office supplies, photocopying, shipping, and typing.

Cable Standard cable service; "premium" indicates that HBO, Disney, Showtime, or similar cable services are available.

Ck-in, ck-out Check-in time, check-out time.

Coin lndry Self-service laundry.

Complete meal Soup and/or salad, entree, and dessert, plus nonalcoholic beverage.

Continental bkfst Usually coffee and a roll or doughnut.

Cr cds: A, American Express; C, Carte Blanche; D, Diners Club; DS, Discover; ER, enRoute; JCB, Japanese Credit Bureau; MC, MasterCard; V, Visa.

D Followed by a price, indicates room rate for a "double"—two people in one room in one or two beds (the charge may be higher for two double beds).

Downhill/X-country ski Downhill and/or cross-country skiing within 20 miles of property.

Each addl Extra charge for each additional person beyond the stated number of persons at a reduced price.

Early-bird dinner A meal served at specified hours, typically around 4:30-6:30 pm.

Exc Except.

Exercise equipt Two or more pieces of exercise equipment on the premises.

Exercise rm Both exercise equipment and room, with an instructor on the premises.

Fax Facsimile machines available to all guests.

Golf privileges Privileges at a course within ten miles.

Hols Holidays.

In-rm modem link Every guest room has a connection for a modem that's separate from the phone line.

Kit. or **Kits.** A kitchen or kitchenette that contains stove or microwave, sink, and refrigerator and that is either part of the room or a separate room. If the kitchen is not fully equipped, the listing will indicate "no equipt" or "some equipt."

Luxury level A special section of a lodging, covering at least an entire floor, that offers increased luxury accommodations. Management must provide no less than three of these four services: separate check-in and check-out, concierge, private lounge, and private elevator service (key access). Complimentary breakfast and snacks are commonly offered.

MAP Modified American plan (lodging plus two meals).

Movies Prerecorded videos are available for rental.

No cr cds accepted No credit cards are accepted.

No elvtr In hotels with more than two stories, it's assumed there are elevators; only their absence is noted.

No phones Phones, too, are assumed; only their absence is noted.

Parking There is a parking lot on the premises.

Private club A cocktail lounge or bar available to members and their guests. In motels and hotels where these clubs exist, registered guests can usually use the club as guests of the management; the same is frequently true of restaurants.

Prix fixe A full meal for a stated price; usually one price is quoted.

Res Reservations.

S Followed by a price, indicates room rate for a "single," i.e., one person.

Serv bar A service bar, where drinks are prepared for dining patrons only.

Serv charge Service charge is the amount added to the restaurant check in lieu of a tip.

Table d'hôte A full meal for a stated price, dependent upon entree selection; no a la carte options are available.

Tennis privileges Privileges at tennis courts within five miles.

TV Indicates color television.

Under certain age free Children under that age are not charged if staying in room with a parent.

Valet parking An attendant is available to park and retrieve a car.

VCR VCRs in all guest rooms.

VCR avail VCRs are available for hookup in guest rooms.

Special Information for Travelers with Disabilities

The *Mobil Travel Guides* Ⓓ symbol shown in accommodation and restaurant listings indicates establishments that are at least partially accessible to people with mobility problems.

The *Mobil Travel Guides* criteria for accessibility are unique to our publication. Please do not confuse them with the universal symbol for wheelchair accessibility. When the Ⓓ symbol appears following a listing, the establishment is equipped with facilities to accommodate people using wheelchairs or crutches or otherwise needing easy access to doorways and rest rooms. Travelers with severe mobility problems or with hearing or visual impairments may or may not find facilities they need. Always phone ahead to make sure that an establishment can meet your needs.

All lodgings bearing our Ⓓ symbol have the following facilities:

- ISA-designated parking near access ramps
- Level or ramped entryways to building
- Swinging building entryway doors minimum 39"
- Public rest rooms on main level with space to operate a wheelchair; handrails at commode areas
- Elevators equipped with grab bars and lowered control buttons
- Restaurants with accessible doorways; rest rooms with space to operate wheelchair; handrails at commode areas
- Minimum 39" width entryway to guest rooms
- Low-pile carpet in rooms
- Telephone at bedside and in bathroom
- Bed placed at wheelchair height
- Minimum 39" width doorway to bathroom
- Bath with open sink—no cabinet; room to operate wheelchair
- Handrails at commode areas; tub handrails

- Wheelchair-accessible peephole in room entry door
- Wheelchair-accessible closet rods and shelves

All restaurants bearing our Ⅾ symbol offer the following facilities:

- ISA-designated parking beside access ramps
- Level or ramped front entryways to building
- Tables to accommodate wheelchairs
- Main-floor rest rooms; minimum 39" width entryway
- Rest rooms with space to operate wheelchair; handrails at commode areas

In general, the newest properties are apt to impose the fewest barriers.

To get the kind of service you need and have a right to expect, do not hesitate when making a reservation to question the management in detail about the availability of accessible rooms, parking, entrances, restaurants, lounges, or any other facilities that are important to you, and confirm what is meant by "accessible." Some guests with mobility impairments report that lodging establishments' housekeeping and maintenance departments are most helpful in describing barriers. Also inquire about any special equipment, transportation, or services you may need.

MAKING THE MOST OF YOUR TRIP

A few hardy souls might look with fondness upon the trip where the car broke down and they were stranded for a week. Or maybe even the vacation that cost twice what it was supposed to. For most travelers, though, the best trips are those that are safe, smooth, and within their budget. To help you make your trip the best it can be, we've assembled a few tips and resources.

Saving Money

ON LODGING

After you've seen the published rates, it's time to look for discounts. Many hotels and motels offer them—for senior citizens, business travelers, families, you name it. It never hurts to ask—politely, that is. Sometimes, especially in late afternoon, desk clerks are instructed to fill beds, and you might be offered a lower rate, or a nicer room, to entice you to stay. Look for bargains on stays over multiple nights, in the off-season, and on weekdays or weekends (depending on location). Many hotels in major metropolitan areas, for example, have special weekend package plans that offer considerable savings on rooms; they may include breakfast, cocktails, and meal discounts. Prices can change frequently throughout the year, so phone ahead.

Another way to save money is to choose accommodations that give you more than just a standard room. Rooms with kitchen facilities enable you to cook some meals for yourself, reducing restaurant costs. A suite might save money for two couples traveling together. Even hotel luxury levels can provide good value, as many include breakfast or cocktails in the price of the room.

State and city sales taxes, as well as special room taxes, can increase your room rates as much as 25 percent per day. We are unable to include this specific information in the listings, but we strongly urge that you ask about these taxes when placing reservations to understand the total cost of your lodgings.

Watch out for telephone-usage charges that hotels frequently impose on long-distance calls, credit-card calls, and other phone calls—even those that go unanswered. Before phoning from your room, read the information given to you at check-in, and then be sure to read your bill carefully before checking out. You won't be expected to pay for charges that they did not spell out. (On the other hand, it's not unusual for a hotel to bill you for your calls after you return home.) Consider using your cell phone; or, if public telephones are available in the hotel lobby, your cost savings may outweigh the inconvenience.

ON DINING

There are several ways to get a less expensive meal at a more expensive restaurant. Early-bird dinners are popular in many parts of the country and offer considerable savings. If you're interested in sampling a 4- or 5-star establishment, consider going at lunchtime. While the prices then are probably relatively high, they may be half of those at dinner and come with the same ambience, service, and cuisine.

ON PARK PASSES

Although many national parks, monuments, seashores, historic sites, and recreation areas may be used free of charge, others charge an entrance fee (ranging from $1 to $6 per person to $5 to $15 per carload) and/or a "use fee" for special services and facilities. If you plan to make several visits to federal recreation areas, consider one of the following National Park Service money-saving programs:

Park Pass. This is an annual entrance permit to a specific unit in the National Park Service system that normally charges an entrance fee. The pass admits the permit holder and any accompanying passengers in a private noncommercial vehicle or, in the case of walk-in facilities, the holder's spouse, children, and parents. It is valid for entrance fees only. A Park Pass may be purchased in person or by mail from the National Park Service unit at which the pass will be honored. The cost is $15 to $20, depending upon the area.

Golden Eagle Passport. This pass, available to people who are between 17 and 61, entitles the purchaser and accompanying passengers in a private noncommercial vehicle to enter any outdoor National Park Service unit that charges an entrance fee and admits the purchaser and family to most walk-in fee-charging areas. Like the Park Pass, it is good for one year and does not cover use fees. It may be purchased from the National Park Service, Office of Public Inquiries, Room 1013, US Department of the Interior, 18th and C sts NW, Washington, D.C. 20240, phone 202/208-4747; at any of the ten regional offices throughout the country; and at any National Park Service area that charges a fee. The cost is $50.

Golden Age Passport. Available to citizens and permanent residents of the United States 62 years or older, this is a lifetime entrance permit to fee-charging recreation areas. The fee exemption extends to those accompanying the permit holder in a private noncommercial vehicle or, in the case of walk-in facilities, to the holder's spouse and children. The passport also entitles the holder to a 50 percent discount on use fees charged in park areas but not to fees charged by concessionaires. Golden Age Passports must be obtained in person. The applicant must show proof of age, i.e., a driver's license, birth certificate, or signed affidavit attesting to age (Medicare cards are not acceptable proof). These passports are available at most park service units where they're used, at National Park Service headquarters (see above), at park system regional offices, at National Forest Supervisors' offices, and at most Ranger Station offices. The cost is $10.

Golden Access Passport. Issued to citizens and permanent residents of the United States who are physically disabled or visually impaired, this passport is a free lifetime entrance permit to fee-charging recreation areas. The fee exemption extends to those accompanying the permit holder in a private noncommercial vehicle or, in the case of walk-in facilities, to the holder's spouse and children. The passport also entitles the holder to a 50 percent discount on use fees charged in park areas but not to fees charged by concessionaires. Golden Access Passports must be obtained in person. Proof of eligibility to receive federal benefits is required (under programs such as Disability Retirement, Compensation for Military Service-Connected Disability, Coal Mine

Safety and Health Act, etc.), or an affidavit must be signed attesting to eligibility. These passports are available at the same outlets as Golden Age Passports.

FOR SENIOR CITIZENS

Look for the senior-citizen discount symbol in the lodging and restaurant listings. Always call ahead to confirm that the discount is being offered, and be sure to carry proof of age. At places not listed in the book, it never hurts to ask if a senior-citizen discount is offered. Additional information for mature travelers is available from the American Association of Retired Persons (AARP), 601 E St NW, Washington, D.C. 20049, phone 202/434-2277.

Tipping

Tipping is an expression of appreciation for good service, and often service workers rely on tips as a significant part of their income. However, you never need to tip if service is poor.

IN HOTELS

Door attendants in major city hotels are usually given $1 for getting you a cab. Bellhops expect $1 per bag, usually $2 if you have only one bag. Concierges are tipped according to the service they perform. It's not mandatory to tip when you've asked for suggestions on sightseeing or restaurants or help in making reservations for dining. However, when a concierge books you a table at a restaurant known to be difficult to get into, a gratuity of $5 is appropriate. For obtaining theater or sporting event tickets, $5-$10 is expected. Maids, often overlooked by guests, may be tipped $1-$2 per days of stay.

AT RESTAURANTS

Coffee shop and counter service waitstaff are usually given 8 percent–10 percent of the bill. In full-service restaurants, tip 15 percent of the bill, before sales tax. In fine restaurants, where the staff is large and shares the gratuity, 18 percent–20 percent for the waiter is appropriate. In most cases, tip the maitre d' only if service has been extraordinary and only on the way out; $20 is the minimum in upscale properties in major metropolitan areas. If there is a wine steward, tip him or her at least $6 a bottle, more if the wine was decanted or if the bottle was very expensive. If your bus person has been unusually attentive, $2 pressed into his hand on departure is a nice gesture. An increasing number of restaurants automatically add a service charge to the bill instead of a gratuity. Before tipping, carefully review your check. If you are in doubt, ask your server.

AT AIRPORTS

Curbside luggage handlers expect $1 per bag. Car-rental shuttle drivers who help with your luggage appreciate a $1 or $2 tip.

Staying Safe

The best way to deal with emergencies is to be prepared enough to avoid them. However, unforeseen situations do happen, and you can prepare for them.

IN YOUR CAR

Before your trip, make sure your car has been serviced and is in good working order. Change the oil, check the battery and belts, and make sure tires are inflated properly (this can also improve gas mileage). Other inspections recommended by the car's manufacturer should be made, too.

Next, be sure you have the tools and equipment to deal with a routine breakdown: jack, spare tire, lug wrench, repair kit, emergency tools, jumper cables, spare fan belt, auto fuses, flares and/or reflectors, flashlights, first-aid kit, and, in winter, windshield wiper fluid, a windshield scraper, and snow shovel.

Bring all appropriate and up-to-date documentation—licenses, registration, and insurance cards—and know what's covered by your insurance. Also bring an extra set of keys, just in case.

En route, always buckle up! In most states it is required by law.

If your car does break down, get out of traffic as soon as possible—pull well off the road. Raise the hood and turn on your emergency flashers or tie a white cloth to the roadside door handle or antenna. Stay near your car. Use flares or reflectors to keep your car from being hit.

IN YOUR LODGING

Chances are slim that you will encounter a hotel or motel fire. The ⊠ in a listing indicates that there were smoke detectors and/or sprinkler systems in the rooms we inspected. Once you've checked in, make sure that any smoke detector in your room is working properly. Ascertain the locations of fire extinguishers and at least two fire exits. Never use an elevator in a fire.

For personal security, use the peephole in your room's door.

PROTECTING AGAINST THEFT

To guard against theft wherever you go, don't bring anything of more value than you need. If you do bring valuables, leave them at your hotel rather than in your car, and if you have something very expensive, lock it in a safe. Many hotels have one in each room; others will store your valuables in the hotel's safe. And of course, don't carry more money than you need; use traveler's checks and credit cards, or visit cash machines.

For Travelers with Disabilities

A number of publications can provide assistance. The most complete listing of published material for travelers with disabilities is available from The Disability Bookshop, Twin Peaks Press, Box 129, Vancouver, WA 98666, phone 360/694-2462.

The Reference Section of the National Library Service for the Blind and Physically Handicapped (Library of Congress, Washington, D.C. 20542, phone 202/707-9276 or 202/707-5100) provides information and resources for persons with mobility problems and hearing and vision impairments, as well as information about the NILS talking program (or visit your local library).

IMPORTANT TOLL-FREE NUMBERS AND ONLINE INFORMATION

Hotels and Motels

Adams Mark   800 444-2326
    www.adamsmark.com

Amerisuites   800 833-1516
    www.amerisuites.com

AMFA Parks & Resorts   800 236-7916
    www.amfac.com

Baymont Inns   800 229-6668
    www.baymontinns.com

Best Western   800 780-7234
    www.bestwestern.com

Budget Host Inn   800 283-4678
    www.budgethost.com

Candlewood Suites   888 226-3539
    www.candlewoodsuites.com

Clarion Hotels   800 252-7466
    www.choicehotels.com

Clubhouse Inns   800 258-2466
    www.clubhouseinn.com

Coast Hotels & Resorts   800 663-1144
    www.coasthotels.com

Comfort Inns   800 252-7466
    www.choicehotels.com

Concorde Hotels   800 888-4747
    www.concorde-hotel.com

Country Hearth Inns   800 848-5767
    www.countryhearth.com

Country Inns   800 456-4000
    www.countryinns.com

Courtyard by Marriott   888 236-2437
    www.courtyard.com

Crown Plaza Hotels   800 227-6963
    www.crowneplaza.com

Days Inn   800 544-8313
    www.daysinn.com

Delta Hotels   800 268-1133
    www.deltahotels.com

Destination Hotels & Resorts
    800 434-7347
    www.destinationhotels.com

Doubletree   800 222-8733
    www.doubletree.com

Drury Inns   800 378-7946
    www.druryinn.com

Econolodge   800 553-2666
    www.econolodge.com

Embassy Suites   800 362-2779
    www.embassysuites.com

Fairfield Inns   800 228-2800
    www.fairfieldinn.com

Fairmont Hotels   800 441-1414
    www.fairmont.com

Family Inns of America   800 251-9752
    www.familyinnsofamerica.com

Forte Hotels   800 300-9147
    www.fortehotels.com

Four Points by Sheraton
    888 625-5144   www.starwood.com

Four Seasons   800 545-4000
    www.fourseasons.com

Hampton Inns   800 426-7866
    www.hamptoninn.com

Hilton   800 774-1500
    www.hilton.com

Holiday Inn   800 465-4329
    www.holiday-inn.com

Homestead Studio Suites   888 782-9473
    www.stayhsd.com

Homewood Suites   800 225-5466
    www.homewoodsuites.com

Howard Johnson   800 406-1411
    www.hojo.com

Hyatt   800 633-7313
    www.hyatt.com

Inn Suites Hotels & Suites
    800 842-4242   www.innsuites.com

Inter-Continental   888 567-8725
    www.interconti.com

Jameson Inns   800 526-3766
    www.jamesoninns.com

Kempinski Hotels   800-426-3135
    www.kempinski.com

Kimpton Hotels   888-546-7866
    www.kimptongroup.com

La Quinta   800-531-5900
    www.laquinta.com

Leading Hotels of the World
    800-223-6800   www.lhw.com

Loews Hotels   800-235-6397
    www.loewshotels.com

Mainstay Suites   800-660-6246
    www.choicehotels.com

Mandarin Oriental   800-526-6566
    www.mandarin-oriental.com

Marriott   888-236-2427
    www.marriott.com

Nikko Hotels   800-645-5687
    www.nikkohotels.com

Omni Hotels   800-843-6664
    www.omnihotels.com

Preferred Hotels & Resorts Worldwide
    www.preferredhotels.com
    800-323-7500

Quality Inn 800-228-5151
www.qualityinn.com
Radisson Hotels 800-333-3333
www.radisson.com
Ramada 888-298-2054
www.ramada.com
Red Lion Inns 800-733-5466
www.redlion.com
Red Roof Inns 800-733-7663
www.redroof.com
Regal Hotels 800-222-8888
www.regal-hotels.com
Regent International 800-545-4000
www.regenthotels.com
Renaissance Hotels 888-236-2427
www.renaissancehotels.com
Residence Inns 888-236-2427
www.residenceinn.com
Ritz Carlton 800-241-3333
www.ritzcarlton.com
Rodeway Inns 800-228-2000
www.rodeway.com
Rosewood Hotels & Resorts
888-767-3966
www.rosewood-hotels.com
Sheraton 888-625-5144
www.sheraton.com
Shilo Inns 800-222-2244
www.shiloinns.com
Shoney's Inns 800-552-4667
www.shoneysinn.com
Sleep Inns 800-453-3746
www.sleepinn.com
Small Luxury Hotels 800-525-4800
www.slh.com
Sofitel 800-763-4835
www.sofitel.com
Sonesta Hotels & Resorts
800-766-3782 www.sonesta.com
SRS Worldhotels 800-223-5652
www.srs-worldhotels.com
Summerfield Suites 800-833-4353
www.summerfieldsuites.com
Summit International 800-457-4000
www.summithotels.com
Swissotel 800-637-9477
www.swissotel.com
The Peninsula Group
www.peninsula.com
Travelodge 800-578-7878
www.travelodge.com
Westin Hotels & Resorts
800-937-8461 www.westin.com
Wingate Inns 800-228-1000
www.wingateinns.com
Woodfin Suite Hotels 800-966-3346
www.woodfinsuitehotels.com
Wyndham Hotels & Resorts
800-996-3426 www.wyndham.com

Airlines

Air Canada 888-247-2262
www.aircanada.ca
Alaska 800-252-7522
www.alaska-air.com
American 800-433-7300
www.aa.com
America West 800-235-9292
www.americawest.com
British Airways 800-247-9297
www.british-airways.com
Continental 800-523-3273
www.flycontinental.com
Delta 800-221-1212
www.delta-air.com
Island Air 800-323-3345
www.islandair.com
Mesa 800-637-2247
www.mesa-air.com
Northwest 800-225-2525
www.nwa.com
Southwest 800-435-9792
www.southwest.com
United 800-241-6522
www.ual.com
US Air 800-428-4322
www.usair.com

Car Rentals

Advantage 800-777-5500
www.arac.com
Alamo 800-327-9633
www.goalamo.com
Allstate 800-634-6186
www.bnm.com/as.htm
Avis 800-831-2847
www.avis.com
Budget 800-527-0700
www.budgetrentacar.com
Dollar 800-800-4000
www.dollarcar.com
Enterprise 800-325-8007
www.pickenterprise.com
Hertz 800-654-3131
www.hertz.com
National 800-227-7368
www.nationalcar.com
Payless 800-729-5377
www.800-payless.com
Rent-A-Wreck.com 800-535-1391
www.rent-a-wreck.com
Sears 800-527-0770
www.budget.com
Thrifty 800-847-4389
www.thrifty.com

Four-Star and Five-Star Establishments in New York and New Jersey

New York

★★★★★ Lodging
The Point, *Saranac Lake*

★★★★ Lodgings
The Castle At Tarrytown, *Tarrytown*
Lake Placid Lodge, *Lake Placid*
Mirbeau Inn & Spa, *Skaneateles*
Rose Inn, *Ithaca*

★★★★ Restaurant
La Panetiere, *White Plains*

New York City

★★★★★ Lodgings
Four Seasons Hotel New York, *Manhattan*
The St. Regis, *Manhattan*
Trump International Hotel & Tower, *Manhattan*

★★★★★ Restaurants
Alain Ducasse, *Manhattan*
Daniel, *Manhattan*
Jean Georges, *Manhattan*
Lespinasse, *Manhattan*

★★★★ Lodgings
The Carlyle, *Manhattan*
Hotel Plaza Athenee, *Manhattan*
The Lowell, *Manhattan*
The Mark, New York, *Manhattan*
Mercer Hotel, *Manhattan*
New York Palace, *Manhattan*
The Peninsula, *Manhattan*
The Pierre New York, a Four Seasons Hotel, *Manhattan*
The Regency Hotel, *Manhattan*
The Regent Wall Street, *Manhattan*
The Ritz-Carlton New York, Battery Park, *Manhattan*
The Stanhope Park Hyatt New York, *Manhattan*

★★★★ Restaurants
Aureole, *Manhattan*
Cafe Boulud, *Manhattan*
Danube, *Manhattan*
The Four Seasons Restaurant, *Manhattan*
Gotham Bar and Grill, *Manhattan*
Gramercy Tavern, *Manhattan*
Kuruma Zushi, *Manhattan*
La Caravelle, *Manhattan*
La Cote Basque, *Manhattan*
La Grenouille, *Manhattan*
Le Bernardin, *Manhattan*
Le Cirque 2000, *Manhattan*
Lutece, *Manhattan*
March, *Manhattan*
Nobu, *Manhattan*
Oceana, *Manhattan*
Picholine, *Manhattan*
Sugiyama, *Manhattan*
Union Pacific, *Manhattan*
Veritas, *Manhattan*

New Jersey

★★★★ Restaurant
Restaurant Serenade, *Chatham*

NEW YORK

Largest of the northeastern states, New York stretches from the Great Lakes to the Atlantic. The falls at Niagara; the gorge of the Genesee, the "Grand Canyon" of the East; the Finger Lakes, carved by glaciers; the Thousand Islands of the St. Lawrence; the Catskills, where Rip Van Winkle is said to have slept for 20 years; the white sand beaches of Long Island; the lakes and forested peaks of the Adirondacks; the stately traprock bluffs along the Hudson—these are a few of the features that attract millions of tourists and vacationers every year.

When Giovanni da Verrazano entered New York Harbor in 1524, the Native Americans of the state were at constant war with one another. But about 1570, under Dekanaw-idah and Hiawatha, they formed the Iroquois Confederacy (the first League of Nations) and began to live in peace. They were known as the Five Nations and called themselves the "Men of Men."

Population: 17,990,456
Area: 54,471 square miles
Elevation: 0-5,344 feet
Peak: Mount Marcy (Essex County)
Entered Union: Eleventh of original 13 states (July 26, 1788)
Capital: Albany
Motto: Ever upward
Nickname: Empire State
Flower: Rose
Bird: Bluebird
Tree: Sugar Maple
Fair: Late August-early September, 2003, in Syracuse
Time Zone: Eastern
Website: www.iloveny.state.ny.us

In 1609 Samuel de Champlain explored the valley of the lake that bears his name, and Henry Hudson sailed up the river that bears his. There was a trading post at Fort Nassau (Albany) in 1614. New Amsterdam (now New York City) was founded in 1625.

Breathtaking Adirondacks scenery

Wars with the Native Americans and French kept the area in turmoil until after 1763. During the Revolutionary War, New York's eastern part was a seesaw of military action and occupation. After the war, Washington was inaugurated president in 1789, and the seat of federal government was established in New York City. As late as 1825, much of New York's central area was swampy wilderness.

Governor DeWitt Clinton envisioned a canal extending from the Hudson River at Albany to Buffalo to develop the state and give needed aid to its western farmers. Started in 1817 and finished in 1825, the Erie Canal became the gateway to the West and was the greatest engineering work of its time, reducing the cost of freight between Buffalo and New York City from $100 to $5 a ton. Enlarged and rerouted, it is now part of the New York State Canal system, 527 miles used mainly for recreational boating.

Industry grew because water power was available; trade and farming grew because of the Erie Canal and its many branches. The state has given the nation four native-born presidents (Van Buren, Fillmore, and both Roosevelts) and two who built their careers here (Cleveland and Arthur).

In addition to being a delightful state in which to tour or vacation, New York has New York City, one of the great cosmopolitan centers of the world.

When to Go/Climate

New York State is large, and the weather is varied. The northern and western parts of the state experience more extreme temperatures—cold, snowy winters and cool summers. Winters are long, especially near the Great Lakes. The Adirondacks, too, can have frigid winters, but fall foliage is magnificent, and summer temperatures and humidity are ideal. Spring thunderstorms frequently travel the Hudson River Valley, and summer here, as well as in New York City and environs, is hot and humid.

AVERAGE HIGH/LOW TEMPERATURES (°F)

NEW YORK CITY

Jan 38/25	**May** 72/54	**Sept** 76/60
Feb 40/27	**June** 80/63	**Oct** 65/50
Mar 50/35	**July** 85/68	**Nov** 54/41
Apr 61/44	**Aug** 84/67	**Dec** 43/31

SYRACUSE

Jan 31/14	**May** 68/46	**Sept** 72/51
Feb 33/15	**June** 77/54	**Oct** 60/41
Mar 43/25	**July** 82/59	**Nov** 48/33
Apr 56/36	**Aug** 79/58	**Dec** 32/21

Parks and Recreation Finder

Directions to and information about the parks and recreation areas below are given under their respective town/city sections. Please refer to those sections for details.

NATIONAL PARK AND RECREATION AREAS

Key to abbreviations. I.H.S. = International Historic Site; I.P.M. = International Peace Memorial; N.B. = National Battlefield; N.B.P. = National Battlefield Park; N.B.C. = National Battlefield and Cemetery; N.C.A. = National Conservation Area; N.E.M. = National Expansion Memorial; N.F. = National Forest; N.G. = National Grassland; N.H.P. = National Historical Park; N.H.C. = National Heritage Corridor; N.H.S. = National Historic Site; N.L. = National Lakeshore; N.M. = National Monument; N.M.P. = National Military Park; N.Mem. = National Memorial; N.P. = National Park; N.Pres. = National Preserve;

CALENDAR HIGHLIGHTS

MARCH

St. Patricks Day Parade (Manhattan). Along Fifth Ave. New York's biggest parade; approximately 100,000 marchers.

APRIL

Central New York Maple Festival (Cortland). A variety of events showing the process of making maple syrup; also arts and crafts, hay rides, and entertainment. Phone 607/849-3812.

MAY

Tulip Festival (Albany). Washington Park. Three-day event. Includes crowning of Tulip Queen. Arts, crafts, food, vendors, children's rides, entertainment. Over 50,000 tulips throughout the park. Phone 518/434-2032.

JULY

Stone House Day (Kingston). In Hurley. Tour of ten privately owned colonial stone houses, led by costumed guides; old Hurley Reformed Church and burying ground; antique show; re-creation of American Revolution military encampment; country fair. Phone 914/331-4121.

Rochester Music Fest (Rochester). Brown Square Park. Three-day celebration of American music. Nationally and internationally known jazz, blues, country, and folk musicians. Phone 800/677-7282.

AUGUST

Erie County Fair (Buffalo). One of the oldest and largest fairs in the nation. Entertainment, rides, games, exhibits, agricultural and livestock shows. Phone 716/649-3900.

US Open Tennis (Queens). The biggest tennis tournament of the year in the United States. Phone box office 718/760-6200.

New York State Fair (Syracuse). State Fairgrounds. The only state fair in New York. Agricultural, animal, and commercial exhibits; midway concerts. Phone 315/487-7711.

SEPTEMBER

Adirondack Canoe Classic (Saranac Lake). Ninety-mile race from Old Forge to Saranac Lake for canoe, kayak, guideboat. Phone Chamber of Commerce, 518/891-1990 or 800/347-1992.

NOVEMBER

NYC Marathon (Manhattan). Major city marathon with more than 25,000 runners. Phone 212/423-2249.

Thanksgiving Day Parade (Manhattan). An R. H. Macy production. Down Broadway to 34th St, from W 77th St and Central Park W. Floats, balloons, television and movie stars. Phone Macy's Special Events, 212/494-4495.

Festival of Lights (Niagara Falls). Downtown. Colored lights, animated displays, decorations, entertainment. Lighting of the Christmas tree. Phone 716/285-2400.

N.R.A. = National Recreational Area; N.R.R. = National Recreational River; N.Riv. = National River; N.S. = National Seashore; N.S.R. = National Scenic Riverway; N.S.T. = National Scenic Trail; N.Sc. = National Scientific Reserve; N.V.M. = National Volcanic Monument.

Place Name	Listed Under
Castle Clinton N.M.	MANHATTAN
Federal Hall N.Mem.	MANHATTAN
Fire Island N.S.	same
Fort Stanwix N.M.	ROME
Gateway N.R.A.	BROOKLYN
General Grant N.Mem. (Grant's Tomb)	MANHATTAN
Hamilton Grange N.Mem.	MANHATTAN
Roosevelt-Vanderbilt N.H.S.	HYDE PARK
Sagamore Hill N.H.S.	OYSTER BAY
Saratoga N.H.	same
Statue of Liberty N.M. and Ellis Island	MANHATTAN
Theodore Roosevelt Birthplace N.H.S.	MANHATTAN
Theodore Roosevelt Inaugural N.H.S.	BUFFALO

STATE PARK AND RECREATION AREAS

Key to abbreviations. I.P. = Interstate Park; S.A.P. = State Archaeological Park; S.B. = State Beach; S.C.A. = State Conservation Area; S.C.P. = State Conservation Park; S.Cp. = State Campground; S.F. = State Forest; S.G. = State Garden; S.H.A. = State Historic Area; S.H.P. = State Historic Park; S.H.S. = State Historic Site; S.M.P. = State Marine Park; S.N.A. = State Natural Area; S.P. = State Park; S.P.C. = State Public Campground; S.R. = State Reserve; S.R.A. = State Recreation Area; S.Res. = State Reservoir; S.Res.P. = State Resort Park; S.R.P. = State Rustic Park.

Place Name	Listed Under
Adirondack Park	same
Allan H. Treman S.M.P.	ITHACA
Allegany S.P.	same
AuSable Point S.P.	PLATTSBURGH
Bear Mountain S.P.	PALISADES INTERSTATE PARKS
Bennington Battlefield S.H.S.	GREENWICH
Bethpage S.P.	BETHPAGE
Bowman Lake S.P.	NORWICH
Burnham Point S.P.	CLAYTON
Buttermilk Falls S.P.	ITHACA
Catskill Park	same
Cayuga Lake S.P.	SENECA FALLS
Cedar Point S.P.	CLAYTON
Chenango Valley S.P.	BINGHAMTON
Chittenango Falls S.P.	CAZENOVIA
Clermont S.H.S.	HUDSON
Coles Creek S.P.	MASSENA
Crown Point S.H.S.	CROWN POINT
Crown Point Reservation S.C.	CROWN POINT
Cumberland Bay S.P.	PLATTSBURGH
Delta Lake S.P.	ROME
Devil's Hole S.P.	NIAGARA FALLS
Evangola S.P.	DUNKIRK
Fair Haven Beach S.P.	OSWEGO

Fillmore Glen S.P.	CORTLAND
Fish Creek Pond S.P.C.	TUPPER LAKE
Fort Niagara S.P.	NIAGARA FALLS
Fort Ontario S.H.S.	OSWEGO
Four Mile Creek S.P.C.	NIAGARA FALLS
Gilbert Lake S.P.	ONEONTA
Glimmerglass S.P.	COOPERSTOWN
Grass Point S.P.	CLAYTON
Green Lakes S.P.	SYRACUSE
Hamlin Beach S.P.	ROCHESTER
Harriman S.P.	PALISADES INTERSTATE PARKS
Herkimer Home S.H.S.	HERKIMER
Hither Hills S.P.	MONTAUK
Jacques Cartier S.P.	OGDENSBURG
James Baird S.P.	POUGHKEEPSIE
John Jay Homestead S.H.S.	MOUNT KISCO
Johnson Hall S.H.S.	JOHNSTOWN
Jones Beach S.P.	same
Keuka Lake S.P.	PENN YAN
Kring Point S.P.	ALEXANDRIA BAY
Lake Eaton S.P.C.	TUPPER LAKE
Lake Erie S.P.	DUNKIRK
Lake Taghkanic S.P.	HUDSON
Letchworth S.P.	same
Long Point on Lake Chautauqua S.P.	BEMUS POINT
Long Point S.P.	WATERTOWN
Lorenzo S.H.S.	CAZENOVIA
Meadowbrook S.P.C.	SARANAC LAKE
Mills Mansion S.H.S.	HYDE PARK
Mills-Norrie S.P.	HYDE PARK
Mine Kill S.P.	STAMFORD
Montauk Point S.P.	MONTAUK
New Windsor Cantonment S.H.S.	NEWBURGH
Niagara Reservation S.P.	NIAGARA FALLS
Olana S.H.S.	HUDSON
Old Erie Canal S.P.	CANASTOTA
Pixley Falls S.P.	BOONVILLE
Putnam Pond S.P.C.	TICONDEROGA (LAKE GEORGE AREA)
Reservoir S.P.	NIAGARA FALLS
Robert H. Treman S.P.	ITHACA
Robert Moses S.P.	same
Rogers Rock S.P.C.	HAGUE
Rollins Pond S.P.C.	TUPPER LAKE
Sackets Harbor Battlefield S.H.S.	SACKETS HARBOR
Sampson S.P.	GENEVA
Schuyler Mansion S.H.S.	ALBANY
Saratoga Spa S.P.	SARATOGA SPRINGS
Selkirk Shores S.P.	OSWEGO
Senate House S.H.S.	KINGSTON
Seneca Lake S.P.	GENEVA

Stony Brook S.P.	HORNELL
Stony Point Battlefield S.H.S.	STONY POINT
Sunken Meadow S.P.	HUNTINGTON
Taconic S.P.	HILLSDALE
Taughannock S.P.	ITHACA
Verona Beach S.P.	ONEIDA
Walt Whitman S.H.S. and Interpretive Center	HUNTINGTON
Washington's Headquarters S.H.S.	NEWBURGH
Waterson Point S.P.	ALEXANDRIA BAY
Watkins Glen S.P.	WATKINS GLEN
Wellesley Island S.P.	ALEXANDRIA BAY
Westcott Beach S.P.	SACKETS HARBOR

Water-related activities, hiking, riding, various other sports, picnicking, and visitor centers, as well as camping, are available in many of these areas. There are more than 200 outdoor state recreation facilities, including state parks, forest preserves, and similar areas. For information on recreation areas within the Adirondack and Catskill forest preserves, contact the Department of Environmental Conservation, 50 Wolf Rd, Albany 12233-4790, phone 518/457-2500. For information on other state parks and recreation areas, contact Office of Parks, Recreation and Historic Preservation, Albany 12238, phone 518/474-0456. The state also provides funds for maintenance of 7,300 miles of trails for snowmobiling. Reservations for all state-operated campgrounds and cabins can be made by calling 800/456-CAMP. There is a $4 fee for boat launching at some state parks. Pets on leash where allowed. The basic fee for camping is $13/night; additional charges for amenities and hookups (electric and sewer). Phone or write for detailed information on individual parks.

SKI AREAS

Place Name	Listed Under
Belleayre Mountain Ski Area	SHANDAKEN
Big Tupper Ski Area	TUPPER LAKE
Bristol Mountain Ski & Snowboard Resort	CANANDAIGUA
Catamount Ski Area	HILLSDALE
Cortina Valley Ski Area	SAUGERTIES
Garnet Hill Ski Lodge	NORTH CREEK
Gore Mountain Ski Area	NORTH CREEK
Greek Peak Ski Area	CORTLAND
Hickory Ski Center	WARRENSBURG
Holiday Mountain Ski Area	MONTICELLO
Hunter Mountain Ski Area	HUNTER
Kissing Bridge Ski Area	EAST AURORA
Labrador Mountain Ski Area	CORTLAND
McCauley Mountain Ski Area	OLD FORGE
Mount Pisgah Municipal Ski Center	SARANAC LAKE
Scotch Valley Resort	STAMFORD
Ski Windham	WINDHAM
Snow Ridge Ski Area	BOONVILLE
Song Mountain Ski Area	CORTLAND
Swain Ski Center	HORNELL
Thunder Ridge Ski Area	BREWSTER
Titus Mountain Ski Area	MALONE

Toggenburg Ski Center	CAZENOVIA
West Mountain Ski Resort	GLENS FALLS
Whiteface Mountian Ski Center	WILMINGTON
White Birches Cross-Country Ski Center	WINDHAM
Willard Mountain Ski Area	GREENWICH
Woods Valley Ski Area	ROME

FISHING AND HUNTING

New York state offers excellent fishing and hunting opportunities, with a wide variety of lengthy seasons. Write or phone for detailed information on fees and regulations. Contact NYS Department of Environmental Conservation, License Sales Office-Room 151, 50 Wolf Rd, Albany 12233-4790, phone 518/457-3521, for the most current fees and a mail order license application and fishing/hunting regulations guides. *The Conservationist* is the department's official illustrated bimonthly periodical on New York State natural resources; contact PO Box 1500, Latham, NY 12110-9983 for subscription ($10/year).

Driving Information

Safety belts are mandatory for all persons in front seat of vehicle. Children under ten years of age must be in an approved passenger restraint anywhere in vehicle: ages four-nine may use a regulation safety belt; age three and under must use an approved safety seat. For further information, phone 518/474-5111.

INTERSTATE HIGHWAY SYSTEM

The following alphabetical listing of New York towns in *Mobil Travel Guide* shows that these cities are within ten miles of the indicated Interstate highways. A highway map should, however, be checked for the nearest exit.

Highway Number	Cities/Towns within ten miles
Interstate 81	Alexandria Bay, Binghamton, Clayton, Cortland, Syracuse, Watertown.
Interstate 84	Brewster, Fishkill, Middletown, Newburgh, Port Jervis.
Interstate 87	Albany, Ausable Chasm, Bolton Landing, Catskill, Diamond Point, Glens Falls, Hartsdale, Hudson, Kingston, Lake George Village, Lake Luzerne, Monroe, Newburgh, New Paltz, New York City, Nyack, Plattsburgh, Poughkeepsie, Rouses Point, Saratoga Springs, Saugerties, Schroon Lake, Spring Valley, Stony Point, Tarrytown, Troy, Warrensburg, Woodstock, Yonkers.
Interstate 88	Bainbridge, Binghamton, Oneonta.
Interstate 90	Albany, Amsterdam, Auburn, Batavia, Buffalo, Canaan, Canajoharie, Canandaigua, Canastota, Dunkirk, Geneva, Herkimer, Ilion, Johnstown, Oneida, Palmyra, Rochester, Rome, Schenectady, Seneca Falls, Syracuse, Troy, Utica, Victor, Waterloo.
Interstate 95	Mamaroneck, White Plains.

Additional Visitor Information

I Love New York Winter Travel & Ski Guide and the *I Love New York Travel Guide* (covering upstate New York, Long Island, and New York City) may be obtained from the State Department of Economic Development, Division of Tourism, PO Box 2603, Albany 12220-0603, phone 518/474-4116 or 800/CALL-NYS (toll-free).

NEW YORK DRIVING TOURS

EXPLORING THE FINGER LAKES REGION

This scenic, rolling region is marked by 11 finger-shaped lakes, named for the tribes of the Six Nations of Iroquois. According to Native American legend, the lakes were formed when God placed his hands on some of the most beautiful land ever created. The landscape features dazzling waterfalls, wild gorges and glens spanned by trestle bridges, steep hills and fairy-tale valleys, spring-fed lakes, sand beaches, and richly forested state parks. Area recreational opportunities include fascinating hiking, boating, and fishing on all 11 lakes.

The towns of the Finger Lakes region have a penchant for classical Greek and Latin names—Romulus, Homer, Etna, Ovid, Camillus, Marcellus, Sparta, Sempronius, Vesper, Scipioville—suggesting rural sophistication and architectural flamboyance. The public buildings and mansions on the wide, shady streets of Ithaca, Skaneateles, Seneca Falls, Penn Yan, Geneva, and Canandaigua celebrate every architectural fad from 1840-1910, including Greek and Gothic revival, Italianate, Georgian, Federal, Queen Anne, Richardsonian Romanesque, Beaux Arts, and Art Deco styles. If architecture isn't your thing, you can attend wine tastings and festivals at local vineyards or learn everything there is to know about enology (the science of winemaking) and viticulture (grape harvesting, fermentation, bottling, riddling racks, French oak barrels, tartrates, and yeasts) by taking the vineyard tours.

From Rochester, head south on Route 96 to Canandaigua, where you will find Sonnenberg Gardens and Mansion and Finger Lakes Race Track. Spend some time exploring the 50-acre estate at Sonnenberg, which includes the 40-room mansion, nine formal gardens, ponds, and a green house conservatory. Continue east on Route 5 to Geneva, which is located on Seneca Lake, the deepest and widest of the Finger Lakes. Seneca Lake is known for its large concentration of lake trout, so this is a great place to cast your fishing lines into the water. If you are traveling over Memorial Day Weekend, you'll catch the National Trout Derby here. Otherwise, head to Seneca Lake State Park, where the kids can take a swim or play at the playground while you try to catch the evening's dinner. From there, follow Route 14 south along Seneca Lake to Penn Yan for a look at the local architecture. The Windmill Farm and Craft Market, where Mennonites arrive in horse and buggy to sell farm produce and hand-made crafts, is also worth a stop. Children will enjoy Fullager Farms Family Farm and Petting Zoo, a working dairy farm that offers such diversions as pony rides, hay rides, and a petting zoo. Farther south on Route 14 is scenic Watkins Glen. Take some time to explore Watkins Glen Gorge, a glacier-made chasm complete with waterfalls. Several foot trails trace the rim of the gorge; stairs and bridges allow you to explore the inside of the chasm. Along the same lines, the nearby town of Montour Falls features 156-foot Chequaga Falls. If you are looking to do more fishing, stop at Catharine Creek where rainbow trout are abundant. From Watkins Glen, head south on 224 and north on 13 to Ithaca on picturesque Cayuga Lake. Visit Cornell Plantations Botanical Gardens, Sapsucker Woods Bird Sanctuary, and Moosewood Café. Those traveling with children might want to check out the Sciencenter, home to over 100 hands-on science exhibits. Take a walk along Sagan Planetwalk, an outdoor scale model of the solar system located on the grounds of Sciencenter—it stretches for almost a mile! Children and adults alike will enjoy a visit to Fall Creek Gorge; the falls here stand almost as high as those at Niagara. This is a good place to pause for a scenic picnic. Round out your tour of the Finger Lakes region by taking 348/90 north and 20 west to Seneca Falls. The big draw here is the Women's Rights National Historic Park, which honors such women's rights activists as Elizabeth Cady Stanton, Amelia Bloomer, Lucretia Mott, and Susan B. Anthony. Return to Rochester via 20 west and 96 west. **(APPROX 220 MI)**

ADIRONDACK PARK

From Albany, take Route 9 north to Glens Falls and Lake George Village. Described as "the most queenly of American lakes," Lake George is 44 square miles of deep blue water dotted with 225 islands; opportunities for water recreation abound in this vacation mecca. Fresh powder awaits winter travelers north on Route 28 at the Gore Mountain Ski Area in North Creek.

Farther north on Route 28 is Adirondack Park, which is bordered by Lake Champlain on the east, the Black River on the west, the St. Lawrence River on the north, and the Mohawk River valley on the south. At six million acres, Adirondack State Park is the largest US Park outside of Alaska (9,000 square miles). Six million acres—that's the size of New Jersey and Rhode Island combined. Just imagine the recreational opportunities available—you could spend days here and not even scratch the surface of all there is to see and do. Whitewater raft on the Hudson, Moose, or Black rivers. Climb one of the 46 peaks in the Adirondack Range. Feeling adventurous? Have a go at Mount Marcy, also known as "Cloud Splitter," which is the highest peak in the range at 5,344 feet. Not a climber? Try canoeing, fishing, or mountain biking instead.

Be sure to make time for a visit to Enchanted Forest/Water Safari (off Route 28 in Old Forge; phone 315/369-6145)—especially if you are traveling with children. After all, there's no better place to spend a hot day than at New York's largest water theme park. Challenging adventure slides are sure to be a hit with older kids, while Tadpole Hole and Pygmy Pond keep the tots cool and happy. Enchanted Forest entertains with the Treetop Skyride and the Enchanted Forest Railroad, and Magical Escapades offers such distractions as bumper cars, a Ferris wheel, and tilt-a-whirl. If that's not enough excitement for one day, stop next door at Calypso's Cove where you will find miniature golf, go-carts, batting cages, bumper boats, and an arcade.

The next stop is Blue Mountain Lake. Take the three-mile trail to the summit of Blue Mountain (3,800 feet) for spectacular views of Adirondack Park. Then head to the Adirondack Museum for a taste of Adirondack history and modes of life. Housed in 20 buildings on 30 acres, the museum also showcases one of the best boat collections in the world, including canoes, steamboats, and the famous Adirondack guide boat.

Head south on Route 28 back to Lake George. Take Route 9N to Bolton Landing and Ticonderoga, home of Fort Mt Hope and Fort Ticonderoga (ca. 1755). Head south on 22 to Whitehall, then follow the Champlain Canal and Hudson River down Route 4. Stop in Saratoga Springs to visit Saratoga National Historical Park, the National Museum of Horse Racing and Hall of Fame, and Saratoga Spa State Park. Continue on Route 4 to return to Albany. **(APPROX 280 MI)**

ESCAPE TO LONG ISLAND

Long Island is a world unto itself—especially off the Long Island Expressway. A mix of city sophistication and rural simplicity, Long Island is a playground for New Yorkers, who find the state parks, wildlife sanctuaries, and small towns refreshing. From New York City, take Southern Parkway 27 to Freeport, then Meadowbrook Parkway south. Stop and visit the beautiful white beaches of Jones Beach State Park for some fun in the sun. Unwind by swimming in the cool waters of the Atlantic, fishing, boating, exploring the nature and bike trails, golfing, or playing softball or shuffleboard. Then continue east on the Parkway along the Atlantic Ocean to JFK Wildlife Sanctuary, Cedar Beach in Gilgo Beach State Park, and Oak Beach. Cross over Robert Moses Bridge for a trip to Robert Moses State Park, located on the western end of Fire Island National Seashore. The pristine white-sand beach here features such amenities as restrooms, showers, lifeguards, concession, and picnic areas. Camping is available farther east at Watch Hill. Ranger-led interpretive canoe programs and nature walks begin at the Watch Hill visitor center. Stop in at the picturesque Fire Island Light Station to visit the ground-floor museum, which houses exhibits on shipwrecks and offshore rescues. (The lighthouse can be toured if reservations are made in advance.) From there, backtrack across the bridge to Robert Moses Causeway. Take Parkway 27A east to Bay Shore to visit 690-acre Bayard Cutting Arboretum. Continue through Islip and East Islip back to Parkway 27 (Sunrise Expressway), connecting with Parkway 27A again to Shinnecock Indian Reservation and Southampton.

One of the oldest English settlements in New York, Southampton was settled in 1640 by colonists from Massachusetts. Today, it is a blue-blood resort, with old, established homes, swanky boutiques, luxurious beach cottages, and Victorian gingerbread mansions along Job's Lane and Main Street. Tour The Olde Halsey House, the oldest English frame house in New York. Parrish Art Museum features 19th- and 20th-century American art, as well as Japanese woodblock prints and changing exhibits. Southampton Historical Museum includes a fantastic collection of Native American artifacts.

Continue on to East Hampton, a fashionable resort town with lots to see and do. Take a guided tour of the 1806 windmill at Hook Mill; visit the Guild Hall Museum for a look at regional art; explore Historic Mulford Farm, a living history farm museum with costumed interpreters; or make an appointment to tour Jackson Pollock's home and studio. The nearby town of Amagansett is home to the Town Marine Museum—sure to be a hit with the anglers in your family. Exhibits explore commercial and sportfishing, whaling, fishing techniques, and underwater archeology. At the very tip of Long Island is Montauk, home to Hither Hills State Park and Montauk Point State Park. Be sure to tour the Montauk Point Lighthouse Museum before taking the Long Island Expressway back to Manhattan. **(APPROX 275 MI)**

THE THOUSAND ISLANDS

From Syracuse, cross the Erie Canal on Route 48. Follow the Oswego Canal route (48 to 481) to the Fort Ontario State Historical Site, where you can explore military life as it was in the 1860s. For more history, head next to the H. Lee White Marine Museum. Continuing on, take 104 east to Mexico Bay, then follow 3 north to Sackets Harbor and Sackets Harbor Battlefield State Historical Site. In nearby Watertown, visit the Sci-Tech Center, a hands-on science museum sure to be a hit with the kids. Ever wonder how maple syrup is made? A visit to the American Maple Museum should answer all your questions about this sweet, sticky stuff. Continue on 12E to Clayton, where three state parks offer swimming, fishing, boating, and camping. Stop in at the Thousand Islands Museum to learn more about the history of this scenic region. The Antique Boat Museum may be of interest to the nautically minded in your group; the Antique Boat Show takes place here in August.

Our last stop is Alexandria Bay and the Thousand Islands. Described by French explorer Count Frontenac as "a Fairyland, that neither pen nor tongue of man may even attempt to describe," these 1,793-odd islands and islets, some only big enough to hold an American flag and others several acres in size, lie along the world's longest unprotected international border. When the International Boundary Commission divided up the islands (1817-1822), Canada got roughly ⅔ of them. The United States got the larger islands, including Wellesley and Grindstone, as well as the deep-water channel to Lake Ontario and the other Great Lakes.

Each of the Thousand Islands in the St. Lawrence River is a little kingdom with a story. On Zavikon, you can see the shortest international bridge in the world. Only ten meters long, the bridge connects a Canadian cottage with an American flag on a pole. On Heart Island, you can tour the melancholy ruins of the half-finished Boldt Castle. Self-made millionaire George Boldt began building the $2,500,000 castle as a gift for his beloved young wife in the 1890s; he abandoned it to ruin when she died in 1904.

What better way to experience the Thousand Islands than out on the water? Boat tours and canoe expeditions explore the sheltered natural wonders of the islands. Sailboat charters and scuba dives are available to see the many shipwrecks off Kingston, including the *Horace Tabor* (1867), a 46-meter sailboat built in Michigan, and the *Steamer Comet* (1848), a 337-ton paddlewheeler built in Portsmouth.

On land, visit the Aqua Zoo (phone 315/482-5771), a privately owned aquarium that displays hundreds of varieties of marine life, including piranhas, alligators, and sharks—oh my! Head up into the air with a hot-air balloon or helicopter ride for gorgeous aerial views of the islands. (**APPROX 215 MI**)

THE HAMPTONS

A series of charming hamlets and pristine villages stud Long Island's east end like jeweled beads strung on a flat, 50-mile-long, farm-green ribbon. These include Bridgehampton, East Hampton, Hampton Bays, Southampton, and Westhampton Beach. Other Hampton communities have less obvious place names: Amagansett, Eastport, East Quogue, Montauk, Sag Harbor, Wainscott, and Water Mill. The strand begins at Eastport—about seventy miles east of Manhattan—and continues eastward out to Montauk on the South Fork, a narrow strip of Long Island bordered by the Atlantic Ocean to the south and by the quiet waters of Peconic Bay and Gardiner's Bay to the north.

The Italian explorer Giovanni da Verrazano first sighted the region in 1524. In 1609, it is likely that Henry Hudson saw it too, but landed instead on western Long Island, closer to what is now New York City. A Dutch trader first stepped ashore at Montauk in 1614, and began to trade with the indigenous Montauket Indians. English settlers, mostly farmers and fishermen, began arriving in 1664 and, during the colonial period that followed, created the wonderful villages that appeal to so many today. Organized around village greens, their shingled saltbox houses have deeply slanted thatched roofs and are separated by low white picket fences. In the 1800s, the whaling, fishing, and ship-building industries flourished and added a new dimension to the trade of the area, especially in the still-scenic port of Sag Harbor, on the northern coast of the South Fork.

The unusual combination of pastoral and marine abundance, along with seaside splendor, attracts an enormously varied population of second-home owners, weekenders, and visitors who join the local farmers, baymen, business owners, and an army of service personnel. Among them are scions, settlers' descendents, trendsetters, has-beens, wannabes, and recognizable names in the worlds of art, communications, design, fashion, finance, industry, media, and politics.

The Hamptons "season" has lengthened beyond its former Memorial Day to Labor Day summer period, although that's unquestionably still the time when beach lovers, boaters, swimmers, surfers, and singles flock eastward. During July and August, the height of the social season, celebrities attract benefactors to charity events, celebrity watchers get an eyeful, and day-trippers seek fun in the sun. During the months before and after summer, there's far less traffic on Route 27 (Montauk Highway, also called Main Street within the villages), the main east/west road.

From early spring through Indian summer, nature lovers hike, ride, boat, walk, shop, and dine in the area's fabulous restaurants (where reservations are recommended year-round). In October, there are vineyards to visit, pumpkins to pick, and Halloween festivals with hayrides, music, and book signings. In times past, shops posted sale signs by late September and closed from fall to spring; now, they are bustling with holiday merchandise in December and filled with shoppers, even on crisp winter weekends. Like many shops, galleries, and antique stores, movies, theatrical performances, and museums are open on weekends from spring until the New Year.

Most visitors drive to the Hamptons from New York City by traveling due east on the Long Island Expressway. Others take the Hampton Jitney (phone 800/936-0440) or the LIRR train (phone 631/231-LIRR or 516/822-LIRR) from Manhattan. Many visitors fly to the Hamptons via Islip MacArthur (ISP) airport on Long Island; JFK International and La Guardia (LGA) in Queens, New York; and Newark Airport in New Jersey (NRK). There are also small, mostly private airfields in Shirley, Westhampton Beach, and East Hampton. Others take ferries to the Hamptons. One ferry departs from Bridgeport, Connecticut and goes to Port Jefferson, Long Island; another departs from New London, Rhode Island via Orient Point to Shelter Island and Sag Harbor; other ferries go to Montauk from Block Island, Newport, New London, and Mystic. Public transportation is ideal for visitors who plan to enjoy the Hamptons mostly on foot or bicycle (taxis are readily available).

WHAT TO SEE AND DO IN THE HAMPTONS

Beaches

The primary Hamptons attraction is the silky-soft, sandy Atlantic Ocean beachfront (the sands facing the bay have a different texture). People head to beaches to walk, jog, and bird-watch and, in some places, to ride; they sunbathe, read, socialize, and play volleyball, and use the beach as a launching pad to swim and surf. The ocean borders one side of the beach; on the other, dusty miller-spotted mounds of dunes separate the beach from stately mansions, grand estates, and private clubs.

Many beaches provide lifeguards, rest rooms, showers, and snack bars; some have volleyball courts. All are open to the public and easily accessible to walkers and bikers. Parking, however, usually requires a vehicular fee for Suffolk County and New York State beaches (and parks with beaches) and a local permit for individual town beaches. (Nonresident permits are available in local communities and some innkeepers even make them available to their guests.)

Natural Parks, Refuges, and Preserves

The rural landscape portrayed by artists who have lived in or visited the Hamptons also lures nature lovers with its sand-swept shores, hiking trails, rivers, ponds, bays, and ocean. Throughout the seasons, about 145 species of birds, including American oystercatchers, greater yellowlegs, egrets and songbirds, terns, willets, and black skimmers can be found on beaches, in nature preserves, and in wildlife refuges. Bird watchers can find endangered piping plovers as well as ospreys in nests on the beaches. Pheasant, geese, wild duck, blue heron, red-tail hawks, and deer also populate nature refuges.

A number of New York State Parks have open camping areas (for the Long Island regional office, phone 631/669-1000 or 631/951-3440); the most popular is Hither Hills State Park, on the ocean in Montauk. Suffolk County Parks span a range from The Theodore Roosevelt County Park (Montauk Highway, Montauk; phone 631/852-7878),which offers horseback riding, biking, canoeing, camping, fishing, seasonal hunting, and beach access, to Shinnecock East County Park (Dune Road, Southampton; phone 631/852-8899), which flanks the eastern border of the Shinnecock Inlet and is a favorite spot for striped bass fishing and outer beach camping. There are parklands in Southampton and East Hampton townships, as well as nature preserves, wildlife refuges, and nature trails. Some of the 28 preserves on the South Fork require a guide to accompany visitors (phone 631/329-7689). The pristine and peaceful Montauk Dunes, Nature and Wildlife Preserves, and hiking trails like the Greenbelt Trail Conference (phone 631/380-0753) are idyllic for hikers.

Boating

The boating season extends more than six months, depending upon the sport, and centers in various harbors, ports, and bays. Offshore fishermen reach the ocean from marinas at the western edge of the Hamptons, at Shinnecock Inlet, and Montauk. Private chartered sportfishing yachts of all sizes, commercial fishing fleets, and public "head" boats are available to visitors. Kayaks, canoes, and small fishing boats are available for rent at many locations, and those who trailer small boats can use public marinas. Sailors dock or moor off Sag Harbor or in Three Mile Harbor and cruise Peconic Bay, Shelter Island; or follow the Atlantic to Block Island, Nantucket, Martha's Vineyard, Cape Cod, or Fire Island.

The Montauk Point Lighthouse

The Montauk Point Lighthouse, the oldest New York State lighthouse, is located within a 724-acre state park at the easternmost point of the South Fork on a site where the Royal Navy used signal bonfires to alert ships during the American Revolution. In 1792, the land, at the edge of a high oceanfront bluff, was purchased for $255.12. The 80-foot sandstone lighthouse, completed in 1796, cost $22,500. Visitors can climb its 137 spiral steps and visit the park's Lost at Sea memorial, museum, and gift shop. Other activities include hiking on the dune-swept nature trails, watching ospreys and bald eagles, and searching for cormorants, loons, and harbor seals.

Farm Stands

Farm-stand shopping is an integral part of Hampton life. Wise shoppers browse the many farm stands for the best produce, including asparagus in May and strawberries in June. Local farms provide a plethora of flowers, homemade pies and jams, and superb fresh produce: berries, peaches, potatoes, greens, melons, pumpkins, and Long Island's succulent white, tiny-kernel sweet corn.

Wineries

When Moses Fournier planted his French grapes during the pre-colonial period, little did he imagine that vintners and visitors would be drawn to the region hundreds of years later for the same qualities that lured him: sunshine and fertile soil. Today, wine tastings and winery tours are popular in the Hamptons, particularly in the fall and on rainy weekends. Winemaking dates back almost 30 years on Long Island, and the region received a special designation as an American Viticultural Area on July 16, 2001. This assures that the grape-growing region has specific, ideal wine-making characteristics, including the right climate and soil conditions. Though there are fewer South Fork wineries than North Fork ones, visiting these wineries is always a pleasant way to spend an afternoon. Channing Daughters Winery (1927 Scuttle Hole Road, Bridgehampton; phone 631/537-7224) is one of the newer wineries and it opened its tasting room in 1998. A large chateau is the home of Duck Walk Vineyards (162 Montauk Highway, Water Mill; phone 631/726-7555) where Dr. Heroditus Damianos of Pindar Vineyards grows local grapes and produces wine. Sagpond Vineyards (Sagg Road, Sagaponack; phone 631/537-5106) was the first winery to produce estate-bottled wines. Finally, Domaine Wolffer Chardonnay is named for its owner, Christian Wolffer, who built a stunning winery where tastings and sales take place under soaring ceilings.

Visitors willing to spend an extra hour (each way) traveling to Long Island's Wine Country on the North Fork will find the experience more than worthwhile. (Beware: this trip can take much longer on busy summer days.) The North Fork's two main roads run for 30 miles west to east, but there are a number of wineries near Greenport. Follow the grape cluster signs on Main Road (Route 25) and on Sound Avenue (North Road/Route 48). Among the top Main Road wineries are Bedell Cellars, Bidwell Vineyards, Corey Creek Vineyards, Gristina Vineyards, Lenz Winery, Paumonok Vineyards, Pellegrini Vineyards, and Pindar Vineyards. Pugliese Vineyards is on Bridge Lane in Cutchogue, one of the many short north/south roads that connects the two east/west arteries. On Sound Avenue, Hargrave Vineyards and Palmer Vineyards offer award-winning selections.

Art in the Hamptons

The history of art in the Hamptons can be traced back to the Montauket and Shinnecock Indians, who transformed seashells into wonderful wampum that they used to trade with 17th-century colonists. By the 1870s, the area's luminous light, fertile farmlands and sandy shores lured painters to a rural countryside that reminded them of Europe. The artists—Winslow Homer, Edwin Austin Abbey, John Twachtman, and William Merritt Chase—called themselves "The Tile Club" and created what became the second-oldest art colony in America. As time passed, artists continued to flock eastward. Childe Hassam arrived in the 1920s. In the 1940s, Jackson Pollock and Lee Krasner, Willem and Elaine de Kooning, and Robert Motherwell reinterpreted the landscape according to their individual sensitivity. Abstract Expression attracted more artists and the first of dozens of art galleries opened. (This first gallery is now known as the Elaine Benson Gallery and Sculpture Garden, on Main Street, Bridgehampton; phone 631/537-5513.) Artists from the New York School displayed their work and exhibitions, including pop artist Larry Rivers, cubist Fernand Leger, abstract painter Harry Kramer, glass artist Dale Chihuly, sculptor Louise Nevelson, ceramist Toshiko Takaezu, and jeweler David Yurman.

Most of the art galleries are found in the villages of Southampton, Westhampton Beach, and, primarily, in East Hampton. On just one tiny passageway between Main Street and the public parking lot in East Hampton, art lovers can stop in to Vered (68 Park Place Passage; phone 631/324-3308) and see work by Marc Chagall, Pablo Picasso, Henri Matisse, Ben Shahn, David Hockney, and Louise Nevelson. The Wallace Gallery, across the passage (37A Main Street; phone 631/329-4516), displays a retrospective of local landscapes and seascapes that reflect the authentic history of the region, including work by east-end artists Edward Lamson Henry, Thomas Moran, and Childe Hassam.

Guild Hall (158 Main Street, East Hampton; phone 631/324-0806) provides exciting lectures, films, music, and live theatrical performances at the John Drew Theater. Its fine art exhibitions often focus on regional artists. Parrish Art Museum, (25 Job's Lane, Southampton; phone 631/283-2118) has the largest public collection of the works of William Merritt Chase and Fairfield Porter. This leading cultural institution offers changing exhibitions, lectures, films, and concerts, as well as children's events. Its sculpture garden and arboretum provide a pleasant refuge from the shops on Job's Lane. Art aficionados flock to the Ossorio Foundation (164 Mariner Drive, Southampton; phone 631/287-2020) and to the Pollock-Krasner House and Study Center (830 Fireplace Road, East Hampton; phone 631/324-4929).

Antiques

There are antique shops all along Route 27A (Montauk Highway, also called Main Street within the villages). Most display desirably timeless English and French country pieces, such as large tables, chests, armoires and side tables. Many shops also specialize in selling wonderful accessories to furnish fabulous (second) homes designed to entertain guests. Happily, there are also dealers who search out rare and exciting American pieces from the 18th and 19th centuries. The villages of Amagansett and Bridgehampton are especially known for their antique shops.

Theater

The area's cultural life is enriched by local performers who appear in productions at the Westhampton Beach Performing Arts Center (Main Street, Westhampton Beach; phone 631/288-1500), John Drew Theatre at Guild Hall (158 Main Street, East Hampton; phone 631/324-0806), and at Bay Street Theater (Sag Harbor; phone 631/725-9500). Mitzi Pazer of Pazer Production presents a series of four staged readings of new plays followed by refreshments at The Playwright's Theatre of East Hampton (LTV Studios, 75 Industrial Road, Wainscott; phone 631/324-5373). What is particularly special about this production is the cast, which has included such actors as Phyllis Newman, Tammy Grimes, and Ben Gazzara.

Historic Attractions

There are 19 historic districts and 65 houses, buildings, and sites (even a wrecked ship) that are listed on the National Register of Historic Places. East Hampton, considered one of America's most beautiful villages, is a fascinating combination of colonial charm and 21st-century sophistication.

It boasts more than luxurious inns, fabulous shops, art galleries, fine restaurants, and theater. Among its many historic attractions is the Hook Windmill at the eastern edge of town. Although crude windmills were built to grind corn as early as 1664, Nathaniel Dominy IV built this one in 1806, and it still stands as a fine example of the many historic windmills built in the area. The East Hampton Historical Society also conducts walking tours that are highly recommended (phone 631/324-6850) and include Home Sweet Home (14 James Lane; phone 631/324-0713), the boyhood home of John Howard Payne, who wrote his famous poem about this darling saltbox house, which was built in 1650.

Sag Harbor, sometimes called the "unhamptony" Hampton because of its low-key ambiance, has a few more shops today, but maintains its port-town ambiance. The Sag Harbor Whaling and Historical Museum is housed in a gracious Greek Revival mansion (Main and Garden streets; phone 631/725-0770) and features a collection of whaling paraphernalia, ship models, a boat collection, artifacts, and toys.

Special Events

Events in the Hamptons range from traditional small-town parades to sophisticated major productions and appeal to a wide variety of interests. Garden lovers plan their trips for the early spring daffodil season when Jack Lenor Larson opens Longhouse to visitors (Hands Creek Road, East Hampton; phone 631/329-3568). The Longhouse Foundation also operates tours, seminars, workshops, and dance and musical performances.

The summer season traditionally begins in mid-May with an emerging artist show at the Elaine Benson Gallery in conjunction with the John Steinbeck Meet the Writers Book Fair. This is an opportunity to meet many of the famous authors who sign and sell their books to benefit Southampton College's John Steinbeck writing program and library. Memorial Day weekend is the annual Potatohampton local Minithon, a 10k run, in Bridgehampton. In June, on a Sunday afternoon, pleasure boats and commercial fishing vessels parade past a reviewing stand in Montauk for the annual Blessing of the Fleet (phone 516-537-0500). Prize fishing tournaments are held in Montauk throughout the fishing season. Traditional parades with schoolchildren and local fire departments march on July 4th, and spectacular fireworks follow in East Hampton and Montauk. Throughout July, there are countless events in the area. Some of the most popular are the Guild Hall Clothesline Art Sale (158 Main Street, East Hampton; phone 631/324-0806), the annual Quilt Show and Sale (Water Mill; phone 631/726-4625) and The Ladies Village Improvement Society Sale (Gardiner Brown House, 95 Main Street; phone 631/324-1220). The "ladies" raise funds to beautify and safeguard the village of East Hampton at a fabulous flea market that is considered one of the summer's main events. In August, the Artists and Writers Softball Game draws crowds to watch the serious celebrities at bat, and people flock to the Lighthouse Weekend in Montauk (phone 631/688-2544), where there's a festival with a variety of events, including big band music, fife and drum corps, and face painting. The Music Festival of the Hamptons (phone 800/644-4418) is a ten-day period of classical music concert performances.

Throughout August, the Bridgehampton Polo Club matches attract crowds. Labor Day weekend is time for two of the area's most important annual events. The Hampton Classic Horse Show (240 Snake Hollow Road off Route 27; phone 631/537-3177) attracts over 40,000 spectators, including horse aficionados, breeders, trainers, riders, fans, and countless celebrities whose family members compete. They gather on the 60-acre show grounds to watch the 1,200 national competitors—including US Equestrian Team championship riders and Olympic veteran jumpers—strut their stuff. The event goes beyond the competition; there's a petting farm and pony care for kids and a boutique garden with 36 vendors. At the Shinnecock Powwow (Montauk Highway, eight miles east of Hampton Bays, two miles east of Southampton village; phone 631/283-6143), Native Americans gather to demonstrate Tribal rituals, dance, artifacts, and crafts. Some traditional Native American dishes are also served.

In mid-October, along with a number of winery events, the annual Hamptons International Film Festival comes to East Hampton (Sag Harbor Cinema, UA Theater, and Guild Hall, East Hampton; phone 631/324-4600). Venues at The Spotlight Film Series show advance screenings of major films. Sometimes, a star introduces the film, such as when Ed Harris introduced *Pollock*, a movie about Jackson Pollock, an artist who lived in the Hamptons. Roger Ebert taught three master classes about *Citizen Kane* in 2001. Major sections of the festival include American Independent Films (feature length narratives and documentaries plus shorts), World Cinema Films, Cuban Films, and a Student Film Competition. One $25,000 prize goes to the international filmmaker who made the best film about conflict and resolution.

Adirondack Park

(B-7) *See also Blue Mountain Lake, Lake George Village, Lake Placid, Long Lake, Old Forge*

(14 mi NW of Amsterdam on NY 30)

The Adirondack Mountains are protected under an 1885 law establishing the forest preserve and an 1892 law creating Adirondack Park. The state now owns more than two and a half million of the nearly six million acres of the park, a wilderness mountain area with streams and lakes. There are 42 public campgrounds of varying size, a 125-mile canoe route from Old Forge to the Saranacs, and 750 miles of marked foot trails among the pines and spruces. Hunting and fishing are permitted under state regulations. Detailed camping information may be obtained from the Department of Environmental Conservation, Bureau of Recreation, 50 Wolf Rd, Rm 679, Albany 12233-5253. Phone 518/457-2500. Standard fees.

Albany

(E-8) *See also Schenectady, Troy*

Settled 1624 **Pop** 95,658 **Elev** 150 ft
Area code 518
Information Albany County Convention and Visitors Bureau, 25 Quackenbush Sq, 12207; 518/434-1217 or 800/258-3582
Web www.albany.org

Albany is situated on the Hudson River, where Henry Hudson ended the voyage of the *Half Moon* in 1609. It was settled by Dutch-speaking Walloons from Holland, Norwegians, Danes, Germans, and Scots during the patronship of Kiliaen Van Rensselaer and was named in honor of the Duke of Kent and Albany when the British took over the city in 1664. Despite the French and Indian War, Albany was a thriving fur-trading center in 1754. Albany's General Philip Schuyler commanded the northern defenses in the Revolution and, according to Daniel Webster, was "second only to Washington in the services he performed for his country."

Albany has been a transportation center since

Jacob's Ladder, Adirondack Park

Native American trail days. Robert Fulton's steamboat, the *Clermont,* arrived here from Jersey City in 1807. The Erie Canal opened in 1825; by 1831, 15,000 canal boats and 500 ocean-going ships crowded Albany's docks.

Politics is a colorful part of the business of New York's capital city. Located on the western bank of the Hudson River and at the crossroads of major state highways, Albany is now a hub of transportation, business, industry, and culture.

What to See and Do

Albany Institute of History and Art. Victorian salon, colonial exhibits, traveling and changing exhibits; Hudson-Mohawk Valley paintings and sculpture; contemporary art; changing exhibits and programs promote fine arts as well as regional history; research library with archival material. (Wed-Sun, closed hols) 125 Washington Ave, 1 blk W of capitol. Phone 518/463-4478. **FREE** ¢¢

Crailo State Historic Site. Eighteenth-century Dutch house, now a museum of Dutch culture in the Hudson Valley. Exhibits and audiovisual presentation explain the history and development of Dutch settlements in America. (Early-Apr-Oct, Wed-Sun) 9½ Riverside Ave in Rensselaer, 1½ blks S of US 9 and 20. Phone 518/463-8738. ¢¢

Dutch Apple Cruises Inc. Scenic cruises on the Hudson River with view of the Capital District. Sightseeing, dinner/entertainment, and Sun brunch cruises (by appt). (May-Oct, daily) Broadway at Quay. Contact PO Box 395, 12201-0395. Phone 518/463-0220. ¢¢

Empire State Plaza. A 98-acre, 11-building complex providing office space for state government, cultural, and convention facilities; New York State Modern Art Collection on view. On 42nd floor is the Tower Building observation deck (daily). NY State Thrwy, exit 23. Phone 518/474-2418. **FREE**

Historic Cherry Hill. (1787) Georgian-style farmhouse built for Philip Van Rensselaer, a prominent merchant farmer. Lived in by four generations of descendants until 1963. Nine period rms of original furnishings and personal belongings from the 18th-20th centuries. Gardens. Tours (Tues-Sun; closed hols, Jan). 523½ S Pearl St. Phone 518/434-4791. ¢¢

New York State Museum. Life-size dioramas, photo murals, and thousands of objects illustrate the relationship between people and nature in New York State. Three major halls detailing life in metropolitan New York, the Adirondacks, and upstate New York. Special exhibits of photography, art, history, nature, science, and Native Americans. Working carousel. Memorial to the World Trade Center. Cafeteria. Entertainment, classes, and films. (Daily; closed Jan 1, Thanksgiving, Dec 25) Empire State Plaza, Cultural Education Center. Phone 518/474-5877. **Donation**

Rensselaerville. Village, established in 1787, has restored homes, inns, churches, gristmill. Nature preserve and biological research station. Also here is the Rensselaerville Institute, offering cultural programs and a conference center for educational and business meetings. 27 mi SW via NY 443 to end of NY 85. Phone 518/797-3783.

Schuyler Mansion State Historic Site. (1761) Georgian mansion, home of Philip Schuyler, general of the Revolutionary War and US senator. Alexander Hamilton married Schuyler's daughter here, and other prominent early leaders visited here. Tours (fee). (Apr-Oct Wed-Sun; closed hols exc Memorial Day, July 4, Labor Day) 32 Catherine St. Phone 518/434-0834. ¢¢

Shaker Heritage Society. Located on the site of the first Shaker settlement in America. Grounds, 1848 Shaker Meeting House, orchard, and cemetery where founder Mother Ann Lee is buried. Gift shop. Tours (by appt). (Tues-Sat) Albany-Shaker Rd. Phone 518/456-7890. ¢

State Capitol. A $25,000,000 granite "French" chateau. Legislative session begins the Wed after the first Mon in Jan. Guided tours (daily). Phone 518/474-2418. **FREE**

Ten Broeck Mansion. (1798) Brick Federal house with Greek Revival additions; built by General Abraham Ten Broeck, it was also the home of the prominent Olcott family. Contains collection of period furniture, fine arts, three period bathrms (1890s), and changing exhibits of the Albany County Historical Association; also lawn and herb garden during summer. (May-Dec, Thurs-Sun afternoons; closed hols) 9 Ten Broeck Pl. Phone 518/436-9826. ¢¢

University at Albany, State University of New York. (1844) 13,000 students. A 382-acre campus; art gallery; performing arts center; one million-volume library; nuclear accelerator; atmospheric science research center; carillon tower. Between Washington and Western aves, E of NY State Thrwy exit 24. Phone 518/442-3300.

Special Events

Tulip Festival. Washington Park. Willett St between State St and Madison Ave. Mother's Day wkend. Phone 518/434-2032.

First Night. Celebration of the arts with music performances and fireworks to welcome the new yr. Dec 31. Phone 518/434-2032.

Motels/Motor Lodges

★★ **BEST WESTERN AIRPORT.** *200 Wolf Rd (12205). 518/458-1000; fax 518/458-2807; res 800/528-1234. www.bestwestern.com.* 153 rms, 2 story. S, D $65-$109; each addl $10; under 18 free; wkly, wkend, hol rates. Crib free. TV; cable (premium), VCR avail. Indoor pool. Restaurant 6:30 am-10 pm. Bar 2:30 pm-midnight. Ck-out noon. Meeting rms. Business servs avail. In-rm modem link. Bellhops. Health club privileges. Free airport transportation. Cr cds: A, D, DS, MC, V.

⬛ 🐾 🏋 ⏏ ✈ 🖾 🔥

★★ **BEST WESTERN SOVEREIGN HOTEL-ALBANY.** *1228 Western Ave (12203). 518/489-2981; fax 518/489-8967; res 800/528-1234. www.bestwestern.com.* 195 rms, 5 story. S $95-$105; D $105-$115; each addl $10; suites $150-$195; under 18 free; wkend plan; higher rates special events. Crib free. Pet accepted. TV; cable (premium). Indoor pool. Complimentary full bkfst. Coffee in rms. Restaurant 6:30 am-10 pm. Rm serv 5-9 pm. Bar. Ck-out noon. Meeting rms. Business servs avail. In-rm modem link. Valet serv. Beauty shop. Exercise equipt; sauna. Microwave in suites. Cr cds: A, C, D, DS, ER, JCB, MC, V.

⬛ 🐾 ⏏ 🏋 ✈ 🖾 🔥 SC

★★ **COMFORT INN AND SUITES.** *1606 Central Ave (12205). 518/869-5327; fax 518/456-8971; res 800/228-5150. www.comfortinn.com.* 53 rms. S, D $75; suite $75-$395; under 15 free. Crib free. TV; cable (premium). Complimentary continental bkfst. Restaurant nearby. Meeting rms. Business servs avail. In-rm modem link. Sundries. Exercise equipt. Some refrigerators; microwaves avail. Cr cds: A, C, D, DS, MC, V.

⬛ ⏏ 🏋 ✈ 🖾 🔥 SC

★★ **COURTYARD BY MARRIOTT ALBANY AIRPORT.** *168 Wolf Rd (12205). 518/482-8800; fax 518/482-*

State Capitol, Albany

0001; toll-free 800/321-2211. 78 rms, 3 story. S, D $79-$119; under 18 free. Crib free. TV; cable (premium). Indoor pool. Complimentary coffee in rms. Ck-out noon. Coin lndry. Meeting rms. Business servs avail. In-rm modem link. Valet serv. Sundries. Free airport transportation. Exercise equipt. Refrigerator avail. Cr cds: A, D, DS, MC, V.

⊡ ⇌ 🏋 ⇲ 🔥

★ **ECONO LODGE.** *110 Columbia Tpke, Rensselaer (12144). 518/472-1360; fax 518/427-2924; toll-free 800/477-3123. www.econolodge.com.* 35 rms, 3 kits. S $35-$74; D $39-$89; kit. units $165-$300/wk; higher rates special events. Crib free. TV; cable (premium). Complimentary continental bkfst. Restaurant adj. Ck-out 11 am. Coin lndry. Business servs avail. In-rm modem link. Refrigerators. Cr cds: A, DS, MC, V.

⇲ 🔥

★★★ **GREGORY HOUSE COUNTRY INN.** *Rte 43, Averill Park (12018). 674/674-3774; fax 674/674-8916. www.gregoryhouse.com.* 12 rms, 2 story. S $80-$90; D $85-$95; each addl $5-$10. TV in common rm; cable. Pool. Complimentary continental bkfst. Restaurant (see GREGORY HOUSE). Bar. Ck-out 11 am, ck-in 2 pm. Fireplace in common rm; Oriental rugs, antiques. Some balconies. Cr cds: A, C, D, DS, ER, MC, V.

⇌ 🔥

★★ **HAMPTON INN ALBANY-WOLF ROAD.** *10 Ulenski Dr (12205). 518/438-2822; fax 518/438-2931; toll-free 800/426-7866. www.hamptoninn.com.* 154 rms, 5 story. S, D $87-$94; under 18 free; higher rates special events. Crib free. TV; cable (premium). Pool. Complimentary continental bkfst. Restaurant adj 6 am-midnight. Ck-out noon. Coin lndry. Business servs avail. In-rm modem link. Free airport transportation. Health club privileges. Cr cds: A, C, D, DS, MC, V.

⊡ ⇌ ⇲ 🔥 SC

★★ **HOLIDAY INN ALBANY-TURFON WOLF ROAD.** *205 Wolf Rd (12205). 518/458-7250; fax 518/458-7377; toll-free 800/465-4329. www.holidayinnturf.com.* 309 rms, 2-6 story. S, D $129; suites $150; under 19 free;

some wkend rates; higher rates: Aug, special events. Crib free. TV; cable. 2 pools, 1 indoor; whirlpool, lifeguard. Restaurant 6 am-midnight. Rm serv 6 am-10 pm. Bar 11:30-2 am. Ck-out noon. Meeting rms. Convention facilities. Business servs avail. In-rm modem link. Bellhops. Valet serv. Sundries. Gift shop. Barber, beauty shop. Airport transportation. Lighted tennis. Exercise equipt; sauna. Game rm. Some in-rm whirlpools; refrigerators avail. Cr cds: A, DS, MC, V.

⊡ 🏃 ⇌ 🏋 ✈ ⇲ 🔥

★ **HOWARD JOHNSON .** *416 Southern Blvd (12209). 518/462-6555; fax 518/462-2547; res 518/462-6555. www.hojo.com.* 135 rms, 1-2 story. S $65; D $75; each addl $8; suites $95; under 18 free. Crib free. Pet accepted, some restrictions. TV; cable (premium). Pool; lifeguard. Restaurant open 24 hrs. Bar from 11 am. Ck-out noon. Coin lndry. Meeting rms. Business servs avail. Valet serv. Indoor tennis privileges, pro. Exercise rm. Private patios, balconies. Cr cds: A, D, DS, MC, V.

🏃 ⇲ ⊡ 🐾 ⇌ 🏋 🔥

★ **MICROTEL INN.** *7 Rensselaer Ave, Latham (12110). 518/782-9161; fax 518/782-9162; res 888/771-7171. www.microtelinn.com.* 100 rms, 2 story. S $50-$89; D $53-$89; under 14 free. Crib free. Pet accepted, some restrictions. TV; cable (premium). Complimentary coffee in lobby. Restaurant nearby. Ck-out noon. Meeting rm. Business servs avail. In-rm modem link. Sundries. Some refrigerators; microwaves avail. Cr cds: A, C, D, DS, MC, V.

🐾 ✈ ⇲ 🔥

★★ **RAMADA LIMITED.** *1630 Central Ave (12205). 518/456-0222; fax 518/452-1376; toll-free 800/354-0223. www.ramadaatalbany.com.* 105 rms, 2 story. July-Aug: S $62-$80; D $72-$85; under 18 free; lower rates rest of yr. Crib free. Pet accepted; $50 deposit. TV; cable (premium), VCR (movies). Complimentary continental bkfst, coffee in rms. Restaurant nearby. Ck-out noon. Meeting rms. Business servs avail. Beauty shop. Exercise equipt. Some in-rm whirlpools, refrigerators, microwaves. Cr cds: A, C, D, DS, JCB, MC, V.

⊡ 🐾 🏋 ⇲ 🔥 SC

Hotels

★★★ THE CENTURY HOUSE
HOTEL. *997 New London Rd, Latham (12110). 518/785-0931; fax 518/785-3274; toll-free 888/674-6873. www.the centuryhouse.com.* 68 rms, 2 story. S $95-$129; D $105-$129; each addl $12; suites $125-$225; under 12 free; higher rates: Saratoga racing season, special events. Crib avail. Pet accepted, some restrictions; $5. TV; cable (premium). Pool. Complimentary bkfst buffet. Restaurant 11 am-9:45 pm; Sat 4-10 pm; Sun noon-9 pm. Rm serv 4-9:30 pm. Bar 11 am-11 pm. Ck-out noon. Meeting rms. Business servs avail. In-rm modem link. Valet serv. Tennis. Exercise equipt. Nature trail. Some refrigerators; microwaves avail. Cr cds: A, C, D, DS, MC, V.

★★★ CROWNE PLAZA HOTEL.
State and Lodge Sts (12207). 518/462-6611; fax 518/462-8192. www.bass hotels.com. 386 rms, 15 story. S $95-$155; D $95-$185; each addl $20; suites $125-$450; family, wkend rates. Crib free. Pet accepted; $50. TV; cable, VCR avail. Indoor pool; whirlpool. Coffee in rms. Restaurant 7 am-2 pm, 5-10 pm. Rm serv to noon. Bar 11:30-1 am. Ck-out noon. Meeting rms. Business servs avail. In-rm modem link. Shopping arcade. Covered parking. Free airport, RR station, bus depot transportation. Exercise equipt. Some refrigerators. Cr cds: A, C, D, DS, ER, JCB, MC, V.

★★★ MARRIOTT ALBANY. *189 Wolf Rd (12205). 518/458-8444; fax 518/458-7365; res 800/228-9290.* 359 rms, 7-8 story. S, D $84-$168; suites $250-$350; wkend rates. Crib free. Pet accepted. TV; cable (premium), VCR avail (movies). 2 heated pools, 1 indoor; whirlpool, poolside serv, lifeguard. Restaurant 6:30 am-10 pm. Bar; entertainment wkends. Ck-out noon. Coin lndry. Convention facilities. Business center. In-rm modem link. Gift shop. Free airport transportation. Exercise equipt; sauna. Health club privileges. Refrigerators avail. Luxury level. Cr cds: A, C, D, DS, ER, JCB, MC, V.

B&B/Small Inn

★★ MANSION HILL INN. *115 Philip St at Park Ave (12202). 518/465-2038; fax 518/434-2313; toll-free 888/299-0455. www.mansionhill.com.* 8 rms, 2 story. S $125-$165; D $145-$175; under 17 free; wkend rates. Crib free. Pet accepted. TV; cable (premium), VCR avail (movies). Complimentary full bkfst. Restaurant (see MANSION HILL). Rm serv 5-9 pm. Ck-out 11:30 am, ck-in 4 pm. Luggage handling. Valet serv. Concierge serv. RR station, bus depot transportation. Health club privileges. Cr cds: A, C, D, DS, MC, V.

Conference Center

★★★ DESMOND HOTEL & CONFERENCE CENTER. *660 Albany Shaker Rd (12211). ; fax 518/869-7659; toll-free 800/448-3500. www. desmondhotels.com.* 321 rms, 1-4 story. S $139; D $149; suites $139-$219; under 18 free; wkend rates. Crib free. TV; cable (premium). 2 indoor pools; whirlpool. Coffee in rms. Restaurant 6:30 am-midnight (see also SCRIMSHAW). Bar 11:30-2 am. Ck-out noon. Convention facilities. Business servs avail. In-rm modem link. Bellhops. Valet serv. Concierge. Sundries. Gift shop. Free airport transportation. Exercise equipt; sauna. Game rm. Refrigerators avail. Private patios, balconies. Cr cds: A, C, D, DS, MC, V.

Restaurants

★ BONGIORNO'S. *23 Dove St (12210). 518/462-9176.* Italian menu. Specialties: scaloppine, saltimbocca, pollo cacciatore. Hrs: 11:30 am-2:30 pm, 5-9 pm; Thurs-Sat to 10 pm. Closed Sun; hols. Res accepted. Bar. Lunch $4.75-$9.50, dinner $8.95-$20. Child's menu. Cr cds: A, C, D, ER, MC, V.

★★ CRANBERRY BOG. *56 Wolf Rd (12205). 518/459-5110. www.cranbog. com.* Specializes in steak, fresh seafood, veal. Hrs: 11:30 am-10 pm; Sun 10:30 am-1:30 pm, 4-9 pm; Sun brunch to 1:30 pm. Closed Jan 1, July 4. Res accepted. Bar to 1 am.

Lunch $5.95-$12.95, dinner $12.95-$29.95. Sun brunch $13.95. Child's menu. Entertainment Mon-Sat. Parking. Outdoor dining. Family-owned. Cr cds: A, D, DS, MC, V.

[D] [SC] [⊡]

★★ **DAKOTAS.** *579 Troy Schnectedy Rd, Latham (12110). 518/786-1234. www.dakotarestaurant.com.* Specializes in steak, seafood. Salad bar. Hrs: 4:30-10 pm; Fri to 11 pm; Sat 4-11 pm; Sun 1-9 pm. Bar. Dinner $7.95-$21.95. Child's menu. Rustic decor with hunting lodge theme. Native American artifacts. Cr cds: A, D, DS, MC, V.

[D]

★★★ **GREGORY HOUSE.** *NY 43, Averill Park (12018). 518/674-3774. www.gregoryhouse.com.* Continental menu. Specializes in veal, lamb, seafood. Own baking. Hrs: 5-9 pm; Sun 4-8 pm. Closed Mon; Dec 24-26. Res accepted; required wkends. Bar. Dinner $15.95-$23.95. Parking. Built 1830. Cr cds: A, C, D, DS, ER, MC, V.

★★★ **JACK'S OYSTER HOUSE.** *42 State St (12207). 518/465-8854.* Specializes in seafood, vegetarian dishes, Angus beef. Hrs: 11:30 am-10 pm. Res accepted. Bar. A la carte entrees: lunch $4.95-$9.95, dinner $10.95-$17.95. Child's menu. Parking. Albany's oldest landmark restaurant. Family-owned. Cr cds: A, DS, MC, V.

[D] [⊡]

★★★ **LA SERRE.** *14 Green St (12207). 518/463-6056.* Continental menu. Specialties: medallions of veal, rack of lamb, fresh grilled fish. Own baking. Hrs: 11:30 am-2:30 pm, 5-9 pm; Sat, Sun from 5 pm. Res accepted Sat, Sun (dinner). Bar. Lunch $6.95-$9.95, dinner $12.95-$22.95. Child's menu. Outdoor dining. Built 1829; formerly a stove factory. Cr cds: A, D, MC, V.

[D] [SC] [⊡]

★★ **L'ECOLE ENCORE.** *337 Fuller Rd (12203). 518/437-1234.* Continental menu. Specialties: artichokes French, chicken broccoli strudel, angel hair shrimp fra diavalo. Hrs: 11:30 am-3 pm, 5-10 pm; Sat from 5 pm; Sun 4-9 pm. Closed hols. Res accepted. Bar. Lunch $6.95-$9.95, dinner $14.95-$20.95. Jazz Thurs. Parking. Outdoor dining. Casual dining with intimate atmosphere. Cr

cds: A, DS, MC, V.

[⊡]

★★★ **MANSION HILL.** *115 Philip St (12205). 518/465-2038. www.mansion hill.com.* Specializes in seasonal, vegetarian and pasta dishes. Hrs: 5-9 pm. Closed Sun; hols. Res accepted. Bar. Wine list. Dinner $13-$21. Child's menu. Outdoor dining. In 1861 building. Cr cds: A, D, DS, MC, V.

[D]

★★★ **OGDEN'S.** *42 Howard St (12207). 518/463-6605.* Continental menu. Specializes in fresh seafood, veal, aged Angus steak. Hrs: 11:30 am-9 pm; Sat from 5:30 pm. Closed Sun; hols. Res accepted. Bar. Wine list. Lunch $5.95-$11.95, dinner $15.95-$24.95. Restored historic building (1903); oak woodwork. Cr cds: A, MC, V.

[⊡]

★★★ **SCRIMSHAW.** *660 Albany-Shaker Rd (12211). 518/869-8100. www.desmondny.com.* Continental menu. Specialties: steak au poivre, shrimp scampi, veal Oscar. Hrs: 5:30-10 pm. Closed Sun; Memorial Day, July 4, Labor Day, Dec 25. Res accepted. Bar. Wine list. Dinner $16-$25. Child's menu. Pianist. Parking. Nautical theme; Colonial atmosphere. Jacket. Cr cds: A, DS, MC, V.

[D]

★★★ **SHIPYARD.** *95 Everett Rd (12205). 518/438-4428.* Specializes in fresh fish, rack of lamb, beef tenderloin. Hrs: 5-9:30 pm; Sat, Sun 5-9 pm. Closed hols. Res accepted. Bar. Wine list. Dinner $12.95-$23. Prix fixe: dinner $20-$25. Parking. Country garden elegence. Cr cds: A, D, DS, MC, V.

[D] [⊡]

★ **VEEDER'S.** *2020 Central Ave (12205). 518/456-1010.* Continental menu. Specializes in leg of lamb, prime rib, scallops. Hrs: 11:30 am-9 pm; Sun noon-8 pm; early-bird dinner 4-7 pm. Closed Mon; Dec 24. Res accepted. Lunch $4.95-$7.50, dinner $8.50-$18. Child's menu. Parking. Family-owned. Cr cds: A, DS, MC, V.

[⊡]

★★★ **YONO'S.** *64 Colvin Ave (12206). 518/436-7747. www.yonos center.com.* Indonesian, continental menu. Specialties: sate, shrimp simmered in coconut milk, chicken au pistaches. Own desserts. Hrs: 5:30-10 pm. Closed Sun, Mon; Thanksgiving, Dec 25. Res accepted. Bar to midnight. Dinner $13.95-$21.95. Complete meals: dinner $32.50. Entertainment Fri. Outdoor dining. Cr cds: A, C, D, DS, ER, MC, V.

D SC

Alexandria Bay (Thousand Islands)

(B-5) *See also Clayton (Thousand Islands), Kingston*

Pop 1,088 **Elev** 284 ft **Area code** 315 **Zip** 13607

Information Chamber of Commerce, 11 Market St, Box 365; 315/482-9531, 800/541-2110, or 888-HEART-TI

Web www.alexbay.org

Resort center of the Thousand Islands, Alexandria Bay overlooks a cluster of almost 1,800 green islands divided by intricate waterways. The islands range in size from a few square inches, a handful of rocks with a single tree, to several miles in length.

What to See and Do

Boat Trips.

Rockport Boat Lines. A one-hr tour through the islands. (May-Oct, daily) 2 mi E of Thousand Islands International Bridge, off Thousand Islands Pkwy E in Rockport, Ontario. Phone 613/659-3402.

Uncle Sam Boat Tours. Two-hr cruises wind through scenic islands; dinner and luncheon cruises (May-Oct). All tours stop at Boldt Castle. 47 James St. Phone 315/482-2611.

Boldt Castle. George C. Boldt came from Prussia in the 1860s and became the most successful hotel magnate in America, managing the Waldorf-Astoria in New York City and owning the Bellevue-Stratford in Philadelphia. The castle was a

$2,500,000 present to his wife, who died in 1904; the castle was never completed. Other structures here incl the dove cote, which housed fancy fowl; Italian garden, Alster Tower power house, and the yacht house. (Fee) Slide show in main castle; craft demonstrations and exhibits on first floor. (Mid-May-early Oct) On Heart Island. Phone 315/482-9724. ¢¢

Kring Point State Park. Swimming beach, bathhouse, fishing, boating (launch, dock); picnicking, cabins, tent and trailer sites, x-country skiing. (Early May-Columbus Day) Standard fees. 6 mi NE on NY 12, then W on Kring Point Rd. Phone 315/482-2444.

Thousand Islands Skydeck. Between the spans of the Thousand Islands International Bridge, on Hill Island, Lansdowne, Ontario. (See GANANOQUE, ONTARIO) Phone 613/659-2335.

Wellesley Island. On the island are three state parks: **Wellesley Island.** Swimming beach, bathhouse, fishing, boating (ramp, marina); nature center, hiking, golf, x-country skiing, snowmobiling, picnicking, playground, concession, trailer sites. Standard fees. **DeWolf Point.** Swimming, fishing, boating (ramp); tent and trailer sites, cabins. Standard fees. **Waterson Point.** Accessible only by boat. Fishing, boat anchorage; camping, picnicking. Across Thousand Islands International Bridge. Phone 315/482-2722.

Motels/Motor Lodges

★★ **CAPTAIN THOMSON'S RESORT ALEXANDRIA.** *45 James St, Alexandria Bay (13607). 315/482-9961; fax 315/482-5013; toll-free 800/253-9229. www.captthomsons. com.* 117 rms, 2 story, 2 kits. Mid-June-Labor Day: S $65-$104; D $76-$115; each addl $10; kit. units $165; under 12 free; lower rates May-mid-June and after Labor Day-Oct. Closed rest of yr. Crib free. TV; cable, VCR avail. Pool; wading pool. Restaurant 7 am-10 pm. Ck-out 11 am. Balconies. On seaway; dock. Cr cds: A, DS, MC, V.

🐕 ⇌ 🚫 🔥

★ **LEDGES RESORT MOTEL ALEXANDRIA BAY.** *71 Anthony St,*

Alexandria Bay (13607). 315/482-9334; fax 315/482-9334. www. thousandislands.com/ledges. 27 rms. Late June-Labor Day: D $88-$108; each addl $8; lower rates early May-late June and after Labor Day-mid-Oct. Closed rest of yr. Crib $8. Pet accepted. TV; cable. Heated pool. Restaurant adj 7:30-11 am, noon-2 pm, 5-10 pm. Ck-out 11 am. Free bus depot transportation. Refrigerators avail. Picnic tables, grills. Private dock. Cr cds: A, C, D, DS, MC, V.

★ **ROCK LEDGE MOTEL, COT-TAGES & EFFICIENCY.** *NY Rte 12, Alexandria Bay (13607). 315/482-2191; toll-free 800/977-9101. www. rockledgemotel.com.* 14 motel rms, 6 cabins. Late June-mid-Sept: S $30-$68; D $40-$68; cabins $35-$55; lower rates mid-Apr-late June and mid-Sept-mid-Oct. Closed rest of yr. TV; cable. Complimentary continental bkfst. Restaurant nearby. Ck-out 11 am. Cr cds: DS, MC, V.

Resorts

★★★ **BONNIE CASTLE HOTEL & RESORT.** *Outer Holland St, Alexandria Bay (13607). 315/482-4511; fax 315/482-9600; toll-free 800/955-4511. www.bonniecastle.com.* 129 rms, 1-3 story. No elvtr. Mid-May-Labor Day: S, D $89-$185; each addl $10; suites $119-$275; under 12 free; lower rates rest of yr. TV; cable (premium). 2 pools, 1 indoor; whirlpool. Complimentary coffee in rms. Restaurant 7 am-2 pm, 5-10 pm (see also BONNIE CASTLE MANOR). Bar noon-2 am; entertainment. Ck-out 11 am, ck-in 2 pm. Business servs avail. Bellhops. Concierge. Sundries. Gift shop. Airport transportation. Tennis. Golf privileges, driving range. Exercise equipt; sauna. Miniature golf. Refrigerators, bathrm phones; some in-rm whirlpools. Private patios, balconies. Built circa 1875; extensive grounds; on river, boat dockage. Cr cds: A, C, D, DS, ER, MC, V.

★ **EDGEWOOD RESORT.** *Edgewood Park Dr, Alexandria Bay (13607). 315/482-9922; fax 315/482-5210; toll-free 800/334-3996.* 160 rms, 1-2 story. Mid-May-Labor Day: S, D $79-$149; each addl $10; suites $250; lower

rates rest of yr. Crib free. TV. Pool; poolside serv. Playground. Restaurant 7 am-10 pm. Bar noon-2 am; entertainment. Meeting rms. Ck-out 11 am. Business servs avail. Sundries. Gift shop. Lawn games. Many balconies; some private patios. Built 1886; extensive grounds on riverfront; boat tours. Cr cds: A, D, DS, MC, V.

★ **NORTH STAR RESORT.** *116 Church St, Alexandria Bay (13607). 315/482-9332; fax 315/482-5825; toll-free 877/417-7827. www.northstar resort.com.* 70 rms. S $29-$89; D $39-$109; each addl $10. Crib $10. Pet accepted. TV; cable. Pool. Playground. Restaurant 6 am-9 pm. Ck-out 11 am. Some refrigerators. Boat launch, docks. Cr cds: A, DS, MC, V.

★★ **PINE TREE POINT RESORT.** *70 Anthony St, Alexandria Bay (13607). 315/482-9911; fax 315/482-6420; toll-free 888/756-3229. www.pinetreepoint resort.com.* 83 rms in resort and chalets. July-Labor Day: S, D $65-$145; each addl $10; suites $190; under 12 free; lower rates May-June and after Labor Day-Oct. Closed rest of yr. TV; cable, VCR avail (movies). Pool; whirlpool. Sauna. Restaurant 7 am-2 pm, 6-10 pm. Bar noon-2 am; entertainment. Ck-out 11 am. Meeting rms. Business servs avail. Bellhops. Sundries. Gift shop. Valet parking. Lawn games. Many balconies. Dockage. Cr cds: A, C, D, DS, MC, V.

★★★ **RIVEREDGE RESORT HOTEL.** *17 Holland St, Alexandria Bay (13607). 315/482-9917; fax 315/482-5010; toll-free 800/365-6987. www. riveredge.com.* 129 rms, 4 story. June-Labor Day: S, D $174-$218; each addl $20; suites $178-$238; under 12 free; AP, MAP avail; ski, golf plans; lower rates rest of yr. Crib free. Pet accepted. TV; cable. 2 pools, 1 indoor; whirlpool, poolside serv. Dining rm 6:30 am-10 pm (see also JACQUES CARTIER). Bar 11-2 am; entertainment. Ck-out 11 am, ck-in 3 pm. Grocery, package store 1 blk. Coin lndry. Convention facilities. Business servs avail. Bellhops. Valet serv. Concierge. Gift shop. 9-hole golf privileges. Boats, dockage, water-

skiing. X-country ski 5 mi. Snowmobiling, sleighing. Hiking. Lawn
games. Exercise equipt; sauna. Massage. Fishing/hunting guides. Bathrm
phones, minibars. Balconies. On
river. Luxury level. Cr cds: A, C, D,
DS, MC, V.

Restaurants

★ ★ **ADMIRALS' INN.** *20 James St,
Alexandria Bay (13607).* 315/482-
2781. Specializes in prime rib, fresh
fish, fresh roasted turkey. Hrs: 11 am-
10 pm; Fri, Sat to 11 pm; Sun to 9
pm. Closed Oct-Mar. Res accepted.
Bar to 2 am. Lunch $3.50-$8.95, dinner $8.95-$25.95. Child's menu. Outdoor dining. Victorian house;
nautical theme, antiques. Cr cds: A,
C, D, DS, ER, MC, V.

★ ★ ★ **BONNIE CASTLE MANOR.**
Holland St, Alexandria Bay (13607).
315/482-4511. www.bonniecastle.com.
Continental menu. Specializes in
prime rib, seafood, veal. Own baking.
Hrs: 7 am-2 pm, 5-10 pm; Fri, Sat to
11 pm. Closed Dec 25. Res accepted.
Bar noon-2 am. Wine list. Bkfst
$4.95-$12.95, lunch $5.95-$12.95,
dinner $13.95-$21.95. Child's menu.
Entertainment. Outdoor dining
(lunch). View of river. Cr cds: A, C,
D, DS, ER, MC, V.

★ ★ **CAVALLARIO'S STEAK &
SEAFOOD HOUSE.** *24 Church St,
Alexandria Bay (13607).* 315/482-
9867. Continental menu. Specializes
in prime rib, live Maine lobster, veal.
Hrs: 5-10 pm; Sat to 11 pm; Sun 3-10
pm; early-bird dinner Mon-Fri 4-6
pm. Closed early Nov-mid-Apr. Res
accepted; required Sat and hols. Bar
to 2 am. Dinner $12.95-$28.50.
Child's menu. Entertainment Fri-Sat.
Valet parking. Medieval decor.
Family-owned. Cr cds: A, DS, MC, V.

★ ★ ★ **JACQUES CARTIER.** *17 Holland St, Alexandria Bay (13607).*
315/482-9917. www.riveredge.com.
Specializes in veal, seafood. Own pastries. Hrs: 6-10 pm; Sun brunch seasonal (July 4 to Labor Day) 10:30
am-2:30 pm. Closed Dec 25. Res
accepted. Wine cellar. Dinner $21-

$25. Prix fixe: dinner $45. Sun
brunch $15.95. Child's menu.
Harpist. Valet parking. On St.
Lawrence River. Cr cds: A, D, DS,
MC, V.

Allegany State Park

(F-2) *See also Olean*

(At Salamanca on NY 17)

This 65,000-acre park is one of the
most complete recreation areas in the
United States. It borders on the Allegany Indian Reservation and the
Kinzua Reservoir in New York and the
Allegheny National Forest in Pennsylvania. It has more than 85 miles of
hiking trails and many scenic drives
through rolling hills. The park is open
all year and has a museum, seasonal
stores, and two restaurants. Swimming at Quaker and Red House lakes,
bathhouses, boat rentals, fishing;
hunting, sports fields, tennis, 25 miles
of groomed cross-country ski trails, 55
miles of snowmobile trails, tobogganing; picnicking, refreshment stands;
tent and trailer sites (April-December,
most with electricity), cabins. Standard fees. Contact Allegany State Park
Region, Salamanca 14779; 716/354-
9121.

Amagansett (L. I.)

(G-4) *See also East Hampton (L.I.), Montauk (L.I.), Sag Harbor (L.I.)*

Pop 1,067 **Elev** 40 ft **Area code** 631
Zip 11930

Information East Hampton Chamber
of Commerce, 79A Main St, East
Hampton 11937; 516/324-0362

Web www.easthamptonchamber.com

What to See and Do

Miss Amelia's Cottage Museum. (1725) Built by Jacob Schellinger; preserved and furnished to allow visitors a glimpse of of how people lived from the earliest colonial times through the early 19th century. A changing series of exhibits show specific aspects of everyday life in the area. (June-Sept, Fri-Sun afternoons) Phone 631/267-3020. **Donation**

Town Marine Museum. Exhibits on commercial and sport fishing, offshore whaling from colonial times to present; underwater archaeology, sailing, aquaculture, commercial fishing techniques; garden; picnicking. Programs administered by the East Hampton Historical Society. (July-Aug, daily; June and Sept, wkends only) Bluff Rd, ½ mi S of NY 27 on ocean. Phone 631/267-6544. ¢

Motel/Motor Lodge

★★ **SEA CREST ON THE OCEAN.** *2166 Montauk Hwy (11930). 631/267-3159; fax 631/267-6840.* 74 kit. units, 2 story. S, D $60-$110. Crib $15. TV; cable (premium). Heated pool; lifeguard. Restaurant nearby. Ck-out 11 am. Coin lndry. Business servs avail. Tennis privileges. Refrigerators. Private patios, balconies. Picnic tables, grills. On ocean, beach. Cr cds: DS, MC, V.

B&B/Small Inn

★★ **MILL GARTH COUNTRY INN.** *23 Windmill Ln (11930). 631/267-3757; fax 631/267-3675.* 12 kit. units, 3 A/C, 2 story. 4 suites, 5 cottages. Memorial Day-Oct: S, D $135-$465; each addl $25; suites $165-$300; studio rms $145-$185; cottages $225-$300; family, wkly rates; lower rates rest of yr. Crib avail. TV in sitting rm. Complimentary continental bkfst. Ck-out 11 am, ck-in 3 pm. Business servs avail. Health club privileges. Lawn games. Private patios. Picnic tables, grills. Antiques. Built 1840, became inn late 1800s; stone originally from ancient windmill. Cr cds: MC, V.

Restaurants

★★ **GORDON'S.** *Montauk Hwy (11930). 631/267-3010.* Continental menu. Specializes in seafood, veal. Hrs: noon-2:30 pm, 6-10 pm; July-Aug from 6 pm. Closed Mon; Thanksgiving, Dec 25; Feb. Bar. A la carte entrees: lunch $11.75-$15.75, dinner $15.75-$23.75. Complete meals: lunch $12.50, dinner $21. Cr cds: A, D, DS, MC, V.

★ **LOBSTER ROLL.** *1980 Montauk Hwy, Amagansett, L. I. (11930). 631/267-3740. www.lobsterroll.com.* Specialties: char-broiled fish, clam chowder, lobster rolls. Hrs: 11:30 am-10 pm. Closed Nov-Apr; also wkdays May and Oct. Wine, beer. A la carte entrees: lunch $5-$10, dinner $10-$15. Child's menu. Outdoor dining. Nautical decor. Family-owned. Cr cds: MC, V.

Amityville (L.I.)

Pop 18,355 **Elev** 25 ft **Area code** 631 **Zip** 11701

Information Chamber of Commerce, PO Box 885; 631/598-0695

Web www.amityville.com

Amityville is a town on the Great South Bay noted for antiques, craftspeople, and its many restored houses.

What to See and Do

Lauder Museum. Permanent and changing exhibits reflect Amityville's heritage and that of surrounding communities; research library, genealogical files. (Tues, Fri, Sun) 170 Broadway. Phone 631/598-1486. **FREE**

Restaurant

★★★ **AMATO'S.** *330 Merrick Rd, Amityville, L.I. (11701). 631/598-2229.* Italian, American menu. Specialties: chicken Shoemaker, lobster Fra Diavolo. Own pastries. Hrs: 11:30 am-9:30 pm; Fri to 10 pm; Sat 1-4 pm, 5-10:30 pm; Sun 1-9 pm; Sun brunch to 5 pm. Closed Mon; July 4, Thanksgiving, Dec 25. Serv bar. Wine cellar. Lunch, dinner $9.75-$40. Complete meals: lunch $9-$15, dinner $17.95-$35. Sun brunch $14-$17.50. Cr cds: A, DS, MC, V.

Amsterdam

(D-7) *See also Johnstown, Schenectady*

Settled 1785 **Pop** 18,355 **Elev** 450 ft
Area code 518 **Zip** 12010
Information Montgomery County Chamber of Commerce, 366 W Main St, PO Box 309; 518/842-8200 or 800/743-7337

Located on the Mohawk River and New York Barge Canal, this city manufactures clothing, novelties, toys, and electronic equipment.

What to See and Do

Erie Canal. Site of last remaining section of original canal (built in 1822). 6 mi W on NY 5 S at Fort Hunter. Phone 518/842-8200. **FREE**

Guy Park State Historic Site. (1773) Former home of Guy Johnson, Superintendent of Indian Affairs, who remained loyal to King George III; abandoned by Johnson in 1775. Served as a tavern for many yrs. Exhibits on Native Americans and on Erie Canal and its impact on westward expansion. (Mon-Fri; closed hols) 366 W Main St. Phone 518/842-8200. **FREE**

National Shrine of the North American Martyrs. Site of Ossernenon, 17th-century Mohawk settlement, where Father Isaac Jogues and companions, the first canonized martyrs of the US, were put to death. Birthplace of Blessed Kateri Tekakwitha. Coliseum-type chapel seats 6,500. Native American museum; cafeteria. (Early May-Nov 1, daily) 6 mi W on NY 5 S in Auriesville, Dewey Thrwy exit 27. Phone 518/853-3033. **FREE**

Schoharie Crossing State Historic Site and Visitors Center. Seven arches of the Schoharie Aqueduct; remains of original canal locks; canals from 1825 and 1840s and barge canal can be seen. Park, boat launch; historic site markers, picnic tables; hiking paths; wagon rides; tours. (Mid-May-Oct, Wed-Sat, also Sun afternoons) 5 mi W, just off NY 5 S, in Fort Hunter. Contact PO Box 140, Fort Hunter 12069. Phone 518/829-7516.

Walter Elwood Museum. Exhibits of history, natural science, and ethnology; changing exhibits in gallery; research library. (July-Aug, Mon-Thurs; rest of yr, Mon-Fri; closed hols) 300 Guy Park Ave. Phone 518/843-5151. **Donation**

Motels/Motor Lodges

★★ **BEST WESTERN.** *10 Market St (12010). 518/843-5760; fax 518/842-0940; res 800/328-1234.* 125 rms, 5 story. S $55-$72; D $58-$89; each addl $6; under 18 free; wkly rates; higher rates Aug. Crib $6. Pet accepted, some restrictions. TV; cable, VCR avail (movies). Indoor pool. Restaurant 6:30 am-10 pm. Bar 11-12:30 am. Ck-out noon. Meeting rms. Business servs avail. In-rm modem link. Valet serv. Sundries. Refrigerator avail. Cr cds: D, DS, MC.
🔡 🔥 ⬆ ⬌ 🔲 🔥 ⬜

★ **SUPER 8 MOTEL.** *Rte 30 S (12010). 518/843-5888; fax 518/843-5888.* 67 rms, 2 story. S $48.88-$60.88; D $54.88-$64.88; each addl $4; under 12 free; higher rates: Aug, special events. Crib $4. TV; cable, VCR avail (movies). Complimentary continental bkfst. Restaurant adj 6 am-11 pm. Ck-out 11 am. Meeting rms. Business servs avail. Cr cds: A, C, D, DS, MC, V.
🔡 ⬆ 🔲 ⬜

Restaurant

★★★ **RAINDANCER STEAK PARLOUR.** *4582 State Hwy 30 (12010). 518/842-2606.* Specializes in steak, chops, seafood. Salad bar. Own baking. Hrs: 11:30 am-10 pm; Sun 1-9 pm; early-bird dinner Mon-Sat 4:30-6 pm, Sun 1-3 pm. Closed Super Bowl Sun, Dec 24, 25. Res accepted; required hols. Bar. Lunch $4.95-$12.95, dinner $10.50-$28.95.

Child's menu. Country decor; garden rm. Cr cds: A, D, DS, MC, V.

Arcade

Pop 4,184 **Elev** 1,497 ft
Area code 716 **Zip** 14009

What to See and Do

Arcade and Attica Railroad. Steam train ride (1½-hr) through scenic countryside. (Late May-Oct, Sat, Sun, and hols; July-Aug, also Wed) 278 Main St. Phone 716/496-9877. ¢¢¢

B&B/Small Inn

★★ **THE INN AT HOUGHTON CREEK.** *9722 Genesee St, Houghton (14744). 716/567-8400; fax 716/567-4842.* 17 rms, 2 story. S $59; D $64; each addl $5; under 5 free; higher rates college events (2-day min). Crib $5. TV; cable. Ck-out 11 am, ck-in 3 pm. Business servs avail. Luggage handling. X-country ski on site. Health club privileges. Country decor. Totally nonsmoking. Cr cds: A, DS, MC, V.

Auburn

(D-4) *See also Seneca Falls, Syracuse*

Settled 1793 **Pop** 28,574 **Elev** 708 ft
Area code 315 **Zip** 13021
Information Cavuga County Office of Tourism, 131 Genesee St; 315/255-1658 or 800/499-9615
Web www.cayuganet.org

On Owasco Lake, Auburn is one of the largest cities in the Finger Lakes region. Harriet Tubman, whose home was a link in the Underground Railroad, lived here. A resort and farm center, Auburn's products include electronics, auto parts, air conditioners, wire, plastics, diesel engines, steel, bottles, and aviation spark plugs.

What to See and Do

Cayuga Museum/Case Research Lab Museum. The Cayuga Museum is housed in Greek Revival Willard-Case Mansion (1836); 19th-century furnishings; local industrial history; Bundy Monumental clock; Civil War exhibit. The Case Research Lab Museum is the restored lab where T. W. Case and E. I. Sponable invented sound film; permanent exhibits of lab, Fox Movietone, and sound studio. (Tues-Sun afternoons; also Mon hols; closed Jan) 203 Genesee St. Phone 315/253-8051. **Donation** Adj is

Schweinfurth Memorial Art Center. Classical and contemporary fine art, photography, folk art, and quilting exhibit; concerts, lectures, museum shop. (Feb-Dec, Tues-Sun; closed hols) 205 Genesee St. Phone 315/255-1553. ¢

Emerson Park. Swimming, boating (launch); ball fields, playground, picnicking. Agricultural museum. (Mid-May-mid-Sept, daily) 3 mi S on NY 38A, at head of Owasco Lake. Phone 315/253-5611. ¢ In park is

Cayuga Museum Iroquois Center. Permanent and changing exhibits on traditional Northeast Woodlands Native people's arts and culture; emphasis on Iroquois cultures of central New York. (June wkends, July-Aug Wed-Sun) Phone 315/253-8051. **FREE**

Fort Hill Cemetery. Site was used for burial mounds by Native Americans as early as 1100 A.D. Burial sites of William Seward and Harriet Tubman are here. (Daily) 19 Fort St. Phone 315/253-8132. **FREE**

Harriet Tubman Home. Born a slave, Harriet Tubman escaped in 1849 and rescued more than 300 slaves via the Underground Railroad. She later assisted the Union Army during the Civil War and, settling in Auburn after the war, continued to pursue other humanitarian endeavors. (Tues-Sat; closed hols) 180 South St. Phone 315/252-2081. ¢¢¢

Hoopes Park Flower Gardens. Band concerts (July and Aug, wkly); rollerblading; ice-skating (winter). Park (daily). E Genesee St, on US 20. Phone 315/252-9300. **FREE**

Seward House. (1816-1817) Home of William Henry Seward, governor of

New York, US senator, and Lincoln's and Andrew Johnson's secretary of state, who was instrumental in purchasing Alaska. Civil War relics, original Alaskan artifacts, costumes, furnishings. (Apr-Dec, Tues-Sat afternoons; closed hols) 33 South St. Phone 315/252-1283. ¢¢

Willard Memorial Chapel & Welch Memorial Building. (1894) These grey and red stone Romanesque Revival buildings were once part of the Auburn Theological Seminary. The chapel's interior was designed and handcrafted by the Tiffany Glass and Decoration Company, and is the only complete and unaltered Tiffany chapel known to exist. Tiffany Concert Series in the chapel (July and Aug, Wed noon). Tours (Tues-Fri afternoons or by appt; closed hols). 17 Nelson St. Phone 315/252-0339. ¢

Motels/Motor Lodges

★ **DAYS INN.** 37 William St (13021). 315/252-7567; toll-free 800/329-7466. 51 rms, 2 story. May-Sept: S $52; D $62; each addl $5; under 12 free; higher rates graduation; lower rates rest of yr. Crib free. Pet accepted. TV; cable. Complimentary continental bkfst. Restaurant nearby. Ck-out 11 am. Coin lndry. Meeting rms. Business servs avail. In-rm modem link. Health club privileges. Cr cds: A, C, DS, MC, V.
🅳 🐾 ⛱ 🔥 SC

★★ **HOLIDAY INN.** 75 North St (13021). 315/253-4531; fax 315/252-5843; toll-free 800/465-4329. www. holiday-inn.com. 166 rms, 5 story. S, D $69-$129; suites $150-$300; under 19 free; higher rates special events. Crib free. TV; cable (premium). Indoor pool. Coffee in rms. Restaurant 6:30 am-2 pm, 5-10 pm; Sat, Sun from 6:30 am. Bar 11:30-2 am; entertainment Fri, Sat. Ck-out 11 am. Coin lndry. Meeting rms. Business servs avail. Bellhops. Beauty shop. Exercise equipt. Many balconies. Cr cds: A, C, D, DS, JCB, MC, V.
🅳 ⛱ 🕍 ⛱ 🔥 SC

★★ **SPRINGSIDE INN.** 6141 W Lake Rd (13021). 315/252-7247; fax 315/252-8096. www.springsideinn.com. 8 rms, 5 with bath, 3 story. No rm phones. S $47; D $65; each addl $10;

wkend rates. Complimentary continental bkfst. Restaurant (see SPRING-SIDE INN). Ck-out noon, ck-in 2 pm. Built in 1830 as a boy's school; antiques, sitting rm. Cr cds: MC, V.
🅳 🐾 ⛱ ⛱ 🔥

★ **SUPER 8 MOTEL.** 9 McMaster St (13021). 315/253-8886; fax 315/253-8329; res 800/805-8000. www.super8. com. 48 rms, 2 story. May-Oct: S $40-$65; D $50-$75; each addl $5; under 18 free; higher rates special events. Crib free. TV; cable. Complimentary continental bkfst. Restaurant nearby. Ck-out 11 am. Meeting rms. Business servs avail. In-rm modem link. Cr cds: A, D, DS, MC, V.
🅳 ⛱ 🔥

Restaurants

★★ **LASCA'S.** 252 Grant Ave (13021). 315/253-4885. Italian, Amer menu. Specializes in fresh seafood, steak, veal. Hrs: 11:30 am-2 pm, 5-9 pm; Fri, Sat to 10 pm; Sun from 4 pm. Closed Mon; hols; also 1st 2 wks Feb. Res accepted. Bar. Lunch $2.75-$5.95, dinner $7.95-$18.95. Child's menu. Cr cds: DS, MC, V.
🅳 ⛱

★★ **SPRINGSIDE INN.** 6141 W Lake Rd (13021). 315/252-7247. www. springsideinn.com. Specialties: duckling flambe, lobster Newburg, prime rib. Hrs: 5-10 pm; Sun 1-7 pm; Sun brunch 10:30 am-2 pm. Closed hols; Res accepted. Bar. Dinner $8.95-$21.95. Sun brunch $12.99. Child's menu. Entertainment Sat; jazz Wed. Colonial decor. Built in 1830. Owasco Lake opp. Family-owned. Cr cds: MC, V.
🅳 SC

Ausable Chasm

(B-8) See also Plattsburgh

(1 mi N of Keesville; 12 m S of Plattsburgh off I-87)

Information Ausable Chasm Co, US 9, PO Box 390, 12911; 518/834-7454

This scenic gorge, accessible from US 9, was opened to the public in 1870. It is one of the oldest tourist attractions in the United States. Ausable (Aw-SAY-bl) Chasm leads eastward toward Lake Champlain for about a mile and a half. This spectacular gorge is 20 to 50 feet wide and from 100 to 200 feet deep. The Ausable River plunges in falls and rapids past curious rock formations, each with its own name: Pulpit Rock, Elephant's Head, Devil's Oven, Jacob's Well, the Cathedral. Paths and bridges crisscross the chasm. Camping is available on the grounds.

What to See and Do

Activities. Game rm, glass-blower's shop, craft shops, picnic area, and playground. (July-Aug, daily) X-country ski center (winter).

⭐ **Self-guided walking tour.** To mid-way point of stream and guided boat ride through "flume" rapids. (Memorial Day wkend-Columbus Day, daily) ¢¢¢¢

Ausable Chasm

exhibits of antique horse carriages. Gallery of Sporting Art has over 700 pieces of wildlife art. (Mid-May-mid-Oct, Tues-Sun) 8 mi NW via NY 5 to NY 36 in Mumford, on Flint Hill Rd. Phone 716/538-6822. ¢¢¢¢

Avon

(D-3) *See also Geneseo, Rochester*

Pop 6,443 **Elev** 651 ft **Area code** 716 **Zip** 14414

Originally a health resort with sulphur springs, Avon has since become a farming, food processing, and horse-breeding center.

What to See and Do

Genesee Country Village and Museum. A 19th-century village representing life in the Genesee River valley. Fifty-seven buildings, incl a log cabin and a Greek Revival mansion. Small-scale farm, blacksmith, pottery, print, and tinsmith shops and a general store are in daily operation by museum guides dressed as 19th-century villagers. Replication of 19th century baseball with ballpark and authentic teams. Permanent

Motel/Motor Lodge

★★ **AVON INN.** *55 E Main St (14414). 716/226-8181; fax 716/226-8185.* 15 rms, 2 story. S, D $65-$75; suites $85; family rates; package plans. TV. Complimentary continental bkfst. Dining rm Wed, Thurs 4:30-9 pm; Fri, Sat 5-10 pm; Sun 9 am-8 pm. Ck-out 11 am, ck-in 3 pm. Business servs avail. Historic inn (1820); antiques; fireplace. Gazebo and fountain in rear. Cr cds: A, C, D, DS, MC, V.
🔲 🖼

Bainbridge

(E-6) *See also Deposit, Oneonta*

Pop 3,401 **Elev** 1,006 ft
Area code 607 **Zip** 13733

Information Chamber of Commerce, PO Box 2; 607/967-8700

Special Event

General Clinton Canoe Regatta. World championship flat water canoe race, arts and crafts show. Midway show. Entertainment. Phone 607/967-8700. One week in late May.

Motel/Motor Lodge

★ **SIDNEY SUPER 8 MOTEL.** *4 Mang Dr, Sidney (13838). 607/563-8880; fax 607/563-8989; res 800/800-8000.* 39 rms, 2 story. Apr-Sept: S $48.88; D $54.88; under 12 free; higher rates: Regatta, graduation, Baseball Hall of Fame events; lower rates rest of yr. Crib free. TV; cable, VCR avail (movies). Complimentary coffee in lobby. Restaurant adj 6:30 am-10 pm. Ck-out 11 am. Business servs avail. Cr cds: A, D, DS, MC, V.

Restaurants

★ **JERICHO TAVERN.** *4 N Main St (13733). 607/967-5893.* Hrs: Wed-Sat 11:30 am-2 pm, 5-8 pm; Sun noon-7 pm. Closed Mon, Tues; Dec 25. Res accepted. Bar. Lunch $5.95-$10.95, dinner $10.95-$27.95. Buffet: lunch $6.95; dinner (Fri-Sun) $14.95. Child's menu. Early American decor.

In 1793 tavern; player piano, nickelodeon. Family-owned. Cr cds: A, MC, V.

★★ **RIVER CLUB.** *1 Maple St, Afton (13730). 607/639-3060. www.riverclub rest.com.* Continental menu. Specializes in prime rib, fresh seafood, steak. Own desserts. Hrs: Thurs and Sat 4-9 pm; Fri 4:30 - 9 pm; Sun 10 - 5 pm. Closed Mon-Wed; Dec 25. Res accepted. Bar. A la carte: dinner $9.95-$17.95. Child's menu. Outdoor dining. Converted railroad depot overlooking river. Cr cds: A, DS, MC, V.

★★ **SILO.** *203 Moran Rd, Greene (13778). 607/656-4377.* Specializes in veal, seafood, chicken. Salad bar. Hrs: 4-10 pm; Fri, Sat to 10:30 pm; Sun 10 am-8 pm; Sun brunch to 2 pm. Closed hols. Res accepted. Bar. Dinner $9.95-$25.95. Sun brunch $13.95. Folk guitarist Fri. Country setting; view of gardens. Overnight stays avail. Cr cds: A, C, D, DS, ER, MC, V.

★ **UNADILLA HOUSE.** *63 Main St, Unadilla (13849). 607/369-7227.* Continental menu. Hrs: 11 am-2 pm, 5-9 pm; Fri, Sat to 9:30 pm. Closed Sun; hols. Res accepted. Bar to 1 am; wkends to 2 am. Lunch $4.50-$7.95,

Historic reenactment at Genesee Country Village and Museum

dinner $9.95-$20.95. Child's menu. Country decor, many antiques. Restored 19th-century hotel. Cr cds: A, DS, MC, V.

D ⊣

Barryville

See also Middletown, Port Jervis

Pop 600 **Elev** 600 ft **Area code** 914 **Zip** 12719

What to See and Do

Fort Delaware Museum of Colonial History. Replica of 1755 stockade, cabins, blockhouses, gardens; exhibits, film, and demonstrations depict life of early settlers. Colonial military encampments (July-Aug). Picnic area; snacks. (Last wk June-Labor Day, daily; Memorial Day-late June, Sat and Sun only) On NY 97 in Narrowsburg. Phone 845/252-6660.

Lander's Delaware River Trips. Canoe, raft, and kayak trips on whitewater and calm water; campground along river. (Mid-Apr-mid-Oct, daily) One- and two-day package plans. 2 mi N via NY 97 in Minisink Ford. Contact 1336 NY 97, Department M, Narrowsburg 12764. Phone 800/252-3925. ¢¢¢¢

★ **Zane Grey Museum.** Former home of author; items incl Grey's books, photographs, oil paintings for book jackets; original furnishings and utensils. Guided tours (Schedule varies, call for hrs) 4 mi NW on NY 97, left across Roebling Bridge then right, in Lackawaxen, PA. Phone 570/685-4871. **FREE**

Batavia

(D-3) *See also Buffalo, Rochester*

Founded 1801 **Pop** 16,256 **Elev** 895 ft **Area code** 585 **Zip** 14020
Information Genesee County Chamber of Commerce, 210 E Main St; 585/343-7440 or 800/622-2686
Web www.geneseeny.com/chamber

Established at the crossing of two Native American trails by Joseph Ellicott, an agent of the Holland Land Company, which purchased 3,300,000 acres from Robert Morris, Batavia was named for a province of the Netherlands. The brisk rate of sales of this western New York State land is said to have inspired the phrase "doing a land-office business." Batavia today is a lively farm area producing potatoes, onions, fruit, and dairy products. Industrial items include heat exchange equipment, alloy castings, and shoes. The New York State School for the Blind is here.

What to See and Do

Batavia Downs Race Track. Oldest pari-mutuel harness track in North America. Clubhouse, open-air and enclosed grandstands. (Early Aug-late Nov, daily) Park Rd, I-90 to exit 48. Phone 585/343-3750. ¢

Holland Land Office Museum. (1815) Building from which deeds to the lands in the Holland Purchase were issued. This stone office was built by Joseph Ellicott, land agent. Local Native American and pioneer artifacts, period furniture and costumes; Civil War, medical and surgical collections (Summer Mon-Sat; Tues-Sat rest of yr; closed hols). 131 W Main St. Phone 585/343-4727. **Donation**

Iroquois National Wildlife Refuge. Migratory waterfowl, especially geese, visit here in large numbers during the spring migration. Overlooks, trails, illustrated talks (res); fishing, hunting (in season). Office (Mon-Fri; closed hols). 15 mi NW of town via NY 63, on Casey Rd in Alabama, NY. Phone 585/948-5445.

Le Roy House. Early 19th-century house with furnishings of the period; nine rms open to the public. Also home of Le Roy Historical Society. (Tues-Fri, mid-morning-mid-afternoon; also Sun afternoons; closed hols) ½ mi E of jct NY 19 and 5; 7 mi S of NY State Thrwy exit 47, at 23 E Main St in Le Roy. Phone 716/768-7433. **Donation**

Six Flags Darien Lake. Family entertainment complex is NY's largest. Features five roller coasters, a million-gallon wave pool and sun deck, 40,000-square-ft water adventure park, and performing arts center; 2,000-site campground. (Late May-early Sept, daily; rest of Oct, wkends) I-90 to exit 48A, S on NY 77 in Darien Center. Phone 585/599-4641. ¢¢¢¢

Special Events

Genesee County Agricultural Fair. Tractor pull, demolition derby, livestock show, entertainment. Phone 585/344-2424. Late July-Aug.

Wing Ding Weekend. Ethnic festival, block party, food, games, entertainment. Third wkend Aug.

Motels/Motor Lodges

★★ **BEST WESTERN BATAVIA INN.** *8204 Park Rd (14020). 716/343-1000; fax 716/343-8608; res 800/528-1234.* 75 rms, 2 story. Mid-June-mid-Sept: S $74-$84; D $79-$99; each addl $6; under 18 free; lower rates rest of yr. Crib free. Pet accepted, some restrictions. TV; cable (premium), VCR avail. Heated pool; poolside serv, lifeguard. Restaurant 6:30 am-2 pm, 5-9 pm. Bar 11-2 am; entertainment Fri, Sat. Ck-out noon. Meeting rms. Business servs avail. In-rm modem link. Valet serv. Lawn games. Cr cds: A, C, D, DS, MC, V.

★ **DAYS INN.** *200 Oak St (14020). 716/343-1440; fax 716/343-5322.* 120 rms, 2 story. May-Sept: S $62-$82; D $69-$99; each addl $7; under 18 free; lower rates rest of yr. Crib free. Pet accepted. TV; cable (premium). Pool; lifeguard. Complimentary continental bkfst. Restaurant nearby. Ck-out noon. Meeting rms. Business servs avail. Health club privileges. Cr cds: A, C, D, DS, JCB, MC, V.

Hotel

★ **PARK OAK MOTEL.** *301 Oak St (14020). 716/343-7921; fax 716/343-6701.* 23 rms, 2 story. S $39-$79; D $42-$79; each addl $6-$15; higher rates special events. TV; cable. Complimentary continental bkfst. Restaurant adj 6:30 am-8:30 pm. Ck-out 11 am. Business servs avail. Totally nonsmoking. Cr cds: A, DS, MC, V.

Restaurant

★★ **SUNNY'S.** *Genesee Country Mall (14020). 716/343-4578.* Italian, Amer menu. Specializes in seafood, steak. Hrs: 11-2 am; early-bird dinner 4-6 pm. Closed Sun; hols. Res accepted. Bar. Lunch $4.25-$5.50, dinner $5.85-$17.95. Child's menu. Family-owned. Cr cds: A, C, D, DS, ER, MC, V.

Bath

(E-4) See also Hammondsport

Pop 12,097 **Elev** 1,106 ft
Area code 607 **Zip** 14810

Motels/Motor Lodges

★ **CABOOSE MOTEL.** *8620 State Rte 415, Avoca (14809). 607/566-2216; fax 607/566-3817. www.caboosemotel. net.* 23 units, 1 story, 5 caboose rms. Mid-Apr-mid-Oct: S, D $45-$70; each addl $7; higher rates: college events, racing season; lower rates mid-Oct-Nov and May-late June. Closed Nov-Mar. Crib $5. Pet accepted, some restrictions. TV; cable (premium). Heated pool. Playground. Complimentary coffee in rms. Restaurant opp 6 am-8 pm. Ck-out 11 am. Business servs avail. In-rm modem link. Gift shop. Lawn games. Refrigerators avail. Picnic tables, grills. Five antique cabooses (1916), set on track laid adj to motel, provide unique accommodations; interiors, incl intact bunks, air brakes, torpedo boxes, are in near-original condition. Cr cds: MC, V.

★ **DAYS INN BATH.** *330 W Morris (14810). 607/776-7644; fax 607/776-7650; res 400/329-7466. www.daysinn. com.* 104 rms, 5 story. June-Oct: S $50-$70; D $65-$85; each addl $5; under 18 free; lower rates rest of yr. Crib free. Pet accepted. TV; cable (premium), VCR avail (movies). Indoor pool. Restaurant 11 am-10 pm. Bar. Ck-out 11 am. Coin lndry.

Meeting rms. Business servs avail. Cr cds: A, C, D, DS, JCB, MC, V.

★ **HOLLAND AMERICAN COUNTRY INN.** *6632 Rte 415 S (14810). 607/776-6057; fax 607/776-6407.* 15 rms. S $32; D $36-$38; each addl $5; under 18 free. Crib $5. TV; cable. Coffee in lobby. Ck-out 11 am. Cr cds: A, DS, MC, V.

★ **SUPER 8 MOTEL.** *333 W Morris St (14810). 607/776-2187; fax 607/776-3206; toll-free 800/800-8000. www. super8.com.* 50 rms, 3 story. No elvtr. June-Aug: S $42.88-$47.88; D $48.88-$53.88; each addl $5; under 12 free; lower rates rest of yr. Crib free. TV; cable (premium), VCR avail (movies). Complimentary continental bkfst, coffee in lobby. Restaurant nearby. Ck-out 11 am. Business servs avail. Cr cds: A, D, DS, MC, V.

Bay Shore (L.I.)

(G-2) See also Sayville (L.I.)

Founded 1708 **Pop** 23,852 **Elev** 15 ft
Area code 516 **Zip** 11706

What to See and Do

Bayard Cutting Arboretum. Approx 690 acres; many broadleaf trees and coniferous evergreens, wildflowers, shrubs; aquatic birds; nature walks. (Tues-Sun; closed Jan 1, Dec 25) 6 mi E on Montauk Hwy (NY 27A). Phone 631/581-1002. ¢¢

Robert Moses State Park. (see)

Sagtikos Manor. Apple Tree Wicke (1692), served as headquarters for General Henry Clinton; original kitchen, parlor; Thompson music rm and dining rm added ca 1890; antiques. (July-Aug, Wed, Thurs, and Sun; June and Sept, Sun only) 3 mi W on Montauk Hwy (NY 27A). ¢¢

Motel/Motor Lodge

★★ **HAMPTON INN LONG ISLAND.** *1600 Veterans Memorial Hwy, Islandia (11722). 631/234-0400;* *fax 631/234-0415. www.hamptoninn. com.* 121 rms, 4 story. S, D $99-$115; under 18 free. Crib free. TV; cable (premium). Complimentary continental bkfst. Restaurant nearby. Ck-out noon. Business servs avail. Valet serv Mon-Fri. Free airport, RR station transportation. Exercise equipt. Health club privileges. Cr cds: A, C, D, DS, JCB, MC, V.

Restaurants

★ **MOUNTAINVIEW.** *839 Shandelee Rd, Livingston Manor (12758). 845/439-5070.* Continental menu. Specializes in seafood, vegetarian dishes. Hrs: 11:30 am-2 pm, 5 pm-closing; Sat from 5 pm; from 5 pm in July. Closed Sun; hols; also Mon. Res accepted; required hols. Bar. Lunch $4.50-$8.50, dinner $8.95-$15.95. Post-Revolutionary tavern (1798); early Colonial decor. Cr cds: C, D, DS, MC, V.

★ **PORK'S & GLENN'S SEAFOOD HOUSE.** *28 Cottage Ave (11706). 631/666-2899. www.porkysandglenns. com.* Specializes in fresh seafood, prime rib. Hrs: 11:30 am-9 pm; Fri, Sat to 10 pm; summer 11:30 am-10 pm; Fri, Sat to 11 pm; Closed Dec 25. Res accepted. Bar. A la carte entrees: lunch $7.95-$9.95, dinner $12.95-$30. Child's menu. Outdoor dining. Deck overlooks Great South Bay. Family-owned. Cr cds: A, DS, MC, V.

Bear Mountain

(see Palisades Interstate Parks)

Bemus Point

See also Chautauqua, Jamestown

Pop 340 **Elev** 1,320 ft **Area code** 716
Zip 14712

What to See and Do

Long Point on Lake Chautauqua State Park. Swimming, fishing, boating (marina), ice fishing; snowmobiling, x-country skiing, picnicking. (Mid-May-Columbus Day) 1 mi W off NY 17. Phone 716/386-2722. ¢¢

Hotel

★★ **LENHART HOTEL.** *20 Lakeside Dr (14712). 716/386-2715.* 54 rms, 34 with bath, 4 story. MAP, late May-mid-Sept: S $47-$90; D $91-$140; family rates. Closed rest of yr. Restaurant 8:30-10 am, 12:30-1:30 pm, 6:30-7:30 pm; closed off-season. Bar. Ck-out 2 pm. Meeting rms. Business servs avail. Airport transportation. Tennis. Opp lake, swimming beach. Boat dockage. Family-owned since 1880. Cr cds: A, DS, MC, V.

Restaurant

★★ **YE HARE N' HOUNDS INN.** *64 Lakeside Dr (14712). 716/386-2181. www.restaurant.com/hareandhounds.* Continental menu. Specializes in seafood, beef, veal. Own desserts. Hrs: 5-10 pm; Sun to 9 pm; Sun in winter from 4 pm. Closed Dec 24, 25. Res accepted. Bar. Dinner $15.95-$39.95. Outdoor dining. English-style inn (1915); fireplaces. Cr cds: A, MC, V.

Bethpage (L.I.)

See also Plainview (L.I.)

Pop 16,543 **Elev** 106 ft **Area code** 516 **Zip** 11714

What to See and Do

Bethpage State Park. On 1,475 acres. Hiking, biking, golf (five 18-hole courses), tennis, bridle paths, game fields, picnicking, x-country skiing. Standard fees. E off Bethpage Pkwy. Phone 516/249-0700. **FREE**

Old Bethpage Village Restoration. More than 25 pre-Civil War buildings incl carpentry and hat shops, general store, tavern, schoolhouse, church, homes; working farm and craftsmen

depict life of mid-1800s; film. Picnic area. (Mar-Dec, Wed-Sun; closed winter hols) Round Swamp Rd, 1 mi S of Long Island Expy, exit 48. Phone 516/572-8401. ¢¢¢

Restaurant

★ **56TH FIGHTER GROUP.** *110 E Farmingdale, E Farmingdale (11735). 631/694-8280.* Continental menu. Specializes in seafood. Hrs: 11 am-3 pm, 4-10 pm; Fri, Sat to midnight; Sun from 4 pm; Sun brunch noon-2 pm. Res required. Bar 11 am-midnight; wkends to 3:30 am. A la carte entrees: lunch $5.95-$9.95, dinner $10.95-$29.95. Sun brunch $19.95. Child's menu. Outdoor dining. WWII theme; airplanes, jeeps, and pictures. Cr cds: A, C, D, DS, ER, MC, V.

Binghamton

(F-5) *See also Endicott*

Settled 1787 **Pop** 47,380 **Elev** 860 ft **Area code** 607

Information Broome County Convention and Visitors Bureau, 49 Court St, Box 995, 13902; 607/772-8860, 800/836-6740, or 607/772-8945 (recording)

Web www.broome-ny.com

Largest of the Triple Cities (Johnson City and Endicott branched off later), Binghamton lies at the junction of the Chenango and Susquehanna rivers. Completion of the Chenango Canal in 1837 made it an important link between the coal regions of Pennsylvania and the Erie Canal.

What to See and Do

Binghamton University, State University of New York. (1946) 12,000 students. Anderson Center for the Arts offers performing arts events incl dance, music, and theater. Foreign films, lectures, art museum (academic yr, Tues-Sun; closed hols). Tours of campus. 2 mi W on Vestal Pkwy E, NY 434. Phone 607/777-2000 (university information) or 607/777-3535 (recording of events). Phone 607/777-ARTS.

Chenango Valley State Park. Swimming beach, bathhouse, fishing, boat rentals; hiking, biking, nature trails, 18-hole golf (fee), x-country skiing, picnicking, playground, concession, tent and trailer sites, cabins (closed winter). Standard fees. 13 mi NE via I-88. Phone 607/648-5251.

"Day of a Playwright." Theater has exhibit honoring Syracuse-born Rod Serling (1925-1975), who grew up in Binghamton and created "The Twilight Zone" TV series; incl photos and documents highlighting his career in TV and films. (Mon-Fri and during Forum performances) The Forum, 236 Washington St. Phone 607/778-2480.

Discovery Center of the Southern Tier. Hands-on museum allows children to experience a simulated flight in an airplane, crawl through a culvert, and stand inside a bubble, in addition to exploring other interactive exhibits. (July and Aug, daily; rest of yr, Tues-Sun) 60 Morgan Rd. Phone 607/773-8661. ¢¢

Roberson Museum and Science Center. Regional museum with collections in art, history, folk art, and science. Incl turn-of-the-century mansion; changing exhibits; planetarium (fee). (Daily; closed hols) 30 Front St. Phone 607/772-0660. ¢¢¢

Ross Park Zoo. Operated by the Southern Tier Zoological Society. A 75-acre park (free); 25-acre zoo with Wolf Woods, tiger, snow leopard, spectacled bear exhibits, petting zoo, and aviary. (Apr-Oct, daily) Playground, picnicking. 185 Park Ave. Phone 607/724-5461. ¢¢

Special Events

B.C. Open PGA Golf Tournament. Phone 607/754-2482. July.

Balloon Rally. Phone 607/761-2475. Early Aug.

Broome County Performing Arts Theater, the Forum. Broadway shows, center for dramatic and musical comedy productions by professional performers. Phone 607/778-2480.

Broome County Veterans Memorial Arena & Convention Center. Professional hockey (B.C. Icemen, UHL; winter); national shows and concerts. Phone 607/778-6626.

Motels/Motor Lodges

★★ **BEST WESTERN BINGHAMTON REGENCY HOTEL & CONFERENCE CENTER.** *1 Sarbro Sq (13901). 607/722-7575; fax 607/724-7263; toll-free 800/723-7676. www.bingregency.com.* 204 rms, 9 story. S, D $69; each addl $10-$25; suites $109-$169; under 12 free; wkend rates. TV; cable (premium). Indoor pool; lifeguard. Restaurant 7 am-9 pm. Bar. Ck-out noon. Meeting rms. Business center. In-rm modem link. Bellhops. Valet serv. Sundries. Free covered parking. Exercise equipt. Health club privileges. Some bathrm phones, refrigerators. Cr cds: A, C, D, DS, MC, V.

🄳 🛏 🕎 🛌 🔥 🏃

★★ **COMFORT INN.** *1156 Front St (13905). 607/722-5353; fax 607/722-1823; res 800/228-5150. www.choicehotels.com.* 67 rms, 2 story. S $55-$70; D $60-$75; each addl $10; kit. suites $60-$105; under 18 free; higher rates special events. Crib $8. Pet accepted; deposit. TV; cable (premium). Complimentary continental bkfst. Restaurant adj 7 am-11 pm. Ck-out noon. Coin lndry. Meeting rm. Business servs avail. In-rm modem link. Microwave in suites. Cr cds: A, C, D, DS, ER, JCB, MC, V.

🄳 🐾 🕎 🛌 🆂🅲

★ **DAYS INN.** *1000 Front St (13905). 607/724-3297; fax 607/771-0206; toll-free 800/469-7009. www.daysinn.com.* 106 rms, 4 story. S $65-$100; D $75-$110; each addl $8; under 18 free; some wkend rates; higher rates college events. Crib free. TV; cable (premium), VCR avail. Pool; lifeguard. Complimentary continental bkfst. Restaurant adj open 24 hrs. Ck-out 11 am. Meeting rms. Business servs avail. In-rm modem link. Valet serv. Sundries. Refrigerators avail. Picnic tables, grills. Cr cds: A, C, D, DS, ER, JCB, MC, V.

🄳 🛏 🕎 🛌

★★ **HOLIDAY INN.** *2-8 Hawley St (13901). 607/722-1212; fax 607/722-6063; toll-free 800/465-4329. www.holiday-inn.com.* 241 rms, 8 story. S, D $93-$99; each addl $10; suites $130; under 19 free; wkend plans.

Crib free. Pet accepted; $15. TV; cable (premium). Indoor pool; lifeguard. Coffee in rms. Restaurant 6:30 am-10 pm. Bar noon-1 am; Fri, Sat to 2 am; entertainment wkends. Ck-out noon. Coin lndry. Convention facilities. Business servs avail. In-rm modem link. Shopping arcade. Airport transportation. Health club privileges. Some refrigerators. Cr cds: A, C, D, DS, JCB, MC, V.

★ **HOWARD JOHNSON EXPRESS INN.** *690 Front St (13905). 607/724-1341; fax 607/773-8287; toll-free 800/446-4656. www.hojo.com.* 107 rms, 2 story. S $40-$60; D $46-$70; each addl $5; higher rates special events. Crib free. Pet accepted, some restrictions. TV; cable, VCR. Complimentary continental bkfst. Coffee in rms. Restaurant nearby. Ck-out noon. Meeting rms. Business servs avail. Health club privileges. Balconies. Cr cds: A, C, D, DS, MC, V.

★★ **PARKWAY MOTEL OF VESTAL.** *900 Vestal Pky 434E, Vestal (13858). 607/785-3311; fax 607/785-8117.* 58 rms, 10 kits. S $30-$45; D $38-$60; each addl $5-$10; family, wkly, wkend rates. Crib $5-$8. TV; cable. Pool. Restaurant nearby. Bar 11 am-midnight. Ck-out 11 am. Health club privileges. Refrigerators, microwaves avail. Cr cds: A, C, D, DS, ER, MC, V.

Hotel

★★★ **THE HISTORIC GRAND ROYALE.** *80 State St (13901). 607/722-0000; fax 607/722-7912; res 800/295-5599. www.villager.com.* 61 rms, 6 story. S $75-$95; D $85-$95; each addl $7; suites $150; under 18 free. Crib avail. Pet accepted, some restrictions. TV; cable (premium). Complimentary bkfst. Bar. Ck-out noon. Meeting rms. Business servs avail. In-rm modem link. Valet parking. X-country ski 5 mi. Health club privileges. Renovated city hall (1897). Cr cds: A, C, D, DS, ER, JCB, MC, V.

Restaurants

★ **ARGO.** *117 Court St (13901). 607/724-4692.* Specializes in seafood, Greek and Italian dishes. Own desserts. Hrs: 6 am-9 pm. Closed Jan 1, Thanksgiving, Dec 25. Wine, beer. Bkfst $1.75-$7.25, lunch $3-$14, dinner $6.50-$14.95. Child's menu. Family-owned. Cr cds: A, MC, V.

Adirondack Mountain Museum, Blue Mountain Lake

★★★ **NUMBER FIVE.** *33 S Washington (13903). 607/723-0555. www. number5restaurant.com.* Continental menu. Specializes in steak, seafood, poultry. Hrs: 4-10 pm; Fri, Sat to 11 pm; Sun noon-9 pm; early-bird dinner 4-5:45 pm, Sun to 5 pm. Closed Dec 25. Res accepted. Bar. Wine list. Dinner $17-$21. Child's menu. Entertainment Fri, Sat. Former fire station (1897); firehouse memorabilia. Cr cds: A, D, DS, MC, V.

★ **SPOT.** *1062 Upper Front St (13905). 607/723-8149.* Greek, Amer menu. Specializes in seafood, prime rib, pastries. Open 24 hrs. Res accepted. Bar 8-1 am. Bkfst $2-$8.25, lunch $4.95-$9, dinner $6.50-$27.95. Child's menu. Cr cds: A, D, DS, MC, V.

Blue Mountain Lake

(C-7) See also Long Lake

Pop 250 **Elev** 1,829 ft **Area code** 518 **Zip** 12812

This central Adirondack resort village has mountain trails, splendid views, interesting shops, water sports, good fishing, and hunting.

What to See and Do

Adirondack Lakes Center for the Arts. Concerts, films, exhibitions, theater, community center. In village, next to post office. Phone 518/352-7715.

Adirondack Museum. On slope of Blue Mtn overlooking lakes, mountains, and village. Noted for landscaping; indoor and outdoor displays. Exhibits explore logging, transportation, boating, mining, schooling, outdoor recreation, and rustic furniture. Gift shop. (Memorial Day-mid-Oct, daily) 1 mi N on NY 30. Phone 518/352-7311. ¢¢¢

Adirondack Park. (see)

Blue Mountain. Three-mi trail to 3,800-ft summit; 35-ft observation tower overlooks Adirondack Park (see). Blue Mtn Lake Association has map of trails. 1½ mi N.

Motel/Motor Lodge

★★ **HEMLOCK HALL HOTEL.** *Maple Lodge Rd (12812). 518/352-7706.* 22 rms in lodge, motel and cottages, 20 baths, 10 kits. No A/C. No rm phones. MAP, mid-June-Oct: D $92-$115; each addl $35, under 8, $25; kit. cottages for 2, $125-$135; lower rates late-May-mid-June. Closed rest of yr. Serv charge 12 percent. Crib free. Playground. Dining rm (public by res) sittings 8:30 am and 6 pm. Ck-out 11 am. Game rm. Rec rm. Lawn games. Some private patios. Library. Many antiques. Secluded resort inn near woods on lakeshore. Private sand beach. No cr cds accepted.

Bolton Landing (Lake George Area)

(C-8) See also Diamond Point, Glens Falls, Warrensburg

Pop 1,600 **Elev** 360 ft **Area code** 518 **Zip** 12814
Information Chamber of Commerce, Lakeshore Dr, PO Box 368; 518/644-3831

Bolton Landing, on the shores of Lake George, has been home to musicians, artists, authors, and people of great wealth. Today most of the estates are resorts, but the cultural atmosphere lives on.

What to See and Do

Recreation. Veterans Memorial Park. North end of town. **Rogers Memorial Park.** Center of town on NY 9 N. Beaches (parking fee), tennis, picnicking, arts and crafts instruction; swimming lessons (all free). Phone 518/644-3831.

Motel/Motor Lodge

★★ **VICTORIAN VILLAGE RESORT MOTEL.** *4818 Lake Shore Dr, Bolton Landing (12814). 518/644-9401; fax 518/644-2692.* 33 rms. No A/C. Late June-Labor Day (3-day min): D $69-

$77; each addl $12; lower rates mid-Apr-late June, after Labor Day-Nov. Closed rest of yr. TV; cable. Restaurant nearby. Ck-out 11 am. Tennis. Lawn games. Rec rm. Private sand beach. Cr cds: MC, V.

Resorts

★ **BONNIE VIEW RESORT.** *4654 Lake Shore Dr, Bolton Landing (12814). 518/644-5591. www.bonnieviewlakegeorge.com.* 22 rms, 28 kit. cottages (1-3 bedrm). Mid-July-late Aug: D $86-$101; each addl $7; kit. units for 2-8, $545-$1,117/wk; 3-4-day min stay July-Aug; lower rates mid-May-mid-July, late Aug-mid-Sept. Closed rest of yr. Crib avail. TV; cable. Heated pool. Playground. Complimentary coffee in motel rms. Restaurant nearby. Ck-out 10 am. Tennis. Lawn games. Some fireplaces. Picnic tables, grills. Private beach; boats. Cr cds: DS, MC, V.

★★ **MELODY MANOR RESORT.** *4610 Lakeshore Dr, Bolton Landing (12814). 518/644-9750; fax 518/644-9750. www.melodymanor.com.* 40 rms, 1-3 story. Late June-Labor Day: D $107-$125; each addl $10; wkly rates; lower rates mid-May-late June, after Labor Day-Oct. Closed rest of yr. TV; cable. Heated pool. Restaurant 8 am-noon, 5-10 pm. Bar 5-11 pm. Ck-out 11 am. Tennis. Rec rm. Lawn games. Rowboat, paddleboat. Some balconies. Picnic tables, grills. On 9 acres, 300-ft lakefront; private sand beach. Cr cds: A, MC, V.

★ **NORTHWARD HOTEL RESORT.** *4648 Lake Shore Dr, Bolton Landing (12814). 518/644-2158; fax 518/644-3117. northwardho.com.* 17 motel rms, 10 kits., 8 kit. cottages. Early July-Labor Day: motel: S, D $50-$88; each addl $10; kits. $90-$95; kit. cottages $810-$960/wk; wkends (3-day min); lower rates after Labor Day-Nov, Apr-early July. Closed rest of yr. Crib avail. TV; cable. Pool. Playground. Ck-out 11 am. Game rm. Lawn games. Sun deck. Refrigerators. Picnic tables, grills. Private beach. Cr cds: A, DS, MC, V.

★★★ **THE SAGAMORE.** *110 Sagamore Rd, Bolton Landing (12814). 518/644-9400; fax 518/644-2626; toll-free 800/358-3585. www.thesagamore.com.* 100 rms in main hotel bldg, 3 story, 130 suites in lodge, 2 story. July-Aug: S, D $155-$380; each addl $12; 6-17 yrs $5; under 6 free; suites $360-$430; MAP avail; package plans; lower rates rest of yr. Serv charge $5/person. Crib free. TV; cable (premium). Indoor pool; whirlpool. Playground. Supervised children's activities (July-Aug; rest of yr wkends only); ages 3-12. Dining rm (public by res) 6:30 am-11 pm (see also TRILLIUM). Box lunches. Rm serv 24 hrs (summer). Bar 11 am-midnight. Ck-out noon, ck-in 4 pm. Package store nearby. Convention facilities. Business center. In-rm modem link. Bellhops. Concierge. Gift shop. Beauty shop. Valet parking. Airport, RR station, bus depot transportation; horse-drawn carriages. Lighted and indoor tennis, pro. 18-hole golf privileges, pro, putting green. Private beach. Boats, motors; sightseeing boats, dinner cruises avail; dockage. Downhill ski 18 mi; x-country ski on site. Ski store, rentals; ice-skating. Nature trail. Bicycles. Soc dir; entertainment. Game rm. Racquetball court. Exercise rm; sauna, steam rm. Spa. Many refrigerators, wet bars, fireplaces; microwaves avail. Some private patios, balconies. Cr cds: A, C, D, DS, ER, MC, V.

Restaurant

★★★ **TRILLIUM.** *110 Sagamore Rd, Bolton Landing (12814). 518/644-9400. www.thesagamore.com.* Gourmet cuisine; own baking, ice cream. Hrs: 6-9:30 pm. Res required. Bar. Wine cellar. A la carte entrees: dinner $18-$34. Serv charge 17 percent. Valet parking. Elegant Greek-revival decor, furnishings. Two-level dining area; view of lake. Jacket. Cr cds: A, D, DS, MC, V.

Boonville

(C-6) *See also Rome*

Pop 4,572 **Elev** 1,146 ft
Area code 315 **Zip** 13309
Information Boonville Area Chamber of Commerce, 122 Main St, PO Box 163; 315/942-5112 or 315/942-6823 (recording)
Web www.cybervillage.com/bac

This rural community is nestled in the divide between the Mohawk and Black rivers on the southeastern portion of the Tug Hill Plateau. Pioneers cleared the forests of this area for their dairy farms; it has since become the dairy center of the region.

What to See and Do

Constable Hall. (ca 1820) Limestone Georgian residence built by William Constable, son of one of New York's most prominent merchants; he joined Alexander MaComb and William McCormick in the MaComb Purchase, which consisted of one-tenth of the state. Memorabilia of five generations of Constable family. (June-mid-Oct, Tues-Sun) 7 mi NW via NY 12D, unnumbered road. Phone 315/397-2323. ¢¢

Dodge-Pratt-Northam Art and Community Center. Victorian mansion (1875) features changing art exhibits; tour and a variety of workshops and courses. Gift shop. (Mar-late Dec, Tues-Sat; closed Thanksgiving, Dec 25) 106 Schuyler St. Phone 315/942-5133. **FREE**

Erwin Park. Swimming pool (June-Aug); tennis and basketball courts, picnicking, playground. (Mid-May-mid-Oct) On NY 12. **FREE**

Pixley Falls State Park. Fishing; hiking, picnicking, playground, tent and trailer sites. (May-Sept) Standard fees. 6 mi S on NY 46. Phone 315/942-4713. ¢¢

Skiing. Snow Ridge Ski Area. Four double chairlifts, two T-bars, bunny tow; patrol, school, ski shop, rentals, snowmaking; babysitting, restaurant, cafeteria, bar. (Thanksgiving-Apr, daily) X-country trails. 11 mi N via

NY 12D, 26, in Turin. Phone 315/348-8456. ¢¢¢¢

Special Events

Oneida County Fair. Phone 315/942-2251. Fourth wk July.

NY State Woodsmen's Field Days. Forest industry exhibits; competition. Phone 315/942-4593. Third wkend Aug.

Fall Arts Fest. Craft fair, demonstrations, art show. Second wkend Oct.

Motel/Motor Lodge

★★ **HEADWATERS MOTOR LODGE.** *13524 Rr 12 (13309). 315/942-4493; fax 315/942-4626; toll-free 877/787-4606. www.headwaters motorlodge.com.* 37 rms, 1-2 story, 4 kits. S $45; D $55; each addl $8; under 12 free. Crib $5. Pet accepted, some restrictions. TV; cable (premium). Complimentary continental bkfst. Restaurant nearby. Ck-out 11 am. Meeting rms. In-rm modem link. Game rm. Downhill/x-country ski 9 mi. Health club privileges. Refrigerators. Cr cds: A, DS, MC, V.
D ⬛ ⬛ ⬛ ⬛ SC

Restaurant

★ **HULBERT HOUSE.** *106 Main St (13309). 315/942-4318. www.hulbert house.com.* Specializes in prime rib, seafood. Salad bar. Hrs: 11:30 am-2 pm, 5-9 pm; Sun 11:30 am-8 pm; Fri buffet (seasonal) 5-9 pm. Closed Election Day, Dec 25. Res accepted. Bar from 11 am. Lunch $2-$5, dinner $9.95-$15. Buffet: dinner $8.75. Child's menu. Early American decor; antiques; established 1812. Cr cds: A, MC, V.
D SC ➡

Brewster

See also Mahopac, Mt Kisco, White Plains

Settled 1730 **Pop** 2,162 **Elev** 395 ft
Area code 845 **Zip** 10509

Information Chamber of Commerce; 845/279-2477

Web www.brewsterchamber.com

What to See and Do

Skiing. Thunder Ridge Ski Area. Three chairlifts, rope tow, Mighty Mite; patrol, school, ski and snowboard rentals; snowmaking; cafeteria, bar. Longest run one mi; vertical drop 500 ft. Night skiing. (Dec-Mar, daily; closed Jan 1, Dec 25 morning) Half-day rates. 10 mi N on NY 22. Phone 845/878-4100. ¢¢¢¢¢

Southeast Museum. Located in the 1896 Old Town Hall of Southeast. Borden dairy condensary, circus and railroad artifacts; Trainer collection of minerals from Tilly Foster Mine; seasonal exhibits and activities. (Apr-Dec, Wed, Sat, and Sun afternoons; closed hols) 67 Main St. Phone 845/279-7500. **FREE**

Restaurants

★ ★ ★ **ARCH.** *NY 22 (10509). 845/279-5011. www.archrestaurant. com.* French, continental menu. Specializes in seafood, veal, lamb. Hrs: noon-2:30 pm, 6-10 pm; Sat from 6 pm; Sun 2:30-8 pm; Sun brunch noon-2:30 pm. Closed Mon, Tues; Jan 1. Res accepted. Bar. Wine cellar. Complete meals: $54. Sun brunch $28. Child's menu. Outdoor dining.

Elegant French country inn; stone fireplace. Family-owned. Cr cds: A, C, D, DS, MC, V.

★ ★ ★ **AUBERGE MAXIME.** *721 Titicus Rd, North Salem (10560). 914/669-5450. www.aubergemaxime. com.* French menu. Specializes in duck, souffles. Hrs: noon-3 pm, 6-9 pm; Sun noon-9 pm. Closed Wed. Res accepted. Bar. Prix fixe: 3-course lunch $19.95. Complete meals: dinner $29.98. Child's menu. Valet parking. Outdoor dining in season. Cr cds: A, D, MC, V.

Bronx, Brooklyn

(Follows New York City)

Buffalo

(D-2) *See also East Aurora, Niagara Falls*

Pop 292,648 **Elev** 600 ft
Area code 716

Allentown

Information Buffalo Niagara Convention & Visitors Bureau, 617 Main St, Suite 400; 716/852-0511 or 888/2BUFF-NY
Web www.buffalocvb.org

Buffalo, at the eastern end of Lake Erie, is New York's second-largest city and one of the largest railroad centers in America. Fifteen freight depots and one passenger terminal handle more than 25,000 trains annually. Major products are metal alloys and abrasives; automobile parts and tires; aerospace and defense products; medical, dental, and pharmaceutical devices and products; chemicals and dyes; and food products.

Planned by Joseph Ellicott (agent of the Holland Land Company) in 1803-1804, the city was modeled after Washington, D.C., which was laid out by his brother, Major Andrew Ellicott. Buffalo radiates from Niagara Square, dominated by a monument to President William McKinley, who was assassinated here while attending the Pan-American Exposition in 1901. The area also includes a $7 million city hall, state, and federal buildings. The Buffalo Philharmonic Orchestra, Albright-Knox Art Gallery, and many nightclubs cater to the varied interests of residents and visitors. The city is ringed with 3,000 acres of parks, which offer swimming, boating, tennis, golf, and riding.

In 1679, when Buffalo was claimed by the French, La Salle built the first boat to sail the Great Lakes, the wooden *Griffon.* During the War of 1812, Buffalo was burned by the British, but its 500 citizens returned a few months later and rebuilt. In 1816, *Walk-on-the-Water,* the first steamboat to ply the Great Lakes, was launched here. The opening of the Erie Canal in 1825 made Buffalo the major transportation break between east and west and brought trade and prosperity. Joseph Dart's invention in 1843 of a steam-powered grain elevator caused Buffalo's grain-processing industry to boom.

Since completion of the St. Lawrence Seaway in 1959, Buffalo has been one of the top Great Lakes ports in import-export tonnage.

Transportation
Car Rental Agencies. See IMPORTANT TOLL-FREE NUMBERS.
Public Transportation. Buses and trains (Metro), phone 716/855-7211.
Rail Passenger Service. Amtrak 800/872-7245.

Airport Information
Buffalo/Niagara International Airport. Information 716/630-6000; lost and found 716/630-6150; cash machines, gateway and baggage claim areas.

What to See and Do
Albright-Knox Art Gallery. Eighteenth-century English, 19th-century French and American, 20th-century American and European paintings; works by Picasso, Matisse, Monet, Renoir, and Van Gogh; sculpture from 3000 B.C.-present. Changing exhibits. (Tues-Sun; closed Jan 1, Thanksgiving, Dec 25) 1285 Elmwood Ave. Phone 716/882-8700. ¢¢¢

Allentown. Historic preservation district containing Victorian-era structures of every major style. Many restaurants, antique stores, art galleries, and boutiques.

✪ **Architecture in Buffalo.** Among the works of famous figures in American architecture are

Frank Lloyd Wright houses. 125 Jewett Pkwy, 118 Summit, 285 Woodward, 57 Tillinghast Pl, and 76 Soldiers Pl. Phone 716/829-3543.

Prudential Building. (1895-1896) Designed by Dankmar Adler and Louis Sullivan, the Prudential Building is an outstanding example of Sullivan's ideas of functional design and terra-cotta ornament; one of America's great skyscrapers. 28 Church St. Phone 716/829-3543.

Boat trips. Buffalo Charter Cruises. *Miss Buffalo II* (200 capacity) leaves Naval and Military Park, foot of Main St, for afternoon or eve cruise of harbor, Niagara River, and Lake Erie. (July and Aug, daily; June and Sept, Sat and Sun; also eve cruises) *Niagara Clipper* leaves from North Tonawanda for lunch, brunch, and dinner cruises around Grand Island. (May-Oct) Phone 716/856-6696. ¢¢¢

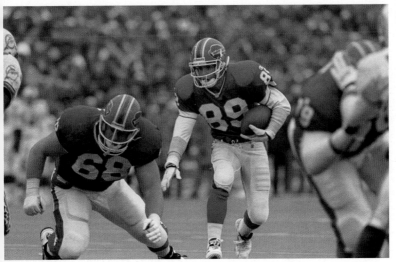

Buffalo Bills

Buffalo & Erie County Botanical Gardens. A 150-acre park with Victorian conservatory and outdoor gardens. Eleven greenhouses with desert, rainforest, and Mediterranean collections. Seasonal shows. (Daily; closed Dec 25) 4 mi SE, 2 mi off NY State Thrwy I-90, exit 55 W Ridge Rd, to 2655 S Park Ave. Phone 716/827-1584. **FREE**

Buffalo & Erie County Historical Society. A Pan-American Exposition building (1901). Exhibits incl history of western New York, pioneer life; 1870 street. (Wed-Sun) 25 Nottingham Ct, at Elmwood. Phone 716/873-9644. ¢¢

Buffalo & Erie County Naval & Military Park. Largest inland naval park in the nation. Cruiser USS *Little Rock,* destroyer USS *The Sullivans,* and submarine USS *Croaker;* aircraft, PT boat, tank, and other WWII equipt; museum, video presentations; gift shop. (Apr-Oct, daily; Nov, wkends) 1 Naval Park Cove. Phone 716/847-1773. ¢¢

Buffalo Museum of Science. Birds of western New York, Gibson Hall of Space, Bell Hall of Space Exploration, Dinosaurs & Company, Insects Magnified World, exhibits on astronomy, botany, geology, zoology, anthropology, and natural sciences; research library, Discovery Room for children. Lectures. (Tues-Sun; closed hols) 1020 Humboldt Pkwy. Phone 716/896-5200. ¢¢

Buffalo Raceway. Pari-mutuel harness racing (Feb-July). Erie County Fairgrounds, 5600 McKinley Pkwy, Thrwy (I-90) exit 56 in Hamburg. Phone 716/649-1280. **FREE**

Buffalo State College. (1867) 11,000 students. On campus are Burchfield Penney Art Center (Tues-Sun; closed hols) Upton Gallery in Upton Hall (academic yr, Mon-Fri). 1300 Elmwood Ave. Phone 716/878-6011 or 716/878-4000.

Buffalo Zoological Gardens. More than 2,200 animals in 23½-acre park; indoor and outdoor exhibits; gallery of Boehm wildlife porcelains; tropical gorilla habitat; outdoor lion and tiger exhibit; children's zoo. (Daily; closed Thanksgiving, Dec 25) 300 Parkside Ave, in Delaware Park. Phone 716/837-3900. ¢¢

City Hall/Observation Tower. Panoramic view of western New York, Lake Erie, and Ontario, Canada. (Mon-Fri; closed hols) Niagara Sq, 28th floor. **FREE**

Gray Line bus tours. 3466 Niagara Falls Blvd, North Tonawanda 14120. Phone 800/365-3609.

Professional sports.

    Buffalo Bills (NFL). Ralph Wilson Stadium, 1 Bills Dr. Orchard Park, NY 14127. Phone 716/648-1800.

Buffalo Sabres (NHL). HSBC Arena, 1 Seymour H. Knox III Plaza. Phone 716/855-4444.

Q-R-S Music Rolls. World's largest and oldest manufacturers of player-piano rolls. Tours twice a day (Mon-Fri). Several steep stairways may pose a problem for some visitors. 1026 Niagara St. Phone 716/885-4600. ¢

Shea's Performing Arts Center. (1926) Broadway shows, theater, dance, opera, music, and family programs. 646 Main St. Phone 716/847-0850. ¢¢¢

State University of NY at Buffalo. (1846) 25,000 students. Buffalo Materials Research Center, National Center for Earthquake Research, rare library collections; art exhibits. Music, theater, dance performances. Campus tours. I-90 to Millersport Hwy, N to SUNY-Buffalo exit. Also at 3435 Main St, near Bailey Ave in Buffalo. Phone 716/645-2000.

Studio Arena Theatre. Regional professional theater presents world premieres, musicals, classic dramas, and contemporary works. (Sept-May, Tues-Sun eve) 710 Main St. Phone 716/856-5650. ¢¢¢¢

Theodore Roosevelt Inaugural National Historic Site. (Wilcox Mansion) Theodore Roosevelt was inaugurated in this classic Greek Revival house in 1901 following the assassination of President McKinley. Audio-visual presentation; tours; Victorian herb garden. Self-guided two-mi architectural walking tours (fee). (Daily) 641 Delaware Ave. Phone 716/884-0095. ¢¢

Special Events

Taste of Buffalo. Main St. July. Phone 716/831-9376.

Erie County Fair. NY thruway to exit 56 right onto Mile Strip Rd, left South Park Ave. Phone 716/649-3900. Aug.

Buffalo Philharmonic Orchestra. Kleinhans Music Hall, 370 Pennsylvania Ave (box office). Classical and pop concert series; children's and family programs. Summer season also. Phone 716/885-5000. July.

Motels/Motor Lodges

★★ **BEST WESTERN INN-ON THE AVE.** *510 Delaware Ave (14202). 716/886-8333; fax 716/884-3070; toll-free 888/868-3033. www.innonthe avenue.com.* 61 rms, 5 story. S $69-$79; D $71-$95; each addl $7; suites $198-$250; under 18 free. Crib $7. TV; cable. Ck-out noon. Meeting rm. Business servs avail. Valet serv. Health club privileges. Wet bar in suites. Cr cds: A, C, D, DS, ER, JCB, MC, V.

★★ **COMFORT SUITES.** *901 Dick Rd (14225). 716/633-6000; fax 716/633-6858; res 800/517-4000.* 100 suites, 2 story. S $67-$80; D $72-$88; each addl $7; family rates; ski plan;

Theodore Roosevelt Inaugural N.H.S.

higher rates sporting events. Crib free. TV; cable (premium), VCR avail. Indoor pool; whirlpool, lifeguard. Complimentary continental bkfst, coffee in rms. Restaurant nearby. Ck-out noon. Coin lndry. Meeting rms. Business servs avail. In-rm modem link. Sundries. Valet serv. Free airport, RR station transportation. Tennis privileges. Golf privileges. Downhill/x-country ski 20 mi. Exercise equipt. Game rm. Refrigerators, microwaves. Cr cds: A, C, D, DS, MC, V.

★ **DAYS INN BUFFALO AIRPORT.**
4345 Genesee St (14225). 716/631-0800; fax 716/631-7589; res 800/329-7466. www.daysinn.com. 130 rms, 6 story. S $55-$75; D $65-$85; each addl $8; family rates. Crib free. TV; cable (premium). Pool; lifeguard. Complimentary continental bkfst, coffee in rms. Restaurant 6:30 am-10:30 pm. Ck-out noon. Meeting rms. Business center. In-rm modem link. Free airport, RR station transportation. Health club privileges. Microwaves avail. Cr cds: A, C, D, DS, ER, JCB, MC, V.

★★ **HAMPTON INN.** *10 Flint Rd, Amherst (14226). 716/689-4414; fax 716/689-4382; toll-free 800/426-7866. www.harthotels.com.* 198 rms, 4 story. S $80-$90; D $90-$100; under 18 free. Crib free. TV; cable (premium). Indoor pool. Complimentary continental bkfst. Restaurant opp 8 am-11 pm. Ck-out noon. Meeting rms. Business servs avail. In-rm modem link. Free airport, RR station transportation. Exercise equipt. Cr cds: A, C, D, DS, MC, V.

★★ **HOLIDAY INN.** *620 Delaware Ave (14202). 716/886-2121; fax 716/886-7942; toll-free 800/465-4329. www.harthotels.com.* 168 rms, 8 story. S, D $84-$99; each addl $10; under 18 free. Crib free. Pet accepted, some restrictions. TV; cable (premium). Heated pool; wading pool, lifeguard. Complimentary bkfst. Restaurant 6:30 am-10 pm. Bar 11 am-midnight. Ck-out noon. Coin lndry. Meeting rms. Business servs avail. In-rm modem link. Bellhops. Valet serv. Free airport transportation. Health club privileges. Cr cds: A, C, D, DS, JCB, MC, V.

★ **MICROTEL.** *1 Hospitality Centre Way, Tonawanda (14150). 716/693-8100; fax 716/693-8750; toll-free 800/227-6346. www.microtelinn.com.* 100 rms, 2 story. Mid-June-early Sept: S $45.95-$60.95; D $50.95-$65.95; under 18 free; lower rates rest of yr. Crib free. Pet accepted, some restrictions. TV; cable. Complimentary continental bkfst. Ck-out noon. Cr cds: A, C, D, DS, JCB, MC, V.

★ **RED ROOF INN.** *42 Flint Rd, Amherst (14226). 716/689-7474; fax 716/689-2051. www.redroof.com.* 108 rms. June-Aug: S $69.99-$79.99; D $79.99-$89.99; under 18 free; higher rates special events; lower rates rest of yr. Crib free. Pet accepted, some restrictions. TV; cable (premium). Complimentary coffee. Restaurant nearby. Ck-out noon. Business servs avail. Cr cds: A, C, D, DS, MC, V.

★ **SUPER 8.** *1 Flint Rd, Amherst (14226). 716/688-0811; fax 716/688-2365; toll-free 800/800-8000. www. super8.com.* 103 rms, 4 story. S $29-$92; D $34-$92; each addl $5; under 12 free; higher rates special events. TV; cable (premium), VCR avail (movies). Complimentary continental bkfst. Restaurant nearby. Ck-out 11 am. Microwaves avail. Cr cds: A, C, D, DS, ER, MC, V.

★★ **THE VICTORIAN MANOR HOTEL.** *8261 Main St, Williamsville (14221). 716/633-4900; res 800/283-3899. www.newyorklodging.com.* 53 rms, 2 story, 9 kit. units. S $52.95-$68.95; D $58.95-$75.95; kit. units $58.95-$88.95; each addl $7; under 18 free. Crib $7. Pet accepted, some restrictions. TV; cable. Complimentary continental bkfst. Ck-out noon. Valet serv. Free airport, RR station transportation. Refrigerator, microwave in kit. units. Picnic tables. Cr cds: A, C, DS, MC, V.

Hotels

★★ **ADAM'S MARK.** *120 Church St (14202). 716/845-5100; fax 716/845-5377. www.adamsmark.com.* 483 rms, 9 story. S $99-$159; D $119-$179; each addl $16; suites $225-$925; family, wkend rates. Crib free. Garage parking (fee). TV; cable (premium), VCR avail. Indoor pool; poolside serv. Restaurants 6:30 am-midnight. Bars; entertainment. Ck-out 11 am. Convention facilities. Business center. In-rm modem link. Concierge. Gift shop. Exercise equipt. Refrigerator avail in some suites. Some private patios, balconies. Cr cds: A, C, D, DS, ER, JCB, MC, V.

★★★ **HYATT REGENCY BUF-FALO.** *2 Fountain Plaza (14202). 716/856-1234; fax 716/852-6157; res 800/233-1234. www.buffalo.hyatt.com.* 395 rms, 16 story. S, D $119-$190; each addl $25; suites $345-$495; under 18 free; wkend rates. Crib free. Garage $5.95. TV; cable (premium), VCR avail. Restaurant 6:30-11 pm. Bar 11:30 am-11 pm. Coffee in rms. Ck-out noon. Convention facilities. Business center. In-rm modem link. Gift shop. Beauty shop. Exercise equipt. Health club privileges. Valet serv. Refrigerators, microwaves avail. Bathrm phone, whirlpool in suites. Cr cds: A, C, D, DS, MC, V.

★★ **LENOX HOTEL & SUITES.** *140 North St (14201). 716/884-1700; fax 716/885-8636; res 800/825-3669.* 149 rms, 9 story, 129 kits. S $59; D $69; each addl $10; suites $70-$100; under 12 free; wkly, monthly rates. Crib free. TV; VCR avail. Ck-out noon. Coin lndry. Meeting rms. Business center. In-rm modem link. Microwaves avail. Built in late 1800s. Cr cds: A, C, D, DS, MC, V.

★ **LORD AMHERST MOTOR HOTEL.** *5000 Main St, Amherst (14226). 716/839-2200; fax 716/839-1538; toll-free 800/544-2200.* 101 rms, 2 story. May-Sept: S $59-$75; D $69-$89; each addl $7; suites $95-$160; kit. units $75-$150; under 18 free; lower rates rest of yr. Crib free. Pet accepted, some restrictions. TV; cable. Heated pool; lifeguard. Complimentary full bkfst. Restaurant 7 am-midnight. Bar 11 am-2 am. Ck-out 1 pm. Coin lndry. Meeting rms. Business servs avail. In-rm modem link. Valet serv. Game rm. Exercise equipt. Microwaves avail. Colonial decor. Cr cds: A, C, D, DS, MC, V.

★★★ **MARRIOTT BUFFALO NIA-GARA.** *1340 Millersport Hwy (14221). 716/689-6900; fax 716/689-0483; res 800/334-4040. www.marriott.com.* 356 rms. 10 story. S, D $79-$181; each addl $10; suites $200; under 18 free; wkend plans. Crib free. Pet accepted, some restrictions; $50. TV; cable (premium). Indoor/outdoor pool; whirlpool; lifeguard; poolside serv. Restaurant 6:30 am-2 pm, 5-10 pm. Bar noon-3 am. Coffee in rms. Ck-out noon. Convention facilities. Business center. In-rm modem link. Valet serv. Concierge. Gift shop. Free airport transportation. Exercise equipt; sauna. Game rm. Some bathrm phones. Refrigerators, microwaves avail. Some poolside patios. Luxury level. Cr cds: A, C, D, DS, JCB, MC, V.

★★★ **RADISSON HOTEL & SUITES- AIRPORT.** *4243 Genesee St, Cheektowaga (14225). 716/634-2300; fax 716/632-2387; res 800/333-3333. www.radisson.com.* 274 rms, 4 story, 54 suites. S, D $94-$150; each addl $10; suites $170; under 18 free; wkend rates. Valet parking avail. Crib free. TV; cable (premium), VCR avail. Heated indoor pool; whirlpool, lifeguard. Restaurant 6 am-midnight. Bar noon-4 am; entertainment. Coffee in rms. Ck-out noon. Convention facilities. Business servs avail. In-rm modem link. Concierge. Gift shop. Free airport, RR station transportation. Exercise equipt; sauna, steam rm. Valet serv. Many bathrm phones; some wet bars. Luxury level. Cr cds: A, C, D, DS, ER, JCB, MC, V.

★★★ **RADISSON SUITES.** *601 Main St (14203). 716/854-5500; fax 716/854-4836; res 800/333-3333. www.radisson.com.* 146 suites, 7 story. S, D $99-$169; each addl $10; under 18 free; family rates. Crib $15. TV; cable (premium). Complimentary continental bkfst, coffee in rms. Restaurant 6:30 am-midnight. Bar 11 am-midnight. Ck-out noon.

Meeting rms. Business servs avail. In-rm modem link. Valet serv. Downhill/x-country ski 15 mi. Exercise equipt. Refrigerators, wet bars; some microwaves. Cr cds: A, C, D, DS, JCB, MC, V.

🔊 🄳 🏋 ☁ 🏊 SC

B&Bs/Small Inns

★ ★ ★ **ASA RANSOM HOUSE.**
10529 Main St, Clarence (14031). 716/759-2315; fax 716/759-2791; toll-free 800/841-2340. www.asaransom. com. 9 rms, 1 with shower only, 2 story, 2 suites. D $95-$125; each addl $20; suites $145; higher rates Sat, hols; lower rates Nov-Dec, Feb-Mar. Closed Jan. Crib free. TV; cable, VCR. Complimentary full bkfst. Restaurant (see ASA RANSOM HOUSE). Serv bar. Ck-out 11 am (Sat, Sun noon), ck-in 2-10 pm. Free RR station transportation. Meeting rm. Business servs avail. In-rm modem link. Luggage handling. Many fireplaces, refrigerators, balconies. Built 1853; antiques. Gift shop. Herb garden. Library. Each rm decorated to distinctive theme. Totally nonsmoking. Cr cds: DS, MC, V.

🄳 ☁ 🔥

★ ★ **VILLAGE HAVEN MOTEL.**
9370 Main St, Clarence (14031). 716/759-6845; fax 716/759-6847. www.newyorklodging.com. 30 rms, 4 kits. Late May-early Sept: S $55-$67; D $62-$72; each addl $7; wkly rates off-season; higher rates hols; lower rates rest of yr. Crib $7. TV. Pool; lifeguard. Playground. Complimentary continental bkfst, coffee in rms. Restaurant nearby. Ck-out 11 am. Business servs avail. Some fireplaces; refrigerators, microwaves avail; whirlpool in suites. Picnic tables. Cr cds: A, MC, V.

🄳 ☁ 🏋 🔥

Extended Stay

★ ★ **RESIDENCE INN BY MARRIOTT.** *100 Maple Rd, Williamsville (14221). 716/632-6622; fax 716/632-5247; res 800/331-3131. www.residenceinn.com/bufam.* 112 kit. suites, 2 story. Kit. suites $109-$159. Crib free. Pet accepted, some restrictions; $6/day. TV; cable, VCR avail. Heated pool. Complimentary continental

bkfst. Ck-out noon. Coin lndry. Business servs avail. In-rm modem link. Valet serv. Free airport transportation. Exercise equipt. Health club privileges. Microwaves. Cr cds: A, C, D, DS, JCB, MC, V.

🄳 🔊 ☁ 🏋 ✈ ☁ 🔥

Restaurants

★ ★ ★ **ASA RANSOM HOUSE.**
10529 Main St, Clarence (14031). 800/841-2340. www.asaransom.com. Hrs: 4-8 pm; Wed 11:30 am-2:30 pm, 4-8 pm; early-bird dinner Tues-Thurs 4-5:30 pm. Closed Dec 25; also Jan-Feb 10. Specialties: grilled salmon steak, roast chicken, smoked corned beef with apple raisin sauce. Own baking, ice cream. Res accepted; required hols. Lunch $7-$13, dinner $9.95-$26.95. Child's menu. Parking. Outdoor dining. Built in 1853. Early American decor; library-sitting rm, antiques. Fresh herb garden. Braille menu. Cr cds: DS, MC, V.

🄳

★ ★ ★ **DAFFODIL'S.** *930 Maple Rd, Williamsville (14221). 716/688-5413. www.daffodilsrestaurant.com.* Specializes in seafood, beef, lamb. Hrs: 11:30 am-2:30 pm, 5-11 pm; Sun 4-9 pm. Res accepted. Bar. A la carte entrees: lunch $6.95-$11.95, dinner $15-$59. Children's menu. Pianist Fri, Sat. Valet parking. Victorian decor. Cr cds: A, DS, MC, V.

🄳

★ ★ **OLD RED MILL INN.** *8326 Main St, Williamsville (14221). 716/633-7878. www.redmillinn.com.* Hrs: 11:30 am-9 pm; Sun 11 am-9 pm; Sun brunch to 2 pm. Closed Mon; also Dec 25. Specializes in prime rib, steaks, seafood combination plates. Res accepted. Bar. Lunch $7.50-$9.95, dinner $10.29-$23.75. Sun brunch $13.95. Children's menu. Parking. Fireplaces; country inn built in 1858. Caboose and Union Pacific dining cars. Cr cds: A, C, D, DS, MC, V.

SC 🍽

★ ★ ★ **SALVATORE'S ITALIAN GARDENS.** *6461 Transit Rd (14043). 716/683-7990.* Hrs: 5-11 pm; Sun from 3 pm. Closed Dec 24, 25. Italian, American menu. Own pastries. Res accepted. Bar. Wine list. Dinner

$12.95-$45. Child's menu. Entertainment Fri, Sat. Parking. Courtyard and gardens. Family-owned. Cr cds: A, D, DS, MC, V.

D

★ **SIENA.** *4516 Main St, Amherst (14226). 716/839-3108.* Hrs: 11:30 am-3 pm, 5-10 pm; Fri, Sat to midnight; Sun 4:30-9 pm. Closed hols. Italian menu. Specializes in wood-oven pizza, ossbucco. Bar. A la carte entrees: lunch $6.25-$8.75, dinner $10-$25. Parking. Italian bistro decor. Cr cds: A, MC, V.

D

Unrated Dining Spots

JENNY'S ICE CREAM. *78 E Spring St, Williamsville (14221). 716/633-2424.* Specializes in homemade ice cream creations, yogurt, sorbet. Hrs: 11 am-9:30 pm; July-Aug to 11 pm. Closed Nov-Mar. Former stable, built in 1807. Old-fashioned decor. Totally nonsmoking.

D

OLD MAN RIVER. *375 Niagara St, Tonawanda (14150). 716/693-5558.* Specialties: charcoal-broiled hot dogs, chicken and sausage, sweet potato french fries. Clam and lobster bar in summer. Own apple dumplings, soups, cookies. Hrs: 8 am-11 pm; Oct-Apr to 9 pm. Closed Jan 1, Thanksgiving, Dec 25. A la carte entrees: bkfst, lunch, dinner $3-$6. Child's menu. All counter serv. Parking. Overlooks Niagara River; reproduction of 18th-century sailing ship for children to play on. Cr cds: A, DS, MC, V.

D SC ⇥

PRIMA PIZZA PASTA. *396 Pearl St (14202). 716/852-5555.* Italian, Amer menu. Specializes in pizza, calzones, chicken wings. Hrs: 9:30 am-midnight; Thurs 9-1 am; Fri, Sat to 3 am; Sun 3-9 pm. Closed Dec 25. Serv bar. A la carte entrees: lunch, dinner $2.75-$10. Two-story; cafe style downstairs, upstairs dining area overlooking street. Cr cds: A, DS, MC, V.

Cairo

(E-7) *See also Catskill, Windham*

Pop 6,355 **Elev** 380 ft **Area code** 518 **Zip** 12413

What to See and Do

Durham Center Museum. Schoolhouse used from 1825-1940; displays of progress of the Catskill Valley; folk art; Native American artifacts; fossils; minerals; railroad and turnpike relics; antiques, household and business equipt. (Memorial Day-Columbus Day, Thurs-Sun; other times by appt) 9 mi on Rte 145 just outside East Durham. Phone 518/239-8461. ¢¢

Zoom Flume Waterpark. Featuring water slides and other rides and attractions. Gift shop; restaurant, snack bar. (Mid-June-Labor Day, daily) Exit 21 off NY State Thrwy, W on NY 23 to NY 145W, 1 mi off NY 145 on Shady Glen Rd in East Durham. Phone 518/239-4559. ¢¢¢¢

Motels/Motor Lodges

★ **PICKWICK LODGE.** *Winter Clove Rd, Round Top (12473). 518/622-3364. www.pickwicklodge.com.* 50 rms, 42 with bath, 3 story. No elvtr. No rm phones. Apr-Nov: S $255-$395/person/wk; $120-$140/person for 2 days; family rates; Closed rest of yr. Crib free. TV in some rms. Pool. Dining rm (public by res) 8-9:15 am, 12:30-2 pm, 6-7:30 pm. Bar 11:30 am-midnight. Ck-out, ck-in 11 am. Meeting rms. Gift shop. Tennis. Putting green. Hiking trails. Lawn games. Rec rm. Large private stocked pond and creeks. Cr cds: MC, V.

D ⬤ ⚐ ⤚ ⇌ ⬱ ⚒

★★ **WINTER CLOVE INN ROUND TOP.** *Winter Clove Rd, Round Top (12473). 518/622-3267. www.winterclove.com.* 40 rms, 4 story. No A/C. No elvtr. No rm phones. AP: $72-$82/person; under 4 free; wkly rates; wkends (2-day min). Closed first 3 wks Dec. Crib avail. TV in sitting rm. Indoor/outdoor pools. Playground. Supervised children's activities in season. Dining rm (public by res) 8 am-9 am, 12:30-1:30 pm, 6-7 pm. Ck-out 11 am, ck-in 1 pm. Free RR station transportation. Lighted tennis. 9-hole golf course. Downhill ski 15 mi;

x-country ski on site. Game rm. Rec rm. Lawn games. Bowling alley. Inn since 1838; antiques. Cr cds: MC, V.

Resort

★ **GAVIN'S GOLDEN HILL RESORT.** *Rte 145 and Golden Hill Rd, East Durham (12423). 518/634-2582; fax 518/634-2531. www.gavins.com.* 60 rms, 2 story. July-Aug, AP: S $70-$80/person; D $99-$112/person; family, wkend, wkly rates; lower rates Sept-Oct, May-June. Closed rest of yr. Crib free. TV; cable, VCR avail (movies). Pool. Playground. Complimentary full bkfst. Restaurant sittings 8:30-10 am, 12:30 pm, 5:30-6:30 pm. Bar; entertainment seasonal. Ck-out 11 am. Downhill ski 20 mi. Lawn games. Cr cds: A, DS, MC, V.

B&B/Small Inn

★★★ **GREENVILLE ARMS 1889 INN.** *Rte 32 South St, Greenville (12083). 518/966-5219; fax 518/966-8754. www.greenvillearms.com.* 13 rms, 2 story. No rm phones. Jan-Nov: S, D $115; each addl $30; wkly rates (MAP); hols (2-day min). Closed Dec. Children over 12 yrs only. TV in sitting rm; cable. Pool. Complimentary full bkfst. Ck-out 11 am, ck-in 3 pm. Business servs avail. Luggage handling. Downhill ski 20 mi. Lawn games. Built 1889 for William Vanderbilt. Original artwork. On seven acres; flower gardens. Cr cds: MC, V.

Canaan

See also Albany, Coxsackie

Pop 1,820 **Elev** 847 ft **Area code** 518 **Zip** 12029

B&Bs/Small Inns

★★ **INN AT SILVER MAPLE FARM.** *NY 295 (12029). 518/781-3600; fax 518/781-3883. www.silvermaplefarm. com.* 9 rms. Some rm phones. S, D $95-$155; each addl $20. Children over 12 yrs only. TV; cable, VCR avail. Whirlpool. Complimentary full bkfst. Ck-out 11 am, ck-in 3 pm. Luggage handling. Gift shop. Downhill ski 11 mi; x-country ski 5 mi. Lawn games. Refrigerators. Converted barn and carriage house. Totally nonsmoking. Cr cds: A, DS, MC, V.

★★ **MILLHOUSE INN.** *Rte 43, Stephentown (12168). 518/733-5606; fax 518/733-6025; toll-free 800/563-8645. www.themillhouseinn.com.* 12 rms, 2 story, 5 suites. S $90; D $105; each addl $15; suites $105-$140; package plans; 2-day min stay hols, wkends July-Aug. Closed mid-Mar-mid-May, Sept and Nov. Crib free. TV in some rms, sitting rm. Pool. Complimentary continental bkfst. Ck-out 11 am, ck-in 2:30 pm. Early 1900s sawmill redone in central European manner; many antiques. Totally nonsmoking. Cr cds: A, MC, V.

Canajoharie (D-7)

Settled 1730 **Pop** 3,797 **Elev** 311 ft **Area code** 518 **Zip** 13317

Located on the south bank of the Mohawk River, Canajoharie is in the center of the scenic and industrial Mohawk Valley. Named for a native word meaning "pot that washes itself," the town is near Canajoharie Gorge, which has a creek that winds down to a waterfall. There are many interesting buildings in the area.

What to See and Do

Fort Klock. (1750) Restored farmhouse (1750) and Native American trading post fortified during the Revolutionary War; also Dutch barn schoolhouse, blacksmith shop, carriage house, herb garden; picnicking. (Memorial Day-mid-Oct, Tues-Sun) 1 mi N, then 8 mi W of NY Thrwy exit 29 on NY 5, in St. Johnsville. Phone 518/568-7779.

Fort Plain Museum. Site of fort and blockhouse (1780-1786) used in defense of the Mohawk Valley during the Revolutionary War. Museum contains local history and archaeological artifacts. (May-Sept, Wed-Sun; rest of yr, by appt) Rte 5S on Western edge of Fort Plain. Phone 518/993-2527.

Library and Art Gallery. Paintings by Sargent, Inness, Whistler, the Wyeths, Stuart; large Winslow Homer collection; Korean ceramics. (Mon-Sat; closed hols) 2 Erie Blvd. Phone 518/673-2314. **FREE**

Motel/Motor Lodge

★ **RODEWAY INN.** *93 E Grand St, Palatine Bridge (13428). 518/673-3233; fax 518/673-5011. www.rodeway inn.com.* 30 rms, 3 kits. May-Oct: S $45-$75; D $50-$85; each addl $8; kit. units $60-$125; family, wkly rates; lower rates rest of yr. Crib $5. TV; cable. Complimentary continental bkfst, coffee in rms. Restaurant nearby. Ck-out 11 am. Business servs avail. Downhill/x-country ski 10 mi. Overlooks Mohawk River. Cr cds: A, C, D, DS, ER, JCB, MC, V.

⬚ ⬚ ⬚ ⬚ ⬚ **SC**

Canandaigua

(D-3) *See also Geneva, Naples, Rochester, Victor*

Pop 11,264 **Elev** 767 ft **Area code** 585
Information Chamber of Commerce, 113 S Main St, 14424; 585/394-4400
Web www.canandaigua.com/chamber

This is a resort city on Canandaigua Lake (westernmost of the Finger Lakes).

What to See and Do

Canandaigua Lady. Replica of 19th-century paddlewheel steamboat offers variety of cruises, incl lunch, brunch, dinner, and special events. (May-Oct daily) 205 Lakeshore Dr. Phone 585/396-7350.

Finger Lakes Race Track. Thoroughbred racing (Apr-Nov, Mon, Tues, Fri-Sun). 7 mi NW on NY 332 at jct NY 96; I-90, exit 44. Phone 585/924-3232. ¢¢

Granger Homestead. (1816) and **Carriage Museum.** Home of Gideon Granger, Postmaster General under presidents Jefferson and Madison; nine restored rms; original furnishings. Carriage museum in two buildings; more than 50 antique horse-drawn vehicles; incl coaches, cutters, surreys, sleighs, hearses. Tours (by appt). (June-Aug, Tues-Sun; mid-May-late May and Sept-mid-Oct, Tues-Fri) 295 N Main St. Phone 585/394-1472. ¢¢

Ontario County Historical Society. Museum and archives relating to the history of Ontario County; changing exhibits; research library for genealogical studies. Bookstore. (Tues-Sat; closed hols) 55 N Main St. Phone 585/394-4975. ¢

Skiing. Bristol Mountain Ski & Snowboard Resort. Two quad, two triple, double chairlifts; tow rope; patrol, school, rentals; snowmaking; cafeteria, bar. Longest run two mi, vertical drop 1,200 ft. (Mid-Nov-Apr, daily) 12 mi SW on NY 64.

Sonnenberg Gardens. A 50-acre Victorian garden estate with 1887 mansion; conservatory; nine formal gardens incl Italian, Japanese, colonial, rock, rose, and blue and white pansy. Tours. (Mid-May-mid-Oct, daily) Off Rte 21 on Charlotte St. Phone 585/394-4922. ¢¢¢

Special Events

Ontario County Fair. Hopewell Townline Rd. July. Phone 585/394-4987.

SummerMusic. Rochester Philharmonic Orchestra, Finger Lakes Performing Arts Center. Symphonic, classical, and pops concerts. Indoor/outdoor seating. Picnic sites. Contact 108 East Ave, Rochester 14604. Phone 716/454-2620. July.

Pageant of Steam. 3 mi E on Gehan Rd. Working steam engines and models; parade. Four days Aug. Phone 585/394-8102.

Ring of Fire. Re-enactment of Native American ceremony. Sat before Labor Day.

Motel/Motor Lodge

★ **ECONO LODGE CANANDAIGUA.** *170 Eastern Blvd (14424). 716/394-9000; fax 716/396-2560; res 800/553-2666. www.econo lodge.com.* 65 rms, 2 story. May-Oct: S $42-$80; D $49-$90; each addl $10; under 18 free; lower rates rest of yr. Crib free. Pet accepted, some restrictions. TV; cable (premium), VCR avail (movies). Complimentary coffee in lobby. Restaurant adj open 24 hrs. Ck-out 11 am. Coin lndry. Business servs avail. Downhill ski 12 mi. Opp lake. Cr cds: A, D, DS, MC, V.
[D] [icons] [SC]

B&Bs/Small Inns

★★ **ACORN INN B & B.** *4508 NY 64 (14424). 716/229-2834; fax 716/229-5046; toll-free 888/245-4134. acorninnbb.com.* 4 rms, 2 story. May-Oct: S $100; D $100-$115; each addl $25; ski plans; wkends 2-day min; higher rates hols; lower rates rest of yr. Children over 14 yrs only. TV; cable (premium), VCR (movies). Complimentary full bkfst; refreshments. Ck-out 11 am, ck-in 3 pm. Business servs avail. Luggage handling. Downhill/x-country ski 5 mi. Some fireplaces. Built in 1795; originally was a stagecoach inn. Federal style; antiques. Totally nonsmoking. Cr cds: A, DS, MC, V.
[icons]

★★★ **CANANDAIGUA INN ON THE LAKE.** *770 S Main St (14534). 716/394-7800; fax 716/394-5003. www.hudsonhotels.com.* 134 rms, 2 story, 44 suites. May-Nov: S $98-$145; D $108-$155; each addl $10; suites $152-$295; under 18 free; package plans; lower rates rest of yr. Crib free. Pet accepted. TV; cable, VCR avail (movies). 2 heated pools, 1 indoor; whirlpool, lifeguard. Restaurant 6:30 am-9 pm; wkends to 10 pm. Bar 11-1 am. Ck-out 11 am. Coin lndry. Meeting rms. Business servs avail. In-rm modem link. Exercise equipt. Downhill ski 20 mi. Refrigerators in suites. Some balconies. Picnic tables. On lake. Cr cds: A, D, DS, MC, V.
[D] [icons]

★★★ **GREENWOODS BED & BREAKFAST.** *8136 Quayle Rd, Honeoye (14471). 716/229-2111; toll-free 800/914-3559. www.greenwoods inn.com.* 5 rms, 3 story. No rm phones. S $100-$110; D $105-$115; each addl $15; ski plans. Children over 12 yrs only. TV. Whirlpool. Complimentary full bkfst. Ck-out 11 am, ck-in 3 pm. Business servs avail. Downhill ski 7 mi; x-country ski 8 mi. Picnic tables. Log building in rural setting with three porches. Totally nonsmoking. Cr cds: A, DS, MC, V.
[icons]

★★★ **MORGAN SAMUELS INN.** *2920 Smith Rd (14424). 716/394-9232; fax 716/394-8044. www.morgan samuelsinn.com.* 5 rms, 2 story, 1 suite. Mid-May-mid-Nov, wkend rates: S $69-$99; D $139-$199; each addl $20; suite $195; lower rates rest of yr. Crib free. TV; VCR avail. Complimentary full bkfst. Ck-out 11 am, ck-in 3 pm. Business servs avail. Tennis. Downhill ski 11 mi; x-country ski on site. Health club privileges. Balconies. Stone and brick farmhouse (1810); library, fireplaces, antiques, original artwork. Extensive grounds. Totally nonsmoking. Cr cds: DS, MC, V.
[icons]

★★ **SUTHERLAND HOUSE BED & BREAKFAST.** *3179 State Rt 21 S (14424). 716/396-0375; toll-free 800/396-0375. www.sutherlandhouse. com.* 5 rms, 1 suite. Some rm phones. S $85; D $150; each addl $20; suites $170; package plans. TV; cable, VCR (movies). Complimentary full bkfst; afternoon refreshments. Ck-out 11 am, ck-in 3-6 pm. Business servs avail. Luggage handling. Concierge serv. Gift shop. Donwhill ski 10 mi; x-country ski 20 mi. Many fireplaces; some in-rm whirlpools, refrigerators. Built in 1885; country Victorian inn. Antiques. Totally nonsmoking. Cr cds: A, DS, MC, V.
[icons]

Restaurants

★★★ **HOLLOWAY HOUSE.** *29 State St, East Bloomingfield (14443). 585/657-7120.* Specialties: Sally Lunn bread, roast turkey. Own baking. Hrs: 11:30 am-2 pm, 5-8:30 pm; Sat to 9 pm; Sun noon-7:30 pm. Res accepted. Closed Mon; also late Dec-Mar. Bar. Lunch $6.95-$10.95, dinner $11.95-$22.95. Child's menu. Parking. Inn and stagecoach stop established 1808. Family-owned. Cr cds: A, DS, MC, V.

★ **KELLOGG'S PAN-TREE INN.** *130 Lakeshore Dr (14424). 716/394-3909. www.stegalls.com/kelloggs.* Specialties: griddle cakes, chicken pie, creamed codfish. Own baking. Hrs: 7:30 am-7:30 pm; Sun from 8 am. Closed Nov-mid-Apr. Bkfst $4-$6.25, lunch $4.50-$14.95, dinner $8-$14.25. Childen's meals. Parking. Overlooks park, lake. Family-owned. Cr cds: MC, V.

★ ★ ★ **LINCOLN HILL INN.** *3365 E Lake Rd, Canadaigua (14424). 716/394-8254. www.lincolnhill.com.* Continental menu. Specializes in seafood, beef, chicken. Hrs: 5-10 pm. Closed Sun, Mon mid-Oct-mid-Apr; Dec 25. Res accepted. Bar. Dinner $9.95-$20.95. Child's menu. Outdoor dining. Early Finger Lakes homestead, built 1804. Cr cds: A, MC, V.

★ **MANETTI'S.** *20 Maur St (14424). 716/394-1915.* Italian, Amer menu. Specializes in veal, pasta. Salad bar. Hrs: 4-10 pm; Sun from noon; 4-11 pm summer. Closed Thanksgiving, Dec 25. Res accepted. Bar to 1 am; Sat to 2 am. Dinner $7.25-$21.95. Child's menu. Parking. Solarium. Cr cds: A, D, MC, V.

Canastota

(D-6) *See also Rome, Syracuse, Utica*

Settled 1810 **Pop** 4,425 **Elev** 420 ft **Area code** 315 **Zip** 13032

In 1820, when the first packetboat run was established on the Erie Canal from here to Rome, Canastota became a canal town. Some of the original structures still exist along the canal, which bisects the village.

What to See and Do

Canastota Canal Town Museum. Displays trace growth of Erie Canal and its effect on Canastota and western

New York. Adj to state park. (Apr-Oct Mon-Sat; closed hols) 122 Canal St. Phone 315/697-3451. **Donation**

Canton

(A-6) *See also Ogdensburg (Thousand Islands), Potsdam*

Pop 10,334 **Elev** 380 ft **Area code** 315 **Zip** 13617
Information Chamber of Commerce, Municipal Building, PO Box 369; 315/386-8255

Canton, which lies on the Grass River, was settled in the early 1800s by Vermonters. Canton College of Technology is located here.

What to See and Do

St. Lawrence University. (1856) 2,000 students. On campus are the Griffiths Arts Center, Gunnison Memorial Chapel, Owen D. Young Library, Augsbury-Leithead Physical Education Complex. Campus tours. Phone 315/229-5261.

Silas Wright House and Museum. (St. Lawrence County Historical Association) Greek Revival residence (1832-1844) of the US senator and New York governor. First floor restored to 1830-1850 period; second floor gallery for temporary exhibits on local history. Gift shop. Library, archives, museum (Tues-Sat; closed hols). 3 E Main St. Phone 315/386-8133. ¢¢

Motels/Motor Lodges

★ ★ **BEST WESTERN UNIVERSITY INN.** *90 E Main St (13617). 315/386-8522; fax 315/386-1025; toll-free 888/386-8522. www.bwcanton.com.* 98 rms, 3 story. No elvtr. May-Oct: S $75-$120; D $85-$130; under 12 free; golf plan; lower rates rest of yr. Crib free. Pet accepted. TV; cable (premium). Pool. Coffee in rms. Restaurant 6:30 am-9 pm. Bar 11-2 am. Ck-out noon. Meeting rms. Business servs avail. X-country ski on site. Exercise equipt. Some refrigerators, microwaves. Cr cds: A, D, DS, MC, V.

★ **CLEARVIEW MOTEL & RESTAU-RANT.** *1180A US Hwy 11, Gouverneur (13642).* 315/287-2800; fax 315/287-0534. 34 rms. S $41-$47; D $45-$58; each addl $6; under 12 free. Crib free. TV; cable. Pool. Complimentary coffee in lobby. Restaurant adj 11 am-11 pm. Ck-out 11 am. Meeting rms. Sundries. 18-hole golf privileges, pro. Picnic tables, grills. Cr cds: A, DS, MC, V.
🄳 🛠 ⩳

Restaurant

★ **MCCARTHY'S.** *5821 US 11 (13617).* 315/386-2564. Specializes in chicken and biscuits, soups. Own cinnamon rolls. Salad bar. Hrs: 7 am-9 pm. Closed hols. Res accepted. Bar. Bkfst $3.75-$6.50, lunch $2.95-$9.50, dinner $8.25-$12.95. Sun brunch $6.25. Child's menu. Cr cds: D, DS, MC, V.
🄳

Catskill

(E-8) *See also Hillsdale, Hudson, Hunter*

Settled 1662 **Pop** 11,849 **Elev** 47 ft
Area code 518 **Zip** 12414
Information Greene County Promotion Dept, NY Thrwy exit 21, PO Box 527; 518/943-3223 or 800/355-CATS
Web www.greene-ny.com

This is the eastern entrance to the Catskill Mountains resort area. The town is at the west end of the Rip Van Winkle Bridge, over the Hudson River across from the manufacturing town of Hudson (see). The legendary Rip is said to have slept for 20 years near here.

What to See and Do

Catskill Game Farm. Children may feed tame deer, donkeys, llamas, other animals. Rides; picnic grounds; cafeteria. (May-Oct, daily) 8 mi W on NY 23, 5 mi S on NY 32. Phone 518/678-9595. ¢¢¢¢

Zoom Flume Waterpark. Catskill's largest water park. Gift shop. Restaurant. (Mid-June-Labor Day daily) 13 mi from Exit 21 off NY state thruway. Phone 518/239-4559. ¢¢¢¢

Motels/Motor Lodges

★★ **CARL'S RIP VAN WINKLE.** *810 Rte 23B, Leeds (12451).* 518/943-3303; fax 518/943-2309. www.ripvanwinkle motorlogde.com. 41 units, 27 cabins, 6 kits. Many rm phones. July-Aug: S, D $48-$65; each addl $5-$15; kit. units to 4, $425-$450/wk; lower rates mid-Apr-June, Sept-mid-Nov. Closed rest of yr. Crib $5. TV; cable (premium). Pool; wading pool. Playground. Restaurant adj 7:30-11 am, 4:30-9 pm. Ck-out 11 am. Hiking trails. Lawn games. Some refrigerators; fireplace in some cabins. Picnic tables, grill. On 160 wooded acres. Cr cds: A, MC, V.
⩳ 🔥 ⩳

★★ **CATSKILL MOUNTAIN LODGE.** *334 Rte 32A, Palenville (12463).* 518/678-3101; fax 518/678-3103; res 800/686-5634. www.thecat skills.com/catmtldg.htm. 42 units, 2 kit. units, 2 cottages. Late-June-Labor Day: S, D $60-$95; kit. units $425/wk; cottages $625/wk; under 6 free; family, wkly rates; wkends (min stay required); higher rates hols; lower rates rest of yr. Crib $7.50. TV; cable. Restaurant adj 7 am-10 pm. Bar. Ck-out 11 am. Valet serv. Sundries. RR station transportation. Pool; wading pool. Playground. Game rm. Lawn games. Some refrigerators. Cr cds: A, C, D, DS, MC, V.
🄳 ⩳ 🔥 🅂🄲

★★ **RED RANCH.** *4555 NY 32 (12414).* 518/678-3380; toll-free 800/962-4560. www.redranchmotel. com. 39 rms, 2 story, 4 kits. July-Labor Day: S, D $45-$68; kit. units up to 6, $72-$90; wkly rates; ski plans; higher rates: Hunter Mtn festivals, hol wkends; lower rates rest of yr. Crib $6. TV; cable (premium). Pool; wading pool. Playground. Restaurant adj 7:30 am-10 pm. Ck-out 11 am. Downhill/x-country ski 10 mi. Game rm. Lawn games. Refrigerators avail. Picnic tables. Cr cds: A, D, DS, MC, V.
🄳 🔥 ⩳

Catskills

Resorts

★★★ **FRIAR TUCK RESORT AND CONVENTION CENTER.** *4858 State Rte 32 (12414). 518/678-2271; toll-free 800/832-7600. www.friartuck. com.* 525 rms, 2-5 story. MAP, June-Aug: D $95-$145/person; suites $150-$250/person; under 12 free; wkly rates; ski, golf plans; lower rates rest of yr. Crib free. TV; cable (premium). 3 pools, 1 indoor; whirl-pool, lifeguard. Playground. Super-vised children's activities (summer, winter). Dining rm 8 pm-midnight. Bar from 11 am; entertainment. Ck-out noon, ck-in 3 pm. Coin lndry. Convention facilities. Business cen-ter. Bellhops. Gift shop. Airport, bus depot transportation. Lighted ten-nis. Downhill/x-country ski 12 mi. Soc dir. Game rm. Rec rm. Exercise rm; sauna, steam rm. Theater. On lake. Cr cds: A, MC, V.

★★ **WOLFFIS MAPLE BREEZE** *Resort. 360 Cauterskill Rd (12414). 518/943-3648; fax 518/943-9335; toll-free 800/777-9653. www.wolffs resort.com.* 42 rms, 1-2 story. MAP, July-Aug: S $70/person; D $80-$120/person; suites $75-$95; wkly: $362-$415/person; family rates; lower rates May-June, Sept-Oct.

Closed rest of yr. Crib free. TV; cable (premium). Pool; lifeguard. Playground. Supervised children's activities. Dining rm (public by res) 8:30-10 am, 5:30-6:30 pm. Snack bar. Bar; entertainment. Ck-out 11 am, ck-in 1 pm. Business servs avail. Grocery, coin lndry, package store 3 mi. Tennis. Boats, rowboats. Lawn games. Soc dir. Game rm. Refrigerators. Spacious grounds. Three lakes. Hayrides. Cr cds: MC, V.

B&B/Small Inn

★★ **STEWART HOUSE.** *2 N Water St, Athens (12015). 800/339-4622. www.stewarthouse.com.* 5 rms, 4 with shower only, 2 story. No rm phones. S, D $90; higher rates Dec 31. Complimentary full bkfst. Restaurant. Ck-out noon, ck-in after 3 pm. On Hudson River. Built in 1883; antiques. Cr cds: A, MC, V.

Restaurants

★★ **FERNWOOD.** *341 Malden Ave, Palenville (12463). 518/678-9332.* Continental menu. Specialties: chicken Rebecca, shrimp scampi, linguini bucaniera. Hrs: 5-10 pm. Closed Mon, Tues; Dec 25. Res accepted. Bar. Dinner $11.50-$30. Child's menu. Outdoor dining. Family-owned since 1966. Cr cds: A, DS, MC, V.

★★ **STEWART HOUSE.** *2 N Water St, Athens (12015). 518/945-1357.* Specialties: rack of lamb, penne and smoked Salmon, chocolate terrine. Hrs: 11:30 am-9 pm; Fri to 10 pm; Sat 2-10 pm; Sun 10 am-9 pm; Sun brunch to 2 pm. Res accepted. Wine list. Lunch $5.95-$11.95, dinner $11.95-$21.95. Sun brunch $13.95. Outdoor dining. Restored to 1905 arts-and-crafts style. Totally non-smoking. Cr cds: A, MC, V.

Catskill Park

(E-7 - F-7) *See also Cairo, Hunter, Shandaken, Woodstock*
Web www.fortmyersbeach.org

The 705,500-acre Catskill Park includes some of the wildest country south of Maine. More than 200 miles of marked trails wind through its woods. More than 272,000 acres are owned by the state and comprise the Forest Preserve. This includes seven campgrounds: **North/South Lake**, off NY 23A, 3 mi NE of Haines Falls, 518/589-5058; **Devil's Tombstone**, NY 214, 4 mi S of Hunter, 914/688-7160; **Woodland Valley**, off NY 28, 6 mi SW of Phoenicia, 914/688-7647; **Mongaup Pond**, off NY 17, 3 mi N of DeBruce, 914/439-4233; **Little Pond**, off NY 17, 14 mi NW of Livingston Manor, 914/439-5480; **Beaverkill**, off NY 17, 7 mi NW of Livingston Manor, 914/439-4281; **Kenneth L. Wilson**, off NY 28, 4 mi E of Mount Tremper on County 40, 914/679-7020. Nearby is **Bear Springs Mountain** (outside Catskill Park), 5 mi SE of Walton off NY 206, 607/865-6989. Standard fees. Skiing at Belleayre Mountain (see SHANDAKEN), chairlift operating to 3,400 feet. Phone 914/254-5600.

Cazenovia

(D-5) *See also Syracuse*

Pop 6,481 **Elev** 1,224 ft
Area code 315 **Zip** 13035

What to See and Do

Chittenango Falls State Park. Has 167-ft waterfall. Fishing; hiking, picnicking, playground, tent and trailer sites. Standard fees. (May-Oct, daily) 4 mi N on NY 13. Phone 315/655-9620.

Lorenzo State Historic Site. (1807) Elegant Federal-period mansion built by John Lincklaen; original furnishings; garden, arboretum. (May-Oct, Wed-Sun) ¾ mi S on NY 13. Phone 315/655-3200. ¢¢

Skiing. Toggenburg Ski Center. Triple, double chairlifts; two beginners' lifts, two T-bars; patrol, ski school, rentals; snowmaking; cafeteria, bar; nursery. Night skiing. (Dec-early Apr, daily; closed Dec 25) X-country trails in Highland Forest, approx 2 mi W on NY 80. 6 mi W on US 20, then 6 mi S on Pompey Center Rd. Phone 315/683-5842 or 800/720-TOGG. ¢¢¢¢

Motels/Motor Lodges

★★★ **BREWSTER INN.** *6 Ledyard Ave Rte 20 (13035).* 315/655-9232; fax 315/655-2130. www.cazenovia.com/brewsterinn. 17 rms, 3 story. S, D $75-$225; each addl $10. TV; cable (premium). Complimentary continental bkfst. Restaurant (see BREWSTER INN). Bar 5 pm-midnight. Ck-out 11 am, ck-in 2 pm. Business servs avail. 18-hole golf privileges. Exercise equipt. Victorian summer home (1890); elegant antique furnishings; library; fireplaces. Extensive grounds; elaborate landscaping. Cr cds: C, D, DS, MC, V.
🄳 🕃 🖼 🐾 🏋 🏌

★★★ **LINCKLAEN HOUSE.** *79 Albany St (13035).* 315/655-3461; fax 315/655-5443. www.cazenovia.com. 18 rms, 3 story. S, D $99-$140; suites $120-$140. Crib free. Pet accepted. TV. Complimentary continental bkfst. Ck-out 11 am, ck-in 2 pm. Meeting rms. Business servs avail. Built in 1835. Cr cds: A, MC, V.
🄳 🐾 🕃 🔔 🖼 🏌

B&B/Small Inn

★★ **BRAE LOCH INN.** *5 Albany St (13035).* 315/655-3431; fax 315/655-4844. www.cazenovia.com/braeloch. 14 rms. S, D $70-$100; each addl $15; under 12 free. Crib free. TV. Complimentary continental bkfst. Restaurant (see BRAE LOCH INN). Ck-out 11 am, ck-in 2 pm. Gift shop. Located opp a swimming beach. Inn built ca 1805; many antiques. Cr cds: A, DS, MC, V.
🔔 🖼 🌊

Restaurants

★★ **BRAE LOCH INN.** *5 Albany St (13035).* 315/655-3431. www.cazenovia.com/braeloch. Continental menu. Specialties: Angus Dundee, prime rib. Own baking. Hrs: 5-9:30 pm; Sat to 10 pm; Sun 11 am-9 pm; Sun brunch (Sept-June) to 2 pm. Closed Dec 24, 25. Res accepted. Bar. Dinner $9.95-$18.95. Sun brunch $12.95. Child's menu. Scottish pub atmosphere; downstairs pub dining. Family-owned. Cr cds: A, MC, V.

★ ★ ★ **BREWSTER INN.** *6 Ledyard Ave (13035). 315/655-9232. www. cazenovia/brewsterinn.com.* Continental menu. Specializes in roast duck, fresh seafood, lamb. Own baking. Hrs: 5-9 pm; Sun brunch 11 am-2 pm. Closed hols. Res accepted. Bar. Wine list. Dinner $17-$20. Sun brunch $16. Outdoor dining. Victorian mansion; many antiques, 4 fireplaces. Overlooks lake. Cr cds: C, D, DS, MC, V.

Chautauqua

(E-1) *See also Bemus Point, Jamestown*

Founded 1874 **Pop** 4,666 **Elev** 1,360 ft **Area code** 716 **Zip** 14722

Chautauqua Institution is a lakeside summer center for the arts, education, religion, and recreation. Programs are offered to adults and children. Summer population swells to more than 10,000.

The community began as a Sunday school teachers' training camp and developed into a cultural center that originated nationwide book clubs and correspondence schools. It has provided a platform for presidents and political leaders, as well as great musical artists and popular entertainers.

What to See and Do

Boat cruise. *Chautauqua Belle.* Replica of a 19th-century paddle-wheel steamboat cruises on Chautauqua Lake; incl narrative of history of the area and wildlife around the lake. (Memorial Day-Labor Day, daily) Phone 716/753-2403.

The Chautauqua Institution. Summer center for arts, education, religion, and recreation. Nine-wk season (late June-late Aug, daily) features a

lecture platform as well as performing arts events. Along NY 394 on the W shore of Chautauqua Lake. Phone 716/357-6200.

Chautauqua Amphitheater. Contains 5,000 seats, home of Chautauqua Symphony Orchestra; recitals, ballet, lectures, special popular musical events. Phone 716/357-6200.

Miller Bell Tower. Campanile on the shore of Chautauqua Lake.

Norton Memorial Hall. Four operatic productions are presented in English each season by the Chautauqua Opera Company.

Palestine Park. Outdoor walk-through model of the Holy Land. Tours Mon eve, Sun afternoon.

Recreation. Swimming, boating, sailing, fishing; tennis, 27-hole golf (fee), x-country skiing (winter). Phone 716/357-6200.

Motels/Motor Lodges

★ ★ ★ **ST. ELMO ACCOMMODA-TIONS.** *1 Pratt Ave (14722). 716/357-3566; fax 716/357-3317; toll-free 800/507-5005. www.chautauquaarea. com.* 21 kit. suites, 4 story. Kit. suites $65-$150; wkly rates; ski plans. Gate fee for Institution grounds (late June-late Aug). Crib free. TV; cable (premium), VCRs/CDs avail. Ck-out 10 am. Coffee in rms. Coin lndry. Business servs avail. Shopping arcade. Tennis. Golf course, greens fee $15-$30, pro, putting green, driving range. Downhill ski 20 mi; x-country ski on site. Microwaves. Balconies. Victorian hotel on Chautauqua Lake. Cr cds: A, DS, MC, V.

★ ★ ★ **WILLIAM SEWARD INN.** *6645 S Portage Rd, Westfield (14787). 716/326-4151; fax 716/326-4163. www.williamsewardinn.com.* 12 rms, 7 with shower only, 2 story. No rm phones. Jun-Oct: S, D $80-$185; each addl $15; wkends, hols (2-day min). Children over 12 yrs only. Pet accepted, some restrictions. TV; cable in library. Restaurant Wed-Sun (res only). Complimentary full bkfst; afternoon refreshments. In-rm modem link. Ck-out 11 am, ck-in 2-8 pm. Downhill ski 20 mi; x-country ski 7 mi. Some fireplaces, in-rm whirlpools, balconies. 3 mi to lake. Restored Greek Revival mansion built

1837; antiques. Totally nonsmoking. Cr cds: A, DS, MC, V.

Hotel

★★★ **ATHENAEUM HOTEL.** *Lake Dr (14722).* 716/357-4444; fax 716/357-4175; toll-free 800/821-1881. *www.athenaeum-hotel.com.* 156 rms. AP, late June-late Aug: S $173-$269; D $210-$382; each addl $75; suites $300-$420. Closed rest of yr. Gate fee for Institution grounds (late June-late Aug). Crib free. TV; cable (premium). Valet parking $10/day. Supervised children's activities (June-Sept). Complimentary continental bkfst. Restaurant (see ATHENAEUM). Ck-out 10 am. Meeting rms. Business servs avail. Tennis. Golf. Bellhops. Lawn games. Gift shop. Nature walks. Sun deck. Concerts. Restored Victorian hotel (1881). Cr cds: A, DS, MC, V.

Resort

★★ **WEBBS YEAR ROUND LAKE RESORT.** *Rt 394, Mayville (14757).* 716/753-2161; fax 716/753-1383. *webbsworld.com.* 52 rms, 2 story. S, D $66-$69. Crib $5. TV. Heated pool. Restaurant 11:30 am-2 pm, 5-10 pm; Sun noon-9 pm. Bar to midnight. Ck-out 11 am. Coin lndry. Meeting rm. Business servs avail. Sundries. Exercise equipt. Game rm. Lawn games. Open-air deck 11 am-midnight. Cr cds: A, MC, V.

Restaurants

★★★ **ATHENAEUM.** *South Lake Dr (14722).* 716/357-4444. *www. athenaeum-hotel.com.* Continental menu. Specializes in seafood, veal. Hrs: 8-9:30 am, noon-1:30 pm, 5-7:30 pm. Closed Sept-May. Res required. Complete meals: bkfst $13.20, lunch $18, dinner $32.50. Child's menu. Valet parking. Outdoor dining. Victorian dining rm with many antiques. Jacket and tie (dinner). Cr cds: A, D, MC, V.

★ **SADIE J'S CAFE.** *15-17 Ramble Ave (14722).* 716/357-5245. Specializes in vegetarian sandwiches, soup,

muffins. Hrs: 9 am-4 pm; June-Aug 7 am-11 pm. Closed Nov 1-Apr 1. A la carte entrees: bkfst $2.25-$3.25, lunch, dinner $3.95-$6.75. Totally nonsmoking. Cr cds: A, MC, V.

★★ **WEBB'S-THE CAPTAIN'S TABLE.** *NY 394, Mayville (14757).* 716/753-3960. *www.webbsworld.com.* Specializes in beef, seafood, chicken. Hrs: 11 am-3 pm, 5-9 pm; wkends noon-10 pm. Res accepted. Bar. Lunch $5.95-$10.95, dinner $13.95-$25.95. Closed Thanksgiving, Dec 24, 25. Child's menu. Parking. Outdoor dining on deck. Intimate dining. Family-owned. Cr cds: A, DS, MC, V.

Clayton (Thousand Islands)

(B-5) *See also Alexandria Bay (Thousand Islands), Kingston*

Pop 4,817 **Elev** 260 ft **Area code** 315 **Zip** 13624

Information Chamber of Commerce, 510 Riverside Dr; 315/686-3771 or 800/252-9806

Web www.thousandislands.com/ claytonchamber

Clayton juts into the St. Lawrence River in the midst of the Thousand Islands resort region. Pleasure boats line the waterfront docks.

What to See and Do

The Antique Boat Museum. Displays of antique boats and motors; nautical exhibits. (Mid-May-mid-Oct, daily) 750 Mary St. Phone 315/686-4104. ¢¢

Burnham Point State Park. Fishing, boating (launch, dock); picnicking, playground, camping. (Mid-May-Labor Day) Standard fees. 10 mi W on NY 12 E. Phone 315/654-2324.

Cedar Point State Park. Swimming beach, bathhouse, fishing, boating (ramp, marina); picnicking, playground, recreation programs, camping. (Mid-May-mid-Oct) Standard fees. 6 mi W on NY 12 E. Phone 315/654-2522.

Grass Point State Park. Swimming beach, bathhouse, fishing, boating (launch, marina); picnicking, playground, camping. (Mid-May-late-Sept) Standard fees. 6 mi E on NY 12, 1 mi W of I-81. Phone 315/686-4472.

Thousand Islands Museum. History of the region; replica of turn-of-the-century Clayton. (Mid-May-Labor Day, daily) Old Town Hall, 403 Riverside Dr. Phone 315/686-5794. **Donation**

Uncle Sam Boat Tours. A 40-mi cruise of the Thousand Islands, traveling through Canadian and American waters, the St. Lawrence Seaway; stop at Boldt Castle and Alexandria Bay. (Mid-May-Oct, daily) 604 Riverside Dr. Phone 315/686-3511. ¢¢¢¢

Special Events

Duck, Decoy, and Wildlife Art Show. East Line Rd, Recreation Park Arena. Third wkend July.

Antique Boat Show. The Antique Boat Museum. More than 150 restored antique craft; sailing race; boat parade. Phone 315/686-4104. First wkend Aug.

Model Train Show. Recreation Park Arena. Second wkend Sept.

Motels/Motor Lodges

★ **BERTRAND'S MOTEL.** *229 James St, Clayton (13624). 315/686-3641; toll-free 800/472-0683.* 28 rms, 1-2 story, 5 kits. July-Labor Day: S $50; D $60-$62; each addl $7; kit. units $65-$70; family, wkly rates off-season; lower rates rest of yr. Crib free. TV; cable. Restaurant opp 6 am-10 pm. Ck-out 11 am. Picnic tables, grills. Cr cds: A, DS, MC, V.
🔥

★ **BUCCANEER MOTEL.** *230 N Point St, Cape Vincent (13618). 315/654-2975.* 10 rms. Mid-June-Labor Day: S, D $75-$85; each addl $10; under 12 free; lower rates rest of yr. Crib free. TV; cable. Restaurant nearby. Ck-out 11 am. On river; dockage. Cr cds: MC, V.
⬆️ 🔀 🔥

★ **WEST WINDS MOTEL & COTTAGES.** *38267 Rte 12E, Clayton (13624). 318/686-3352; res 888/937-8963. www.thousandislands.com/westwinds.* 12 motel rms, 5 kit. cabins, 4 kit. cottages. Late June-early Sept: S $38-$60; D $48-$67; each addl $6; kit. Cabins for 2, $520/wk; kit. Cottages for 2, $760-$880/wk; each addl $50; lower rates mid-May-late June, early Sept-mid-Oct. Closed rest of yr. Crib $5. Pet accepted; fee. TV; cable (premium). Heated pool. Complimentary coffee. Restaurant nearby. Ck-out 10 am. Game rm. Picnic tables, grills. Boats; dockage. On 5 acres; gazebo. Cr cds: MC, V.
🔀 ⬆️ 🔀 🔥

Resort

★ **FAIR WIND LODGE.** *38201 Rte 12E, Clayton (13624). 315/686-5251; fax 315/686-5253; toll-free 800/235-8331.* 10 rms, 8 cottages, 6 kit. cottages. Mid-June-early Sept: S, D $48-$66; each addl $6; kit. cottages for 2, $495/wk, each addl $25; lower rates mid-May-mid-June, early Sept-mid-Oct. Closed rest of yr. Crib free. TV; cable (premium). Heated pool. Complimentary coffee in lobby. Restaurant nearby. Ck-out 10 am. Picnic tables. 45-ft dock. Cr cds: A, DS, MC, V.
🄳 ⬆️ 🔀 🔥

Restaurants

★★ **CLIPPER INN.** *126 State St (NY 12), Clayton (13624). 315/686-3842.* Continental menu. Specializes in veal, scampi, fresh fish. Hrs: 5-10 pm; early-bird dinner 5-6 pm. Closed Nov-Mar. Res accepted. Bar 4 pm-2 am. Dinner $10.95-$21.95. Child's menu. Nautical decor. Cr cds: A, D, DS, MC, V.
🄳 🔀

★★ **THOUSAND ISLANDS INN.** *335 Riverside Dr, Clayton (13624). 315/686-3030. www.1000-slands.com.* Specializes in freshwater fish, wild game, prime rib, quail, seafood. Hrs: 7 am-1:30 pm; 5:30-9 Sun-Thurs, 5:30-10 Fri and Sat. Early-bird dinner 5:30-6 pm. Closed Oct-mid-May. Res accepted. Bar from 11 am. Bkfst $2.95-$7.95, lunch $3.95-$7.95, dinner $8.95-$24.95. Child's menu. Small hotel since 1897; Thousand

Island dressing first created and served here. Cr cds: A, C, D, DS, MC, V.

Cooperstown

(E-6) *See also Oneonta*

Founded 1786 **Pop** 2,032 **Elev** 1,264 ft **Area code** 607 **Zip** 13326
Information Chamber of Commerce, 31 Chestnut St; 607/547-9983
Web www.cooperstownchamber.org

Founded by James Fenimore Cooper's father, Judge William Cooper, Cooperstown is in the center of the "Leatherstocking" country. Here in 1839, on the south end of Otsego Lake, legend has it that Abner Doubleday devised modern baseball. The National Baseball Hall of Fame and Museum is located here, on Main Street.

What to See and Do

The Farmers' Museum and Village Crossroads. Outdoor museum of rural life in early times. Craftspeople present printing, weaving, and blacksmithing in historic setting. Village of historic buildings and barn filled with exhibits. Famous "Cardiff Giant," a 10-ft statue presented to the public in 1869 as a petrified prehistoric man, is here. (Apr-Oct, daily) Special events held throughout the yr. Inquire about combination ticket with Fenimore House and/or National Baseball Hall of Fame and Museum. 1 mi N on NY 80. Phone 888/547-1450.

Fenimore Art Museum. Museum and headquarters of NY State Historical Association. Large American folk art collection, exhibits of Native American art and artifacts, James Fenimore Cooper memorabilia, academic and decorative arts of Romantic Era, 1800-1850; research library. (June-Sept, daily; Apr-June, Tues-Sun) Inquire about combination ticket with Farmers' Museum and/or National Baseball Hall of Fame. 1 mi N on NY 80. Phone 607/547-1400.

Glimmerglass State Park. Swimming beach, bathhouse, fishing; hiking, biking, x-country skiing, picnicking, playground, tent and trailer sites. (Daily; closed Jan 1, Dec 25) Standard fees. Also here is Hyde Hall, Clarke family mansion with view of Otsego Lake; Classical Revival architecture (summer daily). 6 mi N on E Lake Rd. Phone 607/547-8662. ¢¢

⭐ **National Baseball Hall of Fame and Museum.** Nationally known museum dedicated to the game and

National Baseball Hall of Fame

its players. The Hall of Fame Gallery contains plaques honoring the game's all-time greats. The museum features displays on baseball's greatest moments, the World Series, All-Star Games, ballparks, and a complete history of the game. Theater presents special multimedia show. Gift shop. Inquire about combination ticket with Farmers' Museum and/or Fenimore House. (Daily; closed Jan 1, Thanksgiving, Dec 25) Main St. Phone 607/547-7200. ¢¢¢

Special Events

Glimmerglass Opera. Alice Busch Opera Theater. Four productions, 28 performances. Phone 607/547-2255. July-Aug.

Cooperstown Concert Series. Sterling Auditorium, Cooperstown High School. Several performances per season by classical and jazz musicians, folk artists, dancers, actors. Phone 607/547-1812. Sept-May.

Autumn Harvest Festival. The Farmers' Museum and Village Crossroads. Mid-Sept. Phone 888/547-1450.

Motels/Motor Lodges

★ **BAYSIDE INN & MARINA.** *7090 State Hwy 80 (13326). 607/547-2371; fax 607/547-5856. www.cooperstown. net/bayside.* 19 rms, 1-2 story, 10 kit. cottages. Late June-Labor Day: S $59-$129; D $69-$139; kit. cottages $650-$1,200/wk; lower rates after Labor Day-Oct, May-mid-June. Closed rest of yr. Crib $10. TV; cable (premium). Ck-out 11 am. Game rm. Lawn games. Microwave in cottages. Picnic tables, grills. Sand beach, marina. Cr cds: DS, MC, V.
🄳 ♨ ➷ 🐾

★★ **BEST WESTERN INN & SUITES.** *50 Commons Dr (13326). 607/547-9439; fax 607/547-7082; res 800/780-1234.* 62 rms, 2 story. June-Sept: S $75-$205; D, suites $85-$225; each addl $10; under 12 free; higher rates special events; lower rates rest of yr. Crib free. TV; cable (premium), VCR avail (movies). Indoor pool; whirlpool. Playground. Complimentary continental bkfst. Restaurant adj 6 am-midnight. Ck-out 11 am. Coin lndry. Meeting rm. Business servs avail. In-rm modem link. Shopping arcade adj. Barber shop. Exercise

equipt. Game rm. Refrigerator, microwave in suites. Picnic tables. Cr cds: A, D, DS, MC, V.
🄳 ♨ 🏋 ➷ 🐾

★ **HICKORY GROVE MOTOR INN.** *6854 State Hwy 80 (13326). 607/547-9874; fax 607/547-8567; toll-free 877/547-9874. www.cooperstown.net/ hickorygrove.* 12 rms. Mid-June-Labor Day: S $50-$100; D $55-$110; each addl $5; higher rates special events; lower rates mid-Apr-mid-June, Sept-mid-Oct. Closed rest of yr. TV; cable. Complimentary coffee. Restaurant nearby. Ck-out 11 am. Picnic tables, grills. Boat rentals. Cr cds: A, DS, MC, V.
⬆ ✈ ➷

★★ **LAKE FRONT MOTEL & RESTAURANT.** *10 Fair St (13326). 607/547-9511; fax 607/547-2792. www.cooperstown.net.* 44 rms, 15 with shower only, 2 story. Late June-Aug: S, D $60-$105; lower rates rest of yr. TV; cable (premium). Restaurant May-Oct: 7:30 am-9 pm. Bar. Ck-out 11 am. Business servs avail. Sundries. Gift shop. On lake. Cr cds: MC, V.
⬆ ➷ 🐾

★★ **LAKE 'N PINES MOTEL.** *7102 NY 80 (13326). 607/547-2790; fax 607/547-5671; toll-free 800/615-5253. www.cooperstown.net/lake-n-pines.* 24 rms, 1-2 story, 3 cottages. June-Labor Day: S $90; D $122; each addl $7; cottages $150; wkend rates; wkly rates off-season; lower rates Apr-May, after Labor Day-late Nov. Closed rest of yr. TV; cable (premium). 2 heated pools, 1 indoor; whirlpool. Sauna. Complimentary coffee. Restaurant nearby. Ck-out 11 am. Game rm. Refrigerators, microwaves in cottages. Some balconies. Picnic tables, grill. Observation deck. Rowboats, paddleboats. View of lake. Cr cds: A, DS, MC, V.
🄳 ⬆ ♨ 🐾

★★ **LAKE VIEW MOTEL AND COTTAGES.** *6805 NY 80 (13326). 607/547-9692; fax 607/547-5080; toll-free 888/452-5384. www.cooperstown vacations.com.* 19 rms, 7 kit. cottages. June-Aug: S $55-$99; D $59-$135; each addl $7; kit. cottages $160; lower rates Apr-May, Sept-mid-Nov. Closed rest of yr. TV; cable (premium). Complimentary coffee. Ck-out 11 am. Some microwaves. Patios.

NEW YORK WALKING TOURS:

A BASEBALL KIND OF TOWN

Cooperstown is best known as the home of the Baseball Hall of Fame, and anyone who has any affinity for the game will love being immersed in it here. Not a baseball fan? Don't worry—the town also offers a variety of entertaining historic sites, activities, shops, and restaurants.

Start by picking up a copy of the self-guided walking tour at the information kiosk in the Chamber of Commerce office (31 Chestnut Street). From there, turn right and walk into the heart of town. At the corner of Chestnut and Main, you'll encounter the Cooper Inn, which was built in 1813 and is surrounded by its own pocket park. Peek at the entrance hall and lobby, highlighted by paintings from the Fenimore Art Museum. Return to Main Street and walk east. On the right is Doubleday Field where, if your timing is right, a baseball game might be in progress. Both sides of Main Street are lined with shops, many of which have baseball themes. Among the baseball-themed shops to visit are Cooperstown Bat Company (66 Main Street), America's Game (75 Main Street), National Pastime (81 Main Street), Third Base (83 Main Street), "Where It All Began" Bat Company (87 Main Street), The Cap Company (108 Main Street), Collectors World (139 Main Street), and Grand Slam Collectibles (134 Main Street). Other Main Street shops of note are the Cooperstown General Store (45 Main Street) and Cooperstown Kid Co. (131 Main Street). Take a left onto alleylike Hoffman Lane, and visit the Cooperstown Book Nook (1 Hoffman Lane). Then stop in next door for a meal at Hoffman Lane Bistro, a modern cafe with outdoor dining.

Return to Main Street, turn left and visit the National Baseball Hall of Fame (25 Main Street); this takes some time, but daily admission allows visitors to come and go as often as they please. No food is served in the Hall, but the nearby Doubleday Café (93 Main Street) serves up good homemade food in a real small-town atmosphere. Leaving the Hall, head north on First Street and follow it to the end for nice views of Otsego Lake. Head west on Lake Street for two blocks to Lake Front Park at the foot of Pioneer Street—a good spot for a picnic. From there, walk about two more blocks to the Otesaga Resort Hotel—it's the huge building on your right with the three-story columns guarding the entry portico. The lobby is immense and decorated with fine art. Peek into the ballroom, decorated with circa-1910 murals by Blendon Campbell, and lounge on the back veranda overlooking the lake. The food here is excellent, too.

Continue walking—or hop on the village trolley—up Lake Street (now Route 80) for about ½ mile, where the Fenimore Art Museum appears on the right and the Farmers' Museum is on the left. One to three hours can be spent at each of these. The Art Museum contains an outstanding collection of New York State-based art, excellent works from the Hudson River School, and an American Indian Wing. The Farmers' Museum is a 19th-century living history installation and working farm. Ride the village trolley back to town and visit the art galleries on Pioneer Street: the Smithy-Pioneer Gallery and the Leatherstocking Brush and Palette Club.

Private beach; swimming. Free paddle boats, row boats, dockage. Cr cds: DS, MC, V.

B&B/Small Inn

★ ★ **INN AT COOPERSTOWN.** *16 Chestnut St (13326). 607/547-5756; fax 607/547-8779. www.cooperstown. net/theinn.* 18 rms, 3 story. No A/C. No rm phones. May-Oct: S $95-$135; D $110-$155; each addl $20; lower rates rest of yr. TV in sitting rm. Complimentary continental bkfst; afternoon refreshments. Restaurants nearby. Ck-out 11 am, ck-in early afternoon. Business servs avail. Trolley stop nearby. Former annex to Fenimore Hotel, built 1874. Some antiques. Common rm with fireplace, Victorian furnishings. Cr cds: A, D, DS, V.

Restaurants

★ ★ ★ **GABRIELLA'S ON THE SQUARE.** *161 Main St (13326). 607/547-8000.* Hrs: 5-9 pm; hrs vary June-Oct. Closed Mon, exc summer. Res accepted. Dinner $14.95-$19.95. Child's menu. Wine cellar. Specialties: rack of lamb with encrusted dijon mustard and mushroom risotto, tuna steak au poivre. Own desserts. Outdoor dining. Formal dining. Cr cds: A, D, DS, MC, V.

★ ★ **PEPPER MILL.** *NY 28 (13326). 607/547-8550.* Specializes in beef, chicken, seafood. Own pastries. Hrs: 4-10 pm. Closed Dec 25; Jan-Mar. Res accepted. Bar. Dinner $6.95-$24.95. Child's menu. Cr cds: A, DS, MC, V.

Corning

(F-4) *See also Elmira, Watkins Glen*

Settled 1833 **Pop** 10,842 **Elev** 937 ft
Area code 607 **Zip** 14830
Information Chamber of Commerce, 1 Baron Steubing Pl; 607/936-4686
Web www.corningny.com

This world glass center began to grow when completion of the Chemung Canal brought plentiful Pennsylvania anthracite. In 1868 lower fuel and materials costs attracted the Brooklyn Flint Glass Works, incorporated in 1875 as the Corning Glass Works. Mass production of bulbs for Thomas A. Edison's electric light soon began. Dresser-Rand makes compressors at Painted Post, near Corning. The city's central shopping district has been restored to its 1890s appearance.

What to See and Do

Benjamin Patterson Inn Museum Complex. Central attraction is restored and furnished 1796 inn, built to encourage settlement in the Genesee Country. Incl public rm and kitchen on first floor; ballrm and two bedrms on second floor. Also on site is DeMonstoy Log Cabin (ca 1785), Browntown one-rm schoolhouse (1878), Starr Barn with agricultural exhibit (ca 1860), and blacksmith shop (ca 1820). (Mon-Fri) 59 W Pulteney St. Phone 607/937-5281. ¢

◪ **The Corning Museum of Glass.** More than 25,000 objects on display, incl outstanding pieces of both antique and modern Steuben and an 11-ft-high leaded glass window designed by Tiffany Studios in 1905. Library has most complete collection of materials on glass in the world. **The Innovations Gallery** showcases optics, vessels, and windows. **The Steuben Factory** features skilled craftsmen transforming hot molten glass into fine crystal; only factory in the world that produces Steuben crystal. Retail stores. (Daily; closed hols) On Centerway. Phone 607/937-5311. ¢¢¢¢

The Rockwell Museum. Largest collection of American Western art in the East, incl paintings by Remington, Russell, Bierstadt, Catlin, others; antique firearms. Changing exhibits. (Daily; closed hols) 111 Cedar St. Phone 607/937-5386. ¢

Motels/Motor Lodges

★ ★ **COMFORT INN.** *66 W Pulteney St (14830). 607/962-1515; fax 607/962-1899; res 800/228-5150. choicehotels.com.* 62 rms, 2 story. May-Oct: S $75-$85; D $85-$95; each addl $6; under 18 free; higher rates: LPGA Corning Classic, racing events; lower rates rest of yr. Crib free. TV; cable. Indoor pool. Complimentary continental bkfst. Restaurant nearby. Ck-out 11 am. Business servs avail. In-rm modem link. Exercise equipt; sauna. Some refrigerators. Cr cds: A, C, D, DS, ER, JCB, MC, V.

★ **CORNING DAYS INN.** *23 Riverside Dr (14830). 607/936-9370; fax 607/936-0513; res 800/329-7466. www.daysinn.com.* 56 rms, 2-3 story. May-Oct: S $55-$72; D $62-$82; each addl $5; suites $85-$95; under 18 free; lower rates rest of yr. Crib free. TV; cable (premium). Indoor pool. Coffee in rms. Restaurant 7 am-10 pm. Ck-out 11 am. Business servs avail. In-rm modem link. Parking. Health club privileges. Cr cds: A, D, DS, MC, V.

★ **GATE HOUSE MOTEL.** *145 E Corning Rd (14830). 607/936-4131.* 20 rms, 6 with shower only. Mid-May-mid-Nov: S $33-$40; D $38-$52; each addl $6; under 21 free; higher rates: auto races, LPGA; lower rates rest of yr. Crib free. TV; cable. Restaurant 6 am-11 am. Ck-out 11 am. Coin lndry. Cr cds: A, MC, V.

★ **KNIGHTS INN.** *2707 Westinghouse Rd, Horseheads (14904). 607/739-3807; fax 607/796-5293; toll-free 800/418-8977. www.knightsinn. com.* 40 rms. Apr-Oct: S, D $32.95-$95.95; under 12 free; family rates; package plans; wkends 2-day min; higher rates special events; lower rates rest of yr. Crib free. Pet accepted, some restrictions; $5 and $25 deposit. TV; cable (premium), VCR avail (movies). Complimentary continental bkfst. Restaurant nearby. Business servs avail. In-rm modem link. Valet serv. Coin lndry. Pool. Some refrigerators, microwaves. Picnic tables, grills. Cr cds: A, D, DS, MC, V.

★ **STILES MOTEL.** *9239 Victory Hwy, Painted Post (14870). 607/962-5221; toll-free 800/331-3920. www. stilesmotel.com.* 15 rms. May-Nov: S $32-$42; D $42-$52; each addl $5; family rates; wkly rates Dec-Apr; lower rates rest of yr. Crib $1. TV; cable. Playground. Complimentary coffee in rms. Ck-out 10:30 am. Refrigerators avail. Picnic tables. Country surroundings. Gazebo. Cr cds: DS, MC, V.

Hotel

★★★ **RADISSON HOTEL.** *125 Denison Pkwy E (14830). 607/962-5000; fax 607/962-4166; toll-free 800/333-3333. www.radisson.com/ corningny.* 177 rms, 3 story. S $107-$141; D $117-$151; each addl $10; suites $175-$255; under 18 free; wkend rates. Crib free. Pet accepted, some restrictions. TV; cable. Indoor pool; lifeguard. Coffee in rms. Restaurant 7 am-9:30 pm. Rm serv. Bar 11-12:30 am; entertainment Fri, Sat. Ck-out 1 pm. Meeting rms. Business servs avail. Bellhops. Cr cds: A, D, DS, JCB, MC, V.

B&B/Small Inn

★★★ **ROSEWOOD INN.** *134 E 1st St (14830). 607/962-3253. www. rosewoodinn.com.* 7 rms, 2 story. S $85-$115; D $90-$125; each addl $20; suite $145; off-season rates. TV in some rms. Complimentary full bkfst. Ck-out 11 am, ck-in 3 pm. Restored Victorian home (1855); antiques. Rms individually decorated. Fireplace in parlor. Totally nonsmoking. Cr cds: A, C, D, DS, MC, V.

Restaurants

★ **BOOMERS.** *35 E Market St (14830). 607/962-6800.* Specializes in pasta, seafood, hamburgers. Hrs: 8 am-11 pm; Sun 8 am-8 pm. Closed Thanksgiving, Dec 25. Beer, wine. Bkfts 65¢ -$4.45, lunch $2.95-$5.45, dinner $5.45-$11.95. Child's menu. 19th-century building; memorabilia, antique tools on display. Cr cds: A, DS, MC, V.

★★ **LONDON UNDERGROUND CAFE.** *69 E Market St (14830). 607/962-2345.* Continental menu.

Specialties: marinated ostrich steak, fresh seafood, house-baked desserts. Hrs: 11:30 am-9 pm; Sun noon-5 pm. Closed hols. Res accepted. Beer, wine. A la carte entrees: lunch $5.75-$8.25. Dinner $15.25-$22.95. Child's menu. Pianist Sat eves. Outdoor dining. Cr cds: A, D, DS, MC, V.

D ⬛

★ **SPENCER'S.** *359 E Market St (14830). 607/936-9196. www.spencers restaurant.com.* Italian, Amer menu. Specializes in pasta. Own desserts. Hrs: 11 am-10 pm; early-bird dinner 4-6:30 pm (Mon-Thurs). Closed Thanksgiving, Dec 25. Res accepted. Bar. A la carte entrees: lunch $1.75-$5.95. Dinner $6.45-$23.95. Child's menu. Parking. Outdoor dining. Rustic decor. Unique gift shop. Cr cds: A, DS, MC, V.

D ⬛

Cortland

(E-5) *See also Ithaca*

Settled 1791 **Pop** 18,740 **Elev** 1,120 ft
Area code 607 **Zip** 13045
Information Cortland County Convention and Visitors Bureau, 34 Tompkins St; 607/753-8463 or 800/859-2227
Web www.cortlandtourism.com

Cortland lies in the midst of rich farming country. This is the home of the State University College at Cortland.

What to See and Do

Country Music Park. Hall of Fame museum, memorial garden, concerts, dinner theater, line dancing classes, playground, camping. On NY 13 N. Phone 607/753-0377.

1890 House Museum. Former mansion of industrialist Chester F. Wickwire. Built in a style known as Victorian chateauesque, the building has four stories and 30 rms. Handcarved cherry and oak woodwork, stained and painted glass windows, parquet floors, and elaborate stenciling. The house remained in the Wickwire family until 1974. (Tues-

Sun; closed hols) 37 Tompkins St. Phone 607/756-7551. ¢¢

Fillmore Glen State Park. Replica of President Millard Fillmore's birthplace cabin. Flow-through natural pool, bathhouse; hiking trails, picnicking, playground area, x-country skiing, snowmobiling, tent and trailer sites, cabins (mid-May-mid-Oct). Standard fees. 14 mi W on NY 90, then 3 mi N on NY 38, near Moravia. Phone 315/497-0130.

Ski areas.

Greek Peak. Eight chairlifts, one tubing lift; patrol, school, adaptive ski program, rentals; snowmaking; cafeteria, restaurants, lounges; ski shop, nursery. Lodging (yr-round). Longest run 1½ mi; vertical drop 952 ft. X-country trails. (Dec-Apr, daily, depending on weather conditions) 6 mi S on NY 392, off I-81. Phone 800/955-2754. ¢¢¢¢

Labrador Mountain. Triple, two double chairlifts; T-bar; snowboarding; two ski shops, patrol, school, rentals; snowmaking; cafeterias, restaurant, bar; nursery. Longest run 1½ mi; vertical drop 700 ft. Twenty-four slopes. (Dec-Mar, daily; closed Dec 25) 10 mi NE on NY 13 to Truxton, then 2 mi N on NY 91. Phone 607/842-6204. ¢¢¢¢

Song Mountain. Double and triple chairlifts, two T-bars, J-bar; patrol, school, rentals; snowmaking; restaurant, cafeteria, bar. Longest run one mi; vertical drop 700 ft. (Dec-Mar, daily) Summer: 3,000-ft Alpine Slide (mid-June-Labor Day, daily; late May-mid-June and rest of Sept, wkends only); miniature golf; water slide; some fees. Approx 15 mi N off I-81, near Preble. Phone 315/696-5711. ¢¢¢¢

Suggett House Museum and Kellogg Memorial Research Library. Headquarters of the Cortland County Historical Society; museum (ca 1880) houses vignettes of home arts of 1825-1900; 1882 kitchen; military memorabilia, local art, children's rm, and changing exhibits. Library has local history and genealogy material (additional fee per hr). (Tues-Sat, afternoons; other times by appt; closed hols) 25 Homer Ave. Phone 607/756-6071. ¢

Special Events

Central New York Maple Festival. 13 mi S, I-81, exit 9, in Marathon. A variety of events showing the process of making maple syrup; also arts and crafts, hay rides, and entertainment. Phone 607/849-3812. Early Apr.

Cortland Repertory Theatre. Dwyer Memorial County Park Pavilion Theatre, 10 mi N on NY 281 in Little York. Musicals, comedies and drama. Phone 607/753-6161. Tues-Sun eves. Mid-June-early-Sept.

Motels/Motor Lodges

★★ **COMFORT INN.** *2 1/2 Locust Ave (13045).* 607/753-7721; *fax 607/753-7608; toll-free 800/221-2222. www.comfortinn.com.* 66 rms, 2 story. May-Nov: S, D $79-$139; under 18 free; ski plans; higher rates special events; lower rates rest of yr. Crib free. Pet accepted. TV; cable. Complimentary continental bkfst. Restaurant nearby. Ck-out 11 am. Business servs avail. In-rm modem link. Exercise equipt. Game rm. Microwaves avail. Cr cds: A, C, D, DS, ER, JCB, MC, V.

[D] [⟲] [⤢] [🔥] [SC] [⚗]

★ **DOWNES MOTEL.** *10 Church St (13045).* 607/756-2856; *res 800/800-0301.* 42 rms, 2 story. S $35-$45; D $45-$55; each addl $8; kit. units $126-$136/wk; under 12 free; higher rates: wkends, special events. Crib free. TV; cable (premium), VCR avail (free movies). Complimentary coffee in lobby. Restaurant nearby. Ck-out 11 am. Business servs avail. Downhill/x-country ski 9 mi. Some refrigerators; microwaves avail. Patios, balconies. Cr cds: A, D, DS, MC, V.

[D] [⤢] [⤢] [🔥]

B&B/Small Inn

★★★ **BEN CONGER INN.** *206 W Cortland St, Groton (13073).* 607/898-5817; *fax 607/898-5818.* 5 rms. S, D $90-$220; each addl $25. TV; cable (premium), VCR avail (movies). Complimentary full bkfst; afternoon refreshments. Dining rm (public by res) 5:30-9 pm. Bar. Ck-out 11 am, ck-in 2 pm. Airport, bus depot transportation. Golf privileges. Downhill ski 15 mi; x-country ski on site.

Health club privileges. Greek Revival mansion (1921); former home of Benn Conger, founder of Smith Corona. Antiques; handmade quilts. Winding staircase; library; glass-enclosed conservatory. Located on 18 acres, hiking trails. Cr cds: A, C, D, MC, V.

[⚗] [⟲] [🔥] [⤢] [⤢] [🔥]

Restaurants

★★★ **BEN CONGER INN.** *206 W Cortland St, Groton (13073).* 607/898-5817. Mediterranean menu. Specialties: grilled pork tenderloin; shrimp, scallops and mussels with tomatoes; rack of lamb. Hrs: 5:30-9 pm. Closed Mon, Tues. Res required. Bar. Wine cellar. Dinner $14-$24. Child's menu. Antique decor. Cr cds: A, D, MC, V.

★ **ROCCI'S.** *294 Tompkins St (NY 13W) (13045).* 607/753-0428. Italian, Amer menu. Specializes in pasta, beef, seafood. Salad bar. Hrs: 11:30 am-9 pm; Sun brunch 11:30 am-2:30 pm. Closed Jan 1, Dec 25. Res accepted. Bar. Lunch $5-$7, dinner $10-$15. Sun brunch $6.50. Greenhouse/solarium atmosphere. Cr cds: A, D, MC, V.

[D] [SC] [⤙]

★ **RUSTY NAIL.** *3993 West Rd (13045).* 607/753-7238. Specializes in fresh cut prime rib, steak, fresh seafood. Hrs: 11:30 am-10 pm; Fri, Sat to 11 pm; Sun 4-9 pm. Closed Jan 1, Thanksgiving, Dec 25. Res accepted. Bar. Lunch $3.50-$8.25, dinner $8.95-$29.95. Child's menu. Entertainment Sat. Rustic country decor. Cr cds: A, C, D, DS, ER, MC, V.

[D] [⤙]

Coxsackie

(E-8) *See also Albany, Catskill, Hudson*

Pop 8,884 **Elev** 50 ft **Area code** 518 **Zip** 12051

What to See and Do

Bronck Museum. (1663) Built by Pieter, brother of Jonas Bronck, whose 500-acre "bouwerie" became New York City's Bronx. Complex of early Dutch houses dated 1663, 1685, and 1738 with outbuildings, incl 13-sided barn. Antique furniture, china, glass, silver, paintings, quilts, and agricultural equipt. (Memorial Day wkend-mid-Oct, Tues-Sun) 4 mi S of Coxsackie Thrwy exit 21B on US 9 W, then right on Pieter Bronck Rd. ¢¢

Restaurant

★★ **REDS.** *12005 Rte 9W, West Coxsackie (12192). 518/731-8151.* Specializes in fresh seafood, shellfish-pasta, hand-cut steak. Hrs: 11:30 am-9 pm; Sun brunch 10:30 am-2 pm. Closed Mon. Bar. Lunch $4.90-$10.90, dinner $9.90-$29. Sun brunch $12.95. Parking. Lobster tank. Family-owned. Cr cds: A, D, DS, MC, V.
D ➔

Crown Point

(B-8) *See also Hague, Ticonderoga (Lake George Area)*

Pop 2,119 **Elev** 200 ft **Area code** 518 **Zip** 12928

Information Ticonderoga Area Chamber of Commerce, 94 Montcalm, Ticonderoga 12883; 518/585-6619

Located on a peninsula that forms the northernmost narrows of Lake Champlain, the Point was a strong position from which to control the trade route between New York and Canada during the French and Indian War. In the 19th century, agriculture and ironworks dominated the area.

What to See and Do

Crown Point Reservation State Campground. Fishing, boating (launch); picnic area, camping (fee). (Mid-Apr-mid-Oct) Across highway from Crown Point State Historic Site. Phone 518/597-3603. ¢¢

Crown Point State Historic Site. Preserved ruins of fortifications occupied by French, British, and American forces during the French and Indian and Revolutionary wars: Fort St. Frederic (1734) and Fort Crown Point (1759). Site museum with exhibits and audiovisual presen-

tation on history of area. Self-guided tours; events. (Grounds: May-Oct, daily; Museum: Mon, Wed-Sun) N on NY 9 N/22, 4 mi E at Champlain Bridge. Phone 518/597-3666. **FREE**

Penfield Homestead Museum. Site of first industrial use of electricity in US. Museum of local history, Adirondack iron industry; self-guided tour through ironworks ruins. (Mid-May-mid-Oct, Wed-Sun) 6 mi W, in Ironville Historic District. Phone 518/597-3804. ¢

B&B/Small Inn

★★ **CROWN POINT BED & BREAKFAST.** *3A Main St (12928). 518/597-3651; fax 518/597-4451. www.crownpointbandb.com.* 5 rms, 1 with shower only, 2 story, 1 suite. No A/C. No rm phones. D $60-$75; each addl $12; suite $120; hols (2-day min). Closed Thanksgiving, Dec 25. Crib free. TV in parlor; cable. Complimentary continental bkfst. Restaurant nearby. Ck-out 11 am, ck-in 4 pm. Victorian house built 1886 for banker; many antiques. Totally nonsmoking. Cr cds: A, D, DS, MC, V.

Deposit

(F-6) *See also Bainbridge, Binghamton*

Settled 1789 **Pop** 1,824 **Elev** 991 ft **Area code** 607 **Zip** 13754

Information Chamber of Commerce, PO Box 222; 607/467-2556

Resort

★★ **SCOTT'S OQUAGA LAKE HOUSE.** *Oquaga Lake (13754). 607/467-3094; fax 607/467-2370. www.scottsfamilyresort.com.* 148 rms, 138 baths, 3 story, 4 cottages. No A/C. AP, late May-mid-Oct: S $117-$135; D $101-$111/person; cottages (EP) $185-$269/day; family, wkly rates. Closed rest of yr. Crib avail. Supervised children's activities. Dining rm 8-9 am, 12:45-1:30 pm, 6:15-7:15 pm. Soda fountain. Wkly cookouts. Ck-out 2 pm, ck-in 4 pm. Coin lndry. Grocery 2 mi. Meeting rms. Bellhops. Free bus depot transportation. Sports dir. Indoor/outdoor tennis. 18-hole golf, putting green, pitch and putt. Private waterfront; speedboats, canoes, sailboats, water-skiing. Lawn games. Bicycles. Soc dir. Stage entertainment. Rec rm. Tours. Showboat cruises; concerts, bowling. Some fireplaces. On 1,000-acre estate. Family-owned since 1869. Cr cds: DS, MC, V.

B&B/Small Inn

★★ **CHESTNUT INN AT OQUAGA LAKE.** *498 Oquaga Lake Rd (13754). 607/467-2500; fax 607/467-5911; toll-free 800/467-7676.* 30 rms, 20 share bath, 3 story, 5 suites. No rm phones. S, D $69-$149; each addl $15; suites $99-$209; under 12 free; golf plans. Crib free. TV, cable. Lake swimming. Dining rm 7 am-2 pm, 5-10 pm. Bar. Ck-out 11 am. Meeting rm. Business servs avail. Bellhops. Tennis privileges. Golf privileges. Lawn games. Massage. Valet parking. Built 1928; antiques. On Oquaga Lake. Cr cds: A, DS, MC, V.

Diamond Point (Lake George Area)

(C-8) *See also Glens Falls, Lake Luzerne, Warrensburg*

Pop 400 **Elev** 354 ft **Area code** 518 **Zip** 12824

This town is located on the south-western shore of Lake George (see).

Motel/Motor Lodge

★ **TREASURE COVE RESORT MOTEL.** *3940 Lake Shore Dr (12824). 518/668-5334; fax 581/668-9027. www.treasurecoveresort.com.* 50 rms, 14 kit. cottages, A/C in some cottages. July-Labor Day: S, D $90-$121; each addl $10; kit. units $100-$121; kit. cottages (to 4 persons) $975-$1,160/wk; lower rates mid-Apr-June, after Labor Day-mid-Oct. Closed rest of yr. Crib $5. TV; cable.

Pools. Playground. Complimentary coffee. Restaurant nearby. Ck-out 10 am. Game rm. Lawn games. Boat rentals; fishing charters. Refrigerators; some fireplaces. Picnic tables, grills. Private beach. Cr cds: MC, V.

Resorts

★★★ **CANOE ISLAND LODGE.** *Lakeshore Dr (12824). 518/668-5592. www.canoeislandlodge.com.* 30 rms in cottages, 18 rms in 2-story lodges, 6 mini-chalets, 67 A/C. MAP, May-Oct: D $85-$160/person; family rates. Closed rest of yr. Crib avail. TV; cable. Playground. Supervised children's activities (July-Aug); ages 3 and up. Dining rm 8-10 am, noon-2:30 pm, 6:30-8:30 pm. Box lunches. Bar 5 pm-midnight. Ck-out 11 am, ck-in 1-4 pm. Business servs avail. Free bus depot transportation. Tennis. Beach; waterskiing, boats, sailboats, rides; dockage. Lawn games. Rec rm. Entertainment; dancing. Barbecues on island. Some fireplaces in cottages. Some balconies. Rustic atmosphere. Cr cds: MC, V.

★ **JULIANA MOTEL.** *3842 Lakeshore Dr (12824). 518/668-5191; fax 518/668-3294. www.capital.net.* 26 motel rms, 1-2 story, 9 kits., 7 kit. cottages. Late June-Labor Day: S $62-$72; D $72-$135; each addl $5; kit. units $82-$97; kit. cottages $500-$625/wk; lower rates late May-late June. Closed rest of yr. Crib avail. TV; cable (premium). Pool. Playground. Restaurant nearby. Ck-out 10 am. Rec rm. Picnic tables, grills. Sun deck. Private beach; rowboat. Cr cds: MC, V.

Dunkirk (E-2)

Pop 13,989 **Elev** 598 ft **Area code** 716 **Zip** 14048

Information Northern Chautauqua Chamber of Commerce, 212 Lake Shore Dr W; 716/366-6200

Web www.clweb.com/nccc

A pleasant industrial and vacation city southwest of Buffalo on the shores of Lake Erie, about 35 miles from the Pennsylvania border, this was the birthplace of author-historian Samuel Hopkins Adams.

What to See and Do

Boating. One of three small boat harbors of refuge on Lake Erie between Erie, PA and Buffalo, NY. Launch; protected inner harbor; mooring. Breakwater.

Dunkirk Lighthouse. (1875) Built in 1875; ten rms in lighthouse with a rm dedicated to each branch of the military service, lighthouse keeper's rm, Victorian furnishings in kitchen and parlor. Guided tour incl tower and history of the Great Lakes. (June-Sept, daily; Apr-June and Sept-Oct, Mon-Tues and Thurs-Sat) Off NY 5, on Point Dr N. Phone 716/366-5050. ¢¢

Evangola State Park. Swimming, 4,000-ft sand beach, bathhouse, lifeguards, fishing; nature trails, hiking, x-country skiing, snowmobiling, picnicking (fee), playground, game areas, tent and trailer sites (fee). 17 mi N on NY 5. Phone 716/549-1802. ¢¢

Historical Museum of the Darwin R. Barker Library. Period furniture, 1880s parlor; exhibits on Fredonia and Pomfret; documents, photos, portraits, and genealogical material; children's museum, education programs. (Tues, Thurs, also Wed, Fri-Sat afternoons) 20 E Main St, 3 mi S in Fredonia. Phone 716/672-2114. **FREE**

Lake Erie State Park. Fishing; nature trails, hiking, x-country skiing, snowmobiling, picnicking, playground, tent and trailer sites, cabins (fee). (May-mid-Oct, daily) 7 mi W on NY 5. Phone 716/792-9214. ¢¢

Swimming. Point Gratiot Park Beach and Wright Park Beach. (Mid-June-Labor Day, daily) Bathhouses. Phone 716/366-6901.

Special Event

Chautauqua County Fair. Last wk July. Phone 716/366-4752.

Motels/Motor Lodges

★ ★ **BEST WESTERN.** 3912 Vineyard Dr (14048). 716/366-7100. www.best western.com. 61 rms, 2 story. S $59-$79; D $69-$109; each addl $4; under 17 free. Crib free. Pet accepted. TV; cable (premium). Pool; lifeguard. Playground. Ck-out noon. Meeting rms. Business servs avail. Health club privileges. Cr cds: A, D, DS, MC, V.
D ➘ ≋ ⊠ ⓧ SC

★ **DAYS INN DUNKIRK FREDO-NIA.** 10455 Bennett Rd, Fredonia (14063). 716/673-1351; fax 716/672-6909; res 800/329-7466. www.daysinn. com. 132 rms, 2 story. Apr-Sept: S $51-$69; D $59-$79; each addl $7; under 18 free; lower rates rest of yr. Crib free. Pet accepted, some restrictions. TV; cable (premium), VCR avail. Ck-out 11 am. Lndry facilities. Meeting rms. Business servs avail. Valet serv. Downhill/x-country ski 20 mi. Cr cds: A, DS, MC, V.
D ➘ ⋗ ⊠ ⓧ SC

★ ★ **FOUR POINTS BY SHERA-TON.** 30 Lake Shore Dr E (14048). 716/366-8350; fax 716/366-8899; res 800/325-3535. www.fourpoints.com. 132 rms, 4 story. June-mid-Sept: S $49-$109; D $59-$119; each addl $10; suites $121-$131; under 17 free; ski plans; lower rates rest of yr. Crib free. Pet accepted. TV; cable. Indoor/outdoor pool; whirlpool, poolside serv, lifeguard. Complimentary coffee in lobby. Restaurant 7 am-10 pm. Bar 11 am-midnight. Ck-out noon. Meeting rms. Business servs avail. In-rm modem link. Downhill/x-country ski 15 mi. Exercise equipt; sauna. Some refrigerators, wet bars. On Lake Erie. Cr cds: A, C, D, DS, MC, V.
D ➘ ⓛ ⋗ ≋ ⋔ ⊠ ⓧ SC

★ **SOUTHSHORE MOTOR LODGE.** 5040 W Lake Rd (14048). 716/366-2822. 9 rms, 7 kits., 12 kit. cottages. July-Aug: D, kit. units, kit. cottages $48-$95; wkly rates; lower rates rest of yr. Pet accepted, some restrictions. TV; VCR avail. Heated pool. Playground. Ck-out 10 am. Guest lndry. Lawn games. Refrigerators. Picnic tables, grill. Cr cds: MC, V.
➘ ≋ ⓧ

B&B/Small Inn

★ ★ ★ **WHITE INN.** 52 E Main St, Fredonia (14063). 716/672-2103; fax 716/672-2107. www.whiteinn.com. 23 rms, 3 story, 11 suites. May-Oct: S, D

$69-$109; suites $109-$129; each addl $10; under 12 free. Crib free. TV; cable, VCR avail. Complimentary full bkfst. Restaurant (see THE WHITE INN). Bar 11:30-2 am; Sun noon-10 pm. Ck-out 11 am, ck-in 3 pm. Meeting rms. Business servs avail. Valet serv. Health club privileges. Some refrigerators, fireplaces. Built 1868; Victorian atmosphere. Antiques. Cr cds: A, C, D, DS, MC, V.

Restaurant

★ ★ ★ **THE WHITE INN.** *52 E Main St, Fredonia (14063). 716/672-2103. www.whiteinn.com.* Specialties: Gaelic strip steak, lamb a la Madeline. Hrs: 7-10 am, 11:30 am-2 pm, 5-8:30 pm; Fri, Sat to 9 pm; Sun 8-11 am, 12:30-8 pm. Res accepted. Bar. A la carte entrees: bkfst $2.75-$7.95, lunch $3.95-$8.25, dinner $14.95-$21.95. Buffet lunch $5.95. Outdoor dining. Authentic Victorian decor. Cr cds: A, D, DS, MC, V.

D

East Aurora

(E-2) *See also Arcade, Buffalo*

Pop 6,673 **Elev** 917 ft **Area code** 716 **Zip** 14052

Information Greater East Aurora Chamber of Commerce, 431 Main St; 716/652-8444 or 800/441-2881

Web www.eanycc.com

East Aurora lies very close to the large industrial and commercial center of Buffalo. In the early 1900s, Elbert Hubbard, author of *A Message to Garcia,* lived here and made it the home of the Roycrofters, makers of fine books, copper and leather ware, and furniture. The Roycroft campus is still operating, and it is the only continuous operation of its kind in America today. East Aurora is also the headquarters of Fisher-Price toys. The Baker Memorial Methodist Church, which has hand-signed Tiffany windows, is located here.

What to See and Do

The Elbert Hubbard Museum. A five-bedrm, 1910 Craftsman period home built by and for the Roycrofters. Contains Roycroft furniture, modeled leather, hammered metal, leaded glass, books, pamphlets, and other artifacts from 1895-1938. Also here is material on Elbert Hubbard, author of the famous essay *The Message to Garcia.* (June-mid-Oct, Wed, Sat and Sun afternoons; tours by appt) 363 Oakwood Ave, located in the ScheideMantel House. Phone 716/652-4735.

Millard Fillmore Museum. House (ca 1825) Fillmore built for his wife contains memorabilia, furnishings. 1830s herb and rose garden. Carriage house (ca 1830) built of lumber from the former Nathaniel Fillmore farm; antique tools, Fillmore sleigh. (June-mid-Oct, Wed, Sat, and Sun; rest of yr, by appt) 24 Shearer Ave. Phone 716/652-8875. ¢¢

Skiing. Kissing Bridge Ski Area. Two quad, four double chairlifts; two T-bars, J-bar, and handle tow; patrol, school, rentals; snowmaking; bars, cafe; nursery. Longest run 3,500 ft; vertical drop 550 ft. Night skiing. (Dec-Mar, daily) 9 mi W on US 20A, then 17 mi S on US 219 Expy S, exit at Armor Duells Rd to NY 240 S; follow signs. Phone 716/592-4963. ¢¢¢¢

Special Events

Roycroft Summer Festival of Arts & Crafts. Roycroft artisans and members of the art society display their arts and crafts. Phone 716/655-7252. Last wkend June.

Toy Festival. Celebration commemorating Fisher-Price Toy Company's establishment here in the 1930s. Last wkend Aug. Phone 716/687-5151.

Hotel

★ ★ ★ **ROYCROFT INN.** *40 S Grove St (14052). 716/652-5552; fax 716/655-5345; res 800/267-0525. www.roycroftinn.com.* 22 suites, 3 story. Suites $120-$210; under 12 free; ski plans. Crib free. TV; cable, VCR. Complimentary continental bkfst. Restaurant (see ROYCROFT INN). Bar 11:30 am-9 pm. Ck-out 11

am. Meeting rms. Business
servs avail. In-rm modem
link. Downhill/x-country
ski 10 mi. Health club privileges. In-rm whirlpools.
Totally nonsmoking. Cr cds:
A, D, DS, MC, V.

B&B/Small Inn

★★ **GREEN GLEN BED &
BREAKFAST.** *898 Main St
(14052). 716/655-2828.* 4
rms, 3 with bath, 2 story. 3
A/C. No rm phones. S, D
$65-$75; each addl $15. TV
in lounge; VCR avail. Complimentary full bkfst.
Restaurant nearby. Ck-out
noon, ck-in 3 pm. Luggage
handling. Downhill ski 8
mi; x-country ski 7 mi.
Health club privileges.
Queen Anne-style house
(1890); many antiques.

Restaurants

★★★ **OLD ORCHARD
INN.** *2095 Blakeley Rd
(14052). 716/652-4664.* Specializes in fish, chicken fricas-
see with biscuits. Own dressings. Hrs:
11:30 am-2:30 pm, 5-9 pm; Sun
noon-9 pm; early-bird dinner 5-6
pm; Sun noon-2 pm. Closed Dec 25.
Res accepted. Bar. lunch $6.95-
$12.85, dinner $13.95- up. Child's
menu. Outdoor dining. Fireplaces.
Duck pond; wooded countryside.
Family-owned. Cr cds: A, MC, V.

★★★ **ROYCROFT INN.** *40 S Grove
St (14052). 716/652-5552. www.
roycroftinn.com.* Specialties: steaks, rack
of pork, lamb chops and vegetarian
dishes; chocolate terrine. Hrs: 11:30
am-9 pm; Fri to 10 pm; Sat 5-10 pm;
Sun 10 am-2 pm and 5-9pm; Sun
brunch to 2 pm. Res accepted. Wine
list. Lunch $5.95-$11.95, dinner
$11.95-$24.95. Sun brunch $16.95.
Outdoor dining. Restored to 1905
Arts and Crafts style. Totally nonsmoking. Cr cds: A, D, DS, MC, V.

Old Hook Mill, East Hampton

East Hampton (L.I.)

*(G-4) See also Amagansett, Sag Harbor
(L.I.), Southampton (L.I.)*

Settled 1648 **Pop** 19,719 **Elev** 36 ft
Area code 516 **Zip** 11937

Information East Hampton Chamber
of Commerce, 79A Main St; 631/324-
0362

Web www.easthamptonchamber.com

East Hampton is an old Long Island
village, founded in 1648 by a group
of farmers. Farming was the main
livelihood until the mid-1800s, when
the town began to develop into a
fashionable resort.

What to See and Do

Guild Hall Museum. Regional art
exhibits; changing shows. Art and

poetry lectures, classes. Library covering art and artists of the region. June-Sept, daily; rest of yr, Wed-Sun; closed Thanksgiving, Dec 25) 158 Main St. Phone 631/324-0806. **Donation** Also here is

John Drew Theater at Guild Hall. A 382-seat theater for films, plays, concerts, lectures, children's performances. Phone 631/324-4050.

Historic Mulford Farm. (1680) Living history farm museum; 18th-century New England architecture; colonial history; period rms; costumed interpretation. (Afternoons: July and Aug, daily; June and Sept, wkends only; rest of yr, by appt) James Ln, adj to Payne House. Phone 631/324-6850. ¢ Nearby is

Historic Clinton Academy. (1784) First preparatory school in New York. Now museum housing collection of artifacts of Eastern Long Island. (Afternoons: July and Aug, daily; June and Sept, wkends only) 151 Main St. Phone 631/324-6850. ¢

"Home Sweet Home" House. (1680) **and Windmill** (1804). Childhood home of John Howard Payne (1791-1852), who wrote "Home, Sweet Home." Three centuries of American furniture, 18th- and 19th-century English china, mementos. Gallery with special and changing exhibits. Windmill in rear. Tours. (May-Sept daily, Oct-Nov wkends) 14 James Ln. Phone 631/324-0713. ¢¢

Hook Mill. 36 N Main St, on Montauk Hwy. Completely equipped 1806 windmill. Guided tours. (Memorial Day-Labor Day, Wed-Mon) ¢

Pollock-Krasner House and Study Center. Jackson Pollock's studio and house plus a reference library on 20th-century American art. (May-Oct, Thurs-Sat, by appt only) 830 Fireplace Rd. Phone 631/324-4929. ¢¢

Motels/Motor Lodges

★★ **EAST HAMPTON HOUSE.** 226 Pantigo Rd (11937). 631/324-4300; fax 631/329-3743. www.theeasthampton house.com. 52 rms, 2 story, 32 kits. July-Labor Day: D $125-$220; each addl $15; lower rates rest of yr. TV; cable (premium). Heated pool; wading pool, lifeguard. Ck-out 11 am.

Business servs avail. Tennis. Private patios, balconies. Grill. Cr cds: A, DS, MC, V.

★★★ **MAIDSTONE ARMS.** 207 Main St (11937). 631/324-5006; fax 631/324-5037. www.theeasthampton house.com. 12 rms, 3 story, 4 suites, 3 cottages. D $195-$225; each addl $25; suites $265; cottages $325-$350; lower rates off season. Complimentary continental bkfst. Dining rm (see MAIDSTONE ARMS). Rm serv 8 am-10 pm. Bar noon-midnight. Ck-out 11 am, ck-in after 3 pm. Sitting area. Cr cds: A, D, MC, V.

Hotel

★★★ **CENTENNIAL HOUSE.** 13 Woods Ln (11937). 631/324-9414; fax 631/324-0493. www.centhouse.com. 4 rms, 2 story, 1 cottage. May-Oct: D $225-$395; cottage $500; higher rates wkends and hols (3-6-day min); lower rates rest of yr. Children over 12 yrs only. Pet accepted. TV; cable. Pool. Complimentary full bkfst. Restaurant nearby. Ck-out 11 am, ck-in 2 pm. Business servs avail. Exercise equipt. Some fireplaces. Built 1876 by local craftsman. Period furnishings. Totally nonsmoking. Cr cds: MC, V.

B&Bs/Small Inns

★★ **HEDGES INN.** 74 James Ln (11937). 631/324-7100; fax 631/324-5816. 11 rms, 3 story. No rm phones. May-Sep: D $145-$195; higher rates: wkends (3-day min), hols (5-day min); lower rates rest of yr. TV; cable (premium) in main rm. Complimentary continental bkfst. Restaurant. Ck-out noon, ck-in 2 pm. Business servs avail. Tennis privileges. 9-hole golf privileges, pro, putting green, driving range. Victorian house built (ca 1870) with wraparound porch. Cr cds: A, C, D, MC, V.

★★ **HUNTING INN.** 94 Main St (11937). 631/324-0410; fax 631/324-6122. 19 rms, 3 story. May-Sept: S $125; D $150-$250; each addl $15; suites $300; wkends; 5-day min July

4, Labor Day; lower rates rest of yr. TV. Complimentary continental bkfst. Dining rm (see PALM). Ck-out noon, ck-in 2 pm. Business servs avail. Luggage handling. Tennis privileges. Established in 1751; English country garden. Cr cds: A, C, D, MC, V.

★★★ **J. HARPER POOR COTTAGE.** *181 Main St (11937). 631/324-4081; fax 631/329-5931. www.jharper poor.com.* 4 rms, 2 story. May-Oct (2-day min): D $275-$350; 3-day min July-Labor Day; lower rates rest of yr. TV; cable. Pool. Complimentary full bkfst. Restaurants nearby. Ck-out 11:30 am, ck-in 2 pm. Business servs avail. Original house built 1650. English garden. Cr cds: A, D, MC, V.

Hook Mill Windmill

★★ **THE 1770 HOUSE.** *143 Main St (11937). 631/324-1770; fax 631/324-3504; res 631/324-1770. www.1770 house.com.* 7 rms, 2 story. S $120-$230; D $195-$250. Children over 12 yrs only. Complimentary full bkfst. Restaurant. Ck-out 11:30 am, ck-in 2 pm. Business servs avail. Restored 18th-century house; antique furnishings. Cr cds: A, MC, V.

Restaurants

★★ **EAST HAMPTON POINT.** *295 Three Mile Harbor (11937). 631/329-2800. www.easthamptonpoint.com.* Specializes in seafood. Hrs: noon-midnight; to 11 pm summer. Res required. A la carte entrees: lunch $9-$16, dinner $19-$30. Child's menu. Valet parking. Outdoor dining. Sunset views. Cr cds: A, MC, V.
D

★★ **JAMES LANE CAFE AT THE HEDGES.** *94 Main St (11937). 631/324-7100.* Italian, American menu. Specializes in fresh local produce. Hrs: 5-10 pm. Closed Tues and Wed (Oct-May). Res accepted. A la carte entrees: dinner $15-$30. Valet

parking. Outdoor tented dining. In 1870s Victorian home. Cr cds: A, D, MC, V.
D

★★ **LAUNDRY.** *31 Race Ln, East Hampton (11937). 631/324-3199.* Specializes in fish. Hrs: 5:30 pm-midnight; winter to 11 pm. Closed Wed after Labor Day; Thanksgiving, Dec 25. A la carte entrees: dinner $16.50-$24. Parking. Once operated as a commercial laundry; courtyard, garden. Cr cds: A, C, D, DS, ER, MC, V.
D

★★★ **MAIDSTONE ARMS.** *207 Main St (11963). 631/324-5006. www. themaidstonearms.com.* Own baking. Hrs: 8-10:30 am, noon-2:30 pm, 6-10 pm; Sat to 10:30 pm; Sun brunch noon-2:30 pm. Res accepted. Bar. Wine cellar. A la carte entrees: bkfst $6-$10, lunch $9.50-$16.50, dinner $19.50-$30. Sun brunch $10.50-$16. Parking. Cr cds: A, D, MC, V.

★★ **MARYJANE'S IL MONASTERO.** *128 N Main St (11937). 631/324-8008.* Italian, American menu. Hrs: 5-10 pm. Closed Thanksgiving, Dec 25. Res accepted. Bar. A la carte

ntrees: dinner $11.95-$18.95.
Child's menu. Parking. 3 dining rms.
Original art, Tiffany-style lamps. Cr
ds: A, MC, V.

🅓

★★ **MICHAEL'S.** *28 Maidstone Park
Rd, East Hampton (11937). 631/324-
0725.* Continental menu. Specializes
in fresh seafood, marinated boneless
teak. Hrs: 5-10 pm; wkends to 11
pm. Closed Wed off-season; Dec 25.
Res accepted. Bar. Dinner $9.95-
$18.95. Casual, country atmosphere.
Cr cds: A, MC, V.

🅓

★★ **NICK & TONI'S.** *136 N Main St,
East Hampton (11937). 631/324-3550.*
Mediterranean menu. Wood-burning
oven specials. Own baking. Hrs: 6-
10:30 pm; Fri, Sat to 11:30 pm; off
season to 9:30 pm; Sun brunch 11:30
am-2:30 pm. Closed Dec 25. Res
required. Bar. A la carte entrees: dinner $15-$28. Sun brunch $14. Park-
ng. Contemporary decor, folk art. Cr
cds: A, MC, V.

🅓

★★ **PALM.** *94 Main St, East Hampton
(11937). 631/324-0411.* Continental
menu. Specializes in steak, lobster,
seafood. Hrs: 5-11 pm. Bar. A la carte
entrees: dinner $15-$30. Turn-of-the-
century decor. Cr cds: A, D, MC, V.

🖃

Ellenville

(F-7) *See also Kingston, Liberty, New
Paltz*

Pop 4,130 **Elev** 330 ft **Area code** 914
Zip 12428

Information Chamber of Commerce,
PO Box 227; 914/647-4620

Center of the Ulster County resort
area, Ellenville offers abundant
scenic beauty. Hang gliding is popular here.

Resorts

★★ **HUDSON VALLEY RESORT.**
*400 Granite Rd, Kerhonkson (12446).
845/626-8888; fax 845/626-2595; toll-
free 888/684-7264. www.hudsonvalley*

resort.com. 296 rms, 8 story. AP: D
$77-$118/person; MAP avail July-
Aug; higher rates: wkends, hols. TV;
cable. 2 pools, 1 indoor; whirlpool,
poolside serv, lifeguard. Supervised
children's activities; ages 4-13.
Restaurants 7-11 am, noon-3 pm, 6-
11 pm. Bar 11-3 am. Ck-out 11 am,
ck-in 4 pm. Meeting rms. Business
servs avail. Bellhops. Valet serv.
Sports dir. Tennis. 18-hole golf,
greens fee $23. Rowboats. Down-
hill/x-country ski on site. Indoor/
outdoor games. Soc dir; nightclubs;
entertainment. Exercise rm; sauna,
steam rm. Cr cds: A, D, DS, MC, V.

🅓 ⛹ 🏂 🎣 🎿 🏊 🏇 ✈ 🚣 🧖

★★ **NEVELE GRANDE RESORT.** *1
Nevele Rd (12428). 845/647-6000; fax
845/647-9884; toll-free 800/647-
6000. www.nevele.com.* 700 rms in
main building and annexes, 10
story. AP (2-day min wkends, hols,
or $10 addl), late June-early Sept: D
$97-$148/person; family rates; varied rates rest of yr. Crib free. TV;
cable, VCR avail (movies). 6 pools, 2
indoor; whirlpools, poolside serv,
lifeguard. Supervised children's
activities (July-early Sept, also
wkends); ages 3-12. Dining rm (hrs
flexible). Snack bar. Bar noon-4 am.
Ck-out 1 pm, ck-in 3 pm. Coin
lndry ½ mi. Business center. In-rm
modem link. Bellhops. Valet serv.
Shopping arcade. Bus depot transportation. Sports dir. Lighted tennis,
pro. 36-hole golf, greens fee $35-
$50, pro, indoor miniature golf. Pri-
vate lakes; boats, rowboats.
Downhill/x-country ski on site. Ice
rink, tobogganing, sleighing. Lawn
games. Ball fields. Soc dir; stage productions, entertainment, dancing. 2
rec rms. Exercise rm; sauna, steam
rm. Spa. Contemporary design,
decor; on 1,000-acre estate. Cr cds:
A, D, DS, MC, V.

🅓 ⛹ 🏂 🎣 🎿 🏊 🏇 🚣 🧖 🏂

Elmira

(F-4) *See also Corning, Watkins Glen*

Settled 1788 **Pop** 30,940 **Elev** 859 ft
Area code 607

Information Chemung County Chamber of Commerce, 400 E Church St, 14901; 607/734-5137 or 800/627-5892

Web www.chemungchamber.org

Elmira is on both shores of the Chemung River—on a site where, in 1779, the Sullivan-Clinton expedition found a Native American village. By the mid-19th century the railroads and canals were opening new fields of industry; first lumber, later metalworking and textiles.

Samuel Clemens (Mark Twain) spent more than 20 summers at Quarry Farm, the Elmira country home of his wife's sister, Susan Crane. Elmira also was the birthplace of noted filmmaker Hal Roach, first United States woman space pilot Eileen Collins, and fashion designer Tommy Hilfiger.

What to See and Do

Arnot Art Museum. An 1833 mansion with three-story wing. Incl 17th- and 19th-century European paintings displayed in 1880 gallery; 19th-century American gallery; also changing exhibits. (Tues-Sun; closed hols) 235 Lake St. Phone 607/734-3697. ¢¢

Chemung Valley History Museum. Local history displays, Mark Twain exhibit, research library; special events. (Tues-Sun; closed hols) 415 E Water St. Phone 607/734-4167. **Donation**

Elmira College. (1855) 1,100 students. Liberal arts. Coeducational since 1969, Elmira College was the first (1855) to grant women degrees equal to those of men. Mark Twain Study at Park Pl was presented to the college by the Langdon Family in 1952; Clemens did much of his writing here, incl *The Adventures of Huckleberry Finn*. Mark Twain exhibit in Hamilton Hall has memorabilia and a 20-min video. Study and exhibit (summer, Mon-Sat; rest of yr, by appt). Park Pl. Phone 607/735-1941. **FREE**

National Soaring Museum and Harris Hill Soaring Site. "Soaring Capital of America." Museum has collection of historic and contemporary sailplanes; meteorology, aerodynamic, and aviation exhibits; films; soaring memorabilia and WWII gliders.

Sailplane rides (June-early Sept, daily Apr-May and early Sept-Oct, wkends only; additional fee). Pool; playground, kiddie rides, picnicking, and golf (early May-late Sept, daily). Museum (daily; closed Jan 1, Thanksgiving, Dec 25). 8 mi NW in Harris Hill Park, off NY 17 exit 51. Phone 607/734-3128.

National Warplane Museum. Dedicated to preserving the planes, engines, and memories of those who molded aviation heritage. Museum houses interactive displays, exhibits, aircrafts. Gift shop. (Daily) Elmira-Corning Regional Airport, off NY 17 exit 51. Phone 607/739-8200. ¢¢¢

Replica Trolley Tours. Guided tours (60 min) of Chemung County's tourist attractions aboard a replica trolley. (July-Labor Day; Tues-Sat) Depart on E Water. Phone 607/734-5137. ¢

Woodlawn Cemetery. Graves of Samuel Clemens (Mark Twain) and Hal Roach. N end of Walnut St. Nearby is

Woodlawn National Cemetery. Graves of 2,000 Confederate prisoners of war who died in Elmira.

Special Events

Baseball. Elmira Pioneers. Affiliate of the Northeast League. Mid-May-Labor Day. Phone 607/734-1270.

Chemung County Fair. In Horseheads. Early Aug. Phone 607/734-1203.

NASCAR Race Day. Contests, drivers, entertainment. Early Aug. Phone 607/535-2481.

Motels/Motor Lodges

★★ **BEST WESTERN MARSHALL MANOR.** *3527 Watkins Rd, Horseheads (14845). 607/739-3891; toll-free 800/528-1234. www.bestwestern.com.* 40 rms. S $38-$69; D $42-$69; each addl $5; under 18 free; higher rates special events. Crib $2. Pet accepted; $4. TV; cable, VCR avail. Pool. Complimentary continental bkfst, coffee in rms. Restaurant 4-10 pm. Bar to 1 am. Ck-out 11 am. In-rm modem link. Refrigerators, microwaves avail. Cr cds: A, C, D, DS, MC, V.

⊠ ⬛ ⬛ **SC**

★ **COACHMAN MOTOR LODGE.** *908 Pennsylvania Ave (14904).*

607/733-5526; fax 607/733-0961. www.coachmanmotorlodge.com. 18 kit. units, 2 story. Apr-Nov: S $40-$55; D $50-$65; under 18 free; each addl $5; wkly rates; lower rates rest of yr. Crib free. Pet accepted. TV; cable. Complimentary coffee in rms. Restaurant nearby. Ck-out noon. Coin lndry. Business servs avail. Sundries. Health club privileges. Microwaves avail. Some balconies. Picnic table, grill. Cr cds: A, DS, MC, V.

⊡ 🕭 ⌦ 🔥 SC

★ **ECONO LODGE.** *871 NY 64 (14903). 607/739-2000; fax 607/739-3552; res 800/553-2666. www.econo lodge.com.* 48 rms, 2 story. May-Oct: S $58; D $71; each addl $7; under 18 free; higher rates: racing events, college graduation; lower rates rest of yr. Crib free. TV; cable. Whirlpools. Complimentary continental bkfst. Ck-out 11 am. Coin lndry. In-rm modem link. Health club privileges. Refrigerators, microwaves. Cr cds: A, C, D, DS, ER, JCB, MC, V.

⊡ ✕ ⌦ 🕭

★★ **HOLIDAY INN ELMIRA RIVERVIEW.** *760 E Water St (14901). 607/734-4211; fax 607/734-3549; res 800/465-4329. www.holiday-inn.com/ elm-riverview.* 150 rms, 2 story. S, D $79-$119; under 19 free; higher rates special events. Crib free. Pet accepted. TV; cable (premium), VCR avail. 2 pools, 1 indoor (winter); wading pool. Restaurant 6:30 am-2 pm, 5-10 pm; wkends from 7 am. Rm serv. Bar 4 pm-midnight. Ck-out noon. Coin lndry. Meeting rms. Business servs avail. In-rm modem link. Valet serv. Sundries. Exercise equipt. Health club privileges. Refrigerators, microwaves avail. Cr cds: A, C, D, DS, JCB, MC, V.

⊡ 🕭 ⌦ 🏋 🕭 SC

★ **HOWARD JOHNSON INN.** *2671 Corning Rd, Horseheads (14845). 607/739-5636; fax 607/739-8630; res 800/446-4656. www.hojo.com.* 76 rms, 1-2 story. May-mid-Nov: S $48-$70; D $58-$80; each addl $8; studio rms avail; under 18 free; lower rates rest of yr. Crib free. Pet accepted. TV; cable (premium). Pool. Coffee in rms. Restaurant 6:30 am-11 pm; Fri, Sat to midnight. Ck-out noon. In-rm modem link. Valet serv. Sundries. Some refrigerators; microwaves avail.

Private patios, balconies. Cr cds: A, DS, JCB, MC, V.

⊡ 🕭 ⌦ 🕭 🔥

Restaurant

★★ **HILL TOP INN.** *171 Jerusalem Hill Rd (14901). 607/732-6728. www.hill-top-inn.com.* Specializes in lamb, steak, fresh seafood. Hrs: 5-10 pm. Closed hols; also 4 wks in Feb. Res accepted. Bar to 1 am. Dinner $8.95-$19.95. Child's menu. Outdoor dining in season. View of Elmira. Family-owned. Cr cds: A, C, D, DS, ER, MC, V.

⊡ ⊟

Endicott

See also Binghamton, Owego

Settled 1795 **Pop** 13,038 **Elev** 840 ft
Area code 607 **Zip** 13760

Endicott is a center of industry. With Binghamton (see) and Johnson City it makes up the "Triple Cities."

Motels/Motor Lodges

★ **EXECUTIVE INN.** *1 Delaware Ave (13760). 607/754-7575; fax 607/754-7578; toll-free 800/393-2466.* 135 rms, 40 suites, 60 kits. S $44-$59; D $54-$59; suites $59-$89; kits. $79-$89; under 16 free; wkly, wkend, hol rates; higher rates special events. Crib free. Pet accepted, some restrictions; $50 refundable. TV; cable (premium), VCR avail (movies). Restaurant adj. Ck-out noon. Meeting rms. Business servs avail. Some refrigerators; microwaves avail. Cr cds: A, C, D, DS, MC, V.

⊡ 🕭 🕭 🔥 SC

★ **KINGS INN.** *2603 E Main St, Endwell (13760). 607/754-8020; fax 607/754-6768; toll-free 800/531-4667.* 60 rms, 1-2 story. S $52.50; D $57-$62; each addl $7; under 12 free; higher rates B.C. Open. Crib free. TV; cable (premium). Indoor pool. Restaurant 7-9:30 am; Sat, Sun to 11 am. Ck-out noon. Business servs avail. In-rm modem link. Valet serv.

Lighthouse at Fire Island National Seashore

Sundries. Exercise equipt; sauna. Health club privileges. Cr cds: C, D, DS, MC, V.

[icons]

Finger Lakes

(E-4) *See also Auburn, Canandaigua, Corning, Cortland, Elmira, Geneseo, Geneva, Hammondsport, Ithaca, Owego, Penn Yan, Rochester, Skaneateles, Syracuse, Waterloo, Watkins Glen*

Scientists say the Finger Lakes were scooped out by glaciers, resulting in one of the most delightful landscaping jobs in America. There are 11 lakes in all; Canandaigua, Keuka, Seneca, Cayuga, Owasco, and Skaneateles are the largest. The smaller lakes also have the characteristic finger shape. Seneca is the deepest at 630 feet and Cayuga the longest at 40 miles. The region has many glens and gorges with plunging streams. Hundreds of recreation spots dot the shores, offering every imaginable sport. The famous New York State wine grapes grow in the many miles of vineyards in the area.

This scenic area boasts 25 state parks, many waterfalls, camping and picnicking areas, and other features.

Fire Island National Seashore

(G-3) *See also Bay Shore (L.I.), Riverhead (L.I.)*

Five areas of the Fire Island National Seashore are open. **Otis Pike Wilderness Visitor Center,** reached via William Floyd Parkway and Smith Point Bridge (phone 516/281-3010); self-guided nature walk and boardwalk trail for the disabled. Parking (May-September, fee) and swimming at adjacent county park. **Sailors Haven/Sunken Forest,** reached by ferry from Sayville (begins running mid-May, phone 516/589-8980), has swimming, lifeguards, marina, picnicking, concession, visitor center, nature walk, self-guided tours, naturalist programs (June-Labor Day). **Watch Hill,** reached by ferry from Patchogue (phone 516/475-1665), offers the same facilities as Sailors Haven plus 26 family campsites (lottery reservations required, phone 516/597-6633 after May 1). **Fire Island Lighthouse** (1858) area, reached by Robert Moses Causeway, has boardwalk leading to lighthouse; nature trail (all year); former lightkeeper's quarters are a visitor center with exhibits (April-June, Labor Day-December, weekends; July-Labor Day, Wednesday-Sunday; phone 516/661-4876). Parking at adjacent Robert Moses State Park (field #5). Headquarters is at 120 Laurel Street, Patchogue 11772; 516/289-4810.

Located on Washington Avenue in Mastic Beach is the restored estate of one of the signers of the Declaration of Independence, William Floyd (July 4-Labor Day, weekends). Phone 516/399-2030 for tour schedule. No pets allowed.

Fishkill

See also Newburgh, Poughkeepsie

Pop 20,258 **Elev** 223 ft **Area code** 845 **Zip** 12524

Information Dutchess County Tourism Promotion Agency, 3 Neptune Rd, Suite M-17, Poughkeepsie 12601; 914/463-4000 or 800/445-3131

Web www.dutchesstourism.com

What to See and Do

Madam Brett Homestead. (1709) Oldest standing structure in Dutchess County. Period furnishings of seven generations, from Dutch Colonial through Federal and Victorian eras. Garden. Occupied by same family from 1709-1954. (May-Dec, first Sun every month, afternoons or by appt) SW on I-84, exit NY 52, then W 3 mi at 50 Van Nydeck Ave in Beacon. Phone 845/831-6533. ¢¢

Mount Gulian Historic Site. (1730-1740) Headquarters of Baron von Steuben during the final period of the Revolutionary War; birthplace of the Order of the Society of Cincinnati—the first veteran's organization; Dutch barn and restored garden. (Apr-Oct, Wed-Fri, Sun; Nov-Dec, Wed, Sun; also by appt) 145 Sterling St, off NY 9D N. Phone 845/831-8172. ¢¢

Van Wyck Homestead Museum. (1732) Once requisitioned by the Continental Army as headquarters, orders for the army were issued from the house. Also site of court-martials, incl that of Enoch Crosby, counterspy for the American forces. Notables incl Washington, Lafayette, and von Steuben visited here. Library. Collection of Hudson Valley Folk Art; also changing exhibits. (Memorial Day-Oct, Sat and Sun, also by appt) S of town, at jct US 9, I-84. Phone 845/896-9560. ¢¢

Hotel

★ ★ **WELLSLEY INN.** *20 Schuyler Blvd (12524).* 845/896-4995; fax 845/896-6631; res 800/444-8888. *www.wellsleyinnsandsuites.com.* 82 rms, 4 story. Apr-Oct: S, D $89-$109; each addl $2; suites $95-$150; under 17 free; wkly rates; package plans; higher rates special events; lower rates rest of yr. Crib $5. Pet accepted; $5. TV; cable (premium). Complimentary continental bkfst, coffee in rms. Restaurant adj open 24 hrs. Bar noon-11 pm. Ck-out 11 am. In-rm modem link. Health club privileges. Sundries. Some refrigerators; microwaves avail. Cr cds: A, C, D, DS, MC, V.

Extended Stay

★ ★ **RESIDENCE INN BY MARRIOTT.** *14 Schuyler Blvd (12524).* 845/896-5210; fax 845/896-9689; toll-free 800/331-3131. *www.residenceinn. com.* 136 suites, 2 story. S $125-$139; D $129-$155; Suites $150-$279. Crib free. Pet accepted; $150. TV; cable (premium), VCR avail (movies). Pool; whirlpool. Complimentary continental bkfst. Restaurant adj. Ck-out noon. Coin lndry. Meeting rm. Business servs avail. In-rm modem link. Coin lndry. Valet serv. Sundries. Exercise equipt. Health club privileges. Lawn games. Refrigerators, microwaves. Basketball, volleyball. Cr cds: A, D, DS, JCB, MC, V.

Restaurants

★★ **HARRALDS.** *3760 Rte 52, Stormville (12582). 845/878-6595.* International menu. Specialties: truite au bleu, Zurcher rahm schnitzel, poached fresh North Atlantic salmon. Own baking. Hrs: 6 pm-midnight. Closed Sun-Tues; Dec 24, 25; also Jan. Res required. Bar. Wine cellar. Prix fixe: dinner $65. Chef-owned. Jacket.

★★ **HUDSON'S RIBS & FISH.** *1099 Rte 9 (12524). 845/297-5002.* Seafood menu. Specializes in fresh seafood, hand-cut meat, babyback ribs. Own baking. Hrs: 4-10 pm; Fri, Sat to 11 pm; Sun to 9 pm. Bar. Dinner $12-$18. Child's menu. New England nautical decor; lobster traps, fish nets, and picture windows abound. Cr cds: A, D, DS, MC, V.

★★★ **INN AT OSBORNE HILL.** *150 Osborne Hill Rd (12524). 845/897-3055. www.osbornehill.com.* Specialties: breast of duck, loin of veal. Hrs: 11:30 am-2:30 pm, 5-9 pm; Fri, Sat 5-10 pm. Closed Sun; hols. Res accepted. Bar. Wine list. Lunch $6-$9.95, dinner $11.95-$21.95. Child's menu. Outdoor dining. Built in 1935 as summer boarding house. Cr cds: A, D, MC, V.

Floral Park (L.I.)

See also Garden City (L.I.), Hempstead (L.I.), New York City

Pop 15,967 **Elev** 95 ft **Area code** 516

John Lewis Childs started a florist and seed business here in the 1870s. He planted the village with acres of flowers, which even lined the railroad tracks for over a mile, and had

the town's name changed from East Hinsdale to Floral Park.

Motel/Motor Lodge

★★ **FLORAL PARK MOTOR LODGE.** *30 Jericho Tpke (11001). 516/775-7777; fax 516/775-0451; toll-free 800/255-9680. www.floralpark motorlodge.com.* 107 rms, 3 story. S $120-$140; D $160-$184; under 18 free; higher rates Belmont races. Crib free. TV; cable (premium), VCR avail. Complimentary continental bkfst. Restaurant nearby. Ck-out noon. Meeting rms. Business servs avail. Health club privileges. Cr cds: A, C, D, DS, JCB, MC, V.

Restaurants

★★ **ARTUROS ITALIAN RESTAURANT.** *246-04 Jericho Tpke, Bellerose (11001). 516/352-7418.* Italian menu. Specialties: rigatoni with porcini mushrooms, Dover sole, veal chop. Own baking. Hrs: noon-3 pm, 5:30-10 pm; Fri, Sat to 11:30 pm; Sun 3-9:30 pm. Closed Easter, Thanksgiving, Dec 25. Res accepted. Bar. Lunch, dinner $9-$26. Cr cds: A, C, D, DS, MC, V.

★ **CRABTREE'S.** *226 Jericho Tpke (11001). 516/326-7769.* Specializes in fish, fresh pasta, fresh seafood. Hrs: noon-10 pm; Fri, Sat to 11 pm; Sun brunch noon-4 pm. Closed Mon; Jan 1, Thanksgiving, Dec 25. Res accepted. Bar to midnight. A la carte entrees: lunch $5.95-$11.95, dinner $9.95-$18.95. Outdoor dining. Cr cds: A, D, DS, MC, V.

★ **STELLA RISTORANTE.** *152 Jericho Tpke (11001). 516/775-2202.* Italian menu. Specialty: osso buco. Own pasta, Hrs: 11:30 am-3 pm, 4-10 pm; Fri to 11 pm; Sat 4-11 pm; Sun 1-9:30 pm. Closed Mon; Thanksgiving, Dec 25. Res accepted. Bar. A la carte entrees: dinner $8.95-$22.95. Parking. Italian artwork. Family-owned. Cr cds: A, C, D, DS, ER, MC, V.

★ **VICTOR KOENIG'S.** *86 S Tyson Ave (11001). 516/354-2300.* German, American menu. Specialties: sauerbraten, Wiener schnitzel, L.I. duckling. Hrs: noon-11 pm; Fri, Sat to 1

m. Res required wkends. Bar. A la
arte entrees: lunch $4.25-$8.50.
Complete meals: dinner $9.25-$18.
Child's menu. Parking. Cr cds: A, D,
MC, V.

Fulton

D-5) *See also Oswego, Syracuse*

Pop 11,855 **Elev** 360 ft **Area code** 315
Zip 13069
Information Chamber of Commerce,
1 S Second St, Box 148; 315/598-
2231

What to See and Do

Battle Island State Park. N on NY 48.
Eighteen-hole golf (fee). X-country
skiing. Concession. Phone 315/593-
3408.

Motel/Motor Lodge

★ **KNIGHTS INN.** *163 S First St
(13069).* 315/598-6100; fax 315/592-
4738; res 800/843-5644. 70 rms, 2
story. S $48-$79; D $55-$90; each
addl $8; suites $72-$92. Crib free. Pet
accepted. TV; cable (premium). Pool.
Complimentary full bkfst. Ck-out
noon. Meeting rms. Business servs
avail. Valet serv. Exercise equipt.
Business servs avail. Bathrm phones;
refrigerators. Cr cds: A, C, D, DS,
MC, V.

Restaurant

★★ **LOCK III.** *24 S 1st St Canal
Landing (13069).* 315/598-6900. Con-
inental menu. Specializes in steak,
chicken, seafood. Salad bar. Hrs:
11:30 am-2:30 pm, 4:30-10 pm; Sun
noon-9 pm; early-bird dinner Mon-
Sat 4:30-6 pm. Closed Memorial Day,
July 4, Dec 25. Res accepted; required
hols. Bar to 2 am. Lunch $3.95-
$5.95, dinner $10.95-$14.95. Child's
menu. Jazz Fri. Outdoor dining. Din-
ng rm has view of river; overlooks
Barge Canal. Cr cds: A, C, D, DS, ER,
MC, V.

Garden City (L.I.)

*See also Floral Park (L.I.), Hempstead
(L.I.), New York City, Westbury (L.I.)*

Pop 21,672 **Elev** 90 ft **Area code** 516
Zip 11530
Information Chamber of Commerce,
230 Seventh St; 516/746-7724

Special Event

Antique Car Parade. Franklin Ave.
More than 300 antique and vintage
cars. Easter Sun. Contact the Chamber of Commerce.

Hotels

★★★ **GARDEN CITY HOTEL.** *45
7th St (11530).* 516/747-3000; fax
516/747-1414; toll-free 800/547-0400.
www.gch.com. 273 rms, 16 kits. S
$225-$385; D $205-$385; each addl
$20; suites $485-$1,650; under 12
free; wkly, wkend rates. Crib free. Pet
accepted. TV; VCR avail. Indoor pool;
lifeguard. Restaurant 6:30 am-11 pm.
Rm serv 24 hrs. Bar 11:30-2 am;
entertainment. Ck-out noon. Convention facilities. Business servs
avail. In-rm modem link. Concierge.
Shopping arcade. Beauty shop. Free
parking. Exercise rm; sauna. Massage.
Bathrm phones; some refrigerators.
Balconies. Cr cds: A, C, D, DS, JCB,
MC, V.

★★★ **MARRIOTT HOTEL & CON-
FERENCE CENTER LONG ISLAND.**
*101 James Doolittle Blvd, Uniondale
(11553).* 516/794-3800; fax 516/794-
5936; res 800/228-9290. 617 rms, 11
story. S, D $209; each addl $20;
suites $350-$650; under 18 free;
wkend rates. Crib free. Pet accepted,
some restrictions. TV; cable (premium), VCR avail. Indoor pool;
whirlpool, poolside serv, lifeguard.
Restaurant 6:30 am-11 pm. Rm serv
to midnight. Bar 11-2 am. Ck-out
noon. Convention facilities. Business center. In-rm modem link. Barber, beauty shop. Exercise equipt;
sauna. Game rm. Refrigerators,

microwaves avail. Balconies. Adj Nassau Coliseum. Cr cds: A, C, D, DS, JCB, MC, V.

⬛ 🐕 ⛱ 🏋 🎿 🔥 SC 🚶

Restaurants

★★ **AKBAR.** *1 Ring Rd W 1 (11530). 516/248-5700.* Northern Indian menu. Hrs: noon-3 pm, 5:30-10 pm; Fri, Sat to 11 pm; Sun noon-3 pm, 5-10 pm; Sun brunch to 3 pm. Res required. Serv bar. Buffet: lunch $8.99, dinner (Sun) $15.99. A la carte entrees: dinner $9.95-$21.95. Indian decor. Cr cds: A, DS, MC, V.
⬛

★★ **ORCHID.** *730 Franklin Ave (11530). 516/742-1116.* Chinese menu. Specializes in Hunan and Szechwan dishes. Hrs: 11:30 am-10 pm; Fri to 11 pm; Sat noon-11 pm; Sun 1-10 pm. Closed Thanksgiving. Res required. Bar. A la carte entrees: lunch $6.25-$8.95, dinner $15-$20. Elaborate decor; etched glass and murals. Cr cds: A, MC, V.
⬛

Garrison

See also Fishkill, Mahopac, Peekskill

Pop 800 **Elev** 21 ft **Area code** 845 **Zip** 10524

What to See and Do

Foundry School Museum. Old-fashioned schoolrm; West Point Foundry memorabilia, paintings, Native American artifacts, antiques; changing exhibits; genealogy and historical research library. Maintained by the Putnam County Historical Society. (Mar-Dec, Tues-Thurs and Sat-Sun, also by appt) 4 mi N on NY 9D, at 63 Chestnut St in Cold Spring. Phone 845/265-4010. **Donation**

B&Bs/Small Inns

★★ **THE BIRD & BOTTLE.** *1123 Old Albany Post Rd (10524). 845/424-3000; fax 845/424-3283; toll-free 800/782-6837. www.birdbottle.com.* 4 rms, 1-2 story. No rm phones. MAP: S, D $210-$240. Children over 12 yrs only. Complimentary full bkfst. Restaurant (see also BIRD & BOTTLE INN). Ck-out noon, ck-in 2 pm. Business servs avail. Restored Colonial building (1761); many antique furnishings. Cr cds: A, D, DS, MC, V.
🎿 🔥 SC

★★ **HUDSON HOUSE RIVER INN.** *2 Main St, Cold Spring (10516). 845/265-9355; fax 845/265-4532. www.hudsonhousinn.com.* 13 rms, 2 story, 1 suite. No rm phones. Apr-Dec, MAP: D $150; each addl $15; suite $180; lower rest of yr. Crib free. TV in sitting rm; cable, VCR avail. Complimentary full bkfst. Restaurant (see HUDSON HOUSE). Ck-out 11 am, ck-in 3 pm. Business servs avail. X-country ski 10 mi. Balconies. Picnic tables. Country inn (1832) on banks of Hudson River. Cr cds: A, D, MC, V.
♿ ⛱ 🎿 🔥

Restaurants

★★ **BIRD & BOTTLE INN.** *1123 Old Albany Post Rd (10524). 845/424-3000. www.birdbottle.com.* Continental menu. Specializes in fresh fish, chicken. Hrs: noon-3 pm, 6-9 pm; Sat 2 sittings 6 and 9 pm; Sun 4:30-7 pm; Sun brunch noon-2 pm. Closed Mon, Tues. Res accepted. Bar. Complete meal: dinner $36.95-$51.95. Sun brunch $16.95-$23.95. Outdoor dining. Fireside dining in restored 18th-century tavern. Cr cds: A, D, DS, MC, V.
⬛

★★ **HUDSON HOUSE.** *2 Main St, Cold Spring (10516). 845/265-9355. www.hudsonhouseinn.com.* Specializes in fresh fish, game, smoked foods. Own desserts. Hrs: 11:30 am-3:30 pm, 5:30-9 pm; Fri, Sat to 10 pm; Sun 11:30 am-8 pm. Closed Dec 25. Res accepted; required wkends. Bar. Lunch $7.50-$16.95, dinner $17.50-$26.75. Child's menu. Built 1832. Overlooks river. Cr cds: A, MC, V.
⬛

★★★ **PLUMBUSH INN.** *1656 US 9D, Cold Spring (10516). 845/265-3904.* Continental menu. Specialties: trout, Swiss apple fritters, medallions of veal. Own baking. Hrs: noon-2 pm, 5:30-9:30 pm; Sun noon-8 pm; Sun brunch to 3 pm. Closed Mon, Tues. Res accepted; required wkends.

Bar. Lunch $8.50-$11.95. Complete meals: dinner from $32.50. Sun brunch $16.50. Valet parking. Fireplaces. Paintings by local artists displayed. 3 guest rms avail. Cr cds: A, MC, V.

D

★ ★ ★ **XAVIAR'S RESTAURANT.** *Rte 9 D (10524). 845/424-4228. www. xaviars.com.* Continental menu. Specializes in contemporary cuisine. Hrs: 5-9 pm; Sun brunch 11:30 am-2 pm. Closed Mon-Thurs; hols; also mid-Jan-mid-Feb. Res required. Serv bar. Wine cellar. Prix fixe: dinner $75. Sun brunch $32. Child's menu. Entertainment Fri, Sat.

D

Geneseo

D-3) *See also Avon*

Pop 9,654 **Elev** 800 ft **Area code** 716 **Zip** 14454

What to See and Do

Letchworth State Park. (see) 1 Hall of Fame Dr. Phone 315/697-7095. ¢¢
Livingston County Historical Museum. Pioneer exhibits, antique toys, Native American artifacts housed in Cobblestone School (1838); Shaker Colony Fountain Stone, farm items; antique fire equipt. (May-Oct, Sun and Thurs afternoons; summer, also Tues eves) 30 Center St. Phone 716/243-9147. **Donation**

Motel/Motor Lodge

★ **DAYS INN.** *4242 Lakeville Rd, Rte 20A (14454). 716/243-0500; fax 716/243-9007; toll-free 800/329-7466. www.daysinn.com.* 76 rms, 1-2 story. S $59-$74; D $65-$80; each addl $8; under 18 free; ski plan. Crib free. TV; cable (premium). Pool. Restaurant adj open 24 hrs. Ck-out noon. Meeting rms. Business servs avail. Sundries. X-country ski 6 mi. Cr cds: A, C, D, DS, JCB, MC, V.

D ⊠ ⊠ ⊠ ⊠ SC

Geneva (D-4)

Settled 1788 **Pop** 13,617 **Elev** 460 ft **Area code** 315 **Zip** 14456
Information Chamber of Commerce, 35 Lakefront Dr, Box 587; 315/789-1776
Web www.genevany.com

In the 19th century Geneva attracted large numbers of retired ministers and spinsters and became known as "the saints' retreat and old maids' paradise." Today, Geneva is known as a "fisherman's paradise." Located at the foot of Seneca Lake, the deepest of the Finger Lakes, the town is surrounded by rich farmland with nurseries on the outskirts of the city.

What to See and Do

Geneva Historical Society Museum. (Prouty-Chew House) 1829 Federal-style home with items of local history; changing exhibits. (July and Aug, Tues-Sun; rest of yr, Tues-Sat; closed hols) 543 S Main St. Phone 315/789-5151. **FREE**
Rose Hill Mansion. (1839) Elegant country estate; Greek Revival architecture; Empire furnishings. Guided tours (May-Oct, Mon-Sat, also Sun afternoons). 3 mi E on NE shore of Seneca Lake on NY 96A, just S of US 20, use NY Thrwy exit 41 or 42. Phone 315/789-3848. ¢¢
Sampson State Park. Swimming beach, bathhouse, fishing, boating (launch, marina); hiking, tennis, picnicking, playground, tent and trailer sites (mid-Apr-late Nov). 11 mi S on NY 96A. Phone 315/585-6392. ¢¢
Seneca Lake State Park. Swimming beach, bathhouse, fishing, boating (launch, marina); picnicking, playground. 1 mi E on US 20 (NY 5). Phone 315/789-2331. ¢¢
Smith Opera House for the Performing Arts. (1894) Alternates films with theater, concerts, children's shows. Tours. (Mon-Fri) 82 Seneca St. ¢¢

Special Events

National Trout Derby. Memorial Day wkend. Phone 315/789-1776.
Seneca Lake Whale Watch. Lakeshore Park. Three days of music,

arts and crafts, food. Aug. Phone 315/781-0820.

Hotel

★★★ GENEVA ON THE LAKE.
1001 Lochland Rd; Rte 14 S (14456). 315/789-7190; fax 315/789-0322; toll-free 800/343-6382. www.genevaonthe lake.com. 30 kit. suites, 3 story. June 1-Nov 21: kit. suites $193-$495; each addl over 18, $30; 13-17, $10; under 12 free; wkly rates; lower rates rest of yr. Crib avail. TV; cable (premium), VCR avail (movies). Pool. Complimentary continental bkfst. Ck-out noon, ck-in 3 pm. Meeting rms. Business servs avail. Luggage handling. Valet serv. Gift shop. Tennis privileges. 18-hole golf privileges. Health club privileges. Private lakefront, sailboats. Refrigerators; some fireplaces. Some private patios, balconies. Picnic tables, grills. Italianate Renaissance villa (1912) overlooks Seneca Lake. Many antiques. Cr cds: A, DS, MC, V.

B&B/Small Inn

★★★ BELHURST CASTLE. *Rte 14 S (14456). 315/781-0201. www. belhurstcastle.com.* 13 rms, 3 story. May-Oct: S, D $105-$220; suites $240-$315; lower rates rest of yr. Crib $10. TV; cable. Restaurant (see BEL-HURST CASTLE). Bar 11-1 am. Ck-out 11 am, ck-in 3 pm. Balconies. Turreted, Romanesque mansion (1885) on Seneca Lake; extensive grounds, elaborate landscaping. Elegant antique furnishings; stained-glass windows. Cr cds: MC, V.

Restaurants

★★★ BELHURST CASTLE. *Rte 14 S, Lochland Rd (14456). 315/781-0201. www.belhurstcastle.com.* Continental menu. Specializes in veal, seafood, prime rib. Hrs: 11 am-2 pm, 5-9:30 pm; Sun 3:30-9 pm; Sun brunch 11 am-2 pm. Res accepted. Bar to 1 am. Wine list. Lunch $5.95-$7.95, dinner $16-$30. Sun brunch $14.95. Child's menu. 19th-century Romanesque mansion with view of lake and gardens; was speakeasy and casino during Prohibition. Cr cds: MC, V.

★★ EMILE'S. *E North St (14456). 315/789-2775.* Continental menu. Specialties: prime rib, baby back ribs. Salad bar. Hrs: 11 am-2 pm, 5-9 pm; Fri, Sat to 10 pm. Closed Mon; Thanksgiving, Dec 25. Res accepted. Bar. Lunch $3-$5.95, dinner $7.95-$17.95. Child's menu. Casual dining. Cr cds: A, C, DS, ER, MC, V.

Glen Cove (L.I.)

See also Jericho (L.I.), Oyster Bay (L.I.), Port Washington (L.I.)

Pop 26,622 **Elev** 133 ft **Area code** 516 **Zip** 11542

Information Chamber of Commerce, 14 Glen St, Suite 303, PO Box 721; 516/676-6666

Web www.glencove-li.com

What to See and Do

Garvies Point Museum and Preserve. Exhibits devoted to regional geology and Native American archaeology. The preserve incl 62 acres of glacial moraine covered by forest; high cliffs along the shoreline of Hempstead Harbor. There are five mi of trails throughout the preserve. (Tues-Sun; closed hols) 50 Barry Dr. Phone 516/571-8010. ¢

Restaurants

★★ BARNEY'S RESTAURANT. *315 Buckram Rd, Locust Valley (11560). 516/671-6300.* Specialties: L.I. duck, rack of lamb, crab cakes. Hrs: 5:30-10 pm; Fri, Sat to 11 pm; Sun 5-9 pm. Closed Mon; Dec 25. Res accepted Sat. Bar 5-10 pm, wkends to 1 am. A la carte entrees: dinner $20-$30. Prix fixe: 3 courses $25. Menu changes seasonally. Firehouse antiques and memorabilia. Cr cds: A, MC, V.

★★ LA BUSSOLA. *40 School St, Glen Cove, L.I. (11542). 516/671-2100.* Italian menu. Specializes in veal, pasta, seafood. Hrs: noon-10 pm; Sat 5-11 pm; Sun 3-9 pm. Closed hols. Res accepted. Bar. A la carte

entrees: lunch $7-$19.50, dinner
$11-$25. Cr cds: A, DS, MC, V.
D

★ ★ ★ **LA PACE.** *51 Cedar Swamp Rd,
Glen Cove (11542). 516/671-2970.*
Northern Italian menu. Own baking.
Hrs: noon-2:30 pm, 6-10 pm; Sat 6-
11 pm; Sun 4-10 pm. Closed Easter,
Dec 25. Res accepted. Bar. Wine cel-
lar. A la carte entrees: lunch, dinner
$14.95-$21.95. Prix fixe: dinner $25.
Valet parking. Fireplaces. Cr cds: A,
C, D, ER, MC, V.
D

★ ★ ★ **VERANDA.** *75 Cedar Swamp
Rd, Glen Cove (11542). 516/759-0394.*
Northern Italian menu. Specializes in
chicken, veal, fish. Hrs: noon-3 pm,
5:30-10 pm; Sat to 11 pm; Sun 2-10
pm. Closed Jan 1, Dec 25. Res
required. Bar. Wine list. A la carte
entrees: lunch $7.95-$13.95, dinner
$14.95-$26.95. Complete meals
(Mon-Fri, Sun): dinner $20-$25. Valet
parking. Fireplace, artwork. Cr cds: A,
C, D, DS, MC, V.
D

Glens Falls

*(D-8) See also Lake George Village, Lake
Luzerne, Saratoga Springs*

Settled 1763 **Pop** 14,354 **Elev** 340 ft
Area code 518 **Zip** 12801
Information Adirondack Regional
Chambers of Commerce, 136 Warren
St; 518/798-1761

The Iroquois called what is now
Glens Falls "Chepontuc," a word
meaning "a difficult place to get
around." Surrounded by the Adirondack Mountains and adjacent to the
60-foot drop in the Hudson River,
the area was settled by Abraham
Wing, a Quaker.

What to See and Do

The Chapman Historical Museum.
Victorian/Second Empire home
(1868). Major portion has been
redecorated as a period home reflecting 1865 and 1910. Gallery with

rotating exhibits on Glens Falls,
Queensbury, and the southern
Adirondacks. Large photographic
library featuring collection of Seneca
Ray Stoddard. (Tues-Sat; closed hols)
348 Glen St. Phone 518/793-2826.

Cross-country skiing. Glens Falls
International X-Country Ski Trails,
contact Recreational Department.
Phone 518/761-3813. **FREE**

Hyde Collection. Art museum in
original collector's home. Emphasis
on 15th-20th century art, incl Rembrandt, Rubens, Picasso, El Greco;
sculptures, antique furniture; films
and lectures. (Tues-Sun; closed hols)
161 Warren St. Phone 518/792-1761.
FREE

Skiing. West Mountain Ski Resort.
Triple, two double chairlifts; two
rope tows; night skiing; patrol,
school, rentals; snowmaking; cafeterias, bar; shop, lodge. Longest run
approx 1½ mi; vertical drop 1,010 ft.
(Dec-Apr, daily; closed Dec 25) I-87
exit 18, 3 mi W on Corinth Rd, then
¼ mi N on West Mtn Rd. Phone
518/793-6606. ¢¢¢¢

Motels/Motor Lodges

★ **ALPENHAUS.** *851 Rte 9 Lake
George Rd, Queensbury (12804).
518/792-6941.* 15 rms. Late June-
early Sept: S $65-$80; D $72-$88;
each addl $5; higher rates racing sea-
son; lower rates rest of yr. Crib $5.
TV; cable. Restaurant nearby. Ck-out
11 am. Downhill ski 5 mi; x-country
ski 1 mi. Alpine decor. Cr cds: A,
MC, V.
🐾 ⚡ ☝ 🖼 🔥

★ ★ **GRAYCOURT MOTEL.** *1082 Rte
9, Queensbury (12804). 518/792-0223;
fax 518/792-2003.* 25 units, 4 with
shower only, 5 cottages. July-Labor
Day: S $50-$95; D $60-$98; each addl
$5; cottages $120-$140; under 12
free; lower rates rest of yr. Closed late
Sept-Memorial Day. Crib $5. TV;
cable. Complimentary coffee in rms.
Restaurant adj 7 am-5:30 pm. Ck-out
11 am. Heated pool. Playground.
Many refrigerators. Picnic tables,
grills. Cr cds: A, DS, MC, V.
✈ 🖼 🔥 🏊

★ ★ **LANDMARK MOTOR INN.** *Rte
9 & Rte 197 (12801). 518/793-3441;
fax 518/761-6909; toll-free 800/541-*

3441. 74 rms. Mid-July-Aug: S $85-$90; D $95-$105; each addl $5; higher rates hols, racing season; lower rates rest of yr. Crib $3-$5. TV; cable (premium). 2 pools, 1 indoor; whirlpool. Playground. Restaurant adj 6 am-11 pm. Ck-out 11 am. Meeting rm. Business servs avail. Airport, bus depot transportation. Putting green. Downhill ski 6 mi; x-country ski 3 mi. Rec rm. Exercise equipt. Game rm. Lawn games. Refrigerators avail. Picnic tables, grills. Cr cds: A, C, D, DS, MC, V.

★ ★ **RAMADA INN GLENS FALLS.** *Abby Ln, Queensbury (12804). 518/793-7701; fax 518/792-5463; res 888/298-2054. www.ramada.com.* 110 rms, 2 story. Late July-early Sept: S $49-$99; D $59-$109; each addl $10; under 17 free; higher rates racing season; lower rates rest of yr. Crib free. TV; cable (premium). Indoor pool. Complimentary coffee in rms. Restaurant 6:30 am-10 pm. Bar 5 pm-midnight. Ck-out noon. Meeting rms. Business servs avail. In-rm modem link. X-country ski 2 mi. Health club privileges. Microwaves avail. Picnic tables. Cr cds: A, C, D, DS, MC, V.

★ **SUPER 8 MOTEL.** *191 Corinth Rd, Queensbury (12804). 518/761-9780; fax 518/761-1049; toll-free 800/800-8000.* 59 rms, 2 story. July: S $48-$50; D $55-$57; each addl $6; under 12 free; higher rates: wkends, special events; lower rates rest of yr. Crib free. TV; cable, VCR avail (movies). Complimentary coffee in lobby. Restaurant nearby. Ck-out 11 am. Downhill/x-country ski 10 mi. Cr cds: A, D, DS, MC, V.

Hotels

★ **BROWN'S WELCOME INN HOTEL.** *932 Lake George Rd Rt 9, Queensbury (12804). 518/792-9576; fax 518/792-8072. www.browns welcomeinn.com.* 20 rms, 5 with shower only. July-Labor Day: S $65-$85; D $65-$95; each addl $5; lower rates mid-May-June, Labor Day-mid-Oct. Closed rest of yr. Crib $5. TV; cable (premium). Pool. Playground. Complimentary coffee in rms. Restaurant adj 8 am-10 pm. Ck-out

10:30 am. Some refrigerators. Picnic tables. Cr cds: A, DS, MC, V.

★ ★ ★ **QUEENSBURY HOTEL.** *88 Ridge St (12801). 518/792-1121; fax 518/792-9259. www.queensburyhotel. com.* 126 rms, 5 story. Aug: S $79-$99; D $119-$109; suites $215-$325; under 18 free; lower rates rest of yr. Crib $10. TV; cable. Indoor pool; whirlpool. Restaurant 7 am-9 pm. Bar 11:30-1 am. Ck-out noon. Meeting rms. Business servs avail. Barber. Downhill ski 4 mi; x-country ski 1 mi. Exercise equipt. Massage. Health club privileges. Cr cds: A, C, D, DS, MC, V.

Goshen

(G-7) *See also Monroe, Newburgh*

Settled 1714 **Pop** 12,913 **Elev** 440 ft
Area code 914 **Zip** 10924

Information Chamber of Commerce, 44 Park Pl, PO Box 506; 914/294-7741 or 800/884-2563

Web www.goshennychamber.com

This town, in the center of dairying and onion-growing country, has long been famous for harness racing.

What to See and Do

Brotherhood Winery. (America's Oldest Winery) Tours, wine tasting. (May-Oct, daily; rest of yr, wkends; closed Jan 1, Dec 25) NY Thrwy to exit 16, NY 17 W to exit 130, NY 208 N to Washingtonville. Phone 845/496-9101. ¢¢

Goshen Historic Track. Harness racing's oldest track dates to 1838. Self-guided walking tour. (Daily) (See SPECIAL EVENTS) 44 Park Pl. Phone 845/294-5333. **FREE**

Harness Racing Museum and Hall of Fame. Home of the Hall of Fame of the Trotter; incl Currier and Ives trotting prints; paintings; statues; dioramas of famous horses; library. Harness racing simulator; interactive exhibits. Self-guided tours. (Daily; closed Jan 1,

Thanksgiving, Dec 25) 240 Main St. Phone 845/294-6330. ¢¢¢

Special Events

Racing. Goshen Historic Track. Grand Circuit; County Fair Sire Stakes; matinee racing. Phone 845/294-5333. Three Sat June and four days early July.

Great American Weekend. Arts and crafts, entertainment, rides, races. July 3-4. Phone 845/294-7741.

Great Neck (L.I.)

(G-2) *See also New York City, Port Washington (L.I.)*

Pop 9,538 **Elev** 100 ft **Area code** 516
Information Chamber of Commerce, 643 Middleneck Rd, 11023; 516/487-2000

Consisting of nine villages and an unincorporated area, the population would be approximately 41,500 if added together.

What to See and Do

US Merchant Marine Academy. (1943) 950 midshipmen. Memorial Chapel honoring war dead. Visitors welcome (daily; closed hols and July). Regimental Reviews (spring and fall, Sat; schedule varies). The American Merchant Marine Museum is open (Mon-Fri). At Kings Point. Phone 516/773-5000. **FREE**

Hotel

★★★ **INN AT GREAT NECK.** *30 Cutter Mill Rd, Great Neck (11021). 516/773-2000. www.innatgreatneck. com.* 85 rms, 2 story. S, D $195-$250; suites $250-$450. TV; cable (premium), VCR avail. Coffee in rms. Restaurants 6:30 am-midnight. Bar 11 am-midnight. Ck-out noon. Meeting rms. Business servs avail. In-rm modem link. Concierge. Gift shop.

Exercise equipt. Cr cds: A, D, DS, MC, V.

Restaurants

★★ **BEVANDA RISTORANTE.** *570 Middle Neck Rd, Great Neck (11023). 516/482-1510.* Italian menu. Specialties: cold and hot antipasto, chicken giardino, salmon Dijon. Own pasta. Hrs: noon-10 pm; Sat 4:30-10:30 pm; Sun 3-9:30 pm. Res required. Bar. A la carte entrees: lunch $10-$16, dinner $15.50-$22.50. Complete meals: lunch $14.95. Old World atmosphere; traditional paintings. Cr cds: A, C, DS, MC, V.
D

★★ **BRUZELL'S.** *451 Middle Neck Rd, Great Neck (11023). 516/482-6600.* Continental menu. Specializes in steak, fresh fish. Hrs: noon-2:30 pm, 5-10 pm; wkend hrs vary; Mon from 5 pm; early-bird dinner 5-6 pm. Closed Jan 1, Dec 25. Res accepted. Bar. A la carte entrees: lunch $9.95-$11.95, dinner $13.95-$24.95. Complete meals: lunch $10.95, dinner $16.50. Child's menu. Valet parking wkends. Bilevel dining with art deco decor. Cr cds: A, DS, MC, V.
D

★★ **MILLIE'S PLACE.** *25 Middle Neck Rd, Great Neck (11021). 516/482-4223.* Continental menu. Specializes in pasta with seafood. Hrs: 11:30 am-11 pm; Sun brunch to 4 pm. Closed Thanksgiving, Yom Kippur. Bar. Lunch $10-$23, dinner $12-$23. Outdoor dining. Antique mirrors, paintings. Cr cds: A, MC, V.

Greenport (L.I.)

(F-4) *See also Riverhead (L.I.), Shelter Island, Southold (L.I.)*

Pop 4,180 **Elev** 10 ft **Area code** 516
Zip 11944

Greenport is a bit of New England on Long Island. There are clean, uncrowded beaches visitors can enjoy, as well as several wineries.

What to See and Do

Orient Point, NY-New London, CT, Ferry. Ninety-min crossing. (Daily; closed Dec 25) One-day round trips. Res required for vehicle. 8 mi NE at end of NY 25 in Orient Point. Phone 631/323-2525. ¢¢¢¢

Special Event

Greenport Maritime Festival. Wooden boat regatta, fishing tournament, whale boat race; clam chowder tasting contest. Phone 516/477-0004. Late Sept.

Motels/Motor Lodges

★ **SILVER SANDS MOTEL.** *1 Silvermere Rd (11944). 631/477-0011; fax 631/477-0922. www.silversands-motel. com.* 35 rms, 15 kit. cottages. Mid-June-mid-Sept: S, D $100-$150; each addl $15; kit. cottages $850-$1,500/wk; wkly rates; lower rates rest of yr. Crib avail. TV; cable. Heated pool; lifeguard. Complimentary continental bkfst. Restaurant nearby. Ck-out 11 am. Game rm. Picnic tables, grills. On bay. Cr cds: A, D, DS, MC, V.

★★ **SOUND VIEW INN.** *57185 N Rd (11944). 631/477-1910; fax 631/477-9436.* 49 rms, 1-2 story, 31 kit. suites. Late June-early Sept: S, D $99; each addl $10; kit. suites $130-$275; lower rates rest of yr. TV; cable, VCR avail. Pool. Restaurant noon-10 pm. Bar; entertainment wknds, dinner theater Wed eves in season. Ck-out noon. Meeting rms. Tennis. Golf privileges. Sauna. Refrigerators. On beach. Cr cds: A, C, D, DS, MC, V.

★ **SUNSET MOTEL.** *62005 N Rd Rte 48 (11944). 631/477-1776.* 11 rms, 1-2 story, 11 kits. Mid-June-mid-Sept, Memorial Day wkend (3-day min; hol wkends 4-day min): D $95-$160; each addl $10; kit. units $115-$160; lower rates mid-Apr-mid-June, mid-Sept-Oct. Closed rest of yr. Crib free. TV; cable. Restaurant nearby. Ck-out 11 am. Tennis privileges. Lawn games. Porches. Picnic tables, grills. Private beach. Cr cds: DS, MC, V.

Restaurants

★ **CHOWDER POT PUB.** *104 3rd St (11944). 631/477-1345.* Specialties: New England and Manhattan chowders. Hrs: noon-2:30 pm, 5-9 pm; Fri, Sat to 10 pm. Closed Mon; also winter wkdays. Res accepted. Bar. Lunch $3.75-$12.50, dinner $12.95-$15.75. Outdoor dining. Cr cds: A, MC, V.

★★ **CLAUDIO'S.** *111 Main St (11944). 631/477-0627. www.claudios. com.* Specializes in seafood, steak. Hrs: 11:30 am-10 pm; Fri, Sat to 11 pm. Res accepted. Bar. Lunch $9.95-$12.95, dinner $14.95-$22.95. Entertainment. Parking. Outdoor dining. Clam bar on dock. Souvenirs of America's Cup defenders decorate walls. View of fishing harbor. Family-owned for more than 100 yrs. Cr cds: MC, V.
Ⓓ

Greenwich

(G-2) See also Saratoga Springs

Pop 4,896 **Elev** 360 ft **Area code** 518 **Zip** 12834

What to See and Do

Bennington Battlefield State Historic Site. Battlefield where militiamen under Brigadier General John Stark stopped a force of British sharpshooters, mercenaries, Loyalists, and Native Americans in Aug 1777. Hilltop view; relief map, picnic tables. View of monument in Vermont. (May-Oct, daily) 7 mi SE via NY 372, 6 mi S on NY 22, and 2 mi E on NY 67, E of N Hoosick, in the town of Walloomsac. **FREE**

Skiing. Willard Mountain Ski Area. Chairlift, T-bar, pony lift; patrol, school, rentals; snowmaking; bar, cafeteria, snack bar; ski shop. Longest run 3,500 ft; vertical drop 550 ft. Night skiing. (Early Dec-late Mar, daily; closed Thanksgiving, Dec 25) 6 mi S on NY 40. Phone 518/692-7337. ¢¢¢¢

Restaurant

★ **WALLIE'S OF GREENWICH.** *56 Main St (12834). 518/692-7823.* Specializes in prime rib, seafood. Hrs: 4-9 pm; Fri, Sat to 10 pm; Sun noon-9 pm; early-bird dinner Wed-Sat 4-6 pm. Closed Mon; Dec 24, 25. Bar. Complete meals: dinner $9.95-$23.95. Child's menu. Cr cds: A, DS, MC, V.

Hague (Lake George Area)

See also Crown Point

Pop 854 **Elev** 328 ft **Area code** 518 **Zip** 12836
Information Chamber of Commerce; 518/543-6353

Hague is a resort community on the western shore of Lake George, near its northern tip.

What to See and Do

Rogers Rock State Public Campground. Boating (launch, motors), fishing, swimming, bathhouse, lifeguards; camping (dump station; fee), picnicking. (Early May-mid-Oct) 3 mi N on NY 9 N, in Adirondack Park (see). Phone 518/585-6746. ¢¢

Resort

★★ **TROUT HOUSE VILLAGE RESORT.** *Lake Shore Dr - Rte 9 N (12836). 518/543-6088; res 800/368-6088. www.trouthouse.com.* 22 rms in motel, lodge, 3 kits., 5 kit. cottages, 10 kit. chalets, 1-3 story. No A/C. Mid-June-mid-Sept: S, D $69-$125; each addl $5; kit. units to 4, $92-$300, cabins $750-$2,100/wk; ski rates; lower rates rest of yr. Crib free. TV; cable. Ck-out 11 am. Putting green. X-country ski 2 mi. Rec rm. Lawn games. Some fireplaces, in-rm whirlpools. Picnic tables, grill. 400-ft swimming beach; dockage. View of lake. Cr cds: A, DS, MC, V.

Hamilton

(D-1) *See also Cazenovia, Oneida*

Settled ca 1794 **Pop** 5,733 **Elev** 1,126 ft **Area code** 315 **Zip** 13346

What to See and Do

Colgate University. (1819) 2,650 students. A handsome campus with buildings dating from 1827. The Charles A. Dana Arts Center, designed by Paul Rudolph, houses the Picker Art Gallery (academic yr, daily; closed hols). On NY 12B. Campus tours: contact Admission Office, Administration Building. Phone 315/228-7401.

Rogers Environmental Education Center. On 600 acres; trout ponds; visitor center, 350 mounted birds, outdoor exhibits, six mi of nature trails, x-country skiing, observation tower, picnicking. Buildings (June-Aug, daily; rest of yr, Mon-Sat). Center (daily; closed hols). Approx 12 mi S on NY 12 or NY 12B to Sherburne, then 1 mi W on NY 80. Phone 607/674-4017. **FREE**

Motel/Motor Lodge

★★ **COLGATE INN.** *1-5 Payne St (13346). 315/824-2300; fax 315/824-4500.* 46 rms, 3 story. S $79-$109; D $89-$119; each addl $10; suites $150-$175; under 11 free. Crib free. TV; cable. Complimentary continental bkfst. Restaurant (see PAYNE STREET CORNER). Bar 11:30 am-midnight. Ck-out 11 am, ck-in 3 pm. Meeting rms. Business servs avail. Recreational facilities of Colgate University avail to guests. Some in-rm whirlpools. Cr cds: A, D, DS, MC, V.

Restaurant

★★ **PAYNE STREET CORNER.** *1-5 Payne St (13346). 315/824-2300.* Specializes in fresh seafood, hand-cut steaks. Hrs: 11:30 am-8:30 pm; Fri, Sat to 9:30 pm; Sun brunch 10 am-1 pm. Res accepted. Bar 11:30 am-midnight. Lunch $4.95-$8.95, dinner $9.95-$15.95. Buffet: lunch $5.95. Sun brunch $12.95. Child's menu. Outdoor dining. Early American tavern; fireplace. Cr cds: A, C, D, DS, ER, MC, V.

Hammonds-port

See also Bath, Penn Yan

Pop 731 **Elev** 743 ft **Area code** 607 **Zip** 14840

This is the center of the New York State wine industry, at the southern tip of Keuka Lake. The grape growers are mainly of German and Swiss origin. They have more than a century of viniculture in New York State behind them, dating from 1829, when the Reverend William Bostwick planted the first vineyard. Glenn H. Curtiss, a pioneer aviator, was born here; most of his early experimental flights took place in this area.

What to See and Do

Glenn H. Curtiss Museum. Curtiss memorabilia; historical aircraft; local history exhibits 1860-1948. Changing exhibits, restoration shop. (Apr-Dec, daily; winter hrs vary; closed hols) NY 54. Phone 607/569-2160. ¢¢¢

Wine & Grape Museum of Greyton H. Taylor. Vineyard equipt, exhibits on early champagne, wine, and brandy production; presidential wine glass collection; barrel-making housed in old area winery (1880-1920). Tours. (May-Oct, daily) 8843 G .H. Taylor Memorial Dr, 2 mi N off NY 54A, W side of Keuka Lake. Phone 607/868-4814. **Donation**

Motel/Motor Lodge

★ **HAMMONDSPORT MOTEL.** *William St (14840). 607/569-2600.* 17 rms. Apr-mid-Nov: S $55; D $60; each addl $9. Closed rest of yr. Crib $9. TV; cable. Ck-out 11 am. Dock, boat launch. On Keuka Lake; swimming. Cr cds: MC, V.

B&B/Small Inn

★★ **BLUSHING ROSE BED & BREAKFAST.** *11 William St (14840). 607/569-3402; toll-free 800/982-8818. www.blushingroseinn.com.* 4 rms, 3 with shower only. No rm phones. S $75-$85; D $85-$105; each addl $15; wkends 2-day min. Children over 12 yrs only. TV in common rm; cable (premium), VCR avail. Complimentary full bkfst; afternoon refreshments. Restaurant nearby. Ck-out 11 am, ck-in 3 pm. Luggage handling. Built in 1843; antiques. Totally nonsmoking.

Hampton Bays (L.I.)

(G-4) *See also Riverhead (L.I.), Southampton (L.I.), Westhampton Beach*

Pop 12,236 **Elev** 50 ft **Area code** 516 **Zip** 11946

Restaurant

★★ **VILLA PAUL.** *162 W Montauk Hwy, Hampton Bays (11946). 631/728-3261.* Italian, American menu. Hrs: 4:30-10 pm. Closed Dec 25. Res accepted. Bar. A la carte entrees: dinner $11.50-$20.95. Late 1800s building; original woodwork in dining area. Family-owned. Cr cds: A, MC, V.

Hartsdale

See also White Plains

Pop 9,830 **Elev** 182 ft **Area code** 914 **Zip** 10530

Restaurant

★★★ **AUBERGE ARGENTEUIL.** *42 N Healy Ave (10530). 914/948-0597.*

French menu. Specialties: rack of amb, filet with peppercorn, lobster bisque. Own baking. Hrs: noon-2 pm, 6-9 pm; Sat 6-10 pm; Sun 1-8 pm. Closed Mon; Jan 1, 2. Res accepted; required Fri, Sat. Bar. A la carte entrees: lunch $6.75-$20. Prix ixe: dinner $38. Country French decor. Cr cds: A, D, MC, V.

Hawthorne

See also White Plains

Pop 5,083 **Elev** 258 ft **Area code** 914 **Zip** 10532

Restaurant

★★ **GASHO OF JAPAN.** *2 Sawmill River Rd (NY 9A) (10532).* 914/592-5900. Japanese menu. Specialties: teriyaki swordfish with broccoli, filet mignon and hibachi chicken combination. Hrs: 11:30 am-2:30 pm, 5-9:30 pm; Fri to 10 pm; Sat noon-2:30 pm, 5-10:30 pm; Sun noon-9 pm. Res required. Bar. Lunch $5.95-$19.95, dinner $12.95-$24.75. Child's menu. Tableside cooking. Building moved from Japan; Japanese gardens. Cr cds: A, D, DS, MC, V.
D **SC** ⊟

Hempstead (L.I.)

(G-2) *See also Bethpage (L.I.), New York City, Rockville Centre (L.I.)*

Pop 56,554 **Elev** 60 ft **Area code** 516 **Information** Chamber of Commerce, 1776 Nicholas Ct, 11550; 516/483-2000

What to See and Do

African-American Museum. Depicts the scope and depth of the story of African-American people on Long Island and their contributions to the development of its history. Collection of African-American artifacts; changing exhibits. Workshops, seminars, films. (Tues-Sun; closed hols) 110 N Franklin St.

Hofstra University. (1935) 13,400 students. The Hofstra Museum presents exhibitions in the Emily Lowe Gallery, David Filderman Gallery, Hofstra's Cultural Center, and in nine other areas on campus. (Daily; closed hols) Concerts, lectures, drama productions, arboretum tours, and sports events. Campus tours (Mon-Fri). Phone 516/463-6600.

Nassau Veterans Memorial Coliseum. Arena seats 17,000; 60,000 square ft of exhibition space. Home of the New York Islanders (hockey) and New York Saints (lacrosse); facilities for basketball; ice shows; concerts, stage shows. 2 mi E, on Hempstead Tpke (NY 24).

Restaurant

★★ **CHURRASQUEIRA BAIRRADA.** *144 Jericho Tpke, Mineola (11501).* 516/739-3856. Portuguese barbecue menu. Specializes in all-you-can-eat barbecue. Hrs: 11:30 am-10:30 pm. Closed Mon. Serv bar. Lunch $7.95-$12.95, dinner $8.95-$19.95. Hanging lamps, wall-to-wall mirrors. Cr cds: A, MC, V.
D **SC**

Herkimer

(D-6) *See also Ilion, Utica*

Settled 1725 **Pop** 9,962 **Elev** 407 ft **Area code** 315 **Zip** 13350
Information Herkimer County Chamber of Commerce, 28 W Main St, PO Box 129, Mohawk 13407; 315/866-7820
Web herkimer.org

Herkimer is a town that retains pride in its history. General Nicholas Herkimer marched from the fort here to the Battle of Oriskany, one of the Revolutionary War's bloodiest, which took place August 4, 1777. The Gillette trial, basis for Theodore

Japanese Gardens

Dreiser's *An American Tragedy,* was held in the Herkimer County Courthouse.

What to See and Do

Herkimer County Historical Society. Mansion contains exhibits of county history. (July-Aug, Mon-Sat; rest of yr, Mon-Fri; closed hols) 400 N Main St at Court St, on site of Fort Dayton (1776). Phone 315/866-6413. **FREE**

Herkimer Home State Historic Site. (1764) General Nicholas Herkimer lived here; 18th century furnishings. Family cemetery and General Herkimer Monument. Visitor center; picnic area. 8 mi E on NY 169 off NY 5 S. Phone 315/823-0398. **FREE**

Motels/Motor Lodges

★★ **BEST WESTERN.** *20 Albany St, Little Falls (13365).* 315/823-4954; fax 315/823-4507; res 800/528-1234. *www.bestwestern.com.* 56 rms, 2 story. May-Sept: S $57-$67; D $70-$80; each addl $6; under 12 free; lower rates rest of yr. Crib free. Pet accepted, some restrictions; $10 refundable. TV; cable. Restaurant 6:30 am-2 pm, 5-9 pm; Sun 7 am-1 pm, 5-9 pm. Bar 11 am-2 pm, 5-11 pm. Ck-out noon. Meeting rms. Business servs avail. Game rm. Cr cds: A, C, D, DS, MC, V.

★ **HERKIMER MOTEL.** *100 Marginal Rd (13350).* 315/866-0490; fax 315/866-0416; toll-free 877/656-6835. 61 rms, 2 story, 16 kits. July-early Sep: S $49-$54; D $59-$68; each addl $7; kit. units, studio rms $75-$83; under 13 free; wkly rates; lower rates rest of yr. Crib free. Pet accepted, some restrictions. TV; cable. Heated pool. Restaurant adj open 24 hrs. Ck-out 11 am. Coin lndry. Meeting rms. Business servs avail. Sundries. Downhill/x-country ski 7 mi. Picnic tables. Cr cds: A, D, DS, MC, V.

Restaurant

★★★ **CANAL SIDE INN.** *395 S Ann St, Little Falls (13365).* 315/823-1170. *www.canalsideinn.com.* French provincial, continental menu. Specializes in duck, seafood, lamb. Own pastries. Hrs: 5-10 pm. Closed Sun, Mon; hols; also Feb-mid-Mar. Res accepted. Bar. Wine list. Dinner $14.50-$19. Chef-owned. Cr cds: D, DS, MC, V.

Hillsdale

See also Catskill, Coxsackie, Hudson

Pop 1,744 **Elev** 700 ft **Area code** 518
Zip 12529

Information Columbia County
Tourism Department, 401 State St,
Hudson 12534; 800/724-1846

What to See and Do

Skiing. Catamount Ski Area. Four
double chairlifts, tow, J-bar; patrol,
school, rentals; snowmaking; cafeteria, bar; nursery. Longest run two mi;
vertical drop 1,000 ft. Night skiing.
(Dec-Mar, daily) Half-day rates. 2 mi
E of NY 22 on NY 23. Phone
518/325-3200 or 413/528-1262.
¢¢¢¢

Taconic State Park. More than 4,800
acres. Bash Bish Stream and Ore Pit
Pond are in the park. Swimming
beach, bathhouse, fishing; hiking,
picnicking (all yr), x-country skiing,
tent and trailer sites. At Rudd Pond,
also boating (launch, rentals); ice-
skating. S edge of town. Phone
518/789-3993. ¢¢¢

Resort

★★ **SWISS HUTTE.** Rt 23 (12529).
518/325-3333; fax 413/528-6201.
www.swisshutte.com. 15 rms, 2 story.
MAP: S, D $75-$110; lodge suites
$95/person; EP avail; wkly rates;
lower rates Mar-Apr, Nov. Pet
accepted, some restrictions. TV;
cable. Heated pool. Restaurant (see
SWISS HUTTE). Bar noon-11:30 pm.
Ck-out 11 am, ck-in 2 pm. Meeting
rms. Business servs avail. Tennis.
Downhill/x-country ski adj. Lawn
games. Refrigerators avail. Private
patios, balconies. Cr cds: MC, V.

B&Bs/Small Inns

★★★ **LINDEN VALLEY.** Rt 23 PO
Box 157 (12529). 518/325-7100; fax
518/325-4107. 7 rms, 6 with shower
only. July-Aug: S $95-$135; D $145-
$155; wkends (3-day min); lower
rates rest of yr. Pet accepted, some

restrictions. TV; cable. Complimentary full bkfst, coffee in rms. Restaurant adj 6-9 pm. Ck-out 1 pm, ck-in 1
pm. Tennis. Downhill ski adj. Refrigerators, minibars. Some balconies.
Large spring-fed pond with sand
beach; swimming. Cr cds: MC, V.

★★★ **SIMMON'S WAY VILLAGE
INN.** 53 Main St, Millerton (12546).
518/789-6235; fax 518/789-6236.
www.simmonsway.com. 10 rms, 3
story. No rm phones. S, D $145-$175
(2-day min wkends); Nov-May: MAP
$125/person; ski plans. Crib free. TV
in sitting rm; cable, VCR. Complimentary bkfst; afternoon refreshments. Restaurant (see SIMMON'S
WAY). Ck-out noon, ck-in 2 pm.
Business servs avail. Concierge. X-
country skiing. Game rm. Lawn
games. European-style inn (1854);
original antique furnishings, fireplaces, library. Village setting. Cr cds:
A, D, DS, MC, V.

Restaurants

★★★ **AUBERGINE.** NY 22 & NY
23 (12529). 518/325-3412. www.
aubergine.com. French, American
menu. Specialties: Maine scallop
cakes, hot souffles, seasonal specialties. Own baking. Hrs: from 5:30 pm.
Closed Mon, Tues. Res accepted. Bar.
Wine cellar. A la carte entrees: dinner
$17-$23. Guest rms avail. Chef-
owned. Cr cds: A, D, MC, V.

★★★ **SIMMON'S WAY.** 53 Main St,
Millerton (12546). 518/789-6235.
www.simmonsway.com. Eclectic, inter-
national menu. Specializes in
regional dishes, seasonal game. Own
baking. Menu changes frequently.
Hrs: 6-8 pm; Fri, Sat 5:30-9:30 pm;
Sun brunch 11:30 am-2:30 pm.
Closed Mon, Tues. Res accepted. Bar.
Wine cellar. Dinner $16.95-$27.95.
Sun brunch $7.50-$12.95. Outdoor
dining. Former industrialist's house
(1854) with country inn ambience.
Cr cds: A, C, D, DS, MC, V.

★★★ **SWISS HUTTE.** Rte 23
(12529). 518/325-3333. www.swiss
hutte.com. Hrs: noon-2 pm, 5:30-9
pm; Mon-Wed from 5:30 pm; Sat to
9:30 pm; Sun noon-3 pm, 5-9 pm.

Closed Mon, Tues in winter; also 1 wk in Nov and 1 wk in Mar. Res accepted. Continental menu. Lunch $8.50-$14, dinner $17-$28. Child's menu. Specialties: Wiener schitzel, rack of lamb, steak au poivre. Own baking. Outdoor dining. Swiss Alpine decor; brick fireplace. Cr cds: MC, V.

[D] [⊡]

Hornell

(E-3) *See also Bath*

Settled 1799 **Pop** 9,019 **Elev** 1,160 ft **Area code** 607 **Zip** 14843
Information Hornell Area Chamber of Commerce, 40 Main St; 607/324-0310. A Tourist Information booth is located just off NY 17 at exit 34 and jct NY 36 and 21
Web www.hornellny.com

Also known as the "Maple City," Hornell is a scenic and popular gateway to the Finger Lakes Region. Fishing, hunting, and outdoor recreation contribute to the town's offerings. Fall foliage is especially brilliant in September and October, in and around Hornell.

What to See and Do

Almond Dam Recreation Area. Incl a 125-acre lake; provides swimming, fishing, boating; hunting, camping facilities (fee). Just W of town, accessible by NY 21 and NY 36, just off County Rd 66. Contact Chamber of Commerce for details. Phone 607/776-9631. **FREE**

Skiing. Swain Ski Center. Three quad, double chairlifts; patrol, school, rentals; snowmaking; restaurants, cafeteria, bar. Longest run one mi; vertical drop 650 ft. Night skiing. (Nov-Mar, daily) 8 mi N on NY 36, then 7 mi NW on NY 70 in Swain. Phone 607/545-6511. ¢¢¢¢

Stony Brook State Park. Swimming beach, bathhouse; hiking, tennis, x-country skiing, picnicking, playground, concession, tent and trailer sites (May-late-Oct). Standard fees. 13 mi N on NY 36, 3 mi S of Dansville. Phone 716/335-8111. ¢¢

Motels/Motor Lodges

★★ **COMFORT INN.** *1 Canisteo Sq (78501). 607/324-4300; fax 607/324-4311; res 800/228-5150. www.comfort inn.com.* 62 rms, 2 story. S $52-$75; D $59-$85; each addl $5; suites $76-$101; under 18 free; higher rates auto racing. Crib free. TV; cable (premium). Indoor pool. Complimentary continental bkfst. Restaurant nearby. Ck-out 11 am. Coin lndry. Meeting rm. Business servs avail. Valet serv. Downhill ski 15 mi. Exercise equipt. Refrigerators avail. Cr cds: A, C, D, DS, JCB, MC, V.

[D] [🐾] [🍴] [⊠] [≈] [🏋] [🎿] [🔥] [⊡]

★ **HORNELL ECONO LODGE.** *7462 Seneca Rd N (14843). 607/324-0800; fax 607/324-0905. www.econo lodge.com.* 67 rms, 2 story. S $39-$45; D $45-$55; each addl $3. Pet accepted. TV; cable, VCR avail (movies). Complimentary continental bkfst. Restaurant 5-10 pm; Sun brunch 11 am-3 pm. Bar from 4:30 pm. Ck-out 11 am. Meeting rms. Business servs avail. In-rm modem link. Downhill ski 10 mi. Picnic tables. Cr cds: A, D, DS, MC, V.

[D] [🐾] [≈] [✈] [🐾]

★★★ **SAXON INN.** *1 Park St, Alfred (14802). 607/871-2600; fax 607/871-2650. www.alfred.edu.* 26 rms, 2 story, 6 suites. S, D $85-$110; each addl $10; suites $110; under 12 free; higher rates university events. Crib free. TV; cable. Pool privileges. Complimentary continental bkfst. Ck-out 11 am. Meeting rms. Business servs avail. Tennis privileges. Some refrigerators. Cr cds: A, C, D, DS, MC, V.

[🎿] [D] [≈] [⊠] [🐾]

Howes Cave

(E-7) *See also Albany, Schenectady, Stamford*

Pop 150 **Elev** 801 ft **Area code** 518 **Zip** 12092

What to See and Do

Howe Caverns. Elaborately developed series of caverns with underground river and lake, unique rock formations 160-200 ft below the surface; reached by elevators; 52°F in caverns. (Daily; closed Thanksgiving, Dec 25) Tour combined with boat trip. Snack bar. Restaurant. Picnic area. On NY 7. Phone 518/296-8990. ¢¢¢

Old Stone Fort Museum Complex. Church built in 1772 was fortified against raids by Tories and Native Americans during the Revolutionary War and became known as Lower Fort. Major attack came in 1780; building restored to house of worship in 1785; now houses exhibits on Revolutionary War and Schoharie Valley history; firearms, Native American artifacts, and period furniture; local historical and genealogical library. Badgley Museum and Carriage House, annex built in style of fort. Furnishings, tools, farm implements, 1901 Rambler, fire engines. (July-Aug, daily; May-Oct, Tues-Sun) 3 mi SE via NY 7, 30 in Schoharie. Phone 518/295-7192. ¢¢

Secret Caverns. Cave with natural entrance, 100-ft underground waterfalls, fossilized sea life; 50°F in caverns. (Late Apr-Oct, daily) ½-mi tour. On Secret Caverns Rd. Phone 518/296-8558. ¢¢¢¢

Motels/Motor Lodges

★ ★ **BEST WESTERN INN OF COBLESKILL.** 12 Campus Dr Extension, Cobleskill (12043). 518/234-4321; fax 518/234-3869; res 800/528-1234. www.bestwestern.com. 76 rms, 2 story. S, D $69-$119; under 12 free. Crib free. Pet accepted, some restrictions. TV; cable (premium), VCR avail (movies $7). Indoor pool; wading pool. Coffee in rms. Restaurant 7 am-9 pm. Bar 4-10 pm. Ck-out 11 am. Meeting rms. Business servs avail. Game rm. Bowling lanes. Refrigerators, microwaves avail. Cr cds: A, C, D, DS, MC, V.

D 🐾 🐘 🐦 ⛱ 🐕 🐾

★ **HOWE CAVERNS MOTEL.** RR 1 Box 107 (12092). 518/296-8950. www.howecaverns.com. 21 rms. July-Labor Day: S $68-$78; D $85-$95; each addl $10; lower rates late Apr-June, after Labor Day-Oct. Closed rest of yr. TV. Pool. Coffee in rms. Restaurant hrs vary. Ck-out 10:30 am. On hillside with view of valley. Cr cds: DS, MC, V.

D ⛱ 🐦 🐾

Restaurant

★ ★ **BULLS HEAD INN.** 2 Park Pl, Cobleskill (12043). 518/234-3591. Specializes in steak, prime rib, seafood. Hrs: 11:30 am-2 pm, 5-9 pm; Fri to 10 pm; Sat 5-10 pm; Sun 1-8 pm. Closed Mon; Jan 1, Dec 25. Res accepted. Bar to midnight. Lunch $3.95-$8.75, dinner $10.95-$26.95. Open hearth cooking, brewery on premises. Historic building (1802). Cr cds: A, MC, V.

D 🗠

Hudson

(E-8) See also Cairo, Catskill, Coxsackie, Hillsdale

Settled 1783 **Pop** 7,524 **Elev** 80 ft
Area code 518 **Zip** 12534
Information Columbia County Tourism Department, 401 State St; 800/724-1846
Web www.columbiacountyny.org

What to See and Do

American Museum of Fire Fighting. Antique fire-fighting equipt incl 1725 Newsham fire engine; memorabilia, art gallery. (Daily; closed hols) Harry Howard Ave. Phone 518/828-7695. **FREE**

🟥 **Clermont State Historic Site.** The ancestral home of Robert R. Livingston, one of five men elected to draft the Declaration of Independence, who later, as chancellor of New York, administered the oath of office to George Washington. Lived in by seven generations of the Livingston family, the grounds and mansion retain their 1930 appearance, illustrating 200 yrs of changing tastes. Centerpiece of a 485-acre estate on the eastern shore of the Hudson River, the home features period furnishings, restored gardens, guided tours, nature trails, and special events. Visitor center, museum store (May-Oct, Tues-Sun). Grounds open all yr for hiking, riding, x-country skiing, picnicking. 16 mi S on NY

9G, then W on County Rte 6. Phone 518/537-4240. ¢¢

James Vanderpoel House. Federal period house built around 1820, now a museum with 19th-century furnishings and art. Maintained by the Columbia County Historical Society. (Memorial Day-Labor Day, Wed-Sun) 11 mi N on US 9 in Kinderhook. Phone 518/758-9265. ¢¢ The society also maintains

> **Luykas Van Alen House.** (1737) Restored house is a museum of Dutch domestic culture during the 18th century. 3 mi S of Kinderhook on NY 9H. ¢¢

Lake Taghkanic State Park. On 1,569 acres. Swimming beaches, bathhouses, fishing, boating (launch, rentals); hiking trails, x-country skiing, snowmobiling, ice-skating, picnicking, playground, concession, tent and trailer sites, cabins, cottages. Also 177-acre lake. 11 mi SE via NY 23, 82. Phone 518/851-3631. ¢¢¢

Martin Van Buren National Historic Site. Retirement house of America's eighth president. The estate, Lindenwald, was purchased by Van Buren from General William Paulding in 1839. The house, on 20 acres, contains 36 rms. Tours (Schedule varies). 2 mi S of Kinderhook on NY 9H. Phone 518/758-9689.

Olana State Historic Site. (1870) A 250-acre hilltop estate with views of the Hudson River and Catskill Mtns, incl Persian/Moorish mansion and grounds landscaped in Romantic style, all designed by Hudson River School artist Frederic Edwin Church as a multidimensional work of art. Decorative Asian arts and furnishings collected by the artist; also paintings by Church. 5 mi of carriage roads for walking with views planned by the artist. Grounds (daily). House Museum (Apr-Oct, Wed-Sun): entrance by guided tour only—tours limited. Res recommended. 5 mi S on NY 9G. Phone 518/828-0135. ¢¢

Shaker Museum and Library. One of the largest collections of Shaker culture; 26 galleries in three buildings. Exhibits incl furniture, crafts, basketry, agricultural and industrial tools. Library (by appt only). Picnic area, cafe. Gift shop. (Late Apr-Oct, Mon, Wed-Sun) 88 Shaker Museum Rd, 18 mi NE via NY 66, County 13. Phone 518/794-9100. ¢¢¢

Hotel

★ ★ ★ **ST. CHARLES.** *16-18 Park Pl (12534). 518/822-9900; fax 518/822-0835. www.stcharleshotel.com.* 34 rms, 3 story, 6 suites. S, D $79-$99; each addl $10; suites $99; under 18 free; ski plans. Crib free. Pet accepted. TV; cable, VCR avail. Complimentary continental bkfst. Restaurants 11:30 am-10 pm (see also REBECCA'S). No rm serv. Bar to midnight; entertainment. Ck-out noon. Meeting rms. Business servs avail. No bellhops. Tennis privileges. Health club privileges. Cr cds: A, D, DS, MC, V.

Restaurant

★ ★ **REBECCA'S.** *16-18 Park Pl (12534). 518/822-9900. www.stcharles hotel.com.* Hrs: 5:30-10 pm. Closed Sun-Tues; Jan 1, Thanksgiving, Dec 25. Res accepted. Continental menu. Bar 11:30 am-midnight. Dinner $12.95-$22.95. Child's menu. Specialties: beef Wellington, salmon en croûté, herb-encrusted spring lamb chops. Colonial decor with fireplace. Totally nonsmoking. Cr cds: A, D, DS, MC, V.

Hunter

See also Cairo, Catskill Park, Shandaken, Windham, Woodstock

Pop 490 **Elev** 1,603 ft **Area code** 518 **Zip** 12442

Information Greene County Promotion Department, NY Thrwy exit 21, PO Box 527, Catskill 12414; 518/943-3223 or 800/355-CATS

Web www.greene-ny.com

What to See and Do

Skiing. Hunter Mountain Ski Resort. Three quad, two triple, five double chairlifts. Offers 53 slopes and trails. Patrol, school, rentals; snowmaking; bar, restaurant, cafeteria; nursery. Longest run two mi; vertical drop 1,600 ft. (Early Nov-late Apr, daily) NY 23A. Phone 518/263-4223. ¢¢¢¢

Hotel

★★ **HUNTER INN.** *Rte 23A (12442).*
518/263-3777; fax 518/263-3981.
www.hunterinn.com. 41 rms, 2-3 story.
No elvtr. Mid-Nov-mid-Apr: S, D
$100-$150; each addl $10-$15; suites
$115-$185; under 17 free; hols (3-day
min); wkend, package plans; higher
rates hols; lower rates rest of yr. Crib
free. Pet accepted; $10. TV; cable.
Whirlpool. Complimentary continental bkfst. Ck-out 11 am. Meeting
rm. Business servs avail. Sundries.
Exercise equipt. Downhill/x-country
ski1/2mi. Cr cds: A, DS, MC, V.
D ⬆ ⯈ 🏃 🔄 🐾 SC

Resort

★★★ **SCRIBNER HOLLOW
LODGE.** *Route 23A (12442). 518/263-
4211; fax 518/263-5266; toll-free
800/395-4683. www.scribnerhollow.
com.* 38 rms, 3 story, 22 suites, 36
townhouses. MAP, Thanksgiving-
Mar: S $120-$195; D $170-$270;
suites $200-$450; townhouses $200-
$350; family, wkly rates; ski, golf
plans; higher rates some hols, special
events; lower rates rest of yr. Closed
Apr-mid May. Crib free. TV; cable. 2
pools; 1 indoor pool; wading pool,
whirlpool, poolside serv. Restaurant
(see also THE PROSPECT). Bar; entertainment. Ck-in 3 pm, ck-out noon.
Meeting rms. Business servs avail.
Bellhops. Valet serv. Concierge. Sundries. Free bus depot transportation.
Tennis. Downhill ski adj; x-country
ski on site. Sauna. Rec rm. Lawn
games. Refrigerators. Rustic atmosphere blended with modern facilities;
features underground grotto with
waterfalls, alcoves, fireplace. Cr cds:
A, DS, MC, V.
D ⯈ 🏃 ⛷ 🔄 🐾

B&B/Small Inn

★★ **EGGERY COUNTRY INN.**
County Rd 16, Tannersville (12485).
*518/589-5363; fax 518/589-5774; toll-
free 800/785-5364. www.eggeryinn.
com.* 15 rms, 3 story. 9 A/C. July-Mar:
S $90-$99; D $110-$125; each addl
$20-$30; wkends, fall season (2-day
min); special events (3-day min);
lower rates rest of yr. TV; cable. Complimentary full bkfst. Ck-out 11 am,
ck-in 1 pm. Lawn games. Antique

furnishings. Restored farmhouse inn
built 1900. Facing Hunter Mtn. Cr
cds: A, MC, V.
⬆ 🔄 ⛷ 🐾

Restaurants

★★★ **CHATEAU BELLEVIEW.** *Rte
23A, Tannersville (12485). 518/589-
5525.* Hrs: 5-10 pm; Sun from 1 pm.
Closed Tues; also 2 wks Apr, 2 wks
Nov. Res accepted. French menu. Bar.
Dinner $14.95-$22.95. Child's menu.
Specialties: fish with herbs or Cajun
spices, duckling, beef bourguignon.
Outdoor dining. View of Catskills. Cr
cds: A, DS, MC, V.
D

★★ **MOUNTAIN BROOK.** *Main St
(12442). 518/263-5351.* Hrs: 5-10:30
pm; Sun brunch 11 am-3 pm (Mid-
Dec-mid-Mar). Closed Tues in ski
season, July, Aug; also Dec 25. Res
required Sat. Some A/C. Bar. A la
carte entrees: dinner $10.75-$18.75.
Child's menu. Specialties: radicchio
and endive salad with melted goat
cheese; homemade meatloaf with
rich veal stock gravy; grilled filet of
tuna, wasabi soy ginger marinade.
Sun brunch prices vary. Parking. Outdoor dining. Cr cds: C, MC, V.
D ⬄

★★ **THE PROSPECT.** *Main St (NY
23A) (12442). 518/263-4211. www.
scribnerhollow.com.* Hrs: 8-10 am, 5-10
pm; wkends 8 am-11 pm. Res
accepted. Continental, contemporary
American menu. Bar. Bkfst $7.95-$9,
dinner $13.95-$19.95. Specializes in
fresh fish, vegetarian specials, wild
game. Child's menu. jazz wkends.
Wine tasting dinner. Overlooks
Hunter Mtn. Family-owned. Cr cds:
A, C, D, DS, MC, V.

★★ **VESUVIO.** *Goshen Rd, Hen-
sonville (12439). 518/734-3663.*
Regional Italian menu. Specializes in
veal, lobster steak, fresh pasta. Own
pastries, pasta. Hrs: 4-10 pm; Fri, Sat
to 11 pm; early-bird dinner 4-8 pm,
Sat to 6 pm. Res accepted. Bar. A la
carte entrees: dinner $10.95-$21.95.
Complete meals (Sun-Fri): dinner
$10.95. Child's menu. Pianist

wkends. Outdoor dining. Fireplace. Family-owned. Cr cds: MC, V.

Huntington (L.I.)

See also Northport (L.I.), Oyster Bay (L.I.), Plainview (L.I.)

Settled 1653 **Pop** 195,289 **Elev** 60 ft
Area code 516 **Zip** 11743
Information Huntington Township Chamber of Commerce, 288 Main St; 516/423-6100
Web www.huntingtonchamber.com

Although the expanding suburban population of New York City has reached Huntington, 37 miles east on Long Island, it still retains its rural character. Huntington is a township including 17 communities, in which there are more than 100 industrial plants. The area has five navigable harbors and 51 miles of shorefront.

What to See and Do

Cold Spring Harbor Whaling Museum. Fully equipped 19th-century whale boat from the brig *Daisy* is on display. Marine paintings, scrimshaw, ship models, changing exhibit gallery. "Mark Well the Whale" permanent exhibit documents Long Island's whaling industry. Permanent exhibit "The Wonder of Whales" incl a hands-on whale bones display, a killer whale skull, and whale conservation information. (Memorial Day-Labor Day, daily; rest of yr, Tues-Sun) Main St, 2 mi W on NY 25A, in Cold Spring Harbor. Phone 631/367-3418. ¢¢

David Conklin Farmhouse. (ca 1750) Four generations of Conklin family lived here. Period rms (Colonial, Federal, Victorian). (Tues-Fri and Sun; closed hols) 2 High St at New York Ave. Phone 631/427-7045. ¢¢ Other historic buildings incl

Huntington Trade School. (1905) School building houses the offices of the Huntington Historical Society and a history research library. (Tues-Fri) 209 Main St. Phone 631/427-7045. ¢¢

Kissam House. (1795) Federal house, barn, sheepshed, and outbuildings; home of early Huntington physicians. Period rms (1800-1850). (Sun afternoons; closed hols) 434 Park Ave. ¢¢

Heckscher Museum of Art. Permanent collection of European and American art dating from 16th century; changing exhibits. (Tues-Sun; closed Thanksgiving, Dec 25) Heckscher Park, Prime Ave and NY 25A (Main St). Phone 631/351-3250. **Donation**

Walt Whitman Birthplace S.H.S.

Joseph Lloyd Manor House. (1767) Large Colonial manor house, elegantly furnished; 18th-century garden. (Memorial Day-mid-Oct, Sat and Sun afternoons) Lloyd Ln, 3 mi N in Lloyd Harbor. Phone 631/271-7760. ¢

Sunken Meadow State Park. Swimming beach, bathhouse, fishing (all yr); nature, hiking, and biking trails; three 9-hole golf courses (fee), picnicking, playground, concession, x-country skiing. Recreation programs. Standard fees. Approx 9 mi E of town on NY 25A. Phone 631/269-4333. ¢¢¢

Target Rock National Wildlife Refuge. An 80-acre refuge with hardwood forest, pond, and beach. Fishing; photography, nature trail, wildlife nature study, and environmental education. (Daily) 8 mi N via West Neck Rd, follow onto Lloyd Harbor Rd. Phone 631/286-0485. ¢¢

Walt Whitman Birthplace State Historic Site. Boyhood home of the poet; 19th-century furnishings; Whitman's schoolmaster's desk; his voice on tape; exhibits, sculpture; museum, research library (by appt); audiovisual presentation. Gift shop, picnic facilities. Guided tours (groups by appt). Interpretive Center. (Wed-Sun; closed hols) 246 Old Walt Whitman Rd, across from Walt Whitman Mall. 1 mi from Long Island Expy. Phone 631/427-5240. ¢

Special Events

Huntington Summer Arts Festival. Heckscher Park amphitheater. Local, national, and international artists perform dance, folk, classical, jazz, theater, and family productions. Phone 631/271-8442. Late June-mid-Aug, Tues-Sun.

Long Island Fall Festival at Huntington. Heckscher Park. Entertainment, carnival, sailboat regatta, food, wine tasting, family activities. Phone 631/423-6100. Mid-Oct.

Hotels

★★★ **HILTON HOTEL.** 598 Broad Hollow Rd, Melville (11747). 631/845-1000; fax 631/845-1223; toll-free 800/445-8667. www.hilton.com. 302 rms, 5 story. S $159; D $169; each addl $20; suites $225-$550. Crib free. TV; cable (premium), VCR avail

(movies). 2 pools, 1 indoor; whirlpool, poolside serv, lifeguard. Restaurant 6:30 am-11 pm. Bar 11-2 am; entertainment. Ck-out noon. Convention facilities. Business servs avail. In-rm modem link. Concierge. Gift shop. Lighted tennis. Exercise equipt. Bathrm phones, minibars; wet bar in suites. Cr cds: A, C, D, DS, JCB, MC, V.

🄳 🏌 ≈ 🛉 🔜 🔥

★★ **HUNTINGTON COUNTRY INN HOTEL.** 270 W Jericho Tpke, Huntington St (11746). 631/421-3900; fax 631/421-5287; res 800/739-5777. www.huntingtoncountryinn.com. 64 rms, 2 story. S $99-$109; D $109-$119; each addl $10; suite $150; under 16 free. Crib free. Pet accepted. TV; cable (premium). Pool; lifeguard. Complimentary continental bkfst, coffee in rms. Restaurant adj noon-10 pm. Ck-out noon. Health club privileges. Some refrigerators, microwaves. Cr cds: A, C, D, DS, JCB, MC, V.

🄳 🐾 🏌 ≈ 🛉 🔜 🐾 🆂🅲

Restaurants

★★ **ABEL CONKLIN'S.** 54 New St (11743). 631/385-1919. Specializes in aged steak. Hrs: noon-10 pm; Fri to 11 pm; Sat, Sun 4:30-11 pm. Closed hols. Res required. Bar. Complete meals: lunch $8-$12. A la carte entrees: dinner $10-$22. Built in 1830; etched glass, fireplace. Cr cds: MC, V.

🄳 🔜

★★★ **FOX HOLLOW.** 7725 Jericho Tpke, Woodbury (11797). 516/921-1415. www.scottobrothers.com. Northern Italian menu. Hrs: 11:30 am-3 pm, 5-10 pm; Sat from 5 pm. Closed Sun; Dec 25. Res required. Bar. A la carte entrees: lunch $6.50-$16.25, dinner $14.75-$31. Piano bar. Valet parking. Patio dining (in season). Rustic surroundings in wooded area. Jacket. Family-owned. Cr cds: A, D, MC, V.

🄳

★★ **FREDERICK'S.** 1117 Walt Whitman Rd, Melville (11747). 631/673-8550. Continental menu. Blackboard specials change daily. Hrs: 11:30 am-2 pm, 5-9 pm; Sat 5-9 pm. Closed Sun. Res accepted. Serv bar. A la carte entrees: lunch $13.95-$24.75, dinner $14.95-$24.75. Parking. Cr cds: A, D, MC, V.

★★ **INN ON THE HARBOR.** *105 Harbor Rd, Cold Spring Harbor (11724). 631/367-3166. www.innontheharbor. net.* French, continental menu. Own baking. Hrs: 11:30 am-2:30 pm, 4:30-9:30 pm; Fri, Sat to 10:30 pm; Sun brunch 11:30 am-2:45 pm. Closed Dec 25. Res accepted. Bar. A la carte entrees: lunch $6.95-$14.95, dinner $16.95-$26.95. Sun brunch $21.95. Valet parking. Fireplaces. Overlooks Cold Spring Harbor. Cr cds: A, D, MC, V.
D

★ **PETITE ON MAIN.** *328 Main St (11743). 631/271-3311.* International menu. Specialties: grilled chicken with salsa, filet mignon, marinated skirt steak. Hrs: 5-9:30 pm; Fri, Sat to 10:30 pm; Sun to 8:45 pm. Closed Mon; hols. Res required wkends. Setups. A la carte entrees: dinner $13-$23. Prix fixe Sun-Thurs: dinner $22. Casual country decor. Cr cds: A, MC, V.

Unrated Dining Spot

WYLANDS COUNTRY KITCHEN. *55 Main St, Cold Spring Harbor (11724). 631/692-5655.* Specializes in flounder, shrimp. Own pastries. Hrs: 11 am-4:30 pm; Sat to 3:45 pm. Closed Sun, Mon; major hols; also late Feb-early Mar. Serv bar. A la carte entrees: lunch $6.50-$8.75. Child's menu. Casual dining. Family-owned. Cr cds: A, D, DS, MC, V.

Hyde Park

See also New Paltz, Poughkeepsie, Rhinebeck

Settled 1740 **Pop** 20,851 **Elev** 188 ft **Area code** 845 **Zip** 12538
Information Dutchess County Tourism Promotion Agency, 3 Neptune Rd, Ste M-17, Poughkeepsie 12601; 845/463-4000 or 800/445-3131
Web www.dutchesstourism.com

Hyde Park was named for Edward Hyde, Lord Cornbury, provincial governor of New York, who in 1705 presented a parcel of land along the river to his secretary. Hyde's name was given to an estate on that property and later to the town itself. The area, noted for the varying scenery from rock outcroppings to scenic water views, is best known as the site of Springwood, the country estate of Franklin Roosevelt.

What to See and Do

Mills-Norrie State Park. Fishing, boat basin (marina, dock, launch); nature and hiking trails, 18-hole golf (fee), x-country skiing, picnicking, tent and trailer sites, cabins. Environmental education programs, concert series. Standard fees. 4 mi N on US 9 in Staatsburg. Phone 845/889-4646. In park is

  Mills Mansion State Historic Site. Built in 1832, the Greek Revival mansion was remodeled and enlarged in 1895 by prominent architect Stanford White into a 65-rm, neo-Classical country residence for Ogden Mills. Furnished in Louis XIV, Louis XV, and Louis XVI styles; tapestries, art objects, marble fireplaces, gilded plasterwork. Park overlooks the Hudson. (Mid-Apr-Oct, Wed-Sun; also last two wks in Dec) Phone 845/889-8851. ¢¢

🗹 **Roosevelt-Vanderbilt National Historic Sites.** (Daily) 1 mi S on US 9. Phone 845/229-9115. Here is

  Eleanor Roosevelt National Historic Site at Val-Kill. Dedicated as a memorial to Mrs. Roosevelt on Oct 11, 1984, the 100th anniversary of her birth, Val-Kill was her country residence from the 1920s until her death. The original house on the property, Stone Cottage (1924), is now a conference center. Her second house at Val-Kill was originally a furniture and crafts factory that Mrs. Roosevelt sponsored in an effort to stimulate rural economic development. After closing Val-Kill Industries, she had the factory remodeled to reflect her tastes and humanitarian concerns; here, she entertained family, friends, and heads of state from around the world. Film; tour. 2 mi E of Roosevelt estate.

Franklin D. Roosevelt N.H.S.

Franklin D. Roosevelt Presidential Library and Museum. First of the public presidential libraries, it has exhibits covering the private lives and public careers of Franklin and Eleanor Roosevelt. Research library contains family artifacts and documents and presidential archives. Library, museum, and home. Phone 845/229-8114.

Home of Franklin D. Roosevelt National Historic Site. The Hyde Park estate, Springwood, was President Roosevelt's birthplace and lifelong residence. The central part of the building, the oldest section, dates from about 1826. The house was bought in 1867 by FDR's father and was extensively remodeled and expanded in 1915 by FDR and his mother, Sara Delano Roosevelt. At that time the frame, Victorian house took on its present brick and stone, neo-Georgian form. The interior is furnished exactly as it was when FDR died. Roosevelt's grave and that of Anna Eleanor Roosevelt are in the rose garden. Home, library, and museum.

Vanderbilt Mansion National Historic Site. Beaux-arts mansion (1898) designed by McKim, Mead, and White for Frederick W. Vanderbilt is a prime example of the "American-millionaire palaces" typical of the period; the interior retains most of the original furnishings as designed by turn-of-the-century decorators. The grounds offer superb views up and down the Hudson River; many ancient trees; restored formal Italian gardens. Phone 845/229-9115.

Motels/Motor Lodges

★ **ROOSEVELT INN.** *4360 Albany Post Rd (12538). 845/229-2443; fax 845/229-0026.* 26 rms, 2 story. May-Oct: S $45-$55; D $48-$68; each addl $4; under 17 free; lower rates rest of yr. TV; cable (premium), VCR avail. Restaurant 7-11 am. Ck-out 11 am. X-country ski 5 mi. Business servs avail. Some refrigerators. Balconies. Cr cds: A, DS, MC, V.
D ⚓ ➘ 🐾

★ **SUPER 8 MOTEL.** *528 Albany Post Rd (12538). 845/229-0088; fax 845/229-8088; res 800/800-8000. www.super8.com.* 61 rms, 2 story. Apr-Oct: S $45-$74; D $55-$94; each addl $4; higher rates special events; lower rates rest of yr. Crib $5. TV; cable (premium). Complimentary continental bkfst. Restaurant nearby. Business servs avail. In-rm modem link. Sundries. Microwaves, refrigerators avail. Cr cds: A, D, DS, MC, V.
D 🐾 🖐 ➘ 🐾

Restaurants

★ **EASY STREET CAFE.** *3957 Albany Post Rd US 9 (12538).* *845/229-7969.* Specializes in prime rib, veal, seafood. Hrs: 11 am-10 pm; Sun noon-9 pm. Closed Dec 25. Res accepted. Bar. Lunch $4.95-$9.50, dinner $9.50-$18.75. Country atmosphere. Cr cds: A, D, DS, MC, V.
D

★ ★ **ST. ANDREW'S CAFE.** *433 Albany Post Rd US 9 (12538).* *845/471-6608. www.ciachef.edu.* Contemporary American menu. Own baking. Hrs: 11:30 am-1 pm, 6:30-8:30 pm. Closed Sat, Sun; hols; also 3 wks July, 2 wks Dec. Bar. Lunch $8-$13.50, dinner $8.95-$17. Outdoor dining. Dining rm opens onto courtyard; original regional watercolors; fireplace. Cr cds: A, D, DS, MC, V.
D

Unrated Dining Spots

AMERICAN BOUNTY. *433 Albany Post Rd US 9 (12538).* *845/471-6608. www.ciachef.edu.* Regional American menu. Own baking. Hrs: 11:30 am-1 pm, 6:30-8:30 pm. Closed Sun, Mon; hols; also 3 wks July, 2 wks Christmas. Res accepted. Bar 11:30 am-11 pm. Wine cellar. A la carte entrees: lunch $10.95-$14.95, dinner $16.50-$23. In former St. Andrew-on-Hudson Jesuit Seminary on 150 acres, high above Hudson River. Cr cds: A, D, DS, MC, V.
D

THE ESCOFFIER. *433 Albany Post Rd US 9 (12538).* *845/471-6608. www.ciachef.edu.* Classical French cuisine. Specialties: duck, Dover sole, crevette Madagascar. Own baking. Hrs: 11:30 am-1 pm, 6:30-8:30 pm. Closed Sun, Mon; hols; also 3 wks July, 2 wks Christmas. Res accepted. Serv bar. Wine list. A la carte entrees: lunch $14.50-$18.50, dinner $20.50-$23. Table d'hôte: lunch $23. One of four restaurants of the Culinary Institute of America, the country's foremost restaurant school. Student chefs prepare dishes that their peers serve in the dining room. Some dishes prepared at table. Cr cds: A, D, DS, MC, V.
D

Ilion (D-6)

Pop 8,610 **Elev** 410 ft **Area code** 315 **Zip** 13357

Restaurant

★ ★ **MOHAWK STATION.** *100 E Main St, Mohawk (13407).* *800/772-4396. www.mohawkstation.com.* Specializes in prime rib, seafood, poultry. Hrs: 11 am-9 pm; Fri, Sat to 10 pm; Sun 11 am-8 pm. Sun brunch to 2:30 pm. Closed Dec 25. Res accepted. Bar. Lunch $3.95-$7.95, dinner $6.95-$26.95. Sun brunch $9.95. Child's menu. Railroad theme; original caboose for dining area. Cr cds: DS, MC, V.
D SC ⊸

Ithaca

(E-5) *See also Binghamton, Cortland*

Settled 1789 **Pop** 29,287 **Elev** 405 ft **Area code** 607 **Zip** 14850

Information Ithaca/Tompkins County Convention & Visitors Bureau, 904 East Shore Dr; 607/272-1313 or 800/284-8422

Web www.visitithaca.com

Ithaca climbs from the plain at the head of Cayuga Lake up the steep slopes of the surrounding hills. Creeks flow through town and cut picturesque gorges with cascading waterfalls. Named for Grecian Ithaca by Simeon De Witt, surveyor-general under Washington, Ithaca is a center of inland water transportation and an educational center of New York State.

What to See and Do

Cornell University. (1865) 20,000 students. A 745-acre campus overlooks Cayuga Lake and incl Beebe Lake, gorges, waterfalls. Founded both as a land-grant and privately endowed college by Ezra Cornell (1807-1874) and Andrew Dickson White (1832-1918). There are 13 colleges, four of which are state supported; 11 schools and colleges are in Ithaca, two in New York City. E side of town. On campus are Willard Straight Hall; Laboratory of Ornithology (daily). Phone 607/254-6072.

DeWitt Historical Society & Museum. Local historical exhibits; large photography collection; local history library. (Tues-Sat; closed hols) 401 E State St. Phone 607/273-8284. **FREE**

Ithaca College. (1892) 6,400 students. Liberal arts and professional programs. Music, art exhibits, drama, lectures, and athletic programs. Handwerker Gallery. Campus overlooks city, Cayuga Lake. Tours of campus. ½ mi S on NY 96B. Phone 607/274-3011.

Recreation areas. Stewart Park. James L. Gibbs Dr. Picnicking, tennis, playground, concession. **Cass Park.** 701 Taughannock Blvd. Pool, wading pool; ice-skating rink, tennis, ball fields (four lighted), playground, picnicking, concession. Fees for some activities. Phone 607/273-1090.

Sciencenter. 200 hands-on interactive science exhibits and outdoor science park; lectures; special events. (Tues-Sun; closed hols) 601 First St. Phone 607/272-0600. ¢¢ On grounds is the

Sagan Planetwalk. Scaled model of the solar system built in remembrance of Carl Sagan. (Daily) 601 First St. Phone 607/272-0600. **FREE**

Six Mile Creek Vineyard. Family-operated winery. Tours, tastings. (Daily, afternoons) NY 79 E, 1551 Slaterville Rd. **FREE**

State parks.

Allan H. Treman State Marine Park. Fishing, boating (launch, marina); picnicking. (Apr-late Oct) Standard fees. 3 mi N on NY 89. Phone 607/273-3440.

Buttermilk Falls. Swimming, bathhouse; hiking trails, picnicking, playground, concession, tent and trailer sites, cabins. (Mid-May-Columbus Day) Standard fees. On NY 13. Phone 607/273-5761.

Robert H. Treman. Swimming, bathhouse; hiking trails, picnicking, playground, cabins, recreation programs, tent and trailer sites. (Mid-May-late Nov) Standard fees.

5 mi S on NY 13. Phone 607/273-3440. ¢¢¢

Taughannock Falls. Swimming, bathhouse, fishing, boating (marina, launch); nature trails, hiking trails, x-country skiing, picnicking, playground, concession, tent and trailer sites, cabins. Standard fees. 8 mi N on NY 89. Phone 607/387-6739.

Special Events

Ithaca Festival. Ithaca Commons and Stewart Park. First wkend June. Phone 607/273-3646.

Hangar Theatre. Professional summer theater in park setting adj to Treman Marina. Five main stage productions; dramas, comedies, and musicals (Tues-Sat eves, also Sat and Wed afternoons). Children's theatre (Thurs-Sat mornings). For tickets phone 607/273-4497 or 607/273-8588. Late June-Labor Day wkend.

Grassroots Festival. Trumansburg Fairground. Third wkend July. Phone 607/387-5098.

Finger Lakes Antique Show. Women's Community Building. N Cayuga and Seneca Sts. First wkend Oct. Phone 607/272-1247.

Apple Harvest Festival. Downtown Ithaca Commons. First wkend Oct.

Motels/Motor Lodges

★★ **BEST WESTERN UNIVERSITY INN.** *1020 Ellis Hollow Rd (14850).* *607/272-6100; fax 607/272-1518; res 800/528-1234. www.bestwestern.com.* 94 rms. S, D $79-$99; each addl $10; suites $109-$179; under 17 free; wkly rates. Crib free. Pet accepted, some restrictions; $10. TV; VCR (movies). Pool; lifeguard. Restaurant 7 am-5 pm; Sun to 2 pm. Ck-out noon. Meeting rms. Business servs avail. Valet serv. Airport transportation. Refrigerators; microwaves avail. Cr cds: A, C, D, DS, ER, JCB, MC, V.

★ **ECONO LODGE.** *2303 N Triphammer Rd (14850). 607/257-1400; fax 607/257-6359; toll-free 800/424-4777. www.econolodge.com/ hotel/ny127.* 72 rms, 2 story. May-Sept: S $51-$71; D $66-$76; each addl $5; suites $85-$102; under 18 free; lower rates rest of yr. Crib free.

SMALL-TOWN NEW YORK

Ithaca offers the best of small-town America with a college-town sophistication, plus the spectacular natural sites of Cayuga Lake and a variety of gorges and waterfalls. This walk explores Ithaca's center with a stroll to nearby falls. For those who really love to hoof it, other options include the Cornell University Plantations, an arboretum and botanical gardens, and, on the other end of town, Stewart Park along Cayuga Lake's shoreline.

Start at the public parking garage on Green Street and walk west to Cayuga Street. City Hall is on the right. Stop in here to obtain visitor information and a city map. Turn right and walk ½ block to The Commons, home to a wide variety of shops, restaurants, cafes, and a gallery. Duck into the Susan Titus Gallery and ask about the Ithaca Art Trail—a guide to galleries and artists' studios throughout the region. Other shops of interest at the Commons are Autumn Leaves, Ithaca Books, Angleheart Designs, Handblock and Harold's Army Navy, and The Outdoor Store. The Home Dairy Bakery is a great place to grab a snack. Here, too, begins the Sagan Planet Walk. Named after astronomer Carl Sagan, this is an outdoor, scale model of the solar system that stretches ¾ mile from the Commons to the Sciencenter on Second Street.

Leaving the west end of the Commons, turn right on Cayuga. The Clinton House Art Space is located at 116 Cayuga, and DeWitt Mall is on the next block on the right. More shopping and eating await you here; highlights include the famous Moosewood Restaurant, Calhouns Antiques, and the Sola Gallery. Continue up Cayuga past DeWitt Park, and turn left on Cascadilla Street. Go four blocks and turn right onto First Street. After two more blocks, you will reach the Sciencenter, an imaginative hands-on science "exploratorium." After visiting the Sciencenter, return along First Street, and go left on Adams, which eventually merges to the right with East Lewis Street. Follow East Lewis three blocks to Tioga and turn left. The walk travels here through a pleasant residential neighborhood. After three blocks, turn right onto Falls Street, and walk two blocks to Lake Street to arrive at Ithaca Falls and Fall Creek Gorge. These falls stand almost as high as Niagara. Pause for a picnic, play on the rocks in the stream, or just admire the view. The energetic can follow the hiking trail into the upper areas of Fall Creek Gorge and onto the Cornell University campus, where a variety of trails lead to several waterfalls and Beebe Lake.

Return to Falls Street and, for diversity's sake, follow Aurora Street back into the town center. Just two blocks before arriving back at the Commons, note the William Henry Miller Inn, a circa-1880 historic home turned bed-and-breakfast, at the corner of Buffalo Street. If more walking is in order, turn left onto Court Street, and follow the trail in Cascadilla Glen (where Court meets Linn Street and University Avenue), an uphill clamber that will yield several waterfalls and views. For a more serene walk addition, drive west on Seneca Street (Route 79), turn right onto Routes 34/13, and head into Stewart Park where miles of paths skirt Cayuga Lake. Or, simply return to the Commons for a rest and some food.

Pet accepted; $10. TV; cable. Continental bkfst. Restaurant nearby. Ck-out 11 am. Meeting rm. Business servs avail. In-rm modem link. Microwaves avail. Cr cds: A, D, DS, MC, V.

★★ **HOLIDAY INN.** *222 S Cayuga St (14850). 607/272-1000; fax 607/277-1275; res 800/465-4329. www.holiday-inn.com.* 178 rms, 10 story. S, D $99-$109; each addl $10; suites $120-$190; under 19 free; higher rates special events. Crib free. Pet accepted, some restrictions; $15. TV; cable (premium). Indoor pool. Coffee in rms. Restaurant 7-11 am, 5-10 pm. Bar 5 pm-1 am. Ck-out noon. Meeting rms. Business servs avail. Bellhops. Sundries. Free airport, bus depot transportation. Exercise equipt. Some bathrm phones. Cr cds: A, C, D, ER, CB, MC, V.

★★ **RAMADA INN AIRPORT & CONFERENCE CENTER.** *2310 N Triphammer Rd (14850). 607/257-3100; fax 607/257-4425; toll-free 888/298-2054. www.ramada.com.* 121 rms, 2 story. S, D $99-$149; each addl $5; suites $95-$150; under 18 free; higher rates: wkends, special events. Crib free. Pet accepted, some restrictions. TV; cable, VCR avail (movies). 2 pools, 1 indoor; wading pool, whirlpool, poolside serv, lifeguard. Restaurant 6:30 am-2 pm, 5-10 pm. Bar 4:30 pm-1 am. Ck-out noon. Meeting rms. Business servs avail. In-rm modem link. Valet serv. Game rm. Free airport, bus depot, transportation. Exercise equipt; sauna. Refrigerators, microwaves avail. Cr cds: A, C, D, DS, ER, JCB, MC, V.

★ **SUPER 8 MOTEL.** *400 S Meadow St (14850). 607/273-8088; fax 607/273-4832; res 800/800-8000. www.super8.com.* 63 rms, 2 story. Apr-Sept: S $44.88-$75.88; D $55-$75.88; under 12 free; higher rates special events; lower rates rest of yr. Crib free. TV; cable (premium). Complimentary coffee. Ck-out 11 am. Cr cds: A, D, DS, MC, V.

Hotels

★★ **CLARION UNIVERSITY HOTEL & CONFERENCE CENTER.** *One Sheraton Dr (14850). 607/257-2000; fax 607/257-3998; toll-free 800/257-6992. www.choicehotels.com.* 106 rms, 3 story. S, D $99-$149; each addl $10; suites $135-$225; under 18 free; package plans; higher rates special events. Crib free. TV; cable. Indoor pool; lifeguard. Restaurant 7 am-2 pm. Ck-out noon. Meeting rms. Business servs avail. Bellhops. Valet serv. Free airport transportation. Sauna. Refrigerators avail. Cr cds: A, C, D, DS, ER, JCB, MC.

★★ **THE STATLER HOTEL.** *11 East Ave, Cornell University (14853). 607/257-2500; fax 607/257-6432; toll-free 800/541-2501.* 150 rms, 9 story,

18 suites. S $125-$160; D $135-$170; suites $175-$375. Crib free. Valet, lot parking in/out $5.50/day. TV; cable. Pool privileges. Coffee in rms. Restaurant 7 am-9 pm. Rm serv to 10 pm. Bar from 4:30 pm. Ck-out noon. Convention facilities. Business servs avail. In-rm modem link. Gift shop. Free airport transportation. Tennis privileges. 18-hole golf privileges. Downhill/x-country ski 17 mi. Health club privileges. Bathrm phones, refrigerators; microwaves avail. Access to recreational facilities of the university. Marriott Executive Education Center located on the 1st floor of the hotel. Cr cds: A, C, D, DS, MC, V.

B&Bs/Small Inns

★★★ **LA TOURELLE COUNTY ✓ INN.** *1150 Danby Rd, Rte 96B (14850). 607/273-2734; fax 607/273-4821; toll-free 800/765-1492. www. latourelleinn.com.* 35 units, 3 story. S, D $99-$225. Crib $10. Pet accepted, some restrictions. TV; cable, VCR (free movies). Restaurant adj. Ck-out noon, ck-in 3 pm. Meeting rm. Business servs avail. In-rm modem link. Luggage handling. Valet serv. Tennis. X-country ski on site. Hiking trails. Refrigerators. Some fireplaces, balconies. European inn atmosphere. Located on 70 acres. Buttermilk Falls State Park adj. Cr cds: A, C, D, MC, V.

★★★★ **ROSE INN.** *813 Auburn Rd (14851). 607/533-7905; fax 607/533-7908; res 607/533-7905. www.roseinn. com.* Ornate gardens surround this Italianate mansion in the heart of the Finger Lakes district. Inside, the gorgeous circular staircase of carved wood is the focal point. Guests enjoy a thoroughly civilized stay, from drinks in the parlor, to sumptuous breakfasts and dinners in one of the dining rooms, to feather beds and period furnishings in the guest rooms. 10 rms, 2 story, 12 suites. D $125-$200; suites $260-$330; wkends (2-day min), hols, special events (3-day min); each addl $30. Children over 6 yrs only (or with advance arrangements). TV in public rm and in 2 suites. VCR avail. Complimentary full bkfst. Dining rm: 1 sitting (res required) Tues-Sat 7 pm. Rm serv on request. Bar; entertainment Fri, Sat. Wine cellar. Ck-out 11 am, ck-in 3 pm. Meeting rm (1850s carriage house). Business servs avail. Luggage handling. Some in-rm whirlpools, fireplaces. Totally nonsmoking. Cr cds: A, MC, V.

D ⬛ 🔥

Restaurants

★★ **ANGELINA CENTINI'S.** *124 Coddington Rd (14850). 607/273-0802. www.angelinacentinis.com.* Hrs: 11 am-2 pm, 5-9 pm; Fri, Sat to 10 pm; Sun 4-9 pm. Closed Thanksgiving, Dec 25. Res accepted. Italian menu. Bar. Lunch $2.95-$9.95, dinner $7.50-$16.95. Child's menu. Specializes in homemade pasta and sauces. Parking. Outdoor dining. Italian decor. Terrace dining overlooks city and lake. Family-owned. Cr cds: A, D, DS, MC, V.

D

★★★ **DANO'S ON CAYUGA.** *113 S Cayuga St (14850). 607/277-8942. www.fingerlakes.net/danos.* Continental menu. Specialties: chicken paprikash, house-smoked salmon with cabbage and potato pierogi, creme brulee. Hrs: 5:30-10 pm. Closed Sun, Mon; hols. Res accepted. Bar. Wine list. A la carte entrees: dinner $12.95-$24.95. Formal dining. Artwork. Totally nonsmoking. Cr cds: A, D, DS, MC, V.

D

★★★ **JOHN THOMAS STEAK HOUSE.** *1152 Danby Rd (14850). 607/273-3464.* Hrs: 5:30-10 pm; Fri, Sat to 11 pm. Closed hols. Res accepted. Bar. A la carte entrees: dinner $14.95-$29.95. Specialities: prime dry-aged beef, fresh seafood. Own baking. Parking. Restored 1828 farmhouse with variety of dining rms. Pond with ducks. Cr cds: A, D, DS, MC, V.

D ⬛

★ **MOOSEWOOD.** *215 N Cayuga St (14850). 607/273-9610. www.moosewoodrestaurant.com.* Hrs: 11:30 am-4 pm, 5:30-9 pm; winter to 8:30 pm; summer wknds to 9:30 pm. Gourmet vegetarian, seafood menu. Menu changes twice a day; daily vegan menu. Wine, beer. Lunch $6.50, dinner $12-$14. Serv charge 15 percent. Outdoor dining. Totally nonsmoking. Cr cds: MC, V.

D SC

★★ **STATION.** *806 W Buffalo St (14850). 607/272-2609. www.ithacastation.com.* Hrs: 4-9 pm; Sun noon-8 pm; early-bird dinner Tues-Fri 4-6 pm, Sun 12-4 pm. Closed Jan 1, Thanksgiving, Dec 25; also Mon Sept-June and 1st 2 wks Jan. Res accepted. Bar. Dinner $9.95-$18.95. Child's menu. Specializes in prime rib, seafood, veal. Salad bar. Parking. Converted 1886 railroad station. Ticket-punch menus. Family-owned. Cr cds: A, D, DS, MC, V.

Jamestown

(F-I) *See also Bemus Point, Chautauqua*

Settled 1811 **Pop** 31,730 **Elev** 1,370 ft
Area code 716 **Zip** 14701

Information Chamber of Commerce, 101 W 5th St; 716/484-1101

Jamestown made its mark early in the nineteenth century in the manufacture of metal products and furniture. These industries still flourish in this city at the southern end of Chautauqua Lake. Tourism and farming are important to the economy as well.

What to See and Do

Allegany State Park. (see) Approx 30 mi E on NY 17.

Fenton Historical Center. Home of post-Civil War governor; memorabilia of Chautauqua Lake area, Fenton family, Victorian era; re-created Victorian drawing rm. Archival and genealogical library; Swedish and Italian heritage, Civil War exhibit. (Mon-Sat; closed Thanksgiving, Dec 25) 67 Washington St. Phone 716/664-6256. ¢¢

Lucy-Desi Museum. Interactive exhibits provide a look into the lives and careers of Lucille Ball and Desi Arnaz. Video presentation. Gift shop. (May-Oct daily, Nov-Apr wkends) 212 Pine St. Phone 716/484-0800. ¢¢

Panama Rocks Park. Massive rock outcrop (25 acres) of a primeval seashore formation; cliffs, caves,

Lucy-Desi Museum

crevices, and passages. Rare mosses, wildflowers, ferns; unusually shaped tree roots. Self-guided tours; hiking trail; picnicking. (May-late-Oct, daily) (See SPECIAL EVENT) 14 mi W via NY 394, then 6 mi S of exit 7 on I-86. Phone 716/782-2845. ¢¢¢

Special Event

Panama Rocks Folk Fair. Panama Rocks Park. Second Fri-Sun July. Phone 716/782-2825.

Motels/Motor Lodges

★★ **COMFORT INN.** *2800 N Main St Extension (14701). 716/664-5920; fax 716/664-3068; res 800/228-5150. www.comfortinn.com.* 101 rms, 2 story. June-mid-Sept: S $50-$139; D $64-$139; each addl $5; under 18 free; lower rates rest of yr. Crib free. Pet accepted, some restrictions. TV; cable (premium), VCR avail. Complimentary continental bkfst. Restaurant adj. Bar. Ck-out noon. Meeting rm. Business servs avail. Downhill ski 20 mi. Health club privileges. Some in-rm whirlpools. Microwaves avail. Cr cds: A, D, MC, V.

D ✈ ➤ ⇗ ⊠ SC

★★ **HOLIDAY INN.** *150 W Fourth St (14701). 716/664-3400; fax 716/484-3304; res 800/465-4329. www.holiday-inn.com.* 146 rms, 8 story. S, D $79-$249; under 18 free; ski plans; wknd rates. Crib free. TV; cable (premium). Indoor pool. Complimentary coffee in rms. Restaurant 6:30 am-2 pm, 5:30-10 pm. Bars 5 pm-midnight. Ck-out noon. Coin lndry. Meeting rms. Business servs avail. In-rm modem link. Bellhops. Cr cds: A, C, D, DS, JCB, MC, V.

D ♿ ➤ ⇗ ⊠

Restaurants

★★ **HOUSE OF PETILLO.** *382 Hunt Rd (14701). 716/664-7457.* Continental menu. Specializes in veal, seafood, pasta. Hrs: 5 pm-midnight. Closed Sun, Mon; hols. Res accepted. Bar. Dinner $11.95-$21.95. Child's menu. Fireplaces. Stein collection. Family-owned. Cr cds: A, DS, MC, V.
⊠

★★ **IRONSTONE.** *516 W 4th St (14701). 716/487-1516.* Specializes in rack of lamb, flatbread. Hrs: 11:30 am-2 pm, 5-9 pm; Sat from 5 pm. Closed Sun; Jan 1, Dec 24, 25. Bar. Lunch $4.25-$6.95, dinner $12-$39.95. Victorian decor. In 1884 building. Family-owned. Cr cds: A, C, D, DS, MC, V.
D ⊠

★★★ **MACDUFF'S.** *317 Pine St (14701). 716/664-9414.* Hrs: 5:30-10 pm. Closed Sun; hols. Continental menu. Specialties: twin tournedoes of beef with port and Stilton sauce, salmon stuffed with pike. Own baking, ice cream. Res accepted. Bar.

Wine list. Dinner $17.95-$25.95. Intimate dining. Cr cds: A, MC, V.
[D]

Jericho (L.I.)

See also Oyster Bay (L.I.), Plainview (L.I.), Westbury (L.I.)

Pop 13,045 **Elev** 180 ft **Area code** 516 **Zip** 11753

Restaurants

★ ★ **CAPRICCIO.** *399 Jericho Tpke (11753). 516/931-2727.* French, Italian menu. Specialties: chicken Riviera, roast L. I. duck, veal chop with fresh herbs. Own pastries. Hrs: 11:30 am-2:30 pm, 5:30-10 pm; Sat 5:30-11 pm. Closed Sun; hols. Bar. Wine list. A la carte entrees: lunch $10.95-$18.95, dinner $16.95-$25.95. Valet parking. Cr cds: A, D, MC, V.
[D]

★ **FRANK'S STEAKS.** *4 Jericho Tpke (11753). 516/338-4595.* Specializes in steak, chicken, seafood. Hrs: 11:30 am-10 pm; Fri to 11 pm; Sat 4-11:30 pm; Sun 4-9 pm. Closed Easter, Thanksgiving, Dec 25. Res accepted wkends. Bar. A la carte entrees: lunch $6.95-$15.95, dinner $14.95-$25. Cr cds: A, C, D, DS, ER, MC, V.
[D] [⊒]

★ ★ **MAINE MAID INN.** *Rte 106 Jericho Tpke (11753). 516/935-6400. www.lirestaurants.com/mainemaid.* Continental menu. Specialties: L. I. duckling, prime rib. Hrs: 11:30 am-10 pm; Fri, Sat to 11 pm; Sun to 9 pm; early-bird dinner Wed-Sat 4-6 pm. Closed Mon; hols. Res accepted. Bar. Complete meals: lunch $6.95-$14, dinner $12.95-$28.50. Child's menu. Built in 1789; Federal-period decor. Cr cds: A, C, D, DS, ER, MC, V.
[D]

★ ★ **MILLERRIDGE INN.** *585 N Broadway, Jericho (11753). 516/931-2201.* Specialties: prime rib, pot roast, sauerbraten. Hrs: 11:30 am-9:30 pm; Fri to 10 pm; Sat to 11 pm; Sun to 9 pm; early-bird dinner Mon-Fri 3:30-6:30 pm. Closed Dec 25.

Complete meals: lunch $9.95-$14.95, dinner $14.95-$22.95. Sun brunch $9.95-$14.95. Child's menu. Colonial inn (1672); fireplaces, antiques. Adj to Colonial Village. Family-owned. Cr cds: A, C, D, DS, ER, MC, V.
[D]

Johnstown

(D-7) *See also Amsterdam, Canajoharie, Schenectady*

Founded 1723 **Pop** 8,511 **Elev** 691 ft **Area code** 518 **Zip** 12095
Information Fulton County Regional Chamber of Commerce and Industry, 2 N Main St, Gloversville 12078; 518/725-0641 or 800/676-3858
Web www.fultoncountyny.org

A center of leather tanning and related industries, Johnstown often is called a twin city to Gloversville, which it adjoins. A Revolutionary War battle was fought here six days after Cornwallis surrendered at Yorktown. Women's rights pioneer Elizabeth Cady Stanton was born here in 1815.

What to See and Do

Johnson Hall State Historic Site. (1763) Residence of Sir William Johnson, first baronet of New York colony; Native Americans and colonists held meetings here. Site incl hall with period furnishings; stone blockhouse; interpretation center; dioramas depicting history of the estate; tours; special events. (Mid-May-Oct, Wed-Sat, also Sun afternoons) Contact Site Manager, Hall Ave. Phone 518/762-8712. ¢¢

Motel/Motor Lodge

★ ★ **HOLIDAY INN.** *308 N Comrie Ave (12095). 518/762-4686; fax 518/762-4034; toll-free 800/465-4329. www.holiday-inn.com.* 100 rms, 3 story. No elvtr. S $62-$72; D $68-$78; under 19 free; higher rates Aug. Crib free. Pet accepted, some restrictions. TV; cable (premium), VCR avail (movies). Heated pool. Coffee in rms. Restaurant 6:30 am-10 pm. Rm serv 8 am-10 pm. Bar 11 am- midnight; entertainment wkends. Ck-out 11

m. Coin lndry. Meeting rms. Business servs avail. In-rm modem link. Valet serv. Downhill/x-country ski 15 mi. Cr cds: A, C, D, DS, JCB, MC, V.

Restaurant

★★ UNION HALL INN. *2 Union Pl 12095). 518/762-3210.* Continental menu. Specializes in fresh seafood, vegetarian dishes. Hrs: (no lunch in summer) Tues-Sat 5 pm-closing; Closed Sun, Mon; hols. Res accepted; required hols. Bar. Lunch $4.50-$8.50, dinner $8.95-$15.95. Post-Revolutionary tavern (1798); early Colonial decor. Cr cds: A, MC, V.

Jones Beach State Park

G-2) See also New York City

On south shore of Long Island via pkwys)

For millions of New Yorkers, summer means Jones Beach, a fabulous recreation area that can accommodate hundreds of thousands of people on its more than 2,400 acres.

Recreational facilities include swimming in the ocean, Zach's Bay, and freshwater pools; bathhouse, fishing in ocean and bay, boating (dock). Nature, biking trails; 18-hole pitch-and-putt golf course, miniature golf, softball fields (with permit), shuffleboard; recreation programs. Restaurant, snack bars. Gift shop. Fees vary. Phone 516/785-1600.

Special Event

Jones Beach Theatre. Concerts ranging from country to rock; top entertainers. 14,000-seat outdoor theater. Contact Box 1000, Wantagh 11793. Phone 516/221-1000.

Kingston

(B-5) See also New Paltz, Rhinebeck, Saugerties, Woodstock

Settled 1652 **Pop** 23,456 **Elev** 200 ft
Area code 845 **Zip** 12401
Information Chamber of Commerce of Ulster County, 1 Albany Ave; 914/338-5100
Web www.ulsterchamber.org

In more than 300 years, Kingston has had several names, including Esopus and Wiltwyck, and has been raided, burned, and fought over by Native Americans, Dutch, British, and Americans. It was the first capital of New York. The Delaware and Hudson Canal and then the railroads brought prosperity. A huge cement industry bloomed and died on Rondout Creek harbor in the 19th century.

What to See and Do

Delaware & Hudson Canal Museum. Dioramas, canalboat models, photographs, and memorabilia. Tours. (May-Oct Mon, Thurs-Sun; closed Nov-Apr) 15 mi S, NY Thrwy exit 19, then S on NY 209, turn left on NY 213 in High Falls. Phone 845/687-9311. ¢¢

Hudson River Maritime Museum. Models, photographs, and paintings depict bygone era of river commerce; outdoor area features steam tug and a variety of antique and modern pleasure boats. (Daily) 1 Rondout Landing, at the foot of Broadway. Phone 845/338-0071. ¢

Old Dutch Church. (Congregation established 1659) A 19th-century church; buried on grounds is George Clinton, first governor of New York and vice president under Madison and Jefferson. Church and museum tours by appt. Main and Wall sts. Phone 845/338-6759. **Donation**

Senate House State Historic Site. (1676) Stone residence in which the first New York State Senate met in 1777. Furnished in 18th-century Dutch style; delft tiles, Hudson Valley furniture. Paintings by John Vanderlyn and others in adj museum; boxwood garden. Also library of regional history (by appt only), displays, special events. (Mid-Apr-Oct, Wed-Sat, also Sun afternoons) 312 Fair St, in Stockade District. Phone 845/338-2786. ¢¢

Ulster Performing Arts Center. Historic Vaudeville theater (1927) presents professional Broadway touring companies, dance, contemporary music, comedy, and children's productions. 601 Broadway. Phone 845/339-6088.

Special Event

Stone House Day. Approx ½ mi NW on NY 28, then 2 mi S on US 209 in Hurley. Tour of eight privately owned colonial stone houses, led by costumed guides; Hurley Reformed Church and old burial ground; antique show; re-creation of Revolutionary War military encampment; country fair. Phone 845/331-4121. Second Sat July.

Motels/Motor Lodges

★★ **HOLIDAY INN.** *503 Washington Ave (12401). 845/338-0400; toll-free 800/465-4329. www.holidayinn kingston.com.* 212 rms, 2 story. S, D $109-$149; suites $119-$149; under 19 free; higher rates wkends (May-Oct). Crib free. Pet accepted. TV. Indoor pool; wading pool; whirlpool. Coffee in rms. Restaurant 6 am-10 pm. Bar from 11:30 am; entertainment Wed-Sat. Ck-out noon. Coin lndry. Meeting rms. Business servs avail. Bellhops. Sundries. Sauna. Game rm. Refrigerators avail. Balconies. Cr cds: A, C, D, DS, ER, JCB, MC, V.
🄳 🕊 ⇌ 🖎 🐾 SC

★★ **RAMADA INN.** *114 Rte 28 (12401). 845/339-3900; fax 845/338-8464; res 800/272-6232.* 147 rms, 2 story. S, D $75-$130; each addl $10; suites $95-$130; under 18 free. Crib free. TV; cable (premium). Indoor pool; lifeguard. Restaurant 7 am-10 pm. Bar. Ck-out noon. Meeting rms. Business servs avail. Bellhops. Valet serv. Sundries. Downhill ski 20 mi. Exercise equipt. Health club privileges. Game rm. Refrigerators avail. Cr cds: A, D, DS, MC, V.
🕴 🄳 ⇙ ⇌ 🐾

★ **SUPER 8 MOTEL.** *487 Washington Ave (12401). 845/338-3078; toll-free 800/800-8000. www.super8.com.* 84 rms, 2 story. June-Oct: S $54.88; D $58.88-$63.88; each addl $6; under 12 free; lower rates rest of yr. Crib free. Pet accepted, some restrictions. TV; cable, VCR avail (movies). Complimentary continental bkfst. Restaurant adj open 24 hrs. Ck-out 11 am. Coin lndry. Sundries. Valet serv. Business servs avail. Refrigerators, microwaves avail. Cr cds: A, C, D, DS, MC, V.
🄳 🕊 ⇌ 🐾 SC

Restaurant

★★ **LE CANARD ECHAINE.** *276 Fair St (12401). 845/339-2003.* Hrs: 11:30 am-10 pm; Fri-Sun to 11 pm. Closed Dec 25. Res accepted. Classical French menu. Bar. A la carte entrees: lunch $5-$9, dinner $15-$21. Specialty: roasted duck. Street parking. French bistro atmosphere. Cr cds: A, C, DS, ER, MC, V.
🄳 ⇘

Lake George Area

(C-8) *See also Bolton Landing (Lake George Area), Diamond Point, Hague, Lake George Village, Ticonderoga (Lake George Area)*

Early explorers and settlers knew Lake George as Lac du St. Sacrement—the name given it when a Jesuit missionary, Father Isaac Jogues reached the southern tip of the lake on the eve of Corpus Christi Day in 1646. In the foothills of the Adirondacks, the area is a center for winter as well as summer sports; there are many miles of snowmobile trails. The area is rich in memories of battles that played a major role in the future of the nation.

Lake George Village

(C-8) *See also Glens Falls, Lake Luzerne*

Pop 985 **Elev** 353 ft **Area code** 518
Zip 12845

Information Chamber of Commerce,
PO Box 272; 518/668-5755 or
800/705-0059

Web www.lgchamber.org

This village, located on the 32-mile
lake, is in a popular resort area well
known for fishing, swimming, boating, golf, and winter sports.

What to See and Do

Fort William Henry Museum. A
1755 fort rebuilt from original plans;
French and Indian War relics; military drills, musket firings, bullet
molding, and cannon demonstrations. Replica of fort used in filming
of the movie *Last of the Mohicans*.
Tours (July and Aug). (May-Oct,
daily) 48 Canada St, S edge of village
on US 9, NY 9 N. Phone 518/668-
5471. ¢¢

**The Great Escape and Splashwater
Kingdom Fun Park.** State's largest
theme park has over 120 rides, live
shows, and attractions, incl numer-
ous roller coasters, Raging River Raft
Ride, All-American High-Dive Show,
Storytown themed children's area.
Splashwater Kingdom water park fea-
tures giant wavepool, water slides,
Adventure River, and kiddie pools.
(Memorial Day-Labor Day, daily) NY
9, between exits 19 and 20 off I-87.
Phone 518/792-3500. ¢¢¢¢

Lake excursions. MV *Mohican, Lac de
t. Sacrement,* and the paddlewheeler
Minne-Ha-Ha cruise Lake George.
Trips vary from one-hr shoreline
cruise to 4½-hr full-length cruise of
Lake George; also lunch, dinner,
moonlight, and Sun brunch cruises
(late June-Labor Day, daily; limited
schedule spring and fall). Lake
George Steamboat Company, Beach
Rd. Phone 518/668-5777. ¢¢¢¢

Lake George Battlefield Picnic Area.
Site of Battle of Lake George (1755);
ruins of Fort George. Picnic tables,
fireplaces, charcoal grills, water.

(Mid-June-Labor Day, daily; May-
mid-June, wkends) 1 mi S off US 9.
Phone 518/668-3352. ¢¢

Prospect Mountain State Parkway.
(1969) A 5½-mi paved road up
Prospect Mtn (2,100 ft); buses (free)
from parking lot near top to crest.
(Mid-May-mid-Oct, daily) ½ mi S
on US 9. Phone 518/668-3352. ¢¢

Swimming. Lake George Million Dol-
lar Beach. In Adirondack Park (see).
Bathhouse, lockers, lifeguards. (Mid-
June-Labor Day, daily) ¼ mi E off
US 9. Beach Phone 518/668-5755.

Water Slide World. Water fun park
incl wave pool, 13 water slides,
Activity Pool, Lazy River, and Toddler
Lagoon play area. (Late June-Labor
Day, daily) US 9. Phone 518/668-
4407. ¢¢¢¢

Special Events

Winter Carnival. Wkends Feb. Phone
518/668-5755.

Americade. Annual touring motorcycle event incl seminars, exhibits,
shows, guided scenic tours. Phone
518/668-5755. Second wk June.

Family Festival. Shepard Park,
Canada St. Craft show, family enter-
tainment, game booths, music, food.
Phone 518/668-5771. Third wk Aug.

Jazz Festival. Shepard Park Band-
stand. Regional jazz bands; lawn
seating. Phone 518/668-5771. Mid-
Sept.

Lakeside Festival. Beach Rd. Juried
craft show; boat show with demo
rides; food, music, fireworks. Phone
518/668-5771. Third wkend Sept.

Motels/Motor Lodges

★★ **BEST WESTERN OF LAKE
GEORGE.** *Exit 21 at I-89 (12845).*
*518/668-5701; fax 518/668-4926; res
800/528-7234. www.bestwestern.com.*
87 rms, 2 story. July-Labor Day: S, D
$99-$140; each addl $10; suites $166-
$265; under 12 free; higher wkend
rates in season; lower rates rest of yr.
Crib free. TV; cable, VCR avail. 2
pools, 1 indoor; wading pool, whirlpool. Complimentary coffee. Ck-out
11 am. Business servs avail. Downhill
ski 10 mi; x-country ski 8 mi. Fireplace in some suites. Balconies. Cr
cds: A, C, D, DS, ER, MC, V.

★ **COLONEL WILLIAMS MOTOR INN.** *RR 9 (12845). 518/668-5727; fax 518/668-2996; toll-free 800/334-5727. www.colonelwilliamsresort.com.* 40 rms. July-Labor Day: S, D $85-$125; each addl $8; suites $130-$160; family, wkly rates; lower rates mid-May-June, after Labor Day-late Oct. Closed rest of yr. Crib free. TV; cable. Indoor/outdoor pool; whirlpool. Playground. Restaurant nearby. Ck-out 11 am. Lndry facilities. Meeting rm. Exercise equipt; sauna. Game rm. Lawn games. Refrigerators, microwaves avail. Picnic tables, grill. Cr cds: A, DS, MC, V.

★★ **COLONIAL MANOR.** *2200 State Rte 9 (12845). 518/668-4884; toll-free 800/447-0221. www.colonial manorlg.com.* 35 motel rms, 1-2 story, 9 cottages, 17 kit. cottages (1-4-bedrm). Late June-Labor Day: S, D $68-$150; each addl $6-$10; under 12 free (motel only); kit. units to 4, $650-$1,450/wk; each addl $50-$100; lower rates May-late June, after Labor Day-mid-Oct. Closed rest of yr. Crib free. TV; cable. Heated pool; whirlpool. Playground. Restaurant opp open 24 hrs. Ck-out 11 am, kit. cottages 10 am. Lawn games. Refrigerators. Cottages with porches. Picnic tables, grill for kit. units. Shaded grounds. Cr cds: A, DS, MC, V.

★ **DAYS INN LAKE GEORGE.** *1454 State Rte 9 (12845). 518/793-3196; fax 518/793-6028; res 800/329-7466. www.daysinnlalakegeorge.com.* 109 rms, 2 story. July-Sept: S, D $58-$146; each addl $5; under 12 free; lower rates rest of yr. Crib free. TV; cable (premium). Indoor pool; whirlpool. Restaurant 7 am-11 pm. Ck-out 11 am. Business servs avail. Game rm. Some balconies. Cr cds: A, D, DS, MC, V.

★ **DUTCHESS MOTEL.** *3029 Lake Shore Dr (12845). 518/668-5264; toll-free 800/785-9558. www.dutchess motel.com.* 14 rms, 1-2 story, 5 kits. July-Aug: S, D $65-$70; each addl $4-$8; kit. units $70-$75 ($460-$510/wk); lower rates rest of yr. Crib free. TV; cable. Pool. Playground. Coffee in lobby. Restaurant opp 8 am-9 pm. Ck-out 10 am. Tennis. Downhill/x-country ski 10 mi. Rec

rm. Lawn games. Refrigerators. Picnic tables, grills. Cr cds: A, MC, V.

★ **ECONO LODGE.** *439 Canada St (12845). 518/668-2689; fax 518/798-3455; toll-free 800/477-3529. www. econolodge.com.* 50 rms, 3 story. Mid-June-Labor Day: S, D $57-$114; each addl $10; under 18 free; lower rates May-mid-June, after Labor Day-Oct. Closed rest of yr. Crib free. TV; cable. 2 pools, 1 indoor; whirlpool. Restaurant opp 6 am-10 pm. Ck-out 10 am. Meeting rm. Business servs avail. Game rm. Refrigerators avail. Balconies. Cr cds: A, D, DS, MC, V.

★★ **GEORGIAN MOTEL.** *384 Canada St (12845). 518/668-5401; toll-free 800/525-3436. www.georgian resort.com.* 164 rms, 2 story. Late June-Labor Day: S, D $99-$199; each addl $10; suites $199-$299; under 5 free; wkend plans; lower rates rest of yr. Crib $7. TV; cable (premium), VCR avail. Underground garage parking. Heated pool; poolside serv, lifeguard. Coffee in rms. Restaurant 7 am-9 pm. Bar 5 pm-1 am. Ck-out 11 am. Meeting rms. Business servs avail. Bellhops. Valet serv. Airport, RR station transportation. Downhill/x-country ski 8 mi. Game rm. Refrigerators in suites, avail for rms (fee). Some balconies. Cr cds: A, C, D, DS, MC, V.

★ **THE HERITAGE OF LAKE GEORGE.** *419 Canada St (12845). 518/668-3357; fax 518/668-9784; toll-free 800/883-2653. heritageoflake george.com.* 38 rms, 7 with shower only, 2 story. July-Labor Day: S, D $55-$100; each addl $10; kit. units (wkly) $775-$1,075; under 16 free; wkends, hols (2-day min); lower rates mid-May-June, Labor Day-mid-Oct. Closed rest of yr. Crib free. TV; cable. Heated pools. Complimentary coffee in lobby. Restaurant opp 6:30 am-10 pm. Ck-out 11 am. Business servs avail. Refrigerators; microwaves avail. Picnic tables, grills. Cr cds: A, DS, MC, V.

★★ **LAKE CREST MOTEL.** *366 Canada St (12845). 518/668-3374. www.lakecrestmotel.com.* 40 rms, 1-2 story. Late June-early Sept: S, D $98-

176; each addl $9; suites $158-$176; under 6 free; lower rates mid-Apr-late June, early Sept-mid-Oct. Closed rest of yr. Crib $6. TV; cable. Heated pool. Restaurant 7:30 am-noon in season; closed rest of yr. Ck-out 11 am. Business servs avail. Sundries. Private sand beach. Terraces. Cr cds: MC, V.

★ **MOHAWK MOTEL AND COTTAGE.** 435 Canada St (12845). 518/668-2143; fax 518/668-3025; res 800/795-6680. www.mohawkmotel. com. 60 rms, 8 kits., 7 kit. cottages. Late June-Labor Day: S $49-$129; D $55-$129; each addl $8; kit. units (3-day min), cottages $650-$975/wk; lower rates rest of yr. Crib free. TV; cable. Indoor pool; whirlpool. Playround. Restaurant opp 9 am-11 pm. Ck-out 11 am, kit. units 10 am. Guest lndry. Downhill/x-country ski 5 mi. Game rm. Lawn games. Some in-rm whirlpools, fireplaces. Picnic tables, grills. Cr cds: DS, MC, V.

★★ **MOHICAN MOTEL.** 1545 State Rte 9 (12845). 518/792-0474; fax 518/761-4089. www.mohicanmotel. com. 43 rms, 13 kit. units. Late June-Labor Day: S $98; D $115-$140; kit. units $140-$185; lower rates rest of yr. Crib $5. TV; cable (premium). 2 pools, 1 indoor; wading pools, whirlpools. Playground. Restaurant 7:30 am-4 pm. Ck-out 11 am. Coin lndry. Sundries. Downhill ski 15 mi; x-country ski 4 mi. Sauna. Game rm. Lawn games. Refrigerators. Picnic tables, grills. Cr cds: A, MC, V.

★ **NORDICK'S MOTEL.** 2895 Lake Shore Dr (12845). 518/668-2697; res 800/368-2697. www.nordicks.com. 21 rms. Mid-July-Labor Day, hol wkends: S $44-$89; D $44-$104; under 16 free; lower rates May-July 1, after Labor Day-late Oct. Closed rest of yr. Crib free. TV; cable. Heated pool. Complimentary coffee. Restaurant 7 am-10 pm. Bar. Ck-out 10 am. Health club privileges. Refrigerators avail. Patios, balconies. Cr cds: A, DS, MC, V.

★★★ **ROARING BROOK RANCH & TENNIS RESORT.** Rte 9N S (12845). 518/668-5767; fax 518/668-4019. www.roaringbrookranch.com. 142 rms, 2 story. MAP (2-day min) (riding optional): July-Labor Day: D $81-$86/person; suites $106/person; wkly rates 10 percent less; family rates; golf, tennis, riding plans; lower rates Jan-Feb, mid-May-June, after Labor Day-mid-Oct. Closed rest of yr. Crib free. TV. 3 pools, 1 indoor; poolside serv. Free supervised children's activities (summer); ages 4-7. Restaurant 8-10 am, 6-7:30 pm. Snack bar. Cookouts in summer season. Bars 11-3 am. Ck-out 11 am, ck-in 3 pm. Coin lndry. Meeting rms. Business servs avail. Free bus depot transportation. Sports dir. 5 tennis courts, pro in season. Golf privileges. Downhill ski 10 mi; x-country ski 6 mi. Snowmobile, nature trails. Lawn games. Entertainment; movies. Rec rm. Game rm. Exercise equipt; saunas. On 500 acres. Cr cds: MC, V.

★★ **SUN CASTLE MOTEL AND VILLAS.** 378 Lake Shore Dr (12845). 518/668-2085; res 518/745-7163. www.suncastleresort.com. 16 kit. villas (1-2 bedrm). Mid-June-Labor Day: villa (up to 4) $800-$1,375/wk; lower rates Memorial Day wkend-mid-June, after Labor Day-mid-Oct. Closed rest of yr. Crib free. Maid serv twice wkly (fee). TV; cable (premium). Heated pool. Restaurant nearby. Ck-out 11 am. Tennis. Wood-burning stoves (free firewood). Private patios, balconies. Picnic table, grills. Private beach; dock privileges, rowboats. Original mansion house on grounds. Cr cds: MC, V.

★★ **TALL PINES MOTEL.** 1747 Hwy 9 S, Lake George (12845). 518/668-5122; toll-free 800/368-5122. www.tall pinesmotel.com. 26 rms, 1-2 story. Mid-July-Labor Day: S, D $108-$118; each addl $10; family, wkly rates; lower rates Memorial Day-mid-July. Closed rest of yr. Crib free. TV; cable. Pool; wading pool, whirlpool. Playground. Complimentary continental bkfst. Ck-out 11 am. Sauna. Refrigerators. Picnic table, grills. Cr cds: DS, MC, V.

Resorts

★ CRESTHAVEN RESORT MOTEL LAKE GEORGE. *3210 Lake Shore Dr (12845). 518/668-3332; fax 518/668-0324; toll-free 800/853-1632. www. lakegeorgelodges.com.* 12 kit. units in motel (3-day min July-Aug), 15 kit. cottages, 20 cabins. Late June-Labor Day: S $75-$115; D $75-$215; each addl $10-$20; kit. units, cottages (up to 4 persons) $950-$1,299/wk; lower rates mid-May-late June, after Labor Day-mid-Oct. Closed rest of yr. Crib free. TV; cable. Pool; wading pool. Playground. Restaurant 8 am-11 pm (in season). Ck-out 10 am. Private beach. Rec rm. Lawn games. Fireplace in cottages. Picnic tables, grills. Cr cds: MC, V.

★★ DUNHAMS BAY LODGE. *2999 NY 9L (12845). 518/656-9242; fax 518/656-9250; toll-free 800/795-6343. www.dunhamsbay.com.* 20 rms in main building, 24 motel units, 1-2 story, 10 kit. cottages. No A/C in cottages. July-Labor Day: S $80-$135; D $90-$155; each addl $20-$25; kit. cottages $850-$1,050; wkends (3-day min); family, wkly rates; lower rates mid-May-late June, after Labor Day-mid-Oct. Closed rest of yr. Crib free. TV; cable. Indoor pool; wading pool, whirlpool. Playground. Complimentary continental bkfst. Restaurant 8:30-10 am, Sun to 11 am. Bar. Ck-out 10 am, ck-in 3 pm. Business servs avail. Tennis. Boat rentals, dockage. Lawn games. Game rm. Some refrigerators. Some balconies. Picnic tables, grills. 150 acres on lake. Cr cds: A, MC, V.

★★ FORT WILLIAM HENRY RESORT. *48 Canada St (12845). 518/668-3081; fax 518/668-4926; toll-free 800/234-6686. www.fortwilliam henry.com.* 99 rms, 2 story. Late June-Labor Day: S, D $140-$159; each addl $15; suite $200-$255; under 12 free; hol wkends (2-day min); lower rates rest of yr. Crib free. Pet accepted, some restrictions. TV; cable, VCR avail (movies). 2 pools, 1 indoor; whirlpool, poolside serv. Playground. Restaurant in season 7 am-10 pm. Bar noon-1 am, closed off-season. Ck-out 11 am. Meeting rms. Business servs avail. Downhill ski 20 mi; x-country ski 8 mi. Sauna.

Bicycle rentals. Cr cds: A, C, D, DS, ER, MC, V.

★★ HOLIDAY INN TURF. *Rte 9 Canada St (12845). 518/668-5781; fax 518/668-9213; res 800/465-5329. www.holiday-inn.com.* 105 rms, 2 story. July-Labor Day: S, D $75-$225; each addl $10; under 19 free; higher rates special events; lower rates rest of yr. Crib avail. TV; cable (premium). 2 pools, 1 indoor; wading pool, lifeguard in season. Playground. Restaurant 6:30 am-2 pm, 5-10 pm. Bar. Ck-out 11 am. Coin lndry. Meeting rms. Business servs avail. Gift shop. Exercise equipt. Game rm. Miniature golf. Refrigerators. Cr cds: A, D, DS, MC, V.

★ HOWARD JOHNSON RESORT HOTEL. *2 Canada St (12845). 518/668-5744; fax 518/668-3544; toll-free 888/843-8454. www.tikiresort.com.* 110 rms, 2 story, 20 suites, 10 kit. units. July-Labor Day: S, D $80-$130; each addl $10; suites, kit. units $139-$199; under 18 free; hols (2-day min); lower rates rest of yr. Closed Dec-Mar. Crib $10. TV; cable (premium). 2 pools, 1 indoor; wading pool. Complimentary coffee in lobby. Restaurant 7 am-noon, 6-10 pm. Bar 5 pm-1 am; entertainment Thurs-Sun. Meeting rms. Business servs avail. Downhill/x-country ski 15 mi. Exercise equipt. Refrigerators avail. In-rm whirlpool in some suites. Picnic tables, grills. Cr cds: A, C, D, DS, MC, V.

★★ STILLBAY RESORT. *Bolton Rd; Rte 9N (12845). 518/668-2584; toll-free 800/521-7511. www.stillbay.com.* 22 rms, 1-2 story, 4 kits., 2 kit. units (2-bedrm). July-Labor Day: D $98-$120; each addl $15; kit. units $115-$135; wkly rates; lower rates late May-June, Sept-mid-Oct. Closed rest of yr. Crib free. TV; cable. Complimentary buffet bkfst July-Labor Day. Restaurant nearby. Ck-out 11 am. Lawn games. Refrigerators avail. Picnic tables, grills. Private beach, boathouse, dockage, rowboats, paddle boats. Cr cds: MC, V.

B&B/Small Inn

★★ **BAYFRONT COTTAGES.** *3224 Lake Shore Dr (12846). 518/668-9579; fax 518/668-4143.* 4 kit. units, 6 kit. cottages. Late June-Labor Day: up to 4, $850-$1,200/wk; lower rates Memorial Day wkend-late June, after Labor Day-mid-Oct. Closed rest of yr. Crib free. TV; cable (premium). Playground. Restaurant nearby. Ck-out 10 am. Porches. Picnic tables, grills. Beach, dockage. Rustic setting on lake. Cr cds: A, MC, V.
🏊

Cottage Colonies

★ **ALPINE VILLAGE RESORT.** *Lake Shore Dr (12845). 518/668-2193. www.alpinelg.com.* 15 rms in lodge, guesthouse, 1-2 story; 24 rms in cabins, 18 A/C. Late June-Labor Day: D $72-$105; each addl $8-$10; cabins $460-$760/wk; under 3 free; wkly rates; 3-day min in season; lower rates rest of yr. TV. Heated pool. Playground. Snack bar. Ck-out 11 am, ck-in 3 pm. Package store ½ mi. Meeting rms. Free bus depot transportation. Tennis. Private beach, rowboats, canoes. Downhill/x-country ski 13 mi. Ice-skating. Lawn games. Rec rm. Entertainment. Grills. Fireplace in cabin units. Landscaped grounds; on lakeshore. Cr cds: A, DS, MC, V.
🏊 🚣 ⛷ 🛥 🔥

★★ **O'CONNOR'S RESORT COTTAGES.** *3454 Lake Shore Dr (12845). 518/668-3367; fax 518/668-9510.* 32 kit. cottages (2-3 bedrm). Late June-Labor Day, wkly: from $860, kit. cottages for 2 from $644; lower rates rest of yr. Crib free. TV; cable. Playground. Restaurant nearby. Ck-out 10 am, ck-in 3:30 pm. Miniature golf. Private beach; float, dockage; paddleboats, rowboats. Lawn games. Picnic tables, grill. Wooded grounds. Cr cds: MC, V.
🏊 🔥

Restaurants

★★ **THE LOG JAM.** *1484 NY 9, Site 1 (12845). 518/798-1155.* Specializes in steak, seafood, prime rib. Salad bar. Hrs: 11:30 am-9:30 pm; July, Aug: Fri, Sat to 10 pm. Closed Thanksgiving, Dec 25. Res accepted. Bar. Lunch $5.95-$10.50, dinner $13.95-$19.95. Child's menu. Lobster tank. Rustic decor. Cr cds: A, C, D, DS, MC, V.
D SC ⛏

★★★ **MONTCALM SOUTH.** *1415 NY 9 (12845). 518/793-6601. www. menumart.com/montcalm.* Continental menu. Specializes in veal, prime rib, seafood. Own baking. Hrs: 11:45 am-2:30 pm, 5-9:45 pm; Sun 11:45 am-9:30 pm. Closed hols. Res accepted. Bar. Wine list. Lunch $4.95-$7.95, dinner $11.95-$29.95. Child's menu. Fireplace. Family-owned. Cr cds: A, C, D, DS, MC, V.
D

Lake Luzerne

See also Glens Falls, Lake George Village

Pop 3,219 **Elev** 610 ft **Area code** 518 **Zip** 12846

Information Chamber of Commerce, 79 Main St, PO Box 222; 518/696-3500

Web www.lakeluzernechamber.org

Lumbering and papermaking formed the economic background of Lake Luzerne, now an all-year resort. In addition to being on the small lake for which it is named, it is near Great Sacandaga Lake, another popular area for summer and winter sports.

What to See and Do

Bow Bridge. Parabolic bridge (1895) spans the Hudson and Sacandaga rivers. The only remaining semideck lenticular iron truss bridge, typical of the late 19th-century iron bridges in New York State. Phone 518/696-3500.

Rockwell Falls & Chasm. Hudson River flows over rocks causing a great rush of water; joins the Sacandaga River at the end of the falls and chasm. Viewed from bridge. SE of town via Northway, exit 21.

Swimming, boating, fishing. On Lake Vanare, Lake Luzerne, and Great

Sacandaga Lake. Boat launching sites (free) on the Hudson River, at Fourth Lake Campground and on the Sacandaga, North Shore Rd. Phone 518/582-4451.

White water rafting. Down the Sacandaga River. Several outfitters operate in the area. Seasons usually Memorial Day-Labor Day; inquire locally.

Motels/Motor Lodges

★ **ISLAND VIEW MOTEL.** *302 Lake Ave (12846). 518/696-3079. www. islandviewmotel.com.* 10 rms, 4 kits. June-Sept: S, D $65-$75; each addl $5; kit. units $70-$73; under 12 free; wkly rates; lower rates rest of yr. Crib free. TV; cable. Complimentary coffee. Restaurant nearby. Ck-out 11 am. Lawn games. Some refrigerators. Picnic tables, grills. Private beach, boats. Cr cds: A, DS, MC, V.
🐾 🏋 🏊 🔥

★★ **SARATOGA ROSE.** *4274 Rockwell St, Hadley (12835). 518/696-2861; toll-free 800/942-5025. www. saratogarose.com.* 6 rms, shower only, 2 story. No rm phones. Mid-June-Labor Day: S, D $85-$175; each addl $8.50-$17.50; ski, golf plans; wkends, hols (2-day min); lower rates rest of yr. Children over 10 yrs only. TV in common rm; VCR avail (movies). Complimentary full bkfst. Restaurant from 5 pm. Ck-out 11 am, ck-in 3 pm. Business servs avail. Downhill ski 12 mi; x-country ski 15 mi. Many in-rm whirlpools, fireplaces. Built in 1885 as wedding gift for a town founder's daughter. Antiques. Cr cds: A, DS, MC, V.
🅳 🐾 🏋 🏊 🏊 🔥

B&B/Small Inn

★★★ **LAMPLIGHT INN BED & BREAKFAST.** *231 Lake Ave (12846). 518/696-5294; fax 518/696-5256; toll-free 800/262-4668. lamplightinn.com.* 15 rms, 2 story, 5 suites. MAP: S $89-$135; D $95-$155; each addl $25; wkly rates. Children over 12 yrs only. TV in sitting rm; cable (premium). Complimentary full bkfst; afternoon refreshments. Dining rm Sun 10:30 am-1 pm. Ck-out 11 am, ck-in 3 pm. Meeting rm. Business servs avail. Gift shop. Lawn games. Some fireplaces, in-rm whirlpools. Picnic tables. Victorian house (1890) with 12-ft beamed ceilings, chestnut woodwork, chestnut keyhole staircase crafted in England; wrap-around porch; antiques; library. Lake, beach 1 blk. Cr cds: A, MC, V.
🅳 🐾 🏋 🏊 🔥

Cottage Colony

★ **PINE POINT COTTAGES & MOTEL.** *1369 Lake Ave (12846). 518/696-3015.* 8 rms in motel, 7 A/C, 10 kit. cottages. Mid-May-late Oct: S $53-$59; D $59-$66; each addl $3-$5, kit. cottages for 2-4, $70-$96; wkly rates. Closed rest of yr. Crib free. TV; cable. Playground. Restaurant nearby. Ck-out 10 am. Free airport, bus depot transportation. Downhill ski 15 mi; x-country ski 1 mi. Lawn games. Many fireplaces. Porches. Picnic tables, grills. Private sand beach. Cr cds: MC, V.
🐾 🏊 🔥

Restaurants

★ **CIRO'S.** *1439 Lake Ave (12846). 518/696-2556. www.menumart.com/ ciros.* Italian, American menu. Specialties: fettucine Alfredo with frutti di mare, veal Anthony parmigiana. Soup bar. Hrs: 5-10 pm; winter 5-9 pm. Closed Thanksgiving, Dec 25; also Tues, Wed in winter. Res accepted. Bar. Dinner $6.95-$18.95. Child's menu. Cr cds: MC, V.
🅳

★ **DE FINO'S HERITAGE INN.** *61 Northwood Rd (12846). 518/696-3733.* Italian, American menu. Specialties: linguine with white or red clam sauce, stuffed cabbage, beef pot roast. Hrs: 5-10 pm; Sun 4-9 pm. Closed Mon-Tues; mid-Oct-mid-May, Mon-Thurs in May and June and after Labor Day-Columbus Day. Res accepted. Bar. Dinner $7.95-$14.95. Child's menu. Candlelight dining; fireplaces. Chef-owned. Cr cds: MC, V.
🅳 ➖

★ **WATERHOUSE.** *85 Lake Ave (12846). 518/696-3115. www. menumart.com/waterhouse.* Specializes in prime rib, seafood. Own pies. Hrs: 11:30 am-10 pm. Closed Thanksgiving, Dec 25. Res accepted. Bar. Lunch $1.95-$6.95, dinner $8.95-$18.95.

Child's menu. Outdoor dining. Family-owned. Cr cds: MC, V.

Lake Placid

(B-7) *See also Saranac Lake, Wilmington*

Pop 2,638 **Elev** 1,882 ft
Area code 518 **Zip** 12946
Information Essex County Visitors Bureau, Olympic Center, 216 Main St; 518/523-2445 or 800/447-5224
Web www.lakeplacid.com

Mount Marcy, the highest mountain in New York State (5,344 ft) rises in the Adirondack peaks that surround the town. On Lake Placid, the village also partly surrounds Mirror Lake. This is one of the most famous all-year vacation centers in the East and the site of the 1932 and 1980 Winter Olympics. The Intervale Olympic Ski Jump Complex has 229-foot and 296-foot ski jumps constructed for the 1980 games, now open to the public and used for training and competition.

What to See and Do

John Brown Farm Historic Site. Brown's final home; graves of the noted abolitionist, two sons, and ten others who died in the struggle to end slavery. (Late May-late Oct, Mon, Wed-Sun) John Brown Rd, 2 mi S, 1 mi off NY 73. Phone 518/523-3900. ¢

Lake Placid Center For the Arts. Concerts, films, art exhibits. Gallery (Tues-Sun). 91 Saranac Ave at Fawn Ridge. Phone 518/523-2512. **FREE**

Lake Placid Marina. One-hr scenic cruises. (Mid-May-mid-Oct) Lake St, 1 mi N on NY 86 to Mirror Lake Dr. Phone 518/523-9704. ¢¢¢

Olympic Arena and Convention Center. Built for the 1932 Winter Olympics and renovated for the 1980 Winter games. Winter and summer skating shows, family shows, hockey; public skating, concerts. Main St. Phone 518/523-1655.

Olympic Sports Complex (Mount Van Hoevenberg Recreation Area). Site of

1980 Winter Olympic Games. Bob-sled, luge, x-country, biathlon events. Championship bobsled and luge races most wkends in winter. X-country trails (33 mi) open to the public when not used for racing. Bobsled rides (mid-Dec-early Mar, Tues-Sun; fee); luge rides (mid-Dec-early Mar, wkends; fee). 7 mi SE on NY 73. Phone 518/523-1655.

Uihlein Sugar Maple Research-Extension Field Station. 4,000-tap sugar bush; maple syrup demonstrations, exhibits in Sugar House. Owned and operated by NY State College of Agriculture at Cornell University. (July-Labor Day, Tues-Fri; mid-Sept-mid-Oct, Fri; closed July 4) Schedule may vary. Bear Cub Rd. Phone 518/523-9337. **FREE**

Motels/Motor Lodges

★ **ALPINE AIR MOTEL.** *99 Saranac Ave (12946). 518/523-9261; fax 518/523-9273; toll-free 800/469-3663.* 24 rms, 6 with shower only, 1-2 story. Late-June-mid-Oct: S, D $50-$90; each addl $8; under 12 free; ski plans; wkends, hols (2-day min); lower rates rest of yr. Crib $8. TV; cable. Complimentary coffee in rms. Restaurant nearby. Ck-out 10:30 am. Downhill ski 8 mi; x-country ski 1 mi. Heated pool. Some balconies. Picnic tables. Cr cds: DS, MC, V.

★★ **ALPINE MOTOR INN.** *Rte 86 Wilmington Rd (12946). 518/523-2180; fax 518/523-1724. www.alpine-inn.com.* 18 rms, 2 story. July-Aug, ski season: S, D $56-$78; kit. units $68-$82; under 12 free; lower rates rest of yr. Crib $3. TV; cable (premium). Heated pool. Restaurant 5-9:30 pm. Bar 3 pm-midnight. Ck-out 11 am. 45-hole golf privileges opp. Downhill ski 8 mi; x-country ski 1 mi. Sun deck. Some refrigerators. Balconies. Cr cds: A, D, DS, MC, V.

★★ **ART DEVLINS OLYMPIC MOTOR INN.** *348 Main St. (12946). 518/523-3700; fax 518/523-3893. artdevlins.com.* 40 rms, 2 story. S, D $48-$108; each addl $6; higher rates special events. Crib free. Pet accepted. TV; cable. Pool; wading pool. Complimentary continental

Lake Placid

bkfst. Ck-out 11 am. Airport, bus depot transportation. Downhill ski 8 mi; x-country ski 2 mi. Refrigerators; some in-rm whirlpools. Some balconies. Sun deck. Cr cds: A, D, DS, MC, V.

★ **THE BARK EATER INN.** *Alstead Hill Rd, Keene (12942). 518/576-2221; fax 518/576-2071; toll-free 800/232-1607. www.barkeater.com.* 19 rms, 7 share baths, 3 buildings, 1-2 story. No rm phones. D $75-$136; each addl $36; under 3 free; MAP avail; wkly rates; ski, riding packages. Crib free. TV in living rm; cable (premium). Complimentary full bkfst. Dining rm 8-9 am, dinner (1 sitting) 7 pm. Box lunches. Setups. Ck-out 11 am, ck-in 1 pm. Business servs avail. Downhill ski 15 mi; x-country ski on site, rentals. Picnic tables, grills. Former stagecoach stop built in early 1800s; antiques. Spacious farm with 5-acre pond. Horse stables. Polo field. Family-owned since 1936. Totally nonsmoking. Cr cds: A, D, DS, MC, V.

★★ **BEST WESTERN GOLDEN ARROW.** *150 Main St (12946). 518/523-3353; fax 518/523-8063; res 800/528-1234. www.golden-arrow. com.* 130 rms, 2-4 story. July-mid-Oct, late Dec-Mar: S $69-$139; D $89-$159; each addl $10; suites $99-$220; under 12 free; MAP avail; ski plans; lower rates rest of yr. Crib $6. Pet accepted; $25. TV; cable. Indoor pool; wading pool, whirlpool. Restaurant 7 am-9 pm. Bar 11-2 am; entertainment Wed-Sat (in season). Ck-out 11 am. Meeting rms. Business servs avail. In-rm modem link. Shopping arcade. Covered parking. Free airport transportation. Downhill ski 9 mi; x-country ski on site. Exercise rm; sauna. Racquetball. Paddle boats, canoes. Rec rm. Some fireplaces; refrigerators avail. Private patios, balconies. Picnic tables, grill. Private beach. Cr cds: A, C, D, DS, ER, MC, V.

★ **ECONO LODGE.** *Cascade Rd (12946). 518/523-2817; res 800/553-2666. www.econolodge.com.* 61 rms, 2 story. Mid-June-mid-Oct, late Dec-Mar: S $55-$95; D $65-$105; each addl $5; under 18 free; lower rates rest of yr. Crib free. TV; cable. Indoor pool; whirlpool. Complimentary coffee in lobby. Restaurant nearby. Ck-out 11 am. Coin lndry. Meeting rm. Business servs avail. Downhill/x-country ski 1 mi. Game rm. Balconies. Picnic tables. Cr cds: A, C, D, DS, JCB, MC, V.

★ **MOUNTAIN VIEW.** *140 Main St (12946). 518/523-2439; fax 518/523-8974; toll-free 800/499-2668. lake placidlodging.com.* 18 rms, 2 story. July-Oct, ski season: S, D $78-$105; each addl $5-$10; higher rates hols, special events; lower rates rest of yr. Crib free. TV; cable. Restaurant nearby. Ck-out 11 am. Health club privileges. Refrigerators; microwaves avail. Balconies. Overlooks Lake Placid Village and Mirror Lake. Cr cds: A, D, DS, MC, V.
🏊 ✈ 🛶 🔥 SC

★ **NORTHWAY MOTEL.** *5 Wilmington Rd (12946). 518/523-3500.* 14 rms. No A/C. Mid-June-mid-Oct, mid-Dec-Mar: S, D $65-$80; each addl $5; family units $75; under 14 free; lower rates rest of yr. Crib free. TV; cable. Pool. Playground. Complimentary coffee in lobby. Restaurant nearby. Ck-out 11 am. Downhill ski 9 mi; x-country ski adj. Lawn games. Cr cds: A, DS, MC, V.
D 🏊 🎿 🛶 🛶 🔥

★★ **RAMADA INN.** *8-12 Saranac Ave (12946). 518/523-2587; fax 518/523-2328; res 888/298-2054. www.ramada.com.* 90 rms, 3 story. Mid-July-early Sept, late Sept-mid-Oct, late Dec-early Jan: S $55-$130; D $60-$140; each addl $10; under 18 free; ski, golf plans; higher rates hols; lower rates rest of yr. Crib free. Pet accepted, some restrictions. TV; cable, VCR avail. Indoor pool; whirlpool. Coffee in rms. Restaurant 7 am-10 pm. Bar 4:30 pm-1 am. Ck-out noon. Business servs avail. In-rm modem link. Downhill ski 10 mi; x-country ski 1 mi. Exercise equipt. Game rm. Some balconies. Cr cds: A, C, D, DS, MC, V.
D 🏊 🎿 🛶 🛶 🎿 🛶 🔥

★ **SCHULTE'S HOTEL.** *Rte 73 Cascade (12946). 518/523-3532.* 30 units, 14 with shower only, 15 kit. cottages. Some A/C. Some rm phones. Mid-June-mid-Sept, mid-Dec-mid-Mar: S, D $68-$78; each addl $9; kit. cottages $48-$85; under 13 free; wkly rates; higher rates some hols; lower rates rest of yr. Crib free. Pet accepted, some restrictions; $5. TV; cable. Restaurant nearby. Ck-out 11 am. Downhill ski 7 mi; x-country ski 2 mi. Pool. Playground. Lawn games.

Many refrigerators. Some balconies. Picnic tables, grills. Cr cds: A, MC, V.
🛶 🎿 🛶 🔥

★ **TOWN & COUNTRY MOTOR INN.** *65-67 Saranac Ave (12946). 518/523-9268; fax 518/523-8058; toll-free 888/523-6640. www.tcmotorinn.com.* 24 rms, 2 story. June-Oct, Dec-Mar: S $52-$72; D $62-$82; each addl $5; cottage/apt $140; family rates; golf plans; lower rates rest of yr. Crib $5. TV; cable. Heated pool. Complimentary bkfst. Restaurant nearby. Ck-out 11 am. Downhill ski 8 mi; x-country ski ½ mi. Refrigerators. Balconies. Picnic tables, grills. Cr cds: A, DS, MC, V.
🛶 🎿 🛶 🎿 🛶 🛶 🔥

★★ **WILDWOOD ON THE LAKE.** *88 Saranac Ave (12946). 518/523-2624; fax 518/523-3248; toll-free 800/841-6378. wildwoodmotel.com.* 35 rms, 1-2 story, 6 kit. cottages. July-Oct: S, D $48-$88; suites, kit. units $58-$150; each addl $6; cottages $860-$900/wk; under 15 free; higher rates: hol wkends, special events; lower rates rest of yr. Crib free. TV; cable. Heated pool; outdoor natural pool, wading pool, whirlpool. Playground. Complimentary coffee in rms. Restaurant adj 6 am-10 pm; open 24 hrs in season. Ck-out 11 am. Downhill ski 10 mi; x-country ski ½ mi. Sauna. Lawn games. Rowboats, paddle boats, canoes free to guests. Refrigerators; some in-rm whirlpools, some fireplaces. Private patios, balconies. Picnic tables, grill. On beach. Cr cds: A, C, D, DS, MC, V.
🛶 🎿 🛶 🛶 🔥

Hotels

★★ **ADIRONDACK INN BY THE LAKE.** *217 Main St (12946). 518/523-2424; fax 518/523-2425; toll-free 800/556-2424. www.lakeplacid.com/adkinn.* 49 rms, 2 story. Wkends late Dec-mid-Mar, early July-Oct: S $59-$144; D $69-$154; each addl $12; suites $150-$200; kit. unit $99-$130; ski, golf plans; lower rates rest of yr. Crib $10. TV; cable. 2 pools, 1 indoor; whirlpool. Playground. Restaurant 7 am-10 pm. Bar 5 pm-1 am in season. Ck-out 11 am. Meeting rms. Business servs avail. Downhill ski 8 mi; x-country ski 1 mi. Exercise equipt; sauna. Rec rm. Refrigerators. Many balconies. Opp Olympic Arena and Convention Hall. Cr cds: A, D, MC, V.

D ⊠ ⊠ ⚡ ⊠ ⊠

Resorts

★★★ HILTON LAKE PLACID
RESORT. *1 Mirror Lake Dr (12946). 518/523-4411; fax 518/523-1120; res 800/445-8667. lphilton.com.* 176 rms, 5 story. Mid-June-mid-Oct: S $59-$149; D $69-$159; each addl $12; family rates; ski, golf plans; lower rates rest of yr. Pet accepted. TV. 4 pools, 2 indoor; whirlpools, poolside serv. Restaurant 7-10:30 am, noon 2 pm, 5:30-9 pm. Rm serv 7 am-9 pm. Bar 11-2 am; entertainment Fri, Sat. Ck-out noon. Meeting rms. Business servs avail. Bellhops. Covered parking. Downhill ski 8 mi; x-country ski 1 mi. Exercise equipt. Boats. Game rm. Rec rm. Many balconies. Some rms on beach. Cr cds: A, C, D, DS, ER, JCB, MC, V.

D ⚡ ⚡ ⚡ ⊠ ⚡ ⊠ ⊠ SC

★ HOWARD JOHNSON RESORT
INN. *90 Saranac Ave (12946). 518/523-9555; fax 518/523-4765; res 800/446-4656. www.hojo.com.* 92 rms, 2 story. July-mid-Sept and mid-Dec-Mar: S, D $85-$140; each addl $10; suites $110-$150; under 18 free; golf plans; lower rates rest of yr. Crib free. Pet accepted. TV; cable (premium). Indoor pool; whirlpool. Coffee in rms. Restaurant 7 am-11 pm. Bar from noon. Ck-out noon. Coin lndry. Meeting rms. Business servs avail. Sundries. Tennis. Downhill ski 10 mi; x-country ski on site. Rec rm. Lawn games. Balconies. Picnic tables, grills. Cr cds: A, D, DS, MC, V.

D ⚡ ⚡ ⊠ ⊠ ⚡ ⚡

★★★★ LAKE PLACID LODGE.
Whiteface Inn Rd (12946). 518/523-2700; fax 518/523-1124. www.lake placidlodge.com. This lakeside lodge, a sister to The Point, is a charming Adirondack retreat. Beautifully appointed guest rooms have down comforters and working fireplaces. A fine restaurant offers indoor or outdoor seating. Special programs include tai chi, taught in the mornings on the dock. 17 cabins. No elvtr. S, $300; D $800; each addl $50; cabins $300-$650; wkends (2-day min), hols (3-day min). Crib free. Pet

accepted; $50/day. Complimentary full bkfst, coffee in lobby. Restaurant (see LAKE PLACID LODGE). Box lunches. Bar. Ck-out noon. Meeting rms. Business servs avail. In-rm modem link. Bellhops. Concierge. Gift shop. Tennis privileges. Golf privileges. Downhill ski 10 mi; x-country ski on site. Game rm. Refrigerator, wet bar in cabins; some fireplaces. Some balconies. Picnic tables, fire pit. Cr cds: A, MC, V.

D ⚡ ⚡ ⚡ ⊠ ⚡ ⚡ ⊠ ⊠ ⊠

★★ LAKE PLACID RESORT HOLI-
DAY INN. *1 Olympic Dr (12946). 518/523-2556; fax 518/523-9410; toll-free 800/874-1980. www.lakeplacid resort.com.* 199 rms, 4 story. July-Aug: S, D $59-$199; each addl $10; under 19 free; MAP avail; wkend rates; ski, golf plans; varied lower rates rest of yr. Crib free. Pet accepted. TV; cable. Heated pool; whirlpool. Playground. Coffee in rms. Restaurant 7 am-10 pm. Bar 11-2 am. Ck-out 11 am. Meeting rms. Business servs avail. In-rm modem link. Gift shop. Rec rm. Tennis. Golf privileges, putting green. Downhill ski 9 mi; x-country ski on site. Exercise rm; sauna. Refrigerators, microwaves. Many balconies. On hilltop overlooking lake. Cr cds: A, C, D, DS, ER, JCB, MC, V.

D ⚡ ⚡ ⚡ ⊠ ⚡ ⚡ ⚡ ⊠ ⚡ ⊠ ⊠ SC

★★★ MIRROR LAKE INN RESORT
AND SPA. *5 Mirror Lake Dr (12946). 518/523-2544; fax 518/523-2871. www.mirrorlakeinn.com.* 128 inn rms, 4 story, 17 rms in lakeside bldg. S, D $155-$240; each addl $15; suites $275-$345; under 18 free; MAP avail; ski plans. Crib free. TV; cable. 2 heated pools, 1 indoor; wading pool, whirlpool. Complimentary coffee; afternoon refreshments. Dining rm (see AVERILL CONWELL DINING ROOM). Bar noon-2 am. Ck-out noon. Meeting rm. Business servs avail. Valet serv. Gift shop. Beauty shop. Tennis. Downhill ski 10 mi; x-country ski 1 mi. Row boats, paddle boats, canoeing. Exercise equipt; sauna. Rec rm. Refrigerators, fireplaces. Some balconies. Private sand beach. On 8 acres. Cr cds: A, C, D, DS, MC, V.

D ⚡ ⚡ ⚡ ⊠ ⚡ ⊠ ⊠ ⊠ ⚡

B&Bs/Small Inns

★★ INTERLAKEN LODGE & RESTAURANT. *15 Interlaken Ave (12946).* 518/523-3180; fax 518/523-0117; toll-free 800/428-4369. *www. selectregistry.com.* 11 rms, 3 story. No A/C. No rm phones. S $130; D $150; each addl $15; MAP avail; wkends (2-day min), hol wkends (3-day min). Children over 5 yrs only. Pet accepted, some restrictions. TV in sitting rm; cable. Complimentary full bkfst; afternoon refreshments. Dining rm 6-9 pm; closed Tues, Wed. Ck-out 11 am, ck-in 3 pm. Gift shop. Downhill/x-country ski 8 mi. Health club privileges. Some balconies. Picnic tables. Built in 1906; turn-of-the-century furnishings. Cr cds: A, MC, V.

★ ★ ★ ★ ★ ★

★ PLACID BAY INN ON LAKE PLACID. *70 Saranac Ave (12946).* 518/523-2001; fax 518/523-2001. *www.placidbay.com.* 20 rms, 2 story, 8 kit. units, 2 cottages. Late June-Labor Day, hol wks and winter wkends: S $55-$75; D $65-$85; each addl $5; kit. units $68-$98; cottages (1-3 bedrm) $130-$200; family, wkly rates; lower rates rest of yr. Crib free. TV; cable. Heated pool. Playground. Restaurant nearby. Ck-out 11 am. Bus depot transportation. Picnic tables, grill. Fishing charters and guide serv. Paddleboats, canoes. Cr cds: A, DS, MC, V.

D ★ ★ ★ ★ ★ SC

Restaurants

★★★ AVERIL CONWELL DINING ROOM. *5 Mirror Lake Dr (12946).* 518/523-2544. *www.mirrorlakeinn. com.* Specializes in roasted rack of lamb, venison sirloin saddleback, hickory-style home-smoked shrimp. Own baking. Hrs: 7:30-10 am, 5:30-9 pm; Sat, Sun 7:30-11 am, 5:30-9 pm. Res accepted. Bar. A la carte entrees: bkfst $3.50-$9.95, dinner $16.95-$29.95. Child's menu. Pianist Fri and Sat. Outdoor dining. Formal, early American decor; view of lake. Family-owned. Totally nonsmoking. Cr cds: A, D, DS, MC, V.

D

★★★ LAKE PLACID LODGE. *Whiteface Inn Rd (12946).* 518/523-2700. *www.lakeplacidlodge.com.* Contemporary American menu. Hrs: 7:30-10:30 am, noon-2:30 pm, 6-9 pm; Fri, Sat 6-10 pm. Res accepted. Bar. A la carte entrees: bkfst $12.95, lunch $7.95-$14.95, dinner $16-$31. Outdoor dining. View of lake. Cr cds: A, MC, V.

D

★★ LE BISTRO LALIBERTE. *51 Main St (12946).* 518/523-3680. French menu. Specializes in lamb, fresh seafood. Hrs: 5-10 pm; summer also 11:30 am-3 pm. Closed Easter, Thanksgiving, Dec 25; Mon in Nov; also Apr. Res accepted. Bar. Lunch $5.50-$8.95, dinner $15-$22. Child's menu. Street parking. Outdoor dining. Bistro atmosphere; open kitchen. Cr cds: C, D, DS, MC, V.

★

Letchworth State Park

(E-3) *See also Avon, Geneseo*

(Entrances at Castile, Mount Morris, Perry, and Portageville)

In this 14,344-acre park are 17 miles of the Genesee River Gorge, sometimes called the Grand Canyon of the East. Sheer cliffs rise 600 feet at some points, and the river roars over three major falls, one of them 107 feet high. The park has a variety of accommodations, including an inn and motel, a 270-site tent and trailer camping area, and 82 camping cabins (ranging from one room to family size). Standard fees.

Swimming pools with bathhouses (mid-June-Labor Day), fishing, whitewater rafting, hot-air ballooning, nature and hiking trails (year-round), outstanding fall foliage. Cross-country skiing, snowmobiling, snow-tubing, picnicking at eight areas with tables, fireplaces, shelters, rest rooms; playground. Recreation programs. No pet in cabin areas and part of camping area. Standard fees.

The William Pryor Letchworth Museum, the grave of Mary Jemison, and a restored Seneca Indian Council

House are in the park (mid-May-Oct, daily; donation).

For detailed information contact Letworth State Park, 1 Letchworth State Park, Castile 14427; 716/493-3600.

B&Bs/Small Inns

★ **BROMAN'S GENESEE FALLS INN.** *Main and Hamilton sts, Portageville (14536). 716/493-2484; fax 716/468-5654.* 10 rms, 3 story. No rm phones. S, D $57-$77; each addl $15. Complimentary full bkfst. Restaurant (see BROMAN'S GENESEE FALLS INN). Bar. Ck-out 11 am, ck-in 2 pm. Inn since 1870s. Cr cds: MC, V.

★★★ **GLEN IRIS INN.** *7 Letchworth State Pk, Castile (14427). 716/493-2622; fax 716/493-5803. www.glenirisinn.com.* 16 rms in inn, 3 story, 7 kit. No rm phones. Apr-Oct: S, D $70; each addl $7.50; suites $125-$135; kit. units for 2, $60. Closed rest of yr. TV in motel rms; also in library of main building; VCR avail. Playground. Restaurant (see GLEN IRIS INN). Serv bar. Ck-out noon, ck-in 2 pm. Meeting rms. Business servs avail. Gift shop. Some refrigerators. Picnic tables, grill. Former residence of William Pryor Letchworth (1860s); antiques. Overlooks falls. Cr cds: A, MC, V.

★★ **JUST A PLANE BED & BREAKFAST.** *11152 Rte 19A, Fillmore (14735). 716/567-8338.* 4 rms, 1 A/C, 3 with shower only, 3 story, 1 suite. No rm phones. S $45; D $57; each addl $12; suites $57; under 2 free. TV in common rm; VCR avail (movies). Complimentary full bkfst. Ck-out 11 am, ck-in 4 pm. X-country ski on-site. Picnic tables, grills. Built in 1926; family-owned farmhouse. Totally nonsmoking. Cr cds: A, MC, V.

Restaurants

★ **BROMAN'S GENESEE FALLS INN.** *Main and Hamilton sts at Hwy 436 (14536). 716/493-2484.* Continental menu. Specializes in seafood, steak. Hrs: 8:30-1:30 am. Res accepted. Bar 11-2 am; Sun to 1 am. Bkfst $5, lunch $3.95-$8.95, dinner $11.95-$21. Child's menu. Victorian decor; antiques. Cr cds: MC, V.

★★★ **GLEN IRIS INN.** *7 Letchworth State Park (14427). 716/493-2622. www.glenirisinn.com.* Continental menu. Specializes in prime rib, venison, seafood. Hrs: 8-10 am, noon-2 pm, 5:30-8 pm; Fri, Sat 9 pm. Closed 1st wkend Nov-Easter. Serv bar. Bkfst $5.95-$8.95; lunch

Genesee River Gorge at Letchworth State Park

$5.50-$9, dinner $15-$25. Child's
menu. Cr cds: A, MC, V.

D

★★ **OLD HEIDELBERG.** *3755 S
Main, Warsaw (14569). 716/786-5427.*
German, American menu. Specialties:
Kasseler rippchen, rouladen, sauerbraten. Hrs: 11:30 am-2 pm, 5-9 pm;
Fri to 10 pm; Sat 5-10 pm; Sun noon-
7 pm. Closed Mon; Jan 1, Thanksgiving, Dec 24-25. Res accepted. Serv
bar. Lunch $4.25-$8.50, dinner
$10.50-$18.95. Child's menu. Extensive selection of German beers. Cr
cds: A, MC, V.

D

Liberty

(F-7) *See also Catskill Park, Monticello,
Roscoe*

Pop 9,632 **Elev** 1,509 ft
Area code 845 **Zip** 12754
Information Chamber of Commerce,
PO Box 147; 845/292-1878

Near the junction of the Willowemoc
and Beaverkill rivers and on the edge
of the Catskill Forest Preserve, this
area offers good hunting and trout
fishing, camping, hiking, and sightseeing.

What to See and Do

NY State Catskill Fish Hatchery.
Ponds featuring trout of various sizes
as well as breeder trout. (Oct-mid-
June daily, mid-June-Sept wkend
mornings) 11 mi NW on Fish Hatchery Rd near DeBruce. Phone 845/439-
4328. **FREE**

Motels/Motor Lodges

★ **DAYS INN.** *25 Sullivan Ave
(12754). 845/292-7600; fax 845/292-
3303; toll-free 800/329-7466. www.
daysinn.com.* 120 rms, 2 story. June-
Sept: S, D $70-$85; each addl $6;
under 12 free; lower rates rest of yr.
Crib free. TV; cable (premium). 2
pools; 1 indoor. Complimentary continental bkfst. Restaurant 11:30 am-3
pm, 5-10 pm. Bar; entertainment Fri,

Sat. Ck-out 11 am. Meeting rms.
Business servs avail. Downhill/x-
country ski 15 mi. Game rm. Cr cds:
A, C, D, DS, MC, V.

★ **LANZA'S COUNTRY INN.** *839
Shandelee Rd, Livingston Manor
(12758). 845/439-5070; fax 845/439-
5003.* 8 air-cooled rms, 2 story. No
rm phones. S $54-$62; D $75-$84;
each addl $15; under 5 free. TV in
sitting rm. Complimentary full bkfst.
Restaurant. Ck-out, ck-in noon.
Downhill ski 10 mi; x-country ski on
site. Picnic tables. Built 1900; many
antiques. Greenhouse sitting room.
Cr cds: D, DS, MC, V.

Restaurant

★ **VILLAGE SQUARE CAFE.** *1980
NY 52 (12754). 845/292-2233.* Hrs:
11 am-3 pm. Closed Sun; also Jan 1,
Thanksgiving, Dec 25. Res required
July, Aug. Wine, beer. A la carte
entrees: lunch $6.50-$10.25. Specializes in chicken, pasta. Child's menu.
Parking. Outdoor dining. Totally
nonsmoking. Cr cds: DS, MC, V.

D

Lockport

(D-2) *See also Batavia, Niagara Falls*

Settled 1816 **Pop** 22,279 **Elev** 600 ft
Area code 716 **Zip** 14094
Information Chamber of Commerce,
151 W Genessee St; 716/433-3828

The town was originally settled
around a series of locks of the Erie
Canal, now the New York State Barge
Canal.

What to See and Do

Canal Bridge. Claimed to be one of
the widest single-span bridges (399½
ft) in the world. View of the locks'
operation, raising and lowering
barges and pleasure craft more than
60 ft. Cottage St.

Colonel William Bond House. Pre-Victorian home (1824) was built with bricks made on site. Restored, with 12 furnished rms; of special interest are the kitchen and the children's garret. (Mar-Dec, Thurs, Sat, and Sun afternoons) 143 Ontario St. Phone 716/434-7433. **FREE**

Kenan Center. Art gallery and recreation/sports arena. Gallery (Sept-May, daily; June-Aug, Mon-Fri and Sun); Taylor Theater (fee); garden and orchard, herb garden. 433 Locust St. Phone 716/433-2617. **Donation**

Niagara County Historical Center. An 1860 brick house with antiques; Erie Canal artifacts. Pioneer Building contains Native American collection, pioneer artifacts; Washington Hunt Law Office (1835); Niagara Fire Company #1, with 1834 and 1836 pumpers. 19th-century farming equipt. (Thurs-Sun; closed hols) 215 Niagara St. Phone 716/434-7433. **FREE**

Motel/Motor Lodge

★ ★ **LOCKPORT MOTEL.** *315 S Transit St (14094). 716/434-5595; fax 716/433-0105. www.lockportmotel. com.* 65 rms. S $54-$66; D $60-$80; each addl $2; suites $99-$150. Crib $5. TV; VCR avail (free movies). Pool; lifeguard. Complimentary coffee. Restaurant 6 am-10 pm. Ck-out 11 am. Business servs avail. In-rm modem link. Refrigerators, microwaves. Whirlpool in suites. Cr cds: A, C, D, DS, MC.

🄳 🛉 ⚡ 🌊 🛏 🔥

Restaurant

★ **GARLOCK'S.** *35 S Transit St (14094). 716/433-5595.* Specializes in prime rib, steak, seafood. Hrs: 5 pm-midnight; Sun 3-10 pm. Closed Thanksgiving, Dec 25. Res accepted. Bar to 1 am. Dinner $8.95-$29.95. Child's menu. In mid-1800s building. Collection of decanters. Cr cds: A, DS, MC, V.

🄳 🍽

Long Island (G-I - F-4)

Long Island stretches 118 miles east by northeast from the edge of Manhattan to the lonely dunes of Montauk. Much of the island is ideal resort country, with vast white beaches, quiet bays, coves, and woods.

At the eastern tip, Montauk Light stands on its headland; on the southwestern shore is Coney Island. New York City sprawls over the whole of Long Island's two westernmost counties—Queens and Kings (boroughs of Queens and Brooklyn).

Nassau County, adjoining the city, is made up of suburbs filled with residential communities. Eastward in Suffolk County, city influence eases, and there are firms that have attracted substantial local populations. Potatoes and the famous Long Island duckling are still raised here alongside farms for horse-breeding and the vineyards producing Long Island wines.

Long Island has many miles of sandy barrier beaches along the south shore, with fine swimming and surf casting. The bays behind these make natural small-boat harbors. On the more tranquil waters of the north shore is a series of deeper harbors along Long Island Sound, many of them with beaches and offering good sailing opportunities. The island has played a major role in US history from the early 17th century; the record of this is carefully preserved in many buildings, some 300 years old. Few regions offer such varied interests in so small an area. The Long Island Railroad conducts tours to points of interest on the island (late May-early November). For information on these escorted day excursions, write to the Long Island Railroad, Sales and Promotion Department, #1723, Jamaica 11435; phone 718/217-LIRR. For further information and special events contact the Long Island Convention & Visitors Bureau, 350 Vanderbilt Motor Pkwy, Suite 103, Hauppage 11788; 800/441-4601.

Long Island towns listed in *Mobil Travel Guide* are Amagansett, Amityville, Bay Shore, Bethpage, East Hampton, Fire Island National Seashore, Floral Park, Garden City, Glen Cove, Great Neck, Greenport, Hampton Bays, Hempstead, Huntington, Jericho, Jones Beach State Park, Massapequa Park, Montauk, Northort, Oyster Bay, Plainview, Port Jefferson, Port Washington, Riverhead, Robert Moses State Park, Rockville Centre, Roslyn, Sag Harbor, Sayville, Shelter Island, Smithtown, Southampton, Southold, Stony Brook, Westbury, and Westhampton Beach.

What to See and Do

P.S. I Contemporary Art Center. A premier center for art on the cutting edge; specializes in the avant-garde, conceptual, and experimental; housed in a newly renovated, four-story building that was once a public school; changing exhibits. (Mon, Thurs-Sun; closed hols) 22-25 Jackson Ave, at 46th Ave, Long Island City. Phone 718/784-2084. ¢¢

Long Lake

(B-7) *See also Blue Mountain Lake, Tupper Lake*

Pop 852 **Elev** 1,683 ft **Area code** 518 **Zip** 12847

Located in the heart of the Adirondack Park, this area is a wilderness setting for water sports, hunting, fishing, cross-country skiing, and snowmobiling.

Motels/Motor Lodges

★ **LONG LAKE MOTEL.** *Boat Landing Rd (12847). 518/624-2613; fax 518/624-2576. www.motellonglake. com.* 8 motel rms, 9 cottages, 7 kits. No A/C. S, D $70; each addl $10; kit. cottages for 2-4, $475-$800/wk. Closed mid-Oct-mid-May. Crib $7.50. TV; cable. Coffee in rms. Restaurant nearby. Ck-out 10:30 am; cottages 10 am. Lawn games. Picnic tables, grills. Private sand beach. Private screened patios overlook woods, lake. Cr cds: A, MC, V.
🐾 ⚡ ✈ 🔥

★ **SANDY POINT.** *Rtes 28 and 30 N (12847). 518/624-3871. www.sandy pointmotel.com.* 11 rms, 2 story, 6 kits. No A/C. Mid-June-Labor Day, fall foliage season: S, D $75; each addl $10; kit. units $12 addl (4-7-day min); higher rates special events;

lower rates rest of yr. Crib free. TV; cable. Complimentary coffee in rms. Restaurant nearby. Ck-out 10:30 am. Sauna. Screened-in patios, balconies. Private sand beach, dockage, boat rentals. Cr cds: A, DS, MC, V.
🐾 ⚡ 🔥

★ **SHAMROCK.** *Rtes 28 N and 30 (12847). 518/624-3861; fax 518/624-9803.* 10 motel rms, 7 kit. cottages (3-day min). No A/C. Memorial Day-Labor Day: S, D $50-$65; each addl $10; cottages for 2-6, $475-$600/wk; family rates; higher rates special events; lower rates after Labor Day-Oct. Closed rest of yr. Crib $5. TV, some B/W. Playground. Complimentary coffee in rms. Ck-out 10:30 am. Coin lndry. Rec rm. Lawn games. Refrigerators. Picnic tables, grill. Private sand beach. Paddle boats, canoes. Cr cds: A, DS, MC, V.
D 🐾 🔥

Mahopac

(G-8) *See also Brewster, Garrison, Peekskill, Tarrytown, West Point (US Military Academy), White Plains*

Pop 8,478 **Elev** 650 ft **Area code** 914 **Zip** 10541

What to See and Do

Mahopac Farm and Museum. Collection of antiques and memorabilia dating from 1800s to early 1900s displayed in a barn on a 31-acre working farm. (Daily; closed hols) NY 6 and Baldwin Place Rd, in Baldwin Place. Phone 845/628-9298. ¢ Adj and incl in admission is

Old Borden Farm. Country store, museum, farm animals. (Daily; closed hols)

Restaurant

★ **HEIDI'S BRAUHAUS.** *241 US 6N (10541). 914/628-9795. www.heidis brauhaus.com.* German, American menu. Specialties: sauerbraten, Wiener schnitzel, jagerschnitzel. Salad bar. Hrs: 5-9 pm; Fri, Sat from 4-10 pm; Sun 3-9 pm; Sun brunch

11:30 am-2:30 pm. Closed Mon, Tues. Res accepted; required hols. Bar. Dinner $10.95-$16.95. Sun brunch $9.95. Child's menu. German artifacts on walls. Cr cds: A, MC, V.

Malone

(A-7) *See also Adirondack Park*

Pop 14,981 **Elev** 722 ft
Information Chamber of Commerce, 170 E Main St; 518/483-3760

What to See and Do

Franklin County Historical & Museum Society. Country store, craft rms; kitchen; exhibits, Victorian parlor. Kilburn Library, genealogical collection. (Sat afternoons or by appt) 51 Milwaukee St. Phone 518/483-2750. **Donation**

Skiing. Titus Mountain Ski Area. Two triple, five double chairlifts; handle tow; school, rentals. Snowmaking. Lodge. Twenty-six trails, longest run 3½ mi, vertical drop 1,350 ft. (Nov-Apr, daily) Duane Street Rd, 7 mi S. Phone 518/483-3740 or 800/848-8766. ¢¢¢¢

Special Event

Franklin County Fair. Malone Fairgrounds. Early-mid-Aug. Phone 518/483-0720.

Motels/Motor Lodges

★ **ECONO LODGE.** *227 W Main St (12953). 518/483-0500; fax 518/483-4356; toll-free 800/553-2666. www.maloneeconolodge.com.* 45 rms, 1-2 story. S $42-$47; D $48-$52; each addl $5. Crib $5. Pet accepted. TV; cable. Pool. Complimentary continental bkfst. Restaurant nearby. Ck-out 11 am. Meeting rms. Cr cds: A, D, DS, MC, V.

★ **FOUR SEASONS MOTEL.** *236 W Main St (12953). 518/483-3490; fax 518/483-3480; toll-free 877/299-3448. fourseasonsmalone.com.* 26 rms. S $38-$55; D $42-$65; each addl $5; golf, ski plans. TV; cable (premium). Pool. Complimentary continental bkfst. Cr

cds: A, C, D, DS, MC, V.

Hotel

★★ **CROSSROADS RESTAURANT HOTEL.** *Main St, Moira (12957). 518/529-7372; fax 518/529-6755.* 43 rms. S $40-$52; D $48-$55; each addl $8; under 12 free; wkend rates; golf, ski plans. Crib $10. TV; cable. Pool. Restaurant 7 am-midnight. Bar 5 pm-1 am; entertainment, dancing Tues-Sun. Ck-out 11 am. Meeting rms. Gift shop. Barber, beauty shop. Downhill ski 15 mi; x-country ski 20 mi. Cr cds: A, D, DS, MC, V.

Mamaroneck

(G-2) *See also New Rochelle, New York City, White Plains, Yonkers*

Pop 28,967 **Elev** 50 ft **Area code** 914 **Zip** 10543

Restaurants

★★ **ABIS JAPANESE RESTAURANT.** *406 Mamaroneck Ave (10543). 914/698-8777.* Japanese menu. Specializes in sushi, steak, seafood. Hrs: 11:30 am-2:30 pm, 5:30-9:30 pm; Fri to 10:30 pm; Sun brunch to 2:30 pm. Res accepted. Bar. Lunch $5.75-$10.50, dinner $9.95-$37. Sun brunch $16.95. Cr cds: A, D, MC, V.

★★ **CHEF ANTONIO.** *551 Halstead Ave (10543). 914/698-8610.* Italian menu. Specializes in pasta, seafood. Own desserts. Hrs: 11:30 am-10:30 pm; Fri to 11:30 pm; Sat 4-11:30 pm; Sun 1-10 pm. Closed Thanksgiving, Dec 25. Res accepted. Bar. Lunch $5.95-$10.95, dinner $13.95-$20.95. Child's menu. Modern Italian decor; archways and artwork. Cr cds: A, D, DS, MC, V.

★★ **LE PROVENCAL.** *436 Mamaroneck Ave (10543). 914/777-2324.* French menu. Specialties: sweetbread with olives and mushrooms, veal tenderloin, steak au poivre. Hrs: noon-2:30 pm, 6-10 pm; Fri to 11

m; Sat 6-11 pm; Sun 5-9 pm. Closed
Mon; also Jan 1, Dec 25. Res
accepted. Bar. Lunch $7.50-$17.50,
dinner $15.50-$24.50. Child's menu.
treet parking. Outdoor dining.
otally nonsmoking. Cr cds: A, DS,
MC, V.

0

Massapequa Park (L.I.)

3-2) *See also Amityville (L.I.), Bethpage
L.I.)*

Pop 17,499 **Elev** 20 ft **Area code** 516
Zip 11762

What to See and Do

Tackapausha Museum & Preserve.
Museum devoted to living things.
Small collection of live animals. An
80-acre tract of glacial outwash plain
maintained in natural state; many
small mammals. (Tues-Sat, also Sun
afternoons; closed hols) 4 mi SW on
Washington Ave in Seaford. Phone
516/571-7443. ¢

Massena

A-6) *See also Potsdam*

Settled 1792 **Pop** 13,121 **Elev** 210 ft
Area code 315 **Zip** 13662

Information Chamber of Commerce,
50 Main St; 315/769-3525

Web www.massenany.com

This is the site of the largest power
plant on the St. Lawrence Seaway.
Massena has two aluminum plants
and a major foundry.

As far back as 1903, a canal linking
the Grasse River and the St.
Lawrence Seaway has provided
70,000 horsepower for Massena-
based Alcoa operations.

What to See and Do

Akwesasne Museum. Museum is
devoted to the evolving cultural heritage of the Akwesasne Mohawk people. Incl clothing, tools, beadwork,
display of Mohawk basketry. Gift
shop. (Mon-Fri) 321 NY 37, Hogans-
borg. Phone 518/358-2461. ¢

Coles Creek State Park. Beach swimming, fishing (all yr), boating
(launch, marina, dock), picnicking,
playground, concession, tent and
trailer sites. (Mid-May-Labor Day)
Standard fees. 16 mi W on NY 37.
Phone 315/388-5636. ¢¢¢

Eisenhower Lock. Visitors view vessels navigating the lock, lock operations, as well as the vehicular
tunnel traffic under the lock. Interpretive center with films, photos.
Viewing deck. Picnic tables. (May-
Columbus Day, daily) E on NY 37,
then N on NY 131, W end of Wiley-
Dondero Ship Channel. Phone
315/769-2422. ¢

Robert Moses State Park. A different
state park with the same name (see)
is located on Fire Island, on the
south shore of Long Island. Overlook
from which Moses-Saunders Power
Dam can be viewed. Barnhart Island
Power House at main dam. Visitors
gallery and exhibit hall. Swimming
beach, bathhouse, fishing, boating
(launch, rentals, marina); x-country
skiing, picnicking, playground, tent
and trailer sites, cabins. Recreation
programs. (Mid-May-mid-Oct, daily)
Standard fees. E of town, 3 mi N of
NY 37. Contact PO Box 548. Phone
315/769-8663.

The St. Lawrence Seaway. A joint
project of the United States and
Canada, this is one of the world's
great public works and provides a
route for ocean ships from more
than 60 countries around the world
into mid-America—a "fourth coast."
Ships traverse seaway from Apr-Dec.
Locks can accommodate ships 730 ft
long and 76 ft wide. Ocean and lake
vessels carry bulk and general cargoes
of iron ore, grain, and coal to and
from points along the seaway's
8,300-mi shoreline. The seaway was
formally dedicated June 26, 1959, by
Queen Elizabeth II and President
Eisenhower.

Special Events

Heritage Festival. Massena Arena, NY 37. Antique and craft show; parade, entertainment, casino. First Sat June. Phone 315/769-3525.

Folklife Festival. Robert Moses State Park. Demonstrations, music, storytelling; ethnic foods. Second Sat Aug. Phone 315/769-3525.

Massena Car Show. Robert Moses State Park. Classic and antique car show. Late Aug. Phone 315/769-8663.

Motels/Motor Lodges

★ **ECONO LODGE.** *15054 State Hwy 37 (13662). 315/764-0246; fax 315/764-9615; toll-free 800/553-2666. www.econolodge.com.* 52 rms, 2 story. S $68; D $78-$80; suites $80-$100; under 18 free. Crib free. TV; cable (premium). Coffee in rms. Restaurant in season 6:30-10:30 am, 5-10 pm; Sun 7 am-2 pm. Ck-out 11 am. Meeting rm. Business servs avail. In-rm modem link. Exercise equipt. Refrigerators. Cr cds: A, D, DS, JCB, MC, V.

★ **SUPER 8.** *84 Grove St (13662). 315/764-1065; fax 315/764-9701; toll-free 800/800-8000. www.super8.com.* 42 rms, 3 story. No elvtr. June-Sept: S $48; D $56; under 12 free; lower rates rest of yr. Crib free. TV; cable, VCR avail. Complimentary coffee in lobby. Ck-out 11 am. Meeting rm. Business servs avail. In-rm modem link. Cr cds: A, D, DS, MC, V.

Restaurant

★★ **VILLAGE INN.** *Outer Maple St (13662). 315/769-6910.* Continental menu. Specializes in fresh fish, veal, prime rib. Hrs: 11:30 am-10 pm; Sun 4-9 pm. Closed Mon, Tues; Dec 25. Res accepted. Bar 11 am-midnight. Lunch $4.25-$12, dinner $9.50-$19.50. Child's menu. Family-owned. Cr cds: A, MC, V.

Middletown

(F-7) See also Goshen, Monroe, Monticello, Newburgh, Port Jervis

Pop 25,388 **Elev** 500 ft **Area code** 845 **Zip** 10940

Information Orange County Tourism, 30 Matthews St, Suite 111, Goshen 10924; 845/928-2946 or 800/762-8687.

Web www.orangetourism.org

Special Event

Orange County Fair. Agricultural and industrial exhibits, stock-car races, entertainment. Phone 845/343-4826. Mid-late July.

Motel/Motor Lodge

★ **SUPER 8 MOTEL.** *563 Rte 211 E (10940). 845/692-5828; res 800/800-8000. www.super8.com.* 82 rms, 2 story. S $60-$80; D $68-$90; each addl $7; under 12 free; higher rates: special events, wkends. Pet accepted. TV. Complimentary continental bkfst. Ck-out 11 am. Downhill/x-country ski 15 mi. Some in-rm whirlpools. Cr cds: A, D, DS, MC, V.

Restaurants

★ **CASA MIA.** *NY 211 E (10940). 845/692-2323.* Italian, American menu. Specializes in seafood, pasta, steak. Own desserts. Hrs: 11:30 am-10 pm. Closed Mon; Thanksgiving, Dec 24, 25. Res accepted. Bar. Lunch $3.50-$8.50, dinner $8.50-$22.95. Child's menu. Cr cds: A, D, DS, MC, V.

★ **RUSTY NAIL.** *50 Dunning Rd (10940). 845/343-8242.* Specializes in steak, seafood, pasta. Salad bar. Hrs: 11:30 am-10 pm; Fri, Sat to 11 pm; Sun 3-9 pm. Res accepted; required Fri, Sat. Bar to midnight; wkends to 3 am. Lunch $4.95-$9.95, dinner $11.95-$26.95. Child's menu. Entertainment Fri,

...at. Rustic decor; restored RR station. Cr cds: A, DS, MC, V.

Monroe

(G-7) See also Goshen, Middletown, Newburgh, West Point (US Military Academy)

Pop 31,407 **Elev** 679 ft **Area code** 914 **Zip** 10950

What to See and Do

Museum Village. Outdoor living history museum of over 25 buildings depicting the crafts and technology of 19th-century America. Exhibit/demonstration buildings incl print shop, log cabin, drug store, general store, schoolhouse. Broom maker, candle maker, blacksmith, weaver; farm animals; historical gardens. Shops, food service, picnic area. (May-Nov, Tues-Sun; closed Thanksgiving) Museum Village Rd, W on NY 17M; US 6, NY 17 exit 129. Phone 845/782-8247. ¢¢¢

Montauk (L.I.)

(F-4) See also Amagansett, East Hampton (L.I.)

Pop 3,851 **Elev** 18 ft **Area code** 631 **Zip** 11954

Information Chamber of Commerce, PO Box 5029; 631/668-2428

This is a lively fishing town on Long Island, with a big business in deep-sea fishing (tuna, shark, marlin, striped bass, and other varieties). Boats can be rented, and there are miles of uncrowded sandy beaches to enjoy.

What to See and Do

Hither Hills State Park. Swimming beach, bathhouse, lifeguards, fishing; nature and hiking trails, picnicking,

playground, concession, tent and trailer sites (mid-Apr-Nov; res required). Standard fees. 3 mi W on NY 27. Phone 631/668-2554.

Montauk Point State Park. Barren moor with sea view. Montauk Lighthouse, built 1795; museum, tours (summer wkends; fee). Fishing; hiking, biking, picnicking, concession. Standard fees. 6 mi E on NY 27; easternmost tip of Long Island. Phone 631/668-2554.

Motels/Motor Lodges

★ ★ **BURCLIFFE BY THE SEA.** *397 Old Montauk Hwy, Montauk (11954). 631/668-2880; fax 631/668-3129.* 7 kit. units, 5 with shower only. July-Sept: S, D $100-$120; each addl $20-$25; cottages $125-$225; wkly rates; higher rates wkends and hols (2-day min); lower rates rest of yr. Crib free. TV; cable (premium). Restaurant nearby. Ck-out 10 am. Tennis privileges. 18-hole golf privileges. Picnic tables, grills. Microwaves. Swimming beach. Cr cds: MC, V.
🏋 🖙 🐾

★ ★ **DRIFTWOOD MOTEL & COTTAGES.** *2718 Montauk Hwy, Montauk (11954). 631/668-5744; fax 631/267-3081; toll-free 800/643-7438. www. duneresorts.com.* 57 units in 7 buildings, 1-2 story, 21 suites, 2 cottages. Late June-early Sept: S, D $143-$185; each addl $15; suites $163-$210; kit. units $148-$198; cottages $295; wkly plans; lower rates May-late June, early Sept-Oct. Closed rest of yr. TV; cable (premium), VCR avail (movies free). Heated pool; lifeguard. Playground. Complimentary coffee in rms. Restaurants opp. Ck-out 11 am. Coin laundry. Business servs avail. Tennis. Refrigerators. Balconies. Picnic tables, grills. On beach. Cr cds: A, DS, MC, V.
🅳 🐾 🖙 🛏 🐾

★ ★ **ROYAL ATLANTIC BEACH RESORT.** *S Edgemere St, Montauk (11954). 631/668-5103; fax 631/668-4172.* 152 kit. units, 2 story. Mid-June-Labor Day: S, D $129-$165; each addl $10-$25; suites $155-$185; town houses $360; lower rates Apr-mid-June, after Labor Day-Oct. Most units closed rest of yr. TV; cable (premium). Heated pools; poolside serv, lifeguard. Restaurant 4-10 pm. Bar 4:30 pm-midnight. Ck-out 11 am. Business servs avail. Rec rm. Refrigerators. Balconies. Picnic tables. Private beach. Cr cds: A, C, D, DS, MC, V.

🄳 ➿ 🔥

★ **SANDS MOTEL.** *S Emerson Ave and S Emery St, Montauk (11954).* *631/668-5100.* 42 rms, 1-2 story, 22 kits. June-Aug: S, D $99-$140; each addl $12-$25; suites $110-$185; kit. cottages $650-$1,195/wk; higher rates: wkends of Memorial Day, July 4, Labor Day; lower rates Sept-Nov, Apr-May. Closed rest of yr. Crib free. TV; cable (premium), VCR avail. Pool; lifeguard. Playground. Restaurants nearby. Ck-out 11 am. Business servs avail. Lawn games. Refrigerators. Some balconies. Picnic tables, grills. Cr cds: A, DS, MC, V.

👤 ⚕ ➿ 🔥

★ **WAVE CREST RESORT.** *170 Old Montauk Hwy, Montauk (11954).* *631/668-2141; fax 631/668-2337.* 65 kit. units, 2 story. No elvtr. July-Aug (wkends, 3-day min): S, D, studio rms $125-$155; each addl $15; suites $155; lower rates May-June, Sept-Oct. Closed rest of yr. Crib free. TV; cable (premium), VCR (movies). Indoor pool; lifeguard. Ck-out 11 am. Business servs avail. Private patios, balconies. On hilltop and dune, overlooking ocean, beach. Hither Hills State Park adj. Cr cds: A, DS, MC, V.

👤 ➿ 🔥

Hotel

★★ **PANORAMIC VIEW.** *272 Old Montauk Hwy, Montauk (11954).* *631/668-3000; fax 631/668-7870.* 118 kit. units, 1-3 story, 14 suites, 3 cottages. Late June-early Sept: S, D $124-$172; each addl $15; suites $148-$198; cottages $398; wkend rates; lower rates Apr-late June, early Sept-Nov. Closed rest of yr. Children over 10 yrs only. TV; cable (premium), VCR avail. Pool; lifeguard. Restaurant nearby. Ck-out 11 am, ck-in 2 pm. Coin lndry. Meeting rms. Business servs avail. In-rm modem link. Game rm. Refrigerators. Grills. On beach. Cr cds: MC, V.

🄳 👤 ➿ 🔥

Resorts

★★ **BEACHCOMBER RESORT.** *727 Old Montauk Hwy, Montauk (11954).* *631/668-2894; fax 631/668-3154.* 88 kit. suites, 2 story. Mid-June-Labor Day: S, D $155-$285; each addl $15; higher rates wkends and hols (3-day min); lower rates Apr-mid-June, Labor Day-late Oct. Closed rest of yr. Crib free. TV; cable (premium), VCR (movies). Heated pool. Sauna. Restaurant nearby. Ck-out 11 am. Coin lndry. Business servs avail. Swimming beach. Cr cds: A, C, D.

🄳 👤 ⚕ ➿ 🔄 🔥

★★ **GURNEY'S INN RESORT AND SPA.** *290 Old Montauk Hwy, Montauk (11954).* *631/668-2345; fax 631/668-3576; toll-free 800/445-8062.* *www.gurneys-inn.com.* 109 rms, 1-4 story, 5 cottages. No elvtr. MAP, Memorial Day-Labor Day, wkends: S, D $290-$340; each addl $90; suites $340-$400; cottages (1-3 bedrm) $380-$1,080; serv charge 15 percent; lower rates rest of yr. TV; cable (premium), VCR. Indoor sea water pool; whirlpool; lifeguard. Dining rm 7:30-10 am, noon-3 pm, 6-10 pm. Box lunches, snacks. Fisherman's bkfst from 4 am on request. Bar noon-4 am; entertainment. Ck-out 11:30 am, ck-in 3:30 pm. Meeting rms. Business servs avail. Bellhops. Drugstore. Barber, beauty shop. Airport, RR station, bus depot transportation. Rec rm. Exercise rm; sauna, steam rm. Refrigerators. Patios; many terraces. Resort-type inn on 1,000-ft private beach. Cr cds: A, DS, MC, V.

👤 ➿ 🚶 🔥

★★★ **MONTAUK YACHT CLUB RESORT AND MARINA.** *32 Star Island Rd, Montauk (11954).* *631/668-3100; fax 631/668-3303; toll-free 800/692-8668.* *www.montaukyachtclub.com.* 84 rms, 2 story, 23 villas. Late Apr-Oct: S, D $149-$299; each addl $25; lower rates Apr, Oct. Closed rest of yr. Crib free. TV; cable (premium). 3 pools, 1 indoor; lifeguard. Dining rms 7 am-11 pm. Bar noon-2 am; entertainment Fri, Sat. Ck-out 11 am, ck-in 3 pm. Meeting rms. Business servs avail. Bellhops. Local airport, RR station, bus depot transportation. Tennis. Rec rm. Exercise equipt; sauna. Bathrm phones. Private patios, balconies. Marina;

ailing, waterskiing. Golf nearby. Cr
cds: A, C, D, DS, MC, V.

Restaurants

★★ DAVE'S GRILL. *468 W Lake Dr, Montauk (11954). 631/668-9190. www.davesgrill.com.* Specializes in seafood, pasta. Own pastries. Hrs: 5:30-10:30 pm. Closed Wed; also Nov-Apr. Bar. A la carte entrees: dinner $14.95-$19.95. Parking. Outdoor dining. Casual; located on fishing docks. Cr cds: A, D, DS, MC, V.
D

★★ GOSMAN'S. *500 W Lake Dr, Montauk (11954). 631/668-5330.* Specializes in fresh seafood. Own pastries. Hrs: noon-10 pm. Closed Nov-Mar. Bar noon-2 am. A la carte entrees: lunch, dinner $13.95-$25. Child's menu. Outdoor dining. On dock; view of boats. Cr cds: A, MC, V.
D

★★ HARVEST. *11 S Emory St, Montauk (11954). 631/668-5574.* Specializes in fresh seafood, pasta, grilled pizzas. Hrs: Thurs 5:30-10 pm; Fri, Sat to 11 pm. Closed Thanksgiving, Dec 25. Res accepted. Bar. A la carte entrees: dinner $16-$28. Parking. Outdoor dining in herb garden. Bacci courts. Original artwork. Overlooks large pond with swans; rooftop lounge overlooks ocean and pond. Cr cds: A, DS, MC, V.
D

★★ RUSCHMEYER'S. *161 Second House Rd, Montauk (11954). 631/668-2877. www.ruschmeyers.com.* Menu changes daily. Hrs: 5-10 pm; May-Memorial Day, mid-Sept-Columbus Day Fri-Sun 5-9 pm; early-bird dinner 5-6 pm. Closed rest of yr. Res accepted. Bar. Dinner $12-$19. Child's menu. Pianist Fri, Sat. Parking. Outdoor dining. Comfortable atmosphere. Cr cds: A, D, DS, MC, V.
D

★ SHAGWONG RESTAURANT. *774 Montauk Hwy, Montauk (11954). 631/668-3050. www.shagwong.com.* Menu changes daily. Specializes in fresh seafood. Hrs: noon-midnight; early-bird dinner 4:30-6 pm; Sun 10 am-2 pm (brunch), 6-10 pm. Bar. Lunch $6-$10, dinner $12-$20. Sun

brunch $7-$10. Parking. Covered patio dining. Photographs of Old Montauk and celebrity guests. Original tin ceiling (1927). Family-owned. Cr cds: A, D, DS, MC, V.
D

Monticello

(F-7) *See also Barryville, Liberty*

Pop 6,512 **Elev** 1,520 ft
Area code 914 **Zip** 12701
Information Sullivan County Visitors Association, Inc, 100 North St; 914/794-3000 or 800/882-2287
Web www.scva.net

As the center of the Sullivan County Catskills resort region, Monticello offers visitors a wide selection of activities: summer theaters, children's camps, summer cottages, fishing, hunting, swimming, canoeing, skiing, tennis, golf, or just basking in the sun. Nearby lakes offer many water sports.

What to See and Do

Monticello Raceway. Harness racing. Pari-mutuel betting. 1 mi W on NY 17B, Quickway exit 104. Phone 914/794-4100.

Skiing. Holiday Mountain Ski Area. Triple, two double chairlifts; Poma-lift, two rope tows; patrol, school, rentals; snowmaking; cafeteria, bar, ski shop. Longest run 3,500 ft; vertical drop 400 ft. Night skiing. (Dec-Mar, daily) 3 mi E off NY 17 exit 107 at 99 Holiday Mtn Rd. Phone 845/796-3161. ¢¢¢¢

Woodstock Music Festival Monument. Monument to the 1969 music festival, which was held here on Yasgur's farm. W on NY 17B to Hurd Rd in Bethel.

Mount Kisco

(G-8) *See also New York City, Peekskill, Pound Ridge, White Plains*

Pop 9,983 **Elev** 289 ft **Area code** 914 **Zip** 10549
Information Chamber of Commerce, 3 N Moger Ave; 914/666-7525

What to See and Do

Caramoor Center for Music and the Arts. European-style villa built during 1930s with rms from European villas and palaces. Collections of Chinese art, Italian Renaissance furniture; European paintings, sculptures, and tapestries dating from the Middle Ages through the 19th century; formal gardens. Tours (June-mid-Nov, Thurs, Sat and Sun afternoons, also Wed, Fri, by appt; rest of yr, by appt). Also Summer Music Festival (late June-mid-Aug). 5 mi NE via Saw Mill River Pkwy to Katonah-Cross River exit 6, then ½ mi E on NY 35, right onto NY 22 to jct with Girdle Ridge Rd; follow signs. Phone 914/232-5035. ¢¢

John Jay Homestead State Historic Site. Estate of the first chief justice of the US and four generations of his descendants; period furnishings, American portrait collection, gardens, farm buildings and grounds. Visits by guided tour only. (Early-Apr-Nov, Wed-Sat, also Sun afternoons) Phone 914/232-5651. **FREE**

Northern Westchester Center for the Arts. Home to a variety of programs and classes in music, dance, theater, and visual arts. Participants in the various programs range from budding ballerinas to octogenarian actors all studying under faculty members who are accomplished in their fields; past performers incl Vanessa Williams, Glenn Close, Gregory Hines, Alan Menken, Chevy Chase, and Blythe Danner. 272 N Bedford Rd. Phone 914/241-6922.

Motel/Motor Lodge

★★ **HOLIDAY INN MOUNT KISCO.** *1 Holiday Inn Dr (10549). 914/241-2600; fax 914/241-4742; toll-free 888/452-5771.* 122 rms, 2 story. S, D $139-$159; under 12 free; wkend plans. Crib. Pet accepted. TV; cable (premium), VCR avail. Pool; lifeguard. Coffee in rms. Restaurant 6:30 am-10 pm. Bar 2 pm-1 am, wkends to 3 am; entertainment. Ck-out 11 am. Coin lndry. Meeting rms. Business center. In-rm modem link. Beauty shop. Health club privileges. Refrigerators avail. Cr cds: A, C, D, DS, JCB, MC, V.

Restaurants

★★★ **CRABTREE'S KITTLE HOUSE.** *11 Kittle Rd, Chappaqua (10514). 914/666-8044.* Specializes in game. Hrs: noon-2:30 pm, 5:30-9:30 pm; Fri to 11 pm; Sat 5:30-11 pm; Sun noon-2:30 pm (brunch), 3-9 pm. Closed Dec 25. Res accepted. Bar. Wine list. Lunch $7.50-$13.50, dinner $16.50-$26.50. Sun brunch buffet: $19.95. Child's menu. Valet parking. Elegant country decor. Picture windows overlook lawn. Cr cds: A, C, D, DS, MC, V.

★★★ **LA CAMELIA.** *234 N Bedford Rd (10549). 914/666-2466.* Spanish menu. Specializes in tapas. Own desserts. Hrs: noon-3 pm, 6-9:30 pm; Sat, Sun 6-10 pm; Sun brunch noon-3 pm. Closed Mon; also Jan 1, Thanksgiving, Dec 25. Res accepted. Bar. Wine list. Lunch $12-$23, dinner $18-$30. Sun brunch $22. Child's menu. Parking. Elegant dining. Cr cds: A, C, D, DS, MC, V.

★★★ **TRAVELER'S REST.** *Rte 100, Ossining (10546). 914/941-7744.* German, Amer menu. Specialty: jaegerschnitzel. Hrs: 5-9:30 pm; Fri, Sat to 10 pm; Sun 1-9 pm. Closed Tues; Dec 24. Res accepted. Bar. Wine list. Complete meals: dinner $27.95-$32.95. Child's menu. Built 1880s; extensive grounds, gardens, waterfalls, pond; fireplaces. Family-owned. Cr cds: MC, V.

Naples

(E-4) *See also Canandaigua, Penn Yan*

Pop 2,441 **Elev** 800 ft **Area code** 716 **Zip** 14512

At the south end of Canandaigua Lake, one of the Finger Lakes, Naples is the center of a grape growing, winemaking area. Many of its residents are descendants of Swiss and German winemakers.

What to See and Do

Cumming Nature Center of the Rochester Museum & Science Center. A 900-acre living museum; nature trails, natural history programs; conservation trail with operating sawmill; x-country skiing (rentals) and snowshoeing. Visitors building with theater and exhibit hall. (Late Dec-mid-Nov, Wed-Sun) 6472 Gulick Rd. Phone 716/374-6160. ¢¢

Widmer's Wine Cellars. Tours, wine tastings (Daily, afternoons). 1 Lake Niagara Ln. Phone 716/374-6311. ¢

Motel/Motor Lodge

★★★ **THE VAGABOND INN.** 3300 Sliter Hill Rd (14512). 716/554-6271. www.thevagabondinn.com. 5 rms. No A/C. No rm phones. S, D $115-$225; each addl $25; package plans. Children over 13 yrs only. TV; VCR (movies). Complimentary full bkfst, coffee in rms. Ck-out 11:30 am, ck-in 2:30 pm. 9-hole golf privileges, greens fee $8-$18. Downhill ski 12 mi; x-country ski ⅛ mi. Massage. Pool; whirlpool. Many in-rm whirlpools, fireplaces. Many balconies. Picnic tables, grills. Contemporary inn; antiques, art from around the world. On 65 acres. Totally nonsmoking. Cr cds: MC, V.

Restaurants

★★ **BOB & RUTH'S VINEYARD.** 204 Main St (14512). 716/374-5122. Specializes in homemade soups and pies. Salad bar. Hrs: 6 am-8 pm. Closed Nov-Mar. Res accepted. Bar. Bkfst $2-$4.25, lunch $2.95-$10, dinner $9.95-$18.95. Child's menu. Wine wall. Outdoor dining. Family-owned. Cr cds: MC, V.

★★ **NAPLES HOTEL.** 111 S Main St (14512). 716/374-5630. German menu. Specialties: prime rib, sauer-braten, lobster bisque. Hrs: 11 am-2:30 pm; Fri, Sat to 9 pm; Sun noon-7 pm; hrs vary July-Labor Day. Res accepted. Bar to 1 am. Lunch $3.95-$5.95, dinner $8.50-$19.95. Child's menu. Pianist Fri, Sat eves. Built in 1895; antiques. Guest rms avail. Cr cds: A, DS, MC, V.

★★ **REDWOOD.** 6 Cohocton St (14512). 716/374-6360. Specializes in steak, seafood. Salad bar. Hrs: 6 am-8 pm; Fri, Sat to 9 pm; Sun 7 am-8 pm. Closed Mon; Dec 24, 25. Res accepted. Bar from noon. Bkfst $1.85-$5.95, lunch $2.50-$6.95, dinner $6.95-$25.95. Child's menu. Cr cds: A, DS, MC, V.

Newburgh

(G-8) *See also Fishkill, New Paltz, Poughkeepsie, West Point (US Military Academy)*

Settled 1709 **Pop** 28,259 **Elev** 139 ft
Area code 845 **Zip** 12550
Information Chamber of Commerce of Orange County, Inc, 47 Grand St; 845/562-5100 or 845/782-2007 (Monroe office)
Web www.orangeny.org

This manufacturing city was General George Washington's headquarters from April 1, 1782, until August 18, 1783. He announced the end of the Revolutionary War here, and officially disbanded the army.

Newburgh is the small urban center of eastern Orange County. West Point, the US Military Academy, lies 12 miles south of town (see).

What to See and Do

New Windsor Cantonment State Historic Site. (1782) The Cantonment was the last winter encampment (1782-1783) of the Continental Army. Featured are demonstrations of 18th-century military life, incl muskets and artillery, woodworking, blacksmithing, and camp life activities. Exhibit buildings and picnic area. (Mid-Apr-Oct, Wed-Sat, also Sun afternoons) Special events. On Temple Hill Rd (NY 300); 2 mi S of NY Thrwy exit 17 in Vails Gate. Phone 845/561-1765. **FREE**

Storm King Art Center. A 400-acre sculpture park and museum with permanent collection of 20th-century sculpture. Guided tours. (Apr-mid-Nov, daily). 6 mi S via NY 32, Old Pleasant Hill Rd, in Mountainville. Phone 845/534-3115. ¢¢¢

Washington's Headquarters State Historic Site. Jonathan Hasbrouck house (1750); General George Washington's headquarters for 16½ months at the close of the Revolutionary War (Apr 1782-Aug 1783). Dutch vernacular fieldstone house furnished as headquarters. Adj museum has permanent and changing exhibits, audiovisual program. Tours, special events. (Mid-Apr-Oct, Wed-Sun; inquire for winter schedule) 84 Liberty St. Phone 845/562-1195. ¢

Motels/Motor Lodges

★★ **COMFORT INN.** 5 Lakeside Rd (12550). 845/567-0567; fax 845/567-0582; res 800/228-5150. www.comfort inn.com. 130 rms, 3 story, 2 suites. May-late Nov: S $59-$95; D $63-$125; each addl $10; under 18 free; higher rates West Point graduation; lower rates rest of yr. Crib $6. TV; cable, VCR avail (movies). Complimentary continental bkfst. Restaurant nearby. Ck-out 11 am, ck-in 3 pm. Coin lndry. Meeting rms. Business servs avail. In-rm modem link. Free airport, bus depot transportation. Cr cds: A, C, D, DS, MC, V.

🆔 🏃 📠 🏊 🔥

★★ **HOLIDAY INN.** 90 NY Rte 17K (12550). 845/564-9020; fax 845/564-9040; toll-free 800/542-7978. www.holiday-inn.com. 122 rms, 2 story. S, D $85-$95; each addl $10; under 18 free. Crib free. TV; cable (premium). Pool; lifeguard. Coffee in rms. Restaurant 6:30 am-10 pm. Bar 4 pm-1 am; entertainment Fri, Sat. Ck-out noon. Meeting rms. Business servs avail. In-rm modem link. Free airport transportation. Exercise equipt. Some bathrm phones. Cr cds: A, D, DS, JCB, MC, V.

🆔 🏊 🏃 📠 🔥

★ **HOWARD JOHNSON INN.** 95 Rte 17K (12550). 845/564-4000; fax 845/564-0620; res 800/446-4656. 74 rms, 2 story. May-Nov: S $69-$89; D $79-$99; each addl $8; under 18 free; higher rates special events; lower rates rest of yr. Crib free. Pet accepted. TV; cable (premium). Pool. Complimentary continental bkfst. Restaurant nearby. Ck-out noon. Coin lndry. Meeting rms. Business servs avail. Tennis. Downhill/x-country ski 15 mi. Health club privileges. Microwaves, refrigerators avail. Private patios, balconies. Cr cds: A, C, D, DS, MC, V.

🆔 🏃 📠 ✈ 📠 🔥 SC ✈

★★ **RAMADA INN.** 1289 Rte 300 (12550). 845/564-4500; fax 845/564-4524. www.ramada.com. 164 rms, 2 story. S, D $82-$92; each addl $10; suites $100-$130; under 18 free. Crib free. TV; cable. Pool; poolside serv. Complimentary full bkfst. Restaurant 6:30 am-10 pm. Bar 11-2 am; entertainment Wed, Fri, Sat. Ck-out noon. Meeting rms. Business servs avail. In-rm modem link. Free airport transportation. Exercise equipt. Game rm. Refrigerators, microwaves avail. Cr cds: A, C, D, DS, MC, V.

🆔 📠 🏃 📠 🔥

★ **SUPER 8 MOTEL.** 1287 Rte 300 (12550). 845/564-5700; fax 845/564-7338; toll-free 800/800-8000. www.super8.com. 108 rms, 2 story. S $52.88-$61.88; D $69.88; each addl $7; under 12 free. TV; cable (premium). Complimentary continental bkfst. Restaurant opp open 24 hrs. Ck-out 11 am. Business servs avail. Cr cds: A, C, D, DS, MC, V.

🆔 📠 🔥 SC

Restaurants

★ **BANTA'S STEAK & STEIN.** 935 Union Ave, New Windsor (12553). 845/564-7678. Specializes in steak, prime rib, seafood combo. Salad bar. Hrs: 4-10 pm; Fri, Sat to 11 pm; Sun from noon. Closed Thanksgiving, Dec 25. Bar. Dinner $7.95-$23.95. Child's menu. Family-owned. Cr cds: A, D, MC, V.

🆔 SC 📠

★ **COSIMO'S ON UNION.** 1217 Rte 300 Union Ave (12550). 845/567-1556. www.cosimosonunion.com. Hrs: 11:30 am-10 pm; Fri, Sat to 11 pm;

Sun from noon. Closed Easter, Thanksgiving, Dec 25. Res accepted. Italian menu. Wine, beer. Lunch $5.25-$8.95, dinner $7.95-$16.95. Child's menu. Specializes in wood-fired pizza, pasta, steak. Parking. Outdoor dining. Cr cds: A, D, DS, MC, V.

★★ **SCHLESINGER'S STEAK HOUSE.** *475 Temple Hill Rd, New Windsor (12553). 845/561-1762.* Specializes in steak, seafood, barbecue ribs. Hrs: 11:30 am-9 pm; Sat 4:30-10 pm; Sun 3-9 pm. Closed Thanksgiving, Dec 25. Bar. Lunch $4.95-$12, dinner $5.95-$29.95. Child's menu. Two dining rms in original Colonial building (1762). Cr cds: A, D, MC, V.

★★★ **YOBO.** *1297 NY 300 (12550). 845/564-3848.* Far Eastern menu. Specialties: Peking duck, hibachi steak, sushi. Hrs: 11:30 am-10 pm; Fri to 11 pm; Sat 12:30-11 pm; Sun 12:30-10 pm. Closed Thanksgiving. Res accepted. Lunch $4.50-$8.50, dinner $9-$24.50. Japanese architect constructed building by hand; 5 dining rms; waterfalls, palm trees, teak statues. Cr cds: A, MC, V.

New Paltz

(F-7) See also Kingston, Newburgh, Poughkeepsie

Founded 1678 **Pop** 12,830 **Elev** 196 ft
Area code 845 **Zip** 12561
Information Chamber of Commerce, 124 Main St; 845/255-0243 or 845/255-0411
Web www.newpaltzchamber.org

New Paltz was founded by a dozen Huguenots who were granted land by the colonial governor of New York. The town is surrounded by the fertile farmlands of the Wallkill River Valley, with apple orchards and vineyards.

What to See and Do

Huguenot Street Old Stone Houses. Six original stone dwellings (1692-1712), a reconstructed French church (1717); Jean Hasbrouck House (1694) of medieval Flemish stone architecture. All houses furnished with heirlooms of descendants. (May-Oct, Tues-Sun) Visitor center at DuBois Fort on Hugnenot. Phone 914/255-1660.

Locust Lawn. Federal mansion of Josiah Hasbrouck (1814). Incl smokehouse, farmers' museum; Terwilliger Homestead (1738); bird sanctuary. (By appt) 4 mi S on NY 32. Phone 845/255-1660.

State University of New York College at New Paltz. (1828) 8,129 students. Art gallery (usually Mon-Fri, Sun); concerts, plays. Language immersion program in 15 languages (summers and wkends); Music in the Mountains, contemporary music series (summer); Repertory Theatre (see SPECIAL EVENTS). Campus tours by appt. On NY 32 S, 1 mi W of NY State Thrwy exit 18. Phone 845/257-2121.

Special Events

SUNY College Summer Repertory Theatre. State University of New York College at New Paltz. Phone 845/257-3872. June-Aug.

Ulster County Fair. Fairgrounds, 2 mi SW on Libertyville Rd. Contact Ulster County Public Information Office, Box 1800, Kingston 12401. Phone 845/340-3000. First wk Aug.

Apple Festival. Huguenot St. Second Sat in Oct.

Motel/Motor Lodge

★ **DAYS INN.** *601 Main St; Rte 299 (12561). 845/883-7373; fax 845/883-7383. www.daysinn.com.* 21 rms. S, D $49-$99; each addl $6; under 12 free; higher rates special events, wkends. Crib $6. TV; cable. Complimentary coffee. Restaurant nearby. Ck-out 11 am. X-country ski 5 mi. Cr cds: A, C, D, DS, MC, V.

Resorts

★ ★ ★ **MOHONK MOUNTAIN HOUSE.** *1000 Mountain Rest Rd (12561). 845/255-1000; fax 845/256-2161. www.mohonk.com.* 261 rms, 6-7 story. No A/C. AP: S $180-$550; D $310-$650; each addl $100; 4-12 yrs, $65; under 4 free; wkly, seasonal, special events rates. Crib free. Serv charge 13 percent per person. TV in lobby; cable. Supervised children's activities. Dining rm (public by res) 8-9:30 am, 12:30-2 pm, 6:30-8 pm; Fri to 10 pm. Box lunches, snack bar, picnics. Serv bar at lunch and dinner. Ck-out 2 pm, ck-in 4 pm. Coin lndry. Meeting rms. Bellhops. Valet serv. Gift shop. Resident doctor daily in summer, wkends rest of yr. Airport, RR station, bus depot transportation. Sports dir. Tennis. 9-hole golf, greens fee $12, putting green. Swimming from lake beach, lifeguard. Boats. X-country ski on site. Ice-skating. Lawn games. Hayrides, carriage rides, picnics. Soc dir. Movies, concerts, lectures, square dancing, theme wkends. Rec rm. Exercise rm; sauna. Many fireplaces. Many private balconies. Library. Resort since 1869; gardens, many gazebos. More than 2,000 mountainous acres, surrounded by 5,500-acre natural preserve. More than 90 mi of carriage roads, hiking trails. Cr cds: A, C, D, DS, MC, V.

★ ★ **ROCKING HORSE RANCH RESORT.** *600 Rte 44-55, Highland (12528). 845/691-2927; fax 845/691-6434; toll-free 800/647-2624. www.rhranch.com.* 120 rms, 2 story. MAP, July-early Sept, wkly: S $100-$155; D $200-$300; each addl $320-$345; under 4 free; package plans; wkends, hols (2-day min); lower rates rest of yr. Crib $5/day. Maid serv twice wkly. TV; cable, VCR avail (movies). Complimentary coffee in rms. Box lunches. Snack bar. Picnics. Bar noon-midnight; entertainment. Ck-out noon, ck-in 3 pm. Grocery 2 blks. Meeting rms. Business servs avail. Bellhops. Valet serv. Concierge. Aiport, RR station, bus depot transportation. Lighted tennis. 18-hole golf privileges, greens fee $45. Boats. Waterskiing. Downhill ski on site. Sleighing. Hiking. Lawn games. Soc dir. Rec rm. Game rm. Exercise rm; sauna, spa. Massage. Fishing guides. 3 pools, 1 indoor; wading pool, whirlpool, poolside serv, lifeguard. Playground. Supervised children's activities; ages 4-12. Some refrigerators. Picnic tables, grills. On lake. Cr cds: A, D, DS, MC, V.

Restaurant

★ ★ ★ **LOCUST TREE.** *215 Huguenot St (12561). 914/255-7888.* American regional menu. Specialties: local produce, game, fish. Own desserts. Hrs: 11:30 am-2:30 pm, 5:30-10 pm; Sat 5:30-10 pm; Sun 3:30-8 pm; Sun brunch 11 am-2 pm. Closed Mon; Dec 25. Res accepted. Bar. Wine cellar. Lunch $6.95-$10.95, dinner $14.95-$21.95. Sun brunch $13. Parking. Outdoor dining. Dutch stone and frame house (portion dates from 1759) overlooking pond, 9-hole golf course; many antiques, fireplaces. Cr cds: A, MC, V.

New Rochelle

(G-2) *See also New York City, White Plains*

Pop 72,182 **Elev** 100 ft **Area code** 914
Information Chamber of Commerce, 459 Main St, 10801; 914/632-5700

New Rochelle was founded in 1688 by a group of Huguenot families. Prior to the Europeans who settled here, the area was home to the Siwanoys, a part of the Mohegans stemming from the Algonquins. Boat building was the trade of many of the early settlers, and their boats carried goods to and from New York City and other towns and ports on the coast.

What to See and Do

Thomas Paine National Historical Association. Museum containing original writings and artifacts of Thomas Paine, author of *Common Sense;* also histories of the Huguenots and New Rochelle. (Fri-Sun, also by appt; closed winter) 983 North Ave. Phone 914/632-5376. ¢¢

Thomas Paine Cottage. This is the house where Paine lived upon his return from Europe. The cottage is now a museum containing Paine artifacts and memorabilia. (Fri-Sun, also by appt; closed winter) 20 Sicard. Phone 914/632-5376.

Motel/Motor Lodge

★★ **RAMADA PLAZA HOTEL.** *1 Ramada Plaza (10801). 845/576-3700; fax 845/576-3711; toll-free 888/298-2054.* 130 rms, 2 suites, 10 story. Apr-Oct: S $122; D $157; suites $225; under 18 free; wkly, wkend, hol rates; higher rates special events; lower rates rest of yr. Crib free. TV; cable (premium), VCR avail (movies). Pool; poolside serv, lifeguard. Complimentary coffee in lobby. Restaurant 6:30-10 pm; Sat from 7:30 pm; Sun 7:30-9 pm. Bar. Ck-out noon. Meeting rms. Business center. In-rm modem link. Bellhops. Valet serv. Sundries. Gift shop. Exercise equipt. Health club privileges. Some refrigerators. Cr cds: A, C, D, DS, ER, MC, V.
🅓 ⊠ 🏋 ⊴ 🔥 SC 🏃

New York City

(Follows Yonkers at end of New York State)

Niagara Falls

(D-1, D-2) *See also Buffalo, Lockport, Niagara Falls*

Settled 1806 **Pop** 55,593 **Elev** 610 ft
Area code 716
Information Convention & Visitors Bureau, 310 4th St, 14303; 716/285-2400 or 800/421-5223
Web www.nfcvb.com

There are higher falls, but Niagara still puts on a first-class performance. On the border with Canada, the American Falls are 184 feet high, the Canadian Horseshoe, 176 feet. The two are separated by Goat Island. For several hours in the evening the beauty of the falls continues in a display of colored lights playing over the water.

Originally, after the glacial period, the falls were seven miles downstream at the Niagara escarpment. Rocks have crashed from top to bottom, causing the falls to retreat at a rate averaging about one foot per year.

With a flow of more than 200,000 cubic feet of water per second, Niagara has a power potential of about 4,000,000 horsepower. Electrical production is controlled by agreements between the US and Canada so that each receives a full share while the beauty of the cataracts is preserved.

The industries nourished by these waters include aircraft, aerospace equipment (Bell), abrasives (Carborundum), food products, paper, chemicals, and a tremendous tourist business. (For Border Crossing Regulations see MAKING THE MOST OF YOUR TRIP.)

What to See and Do

Aquarium of Niagara Falls, NY. Sea lions; more than 2,000 marine creatures, incl sharks, otters, piranha, penguins, exotic fish. Free outdoor sea lion pool; largest collection of freshwater gamefish in the Northeast. (Daily; closed Thanksgiving, Dec 25) 701 Whirlpool St. Phone 716/285-3575. ¢¢¢

Artpark. A 150-acre state park and summer theater devoted to visual and performing arts. Events at 2,300-seat theater with lawn seating incl musicals, classical concerts by Buffalo Philharmonic Orchestra, dance programs, and jazz and pop music concerts. 7 mi N on Robert Moses Pkwy, in Lewiston. For schedule, contact PO Box 371, Lewiston 14092. Phone 716/754-9000.

Castellani Art Museum. Over 3,000 artworks ranging from the Hudson River School to contemporary sculpture; first-rate Folk Arts Program, incl exhibits, artist demonstrations, and performances; changing exhibits. (Wed-Sun; closed hols) Senior Dr, Niagara University. Directly across from Devil's Hole State Park. Phone 716/286-8200. **FREE**

Devil's Hole State Park. View of Lower Rapids and Power Authority generating plant. Nature and hiking trail, picnicking. 4½ mi N of falls. Phone 716/278-1770. **FREE**

Fantasy Island. An 80-acre family theme park with more than 100 attractions, incl water park, thrill rides, children's rides, and western town; live shows; picnic area. (Mid-June-early Sept, daily; also wkends Mid-May-mid-June) 2400 Grand Island Blvd, S on I-190 in Grand Island. Phone 716/773-7591. ¢¢¢¢

Fort Niagara State Park. Swimming pool (fee), bathhouse, fishing, boating (launch); nature and hiking trails, tennis, x-country skiing, snowmobiling. (Daily; closed Jan 1, Thanksgiving, Dec 25) Standard fees. 14 mi N on Robert Moses Pkwy, in Youngstown. Phone 716/745-7273. Here is

>   **Old Fort Niagara.** (1726) Restored fort played important role in French and Indian War and in War of 1812. Museum, French "Castle," other buildings. Military drills, ceremonies in summer. (Daily) Phone 716/745-7611.

Four Mile Creek State Park Campground. On Lake Ontario. Fishing; hiking, playground, 266 tent and

trailer sites. (Mid-Apr-Oct) Standard fees. Phone 716/745-7273.

Niagara Falls Convention & Civic Center. Sports events, concerts, conventions, trade shows. 305 4th St. Phone 716/286-4769.

Niagara Power Project Visitor Center. Glass-enclosed observation building with outdoor balcony; view of Niagara River Gorge, hydroelectric projects on both sides of river; displays explain power generation; Father Louis Hennepin mural; museum shows development of power and industry at Niagara Falls with hands-on displays. (Daily; closed hols) 5777 Lewiston Rd (NY 104), 4½ mi N of the falls. Phone 716/285-3211. **FREE**

✪ **Niagara Reservation State Park.** Provides many views of Niagara Falls and the rapids above and below the cataract from Prospect and Terrapin points, Luna Island, and many other locations. Fishing; nature and hiking trails. Restaurant. Visitor center; recreation programs. Standard fees. 4 mi W of I-190 via Robert Moses Pkwy. Phone 716/278-1770. ¢¢ Includes

>   **Boat ride.** *Maid of the Mist* takes passengers close to the falls. (Mid-May-mid-Oct, daily, approx every

Niagara Falls

30 min) Fee incl use of waterproof clothing. Phone 716/284-4233. ¢¢¢

Cave of the Winds Trip. Elevators from Goat Island. Walk through the spray at the base of the American Falls. Waterproof garments supplied. (Mid-May-mid-Oct, daily) Phone 716/278-1770. ¢¢¢

Goat Island. Separates the Canadian Horseshoe and American Falls. Drives and walks in 70-acre park; closest possible views of falls and upper rapids. Picnic areas; restaurant, snack bar. Smaller Luna Island and Three Sister Islands can be reached by footbridge. Phone 716/278-1762.

Niagara Scenic Trolley. Miniature train ride from Prospect Point to Goat Island and return with seven stopovers incl Cave of the Winds, *Maid of the Mist*, Terrapin Point, and Three Sister Islands. (Apr-Oct, daily) Phone 716/278-1730. ¢¢

Prospect Park Visitor Center. Information desk, video displays; wide-screen theater featuring movie *Niagara Wonders;* Great Lakes Garden. (Daily) Phone 716/278-1796. **FREE**

Prospect Point Observation Tower. The 282-ft tower rises adj to American Falls. Elevator to gorge below and *Maid of the Mist*. (Daily) Prospect Park. Phone 716/278-1770. ¢

Schoellkopf Geological Museum. Spiral-shaped building houses exhibits relating to geological formation and history of the falls. Audiovisual presentation. Rock garden, gorge overlook. (Memorial Day-Oct, daily; rest of yr, Thurs-Sun; closed Jan 1, Thanksgiving, Dec 25) Phone 716/278-1780. ¢

Niagara's Wax Museum of History. Life-size wax figures depict history of the area; historic items. (Daily) 303 Prospect St, at Old Falls St. Phone 716/285-1271. ¢¢

Reservoir State Park. Overlook at the Robert Moses Power Plant Reservoir. Tennis, picnicking, playground, ball field, x-country skiing, snowmobiling. 4 mi NE at jct NY 31, 265. Phone 716/278-1762.

Whirlpool State Park. Splendid view of the famous Niagara River Gorge whirlpool and rapids. Ongiara Trail,

nature and hiking trails, picnicking, playground. 3 mi N of falls on Robert Moses Pkwy. Phone 716/278-1770. **FREE**

Wintergarden. A seven-story indoor tropical park. Over 7,000 trees, shrubs, and flowers; glass elevators, and elevated walkways. Adj to falls and Convention Center. (Daily; closed Dec 25) Rainbow Blvd. Phone 716/286-4940. **FREE**

Motels/Motor Lodges

★ ★ **BEST WESTERN INN ON THE RIVER.** *7001 Buffalo Ave (14304). 716/283-7612; fax 716/283-7631; toll-free 800/780-7234. www.bestwestern. com.* 150 rms, 8 story. Late May-Sep: S $78-$118; D $88-$128; each addl $10; under 18 free; mid-wk, wkend rates; lower rates rest of yr. Crib free. TV; VCR avail. Indoor pool. Sauna. Restaurant 7 am-2 pm, 4:30-9 pm. Bar noon-midnight; entertainment. Ck-out noon. Coin lndry. Meeting rms. Business servs avail. Game rm. Boat docking. On Niagara River. Cr cds: A, C, D, DS, ER, JCB, MC, V.

☒ ☒ ☒ **SC**

★ ★ **BEST WESTERN SUMMIT INN.** *9500 Niagara Falls Blvd (14304). 716/297-5050; fax 716/297-0802; toll-free 800/404-8217. www.bestwestern. com.* 88 rms, 2 story. July-early Oct: S $68-$88; D $88-$98; each addl $10; under 18 free; wkly and wkend rates; lower rates rest of yr. Crib free. Pet accepted, some restrictions. TV; VCR avail (movies). Indoor pool. Sauna. Restaurant 7-11 am, 4-9 pm. Bar 4-9 pm. Ck-out 11 am. Meeting rms. Business servs avail. Game rm. Cr cds: A, C, D, DS, MC, V.

☒ ☒ ☒ ☒ ☒

★ **CHATEAU MOTOR LODGE.** *1810 Grand Island Blvd, Grand Island (14072). 716/773-2868; fax 716/773-5173.* 17 rms, 4 kits. June-Sept: S $59; D $69; under 8 free; wkly rates; lower rates rest of yr. Crib free. Pet accepted, some restrictions. TV. Restaurant nearby. Ck-out 11 am. Refrigerators, microwaves avail. Cr cds: A, DS, MC, V.

D ☒ ☒ ☒

★ ★ **COMFORT INN THE POINTE.** *1 Prospect Pointe (14303). 716/284-6835; fax 716/284-5177; res 800/228-*

NIAGARA RESERVATION STATE PARK

Niagara Falls is almost an American tourist cliche. But, it's still one of the most spectacular natural sites in the country, and Niagara Reservation State Park—the oldest state park in the United States—offers a wonderful walking opportunity. In warmer months, tickets can be purchased for a ride on the Viewmobile, which tours the entire park, so that at any given point walking can be abandoned for a respite ride.

Start at the Visitor Center to obtain maps of the park, watch a wide-screen film about the falls, and purchase a Niagara Master Pass. The Pass allows savings on all the major attractions in the park, including the Observation Tower, the geological museum, a guided walking tour, the boat tour, and more. From the Visitor Center walk toward the river to the Observation Tower (closed in winter). The tower rises some 200 feet above the base of the gorge and presents terrific views of all three falls—Horseshoe, American, and Bridal Veil. The glass elevator ride is fun, too. The elevator goes down to the dock from which the *Maid of the Mist* boat tour departs. This narrated 30-minute boat ride, in operation since 1846, goes to the base of American Falls and into the ring of Horseshoe Falls.

From the Tower turn right and follow the pedestrian walkway to the edge of American Falls. Follow the walkway upriver and cross the Goat Island Pedestrian Bridge. On Goat Island are picnic grounds, a restaurant, a gift shop, and snack bars. Follow the path to the Bridal Veil Falls overlook. Here, too, is the Cave of the Winds attraction, a boardwalk that leads right into the Bridal Veil Falls themselves. Continue around the downriver point of the island to Terrapin Point. This overlook sits just a few yards from the top of Horseshoe Falls and reveals the full power of the rushing water. From there, walk up the side of the island and follow the pedestrian bridge onto Three Sisters Island. This trio of small islands yields an excellent view of the river's upper rapids.

Coming off Three Sisters, either turn right and continue the Goat Island loop, or turn left and follow the midisland pathways back to the pedestrian bridge. Continue back past the Visitor Center and onto Main Street. A short way up Main stands the Aquarium of Niagara (701 Whirlpool Street). The aquarium houses an international collection of fish, a unique colony of endangered Peruvian penguins, and California sea lions that perform every 90 minutes. Leaving the aquarium, cross the highway via the pedestrian bridge, and visit The Schoellkopf Geological Museum (Robert Moses Parkway at Main Street), which offers a multifaceted look at the Niagara Gorge and its 12,000-year-old waterfalls. To reap the fullest experience, leave the museum along the riverside walkway and stroll across Rainbow Bridge, which leads to Canada. The bridge yields another spectacular view of all the falls.

5150. *www.comfortinn.com.* 118 rms, 6 story. June-Oct: S $82-$132; D $92-$142; each addl $10; suites $165-$300; under 18 free; lower rates rest of yr. Crib free. TV; cable (premium). Complimentary continental bkfst. Restaurant 7 am-11 pm. Ck-out 11 am. Meeting rms. Business servs avail. Sundries. Gift shop. Cr cds: A, C, D, DS, ER, JCB, MC, V.
[D] [⌫] [🔥]

★ **DAYS INN AT THE FALLS.** 443 *Main St (14301). 716/284-8801; fax 716/284-8633; res 800/329-7466. www.daysinn.com.* 168 rms, 8 story. Mid-June-mid-Sept: S, D $89-$129; each addl $10; under 18 free; wkend rates; lower rates rest of yr. Crib free. TV; cable. Indoor pool. Sauna. Restaurant open 24 hrs. Bar 4 pm-2 am. Ck-out 11 am. Coin lndry. Meeting rms. Business servs avail. Sundries. Game rm. Cr cds: A, D, DS, MC, V.
[D] [⌫] [🔥]

★ **DRIFTWOOD.** 2754 *Niagara Falls Blvd (14304). 716/692-6650.* 20 rms. S, D $32-$87. TV. Pool. Restaurants nearby. Ck-out 10 am. Some refrigerators, microwaves. Cr cds: A, D, DS, MC, V.
[⌂] [⌙] [⌫] [🔥]

★ **ECONO LODGE NIAGARA FALLS.** *7708 Niagara Falls Blvd (14304). 716/283-0621; fax 716/283-2121; res 800/553-2666. www.tkis.com/econolodge.* 70 rms, 2 story. June-Labor Day: S $39-$99; D $45-$109; each addl $7; under 18 free; wkly rates; higher rates hols; lower rates rest of yr. Crib $7. TV; VCR avail (movies). Heated pool. Complimentary coffee in lobby. Restaurants nearby. Ck-out 11 am. Gift shop. Microwaves avail. Cr cds: A, C, D, DS, ER, JCB, MC, V.

🄳 👜 🔜 📳 🔥 **SC**

★★ **FOUR POINTS BY SHERATON.** *114 Buffalo Ave (14303). 716/285-2521; fax 716/285-0963; res 800/325-3535. www.lodgian.com.* 200 rms, 7 story. June-Aug: S, D $39-$149; each addl $10; suites $175-$279; under 19 free; lower rates rest of yr. Crib free. TV; cable (premium). Indoor pool; whirlpool, lifeguard. Complimentary coffee in rms. Restaurant 6:30 am-10 pm. Bar noon-2 am. Ck-out noon. Coin lndry. Business servs avail. In-rm modem link. Bellhops. Valet serv. Exercise equipt; sauna. Game rm. Cr cds: A, DS, MC, V.

🄳 🔜 📳 🔥

★★ **HOLIDAY INN GRAND ISLAND.** *100 Whitehaven Rd, Grand Island (14072). 716/773-1111; fax 716/773-1229; res 800/465-4329. www.basshotels.com.* 262 rms, 5 suites, 6 story. Mid-June-early Sept: S, D $99-$129; suites $159; each addl $10; under 19 free; wkend plan; lower rates rest of yr. Crib free. TV; cable (premium). 2 pools, 1 heated indoor; whirlpool, wading pool, lifeguard. Playground. Supervised children's activities (June-Sept). Complimentary coffee in rms. Restaurant 6:30 am-2 pm, 5-10 pm; Sat, Sun from 7 am, 5-10 pm. Bar 5-10 pm; Sat 2-10 pm. Coffee in rms. Ck-out noon. Meeting rms. Business servs avail. Gift shop. Tennis. Golf adj. Coin lndry. Valet serv. Exercise rm; sauna. Massage. Rec rm. Game rm. Lawn games. Balconies. Some refrigerators. On Niagara River. Marina. Luxury level. Cr cds: A, C, D, DS, MC, V.

🄳 🏂 👜 📳 🔥

★★ **HOLIDAY INN SELECT.** *300 Third St (14303). 716/285-3361; fax 716/285-3900; res 800/465-4329. www.holiday-inn.com.* 397 rms, 28 suites, 6 story. Mid-June-mid-Sept: S, D $85-$139; each addl $10; suites $175-$375; lower rates rest of yr. Crib free. Pet accepted, some restrictions; $50 refundable. Free garage parking. TV; cable (premium), VCR avail. Indoor pool. Sauna. Restaurant 6:30 am-11 pm. Bar noon-midnight; Sat to 3 am. Ck-out noon. Convention facilities. Business servs avail. Gift shop. Exercise equipt. Game rm. Some refrigerators. Walkway to International Convention and Civic Center and Rainbow Center. Cr cds: A, C, D, DS, ER, JCB, MC, V.

🔜 🄳 🔜 📳 🔥

★ **HOWARD JOHNSON HOTEL.** *454 Main St (14301). 716/285-5261; fax 716/285-8536; toll-free 800/282-5261. www.hojo.com.* 80 rms, 5 story. June-Labor Day: S $80-$140; D $90-$150; each addl $8-$10; under 18 free; wkly, wkend rates; higher rates: hols, special events; lower rates rest of yr. Crib free. TV; cable. Indoor pool. Sauna. Restaurant 6:30 am-11 pm. Ck-out noon. Coin lndry. Business servs avail. Sundries. Game rm. Some in-rm whirlpools. Near falls. Cr cds: A, C, D, DS, ER, JCB, MC, V.

🄳 👜 🔜 📳 🔥

★ **PORTAGE HOUSE.** *280 Portage Rd, Lewiston (14092). 716/754-8295.* 21 rms, 2 story. No rm phone. May-Nov: S $57-$80.25; D $61-$80.25; each addl $7; under 12 free; lower rates rest of yr. Crib free. Pet accepted. TV; cable. Restaurant nearby. Ck-out 11 am. Cr cds: A, DS, MC, V.

🔜 👜 📳 🔥

★★ **RAMADA INN AT THE FALLS.** *240 Rainbow Blvd (14303). 716/282-1212; fax 716/282-1216. www.businessvillage.com/ramada.htm.* 217 rms, 4 story. Memorial Day-Labor Day: S, D $69-$139; each addl $10; suites $90-$150; under 18 free; lower rates rest of yr. TV; VCR avail (movies). Indoor pool; whirlpool. Restaurant 6:30 am-10 pm. Bar 3 pm-1 am. Ck-out noon. Meeting rms. Business servs avail.

Bellhops. Shopping mall adj. Cr cds: A, C, D, DS, MC, V.

D ⛱ ❄ 🔥 SC

★★ **RAMADA INN BY THE FALLS.** *219 4th St and Rainbow Blvd (14303). 716/282-1734; fax 716/282-1881; toll-free 800/333-2557. www.ramadainn bythefalls.com.* 112 rms, 2 story. Apr-Oct: S, D $49-$199; each addl $8-$12; lower rates rest of yr. Crib free. TV; cable (premium). Heated indoor pool; whirlpool. Complimentary continental bkfst. Restaurant 6:30 am-11 pm. Ck-out 11 am. Coin lndry. Concierge. Valet serv. Gift shop. Airport transportation. Meeting rm. Business servs avail. In-rm modem link. Some coffeemakers. Cr cds: A, C, D, DS, MC, V.

D 🛈 ⛱ ❄ 🔥

★ **THRIFTLODGE AMERICANA.** *9401 Niagara Falls Blvd (14304). 716/297-2660; fax 716/297-7675; toll-free 800/283-4678.* 45 rms. June-Labor Day: S $39-$69; D $45-$79; each addl $5-$10; kit. suites $45-$129; under 18 free; higher rates American and Canadian hols; lower rates rest of yr. Crib free. TV; cable (premium). Heated pool. Restaurant opp 7-3 am. Ck-out 11 am. Coin lndry. Business servs avail. Some in-rm whirlpools, refrigerators. Picnic tables. Cr cds: A, C, D, DS, MC, V.

D ⛱ ❄ 🔥 SC

★ **TRAVELODGE FALLS VIEW.** *201 Rainbow Blvd (14303). 716/285-9321; fax 716/285-2539.* 193 rms, 12 story. Mid-June-early Sept: S, D $59-$118; each addl $8; under 16 free; lower rates rest of yr. Crib free. Pet accepted. TV; VCR avail (movies). Restaurant 6:30 am-10 pm. Bar 11-2 am. Ck-out 11 am. Meeting rms. Business servs avail. Game rm. Some refrigerators; microwaves avail. Overlooks rapids. Cr cds: A, D, DS, MC, V.

🐾 ❄ 🔥 SC

B&B/Small Inn

★★★ **THE RED COACH INN.** *2 Buffalo Ave (14303). 716/282-1459; fax 716/282-2650; toll-free 800/282-1459. www.redcoach.com.* 14 rms, 3 story, 12 kit. suites. S, D $139-$299; kit. suites $$299; package plans. TV; cable (premium), some VCRs. Complimentary continental bkfst, coffee in rms. Restaurant (see also RED COACH INN). Bar 11:30 am-10 pm. Ck-out 11 am, ck-in 3 pm. Meeting rms. Business servs avail. In-rm modem link. Luggage handling. Valet serv. Refrigerators. Some fireplaces. Microwaves avail. X-country ski 5 mi. View of Upper Rapids. Built 1923; authentic Old English atmosphere. Cr cds: DS, MC, V.

D 🐾 ❄ 🔥

Restaurants

★ **ALPS CHALET.** *1555 Military Rd (14304). 716/297-8990.* Greek, American menu. Specializes in steak, seafood. Hrs: 11-2 am; Sat noon-3 am; Sun brunch 11 am-2 pm. Closed Mon. Res accepted. Bar. Lunch $3-$5, dinner $8.95-$20.95. Child's menu. Parking. Chalet-type decor. Family-owned. Cr cds: A, DS, MC, V.

D ⌐

★★ **CLARKSON HOUSE.** *810 Center St, Lewiston (14902). 716/754-4544.* Specializes in charbroiled steak, lobster. Hrs: 5-11 pm; Sun 3-9 pm. Closed Dec 25. Res accepted; required Sat, Sun. Bar. Dinner $12.95-$45. Child's menu. Parking. Open-hearth cooking. 1818 house. Family-owned. Cr cds: A, D, MC, V.

D SC ⌐

★★ **COMO.** *2220 Pine Ave (14301). 716/285-9341.* Italian, Amer menu. Specialties: veal parmigiana, fettucine Alfredo, ravioli. Hrs: 11:30 am-11 pm; early-bird dinner Mon-Thurs 3-5 pm. Closed hols. Res accepted. Bar. Lunch $4-$7, dinner $8-$28. Child's menu. Parking. Statuary reproductions. Family-owned. Cr cds: A, DS, MC, V.

D SC ⌐

★★ **JOHN'S FLAMING HEARTH.** *1965 Military Rd (14304). 716/297-1301.* Specializes in steak, lobster. Own ice cream. Hrs: 11:30 am-10 pm; Sun noon-9 pm; early-bird dinner Mon-Fri 4-6 pm. Res accepted. Bar. Lunch $3-$7.50. Complete meals: dinner $11.95-$42.95. Child's menu. Entertainment Sat. Parking. Family-owned. Cr cds: A, C, D, DS, MC, V.

D SC ⌐

★★ **RED COACH INN.** *2 Buffalo Ave (14303). 716/282-1459. www.redcoach.*

om. Specializes in prime rib. Hrs: 11:30 am-10 pm; Fri, Sat to 11 pm. Closed Dec 25. Bar. Lunch $3.95-$8.95, dinner $7-$24. Child's menu. Parking. Glassed-porch dining overlooking Upper Rapids. English inn decor and atmosphere. Cr cds: DS, MC, V.

D SC

★ ★ **RIVERSIDE INN.** *115 S Water St, Lewiston (14092). 716/754-8206. www.riversideinn.net.* Specializes in lamb shanks. Hrs: 11:30 am-3 pm, 4-11 pm; Fri and Sat to midnight; winter hrs vary; early-bird dinner 4-5 pm, Sun noon-8 pm. Res accepted. Bar. Lunch $4.95-$12.95, dinner $8.99-$24.99. Child's menu. Entertainment Thurs-Mon; also Sun in summer. Parking. Outdoor dining. Built 1871; riverboat atmosphere. Family-owned. Cr cds: A, C, D, DS, JCB, MC, V.

D SC →

★ **VILLA COFFEE HOUSE.** *769 Cayuga St, Lewiston (14092). 716/754-2660.* Specializes in egg dishes, pancakes, soup. Hrs: 7 am-2 pm. Closed Jan 1, Thanksgiving, Dec 25. Bkfst, lunch $2.40-$9.95. Child's menu.

D →

North Creek

See also Schroon Lake, Warrensburg

Pop 950 **Elev** 1,028 ft **Area code** 518 **Zip** 12853

Information Gore Mountain Region Chamber of Commerce Accommodation and Visitors Bureau, 295 Main St, PO Box 84; 518/251-2612 or 800/880-GORE

Web www.goremtnregion.org

What to See and Do

Adirondack Park. (see)

Gore Mountain Mineral Shop. Tours of open-pit garnet mine; opportunity to collect loose gem garnets. (Mid-June-Labor Day, daily) Barton Mine Rd. Phone 518/251-2706.

Rafting. Sixteen-mi whitewater rafting trips from Indian Lake to North

River. (Apr-Nov) Contact Gore Mtn Region Chamber of Commerce.

Ski areas.

Garnet Hill Lodge, Cross-Country Ski Center, and Mountain Bike Center. Approx 35 mi of groomed x-country trails adj state wilderness trails; tennis courts, mountain biking (rentals), hiking trails, fishing, beach and boat rentals on 13th Lake, site of abandoned garnet mine. Restaurant. (Daily) 5 mi NW via NY 28, at the top of 13th Lake Rd. Phone 518/251-2444 or 518/251-2821. ¢¢¢¢

Gore Mountain. Gondola; two quad, triple, three double chairlifts; two surface lifts; x-country trails; patrol, school, rentals; cafeteria, restaurant, bar; nursery; lodges; snowmaking. Longest run three mi; vertical drop 2,100 ft. (Nov-Apr, daily; also fall wkends for gondola) Approx 2 mi NW off NY 28. Phone 518/251-2411. ¢¢¢¢

Special Events

White Water Derby. Hudson River. Canoe and kayak competition. First wkend May. Phone 518/523-1855.

Adirondack Artisans Festival. Gore Mtn Ski Area. First wkend Aug.

Teddy Roosevelt Celebration. Townwide. Sept. Phone 518/582-4451.

Motel/Motor Lodge

★ ★ **BLACK MOUNTAIN SKI LODGE & MOTEL.** *2999 NY 8 (12853). 518/251-2800; fax 518/251-5326; toll-free 888/846-4858. blackmountainskilodge.com.* 25 rms. Mid-Dec-mid-May: S $35-$45; D $55-$75; each addl $5; Apr-May: family, wkly rates; skiing, hiking, canoeing, rafting packages; lower rates rest of yr. Crib $5. Pet accepted. TV; cable. Pool. Playground. Restaurant 7-10 am. Ck-out 11 am. Sundries. Downhill/x-country ski 5 mi. Rec rm. Some refrigerators. Cr cds: A, DS, MC, V.

🐾 🏊 ⛷ 🎿

B&B/Small Inn

★ **GARNET HILL LODGE.** *13 Lake Rd, North River (12856). 518/251-2444; fax 518/251-3089; toll-free 800/497-4207. www.garnet-hill.com.*

29 rms, 26 with bath, 2 story. MAP: S $82-$135; D $62-$95/person; each addl $45; family, wkly rates; skiing, rafting packages. TV rm; VCR (movies). Dining rm 7:30-9:30 am, noon-2:30 pm, 5-9 pm. Ck-out 11 am, ck-in 4 pm. Business servs avail. Airport transportation, free bus depot transportation. Tennis. Downhill ski 15 mi; x-country ski on site, instructor, rentals. Nature trails. Mountain bicycles. Rec rm. Exercise rm; sauna. Some balconies. Private beach; swimming. Fishing guides. Stocked lake. Rustic setting. Cr cds: MC, V.

D 🐾 📷 ⛳ 🎿 SC

Northport (L.I.)

(G-2) *See also Huntington (L.I.), Smithtown (L.I.), Stony Brook (L.I.)*

Settled 1656 **Pop** 7,606 **Elev** 100 ft
Area code 516 **Zip** 11768

An early English Puritan settlement, the land in and around Northport was purchased from the Matinecock.

What to See and Do

Eaton's Neck Lighthouse. (1798) Second lighthouse built in the US. A 73-ft-high beacon warns ships more than 17 mi out at sea. Lighthouse Rd.

Northport Historical Museum. Changing exhibits of local history; photographs, artifacts, costumes, and shipbuilding memorabilia. (Tues-Sun; closed hols) Walking tours of village on some Sun afternoons in spring and summer. 215 Main St. Phone 516/757-9859. **Donation**

Suffolk County Vanderbilt Museum. Marine science and natural history exhibits, habitat groups; original fine and decorative arts; Spanish Revival 21-rm mansion, 43 landscaped acres. (Tues-Sun; closed hols) On Little Neck Rd in Centerport, about 1 mi N of NY 25A. Phone 516/854-5555. ¢¢¢ Also here is

Vanderbilt Museum Planetarium. Sky shows (Tues-Sun). Phone 516/854-5555.

North Salem

(see Brewster)

Norwich

(E-6) *See also Hamilton, Oneonta*

Pop 7,355 **Elev** 1,015 ft
Area code 607 **Zip** 13815
Information Chenango County Chamber of Commerce, 19 Eaton Ave; 607/334-1400 or 800/556-8596
Web www.chenangony.com

What to See and Do

Bowman Lake State Park. This 660-acre park borders on 11,000 acres of state forest land. Swimming beach, fishing, paddleboats, rowboats (rentals); nature and hiking trails, x-country skiing, snowmobiling, picnicking. NY 220 W, in Oxford. Phone 607/334-2718. ¢¢

Northeast Classic Car Museum. Features the largest collection of Franklin autos in the world; Duesenbergs, Cords, Auburns, Packards, and more. All are restored, preserved, and fully operational. (Daily; closed Jan 1, Thanksgiving, Dec 25) 24 Rexford St. ¢¢

Special Events

General Clinton Canoe Regatta. General Clinton Park, Rte 7 in Bainbridge. Phone 607/967-8700. Memorial Day wkend.

Chenango County Fair. Chenango County Fairgrounds, W Main St. Phone 607/334-9198. Mid-Aug.

Motels/Motor Lodges

★ **HOWARD JOHNSON HOTEL.** 75 N Broad St (13815). 607/334-2200; fax 607/336-5619. www.norwich.net/~hojos. 86 units, 3 story. S $79-$149; D $89-$159; each addl $10; suites $75-$125; some wkend rates; higher rates special events. Crib free. Pet accepted, some restrictions; $5. TV; cable (premium). Indoor pool. Coffee in rms. Restaurant 8 am-11 pm. Bar. Ck-out 11 am. Meeting rms. Business servs avail. Health club privileges. In-rm whirlpools; some refrigerators; microwaves avail. Cr cds: A, D, DS, MC, V.

★ **SUPER 8.** *6067 State Hwy 12 (13815). 607/336-8880; fax 607/336-2076; toll-free 800/800-8000. www.super8.com.* 42 rms, 3 story. June-Aug: S, D $48-$170; each addl $5; suites $100-$200; under 12 free; wkend rates; higher rates special events; lower rates rest of yr. Crib free. TV; cable (premium). Complimentary continental bkfst. Restaurant opp 6 am-10 pm. Ck-out 11 am. Meeting rm. Refrigerator in suites. Picnic tables. Cr cds: A, C, D, DS, JCB, MC, V.

Restaurant

★★ **HANDS INN.** *S Broad St (13815). 607/334-8223.* Specializes in steak, seafood, pasta. Hrs: 11 am-2 pm, 5-9:30 pm. Closed Sun; Memorial Day, July 4, Labor Day. Res accepted; required hols. Bar 11 am-10 pm. Lunch $4-$11.95, dinner $6.95-$25. Buffet: lunch $5.95. Child's menu. Family-owned. Cr cds: A, C, D, DS, MC, V.

Nyack

See also White Plains

Pop 6,737 **Elev** 70 ft **Area code** 845 **Zip** 10960

Information Chamber of Commerce, PO Box 677; 845/353-2221

Many outstanding Victorian-style homes and an Edward Hopper art gallery grace this village.

What to See and Do

Antiques on the Hudson. A collection of more than 75 art, crafts, and antique shops located in upper Nyack on the Hudson. (Tues-Sun) W side of Tappan Zee Bridge; NY State Thrwy N exit 10 or 11; or Thrwy S exit 11. Phone 845/358-3751.

Hudson Valley Children's Museum. Interactive, hands-on exhibits focus on arts and sciences. Exhibits incl Early Childhood, Royal Bubble Factory, Gadget Garage, Creation Station, and others with social and educational themes. Museum shop. (Mon-Sat) 21C Burd St, Nyack Seaport. Phone 845/358-2191. ¢¢

Motels/Motor Lodges

★★ **BEST WESTERN NYACK ON HUDSON.** *26 Rte 59 (10960). 845/358-8100; fax 845/358-3644; res 800/528-1234. www.bestwestern.com.* 80 rms, 2 story. S, D $95; each addl $5; under 18 free. Crib $10. TV; cable (premium). Restaurant open 24 hrs. Bar 4:30 pm-2 am; entertainment. Ck-out noon. Meeting rms. Business servs avail. In-rm modem link. Cr cds: A, D, DS, MC, V.

★ **SUPER 8 MOTEL.** *47 NY 59 (10960). 845/353-3880; fax 845/353-0271; toll-free 800/800-8000.* 43 rms, 2 story. May-Sep: S $62.88; D $64.88; each addl $3; under 12 free; higher rates: West Point graduation, some hols; lower rates rest of yr. Crib free. TV; cable (premium). Complimentary coffee in lobby. Restaurant adj 5 am-10 pm. Ck-out 11 am. Business servs avail. In-rm modem link. Cr cds: A, D, DS, MC, V.

Restaurants

★ **ICHI RIKI.** *110 Main St (10960). 845/358-7977.* Japanese menu. Specializes in sushi, Japanese dishes. Hrs: noon-2:30 pm, 5:30-10 pm; Fri to 11 pm; Sat 5-11 pm; Sun 5-9:30 pm. Closed Mon; Thanksgiving, Dec 25. Res accepted. Bar. Lunch $7.95-$18.95, dinner $12.50-$27.50. Cr cds: A, C, D, MC, V.

★ **KING & I.** *93 Main St (10960). 845/353-4208.* Thai menu. Specialties: curried duck, whole crispy fish flambe, chicken with peanut sauce. Hrs: 11:30 am-3 pm, 5-10 pm; Fri to

11 pm; Sat 11:30 am-11 pm; Sun 11:30 am-10 pm. Closed hols. Res accepted. Bar. Lunch $7.50-$8.50, dinner $10.95-$17.95. Cr cds: A, MC, V.

D

★★ **THE MARINER.** *701 Piermont Ave, Piermont (10968).* 845/365-1360. Seafood menu. Specializes in lobster. Own desserts. Hrs: 11:30 am-10 pm; Fri, Sat to 11 pm; Sun to 9 pm. Res accepted. Bar. A la carte entrees: lunch $3.95-$17.95, dinner $4.95-$17.95. Pianist Sat. Parking. Outdoor dining. Tiered dining rm overlooking the river; view of Tappan Zee Bridge. Cr cds: A, MC, V.

D

★★★ **RESTAURANT X AND BULLY BOY BAR.** *117 N Rte 303, Congers (10920).* 845/268-6555. *www. xaviars.com.* International menu. Own baking. Hrs: noon-2:30 pm, 5:30-10 pm; Sun 2-9 pm. Closed Mon; also Dec 25 and Jan 1. Res accepted. Bar. A la carte: lunch $10-$15, dinner $18-$27. Parking. 3 fireplaces. Overlooks pond and gardens. Cr cds: A, MC, V.

D ⌐

★★ **RIVER CLUB.** *11 Burd St (10960).* 845/358-0220. Specializes in steak, seafood, ribs. Hrs: noon-midnight; Fri, Sat to 1 am; Sun brunch 11:30 am-3 pm. Closed Thanksgiving, Dec 25. Res accepted. Bar. A la carte entrees: lunch $6.95-$10.95, dinner $9.95-$21.95. Sun brunch $4.95-$9.95. Parking. Outdoor dining. Nautical decor; view of river, marina. Cr cds: A, C, D, DS, MC, V.

D ⌐

Ogdensburg (Thousand Islands)

(A-6) *See also Canton*

Settled 1749 **Pop** 12,364 **Elev** 280 ft
Area code 315 **Zip** 13669
Information Greater Ogdensburg Chamber of Commerce, 1020 Park St, PO Box 681; 315/393-3620
Web www.ogdensburgny.com

On the St. Lawrence Seaway, at the mouth of the Oswegatchie River, this busy port and industrial town had its beginnings as an outpost of New France, where the Iroquois were converted to Christianity. In 1837, it was the base from which American sympathizers worked "to free Canada from the yoke of England" in the abortive Patriots' War.

What to See and Do

Fort Wellington National Historic Site. Built during War of 1812 to protect communications link between Montreal and Kingston; rebuilt 1838-1839 in response to the Canadian Rebellions of 1837-1838. Restored blockhouse, officers' quarters, guides in period costume, demonstrations of 1846 life at the fort. (Mid-May-Sept, daily; rest of yr, by appt) 379 Van-Koughnet St in Prescott, Ontario, Canada, 4 mi W of International Bridge. Phone 613/925-2896.

✪ **Frederic Remington Art Museum.** Largest single collection of paintings, sculpture, drawings by Frederic Remington, foremost artist of the Old West; re-created studio; Belter furniture, glass, china, silver. (May-Oct, daily; rest of yr, Wed-Sat; closed legal hols) 303 Washington St. Phone 315/393-2425. ¢¢

Greenbelt Riverfront Park. Deepwater marina, launching ramp; picnicking, barbecue pits, lighted tennis courts. (Daily) Riverside Ave. Phone 315/393-1980.

Jacques Cartier State Park. Swimming beach, bathhouse, fishing, boating (launch, anchorage); picnicking, playground, tent and trailer sites. (Late May-early Oct) Standard fees. 3 mi SW via NY 12, near Morristown. Phone 315/375-6371.

Ogdensburg, NY-Johnstown, Ontario International Bridge. 13,510 ft long; opened Sept 1960. View of St. Lawrence Valley and Seaway marine terminal. Duty-free shop. Connects NY 37 and 812 with Hwys 2, 16, and 401 in Canada. Contact Bridge Plaza. Phone 315/393-4080. ¢

Swimming Beaches. Municipal Beach. At Bridge Plaza. **Lisbon Beach.** 5 mi N on NY 37. **FREE**

War of 1812 Battlefield Walking Tour. Walking tour along site of the Battle of Ogdensburg. ½ mi of paved walkways on waterfront; plaques located along the path detail the action. In Greenbelt Riverfront Park.

Special Event

International Seaway Festival. Concerts, fireworks, parade, canoe race. Last full wk July. Phone 315/393-3620.

Motels/Motor Lodges

★★ **QUALITY INN GRAN VIEW.** *6765 NY 37 (13669). 315/393-4550; fax 315/393-3520; res 800/228-5151. www.qualityinn.com.* 48 rms, 2 story. Mid-May-mid-Sep: S $45-$55; D $57-$72; each addl $8; under 18 free; wkend plans; higher rates special events; lower rates rest of yr. Crib $5. TV; cable. Pool. Coffee in rms. Restaurant. Bar 11-2 am; entertainment. Ck-out 11 am. Meeting rms. Business servs avail. In-rm modem link. Lawn games. Refrigerators avail. Private patios, balconies. Picnic tables, grills. Docking facilities. Overlooks river. Cr cds: A, C, D, DS, ER, JCB, MC, V.

🅳 🖾 🛏 🐾

★★ **RAMADA INN RIVER RESORT.** *119 W River St (13669). 315/393-2222; fax 315/393-9602; toll-free 800/649-1721. www.ramada.com.* 76 rms, 2 story. July-mid-Oct: S $59; D $69-$79; each addl $10; suites $99; under 18 free; higher rates special events; lower rates rest of yr. Crib free. TV; cable (premium), VCR. Indoor pool; lifeguard. Restaurant 7 am-9 pm. Bar. Ck-out 11 am. Coin lndry. Meeting rms. Business servs avail. Exercise equipt. Game rm. Some refrigerators. Minibar in suites. On Oswegatchie River; dockage. Cr cds: A, C, D, DS, MC, V.

🅳 🖾 🛏 🐾 🆂🅲

★ **WINDJAMMER MOTEL.** *5843 A, State Hwy 37 (13669). 315/393-3730; fax 315/393-3520; res 800/392-4550.* 20 rms. July-Sept: S $35; D $45-$49; each addl $5; lower rates rest of yr. Crib $8. TV; cable. Pool. Ck-out 11 am. Sundries. Coffee in rms. Refrigerators avail. Picnic tables. Boat dockage. Overlooks St. Lawrence Seaway. Cr cds: A, C, D, DS, MC, V.

🖾 🐾

Resort

★★ **STONEFENCE LODGING INC.** *7191 State Hwy 37 (13669). 315/393-1545; fax 315/393-1749; res 800/253-1545. www.stonefenceresort. com.* 31 rms, 11 suites. May-Sep: S $69-$89; D $79-$119; each addl $5; suites $79-$145; wkly rates; lower rates rest of yr. Crib $6. Pet accepted; $12. TV; cable. Pool; whirlpool. Sauna. Complimentary coffee in rms. Restaurant 7 am-10 pm. Ck-out 11 am. Coin lndry. Tennis. Putting green. Many refrigerators; some wet bars. Whirlpool in suites. Picnic tables, grills. Gazebo. On river; dockage, boat rentals, beach. Cr cds: A, D, DS, MC, V.

🅳 🐾 🛏 🐾

Restaurant

★ **SHOLETTE'S STEAK & ALE.** *1000 Linden St, Ogdensburg (13669). 315/393-5172.* Italian, Mexican, American menu. Specializes in steak, lasagne, seafood. Salad bar. Hrs: 10-2 am; Sat from 11 am; Sun from 11 am. Closed hols. Res accepted. Bar. A la carte entrees: lunch $3-$7.50, dinner $6.50-$25.95. Child's menu. Family-owned. Cr cds: A, DS, MC, V.

🅳 🖾

Old Forge

Pop 1,060 **Elev** 1,712 ft
Area code 315 **Zip** 13420
Information Visitor Information Center, NY 28, PO Box 68; 315/369-6983

In almost any season there is fun in this Adirondack resort town, located in the Fulton Chain of Lakes region—everything from hunting, fishing, snowmobiling, and skiing to basking on a sunny beach.

What to See and Do

Adirondack Park. (see)
Canoeing. An 86-mi canoe trip to the hamlet of Paul Smiths (north of the Saranac Lakes). For information on Adirondack canoe trips contact Department of Environmental Con-

servation, Albany 12233-4255. Phone 518/457-7433.

Enchanted Forest/Water Safari. A 60-acre water-theme park complex featuring 23 water attractions and 14 traditional amusement rides; circus performances. (June-Labor Day) ½ mi N on NY 28. Phone 315/369-6145. ¢¢¢¢

Fern Park. Hiking, x-country skiing, showshoeing, biking, ice-skating, baseball, volleyball, basketball; special events. 15 mi NW in Inlet. Phone 315/357-5501. **FREE**

Forest Industries Exhibit Hall. Samples of products of forest industries; dioramas; film on managed forests. (Late May-Labor Day, Mon, Wed-Sun; after Labor Day-Columbus Day, wkends only) 1 mi N on NY 28. Phone 315/369-3078. **FREE**

Old Forge Lake Cruise. Cruises on Fulton Chain of Lakes (28 mi). (Memorial Day-Columbus Day) Also showboat and dinner cruises. Contact Box 1137. Phone 315/369-6473. ¢¢¢

Public beach. Swimming; lifeguards, bathhouse. (Early June-Labor Day, daily) Tourist Information Center is located here (daily). On NY 28. ¢

Skiing. McCauley Mountain. Double chairlift, two T-bars, two rope tows, pony lift; patrol, school, rentals; snowmaking; cafeteria. Longest run ¾ mi; vertical drop 633 ft. (Thanksgiving-Apr, Mon and Wed-Sun) Half-day rates. Chairlift to top of McCauley Mtn also operates June-Oct (daily). Picnic area. 2 mi S off NY 28. ¢¢¢¢

Motels/Motor Lodges

★★ **BEST WESTERN.** *NY 28 (13420). 315/369-6836; fax 315/369-2607; toll-free 800/780-7234. www.bestwestern.com.* 52 rms, 1-2 story. Late June-Labor Day, late Dec-early Apr: S, D $79-$135; each addl $10, under 13 free; lower rates rest of yr. Crib $6. Pet accepted. TV; cable (premium). Indoor pool; whirlpool. Sauna. Playground. Complimentary continental bkfst. Restaurant nearby. Ck-out 11 am. Lndry facilities. Tennis. Golf opp. Downhill ski 3 mi; x-country ski opp. Some balconies. Picnic area, gazebo, grill. Cr cds: A, DS, MC, V.

★ **COUNTRY CLUB MOTEL.** *Hwy 28 (13420). 315/369-6340.* 27 rms. Jan-Feb, late June-Labor Day: S, D $70-$85; each addl $5; wkly rates; under 12 free; lower rates rest of yr. Crib $5. TV; cable (premium). Heated pool. Complimentary coffee in rms. Restaurant nearby. Ck-out 11 am. Downhill ski 2 mi; x-country ski adj. Lawn games. Many refrigerators, microwaves. Cr cds: A, C, D, DS, JCB, MC, V.

Hotel

★ **19TH GREEN.** *NY 28 (13420). 315/369-3575.* 13 rms. Late June-Sept, Dec-Mar: S, D $55-$80; each addl $5; lower rates rest of yr. Crib $5. TV; cable. Pool. Coffee in rms. Restaurant nearby. Ck-out 10 am. Downhill ski 3 mi; x-country ski adj. Game rm. Lawn games. Refrigerators, microwaves. Picnic tables. Golf course adj. Cr cds: A, D, DS, MC, V.

Cottage Colony

★ **COVEWOOD LODGE.** *Big Moose Lk, Eagle Bay (13331). 315/357-3041; fax 315/357-5902; toll-free 800/357-7530. www.covewoodlodge.com.* 3 kit. apts (2-bedrm), 1-2 story, 17 kit. cottages. No A/C. No rm phones. Kit. apts $705-$810/wk; kit. cottages for 2-12, $600-$1,600/wk. Kit. apts and 3 cottages closed in winter. Crib free. Playground. Ck-out 10:30 am. Coin lndry. Tennis. Downhill ski 15 mi; x-country ski on site. Game rms. Lawn games. Lake swimming. Fireplaces. Library. Private porches. Grills. Dock.

Restaurant

★★ **OLD MILL.** *RR 28 (13420). 315/369-3662.* Specializes in steak, seafood. Hrs: 4:30-9:30 pm; Fri, Sat to 10 pm; Sun 1-9 pm. Closed 2nd wkend Mar; also Nov-Dec. Bar. Dinner $10.95-$17.95. Child's menu. Converted gristmill. Cr cds: MC, V.

Olean (F-2)

Settled 1804 **Pop** 15,347 **Elev** 1,451 ft
Area code 716 **Zip** 14760

Information Greater Olean Chamber of Commerce, 120 N Union St; 716/372-4433

Web www.oleanny.com

Only seven years after the landing of the Pilgrims, a Franciscan father was led by Native Americans to a mystical spring near the present city of Olean. There he found what he called "thick water which ignited like brandy." It was petroleum. Olean (from the latin *oleum,* meaning "oil") was once an oil-boom town; now it is a manufacturing and retail center.

What to See and Do

Allegany State Park. (see) 15 mi E on NY 17.

Friedsam Memorial Library. Paintings by Rembrandt, Rubens, and Bellini; works by 19th-century and contemporary artists; American southwest and pre-Columbian pottery, porelain collection; rare books. Sept-mid-June, Mon-Sat; rest of yr, Mon-Fri; closed school hols) On campus of St. Bonaventure University, St. Bonaventure. Phone 716/375-2323. **FREE**

Motel/Motor Lodge

★★ **CASTLE INN.** *3168 Rte 417 (14760). 716/372-1050; fax 716/372-745; toll-free 800/422-7853. www.castleolean.com.* 160 rms, 2 story. S $45-$74; D $52-$81; each addl $6; suites $71-$86; under 18 free; ski, wkend plans. Crib free. TV; cable. Heated pool. Complimentary full bkfst Sun-Thurs. Restaurant 6-11 am, 5-9 pm; Sat to noon; Sun 6 am-2 pm. Bar 5 pm-2 am; entertainment. Ck-out noon. Meeting rms. Business servs avail. Valet serv. 9-hole, par 3 golf. X-country ski 20 mi. Exercise equipt. Health club privileges. Bicycles. Lawn games. Some refrigerators. Private patios, balconies. Picnic tables. Cr cds: A, D, DS, MC, V.

B&B/Small Inn

★★ **OLD LIBRARY B & B.** *120 S Union St (14760). 716/373-9804; fax 716/373-2462; toll-free 877/241-4348. www.oldlibraryrestaurant.com.* 7 rms, 3 story, 2 suites. S $65; D $75; each addl $20; suites $115-$125. TV; cable, VCR avail. Complimentary full bkfst. Restaurant (see also OLD LIBRARY). Ck-out 11 am, ck-in 3 pm. Meeting rm. Business servs avail. In-rm modem link. Health club privileges. House built in 1895. Antique furnishings; sitting rm with fireplace. Cr cds: A, D, DS, MC, V.

Restaurants

★★ **BEEF 'N BARREL.** *146 N Union St (14760). 716/372-2985.* Specializes in beef, pie. Hrs: 11 am-11 pm. Closed hols. Bar. Lunch $4.25-$9.95, dinner $4.95-$18.95. Child's menu. Colonial decor. Family-owned. Cr cds: A, C, D, DS, MC, V.

★★ **OLD LIBRARY.** *116 S Union St (14760). 716/372-2226. www.oldlibraryrestaurant.com.* Continental menu. Specializes in prime rib, scampi, veal. Own pastries. Hrs: 11 am-10 pm; Sun brunch to 2:30 pm. Closed hols. Res accepted. Bar. Wine cellar. Lunch $4.50-$9.95, dinner $9.95-$24.95. Sun brunch $9.95. Child's menu. Historic landmark; former Andrew Carnegie library (1909). Some original furnishings; many antiques; rotunda; marble frieze extends through the foyer; leaded glass. Cr cds: A, DS, MC, V.

Unrated Dining Spot

NO MATCH SOUTHERN COOKIN'. *1615 W State St (14760). 716/373-7181.* Specializes in Southern style chicken steak dinner, southern barbeque salad, ribs, catfish. Hrs: 11:30 am-7:30 pm, Sun 11:30 am-5:30 pm. Closed Wed. Lunch, dinner $3.95-$7.95.

Oneida

(D-6) *See also Canastota, Cazenovia, Herkimer, Ilion, Rome, Skaneateles, Syracuse, Utica*

Settled 1834 **Pop** 10,987 **Elev** 443 ft
Area code 315 **Zip** 13421
Information The Greater Oneida Chamber of Commerce, 136 Lenox Ave; 315/363-4300
Web www.oneidachamber.org

Perhaps the best known of the 19th-century American "Utopias" was established at Oneida (o-NYE-dah) in 1848 by John Humphrey Noyes, leader of the "Perfectionists." The group held all property in common, practiced complex marriage, and undertook other social experiments. Faced with hostile attacks by the local population, the community was dissolved in 1880. In 1881 the Oneida Community became a stock corporation. The silverware factory it built remains a major industry, making "Community Plate" and William A. Rogers silver.

What to See and Do

Madison County Historical Society, Cottage Lawn Museum. An 1849 Gothic-revival cottage designed by Alexander Jackson Davis. Victorian period rms; historical and traditional craft archives; changing exhibits; 1862 stagecoach, 1853 gym, and adj agricultural museum. (June-Aug, Mon-Sat; Sept-May, Mon-Fri) 435 Main St at Grove St. Phone 315/363-4136. ¢

The Mansion House. The communal home built in the 1860s. Tours (Wed-Sat, morning and afternoon tours, also Sun afternoon tours). Phone 315/361-3671. ¢¢

Vernon Downs. Harness racing; glass-enclosed grandstand and clubhouse. (Feb-early Nov) 8 mi E on NY 5, S of I-90 exit 33, on NY 31 in Vernon. Phone 315/829-2201. ¢

Verona Beach State Park. Swimming beach, bathhouse, fishing; hiking (all yr), x-country skiing, snowmobiling, picnicking, baseball, basketball, fishing, horse trails, playground, concession, tent and trailer sites. Standard fees. N on NY 46, W on NY 31, then N on NY 13, on Oneida Lake. Phone 315/762-4463. ¢¢

Special Events

Craft Days. Madison County Historical Society Museum. Traditional craftsmen demonstrate their skills; food, entertainment. First wkend after Labor Day wkend. Phone 315/363-4136.

Madison County Hop Fest. Phone 315/363-4136.

Motels/Motor Lodges

★★ **COMFORT SUITES.** *4229 Stuhlman Rd, Vernon (13476). 315/829-3400; fax 315/829-3787.* 175 suites, 7 story. S $69-$119, D $79-$129; under 16 free; higher rates wkends, special events. Crib free. TV; cable (premium). Indoor pool; whirlpool, lifeguard. Complimentary continental bkfst, coffee in rms. Restaurant 6:30-10 am, 11:30 am-2:30 pm, 4:30-11 pm. Bar 4 pm-1 am. Ck-out noon. Meeting rms. In-rm modem link. Exercise rm; sauna. Gift shop. Game rm. Refrigerators, microwaves, some in-rm whirlpools. Cr cds: A, C, D, DS, JCB, MC, V.
⊡ ⬥ ⚡ ⌷ 🏃 🐾 SC

★ **SUPER 8 MOTEL.** *215 Genesee St (13421). 315/363-5168; fax 315/363-4628; res 800/800-8000. www.super8.com.* 39 rms, 2 story. June-Sept: S $40-$70; D $40-$80; each addl $5; under 12 free; higher rates some wkends, special events; lower rates rest of yr. Crib free. TV; cable (premium). Complimentary continental bkfst in lobby. Restaurant adj 7 am-11 pm. Ck-out 11 am. In-rm modem link. Cr cds: A, C, D, DS, JCB, MC, V.
⊡ ⬚ 🐾

B&B/Small Inn

★ **INN AT TURNING STONE.** *5558 Main St, Verona (13478). 315/363-0096; fax 315/361-7999; res 800/771-7711.* 63 rms, 2 story. S $45-$65; D $55-$80; each addl $5; under 12 free wkend rates; higher rates special events. TV; cable (premium). Complimentary continental bkfst. Restaurant nearby. Ck-out 11 am. Cr cds: A, D, DS, MC, V.
⊡ ⬥ ⬚ 🐾

Oneonta

E-6) See also Cooperstown, Norwich, Stamford

Settled 1780 **Pop** 13,292 **Elev** 1,085 ft
Area code 607 **Zip** 13820
Information Otsego County Chamber of Commerce, 12 Carbon St; 607/432-4500 or 800/843-3394
Web www.otsegocountychamber. com

Oneonta lies deep in the hills at the western edge of the Catskills. It was here in 1883 that the Brotherhood of Railroad Trainmen had its beginnings. A branch of the State University College of New York is located here.

What to See and Do

Gilbert Lake State Park. Swimming, fishing, boating; picnicking, playground, concession, tent and trailer sites, cabins. Standard fees. (Mid-May-mid-Oct, daily) 7½ mi N on NY 205 to Laurens, then County 12 to park. Phone 607/432-2114. ¢¢

Hanford Mills Museum. Water-powered sawmill, gristmill, and woodworking complex dating from a 1840. Ten-ft diameter by 12-ft width overshot waterwheel drives machinery. Demonstrations of antique machine collection, tours. Special events. Picnicking. (May-Oct, daily) 11 mi E via NY 23, on County 10, in East Meredith. Phone 607/278-5744. ¢¢

Hartwick College. (1797) 1,400 students. Library and archives house collections of works by Willard Yager, Judge William Cooper, and John Christopher Hartwick papers. Hall of Science with display of fresh and saltwater shells and Hoysradt Herbarium. Anderson Center for the Arts. Yager Museum contains more than 10,000 Native American artifacts and the VanEss Collection of Renaissance and Baroque Art (Sept-May, daily; rest of yr, by appt only). Oyaron Hill. Phone 607/431-4200.

National Soccer Hall of Fame. Displays and exhibits range from youth, amateur, and collegiate to professional soccer; trophies, mementos, historical items, uniforms. Interactive games. Video theater with soccer films dating from 1930s. (Daily; closed hols) 18 Stadium Cir. Phone 607/432-3351. ¢¢

Motels/Motor Lodges

★ ★ **HOLIDAY INN.** *Rte 23 Southside (13820).* 607/433-2250; fax 607/432-7028; toll-free 800/465-4329. www. holiday-inn.com. 120 rms, 2 story. S, D $77-$199; under 19 free; higher rates special events. Crib free. Pet accepted, some restrictions. TV; cable (premium). Pool; wading pool. Coffee in rms. Restaurant 7 am-9 pm. Bar noon-midnight; entertainment Wed, Fri, Sat. Ck-out 11 am. Coin lndry. Meeting rms. In-rm modem link. Game rm. Refrigerators, microwaves avail. Picnic tables. Cr cds: A, C, D, DS, MC, V.
D ◨ ◨ ◨ ◨ SC

★ **KNOTT'S MOTEL ON THE LAKE.** *2306 Ny 28 (13820).* 607/432-5948; fax 607/433-2266. www.coopers townchamber.org/knotts. 25 rms, 10 kit. units. Some rm phones. S $84; D $62-$94, kit. units $76-$94; each addl $8; wkly rates. Crib free. TV; cable. Complimentary coffee. Restaurant nearby. Ck-out 11 am. Tennis. Lawn games. Waterskiing; sailboats avail. Picnic tables, grill. Private beach. Cr cds: DS, MC, V.
D ◨ ◨ ◨ ◨

★ **SUPER 8.** *4973 NY 23 (13820).* 607/432-9505; res 800/800-8000. www.super8.com. 60 rms, 2 story. July-Aug: S $53-$103; D $63-$107; each addl $5; under 12 free; higher rates wkends, special events; lower rates rest of yr. Crib $3. Pet accepted, some restrictions. TV; cable, VCR avail (movies). Complimentary continental bkfst. Restaurant adj 7 am-10 pm. Ck-out 11 am. Coin lndry. Business servs avail. Cr cds: A, C, D, DS, MC, V.
D ◨ ◨ ◨

B&B/Small Inn

★ ★ ★ **CATHEDRAL FARMS COUNTRY INN.** *4158 NY Hwy 23 (13820).* 607/432-7483; fax 607/432-7483; toll-

free 800/327-6790. www.cathedral farms.com. 19 rms, 2 story, 4 suites. D $75-$125; suites $120-$250; under 18 free; wkly rates. Crib free. TV; cable. Heated pool; whirlpool. Complimentary coffee in rms. Restaurant (see also CATHEDRAL FARMS). Ck-out noon, ck-in 3 pm. Business servs avail. Lawn games. Balconies. Inn was once servants' house built in the 1930s. Totally nonsmoking. Cr cds: A, C, D, MC, V.

🄳 🌢 🖼 🖼

Restaurants

★★★ **CATHEDRAL FARMS RESTAURANT.** *4158 NY Hwy 23 (13820). 607/432-7483. www.cathedral farms.com.* Continental menu. Specializes in fresh seafood, hand-cut prime beef, free-range chicken. Own baking, soups. Hrs: 3-9 pm; Fri, Sat to 10 pm; Sun 11 am-8 pm; Sun brunch 11 am-3 pm. Closed Mon, Tues. Res accepted. Bar to midnight. Wine cellar. Dinner $13.95-$22.95. Sun brunch $8.95-$16.95. Child's menu. Parking. Former estate (1915); extensive grounds. Peacocks on premises. Cr cds: A, MC, V.

🄳 🖼

★ **CHRISTOPHER'S.** *NY 23 (13820). 607/432-2444. www.cathedralinn.com.* Continental menu. Specializes in steak, barbecued ribs, fresh seafood. Salad bar. Hrs: 11 am-10 pm; Sun noon-9 pm. Closed Dec 25. Res accepted. Bar to midnight. Lunch $4.50-$7.95, dinner $8.95-$18.95. Child's menu. Parking. Rustic decor. Fireplace. Guest rms avail. Cr cds: A, C, D, MC, V.

🄳 🖼

★★ **FARMHOUSE.** *Rte 7 (13820). 607/432-7374. www.farmhouse restaurant.com.* Continental menu. Specializes in prime rib, seafood, chicken. Salad bar. Hrs: 3-9 pm; Fri, Sat to 9:30 pm; Sun noon-9 pm; winter hrs vary; Sun brunch to 3 pm. Closed Dec 25. Res accepted. Serv bar. Dinner $10.95-$17.95. Sun brunch $6.95. Child's menu. Parking. Restored farmhouse built 1780s. Cr cds: A, MC, V.

🄳 🖼

★★ **SABATINI'S LITTLE ITALY.** *Rte 28 Southside (13820). 607/432-3000. www.cathedralinn.com.* Italian, American menu. Specializes in homemade mozzarella, authentic Italian dishes. Hrs: 4-9 pm; Fri, Sat to 10 pm. Closed Thanksgiving, Dec 25. Bar. A la carte entrees: dinner $8-$22.95. Parking. Italian decor. Cr cds: A, C, D, MC, V.

🄳 🖼

Oswego

(C-5) *See also Fulton*

Pop 17,954 **Elev** 298 ft **Area code** 315 **Zip** 13126

Information Chamber of Commerce, 156 W 2nd St; 315/343-7681

Web www.oswegochamber.com

Oswego's location on Lake Ontario, at the mouth of the Oswego River, made it an important trading post and a strategic fort as early as 1722. Today, as a seaway port and northern terminus of the State Barge Canal, Oswego carries on its industrial and shipping tradition. The town has the largest US port of entry on Lake Ontario.

What to See and Do

Fair Haven Beach State Park. Swimming beach, bathhouse, fishing, boating (rentals, launch, anchorage); hiking trails, x-country skiing, picnicking, playground, concession, camping, tent and trailer sites, cabins. (Late Apr-early Nov) Standard fees. Approx 15 mi SW via NY 104, 104A. Phone 315/947-5205.

Fort Ontario State Historic Site. The original fort was built by the British in 1755, taken by the French and eventually used as a US Army installation (1840-1946). Strategic fort commanded the route from the Hudson and Mohawk valleys to the Great Lakes. Restored site re-creates life at a military installation during the 1860s. Exhibits; guided and self-guided tours. Picnic area. Drills (July-Labor Day). Special programs. Park (Memorial Day-Labor Day, Wed-Sun) Foot of E 7th St. Phone 315/343-4711. ¢¢

H. Lee White Marine Museum. Museum features 12 rms of artifacts, models, documents, and paintings

elating to 300 yrs of Oswego Harbor
nd Lake Ontario history. (Mid-May-
Dec, daily afternoons, Jan-Apr, Mon-
at afternoons) W First St at end of
Pier. Phone 315/342-0480. ¢¢

Oswego County Historical Society.
Richardson-Bates House Museum incl
local historical material; period fur-
nishings; changing exhibits. (Tues-
Fri; Sat, Sun afternoons) 135 E 3rd St.
Phone 315/343-1342. ¢¢

Selkirk Shores State Park. Beach,
ishing, canoeing; hiking, x-country
kiing, picnicking, playground, con-
ession, tent and trailer sites (fee),
abins. Standard fees. 17 mi NE via
NY 104, 3. Phone 315/298-5737. ¢¢

State University of New York. (1861)
8,000 students. Campus overlooks
Lake Ontario. On NY 104. Campus
ours, contact Office of Admissions.
Phone 315/341-2250.

Special Event

Oswego Speedway. 300 E Albany, off
NY 104 E. ⅝th's asphalt racing facil-
ty. Short-track racing; supermodi-
eds and limited supermodifieds.
Phone 315/342-0646. Early May-
Labor Day.

Motels/Motor Lodges

★★ **BEST WESTERN CAPTAIN'S
QUARTERS HOTEL.** *26 E 1st St
(13126). 315/342-4040; fax 315/342-
4454; toll-free 800/780-7234. www.
bestwestern.com.* 93 units, 4 story. S
$76-$138; D $88-$150; each addl
$12; under 12 free; higher rates: sum-
mer wkends, college events, Harbor
est, Labor Day. Crib free. TV; cable.
ndoor pool; whirlpool. Complimen-
ary continental bkfst Mon-Fri. Complimentary coffee. Restaurant opp
11:30 am-10 pm; wkends from 8 am.
Ck-out 11 am. Meeting rms. Business
ervs avail. In-rm modem link. Exer-
ise equipt; sauna. View of river. Cr
ds: A, C, D, DS, MC, V.

★ **DAYS INN.** *101 NY 104 (13126).
315/343-3136; fax 315/343-6187; res
800/325-2525. www.daysinn.com.* 44
rms, 2 story. S $49-$70; D $59-$100;
each addl $5; suites $89; under 13
ree; wkly rates; higher rates special
vents. Crib avail. Pet accepted. TV;
able. Complimentary continental

bkfst. Restaurant adj open 24 hrs.
Ck-out 11 am. Business servs avail.
Refrigerators. Cr cds: A, C, ER.

Hotel

★ **OSWEGO.** *180 E 10th St (13126).
315/342-6200; fax 315/343-6234; res
800/721-7341. www.pos.net/oswego/
inn.* 13 rms, 2 story. May-Oct: S $45;
D $55; each addl $10; under 12 free;
wkly, monthly rates; higher rates special events; lower rates rest of yr. Crib
$10. TV; cable (premium). Compli-
mentary continental bkfst. Ck-out 11
am, ck-in 2 pm. Business servs avail.
In-rm modem link. X-country ski 3
mi. Refrigerators. Totally nonsmoking. Cr cds: A, C, D, DS, MC, V.

Restaurant

★★ **VONA'S.** *W 10th and Utica St S
(13126). 315/343-8710.* Italian, American menu. Specializes in veal, New
York steak. Own pasta. Hrs: 11:30
am-2:30 pm, 4:30-10:30 pm; Sat, Sun
4-10 pm. Closed July 4, Thanksgiving, Dec 24-25. Res accepted. Bar
11:30-2 am. Lunch $5-$8, dinner
$7.50-$15.95. Child's menu. Family-
owned. Cr cds: A, DS, MC, V.

Owego

(F-5) *See also Binghamton, Elmira, Endicott*

Pop 20,365 **Elev** 817 ft **Area code** 607
Zip 13827

Information Tioga County Chamber
of Commerce, 188 Front St; 607/687-
2020

Web www.tiogachamber.com

What to See and Do

**Tioga County Historical Society
Museum.** Native American artifacts,
folk art; pioneer crafts; exhibits on
early county commerce, industry,
and military history. (Tues-Sat; closed

hols) 110 Front St. Phone 607/687-2460. **FREE**

Tioga Gardens. Tropical plant conservatory with solar dome. Greenhouses; two-acre water garden with water lilies; Japanese garden. (Daily) NY 17C. Phone 607/687-5522. **FREE**

Tioga Scenic Railroad. Scenic rail excursions avail. (Early May-late Oct) Phone 607/687-6786. ¢¢¢¢

Special Events

Owego Strawberry Festival. Phone 607/687-6305. Mid-June.

Tioga County Fair. Phone 607/687-1308. Mid-July.

Motel/Motor Lodge

★ **SUNRISE MOTEL.** *3778 Waverly Rd (13827).* 607/687-5666; fax 607/687-5667; res 800/806-9074. 20 rms. S $43; D $47; each addl $4. Crib $3. Pet accepted, some restrictions; $5. TV; cable. Ck-out 11 am. Picnic tables. Cr cds: A, C, D, DS, MC, V.
D 🐾 🐾 ⛽ 🐾 SC

Hotel

★★ **OWEGO TREADWAY INN.** *1100 NY Rte 17C (13827).* 607/687-4500; fax 607/687-2456. www.owego treadway.com. 96 rms, 2 story. S, D $85-$94; each addl $5; under 18 free; wkend rates. TV; cable. Indoor pool. Restaurant 6:30 am-10 pm. Bar 11:30-1 am; entertainment Fri, Sat. Ck-out noon. Meeting rms. Valet serv (Mon-Fri). Sundries. 18-hole golf privileges, pro. Exercise equipt. Some private patios, balconies. On river. Cr cds: A, C, D, DS, MC, V.
D 🐾 ⛽ 🐾 🐾 🐾 🐾 SC

Oyster Bay (L.I.)

See also Glen Cove (L.I.), Huntington (L.I.), Jericho (L.I.), New York City

Settled 1653 **Pop** 6,826 **Elev** 20 ft
Area code 516 **Zip** 11771

Information Chamber of Commerce, 120 South St, PO Box 21; 516/922-6464

What to See and Do

Planting Fields Arboretum. A 400-acre estate of the late William Robertson Coe. Landscaped planting (150 acres); large collections of azaleas and rhododendrons; self-guided tour; guided tours avail; nature trails; greenhouses. (May-Labor Day, daily; rest of yr, wkends) Planting Fields Rd 1½ mi W, off NY 25A. Phone 516/922-9201. ¢ Per vehicle parking ¢¢ Located in center of Arboretum is

Coe Hall. (1918) Tudor-revival mansion (65 rms) was a country estate for Coe and his family. Various 16th- and 17th-century furnishings imported from Europe contribute to its atmosphere of a historic English country house. Guided tours. (Daily) Phone 516/922-0479. ¢¢

Raynham Hall Museum. Historic colonial house museum with Victorian wing. Home of Samuel Townsend, a prosperous merchant; headquarters for the Queens Rangers during the Revolutionary War. Victorian garden. (Tues-Sun) 20 W Main St. Phone 516/922-6808. ¢

🔲 **Sagamore Hill National Historic Site.** Theodore Roosevelt summer house has original furnishings and many historic items; summer White House from 1901 to 1909, the rambling Queen Anne/Victorian mansion incl famous trophy rm with mounted species and presidential memorabilia. Guided tours. Film on Roosevelt's life shown at Old Orchard Museum on grounds. House (daily; closed hols). Golden Eagle Passport (see MAKING THE MOST OF YOUR TRIP). 2 mi NE via Cove Neck Rd. Contact the Superintendent, 20 Sagamore Hill. Phone 516/922-4447. ¢¢

Theodore Roosevelt Sanctuary & Audubon Center. Owned by the National Audubon Society, the memorial contains 12 acres of forest and nature trails. The sanctuary serves as a memorial to Theodore Roosevelt's pioneering conservation achievements. Museum contains displays on Roosevelt and the conservation movement; bird exhibits. Adj in Young's Cemetery is **Theodore Roo-**

evelt's grave. Trails, bird-watching, library. (Daily) Cove Rd. Phone 516/922-3200. **FREE**

Special Event

Oyster Festival. Street festival, arts and crafts. Phone 516/922-6464 or 516/624-8082. Usually wkend after Columbus Day.

Motel/Motor Lodge

★ ★ ★ **EAST NORWICH INN.** 6321 Northern Blvd, East Norwich (11732). 516/922-1500; fax 516/922-1089; toll-free 800/334-4798. www.eastnorwich-inn.com. 65 rms, 5 suites, 2 story. S $120; D $135; each addl $10; under 6 free. Crib free. TV; cable (premium). Heated pool; lifeguard. Complimentary continental bkfst. Ck-out noon. Meeting rms. Business servs avail. In-rm modem link. Valet serv. Exercise equipt; sauna. Cr cds: A, C, D, DS, MC, V.

Restaurants

★ ★ ★ **CAFE GIRASOLE.** 1053 Oyster Bay Rd, East Norwich (11732). 516/624-8330. Italian menu. Specializes in pasta, fresh fish. Hrs: noon-10 pm; Sat 5-11 pm; Sun 4-9 pm. Closed hols. Res required Fri, Sat. Bar. A la carte: lunch $11.50-$16.50, dinner $13-$24.50. Outdoor dining. Casual trattoria. Cr cds: A, C, D, MC, V.

★ **CANTERBURY ALES OYSTER BAR & GRILL.** 46 Audrey Ave (11771). 516/922-3614. Specializes in mesquite-grilled seafood. Hrs: 11:30 am-11 pm; Fri, Sat to 1 am; Sun brunch to 3 pm. Closed Thanksgiving, Dec 25. Res accepted. Bar. Lunch $4.95-$13.95, dinner $7.50-$19.95. Sun brunch $5.95-$14.95. Child's menu. Parking. New England fish house atmosphere with bistro flair. Historic Teddy Roosevelt library in rear, includes photos. Cr cds: A, C, D, MC, V.

★ ★ **MILL RIVER INN.** 160 Mill River Rd (11771). 516/922-7768. Specializes in grilled fish, steak. Menu changes daily. Hrs: 6-10 pm; Sun 5-10 pm. Closed Dec 25. Res required. Bar. A la carte entrees (Sun-Thurs):

$29-$38. Prix fixe: dinner (Fri) $48, (Sat) $58. Parking. Contemporary decor. Fireplace. Cr cds: A, D, MC, V.

★ ★ ★ **STEVE'S PIER I.** 33 Bayville Ave, Bayville (11709). 516/628-2153. Specializes in Nova Scotia lobster, seafood, steak. Own baking. Hrs: noon-10 pm; Mon to 9:30 pm; Fri to 11 pm; Sat to 11:30 pm; Sun and hols 1-9:30 pm. Bar. Wine cellar. Complete meals: lunch $11.95-$14.95, dinner $17.95-$23. Child's menu. Valet parking. Outdoor dining. On L.I. Sound. Cr cds: A, C, D, MC, V.
D

Palisades Interstate Parks

See also New York City, Yonkers

This system of conservation and recreation areas extends along the west side of the Hudson River from the George Washington Bridge at Fort Lee, NJ, to Saugerties, NY, and covers 81,008 acres. The main unit is the 51,680-acre tract of Bear Mountain and Harriman state parks. Included in the system are 17 parks and six historic sites.

Bear Mountain (5,067 acres) extends westward from the Hudson River opposite Peekskill. Only 45 miles from New York City via the Palisades Interstate Parkway, this is a popular recreation area, with all-year facilities, mainly for one-day visits. Bear Mountain has picnic areas, hiking trails, swimming pool with bathhouse, boating on Hessian Lake, fishing, and an artificial ice rink. Perkins Memorial Drive goes to the top of Bear Mountain, where there is a picnic area and a sightseeing tower. Near the site of Fort Clinton, just west of Bear Mountain Bridge, is Trailside Museums and Wildlife Center, with native animals and exhibit buildings (daily). Phone 914/786-2701. ¢¢

Harriman (46,613 acres), southwest of Bear Mountain, consists of wilder country. Fishing, boating,

Sagamore Hill

scenic drives, lakes, bathing beaches at Lakes Tiorati, Welch and Sebago; tent camping at Lake Welch and cabins (primarily for family groups) at Lake Sebago. The **Silver Mine Area**, four miles west of Bear Mountain, has fishing, boating, picnicking. (All year)

Charges for parking and for most activities change seasonally. Further information can be obtained from Palisades Interstate Parks Commission, Administration Building, Bear Mountain 10911-0427; 914/786-2701.

Hotel

★★ **BEAR MOUNTAIN INN.** *Bear Mountain Complex (10911). 845/786-2731; fax 845/786-2543.* 12 rms in inn, 48 rms in 5 lodges. S, D $89; each addl $10. Crib $10. TV. Pool; lifeguard. Complimentary continental bkfst. Restaurant 11 am-3 pm, 5-9 pm; wkends to 10 pm. Bar 11 am-11 pm. Ck-out 11 am. Meeting rms. Business servs avail. Sundries. Balconies. Picnic tables. Cr cds: A, DS, MC, V.

Palmyra

(D-4) *See also Canandaigua, Rochester, Victor*

Founded 1789 **Pop** 7,672 **Elev** 472 ft
Area code 315 **Zip** 14522

In 1820, in the frontier town of Palmyra, 15-year-old Joseph Smith had a vision that led to the founding of a new religious group—the Church of Jesus Christ of Latter-day Saints, better known as the Mormon Church.

What to See and Do

Alling Coverlet Museum. Largest collection of American Jacquard and handwoven coverlets in the country (June-Sept, daily, afternoons, or by appt) 122 William St. Phone 315/597-6737. **FREE**

Mormon Historic Sites and Bureau of Information. Hill Cumorah, 4 mi S on NY 21, near I-90 exit 43. Guides. (Daily) Phone 315/597-5851. **FREE** Incl

Book of Mormon Historic Publication Site. Between June 1829 and March 1830, the first edition of 5,000 copies of the *Book of Mormon* was printed here at a cost of $3,000. (Daily; also summer eves) 217 E Main St. Phone 315/597-5982.

Hill Cumorah. Where the golden plates from which Joseph Smith translated the Book of Mormon were delivered to him. A monument to the Angel Moroni now stands on the hill. Visitor center has religious exhibits and films. (Daily; also summer eves) Phone 315/597-5851.

Joseph Smith Home. Where Smith lived as a young man; period decor (1820-1830). Nearby is the Sacred Grove where he had his first vision. Stafford Rd. Phone 315/597-4383.

Palmyra Historical Museum. Display of 19th-century items incl furniture, toys, and household items. (June-Sept, Sat and Sun afternoons, or by appt) 132 Market St. Phone 315/597-5981. **FREE**

Phelps General Store Museum. Contains displays of turn-of-the-century merchandise and household furnishings. (June-Sept, Sat and Sun afternoons, or by appt) 140 Market St. Phone 315/597-6981. **FREE**

Special Event

The Hill Cumorah Pageant. At Hill Cumorah; seating for 6,500. Phone 315/597-6808. Early-mid-July.

Motels/Motor Lodges

★★ **QUALITY INN NEWARK.** *125 N Main St, Newark (14513). 315/331-9500; fax 315/331-5264; res 800/228-5151.* 107 rms, 2 story. S $68-$88; D $78-$108; each addl $10; under 18 free; monthly rates; ski plans. Crib free. Pet accepted. TV; cable (premium). Pool. Sauna. Restaurant 6:30 am-9 pm; wkend hrs vary. Bar 11-2 am. Ck-out 11 am. Meeting rms. Business servs avail. Downhill ski 8 mi; x-country ski 9 mi. Some refrigerators, microwaves. Picnic tables. On large canal. Cr cds: A, C, D, DS, JCB, MC, V.

★ **WAYNE VILLA MOTEL.** *344 NY 31, Macedon (14502). 315/986-5530; toll-free 800/564-8927.* 14 rms, 1 kits, 2 apts. S $40; D $50. Crib free. TV; cable. Playground. Restaurant nearby. Ck-out 11 am. Picnic tables, grill. Cr cds: A, DS, MC, V.

Peekskill

(G-8) See also Mahopac, Mount Kisco, Tarrytown, West Point (US Military Academy)

Pop 22,441 **Elev** 132 ft **Area code** 914 **Zip** 10566
Information Peekskill/Cortlandt Chamber of Commerce, 1 S Division St; 914/737-3600
Web www.pcccweb.net

This city is named for Jan Peek, a Dutchman who set up a trading post on the creek that runs along the northern edge of town.

Hotel

★★ **PEEKSKILL INN.** *634 Main St (10566). 914/739-1500; fax 914/739-7067; toll-free 800/526-9466. www.peekskillinn.* 53 rms, 2 story. S $89-$102; D $95-$110; suite $125-$159; higher rates West Point graduation. Crib free. Pet accepted, some restrictions. TV; cable (premium). Complimentary continental bkfst; full bkfst on wkends. Restaurant 11:30 am-10 pm; wkends 8 am-11 pm. Bar noon to 2 am. Ck-out 11 am. Business servs avail. Pool; lifeguard. Refrigerators avail. Some balconies. Grills. Cr cds: A, C, D, DS, MC, V.

Restaurants

★★ **CRYSTAL BAY.** *5 John Walsh Blvd (10566). 914/737-8332. www.crystal-bay.com.* Eclectic menu. Specializes in seafood. Hrs: 11:30 am-3 pm, 5-10 pm; Sun brunch, 2 seatings, 11 am-1:30 pm. Closed Dec 25. Res accepted. Bar. A la carte entrees: lunch $7.95-$16.95, dinner $15-$30.

Seafood buffet: dinner (Wed) $22.95. Sun brunch $18.95. Child's menu. Entertainment Fri, Sat. Outdoor dining. On the Hudson River. Cr cds: A, C, D, DS, MC, V.

★★★ **MONTEVERDE RESTAU-RANT AT OLDSTONE.** *Rtes 6 and 202 W (10566).* 914/739-5000. Continental menu. Specializes in French and Italian dishes. Hrs: noon-2:30 pm, 5:30-9:30 pm; Fri to 10:30 pm; Sat 5-11 pm; Sun noon-8:30 pm. Closed Tues. Res accepted; required Sat, hols. Bar. A la carte entrees: lunch $14.75-$17.75, dinner $16.75-$27.75. Outdoor dining. 18th-century mansion with outdoor terrace overlooking Hudson River. Victorian furnishings; wrought iron lamps and chandeliers. Cr cds: A, D, MC, V.

★★ **SUSAN'S.** *12 N Division St (10566).* 914/737-6624. Specialties: salmon strudel, chocolate dream cake. Hrs: noon-2:30 pm, 5:30-9 pm; Fri, Sat to 10 pm. Res accepted. Bar. Lunch $5.75-$8.50, dinner $12.50-$17.50. Child's menu. French country furnishings. Cr cds: A, C, D, MC, V.

Penn Yan

(E-4) *See also Canandaigua, Geneva, Hammondsport, Watkins Glen*

Founded 1787 **Pop** 5,219 **Elev** 737 ft **Area code** 315 **Zip** 14527
Information Yates County Chamber of Commerce, 2375 Rte 14A; 315/536-3111 or 800/868-YATES
Web www.yatesny.com

Legend has it that the first settlers here, Pennsylvanians and Yankees, could not agree on a name for their town and finally compromised on Penn Yan. The town lies at the north end of Y-shaped Keuka Lake, in resort country; nearby is Keuka College.

What to See and Do

Fullager Farms Family Farm & Petting Zoo. Working dairy farm tour. Pony rides, hay rides, walking trails, and picnic area. Petting zoo incl llamas, miniature donkey, rabbits, sheep, and goats in addition to dairy cattle. (July-mid Sept, Tues-Sun; May June and mid-Sept-Oct, wkends, also wkdays by appt) 3202 Bath Rd (County Rd 17). Phone 315/536-3545. ¢¢

Keuka Lake State Park. Swimming beach, bathhouse, fishing, boating (launch); hiking, x-country skiing, playground, tent and trailer sites (May-Oct). Standard fees. 6 mi SW off NY 54A. Phone 315/536-3666. ¢¢

Oliver House Museum. (1852) Brick house that originally belonged to the Oliver family, distinguished by three generations of physicians. Now headquarters for the Yates County Genealogical and Historical Society, operated as a local history museum. Incl period rms, changing local history exhibits, research rm. (Mon-Fri; Sat by appt) 200 Main St. Phone 315/536-7318. **Donation**

The Outlet Trail. Six-mi trail that follows an abandoned railroad path built in 1884. The Outlet drops almost 300 ft between Keuka and Seneca lakes, with waterfalls, wildlife and remains of early settlements and mills to be found along the way. Keuka St in Penn Yan to Seneca St, in Dresden.

Motel/Motor Lodge

★★★ **FOX INN.** *158 Main St (14527).* 315/536-1100; toll-free 800/901-9779. 5 rms, 1 with shower only, 2 story, 1 suite. No rm phones. June-Oct: S $70-$80; D $75-$85; each addl $15; suite $125; under 5 free; wkly rates; wkends (2-day min); lower rates rest of yr. Crib free. TV; cable, VCR avail (movies). Complimentary full bkfst. Restaurant adj 6 am-9 pm. Ck-out noon, ck-in 3 pm. Luggage handling. X-country ski ¼ mi. Picnic tables. Built in 1820. Totally nonsmoking. Cr cds: A, MC, V.

Resort

★★ **VIKING RESORT.** *680 E Lake Rd (14527). 315/536-7061; fax 315/536-0737. www.vikingresort.com.* 31 rms, 2 story, 24 kits. S $48; D $65; each addl $15; kit. units $75-$160; family, wkly rates. Closed mid-Oct-mid-May. Crib free. Pet accepted; $20. TV; cable. Pool; whirlpool. Restaurant nearby. Ck-out 11 am. Lawn games. Refrigerators. Private patios, balconies. Picnic tables, grills. On Keuka Lake; private beach, daily cruises. Rental boats. Cr cds: DS, MC, V.

Plainview (L.I.)

See also Bethpage (L.I.)

Pop 25,637 **Elev** 180 ft **Area code** 516 **Zip** 11803

Hotel

★★★ **MARRIOTT LONG ISLAND MELVILLE.** *1350 Old Walt Whitman Rd, Melville (11747). 631/423-1600; fax 631/423-1790; toll-free 800/228-9290. www.marriott.com.* 370 rms, 24 stes, 4 story. S $149-$159; D $159; each addl $10; suites $169-$553; under 18 free; wkly, wkend and hol rates. Crib free. TV; cable. Indoor pool; whirlpool, lifeguard. Restaurant 6:30 am-10 pm; Sat to 11 pm. Bar; entertainment Fri, Sat. Ck-out 11 am. Convention facilities. Business center. In-rm modem link. Bellhops. Sundries. Gift shop. Exercise equipt. Game rm. Cr cds: A, C, D, DS, ER, CB, MC, V.

Plattsburgh

(A-8) *See also Ausable Chasm, Rouses Point*

Pop 18,816 **Elev** 135 ft **Area code** 518 **Zip** 12901

Information Plattsburgh-North Country Chamber of Commerce, 7601 Rte 9, PO Box 310; 518/563-1000
Web northcountrychamber.com

The Cumberland Bay area of Lake Champlain has been a military base since colonial days. Plattsburgh, at the mouth of the Saranac River, has a dramatic history in the struggle for US independence. The British won the Battle of Lake Champlain off these shores in 1776. Here, in 1814, Commodore Thomas Macdonough defeated a British fleet from Canada by an arrangement of anchors and winches that enabled him to swivel his vessels completely around, thus giving the enemy both broadsides. While this was going on, US General Alexander Macomb polished off the Redcoats on shore with the help of school boys and the local militia. Today, Plattsburgh accommodates both industry and resort trade.

What to See and Do

Adirondack Park. (see) S on I-87.

Alice T. Miner Colonial Collection. Antiques, colonial household items and appliances in 1824 house; sandwich glass collection; gardens. (Tues-Sat; closed Jan, Dec 25) 12 mi N on NY 9 in Chazy. Phone 518/846-7336. ¢¢

Boat excursion. M/V *Juniper.* Leaves from foot of Dock St and cruises Lake Champlain, circling Valcour Island. (May-Sept, two daily departures; also sunset and dinner cruises nightly) Contact Heritage Adventures Inc, 69 Miller St. Phone 800/388-8970.

Champlain Monument. Statue of the explorer. Cumberland Ave.

Kent-Delord House Museum. (1797) Historic house; British officers' quarters during the Battle of Plattsburgh (War of 1812); period furnishings. Tours (Mar-Dec, Tues-Sat afternoons; rest of yr, by appt only; closed Jan 1, Thanksgiving, Dec 25). 17 Cumberland Ave. Phone 518/561-1035. ¢¢

Macdonough Monument. Obelisk commemorates the naval encounter. City Hall Place at City Hall. Phone 518/563-7701.

State University of New York College at Plattsburgh. (1889) 6,400 students. On campus is SUNY Plattsburgh Art Museum, comprised of Meyers Fine Arts Gallery and Winkel Sculpture Court; also Rockwell Kent Gallery, with extensive collection of paintings, drawings, prints, and book engravings by American artist Rockwell Kent, famous for his illustrated Shakespeare and *Moby Dick* (Mon-Thurs, Sat, Sun). Phone 518/564-2813.

Swimming. Municipal Beach. AuSable Point State Park. 12 mi S on US 9. Beach, fishing, boating; camping. Phone 518/561-7080. **Cumberland Bay State Park.** Adj to Municipal Beach. Phone 518/563-5240. All areas (Memorial Day-Oct). Admission fee. Phone 518/563-4431. Bathhouse, lifeguard; picnicking, concession. 1¼ mi N on US 9, 1 mi E on NY 314.

Motels/Motor Lodges

★★ **BEST WESTERN INN AT SMITHVILLE.** *446 Cornelia St (12901). 518/561-7750; fax 518/561-9431; toll-free 800/780-7234. www.bestwestern.com.* 120 rms, 2 story. June-Labor Day: S, D $89-$99; each addl $10; under 18 free; higher rates some special events, hols; lower rates rest of yr. Crib free. Pet accepted. TV; cable (premium), VCR avail. Indoor pool; poolside serv. Coffee in rms. Restaurant 6 am-11 pm. Bar 3 pm-midnight, wkends to 1 am. Ck-out noon. Coin lndry. Meeting rms. Business servs avail. In-rm modem link. Exercise equipt. Rec rm. Refrigerators avail. Some private patios, balconies. Shopping mall adj. Cr cds: A, C, D, DS, JCB, MC, V.

D ➼ ⩲ 🕴 ⤴ 🔥 SC

★ **DAYS INN - PLATTSBURGH.** *8 Everleth Dr (12901). 518/561-0403; fax 518/561-4192; res 800/544-8313. www.daysinn-plattsburgh.com.* 112 rms, 3 story. Late June-mid-Oct: S $55-$65; D $65-$75; each addl $8; under 18 free; wkly rates off-season; higher rates college events; lower rates rest of yr. Crib free. TV; cable (premium). Indoor pool; whirlpool. Restaurant opp. Ck-out noon. Meeting rm. Business servs avail. Exercise equipt. Picnic table. Cr cds: A, C, D, DS, JCB, MC, V.

D ⩲ 🕴 ✈ ⤴ 🔥 SC

★★ **HOLIDAY INN.** *412 NY Rte 3 (12901). 508/561-0403; fax 518/562-2974. www.holiday-inn.com.* 102 rms, 4 story. Mid-June-mid-Oct: S, D $79-$99; each addl $10; under 19 free; lower rates rest of yr. Crib free. Pet accepted, some restrictions. TV; cable. Indoor pool; wading pool; whirlpool. Complimentary bkfst. Restaurant 6:30 am-1 pm, 5-9 pm. Bar from 4 pm. Ck-out noon. Meeting rms. Business servs avail. In-rm modem link. Sundries. Exercise equipt. Game rm. Cr cds: A, C, D, DS, JCB, MC, V.

D ⩲ 🕴 ⤴ 🔥 🐾

★ **STONEHELM LODGE.** *72 Spellman Rd (12901). 518/563-4800; fax 518/562-1380; toll-free 800/443-4344.* 40 rms. July-Aug: S $35-$45; D $40-$50; each addl $5; lower rates rest of yr. Crib free. TV; cable. Restaurant 7:30 am-2 pm. Ck-out 11 am. Many refrigerators. Picnic tables, grills. Cr cds: A, DS, MC, V.

D ⤴ 🔥

Restaurants

★★ **ANTHONY'S.** *538 Rte 3 (12901). 518/561-6420.* Continental menu. Specialties: roast L.I. duckling, steak au poivre, roast rack of lamb. Hrs: 11:30 am-2:30 pm, 5-9:30 pm; wkends 5-10 pm. Closed hols. Res accepted. Bar to 11 pm. Lunch $4.95-$9.95, dinner $9.95-$23.95. Child's menu. Piano bar wkends. Country elegance. Cr cds: A, C, D, DS, MC, V.

⤴

★★ **ROYAL SAVAGE INN.** *4107 Rte 9 (12901). 518/561-5140.* Specialties: baked stuffed shrimp, chicken Hawaiian. Hrs: 11:30 am-9 pm; Sun from noon. Closed Jan-Easter. Res accepted. Bar. Lunch $5.50-$9.95, dinner $8.95-$18.95. Complete meals: dinner $8.95-$14.95. Child's menu. Converted hay barn; many antiques. Fireplace in lobby, bar. Gift shop. View of Salmon River. Cr cds: A, D, DS, MC, V.

D

Port Jefferson (L.I.)

(G-3) *See also Smithtown (L.I.), Stony Brook (L.I.)*

Pop 7,527 **Elev** 50 ft **Area code** 631 **Zip** 11777

Information Greater Port Jefferson Chamber of Commerce, 118 W Broadway; 631/473-1414

Web www.portjeffchamber.com

What to See and Do

Ferry to Bridgeport, CT. Car and passenger service. (Daily) For fees and schedule contact Bridgeport and Port Jefferson Steamboat Company, 102 W Broadway. Phone 631/473-0286.

Thompson House. (ca 1700) Historian Benjamin F. Thompson was born in this saltbox house in 1784; authentically furnished to depict 18th-century life on rural Long Island. Herb garden. (Memorial Day-Columbus Day, Fri-Sun) 4 mi W on NY 25A, on North Country Rd in Setauket. Phone 631/692-4664. ¢

B&B/Small Inn

★★★ DANFORDS INN. *25 E Broadway (11777). 631/928-5200; fax 631/928-3598; toll-free 800/332-6367.* 85 rms, 3 story, 7 suites, 3 kits. D $145-$300; each addl $10; suites $200-$400; kit. units $160; package plans. Crib free. TV; cable. Restaurant. Ck-out 11 am, ck-in 2 pm. Business servs avail. Bellhops. Valet serv. Concierge (wkends). Exercise equipt. Health club privileges. Balconies. On Long Island Sound. Library; Oriental rugs, antiques, fireplace. Cr cds: A, C, D, DS, MC, V.
ᗒ ⚓ 🏋 🖼 🐾 SC

Restaurants

★ DOCKSIDE. *111 W Broadway, Port Jefferson (11777). 631/473-5656.* German, American menu. Specializes in German dishes, seafood. Hrs: noon-midnight. Res accepted. Bar. A la carte entrees: lunch $4.95-$17.95, dinner $12.50-$21.50. Child's menu. Pianist Fri-Sun. Outdoor dining over-

looking harbor. Nautical theme. Cr cds: A, D, MC, V.
D

★★ 25 EAST AMERICAN BISTRO. *25 E Broadway, Port Jefferson (11777). 631/928-5200.* Specializes in fresh seafood, prime meats. Hrs: 7 am-10 pm; Fri, Sat to 11 pm; Sun 8 am-10 pm; Sun brunch 11:30 am-3 pm. Res accepted. Bars. A la carte: bkfst, lunch $7.50-$16.95, dinner $14-$24. Sun brunch $21.95. Child's menu. Entertainment Fri, Sat eves. Outdoor dining. Built in 1890 as a chowder house. Cr cds: A, D, DS, MC, V.
D SC

★ VILLAGE WAY. *106 Main St, Port Jefferson (11777). 631/928-3395.* Specializes in seafood, beef, pasta. Hrs: 11-1 am; Fri, Sat to 2 am; early-bird dinner Mon-Fri 4-6 pm; Sun brunch 10 am-1 pm. Closed Thanksgiving, Dec 25. Res accepted. Bar. Lunch $5.50-$9.95, dinner $9.95-$15.95. Sun brunch $3.50-$9. Childs meals. Outdoor dining. Cr cds: A, D, DS, MC, V.
D

Port Jervis

(G-7) *See also Barryville, Middletown*

Pop 8,860 **Elev** 440 ft **Area code** 845 **Zip** 12771

Information Tri-State Chamber of Commerce, 5 S Broome St, PO Box 121; 845/856-6694 or 845/856-6695

Web www.tristatechamber.org

Port Jervis is a popular area for whitewater canoeing and rafting. Fishing, nature trails, and hot-air ballooning are highlights of the area.

What to See and Do

Gillander Glass Factory Tours and Store . Observe skilled craftsmen at work as they transform molten glass into beautiful glass objects. Tours, museum, store. (Mon-Fri; wkends seasonal; closed hols) Erie and Liberty sts. Phone 845/856-5375. ¢¢

Restaurants

★★ **CORNUCOPIA.** *176 US 209 (12771).* 845/856-5361. Continental, German menu. Specializes in German dishes. Salad bar. Hrs: noon-2 pm, 5-9 pm; Sat from 5-10pm; Sun 1-8 pm. Closed Mon. Res accepted. Bar. Lunch $5.95-$10.95, dinner $12.95-$16.95. Country inn built 1892; chalet decor. Guest rms avail. Cr cds: A, C, D, DS, MC, V.

★★ **FLO-JEAN.** *Rte 6 & 209 (12771).* 845/856-6600. Specializes in prime rib, fresh seafood, roast turkey. Own desserts. Hrs: 11:30 am-9 pm; Fri, Sat to 10 pm. Closed Mon; Tues, Wed Oct-May. Res accepted. Bar. Lunch $3.95-$8.95, dinner $8.95-$18.95. Child's menu. Entertainment wkends. Outdoor dining. Overlooks Delaware River; antiques, doll collection. Cr cds: A, D, DS, MC, V.

Port Washington (L.I.)

(G-2) *See also Glen Cove (L.I.), Great Neck (L.I.), New York City*

Pop 15,215 **Elev** 140 ft **Area code** 516 **Zip** 11050

Restaurants

★★ **DIWAN.** *37 Shore Rd, Port Washington (11050).* 516/767-7878. www.diwanonline.com. Indian menu. Specializes in tandoori lamb, chicken. Hrs: noon-2:30 pm, 5:30-10 pm; wkends noon-3 pm, 5:30-10:30 pm; Sat, Sun brunch noon-3 pm. Res required. Bar. Complete meals: lunch $9.95. A la carte entrees: dinner $10.95-$19.95. India motif. Overlooks mill pond and marina. Cr cds: A, D, DS, MC, V.

★ **YAMAGUCHI.** *63 Main St, Port Washington (11050).* 516/883-3500. Japanese menu. Specializes in sushi, casseroles, meat dishes. Sushi bar. Hrs: noon-2:30 pm, 5:30-10 pm; Fri

to 10:30 pm; Sat 5-10:30 pm; Sun 5-9:30 pm. Closed Mon; Jan 1, Thanksgiving, Dec 25. Res required wkends. Bar. Lunch $6.50-$13.50, dinner $9.50-$22. Japanese lanterns and screens. Cr cds: A, C, D, MC, V.

Potsdam

(A-6) *See also Canton, Massena, Ogdensburg (Thousand Islands)*

Founded 1802 **Pop** 15,957 **Elev** 433 ft **Area code** 315 **Zip** 13676
Information Chamber of Commerce, PO Box 717; 315/265-5440
Web www.potsdam.ny.us

What to See and Do

Adirondack Park. (see) S on NY 56.

Potsdam College of the State University of New York. (1816) 4,450 students. Founded as St. Lawrence Academy. Gibson Art Gallery; Crane School of Music; planetarium; summer programs. Campus tours. Phone 315/267-2000.

Potsdam Public Museum. Collection of English pottery; local history and decorative arts displays; changing exhibits. Walking tour brochures avail. (Memorial Day-Labor Day, Tues-Fri afternoons, rest of yr, Tues-Sat afternoons; closed hols) Civic Center, Elm and Park sts. Phone 315/265-6910. **FREE**

Motels/Motor Lodges

★ **SMALLING MOTEL.** *6775 State Hwy 56 (13676).* 315/265-4640; fax 315/265-4614. 15 rms. S $39; D $44-$49; each addl $5; under 5 free. Crib $5. TV; cable (premium). Pool. Complimentary coffee. Ck-out 11 am. Picnic tables. Cr cds: A, MC, V.

★ **WEDGEWOOD INN.** *6570 State Hwy 56 (13676).* 315/265-9100. 15 rms. S $44.50-$74.50; D $46.50-$86.50; each addl $8; wkly rates; higher rates major college events. Crib free. TV; cable, VCR (movies $3). Complimentary coffee in lobby. Restaurant nearby. Ck-out 11 am. Free bus depot transportation. Down

ill/x-country ski 7 mi. Refrigerators.
Cr cds: A, C, D, DS, MC, V.

Hotel

★★★ **THE CLARKSON INN.** *1
Main St (13676). 315/265-3050; fax
315/265-5848; toll-free 800/790-6970.*
40 rms, 2 story. S $75-$99; D $85-
$120; higher rates college events.
Crib $10. TV; cable. Restaurant 6:30-
10 am; also opp 11 am-9 pm. Ck-out
11 am. Meeting rm. Business servs
avail. In-rm modem link. Fireside sitting rm in lobby; turn-of-the-century
atmosphere. Reproduced antique furnishings. Located along Racquette
River and adj park. Cr cds: A, MC, V.

Restaurant

★ **TARDELLI'S.** *141 Market St
(13676). 315/265-8446.* Italian
menu. Specializes in veal, homemade pasta, prime rib. Hrs: 11:30
am-10 pm; Sat from 4 pm. Closed
Sun; hols. Res accepted. Bar to 2 am.
Lunch $2.75-$7.25, dinner $5.95-
$12.95. Child's menu. Family-
owned. Cr cds: A, MC, V.

Poughkeepsie

(F-8) *See also Fishkill, Hyde Park, Newburgh, New Paltz*

Settled 1687 **Pop** 29,871 **Elev** 176 ft
Area code 845

Information Poughkeepsie Area
Chamber of Commerce, 1 Civic Center Plaza, 12601; 845/454-1700

Web www.pokchamb.org

Many people know this Hudson
River town as the site of Vassar College, founded in 1861 by a brewer
named Matthew Vassar. The Smith
Brothers also helped put Poughkeepsie (p'KIP-see) on the map with their
cough drops, once made here. For a
brief time during the Revolutionary
War, this town was the state capital.

It was here in 1788 that New York
ratified the Constitution.

What to See and Do

Bardavon Opera House. (1869) Oldest operating theater in the state presents various dance, theatrical, and
musical performances; also Hudson
Valley Philharmonic concerts. (Oct-
May) 35 Market St. Phone 845/473-
5288.

James Baird State Park. An 18-hole
golf course and driving range, tennis,
hiking trails, x-country skiing, picnicking (shelters), playground,
restaurant, nature center (June-Labor
Day). Standard fees. 9 mi E on NY
55, then 1 mi N on Taconic Pkwy.
Phone 845/452-1489. **FREE**

⭐ Locust Grove. (Young-Morse Historic Site) (ca 1830) Former house of
Samuel F. B. Morse, inventor of the
telegraph; remodeled by him into a
Tuscan villa in 1847. Antiques; Morse
Room, telegraph equipt and memorabilia; alternating exhibits of dolls,
fans, costumes, books, and souvenirs
acquired by Young family (owners
following Morse); paintings, art
objects, and American furnishings.
Wildlife sanctuary and park (150
acres) with hiking trails, picnic area.
Tours (Memorial Day-Sept, Wed-Sun;
Oct, wkends). 2 mi S of Mid-Hudson
Bridge at 370 South Rd (US 9). Phone
845/454-4500. ¢¢

Mid-Hudson Children's Museum.
Interactive children's museum featuring more than 50 exhibits; incl grav-
ity roll, IBM's Da Vinci inventions,
virtual reality, climb-thru-the-heart.
(Tues-Sun; closed hols) Located in
South Hills Mall, Rte 9. Phone
845/471-0589. ¢¢

Vassar College. (1861) 2,250 students. A 1,000-acre campus; coeducational (since 1969) liberal arts
college. Art gallery (free). Raymond
Ave. Phone 845/437-7000.

Windsor Vineyards. Makers of California and New York State wines and
champagnes. Wine tasting. (Daily;
closed hols) Approx 7½ mi S on US
9 from Mid-Hudson Bridge, right on
Western Ave, at Marlboro-on-the-
Hudson. Phone 845/236-4233. **FREE**

Motels/Motor Lodges

★ **BEST INN.** *62 Haight Ave (12603). 845/454-1010; fax 845/454-0127; res 800/237-8466.* 41 rms, 2 story. S, D $65-$71; each addl $5; under 12 free. Crib free. TV; cable (premium). Pool; lifeguard. Complimentary continental bkfst. Restaurant nearby. Ck-out 11 am. Meeting rm. Business servs avail. In-rm modem link. Sundries. Refrigerators avail. Balconies. Vassar College nearby. Cr cds: A, D, DS, MC, V.

★★ **COURTYARD BY MARRIOTT.** *2641 South Rd (12601). 845/485-6336; fax 845/485-6514; res 800/321-2211. www.marriott.com.* 149 rms, 12 suites, 3 story. S, D $69-$129; suites $129-$149; under 18 free; wkly rates. Crib free. TV; cable (premium), VCR avail. Indoor pool; whirlpool. Complimentary coffee in rms. Restaurant 6:30-10 am; Sat, Sun 7 am-noon. Bar 5-10 pm; closed Fri, Sat. Ck-out 1 pm. Coin lndry. Meeting rms. Business center. In-rm modem link. Valet serv (Mon-Fri). Exercise equipt. Refrigerator, microwave in suites. Balconies. Cr cds: A, C, D, DS, ER, JCB, MC, V.

★ **ECONO LODGE.** *2625 South Rd (12601). 845/452-6600; fax 845/454-2210; toll-free 800/553-2666. www.econolodge.com.* 111 rms, 9 kit units, 1-2 story. S, D $99-$110; each addl $5; under 16 free; wkly rates. Crib $5. Pet accepted, some restrictions. TV; cable. Complimentary continental bkfst. Restaurant opp open 24 hrs. Ck-out 11 am. Coin lndry. Meeting rms. Business servs avail. In-rm modem link. Some refrigerators. Cr cds: A, C, D, DS, MC, V.

★★ **HOLIDAY INN EXPRESS.** *2750 South Rd (12601). 845/473-1151; fax 845/485-8127; res 800/465-4329. www.holiday-inn.com.* 121 rms, 4 story. S, D $89-$139; suite $175-$250; each addl $10; under 18 free; higher rates special events. Crib free. Pet accepted. TV; cable (premium). Pool; lifeguard. Complimentary continental bkfst. Ck-out noon. Guest lndry. Meeting rms. Business servs

avail. Exercise equipt. Sundries. Cr cds: A, C, D, DS, ER, JCB, MC, V.

Hotel

★★★ **SHERATON CIVIC CENTER.** *40 Civic Center Plaza (12601). 845/485-5300; fax 845/485-4720; res 800/216-1034. www.sheratoncc.com.* 195 rms, 10 story. S, D $89-$175; suites $250-$350; under 12 free. Crib free. TV; cable (premium). Restaurant 6:30 am-10:30 pm. Bar from noon. Ck-out noon. Meeting rms. Business servs avail. Free garage parking. Exercise equipt. Health club privileges. Cr cds: A, C, D, DS, ER, JCB, MC, V.

B&Bs/Small Inns

★★★ **INN AT THE FALLS.** *50 Red Oaks Mill Rd (12603). 845/462-5770; fax 845/462-5943; toll-free 800/344-1466.* 36 rms, 2 story. S, D $135-$140; suites $165-$170; under 13 free. Crib free. TV; cable, VCR avail. Complimentary continental bkfst. Rm serv (bkfst). Ck-out noon, ck-in 3 pm. Business servs avail. In-rm modem link. Refrigerators. Different period furnishings in every rm. Cr cds: A, C, D, DS, MC, V.

★★★ **OLD DROVERS INN.** *Old Rte 22, Dover Plains (12522). 845/832-9311; fax 845/832-6356. olddrovers inn.com.* 4 rms. No rm phones. D $150-$395; MAP avail wkends $320-$395; higher rates May-Oct (2-day min). Closed Tues, Wed. Pet accepted, some restrictions; $25. TV; VCR avail (free movies). Complimentary full bkfst. Restaurant (see OLD DROVERS INN). Ck-out noon, ck-in 2 pm. Business servs avail. 18-hole golf privileges, greens fee $18-$24. Downhill ski 9 mi. Originally inn for cattle drovers (1750); antiques, fireplaces. Cr cds: D, MC, V.

★★★ **TROUTBECK INN.** *Leedsville Rd, Amenia (12501). 845/373-9681; fax 845/373-7080; res 800/978-7688. www.troutbeck.com.* 42 rms, 2 story. AP: $650-$1,050/couple/wkend. TV in sitting rm; VCR avail (movies). 2 pools, 1 indoor; sauna. Restaurant noon-2 pm, 6:30-9 pm Wed-Sat;

brunch 11:30 am-3:30 pm. Open bar. Ck-out Sun 2 pm, ck-in Fri 5 pm. Meeting rms. Business center. In-rm modem link. Tennis. Downhill/x-country ski 10 mi. Exercise equipt; sauna. Game rm. Lawn games. Cr cds: A, D, MC, V.

Restaurants

★★ **ALLYN'S.** *4258 US 44, Millbrook (12545). 845/677-5888. www.allyns. com.* Continental menu. Specialties: venison, roast duck with port wine and currants. Own baking. Hrs: 11:30 am-9:30 pm; Fri, Sat to 10:30 pm; Sun brunch to 3 pm. Closed Tues; Dec 25. Res accepted. Bar. Wine cellar. Lunch $4.95-$12.50, dinner $10.95-$21.95. Sun brunch $15.95. Child's menu. Parking. Outdoor dining. Renovated church (1790); hunt motif; fireplaces. Cr cds: A, D, MC, V.

★ **BANTA'S STEAK & STEIN.** *1794 South Rd (12590). 845/297-6770.* Specializes in steak, fresh fish, prime rib. Salad bar. Hrs: 4-10 pm; wkends to 11 pm; Sun from noon. Closed Thanksgiving, Dec 25. Bar 4-10 pm; wkends to 11 pm. Dinner $8.95-$26.95. Child's menu. Banjo band Mon. Parking. Fireplaces. Dutch Colonial decor. Family-owned. Cr cds: A, C, D, MC, V.

★★★ **CHRISTOS.** *155 Wilbur Blvd (12603). 845/471-3400. www.christos catering.com.* Continental menu. Specialties: filet of sole, chateaubriand bouquetiere. Own baking. Hrs: 11:30 am-2:30 pm, 5-11 pm; Sat from 5 pm. Closed Sun, Mon; also Aug. Res accepted. Bar. Lunch $8-$15, dinner $17-$25. Child's menu. Parking. Outdoor dining. Cr cds: A, MC, V.

★★★ **LE PAVILLON.** *230 Salt Point Tpke (12603). 845/473-2525.* French menu. Specializes in rack of lamb, seafood, sweetbreads. Own baking. Hrs: 5:30-10 pm. Closed Sun; hols; also 2 wks July. Res accepted. Bar. Wine cellar. A la carte entrees: dinner $16-$19.95. Complete meals: Sat dinner $30. Child's menu. Parking. Patio dining. Brick farmhouse (1790);

many antiques; spacious grounds. Cr cds: A, C, D, DS, MC, V.

★★★ **OLD DROVERS INN.** *Old US 22, Dover Plains (12522). 845/832-9311. www.olddroversinn.com.* Specialties: brown turkey hash, double-cut lamb chops. Hrs: 5-9 pm; Fri noon-3 pm, 5-10 pm; Sat noon-10 pm; Sun noon-3:30 pm. Closed Tues, Wed; Dec 25. Res accepted. Bar. Wine cellar. A la carte entrees: lunch $15-$29, dinner $17-$35. Parking. Outdoor dining. Romantic dining. Colonial decor with stone fireplace and hurricane lamps. Cr cds: D, MC, V.

★ **RIVER STATION STEAK & SEAFOOD.** *1 Water St (12601). 845/452-9207.* Specializes in steak, seafood, pasta. Hrs: 11:30 am-midnight; Fri, Sat to 2 am. Closed Dec 25. Res accepted; required hols. Bar. Lunch $5.50-$7.95, dinner $11.95-$23.95. Child's menu. Parking. Outdoor dining. Oldest food-and-drink establishment in city; view of river, Mid-Hudson Bridge. Cr cds: A, D, DS, MC, V.

Pound Ridge

See also Brewster, Mount Kisco, Stamford, White Plains

Pop 4,726 **Elev** 600 ft **Area code** 914 **Zip** 10576

What to See and Do

Muscoot Farm. This 777-acre park is a turn-of-the-century farm that incl farm animals, buildings, and a 28-rm main house. Demonstrations of sheep-shearing, blacksmithing, bee-keeping, harvesting, and bread-baking (daily). Programs (Sun). Tours (groups only). Phone 914/864-7282. **FREE**

Ward Pound Ridge Reservation. In 4,700-acre park is Trailside Nature Museum (Wed-Sun). X-country ski trails, picnicking, playground, camping in lean-tos (fee). Reservation (daily; closed Jan 1, Thanksgiving, Dec 25). About 4 mi NW on NY 137, then 3½ mi N on NY 121 S, just S of jct NY 35 in Cross River. Phone 914/864-7317. ¢¢¢

Restaurants

★★ **INN AT POUND RIDGE.** *258 Westchester Ave (10576). 914/764-5779. www.innatpoundridge.com.* Specializes in rack of lamb, fresh fish, duck. Hrs: noon-2:30 pm, 6-9:30 pm; Fri, Sat 6-10:30 pm; Sun 4-9 pm; Sun brunch noon-3 pm. Res accepted; required wkends. Bar. A la carte entrees: lunch $8-$21, dinner $19-$29.50. Sun brunch $24. Child's menu. Valet parking. House built 1833; antiques, fireplaces. Cr cds: A, D, MC, V.
D

★★★ **L'EUROPE.** *407 Smlthridge Rd, South Salem (10590). 914/533-2570.* French, continental menu. Specializes in veal chops, rack of lamb, duck. Hrs: noon-2:30 pm, 6-9:30 pm. Closed Mon. Res accepted. Bar. Wine cellar. A la carte entrees: lunch $13-$22, dinner $21.50-$29.50. Prix fixe (Sat): dinner $51. Outdoor dining. Elegant dining in Country French atmosphere. Cr cds: A, C, D, MC, V.
D

Rhinebeck

(F-8) *See also Hyde Park, Poughkeepsie*

Settled 1686 **Pop** 7,762 **Elev** 200 ft
Area code 845 **Zip** 12572
Information Chamber of Commerce, 19 Mill St, Box 42; 845/876-4778
Web www.rhinebecknychamber.org

Rhinebeck was once known as "violet town" because it claimed to produce more hothouse violets than any other town in the United States.

What to See and Do

Hudson River National Estuarine Research Reserve. The Hudson River is an estuary, running from Manhattan to Troy, NY; over 4,000 acres of this estuarine land have been reserved for the study of its life and ecosystems. The Reserve incl Piermont Marsh and Iona Island in Rockland County, Tivoli Bays in Dutchess County, and Stockport Flats in Columbia County. Reserve's headquarters has lectures, workshops, special exhibits, and public field programs. N on NY 9G to Annandale, 1¼ mi N of Bard College Main Gate. Phone 845/758-5193.

Montgomery Place. Estate along Hudson River. Mansion (1805) was remodeled in the mid-1800s in the Classical-revival style. Also on grounds are a coach house, visitor center, greenhouse with rose, herb, perennial, and woodland gardens, museum, and garden shop. Scenic trails and view of cataracts meeting the Hudson. (Apr-Oct, Mon, Wed-Sun; Mar and Nov-Dec, wkends) N on NY 9G to Annandale-on-Hudson. Phone 845/758-5461. ¢¢

Old Rhinebeck Aerodrome. Museum of antique airplanes (1900-1937). Planes from WWI and earlier are flown in air shows (fee) (mid-June-mid-Oct, Sat and Sun). Aerodrome (mid-May-Oct, daily). Picnicking. Barnstorming rides. About 3 mi NE via US 9, at 42 Stone Church Rd. Phone 845/758-8610. ¢¢¢

Special Event

Dutchess County Fair. Fairgrounds. Harness racing, livestock shows, farm machinery exhibits. Late Aug. Phone 845/876-4001.

Motel/Motor Lodge

★★ **VILLAGE INN OF RHINEBECK.** *6260 Rte 9 (12572). 845/876-7000; fax 845/876-4756.* 16 rms. S, D $74; each addl $15; under 12 free; wkly rates. Crib free. TV; cable. Complimentary continental bkfst. Ck-out 11 am. Some refrigerators. Cr cds: DS, MC, V.

Hotel

★★★ **BEEKMAN ARMS.** *6387 Mill St (12572). 845/876-7077; fax 845/876-7077; toll-free 800/361-6517. www.beekmanarms.com.* 59 rms, most A/C, 3 story. S, D $90-$120; each addl $10; suites $125-$150; under 12 free. Crib free. TV; cable. Restaurant (see BEEKMAN 1766 TAVERN). Bar 11-1 am. Ck-out 11 am, ck-in 3 pm. Meeting rms. Business servs avail. Historic inn, opened 1766. Antiques. Cr cds: A, C, D, DS, MC, V.

Restaurants

★★ **BEEKMAN 1766 TAVERN.** *6387 Mill St (12572)*. *845/871-1766*. Specialty: cedar-planked salmon. Hrs: 8-10 am, 11:30 am-3 pm, 5:30-9 pm; Fri, Sat to 9:30 pm; Sun 3:30-8 pm; Sun brunch 10 am-2 pm. Res accepted. Bar. Buffet: bkfst $5.25. Lunch $7.75-$10.95, dinner $10.50-$23.95. Sun brunch $19.95. Child's menu. Parking. Outdoor dining. Several small dining rms in historic inn. Cr cds: A, C, D, DS, MC, V.

★★ **P. J. MCGLYNN'S.** *147 US 9, Red Hook (12571)*. *845/758-3102*. Specializes in freshly cut ribs and steaks. Hrs: 11 am-midnight; Sun brunch to 3 pm. Closed Thanksgiving, Dec 25. Res accepted. Bar; Fri, Sat to 2 am. Lunch $2.95-$6.95, dinner $8.95-$18.95. Sun brunch $4.95-$6.95. Child's menu. Outdoor dining. Casual, Colonial decor in pre-1900 bldg. Cr cds: A, C, D, DS, MC, V.

★★ **RED HOOK INN.** *7460 S Broadway, Red Hook (12571)*. *845/758-8445*. Regional American menu. Specialties: peppercorn-cured salmon with scallion pancakes, local free-range poultry. Own baking. Hrs: 5-10 pm; Sat 11:30 am-3 pm, 5-10 pm; Sun 11 am-3 pm (brunch), 4-9 pm. Closed Mon; Memorial Day, Labor Day; also 2 wks in winter. Res accepted. Bar 4-11 pm. Lunch $4.50-$10.95, dinner $11.95-$18.95. Sun brunch $11.95. Child's menu. Outdoor dining. Country inn (1842) with beamed ceiling, lantern lamps; guest rms avail. Cr cds: A, DS, MC, V.

Richfield Springs

(D-6) *See also Canajoharie, Cooperstown, Herkimer, Ilion*

Pop 1,255 **Elev** 1,315 ft
Area code 315 **Zip** 13439

Motels/Motor Lodges

★ **FOUNTAIN VIEW MOTEL.** *3607 US Route 20 (13439)*. *315/858-1360*. 16 rms. Mid-June-Nov: S, D $55-$90; each addl $5; higher rates: wkends Sept-Nov, Hall of Fame wkend; lower rates wkdays Apr-mid-June. Closed rest of yr. Crib $5. TV; cable (premium). Restaurant nearby. Ck-out 11 am. Lawn games. On hillside. Overlooks illuminated fountain, park, pond. Refrigerators, microwaves. Cr cds: D, ER, JCB.

★ **VILLAGE MOTEL.** *E Main St (13439)*. *315/858-1540; fax 315/858-6702*. 11 rms. June-Sept: S $65; D $75; each addl $5; higher rates hol wkends; lower rates rest of yr. Crib free. TV; cable (premium). Restaurant nearby. Ck-out 11 am. Downhill/x-country ski 15 mi. Picnic tables, grills. Cr cds: A, DS, MC, V.

Riverhead (L.I.)

(G-3) *See also Hampton Bays (L.I.)*

Pop 27,680 **Elev** 19 ft **Area code** 631
Zip 11901

Information Chamber of Commerce, 542 E Main St, PO Box 291; 631/727-7600

Web www.riverheadchamber.com

Suffolk County's thousands of acres of rich farmland, first cultivated in 1690, have made it one of the leading agricultural counties in the United States. Potatoes, corn, and cauliflower are abundant here.

What to See and Do

Brookhaven National Laboratory. The Exhibit Center Science Museum is housed in the world's first nuclear reactor built to carry out research on the peaceful aspects of nuclear science. Participatory exhibits, audiovisual presentations, and historic collections. Tours (Mid-July-Aug, Sun; closed hol wkends). 14 mi W of

Riverhead via NY 24 and NY 495, in Upton. Phone 631/344-2345. **FREE**

Suffolk County Historical Society. Permanent and changing exhibits reflect the history of Suffolk County. Early crafts, ceramics, textiles, china, transportation, whaling, and Native Americans on Long Island are highlighted. Research library specializes in area history and genealogy. Educational programs and tours by advance res. (Tues-Sat afternoons; closed hols) 300 W Main St. Phone 631/727-2881. **FREE**

Special Event

Riverhead Country Fair. Downtown. Agricultural, needlecraft exhibits and competitions; farm animal exhibit; entertainment, midway, music. Mid-Oct. Phone 631/727-1215.

Motels/Motor Lodges

★ **BUDGET HOST INN.** *30 E Moriches Rd (11901).* 631/727-6200; *fax 631/727-6466; toll-free 800/528-1234.* www.budgethost.com. 68 rms, 2 story. S, D $89-$169; each addl $10; under 16 free; kits. $10 addl; higher rates: Memorial Day, July 4, Labor Day wkends; wkly rates. Crib $5. TV; cable (premium). Pool; lifeguard. Ck-out 11 am. Meeting rms. Business servs avail. Sundries. Lighted tennis. Picnic tables, grills. Cr cds: A, C, D, DS, MC, V.

★★ **RAMADA EAST END.** *1830 Rte 25 (11901).* 631/369-2200; *fax 631/369-1202; toll-free 800/272-6232.* 100 rms, 2 story. Mid-May-Sep: S, D $89-$165; each addl $10; under 18 free; lower rates rest of yr. Crib free. TV; cable (premium). Pool; lifeguard. Restaurant 6:30 am-10 pm. Bar noon-midnight. Ck-out 11 am. Meeting rms. Business servs avail. Valet serv. Cr cds: A, C, D, DS, MC, V.

★ **WADING RIVER.** *5890 Middle Country Rd, Wading River (11792).* 631/727-8000; *fax 631/369-8127.* 32 rms, 17 kits. Memorial Day wkend-mid-Sept: S, D $82-$92; each addl $10; kits. $16 addl; higher rates hol wkends; lower rates rest of yr. Crib $5. TV. Heated pool. Ck-out 11 am.

Lawn games. Picnic tables, grill. Sun deck. Cr cds: A, C, D, DS, MC, V.

Restaurant

★ **MEETING HOUSE CREEK INN.** *177 Meeting House Creek Rd, Aquebogue (11931).* 631/722-4220. Specializes in seafood. Hrs: 11:30 am-10 pm; Fri, Sat to 11 pm; Sun brunch to 3 pm. Closed Dec 25. Res accepted. Bar to 2 am. A la carte entrees: lunch $4.95-$9.95, dinner $12.95-$20.95. Sun brunch $12.95. Child's menu. Entertainment wkends. Outdoor dining. French country atmosphere. Overlooks marina. Cr cds: A, DS, MC, V.

Robert Moses State Park

(G-2) *See also Bay Shore (L.I.), New York City*

(On Fire Island, off south shore of Long Island, reached via pkwys)

Reached by the Robert Moses Causeway, the park consists of 875 acres of choice sand at the western end of a 50-mile barrier beach along the south shore of Long Island. The park includes beach swimming, bathhouses; picnic shelter, playground, surf and bay fishing, and a pitch-putt golf course. Standard fees. Headquarters is at Belmont Lake State Park, Babylon, Long Island 11702. For information phone 631/669-1000.

Rochester

(D-3) *See also Avon, Canandaigua*

Founded 1803 **Pop** 219,773 **Elev** 515 ft **Area code** 716

Information Greater Rochester Visitors Association, 45 East Ave, Suite 400, 14604; 716/546-3070 or 800/677-7282

Web www.visitrochester.com

George Eastman House, Rochester

Rochester is a high-tech industrial and cultural center and the third largest city in the state. Its educational institutions include University of Rochester with its Eastman School of Music and Rochester Institute of Technology with its National Technical Institute for the Deaf. The Vacuum Oil Company, a predecessor of Mobil Oil Corporation, was founded here in 1866. The city also has a symphony orchestra and professional theatre.

Rochester has its share of famous citizens too: Susan B. Anthony, champion of women's rights; Frederick Douglass, black abolitionist and statesman; George Eastman, inventor of flexible film; Hiram Sibley, founder of Western Union; and musicians Mitch Miller, Cab Calloway, and Chuck Mangione.

The city is on the Genesee River, near its outlet to Lake Ontario, in the midst of rich fruit and truck-gardening country.

Transportation

Greater Rochester International Airport. Information 716/464-6000; lost and found 716/464-6001; cash machines, Terminal Building.

Car Rental Agencies. See IMPORTANT TOLL-FREE NUMBERS.

Public Transportation. Buses (Regional Transit Service), phone 716/288-1700.

Rail Passenger Service. Amtrak 800/872-7245.

What to See and Do

Genesee Country Village & Museum. 20 mi SW via NY 36, in Mumford (see AVON). Phone 716/538-6822.

George Eastman House. Eastman's 50-rm mansion and gardens contain restored rms with their original 1920s furnishings and decor; exhibit on the house's restoration project; audiovisual shows about George Eastman and on film processes used by Eastman Kodak. Adj to house is the archive building; eight exhibit spaces display extensive collection of 19th- and 20th-century photography representing major photographers of the past 150 yrs. Chronological display presents evolution of photographic and imaging industries. Interactive displays present history of imaging with touch-screens, video stations, and programmed audiovisual shows. Museum tours (twice daily). (Tues-Sun; closed Jan 1, Thanksgiving, Dec 25) 900 East Ave. Phone 716/271-3361. ¢¢¢

Hamlin Beach State Park. Swimming beach (mid-June-Labor Day), fishing; nature, hiking, and biking trails; x-country skiing, snowmobiling, picnicking, playground, concession, tent and trailer area. Recreation programs. Pets allowed in some camping areas. Standard fees. 25 mi W on Lake Ontario State Pkwy. Phone 716/964-2462. ¢¢¢

⭐ **High Falls in the Brown's Race Historic District.** Area between Inner Loop and Platt and State sts, along the Genesee River Gorge. One of Rochester's earliest industrial districts has been renovated to preserve the area where flour mills and manufacturers once operated and Eastman Kodak and Gleason Works originated. Today the district still houses businesses in renovated historic buildings such as the Eastman Technologies Building. **Center at High Falls,** on Brown's Race St, is an interpretive museum with hands-on interactive exhibits on the history of the area as well as information on other attractions to visit in Rochester. **Brown's Race Market** has been transformed from a maintenance facility of the Rochester Gas and Electric Corporation into three levels of attractions incl a night club, a jazz club, and a restaurant. Laser light show can be viewed from the pedestrian bridge that crosses the Genesee River. Phone 716/325-2030.

The Landmark Center (Campbell-Whittlesey House Museum). (1835) Greek Revival home, Empire furniture. Also Hoyt-Potter House with gift shop and exhibit area. Tours (Thrus, Fri afternoons). 123 S Fitzhugh St. Phone 716/546-7029. ¢¢

Memorial Art Gallery (University of Rochester). Permanent collection spanning 50 centuries of art, incl masterworks by Monet, Matisse, and Homer; changing exhibitions. Cafe, gift shop. (Tues-Sun; closed hols) 500 University Ave. Phone 716/473-7720. ¢¢¢

Rochester Historical Society. Headquarters is "Woodside," Greek Revival mansion (1839). Collection of portraits, memorabilia, costumes. Reference library, manuscript collection. Garden. (Mon-Fri, also by appt; closed hols) 485 East Ave. Phone 716/271-2705. ¢¢

Rochester Institute of Technology. (1829) 13,000 students. Seven colleges, National Technical Institute for the Deaf on campus. Also on campus

are the **Bevier Gallery** (academic yr, daily; summer, Mon-Fri) and **Frank Ritter Memorial Ice Arena**. Tours of campus avail. Jefferson Rd at E River Rd. Phone 716/475-2411.

Rochester Museum & Science Center. Complex featuring regional museum of natural science, anthropology, history, and technology. Changing and permanent exhibits. (Daily; closed Thanksgiving, Dec 25) 657 East Ave, at Goodman St. Phone 716/271-4320. ¢¢¢

Strasenburgh Planetarium of the Rochester Museum and Science Center. Star Theatre shows, CineMagic 870 screen with special shows (call for times), educational exhibits. (Daily; closed Dec 24-25) Phone 716/271-1880. ¢¢

Seneca Park Zoo. Animals from all over the world; free-flight bird rm, reptiles, Children's Discovery Center. Rocky Coasts features underwater viewing of polar bears and seals. (Daily) 2222 St. Paul St, at jct NY 104. Phone 716/336-7200. ¢¢

Stone-Tolan House. (ca 1790) Restored pioneer homestead and tavern; four acres of gardens and orchards. (Fri-Sat, afternoons; closed hols) 2370 East Ave, 4 mi SE off I-490 in Brighton. Phone 716/546-7029. ¢¢

Strong Museum. Children's learning center with hands-on exhibits and 25,000 toys, dolls, miniatures, and more. Interactive, 3-D exhibit based on the Children's Television Workshop program *Sesame Street*. Glass atrium features a historic street scene with operating 1956 diner and 1918 carousel. (Mon-Sat, also Sun afternoons; closed Jan 1, Thanksgiving, Dec 25) 1 Manhattan Sq. Phone 716/263-2700. ¢¢¢

Susan B. Anthony House. Susan B. Anthony lived here for 40 yrs; she was arrested here for voting illegally in the 1872 presidential election. Mementos of the women's suffrage movement; furnishings. (Tues-Sun afternoons; closed hols) 17 Madison St. Phone 716/235-6124. ¢¢¢

University of Rochester. (1850) 7,700 students. Medical Center, 601 Elmwood Ave, off Mt Hope Ave. Seven colleges and schools. Tours by appt. River Campus, Wilson Blvd, on Genesee River. Phone 716/275-2121. On campus are

CEK Mees Observatory. On Gannett Hill, in the Bristol Hills. For information on Fri and Sat sunset tours contact the Physics and Astronomy Department. Phone 716/275-4385. **FREE**

Eastman School of Music of the University of Rochester. Concerts, recitals, opera in Eastman Theatre, Howard Hanson Recital Hall, and Kilbourn Hall. 26 Gibbs St. Performances ¢¢¢

Laboratory for Laser Energetics. Pioneering multidisciplinary teaching and research unit in laser and energy studies. Tours by appt. Phone 716/275-5286.

Rush Rhees Library. University of Rochester's central library on River campus. Extensive collection of rare books, manuscripts. (Daily; closed hols) Phone 716/275-4478. **FREE**

Victorian Doll Museum. More than 3,000 dolls from the mid-1800s to he present. Toy circus, puppet show, and dollhouses. Gift shop. (Tues-Sat; closed hols and Jan) W via I-490, exit 4 (NY 259), N to Buffalo Rd (NY 33), urn right (E) ½ blk, at 4332 Buffalo Rd in North Chili. Phone 585/247-0130. ¢¢

Special Events

Lilac Festival. In Highland Park, Highland Ave. More than 500 varieties of lilacs. Parade, art show, entertainment, and tours. Phone 716/256-4960. Mid-May.

Corn Hill Arts Festival. Arts and crafts; entertainment. Phone 716/262-3142. Mid-July.

Monroe County Fair. Monroe County Fairgrounds, 2695 E Henrietta Rd. Agricultural exhibits and displays, amusement rides, games, entertainment. Phone 716/334-4000. Late-July-early-Aug.

Comedies, dramas, and musicals. GeVa Theatre. 75 Woodbury Blvd. Resident professional theater. Phone 716/232-4382. Tues-Sun eves; Sat, Sun matinees. Aug-June.

Clothesline Festival. Grounds of the Memorial Art Gallery, 500 University Ave. Outdoor art show. Phone 716/473-7720, ext 3007. Mid-Sept.

Rochester Philharmonic Orchestra. Eastman Theater, Main and Gibbs. Symphonic concerts. Phone 716/454-2620. Oct-May.

Motels/Motor Lodges

★★ **COMFORT INN WEST.** *1501 Ridge Rd W (14615). 716/621-5700; fax 716/621-8446; res 800/228-5150. www.comfortinn.com.* 83 rms, 5 story. S $48.55-$53.95; D $53.55-$58.95; each addl $5; suites $104.35-$115.95; under 18 free. Crib free. Pet accepted, some restrictions. TV; cable (premium). Continental bkfst. Restaurant nearby. Ck-out noon. Business servs avail. In-rm modem link. Valet serv. Some in-rm whirlpools. Cr cds: A, D, DS, MC, V.

D 🐾 🐾

★★ **COURTYARD BY MARRIOTT.** *33 Corporate Woods (14623). 716/292-1000; fax 716/292-0905; res 800/321-2211. www.marriott.com.* 149 rms, 3 story. S, D $109-$114; suites $120; under 18 free; wkend rates. Crib free. TV; cable (premium), VCR avail. Indoor pool; whirlpool, lifeguard. Complimentary coffee in rms. Restaurant 6:30-10 am; Sat, Sun 7 am-noon. Bar. Ck-out 1 pm. Coin lndry. Meeting rms. Business servs avail. In-rm modem link. Sundries. Free airport transportation. Exercise equipt. Balconies. Cr cds: A, D, DS, MC, V.

D 🏊 🏋 ✈ 🔲 🐾 SC

★ **DAYS INN.** *384 East Ave (14607). 716/325-5010; fax 716/454-3158. www.daysinn.com.* 128 rms, 60 with shower only, 2 story. S $50-$68; D $55-$79; each addl $5; suites $89-$150; under 18 free; family rates. Crib free. TV; cable (premium). Complimentary continental bkfst. Restaurant nearby. Ck-out 11 am. Meeting rms. Business servs avail. In-rm modem link. Valet serv. Free airport, RR station, bus depot transportation. Exercise equipt; sauna. Whirlpool. Cr cds: A, DS, MC, V.

D 🏋 🔲 🐾

★ **ECONO LODGE.** *6575 4th Section Rd, Brockport (14420). 716/637-3157; fax 716/637-0434; toll-free 800/553-2666. www.econolodge.com.* 39 rms, 2 story. S $49-$55; D $53-$60; each addl $5; kit. units $63; under 18 free.

Crib $5. TV; cable (premium). Pool. Playground. Complimentary continental bkfst. Restaurant nearby. Ck-out 11 am. Coin lndry. Business servs avail. Cr cds: A, D, DS, JCB, MC, V.

(icons)

★ **ECONO LODGE ROCHESTER.** *940 Jefferson Rd (14623). 716/427-2700; fax 716/427-8504; res 800/553-2666. www.econolodge.com.* 102 rms, 3 story. S, D $49-$89; each addl $5; suites $89.95-$109.95; under 18 free. Crib free. Pet accepted, some restrictions. TV; cable (premium). Continental bkfst. Restaurant nearby open 24 hrs. Ck-out 11 am. Coin lndry. Business servs avail. Valet serv. Free airport transportation. Some in-rm whirlpools. Cr cds: A, C, D, DS, ER, MC, V.

(icons)

★★ **FOUR POINTS BY SHERATON.** *120 E Main St (14604). 716/546-6400; fax 716/546-3908; res 800/325-3535. www.sheraton.com.* 466 rms, 15 story. S, D $99-$119; suites $125-$350; under 19 free. Crib free. Pet accepted, some restrictions. TV; cable (premium). Heated pool; poolside serv. Complimentary coffee in rms. Restaurant 7 am-10 pm. Bar 11-2 am. Ck-out noon. Coin lndry. Convention facilities. Business servs avail. In-rm modem link. Shopping arcade.

Exercise equipt; sauna. Some balconies. On river. Cr cds: A, D, DS, MC, V.

(icons)

★★ **HAMPTON INN ROCHESTER NORTH.** *500 Center Place Dr (14615) 716/663-6070; fax 716/663-9158; res 800/426-7866.* 118 rms, 4 story. Apr-Sept: S $72-$139; D $75-$179; under 18 free; higher rates special events; lower rates rest of yr. Crib free. Pet accepted. TV; cable (premium). Complimentary continental bkfst, coffee in rms. Restaurant nearby. Ck-out noon. Meeting rms. Business servs avail. In-rm modem link. Bellhops. Valet serv. Exercise equipt. Microwaves avail. Picnic tables. Cr cds: A, C, D, DS, MC, V.

(icons)

★★ **HAMPTON INN SOUTH.** *717 I Henrietta Rd (14623). 716/272-7800; fax 716/272-1211; toll-free 800/426-7866. www.hamptoninn.com.* 113 rms, 5 story. S, D $95; under 18 free. Crib free. Pet accepted, some restrictions. TV; cable. Complimentary continental bkfst. Restaurant adj 11:30 am-midnight. Ck-out noon. Meeting rms. Business servs avail. In-rm modem link. Valet serv. Health club privileges. Cr cds: A, C, D, DS, ER, JCB, MC, V.

(icons)

Susan B. Anthony House

★★ **HOLIDAY INN.** *911 Brooks Ave (14624). 716/328-6000; fax 716/328-1012; toll-free 800/465-4329. www.holiday-inn.com/hotel/rocap.* 280 rms, 3 suites, 2 story. S $99-$119; D $109-$129; each addl $10; suites $200-$250; under 19 free. Crib free. Pet accepted, some restrictions. TV; cable (premium). Indoor pool; whirlpool, lifeguard. Coffee in rms. Restaurant 6 am-2 pm, 5-10 pm. Bar 11-2 am; entertainment. Ck-out noon. Coin lndry. Meeting rms. Business center. In-rm modem link. Bellhops. Concierge. Gift shop. Valet serv. Free airport transportation. Exercise equipt; sauna. Cr cds: A, D, DS, MC, V.

★★ **RAMADA INN ROCHESTER.** *800 Jefferson Rd (14623). 716/475-9190; fax 716/424-2138; toll-free 800/888-8102. www.ramada.com.* 145 rms, 3 story. S $62-$89; D $69-$99; each addl $7; under 18 free. Crib free. Pet accepted, some restrictions. TV; cable (premium), VCR (free movies). Pool; poolside serv, lifeguard. Complimentary bkfst buffet Mon-Fri. Restaurants noon-midnight. Bar. Ck-out noon. Meeting rms. Business servs avail. In-rm modem link. Free airport transportation. Health club privileges. Cr cds: A, C, D, DS, MC, V.

★ **RED ROOF INN.** *4820 W Henriette Rd, Henrietta (14467). 716/359-1100; fax 716/359-1121. www.redroof.com.* 108 rms, 2 story. S $37-$60; D $44-$70; each addl $7; under 18 free. Crib $5. Pet accepted. TV; cable (premium). Restaurant nearby. Ck-out noon. Business servs avail. Cr cds: A, C, D, DS, MC, V.

Hotels

★★★ **BROOKWOOD INN.** *800 Pittsford-Victor Rd, Pittsford (14534). 585/248-9000; fax 585/248-8569.* 108 rms, 4 story. S, D $89-$139; each addl $8; suites $125-$259; under 18 free; wkend rates. Crib free. TV; cable (premium). Heated indoor pool; whirlpool. Restaurant 6:30 am-10 pm; Sat, Sun 7:30 am-10 pm. Bar noon-11 pm; Sat, Sun noon-mid-

night. Coffee in rms. Ck-out noon. Meeting rms. Business servs avail. In-rm modem link. Bellhops. Valet serv. Sundries. Airport transportation. Downhill ski 20 mi. Exercise equipt; sauna. Refrigerators avail. Bicycle path along Erie Canal; bike rentals. Cr cds: A, D, DS, MC, V.

★★★ **CROWNE PLAZA ROCHESTER.** *70 State St (14614). 585/546-3450; fax 585/546-8714; res 800/227-6963. www.crowneplaza.com.* 352 rms, 7 story. S, D $69.95-$139.95; suites $149-$299; under 18 free; family rates; package plans. Crib free. Pet accepted, some restrictions; $25 deposit. Garage parking $3.50/day. TV; cable (premium). Heated pool (June-Sept); lifeguard. Restaurant 6 am-2 pm, 4-10 pm. Bar 3 pm-2 am. Coffee in rms. Ck-out noon. Convention facilities. Business center. In-rm modem link. Valet serv. Concierge. Bellhops. Gift shop. Free airport, RR station, bus depot transportation. Downhill ski 20 mi. Exercise equipt. Game rm. Some minibars. On river. Luxury level. Cr cds: A, C, D, DS, MC, V.

★★★ **HYATT REGENCY ROCHESTER.** *125 E Main St (14604). 585/546-1234; fax 585/546-6777; res 800/233-1234. www.hyatt.com.* 336 rms, 18 suites, 25 story. S, D $89-$179; each addl $25; suites $225-$390; under 18 free; wkly rates. Crib free. Parking garage $3/day. TV; cable (premium). Heated indoor pool; whirlpool. Restaurant 6:30 am-2 pm, 5-10 pm. Bar 3 pm-midnight. Coffee in rms. Ck-out noon. Convention facilities. Business center. In-rm modem link. Concierge. Gift shop. Valet serv. Free airport transportation. Exercise equipt. Bathrm phones. Refrigerator, wet bar in suites. Luxury level. Cr cds: A, C, D, DS, MC, V.

★★★ **MARRIOTT ROCHESTER AIRPORT.** *1890 W Ridge Rd (14615). 716/225-6880; fax 716/225-8188; toll-free 800/228-9290. www.marriott.com.* 210 rms, 7 story. S, D $144-$164; suites $239; under 18 free; wkend, hol rates. Valet parking avail. Crib free. TV; cable (premium), VCR avail.

Heated indoor pool; whirlpool, poolside serv, lifeguard (wkends only). Restaurant 6:30 am-10 pm. Bar 11-midnight. Coffee in rms. Ck-out noon. Meeting rms. Business center. In-rm modem link. Bellhops. Valet serv. Concierge. Sundries. Gift shop. Free airport transportation. Exercise equipt; sauna. Refrigerators in suites. Cr cds: A, C, D, DS, MC, V.

[icons]

★★★ **RADISSON HOTEL ROCHESTER.** 175 Jefferson Rd (14623). 716/475-1910; fax 716/475-9633; res 800/333-3333. www.radisson.com/rochester. 171 rms, 4 story. S, D $79-$149; each addl $10; family, wkend rates. Crib free. TV; cable (premium). Heated indoor pool; lifeguard. Restaurant 6:30 am-10 pm, Sat, Sun 7 am-10 pm. Bar 11 am-11 pm; entertainment Fri, Sat. Coffee in rms. Ck-out 11 am. Meeting rms. Business servs avail. In-rm modem link. Bellhops. Valet serv. Sundries. Free airport transportation. Gift shop. Exercise equipt; sauna. Health club privileges. Lawn games. Balconies. Some refrigerators. Cr cds: A, C, D, DS, ER, JCB, MC, V.

[icons]

★★ **WELLESLEY INN.** 1635 W Ridge Rd (14615). 716/621-2060; fax 716/621-7102; toll-free 800/444-8888. www.wellesleyinnandsuites.com. 97 rms, 1 with shower only, 4 story. Apr-Nov: S, D $55-$69; each addl $5; under 18 free; higher rates some special events; lower rates rest of yr. Crib free. Pet accepted, some restrictions; $3. TV; cable (premium). Complimentary continental bkfst, coffee in rms. Restaurant adj 5:30 am-10:30 pm. Ck-out 11 am. Business servs avail. Health club privileges. Some refrigerators. Cr cds: A, C, D, DS, MC, V.

[icons]

★★ **WELLESLEY INN.** 797 E Henrietta Rd (14623). 716/427-0130; fax 716/427-0903; res 800/444-8888. www.wellesleyinnandsuites.com. 96 rms, 4 story. S $49-$79; D $59-$89; each addl $6; suites $80-$110; under 18 free. Crib free. Pet accepted, some restrictions; $3. TV; cable (premium). Complimentary continental bkfst, coffee in rms. Ck-out 11 am. Business servs avail. In-rm modem link.

Sundries. Health club privileges. Cr cds: A, C, D, DS, ER, JCB, MC, V.

[icons]

B&Bs/Small Inns

★★★ **A B & B AT DARTMOUTH HOUSE.** 215 Dartmouth St (14607). 585/271-7872; fax 585/473-0778. www.dartmouthhouse.com. 4 rms, 3 story. 1 suite. S, D $95-$125; suite $150. Children over 12 yrs only. TV; VCR (movies). Complimentary full bkfst; afternoon refreshments. Ck-out 11 am-noon, ck-in 3-6 pm. Business servs avail. In-rm modem link. Free airport, RR station, bus depot transportation. Library/sitting rm. Health club privileges. Valet serv. English Tudor house (1905); antiques, fireplace. Near International Museum of Photography (George Eastman House). Totally nonsmoking. Cr cds: A, C, D, DS, MC, V.

[icons]

★★★ **GENESEE COUNTRY INN.** 948 George St, Mumford (14511). 716/538-2500; fax 716/538-4565; res 800/697-8297. www.geneseecountryinn.com. 9 air-cooled rms, 3 story. D $105-$160; each addl $15; some wkends (2-day min); package plans. TV; VCR. Complimentary full bkfst; afternoon refreshments. Restaurants nearby; dinner pkgs avail. Ck-out 11:30 am, ck-in 3-7 pm. Gift shop. Picnic table, grill. Restored inn (1830) on 8 wooded acres; fishing in spring-fed trout stream; waterfall. Antiques. Some balconies, fireplaces. Totally nonsmoking. Cr cds: DS, MC, V.

[icons]

★★★ **OLIVER LOUD'S INN.** 1474 Marsh Rd, Pittsford (14534). 716/248-5200; fax 716/248-9970; res 716/248-5200. www.frontiernet.net/~rchi. 8 rms, 2 story. S $125; D $135. Children over 12 yrs only. TV avail; cable. Complimentary continental bkfst in rms; afternoon refreshments. Restaurant (see RICHARDSON'S CANAL HOUSE). Bar 4-10 pm. Ck-out 11 am, ck-in 3 pm. Meeting rms. Business servs avail. In-rm modem link. On Erie Canal. Built 1812; stagecoach inn. Totally nonsmoking. Cr cds: A, D, MC, V.

[icons]

★★ **THE VICTORIAN B&B.** *320 Main St, Brockport (14420). 716/637-7519; fax 716/637-2319. www. victorianbandb.com.* 7 rms, 1 with shower only, 2 story. S $39-$72; D $49-$85; each addl $14; wkly rates; hols 2-day min. TV; cable, VCR avail (movies). Complimentary full bkfst. Restaurant nearby. Ck-out 11 am, ck-in 3 pm. Business servs avail. Golf privileges. Downhill ski/x-country ski 3 mi. Built in 1890; Queen Anne Victorian house. Totally nonsmoking. Cr cds: A, C, D, DS, MC, V.

⬟ ⬟ ⬟ ⬟ ⬟ ⬟ **SC**

All Suite

★★★ **STRATHALLAN HOTEL.** *550 East Ave (14607). 716/461-5010; fax 716/461-3387; toll-free 800/678-7284. www.strathallan.com.* 156 rms, 8-9 story. S, D, suites, kit. units $99-$250; under 18 free; wkend plans. Crib free. TV; cable (premium). Complimentary coffee in rms. Restaurant 6:30 am-10 pm. Bar 11-2 am; entertainment Fri, Sat. Coffee in rms. Ck-out noon. Meeting rms. Business servs avail. In-rm modem link. Beauty shop. Bellhops. Free valet parking. Free airport transportation. Coin lndry. Valet serv. Exercise equipt; sauna. Refrigerators, microwaves. Many balconies, kitchenettes. In sedate residential area. Luxury level. Cr cds: A, C, D, DS, MC, V.

D ⬟ ⬟ ⬟ ⬟ **SC**

Extended Stay

★★ **RESIDENCE INN BY MARRIOTT.** *1300 Jefferson Rd (14623). 716/272-8850; fax 716/272-7822; res 800/331-3131. www.marriott.com.* 112 kit. suites, 2 story. S $99-$135; D $145-$175; under 18 free; wkly, monthly rates. Crib free. Pet accepted, some restrictions; $125 and $6/day. TV; cable (premium), VCR avail (movies). Pool; whirlpool, lifeguard. Complimentary continental bkfst, coffee in rms. Restaurant nearby. Ck-out noon. Coin lndry. Meeting rms. Business servs avail. In-rm modem link. Sundries. Downhill ski 20 mi. Health club privileges. Picnic tables, grills. Cr cds: A, D, DS, MC, V.

⬟ **D** ⬟ ⬟ ⬟ ⬟

Restaurants

★ **BANGKOK.** *155 State St (14614). 585/325-3517.* Thai menu. Specializes in vegetarian dishes, seafood. Hrs: 11 am-10 pm; Fri, Sat to 11 pm. Closed Sun; hols. Res accepted Fri, Sat. Wine, beer. Lunch $4.95-$6.25, dinner $7.95-$12.95. Parking (dinner). Thai decor. Cr cds: DS, MC, V.

★★ **CARTWRIGHT INN.** *5691 W Henrietta Rd, West Henrietta (14586). 716/334-4444.* Specializes in New England clam chowder, prime rib, lobster. Hrs: 11:30 am-10 pm; Sun from 12:30 pm; early-bird dinner 4:30-6:30 pm. Res accepted. Bar to 2 am. Lunch $3.50-$5.95, dinner $10.95-$24.95. Child's menu. Parking. In former stagecoach stop; built 1831. Cr cds: A, D, DS, MC, V.

D ⬟

★ **DINOSAUR BAR-B-QUE.** *99 Court St (14604). 585/325-7090. www. dinosaurbarbque.com.* Specializes in ribs. Hrs: 11 am-midnight; Fri, Sat to 1 am. Closed Sun. Lunch, dinner $6-$30. Cr cds: A, D, DS, MC, V.

D ⬟

★★★ **THE GRILL AT STRATHALLAN.** *550 East Ave (14607). 585/454-1880. www.grill175.com.* Specializes in dry-aged hand-cut steak, sea bass, ahi tuna. Hrs: 11 am-2:30 pm, 5-11 pm; Fri to midnight; Sat 5 pm-midnight. Closed Sun. Lunch $6-$12; dinner $21-$30. Entertainment. Jacket. Tasting menu avail. Cr cds: A, C, D, DS, MC, V.

D **SC**

★★★ **MARIO'S VIA ABRUZZI.** *2740 Monroe Ave (14618). 585/271-1111. www.mariosviaabruzzi.com.* Italian menu. Specializes in grilled calamari. Own pasta. Hrs: 5-10 pm; Fri to 11 pm; Sat 4-11 pm; Sun 4-9 pm; Sun brunch 11 am-2 pm. Closed hols. Res accepted. Bar. Wine cellar. Dinner $10.90-$24. Sun brunch $16.95. Child's menu. Strolling musicians Sat (dinner). Parking. Outdoor dining. Authentic central Italian architecture; original paintings, sculptures. Family-owned since 1979. Totally nonsmoking. Cr cds: A, D, DS, MC, V.

D

★★ **OLIVE TREE.** *165 Monroe Ave (14607). 585/454-3510. www.olivetree restaurant.com.* Greek menu. Specialties: taramosalata. Hrs: 11:30 am-2 pm, 5-9 pm; Sat from 5 pm. Closed Sun; hols. Res accepted. Bar. Lunch $4-$8.50, dinner $10.50-$19.50. Parking. Outdoor dining. Restored dry goods store (1864). Cr cds: A, C, D, DS, MC, V.

D

★ **RAJ MAHAL.** *324 Monroe Ave (14607). 585/546-2315.* Indian menu. Specializes in chicken dishes, vegetarian dishes, seafood, lamb. Hrs: 11:30 am-2:30 pm. Closed Thanksgiving, Dec 25. Res accepted wkends. Bar. Buffet lunch $6.99. Dinner $8-$18. Parking. Traditional Indian decor. Cr cds: A, C, D, DS, MC, V.

D

★★★ **RICHARDSON'S CANAL HOUSE.** *1474 Marsh Rd, Pittsford (14534). 585/248-5000. www.canal house.org.* Contemporary American menu. Specializes in duckling, seafood, beef tenderloin. Own baking. Hrs: 6-9 pm. Closed Sun; hols. Res accepted. Bar 4:30-11 pm; Fri, Sat to midnight. Wine list. Complete meals: dinner $35. Parking. Outdoor dining. Historic inn. Terrace overlooks Erie Canal. Cr cds: A, C, D, MC, V.

D

★★★ **ROONEYS.** *90 Henrietta St (14620). 585/442-0444.* Specializes in plantain crusted shrimp. Own baking. Hrs: 5-10 pm. Closed hols. Res accepted. Wine cellar. Dinner $19-$30. Parking. In tavern built 1860, the original bar is still in use. Cr cds: A, D, DS, MC, V.

★★ **SCOTCH 'N SIRLOIN.** *3450 Winton Pl (14623). 585/427-0808.* Specializes in steak, seafood. Salad bar. Hrs: 5-10 pm; Fri, Sat to 11 pm. Closed Mon; hols. Res accepted. Bar. Dinner $10-$36. Child's menu. Parking. Old West decor; antiques. Cr cds: A, D, DS, MC, V.

D

★ **TOKYO JAPANESE.** *2930 W Henrietta Rd (14623). 716/424-4166.* Japanese, vegetarian menu. Specializes in sushi, hibachi dishes. Hrs: 11:30 am-10 pm; Fri, Sat to 11 pm; Sun 4-10 pm. Closed Thanksgiving. Res accepted. Bar. Lunch $5.25-$8.95, dinner $7.50-$35.95. Child's menu. Parking. Traditional decor. Cr cds: A, DS, MC, V.

D

★ **VILLAGE COAL TOWER.** *9 Schoen Pl, Pittsford (14534). 585/381-7866.* Specializes in potato pancakes. Hrs: 7 am-8 pm; wkends from 8 am. Closed hols. Bkfst $2-$4, lunch $2-$5, dinner $6.95-$9.25. Child's menu. Parking. Outdoor dining. In turn-of-the-century coal storage structure used to service boats on Erie Canal. Cr cds: A, MC, V.

D SC

Rockville Centre (L.I.)

See also Hempstead (L.I.), New York City

Pop 24,568 **Elev** 25 ft **Area code** 516 **Zip** 11570

Information Chamber of Commerce, PO Box 226; 516/766-0666

Incorporated in 1893, Rockville Centre maintains Long Island atmosphere in the midst of a thriving commercial district. The town boasts 200 acres of parkland and is a short ride from several fine beach areas.

What to See and Do

Rock Hall Museum. (1767) Historic house with period furnishings and exhibits. (Sat, Sun afternoons) 5 mi SW on Broadway from Sunrise Hwy W, at 199 Broadway in Lawrence. Phone 516/239-1157. **FREE**

Restaurants

★★ **BUON GIORNO.** *476 Merrick Rd, Lynbrook (11563). 516/887-1945.* Northern Italian menu. Specializes in veal scallopini, fish, chicken. Own pasta. Hrs: noon-3 pm, 5-10 pm; Sat 5-11 pm; Sun 4-9 pm. Closed Mon; hols. Res required wkends. Bar. Lunch $11-$15, dinner $11.95-$22.95. Formal dining. Original artwork. Cr cds: A, C, D, DS, MC, V.

D

★★ **COYOTE GRILL.** *104 Waterview Rd, Island Park (11558). 516/889-8009.* Southwestern menu. Specializes in fresh seafood, venison, rabbit. Hrs: noon-4 pm, 5-10 pm; Mon, Tues from 5 pm; Fri, Sat to 11 pm; Sun brunch to 3 pm. Closed Dec 25. Res accepted. Bar. A la carte entrees: lunch $6-$15, dinner $13-$22. Sun brunch $16-$18. Child's menu. Parking. Outdoor dining. Southwestern artifacts and decor. Cr cds: A, MC, V. **D**

★★ **GEORGE MARTIN.** *65 N Park Ave, Rockville Centre, L.I. (11570). 516/678-7272.* Continental menu. Specializes in grilled meat and seafood. Hrs: 11:30 am-3 pm, 5-11 pm; Fri, Sat to midnight; Sun 5-10 pm. Closed Easter, Thanksgiving, Dec 25. A la carte entrees: lunch $4.95-$12.95, dinner $6.95-$24.95. Bistro-style decor and furnishings. Cr cds: A, MC, V. **D**

★ **MAIER'S BRICK CAFE.** *157 Lakeview Ave, Lynbrook (11563). 516/599-9669.* Specializes in steak. Hrs: 5-10 pm; Fri, Sat to midnight; Sun brunch noon-4 pm. Closed Thanksgiving, Dec 25. Res accepted. Bar. A la carte entrees: dinner $7.50-$19.75. Sun brunch $9.95. Pub atmosphere. Family-owned. Cr cds: A, C, D, DS, MC, V. **D**

★ **RAAY-NOR'S CABIN.** *550 Sunrise Hwy, Baldwin (11510). 516/223-4886.* Specialties: barbecued chicken and ribs, Southern-fried chicken, sugar-cured ham steak. Hrs: noon-9 pm; Sat to 10 pm. Closed Dec 25. Res accepted. Bar. A la carte entrees: lunch $4.95-$7.95; dinner $8.95-$16.50. Child's menu. Parking. Family-style dining in log cabin. Rustic decor. Cr cds: A, C, D, DS, ER, MC, V. **D**

★★ **SCHOONER.** *435 Woodcleft Ave, Freeport (11570). 516/378-7575.* Specializes in seafood, steak, chicken. Hrs: noon-9:30 pm; Fri, Sat to 11 pm; Sun 3-9:30 pm. Closed Dec 25; also 2nd and 3rd wks Jan. Lunch $8.95-$16.95, dinner $13.95-$29.50. Valet parking. Nautical decor; overlooks Woodcleft Canal. Cr cds: A, C, D, DS, ER, MC, V. **D**

Rome

(D-6) *See also Boonville, Canastota, Oneida, Utica*

Settled 1786 **Pop** 34,950 **Elev** 462 ft
Area code 315 **Zip** 13440
Information Rome Area Chamber of Commerce, 139 W Dominick St; 315/337-1700
Web www.romechamber.com

Originally the site of Fort Stanwix, where, during the Revolutionary War, tradition says the Stars and Stripes were first flown in battle. The author of the "Pledge of Allegiance," Francis Bellamy, is buried in Rome. Griffiss Air Force Base is located here.

What to See and Do

Delta Lake State Park. Swimming beach (Memorial Day wkend-mid-June, limited days; mid-June-Labor Day, full-time), bathhouse, fishing, boating (ramp); tent and trailer sites, hiking, biking, x-country skiing, picnicking, playground. Standard fees. 6 mi NE off NY 46. Phone 315/337-4670.

Erie Canal Village. Trips on restored section of the Erie Canal aboard mule-drawn 1840 canal packetboat, *The Chief Engineer.* Buildings of 1840s canal village incl church, blacksmith shop, train station, museums, schoolhouse, Victorian home, stable, settlers house; hotel; orientation center; picnic area, and restaurant. (Mid-May-Labor Day, daily; call for extended schedule) 2½ mi W on NY 49. Phone 315/337-3999. ¢¢¢

Fort Rickey Children's Discovery Zoo. Restoration of 1700s British fort is site of a zoo that emphasizes animal contact. Wide variety of wildlife. Picnic facilities. (Memorial Day-Labor Day, daily; Sept, Sat and Sun only) 3 mi W via NY 49. Phone 315/336-1930.

Fort Stanwix National Monument.
Reconstructed earth-and-log fort on
location of 1758 fort; here the Iroquois signed a treaty opening terri-
tory east of Ohio River to colonial
expansion. In 1777 fort was besieged
by British; General Benedict Arnold
forced their retreat. Costumed
guides; film; museum. (Apr-Dec,
daily; closed Thanksgiving, Dec 25)
Phone 315/336-2090. **FREE**

Skiing. Woods Valley Ski Area. Two
double chairlifts, T-bar; patrol, snowmaking, school, rentals; bar, cafeteria. Longest run 4,000 ft, vertical
drop 500 ft. (Dec-Mar, Tues-Sun;
closed Dec 25) Some eve rates. 8 mi
N on NY 46 in Westernville. Phone
315/827-4721. ¢¢¢¢

**Tomb of the Unknown Soldier of the
American Revolution.** Designed by
Lorimar Rich, who also designed the
tomb at Arlington National Cemetery. 201 N James St.

Special Event

World Series of Bocce. Italian lawn
bowling. Mid-July. Phone 315/339-
3609.

Motels/Motor Lodges

★★ **INN AT THE BEECHES.** *7900
Turin Rd (Rte 26 N) (13440). 315/336-
1775; fax 315/339-2636; toll-free
800/765-7251. www.thebeeches.com.*
75 rms, 1-2 story, 6 kits. S $56-$63; D
$62-$69; each addl $5; kit. units $85-
$99; under 12 free; wkly rates; wkend
rates. Crib free. Pet accepted, some
restrictions; $20 deposit. TV; cable.
Pool. Restaurant 6-10 am; Sat, Sun 8
am-noon. Ck-out 11 am. Business
center. Downhill/x-country ski 8 mi.
Lawn games. Refrigerator, microwaves avail. 52 acres with pond. Cr
cds: A, C, D, DS, MC, V.

★★ **QUALITY INN.** *200 S James
Street (13440). 315/336-4300; fax
315/336-4492; res 800/228-5151.
www.qualityinn.com.* 103 rms, 2 story.
S, D $65-$78; each addl $10; suite
$125; under 18 free. Crib free. TV;
cable. Pool. Complimentary coffee in
rms. Restaurant open 24 hrs. Ck-out
11 am. Coin lndry. Business servs
avail. Game rm. Downhill/x-country

ski 8 mi. Microwaves avail. Cr cds: A,
D, DS, JCB, MC.

Restaurants

★★ **THE BEECHES.** *Turin Rd (NY
26) (13440). 315/336-1700.* Specializes in fresh beef, veal, chicken. Hrs:
11:30 am-2:30 pm, 5-9:30 pm; Sat 5-
10 pm; Sun brunch to 1:30 pm.
Closed Mon; Jan 1, Dec 24, 25. Res
accepted. Bar. Lunch $4.25-$8, dinner $7.50-$19.95. Sun brunch $9.50.
Child's menu. Original decor from
'20s estate. Family-owned. Cr cds: A,
D, DS, MC, V.

★★ **SAVOY.** *255 E Dominick St
(13440). 315/339-3166.* Italian, Amer
menu. Specializes in own pasta, fresh
seafood, steak. Hrs: 11:30 am-10 pm;
Sat 5-11 pm; Sun 4-9 pm. Closed
Thanksgiving, Dec 25. Res accepted.
Bar. Lunch from $3.95, dinner $5.95-
$15.95. Child's menu. Pianist Wed,
Fri, Sat. Family-owned. Cr cds: A, C,
D, ER, MC, V.

Roscoe

See also Liberty

Pop 597 **Elev** 1,300 ft **Area code** 607
Zip 12776

Information Roscoe-Rockland Chamber of Commerce, Box 443; 607/498-
6055

Dutch settlers conquered the wilderness in this Catskill area, but in the
process did not destroy it, a practice
continued by those who followed.
Small and large game abound in the
area, and the Willowemoc and
Beaverkill rivers provide excellent
trout fishing. Four unusual and interesting covered bridges are located in
the surrounding countryside.

What to See and Do

Catskill Fly Fishing Center & Museum.
Fishing, hiking, demonstrations,
programs, and events. Interpretive
exhibits featuring the heritage, sci-

ence, and art of the sport. Explore the lives of legendary characters who made angling history. Displays of rods, reels, flies; video rm, library, hall of fame. Visitor center; gift shop. (Apr-Oct, daily; Nov-Mar, Tues-Sat) Old Rte 17, between Roscoe and Livingston Manor. Phone 914/439-4810. ¢¢

Motel/Motor Lodge

★ **ROSCOE MOTEL.** *2045 NY 17 (12776). 607/498-5220; fax 607/498-4643.* 18 rms. S $45; D $60; each addl $10; kit. units $60; Apr-Oct wkends (2-day min). Crib free. Pet accepted. TV; cable. Pool. Complimentary continental bkfst. Ck-out 11 am. Some refrigerators. Picnic tables, grill. On Beaverkill River. Cr cds: A, MC, V.

B&B/Small Inn

★★★ **THE GUEST HOUSE.** *408 Debruce Rd, Livingston Manor (12758). 845/439-4000; fax 845/439-3344; res 845/439-4000. www.theguesthouse. com.* 7 rms, 4 with shower only, 1-2 story, 2 suites, 1 guest house. Apr-Nov: S $138-$155; D $153-$170; suites $290; guest house $260; package plans; wkends 2-day min; hols 3-day min; lower rates rest of yr. Pet accepted, some restrictions. TV; cable (premium). Complimentary full bkfst,coffee in rms. Restaurant nearby. Ck-out noon, ck-in 11 am. Business servs avail. Luggage handling. Airport transportation. Tennis. X-country ski on site. Exercise equipt. Massage. Indoor pool; whirlpool. On river. Country inn; antiques. Cr cds: A, DS, MC, V.

Roslyn (L.I.)

See also Floral Park (L.I.), Westbury (L.I.)

Pop 2,570 **Elev** 38 ft **Area code** 516
Zip 11576

Hotel

★★★ **ROSLYN CLAREMONT HOTEL.** *1221 Old Northern Blvd (11576). 516/625-2700; fax 516/625-2731; toll-free 800/626-9005. www. roslynclaremonthotel.com.* 76 rms, 3 story. S $179-$209; D $179-$229; suites $275-$395. Crib $15. TV; cable (premium), VCR avail. Coffee in rms. Restaurant 7 am-10 pm. Rm serv 24 hrs. Bar; entertainment. Ck-out noon. Meeting rms. Business servs avail. In-rm modem link. Concierge. Exercise equipt; steam rm. Minibars. Cr cds: A, C, D, DS, MC, V.

Restaurants

★★★ **BRYANT & COOPER STEAK HOUSE.** *2 Middleneck Rd, Roslyn (11576). 516/627-7270.* Specialties: prime steak, jumbo lobster, lamb and veal chops. Own breads. Hrs: noon-10 pm; Fri to 11 pm; Sat 5 pm-midnight; Sun 3-10 pm. Closed Dec 25. Res accepted. Bar. Wine cellar. Lunch $8-$15. A la carte entrees: dinner $14-$28. Valet parking. Cr cds: A, D, V.

★★ **CLASSICO.** *1042 Northern Blvd, Roslyn Estates (11576). 516/621-1870.* Northern Italian menu. Specialties: coniglio al forno, trippa al classico, polenta con quaglie. Hrs: 4-11 pm; Wed-Fri from noon; Sun to 10 pm. Closed Jan 1, Dec 25. Res accepted. Bar. Lunch, dinner $12.50-$25. Complete meal: lunch $14.50. Own baking. Musicians Sat. Valet parking. Italian decor with murals, stucco walls, frosted glass. Cr cds: A, C, D, DS, ER, MC, V.

★★★ **GEORGE WASHINGTON MANOR.** *1305 Old Northern Blvd (11576). 516/621-1200.* Specialties: country-style pot pie, Yankee pot roast. Hrs: 11:30 am-10 pm; Sun brunch 11:30 am-3 pm. Closed Dec 25. Res accepted. Bar. Wine list. Complete meals: lunch $10.95-$14.95, dinner $14-$21.95. Sun brunch $10.95-$14.95. Valet parking. Elegant dining in historic

Colonial mansion (1740). Cr cds: A, DS, MC, V.

★★ **JOLLY FISHERMAN & STEAK HOUSE.** *25 Main St, (11576). 516/621-0055.* Specializes in seafood, steak. Hrs: noon-9 pm; Fri, Sat to 11 pm; Sun 1-9 pm. Closed Mon; Yom Kippur, Thanksgiving. Res accepted. Bar. Dinner $15.95-$25.95. Complete meals: lunch $16.95, dinner $34.95. A la carte entrees: lunch $7.95-$16.95. Child's menu. Valet parking. Nautical decor. Overlooks lake. Family-owned. Cr cds: A, DS, MC, V.
D

★★★ **LA COQUILLE.** *1669 Northern Blvd, Manhasset (11030). 516/365-8422.* French menu. Specializes in veal, chicken, lamb. Hrs: 5-10 pm; Fri, Sat to 11 pm; Sun 5-9 pm. Closed hols. Res required. A la carte entrees: dinner $20-$30. Valet parking. French villa decor. Jacket. Cr cds: A, D, MC, V.
D

★★★ **LA MARMITE.** *234 Hillside Ave, Williston Park (11596). 516/746-1243.* Continental menu. Specialties: roast rack of lamb; ravioli stuffed with shrimp, scallops, and lobster. Own baking, pasta. Hrs: noon-3 pm, 5:30-10 pm; Sat 6-11 pm. Closed Sun; Jan 1, Dec 25. Res accepted. Bar. Wine cellar. A la carte entrees: lunch $5.25-$14.50, dinner $15.75-$25.75. Valet parking. Jacket. Cr cds: A, C, D, DS, MC, V.
D

★ **LA PARMA ITALIAN.** *707 Willis Ave, Williston Park (11596). 516/294-6610. www.laparma.com.* Southern Italian menu. Specializes in lobster, pasta, veal. Hrs: noon-2:30 pm, 5-10 pm; Fri to midnight; Sat 4 pm-midnight; Sun 3-9 pm. Closed Mon. Res accepted hols. Bar. A la carte entrees: lunch $10-$15, dinner $20-$30. Valet parking. Family-style dining. Cr cds: A, C, D, DS, MC, V.
D

★★★ **L'ENDROIT.** *290 Glen Cove Rd (11577). 516/621-6630.* French, continental menu. Specialties: foie de veau Bercy, lamb a L'Endroit, salmon en croûte. Own baking. Hrs: 11:30 am-2:45 pm, 5-10 pm; Fri, Sat to 11 pm. Closed Sun; Jan 1, Thanksgiving, Dec 25. Res accepted; required wkends. Bar. Wine list. A la carte

entrees: lunch $9.50-$22, dinner $14.95-$29.50. Valet parking. Original artwork. Cr cds: A, D, MC, V.
D

Rouses Point

See also Plattsburgh

Pop 2,277 **Elev** 103 ft **Area code** 518 **Zip** 12979

A border town on a main route to Montreal, Rouses Point is a busy customs inspection point. A toll bridge across Lake Champlain goes to Vermont.

What to See and Do

Fort Lennox. Large stone fort built 1819-1829 on an island in the Richelieu River. Tours; picnic area, cafe; ferry (mid-May-early Sept, daily; fee). (For border-crossing regulations, see MAKING THE MOST OF YOUR TRIP.) St-Paul ele aux Noix, Quebec, Canada, 10 mi N off Hwy 223. Phone 450/291-5700. ¢¢

Sackets Harbor

See also Watertown

Settled 1800 **Pop** 1,386 **Elev** 278 ft **Area code** 315 **Zip** 13685

This is a lakeside resort area for the eastern Lake Ontario region. Two major battles of the War of 1812 occurred here. In the first skirmish, the British warships invading the harbor were damaged and withdrew; a landing force was repulsed in the second battle.

What to See and Do

Sackets Harbor Battlefield State Historic Site. War of 1812 battlefield; Federal-style Union Hotel (1818); Commandant's House (1850) (fee); US Navy Yard (1812-1955); visitor center, exhibits; demonstrations; tours. (Mid-May-early Sept, daily) 505 W Washington St, overlooking lake. Phone 315/646-3634. ¢

Westcott Beach State Park. Swimming beach, bathhouse, fishing, boating (launch); hiking and nature trails, x-country skiing, snowmobiling, picnicking, playground, concession, tent and trailer sites. (Mid-May-Columbus Day wkend) Standard fees. 2 mi S on NY 3. Phone 315/938-0083.

Hotel

★ ★ **ONTARIO PLACE HOTEL.** *103 General Smith Dr (13685).* 315/646-8000; toll-free 800/564-1812. www.ontarioplacehotel.com. 38 rms, 3 story, 3 suites. Mid-May-mid-Oct: D $29-59; each addl $10; suites $125-$150; under 14 free; wkly rates; lower rates rest of yr. Crib free. Pet accepted, some restrictions. TV; cable, VCR avail. Restaurant nearby. Ck-out 11 am. Meeting rms. Business servs avail. In-rm modem link. Gift shop. Bicycles avail. Some bathrm phones. Refrigerators avail. Cr cds: A, C, D, DS, MC, V.

Sag Harbor (L.I.)

(G-3) See also Amagansett, East Hampton (L.I.), Shelter Island, Southampton (L.I.)

Settled 1660 **Pop** 2,313 **Elev** 14 ft
Area code 631 **Zip** 11963
Information Chamber of Commerce, PO Box 2810; 631/725-0011
Web www.sagharborchamber.com

This great whaling town of the 19th century provided prototypes from which James Fenimore Cooper created characters for his sea stories. Sheltered in a cove of Gardiners Bay, the economy of Sag Harbor is still centered around the sea.

What to See and Do

Custom House. Served as custom house and post office during the late 18th and early 19th centuries; antique furnishings. (July-Aug, Tues-

Sun; May-June and Sept-Oct, Sat and Sun) Garden St. Phone 631/692-4664. ¢¢

Morton National Wildlife Refuge. A 187-acre sanctuary with sandy and rocky beaches and wooded bluffs. Nature trails; ponds and lagoon for wildlife observation, nature study, photography, and environmental education. (Daily; beach closed Apr-Aug) 4 mi W on Noyack Rd. Phone 631/286-0485.

Sag Harbor Whaling and Historical Museum. Relics of whaling days and historical artifacts in the former home of Benjamin Huntting, local ship owner. (Mid-May-Oct, daily) Garden and Main sts. Phone 631/725-0770. ¢¢

Restaurants

★ ★ ★ **AMERICAN HOTEL.** *Main St (11963).* 631/725-3535. www.theamericanhotel.com. French menu. Hrs: 5-10 pm; Sat, Sun also noon-4 pm. Closed Jan 1, Dec 24, 25. Res accepted. Bar. A la carte entrees: lunch $7.95-$18.50, dinner $17.95-$28.50. Inn built in 1846. Atrium rm. Cr cds: A, DS, MC, V.

★ ★ **IL CAPPUCINO.** *30 Madison St (11963).* 631/725-2747. Northern Italian menu. Hrs: 5:30-10:30 pm; Fri, Sat to 11 pm; Sun 5-10 pm. Closed Thanksgiving, Dec 25. Serv bar. A la carte entrees: dinner $11.95-$15.95. Child's menu. Cr cds: A, D, MC, V.
D

★ ★ **SPINNAKER'S.** *63 Main St (11963).* 631/725-9353. Specializes in lobster, homemade desserts. Hrs: 11:30 am-10 pm; Fri, Sat to 11 pm. Closed Thanksgiving. Res accepted. Bar. A la carte entrees: lunch $5-$8, dinner $12-$20. Sun brunch $6-$9. Child's menu. Piano bar Sat evenings. Dining rm has dark wood and brass accents. Cr cds: A, D, MC, V.
D

Saranac Lake

(B-7) *See also Lake Placid, Tupper Lake*

Settled 1819 **Pop** 5,041 **Elev** 1,534 ft
Area code 518 **Zip** 12983
Information Chamber of Commerce,
30 Main St; 518/891-1990 or
800/347-1997
Web www.saranaclake.com

Surrounded by Adirondack Park
(see), the village of Saranac Lake was
first settled in 1819 when one Jacob
Moody, who had been injured in a
sawmill accident, retired to the
wilderness, built a log cabin at what
is now Pine and River streets, and
raised a family of mountain guides.
The qualities that attracted Moody
and made the town a famous health
resort in the 19th century continue
to lure visitors in search of fresh,
mountain air and a relaxing environment.

What to See and Do

Fishing. More than 130 well-stocked
ponds and lakes plus 600 mi of fishing streams.

**Meadowbrook State Public Camp-
ground.** Tent sites, picnicking. (Mid-
May-mid-Oct) 4 mi E on NY 86, in
Adirondack Park (see). Phone
518/891-4351. ¢¢

**Robert Louis Stevenson Memorial
Cottage.** Where Robert Louis Stevenson lived while undergoing treatment for what is believed to have
been tuberculosis, 1887-1888;
mementos. (July-mid-Sept, Tues-Sun)
Schedule may vary. Phone 518/891-
1462. ¢

Six Nations Indian Museum. Indoor
and outdoor exhibits portray the life
of the Native American, with a council ground, types of fires, ancient and
modern articles; lecture on Native
American culture and history. (July-
Aug, Tues-Sun) On Buck Pond Rd, off
NY 3, in Onchiota. Phone 518/891-
2299. ¢

**Skiing. Mount Pisgah Veterans Memo-
rial Ski Center.** Five slopes, T-bar;
patrol, school, snowmaking; snacks.
Longest run 1,800 ft, vertical drop
300 ft. (Mid-Dec-mid-Mar, Thurs-
Sun) 3 mi NE on NY 86. Phone
518/891-0970. ¢¢¢¢

Special Events

Winter Carnival. Parade; skating, ski
snowshoe, and snowmobile racing.
Phone 518/891-1990. Early Feb.

**Willard Hanmer Guideboat, Canoe,
and War Canoe Races.** Lake Flower
and Saranac River. Phone 518/891-
1990. Early July.

Adirondack Canoe Classic. Ninety-m
race from Old Forge to Saranac Lake
for canoe, kayak, guideboat. Phone
518/891-2744. Second wkend Sept.

Motels/Motor Lodges

★ **ADIRONDACK MOTEL.** *23 Lake
Flower Ave (12983). 518/891-2116; fa
518/891-0380; toll-free 800/416-0117*
14 rms, 1-2 story, 4 kits. S, D $48-
$98; each addl $5; kit. units $60-
$100; wkly rates. Crib $5. Pet
accepted. Complimentary continental bkfst. Restaurant nearby. Ck-out
11 am. Refrigerators. Picnic tables,
grills. Paddle boats, canoes. On lake.
Cr cds: A, DS, MC, V.
🄳 🦮 ⚓ 🔌 🔥 🎿

★ **LAKE FLOWER INN.** *15 Lake
Flower Ave (12983). 518/891-2310;
toll-free 888/628-8900.* 14 rms. Late
June-late Sept: S, D $58-$98; each
addl $10; under 18 free; higher rates
special events; lower rates rest of yr.
Crib free. Pet accepted. TV; cable
(premium). Pool. Ck-out 11 am.
Downhill ski 20 mi; x-country ski 2
mi. Picnic tables. On lake. Cr cds: A,
MC, V.
🦮 ⚓ 🔌 🏊 🔥 🎿

★ **LAKE SIDE MOTEL.** *27 Lake
Flower Ave (12983). 518/891-4333;
fax 518/891-0577; toll-free 877/891-
0577.* 22 rms. July-mid-Oct: S $69; D
$59-$79; each addl $5; kit. units
$79-$99; higher rates: some hol
wkends, special events; lower rates
rest of yr. Crib free. Pet accepted. TV
cable (premium). Heated pool. Com
plimentary coffee in lobby. Restaurant nearby. Ck-out 11 am. Downhi
ski 20 mi; x-country ski 2 mi.
Canoes, rowboats, paddle boats
avail. Patio. Picnic tables, grills.
Overlooks lake; private sand beach.
Cr cds: A, C, D, DS, MC, V.
🦮 ⚓ 🔌 🏊 🔥 🎿

★ ★ **SARA PLACID MOTOR INN.**
*120 Lake Flower Ave (12983).
518/891-2729; fax 518/891-5624; tol*

ee 800/794-2729. sara-placid.com. 18
ms, 3 suites, 7 kits, 1 cottage. Some
/C. Mid-June-mid-Oct: S, D $58-
89; each addl $8; suites, kit. units
58-$175; higher rates: winter carni-
al, hols; lower rates rest of yr. TV;
able (premium), VCR avail. Compli-
nentary bkfst. Restaurant adj. Ck-out
1 am. Tennis. X-country ski on site.
ce-skating. Paddle boats. Picnic
ables, grills. Opp lake. Cr cds: A, D,
S, MC, V.

D 🛌 ⚡ 🎿 🏊 🔥 SC

Hotel

★ ★ **HOTEL SARANAC OF PAUL
SMITH'S COLLEGE.** 101 Main St
12983). 518/891-2200; fax 518/891-
664; toll-free 800/937-0211. www.
otelsaranac.com. 92 rms, 6 story.
Mid-June-mid-Oct: S, D $99; each
ddl $10; under 18 free; golf, ski
lans; lower rates rest of yr. TV;
able, VCR avail (movies). Restaurant
see A. P. SMITH). Bar 11-1 am. Ck-
ut 11 am. Meeting rms. Business
ervs avail. Gift shop. X-country ski 2
ni. Historic hotel (1927); lobby
eplica of foyer in Danvanzati Palace
n Florence, Italy. Cr cds: A, D, DS,
MC, V.

D 🏂 🛌 🏊 🔥

Resort

★ **SARANAC INN GOLF & COUN-
TRY CLUB.** HC1 Box 16 Rte 30
12983). 518/891-1402; fax 518/891-
309. 10 rms. May-Oct: D $220 (incl
olf and cart). Closed rest of yr. TV.
estaurant 7 am-3:30 pm. Bar. Ck-
ut 11 am. 18-hole golf, greens fee
50, putting green, driving range. Cr
ds: A, MC, V.

🏌 🛌 🏊 🔥

B&B/Small Inn

★ ★ ★ ★ **THE POINT.** HC1, Box 65
Y 30 (12983). 518/891-5674; fax
18/891-1152; toll-free 800/255-3530.
ww.thepointresort.com. There are no
igns to lead you to this secluded
dirondack resort, a former hunting
odge of the Rockefellers, because the
wners don't want anyone to find it.
or one all-inclusive and very high
rice, you will have every wish in
he world taken care of: picnics,

boats, cocktails, croquet, books,
moutain bikes, cross-country skis,
you name it. Meals are set around
the property depending on the con-
sensus of the no-more-than 22
guests. 11 rms, 1 story, 4 buildings.
$900-$1,600, incl all meals, wine,
and activities. 18 and over only. Pet
accepted. No TV or telephone in rms.
Restaurant. Bar. Cr cds: A, MC, V.

🐾 🛌 🎿 🏊 ✈ 🔥 🏊

Restaurant

★ ★ **A. P. SMITH.** 101 Main St
(12983). 518/891-2200. Hrs: 7 am-
1:30 pm, 5-9 pm; Sun brunch 10 am-
1:30 pm. Res accepted. Bar 11 am-9
pm; wknds to 10 pm. Bkfst $2.75-
$6.25, lunch $3.95-$7.50, dinner
$9.95-$14.95. Buffet (Thurs): dinner
$12.95. Sun brunch $9.95. Child's
menu. Bakery. College-operated as
training facility. Totally nonsmoking.
Cr cds: A, D, DS, MC, V.

D

Saratoga National Historical Park

(D-8) See also Glens Falls, Saratoga
Springs

(30 mi N of Albany on US 4, NY 32)

Web www.chieflandchamber.com

In two engagements, September 19
and October 7, 1777, American
forces under General Horatio Gates
defeated the army of General John
Burgoyne in the Battles of Saratoga.
This brought France into the war on
the side of the colonies. The battle is
regarded as the turning point of the
Revolutionary War. The scene of this
historic event is the rolling hill country between US 4 and NY 32, five
miles north of Stillwater. Park folders
with auto tour information are available at the Visitor Center. (Daily;
closed January 1, Thanksgiving,
December 25). Phone 518/664-9821.

What to See and Do

Battlefield. Living history demonstrations (Feb-Oct).

General Philip Schuyler House. (1777) Home of patriot officer who commanded Northern Army before Gates. (Mid-May-Labor Day, Wed-Sun) 8 mi N on US 4 in Schuylerville. **FREE**

John Neilson House. Restored American staff headquarters. (Usually June-Sept)

Saratoga Monument. Granite 155-ft obelisk commemorates surrender of Crown forces under Burgoyne to American forces under Gates on Oct 17, 1777. (Mid-May-Labor Day, Wed-Sun) Burgoyne Rd, W of US 4 in Schuylerville. **FREE**

Tour road. Self-conducted; nine mi long; ten stops where exhibits interpret history. (Early Apr-Nov, weather permitting)

Visitor Center and Museum. Visitor orientation. Exhibits and film program explain the battles. **FREE**

Saratoga Springs

(D-8) *See also Glens Falls*

Settled 1773 **Pop** 26,186 **Elev** 316 ft
Area code 518 **Zip** 12866
Information Saratoga County Chamber of Commerce, 28 Clinton St; 518/584-3255
Web www.saratoga.org

Saratoga Springs is a resort city that is rural yet cosmopolitan. Much of the town's Victorian architecture has been restored. Saratoga Springs boasts the springs, geysers, and mineral baths that first made the town famous; internationally recognized harness and thoroughbred racing and polo; respected museums; as well as the Saratoga Performing Arts Center.

What to See and Do

High Rock Spring. Now inactive; the original Saratoga Spring. Rock St at High Rock Ave.

Historic Congress Park. The Museum of the Historical Society and the Walworth Memorial Museum are housed in the old casino (1870). The museums trace the history of the city's growth, highlighting the springs, hotels, gambling, and personalities; also gift shop. Museums (Memorial Day-Labor Day, daily; rest of yr, call for hours). Park (daily). On Broadway. Phone 518/584-6920. ¢¢

National Bottle Museum. Antique bottles, jars, stoneware, and related items; research library on bottle collecting. (June-Oct, daily; rest of yr, Mon-Fri) 6 mi S via NY 50, at 76 Milton Ave in Ballston Spa. Phone 518/885-7589. ¢

National Museum of Dance. Dedicated to American professional dance. Exhibits, hall of fame, museum shop. (Late May-Labor Day, Tues-Sun) 99 S Broadway. Phone 518/584-2225. ¢¢

National Museum of Racing and Hall of Fame. Exhibitions on the history and mechanics of Thoroughbred racing; the stories of racing champs Man o' War, Secretariat, Seattle Slew, and Affirmed; exhibits on Saratoga's gambling heyday. Training track tours in summer (fee). (Daily; closed hols) 191 Union Ave, across from Saratoga Race Course. Phone 518/584-0400. ¢¢¢

Petrified Sea Gardens. Reefs of fossilized organisms; glacial crevices and potholes; sundials, museum. Picnic, hiking, and recreation areas. (Early May-Nov, daily) 3 mi W, off NY 29.

Saratoga Equine Sports Center. Harness racing (Feb-Nov). Nelson Ave. Phone 518/584-2110.

Saratoga Lake. Boating, fishing, waterskiing. Fee. 3 mi E on NY 9P.

Saratoga National Historical Park. (see). Accessible from NY 5 and 46 and I-90 exits 33, 34. Phone 315/687-7821.

★ **Saratoga Spa State Park.** This 2,200-acre park is home to the performing arts center, mineral bath houses, golf, and many other recreational facilities. Visitor center. (Daily) S Broadway, 1 mi S on US 9

r SW on NY 50. Phone 518/584-
535. ¢¢

Lincoln and Roosevelt Baths. Treatments with the mineral waters. Baths, massage, hot packs. Roosevelt (all yr, Wed-Sun); Lincoln (July and Aug, daily). Phone 518/584-2011.

Recreation Center. Swimming, diving, wading pools (June-Labor Day, daily), Victoria Pool, Peerless Pool complex, mineral springs and geysers; two golf courses (Mid-Apr-Nov), picnicking.

Saratoga Performing Arts Center. Amphitheater in natural setting seats 5,000 under cover with space for more on the lawn. The Little Theatre is a 500-seat indoor showcase for chamber music. (See SPECIAL EVENTS)

addo Gardens. An artists' retreat ince 1926, this Victorian Gothic ansion's famous residents have incl lannery O'Connor, Leonard Berntein, and John Cheever. The manion is closed to the general public, ut landscaped gardens are open to ll. (Daily) Union Ave, between the aratoga Race Course and I-87. hone 518/584-0746. **FREE**

Special Events

aratoga Race Course. Union Ave, 4 mi SW from exit 14 off I-87. Thorughbred racing. Phone 518/584-200. Late July-Early-Sept.

olo. Saratoga Polo Association. aratoga Equine Sports Center. June-ug. Also from Broadway St, W on Church St, then N on Seward. Phone 18/584-8108. Aug.

aratoga Performing Arts Center. hone 518/587-3330. New York City Opera, June; New York City Ballet, uly. The Philadelphia Orchestra and aratoga Chamber Music Festival, ug. Jazz festival, summer.

Motels/Motor Lodges

★★ **GRAND UNION MOTEL.** *120 S roadway (12866).* 518/584-9000; fax 18/584-9001. www.grandunionmotel. om. 64 rms. S $149-$189; D $149-199; each addl $10; higher rates pecial events. Crib free. Pet ccepted; $10. TV; cable. Pool; minral bath spa. Sauna. Complimentary

coffee in lobby. Restaurant adj 8 am-10 pm. Ck-out 11 am. Bellhops (seasonal). Sundries. Lawn games. Some refrigerators. Grill. Victorian-style lobby. Only private mineral bath spa in NY. Cr cds: A, MC, V.

D 🐾 🏊 ⊠ 🎿 🔥

★★ **HOLIDAY INN-SARATOGA SPRINGS.** *232 Broadway (Rte 9) (12866).* 518/584-4550; fax 518/584-4417; res 800/465-4329. www.holiday-inn.com. 168 rms, 4 story. S, D $89-$229; each addl $10; suites $199-$459; under 19 free; wkly; ski rates. Crib free. Pet accepted. TV. Heated pool; poolside serv. Restaurant 6:30 am-10 pm. Bar 11-2 am. Ck-out 11 am. Coin lndry. Meeting rms. Business servs avail. In-rm modem link. Bellhops. Valet serv. Downhill ski 20 mi; x-country ski 1 mi. Exercise equipt. Health club privileges. Cr cds: A, C, D, DS, ER, JCB, MC, V.

D 🐾 🏊 ⊠ 🏋 🎿 🔥 SC

★ **SPRINGS MOTEL.** *189 S Broadway (12866).* 518/584-6336; fax 518/587-8164. 28 rms, 2 story. May-mid-July: S $44-$65; D $50-$68; each addl $5; under 16 free; higher rates special events (racing season); varied lower rates rest of yr. Crib $5. TV; cable. Pool. Complimentary coffee in rms. Restaurant nearby. Ck-out 11 am. Refrigerators. Cr cds: A, MC, V.

⊠ 🔥 SC

Hotels

★★ **ADELPHI HOTEL.** *365 Broadway (12866).* 518/587-4688; fax 518/587-0851; res 518/587-4688. www.adelphihotel.com. 39 rms, 3 story. S $105-$225; D $120-$265; each addl $15; suites $130-$400; higher rates racing season (3-day min). Crib free. TV; cable (premium). Pool. Complimentary continental bkfst. Bar 5:30 pm-2 am. Ck-out noon. Meeting rm. Cr cds: A, MC, V.

⊠ 🎿 🔥

★★★ **THE GIDEON PUTNAM HOTEL.** *24 Gideon Putnam Rd (12866).* 518/584-3000; fax 518/584-1354; res 800/732-1560. www.gideonputnam.com. 132 rms, 5 story. Apr-Nov: S, D $130-$150; each addl $15; suites $170-$190; under 16 free; higher rates racing season; lower rates rest of yr. Crib free. TV; cable.

Pool; lifeguard. Restaurant 7-10 am, noon-2 pm, 6-9 pm; Fri and Sat to 10 pm. Bar noon-closing; entertainment (seasonal). Ck-out noon. Meeting rms. Business servs avail. Gift shop. Downhill ski 15 mi; x-country ski on site. Lawn games. Some porches. Mineral bath. Cr cds: A, C, D, DS, MC, V.

🅓 ⛵ ≈ ✈ 🏂 🔥

★ ★ **INN AT SARATOGA.** *231 Broadway (12866). 518/583-1890; fax 518/583-2543; toll-free 800/274-3573. www.theinnatsaratoga.com.* 38 rms, 3 story. Late June-late July: S, D $75-$289; each addl $15; suites $127-$147; under 12 free; higher rates special events (racing season); lower rates rest of yr. TV; cable. Complimentary continental bkfst. Dining rm 5-9 pm. Ck-out 11 am. Meeting rms. Business servs avail. Bellhops (in season). Downhill ski 15 mi; x-country ski 1 mi. Health club privileges. Some refrigerators. Established 1881. Cr cds: A, C, D, DS, ER, JCB, MC, V.

🅓 ⛵ 🏂 🔥

★ ★ ★ **SHERATON SARATOGA SPRINGS.** *534 Broadway (12866). 518/584-4000; fax 518/584-7430; res 800/325-3535. www.sheraton.com.* 240 rms, 5 story. S, D $99-$130; each addl $10; suites $125-$275; under 18 free. Crib free. TV; cable (premium), VCR avail. Indoor pool; lifeguard. Coffee in rms. Restaurant 7 am-10 pm. Bar 11-1 am; entertainment, Wed-Sat (summer). Ck-out noon. Meeting rms. Business center. Concierge. Gift shop. Tennis privileges. 18-hole golf privileges, pro. X-country ski 2 mi. Exercise equipt. Game rm. Some bathrm phones, refrigerators. Some balconies. Luxury level. Cr cds: A, C, D, DS, ER, JCB, MC, V.

🅓 ⛵ 🏋 ⛷ ≈ 🎣 🏂 🔥 🏋 🔥 ⛷

Resort

★ ★ ★ **ROOSEVELT INN & SUITES.** *2961 NY Rte 9, Ballston Spa (12020). 518/584-0980; fax 518/581-8472; toll-free 800/524-9147. www.saratoga.org/roosevelt.* 34 rms, 2 story, 10 suites. June-mid-Oct: S, D $79.50-$89.50, each addl $10; suites $109.50; higher rates special events; lower rates rest of yr. Crib $5. TV; cable (premium), VCR (movies $4). Heated pool. Complimentary continental bkfst. Restau-

rant 7 am-11 pm; Mon, Tues 11 am-10 pm. Bar. Ck-out 11 am. Meeting rms. Business servs avail. Tennis. Refrigerators; some in-rm whirlpools. Balconies. Picnic tables. Cr cds: A, DS, MC, V.

🅓 ⛱ 🏋 ⛷ ≈ 🏋 🔥

B&B/Small Inn

★ ★ **WESTCHESTER HOUSE BED & BREAKFAST.** *102 Lincoln Ave (12866). 518/587-7613; fax 518/583-9562; toll-free 888/302-1717. www.westchesterhousebandb.com.* 7 rms, 2 story. No rm phones. S $95-$205; D $115-$230; wkend rates; higher rates Jazz Festival, racing season, special events. Closed Jan. Complimentary continental bkfst; afternoon refreshments. Restaurant nearby. Ck-out 11 am, ck-in 4 pm. In-rm modem link. Queen Anne Victorian house (1885) in historical residential area. Oriental carpets, antiques. Garden. Totally nonsmoking. Cr cds: A, DS, MC, V.

≈ 🔥

Restaurants

★ ★ ★ **CHEZ PIERRE.** *340 US 9, Gansevoort (12831). 518/793-3350.* French menu. Specialties: steak au poivre, veal Oscar, shrimp Madagascar. Hrs: 5-10 pm. Closed Dec 24-25. Res accepted. Bar. Dinner $14.95-$22.95. Child's menu. Family-owned Cr cds: A, MC, V.

🅓 🍽

★ **OLDE BRYAN INN.** *123 Maple Ave (12866). 518/587-2990. www.oldebryaninn.com.* Specializes in fresh seafood, fettucine, prime rib. Hrs: 11 am-10:30 pm; Fri, Sat to midnight; Sun brunch to 1 pm. Closed Memorial Day, Thanksgiving, Dec 24, 25. Bar. Lunch $3.95-$6.95, dinner $10.95-$17.95. Sun brunch $5.95-$8.95. Child's menu. Outdoor dining. Stone house (1825); fireplaces. Cr cds: A, C, D, DS, ER, MC, V.

🅓

HISTORIC DOWNTOWN SARATOGA SPRINGS

Saratoga Springs was founded in the early 1800s as a high-society spa and gambling resort. The modern downtown holds a multitude of stunning historic buildings, many of which now house shops, cafes, and restaurants.

Begin at the Saratoga Springs Urban Cultural Park Visitor Center (297 Broadway), once a trolley station and later a "drinking hall." Pick up information, brochures, and maps here, or sign up for a guided walking tour. Cross the street and enter Congress Park. Walk to the Canfield Casino, a resplendent Italianate building that was once the height of fashionable gambling spots and is now home to the Saratoga Historical Museum. Seeing the grand ballroom alone is worth a visit. Returning to Broadway, turn right and browse the many shops. Buildings of particular note include the Rip Van Dam Hotel (353 Broadway), an 1840s Federal-style building, and the Adelphi Hotel (365 Broadway), a classic Victorian edifice. Farther along, at 473 Broadway, the Adirondack Trust Building was built in 1916 in the Classic Revival style. Shops of interest along Broadway include: Symmetry (348 Broadway), offering glass artworks; Ye Olde Wishin' Well (353-355 Broadway) for antiques; Impressions of Saratoga (368 Broadway), which sells fine art and collectibles for horse lovers; Celtic Treasures (456 Broadway), offering Irish goods and gifts; and Legends (511 Broadway), a fine art gallery set in an elegant Victorian brownstone showing the work of regional, national, and internationally known artists. Grab a sandwich and dessert at Mrs. London's bakery (464 Broadway), or stop at 43 Phila Bistro, just off Broadway, for excellent, but causal, fine dining. Also on Phila Street, visit the Ballad Bookstore and Café Lena, the oldest continuously run coffeehouse in America, founded in 1960.

Turn back south on Broadway at Lake Street and return past Congress Park. The National Museum of Dance is on the right about three blocks up. This is the only museum in the United States dedicated exclusively to American professional dance. If a break is in order, stop next door at the Lincoln Mineral Baths, offering mineral baths, massages, and herbal wraps; or try The Crystal Spa at 120 South Broadway. Continue south on Broadway to Saratoga State Park, site of the Saratoga Performing Arts Center, which hosts many summer concerts and is the summertime home to the Philadelphia Orchestra and the New York City Ballet. An expansive green space, the park offers abundant walking paths. Or, return north on South Broadway, turn right onto Circular Street, and follow it to Union Avenue. Turn right again and stroll four blocks to the National Museum of Racing and Thoroughbred Hall of Fame, where horse racing is celebrated through displays, paintings, trophies, memorabilia, and interactive activities. The famous Saratoga Race Track lies across the street from the museum, and the Oklahoma Training Track is just a block farther up Union on the left. Also nearby is Bruno's Restaurant (237 Union), a '50s diner that's lots of fun.

Saugerties

(E-8) *See also Cairo, Hudson, Kingston, Woodstock*

Pop 19,868 **Elev** 155 ft **Area code** 845
Zip 12477

At the confluence of Esopus Creek and the Hudson River, Saugerties was a port of call for riverboats. The town was famous for building racing sloops and for the production of fine paper, leather, and canvas.

What to See and Do

Opus 40 & Quarryman's Museum.
Environmental sculpture rising out of an abandoned bluestone quarry. More than 6 acres of fitted bluestone constructed over 37 yrs by sculptor Harvey Fite. Site of Sunset Concert series and other programs. **Quarryman's Museum** houses collection of

tools of quarry workers and others. (Memorial Day-Columbus Day, Fri-Sun; some Sat reserved for special events) 50 Fite Rd. Phone 845/246-3400. ¢¢¢

Motel/Motor Lodge

★★ **COMFORT INN.** *2790 Rte 32 N (12477). 845/246-1565; fax 845/246-1631; res 800/228-5150. www.comfort inn.com.* 66 rms. S $65-$89; D $65-$99; each addl $6; suites, kit. unit $69-$109; under 12 free. Crib free. TV; cable (premium). Complimentary continental bkfst. Restaurant adj 6 am-midnight. Ck-out 11 am. Meeting rms. Business servs avail. Whirlpool in suites. Some refrigerators, microwaves. Cr cds: A, C, D, DS, ER, JCB, MC, V.
🄳 ⬗ ⬗

B&B/Small Inn

★★★ **EMERSON INN AND SPA.** *146 Mt Pleasant Rd (12457). 845/688-7900.* 24 rms, 3 story. S, D $225-$275. TV; cable (premium), VCR avail. Restaurants 6:30 am-midnight. Ck-out noon. Meeting rms. Business servs avail. In-rm modem link. Concierge. Exercise equipt. Spa. Cr cds: A, D, DS, MC, V.
⬗ ⬗

Restaurant

★★★ **CAFE TAMAYO.** *89 Partition St (12477). 845/246-9371. www. tamayo.com.* French, American menu. Specialties: confit of duck, capellini pasta, crème brûlée. Hrs: 5-9:30 pm; Thurs-Sat noon-2:30 pm; Sun brunch 11:30 am-3 pm. Closed Mon, Tues; July 4, Dec 25. Bar. Wine list. Lunch $5.50-$9.50, dinner $12-$20. Outdoor dining. Victorian building (1864). Guest rms avail. Cr cds: DS, MC, V.
⬗

Sayville (L.I.)

See also Bay Shore (L.I.)

Pop 16,735 **Elev** 20 ft **Area code** 631
Zip 11782

Information Chamber of Commerce, Montauk Hwy and Lincoln Ave, PO Box 235; 631/567-5257

What to See and Do

Long Island Maritime Museum. Local maritime exhibits; oyster cull house (ca 1870); Frank E. Penny Boatshop (1900); tug boat *Charlotte* (1888); oyster vessel *Priscilla* (1888); oyster sloop *Modesty* (1923). (Wed-Sun; closed hols) 1 mi W on Montauk Hwy, West Ave, in West Sayville. Phone 631/854-4974. ¢¢

Motels/Motor Lodges

★★ **BEST WESTERN HOTEL.** *1730 N Ocean Ave, Holtsville (11742). 631/758-2900; fax 631/758-2612; toll free 800/528-1234. www.bestwestern. com.* 189 rms, 3 story. S, D $99-$150; suites $179; under 12 free; lower rates in winter. Crib $5. TV; cable (premium). Indoor pool; whirlpool. Complimentary continental bkfst. Restaurant 11 am-11 pm. Bar. Ck-out noon. Meeting rms. Business servs avail. In-rm modem link. Refrigerators avail. Cr cds: A, C, D, DS, MC, V.
🄳 ⬗ ⬗ ⬗ **SC**

★★ **HOLIDAY INN.** *3845 Veterans Memorial Hwy, Ronkonkoma (11779). 631/585-9500; fax 631/585-9550; toll free 800/422-9510. www.holiday-inn. com/ronkonkomany.* 287 rms, 9 suites, 2 story. S $145; D $155; each addl $10; suites $175-$225; under 19 free; wkend packages. Crib free. TV; cable (premium). Pool; lifeguard. Restaurant 6:30 am-10 pm. Bar 11:30-2 am; entertainment. Ck-out noon. Gift shop. Meeting rms. Business servs avail. In-rm modem link. Bellhops. Valet serv. Concierge. Airport, RR station, bus depot transportation. Exercise equipt. Refrigerators avail. Cr cds: A, D, DS, MC, V.
🄳 ⬗ ⬗ ⬗ ⬗

★★ **INN AT MEDFORD.** *2695 Rte 112, Medford (11763). 631/654-3000; fax 631/654-1281; toll-free 800/626-7779.* 76 rms, 2 story. May-Sep: S $89-$99; D $99-$109; each addl $10; suites $140-$175; under 12 free; package plans; higher rates hols; lower rates rest of yr. Crib free. TV; cable, VCR avail (movies $4). Pool. Complimentary continental bkfst. Lounge 4:30 pm-midnight. Ck-out

1 am. Business servs avail. Bellhops. 18-hole golf privileges. Exercise equipt. Health club privileges. Game rm. Cr cds: A, C, D, DS, MC, V.

Restaurants

★★ **BELLPORT.** *159 S Country Rd, Bellport (11713).* 631/286-7550. Specializes in crab cakes, rack of lamb. Hrs: 5:30-10 pm; Fri, Sat to 11 pm; Sun noon-9 pm; Sun brunch to 4:30 pm. Closed Tues; Dec 25. Res accepted. Bar. A la carte entrees: dinner $11.50-$19.50. Cr cds: A, D, DS, MC, V.

★ **BELLPORT CHOWDER HOUSE.** *19 Bellport Ln, Bellport (11713).* 631/286-2343. Specializes in seafood. Hrs: 11:30 am-11 pm; Fri, Sat to midnight; Sun noon-11 pm; Sun brunch to 3 pm. Closed Dec 25. Res accepted. Bar. A la carte entrees: lunch $5.95-$12.95, dinner $12.95-$24.95. Sun brunch $9.95. Parking. Outdoor dining. Cr cds: A, MC, V.

★★ **LE SOIR.** *825 Montauk Hwy, Bayport (11705).* 631/472-9090. French menu. Specializes in seasonal local fare. Own pastries. Hrs: 5-10 pm; Sat 2 sittings: 6:30 pm and 9:15 pm. Closed Mon; July 4, Thanksgiving, Dec 25. Bar. Complete meals: dinner $17.50-$24.95. Parking. Country French chalet. Cr cds: A, MC, V.

★★★ **RIVERVIEW.** *3 Consuelo Pl, Oakdale (11769).* 631/589-2694. Specializes in chateaubriand, live lobster. Hrs: noon-10 pm; Sat 6-11 pm; Sun brunch 11 am-2:30 pm. Res accepted wkends. Bar to 2 am. Wine list. A la carte entrees: lunch $8-$14, dinner $18.50-$26. Complete meals: dinner $19.95. Sun brunch $18.95. Child's menu. Patio dining. Reggae Fri, jazz Sun. Parking. View of Connetquot River. In Commodore Vanderbilt's "tea house." Deep water docking. Cr cds: A, D, DS, MC, V.

★★ **SNAPPER INN.** *500 Shore Dr, Oakdale (11769).* 631/589-0248. Specializes in lobster, fresh seafood. Hrs: noon-10:30 pm Tues-Sun. Sun brunch 11:30-3 pm. Closed Mon;

Dec 25. Res accepted. Bar. Lunch $6.25-$12.50, dinner $15.25-$26.75. Sun brunch $17.75. Child's menu. Parking. Outdoor dining. Overlooks Connetquot River. Family-owned. Cr cds: A, C, D, DS, MC, V.

Schenectady

(D-8) *See also Albany, Amsterdam, Saratoga Springs, Troy*

Settled 1661 **Pop** 61,821 **Elev** 224 ft
Area code 518
Information Schenectady County Chamber of Commerce, 306 State St, 12305; 518/372-5656 or 800/962-8007
Web www.schenectadychamber.org

Schenectady offers a unique blend of the old and the new, from row houses of the pre-Revolutionary War stockade area to the bustle and vitality of the downtown area.

What to See and Do

The Historic Stockade Area. Privately owned houses, some dating to colonial times, many marked with historic plaques. **Schenectady County Historical Society**, 32 Washington Ave, offers guided tours of their building and folder describing walking tour. The society also maintains a historical museum with collection of Sexton and Ames paintings; also 19th-century dollhouse, Shaker collection, genealogical library (fee). (Mon-Sat, afternoons). Downtown. Phone 518/374-0263. ¢

Proctor's Theatre. (1926) Former movie/vaudeville palace is a regional performing arts center hosting Broadway touring shows, dance, opera, and plays. 1931 Wurlitzer theater organ. Seats 2,700. Built by F. F. Proctor and designed by Thomas Lamb, its interior incorporates elegance and grandeur; pastoral mural by A. Lundberg. Free tours by appt. 432 State St. Phone 518/346-6204.

The Schenectady Museum & Planetarium and Schenectady Heritage Area. Exhibits and programs on art, history, science, and technology. (Tues-Sun; closed hols) Planetarium shows and children's planetarium shows (summer, Tues-Sun; rest of yr, Sat, Sun) Nott Terrace Heights, off Nott Terr. Phone 518/382-7890. ¢¢¢

Union College. (1795) 2,000 students. Country's first planned campus; original buildings (1812-1814) by French architect Joseph Jacques Ramée. Nott Memorial (1875), only 16-sided building in the Northern Hemisphere. Also on campus is Jackson Garden, eight acres of landscaped and informal plantings. Tours of campus. Union Ave and Union St. Phone 518/388-6000.

Special Events

Festival of Nations. Second Sat May. Phone 518/382-7890.

Walkabout. Walking tour of six houses and three churches in the Historic Stockade Area. Last wkend Sept.

Motels/Motor Lodges

★ **DAYS INN.** *167 Nott Terr (12308). 518/370-3297; fax 518/370-5948. www.daysinn.com.* 68 rms, 3 story. Apr-Oct: S $75-$79; D $80-$85; each addl $5; under 18 free; lower rates rest of yr. Crib free. TV; cable (premium). Complimentary continental bkfst. Restaurant nearby. Ck-out noon. Business servs avail. Downhill/x-country ski 20 mi. Some in-rm whirlpools, refrigerators. Cr cds: A, D, DS, MC, V.
⊠ ⌦ ⚐

★★★ **HOLIDAY INN.** *100 Nott Terr (12308). 518/393-4141; fax 518/393-4174; res 800/465-4329. www.holiday-inn.com.* 184 rms, 3 suites, 4 story. S $69-$100; D $75-$125; suites $250; under 18 free; higher rates: college events, racing season. Crib free. Pet accepted, some restrictions. TV; cable (premium). Indoor pool; whirlpool. Complimentary bkfst. Restaurant 6:30-10 am, 5-10 pm. Bar 11-1 am; wkends noon-1 am. Ck-out noon. Meeting rms. Business servs avail. In-rm modem link. Valet serv. Coin lndry. Free airport, RR station transportation. Downhill/x-country ski 20 mi. Exercise equipt; sauna. Wet bar in suites. Cr cds: A, C, D, DS, JCB, MC, V.
⊠ Ⓓ ⌦ ⌷ ⌦ ⚐

★★ **RAMADA INN & CONVENTION CENTER.** *450 Nott St (12308). 518/370-7151; fax 518/370-0441. www.ramada.com.* 170 rms, 8 suites, 7 story. S $69-$96; D $79-$106; each addl $10; under 18 free; higher rates Aug. TV; cable, VCR avail (movies). Indoor pool; whirlpool, lifeguard. Restaurant 6:30 am-10 pm. Bar 5 pm-2 am; wkends from 11 am. Ck-out noon. Coin lndry. Meeting rms. Business servs avail. Valet serv. Sundries. Exercise equipt; sauna. Game rm. Refrigerators. Cr cds: A, C, D, DS, ER, JCB, MC, V.
Ⓓ ⌦ ⌷ ⌦ ⚐ SC

B&B/Small Inn

★★★ **GLEN SANDERS MANSION INN.** *1 Glen Ave, Scotia (12302). 518/374-7262; fax 518/374-7391. www.glensandersmansion.com.* 22 rms, 2 story, 2 suites. Aug: S, D $119; suites $175-$275; under 18 free; family rates; lower rates rest of yr. Crib $10. TV; cable (premium). Complimentary continental bkfst. Restaurant (see GLEN SANDERS MANSION). Ck-out 11 am, ck-in 3 pm. Business servs avail. In-rm modem link. Valet serv. Gift shop. Downhill/x-country ski 15 mi. In-rm whirlpool, fireplace in suites. Some balconies. On river. Mansion's kitchen was built in 1600s. Cr cds: A, C, D, DS, MC, V.
Ⓓ ⚐ ⊠ ⌦ ⚐

Restaurant

★★★ **GLEN SANDERS MANSION.** *1 Glen Ave, Scotia (12302). 518/374-7262.* Hrs: 11:30 am-2 pm, 5-10 pm; Sat 5-10 pm; Sun brunch 10:30 am-1:30 pm. Closed hols. Res required Sat, Sun. Continental menu. Bar. Wine cellar. Dinner $6.95-$27.95. Sun brunch $15.95. Specializes in seafood. Parking. Cr cds: A, D, DS, MC, V.
Ⓓ

Schroon Lake

(C-8) *See also Hague*

Pop 1,759 **Elev** 867 ft **Area code** 518
Zip 12870
Information Chamber of Commerce,
PO Box 726; 518/532-7675 or
888/SCHROON
Web www.schroonlake.org

The village extends for two miles
along the west shore of Schroon
Lake. A popular summer resort area,
70 lakes and ponds are within a five-
mile radius. Outdoor recreation
activities are popular all year long.

What to See and Do

Natural Stone Bridge and Caves.
Self-guided tour; underground river,
rock formations, caves; picnicking.
(Memorial Day-Columbus Day, daily)
8 mi S on I-87, exit 26, then 2 mi W,
in Pottersville. Phone 518/494-2283.
¢¢¢

Public campgrounds. Swimming, lifeguards, fishing, boat ramp; picnicking, camping. Phone 518/532-7675.
¢¢¢

Eagle Point. Also bathhouse. (Mid-
May-early Sept) 8 mi S on US 9, N
of Pottersville in Adirondack Forest
Preserve. Phone 518/494-2220.
¢¢¢¢

Paradox Lake. Also boat launch,
bathhouse. (Mid-May-mid-Nov)
On NY 74, 2 mi E of Severance.
Phone 518/532-7451. ¢¢¢

Motel/Motor Lodge

★ **DAVIS MOTEL AND COTTAGE.**
726 Rte 9 (12870). 518/532-7583.
www.adirondack.net/tour/davi. 20 rms,
4 kits. Late June-Labor Day: S, D $40-
$46; each addl $5; kit. units $60; cot-
tages $585-$660/wk; family, wkly
rates; lower rates rest of yr. Crib $3.
TV; cable. Heated pool. Playground.
Restaurant nearby. Ck-out 11 am.
Downhill ski 18 mi; x-country ski on
site, rentals. Boat rentals. Lawn
games. Picnic tables, grills. Cr cds: A,
MC, V.
🐾 🛶 🎿 🏊

Seneca Falls

See also Auburn, Geneva, Waterloo

Settled 1787 **Pop** 9,347 **Elev** 469 ft
Area code 315 **Zip** 13148
Information Seneca County Chamber
of Commerce, NY 5 and 20 W;
315/568-2906 or 800/SEC-1848
Web www.senecachamber.org

The first convention of the US
Women's Suffrage Movement met in
July 1848, in Seneca Falls. The town
was the home of Amelia Jenks
Bloomer, who drew international
attention to women's rights by advo-
cating and wearing the costume that
bears her name. The two great leaders of the movement, Elizabeth Cady
Stanton and Susan B. Anthony, also
worked in Seneca Falls. The Stanton
home has been preserved.

A 50-foot drop in the Seneca River
provided power for local industry.
The rapids have been replaced by the
New York State Barge Canal.

What to See and Do

Cayuga Lake State Park. Swimming,
beach, bathhouse, fishing, boating
(launch, dock); picnicking, playground, tent and trailer sites, cabins
(late Apr-late Oct). Standard fees. 3
mi E on NY 89. Phone 315/568-
5163. ¢¢

Montezuma National Wildlife Refuge.
Federal wildlife refuge; visitor center.
Peak migration for shorebirds (fall),
Canadian geese and ducks (spring
and fall). Refuge (daily daylight hrs).
Office (Mon-Fri; closed hols). 5 mi E
on US 20, NY 5. Phone 315/568-
5987. **FREE**

National Women's Hall of Fame.
Museum and education center honors famous American women, past
and present. (May-Oct, daily; rest of
yr, Wed-Sun) 76 Fall St. Phone
315/568-2936. ¢¢

**Seneca Falls Historical Society
Museum.** A 19th-century, 23-rm Vic-
torian/Queen Anne mansion with
period rm, local history exhibits;
research library, and archives.
Museum shop. Tours (July-Aug,
daily). 55 Cayuga St. Phone 315/568-
8412. ¢¢

State Barge Canal Locks #2 and #3.
Observation point on south side, off
E Bayard St to Seneca St. (May-early
Nov)

**Women's Rights National Historical
Park.** Visitor center with exhibits and
film; talks scheduled daily during
summer. 116 Fall St. Phone 315/568-
2991. ¢¢ Incl in the park are the Wes-
leyan Chapel and the

> **Elizabeth Cady Stanton House.** (ca
> 1830) House where Stanton
> worked and lived from 1847-1862.
> Artifacts incl original china, books,
> and furniture. Changing exhibits.
> Tours (daily). 32 Washington St. ¢

Special Event

Convention Days Celebration. Commemorates first women's rights convention, held July 19 and 20, 1848.
Wkend closest to July 19 and 20.
Phone 315/568-2906.

Shandaken

See also Hunter, Kingston, Woodstock

Pop 3,235 **Elev** 1,070 ft
Area code 845 **Zip** 12480

This Catskill Mountain town carries
the Iroquois name meaning "rapid
waters." Shandaken is a town with
the combination of being in the
Catskills and having easy access to
New York City. Shandaken is home
of the highest peak in the Catskills,
Slide Mountain. It is also the home
of Esopus Creek, one of the finest
wild trout fisheries in the East, also
noted for tubing. Skiing, hiking, and
hunting are popular in this area of
mountains and streams.

What to See and Do

Catskill Park. (see) 7 mi W via NY 5,
on Lakeport Rd in Chittenango.
Phone 315/687-3801. ¢¢

Skiing. Belleayre Mountain. Two
quad, triple, two double chairlifts;
three handle tows; 41 runs; patrol,
school, rentals; snowmaking; cafeterias; nursery. Longest run 2¼ mi;
vertical drop 1,404 ft. (Nov-early
Apr, daily) Half-day rates. Over 5 mi
of x-country trails. 8 mi W, just off

NY 28 at Highmount. Phone
845/254-5600. ¢¢¢¢

Motel/Motor Lodge

★★ **L'AUBERGE DES 4 SAISONS.**
178 Rte 42 (12480). 845/688-2223;
fax 845/668-2739; res 800/864-1877.
30 rms, 10 with shower only. S, D
$75-$185; hols (min stay required);
higher rates hol wkends. Pet
accepted, some restrictions. TV;
cable. Complimentary full bkfst.
Restaurant (see L'AUBERGE DES 4
SAISONS). Bar. Ck-out noon. Tennis.
Pool. Playground. Rec rm. Lawn
games. Many balconies. Picnic tables.
On stream. Cr cds: A, MC, V.
⬛🐾🐕🛏🏂🔥

Hotel

★★★ **THE COOPERHOOD INN &
SPA.** *70-39 NY 28 (12480).* 845/688-
2460; fax 845/688-7484; res 845/688-
2460. www.copperhood.com. 20 rms, 2
story. MAP: S $270-$285; D $310-
$325; children $35; wkly rates. Crib
$15. TV; cable (premium), VCR avail.
Indoor pool; whirlpool. Playground.
Ck-out 11 am, ck-in 3 pm. Meeting
rm. Business servs avail. Tennis.
Downhill ski 8 mi; x-country ski on
site. Exercise rm; sauna. Massage.
Game rm. Lawn games. Picnic tables.
On Esopus Creek surrounded by
Catskills Park. Cr cds: A, MC, V.
🏂🛏🔥🐕🏂🚴

B&Bs/Small Inns

★★ **BIRCH CREEK INN.** *Rte 28 Box
323, Pine Hill (12465).* 845/254-5222;
fax 845/254-5812. 6 rms, 5 with
shower only, 1 cottage, 2 story. No
rm phones. Dec-Mar, June-Oct: S, D
$75-$150; under 12 free; 2-day min
wkends, 3-day min hols; ski plans;
lower rates rest of yr. Crib free. TV in
some rms; cable. Complimentary full
bkfst, coffee in rms. Restaurant
nearby. Ck-out 11 am, ck-in 3 pm.
Downhill ski ½ mi; x-country ski on
site. Some refrigerators. Built in
1896; in Catskill Mtn forest. Totally
nonsmoking. Cr cds: A, DS, MC, V.
🐾🏂🐕🛏🔥

★ **MARGARETVILLE MOUNTAIN
INN BED & BREAKFAST.** *Margaretville Mtn Rd, Margaretville
(12455).* 845/586-3933; fax 845/586-

699. www.catskill.net/mmibnb. 7 air-cooled rms, 2 story. A/C avail. No rm phones. S $75; D $98; each addl $15; suites $110-$130; under 12 free; ski plans; hols (2-3-day min). Crib free. Pet accepted; some restrictions; $10. TV in common rm; cable (premium), VCR avail (movies). Complimentary full bkfst. Ck-out 11 am, ck-in 4-6 pm. Downhill ski 9 mi; x-country ski on-site. Playground. Lawn games. Built in 1886; first commercial cauliflower farm in US. Totally nonsmoking. Cr cds: A, MC, V.

Restaurants

★ ★ **CATAMOUNT CAFE.** *5368 NY 28, Mt Tremper (12457). 845/688-2828. www.catskillcorners.com.* Hrs: 5-10 pm; Sun brunch 11 am-2 pm. Closed Tues, Wed; also Dec 25. Res accepted. Contemporary American menu. Bar. Dinner $12.95-$21.95. Sun brunch $5.95-$8.95. Child's menu. Specialties: Long Island duck breast steak, venison loin and chop with juniper sauce, char-grilled salmon filet. Jazz or classical music Fri-Sun. Parking. Outdoor dining. Adirondacks-style decor; oil paintings. Cr cds: A, DS, MC, V.

★ ★ ★ **L'AUBERGE DES 4 SAISONS.** *178 NY 42 (12480). 845/688-2223.* French menu. Specialties: steak au poivre, roasted duck with wild rice. Hrs: 11:30 am-2:30 pm, 5:30-11 pm. Res accepted. Bar. Complete meals: lunch $7-$24, dinner $15-$38. Country setting in foothills of the Catskills. Cr cds: A, C, MC, V.

Shelter Island

See also East Hampton (L.I.), Sag Harbor (L.I.)

Settled 1652 **Pop** 1,234 **Elev** 50 ft
Area code 631 **Zip** 11964
Information Chamber of Commerce, PO Box 598; 631/749-0399

Quakers, persecuted by the Puritans in New England, settled Shelter Island in Gardiners Bay off the east end of Long Island. The island is reached by car or pedestrian ferry from Greenport, on the north fork of Long Island, or from North Haven (Sag Harbor), on the south. There is a monument to the Quakers and a graveyard with 17th-century stones plus two historical museums; the 18th-century Havens House and the 19th-century Manhanset Chapel. Also 2,200-acre Nature Conservancy's Mashomack Preserve, with miles of trails for hiking and educational programs. The island offers swimming, boating off miles of sandy shoreline, biking, hiking, tennis, and golfing.

Motels/Motor Lodges

★ ★ **DERING HARBOR INN.** *13 Winthrop Rd (11965). 631/749-0900; fax 631/749-2045.* 22 rms, 1-2 story. Memorial Day-Labor Day: S, D $165-$240; each addl $20; kit. cottages $240-$395; under 12 free; wkends (2-day min); lower rates May-Memorial Day and Labor Day-mid-Oct. Closed rest of yr. Crib free. TV; cable. Pool; lifeguard. Complimentary coffee in rms. Ck-out noon. Coin lndry. Business servs avail. Tennis. Lawn games. Refrigerators. Picnic tables. Cr cds: A, DS, MC, V.

★ **PRIDWIN HOTEL AND COTTAGES SHELTER ISLAND.** *81 Shore Rd (11964). 631/749-0476; fax 631/749-2071; toll-free 800/273-2497.* 40 rms, 2-3 story, 8 kit. cottages. No elvtr. July-early Sept: S $79-$199; D $109-$229; each addl $19-$59; kit. cottages $179-$229; family rates; lower rates May-late June, early Sept-Oct. Only cottages open rest of yr. Crib $8. TV. Saltwater pool. Complimentary full bkfst. Restaurant 8-10 am, noon-3 pm, 6-10 pm. Bar noon-midnight; entertainment, dancing Wed, Sat in season. Ck-out noon. Meeting rm. Business servs avail. Tennis. Golf privileges. Game rm. Rec rm. Refrigerator in cottages. Private patios, decks on cottages. Private beach. Dockage. Cr cds: A, DS, MC, V.

★★ **SUNSET BEACH.** *35 Shore Rd, Shelter Island Heights (11965). 631/749-2001; fax 631/749-1843. www.sunsetbeachli.com.* 20 rms, 2 story, 10 kits. Early July-Labor Day: S, D $125-$225; each addl $15-$25; kit. units $20 addl; family rates; lower rates rest of yr. Crib free. TV; cable. Complimentary continental bkfst. Restaurant 8 am-midnight (seasonal). Bar noon-1 am. Ck-out 11 am. Business servs avail. Tennis privileges. Golf privileges. Balconies. Picnic tables, grill. On beach. Cr cds: A, DS, MC, V.

B&B/Small Inn

★★★ **RAM'S HEAD INN.** *108 Ram Island Dr, Shelter Island Heights (11965). 631/749-0811; fax 631/749-0059.* 17 rms, 4 share bath, 2 story. No A/C. S, D $90-$125; each addl $15; suites $195. Crib free. Playground. Complimentary continental bkfst. Restaurant (see also RAM'S HEAD INN). Bar 10 am-midnight. Ck-out noon, ck-in 3 pm. Meeting rms. Tennis. Sauna. Colonial-style inn (1929); extensive grounds; on beach. Totally nonsmoking. Cr cds: A, MC, V.

Restaurants

★★★ **CHEQUIT INN.** *23 Grand Ave (11964). 631/749-0018. www.shelter islandinns.com.* Specializes in seafood, pasta. Hrs: noon-10 pm; wkends from 10 am. Closed Nov-mid-May. Res accepted. A la carte entrees: lunch $4-$9.50, dinner $15-$20. Entertainment wkends. Outdoor dining. Inn was originally built (ca 1870) around a maple tree that, now enormous, still shades the terrace that overlooks Dering Harbor. Cr cds: A, MC, V.

★★★ **RAM'S HEAD INN.** *108 Ram Island Dr (11964). 631/749-0811. www.shelterislandinns.com.* Specializes in duck,seafood. Own baking. Hrs: 5-9 pm; Closed Mon-Wed after Labor Day until Apr. Res accepted. No A/C. Bar. Wine list. A la carte entrees: dinner $18-$28. Outdoor dining. Dining rm with fireplace,

opens to veranda overlooking Coecles Harbor. Cr cds: A, MC, V.

Skaneateles

(D-5) *See also Auburn, Seneca Falls, Syracuse*

Settled 1794 **Pop** 7,323 **Elev** 919 ft
Area code 315 **Zip** 13152

Skaneateles (skany-AT-les) was once a stop on the Underground Railroad. Today it is a quiet resort town at the north end of Skaneateles Lake.

What to See and Do

Boat trips. A 32-mi cruise along shoreline of Skaneateles Lake (July-Aug, Mon-Sat). Lunch cruise (Mon-Fri), dinner cruises (nightly), three-hr excursion (Sun), sightseeing cruise (daily). (May-Sept) Depart Clift Park dock. Contact Mid-Lakes Navigation Co, PO Box 61-M. Phone 800/545-4318. ¢¢¢¢

Special Event

Polo Matches. Skaneateles Polo Club Grounds. 1 mi S, just off NY 41A. Phone 315/685-7373. Sun July-Aug.

Motel/Motor Lodge

★★ **THE BIRD'S NEST.** *1601 E Genesee St and Rte 20 (13152). 315/685-5641. www.skaneateles.com/ birdsnest.* 30 rms, 10 kits. Mid-May-Sept: S, D $45-$95; each addl $5; kit. units $139; under 5 free; wkly rates; lower rates rest of yr. Crib free. Pet accepted. TV; cable. Heated pool. Playground. Complimentary coffee in rms. Restaurant nearby. Ck-out noon. Lawn games. Some refrigerators, whirlpools. Picnic tables, grill. Duck pond. Cr cds: A, C, D, DS, MC, V.

Hotels

★ ★ ★ **MIRBEAU INN & SPA.** *851 N Genesee St (13152). 315/685-5006; fax 315/685-5150; toll-free 877/647-2328. www.mirbeau.com.* This self-contained spa is modeled after a French provincial chateau. Built around a lovely garden with pathways and gardens, the main building and cottage rooms are large and beautifully appointed with wooden furniture, bright yellow accents, and faux beam ceilings. The bathrooms are extraordinary, and feature claw-foot tubs, wooden vanities, and free-standing showers. The spa facility offers many treatments, and just lying in the round relaxing room is enough to restore even the most weary traveler. The ambitious chef serves an elegant four-course tasting menu for dinner, but other meals are less ornate. All in all a delightful respite. 34 rms, 2 story. Late-Apr-early-Nov: S, D $165-$395; suites $400-$1,200. TV; cable (premium), VCR avail. Indoor pool; whirlpool. Restaurants 7:30-10:30 am, 11:30 am-2:30 pm, 6-9 pm. Bar 11 am-11 pm. Coffee in rms. Ck-out noon. Meeting rms. Business servs avail. In-rm modem link. Bellhops. Concierge. Gift shop. Valet serv. Exercise rm; sauna. Spa. Massage. Refrigerators, fireplaces. Patios on first floor. Cr cds: A, MC, V.

★ ★ ★ **SHERWOOD INN.** *26 W Genesee St (13152). 315/685-3405; fax 315/685-8983; toll-free 800/743-7963. www.thesherwoodinn.com.* 24 rms, 11 suites, 3 story. S $85-$170; D $90-$170; suites $170; each addl $15. Crib $10. Complimentary continental bkfst. Dining rm 5-10 pm; informal dining 11:30 am-9 pm, Sat, Sun to 10 pm. Bar 11:30-midnight. Ck-out noon, ck-in 3 pm. Meeting rms. Business servs avail. In-rm modem link. Gift shop. Some fireplaces. Public beach opp. Built 1807; former stage coach stop. Cr cds: A, C, D, MC, V.

B&B/Small Inn

★ ★ ★ **HOBBIT HOLLOW BED & BREAKFAST.** *3061 W Lake Rd (13152). 315/685-2791; fax 315/685-3426. www.hobbithollow.com.* 5 rms, 1 suite. May-Dec: S, D $120-$230; suite $250-$270; each addl $40. Children over 18 yrs only. TV in library. Complimentary full bkfst; afternoon refreshments. Complimentary coffee in rms. Restaurant nearby. Ck-out noon, ck-in 3 pm. Business servs avail. In-rm modem link. Some fireplaces. Built in 1820; country decor. Totally nonsmoking. Cr cds: A, DS, MC, V.

Restaurants

★ ★ ★ **THE DINING ROOM.** *851 Genessee St (13152). 315/685-5006.* Specializes in French country cuisine. Own baking. Hrs: 7 am-10 pm. Bar. Wine cellar. Bkfst $9.95-$15.95. Complete meals: lunch $19.95-$25.95, dinner $25-$32. Cr cds: A, MC, V.

★ **DOUG'S FISH FRY.** *8 Jordan St (13152). 315/685-3288. www.dougsfishfry.com.* Hrs: 11 am-9 pm. Closed major hols; also 2 wks in Jan. Specializes in fresh seafood. Beer. A la carte entrees: lunch, dinner $4-$14.99. Outdoor dining. Cr cds: A, MC, V.

Smithtown (L.I.)

See also Huntington (L.I.), Stony Brook (L.I.)

Pop 115,715 **Elev** 60 ft **Area code** 631 **Zip** 11787

Smithtown includes six unincorporated hamlets and three incorporated villages. The village of Smithtown is situated near several state parks.

Motels/Motor Lodges

★ **ECONO LODGE.** *755 Rte 347, Smithtown (11787). 631/724-9000; fax 631/724-9017; toll-free 800/553-2666. www.econolodge.com.* 39 rms, 2 story. S $60-$65; D $65-$74; each addl $8; under 18 free. Crib $6. TV; cable (premium). Complimentary coffee in lobby. Restaurant nearby. Ck-out 11 am. Cr cds: A, D, DS, MC, V.

★★ **HAMPTON INN.** *680 Commack Rd, Commack (11725). 631/462-5700; fax 631/462-9735; toll-free 800/564-2678. www.hamptoninn.com.* 144 rms, 5 story. S $94; D $110; under 18 free. Crib free. TV; cable (premium), VCR avail. Continental bkfst. Restaurant nearby. Ck-out noon. Meeting rm. Business servs avail. In-rm modem link. Airport transportation. Health club privileges. Some refrigerators, microwaves. Cr cds: A, C, D, DS, MC, V.

Hotels

★★★ **MARRIOTT ISLANDIA.** *3635 Express Dr, Hauppauge (11788). 631/232-3000; fax 631/232-1222. www.marriott.com.* 277 rms, 12 suites, 10 story. S, D $115-$159. Crib free. TV; cable (premium). Indoor pool; whirlpool, lifeguard. Restaurant 6:30 am-2 pm, 5-11 pm. Bar 2 pm-midnight. Ck-out noon. Convention facilities. Business servs avail. Gift shop. Free airport, RR station transportation. Exercise equipt. Game rm. Refrigerators avail. Cr cds: A, D, DS, MC, V.

★★★ **SHERATON SMITHTOWN HOTEL.** *110 Vanderbilt Motor Pkwy (11788). 631/231-1100; fax 631/231-1143; res 800/325-3535. www. sheraton.com.* 209 rms, 6 story. S, D $139; each addl $20; suites $208-$395; wkend rates. Crib avail. TV; cable (premium), VCR avail. Indoor pool; whirlpool, lifeguard. Restaurant 6:30 am-10:30 pm. Bar noon-1 am; entertainment. Ck-out noon. Meeting rms. Business servs avail. In-rm modem link. Bellhops. Valet serv. Sundries. Exercise equipt; sauna, steam rm. Game rm. Refrigerators avail. Cr cds: A, C, D, DS, MC, V.

Restaurants

★★ **BONWIT INN.** *Commack Rd and Vanderbilt Pkwy, Commack (11725). 631/499-2068.* Continental menu. Specializes in seafood, steak.

Hrs: 11 am-midnight; Mon to 10 pm, Sun to 10 pm. Closed Dec 25. Res accepted. Bar. A la carte entrees: lunch $4.95-$13.95, dinner $11-$29. Nautical theme. Fireplaces. Cr cds: A, D, DS, MC, V.

★★★ **LA MASCOTTE.** *3 Crooked Hill Rd, Commack (11725). 631/499-6446.* French menu. Specialties: canard aux airelles, carre d'agneau. Own baking. Hrs: noon-3 pm, 5-10 pm; Fri to 11 pm; Sat, Sun 5-11 pm. Closed Dec 25. Res accepted. Bar. Wine cellar. A la carte entrees: lunch $11.50-$16.50, dinner $15-$26. Complete meals: lunch $15, dinner $24.95. Parking. Cr cds: A, D, DS, MC, V.

★★ **LOTUS EAST.** *416 N Country Rd, St. James (11780). 631/862-6030.* Chinese menu. Specialties: General Tso's chicken, tangerine beef. Hrs: 11:30 am-10:30 pm; Fri, Sat to 11 pm; Sun 11 am-10 pm. Bar. Lunch $4.75-$6.95, dinner $7.75-$17.95. Chinese motif. Cr cds: A, D, MC, V.

★★★ **MIRABELLE.** *404 N Country Rd, St. James (11780). 631/584-5999. www.mirabelle.com.* French menu. Specialties: duck in two courses, ginger almond tarte. Hrs: noon-2 pm, 6-9:30 pm; Sat from 6 pm; Sun from 5 pm. Closed Mon; July 4, Thanksgiving, Dec 25. Res required. Bar. A la carte entrees: lunch $11-$21, dinner $21-$31. Complete meals: lunch $19.95. Parking. Cr cds: A, D, DS, MC, V.

Southampton (L.I.)

(G-4) *See also East Hampton (L.I.), Hampton Bays (L.I.), Riverhead (L.I.)*

Settled 1640 **Pop** 54,712 **Elev** 25 ft
Area code 631 **Zip** 11968

Information Chamber of Commerce, 76 Main St; 631/283-0402

Web www.southamptonchamber. com/

Southampton has many colonial houses. The surrounding dunes and beaches are dotted with luxury estates.

What to See and Do

Old Halsey House. (1648) Oldest English frame house in state. Furnished with period furniture; Colonial herb garden. (Mid-July-mid-Sept, Tues-Sun) S Main St. Phone 631/283-2494. ¢¢

Parrish Art Museum. Incl 19th and 20th-century American paintings and prints; repository for William Merritt Chase and Fairfield Porter; Japanese woodblock prints; collection of Renaissance works; changing exhibits; arboretum; performing arts and concert series; lectures; research library. (Mid-June-mid-Sept, Mon-Tues and Thurs-Sat, also Sun afternoons; rest of yr, Mon and Thurs-Sun; closed hols) 25 Job's Ln, town center. Phone 631/283-2118. ¢

Southampton College of Long Island University. (1963) 1,200 students. Liberal arts, marine science research. Tour of campus. Montauk Hwy (NY 27A). Phone 631/283-4000.

Southampton Historical Museum. Main building formerly was whaling captain's home (1843). Period rms, costumes, china, toys. Large collection of Native American artifacts; one-rm schoolhouse; carriage house; farming and whaling collections. Features 18th-century barn converted to country store. (Tues-Sun) 17 Meeting House Ln, off Main St. Phone 631/283-2494. ¢¢

Water Mill Museum. Restored gristmill, 18th century, houses old tools, other exhibits; craft demonstrations. (Memorial Day-mid-Sept, Mon, Wed, also Sat-Sun afternoons) NE on Old Mill Rd, in Water Mill. Phone 631/726-4625. ¢¢

Special Events

Hampton Classic Horse Show. 240 Snake Hollow Rd, N of NY 27, in Bridgehampton. Horse show jumping event. Celebrities, food, shopping, family activities. Phone 631/537-3177. Last wk Aug.

Powwow. Shinnecock Indian Reservation, just off NY 27A. Dances, ceremonies, displays. Labor Day wkend. Phone 631/283-6143.

Motel/Motor Lodge

★ **SOUTHAMPTON INN.** *91 Hill St, Southampton (11968). 631/283-6500; fax 631/283-6559; toll-free 800/732-6500.* 90 rms, 2 story. June-Sept: S, D $150-$225; each addl $25; wkend packages; lower rates rest of yr. Crib free. TV; cable (premium). Pool; poolside serv, lifeguard. Bar 5 pm-2 am (seasonal); entertainment, dancing Fri, Sat. Ck-out 11 am. Meeting rms. Business servs avail. In-rm modem link. Bellhops. Concierge. Tennis. Lawn games. Some refrigerators. Cr cds: A, MC, V.
⊠ ⊠ 🐾 SC

B&B/Small Inn

★★ **MAINSTAY.** *579 Hill St, Southampton (11968). 631/283-4375; fax 631/287-6240.* 8 rms, 3 share baths, 3 story. No A/C. June-Sept: S, D $95-$350; wkends (2-day min); lower rates rest of yr. TV in some rms. Pool. Complimentary continental bkfst. Restaurant nearby. Ck-out 11 am, ck-in 3 pm. Business servs avail. Restored guest house (1870); antiques. Totally nonsmoking. Cr cds: A, MC, V.
⊠ ⊠ 🐾

Restaurants

★★ **BASILICO.** *10 Windmill Ln (11968). 631/283-7987.* Northern Italian menu. Specializes in pasta, fish, steak. Full vegetarian menu. Hrs: 6-11 pm; Fri-Sun noon-3 pm, 6 pm-midnight. Closed some major hols. Res required. Bar. A la carte entrees: lunch $11-$15, dinner $11-$26. Trattoria; wine racks on walls, many plants, herbs and flowers. Cr cds: A, C, D, DS, ER, MC, V.

★★ **BOBBY VAN'S.** *Montauk Hwy, Bridgehampton (11932). 631/537-0590.* Specializes in aged prime sirloin steak, veal chops, fresh seafood. Hrs: noon-10:30 pm. Res accepted. Bar. A la carte entrees: lunch $8-$19, dinner $16-$29. New York City-style chop house. Cr cds: A, C, D, DS, MC, V.
D

★★ **COAST GRILL.** *1109 Noyack Rd (11968). 631/283-2277.* Specializes in grilled swordfish, lobster, clams. Own pastries. Hrs: 5 pm-2 am. Res accepted. Bar. Dinner $20-$25. Nautical theme; view of Wooley Pond. Cr cds: A, MC, V.
D

★★ **JOHN DUCK JR.** *15 Prospect St (11968). 631/283-0311.* Specializes in L.I. duckling, steak, seafood. Own desserts. Hrs: 11:45 am-10:30 pm; Fri, Sat to midnight. Closed Mon; Dec 24, 25. Res accepted. Bar. Lunch $5.25-$13.50, dinner $14.75-$22. Complete meals: lunch $9.75-$13, dinner (Tues-Thurs) $14-$17.50. Child's menu. Valet parking wkends. Established 1900; 4th generation of ownership. Cr cds: A, D, DS, MC, V.
D

★★ **LE CHEF.** *75 Jobs Ln (11968). 631/283-8581. www.lechefbistro.com.* French, Amer menu. Specializes in grilled fish, French provincial cuisine. Hrs: 11:30 am-10 pm. Res accepted. Bar. Lunch $7-$15. Complete meals: dinner $16.75-$18. Cr cds: A, MC, V.
D

★ **LOBSTER INN.** *162 Inlet Rd, Southampton, L.I. (11968). 631/283-1525.* Specializes in seafood, steak. Salad bar. Hrs: 11:30 am-11 pm. Closed Thanksgiving, Dec 24, 25. No A/C. Bar. Complete meals: lunch $5.75-$12.75, dinner $13.75-$25. Parking. Family-owned. Cr cds: A, MC, V.

★★ **MIRKO'S.** *Water Mill Sq, Water Mill (11976). 631/726-4444. www.mirkosrestaurant.com.* Continental menu. Specializes in pasta, seafood, veal chops. Hrs: 6-11 pm; winter to 10 pm. Closed Tues; Mon-Wed in winter; also Jan. Res required. Bar. A la carte entrees: dinner $17.50-$29. Outdoor dining. Fireplace. Cr cds: A, C, D, MC, V.
D

★★★ **95 SCHOOL STREET.** *95 School St, Bridgehampton (11932). 631/537-5555.* Regional American menu. Specialties: pan-roasted farm chicken, grilled duck breast, pasta with lobster and roasted corn. Hrs: 6-11 pm. Closed Mon, Tues (Labor Day-Memorial Day). Res accepted. Bar. A la carte entrees: dinner $16-$25. Atmosphere of country elegance. Cr cds: A, D, MC, V.
D

★★ **STATION ROAD.** *50 Station Rd, Water Mill (11976). 631/726-3016.* French menu. Specialties: herb-crusted bass, entrecote steak with roasted shallots, baked fruit tarts. Hrs: 6-10 pm; Sat, Sun noon-4 pm; winter hrs vary. Res accepted; required Fri, Sat. Bar. A la carte

The Hamptons

entrees: dinner $18-$25. In former railroad station (1903). Jacket. Cr cds: A, MC, V.

Unrated Dining Spot

GOLDEN PEAR. *99 Main St (11968).* *631/283-8900.* Specialties: pasta, chili, vegetable lasagne. Menu changes daily. Hrs: 8 am-5 pm; Fri-Sun to 6 pm. A la carte entrees: bkfst $4.95-$7.95, lunch $5.95-$10.95. Cr cds: A, DS, MC, V.

Southold (L.I.)

F-3) *See also Greenport (L.I.), Riverhead (L.I.)*

Settled 1640 **Pop** 20,599 **Elev** 32 ft **Area code** 631 **Zip** 11971
Information Greenport-Southold Chamber of Commerce, 1205 Tuthill Rd Extension, 11971; 631/765-3161

What to See and Do

Horton Point Lighthouse & Nautical Museum. (Memorial Day-Columbus Day, Sat and Sun limited hrs) Lighthouse Park, 54325 Main Rd. Phone 631/765-5500. **Donation**

The Old House. (1649) Example of early English architecture; 17th and 18th-century furnishings. Also on Village Green are the **Wickham Farmhouse** (early 1700s) and the **Old Schoolhouse Museum** (1840). (July-Labor Day, Sat-Mon; Sept-Oct, by appt) On NY 25, on the Village Green in Cutchogue. Phone 631/734-7122. **Donation**

Motel/Motor Lodge

★ **SANTORINI'S BEACHCOMBER RESORT MOTEL.** *3800 Duck Pond Rd, Cutchogue (11935).* *631/734-6370; fax 631/734-5579.* 50 rms, 2 story. 11 rm phones. Memorial Day-Labor Day: D $115-$235; each addl $25; wkly rates; 2-day min wkends; lower rates mid-Sept-mid-Oct. Closed rest of yr. TV. Pool; wading pool. Complimentary coffee in rms. Ck-out 11 am. Game rm. Refrigerators. Bal-

conies. Swimming beach. Cr cds: A, DS, MC, V.

Restaurant

★★ **SEAFOOD BARGE.** *62980 Main Rd, Southold, L.I. (11971).* *631/765-3010.* Specializes in lobster, steamers, grilled fish. Hrs: noon-10 pm; mid-Sept-mid-June, hrs vary. Res accepted. Bar. A la carte entrees: lunch $9.50-$13.50, dinner $12-$28. Overlooks Peconic Bay and marina. Family-owned. Cr cds: A, MC, V.

Spring Valley

See also Tarrytown

Pop 25,464 **Elev** 420 ft **Area code** 845 **Zip** 10977

What to See and Do

Historical Society of Rockland County. Museum and publications on county history; Jacob Blauvelt House (1832 Dutch farmhouse), barn. (Tues-Sun afternoons; closed hols) 3 mi N via NY 45, then 3 mi E on New Hempstead Rd, then 2 mi N on Main St to 20 Zukor Rd in New City. Phone 845/634-9629. **Donation**

Motels/Motor Lodges

★★ **HOLIDAY INN.** *3 Executive Blvd, Suffern (10901).* *845/357-4800; fax 845/368-0471; toll-free 800/465-4329.* 241 rms, 3 story. S, D $99-$120; kit. suites $175. Crib free. TV; cable (premium). Complimentary coffee in lobby. Restaurant 7-10:30 am, noon-2 pm, 5-10 pm. Bar 3 pm-midnight. Ck-out noon. Meeting rms. Business center. Bellhops. Valet serv. Sundries. Coin lndry. Exercise equipt; sauna. Indoor pool; whirlpool, lifeguard. Game rm. In-rm whirlpool, refrigerator, microwave in kit. suites. Cr cds: A, C, D, DS, MC, V.

★ **SUSSE CHALET INN.** *100 Spring Valley Marketplace (10977).* *845/426-*

2000; fax 845/426-2008; toll-free 800/524-2538. 105 rms, 4 story. S $73-$78; D $80-$85; each addl $3; under 18 free. Crib $10. TV; cable (premium). Pool; lifeguard. Complimentary continental bkfst. Restaurant nearby. Ck-out 11 am. Coin lndry. Health club privileges. Cr cds: A, D, DS, MC, V.

D ⊠-⊠⚒

Hotels

★★★ **HILTON PEARL RIVER.** *500 Veterans Memorial Dr, Pearl River (10965). 845/735-9000; fax 845/735-9005. www.pearlriver.hilton.com.* 150 rms, 5 story. S $189; D $209; each addl $16; suites $300-$400; family, wkend rates. Crib free. TV; cable (premium). Indoor pool; whirlpool, lifeguard. Restaurant 6:30 am-11 pm; Sat from 7 am. Bar 11-1 am; pianist. Ck-out noon. Coin lndry. Meeting rms. Business center. In-rm modem link. Exercise equipt; sauna. Refrigerators. French chateau style; on 17 acres. Cr cds: A, C, D, DS, ER, JCB, MC, V.

D ⊠ ✕ ⊠ ⊠ ⚒ ★

★★ **WELLESLEY INN.** *17 N Airmont Rd, Suffern (10901). 845/368-1900; fax 845/368-1927; res 800/444-8888.* 95 rms, 4 story. Apr-Oct: S, D $82-$102; each addl $10; suites $110-$160; under 18 free; higher rates West Point graduation, Dec 31; lower rates rest of yr. Crib free. Pet accepted, some restrictions; $5/day. TV; cable (premium). Complimentary continental bkfst, coffee in rms. Restaurant nearby. Ck-out 11 am. Business servs avail. Refrigerators, microwaves avail. Cr cds: A, C, D, DS, MC, V.

D ✎ ⊁ ⊠ ⚒ ⚒

Restaurant

★★ **RAMAPOUGH INN.** *253 NY 59, Suffern (10901). 845/357-0500.* Specializes in lobster, steak, seafood. Hrs: 11:30 am-9:30 pm; Fri to 11 pm; Sat 4-11 pm; Sun 4-9:30 pm. Closed Mon; July 4, Thanksgiving, Dec 25. Res accepted. Bar to 2 am. Lunch $4.95-$11.95, dinner $9.95-$19.95. Child's menu. Cr cds: A, D, DS, MC, V.

D ⊟

Stamford (G-2)

Pop 1,943 **Elev** 1,827 ft
Area code 518 **Zip** 12167

Stamford, located along the west branch of the Delaware River, has a large historical district from the Victorian era.

What to See and Do

Lansing Manor. A 19th-century manor house depicting life of an Anglo-Dutch household of the mid-1800s. (Memorial Day-Columbus Day, Mon, Wed-Sun) 8 mi SE on NY 23, then 8 mi N on NY 30. Phone 607/588-6061. **FREE** Adj is

Visitors Center. Remodeled dairy barn with hands-on exhibits, display on electricity, video presentation, and computers. (Daily; closed Jan 1, Dec 25) Phone 800/724-0309.

Mine Kill State Park. Swimming pool (late June-early Sept; fee), bathhouse, fishing, boating; hiking and nature trails, x-country skiing, snowmobiling, picnicking, playground, concession. Recreation programs. Standard fees. SE on NY 23, 4 mi N on NY 30. Phone 518/827-6111.

Zaddock Pratt Museum. Period furnishings and memorabilia. Tours, exhibits. (Memorial Day-Columbus Day, Wed-Sun afternoons) 1828 Homestead, 13 mi SE via NY 23 in Prattsville. Phone 518/299-3395. ¢ Nearby is

Pratt Rocks. Relief carvings in the cliff face depicting Pratt, his son George, and the tannery. Scenic climb; picnicking; pavilion.

Motel/Motor Lodge

★ **COLONIAL MOTEL.** *Prattsville Rd, Grand Gorge (12434). 607/588-6122; fax 607/588-6495.* 14 rms, 3 A/C, 1-2 story, 3 kits. S $55; D $60; kits. $65. TV; cable (premium). Heated pool. Complimentary coffee. Restaurant adj 6 am-9 pm. Ck-out 11 am. Downhill/x-country ski 8 mi. Lawn games. Picnic tables, grills. Refrigerators. Family-owned. Cr cds: A, DS, MC, V.

⊠ ⊠ ⊠ ⊠ ⚒

Stony Brook (L.I.)

ee also Port Jefferson (L.I.), Smithtown L.I.)

ettled 1655 **Pop** 13,727 **Elev** 123 ft
Area code 631 **Zip** 11790

Originally part of the Three Village area first settled by Boston colonists in the 17th century, Stony Brook became an important center for the shipbuilding industry on Long Island sound in the 1800s.

What to See and Do

The Museums at Stony Brook. Complex of three museums. The Melville Carriage House exhibits 90 vehicles from a collection of horse-drawn carriages. The Art Museum features changing exhibits of American art. The Blackwell History Museum has changing exhibits on a variety of historical themes as well as exhibits of period rms and antique decoys. Blacksmith shop, schoolhouse, other period buildings. Museum store. Wed-Sun and Mon hols; closed other hols) On NY 25A. Phone 631/751-0066. ¢¢

State University of New York at Stony Brook. (1957) 17,500 students. Academic units incl College of Arts and Sciences, College of Engineering and Applied Sciences, and Health Sciences Center. Museum of Long Island Natural Sciences has permanent displays on Long Island natural history. Art galleries in the Melville Library, Staller Center, and the Student Union. Phone 631/689-6000. On campus is

    Staller Center for the Arts. Houses 1,049-seat main theater, three experimental theaters, art gallery, 400-seat recital hall, and electronic music studio. Summer International Theater Festival. Events all yr. Phone 631/632-7235.

Motel/Motor Lodge

★★ **THREE VILLAGE INN.** *150 Main St (11790). 631/751-0555; fax 631/751-0593; toll-free 888/384-4438. www.threevillageinn.com.* 26 rms, 2

story. S $95-$119; D $105-$139; each addl $10. Crib $10. TV; cable. Restaurant (see THREE VILLAGE INN). Bar. Ck-out noon, ck-in 3 pm. Meeting rm. Business servs avail. Picnic tables. Built in late 1700s; some fireplaces. Cr cds: A, D, MC, V.

Restaurants

★★★ **COUNTRY HOUSE.** *NY 25A (11790). 631/751-3332.* Specializes in creative American cuisine. Hrs: noon-3 pm, 5-10 pm. Closed Jan 1, July 4, Dec 25. Res accepted; required dinner. Bar. Prix fixe: lunch $16.75. A la carte entrees: dinner $16-$26. House built in 1710. Cr cds: A, C, D, MC, V.
D

★★ **THREE VILLAGE INN.** *150 Main St (11790). 631/751-0555. www. threevillageinn.com.* Specializes in steak, seafood. Own baking. Hrs: 7-11 am, noon-4 pm, 5-10 pm; Fri, Sat to 11 pm; Sun brunch noon-3 pm. Closed Dec 25. Res accepted. Bar. A la carte entrees: bkfst $1.75-$7.95, lunch $8.95-$16.95. Complete meals: dinner $25.95-$33.95, Fri seafood dinner $23.95. Sun brunch $12.95-$16.95. Child's menu. Colonial homestead built in 1751. Attractive grounds; country dining. Near harbor. Cr cds: A, D, MC, V.
D

Stony Point

(G-8) See also Monroe, Newburgh, Peekskill, West Point (US Military Academy)

Pop 14,244 **Elev** 126 ft **Area code** 914
Zip 10980

What to See and Do

Stony Point Battlefield State Historic Site. Site of Revolutionary War battle in which General "Mad Anthony" Wayne successfully stormed British fortifications, July 15-16, 1779, ending the last serious threat to Washington's forces in the North. Oldest lighthouse (1826) on the Hudson River. Museum with exhibits, audiovisual program. Musket demonstrations. Self-guided walking tour and guided tour. Special events (fee). Picnic area. (Mid-Apr-Oct, Wed-Sun) 2 mi N of town center, off US 9 W, on Park Rd. Phone 845/786-2521. **FREE**

Stormville

(see Fishkill)

Suffern

(see Spring Valley)

Syracuse

(D-5) *See also Auburn, Cazenovia, Skaneateles*

Settled 1789 **Pop** 147,306 **Elev** 406 ft
Area code 315
Information Convention & Visitors Bureau, 572 S Salina St, 13202; 315/470-1910 or 800/284-4797
Web www.syracusecvb.org

Syracuse began as a trading post at the mouth of Onondaga Creek. Salt from wells was produced here from 1796-1900. Industry began in 1793, when Thomas Wiard began making wooden plows. Shortly after 1800, a blast furnace was built that produced iron utensils and, during the War of 1812, cast shot for the Army. When the Erie Canal reached town in the late 1820s, Syracuse's industrial future was assured. Today the city has many large and varied industries.

What to See and Do

Beaver Lake Nature Center. A 600-acre nature preserve that incl ten mi of trails and boardwalks, a 200-acre lake that serves as a rest stop for migrating ducks and geese, and a visitor center that features exhibits. In the winter the preserve is also used

for x-country skiing and snowshoeing. Other programs incl maple sugaring and guided canoe tours. (Daily 12 mi NW via I-690 at 8477 E Mud Lake Rd in Baldwinsville. Phone 315/638-2519. Per vehicle ¢

Erie Canal Museum. Indoor and outdoor exhibits detail the construction and operation of the Erie Canal; 65-f reconstructed canal boat from which exhibits are seen; research library and archives. 318 Erie Blvd E. Phone 315/471-0593. Museum also houses

Syracuse Heritage Area Visitor Center. Video presentation and exhibits here introduce visitors to area attractions. (Daily; closed hols) Weighlock Building, Erie Blvd E and Montgomery St. Phone 315/471-0593. **FREE** The museum also maintains

Everson Museum of Art. First I. M. Pei-designed museum, permanent collection of American art; collection of American ceramics; home of the Syracuse China Center for the Study of American Ceramics; changing exhibits. (Tues-Sun; closed hols) 401 Harrison St. Phone 315/474-6064. **Donation**

Green Lakes State Park. Swimming beach, bathhouse, boat rentals, fishing; hiking and biking trails, 18-hole golf, x-country skiing, picnicking, playground, concession, tent and trailer sites (late May-Columbus Day wkend), cabins. Standard fees. 10 mi E via NY 5 in Fayetteville. Phone 315/637-6111. ¢¢

Landmark Theatre. Built in 1928 as Loew's State Theatre in the era of vaudeville-movie houses. The interior architecture is filled with carvings, chandeliers, and ornate gold decorations. Theater houses concerts, comedy, plays, dance, and classic movies. 362 S Salina St. Phone 315/475-7980.

New York State Canal Cruises. Depart Albany, Syracuse, and Buffalo (June-Oct). Also three-hr dinner cruises (nightly), three-hr excursions (Sun), sightseeing cruises. Phone 800/545-4318.

Onondaga Historical Association Museum. Changing and permanent exhibits illustrate history of central New York. Incl exhibits on sports history, transportation, military history, and industry. (Wed-Sun; closed hols)

21 Montgomery St. Phone 315/428-864. **FREE**

Onondaga Lake Park. Boat launch and marina; picnicking, concession, bicycle rentals, exercise trail, tram rides, children's play area. 2½ mi NW via I-81 to Liverpool exit. Phone 315/453-6712. **FREE** On grounds are

Ste. Marie Among the Iroquois. A 17th-century French mission living history museum. Blacksmithing, cooking, carpentry, and gardening activities. Special programs. (May-Nov, Wed-Sun; Dec-Apr, Tues-Sun) Phone 315/453-6767.

Salt Museum. Re-created 19th-century salt "boiling block"; artifacts and exhibits of Onondaga salt industry. Starting point for history and nature trail around lake. (May-Oct, daily) Phone 315/453-6767. **Donation**

Rosamond Gifford Zoo at Burnet Park. Zoo traces origin of life from 600 million yrs ago; exhibits on animals' unique adaptations and animal/human interaction; gift shop. (Daily; closed Jan 1, Thanksgiving, Dec 25) S Wilbur Ave. Phone 315/435-8511. ¢¢

Syracuse University. (1870) 18,000 students. Major, private graduate-level research and teaching institution. Noted for the Maxwell School of Citizenship and Public Affairs, Newhouse School of Public Communications, College of Engineering, and 50,000-seat Carrier Dome. University Ave at University Pl. Phone 315/443-1870. On the 650-acre campus is

Lowe Art Gallery. Shaffer Art Building. Shows, paintings, sculpture, other art. Phone 315/443-3127. **FREE**

Special Events

Balloon Festival. Jamesville Beach Park. Mid-June. Phone 315/435-5252.

Open-air concerts. In city parks, downtown, and throughout city. Phone 315/473-4330. Early July-late Aug.

Scottish Games. Long Branch Park. Phone 315/470-1800. Mid-Aug.

NY State Fair. State Fairgrounds. Phone 315/487-7711. Late-Aug-early-Sept.

Golden Harvest Festival. Beaver Lake Nature Center. Old-time harvest activities. Wkend after Labor Day. Phone 315/638-2519.

Syracuse Stage. 820 E Genesee St. Original, professional theatrical productions. Phone 315/443-3275. Sept-May.

Motels/Motor Lodges

★★ **BEST WESTERN MARSHALL MANOR.** *Rtes 80 and 11, Tully (13159).* 315/696-6061; fax 315/696-6406; res 800/780-7234. www.best western.com. 44 rms, 2 story. S, D $44-$72; each addl $5; under 12 free; higher rates state fair, Dirt wk. Crib $5. TV; cable. Restaurant 6 am-10 pm. Bar 4 pm-midnight. Ck-out 11 am. Meeting rms. Business servs avail. Downhill ski 2½ mi; x-country ski 10 mi. Cr cds: A, D, DS, JCB, MC, V.

D 🐕 ♿ ➡ ⊠ 🐾

★★ **COMFORT INN FAIR-GROUNDS.** *7010 Interstate Island Rd (13209).* 315/453-0045; fax 315/453-3689; res 800/228-5150. www.comfort inns.com. 109 rms, 4 story. S, D $55-$60; each addl $5; under 18 free; higher rates: state fair, special events. Crib free. TV; cable, VCR avail (movies). Restaurant adj 6 am-11 pm. Ck-out 11 am. Meeting rms. Exercise equipt. Cr cds: A, C, D, DS, MC, V.

D 🏃 ⊠ 🐾

★★ **COURTYARD BY MARRIOTT.** *6415 Yorktown Circle, East Syracuse (13057).* 315/432-0300; fax 315/432-9950; res 800/321-2211. www. courtyard.com/syrca. 149 rms, 12 suites, 3 story. S, D $109; suites $129; under 12 free; wkend rates. Crib free (with res). TV; cable (premium), VCR avail. Heated indoor pool; whirlpool, lifeguard. Complimentary coffee in rms. Restaurant 6:30-10 am. Bar 4-11 pm. Ck-out 11 am. Coin lndry. Meeting rms. Business servs avail. In-rm modem link. Valet serv. Sundries. Exercise equipt. Refrigerator in suites. Balconies. Cr cds: A, C, D, DS, MC, V.

D ≈ 🏃 ⊠ 🐾 SC

★ **ECONO LODGE.** *401 N 7th St, Liverpool (13088).* 315/451-6000; fax 315/451-0193; res 800/553-2666. www.econolodge.com. 83 rms, 4 story. May-Sept: S $42-$59; D $49-$79;

each addl $4; suites $49-$59; under 18 free; higher rates special events; lower rates rest of yr. Crib free. Pet accepted, some restrictions; $3. TV; cable. Complimentary continental bkfst. Restaurant adj 6 am-11 pm. Ck-out 11 am. Business servs avail. Cr cds: A, C, D, DS, MC, V.

★★ **FAIRFIELD INN.** *6611 Old Collamer Rd, East Syracuse (13057). 315/432-9333; toll-free 800/228-2800. www.fairfieldinn.com.* 135 rms, 3 story. June-Oct: S $54-$59; D $60-$70; under 18 free; lower rates rest of yr. Crib free. TV; cable (premium). Pool. Complimentary continental bkfst. Restaurants adj. Ck-out noon. Meeting rm. Business servs avail. In-rm modem link. Cr cds: A, D, DS, MC, V.

★★ **GENESSEE INN EXECUTIVE QUARTERS.** *1060 E Genesee St (13210). 315/476-4212; fax 315/471-4663; toll-free 800/365-4663.* 96 rms, 2 story. S $79-$99; D $89-$109; under 18 free; higher rates university special events. Crib free. Pet accepted. TV; cable. Restaurant 7 am-10 pm. Bar 11:30-1 am. Ck-out 11 am. Meeting rms. Business servs avail. Health club privileges. Cr cds: A, C, D, DS, MC, V.

★★ **HAMPTON INN CARRIER CIRCLE.** *6605 Old Collamer Rd, East Syracuse (13057). 315/432-1080; res 800/426-7866. www.hamptoninn.com.* 116 rms, 4 story. S, D $65.75; suites $85; under 18 free. Crib $10. TV; cable. Complimentary continental bkfst. Ck-out 1 pm. Meeting rm. Business servs avail. In-rm modem link. Valet serv (Mon-Fri). Health club privileges. Cr cds: A, C, D, DS, ER, JCB, MC, V.

★★ **HOLIDAY INN.** *6555 Old Collamer Rd S, East Syracuse (13057). 315/437-2761; fax 315/463-0028; res 800/465-4329. www.holiday-inn.com.* 203 rms, 2 story. S, D $99-$129; under 19 free; wkend rates; higher rates special events. TV; cable. Indoor pool; whirlpool. Complimentary coffee in rms. Restaurant 6 am-2 pm, 5-10 pm. Bar 4 pm-2 am. Ck-out noon. Meeting rms. Business servs avail. In-

rm modem link. Bellhops. Valet serv (Mon-Fri). Exercise equipt; sauna. Cr cds: A, D, DS, MC, V.

★★ **HOLIDAY INN SYRACUSE/LIVERPOOL.** *441 Electronics Pkwy, Liverpool (13088). 315/457-1122; fax 315/451-0675. www.holiday-inn.com.* 280 rms, 2 suites, 6 story. S $99; D $109; each addl $10; under 18 free; wkend rates. Crib free. Pet accepted. TV; cable. Indoor pool; whirlpool, lifeguard. Restaurant 6:30 am-11 pm. Bar 2 pm-2 am; entertainment (seasonal). Ck-out 1 pm. Business servs avail. In-rm modem link. Bellhops. Valet serv Mon-Fri. Sundries. Exercise equipt. Game rm. Patios. Cr cds: A, C, D, DS, MC, V.

★ **KNIGHTS INN.** *430 Electronics Pkwy, Liverpool (13088). 315/453-6330; fax 315/457-9240; res 800/843-5644. www.knightsinn.com.* 82 air-cooled rms, 8 kits. S $39-$44; D $44.95-$51; each addl $5; under 18 free; wkly rates. Crib free. Pet accepted, some restrictions. TV; cable (premium), VCR (movies). Complimentary continental bkfst. Restaurant adj 11 am-10 pm. Ck-out 11 am. Meeting rms. Business servs avail. Downhill ski 20 mi; x-country ski 1 mi. Cr cds: A, D, DS, MC, V.

★★ **RAMADA INN.** *1305 Buckley Rd (13212). 315/457-8670; fax 315/457-8633. www.ramadasyracuse.com.* 150 rms, 2 story. S $99; D $109; each addl $10; suites $129-$150; under 18 free; higher rates state fair, university events. Crib free. TV; cable (premium), VCR avail. Pool; lifeguard. Restaurant 6 am-10 pm. Bar 11:30 am-midnight. Ck-out noon. Meeting rms. Business servs avail. Valet serv. Sundries. Airport transportation. Exercise equipt. Cr cds: A, C, D, DS, ER, MC, V.

★ **RED ROOF INN.** *6614 N Thompson Rd (13206). 315/437-3309; fax 315/437-7865; toll-free 800/843-7663 www.redroof.com.* 115 rms, 3 story. S $31.99-$64.99; D $35.99-$71.99; under 18 free. Crib free. Pet accepted TV; cable (premium). Complimentary coffee in lobby. Restaurant opp open

4 hrs. Ck-out noon. Business servs
vail. Cr cds: A, C, D, DS, MC, V.
🅳 ⛵ 🏊 ⚹ SC

★ **SUPER 8.** *421 N 7th St, Liverpool
(13088). 315/451-8888; fax 315/451-
043; toll-free 800/800-8000. www.
uper8.com.* 99 rms, 4 story. S, D $45-
65; under 18 free; higher rates: state
air, university graduation, special
vents. Crib free. TV; cable. Compli-
nentary continental bkfst. Restau-
ant nearby. Ck-out noon. Business
ervs avail. In-rm modem link.
Downhill/x-country ski 20 mi. Picnic
ables. Cr cds: A, D, DS, MC, V.
🐾 ✈ 🏊

Hotels

★★ **SHERATON SYRACUSE
UNIVERSITY HOTEL & CONFER-
ENCE CENTER.** *801 University Ave
(13210). 315/475-3000; fax 315/475-
266; res 800/325-3535.* 235 rms, 18
uites, 9 story. S, D $99-$275; each
ddl $10; suites $200-$325; under 18
ree; wkend rates; higher rates uni-
ersity events. Parking $3/day. Crib
vail. Pet accepted; $100 (non-
efundable). TV; cable. Indoor pool;
/hirlpool, lifeguard. Coffee in rms.
estaurant 7 am-2 pm, 5-10 pm. Bar
oon-2 am; entertainment. Ck-out
oon. Bellhops. Convention facili-
es. Business center. In-rm modem
nk. Coin lndry. Gift shop. Game
m. Valet serv. Exercise equipt; sauna.
efrigerators avail. Luxury level. Cr
ds: A, C, D, DS, MC, V.
🅳 🐾 ⛵ 🏊 ⚹ ☃

★★ **WYNDHAM SYRACUSE.** *6301
te 298 (13057). 315/432-0200; fax
15/433-1210; toll-free 800/782-9847.
www.wyndham.com.* 250 units, 4-7
tory. S $140; D $165; each addl $10;
uites $275; studio rms $140; under
8 free; wkend rates. Crib free. TV;
able (premium). Indoor/outdoor
ool; whirlpool, poolside serv.
estaurant 6 am-11 pm. Bar noon-2
m; entertainment Fri. Ck-out noon.
oin lndry. Convention facilities.
usiness servs avail. In-rm modem
nk. Bellhops. Valet serv. Sundries.
ift shop. Free airport transporta-
on. Tennis privileges. Golf privi-
eges. Exercise equipt; sauna. Game
m. Some refrigerators. Some private

patios, balconies. Cr cds: A, D, DS,
JCB, MC, V.
🅳 ⛵ ⚹ ☃ 🏊 🐾 ☃

B&Bs/Small Inns

★★ **DICKENSON HOUSE ON
JAMES.** *1504 James St (13203).
315/423-4777; fax 315/425-1965; toll-
free 888/423-4777. www.dickenson
house.com.* 4 rms. S $99; D $115;
each addl $15; hols 2-day min. TV
avail; cable (premium), VCR avail
(movies). Complimentary full bkfst.
Restaurant nearby. Ck-out 11 am, ck-
in 3 pm. Business servs avail. In-rm
modem link. Luggage handling.
Valet serv. Concierge serv. Downhill
ski 15 mi; x-country ski 5 mi. Built
in 1924; English Tudor decor. Totally
nonsmoking. Cr cds: A, DS, MC, V.
🏊 ☃ 🏊

★ **JOHN MILTON INN.** *6578 Thompson Rd (13206). 315/463-8555; fax
315/432-9240.* 54 rms, 2 story. S $30-
$70; D $37-$70; each addl $10;
under 12 free; higher rates special
events. Crib $5. Pet accepted. TV;
cable (premium). Complimentary
continental bkfst. Restaurant adj
open 24 hrs. Ck-out 11:30 am. Business servs avail. Cr cds: A, D, DS,
MC, V.
🐾 🏊 ✈

All Suite

★★★ **EMBASSY SUITES.** *6646 Old
Collamer Rd (13057). 315/446-3200;
fax 315/437-3302; res 800/362-2779.
www.embassysuites.com.* 215 kit.
suites, 5 story. Mar-Nov: S, D $119-
$189; each addl $10; under 18 free;
higher rates university events, state
fair. Crib free. TV; cable (premium).
Heated indoor pool; whirlpool; poolside serv. Complimentary full bkfst,
coffee in rms. Restaurant 11 am-10
pm. Bar to midnight. Ck-out noon.
Coin lndry. Meeting rms. Business
servs avail. In-rm modem link. Valet
serv. Gift shop. Game rm. Airport
transportation. Exercise equipt;
sauna. Refrigerators, wet bars. Cr cds:
A, C, D, DS, MC, V.
🅳 ⛵ ⚹ ✈ ☃ 🏊

Extended Stay

★★ **RESIDENCE INN BY MAR-RIOTT.** *6420 Yorktown Cir, East Syracuse (13057). 315/432-4488; fax 315/432-1042; toll-free 800/331-3131. www.residenceinn.com.* 102 rms, 2 story. S $69-$114; D $89-$129; wkly, wkend rates; higher rates: hols, special events. Crib free. Pet accepted; $100. TV; cable (premium). Pool; whirlpool, lifeguard. Complimentary continental bkfst, coffee in rms. Restaurant nearby. Ck-out noon. Coin lndry. Meeting rms. Business servs avail. Valet serv. Downhill ski 20 mi. Exercise equipt. Health club privileges. Picnic tables. Cr cds: A, C, D, DS, JCB, MC, V.

Restaurants

★★ **COLEMAN'S.** *100 S Lowell Ave (13204). 315/476-1933.* Irish, Continental menu. Specializes in corned beef, beef stew. Own desserts. Hrs: 11:30 am-10 pm. Closed Dec 25. Res accepted. Bar 10-2 am. Lunch $4.95-$8.95, dinner $5.95-$19.95. Child's menu. Entertainment Fri, Sat. Parking. Outdoor dining. Authentic Irish pub; original tin ceiling, mahogany staircase. Family-owned since 1933. Cr cds: A, C, D, DS, MC, V.

★★ **GLEN LOCH MILL.** *4626 North St, Jamesville (13078). 315/469-6969. www.glenloch.net.* Continental menu. Specializes in seafood, veal, prime rib. Raw bar. Hrs: 5-10 pm; Sun 2-9 pm; Sun brunch 10 am-2 pm. Closed Dec 25. Res accepted. Bar 5 pm to midnight. Dinner $13.95-$20.95. Sun brunch $11.95. Child's menu. Dinner theater Fri-Sun. Parking. Outdoor dining. Glen setting, waterwheel. Converted feed mill; built in 1827. Family-owned. Cr cds: A, C, DS, MC, V.

★★★ **INN BETWEEN.** *2290 W Genessee Tpke, Camillus (13031). 315/672-3166. www.inn-between.com.* Continental menu. Specialties: roast duckling, beef Wellington. Own baking. Hrs: 5-10 pm; Sun 2-9 pm. Closed Mon; Jan 1, Dec 24, 25. Res accepted. Bar from 4 pm. Dinner $17.95-$23.95. Child's menu. Park-

ing. Herb garden. In 1880 country house; elegant country decor. Cr cds A, MC, V.

★★ **JUSTIN'S GRILL.** *6400 Yorktown Cir, East Syracuse (13057). 315/437-1461.* Hrs: 11:30 am-10 pm Fri, Sat to 11 pm. Closed Sun; Jan 1 Dec 25. Specializes in dry-aged steaks. Res accepted; required hols. Bar. Lunch $4.50-$12, dinner $11.95-$29.95. Child's menu. Parking. Antiques, objets d'art Cr cds: A C, D, DS, MC, V.

★★★ **PASCALE.** *204 W Fayette St (13202). 315/471-3040.* Continental menu. Specializes in dishes prepared by wood-burning grill, oven and rotisserie. Hrs: 11:30 am-2:30 pm, 5:30-10 pm; Sat from 5:30 pm. Closed Sun; Jan 1, Dec 25. Res accepted. Bar. Wine cellar. Lunch $6 $8, dinner $12-$23. Outdoor dining (summer). Valet parking (dinner). Original paintings. Cr cds: A, D, DS, MC, V.

★ **PHOEBE'S GARDEN CAFE.** *900 E Genessee St (13210). 315/475-5154.* Continental menu. Specializes in scroc Christopher, London broil. Own desserts. Hrs: 11:30 am-10 pm; Mon to midnight; Fri, Sat to 1 am; Sun 4-9 pm; Sun brunch 11 am-4 pm. Closed hols. Res accepted. Bar. A la carte entrees: lunch $2.95-$10.95, dinner $5.95-$20.95. Sun brunch $10.95. Turn-of-the-century building old gaslights. Cr cds: A, MC, V.

★ **PLAINVILLE FARMS.** *8450 Brewerton Rd, Cicero (13039). 315/699-3852. www.plainvillefarms.com.* Hrs: 11 am-9 pm. Closed Dec 25. American menu. Specializes in turkey, steak, seafod. Salad bar. Lunch $2.95 $6.95, dinner $7.95-$11.95. Child's menu. Colonial decor. Totally nonsmoking. Cr cds: DS, MC, V.

Unrated Dining Spots

BROOKLYN PICKLE. *2222 Burnet Ave (13206). 315/463-1851.* Deli menu. Specializes in sandwiches, soups, pickles. Hrs: 9 am-9 pm. Closed Sun; hols. Bkfst $2-$4, lunch dinner $3-$5. Parking. Outdoor din-

g. Family-owned. Totally nonsmok-
g. Cr cds: A, DS, MC, V.

ASTABILITIES. *311 S Franklin St
3202).* 315/474-1153. Continental
enu. Specializes in homemade
asta, antipasto. Hrs: 11 am-3 pm, 5-
0:30 pm; Fri, Sat to midnight.
losed Sun; hols. Bar 5 pm-mid-
ight; Fri, Sat to 2 am. A la carte
ntrees: lunch $4-$6, dinner $6-$18.
afeteria-style serv at lunch, table
erv at dinner. Outdoor dining. In
ld Labor Temple Building (1889).
xtensive Italian and domestic wine
st. Cr cds: A, D, DS, MC, V.

WIN TREES. *1100 Avery Ave
3204).* 315/468-0622. Italian, Amer
enu. Specializes in pizza, Italian
ishes. Hrs: 4-11 pm; Fri, Sat to 1 am.
losed Easter, Thanksgiving, Dec 25.
ar. Dinner $4-$22.95. Child's menu.
amily-owned. Cr cds: A, DS, MC, V.

Tarrytown

-2) *See also New York City, White
lains, Yonkers*

op 11,090 **Elev** 118 ft **Area code** 914
ip 10591

nformation Sleepy Hollow Chamber
f Commerce, 54 Main St, 10591-
660; 914/631-1705

Veb www.hudsonvalley.org

he village of Tarrytown and the
eighboring villages of Irvington and
leepy Hollow were settled by the
utch during the mid-1600s. The
ame Tarrytown was taken from the
utch word "Tarwe," meaning
heat. Here, on September 23, 1780,
he British spy Major John André was
aptured while carrying the detailed
lans for West Point given to him by
enedict Arnold. The village and the
rea were made famous by the writ-
gs of Washington Irving, particu-
arly *The Legend of Sleepy Hollow*,
om which this region takes its
ame.

What to See and Do

**The Historical Society Serving
Sleepy Hollow and Tarrytown.** Victorian house incl parlor, dining rm;
artifacts from archeological dig;
Native American rm; library, map,
and photograph collection; children's rm. (Tues-Thurs, Sat afternoons; closed hols) 1 Grove St.
Phone 914/631-8374. **FREE**

Kykuit, The Rockefeller Estate. This
six-story stone mansion was home to
three generations of the Rockefeller
family; principal first-floor rms open
to the public. Extensive gardens with
spectacular Hudson River views feature an important collection of 20th-
century sculpture acquired by
Governor Nelson A. Rockefeller; carriage barn with collection of antique
cars and horse-drawn vehicles.
Scheduled tours lasting 2½ hrs
depart approx every 15 min from
Philipsburg Manor (mid-Apr-Oct,
Mon and Wed-Sun). In Sleepy Hollow; accessible only by shuttle bus
from Philipsburg Manor. Phone
914/631-9491. ¢¢¢¢

Lyndhurst. (1838) Gothic Revival
mansion built for William Paulding,
mayor of New York City in the
1830s. Approx 67 landscaped acres
overlooking the Hudson. Contains
books, art, and furnishings. Tours.
(Mid-Apr-Oct, Tues-Sun; rest of yr,
Sat and Sun) 635 S Broadway, ½ mi S
of Tappan Zee Bridge on US 9. Phone
914/631-4481. ¢¢

Marymount College. (1907) 800
women. On 25-acre hilltop campus
overlooking the Hudson River. Tours
of campus. Phone 914/631-3200.

Music Hall Theater. (1885) One of
the oldest remaining theaters in the
county; now serves as center for the
arts. 13 Main St. Phone 914/631-
3390.

Old Dutch Church of Sleepy Hollow.
(1685) Church building of Dutch origins built on what was the Manor of
Frederick Philipse. Restored, incl a
replica of the original pulpit. Tours
by appt. (May-Oct, Tues-Sun) Broadway and Pierson (US 9). Phone
914/631-1123.

Philipsburg Manor. Colonial farm
and trading site (1720-1750); also
departure point for tour of Kykuit.
Manor house, barn, animals; restored

operating gristmill, wooden millpond bridge across Pocantico River. A 15-min film precedes tours. Reception center; exhibition gallery; museum shop; picnic area. (Mar-Dec, Mon, Wed-Sun; closed Thanksgiving, Dec 25) In Sleepy Hollow, on US 9, 2 mi N of NY Thrwy exit 9. Phone 914/631-8200. ¢¢¢

Sleepy Hollow Cemetery. Graves of Washington Irving, Andrew Carnegie, William Rockefeller. Adj to Old Dutch Church in Sleepy Hollow. Phone 914/631-0081.

Sunnyside. Washington Irving's Hudson River estate (1835-1859). Contains much of his furnishings, personal property, and library. Museum shop. Landscaped grounds; picnic area. (Mar-Dec, Mon and Wed-Sun; rest of yr, wkends; closed Jan 1, Thanksgiving, Dec 25) On W Sunnyside Ln, W of US 9, 1 mi S of NY Thrwy exit 9. Phone 914/631-8200. ¢¢¢

Van Cortlandt Manor. Post-Revolutionary War estate of prominent Colonial family. Elegantly furnished manor house; ferry house inn and kitchen building on old Albany Post Rd; "Long Walk" with flanking 18th-century gardens; picnic area. Frequent demonstrations of open-hearth cooking, brickmaking, weaving. Museum shop. (Apr-Dec, Mon and Wed-Sun; closed Thanksgiving, Dec 25) In Croton-on-Hudson, at Croton Point Ave exit on US 9, 10 mi N of NY Thrwy exit 9. Phone 914/631-8200. ¢¢¢

Special Events

Sunset Serenades. On Lyndhurst grounds. Symphony concerts (Sat). Phone 914/631-4481. July.

Heritage & Crafts Weekend. Van Cortlandt Manor. Demonstrations and hands-on exhibits of 18th-century crafts and activities. Columbus Day wkend. Phone 914/271-8981.

Candlelight Tours. At Sunnyside, Philipsburg Manor, and Van Cortland Manor. English Christmas Celebration. Phone 914/631-8200 for res (Sunnyside and Philipsburg) or 914/631-4481 for res (Lyndhurst). Dec.

Motels/Motor Lodges

★★ **COURTYARD BY MARRIOTT.** *475 White Plains Rd (10591). 914/631-1122; fax 914/631-1357; toll free 800/321-2211. www.courtyard. com.* 139 rms, 3 story, 19 suites. S, D $149; suites $164-$169; family rates; package plans. Crib free. TV; cable. Indoor pool; whirlpool. Complimentary coffee in rms. Restaurant 6:30-1 am; Sat, Sun 6:30-midnight. Rm serv Mon-Fri 5-10 pm. Bar Mon-Thurs 4-11 pm. Ck-out noon. Coin lndry. Meeting rms. Valet serv. Exercise equipt. Refrigerator in suites; microwaves avail. Cr cds: A, D, DS, MC, V.
⊠ 🏋 🏊

★★ **RAMADA INN.** *540 Saw Mill River Road, Elmsford (10523). 914/592-3300; fax 914/592-3381; res 800/272-6232. www.ramada.com.* 101 rms, 5 story. Mar-Oct: S $89-$159; D $99-$169; each addl $10; under 18 free. Crib free. Pet accepted, some restrictions. TV; cable (premium), VCR. Indoor/outdoor pool; lifeguard Complimentary coffee in rms. Restaurant 6:30 am-10 pm. Bar noon-midnight; entertainment Fri, Sat. Ck-out noon. Meeting rms. Business servs avail. Health club privileges. Cr cds: A, C, D, DS, ER, JCB, MC, V.
🐾 D ⊠ 🔧 🏊

Hotels

★★★ **DOLCE TARRYTOWN HOUSE.** *E Sunnyside Ln (10591). 914/591-8200; fax 914/591-3131. www.dolce.com.* 148 rms in five 2 story bldgs. S, D $139; each addl $15 under 12 free. Crib free. TV; cable (premium). 2 pools; 1 indoor, whirlpool. Complimentary full bkfst, coffee in rms. Dining rm 6:30 am-10 pm. Ck-out 11 am. Business center. In-rm modem link. Concierge. Bellhops. Tennis. Racquetball. Exercise rm; sauna. Balconies. 26-acre estate includes two 19th-century mansions Greek Revival King House and chateau-style Biddle House. Extensiv gardens and wooded areas. Cr cds: A C, D, DS, MC, V.
D ⊠ 🏋 🔧 🏊 🏃 ⛷

★★★ **HILTON TARRYTOWN.** *455 Broadway (10591). 914/631-5700; fax 914/631-0075. www.hilton.com.* 250 rms, 2 story. S $169-$239; D $259-

279; each addl $20; suites $200-
430; family, wkend rates. Crib free.
TV; cable (premium). 2 pools, 1
indoor; wading pool, whirlpool,
poolside serv, lifeguard. Playground.
Restaurant 6:30 am-11 pm. Bar
11:30-2 am; entertainment Fri, Sat.
Ck-out noon. Meeting rms. Business
center. In-rm modem link. Bellhops.
Airport transportation. Tennis. Exer-
ise equipt; sauna. Massage. Private
patios. Cr cds: A, C, D, DS, ER, JCB,
MC, V.

★★ MARRIOTT WESTCHESTER.
670 White Plains Rd (10591).
914/631-2200; fax 914/631-7819; res
800/228-9290. www.marriotthotels.
com. 444 rms, 10 story. S, D $205;
suites $350-$500; family, wkly rates;
wkend rates. Crib free. TV; cable
(premium), VCR avail. Indoor/out-
door pool; whirlpool. Restaurant
6:30 am-11 pm. Bar 11-3 am; entertainment. Ck-out noon. Meeting
rms. Business center. In-rm modem
link. Gift shop. Beauty shop. Exer-
ise rm; sauna. Massage. Some balconies. Luxury level. Cr cds: A, C, D,
DS, JCB, MC, V.

Resort

★★★★ THE CASTLE AT TARRY-
TOWN. 400 Benedict Ave (10591).
914/631-1980; fax 914/631-4612; toll-
free 800/616-4487. www.castleat
tarrytown.com. This elegant chateau
overlooking the Hudson River in
Westchester is a beautiful country
respite less than an hour from Manhattan. Amenities include a fine
restaurant, a marble swimming pool,
manicured grounds, and a lovely terrace on which to enjoy cocktails
while you watch the sunset. 31 rms,
4 story, 10 suites. S, D $285-$305;
each addl $50; suites $325-$625. TV;
cable (premium), VCR (movies). Outdoor pool; hot tub, poolside serv.
Restaurant (see also EQUUS). Rm serv
7 am-11 pm. Bar 11 am-10 pm. Ck-
out noon, ck-in 4 pm. Meeting rms.
Business center. In-rm modem
link/fax. Bellhops. Valet serv.
Concierge. Airport transportation
avail. Tennis privileges. 18-hole golf
privileges. X-country ski 5 mi. Exer-
ise equipt. Massage. Lawn games;
bocce, croquet. Bathrm phones,
refrigerators; some in-rm fireplaces.
Cr cds: A, C, D, MC, V.

B&B/Small Inn

★★★ ALEXANDER HAMILTON
HOUSE. 49 Van Wyck St, Croton On
Hudson (10520). 914/271-6737; fax
914/271-3927. www.alexanderhamilton
house.com. 7 rms, 3 story, 1 kit. unit.
S $100; D $125; each addl child $10,
adult $25; kit. unit $85-$95; family,
wkly rates; wkends (2-day min). TV;
cable (premium), VCR avail. Pool.
Complimentary full bkfst. Ck-out 11
am, ck-in noon. Meeting rm. In-rm
modem link. Free RR station transportation. Health club privileges. X-
country ski 2 mi. Lawn games.
Microwaves avail. Picnic tables, grills.
Victorian house (1889). Victorian
decor. Totally nonsmoking. Cr cds: A,
D, DS, MC, V.

Restaurants

★★ CARAVELA. 53 N Broadway
(10591). 914/631-1863. www.ezpages.
com. Portuguese, Brazilian cuisine.
Specialties: mariscada seafood
combo, paella Valencia, roasted baby
suckling pig. Hrs: 11:30 am-3 pm, 5-
11 pm. Closed Thanksgiving, Dec
25. Res accepted; required wkends.
Bar. Lunch $8.95-$12.95, dinner
$12.50-$23. Child's menu. Parking.
Outdoor dining. Tile floor. Cr cds: A,
DS, MC, V.

★★★ EQUUS. 400 Benedict Ave
(10591). 914/631-3646. www.castleat
tarrytown.com. Continental menu.
Specializes in beef, chicken, seafood.
Hrs: 6:30-10 am, noon-2:30 pm,
6:30-10:30 pm; Sun 6:30-10 am,
(brunch) noon-2:30 pm, 6:30-9 pm.
Res accepted. Bar. Wine cellar. Bkfst
$8-$25, lunch $23-$37, dinner $35-
$50. Sun brunch $29. Child's menu.
Valet parking. Outdoor dining. View
of river. Cr cds: A, D, MC, V.

★★ GAULIN'S. 86 E Main, Elmsford
(10523). 914/592-4213. www.town
link.com. Specializes in pasta, steak
and chops, crab cakes. Own desserts.

Hrs: 11:30 am-3:30 pm, 4-10:30 pm; Fri, Sat to 11 pm; Sun 2-9 pm. Res accepted. Bar. Lunch $5.50-$18.50, dinner $9.50-$23.50. Child's menu. Parking. Outdoor dining. Fireplace. Family-owned. Cr cds: A, C, D, DS, ER, MC, V.

D ▭

★★ **ICHI RIKI.** *1 E Main St, Elmsford (10523). 914/592-2220.* Japanese menu. Specializes in sushi. Hrs: 11:45 am-2:30 pm, 5:30-10 pm; Fri to 11 pm; Sat noon-2:30 pm, 5-11 pm; Sun 5-9:30 pm. Closed Mon; also Thanksgiving, Dec 25. Res accepted. Bar. Lunch $9-$13.25, dinner $14.25-$27.50. Parking. Japanese-style dining. Cr cds: A, C, D, ER, MC, V.

D

★★★ **MAISON LAFITTE.** *25 Studio Hill Rd, Briarcliff Manor (10510). 914/941-5787.* French continental cuisine. Specialties: crépe Riviera, veal cordon bleu, duckling a l'orange. Hrs: noon-2:30 pm, 5-10 pm; Sat 5-11 pm; Sun noon-9 pm. Res accepted; required wkends. Bar. Wine cellar. A la carte entrees: lunch $9.50-$16. Complete meals: dinner $24-$29. Child's menu. Parking. Mansion (1902) overlooks garden, Hudson River; wrought iron doors, marble terrace. Family-owned. Cr cds: A, D, MC, V.

D

★★ **RUDY'S BEAU RIVAGE.** *19 Livingston Ave, Dobbs Ferry (10522). 914/693-3192.* Continental menu. Specializes in seafood. Hrs: noon-3 pm, 5-9 pm; Fri, Sat to 10 pm; Sun noon-8 pm; Sun brunch to 3:30 pm. Closed Mon. Res accepted. Bar. Complete lunch $10, dinner $10.50-$20. Sun brunch $13.50-$16.95. Child's menu. Parking. Victorian decor. On Hudson River. Family-owned. Cr cds: A, DS, MC, V.

D

★★ **SANTA FE.** *5 Main St (10591). 914/332-4452. www.ezpages.com/santefe.* Mexican, Southwestern menu. Specializes in fajitas, taco baskets. Own desserts. Hrs: 11:30 am-10:30 pm; Fri, Sat to 11:15 pm; Sun 1-9:30 pm. Closed Easter, Thanksgiving, Dec 25. Res accepted. Bar. Lunch $3.95-$14.95, dinner $7.50-$16.95.

Child's menu. Southwestern decor; artwork. Cr cds: A, D, DS, MC, V.

D

Thousand Islands (B-5)

(Along the eastern United States-Canadian border)

This group of more than 1,800 islands on the eastern US-Canadian border, at the head of the St. Lawrence River, extends 52 miles downstream from the end of Lake Ontario. Slightly more than half the islands are in Canada. Some of them are five miles wide and extend more than 20 miles in length. These rocky slivers of land are noted for their scenery and numerous parks, including St. Lawrence Islands National Park (see CANADA). The Thousand Islands Bridge and highway (seven miles long) between the New York and Ontario mainlands crosses several of the isles and channels. Many of the Islands were settled during the early 1900s by American millionaires, whose opulent summer residences and private clubs made the area renowned throughout the world.

The Seaway Trail, a 454-mile national scenic byway, runs through the Thousand Islands region along the southeastern shore of Lake Ontario and beside the St. Lawrence area.

Uncluttered villages, boat tours, museums, walks, water sports, and abundant freshwater fishing make the Islands a popular vacation center. For details on recreational activities, contact the Thousand Islands Regional Tourism Development Corporation, PO Box 400, Alexandria Bay 13607; 315/482-2520 or 800/8-ISLAND in US and Canada.

Listed here are the towns and parks in the Thousand Islands included in *Mobil Travel Guide:* Alexandria Bay, Clayton, Ogdensburg in New York; Brockville, Gananoque, Kingston, and St. Lawrence Islands National Park in Ontario.

Ticonderoga (Lake George Area)

(C-8) *See also Crown Point, Hague*

Founded 1764 **Pop** 5,167 **Elev** 154 ft
Area code 518 **Zip** 12883
Information Ticonderoga Area Chamber of Commerce, 121 Montcalm St; 518/585-6619
Web www.ticonderogany.com

This resort area lies on the ancient portage route between Lake George and Lake Champlain. For almost two hundred years it was the site of various skirmishes and battles involving Native Americans, French, British, Canadians, Yankees, and Yorkers.

What to See and Do

Boating. Launching sites, 2 mi E on NY 74, on Lake Champlain; Black Point Rd, on Lake George.

⭐ **Fort Ticonderoga.** (1755) The fort was built in 1755 by the Quebecois, who called it Carillon, and was successfully defended by the Marquis de Montcalm against a more numerous British force in 1758. It was captured by the British in 1759 and by Ethan Allen and the Green Mountain Boys in 1775 (known as the first victory of the Revolutionary War). The stone fort was restored in 1909; the largest collection of cannons in North America is assembled on the grounds. The museum houses collections of weapons, paintings, and articles of daily life of the soldiers garrisoned here during the Seven Year and Revolutionary wars. Costumed guides give tours; cannon firings daily; fife and drum corps parade (July and Aug); special events. Museum shop; restaurant; picnic area. Scenic drive to the summit of Mt Defiance for 30-mi view. (Early May-mid-Oct, daily) 2 mi E on NY 74. Phone 518/585-2821.

Fort Ticonderoga Ferry. (May-Oct, daily) Crosses Lake Champlain to Shoreham, VT. Phone 802/897-7999.

Heritage Museum. Displays of civilian and industrial history of Ticonderoga. Children's workshop. (Late June-Labor Day, daily; Labor Day-mid-Oct, wkends) Montcalm St. Phone 518/585-2696. **Donation**

Putnam Pond State Public Campground. Boating (launch), bathhouse, lifeguards, fishing; hiking, picnicking, tent and trailer sites. (Mid-May-Labor Day) Standard fees. 6 mi W off NY 74, in Adirondack Park (see). Phone 518/585-7280.

Replica of Hancock House. The home of the Ticonderoga Historical Society is a replica of the house built for John Hancock on Beacon St in

Fort Ticonderoga

Boston. It is maintained as a museum and research library. The rms display various period furnishings as well as exhibits presenting social and civil history from the 1700s through the present. Montcalm St, at Moses Cir. Phone 518/585-7868. **Donation**

Motel/Motor Lodge

★ **CIRCLE COURT.** *440 Montcalm St W (12883).* *518/585-7660.* 14 rms. June-mid-Oct: S $51-$55; D $56-$59; each addl $5; wkly rates off-season; lower rates rest of yr. Pet accepted. TV; cable. Complimentary coffee in rms. Restaurant nearby. Ck-out 11 am. Refrigerators. Cr cds: A, MC, V.

Restaurant

★ **HOT BISCUIT DINER.** *428 Montcalm St (12883).* *518/585-3483.* Specializes in homemade biscuits, country dinner plates. Own desserts. Hrs: 6 am-8 pm; Sun 7 am-2 pm. Closed hols. No A/C. Bkfst $1.45-$4, lunch $2.50-$5.95, dinner $6.95-$13.95. Child's menu. 1950s country diner decor; relaxed atmosphere. Cr cds: A, MC, V.

Troy

(E-8) *See also Albany, Schenectady*

Settled 1786 **Pop** 49,170 **Elev** 37 ft
Area code 518

Information Rensselaer County Chamber of Commerce, 31 Second St, 12180; 518/274-7020

Web www.renscochamber.com

What to See and Do

Grave of Samuel Wilson. Meat supplier to the Army in 1812. Because the initials "US" were stamped on his sides of beef that were shipped to Union soldiers, this supplier is regarded as the original "Uncle Sam." By an act of the 87th Congress a resolution was adopted that saluted Wilson as the originator of the national symbol of "Uncle Sam." Oakwood Cemetery, Oakwood Ave.

Junior Museum. Science, natural history, Iroquois, and art exhibits; settlers' cabin, marine aquarium, animals, diorama of beaver pond environment, planetarium shows, "Please Touch" family gallery plus other permanent and changing exhibits. Birthday parties and tours (by appt). (Wed-Sun, afternoons; closed hols) 282 5th Ave. Phone 518/235-2120. ¢¢

Rensselaer County Historical Society. An 1827 town house, the Hart-Cluett Mansion, has period rms furnished with decorative and fine arts; Troy stoves and stoneware. Research library, museum shop. Directions for walking tour of downtown area can also be obtained here. (Tues-Sat; closed hols and Dec 23-Jan 31) 57-59 2nd St. Phone 518/272-7232. ¢¢

Rensselaer Polytechnic Institute. (1824) 6,000 students. Tours begin at Admissions Office in Admissions and Financial Aid Building (Sept-Apr, Mon-Sat; rest of yr, Mon-Fri). 15th St, ¼ mi S off NY 7. Phone 518/276-6216.

Riverspark Visitor Center. Offers visitor information, hands-on exhibits, slide presentation. Driving and walking tour information avail. (Tues-Sat) 251 River St. Phone 518/270-8667. **FREE**

Russell Sage College. (1916) 1,000 women. Established by Margaret Olivia Slocum Sage. Campus tours. Gallery features student art work and changing exhibits. The movie *The Age of Innocence* was filmed in part in the historic brownstones on campus. 45 Ferry St, at 2nd St. Phone 518/244-2214.

Troy Savings Bank Music Hall. (1875) Victorian showplace in Italian Renaissance building. Presents a wide variety of concerts. Tours by appt (Sept-May). State and 2nd St. Phone 518/273-0038.

Special Event

Stars and Stripes Riverfront Festival. Concerts, fireworks, carnival rides, military equipt displays, arts and crafts, food. Phone 518/458-0547. Mid-June.

Motel/Motor Lodge

★ **SUSSE CHALET INN.** *124 Troy Rd, East Greenbush (12061). 518/477-7984; fax 518/477-2382.* 105 rms, 4 story. May-Aug: S $58.70; D $65.70; each addl $3; lower rates rest of yr. Crib free. TV; cable (premium). Pool. Complimentary continental bkfst. Restaurant adj. Ck-out 11 am. Coin ndry. Business servs avail. Sundries. Cr cds: A, C, D, DS, MC, V.

D ⊠ ⊠ 🔥

Restaurants

★ ★ **CAPE HOUSE.** *254 Broadway (12180). 518/274-0167.* Specializes in mesquite swordfish, broiled seafood platter, fresh salmon. Hrs: 11:30 am-2 pm, 5-10 pm; Fri, Sat to 11 pm; Sun 3-9 pm. Closed Mon; hols. Res accepted. Bar to midnight. Lunch $3.50-$5.95, dinner $10.95-$22.95. Built 1871; New England decor. Cr cds: A, C, D, DS, ER, MC, V.

D

★ ★ ★ **TAVERN AT STERUP SQUARE.** *2113 NY 7 (12180). 518/663-5800.* Continental menu. Specializes in fresh seafood, veal, chicken. Hrs: 11 am-11 pm; Sun brunch 10 am-2 pm. Closed Dec 25. Res accepted. Bar. Lunch $7.95-$18.95, dinner $11.95-$37.95. Sun brunch $17.95. Child's menu. Outdoor dining. Modeled after Sterup Square in Sterup, Germany. Cr cds: A, D, DS, MC, V.

D ⊰

★ ★ ★ **VAN RENSSELAER ROOM.** *2113 NY 7 (12180). 518/663-5800.* French, American menu. Specialties: Dover sole, veal Wellington, Birds of a feather. Hrs: 5-11 pm. Closed Dec 25. Res required. Bar. Wine cellar. A la carte entrees: dinner $22.95-$35.95. Prix fixe: dinner $50-$100. Own baking, pastas. Classical music wkends. Valet parking. Formal, elegant dining rm; ice sculptures. Jacket. Totally nonsmoking. Cr cds: A, C, D, DS, ER, MC, V.

D SC

Tupper Lake

(B-7) *See also Lake Placid, Long Lake, Saranac Lake*

Settled 1890 **Pop** 3,935 **Elev** 1,600 ft
Area code 518 **Zip** 12986
Information Chamber of Commerce of Tupper Lake and Town of Altamont, 60 Park St; 518/359-3328 or 888/TUP-LAKE
Web www.tupperlakeinfo.com

In the heart of the Adirondack resort country and surrounded by lakes, rivers, and mountains, Tupper Lake offers hunting, fishing, boating, mountain climbing, skiing, camping, snowmobiling, golf, tennis, and mountain biking amid magnificent scenery.

What to See and Do

Boating. State launching sites on NY 30, S of town, and on the Raquette River, via NY 3, 30. **FREE**

Camping. Fish Creek Pond State Public Campground. Boating (rentals, launch), swimming, bathhouse, lifeguards, fishing; hiking, tent and trailer sites, picnicking. (Apr-Nov) 12 mi E on NY 30, in Adirondack Park (see). Phone 518/891-4560. **Rollins Pond State Public Campground.** 288 campsites, most on waterfront. Same activities as Fish Creek. (Mid-May-early Sept) 12 mi E on NY 30, use Fish Creek entrance. Phone 518/891-3239. **Lake Eaton State Public Campground.** 135 campsites, half on waterfront. Boating (ramp, rentals), swimming, bathhouse, lifeguards, fishing. Fee for some activities. (Mid-May-early Sept) 20 mi S on NY 30. Phone 518/624-2641.

Historic Beth Joseph Synagogue. Built in 1905, this is the oldest synagogue in the Adirondacks and the only synagogue outside of New York City listed in The Register of New York State Historic Buildings. All fixtures and furnishings are the original contents of the building; the two stained-glass rose windows have been restored. (June-Sept, daily and hols; limited hrs) Lake St. Phone 518/359-7229. **Donation**

Raquette River Outfitters. Canoe and kayak outfitting, sales, and rentals in the Adirondack Mtns; guided tours. Contact Box PO 653. Phone 518/359-3228.

Special Events

Flatwater Weekend. Annual canoe races. Mid-June. Phone 888/887-5253.

Woodsmen's Days. Second wkend July. Phone 518/359-9444.

Tinman Triathlon. Swimming, biking, running. Mid-July. Phone 518/359-3328.

Motels/Motor Lodges

★ **SHAHEEN'S.** *314 Park St (12986). 518/359-3384; fax 518/359-3384; toll-free 800/474-2445. www.shaheens motel.com.* 31 rms, 15 A/C, 2 story. July, Aug: S $41-$67; D $45-$71; suites $74-$84; each addl $5; family units up to 6, lower rates rest of yr. Crib $5. TV; cable (premium). Pool. Playground. Complimentary continental bkfst, coffee in rms. Restaurant opp 3-10 pm. Ck-out 11 am. Miniature golf. Downhill/x-country ski 5 mi. Refrigerators. Balconies. Picnic tables. Cr cds: A, C, D, DS, MC, V.

★ **SUNSET PARK.** *71 Demars Blvd (12986). 518/359-3995; fax 518/359-9577.* 11 rms, 4 kits. No A/C. Mid-June-Oct: S $42-$48; D $44-$54; each addl $4; kit. units $56-$62; lower rates rest of yr. Crib free. Pet accepted. TV; cable. Complimentary coffee in rms. Restaurant nearby. Ck-out 11 am. Downhill ski 3 mi. Lawn games. Picnic tables, grills. On Tupper Lake. Private sand beach, dock for small boats. Cr cds: A, DS, MC, V.

★ **TUPPER LAKE MOTEL.** *255 Park St (12986). 518/359-3381; fax 518/359-8549; toll-free 800/944-3585. www.tupperlakemotel.com.* 18 rms. No A/C. Late June-mid-Oct: S $50; D $55-$63; each addl $5; lower rates rest of yr. Crib $5. TV; cable (premium). Pool. Complimentary continental bkfst, coffee in rms. Restaurant nearby. Ck-out 11 am. In-rm modem link. Downhill ski 5 mi;

x-country ski 10 mi. Refrigerators. Cr cds: A, DS, MC, V.

Cottage Colony

★ **PINE TERRACE MOTEL & RESORT.** *1616 State Rte 30 (12986). 518/359-9258; fax 518/359-8340.* 18 cottage units, 11 kits. No A/C. S $45; D $65; each addl $5; kit. units $250-$450/wk; family rates. Crib avail. Pet accepted. TV; cable. Pool; wading pool. Ck-out 11 am. Lighted tennis. Lawn games. Refrigerators. Boats avail. Picnic tables, grills. Private beach opp. View of lake, mountains. Cr cds: A, DS, MC, V.

Utica

(D-6) *See also Herkimer, Ilion, Oneida, Rome*

Pop 60,651 **Elev** 423 ft **Area code** 315

Information Oneida County Convention & Visitors Bureau, PO Box 551, 13503; 315/724-7221 or stop at the Information Booth, just off NY Thrwy exit 31

Web www.oneidacountycvb.com

Near the western end of the Mohawk Trail, Utica has been a manufacturing and trading center since its early days. By 1793 there was stagecoach service from Albany. The opening of the Erie Canal brought new business. The first Woolworth "five and dime" was opened here in 1879.

What to See and Do

Children's Museum. Hands-on exhibits teaching history, natural history, and science. Iroquois exhibit incl section of Long House; local history displays; dress-up area; Playspace; outdoor railroad display; special wkend programs. (July-Labor Day, Tues-Sun; rest of yr, Wed-Sun; closed hols) 311 Main St. Phone 315/724-6128. ¢¢

F. X. Matt Brewing Company. Incl plant tour, trolley ride, and visit to the 1888 Tavern. Free beer or root beer. (Daily; closed hols) Children only with adult. Court and Varick sts. Phone 315/732-0022. ¢¢

Munson-Williams-Proctor Institute. Museum of Art has collection of 18th-20th-century American and European paintings and sculpture; European, Japanese, and American prints; American decorative arts. Adj is **Fountain Elms,** a Victorian house museum, with five mid-19th-century rms; changing exhibits. (Tues-Sun; closed hols) Also **School of Art Gallery** featuring exhibits by visiting artists, faculty, and students. (Mon-Sat; closed hols) 310 Genesee St. Phone 315/797-0000. **FREE**

Oneida County Historical Society. Museum traces Utica and Mohawk Valley history; reference library (fee); changing exhibits. (Tues-Fri; closed hols) 1608 Genesee St. Phone 315/735-3642. **FREE**

Utica College of Syracuse University. (1946) 2,200 students. Campus tour (free). 1600 Burrstone Rd. Phone 315/792-3006.

Utica Zoo. More than 250 exotic and domestic animals. Children's Zoo (Apr-Oct, daily; incl with admission). Snack bar, picnicking. (All yr, daily) Steele Hill Rd. Phone 315/738-0472. ¢¢

Motels/Motor Lodges

★★ **BEST WESTERN GATEWAY INN.** *175 N Genesee St (13502). 315/732-4121; fax 315/797-8265; res 800/780-7234. www.bestwestern.com.* 89 rms, 1-2 story. S $79-$129; D $79-$149; each addl $10; under 12 free; higher rates special events. Crib free. Pet accepted, some restrictions. TV; cable. Complimentary continental bkfst. Coffee in rms. Restaurant adj 10-2 am. Ck-out 11 am. Business servs avail. Sundries. Gift shop. Exercise equipt. Game rm. Refrigerators avail. Cr cds: A, C, D, DS, MC, V.
🄳 🐾 🕅 🔌 🔥

★ **COUNTRY MOTEL.** *1477 Herkimer Rd (13502). 315/732-4628; fax 315/733-8801.* 25 rms. S $32-$36; D $42-$55; each addl $3; higher rates special events. Crib $6. TV; cable. Complimentary coffee in rms. Restaurant nearby. Ck-out 11 am. X-country ski 3 mi. Refrigerators avail.

Picnic tables, grills. Cr cds: A, DS, MC, V.
🄳 🐾 🔌 🔥

★★ **HOLIDAY INN.** *1777 Burrstone Rd, New Hartford (13413). 315/797-2131; fax 315/797-5817; toll-free 800/465-4329. www.holiday-inn.com.* 100 rms, 2 story. S, D $97-$129; under 18 free; higher rates some wkends. Crib free. Pet accepted. TV; cable. Pool; whirlpool. Coffee in rms. Restaurant 6:30 am-10 pm. Bar 4 pm-2 am; entertainment Fri, Sat. Ck-out noon. Coin lndry. Meeting rms. Business servs avail. In-rm modem link. Valet serv. Sundries. Gift shop. Exercise equipt. Game rm. Refrigerators avail. Cr cds: A, C, D, DS, JCB, MC, V.
🄳 🕹 🛏 🕅 🔌 🔥

★★ **RAMADA INN.** *141 New Hartford St, New Hartford (13413). 315/735-3392; fax 315/738-7642. www.ramada.com.* 106 rms, 2 story. S $59-$96; suites $125-$155; under 18 free; wkend rates; higher rates special events. Crib $10. TV; cable. Complimentary coffee in rms. Restaurant 6:30 am-10 pm. Bar to midnight; entertainment wkends. Ck-out noon. Meeting rms. Business servs avail. In-rm modem link. Valet serv. Sundries. Indoor tennis privileges. Exercise equipt. Health club privileges. Heated pool; lifeguard. Microwaves avail. Totally nonsmoking. Cr cds: A, D, DS, MC, V.
🄳 🤾 🛏 🕅 🔌 🔥 **SC**

★ **RED ROOF INN.** *20 Weaver St (13502). 315/724-7128; fax 315/724-7158; res 800/733-7663. www.redroof.com.* 112 rms, 2 story. S $39.99-$59.99; D $47.99-$78.99; each addl $7-$9; under 18 free. Crib free. Pet accepted, some restrictions. TV; cable (premium). Complimentary coffee in lobby. Restaurant nearby. Ck-out noon. Business servs avail. Sundries. Cr cds: A, C, D, DS, MC, V.
🐾 🔌 🔥

Hotel

★★★ **RADISSON HOTEL.** *200 Genesee St (13502). 315/797-8010; fax 315/797-1490; toll-free 800/333-3333. www.radisson.com.* 158 rms, 6 story. S, D $99-$124; suites $175; under 18 free; wkend rates. Crib free. Pet accepted. TV; cable. Indoor pool; life-guard. Coffee in rms. Restaurant 6:30 am-2 pm, 5-10 pm; Sun 7 am-2 pm, 5-9 pm. Bar 3 pm-2 am; entertainment Fri-Sat. Ck-out noon. Meeting rms. Business servs avail. In-rm modem link. Shopping arcade. Gift shop. Barber, beauty shop. Garage parking. Downhill ski 10 mi; x-country ski 5 mi. Exercise rm. Game rm. Some refrigerators. Cr cds: A, C, D, DS, MC, V.

B&B/Small Inn

★ **SUGARBUSH BED & BREAK-FAST.** *8451 Old Poland Rd, Barneveld (13304). 315/896-6860; fax 315/896-8828; toll-free 800/582-5845. www. borg.com/~jmahanna.* 6 air-cooled rms, 3 share bath, 2 story, 1 suite. No rm phones. S $55; D $90; suites $125-$135. Crib $10. TV in some rms, common rm; cable (premium), VCR avail (movies). Complimentary full bkfst. Ck-out 10:30 am, ck-in 2:30 pm. X-country ski on site. Lawn games. Built in early 1800s as a school for boys. Totally nonsmoking. Cr cds: A, DS, MC, V.

Restaurants

★★ **HOOK, LINE & SINKER.** *8471 Seneca Tpke, New Hartford (13413). 315/732-3636.* Specializes in seafood, steak, pasta. Salad bar. Own soups, desserts. Hrs: 11:30 am-3 pm, 4:30-10 pm; Fri, Sat to 11 pm; Sun 1-9 pm. Closed Thanksgiving, Dec 25. Res accepted; required hols. Bar to 2 am. Lunch $4.95-$7.95, dinner $7.95-$24.95. Child's menu. Entertainment Fri. Cape Cod decor. Cr cds: A, C, D, DS, ER, MC, V.

★★★ **HORNED DORSET.** *NY 8, Leonardsville (13364). 315/855-7898.* French menu. Specialties: boneless loin of lamb with black currant sauce, veal Horned Dorset, salmon en cro°te. Hrs: 6-9 pm; Sun 3-7:30 pm. Closed Mon; Jan 1, Dec 25. Res accepted. Serv bar. Wine cellar. Dinner $20-$30. Classical guitarist wkends. Former 19th-century grocery store with Palladian windows. 3 dining rms; Victorian decor, many antiques, view of garden. Recited

menu. Overnight stays avail. Cr cds: A, MC, V.

★ **KITLAS.** *2242 Broad St, Frankfort (13340). 315/732-9616.* Specializes in fresh seafood, babyback ribs, ethnic specials. Hrs: 11:30 am-2 pm, 4:30-8:30 pm; Mon to 2 pm. Closed Sun; hols. Res accepted. Bar. Lunch $3.95-$5.95, dinner $9.50-$13.95. Child's menu. Family-owned. Cr cds: A, DS, MC, V.

Victor

(D-4) *See also Canandaigua, Palmyra, Rochester*

Pop 2,433 **Elev** 587 ft **Area code** 716 **Zip** 14564

What to See and Do

Valentown Museum. A three-story structure built as a community center and shopping plaza in 1879. General store, harness maker and cobbler shops, bakery, schoolrm; Civil War artifacts. (May-Oct, Wed-Sun) 4 mi N on NY 96 to Valentown Sq, in Fishers; ¼ mi N of I-90, exit 45, opp Eastview Mall. Phone 716/924-2645. ¢

Motels/Motor Lodges

★ **EXIT 45.** *7463 NY 96 (14564). 716/924-2121; fax 716/924-0468.* 34 rms. S $45-$58; D $58-$79; each addl $5; wkly rates (winter only). TV; cable (premium). Restaurant adj 6 am-midnight. Bar from 11 am. Ck-out 11 am. Business servs avail. Rural setting. Cr cds: A, DS, MC, V.

★★ **HAMPTON INN & SUITES.** *7637 NY 96 (14564). 716/924-4400; fax 716/924-4478; toll-free 800/426-7866. www.hamptoninn.com.* 123 rms, 3 story, 55 kit. units. May-Oct: S $95-$99; D $105-$109; kit. units $99-$106; under 18 free; lower rates rest of yr. Crib free. TV; cable (premium), VCR avail. Complimentary continental bkfst, coffee in rms. Restaurant nearby 11-1 am. Ck-out noon. Meeting rms. Business servs avail. In-rm

modem link. Valet serv. Gift shop.
Coin lndry. Exercise equipt. Indoor
pool; whirlpool. Some in-rm
whirlpools, fireplaces. Grills. Cr cds:
A, C, D, DS, MC, V.

Hotel

★★ **SUNRISE HILL INN.** *6108
Loomis Rd, Farmington (14425).
716/924-2131; fax 716/924-1876; toll-
free 800/333-0536.* 89 rms, 2 story.
Mid-June-mid-Sept: S $35-$60; $43-
$68; each addl $8; suites $85; under
18 free; lower rates rest of yr. Crib
free. Pet accepted, some restrictions.
TV; cable, VCR avail (movies). Pool.
Bar 5-10 pm Wed-Sat. Ck-out 11 am.
Meeting rms. Business servs avail. In-
rm modem link. Valet serv Mon-Sat.
Health club privileges. Some balconies. Countryside view. Near race
track. Cr cds: A, C, D, DS, ER, JCB,
MC, V.

Restaurant

★★★ **VICTOR GRILLING COM-
PANY.** *75 Coville St (14564).
716/924-1760. www.victorgrilling.com.*
Specialties: Black Angus rib-eye
steak, pasta with shrimp and sun-
dried tomatoes. Hrs: 5:30-10 pm; Fri,
Sat to 10:30 pm; Sun 4-9 pm. Closed
Mon; hols; also 1 wk Jan. Res
accepted Fri, Sat. Bar. Dinner $14-
$24.95. Large microbrewery beer
selection. Cr cds: A, D, DS, MC, V.

Warrensburg

*(C-8) See also Lake George Village, Lake
Luzerne*

Pop 4,255 **Elev** 687 ft **Area code** 518
Zip 12885

Information Chamber of Commerce,
3847 Main St; 518/623-2161

Web www.warrensburgchamber.com

Warrensburg, near Lake George, is an
old-time village in the heart of a
year-round tourist area and is a cen-

ter for campgrounds, dude ranches,
and antique shops. Activities include
canoeing, fishing, golf, swimming,
tubing, skiing, horseback riding, and
biking, among others. The fall foliage
is beautiful here.

What to See and Do

Skiing.Hickory Ski Center. Two
Pomalifts, T-bar, rope tow; school,
rentals; snack bar. Longest run 1¼
mi; vertical drop 1,230 ft. (Dec-Apr,
Sat, Sun, hol wks) 3 mi W on NY
418. Phone 518/623-2825. ¢¢¢¢

**Warrensburg Museum of Local His-
tory.** Exhibits detail the history of
Warrensburg from the time it became
a town to the present. Artifacts of
livelihood, business, industry, and
general living of the residents. (July-
Aug, Tues-Sat) 47 Main St. Phone
518/623-2928. **FREE**

Special Events

Arts & Crafts Festival. Main St and
Stewart Farrar Ave. July 4 wkend.
Phone 518/623-2161.

**World's Largest Garage Sale and
Foliage Festival.** All of Main St and
side sts. First wkend Oct. Phone
518/623-2161.

B&B/Small Inn

★★★ **FRIENDS LAKE INN.** *963
Friends Lake Rd, Chestertown (12817).
518/494-4751; fax 518/494-4616.
www.friendslake.com.* 16 rms, 3 story.
S $190-$330; D $235-$375; MAP: S,
D $175-$325; ski, rafting packages.
TV rm; cable (premium), VCR
(movies). Outdoor whirlpool. Restaurant (see FRIENDS LAKE INN). Ck-
out 11 am, ck-in 2 pm. Meeting rm.
Business servs avail. X-country ski
on site; rentals, instructor. Hiking
trails. Restored Adirondack Inn
(1860). Library. Beach. Cr cds: A, C,
D, MC, V.

Restaurants

★★ **FRIENDS LAKE INN.** *963
Friends Lake Rd, Chestertown (12817).
518/494-4751. www.friendslake.com.*
Specializes in veal, seafood, duck.
Hrs: 8-10:30- am, 5-9 pm; Fri, Sat to
10 pm; Sun 8 am-12:30, 4-9 pm. Bar.

A la carte entrees: bkfst $3.25-$5.95, dinner $17-$32. Built 1860. Cr cds: A, D, MC, V.

D

★★★ **MERRILL MAGEE HOUSE.** *3 Hudson St (12885). 518/623-2449. www.merrillmageehouse.com.* Specialties: rack of lamb, salmon Wellington, crisp roast duckling. Hrs: 5-9:30 pm; Sun 5-8 pm, Closed Dec 25. Res accepted. Bar. Wine list. Dinner $14.50-$23.95. Elegant dining in Victorian atmosphere. Overnight stays avail. Cr cds: A, C, D, DS, MC, V.

D

Waterloo

(D-4) *See also Canandaigua, Geneva, Seneca Falls*

Settled 1800 **Pop** 7,866 **Elev** 455 ft
Area code 315 **Zip** 13165

The Church of Jesus Christ of Latter-day Saints (Mormons) was founded by Joseph Smith and five other men in a small log cabin here on April 6, 1830. The site is commemorated at the Peter Whitmer Farm.

What to See and Do

McClintock House. (1835) Home of the McClintocks, a Quaker family who were active in the planning of the first Women's Rights Convention. Tour (Sat, Sun). 14 E Williams St. Phone 315/568-2991. ¢

Peter Whitmer Farm. This site is where the Church of Jesus Christ of Latter-day Saints (Mormons) was organized in 1830; period furnishings. Tours (20 to 30 min), video presentations. (Daily) 3½ mi S via NY 96. Phone 315/539-2552. **FREE**

Terwilliger Museum. Historical museum housing collections dating from 1875; Native American displays; authentic full-size vehicles and a replica of a general store provides a glimpse of life as it was in the 1920s. Also five rms, each furnished to depict a specific era. (Tues-Fri, afternoons) 31 E Williams St. Phone 315/539-0533. **Donation**

Waterloo Memorial Day Museum. Mementos of Civil War, WWI, WWII, the Korean conflict, Vietnam, and the first Memorial Day in this 20-rm mansion furnished in 1860-1870 period. (July-Labor Day, Mon and Thurs afternoons, also Sat late morning-early afternoon; closed July 4) Under 12 yrs only with adult. 35 E Main St. Phone 315/539-9611. **Donation**

Motel/Motor Lodge

★★ **HOLIDAY INN.** *2468 Mound Rd (13165). 315/539-5011; fax 315/539-8355; toll-free 800/465-4329. www.holidayinn.com.* 148 rms, 2 story. June-mid-Oct: S, D $79-$150; higher rates special events; under 19 free; package plans; lower rates rest of yr. Crib free. Pet accepted. TV; cable (premium), VCR avail. Heated pool; whirlpool. Coffee in rms. Restaurant 6:30 am-10 pm. Bar 11:30-1 am; Fri, Sat to 2 am; Sun to midnight; entertainment Fri, Sat. Ck-out noon. Coin lndry. Meeting rms. Business servs avail. In-rm modem link. Valet serv (Mon-Fri). Tennis. Exercise equipt; sauna. Cr cds: A, DS, MC, V.

D ➶ ⚓ ⛱ ⛵ ☀ ⛷ ⛳ ♿

Watertown

(C-5) *See also Clayton (Thousand Islands)*

Settled 1799 **Pop** 26,705 **Elev** 478 ft
Area code 315 **Zip** 13601
Information Chamber of Commerce, 230 Franklin St; 315/788-4400
Web www.watertownny.com

Watertown lies along the Black River, 11 miles east of Lake Ontario and 22 miles south of the St. Lawrence. Within the city, the river falls more than 100 feet, providing an opportunity for whitewater rafting. During a county fair here in 1878 young Frank W. Woolworth originated the idea of the five-and-ten-cent store.

What to See and Do

American Maple Museum. Displays of maple syrup production; equipt; history of maple production in North America; lumberjack display. (July-mid-Sept, Mon-Sat; mid-May-

June and mid-Sept-mid-Oct, Mon, Fri, Sat; mid-Oct-Nov, by appt) 30 mi SE via NY 12 and NY 812, on Main St in Croghan. Phone 315/346-1107. ¢

Jefferson County Historical Society Museum. Paddock mansion (1876); Victorian mansion with period rms, military rms; Native American artifacts, changing and regional history exhibits; Victorian garden. (Mon-Fri; closed hols) 228 Washington St. Phone 315/782-3491. **FREE**

Long Point State Park. Fishing, boating (launch, dock); picnicking, tent and trailer sites. (May-mid-Sept) Standard fees. NW on Chaumont Bay, via NY 12E, 8 mi W of Three Mile Bay. Phone 315/649-5258.

Roswell P. Flower Memorial Library. Neo-Classic marble building houses murals of local history, French furniture; miniature furniture; geneology and local history. (Mid-June-Labor Day, Mon-Fri; rest of yr, Mon-Sat; closed hols) 229 Washington St. Phone 315/788-2352. **FREE**

Sci-Tech Center. Hands-on science and technology museum for families. More than 40 exhibits, incl laser display and discovery boxes; science store. (Tues-Sat; closed hols) 154 Stone St. Phone 315/788-1340. ¢

Special Event

Jefferson County Fair. Agriculture, livestock, art exhibits; held annually for more than 150 yrs. Mid-July. Phone 315/782-8612.

Motels/Motor Lodges

★★ **BEST WESTERN CARRIAGE HOUSE.** *300 Washington St (13601). 315/782-8000; fax 315/786-2097; res 800/528-1234. www.bestwesternwater townny.com.* 160 rms, 3 story. S $72-$82; D $39-$89; each addl $5; suites $75-$140; under 19 free. Crib free. TV; cable. Indoor pool; poolside serv, sauna. Restaurant 6:30 am-10 pm. Bar 11-2 am; entertainment Mon-Sat. Ck-out noon. Meeting rms. Business servs avail. Bellhops. Valet serv. Barber, beauty shop. Cr cds: A, D, DS, MC, V.
D 🌊 🏕 🐾 SC

★ **DAVIDSON'S MOTEL.** *26177 NY 3 (13601). 315/782-3861; fax 315/786-0599.* 20 rms. May-Sept: S, D $35-$49; each addl $4; lower rates rest of yr. Crib $5. TV; cable (premium). Heated pool. Complimentary coffee in lobby. Ck-out 10 am. Picnic table, grills. Shaded grounds; nature walk. Near Fort Drum. Cr cds: A, DS, MC, V.
🌊 🏕 🐾

★ **DAYS INN.** *1142 Arsenal St (13601). 315/782-2700; fax 315/782-9877.* 135 units, 6 story. Mid-May-mid-Oct: S $55-$75; D $60-$80; each addl $5; suites $99; lower rates rest of yr. Crib avail. TV; cable (premium). Indoor pool. Rm serv 6 am-11 pm. Bar. Ck-out 11 am. Meeting rms. Business servs avail. Exercise equipt. Refrigerator, microwave in suites. Cr cds: A, C, D, DS, ER, JCB, MC, V.
D 🐾 🌊 🏋 🏕 🐾

★★ **THE INN.** *1190 Arsenal St (13601). 315/788-6800; fax 315/788-5366; toll-free 800/799-5224.* 96 rms, 2 story. May-Oct: S $48-$56; D $60-$70; each addl $6; under 18 free; lower rates rest of yr. Pet accepted. TV; cable (premium). Pool. Ck-out noon. Coin lndry. Meeting rms. Game rm. Private patios, balconies. Health club privileges. Cr cds: A, C, D, DS, MC, V.
D 🐾 🏋 🔥 🌊 🏕 🐾

★ **NEW PARROT MOTEL.** *19325 Outer Washington St (13601). 315/788-5080; fax 315/788-5080; toll-free 800/479-9889.* 26 rms. June-Oct: S $34-$36; D $45-$55; each addl $5; family rates off-season; lower rates rest of yr. Crib $5. Pet accepted; $3. TV; cable. Indoor pool. Restaurant adj 6 am-9 pm. Ck-out 11 am. Picnic tables, grills. Cr cds: A, D, DS, MC, V.
🐾 🌊 🐾

★★ **RAMADA INN.** *6300 Arsenal St (13601). 315/788-0700; fax 315/785-9875; toll-free 800/272-6232. www. ramada.com.* 145 rms, 4 story. S, D $49-$80; each addl $6; suites $95; under 18 free; package plans. Crib free. TV; cable (premium). Pool. Restaurants 6:30-11 am, 11:30 am-11 pm; Fri to 1 am; Sat 8-1 am; Sun 8 am-11 pm. Bar 11:30-2 am; entertainment. Ck-out noon. Meeting rms. Business servs avail. In-rm modem link. Sundries. Free airport

transportation. Exercise equipt. Cr
cds: A, D, DS, MC, V.

D 🛗 ➰ 🧍 ✈ 🏊 🔥 SC

★ **REDWOOD MOTOR LODGE.**
*24098 Gifford St (13601). 315/788-
2850.* 27 rms, 2 story. Some rm
phones. May-Sept: S $34; D $42;
each addl $3; under 12 free; wkly
rates off-season; lower rates rest of yr.
Crib $2. TV; cable. Pool. Ck-out 11
am. Cr cds: A, MC, V.

➰ 🏊 🔥

★ **WATERTOWN ECONO LODGE.**
*1030 Arsenal St (13601). 315/782-
5500; fax 315/782-7608; toll-free
800/553-2666. www.econolodge.com.*
60 rms, 2 story. May-Sep: S $59.95-
$64.95; D $69.95-$74.95; each addl
$5; under 18 free; lower rates rest of
yr. Crib free. Pet accepted; $5. TV;
cable (premium). Indoor pool. Complimentary continental bkfst in
lobby. Restaurant adj 11 am-9 pm.
Ck-out 11 am. Coin lndry. Sundries.
Refrigerators. Picnic tables, grills. Cr
cds: A, D, DS, MC, V.

🦐 ➰ 🔥

Restaurants

★ **BENNY'S STEAK HOUSE.** *1050
Arsenal Rd (13601). 315/788-4110.*
Italian, American menu. Specializes
in steak, fresh seafood. Own pasta,
desserts. Hrs: 11 am-11 pm; Sun from
noon. Res accepted. Bar 9-2 am. A la
carte entrees: lunch $2.50-$7.50, dinner $6.95-$21. Child's menu. Entertainment Fri, Sat. Family-owned. Cr
cds: A, C, D, DS, MC, V.

D SC ➡

★ ★ **PARTRIDGE BERRY INN.**
*26561 NY 3 (13601). 315/788-4610.
www.partridgeberryinn.com.* Continental menu. Specializes in prime rib,
veal, fresh fish. Hrs: 6-9 pm; Sun
11:30 am-2:30 pm, 4-8 pm; Sun
brunch to 2:30 pm. Res accepted.
Bar. Dinner $7.95-$29.95. Sun
brunch $12.95. Child's menu. Rustic
decor; 3 large fireplaces. Cr cds: A,
MC, V.

D SC ➡

Watkins Glen

(E-4) *See also Corning, Ithaca, Penn Yan*

Pop 2,149 **Elev** 550 ft **Area code** 607
Zip 14891
Information Schuyler County Cham-
ber of Commerce, 100 N Franklin St;
607/535-4300 or 800/607-4552
Web www.schuylerny.com

Watkins Glen is situated at the
southern end of Seneca Lake, where
the famous tributary gorge for which
it is named emerges in the middle of
the town. Several estate wineries
offering tours and tastings are
located on the southern shores of the
lake, near town.

What to See and Do

Captain Bill's Seneca Lake Cruises.
Two tour boats. Sightseeing, lunch,
dinner, and cocktail cruises. (Mid-
May-mid-Oct, daily) First and
Franklin sts. Phone 607/535-4541.
¢¢¢¢

Montour Falls. Small community
with seven glens nearby; fishing for
rainbow trout in Catharine Creek.
Chequaga Falls (156 ft) plunges into
a pool beside the main street. Municipal marina, N of town, has access to
barge canal system. Trailer site (fee).
2 mi S on NY 14. Phone 607/535-
7367.

Watkins Glen State Park. Stairs and
bridges lead upward through Watkins
Glen Gorge, past the cataracts and
rapids, rising some 600 ft in 1½ mi.
Pool (mid-June-Labor Day, daily),
bathhouse; picnicking, playground,
concession, tent and trailer sites.
(Early-May-Oct) Franklin St; NY
14/414, past the lower entrance.
Phone 607/535-4511. ¢¢ On
grounds is

> **Timespell.** A sound and light show
> in the Watkins Glen Gorge. Laser
> images, panoramic sound, and spe-
> cial effects present the history of
> this majestic wonder. (Mid-May-
> mid-Oct) Phone 607/535-4960.

Winery tours. Twenty-two wineries
dot the hillsides of Seneca Lake. Follow NY 14 or NY 414 for tastings and
tours. Contact the Seneca Lake Wine
Trail for more information. Incl

Finger Lakes

Glenora Wine Cellar. Winery on Seneca Lake; tastings. (Daily) N on NY 14, in Dundee. Phone 607/243-5511. **FREE**

Special Event

Watkins Glen International. 4 mi SW on County 16. IMSA and NASCAR Winston Cup racing. Phone 607/535-2481. Late May-Sept.

Hotel

★ **BELLEVUE.** *3812 NY 14 (14891). 607/535-4232; fax 607/535-9154.* 7 rms, 5 cottages, 1 kit. unit. May-mid-Nov: S, D $59-$75; each addl $10; cottages $49-$65; kit. unit $75-$85; wkly rates. Closed rest of yr. TV. Complimentary continental bkfst. Restaurant nearby. Ck-out 11 am. Refrigerators. Picnic tables, grills. Overlooking lake. Cr cds: A, DS, MC, V.

Restaurants

★ ★ **CASTEL GRISCH.** *3380 County Rd 28 (14891). 607/535-9614. www. fingerlakes-ny.com/castelgrisch.* Alpine, American menu. Specializes in Bavarian dishes, veal, steak. Hrs: 11 am-9 pm; Sun brunch to 2 pm. Closed Jan-

Mar. Res accepted. Wine. A la carte entrees: lunch $3.95-$13.95, dinner $11.95-$21.95. German-Swiss buffet (Fri): dinner $17.95. Sun brunch $13.95. Terrace dining with view of lake. Winery on premises; gift shop. Guest rms avail. Overlooks Seneca Lake. Cr cds: A, DS, MC, V.

★ ★ **FRANKLIN STREET GRILLE.** *413 N Franklin St (14891). 607/535-2007.* Specialties: London broil, vegan specials. Hrs: 11:30-10 pm. Closed Thanksgiving, Dec 25. Res accepted. Lunch $5.95-$7.95, dinner $7.95-$24.95. Child's menu. Outdoor dining. Family-owned. Cr cds: A, MC, V.

★ ★ **SEASONS.** *108 N Franklin St (14891). 607/535-4619.* Specializes in char-broiled steak, seafood, gourmet dinner salads. Hrs: 11 am-10 pm. Closed Dec 25. Res accepted. Bar 11-1 am; Sun noon-9 pm. Lunch $3.95-$6.95, dinner $6.95-$20.95. Child's menu. Originally a hotel (1891). Cr cds: A, MC, V.

★ ★ **WILDFLOWER CAFE.** *301 N Franklin St (14891). 607/535-9797. www.wildflowercafe.com.* Contemporary American cuisine. Specializes in fresh seafood, vegetarian dishes, sauteed dishes. Own desserts, ice cream. Hrs: 11:30 am-10 pm; Fri, Sat to 11 pm. Closed hols. Res accepted. Bar 11:30-1 am. A la carte entrees: lunch $3.95-$8.95, dinner $11.95-$22.95. Totally nonsmoking. Cr cds: MC, V.

Westbury (L.I.)

See also Garden City (L.I.), Jericho (L.I.), New York City

Pop 14,263 **Elev** 100 ft **Area code** 516 **Zip** 11590

What to See and Do

Clark Botanic Garden. The 12-acre former estate of Grenville Clark. Incl Hunnewell Rose Garden; ponds, streams; bulbs, perennials, annuals; wildflower, herb, rock, rhododendron, azalea, and daylily gardens; children's garden; groves of white pine, dogwood, and hemlock. (Daily) 193 I. U. Willets Rd, in Albertson. Phone 516/484-8600.

Old Westbury Gardens. Charles II-style mansion on 160 acres of countryside with formal gardens, allées, ponds, pools, and meadows. House has collection of 17th- and 18th-century English furniture, silver, and paintings. Walled garden, rose garden, lilac and primrose walks. (Apr-Oct, Mon, Wed-Sun; Nov, Sun; Dec, select days) 71 Old Westbury Rd, in Old Westbury. Phone 516/333-0048. ¢¢¢

Westbury Music Fair. Theater-in-the-round; musicals, concerts, children's shows. Brush Hollow Rd, between Northern State Pkwy and Jericho Tpke. Phone 516/334-0800.

Restaurants

★★ **BENNY'S.** *199 Post Ave (11590). 516/997-8111.* Northern Italian menu. Specialties: osso buco, Norwegian salmon, veal chop vadastana. Hrs: noon-3 pm, 5-10 pm; Fri, Sat to 11 pm. Closed Sun; hols; also last 2 wks Aug. Res required. A la carte

entrees: lunch $12.95-$25, dinner $10.50-$27. Parking. Formal atmosphere. Cr cds: A, D, MC, V.

★★ **CAFE BACI.** *1636 Old Country Rd (11590). 516/832-8888.* Italian, American menu. Specializes in pasta, salad, pizza. Hrs: 11:30 am-10 pm; Fri, Sat to midnight; Sun 1-10 pm. Bar. A la carte entrees: lunch, dinner $7.95-$15.95. Parking. Casual dining. Cr cds: A, MC, V.

★★ **CAFE SPASSO.** *307 Old Country Rd, Carle Place (11514). 516/333-1718.* Italian menu. Specializes in pasta, veal, pizza. Hrs: 11:30 am-10 pm; Wed, Thurs to 11 pm; Fri, Sat to midnight; Sun 1-10 pm. Closed Thanksgiving, Dec 25. Bar. A la carte entrees: lunch, dinner $8-$16. Parking. Italian-style café. Cr cds: A, C, D, MC, V.

★★ **GIULIO CESARE.** *18 Ellison Ave (11590). 516/334-2982.* Northern Italian menu. Specialties: chicken cacciatore, stuffed veal chop, pasta primavera. Hrs: noon-3 pm, 5-10 pm; Sat 5-10:30 pm. Closed Sun; hols. Res accepted. Bar. A la carte entrees: lunch, dinner $10.95-$23. Parking. Cr cds: A, D, MC, V.

★★ **RIALTO.** *586 Westbury Ave, Carle Place (11514). 516/997-5283.* Northern Italian menu. Specialties: cold antipasta, rigatoni in vodka sauce, red snapper Sorrentine. Hrs: noon-3 pm, 5-10 pm; Sat from 5 pm. Closed Sun; hols. Res accepted. Bar. A la carte entrees: lunch $8.95-$16.50, dinner $9.50-$21. Parking. Comfortable, elegant atmosphere; many antiques. Cr cds: A, D, MC, V.

★★★ **WESTBURY MANOR.** *1100 Jericho Tpke (11590). 516/333-7117.* Continental menu. Specialties: grilled fresh fish, roast rack of veal. Own baking, pasta. Hrs: noon-3 pm, 5-10:30 pm; Fri to midnight; Sat 5 pm-midnight; Sun 2:30-10 pm. Closed Dec 25. Res accepted. Bar. Wine cellar. A la carte entrees: lunch $8.95-$17.95, dinner $14.75-$28.50. Guitarist Tues; pianist Wed-Sun. Valet parking. On 6 acres of formal gardens that incl fountains, waterfalls, ponds, gazebos. Cr cds: A, D, DS, MC, V.

Westhampton Beach

See also Riverhead (L.I.)

Pop 1,902 **Elev** 10 ft **Area code** 631
Zip 11978

Information Greater Westhampton Chamber of Commerce, 173 Montauk Hwy, PO Box 1228; 631/288-3337

Surrounded by water, this resort area offers fishing and water sports. Nearby are hiking and nature trails.

What to See and Do

Wertheim National Wildlife Refuge.
A 2,600-acre refuge for wildlife incl deer, fox, raccoon, herons, hawks, ospreys, and waterfowl. Fishing, boating, canoeing; walking trail, photography. Environmental education. (Daily) Approx 10 mi W on NY 80 to Smith Rd S, in Shirley. Phone 631/286-0485. **FREE**

Restaurants

★★ **CASA BASSO.** *59 Montauk Hwy, Westhampton (11977).* 631/288-1841. Italian menu. Specializes in veal, seafood. Hrs: 5 pm-midnight. Closed Mon. Res required. Bar. A la carte entrees: dinner $12-$22. Unusual outdoor sculptures; mermaids, horses, lions, and 3 musketeers. Jacket. Cr cds: A, D, MC, V.

★★ **DORA'S.** *105 Montauk Hwy (11977).* 631/288-9723. Specialties: shrimp Dora, L.I. duckling, marinated steak. Hrs: from 5 pm. Closed Thanksgiving, Dec 24, 25; also Mon-Wed Sept-June. Bar. A la carte entrees: dinner $13.45-$24.95. Child's menu. Cr cds: A, C, D, DS, MC, V.

★★ **PATIO.** *54 Main St (11978).* 631/288-4100. www.virtualtouroncampus.com. Specializes in prime meats, fresh seafood. Hrs: 5:30-10:30 pm. Closed Dec 25; also Mon-Thurs mid-Sept-Dec. Bar. A la carte entrees: dinner $20-$32. Outdoor dining. Entertainment Sat (summer). Cr cds: A, MC, V.

★★★ **STARR BOGGS'.** *379 Dune Rd (11978).* 631/288-5250. Specializes in local fish, seasonal vegetables. Hrs: noon-3 pm, 6-10 pm; Fri to 11:30 pm. Closed mid-Oct-mid-May. Res required. Bar. A la carte entrees: lunch $7-$14, dinner $20-$28. Lobster bake $40. Outdoor dining. Original art. Cr cds: A, DS, MC, V.

West Hempstead (L.I.)

(see Hempstead)

West Point (US Military Academy)

(F-8) *See also Monroe, Newburgh, Peekskill, Stony Point*

Established 1802 **Pop** 7,138 **Elev** 161 ft **Area code** 845 **Zip** 10996

West Point has been of military importance since Revolutionary days; it was one of four points on the mid-Hudson fortified against the British. In 1778 a great chain was strung across the river to stop British ships. The military academy was founded by an act of Congress in 1802. Barracks, academic, and administration buildings are closed to visitors.

What to See and Do

Battle Monument. Memorial to the 2,230 officers and men of the Regular Army who fell in action during the Civil War. Nearby are some links from the chain used to block the river from 1778-82. Thayer and Washington rds. Phone 845/938-4011.

Cadet Chapel. (1910) On hill overlooking the campus. Large pipe organ and stained glass. (Daily) Phone 845/938-4011.

Michie Stadium. Seats 42,000. Army home football games. Phone 845/938-4011.

Parades. Inquire at Visitors Center. (Late Apr-May, Sept-Nov) Phone 845/938-2638.

Visitors Center. Displays on cadet training, model cadet rm, films shown, tours. Photo ID required. (Daily; closed Jan 1, Thanksgiving, Dec 25) Just outside Thayer Gate. Phone 845/938-2638.

West Point Museum. Exhibits on history and ordnance. (Daily; closed Jan 1, Thanksgiving, Dec 25) In the Pershing Center at the Visitors Center, just outside Thayer Gate. Phone 845/938-2203. **FREE**

Hotel

★ ★ **HOTEL THAYER.** *Building 674, West Point (10996). 845/446-4731; fax 845/446-0338.* 189 rms, 5 story. S, D $89-$119; each addl $10; suites $110-$185. Crib $10. TV; VCR avail. Restaurant 7-10 am, 11:30 am-2 pm, 5:30-9 pm; Sun from 7:30-9 am. Bar 11:30 am-midnight. Ck-out 11 am (football wkends 10 am). Meeting rms. Business servs avail. Gift shop. Concierge. Downhill ski 2 mi. Outdoor terrace. Overlooks Hudson River. Cr cds: A, C, D, DS, ER, JCB, MC, V.

B&B/Small Inn

★ ★ **CROMWELL MANOR INN.** *174 Angola Rd, Cornwall (12518). 845/534-7136. www.cromwellmanor. com.* 13 rms, 2 story, 3 suites, guest house. No rm phones. S, D $135-$200; suites $225-$275; guest house $650; wkends 2-day min. Premium cable TV in common rm. Complimentary full bkfst. Restaurant nearby. Ck-out 11 am, ck-in 4 pm. Free airport transportation. Many fireplaces. Built in 1820 by descendant of Oliver Cromwell; 7 acres of woodlands/gardens. Antiques. Cr cds MC, V.

Restaurants

★ ★ **CANTERBURY BROOK INN.** *331 Main St, Cornwall (12518). 845/534-9658.* Continental menu. Specializes in veal, salmon, chicken. Hrs: 5-9 pm; Fri, Sat to 9:30 pm; Sun to 8 pm. Closed Mon, Tues; also Dec 25. Res accepted. Bar. Dinner $12.50-$19.95. Fireplaces. View of brook. Cr cds: A, MC, V.

★ **PAINTER'S.** *266 Hudson St, Cornwall-on-Hudson (10996). 845/534-2109. www.winedine.com/painters.* Specializes in pasta, seafood. Hrs: 11:30 am-10 pm; Fri, Sat to 10:30 pm; Sun brunch 10:30 am-3 pm. Closed major hols. Res accepted. Bar to 2 am. Lunch, dinner $5.50-$18. Sun brunch from $6.95. Child's menu. Outdoor dining. Cr cds: A, D, DS, MC, V.

White Plains

(G-2) *See also New Rochelle, New York City, Stamford, Tarrytown, Yonkers*

Settled 1735 **Pop** 53,077 **Elev** 236 ft **Area code** 914

Information Westchester County Office of Tourism, 222 Mamaroneck Ave, 10605; 914/995-8500 or 800/833-9282

In October 1776, General George Washington outfoxed General Lord Howe here. Howe, with a stronger, fresher force, permitted Washington to retreat to an impregnable position; Howe never could explain why he had not pursued his overwhelming advantage.

Cadets at West Point Military Academy

What to See and Do

Miller Hill Restoration. Restored earthworks from the Battle of White Plains (Oct 28, 1776). Built by Washington's troops. Battle diagrams. N White Plains.

Monument. Here the Declaration of Independence was adopted July 1776, and the state of New York was formally organized. S Broadway and Mitchell Pl.

Washington's Headquarters. (1776) Revolutionary War relics; demonstrations, lectures. (By appt) 140 Virginia Rd, in N White Plains. Phone 914/949-1236. **FREE**

Motel/Motor Lodge

★★ **RAMADA INN.** *94 Business Park Dr, Armonk (10504).* 914/273-9090; fax 914/273-4105. *www.ramada.com.* 140 rms, 2 story. S, D $99-$189; each addl $10; suites $169-$225; under 18 free; wkend, hol rates; higher rates Dec 31. Pet accepted, some restrictions. TV; cable (premium). Pool; lifeguard. Complimentary coffee in rms. Restaurant 7 am-10 pm. Bar noon-2 am; entertainment wkends. Ck-out noon. Coin lndry. Meeting rms. Business servs avail. In-rm modem link. Free airport, RR station transportation. Exercise equipt. Some refrigera-

tors; microwaves avail. Picnic tables. Cr cds: A, C, D, DS, ER, JCB, MC, V.

Hotels

★★★ **CROWNE PLAZA.** *66 Hale Ave (10601).* 914/682-0050; fax 914/682-0405. *www.crowneplaza.com.* 402 rms, 12 story. S $189; D $199; each addl $15; suites $475; under 12 free; wkend rates. Crib free. TV; cable (premium), VCR avail (movies). Indoor pool; whirlpool, lifeguard. Coffee in rms. Restaurant 6:30 am-11 pm. Bar noon-midnight. Ck-out noon. Coin lndry. Meeting rms. Business center. In-rm modem link. Gift shop. Garage parking. Free airport, RR station transportation. Exercise equipt. Health club privileges. Refrigerators avail. Luxury level. Cr cds: A, C, D, DS, ER, JCB, MC, V.

★★★ **HILTON.** *699 Westchester Ave, Rye Brook (10573).* 914/939-6300; fax 914/939-5328. *www.hilton.com.* 437 rms. S $179-$279; D $199-$299, poolside rms $185; each addl $20; suites $310-$665; family, wkend rates. Crib $20. TV; cable (premium). 2 pools, 1 indoor; wading pool, whirlpool, lifeguard. Supervised children's activities (July 4-Sept 4); ages 3-15. Coffee in rms. Restaurant 6 am-

11:30 pm. Bar 11-2 am. Ck-out 1 pm. Convention facilities. Business center. In-rm modem link. Concierge. Valet parking. Indoor, outdoor tennis. Exercise equipt; sauna. Lawn games. Private patios, balconies. Cr cds: A, C, D, DS, ER, MC, V.

★ ★ ★ **RENAISSANCE WESTCH-ESTER.** *80 W Red Oak Ln (10604). 914/694-5400; fax 914/694-5616; toll-free 800/468-3571. www.renaissance hotels.com.* 350 rms, 7 suites, 6 story. S $215-$235; D $225-$245; each addl $20; suites $375-$1,500; under 18 free; wkend rates. Crib free. TV; cable. Indoor pool; whirlpool, poolside serv, lifeguard. Complimentary coffee. Restaurant 6:30 am-10 pm. Rm serv 24 hrs. Bar noon-2 am. Ck-out 1 pm. Convention facilities. Business center. In-rm modem link. Concierge. Lighted tennis. Exercise equipt; sauna. Rec rm. Minibars; refrigerators avail. Private patios, balconies. Cr cds: A, C, D, DS, JCB, MC, V.

Conference Center

★ ★ ★ **DORAL ARROWWOOD CONFERENCE RESORT.** *Anderson Hill Rd, Rye Brook (10573). 914/939-5500; fax 914/323-5500. www.doral arrowwood.com.* 274 rms, 5 story. S $300-$325; D $400-$425; golf plans; wkend rates. Crib free. TV; cable (premium). Indoor/outdoor pool; whirlpool, poolside serv, lifeguard. Dining rms (public by res) 6:30 am-10:30 pm. Rm serv 24 hrs. Box lunches, snack bar, picnics. Bar noon-2 am. Ck-out noon, ck-in 5 pm. Conference facilities. Business center. In-rm modem link. Bellhops. Airport, RR station, bus depot transportation. Sports dir. Indoor and lighted tennis, pro. 9-hole golf, greens fee, pro, putting green, driving range. Lawn games. Racquetball. Soc dir; entertainment. Rec rm. Exercise rm; sauna. Massage. Refrigerators, microwaves avail. Some private patios, balconies. On 114 acres; duck pond; trails. Cr cds: A, C, D, DS, MC, V.

Restaurants

★ ★ **DAWAT.** *230 E Post Rd (10601). 914/428-4411.* Indian menu. Special-

ties: leg of lamb, tandoori mixed grill. Hrs: noon-2:45 pm; 5:30-10:15 pm; Fri-Sat 5:30-10:45 pm; Sun 5-9:45 pm. Res accepted. Bar. A la carte entrees: dinner $12.95-$19.95. Lunch buffet $9.95. Parking. Contemporary decor with Indian influence. Cr cds: A, D, MC, V.

★ ★ ★ ★ **LA PANETIERE.** *530 Milton Rd, Rye (10580). 914/967-8140. www. lapanetiere.com.* Country French food served in a country French setting; what more can be said about this Westchester restaurant, located in a cheery house. Professional service and an excellent wine list make for an all-around satisfying evening, about 45 minutes from Manhattan. Hrs: noon-2:30 pm, 6-9:30 pm; Sat from 6 pm; Sun 1-8:30 pm. Lunch $17-$24, dinner $25-$36, 3-course $50. Totally nonsmoking. Bar. Valet. Cr cds: A, D, DS, MC, V.

★ **MICHELANGELO.** *208 Underhill Ave, West Harrison (10604). 914/428-0022.* Italian menu. Specializes in veal, seafood, pasta. Own desserts. Hrs: 11:30 am-3 pm, 4-10 pm; Fri to 11 pm; Sat noon-11 pm; Sun noon-9 pm. Closed hols. Res accepted. Lunch $7.95-$14.95, dinner $9.95-$24.95. Parking. Cr cds: A, C, D, DS, MC, V.

★ ★ **REKA'S.** *2 Westchester Ave (10601). 914/949-1440.* Thai menu. Specializes in seafood, crispy duck, wild boar. Hrs: noon-10 pm; Sat, Sun brunch noon-3 pm. Res accepted; required wkends. Bar. Lunch, dinner $9.95-$19.95. Sat, Sun brunch $14.95. Cr cds: A, D, MC, V.

Wilmington

(B-8) *See also Lake Placid, Saranac Lake*

Pop 1,131 **Elev** 1,020 ft
Area code 518 **Zip** 12997
Information Whiteface Mtn Regional Visitors Bureau, NY 86, PO Box 277; 518/946-2255 or 888/WHITEFACE
Web www.whitefaceregion.com

Gateway to Whiteface Mountain Memorial Highway, Wilmington is made-to-order for skiers and lovers of scenic splendor.

What to See and Do

Adirondack Park. (see)

High Falls Gorge. Deep ravine cut into the base of Whiteface Mtn by the Ausable River. Variety of strata, rapids, falls, and potholes can be viewed from a network of modern bridges and paths. Photography and mineral displays in main building. (Memorial Day-mid-Oct, daily) 5 mi S on NY 86. Phone 518/946-2278.
¢¢¢

Santa's Home Workshop. "Santa's home and workshop," Santa Claus, reindeer, children's rides and shows. (Late-June-mid-Oct, Mon-Wed; Sat, Sun) Reduced rates wkdays spring and fall. 1½ mi W on NY 431, in North Pole. Phone 518/946-2211.
¢¢¢¢

Skiing. Whiteface Mountain Ski Center. Gondola; two triple, seven double chairlifts; snowmaking; patrol, school, rentals; cafeteria, bar, nursery. Longest run 2½ mi; vertical drop 3,350 ft. Chairlift (mid-June-mid-Oct; fee). Lift-serviced mountain biking center; rental, repair shop, guided tours (late June-mid-Oct). (Mid-Nov-mid-Apr, daily) 3 mi SW on NY 86. Phone 800/462-6236. Skiing ¢¢¢¢ Biking ¢¢¢

Whiteface Mountain Memorial Highway. A five-mi toll road to top of mountain (4,867 ft). (Late May-mid-Oct, daily, weather permitting) Trail or elevator from parking area. Views of St. Lawrence River, Lake Placid, and Vermont. Elevator (begins late May). 3 mi W on NY 431. Phone 800/462-6236.

Motel/Motor Lodge

★★ **LEDGE ROCK AT WHITEFACE.** *Rt 86 (12997). 518/946-2302; fax 518/946-7594; res 800/336-4754.* 18 rms, 2 story. Mid-Dec-Mar, mid-June-late Oct: S, D $69-$119. Crib free. Pet accepted; $5. TV; cable. Heated pool; wading pool. Playground. Coffee in rms. Restaurant nearby. Ck-out 11 am. Rec rm. Game rm with fireplace. Refrigerators, microwaves. Some bal-conies. Picnic area, grills. Pond with paddleboats. Cr cds: A, DS, MC, V.
🅳 🈁 🛗 🎿 🏊 🎣 ♿

Hotel

★★ **HUNGRY TROUT MOTOR INN.** *Rte 86 (12997). 518/946-2217; fax 518/946-7418; toll-free 800/766-9137.* 20 rms. Dec-mid-Apr, late June-Labor Day: S, D $69-$89; suites $119-$139; ski, golf, fishing plans; lower rates rest of yr. Closed Apr, Nov. Crib $5. Pet accepted; $4. TV; cable. Pool; wading pool. Playground. Coffee in rms. Restaurant opp 7-10 am. Bar 5-10 pm. Ck-out 11 am. Downhill ski ½ mi; x-country ski 12 mi. On Ausable River. Cr cds: A, DS, MC, V.
🎿 🅳 🈁 🛗 🎣 🏊 ♿

B&B/Small Inn

★★ **WHITEFACE CHALET.** *Spring-field Rd (12997). 518/946-2207; toll-free 800/932-0859.* 16 rms, 15 A/C. June-Oct, mid-Nov-Mar: S, D $45-$70; each addl $5; suites $55-$80; under 12 free; MAP avail; wkly rates; ski plans; lower rates rest of yr. Crib free. Pet accepted. TV; cable. Pool. Playground. Dining rm 8-10 am. Bar noon-1 am. Ck-out 11 am, ck-in 1 pm. Meeting rm. Airport, RR station, bus depot transportation. Tennis. Downhill ski 2 mi; x-country ski 3 mi. Lawn games. Rec rm. Balconies. Fireplace in lounge, living rm. Cr cds: A, DS, MC, V.
🈁 🎣 🎿 🏊 ♿ **SC**

Restaurant

★ **WILDERNESS INN #2.** *NY 86 (12997). 518/946-2391. www.lake placid.net/wildernessinn.* Specializes in fresh seafood, steak. Salad bar. Hrs: 11 am-3 pm (summer and fall), 5-10 pm; winter to 9 pm. Closed Wed in winter; also first 3 wks Nov. Res accepted. Bar. Dinner $10.95-$16.95. Child's menu. Outdoor dining. Fire-place. Guest cottages avail. Family-owned. Cr cds: D, MC, V.
SC 🍽

Windham

See also Cairo, Hunter

Pop 1,660 **Area code** 518 **Zip** 12496

What to See and Do

Skiing. Ski Windham. High-speed detachable quad, double, four triple chairlifts; surface lift; patrol, ski school, rentals; snowmaking; nursery, ski shop, restaurant, two cafeterias, bar. Snowboarding. Longest run 2¼ mi; vertical drop 1,600 ft. (Early Nov-early Apr, daily) 25 mi W on NY 23, exit 21. ¢¢¢¢

White Birches Campsite. Approx 400 acres of Catskill Mtn wilderness, lake. Summer activities incl lake swimming, canoeing (rentals), paddleboats (fee); camping (hook-ups), mountain biking, archery (fee). 2½ mi NE. Phone 518/734-3266. ¢¢

Motel/Motor Lodge

★★ **HOTEL VIENNA.** *107 Rte 296 (12496). 518/734-5300; fax 518/734-4749; toll-free 800/898-5308. www.the hotelvienna.com.* 30 rms, 2 story. S, D $110-$140; each addl $10-$20; higher rates: wkends (2-day min winter), hols. Closed Apr-mid-May. TV; cable. Indoor pool, whirlpool. Complimentary continental bkfst. Restaurant adj 4-10 pm. Ck-out 11 am. Ck-in 2 pm. Business servs avail. Downhill/x-country ski 1 mi. Balconies. Cr cds: MC, V.

Hotel

★★ **WINDHAM ARMS HOTEL.** *Rte 23 Main St (12496). 518/734-3000; fax 518/734-5900.* 51 rms, some A/C, 2-3 story. No elvtr. Apr-early Oct, MAP: $400-$800/person/wk, summer $490-$920; EP: S, D $65-$250; each addl $10; lower rates rest of yr. Crib free. TV; cable. Heated pool. Playground. Restaurant 8-10 am, 5-8 pm. Ck-out 10 am. Coin lndry. Meeting rms. Business servs avail. Bellhops. Bus depot transportation. Tennis. Golf privileges, putting green. Downhill ski ½ mi; x-country ski 1 mi.

Exercise equipt. Game rm. Rec rm. Lawn games. Many balconies. Theater. Cr cds: A, DS, MC, V.

B&B/Small Inn

★★★ **ALBERGO ALLEGRIA.** *State Rte 296 (12496). 518/734-5560; fax 518/734-5570. www.albergousa.com.* 15 rms, 2 story, 6 suites, 1 carriage house. Oct-mid-Mar: S, D $63-$153; each addl $25; suites $95-$225; package plans; lower rates rest of yr. TV; cable, VCR (free movies). Complimentary full bkfst; afternoon refreshments. Restaurant adj 4-10 pm. Ck-out 10:30 am, ck-in 1 pm. Business servs avail. Valet serv. Gift shop. Tennis privileges. Downhill/x-country ski 1 mi. On river; swimming. Library/sitting rm; antiques. Some private decks. Two Queen Anne summer houses (1876) joined with Victorian-style addition. Cr cds: MC, V.

Restaurant

★★ **SIR THETFORD'S SIRLOIN ROOM.** *NY 23 (12496). 518/734-3322.* Continental menu. Specializes in steak, fresh seafood, French sauces. Hrs: 4-10 pm; Fri to 11 pm; Sun 1-9 pm. Closed Mon, Tues Mar-June, Sept-Jan. Res accepted. Bar. Dinner $10.95-$21.95. Child's menu. Colonial atmosphere. Family-owned. Cr cds: A, DS, MC, V.

Woodstock

(F-7) See also Hunter, Kingston, Shandaken

Pop 6,241 **Elev** 512 ft **Area code** 845 **Zip** 12498

Information Chamber of Commerce and Arts, PO Box 36; 845/679-6234

Web www.woodstock-online.com

Woodstock has traditionally been known as an art colony. In 1902 Ralph Radcliffe Whitehead, an Englishman, came from California and set up a home and handcraft community (Byrdcliffe, north of town).

he Art Students' League of New
ork established a summer school
ere a few years later. In 1916 Hervey
White conceived the Maverick Sum-
ner Music Concerts, the oldest
hamber concert series in the coun-
ry. Woodstock was the original site
hosen for the famous 1969 Wood-
tock Music Festival; however, when
he event grew bigger than anyone
magined, it was moved 60 miles
outhwest to a farmer's field near
ethel (see MONTICELLO). Never-
heless, the festival gave Woodstock
otoriety.

What to See and Do

**Woodstock Artists Association
Gallery.** Center of the community
ince 1920. Changing exhibits of
vorks by regional artists. Nationally
ecognized permanent collection. 24
'inker St at Village Green. Phone
45/679-2940. **Donation**

Special Event

Maverick Concerts. Maverick Rd,
etween NY 375 and 28. Chamber
nusic concerts. Phone 845/679-8217.
un June-early Sept.

B&Bs/Small Inns

★ ★ **LA DUCHESSE ANNE.** 1564
Wittenberg Rd, Mt. Tremper (12457).
45/688-5260; fax 845/688-2438.
ww.laduchesseanne.com. 12 rms, 8
hare bath, 2 story. No rm phones. S
65, D $95; suite $120. Complimen-
ary continental bkfst. Restaurant.
ar. Ck-out noon, ck-in 2-11 pm.
uilt as a guest house 1850. Antique
urnishings. Cr cds: A, DS, MC, V.

★ ★ **TWIN GABLES OF WOOD-
STOCK.** 73 Tinker St (12498).
45/679-9479; fax 845/679-5638.
ww.twingableswoodstockny.com. 9
ms, 6 share bath, 2 story. No rm
hones. Memorial Day-Nov: S, D
52-$92; lower rates rest of yr.
estaurant adj. Ck-out 11:30 am, ck-
n noon. Antique furnishings. Fam-
y-owned operated since 1940.
otally nonsmoking. Cr cds: A, DS,
MC, V.

Restaurants

★ ★ **BEAR CAFE.** 295A Tinker St,
Bearville (12409). 845/679-5555.
www.bearcafe.com. Specialties: ravioli
with arugula and radicchio, filet
mignon with port garlic sauce. Hrs:
5-10:30 pm; Fri, Sat to 11 pm. Closed
Tues; Dec 25. Res accepted. Bar. Dinner $11.95-$20.50. Outdoor dining.
Large windows in dining area overlook creek. Cr cds: MC, V.

★ ★ **CATSKILL ROSE.** 5355 Rte 212,
Mt Tremper (12457). 845/688-7100.
www.catskillrose.com. Contemporary
American menu. Specialties: smoked
duckling, chocolate fudge cake with
white chocolate mousse. Hrs: 5-10
pm. Closed Mon, Tues. Res accepted.
Bar. Dinner $13.75-$16.75. Child's
menu. Pianist Sat. Parking. Outdoor
dining. Cr cds: C, D, DS, MC, V.

★ ★ **JOSHUA'S.** 51 Tinker St (12498).
845/679-5533. Continental menu.
Specialties: sesame chicken, vegetarian selections. Hrs: 11 am-10 pm; Fri,
Sat to 11 pm; Sun from 10 am. Res
accepted. Lunch $4-$12.95, dinner
$10.95-$18.95. Guitarist Sat. Family-
owned. Cr cds: A, C, MC, V.

Yonkers (G-2)

Settled 1646 **Pop** 196,086 **Elev** 16 ft
Area code 914
Information Chamber of Commerce,
20 S Broadway, Suite 1207, 10701;
914/963-0332
Web www.yonkerschamber.com

Yonkers, on the New York City line,
was originally puchased by Adriaen
van der Donck in the early 1600s.
His status as a young nobleman from
Holland gave him the nickname
"DeJonkeer," which underwent
many changes until it became "the
Yonkers land" and finally Yonkers.

What to See and Do

**The Hudson River Museum of
Westchester.** Incl Glenview Mansion
(1876), an Eastlake-inspired Hudson

River house overlooking the Palisades; Andrus Planetarium; regional art, history, and science exhibits; changing exhibits of 19th- and 20th-century art in the Glenview galleries and contemporary wing. Changing exhibits, planetarium shows, lectures, jazz festival in summer. (Wed-Sun; closed hols) 511 Warburton Ave. Phone 914/963-4550. Museum ¢¢ Planetarium ¢¢

St. Paul's Church National Historic Site. Setting for historical events establishing basic freedoms outlined in the Bill of Rights. The event that made this site famous, the Great Election of 1733, led to the establishment of a free press in colonial America. Before completion, the fieldstone and brick Georgian St. Paul's Church (1763) served as a military hospital for the British and Hessians during the Revolutionary War. Building was completed after the war and served not only as a church but also as a meeting house and courtrm where Aaron Burr practiced law on at least one occasion. Tours (Mon-Fri, by appt; closed Jan 1, Thanksgiving, Dec 25). 897 S Columbus Ave in Mt Vernon, 10 mi SE via Hutchinson River Pkwy exit 8 (Sandford Blvd). Phone 914/667-4116. **FREE** Also here is

Bill of Rights Museum. Exhibits incl working model of 18th-century printing press and dioramas depicting John Peter Zenger, whose trial and acquittal for seditious libel in 1735 helped establish freedom of the press in America. Series of panels detail history of site, incl the Anne Hutchinson story, the Great Election of 1733, and the Revolutionary period. (Same days as St. Paul's Church) Phone 914/667-4116. **FREE**

Yonkers Raceway. Night harness racing; day simulcasting from NYRA. Yonkers and Central aves in Yonkers, on I-87, between exits 2 and 4. Phone 914/968-4200. ¢¢

Motel/Motor Lodge

★★ **HOLIDAY INN.** 125 Tuckahoe Rd (10710). 914/476-3800; fax 914/423-3555; res 800/465-4329. www.holiday-inn.com. 103 rms, 3 suites, 3 story. S $89-$99; D $89-$106; each addl $7; suites $195; under 18 free; wkend rates. Crib free. TV; cable (premium). Complimentary coffee in rms. Restaurant 7 am-10 pm. Bar 5 pm-midnight; wkends to 2 am; entertainment Thurs-Sat. Ck-out noon. Meeting rms. Business servs avail. In-rm modem link. Exercise equipt. Pool; poolside serv, lifeguard. Many balconies. Cr cds: A, C, D, DS, JCB, MC, V.

D 🏊 🏃 🐾 🔥

Restaurant

★★ **J. J. MANNION'S.** 640 McLean Ave (10705). 914/476-2786. Hrs: 11-1 am; Sun brunch to 3 pm. Closed Dec 25. Bar. Lunch $4.50-$12, dinner $4.50-$22.95. Sun brunch $11.95. Street parking. Irish pub decor. Cr cds: A, C, D, DS, MC, V.

D

NEW YORK CITY

New York is the nation's most populous city, the capital of finance, business, communications, theater, and much more. It may not be the center of the universe, but it does occupy a central place in the world's imagination. Certainly, in one way or another, New York affects the lives of nearly every American. While other cities have everything that New York has—from symphonies to slums—no other city has quite the style or sheer abundance. Nowhere are things done in such a grandly American way as in New York City.

Population: 7,322,564
Elevation: 0-410 ft
Settled: 1615
Nickname: The Big Apple
Time Zone: Eastern

Giovanni da Verrazano was the first European to glimpse Manhattan Island (1524), but the area was not explored until 1609, when Henry Hudson sailed up the river that was later named for him, searching for a passage to India. Adriaen Block arrived here in 1613, and the first trading post was established by the Dutch West India Company two years later. Peter Minuit is said to have bought the island from Native Americans for $24 worth of beads and trinkets in 1626, when New Amsterdam was founded—the biggest real estate bargain in history.

In 1664 the Dutch surrendered to a British fleet, and the town was renamed New York in honor of the Duke of York. One of the earliest tests of independence occurred here in 1734 when John Peter Zenger, publisher and editor of the *New York Weekly-Journal,* was charged with seditious libel and jailed for making antigovernment remarks. Following the Battle of Long Island in 1776, the British occupied the city through the Revolution, until 1783.

Plaza Hotel, overlooking Central Park

On the balcony of Federal Hall at Wall Street, April 30, 1789, George Washington was inaugurated as first president of the United States, and for a time New York was the country's capital.

When the Erie Canal opened in 1825, New York City expanded vastly as a port. It has since consistently maintained its leadership. In 1898 Manhattan merged with Brooklyn, the Bronx, Queens, and Staten Island. In the next half-century several million immigrants entered the United States here, providing the city with the supply of labor needed for its growth into a major metropolis Each wave of immigrants has brought new customs, culture, and life, which makes New York City the varied metropolis it is today.

New York continues to capitalize on its image as the Big Apple, attracting more than 19 million visitors each year, and its major attractions continue to thrive in style. These, of course, are centered in Manhattan; however, vacationers should not overlook the wealth of sights and activities the other boroughs have to offer. Brooklyn has Coney Island, the New York Aquarium, the superb Brooklyn Museum, Brooklyn Botanical Garden, Brooklyn Children's Museum, and the famous landmark Brooklyn Bridge. The Bronx is noted for its excellent Botanical Garden and Zoo and Yankee Stadium. Flushing Meadows-Corona Park, in Queens, was the site of two World's Fairs; nearby is Shea Stadium, home of the New York Mets. Uncrowded Staten Island has Richmondtown Restoration, a re-creation of 18th-century New York; rural farmland; beaches; salt marshes; and wildlife preserves.

Weather

The average mean temperatures for New York are 34°F in winter; 52°F in spring 75°F in summer; and 58°F in fall. In summer the temperature is rarely above 90°F (maximum recorded: 106°F), but the humidity can be high. In winter the temperature is rarely lower than 10°F, but has gone as low as -14°F. Average mean temperatures are listed from surveys taken at the National Weather Bureau station in Central Park.

Theater

New York is theatrical headquarters of the United States, and theater here is an experience not to be missed. Broadway, a 36-square-block area (41st to 53rd streets and 6th to 9th avenues), offers standard full-scale plays and musicals, more than 30 of them on any particular evening. Off-Broadway, not confined to one area, is less expensive and more experimental, giving new talent a chance at exposure and established talent an opportunity to try new and different projects, such as the New York Shakespeare Festival (see SPECIAL EVENTS). Even less expensive and more daring is Off-Off-Broadway, consisting of dozens of small theaters in storefronts, lofts, and cellars, producing every imaginable type of theater.

There are a number of ways to obtain tickets ranging from taking a pre-arranged package theater tour to walking up to the box office an hour before curtain for returned and unclaimed tickets. Ticket Master outlets (phone 212/307-7171), hotel theater desks, and ticket brokers will have tickets to several shows for the box office price plus a service charge. All Broadway theaters accept phone reservations charged to major credit cards. An On Stage Hotline can be reached at 212/768-1818.

The Times Square Ticket Center (a booth with large banners proclaiming "TKTS") at 47th Street and Broadway has same-day tickets at half-price for mos shows (daily) and for matinees (Wednesday, Saturday, Sunday). Same-day half-price tickets to music and dance events may be obtained at the Music & Dance Booth, at 42nd Street and Avenue of the Americas in Bryant Park. *The New Yorker* and *New York* magazines carry extensive listings of the week's entertainment; the Friday edition of *The New York Times* also reports weekend availability of tickets.

Additional Visitor Information

Contact the New York Convention and Visitors Bureau, 810 7th Ave, ground level, 10019; phone 212/484-1222. The bureau has free maps; "twofers" to Broadway shows; bulletins and brochures on attractions, events, shopping, restaurants, and hotels. For events of the week, visitors should get copies of *The New Yorker* and *New York* magazines and *The New York Times.* For those who intend to stay for some time and want to delve more deeply into the city, we suggest browsing in libraries and bookstores for the numerous guidebooks that detail what to see and do.

Transportation

AIRPORTS

La Guardia, in Queens 8 mi NE of Manhattan; *Kennedy International,* in Queens 15 mi SE of Manhattan (for both, see QUEENS—LA GUARDIA AND JFK INTERNATIONAL AIRPORT AREAS); *Newark International,* 16 mi SW of Manhattan in New Jersey.

CAR RENTAL AGENCIES

See IMPORTANT TOLL-FREE NUMBERS.

PUBLIC TRANSPORTATION

Subway and elevated trains, buses (New York City Transit Authority), phone 718/330-3322 or 718/330-1234. The subway system, which carries more than four million people on weekdays, covers every borough except Staten Island, which has its own transportation system. Maps of the system are posted at every station and on every car.

RAIL PASSENGER SERVICE

Amtrak, phone 800/872-7245.

Driving in New York

Vehicular traffic is heaviest during weekday rush hours and on both weekdays and weekends between Thanksgiving and Christmas week—a period of almost continuous rush hour. Most Manhattan avenues and streets are one-way. To assist tourists in finding cross streets nearest avenue addresses, telephone books and several tourist guides contain address locator tables. Because New York traffic is very heavy and parking is both scarce and expensive, many visitors find taxis more convenient and economical than driving.

Sightseeing Tours

For travelers desiring a general overview of the city, a variety of sightseeing tours are available using various forms of transportation (see SIGHTSEEING TOURS under MANHATTAN).

NEIGHBORHOODS

CHINATOWN

The only truly ethnic neighborhood still thriving in Manhattan, Chinatown is filled with teeming streets, jostling crowds, bustling restaurants, exotic markets, and prosperous shops. Once limited to a small enclave contained in the six blocks between the Bowery and Mulberry, Canal, and Worth streets (now known as "traditional Chinatown"), it has burst these boundaries in recent years to spread north of Canal Street into Little Italy and east into the Lower East Side.

Chinatown is the perfect neighborhood for haphazard wandering. In traditional Chinatown, especially, every twist or turn of the small, winding streets brings mounds of shiny fish—live carp, eels, and crabs—piles of fresh produce—cabbage, ginger root, Chinese broccoli—or displays of pretty, colorful objects—toys, handbags, knickknacks. Bakeries selling everything from moon cakes and almond cookies to "cow ears" (chips of fried dough) and pork buns are everywhere, along with the justifiably famous Chinatown Ice Cream Factory (65 Bayard Street, near Mott), selling every flavor of ice cream from ginger to mango.

Chinese men, accompanied by only a handful of women, began arriving in New York in the late 1870s. Many were former transcontinental railroad workers, who came to escape the persecution they were experiencing on the West Coast. But they weren't especially welcomed on the East Coast either, and soon thereafter, the violent "tong wars" between criminal Chinese gangs helped lead to the Exclusion Acts of 1882, 1888, 1902, and 1924, forbidding further Chinese immigration. Chinatown became a "bachelor society," almost devoid of woman and children—a situation that continued until the lifting of immigration quotas in 1965.

Today, Chinatown's estimated population of 100,000 is made up of two especially large groups—the well-established Cantonese community, who have been in New York for over a century, and the Fujianese community, a much newer and poorer immigration group who come from Fujian Province on the southern coast of mainland China. The Cantonese own many of the prosperous shops and restaurants in traditional Chinatown, whereas the Fujianese have set up rice-noodle shops, herbal medicine shops, and outdoor markets along Broadway and neighboring streets between Canal Street and the Manhattan Bridge.

To learn more about the history of Chinatown, visit the Museum of the Chinese in the Americas (70 Mulberry Street, at Bayard). To get a good meal, explore almost any street, with Mott Street—the neighborhood's main thoroughfare—holding an especially large number. Pell Street is especially known for its barber and beauty shops and for its Buddhist Temple (4 Pell Street). The neighborhood's biggest festival is the Chinese New Year, celebrated between mid-January and early February; then, the streets come even more alive than usual with dragon dances, lion dances, and fireworks.

TRIBECA

Short for *Tri*angle *Be*low *Ca*nal, TriBeCa is a former industrial district encompassing about 40 blocks between Canal, Chambers, and West streets, and Broadway. Like SoHo, its considerably more fashionable cousin to the north, the neighborhood discarded its working-class roots years ago and now has its share of expensive restaurants and boutiques. Upper-middle-class residents have replaced factory workers, and avant-garde establishments have replaced sweatshops. Nonetheless, TriBeCa is much quieter than SoHo—and many other sections of Manhattan—and in parts, still retains its 19th-century feel, complete with cobblestone streets and dusty facades. After dark, especially, much of the area seems close to deserted.

TriBeCa's main thoroughfares are Broadway, West Broadway, and Church Street, three wide roads comfortable for strolling. West Broadway was originally built to relieve the congestion of Broadway and is home to a few art galleries, including the SoHo Photo Gallery (15 White Street, at West Broadway), a cooperative gallery featuring the work of 100-plus members. At Church and Walker streets reigns the sleek new TriBeCa Grand, the neighborhood's first upscale hotel.

One of TriBeCa's best-known addresses is the Knitting Factory (74 Leonard Street, between Church Street and Broadway), housed in a former industrial building. Renowned worldwide for avant-garde jazz, the Knitting Factory also books everything from alternative rock to poetry on its four stages spread out over three floors.

Also well known is the TriBeCa Film Center, housed in the landmark Martinson Coffee Company warehouse (375 Greenwich Street, at Franklin Street). The center was started in 1989 by actor Robert DeNiro, who wanted to create a site where filmmakers could talk business, screen films, and socialize. Today, the center houses the offices of several major producers and the TriBeCa Grill, a chic eatery usually filled with more celebrity watchers than celebrities. At Greenwich and Harrison streets stand the Harrison Houses, a group of nine restored Federal-style homes. Several were designed by John McComb, Jr., New York's first architect. East of the houses, at the northwest corner of Harrison and Hudson streets, find the former New York Mercantile Exchange. In this five-story building, complete with gables and a tower, $15,000 worth of eggs would change hands in an hour around the turn of the century. Today, TriBeCa is still the city's distribution center for eggs, cheese, and butter; a few remaining wholesales cluster around Duane Park, one block south of the former exchange, between Hudson and Greenwich streets.

At the southern end of TriBeCa is Chambers Street, where you'll find the Borough of Manhattan Community College (199 Chambers Street, near West Street). At the western end of Chambers, cross over West Street via the TriBeCa Bridge to reach a public recreation center called Pier 25.

SoHo

Short for *So*uth of *Ho*uston, SoHo is New York's trendiest neighborhood, filled with an impossible number of upscale eateries, fancy boutiques, of-the-moment bars, and, most recently, a few astronomically expensive hotels. Contained in just 25 blocks bounded by Houston and Canal streets, Lafayette, and West Broadway, SoHo attracts trend-oids and tourists by the thousands, especially on weekend afternoons, when the place sometimes feels like one giant open-air bazaar.

From the late 1800s to the mid-1900s, SoHo was primarily a light manufacturing district, but starting in the 1960s, most of the factories moved out and artists—attracted by the area's low rents and loft spaces—began moving in. Soon thereafter, the art galleries arrived, and then the shops and restaurants. Almost overnight, SoHo became too expensive for the artists—and, more recently, the art galleries—who had originally settled the place, and a mecca for big-bucks shoppers from all over the world.

Nonetheless, SoHo still has plenty to offer the art lover. Broadway is lined with one first-rate museum after another, while Mercer and Greene streets, especially, boast a large number of galleries. Some top spots on Broadway include the Museum for African Art (593 Broadway), presenting an excellent array of changing exhibits; the New Museum for Contemporary Art (583 Broadway), one of the oldest, best-known, and most controversial art spaces in SoHo; and the Guggenheim Museum SoHo (575 Broadway), a branch of the uptown institution. To find out who's exhibiting what and where in SoHo, pick up a copy of the Art Now Gallery Guide, available at many bookstores and galleries.

SoHo is also home to an extraordinary number of luscious cast-iron buildings. Originally meant to serve as a cheap substitute for stone buildings, the cast-iron facades were an American invention, prefabricated in a variety of styles—from Italian Renaissance to Classical Greek—and bolted onto the front of iron-frame structures. Most of SoHo's best cast-iron gems can be found along Broadway; keep an eye out for the Haughwout Building (488 Broadway), the Singer Building (561 Broadway), and the Guggenheim Museum SoHo.

Top thoroughfares for shopping include Prince and Spring streets, Broadway, and West Broadway. Numerous clothing and accessory boutiques are located along all these streets; West Broadway also offers several interesting bookstores. For antiques and furnishings, check out Lafayette Street; for craft and toy stores, try Greene and Mercer streets.

Restaurants and bars line almost every street in SoHo, but one especially lively nexus is the intersection of Grand Street and West Broadway. West Broadway itself is also home to an especially large number of eateries, some of which offer outdoor dining in the summer.

East Village

Once considered part of the Lower East Side, the East Village is considerably scruffier and more rambunctious than its better-known sister to the West. For years, it was the refuge of immigrants and the working class, but in the 1950s, struggling writers, actors, and artists—forced out of Greenwich Village by rising rents—began moving in. First came such well-known names as Willem de Kooning and W. H. Auden, followed by the beatniks, the hippies, the yippies, the rock groups, the punk musicians, and the fashion designers.

Only in the 1980s did the neighborhood start to gentrify, as young professionals moved in, bringing with them upscale restaurants and smart shops. Ever since, New York's continuously rising rents have forced out many of the younger, poorer, and more creative types that the East Village was known for just two decades ago. Nonetheless, the neighborhood has not completely succumbed and offers an interesting mix between the cutting edge and the mainstream.

The heart of the East Village is St. Mark's Place, an always-thronging thoroughfare where you'll find everything from punked-out musicians to well-heeled business types, leather shops to sleek bistros. Many of the street's noisiest addresses are between Third and Second avenues, many of its most appealing, farther east. At the eastern end of St. Mark's Place stretches Tompkins Square Park, once known for its drug dealers, now for its families and jungle gyms. Some of the best of the many interesting little shops that fill the East Village can be found on Avenue A near the park; others line Seventh and Ninth streets east of Second Avenue.

The neighborhood's second major thoroughfare, Second Avenue, was home to many lively Yiddish theaters early in the 20th century. All are gone now, but the landmark Second Avenue Deli (at 10th Street)—known for its over-stuffed sandwiches—commemorates the street's past with stars in the sidewalk. At Second Avenue and East Tenth Street is St.-Mark's-in-the-Bowery, an historic church where Peter Stuyvesant—the last of the Dutch governors who ruled Manhattan in the 1600s—is buried. The church is also known for its poetry readings, performance art, and leftist politics.

On the western edge of the East Village sprawls Astor Place, home to Cooper Union—the city's first free educational institution, now a design school—and a huge cube sculpture oddly balanced on one corner. On Lafayette Street at the southern end of Astor Place reigns the Joseph Papp Public Theater, housed in an imposing columned building that was once the Astor Library. The theater is renowned for its first-run productions and for Shakespeare in the Park, a free festival that it produces every summer in Central Park.

GREENWICH VILLAGE

Although New York's fabled bohemian neighborhood has gone seriously upscale and more mainstream in recent decades, evidence of its iconoclastic past can still be found in its many narrow streets, Off Broadway theaters, cozy coffee shops, lively jazz clubs, and tiny bars. Stretching from 14th Street south to Houston Street, and from Broadway west to the Hudson River, the neighborhood remains one of the city's best places for idle wandering, people watching, boutique browsing, and conversing over glasses of cabernet or cups of cappuccino.

Washington Square Park anchors the neighborhood to the east and, though it's nothing special to look at, is still the heart of the Village. On a sunny afternoon, everyone comes here: kids hot-dogging on skateboards, students strumming guitars, old men playing chess, and lovers entwined in each other's arms. Bordering the edges of the park are a mix of elegant townhouses and New York University buildings.

Just south and west of Washington Square, find Bleecker and MacDougal Streets, home to coffee shops and bars once frequented by the likes of James Baldwin, Jack Kerouac, Allen Ginsberg, and James Agee. Le Figaro (corner of Bleecker and MacDougal) and the San Remo (93 MacDougal) were favorites back then and still attract crowds today, albeit mostly made up of tourists.

A bit farther west is Seventh Avenue South, where you'll find the Village Vanguard (178 7th Avenue South, at 11th Street)—the oldest and most venerable jazz club in the city. Also nearby are the Blue Note (131 West 3rd Street, near 6th Avenue), New York's premier jazz supper club, and Smalls (183 West 10th Street, near 7th Avenue South), one of the best places to catch up-and-coming talent.

At the corner of Seventh Avenue South and Christopher Street stands Christopher Park, where a George Segal sculpture of two gay couples commemorates the Stonewall Riots, which marked the advent of the gay-rights movement. The Stonewall Inn, where the demonstration began in 1969, once stood directly across from the park at 51 Christopher, and Christopher Street itself is still lined with many gay establishments.

At the corner of Sixth Avenue and West Tenth Street reigns the Gothic towers and turrets of Jefferson Market Library, a stunning maroon-and-white building that dates back to 1876. Across the street from the library is Balducci's (424 Sixth Avenue), a famed gourmet food shop.

The neighborhood's most famous festivals are the Lesbian and Gay Pride Parade, which heads down Fifth Avenue to Greenwich Village in late May, and the Halloween Day Parade, which heads up Sixth Avenue on October 31. Both are outrageous events, attracting thousands of participants, many attired in fantastical fashions or costumes.

CHELSEA

Primarily middle-class residential and still somewhat industrial, Chelsea—stretching between 14th and 30th streets, from Sixth Avenue to the Hudson River—is not the most tourist-oriented of areas. However, the neighborhood does offer an exciting, avant-garde arts scene, as well as many lovely quiet blocks lined with attractive row houses and rustling trees. A new gay community has moved in recently, bringing with it trendy cafes, shops, and bars, while an enormous, state-of-the-art sports complex, the Chelsea Piers, beckons from the river's edge (between 18th and 22nd streets).

Most of Chelsea was once owned by Captain Thomas Clarke, whose grandson, Clement Charles Clarke, laid out the residential district in the early 1800s. Clement Charles was also a scholar and a poet who wrote the famous poem beginning with the line, "'Twas the night before Christmas..." Another of Clement Charles' legacies is the General Theological Seminary, a peaceful enclave of ivy-covered buildings bounded by the block between Ninth and Tenth avenues and 20th and 21st streets.

Also on the western edge of Chelsea are many of the city's foremost art galleries, which began moving here in the early '90s as rents in SoHo—their former home—began skyrocketing. An especially large number can be found on West 21st and 22nd streets between Tenth and Eleventh avenues; among them are the Paula Cooper Gallery (534 West 21st Street), the Max Protech Gallery (511 West 22nd), and the Dia Center for the Arts (548 West 22nd). One of the pioneers of the area, the Dia Center is really more a museum than an art gallery and usually hosts a variety of eye-popping exhibits, along with an open-air sculpture garden on the roof.

Most of Chelsea's thriving shops, restaurants, and bars—some of which are predominantly gay, some not—stand along Sixth and Eighth avenues between 14th and 23rd streets. Some of the neighborhood's prettiest blocks, lined with elegant row houses, are West 20th, 21st, and 22nd streets between Eighth and Tenth avenues. Also, be sure to take a gander at the Chelsea Hotel (222 West 23rd Street, near Eighth Avenue), a maroon-colored landmark that's all black gables, chimneys, and balconies. Built in 1884, the Chelsea has housed dozens of artists, writers, and musicians over the years, including Arthur Miller, Jackson Pollock, Bob Dylan, and Sid Vicious.

Just north of Chelsea lies the underground Pennsylvania Station (Seventh Avenue at 32nd Street), topped with circular Madison Square Garden, and the General Post Office (Eighth Avenue, between 31st and 33rd streets)—a gorgeous building designed by McKim, Mead & White in 1913. The Garment District, centering on Seventh Avenue in the 30s, also begins here.

GRAMERCY PARK AND ENVIRONS

Largely residential, the East Side between 14th and 34th streets is home to two inviting squares—Gramercy Park at Irving Place between 20th and 21st streets, and Union Square at Broadway between 14th and 17th streets. A long line of trendy restaurants and bars beckon along Park Avenue between 17th and 23rd streets, while a bit farther north is Little India, centered on Lexington Avenue between 27th and 29th streets. The neighborhood lacks the vibrancy of some of Manhattan's better-known neighborhoods, but has a quiet charm of its own, with residents ranging from young professionals to middle-class families to the upper-middle-class.

One of the most fashionable squares in the city, Gramercy Park is composed of elegant brownstones and townhouses surrounding an enclosed green to which only residents have the key. At the southern edge of the park stand two especially impressive buildings—the National Arts Club (15 Gramercy Park South) and the Players Club (16 Gramercy Park South). The National Arts Club was once home to New York governor Samuel Tilden, whereas the Players Club once belonged to the great thespian Edwin Booth, the brother of the man who assassinated Abraham Lincoln. Just east of Gramercy Park stands Theodore Roosevelt's Birthplace (28 East 20th Street), a museum filled with the world's largest collection of Roosevelt memorabilia.

Farther south, find Union Square, a booming park surrounded by sleek megastores, upscale restaurants, and fashionable bars. A popular farmers Greenmarket operates in the park on Monday, Wednesday, Friday, and Saturday mornings, and free concerts and other events sometimes take place here during the summer. To the immediate east of the square are several excellent Off-Broadway theaters.

Broadway between Union Square and Madison Square (between 23rd and 26th streets, Fifth and Madison avenues) was once known as the "Ladies Mile," because of the many fashionable department stores located here. Many were housed in extravagant cast-iron buildings, which still stand, now holding more modern emporiums.

At the corner of Broadway and 23rd Street is the famous 1902 Flatiron building, built in the shape of a narrow triangle and only six feet wide at its northern end. Meanwhile, reigning over Madison Park to the east are the enormous art deco Metropolitan Life Insurance Building (Madison Avenue, between 23rd and 25th streets) and the impossibly ornate Appellate Division of the New York State Supreme Court (Madison Avenue at 25th Street).

Still farther north and east lies Little India. Though not as thriving as it once was, it still houses a number of excellent Indian restaurants, sari shops, and spice stores, which attract shoppers from all over the city.

MIDTOWN

Stretching from 34th Street to 57th Street, the Harlem River to the East River, Midtown is the heart of Manhattan. Most of the city's skyscrapers are here, along with most of its offices, major hotels, famous shops, the Empire State Building, Times Square, the Broadway theaters, the Museum of Modern Art, Rockefeller Center, Grand Central Station, and the New York Public Library.

Fifth Avenue is the center of Midtown, dividing the city into east and west. Although nothing more than a line on a map as late as 1811, the thoroughfare had become New York's most fashionable address by the Civil War. It began to turn commercial in the early 1900s and is now lined with mostly shops and office buildings.

Towering over the southern end of Midtown is the Empire State Building (350 Fifth Avenue, at 34th Street), one of the world's most famous skyscrapers. Built in the early 1930s, the building took just 14 months to erect and remains an Art Deco masterpiece.

Forty-second Street is lined with one major attraction after another. On the corner of Third Avenue soars the magnificent Chrysler Building, another Art Deco masterpiece; Grand Central Station, whose magnificent concourse was recently restored to the tune of $200 million, is at Lexington Avenue. At Fifth Avenue beckons the New York Public Library, behind which spreads Bryant Park, where many free events are held during the summer months.

West of Seventh Avenue along 42nd Street begins Times Square, which stretches north to 48th Street along the Seventh Avenue-Broadway nexus. The best time to come here is at night, when the huge state-of-the-art neon lights that line the square begin to shine. Much cleaned up in recent years, Times Square is also a good place to catch street performers and, of course, Broadway theater. Many of the city's most famous theaters are located on the side streets around Times Square.

North and a little east of Times Square, Rockefeller Center reigns as an Art Deco complex stretching between 48th and 51st streets, Sixth and Fifth avenues. Built by John D. Rockefeller during the height of the Depression, Rockefeller Center is home to the landmark Radio City Music Hall, the NBC Studios, and a famed skating rink filled with outdoor enthusiasts during the winter months.

Along Fifth Avenue just south and north of Rockefeller Center, find some of the city's most famous shops—Saks Fifth Avenue, Tiffany's, Steuben Glass, and Cartier's, along with Trump Tower at 56th Street. Between 50th and 51st streets soars the Gothic Saint Patrick's Cathedral, the largest Roman Catholic cathedral in the United States; the Museum of Modern Art, a must-stop for any art lover, is on 53rd Street just west of Fifth.

UPPER EAST SIDE

Long associated with wealth, much of the Upper East Side—stretching from 57th Street north to 106th Street and Fifth Avenue east to the East

River—is filled with elegant mansions and brownstones, clubs and museums. Many of the city's most famous museums—including the Metropolitan Museum of Art—are located here, along with several posh hotels and Gracie Mansion, home to New York City's mayor.

But the neighborhood is about more than just wealth. Remnants of what was once a thriving German community can be found along the 86th Street-Second Avenue nexus, while a Puerto Rican and Latin community begins in the upper 80s, east of Lexington Avenue. At the corner of 96th Street and Third Avenue is a surprising sight—the Islamic Cultural Center, a modern, gold-domed mosque flanked by a skinny minaret.

Many of the Upper East Side's cultural institutions are located on Fifth Avenue, facing Central Park, along what is known as "Museum Mile." The Frick Collection, housing the private art collection of the former 19th-century industrialist Henry Clay Frick, marks the mile's southernmost end, at 70th Street. El Museo del Barrio, dedicated to the art and culture of Latin America, marks the northernmost end, at 104th Street. In between reign the grand Metropolitan Museum of Art (at 82nd Street), huge flags flapping out front, and the circular, Frank Lloyd Wright-designed Guggenheim Museum (at 88th Street)—to name just two.

The Plaza Hotel beckons from the southern end of the Upper East Side (Fifth Avenue, between 58th and 59th streets). This magnificent French Renaissance-style edifice was built in 1907 and is now owned by Donald Trump. Directly across Fifth Avenue from the hotel, F.A.O. Schwartz is an imaginative toy store that's as much fun for adults as it is for kids. Central Park is directly across 59th Street. Horse-drawn hansoms and their drivers congregate along the streets here, waiting hopefully for tourists interested in taking a clip-clopping tour. The small but state-of-the-art Central Park Zoo can be found in the park near Fifth Avenue and 65th Street.

Shoppers will want to take a gander at the many upscale boutiques lining Madison Avenue between 57th and 90th streets, or take a stroll over to Bloomingdale's (Lexington Avenue at 59th Street). Fifty-seventh Street holds numerous world-famous galleries, including PaceWildenstein (32 East 57th Street) and Andre Emmerich (41 East 57th Street), as well as such popular tourist stops as the Warner Brothers Studio Store (57th Street at Fifth Avenue) and Niketown (6 East 57th Street). The infamous St. Patrick's Day Parade, attracting hordes of rowdy revelers, travels down Fifth Avenue from 86th Street to 44th Street every March 17th.

UPPER WEST SIDE

Primarily residential, the Upper West Side has traditionally been known as the liberal-leaning home of writers, intellectuals, musicians, dancers, doctors, lawyers, and other upper-middle-class professionals. A mix of ornate 19th-century landmarks, pre-World War II apartment buildings, and tenement houses, the Upper West Side stretches from 57th Street north to 110th Street and from Fifth Avenue west to the Hudson River. At its eastern border, between Fifth Avenue and Central Park West and 59th and 110th streets, Central Park sprawls out in a vast and beautifully landscaped expanse of green.

Anchoring the neighborhood to the south is one of its best-known addresses—the Lincoln Center for the Performing Arts (Broadway between 62nd and 66th streets), which presents about 3,000 cultural events a year. Centering on a large, circular fountain, the 14-acre complex is home to such renowned institutions as the Metropolitan Opera House and Avery Fisher Hall. Many free outdoor concerts are presented on the plaza during the summer.

Directly across from Lincoln Center beckons a row of attractive restaurants and cafes, many with outdoor seating in summer. The Museum of American Folk Art (Broadway, between 65th and 66th streets), one of the city's smaller and more unusual museums, is also here. Another dozen or so blocks farther north, the Museum of Natural History (Central Park West, at 79th Street) is packed with everything from over 100 dinosaur skeletons to artifacts from peoples around the world. Adjoining the museum on its north side is the state-of-the-art Rose Center for Earth and Space. Completed in 2000, the center is instantly recognizable for its unusual glass architecture revealing a globe within a triangle.

The Upper West Side didn't begin developing until the late 1800s, when a grand apartment building called the Dakota was built at what is now the corner of Central Park West and 72nd Street. At the time, the building was so far north of the rest of the city that New Yorkers said it was as remote as the state of Dakota—and hence the name. Still standing today, the Dakota has been home to many celebrities, including Lauren Bacall, Gilda Radner, Boris Karloff, and John Lennon, who was fatally shot outside the building on December 8, 1980. In Central Park, directly across the street from the Dakota, is Strawberry Fields, a teardrop-shaped acre of land that Yoko Ono had landscaped in her husband's memory.

Central Park can be entered at major intersections all along Central Park West. Near the park's southern end, find Tavern on the Green (near Central Park West and 67th Street), a glittering extravaganza of a restaurant packed with mirrors and chandeliers. A bit farther north, find an odd-shaped body of water simply known as "The Lake" (between 72nd and 77th streets); rowboats can be rented at the Loeb Boathouse at the lake's eastern edge.

HARLEM

Stretching from 110th to 168th streets, between the Harlem and Hudson rivers, Harlem is in the midst of a renaissance. After years of being known primarily for its grinding poverty, drugs, and despair, the historic African American neighborhood is sprucing itself up, attracting mainstream businesses such as Starbucks and Ben & Jerry's, and becoming home once again to the middle class—African American and white.

Harlem can be divided in two: West/Central Harlem, which is primarily African American, and East Harlem, home to many Latinos and a smaller number of Italians. Between 110th and 125th streets west of Morningside Park is Morningside Heights, where Columbia University is located. Washington Heights, north of 155th Street, is home to Fort Tryon Park and the Cloisters, which houses the medieval collection of the Metropolitan Museum of Art.

First a farming community and then an affluent white suburb, Harlem began attracting African American residents after the construction of the IRT subway in 1901, and soon became the nation's premier African American neighborhood. The Harlem Renaissance boomed during the 1920s and 1930s, attracting writers and intellectuals such as Langston Hughes and W.E.B. DuBois, and the streets were packed with nightclubs, dance halls, and jazz clubs. Everything changed, however, with the Depression, when poverty took a strong hold that continues in many parts of the neighborhood today. When exploring Harlem, it's best to stick to the main thoroughfares.

The heart of Harlem is 125th Street, where you'll find a new Magic Johnson Theater complex, several restaurants and sweet shops offering soul food and baked goods, and the famed Apollo Theater (253 West 125th Street). Nearly every major jazz, blues, R&B, and soul artist to come along performed here, and the theater still presents its famed Amateur Night every Wednesday. Just down the street from the Apollo is the Studio Museum of Harlem (144 West 125th Street), a first-class fine arts institution spread over several floors of a turn-of-the-century building.

Another Harlem landmark is the Schomburg Center for Research in Black Culture (Lenox Avenue at 135th Street), founded by Arthur C. Schomburg, a Puerto Rican of African descent who was told as a child that his race had no history. Although primarily a library, the center also houses a large exhibit area where a wide array of changing exhibits is presented.

Not far from Columbia University, which is centered on Broadway and 116th Street, the Cathedral of St. John the Divine (Amsterdam Avenue at 112th Street), is the world's largest Gothic cathedral, said to be big enough to fit both Notre Dame and Chartres inside. Another major attraction nearby is Grant's Tomb (122nd Street at Riverside Drive), an imposing mausoleum sitting high on a bluff overlooking the Hudson.

Brooklyn

The largest borough in population and second largest in area, Brooklyn was a city in its own right—separate from New York—up until 1898. Brooklyn had its own city hall, central park, downtown shops, and cultural attractions, which helps account for the unusual amount the borough has to offer the visitor today. Brooklyn is also home to multiple ethnic groups, socioeconomic groups, and neighborhoods, one of which—Coney Island—is world famous.

Brooklyn Heights and Williamsburg are located at the northern end of Brooklyn, closest to Manhattan. Brooklyn Heights is quiet, upper-middle-class, and dignified, filled with lovely brownstones, historic buildings, and the wide riverside Promenade, which offers magnificent views of the Manhattan skyline and New York Harbor. Williamsburg was once inhabited mostly by Jewish immigrants and is still home to the Satmarer Hasidim, a major orthodox sect. Today the area is better known for its large, young, arts-oriented population. Along Bedford Avenue, especially, find a plethora of lively, inexpensive restaurants, bars, art galleries, and shops.

Bordering Brooklyn Heights is downtown Brooklyn, home to a number of imposing government buildings that date back to the days when Brooklyn was a city in its own right. The Greek Revival Borough Hall, at the intersection of Joralemon, Fulton, and Court streets, was once Brooklyn's City Hall and is still filled with government offices. Not far away is the New York Transit Museum (Schermerhorn Street at Boerum Place), an excellent place to learn the story behind the New York subway.

Near the center of Brooklyn sprawls Prospect Park, one of the city's loveliest retreats. Spread out over 525 acres of forests and meadows, the park was designed by Frederick Law Olmsted and Calvert Vaux, the two men who also planned Central Park in Manhattan. Brooklyn's foremost cultural attractions—the Brooklyn Museum of Art (200 Eastern Parkway, at Washington Avenue) and the Brooklyn Botanic Gardens (1000 Washington Avenue, near Eastern Parkway)—are located on the eastern edge of the park. The northwestern edge is Park Slope, a genteel neighborhood filled with elegant Victorian brownstones, now mostly inhabited by urban professionals with young children.

At the far southern end of Brooklyn, you'll find three most unusual neighborhoods—Coney Island, Brighton Beach, and Sheepshead Bay. Once home to a famed amusement park, Coney Island still beckons with an idiosyncratic collection of creaky historic rides, tawdry newer ones, a first-rate Aquarium for Wildlife Conservation (West Eighth Street, between the Boardwalk and Surf Avenue), and a wide, windswept boardwalk that stretches along a beach. The popular Mermaid Parade, featuring eye-popping costumes, takes place here every June. Next door to Coney Island is Brighton Beach, home to a thriving Russian community, and Sheepshead Bay, a tiny port filled with fishing boats, retirees, and seafood restaurants.

Queens

New York City's biggest borough, Queens is home to many large and vibrant ethnic neighborhoods, as well as to some important cultural and historic gems. It also holds John F. Kennedy International and La Guardia airports and Shea Stadium, the ballpark of the New York Mets.

At the western end of Queens stretch Long Island City and Astoria, both just a stop or two away from Manhattan on the subway. Although largely an industrial area, Long Island City has recently become known for its burgeoning artistic community and holds a number of first-rate galleries and museums. Foremost among them are the Isamu Noguchi Garden Museum (32-37 Vernon Boulevard, at 33rd Road), containing many works of the late great sculptor, and the P.S.1 Contemporary Art Center (22-25 Jackson Avenue, at 46th Street), a premier showcase for art on the cutting edge.

Meanwhile, Astoria is home to a large Greek population, as well as to an increasing number of Pakistani, Italian, and Latino residents. Along 30th Avenue and Broadway between 31st and Steinway streets, you'll find many Greek restaurants, food shops, and bakeries; the American Museum of the Moving Image (34-12 36th Street) is also nearby. Astoria was once the site of the Astoria Movie Studios, which produced such legends as Rudolf Valentino and Gloria Swanson; renovated and reopened in the late 1970s, the studios are now known as the Kaufman-Astoria Studios.

Travel a bit farther east on the No. 7 subway line—the borough's main transportation artery—to find Jackson Heights. Nicknamed the "cornfield of Queens" in the early 1900s, Jackson Heights now holds large Colombian and Indian populations, as well as smaller Peruvian, Uruguayan, Filipino, and Thai populations. A number of excellent Colombian restaurants are located along Roosevelt Avenue near 82nd and 83rd streets; tasty Indian food can be sampled between 70th and 74th streets near Roosevelt Avenue and Broadway.

East of Jackson Heights, Flushing Meadows-Corona Park is an enormous green oasis that housed both the 1939 and 1964 World Fairs. The park's Unisphere—a shining, 140-foot-high hollow globe—dates back to the 1964 fair, as do the buildings that now contain the Queens Museum of Art and the New York Hall of Science. The Queens Wildlife Center and Shea Stadium are also in the park.

Beyond the park, find Flushing, home to a clutch of historic buildings and large Asian communities. The historic buildings include the Bowne House (37-01 Bowne Street), used for illegal Quaker meetings in the 1660s, and the 1785 Kingsland House (143-35 37th Avenue), now the headquarters of the Queens Historical Society. The Asian community is centered on Main and Union streets; Asian restaurants serving delicious, authentic food are everywhere here.

THE BRONX

New York City's second-smallest borough both in size and population, the Bronx is also the only one attached to the mainland. In it you'll discover such legendary New York institutions as the Bronx Zoo, the New York Botanical Gardens, Yankee Stadium, and some of the city's biggest parks.

However, in the 1970s and 1980s, the borough also garnered a reputation for urban decay, as headlining stories involving murder, drugs, and arson seemed to come out of here daily. In more recent years, though, more than $1 billion in public funds has been spent on the South Bronx—where most of the decay occurred—and the place is in better shape now than it has been in years. Elsewhere in the borough, large residential neighborhoods have always flourished, most working- and middle-class (City Island, Co-Op City), a few quite exclusive (Riverdale, Fieldston).

First settled in 1644 by a Scandinavian named Jonas Bronck, the area soon became known as "The Broncks," and remained a predominantly agricultural community up until the late 1800s. But then the Third Avenue Elevated Railway arrived, and by 1900, the borough's population had soared to 200,000. During the 1920s and 1930s, grand Art Deco apartment buildings sprang up along the wide thoroughfare called the

Grand Concourse—a considerably more dilapidated version of which still exists today.

The New York Botanical Garden and Bronx Zoo sit adjacent to each other in the heart of the Bronx. Since they're both enormous, however, it's hard to visit them both in one day. Instead, opt for one of the two, and then head to Belmont, an Italian community just west of the zoo. One of the city's older and more established ethnic neighborhoods, it is packed with Italian restaurants, pastry shops, bakeries, butcher shops, and food markets.

Also in the Bronx is Van Cortlandt Park, which, at two square miles, is one of the city's largest parks. In its northernmost section sits the Van Cortlandt House Museum, a charming 18th-century mansion that once belonged to a wealthy landowner.

Across Jerome Avenue from the park stretches Woodlawn Cemetery, a lush 19th-century burial ground filled with rolling hills, meandering walkways, mausoleums, and tombs. Author Herman Melville, financier Jay Gould, and musicians Duke Ellington and Miles Davis are all buried here.

At the northern end of the Bronx reigns City Island, one of New York City's more unusual communities. A sailors' haven that had once hoped to become an important port, City Island is still home to a small shipbuilding industry. The place has only one main street—City Island Avenue—which is lined with a number of fish restaurants ranging in style from simple to old-fashioned elaborate.

STATEN ISLAND

Significantly more rural and suburban than the four other New York City boroughs, Staten Island is also predominantly white, politically conservative, and mostly working- and middle-class. Many residents own their own homes here, complete with tidy front lawns and garages—something you don't see much in the rest of the city. Unless you have access to a car, Staten Island is also quite difficult to explore. Buses run much less frequently and have more ground to cover than they do elsewhere in the city, making travel a time-consuming affair.

Fourteen miles long by seven miles wide, Staten Island was originally settled by Native Americans who successfully fought off the Dutch until 1661. Later, it became a military camp for the British during the Revolutionary War and then remained predominantly rural throughout the 1800s and early 1900s. Even as late as 1964, when the Verrazano-Narrows Bridge was completed, connecting the borough to the rest of the city, Staten Island was largely undeveloped.

The Staten Island Ferry is the borough's biggest attraction, carrying about 3½ million visitors back and forth every year, with few actually disembarking to explore the Staten Island side. Rides on the ferry are free, and the views they offer of Manhattan and New York Harbor are spectacular, especially at night.

The ferry docks at St. George, a small and often empty town with many deserted storefronts. About a mile away is the Snug Harbor Cultural Center (1000 Richmond Terrace; take the S40 bus), an odd complex of buildings that was once a home for retired sailors. Today, the center holds several galleries, a botanical garden, and a Chinese scholars' garden.

In the center of Staten Island stretches the Greenbelt, a 2,500-acre nature preserve made up of several tracts of woodlands, wetlands, and open fields, interspersed with a golf courses, a considerable amount of human settlement, and a few historic sites. A favorite stop for migrating birds, the Greenbelt also supports diverse flora, thanks to a wide variety of soils deposited here by glaciers about 10,000 years ago.

South of the Greenbelt, find the Jacques Marchais Museum of Tibetan Art (338 Lighthouse Avenue; take the S74 bus), housing what is said to be the largest collection of Tibetan art in the Western world. Within walking distance of the Tibetan Museum is Historic Richmond Town

(441 Clarke Avenue), a re-created historic village filled with 29 buildings, most moved here from elsewhere on the island.

Until recently, Staten Island was also the butt of many jokes, as the city's largest dump, the Fresh Kills landfill, was located here. However, Fresh Kills was closed in early 2001.

MUSEUMS OF NEW YORK

New York is a city of museums. Almost everywhere you go, from the stately Upper East Side of Manhattan to the leafy reaches of Staten Island, you stumble upon them. Some are renowned worldwide: the Metropolitan Museum of Art, the Museum of Modern Art, the Museum of Natural History, the Guggenheim. Others are known only to enthusiasts: the Isamu Noguchi Garden Museum, the Tibetan Museum, the New York City Fire Museum, the Lower East Side Tenement Museum.

Below, find a guide to some of the city's most important, interesting, and/or offbeat museums, arranged by subject matter. If you're short on time, the must-sees are the Metropolitan Museum of Art, the Museum of Modern Art, and the American Museum of Natural History. Following not far behind are the Guggenheim, the Whitney, the Brooklyn Museum of Art, the Studio Museum in Harlem, the Cooper-Hewitt, the National Museum of the American Indian, and the Frick Collection.

Many of New York's major museums are packed with visitors on the weekends, especially in the afternoons or early evenings, because many are open late on Fridays and Saturdays. To avoid the crowds, come during the week or on weekend mornings.

Major Art Museums

Any guide to the Big Apple's museums must start with that most venerable, enormous, and glorious of institutions, the **Metropolitan Museum of Art** (1000 Fifth Avenue, at 82nd Street; phone 212/535-7710). Housed behind an impressive Beaux Arts facade designed by Robert Morris Hunt, the museum holds collections of everything from Egyptian sarcophagi to contemporary American painting. Equally important, it hosts at least two or three major temporary exhibits at any given time.

Founded in 1870, the Met centers on the Great Hall, a vast entrance room with a stately staircase leading to the second floor. Here you'll find the European Paintings galleries, one of the Met's most important collections. Housed in about 20 rooms are works by such masters as Rembrandt, Breughel, Rubens, Botticelli, Goya, and El Greco. Next door are the impressive 19th-century European Galleries, housing works by more modern masters such as van Gogh, Gauguin, Seurat, and Renoir.

Three sides of the Met's original building are flanked by modern glass wings. At the back is the Robert Lehman Collection, containing an exhibit of 19th-century French paintings, among other things. On the south side are the Rockefeller and Acheson Wings, the first holding a South Pacific collection—everything from totem poles to canoes—the second, 20th-century art. On the north side, find the Sacker Wing, best known for its 15th-century-B.C. Temple of Dendur, carved in faded hieroglyphics, and the American Wing, housing exhaustive galleries of decorative arts and paintings by the likes of Thomas Eakins and John Singer Sargent.

The Met's Egyptian collection is one of the largest in the world and a must-stop for history buffs. The Islamic art collection and the new South and Southeast Asian art collection are also among the world's finest. To see the museum's medieval collection, travel north to the **Cloisters** (Fort Tyron Park, 190th Street at Overlook Terrace; phone 212/923-3700). Situated high on a hill with great views of the Hudson River, the Cloisters are housed in a reconstructed medieval monastery that incorporates the actual remains of four medieval cloisters.

The second stop for any serious art lover should be the **Museum of Modern Art** (11 West 53rd Street, between Fifth and Sixth avenues; phone 212/708-9480). Currently in the midst of major expansion (not to be completed until late 2004), the museum houses some 100,000 paintings, sculptures, drawings, prints, and photographs and presents first-rate films—mostly classic, foreign, and experimental—in its comfortable basement auditorium.

Major temporary exhibits usually dominate the museum's first and basement floors, whereas the permanent collections are housed above. On the second floor, find such masterpieces as Cezanne's *The Bather* and van Gogh's *Starry Night*, along with entire rooms devoted to Mondrian, Pollock, Matisse, and Monet's *Water Lilies*. Also on the second floor is a superb photography exhibit. The third floor houses prints and illustrated books and the fourth, architectural drawings and design objects. A jazz concert series is held in the museum's outdoor sculpture garden in the summer.

Another essential stop for the modern art lover is the **Solomon R. Guggenheim Museum** (1071 Fifth Avenue, at 88th Street; phone 212/423-3500). Housed in a circular building designed by Frank Lloyd Wright in 1959, the main gallery is a gentle multileveled spiral circling around a central atrium. The exhibits, all major temporary shows featuring 20th- or 21st-century artists, start at the top of the spiral and wind their way down.

Next door to the main gallery is a rotunda, housing the small but stunning Justin K. Thannhauser Collection, which includes works by such artists as Picasso, Cezanne, Modigliani, and Seurat. A ten-story tower also abuts the main gallery to the back; here, find a mix of temporary and permanent exhibits and an outdoor sculpture garden. This museum boasts a second branch in SoHo, the **Guggenheim Museum SoHo** (575 Broadway, at Prince Street; phone 212/423-3500), which usually houses the work of younger and more cutting-edge artists.

Not far from the Guggenheim is the **Whitney Museum of American Art** (Madison Avenue, at 75th Street; phone 212/570-3676). Most of the exhibits here are temporary and feature the work of one major American artist such as Edward Hooper, Jasper Johns, or Jacques Basquiat. The museum is also known for its superb permanent collection and for its controversial "Biennial" show, presented every two years to showcase the latest work of contemporary American artists.

A few blocks south of the Whitney, find the hushed **Frick Collection** (1 East 70th Street, at Fifth Avenue; phone 212/288-0700). The museum is housed in a lovely 1914 mansion, the former home of 19th-century industrialist Henry Clay Frick, built around a peaceful courtyard. Renowned for its permanent European art collection, the Frick boasts masterpieces by Breughel, El Greco, Vermeer, Rembrandt, and many others. Near the entrance is the Jean-Honore Fragonard Room, where all four walls are covered with *The Progress of Love,* a mural commissioned by Louis XV.

A few blocks north of the Metropolitan beckons another museum housed in a former mansion—the **Cooper-Hewitt National Design Museum** (2 East 91st Street, at Fifth Avenue; phone 212/849-8400). Once home to the 19th-century industrialist Andrew Carnegie, the 64-room building is now a branch of the Smithsonian Institution dedicated to design and the decorative arts. The exhibits are temporary and focus on such subjects as ceramics, furniture, textiles, and metalwork. Out back is a romantic garden, where concerts are sometimes presented.

The **Studio Museum of Harlem** (144 West 125th Street, between Lenox Avenue and Adam Clayton Powell Boulevard; phone 212/864-4500) is located in Harlem. Founded in 1968, the museum is the "principal center for the study of Black art in America," spread out over several well-lit floors of a turn-of-the-century building. The permanent exhibit features works by such masters as Romare Bearden, James VanDerZee, and Jacob Lawrence; the temporary exhibits present a mix of both world-renowned and emerging artists. The Studio is also known for its lively lecture and concert series, presented September through May.

Although often overlooked by tourists, the **Brooklyn Museum of Art** (200 Eastern Parkway, at Washington; phone 718/638-5000) is one of the city's foremost art institutions. Similar to the Metropolitan in some ways, it is housed in a lovely beaux arts building, with collections spanning virtually the entire history of art. Highlights include a large Egyptian wing, a superb Native American collection, and a major permanent assemblage of contemporary art. In addition to staging some of the more unusual and controversial exhibits in town, the museum also hosts a "First Saturday" series (the first Saturday of every month, 5-11 pm), featuring free concerts, performances, films, dances and dance lessons.

SMALLER ART MUSEUMS

In addition to the behemoths above, New York City is home to scores of smaller art museums, many of which are unique gems. No matter where your art interests lie, you're bound to find something that speaks to you.

Photography buffs won't want to miss the **International Center of Photography,** recently relocated from the Upper East Side to Midtown (1133 Sixth Avenue, at 43rd Street; phone 212/768-4682). In these spacious galleries, you'll find changing exhibits featuring everyone from Weegee (Arthur Fellig) to Annie Lebovitz.

Meanwhile, sculpture fans will want to visit the **Isamu Noguchi Garden Museum** in Long Island City, Queens (32-37 Vernon Boulevard, at 33rd Road; phone 718/204-7088), just a short trip from Manhattan. Housed in the sculptor's former studio, complete with an outdoor sculpture garden, the museum is filled with Noguchi stone, metal, and wood work. The museum is only open from April through October, so you will have to time your visit accordingly.

In Murray Hill, find the **Pierpont Morgan Library** (29 East 36th Street, at Madison Avenue; phone 212/685-0610), housed in an elegant neoclassic mansion that was once financier John Pierpont Morgan's personal library and art museum. The library holds a priceless collection of illuminated manuscripts and Old Master drawings; compelling traveling exhibits are frequently on display as well.

In SoHo, the **New Museum of Contemporary Art** (583 Broadway, between Houston and Prince streets; phone 212/219-1222) hosts experimental and conceptual works by contemporary artists from all over the world. Also a premier center for art on the cutting edge is the **P.S.1 Contemporary Art Center** in Long Island City, Queens (22-25 Jackson Avenue, at 46th Street). On the Upper West Side, the **Museum of American Folk Art** (2 Columbus Avenue, between 65th and 66th streets; phone 212/595-9533) showcases everything from quilts and weathervanes to painting and sculpture; admission is always free.

HISTORY MUSEUMS

A good introduction to the history of the Big Apple can be found at the **Museum of the City of New York** (Fifth Avenue, between 103rd and 104th streets; phone 212/534-1672), an eclectic establishment filled with a vast permanent collection of paintings and photographs, maps and prints, Broadway memorabilia and old model ships. Housed in a sprawling neo-Georgian building, the museum also hosts an interesting series of temporary exhibits on such subjects as Duke Ellington or stickball. (Note: the museum will be moving to the Tweed Courthouse on Chambers Street in Lower Manhattan in spring 2003.)

Also devoted to the history of New York is the **New York Historical Society** (2 West 77th Street, at Central Park West; phone 212/873-3400), which has recently reawakened after years of inactivity due to financial troubles. Spread out over many high-ceilinged rooms, the society presents temporary exhibits on everything from the legendary Stork Club—frequented by everyone from Frank Sinatra to JFK—to the small African-American communities that once dotted Central Park.

To find out more about immigration history, visit the **Ellis Island Museum,** a trip that is usually made, via ferry, in conjunction with a jaunt to the Statue of Liberty (for information, call the Circle Line Ferry at 212/269-5755; the ferries leave from Battery Park in Lower Manhattan). The primary point of entry for immigrants to the United States from 1892 to 1924, Ellis Island is a castlelike building, all redbrick towers and white domes, that now houses multiple exhibits on the immigrant experience, along with photographs, films, and taped oral histories. To avoid the crowds that flock here, especially during the summer, arrive first thing in the morning.

Related in theme to Ellis Island is the **Lower East Side Tenement Museum** (97 Orchard Street, between Delancey and Broome streets; phone 212/431-0233; visits by guided tour only, reservations recommended). Deliberately dark and oppressive, the museum re-creates early immigrant life in Manhattan.

The **South Street Seaport Museum** is not so much a museum as it is an 11-block historic district, located in Lower Manhattan where Fulton Street meets the East River. A thriving port during the 19th century, the now-restored area is filled with commercial shops and restaurants, along with dozens of historic buildings—a boat-building shop, a former counting house—and a few historic sailing ships. The ships and some of the buildings require an entrance ticket that can be purchased at the Visitor Center (on Schermerhorn Row, an extension of Fulton Street; phone 212/748-8600).

In the East Village, find the **Merchant's House Museum** (29 East 4th Street, near the Bowery; phone 212/777-1089). This classic Greek Revival home is furnished exactly as it was in 1835, when merchant Seabury Tredwell and his family lived here.

Near Gramercy Park presides **Theodore Roosevelt's Birthplace** (28 East 20th Street, near Broadway; phone 212/260-1616), a handsome four-story brownstone that is an exact replica of the original. Now administered by the National Park Service, the museum houses the largest collection of Roosevelt memorabilia in the country.

CULTURAL MUSEUMS

As befits a city made up of many peoples, New York is home to a number of museums that focus on the culture of one country or area of the world. Some of these are major, professionally assembled institutions; others are small and homespun.

In Lower Manhattan, find the George Gustav Heye Center of the **National Museum of the American Indian** (1 Bowling Green, at State Street and Battery Place; phone 212/668-6624), a branch of the Smithsonian Institution. Housed in a stunning 1907 Beaux Arts building designed by Cass Gilbert, the museum holds some of the country's finest Native American art and artifacts, ranging in date of origin from 3200 B.C. to the 20th century. Admission is always free.

Also in Lower Manhattan is the **Museum of Jewish Heritage** (18 First Place, at Battery Park, Battery Park City; phone 212/968-1800), built in the shape of a hexagon, symbolic of the Star of David. Opened in 1997, the museum features thousands of moving photographs, cultural artifacts, and archival films documenting the Holocaust and the resilience of the Jewish community.

A second Jewish museum, this one devoted to arts, culture, and history, can be found on the Upper East Side. Housed in a magnificent French Gothic mansion, the **Jewish Museum** (1109 Fifth Avenue, at 92nd Street, 212/423-3200) holds an outstanding permanent collection of ceremonial objects and artifacts, while also hosting many major exhibits on everything from "The Dreyfus Affair" to painter Marc Chagall.

Also on the Upper East Side, find the **Asia Society** (502 Park Avenue, at 59th Street; phone 212/517-2742) and **El Museo del Barrio** (1230

Fifth Avenue, between 104th and 105th streets; phone 212/831-7272). The former presents first-rate temporary exhibits, concerts, films, and lectures on various aspects of Asian culture and history. The latter features changing exhibits on both contemporary and historic subjects and houses a superb permanent collection of *santos de palo,* or carved wooden saints.

In Harlem is the **African American Wax Museum** (318 West 115th Street, between Manhattan Avenue and Frederick Douglass Boulevard; phone 212/678-7818; by appointment only), a tiny private place created and run by Haitian-born artist Raven Chanticleer. The museum is filled with wax figures of famous African Americans—Frederick Douglass, Josephine Baker, Nelson Mandela—as well as Chanticleer's own paintings and sculptures.

The **Museum of the Chinese in Americas** in Chinatown (70 Mulberry Street, at Bayard Street, second floor; phone 212/619-4785) is a small but fascinating place, filled with photographs, mementos, and poetry culled from nearly two decades of research in the community. Women's roles, religion, and Chinese laundries are among the subjects covered in the exhibits.

On Staten Island, find the **Jacques Marchais Museum of Tibetan Art** (338 Lighthouse Avenue, at Windsor; phone 718/987-3500). Perched on a steep hill with views of the Atlantic Ocean, the museum houses the collection of Jacqueline Norman Klauber, who became fascinated with Tibet as a child. Highlights of the exhibit include a series of bright colored masks and a large collection of golden *thangkas,* or religious images.

NATURAL HISTORY, SCIENCE, AND TECHNOLOGY MUSEUMS

The must-stop in this category is the enormous **American Museum of Natural History** (Central Park West at 79th Street; phone 212/769-5100), one of the city's greatest museums. Always filled with hundreds of shouting, enthusiastic kids, the museum went through a major renovation in the late 1990s and is now filled with many state-of-the-art exhibits.

At the heart of the museum are its approximately 100 dinosaur skeletons, some housed in the soaring, not-to-be-missed Theodore Roosevelt Memorial Hall. Other highlights include the Mammals Wing, the Hall of Human Biology and Evolution, the Hall of Primitive Vertebrates, and the museum's many dioramas and exhibits devoted to native peoples around the world. Adjoining the museum to the north is the spanking new **Rose Center for Earth and Science,** featuring a planetarium with a Zeiss sky projector capable of projecting 9,100 stars as viewed from earth.

The city's top pure science museum is the **New York Hall of Science** (47-01 111th Street; phone 718/699-0005), located in Flushing Meadows-Corona Park, Queens—best reached from Manhattan via the No. 7 subway. Housed in a dramatic building with undulating walls, the museum is packed with hands-on exhibits for kids and features a large Science Playground out back, where kids can learn about the laws of physics.

Docked at Pier 86 on the western edge of Manhattan is the **Intrepid Sea-Air-Space Museum** (West 46th Street at 12th Avenue; phone 212/245-0072). A former World War II aircraft carrier, the museum is now devoted to military history and includes lots of hands-on exhibits for kids. Small aircraft and space capsules are strewn here and there, and exhibits focus on such subjects as satellite communication and spaceship design.

Also in Midtown is the **Museum of Television and Radio** (25 West 52nd Street, between Fifth and Sixth avenues; phone 212/621-6800), where you can watch your favorite old television show, listen to a classic radio broadcast, or research a pop-culture question. The museum also offers traditional exhibits on such subjects as the history of animation. Be sure to arrive early if you plan to visit on the weekend and want to use one of the museum's 96 semiprivate televisions or radio consoles.

MUSEUMS FOR KIDS

In addition to the natural history, science, and technology museums above, children might also enjoy visiting the **Children's Museum of Manhattan** on the Upper West Side (212 West 83rd Street, between Broadway and Amsterdam Avenue; phone 212/721-1223) or the **Children's Museum of the Arts in SoHo** (182 Lafayette Street, between Broome and Grand streets; phone 212/274-0986). In the former, aimed at ages two to ten, kids can draw and paint, play at being newscasters, or explore the ever-changing play areas; the latter features an "Artists' Studio," where youngsters can try their hand at sand painting, origami, sculpture, and beadwork.

Although not, strictly speaking, a children's museum, the **New York City Fire Museum** in SoHo (278 Spring Street, between Varick and Houston; phone 212/691-1303) has great appeal for kids. Housed in an actual firehouse that was used up until 1959, the museum is filled with fire engines new and old, helmets and uniforms, hoses and lifesaving nets. Retired firefighters take visitors through the museum, reciting fascinating tidbits of fire-fighting history along the way.

Older kids might also enjoy a visit to the **Forbes Magazine Galleries** in Greenwich Village (62 Fifth Avenue, near 12th Street; phone 212/206-5548). Housing the collections of the idiosyncratic media tycoon Malcolm Forbes, the museum includes exhibits of more than 500 toy boats, 12,000 toy soldiers, about a dozen Faberge eggs, and numerous historical documents relating to American history. Admission is free.

Manhattan

Area code 212

When most people think of New York City, they think of Manhattan. When the first colonists arrived in 1626, Manhattan was a rugged, wooded island, inhabited only by a small band of Native Americans at its northern end. A mere three-and-a-half centuries later, it had become our most concentrated definition of the word "city." Only 12½ miles long and 2½ miles wide at its widest point, it is the center of American culture, communications, and business, containing an enormous variety of restaurants, shops, museums, and entertainment.

Many superlatives are needed to describe Manhattan—it has the largest banks, several of the finest streets and avenues, one of the greatest city parks (Central Park), an incredible skyline, the greatest theater district, and the most sophisticated of almost everything. If Manhattanites sometimes forget that there is more to America than this tiny island, perhaps they may be forgiven. Their island is unique.

Airport Information

La Guardia & JFK Intl Airport Areas. *La Guardia,* in Queens eight miles northeast of Manhattan; Kennedy International, in Queens 15 miles southeast of Manhattan (for both, see QUEENS—LA GUARDIA and JFK INTERNATIONAL AIRPORT AREAS); *Newark International,* 16 mi southwest of Manhattan in New Jersey.

What to See and Do

American Bible Society Gallery/Library. Collection of Bibles and unusual current editions; replica of Gutenberg press; changing exhibits. (Mon-Sat; closed hols) 1865 Broadway at 61st St. Phone 212/408-1200. **FREE**

American Craft Museum. Dedicated to the history of American crafts; textiles, ceramics, glasswork; changing exhibits. (Tues, Wed, Fri-Sun; closed hols) 40 W 53rd St, between 5th and 6th aves. Phone 212/956-3535. ¢¢

American Museum of Natural History. Permanent exhibits incl the Hall of Ocean Life, with its 94-ft great blue whale; the Hall of South American Peoples, Asian Peoples, Northwest Coast Indians, Mexico and Central America, and African Peoples; Hall of Reptiles and

The Lake, Central Park

Amphibians; Human Biology and Evolution; skeletal constructions of dinosaurs and other prehistoric life. Changing exhibits. Museum Highlights Tour (daily; free). Demonstration lectures, drama, dance, film. Daily; closed Thanksgiving, Dec 25) IMAX film shown on huge indoor screen. Central Park W at 79th St. Phone 212/769-5100 or 212/769-5034. ¢¢

The Asia Society Galleries. Presents exhibitions of ancient, modern, and contemporary art assembled from public and private collections in Asia and the West; incl as a permanent collection The Mr. and Mrs. John D. Rockefeller III Collection of Asian Art. (Tues-Sun; closed hols) 725 Park Ave. Phone 212/288-6400. ¢¢

Astro Minerals Gallery of Gems. Display of minerals, gems, jewelry; primitive and African art. (Daily; closed Jan 1, Thanksgiving, Dec 25) 185 Madison Ave, at 34th St. Phone 212/889-9000. **FREE**

⭐ **Carnegie Hall.** Completed in 1891, the celebrated auditorium has been home to the world's great musicians for more than a century. Guided one-hr tours (Mon-Fri; fee). 154 W 57th St, at Seventh Ave. Phone 212/247-7800. Performances ¢¢¢¢

Cathedral Church of St. John the Divine. Episcopal. Under construction since 1892. When completed, this will be the largest Gothic cathedral in the world, 601 ft long and 124 ft high. Bronze doors of the central portal represent scenes from the Old and New Testaments. The great rose window, 40 ft in diameter, is made up of more than 10,000 pieces of glass. Cathedral contains tapestry, painting, and sculpture collection. The cathedral and five other buildings are on 13 acres with park and garden areas, incl Biblical Garden. No parking provided. (Daily) Tours Tues-Sat; also Sun following last morning service; no tours religious hols. Amsterdam Ave and 112th St. Phone 212/316-7540. ¢¢

⭐ **Central Park.** Construction of this magnificent 843-acre park, designed by Frederick Law Olmsted and Calvert Vaux, began in 1857; it was the first formally planned park in the country. Topographically rugged, highlights incl a lake with boat and gondola rentals; a lake for sailing miniature boats; a six-acre Wildlife Conservation Center (fee); two skating rinks; a swimming pool; a miniature golf course; a conservatory garden; Strawberry Fields, given to the park by Yoko Ono in memory of John Lennon; the Belvedere Castle; and the Delacorte Theater, where the summer Shakespeare Festival is staged (see SPECIAL EVENTS). Park drives running north and south are closed to vehicular traffic on Sat, Sun, and hols, as well as certain hrs on wkdays (Apr-Oct). The entrances at 59th St and 5th and 6th aves are known for horse-drawn carriages, which can be hired for a ride through the park. 5th Ave to Central Park W (8th Ave) and 59th St to 110th St. Also in the park are

The Dairy. Exhibition/Visitor Information Center. Video on history of the park; time-travel video; gift and book shop. (Tues-Sun) In the Park on 65th St, W of the Central Park Wildlife Conservation Center and the carousel. Phone 212/794-6564. **FREE**

Storytelling in the Park. At Hans Christian Andersen statue in Central Park, near the model boat pond, off 74th St at 5th Ave (June-Sept, Sat). Recommended for children five and older; also in certain playgrounds (July-Aug). Phone 212/360-3444. **FREE**

Children's Museum of Manhattan. Hands-on exhibits for children 1-10; kids can draw and paint, learn crafts, play at being newscasters, listen to stories, or explore changing play areas. (June-Labor Day, Tues-Sun; closed hols) 212 W 83rd St, between Broadway and Amsterdam. Phone 212/721-1234. ¢¢

Chrysler Building. New York's famous Art Deco skyscraper. The graceful pointed spire with triangular windows set in arches is lighted at night. The impressive lobby features beautiful jazz-age detailing. 405 Lexington Ave, at E 42nd St.

City Center. Landmark theater hosts world-renowned dance companies, incl the Alvin Ailey American Dance Theater, the Paul Taylor Dance Company, and Merce Cunningham Dance Company. Also presents American music and theater events. Downstairs, City Center Stages I and II host the Manhattan Theatre Club. 55th St between 6th and 7th aves. Phone 212/581-1212.

City College of New York. (1847) 11,000 students. One of the nation's best-known municipal colleges and the oldest in the city university system. Alumni incl eight Nobel laureates, Supreme Court Justice Felix Frankfurter, and authors Upton Sinclair, Paddy Chayefsky, and Bernard Malamud. Tours (Mon-Thurs, by appt). Convent Ave and W 138th St. Phone 212/650-7000.

The Cloisters. This branch of the Metropolitan Museum of Art has parts of five medieval monasteries, a Romanesque chapel, a 12th-century Spanish apse, extensive gardens, and many examples of sculpture, painting, stained glass, and other art from the 9th-15th centuries. (Tues-Sun; closed Jan 1, Thanksgiving, Dec 25) In Fort Tryon Park, off Henry Hudson Pkwy, 1 exit N of George Washington Bridge. Phone 212/923-3700. ¢¢

Columbia University. (1754) 19,000 students. This Ivy League university was originally King's College; classes were conducted in the vestry rm of Trinity Church. King's College still exists as Columbia College, with 3,000 students. The campus has more than 62 buildings, incl Low Memorial Library, the administration building (which has the Rotunda and the Sackler Collection of Chinese Ceramics), and Butler Library, with more than five million volumes. The university numbers Alexander Hamilton, Gouverneur Morris, and John Jay among its early graduates and Nicholas Murray Butler, Dwight D. Eisenhower, and Andrew W. Cordier among its former presidents. Barnard College (1889), 2,300 women, and Teachers College (1887), 5,000 students, are affiliated with Columbia. Multilingual guided tours. (Mon-Fri exc hols and final exam period) Broadway and 116th St. Phone 212/854-1754. **FREE**

Cooper-Hewitt National Design Museum. A branch of the Smithsonian Institution dedicated to design and the decorative arts. A 64-rm, 1901 Georgian mansion built by industrialist Andrew Carnegie housing permanent exhibits of textiles, metalwork, wallpaper, ceramics, furniture, and architectural design; changing exhibits. (Tues-Sat, also Sun afternoons; closed hols) 2 E 91st St, at 5th Ave. Phone 212/849-8400. ¢¢

Cooper Union. (1859) 1,000 students. All-scholarship college for art, architecture, and engineering. Great Hall, where Lincoln spoke in 1861, is auditorium for readings, films, lectures, and performing arts. Third Ave at 7th St. Phone 212/353-4000.

Dyckman House Park and Museum. (ca 1784) Only 18th-century Dutch

Souvenirs here

© MAPQUEST

farmhouse still on Manhattan Island. Built by William Dyckman; refurnished with some original Dyckman pieces and others of the period. Replica of British officers' hut on landscaped grounds; smokehouse; garden. (Tues-Sun; closed hols) Children only with adult. 4881 Broadway, at 204th St. Phone 212/304-9422. **FREE**

Ellis Island Immigration Museum. The most famous port of immigration in the country. From 1892 to 1954, more than 12 million immigrants began their American dream here. The principle structure is the Main Building with its Great Hall, where the immigrants were processed; exhibits; 28-min film; self-service restaurant. Boat from Castle Clinton on Battery to Statue of Liberty incl stop at Ellis Island. Ellis Island has been incorporated into the monument. Phone 212/363-3200.

Staten Island Ferry. Famous ferry to St. George, Staten Island, offers passengers a close look at both the Statue of Liberty and Ellis Island, as well as extraordinary views of the lower Manhattan skyline. Departs from the ferry terminal at intersection of Whitehall, State, and South sts, just E of Battery Park. ¢¢

El Museo del Barrio. Dedicated to Puerto Rican and other Latin American art, incl paintings, photographs, and sculpture; also films, theater, concerts, and educational programs. Inquire about bilingual tours. (Wed-Sun; closed hols) 1230 5th Ave, between E 104th and 105th sts. Phone 212/831-7272. ¢¢

⭐ **Empire State Building.** (1931) The 1,454-ft-high 1930s-*moderne* skyscraper building that King Kong climbed in the movie classic. Open and enclosed observation platforms on 86th floor (daily). 350 5th Ave, at 34th St. Phone 212/736-3100. ¢¢¢

***Forbes* Magazine Galleries.** Idiosyncratic collections of former media tycoon Malcolm Forbes; permanent exhibits incl a dozen Faberge eggs, more than 500 toy boats, more than 10,000 toy soldiers, more than 200 trophies, and historical documents; changing exhibits. (Tues, Wed, Fri, Sat; closed hols) Phone 212/206-5548.

Fordham University. Idiosyncratic collections of former media tycoon Malcolm Forbes; permanent exhibits include a dozen Faberge eggs, over 500 toy boats, over 10,000 toy soldiers, over 200 trophies, and historical documents; changing exhibits. (Tue, Wed, Fri, Sat; closed hols) 60th St and Columbus Ave, across from St. Paul's Church. Phone 212/636-6000.

Central Park

Cooper Union, home of the American Jazz Orchestra

The Frick Collection. European paintings, bronzes, sculpture, furniture, porcelains, enamels from the 14th-19th centuries exhibited in the Henry Clay Frick mansion. Unusual museum surroundings. (Tues-Sun; closed hols) No children under ten; under 16 only with adult. 1 E 70th St, at 5th Ave. Phone 212/288-0700. ¢¢

The Garment District. This crowded area, heart of the clothing industry in New York, has hundreds of small shops, factories, and streets jammed with trucks and hand-pushed delivery carts. Also in this area is Macy's. 6th Ave to 8th Ave and from 34th St to 42nd St.

General Grant National Memorial. President and Mrs. Ulysses S. Grant are entombed here. (Daily; closed hols) Riverside Dr and W 122nd St. Phone 212/666-1640.

Grand Central Station. (1913) Built in the Beaux Arts style and recently renovated for $200 million, this is one of New York's most glorious buildings. It has a vast 125-ft-high concourse, glassed-in catwalks, grand staircases, shops, restaurants, and a star-studded, aquamarine ceiling. Tours offered Wed by Municipal Art Society; meet at information booth in center of concourse at 12:30pm. 42nd St, between Vanderbilt and Lexington. Phone 212/935-3960. ¢¢

Greenwich Village. An area reaching from Broadway west to Greenwich Ave between 14th St on the north and Houston St on the south. An extension of this area to the East River is known as the East Village. Perhaps most famous as an art and literary center, Greenwich Village was originally settled by wealthy Colonial New Yorkers wishing to escape to the country. Many Italian and Irish immigrants settled here in the late 19th century. Among the famous writers and artists who have lived and worked in this area are Tom Paine, Walt Whitman, Henry James, John Masefield (he scrubbed saloon floors), Eugene O'Neill, Edna St. Vincent Millay, Max Eastman, Arctic explorer-writer Vilhjalmur Stefansson, Franz Kline, e.e. cummings, John Dos Passos, and Martha Graham. It is a colorful area, with restaurants, taverns, book, print, art, and jewelry shops. Greenwich Village is a fashionable and expensive place to live, particularly in the vicinity of

Washington Square. The Washington Arch, completed in 1895 as a commemoration of Washington's first inauguration, is 86 ft high. The park is a local gathering place and the hub of the Village. This area is the site of outdoor art shows by artists from Greenwich

Ellis Island

Village and many other points. East, north, and south of the square is the main campus of New York University (see). At the south end of 5th Ave.

Church of the Ascension. (1840) Episcopal. English Gothic; redecorated 1885-1889 under the direction of Stanford White. John La Farge's mural, *The Ascension of Our Lord,* surmounts the altar; the sculptured angels are by Louis Saint-Gaudens. (Daily) 10th St and Fifth Ave. Phone 212/254-8620.

Joseph Papp Public Theater. Complex of six theaters where Shakespeare, new American plays, new productions of classics, films, concerts, and poetry readings are presented. 425 Lafayette St, in the former Astor Library. Phone 212/260-2400.

Hamilton Grange National Memorial. (1802) Federal-style residence of Alexander Hamilton. (Wed-Sun) 287 Convent Ave, at W 141st St. Phone 212/283-5154. **FREE**

Harlem. An area reaching from 110th St to about 165th St and from the Harlem River to Morningside Ave. Spanish Harlem is toward the east, although Harlem and Spanish

Harlem overlap. Harlem has been called "the black capital of America." Tours: Harlem Spirituals. Phone 212/757-0425.

Horse racing.

   Aqueduct. (see QUEENS)

   Belmont Park. (see QUEENS)

   Meadowlands Sports Complex. Off NJ 3 in East Rutherford, NJ. Phone 888/445-6543.

   Yonkers Raceway. (see YONKERS, NY) Phone 914/968-4200.

International Center of Photography. Changing exhibits represent a wide range of photographic expression; audiovisual presentations; workshops, seminars, lectures. (Tues-Sun; closed hols) Midtown branch is 1133 Avenue of the Americas. Phone 212/860-1777. ¢¢ Midtown branch is

   ICP/Midtown. Changing exhibits; gallery tours; lectures, screening rm; bookstore. 1133 Ave of the Americas. ¢¢

***Intrepid* Sea-Air Space Museum.** The famous aircraft carrier *Intrepid* has been converted into a museum with gallery space devoted to histories of the ship itself, the modern navy, and space technology. Also on display is a nuclear guided submarine and a Vietnam-era destroyer (avail for boarding). Exhibits and film presentations. (Memorial Day-Labor Day, daily; rest of yr, Tues-Sun) Foot of W 46th St; at Pier 86, Hudson River. Phone 212/245-0072. ¢¢¢

Jacob K. Javits Convention Center. One of the world's largest, most technically advanced exposition halls; 900,000 square ft of exhibit space and more than 100 meeting rms can accommodate six events simultaneously. Designed by I. M. Pei, the center is easily recognized by its thousands of glass cubes that mirror the skyline by day. Cafe. 34th-39th sts along Hudson River, on 22-acre site SW of Times Sq. Phone 212/216-2000.

Jewish Museum. Devoted to Jewish art and culture, ancient and modern. Historical exhibits; contemporary painting and sculpture. (Mon-Thurs and Sun, afternoons; closed Jewish hols) 1109 5th Ave at 92nd St. Phone 212/423-3200. ¢¢

Jewish Theological Seminary of America. Extensive collection of Judaica; rare book rm; courtyard with sculpture by Jacques Lipchitz. Special programs. Kosher cafeteria. Tours avail. (Mon-Fri, Sun; closed hols) 3080 Broadway at 122nd St. Phone 212/678-8000.

Lincoln Center for the Performing Arts. New York's premier performing arts center incl Avery Fisher Hall (concerts), New York State Theater (ballet, opera), Vivian Beaumont and Mitzi E. Newhouse Theaters (drama), Metropolitan Opera House, and the Juilliard School, which also houses Alice Tully Hall (films, concerts). Here are 70 Lincoln Center Plaza. Here are

Lincoln Center Guided Tours. Incl Metropolitan Opera House, New York State Theater, and Avery Fisher Hall. Tour Desk is located on the Concourse Level, downstairs from the Plaza. (Daily;

no tours Jan 1, July 4, Thanksgiving, Dec 25). ¢¢

New York Public Library for the Performing Arts. Books, phonograph record collection; exhibits and research library on music, theater, and dance; concerts, films, dance recitals. 40 Lincoln Center Plaza. Phone 212/870-1630. **FREE**

Lower East Side Tenement Museum. Re-creation of early immigrant life, housed in authentic 1863 tenement building; changing exhibits; accessible by guided tour only. (Tues-Sun, call for res; closed hols) 97 Orchard St, at Broome St. Phone 212/431-0233. ¢¢

Madison Square Garden. The Garden has been the site of major sports, entertainment, and special events for well over a century. The present Garden, the fourth building bearing that name, was opened in 1968. (The original Garden was actually on Madison Sq.) It is the home of the New York Knickerbockers and Liberty

Empire State Building

basketball teams, and New York Rangers hockey club. The Garden complex incl the 20,000-seat Arena, Exposition Rotunda, and Bowling Center. Pennsylvania Plaza, above Pennsylvania Station, between 7th and 8th aves, W 31st to W 33rd St. Phone 212/465-MSG1.

⭐ **Metropolitan Museum of Art.** More than two million objects from a period of more than 5,000 yrs make this the most comprehensive collection in America. Egypt, Greece, Italy, the Near and Far East, Africa, the Pacific Islands, pre-Columbian and Native America, Europe, and America are represented. Twentieth-century art galleries, incl rooftop sculpture garden, and Japanese art galleries. To see the entire collection would take days. Special exhibits and programs for children. No strollers Sun or special exhibits. (Tues-Sun; closed Jan 1, Thanksgiving, Dec 25) Recorded tour (fee). Cafeteria; parking (fee). Free lectures, concerts, films, gallery talks. 1000 5th Ave at 82nd St. Phone 212/535-7710. ¢¢¢

Morris-Jumel Mansion. (1765) Built by Colonel Roger and Mary Philipse Morris, this was George Washington's headquarters in 1776 and later became a British command post and Hessian headquarters. Purchased by French merchant Stephen Jumel in

1810, house was the scene of the marriage of his widow, Madame Eliza Jumel, to Aaron Burr in 1833. The mansion is the only remaining Colonial residence in Manhattan. Period furnishings. (Wed-Sun; closed hols) 65 Jumel Terr at W 160th St, ½ blk E of St. Nicholas Ave. Phone 212/923-8008. ¢¢

Museum of American Folk Art. Folk arts of all types, incl painting, sculpture, quilts, needlework, toys, weather vanes, and handmade furniture; changing exhibits; lectures and demonstrations. (Daily; closed hols) Lincoln Sq, 2 Columbus Ave at 66th St. Phone 212/595-9533. **Donation**

Museum of Jewish Heritage. One of New York City's newest museums, dedicated to the Holocaust and the resilience of the Jewish community; housed in a freestanding hexagonal building, symbolic of the Star of David; thousands of photographs, cultural artifacts, and archival films; changing exhibits. (Mon-Fri, Sun; closed hols) Phone 212/509-6130. ¢¢¢ ¢¢¢

The Museum of Modern Art (MOMA). Comprehensive survey of 20th-century paintings, sculptures, drawings, prints, photographs, architectural models and plans, design objects, films, and videos; changing exhibits; free gallery talks; daily

Lincoln Center for the Performing Arts

HISTORIC GREENWICH VILLAGE

Although no longer the "leading edge" of the art world and radicalism, Greenwich Village remains a uniquely dynamic neighborhood. Start in Washington Square Park, lined by New York University buildings and site of the famous arch. The park normally buzzes with street performers, in-line skaters, and playing families. Leave the park from the south side. Judson Memorial Church stands on the corner of West 4th Street and Thompson Street. Designed by Stanford White, the church is noted for its stained glass windows and front marble work. Thompson Street is lined with chess clubs. At Bleecker Street, turn right. Look for Le Figaro (186 Bleecker Street) and Café Borgia (185 Bleecker Street), a pair of old-time coffee houses.

Turn right onto MacDougal Street. Here stand two landmark cafes: Café Reggio (119 MacDougal Street) and Café Wha? (115 MacDougal Street), as well as Minetta Tavern (113 MacDougal Street), an old standby that serves good Italian food. Make a U-turn, turn right onto Minetta Lane, then right onto Minetta Street, both lined with classic Village townhouses. Cross Sixth Avenue and enter the heart of Bleecker's "neighborhood" shopping—including some of the finest Italian bake shops in the city. Continue across Seventh Avenue and turn left onto Barrow Street. This block features a number of classic, redbrick row houses (49 and 51 Barrow Street are Federalist-style) and Chumley's Bar (86 Barrow Street), once a speakeasy and famous writers' hangout. Look for 75 Barrow Street, a strange, narrow house where Edna St. Vincent Millay once lived, and 77 Barrow Street, which was built in 1799, making it the Village's oldest house. Turn right on Bedford, passing a late 19th-century horse stable (95 Bedford), an early 19th-century home with a pair of Tudor-style towers aptly named Twin Peaks (102 Bedford), and a mid-19th-century home built in the Greek Revival style (113 Bedford).

Turn right onto Christopher Street, a throbbing, busy street that's the heart of the Village gay life. Go right onto Bleecker, then left onto Seventh Avenue. Sweet Basil (414 Seventh Avenue) is a famed jazz club, as is Village Vanguard (178 Seventh Avenue South). Turn right on Grove Street and right again on Waverly Place. At 165 Waverly Place stands the Northern Dispensary, built during the 1831 cholera epidemic. Turn left onto Sixth Avenue. The circa-1876, castlelike, Gothic-style Jefferson Market Library is located on 10th Street. Also of note on Sixth Avenue are Balducci's (424 Sixth Avenue), a legendary gourmet food shop, and Bigalow's (414 Sixth Avenue), the city's oldest continuously operating pharmacy. Continue north and turn right onto 11th Street to the minuscule Second Cemetery of the Spanish and Portugese Synagogue. Or, return south and turn left onto 8th Street, another major shopping street.

At Fifth Avenue, turn right. Just before Washington Square Park is the picturesque cul-de-sac Washington Square Mews. For more shopping, continue east on 8th Street and then turn south on Broadway. These blocks, not long ago a forsaken neighborhood of old warehouses and sweatshop factory buildings, now thrive with major retailing chains like Tower Records, the Gap, and more.

---

films; two restaurants set alongside museum's Abby Aldrich Rockefeller Sculpture Garden. (Mon, Tues, Thurs-Sun, extended hrs Fri; closed Thanksgiving, Dec 25) Touch tours for visually impaired. (See SPECIAL EVENTS) 11 W 53rd St, between 5th and 6th aves. ¢¢¢

The Museum of Television & Radio.
Exhibits feature programs from the past and present, news and docu-

mentaries, entertainment, and international TV. Collection of more than 100,000 radio and television programs; theaters; library; lectures and seminars; educational seminars. (Tues-Sun; closed hols) 25 W 52nd St between 5th and 6th aves. Phone 212/621-6800. ¢¢¢

Museum of the City of New York.
Museum on the history of New York City, with paintings, prints, pho-

tographs, ship models, theatrical memorabilia, collection of ten New York dollhouses dating from 1769 to present, firefighting equipt, costumes, and decorative arts. Dutch Gallery covers life in the early Dutch settlement; reconstructed portion of Fort Amsterdam. Multimedia "Big Apple" presentation. Walking tours of the city (Sun, spring-fall; fee). Concerts, gallery talks, and other wkend programs (fee for some). Museum (Wed-Sun; closed hols). 1220 5th Ave, between E 103rd and 104th sts. Phone 212/534-1672. ¢¢¢

New York City Post Office. Guided 90-min tours (Tues-Fri, upon written request to Postmaster, or phone 212/330-2300; one-wk advance res required). No cameras. Children over seven only. 341 9th Ave, between 29th and 30th sts.

MIDTOWN MANHATTAN

Few places pack so much to see and do into so little space as midtown Manhattan. This walk can be as short as two miles or as long as five or six, depending on your stamina and choice of sites.

Start at the Times Square Visitor Center at 1560 Broadway (at Seventh Avenue), and pick up information on theaters, dining, and sightseeing. Walk south to 42nd Street, and go right to the New Amsterdam Theatre (214 West 42nd Street), currently home to the long running hit *The Lion King* but, dating from 1903, the home of the Ziegfeld Follies. Guided tours are offered daily, and the daring Art Nouveau interiors are worth the time. Walk east on 42nd Street, passing the newly renovated Bryant Park, to the corner of Fifth Avenue, site of the New York Public Library Center for the Humanities branch (originally the library's Main Branch). Tours are offered here too; however, if time doesn't allow for a full tour, be sure to at least visit the Main Reading Room. It's a marvel of sumptuous woods and magnificent faux-wood plaster ceilings with a three-part ceiling mural and massive bronzed and arched windows. Returning to 42nd Street, continue east to the Park Avenue and Grand Central Terminal, another landmark that offers guided tours. A stunning example of Beaux Arts architecture, Grand Central's highlight is its huge central hall, lined with 33- by 60-foot windows, palatial marble staircases, and dual balconies. A new gourmet food court can be found in the lower terminal.

Return to Fifth Avenue and turn north (right). The next 15 blocks reveal the crème de la crème of premium shopping, including Saks Fifth Avenue (611 Fifth Avenue), Fortunoff (681 Fifth Avenue), Coca-Cola Fifth Avenue (711 Fifth Avenue), Henri Bendel (712 Fifth Avenue), Bergdorf Goodman (754 Fifth Avenue), Tiffany & Company (727 Fifth Avenue), Trump Tower (at 56th Street), and FAO Schwarz (767 Fifth Avenue). Rockefeller Center stands at 50th Street and Fifth Avenue, home to the famous ice rink, garden and floral displays, Radio City Music Hall, and NBC Studios. Just across from Rockefeller Center on Fifth Avenue stands St. Patrick's Cathedral, the famous English/Gothic seat of the New York City Catholic Archdiocese. At 52nd Street, just a few doors west of Fifth, is the Museum of Television & Radio. On 53rd Street stands the Museum of Modern Art and its signature collection, which includes works by Picasso, Van Gogh, and Matisse, to name just three. The American Craft Museum is found just off Fifth at 40 West 53rd Street.

Turn left (east) onto West 57th Street, where the high-end shopping continues and many art galleries are found. At Seventh Avenue is Carnegie Hall, the city's premier concert hall, which also can be toured. At this point, the southern reaches of Central Park are just two blocks north. Explore the park a bit and emerge on its eastern side. Either walk back downtown or, perhaps more sensibly, hop a bus to 34th Street for a visit to the Empire State Building. Following that, walk west on 34th to Herald Square (at Seventh Avenue) and some more shopping at Macy's, still the world's largest department store. For even more shopping return to Sixth Avenue and 32nd Street for a stop at the Manhattan Mall, home to 80 stores on nine levels.

The New York Historical Society. Variety of exhibits on American history with emphasis on New York (Tues-Sat). Research library (Tues-Sat). 2 W 77th St at Central Park. Phone 212/873-3400.

New York Public Library. One of the best research libraries in the world, with more than ten million volumes. Exhibits of rare books, art materials; free programs at branches. One-hr tours of central building (Mon-Sat), library tours at 11 am and 2 pm. Astor, Lenox, and Tilden foundations. 42nd St and 5th Ave. Phone 212/930-0501 or 212/661-7220. **FREE** Many interesting collections on display at the Central Research Library and The New York Public Library for the Performing Arts (also tours) and the

Schomburg Center for Research in Black Culture. The center's collection covers every phase of black activity wherever black people have lived in significant numbers. Books, manuscripts, periodicals, art, and audiovisual materials. 515 Malcolm X Blvd, at 135th St. Phone 212/491-2200. **FREE**

New York University. (1831) 15,584 students. One of the largest private universities in the country, NYU is known for its undergraduate and graduate business, medical, and law schools, school of performing arts, and fine arts programs. The university has graduated a large number of "Fortune 500" company executives. Most programs, incl the Graduate Business Center, are located on the main campus surrounding Washington Sq Park; the medical and dental schools are on the East Side. Tours Mon-Fri exc hols,

from Admissions Office at 22 Washington Sq N). In Main Building at northeast corner of Washington Sq is Grey Art Gallery and Study Center, with paintings, drawings, sculpture; changing exhibits (Tues-Sat). Renaissance musical instrument collection in Waverly Building (by appt).

Pierpont Morgan Library. Museum/rare book library designed by McKim, Mead, and White; holdings incl medieval and Renaissance manuscripts, early printed books, bookbindings, old master drawings, autograph and musical manuscripts, historical documents, early children's books, and manuscripts. Changing exhibits; permanent exhibits incl Gutenberg Bible, Renaissance paintings and sculpture, medieval gold objects. Glass-enclosed Garden Court. (Tues-Sun; closed hols, also last two wks Aug) 29 E 36th St. Phone 212/685-0610 or 212/685-0008. ¢¢¢

Radio City Music Hall

Macy's Herald Square

Police Museum. Exhibits of police uniforms, badges, and equipt. (Daily; closed hols; schedule may vary) 25 Broadway. Phone 212/301-4440. **FREE**

Professional Sports.

MetroStars (MLS). Giants Stadium, 50 Route 120. East Rutherford, NJ. Phone 201/583-7000.

New York Giants (NFL). Giants Stadium in East Rutherford, NJ. Phone 201/935-8111.

New York Islanders (NHL). Nassau Veterans Memorial Coliseum, Uniondale, NY. Phone 800/882-ISLES. Phone 800/882-4753.

New York Jets (NFL). Giants Stadium, East Rutherford, NJ. Phone 516/560-8200. Phone 516/560-8100.

New York Knicks (NBA). Madison Square Garden, 4 Penn Plaza.

New York Liberty (WNBA). Madison Square Garden, 2 Pennsylvania Plaza. Phone 212/564-WNBA.**New York Mets (MLB).** Shea Stadium (see QUEENS), 123-01 Roosevelt Ave. Phone 718/507-6387.

New York Rangers (NHL). Madison Square Garden, 2 Pennsylvania Plaza. Phone 212/308-NYRS.

New York Yankees (MLB). Yankee Stadium (see BRONX). Phone 718/293-4300.

⭐ **Rockefeller Center.** The largest privately owned business and entertainment center in the world is made up of 19 buildings on 11 acres. The graceful GE (formerly RCA) Building, designed by Raymond Hood, is the highest structure and centerpiece of the complex, which has more than 1,200 tenant firms, 34 restaurants, and 200 shops. The Channel Gardens, at 5th Ave between 49th and 50th sts, has seasonal floral displays, incl a spectacular Christmas tree. The gardens terminate at the gilded Prometheus Fountain. There is an outdoor cafe around the fountain's pool, which in winter is used as an ice rink. Radio City Music Hall, home of the Rockettes, is the world's largest indoor theater (capacity 6,000). (Phone 212/247-4777 for event information). The buildings east of Avenue of the Americas were completed in the 1930s; the Center buildings to the west were primarily completed in the 1960s. Self-guided tours; brochure avail at GE Building or Visitors Bureau. 5th Ave to Avenue of the Americas and beyond, 47th St to 51st St with some buildings stretching to 52nd St. Phone 212/332-3400.

Rose Center for Earth and Space. Opened in February 2000, the Center houses the Cullman Hall of the Universe, the Heilbrunn Cosmic Pathway, Scales of the Universe, and Gottesman Hall of Planet Earth. Also here is the Hayden Planetarium, which closed during a three-yr reconstruction period. The new planetarum centers on a state-of-the-art Zeiss sky projector that has more than 30 motors controlled by 45 computers. It is capable of projecting 9,100 stars as viewed from earth, the planets, and beyond. (Daily; closed Thanksgiving, Dec 25) Central Park W at 81st St. Phone 212/769-5920. ¢¢¢¢

St. Patrick's Cathedral. This famous Gothic Revival cathedral is 330 ft high. The interior can seat 2,400 people. (Daily) 5th Ave and 50th St.

Shopping.

Bloomingdale's. Flagship of famous department store chain. (Daily; closed hols) 1000 3rd Ave, at 59th St and Lexington Ave. Phone 212/705-2000 or 800/472-0788.

Macy's Herald Square. "The world's largest store" has everything from international fashion collections for men and women to antique galleries. (Daily; closed Easter, Thanksgiving, Dec 25) 34th St at Broadway. Phone 212/695-4400.

South Street Seaport. Festival marketplace with more than 100 shops and 40 restaurants in Seaport Plaza, Schermerhorn Row, and Museum Block, and the multifloored Pier 17, which extends into the East River. Fulton and Water sts, at East River. Phone 212/732-7678.

World Financial Center. The center incl more than 40 shops and restaurants on and around the Winter Garden, a 120-ft-high, vaulted glass and steel atrium. West St between Liberty and Vesey sts. Phone 212/945-0505.

Sightseeing Tours.

Adventure on a Shoestring. Walking tours of various neighborhoods, incl SoHo artist area, Haunted Greenwich Village, and Chinatown. Tours yr-round. Contact 300 W 53rd St, 10019. Phone 212/265-2663. ¢¢

Circle Line Sightseeing Yachts. Narrated cruises around Manhattan (three hrs) offer unique views of city (daily). Two-hr express cruise (daily). Harbor Lights cruise (Mar-Nov, nightly); refreshments. Boats depart from Pier 16, W 43rd St at 12th Ave and the Hudson River. Phone 212/563-3200. ¢¢¢¢

Gray Line. For information on a variety of sightseeing tours, incl tours of Manhattan aboard glasstop motor coaches, contact Gray Line of New York. Also day trips and tour packages. 254 W 54th St, 10019. Phone 212/397-2600.

Liberty Helicopters. Offers eight pilot-narrated tours, incl Bird's Eye View, A Taste of New York, Lady Liberty, and Bite of the Apple. Multilingual staff avail. Contact 147 Columbia Tpke, Suite 109, Florham Park, NJ. Phone 973/593-9292. ¢¢¢¢

Rockefeller Center

Prometheus Fountain, Rockefeller Center

SoHo. (For "South of Houston" Street) A neighborhood bounded by Broadway, 6th Ave, Houston (HOUSE-ton), and Canal sts. The city's brothel section in the early 1800s, the area was later razed and hundreds of loft buildings used for light manufacturing and warehouses were built. Zoning changes in 1970 permitted residences in the area. The spacious buildings of this district, many with cast iron facades, are ideal for artists' lofts and galleries. Although still a commercial area, many artists have moved into the 50-blk area, making it another art colony. Galleries, boutiques, and restaurants can be found throughout the area, especially on W Broadway, Prince, Spring, and Greene sts. Contact Friends of Cast Iron Architecture, 235 E 87th St, Rm 6C, 10128. Phone 212/369-6004. East of here is **Little Italy**, with Mulberry its main

street. The colorful festival of San Genarro (mid-or late Sept) is held here (see SPECIAL EVENTS).

Solomon R. Guggenheim Museum. This unique building, designed by Frank Lloyd Wright, has been restored. A ten-story tower based on an earlier Wright design was constructed for new galleries. Museum houses 19th- and 20th-century paintings and sculpture along a spiral ramp more than ¼ mi in length. Wright's intention was that patrons take the elevator to the top and then leisurely descend the gently-pitched spiral. Restaurant. Performance art series. (Mon-Wed, Fri-Sun; closed hols) Fri eves by donation. 1071 5th Ave, between E 88th and 89th sts. Branch museum incl Phone 212/423-3500. ¢¢¢¢ Branch museum includes

Guggenheim Museum SoHo. Facility has 30,000 square ft of exhibition space; also here are offices. (Mon, Thurs-Sun; closed hols) 575 Broadway, at Prince St. Phone 212/423-3500. **FREE**

South Street Seaport Museum. Eleven-blk area restored to display the city's maritime history, with emphasis on South St in the days of sailing vessels. Museum piers now moor the *Ambrose*, a lightship (1908); the *Lettie G. Howard*, a Gloucester fishing schooner (1893); the fully-rigged *Wavertree* (1885); the *Peking*, a German four-masted barque (1911); and the *Pioneer*, a schooner (1885). Permanent and changing maritime exhibits incl models, prints, photos, and artifacts. Tours. Harbor excursions. Children admitted only when accompanied by adult. (Apr-Sept, daily; rest of yr, Mon, Wed-Sun;

closed Jan 1, Thanksgiving, Dec 25)
South and Fulton sts, at the East
River. Phone 212/748-8600. ¢¢ Also
here are

South Street Seaport Events.
Throughout the yr concerts, festivals, and special events are staged
in the seaport area; weather permitting, passengers are taken for a
sail around the harbor aboard the
Pioneer; the museum's Children's
Center hosts a variety of special
programs, workshops, and exhibits.
In the fall, a fleet of classic sailing
vessels is assembled to compete in
a race for the Mayor's Cup.

South Street Seaport Neighborhood. Rows of 19th- and early
20th-century buildings house
almost 100 specialty shops and
museum galleries and more than
40 restaurants and eateries. (Daily)
Along South, Fulton, and Water sts.

☑ **Statue of Liberty National Monument.** A gift from the French, this
statue by Frederic Bartholdi is 152 ft
high and stands on a pedestal of
about the same height.
Made of 3/32 inch-thick
copper on a framework
designed by Gustav Eiffel
(designer of the Eiffel
Tower in Paris), there are
354 steps to the crown.
Snacks, souvenirs on
island (daily). Contact
212/269-5755 Yr round,
Liberty Island. Contact
Interpretive Staff, Liberty
Island, 10004. Phone
212/363-3200. Round trip
¢¢ At the base of the
statue is the

  **Statue of Liberty
  Exhibit.** Photographs,
  artifacts and history,
  dioramas with light and
  sound effects depict the
  construction of the
  Statue of Liberty.

**The Studio Museum in
Harlem.** One of the finest
collections of African-
American art. Changing
exhibits feature master,
mid-career, and emerging
black artists from the US,
the Caribbean, and Africa.
Yearly exhibits showcase
permanent collection.

Workshops, lectures, seminars. (Wed-
Sun afternoons; closed hols) 144 W
125th St. Phone 212/864-4500. ¢

Temple Emanu-El. Largest Jewish
house of worship in the world;
Reform Congregation founded in
1845. Romanesque temple seats
2,500; Beth-El chapel seats 350.
(Daily; no visiting on High Holy
Days) Tours (by appt, upon written
request). Mail requests to 1 E 65th St,
10021. 5th Ave and 65th St. Phone
212/744-1400.

**Theodore Roosevelt Birthplace
National Historic Site.** The reconstructed birthplace of the 26th president, who lived here from 1858-1872.
Tours of five rms restored to 1865
appearance. Audiovisual presentation,
and special events. (Mon-Fri) 28 E
20th St. Phone 212/260-1616. ¢

Times Square and the Theater District. Entertainment center of the
city and theatrical headquarters of
the country offering plays, musicals,
concerts, movies, and exotic entertainments; named for the Times

Guggenheim Museum

Tower at One Times Sq, originally the home of the *New York Times*. (See THEATER in introductory copy.) 6th to 8th aves and 40th to 53rd sts.

Ukrainian Museum. Changing exhibits of Ukrainian folk art, fine art, and history; workshops on wkends in folk crafts. (Wed-Sun; closed hols, Jan 7) 203 2nd Ave, between 12th and 13th sts. Phone 212/228-0110. ¢¢

Soho Art Galleries

United Nations. Four buildings, designed under the direction of Wallace K. Harrison, completed 1950-1952. Regular sessions of the General Assembly start on the third Tues in Sept. Tickets occasionally avail to certain official meetings on a first-come basis. Entrance is on 1st Ave at 46th St, at the north end of the General Assembly Building. In the lobby is an information desk and ticket booth; in the basement are the UN book and gift shops and the UN Post Office, where one can mail letters bearing United Nations stamps. On the fourth floor is the UN Delegates Dining Room. The Conference Building is where the various UN Councils meet. The Secretariat Building is a 550-ft-high rectangular glass-and-steel building; here the day-to-day work of the UN staff is performed. The fourth building is the Dag Hammarskjold Library, open only to UN staff and delegations, or by special permission for serious research.

Guided tours (45 min) leave the public entrance lobby at frequent intervals (daily; closed Thanksgiving and several days during yr-end hol season; also wkends Jan-Feb); no children under five. (Buildings, daily) 1st Ave from 42nd St to 48th St. Phone 212/963-8687. Tours ¢¢¢

Walk through downtown Manhattan. Allow at least three hrs. Start at Battery Park, in which is

Castle Clinton National Monument. (1811) Built as a fort, this later was a place of public entertainment called Castle Garden where Jenny Lind sang in 1850 under P. T. Barnum's management. In 1855 it was taken over by the State of New York for use as an immigrant receiving station. More than eight million people entered the US here between 1855-1890; Ellis Island was opened in 1892. The castle became the New York City Aquarium in 1896, which closed in 1941 and reopened at Coney Island in Brooklyn (see). The site has undergone modifications to serve as the visitor orientation/ferry departure center for the Statue of Liberty and Ellis Island. Ferry ticket booth; exhibits on Castle Clinton, Statue of Liberty, and Ellis Island; visitor center. Contact the Superintendent, Manhattan Sites, 26 Wall St, 10005. Phone 212/344-7220. **FREE** Walk up Broadway, east of the Battery, to

Bowling Green. Originally a Dutch market, this is the city's oldest park, said to be the place where

Peter Minuit purchased Manhattan for $24 worth of trinkets. The park fence dates from 1771. On the south side is the

The George Gustav Heye Center of the National Museum of the American Indian. World's largest collection of materials of the native peoples of North, Central, and South America. (Daily) 1 Bowling Green St. Phone 212/514-3700. **FREE** Go 2 blks S to Whitehall St and 1 blk E on Bridge St to

Fraunces Tavern Museum. (1907) Museum housed in the historic Fraunces Tavern (1719) and four adj 19th-century buildings. The museum interprets history and culture of early America through permanent collection of prints, paintings, decorative arts, and artifacts, changing exhibitions, and period rms, one of which, the Long Room, is the site of George Washington's farewell to his officers at the end of the Revolutionary War (1783). The museum offers a variety of programs and activities incl tours, lectures, and films. (Tues-Sat) Dining rm. (Daily) 54 Pearl St. Phone 212/425-1778. ¢¢

Retrace steps and continue N on Broadway to

Trinity Church. (1846) The third building to occupy this site; original was built in 1697. Its famous graveyard, favorite lunchtime spot of workers in the financial district, contains the graves of Robert Fulton and Alexander Hamilton. The Gothic Revival brownstone church houses a museum. Parish center with dining rm open to the public. Services (daily). Broadway at Wall St. Phone 212/602-0800. **FREE** Directly behind the church is

Wall Street. Walk one blk E to the corner of Broad St (which goes S) and Nassau St (which goes N). At this corner is the

Federal Hall National Memorial. (1842) Greek Revival building on the site of the original Federal Hall, where the Stamp Act Congress met (1765), George Washington was inaugurated (Apr 30, 1789) and the first Congress met (1789-1790). Originally a custom house, the building was for many years the sub-treasury of the US. The JQA Ward statue of Washington is on

United Nations

Interior of St. Patrick's Cathedral

the Wall St steps. (Mon-Fri) Contact the Superintendent, Manhattan Sites, 26 Wall St, 10005. Phone 212/825-6874. **FREE** S of here, on the W side of Broad St, is the

New York Stock Exchange. View the exchange floor in action from the Visitors' Gallery. Audiovisual exhibits and film. Limited number of free admission tickets avail, distributed daily starting at 9 am. (Mon-Fri; closed hols) 20 Broad St, third floor. Phone 212/656-5167. **FREE** Walk 2 blks N up Broad St and through narrow Nassau St to Liberty St. On the N side is the

Federal Reserve Bank of New York. Approx ⅓ of the world's supply of gold bullion is stored here in a vault 80 ft below ground level; cash handling operation and historical exhibit of bank notes and coins. Tours (Mon-Fri; closed hols). Sixteen yrs and older only; no cameras. Tour res required at least one wk in advance. 33 Liberty St. Phone 212/720-6130. **FREE** Walk 2 blks W on Liberty St to Church St. On the right is the

World Trade Center Site. Location of the former 110-story twin towers complex that was destroyed on September 11, 2001.

St. Paul's Chapel. A chapel of Trinity Church, this example of Georgian architecture, finished in 1766, is the oldest public building in continuous use on Manhattan Island. George Washington's pew is in the north aisle; chancel ornamentation by L'Enfant; Waterford chandeliers. Concerts (Mon and Thurs at noon). (Daily) Fulton St and Broadway; chapel faces Church St. 2 blks N is the

Woolworth Building. This neo-Gothic skyscraper by Cass Gilbert was the tallest building in the world (792 ft, 58 stories) when built. Frank W. Woolworth, the dimestore king, paid $13.5 million cash for his "cathedral of commerce" when it was completed in 1913. 233 Broadway. Cross Broadway from here and enter

City Hall Park. Architecturally, City Hall is a combination of American Federalist and English Georgian, with Louis XIV detailing. It is built of marble and brownstone. Directly E is the

Brooklyn Bridge. The first bridge across the East River to Brooklyn, it was a remarkable engineering feat when it opened in 1883. Fine view from bridge of the East River (actually a tidal estuary between Long Island Sound and New York harbor). Also in this area, at the foot of Fulton St and the East River, is the South Street Seaport Museum. From City Hall walk about four blks NE to Chatham Sq and turn left on Mott St to

Chinatown. This colorful area has Chinese shops and restaurants. Mainly on Mott, Pell, and Doyers sts. Phone 212/267-3510. We suggest you walk back to Brooklyn Bridge and City Hall Park, from which a number of subways will take you wherever you next wish to go.

Washington Heights Museum Group. (Audubon Terrace) Clustered around a central plaza and accessible from Broadway, this group incl the American Geographical Society and the American Academy and Institute of Arts and Letters. Broadway and 155th St. Also here are the

American Numismatic Society. Society headquarters; numismatic library; "World of Coins" exhibit; changing exhibits. (Tues-Fri; closed hols) Broadway at 155th St. Phone 212/234-3130. **FREE**

Hispanic Society of America. Art of the Iberian Peninsula from prehistoric times to present. Paintings, sculpture, ceramics, drawings, etchings, lithographs, textiles, and metalwork. (Tues-Sun; closed hols)

Broadway, between W 155th and 156th sts. Phone 212/926-2234. **FREE**

Whitney Museum of American Art. Collection of 20th-century American art, founded by Gertrude Vanderbilt Whitney; changing exhibits; film and video programs; restaurant. (Tues-Sun; closed hols) Free admission Thurs eves. 945 Madison Ave, at E 75th St. Phone 212/570-3676. **¢¢** Branch museums incl

Whitney Museum of American Art at Philip Morris. Gallery and sculpture court. Changing exhibits annually; free lectures, performances. Gallery talks (Mon, Wed, Fri). Gallery (Mon-Fri). Sculpture court (daily). 120 Park Ave at 42nd St. Phone 917/663-2550. **FREE**

Yeshiva University. (1886) 6,300 students. America's oldest and largest university under Jewish auspices. Zysmon Hall, historic main building, has elaborate stone facade and Byzantine domes. Mendel Gottesman Library houses many specialized collections (academic yr, Mon-Fri, Sun; closed hols, Jewish hols; tours by appt). 500 W 185th St. Phone 212/960-5400. On campus is

Yeshiva University Museum. Teaching museum devoted to Jewish art, architecture, history, and culture has permanent exhibits, incl scale models of synagogues from the 3rd to 19th centuries; reproduction of

New York's Financial District

Woolworth Building

frescoes from the Dura-Europos Synagogue; ceremonial objects, rare books; audiovisual presentations; theater; changing exhibits. (Academic yr, Tues-Thurs, Sun; closed hols, Jewish hols) 15 W 16th St. Phone 212/294-8330. ¢¢

Special Events

Chinese New Year. In Chinatown, Mott, Pell, and Doyers sts. Parade with lions, dragons, costumes, firecrackers. Early-mid-Feb.

St. Patrick's Day Parade. Along 5th Ave. New York's biggest parade; approx 100,000 marchers.

Washington Square Art Show. Washington Sq and nearby streets. Outdoor art show. Wkends, late May-June and late-Aug-early Sept.

Ninth Avenue International Food Festival. Mid-May.

Central Park Concerts. Free performances by the New York Philharmonic and the Metropolitan Opera Company on the Great Lawn, mid-park at 81st St. Phone 212/360-3456. June-Aug.

New York Shakespeare Festival & Shakespeare in the Park. At the 2,000-seat outdoor Delacorte Theater in Central Park, near W 81st St. Tues-Sun. Free tickets distributed day of performance. Phone 212/539-8750. June-Sept.

JVC Jazz Festival-New York. World-famous musicians perform in Avery Fisher Hall, Carnegie Hall, Town Hall, and other sites throughout the city. Contact Box 1169, 10023. Phone 212/501-1390. Last two wks in June.

Harbor Festival. Wkend of July 4.

San Gennaro Festival. Little Italy. Mid- or late Sept. Phone 212/768-9320.

Columbus Day Parade. Upper 5th Ave.

Hispanic Day Parade. 5th Ave. Mid-Oct.

NYC Marathon. Usually Nov. Phone 212/860-4455.

Thanksgiving Day Parade. (An R. H. Macy production) Down Broadway to 34th St, from W 77th St and Central Park W. Floats, balloons, television and movie stars, and the arrival of Santa. Phone 212/695-4400.

Christmas Star Show. Hayden Planetarium. Late Nov-early Jan. Phone 212/769-5920.

Christmas season. Rockefeller Center tree, carols, sacred music concerts, animated store displays. Phone 212/484-1222.

Live TV shows. For information regarding availability of regular and/or standby tickets contact NBC's ticket office at 30 Rockefeller Plaza, 10112 (phone 212/664-4000); CBS at 524 W 57th St, 10019 (phone 212/975-2476); or ABC at 77 W 66th St, 10023 (phone 212/456-7777). On the day of the show, the New York Convention and Visitors Bureau at 2 Columbus Cir often has tickets for out-of-town visitors on a first-come, first-served basis. Except for NBC productions, many hotels can get tickets for guests on reasonable notice. (To see an important production, write 4-6 wks in advance; the number of tickets is usually limited.) Most shows restricted to persons over 18 yrs.

Motels/Motor Lodges

★★ **BEST WESTERN INN.** *17 W 32nd St (10001). 212/736-1600; fax 212/563-4007; toll-free 800/567-7720. www.bestwestern.com.* 176 rms, 14 story, 33 suites. S, D $89-$139; each addl $10; suites $149-$319; under 12 free. Crib free. Garage parking $22. TV; cable (premium). Complimentary continental bkfst, coffee in rms. Restaurant open 24 hrs. Bar 11-2 am. Ck-out noon. Meeting rms. Business center. Concierge. Gift shop. Barber, beauty shop. Exercise equipt. Some in-rm whirlpools. Cr cds: A, C, D, DS, ER, JCB, MC, V.

D ⊠ 🐾 SC 🏋 🏃

★★ **BEST WESTERN SEAPORT INN.** *33 Peck Slip (10038). 212/766-6600; fax 212/766-6615; res 800/528-1234. www.bestwestern.com.* 72 rms, 7 story. S, D $189-$199; each addl $10; under 17 free; wkend rates; higher rates special events; lower rates rest of yr. Crib free. Garage parking $20. TV; VCR (movies $6.95). Complimentary continental bkfst. Restaurant nearby. Ck-out 11 am. Business servs avail. In-rm modem link. No bellhops. Health club privileges. Refrigerators. Some balconies. Located in historic district in restored 19th-century building. Cr cds: A, C, D, DS, MC, V.

D ⊠ 🐾 SC

★★ **BEST WESTERN WOODWARD.** *210 W 55th St (10019). 212/247-2000; fax 212/581-2248; res 800/528-1234. www.bestwestern.com.* 175 rms, 20 with shower only, 14 story, 40 suites. S, D $180-$210; each addl $20; suites $220-$350; under 12 free; wkend, hol rates. Crib free. Garage parking $24. TV; cable (premium), VCR avail. Complimentary coffee in rms., newspaper in rms. Restaurant 6:30 am-midnight. Rm serv to 3 am. Ck-out noon. Business servs avail. Concierge. Health club privileges. Cr cds: A, C, D, DS, MC, V.

⊠ 🐾

Fireworks over the Brooklyn Bridge

★ COMFORT INN MANHATTAN.
42 W 35th St (10001). 212/947-0200; fax 212/594-3047; res 800/228-5150. www.comfortinnmanhattan.com. 131 rms, 12 story. S $129-$349; D $129-$229; each addl $15; under 18 free. Crib free. TV; cable. Complimentary continental bkfst. Coffee in lobby. Restaurant 7 am-8 pm. Ck-out noon. In-rm modem link. Some refrigerators, microwaves. Cr cds: A, D, DS, JCB, MC, V.

★ DAYS HOTEL NEW YORK CITY.
790 8th Ave (10019). 212/581-7000; fax 212/974-0291; res 800/329-7466. www.daysinn.com. 367 rms, 15 story. S $89-$197; D $167-$209; each addl $20; suites $240-$365; under 12 free. Parking $20. Crib free. TV; cable. Restaurant 24 hrs. Bar noon-2 am. Rm serv 6 am-10 pm. Ck-out 1 pm. Gift shop. Meeting rm. Business servs avail. Cr cds: A, C, D, DS, ER, JCB, MC, V.

★★ EASTSIDE INN.
201 E 24th St (10010). 212/696-3800; fax 212/696-0077. www.nycityhotels.com. 43 rms, 5 story. Jan-June, Sept-Dec: S $165-$185; D $205-$225; under 18 free; lower rates rest of yr. Crib free. TV; cable (premium), VCR (movies). Complimentary continental bkfst. Restaurant noon-midnight. Rm serv. Bar. Ck-out noon. Business servs avail. In-rm modem link. Valet serv. Concierge. Health club privileges. Bathrm phones; refrigerators avail. Cr cds: A, C, D, DS, JCB, MC, V.

★★ HOLIDAY INN DOWNTOWN.
138 Lafayette St (10013). 212/966-8898; fax 214/363-3978; res 888/535-3187. www.holiday-inn.com. 227 rms, 14 story. S, D $139.95-$289; each addl $15; suites $199-$229; under 18 free. Crib free. Valet parking $27. TV; cable. Complimentary coffee in rms. Restaurant 6:30 am-11 pm. Bar noon-midnight. Ck-out noon. Business servs avail. In-rm modem link. Concierge. Health club privileges. Renovated landmark building. Cr cds: A, C, D, DS, JCB, MC, V.

★ HOWARD JOHNSON PLAZA.
851 8th Ave (10019). 212/581-4100; fax 212/974-7502. www.hojo.com. 300 rms, 11 story. S $140-$202; D $152-$214; each addl $20; under 17 free; wkend rates. Crib free. Garage $15. TV; cable. Restaurant 6 am-midnight. Bar 11-2 am. Ck-out noon. Business servs avail. Gift shop. Refrigerators avail. Cr cds: A, C, D, DS, JCB, MC, V.

★★ MILFORD PLAZA.
270 W 45th St, New York (10036). 212/869-3600; fax 212/944-8357. www.milfordplaza. com. 1,300 rms, 28 story. S $109-$225; D $124-$240; each addl $15; suites $200-$450; under 14 free. Crib free. Parking $20, valet parking avail. TV; cable (premium). Restaurant 7 am-11 pm. Rm serv. Bar from noon. Ck-out noon. Concierge. Gift shop. Convention facilities. Business servs avail. In-rm modem link. Exercise equipt. Refrigerators avail. Cr cds: A, D, DS, JCB, MC, V.

Hotels

★★ ALGONQUIN HOTEL.
59 W 44th St (10036). 212/840-6800; fax 212/944-1419; res 800/555-8000. www.algonquinhotel.com. 165 rms, 12 story. S, D $179.95-$349; suites $299-$529; wkend rates. Crib free. Garage parking $28. TV; cable (premium). Restaurant 7-1 am; Sun from 11:30 am. Bar from 11 am; entertainment. Ck-out noon. Meeting rms. Business center. Exercise equipt. Visited by numerous literary and theatrical personalities. Cr cds: A, C, D, DS, ER, JCB, MC, V.

★★ AMERITANIA HOTEL.
230 W 54th St (10019). 212/247-5000; res 800/922-0330. www.nycityhotels.net. 208 rms, 30 with shower only. S, D $170-$270; each addl $20; suites $275; under 12 free. Crib free. Garage parking $15. TV; cable (premium). Complimentary bkfst. Restaurant 6:30 am-11 pm. Bar noon-1 am. Ck-out noon. In-rm modem link. Concierge. Exercise equipt. Health club privileges. Cr cds: A, D, DS, MC, V.

★★★ **AMSTERDAM COURT.** 226 W 50th St (10019). 212/459-1000; toll-free 800/473-7829. 117 rms, 7 story. S, D $350-$450; each addl $15; suites $450-$650; under 14 free. Crib. TV; cable (premium), VCR avail. Complimentary continental bkfst. Restaurants 6:30 am-midnight. Bar 11 am-midnight. Ck-out noon. Meeting rms. Business center. In-rm modem link. Concierge. Gift shop. Exercise equipt. Cr cds: A, C, D, DS, JCB, MC, V.

★★★ **THE AVALON HOTEL.** 16 E 32nd St (10016). 212/299-7000; fax 212/299-7001. www.theavalonny.com. 100 rms, 12 story, 80 suites. S, D $169.95-$350; each addl $20; suites $250-$600; under 12 free. Crib free. Valet parking $29. Garage parking $23. TV; cable, VCR avail. Complimentary continental bkfst. Complimentary coffee in rms. Restaurant 7 am-11 pm. Bar 4 pm-4 am. Ck-out noon. Meeting rms. Business servs avail. In-rm modem link. Concierge. Bathrm phones, refrigerators; some in-rm whirlpools. Cr cds: A, C, D, DS, JCB, MC, V.

★★★ **THE BENJAMIN.** 125 E 50th St (10022). 212/715-2500; fax 212/715-2525. 209 rooms, 50 percent suites, S, D $225-$465; suites $530-$1600. Crib free. TV (cable); VCR avail. In-rm modem links; high speed Internet access; web TV; private line service, fax, copier, printer in every rm. Ck-out noon. Concierge. Valet serv. Fitness center, complimentary spa 24 hours. Restaurant 7 am-11 pm (see also AN AMERICAN PLACE). Bar noon-1 am. Cr cds: A, C, D, DS, MC, V.

★★ **BOX TREE.** 250 E 49th St (10017). 212/593-9810; fax 212/308-3899. www.theboxtree.com. 13 suites in 2 townhouses, 3 story. MAP (Fri, Sat): D $330-$350; lower rates (AP) wkdays. TV. Complimentary continental bkfst. Restaurant (see also BOX TREE). Fri, Sat dining credit $100 per night incl in MAP rates. Ck-out 11:30 am, ck-in 3 pm. Concierge. Bathrm phones, fireplaces. 1840s brownstones; antique furnishings; imported French ameni-

ties; rms individually decorated. Cr cds: A, D, MC, V.

★★★ **BRYANT PARK.** 40 W 40th St (10018). 212/642-2200; fax 212/869-4446. www.thebryantpart.net. 129 rms, 25 story, 20 suites. S, D $199-$575; suites $900-$3,500; wkend rates. TV; cable (premium), VCR avail. Restaurants 6:30 am-midnight. Bar 5:30 pm-1:30 am. Ck-out noon. Valet parking avail. Meeting rms. Business center. In-rm modem link. Concierge. Gift shop. Exercise equipt. Refrigerators avail. Minibars. Cr cds: A, D, DS, MC, V.

★★★★ **THE CARLYLE.** 35 E 76th St (10021). 212/744-1600; fax 212/717-4682; toll-free 800/227-5737. www.rosewoodhotels.com. Faded New York luxury best describes the decor and atmosphere of this historic Upper East Side hotel. The service remains impeccable, and updated amenities like a new fitness center help make for a pleasant stay. Take in a set by Bobby Short or Woody Allen in the Cafe Carlyle or have a drink at Bemelman's Bar before your night on the town. 180 rms, 35 story. S, D $695-$795; suites (1-2 bedrm) $850-$3,200. Crib free. Pet accepted, some restrictions. Garage $44, valet parking avail. TV; cable (premium), VCR (movies), stereo with CD player. Restaurant. Rm serv 24 hrs. Bar 11-2 am, Sun noon-1 am; Cafe Carlyle 7:30 pm-midnight, entertainment (cover charge $50). Ck-out 1 pm. Meeting rms. Business servs avail. In-rm modem link. Bellhops. Valet serv. Exercise rm; sauna, steam rm. Massage. Bathrm phones, refrigerators, minibars; microwaves avail. Grand piano in some suites. Some terraces. Cr cds: A, C, D, DS, JCB, MC, V.

★★★ **CASABLANCA HOTEL.** 147 W 43rd St (10036). 212/869-1212; fax 212/391-7585; res 888/922-7225. www.casablancahotel.com. 48 rms, 8 with shower only, 6 story. S $225-$245; D $245; suites $325; under 12 free; wkend, hol rates. Crib free. Garage parking $25. TV; cable (premium), VCR (movies). Complimentary continental bkfst; afternoon refreshments.

Restaurant 11 am-11 pm. Ck-out noon. Meeting rms. Business center. In-rm modem link. Concierge. Valet serv. Health club privileges. Bathrm phones, refrigerators, minibars. Cr cds: A, D, DS, MC, V.

D ⊠ SC ⩊

★★★ **CHAMBERS.** *15 W 56th St (10013). 212/974-5656; fax 212/974-5657. www.chambersahotel.com.* 77 rms, 30 story. S, D $350-$500; under 12 free; suites $900-$1,600; wkend rates. TV; cable (premium), VCR avail. Restaurants 6:30 am-midnight. Bar 11 am-midnight. Valet parking avail. Ck-out noon. Meeting rms. Business center. In-rm modem link. Concierge. Valet serv. Gift shop. Exercise equipt. Refrigerators avail. Cr cds: A, D, DS, JCB, MC, V.

⩊ D ⩊

★★ **CLARION HOTEL FIFTH AVENUE.** *3 E 40th St (10016). 212/447-1500; fax 212/213-0972; toll-free 800/252-7466. www.clarionfifthave.com.* 189 rms, 30 story. S, D $225-$275; each addl $15; wkend rates; under 18 free. Crib free. Garage parking $28, valet parking avail. TV; cable (premium). Complimentary coffee in rms. Restaurant nearby. Ck-out noon. Concierge. Business center. In-rm modem link. Health club privileges. Sauna. Cr cds: A, C, D, DS, ER, JCB, MC, V.

D ⊠ ⩊ SC ⩊

★★★ **CROWNE PLAZA.** *1605 Broadway (10019). 212/977-4000; fax 212/333-7393; res 800/243-6969. www.cpmny.com.* 770 rms, 46 story, 17 suites. S, D $150-$289; suites $650-$999 each addl $20; under 19 free. Crib avail. Garage $34. TV; cable (premium), VCR avail (movies). Coffee in rms. Restaurant 6:30 am-2 am; Sun hrs vary. Rm serv 24 hrs. Bar from 11:30 am. Ck-out noon. Gift shop. Convention facilities. Business center. In-rm modem link. Concierge. Valet serv. Pool, health club privileges. Minibars; refrigerators avail. Luxury level. Cr cds: C, D, DS, JCB, MC, V.

D ⊠ ⩊ ⩊

★★★ **CROWNE PLAZA AT THE UNITED NATIONS.** *304 E 42nd St (10017). 212/986-8800; fax 212/986-1758; toll-free 800/227-6963. www. crowneplaza-un.com.* 300 rms in 2 towers, 17 and 20 story. S $228-$347; D $312-$375; each addl $25; suites $325-$490; under 12 free; wkend rates. Crib free. Pet accepted. Garage parking $40. TV; cable, VCR avail. Restaurant 7 am-10:30 am, 5:30-10:30 pm. Rm serv 7 am-11 pm. Bar. Ck-out noon. Meeting rms. Business center. In-rm modem link. Concierge. Exercise equipt; saunas. Massage. Minibars. Some balconies. Cr cds: A, C, D, DS, JCB, MC, V.

D ⩊ ⩊ SC ⩊

★★★ **THE DRAKE-SWISSOTEL.** *440 Park Ave and 56th St (10022). 212/421-0900; fax 212/371-4190; toll-free 800/637-9477. www. swissotel.com.* 387 units, 108 suites, 21 story. S, D $225-$625; one addl $30; 1-, 2-bedrm suites $315-$1,300; under 12 free; wkend rates. Crib free. Pet accepted. Garage $65, valet parking avail. TV; cable, VCR avail. Restaurant 6:30 am-11 pm. Rm serv 24 hrs. Bar noon-1 am. Complimentary coffee in rms. Ck-out noon. Conference facilities. Business center. In-rm modem link. Concierge. Bellhops. Valet serv. Exercise rm $10/day; sauna, steam rm. Spa. Massage. Gift shop. Beauty shop. Shopping arcade. Bathrm phones, minibars. Wet bar in suites. Cr cds: A, C, D, DS, JCB, MC, V.

D ⩊ ⩊ ⩊ ⩊ ⩊

★★ **DUMONT PLAZA HOTEL.** *150 E 34th St (10016). 212/481-7600; fax 212/889-8856; res 800/637-8483. www.mesuite.com.* 247 kit. suites, 37 story. S $259-$309; D $279-$329; each addl $20; suites $499-$519; under 12 free; wkend rates. Crib free. TV; cable, VCR avail. Complimentary coffee in rms. Restaurant 7 am-10 pm. Rm serv 24 hrs. Ck-out noon. Concierge. Coin lndry. Meeting rms. Business servs avail. In-rm modem link. Exercise equipt; sauna. Microwaves. Plaza with fountain. Cr cds: A, D, DS, JCB, MC, V.

⩊ ⩊

★★★ **DYLAN.** *52 E 41st St (10017). 212/338-0500. www.dylanhotel.com.* 108 rms, 20 story. S, D $335-$425; wkend rates. Pet accepted, $45. TV; cable (premium), VCR avail. Restaurants 6:30 am-midnight. Bar 11 am-midnight. Ck-out noon. Meeting rms. Business center. In-rm modem link. Concierge. Gift shop. Exercise equipt. Refrigerators avail. Cr cds: A, D, DS, JCB, MC, V.

★ D ⚑ ⅄ ⤳ ⚿ SC

★★ **EASTGATE TOWER.** *222 E 39th St (10016). 212/687-8000; fax 212/490-2634; toll-free 800/637-8483. www.mesuite.com.* 188 kit. suites, 25 story. S $269-$309; D $289-$329; each addl $20; wkly rates. Garage; valet parking $40. TV; cable (premium). Restaurant. Rm serv 7 am-10 pm. Bar. Concierge. Ck-out noon. Business servs avail. In-rm modem link. Exercise equipt. Microwaves. Cr cds: A, C, D, DS, ER, JCB, MC, V.

D ⅄ ⤳ ⚿

★★ **EMPIRE.** *44 W 63rd St (10023). 212/265-7400; fax 212/315-0349; toll-free 888/822-3555. www.empirehotel. com.* 375 rms, 11 story. S $205-$265; D $225-$285; each addl $20; suites $350-$650; under 14 free. Crib free. Garage $29. TV; cable (premium), VCR (movies). Restaurant 6:30-11 am, 5 pm-midnight. Rm serv 24 hrs. Bar 11 am-midnight. Ck-out noon. Meeting rms. Business servs avail. In-rm modem link. Health club privileges. Concierge. Cr cds: A, C, D, DS, ER, JCB, MC, V.

D ⤳ ⚿

★★★ **ESSEX HOUSE - A WESTIN HOTEL.** *160 South Central Park (10019). 212/247-0300; fax 212/ 315-1839; res 888/645-5687. www. essexhouse.com.* 501 units, 19 story, 81 suites. S, D $175-$525; each addl $25; suites $375-$5,000; under 18 free; wkend rates. Crib free. Valet parking avail. TV; cable (premium), VCR. Restaurants 6:30 am-11 pm. Rm serv 24 hrs. Bar noon-1 am. Ck-out noon. Business center. In-rm modem link, fax. Concierge. Gift shop. Exercise rm; saunas, steam rms. Spa. Minibars. Cr cds: A, C, D, DS, ER, JCB, MC, V.

D ⅄ ⤳ ⚿ ★

★★★ **FITZPATRICK MANHATTAN HOTEL.** *687 Lexington Ave (10022). 212/355-0100; fax 212/355-1371; res 212/784-2520. www.fitzpatrickhotels. com.* 92 rms, 17 story, 52 suites. S $199-$355; D $229-$355; suites $350-$380; each addl in suite $30

wkday, $50 wkend; under 12 free; wkend, hol rates. Crib free. Garage $38. TV; cable (premium), VCR avail. Restaurant 7 am-10:30 pm. Rm serv 24 hrs. Bar noon-2 am. Ck-out noon. Business servs avail. In-rm modem link. Concierge. Airport transportation. Health club privileges. Many refrigerators, wet bars. Cr cds: A, C, D, DS, MC, V.

✈ ⤳

★★★★★ **FOUR SEASONS HOTEL NEW YORK.** *57 E 57th St (10022). 212/758-5700; fax 212/758-5711; res 800/332-3442. www.fourseasons.com.* The geometric design by I. M. Pei uses marble, glass, and light-colored wood to create a sleek, cool environment that is at once chic and thoroughly comfortable. The magestic lobby soars in proportion to the 50-plus-story building. Rooms are generously sized and decorated with a minimalist, almost Japanese aesthetic. Oversized bathrooms feature rapidly filling tubs and fine toiletries. Service is impeccable. Enjoy dinner or cocktails in the sleek Fifty Seven Fifty Seven. 368 rms, 52 story, 63 suites. S, D $595-$755; each addl $50; suites $1,350-$20,000; under 12 free; wkend rates. Crib free. Pet accepted, some restrictions. Garage, valet parking $42. TV; cable (premium), VCR. Restaurant 7 am-10:30 pm (see also FIFTY SEVEN FIFTY SEVEN). Rm serv 24 hrs. Bar noon-1 am. Ck-out noon. Business center. In-rm modem link. Concierge. Extensive exercise rm; sauna, steam rm. Whirlpool. Massage. Health club privileges. Bathrm phones, minibars. Some terraces. Cr cds: A, D, DS, ER, JCB, MC, V.

D ⚑ ⅄ ⤳ ⚿ ★

★★ **FRANKLIN.** *164 E 87th St (10128). 212/369-1000; fax 212/369-8000; toll-free 877/847-4444. www. boutiquehg.com.* 50 rms, 9 story. S, D $159-$179; under 18 free. Garage parking free, in/out $10. TV; cable, VCR (free movies). Complimentary continental bkfst. Restaurant nearby. Ck-out noon. Refrigerators avail. Renovated boutique hotel. Cr cds: A, D, MC, V.

⤳ ⚿

★★★ **GERSHWIN.** *7 E 27th St (10016). 212/545-8000; fax 212/684-5546. www.gershwinhotel.com.* 150 rms, 13 story. S, D $275-$350; suites $250-$450; wkend rates. Crib free. TV; cable (premium). VCR avail. Restaurants 6:30 am-midnight. Bar 11 am-midnight. Ck-out noon. Meeting rms. Business center. In-rm modem link. Concierge. Gift shop. Exercise equipt. Refrigerators avail. Cr cds: A, MC, V.

★★ **GORHAM.** *136 W 55th St (10019). 212/245-1800; fax 212/582-8332; toll-free 800/735-0710. www.gorhamhotel.com.* 115 kit. units, 17 story. S, D $225-$440; each addl $20; suites $255-$575; under 16 free. Crib free. Concierge. TV; cable (premium), VCR avail. Ck-out noon. Restaurant. Business servs avail. In-rm modem link. Exercise equipt. Microwaves. Cr cds: A, C, D, JCB, MC, V.

★★ **GRAND HYATT.** *Park Ave at Grand (10017). 212/883-1234; fax 646/213-6659; res 800/233-1234. www.newyork.hyatt.com.* 1,347 rms, 36 story, 51 suites. S, D $229-$500; each addl $25; suites $600-$3,000; under 18 free; wkend rates. Crib free. Garage $40, valet parking avail. TV; cable (premium). Restaurant 6:30 am-2 pm, 5 pm-1 am. Rm serv 24 hrs. Bar 11 am-2 am; entertainment. Ck-out noon. Complimentary bkfst. Meeting rms. Business center. In-rm modem link. Valet serv. Exercise equipt. Health club privileges. Concierge. Gift shop. Shopping arcade. Refrigerator in suites. Luxury level. Cr cds: A, C, D, DS, ER, JCB, MC, V.

★★ **HELMSLEY MIDDLETOWNE.** *148 E 48th St (10017). 212/755-3000; fax 212/832-0261; res 800/221-4982. www.helmsleyhotels.com.* 192 rms, 18 story. S $170-$260; D $190-$260; each addl $20; suites $215-$375; under 12 free; wkend rates. Crib free. Garage; valet parking $30. Concierge. TV; cable (premium), VCR avail. Complimentary coffee in lobby. Restaurant nearby. Ck-out 1 pm. Business servs avail. In-rm modem link. Health club privileges. Bathrm phones, refrigerators, microwaves,

wet bars. Many balconies. Cr cds: A, C, D, DS, JCB, MC, V.

★★★ **THE HELMSLEY PARK LANE HOTEL.** *36 Central Park S (10019). 212/371-4000; fax 212/521-6666; toll-free 800/221-4982. www.helmsleyhotels.com.* 598 rms, 46 story. S, D $252-$475; each addl $30; suites $425-$2,250; under 12 free; wkend rates. Crib free. Pet accepted, some restrictions. Garage parking $37, valet. TV; VCR avail (movies). Restaurant 7 am-11:30 pm. Rm serv 24 hrs. Bar 11-12:45 am. Ck-out noon. Concierge. Meeting rms. Business center. In-rm modem link. Valet serv. Exercise equipt. Health club privileges. Refrigerators. Cr cds: A, C, D, DS, JCB, MC, V.

★★ **HELMSLEY WINDSOR.** *100 W 58th St (10019). 212/265-2100; fax 212/682-6299; res 800/221-4982. www.helmsleyhotels.com.* 244 rms, 15 story. S $140-$200; D $170-$260; each addl $20; under 12 free; suites $275-$615; summer, wkend rates. Crib free. Garage $28. Valet parking avail. TV; cable (premium). No rm serv. Ck-out 1 pm. Bellhops. Business servs avail. Health club privileges. Serv pantry in suites. Cr cds: A, C, D, DS, JCB, MC, V.

★ **HERALD SQUARE.** *19 W 31st St (10001). 212/279-4017; fax 212/643-9208; res 212/279-4017. www.heraldsquarehotel.com.* 120 rms, some share bath, 9 story. S $85; D $99-$115; each addl $5; under 10 free. Crib free. Garage $13-$21. TV; cable. Restaurant nearby. Ck-out noon. No bellhops. In landmark Beaux Arts building (1893) designed by Carrere and Hastings; was once lived in by Charles Dana Gibson, illustrator who created the Gibson girl; was original headquarters of Life magazine. Hotel interior decorated with Life covers and graphics. Cr cds: A, DS, JCB, MC, V.

★★★ **HILTON NEW YORK.** *1335 Avenue of the Americas (10019). 212/586-7000; fax 212/315-1374; toll-free 212/261-5870. www.newyorktowers. hilton.com.* 1,920 rms, 44 story, 52 suites. S \$209-\$395; D \$239-\$425; each addl \$30; suites \$545-\$2,750; family rates; package plans. Crib free. Pet accepted, some restrictions. Garage \$40. TV; cable (premium), VCR avail. Complimentary coffee in rms. Restaurant 6 am-11 pm. Bar 5:30-11:30 pm. Ck-out noon. Concierge. Supervised children's activities (summer). Convention facilities. Business center. In-rm modem link. Shopping arcade. Barber, beauty shop. Valet serv. Exercise rm; sauna. Minibars. Refrigerators avail. Luxury level. Cr cds: A, C, D, DS, JCB, MC, V.

🏋 🐕 D ⛵ ⛴ 🔥

★★ **HOTEL BEACON.** *2130 Broadway at 75th St (10023). 212/787-1100; fax 212/724-0839; res 800/572-4969. www.beaconhotel.com.* 200 kit. units, 25 story. S \$185-\$195; D \$205-\$225; each addl \$15; suites \$195-\$425; under 17 free. Crib free. Garage parking \$20. TV; cable, VCR avail. Complimentary coffee in rms. Restaurant adj open 24 hrs. Ck-out noon. Coin lndry. Valet serv. Meeting rms. Health club privileges. Microwaves avail. Cr cds: A, D, DS, JCB, MC, V.

D ⛴ 🔥 SC

★★ **HOTEL BEDFORD.** *118 E 40th St (10016). 212/697-4800; fax 212/697-1093; toll-free 800/221-6881. www.bedfordhotel.com.* 136 rms, 17 story, 58 suites. S, D \$135-\$225; each addl \$10; suites \$165-400; under 13 free; wkend rates. Crib free. Garage \$18-\$22. TV; cable (premium). Complimentary continental bkfst. Restaurant noon-11 pm. Bar. Ck-out 11 am Valet serv.. Coin lndry. Business servs avail. In-rm modem link. Cr cds: A, C, DS, ER, JCB, MC, V.

⛴ 🔥

★★ **HOTEL BENTLEY 500.** *500 E 62nd St (10022). 212/644-6000; fax 212/207-4800; toll-free 888/664-6295.* 197 rms, 21 story, 40 suites. S, D \$255-\$375; each addl \$15; suites \$425-\$700; under 16 free. Crib free. Garage parking \$20. TV; cable, VCR avail. Complimentary continental bkfst, coffee in lobby. Restaurant 7 am-10 pm. Bar noon-10 pm. Ck-out noon. Meeting rms. In-rm modem link. Concierge. Health club privileges. Bathrm phones, minibars;

refrigerators avail. Cr cds: A, C, D, DS, MC, V.

D ⛴ 🔥

★★ **HOTEL EDISON.** *228 W 47th St (10036). 212/840-5000; fax 212/596-6850; toll-free 800/637-7070. www.edisonhotelnyc.com.* 1,000 rms, 22 story. S \$150; D \$175; each addl \$15; suites \$190-\$255; family rms \$185-\$230. Crib free. Garage \$18. TV; cable (premium). Complimentary coffee. Restaurant 6:15 am-midnight, Sun to 7 pm. Bar noon-2 am. Ck-out 1 pm. Meeting rm. Business servs avail. Gift shop. Beauty shop. Airport transportation. Cr cds: A, C, D, DS, JCB, MC, V.

D ✈ ⛴ 🔥

★★★ **HOTEL ELYSEE.** *60 E 54th St (10022). 212/753-1066; fax 212/980-9278; res 212/753-1066. www.elyseehotel.com.* 101 rms, 15 story. S, D \$345-\$365; suites \$475-\$1,000; under 12 free. Crib free. TV; cable, VCR avail. Complimentary continental bkfst; afternoon refreshments. Restaurant noon-11:30 pm, Fri, Sat to midnight, Sun to 11 pm. Rm serv 7 am-10:30 pm. Bar noon-2 am. Ck-out 1 pm. Meeting rms. Business servs avail. Health club privileges. Refrigerators, bathrm phones. Microwaves avail. Country French decor, antiques. Cr cds: A, D, MC, V.

D ⛴ 🔥

★★★★ **HOTEL PLAZA ATHENEE.** *37 E 64th St (10021). 212/734-9100; fax 212/772-0958; toll-free 800/447-8800. www.plaza-athenee.com.* Formal French elegance pervades this jewel box of a hotel that feels like it should be in Paris. The staff provides discreet and caring service, making guests feel like they've left the hustle and bustle of Manhattan behind. Sample Le Regence for fancy French food that matches the decor. 152 rms, 17 story. S \$480-\$630, D \$515-\$660; each addl \$35; suites \$1,100-\$4,800. Crib free. Pet accepted. Parking \$45/day. TV; cable (premium), VCR avail. Restaurant 7 am-6:30 pm. Rm serv 24 hrs. Bar 11 am-midnight. Ck-out 1 pm. Meeting rm. Business servs avail. In-rm modem link. Concierge. Bellhops. Bathrm phones. Valet serv. Exercise equipt. Refrigerators. Some suites with private dining rm. Some private patios, glassed-in atriums. Cr cds: A, C, D, DS, ER, JCB, MC, V.

★★ **HOTEL WALES.** *1295 Madison Ave (10128). 212/876-6000; fax 212/860-7000; toll-free 800/428-5252. www.boutiquehg.com.* 92 units, 10 story, 40 suites. S $209, D $259; under 18 free; each addl $20; suites $279. Crib free. Valet parking $28. TV; cable (premium), VCR (free movies). Complimentary continental bkfst; afternoon refreshments. Restaurant 8 am-11 pm. Harpist 5-6 pm Mon-Fri, chamber music 6-8 pm Sun, pianist 8-10 am. Ck-out noon. Business servs avail. Health club privileges. Refrigerators avail. Restored 1902 hotel; original fireplaces. Cr cds: A, D, MC, V.

★★★ **HUDSON.** *356 W 58th St (10019). 212/554-6000.* 1,000 rms, 24 story. S, D $179; suites $375-$450; wkend rates. Crib free. TV; cable (premium). VCR avail. Olympic-size pool. Coffee in rms. Restaurants 6:30 am-midnight. Bar 11 am-midnight. Ck-out noon. Meeting rms. Business center. In-rm modem link. Concierge. Exercise equipt. Refrigerators avail. Cr cds: A, D, DS, MC, V.

★★★ **INTER-CONTINENTAL CENTRAL PARK SOUTH NEW YORK.** *112 Central Park South (10019). 212/757-1900; fax 212/757-9620; res 800/327-0200. www.new-york.interconti.com.* 207 rms, 25 story. S, D $199-$355; suites $775-$5,000. Crib free. Garage $39, valet parking.. Children 17 and under free. TV; cable (premium), VCR avail (in-room movies). Bathrm phones. Restaurant 11 am-10:30 pm. Rm serv. Bar 11-1 am. Ck-out noon. 24-hr. concierge. Meeting rms. Business center. In-rm modem link. Valet serv. Exercise equipt; sauna. Massage. Health club privileges. Refrigerators/in rm bar. Some balconies. Cr cds: A, C, D, DS, ER, JCB, MC, V.

★★★ **INTER-CONTINENTAL THE BARCLAY NEW YORK.** *111 E 48th St (10017). 212/755-5900; fax 212/644-0079; toll-free 877/660-8550. www.new-york.interconti.com.* 603 rms, suites 84, 14 story. S, D $495-$695;

each addl $40; suites $475-$4,000; under 14 free; wkend rates. Crib free. Garage parking $39/day; valet. TV; cable (premium). Restaurant 7 am-11:30 pm. Rm serv. Bar 11:30-1 am. Ck-out noon. Meeting rms. Business center. In-rm modem link. Concierge. Bellhops. Valet serv. Gift shop. Exercise equipt; sauna, steam rm. Health club privileges. Massage. Minibars. Refrigerators, microwaves avail. Cr cds: A, C, D, DS, ER, JCB, MC, V.

★★★ **THE IROQUOIS.** *49 W 44th St (10036). 212/840-3080; fax 212/719-0006; toll-free 800/332-7220. www.iroquoisny.com.* 114 rms, 12 story. S, D $345-$445; under 12 free; suites $570-$645; wkend rates. Crib avail. TV; cable (premium), VCR (movies). Complimentary bkfst. Restaurant 6:30 am-11 pm. Rm serv 24 hrs. Bar to 4 pm-1 am. Ck-out noon. Meeting rms. Business servs avail. In-rm modem link. Concierge. Exercise equipt. Bathrm phones. Minibars. Cr cds: A, MC, V.

★★★ **JOLLY HOTEL MADISON TOWERS.** *22 E 38th St (10016). 212/802-0600; fax 212/447-0747; res 800/221-2626. www.jollymadison.com.* 225 rms, 18 story. S, D $160-$350; each addl $50; suites $450; under 12 free. Crib free. TV; cable (premium). Restaurant 6:30 am-11 pm. Bar 11 am-midnight. Ck-out noon. Business servs avail. In-rm modem link. Concierge. Minibar. Cr cds: A, C, D, DS, JCB, MC, V.

★★★ **KIMBERLY HOTEL.** *145 E 50th St (10022). 212/702-1600; fax 212/486-6915; toll-free 800/683-0400. www.kimberlyhotel.com.* 186 rns, 30 story. S $239-$329; D $259-$349; suites $299-$1000; 2-bedrm $409-$675; under 17 free. Crib free. Garage parking $23. TV; cable (premium), VCR avail. Indoor pool. Restaurant 7 am-11 pm. Bar noon-midnight; entertainment seasonally. Ck-out noon. Business servs avail. Concierge. Health club privileges, sauna. Valet serv. Fully equipped kits.

Little Italy

n some suites. Minibars. Terraces. Cr
ds: A, D, DS, MC, V.

★★★ **THE KITANO HOTEL.** *66
Park Ave (10016). 212/885-7000; fax
212/885-7100; res 800/548-2666.
www.kitano.com.* 149 rms, 18 story, 8
suites. S, D $180-$700; each addl
$25; suites $1,600-$2,100; under 12
free; wkend rates. Crib free. Valet
parking $35. TV; cable (premium),
VCR avail. Complimentary green tea
in rms. Restaurant 7 am-10 pm. Bar 6
pm-midnight; entertainment Wed-
Fri. Ck-out 11 am. Meeting rms. Business servs avail. In-rm modem link,
fax. Concierge. Health club privi-
eges. Minibars. Cr cds: A, D, DS,
CB, MC, V.

★★★ **LE PARKER MERIDIEN.** *118
W 57th St (10019). 212/245-5000; fax
212/307-1776; res 800/543-4300.
www.parkermeridien.com.* 730 rms, 42
story. S, D $325-$550; each addl $30;
suites $450-$3,000; under 12 free;
wkend rates. Crib free. Pet accepted.
Garage parking, valet $40. TV; VCR
avail. Heated indoor pool. Restaurant
6 am-3 pm. Rm serv 24 hrs. Bar 11-3
am. Ck-out noon. Meeting rms. Business center. In-rm modem link. Gift

shop. Valet serv. Refrigerators in
suites. Exercise rm; sauna. Steam rm.
Concierge. Microwaves avail. French
ambience; Italian marble flooring. Cr
cds: A, D, DS, JCB, MC, V.

★★★ **LIBRARY.** *299 Madison Ave
(10017). 212/983-4500. www.library-
hotel.com.* 60 rms, 10 story. S, D
$265-$395; suites $325-$375; wkend
rates. TV; cable (premium), VCR
avail. Complimentary continental
bkfst. Restaurants 6:30 am-midnight.
Bar 11 am-midnight. Ck-out noon.
Meeting rms. Business center. In-rm
modem link. Concierge. Exercise
equipt. Refrigerators avail. Each floor
is named for a slice of the Dewey
Decimal System. Poetry garden
greenhouse. Cr cds: A, D, DS, MC, V.

★★★ **THE LOMBARDY.** *111 E 56th
St (10022). 212/753-8600; fax 212/
754-5683; toll-free 800/223-5254.
www.lombardyhotel.com.* 115 kit.
units, 21 story, 60 suites. S, D $240-
$290; each addl $20; suites $360-
$575; under 12 free; wkend rates
(summer). Crib free. Garage parking
$18. TV; cable (premium), VCR avail.
Restaurant. Rm serv from 6 am. Bar
noon-midnight. Ck-out 1 pm. Meet-

ing rms. Business servs avail. In-rm modem link. Concierge. Exercise equipt. Refrigerators; many microwaves. Some balconies. Cr cds: A, D, DS, MC, V.

[D] [人] [≅] [火]

★★★★ **THE LOWELL.** *28 E 63rd St (10021). 212/838-1400; fax 212/319-4230; toll-free 800/221-4444. www.lhw.com.* Staying at the Lowell is like being given the keys to a friend's apartment--a friend, that is, with impeccable taste and a lot of money. The rooms and suites are decorated with fine antiques and beautiful furnishings, the service is personalized and professional. In fact, many movers and shakers in New York make this hotel their home. It's easy to see why. From the Bulgari products in the bathroom, to the working fireplaces and full kitchens, you feel like you can move in and send for your other things. 68 rms, 17 story, 47 kit. suites. S, D $495-$575; each addl $45; kit. suites $775-$3,900; under 12 free; wkend rates; package plans. Crib free. Valet parking $45. TV; cable (premium), VCR (movies). Restaurants 7 10:30 am; Mon-Fri noon-10:30; Sat, Sun 5:30-10:30 pm. Sat, Sun brunch noon-2:30 pm. Rm serv 24 hrs. Afternoon tea 2-6 pm. Bar noon-11 pm. Ck-out 1 pm, ck-in 3 pm. Meeting rm. Business servs avail. In-rm modem link. Bellhops. Concierge. Valet serv. Exercise equipt. Fitness center. Health club privileges. Bathrm phones, refrigerators, minibars; microwaves avail. Some fireplaces, balconies. Cr cds: A, C, D, DS, ER, JCB, MC, V.

[人] [≅] [火]

★★ **THE LUCERNE HOTEL.** *201 W 79th St (10024). 212/875-1000; fax 212/579-2408; toll-free 800/492-8122. www.newyorkhotel.com.* 250 rms, 14 story, 100 suites. S $140-$260; D $140-$270; each addl $15; suites $175-$410; under 16 free; family rates; package plans. Crib avail. Garage parking $25-35. TV; cable (premium), VCR avail. Complimentary coffee in rms. Restaurant 7-10:30 am, 5 pm-midnight. Bar 5 pm-2 am; entertainment from 8 pm. Ck-out noon. Meeting rms. Business servs avail. In-rm modem link in suites. Concierge. Exercise equipt. Health club privileges. Valet serv. Beauty

salon. Microwaves avail; refrigerator, microwave, wet bar in suites. Cr cds: A, D, DS, MC, V.

[人] [≅] [火]

★★ **LYDEN GARDENS.** *215 E 64th St (10021). 212/355-1230; fax 212/758-7858; toll-free 800/637-8483. www.mesuite.com.* 132 kit. suites, 13 story. S, D $320-$670; each addl $20; under 12 free; wknd rates. Crib free. Valet parking, $32. TV; cable (premium). Complimentary coffee in rms. Restaurant nearby. Rm serv 7:30 am-10:30 pm. Ck-out noon. Business servs avail. Concierge. Valet serv. Exercise equipt. Microwaves. Terraces gardens. Cr cds: A, D, DS, MC, V.

[D] [人] [≅] [火]

★★ **MANSFIELD.** *12 W 44th St (10036). 212/944-6050; fax 212/764-4477; res 877/847-4444. www.mansfield hotel.com.* 124 rms, 36 with shower only, 13 story, 27 suites. S, D $179-$325; each addl $20; under 18 free; suites $229-$875; wknd rates. Crib free. TV; cable (premium), VCR (free movies). Ck-out noon. Rm serv 24 hrs. Restaurant 11 am-10:30 pm. Bar 5 pm-2 am. Business servs avail. Concierge. Valet parking $40. Health club privileges. Refrigerators. Cr cds: A, D, DS, JCB, MC, V.

[D] [✦] [≅] [火] [SC]

★★★★ **THE MARK, NEW YORK.** *25 E 77th St (10021). 212/744-4300; fax 212/744-2749; res 800/843-6275. www.mandarinoriental.com.* Understated European elegance characterizes this upscale hotel, located on a quiet Upper East Side block. Once past the small, marble lobby you'll find guest room suites of generous size with comfortable furnishings. Mark's restaurant provides a sophisticated and sedate meal. 120 rms, 16 story, 60 suites. S $525-$640; D $555-$670; each addl $30; suites $725-$2,500; under 16 free; wkend, hol rates avail. Crib free. Garage $40, valet parking avail. TV; cable (premium), VCR (movies). Restaurant 7 am-10:30 pm. Rm serv 24 hrs. Bar 4 pm-1 am; Sat, Sun to 2 am. Coffee in rms. Ck-out 1 pm. Meeting rms. Business servs avail. In-rm modem link. Concierge. Bellhops. Valet serv. Exercise rm; sauna, steam rm. Bathrm phones, refrigerators. Cr cds: A, JCB, MC, V.

★ ★ **MARRIOTT EAST SIDE.** *525 Lexington Ave (10017). 212/755-4000; fax 212/751-3440; res 800/228-9290. www.marriott.com.* 626 rms, 35 story. S, D $189-$299; suites $450-$900; under 18 free; wkend packages. Crib free. TV; cable (premium). Bellhops. Coin lndry. Valet serv. Concierge serv. Restaurant 7 am-10 pm. Bar noon-1 am. Ck-out noon. Meeting rms. Business center. In-rm modem link. Concierge. Gift shop. Exercise equipt. Valet serv. Bathrm phones, minibars. Airport transportation. Designed by Arthur Loomis Harmon, architect of Empire State Building; hotel was subject of Georgia O'Keefe cityscapes. Cr cds: A, C, D, DS, ER, JCB, MC, V.

★ ★ **MARRIOTT FINANCIAL CENTER.** *85 W St (10006), at Albany St, Financial District. 212/385-4900; fax 212/227-8136; toll-free 800/228-9290. www.marriott.com* 498 rms, 38 story. S, D $239-$299; each addl $20; suites $400-$780; under 18 free; wkend rates. Crib free. Garage parking $30, valet. TV; cable (premium). Heated indoor pool. Restaurant 6:30 am-10 pm. Rm serv. Bar 11 am-midnight. Coffee in rms. Ck-out noon. Convention facilities. Business center. In-rm modem link. Concierge serv. Gift shop. Valet serv. Exercise rm; sauna, steam rm. Luxury level. Walking distance to Wall St, ferry to statue of Liberty. Cr cds: A, D, DS, MC, V.

★ ★ **MAYFLOWER HOTEL ON THE PARK.** *15 Central Park West (10023). 212/265-0060; fax 212/265-0227; res 212/265-0060. www.mayflowerhotelny.com.* 365 rms, 18 story, 200 suites. S $200-$240; D $225-$265; each addl $20; suites $335-$350; under 16 free; package plans; lower rates July, Aug, mid-Dec-Mar 31. Pet accepted. Garage parking, valet $28. TV; cable (premium). Complimentary coffee. Restaurant 7 am-10 pm. Bar 11:30-1 am. Ck-out noon. Meeting rms. Business servs avail. In-rm modem link. Concierge. Exercise equipt. Many

refrigerators. Some terraces. Cr cds: A, C, D, DS, JCB, MC, V.

★ ★ ★ ★ **MERCER HOTEL.** *147 Mercer St (10012). 212/966-6060; fax 212/965-3838; toll-free 888/918-6060. www.mercerhotel.com.* Young, hip, good-looking celebrities have made this hotel, located in stylish SoHo, their home-away-from-home. The decor is strikingly minimalist with neutral tones and clean lines characterizining the guest rooms. Amenities range from CD players and access to all the latest tunes to deep, freestanding marble tubs that are as sculptural as they are luxurious. The scene at the basement restaurant, Mercer Kitchen, is sizzling. 75 rms, 6 story. S, D $350-$875; suites $1,100-$2,200. Crib free. In-rm modem link. Rm serv 24 hrs. Restaurant 8 am-midnight. Bar 8 am-midnight. Valet parkiing $40. Ck-out noon. Concierge. Bellhops. Fireplace. Health club privileges. Refrigerators. Vintage book library. Cr cds: A, D, DS, MC, V.

★ ★ ★ **METROPOLITAN HOTEL.** *569 Lexington Ave (10022). 212/752-7000; fax 212/758-6311; toll-free 800/836-6471. www.metropolitanhotel nyc.com.* 667 rms, 55 suites, 20 story. S, D $120-$325; each addl $25; suites $225-$500; under 14 free; wkend rates. Crib free. Pet accepted, some restrictions. Garage $30. TV; cable (premium). Restaurant 7 am-11:30 pm; Sun to 11 pm. Bar 11:30-2 am; Sun to 1 am. Ck-out noon. Meeting rms. Business center. In-rm modem link. Concierge. Gift shop. Barber. Shopping arcade. Valet serv. Airport transportation. Exercise rm; sauna. Bathrm phones, refrigerators; microwaves avail. Luxury level. Cr cds: A, C, D, DS, ER, JCB, MC, V.

★ ★ ★ **THE MICHELANGELO HOTEL.** *152 W 51st St (10019). 212/765-1900; fax 212/541-6604; toll-free 800/237-0990. www.michelangelo hotel.com.* 178 rms, 7 story, 52 suites. S, D $395-$535; each addl $30; suites $595-$1,735; under 16 free; wkend rates. Crib free. Pet accepted. Valet parking $38/day. TV; cable (premium), VCR avail (movies $5). Complimentary continental bkfst.

Restaurant 6:30 am-11 pm. Rm serv. Bar. Ck-out 1 pm. Meeting rms. Business servs avail. In-rm modem link. Concierge. Valet serv. Exercise equipt. Health club privileges. Bathrm phones; minibars. Refrigerators avail. Cr cds: A, C, D, DS, JCB, MC, V.

★ **MILBURN.** *242 W 76th St (10023). 212/362-1006; fax 212/721-5476; toll-free 800/833-9622. www.milburnhotel.com.* 106 kit. units, 15 story, 55 suites. Mar-Dec: S $129-$179; D $139-$179; suites $169-$239; lower rates rest of yr. Crib free. Garage parking $16. TV; cable, VCR avail (movies). Complimentary coffee in rms. Restaurant nearby. Ck-out noon. Meeting rms. Business servs avail. In-rm modem link. Concierge. Coin lndry. Health club privileges. Bathrm phones; microwaves avail. Cr cds: A, C, D, MC, V.

★★★ **MILLENIUM HOTEL NEW YORK BROADWAY.** *145 W 44th St (10036). 212/768-4400; fax 212/768-0847; toll-free 800/622-5569. www.milleniumbroadway.com.* 750 rms, 52 story. S, D $165; each addl $20; suites $350-$650; under 18 free; wkend rates. Crib free. Valet parking $45. TV; cable (premium), VCR avail. Restaurant 6:30 am-11 pm. Bar 11-1 am. Ck-out noon. Convention facilities. Business center. In-rm modem link. Concierge. Gift shop. Exercise equipt. Minibars. Bathrm phone in suites. Postmodern skyscraper with Moderne setbacks, Deco detailing, incorporates landmark Beaux Arts Hudson Theatre (1903), which has been restored. Cr cds: A, C, D, DS, JCB, MC, V.

★★★ **MILLENNIUM NEW YORK UN PLAZA.** *1 UN Plaza (10017). 212/758-1234; fax 212/702-5051; res 877/866-7529. www.millennium-hotels.com.* 427 rms on floors 28-40. S, D $225-$419; each addl $35; suites $500-$1,500; under 18 free; wkend rates. Crib free. Garage; valet parking $27, wkends $20. TV; cable (premium), VCR avail. Heated indoor pool; lifeguard. Restaurant (see also AMBASSADOR GRILL). Bar

noon-1:30 am. 24-hr rm serv. Ck-out noon. Gift shop. Meeting rms. Business center. In-rm modem link. Indoor tennis. Valet serv. Exercise rm; sauna. Massage. Minibars, bathrm phones; some refrigerators; microwaves avail. Gift shop. Cr cds: A, D, DS, JCB, MC, V

★★★ **MORGANS.** *237 Madison Ave (10016). 212/686-0300; fax 212/779-8352.* 113 rms, 19 story. S, D $250-$375; each addl $30; suites $465-$600; under 12 free; wkend rates. Garage, valet parking $44. TV; cable (premium). Complimentary continental bkfst. Rm serv 24 hrs. Bar 5 pm-4 am; Sun, Mon to 2 am. Ck-out noon Business servs avail. In-rm modem link. Concierge. Health club privileges Bathrm phones, refrigerators, minibars. Andree Putman-designed interiors; combines high-tech ultra-modern look. Cr cds: A, D, DS, MC, V

★★★ **THE MUSE.** *130 W 46th St (10036). 212/485-2400; fax 212/485-2900. www.themusehotel.com.* 200 rms, 19 story. S, D $355-$395; suites $400-$600; wkend rates. TV; cable (premium), VCR avail. Restaurants 6:30 am-midnight. Bar 11-2 am. Ck-out noon. Complimentary continental bkfst, coffee. Meeting rms. Business center. In-rm modem link. Concierge. Gift shop. Exercise equipt Refrigerators avail. Cr cds: A, C, D, DS, JCB, MC, V.

★★ **NEW YORK HELMSLEY HOTEL.** *212 E 42nd St (10017). 212/490-8900; fax 212/867-5992; toll-free 800/221-4982. www.helmsley hotels.com.* 775 rms, 41 story. S, D $230-$315; each addl $30; suites $225-$675; under 12 free; wkend rates. Crib free. Pet accepted, some restrictions. Garage $36/day, valet parking avail. TV; cable, VCR avail (movies). Restaurant 7 am-11:30 pm. Rm serv 24 hr. Bar noon-1 am; entertainment. Ck-out noon. Meeting rms. Business center. In-rm modem link. Concierge. Valet serv. Gift shop. Health club privileges. Bathrm phones. Refrigerators, microwaves avail. 2 blks E of Grand Central Station. Cr cds: A, C, D, DS, ER, JCB, MC, V.

D ◨ ⬚ ⬚ SC ⭣

★ ★ ★ **NEW YORK MARRIOTT MARQUIS.** *1535 Broadway (10036).* *212/398-1900; fax 212/704-8930; res 800/228-9290. www.marriott.com.* 1,946 rms, 50 story, 56 suites. S $183-$290; D $203-$500; suites $425-$3,500; under 18 free; wkend, package plans. Covered parking, valet $45. Crib avail. TV; cable (premium). Complimentary coffee in rms. Restaurants 6 am-11 pm (see also THE VIEW). Rm serv 24 hrs. Bars. Ck-out noon. Convention facilities. Business center. In-rm modem link. Concierge. Gift shop. Valet serv. Beauty shop. Exercise equipt; sauna. Whirlpool. Minibars. Luxury level. Cr cds: A, C, D, DS, JCB, MC, V.

D ⭣ ⬚ ⬚ ⭣

★ ★ ★ **NEW YORK PALACE.** *455 Madison Ave (10022). 212/888-7000; fax 212/303-6000; toll-free 800/697-2522. www.newyorkpalace.com.* Every detail in this large, luxurious hotel, from the speedy room service to the exemplary shoe shine, is carried out with finesse. Home to Le Cirque 2000 and Istana, the Palace is one of the best values in its class in all of New York. 896 rms, 55 story, 104 suites. S, D $450-$550; suites $900-$12,000; under 18 free; wkend rates. Crib free. Garage parking $46. TV; cable, VCR avail (movies). Restaurants 6:30 am-10:30 pm (see also LE CIRQUE 2000). Rm serv 24 hrs. Bars 5:30 pm-1 am. Ck-out 1 pm. Meeting rms. Business center. In-rm modem link. Concierge. Valet serv. Exercise rm; steam rm. Massage. Health club privileges. Refrigerators. Cr cds: A, C, D, DS, JCB, MC, V.

D ⭣ ⬚ ⬚ ⭣

★ **NEW YORK'S HOTEL PENNSYL-VANIA.** *401 7th Ave (10001). 212/736-5000; fax 212/502-8712; toll-free 800/223-8585. www.hotelpenn.com.* 1,705 rms, 22 story. S, D $109-$249; suites $175-$650; each addl $25; under 16 free. Crib free. Garage $26, valet.. TV; cable. Restaurant 6:30-1 am. Bar noon-2 am, entertainment. Ck-out noon. Convention facilities. Business servs avail. In-rm modem link. Shopping

arcade. Barber, beauty shop. Health club privileges. Cr cds: A, D, DS, ER, JCB, MC, V.

⬚ ⬚

★ ★ **NOVOTEL NEW YORK.** *226 W 52nd St (10019). 212/315-0100; fax 212/765-5369; toll-free 800/221-3185. www.novotel.com.* 480 rms, 33 story. S, D $155-$199; each addl $20; under 18 free. Crib $10. Pet accepted. Parking $12. TV; cable (premium). Restaurant 6 am-midnight. Rm serv. Bar 3:30 pm-1 am; entertainment Mon-Sat. Ck-out 1 pm. Meeting rm. Business center. In-rm modem link. Gift shop. Minibars. Exercise equipt. Cr cds: A, D, MC, V.

⭣ ◨ ⬚ ⭣ D

★ ★ ★ **OMNI BERKSHIRE PLACE.** *21 E 52nd St at Madison Ave (10022). 212/753-5800; fax 212/754-5018; toll-free 800/843-6664. www.omnihotels.com.* 396 rms, 21 story, 47 suites. S, D $245-$599; each addl $30; suites $399-$1,150; under 12 free; wkend rates (2-day min). Valet parking $32. Supervised children's activities. TV; cable (premium), VCR avail. Restaurant 7 am-10 pm; wkend hrs vary. Rm serv 24 hrs. Bar 11-1 am. Ck-out noon. Meeting rms. Business center. In-rm modem link. Concierge. Valet serv. Exercise equipt. Minibars. Cr cds: A, C, D, DS, JCB, MC, V.

D ⭣ ⬚ ⬚ ⭣

★ ★ **ON THE AVE HOTEL.** *2178 Broadway at 77th St (10024). 212/362-1100.* 251 rms, 15 story. S, D $120-$295; suites $250-$450; each addl $20; under 12 free; wkend rates. Parking $25 TV; cable (p[remium), VCR avail. Coffee in rms. Restaurants 6:30 am-midnight. Rm serv. Bar 11 am-midnight. Ck-out noon. Meeting rms. Business center. In-rm modem link. Concierge. Valet serv. Exercise equipt. Refrigerators avail. Cr cds: A, D, DS, MC, V.

⭣ ⬚ ⭣ D

★ ★ ★ **PARAMOUNT.** *235 W 46th St (10036). 212/764-5500; fax 212/575-4892; toll-free 800/225-7474.* 608 rms, 19 story. S $150-$270; D $285; each addl $20; suites $425-$650; under 16 free; monthly rates; wkend packages. Crib free. Garage $45. TV; cable (premium), VCR (movies). Restaurant 6:30 am-11:30 pm. Rm serv. Bar 5 pm-midnight.. Ck-out noon. Meeting rms. Business center. In-rm modem link. Concierge. Exercise equipt. Public areas and guest rms designed in a high-tech, futuristic style. Cr cds: A, D, DS, JCB, MC, V.

★ ★ ★ ★ **THE PENINSULA.** *700 5th Ave (10019). 212/956-2888; fax 212/ 903-3949; toll-free 800/262-9467. www.peninsula.com.* This New York branch of the famed Peninsula Hotel group, housed in an ornate beaux-arts buiding, underwent a top-to-bottom refurbishment which has brought it up to the stellar level of its counterparts around the world. Rooms are smartly designed with excellent amenities, including a television in the bathtub, a bedside lighting module, and fine European bed linens. Service at the hotel is top-notch, catering to business travelers and tourists alike. The Penn Top bar, with a stunning view of the city is an excellent place to take in a sunset cocktail; at the spa and fitness center one can be pampered like a princess or whipped into shape by one of the personal trainers. 239 rms, 54 suites, 23 story. S, D $350-$725; suites $775-$9,000; package plans. Crib free. Valet parking; $45. TV; cable (premium), VCR (movies). Indoor pool; whirlpool. Restaurant 7-10:30 am, noon-2:30 pm (Mon-Fri), 6-10 pm (Tues-Sun); Sun brunch 11:30 am-2:30 pm. Rm serv 24 hrs. Bar 11-1 am, Fri, Sat to 2 am, Sun noon-1 am. Complimentary continental bkfst. Ck-out noon. Business center. In-rm modem link. Bellhops. Concierge. Valet serv. Exercise rm; sauna, steam rm. Massage. Barber/beauty salon. TVs inset above tubs in bathrms. Refrigerators in suites. Cr cds: A, C, D, DS, JCB, MC, V.

★ ★ ★ ★ **THE PIERRE NEW YORK, A FOUR SEASONS HOTEL.** *2 E 61st St (10021). 212/838-8000; fax 212/940-8109; toll-free 800/743-7734. www.fourseasons.com.* The charm of this historic hotel on 5th Avenue comes in part from the wealthy New York socialites who make it their home. The rooms are large and decorated in an old-fashioned way with patterned upholstery and feather throw pillows. The elevator operators are full of information about the city Cafe Pierre affords a fine New York dining experience at breakfast, lunch, or dinner. 201 rms, 52 suites, 41 story. S, D $495-$950; 1-bdrm suites $725-$5,475; 2-bdrm suites $1,235-$4,500; 3-bdrm suites $3,490-$5,675; under 18 free. Crib free. Garage $45, 24-hr valet parking. TV; cable (premium), VCR avail (movies). Restaurants 7 am-11 pm. Rm serv 24 hrs. Bar noon-1 am; entertainment 8:30 pm-12:30 am. Ck-out 1 pm. Meeting rms. Business center. In-rm modem link. Concierge. Barber, beauty shop. Gift shop. Exercise equipt. Spa. Massage. Health club privileges. Minibars. Serv pantry in suites. Cr cds: A, C, D, DS, ER, JCB, MC, V.

★ ★ ★ **THE PLAZA.** *5th Ave at Central Park S (10019). 212/759-3000; fax 212/759-3167; toll-free 800/527-4727.* 805 rms, 18 story 60 suites. S, D $275-$800; each addl $35; suites $500-$4,500; under 18 free; wkend rates. Crib free. Pet accepted. Garage $40. TV; cable (premium), VCR avail. Restaurants. Rm serv 24 hrs. Bar 11-2 am. Ck-out noon. Business center. In-rm modem link and fax machine. 2-line speakerphones. Concierge. Gift shop. Barber, beauty shop. Valet serv. Exercise equipt. Health club privileges. Refrigerators on request. Minibars. Fireplaces in deluxe and higher. Cr cds: A, C, D, DS, JCB, MC, V.

★ ★ **PLAZA FIFTY.** *155 E 50th St (10022). 212/751-5710; fax 212/753-1468; toll-free 800/637-8483. www.mesuite.com.* 204 rms, 22 story, 137 suites. S $250; D $320; each addl $20; suites $340-$650; under 12 free; wkend rates. Crib free. Valet parking avail. TV; cable (premium). Coffee in rms. Ck-out noon. Concierge. Valet serv. Business servs avail. In-rm modem link. Exercise equipt. Refrigerators, microwaves. Some balconies. Cr cds: A, C, D, DS, JCB, MC, V.

★ ★ **RADISSON.** *511 Lexington Ave at 48th St (10017). 212/755-4400; fax 212/751-4091; toll-free 800/333-3333.* 700 rms, 27 story, 35 suites. S, D $159-$359; each addl $15; suites

$325-$550. Crib free. TV; cable (premium). Restaurant 6:30 am-midnight; entertainment. Bar 11-1 am. Rm serv. Valet serv. Concierge serv. Bellhops. Ck-out noon. Meeting rm. Business center. Exercise equipt. Refrigerators, microwaves. Near Grand Central Station. Cr cds: A, C, D, DS, ER, JCB, MC, V.

★★★★ **THE REGENCY HOTEL.** *540 Park Ave (10021). 212/759-4100; fax 212/826-5674; res 800/235-6397. www.loewshotels.com.* This aptly named property is indeed fit for a king, or at least a business tycoon, many of whom can be seen engaged in tense power breakfasts in the dining room each morning. In contrast to the hard-as-nails wheeling and dealing are the plush guest rooms awash in a palate of pastels. Service is discreet and attentive enough to make every guest feel like a bigshot. 351 rms, 20 story, 87 kit. suites. S, D $359-$599; suites $569-$3,500; each addl $30; under 17 free; wkend rates. Crib free. Garage $48, valet parking avail. Pet accepted. TV; cable (premium), VCR (movies). Stereo with CD player. Supervised children's activities. Restaurant (see also 540 PARK). Rm serv. Bar noon-1 am. Rm serv 24 hrs. Ck-out noon. Meeting rms. Business center. In-rm modem link. Concierge. Valet serv. Gift shop. Barber, beauty shop. Exercise rm; sauna. Massage. Refrigerators, balconies in suites. Minibars. Cr cds: A, C, D, DS, MC, V.

★★★★ **THE REGENT WALL STREET.** *55 Wall St (10005). 212/845-8600; fax 212/845-8601. www.regenthotels.com.* This property is located in the center of New York's bustling financial district. Guest rooms are spacious and beautifully appointed; the bathrooms are the size of small New York City apartments. Service is superb. The Greek revival masterpiece by architect Isaiah Rogers was completed in 1842 as the Merchant's Exchange. The breathtaking ballroom, formerly the banking hall, was added in 1899 and is breathtaking in design, size and scope. 12,000 square feet with four sets of Corinthian columns, an 80-foot dome with 16 Wedgwood panels

depicting the signs of the zodiac, and a 2,700-pound chandelier. 144 rms, 15 story. S, D $350-$595; suites $525-$995; wkend rates. Pet accepted, some restrictions. TV; cable (premium), VCR avail. Restaurants 7-1 am. Bar 11 am-midnight. Ck-out noon. Meeting rms. Business center. In-rm modem link. Concierge. Bellhops. Valet serv. Exercise equipt, sauna. Refrigerators, minibars. Cr cds: A, D, DS, MC, V.

★★★ **RENAISSANCE NEW YORK TIMES SQUARE.** *714 7th Ave (10036). 212/765-7676; fax 212/765-1962. www.renaissancehotels.com.* 305 rms, 26 story. S, D $229-$400; each addl $20; suites $500-$600; under 12 free; wkend rates. Crib free. Garage $35. TV; cable (premium), VCR. Complimentary coffee in rms. Restaurant 6 am-10 pm. Rm serv 24 hrs. Bar. Ck-out noon. Meeting rms. Business center. In-rm modem link. Concierge. Massage. Valet serv. Exercise equipt. Bathrm phones, minibars. Cr cds: A, D, DS, JCB, MC, V.

★★★★ **THE RITZ-CARLTON NEW YORK, BATTERY PARK.** *2 West St (10004). 212/344-0800; fax 212/344-3801; res 800/241-3333. www.ritzcarlton.com.* This elegant, high-energy property is the only luxury waterfront hotel in Manhattan. Telescope-equipped harbor-view rooms offer panoramic views of New York Harbor, the Statue of Liberty, and Battery Park. 255 rms, 39 story, 43 suites. S, D $465-$850; suites $950-$4,500; each addl $40; under 17 free. Crib free. Parking $40. TV; cable, VCR avail, CD player. Restaurant 6 am-11:30 pm. Rm serv 24 hrs. Bar 4 pm-midnight. Ck-out noon. Meeting rms. Business center. In-rm modem link. Concierge. Bellhops. Gift shop. Valet serv. Exercise rm; sauna. Spa. Massage. Some refrigerators, telescopes. Luxury level. Cr cds: A, C, D, DS, ER, JCB, MC, V.

THE RITZ-CARLTON, NEW YORK, CENTRAL PARK (*Too new to be rated*) *50 Central Park S (10019). 212/308-9100.* 277 rms, 15 story. S, D $325-$425; suites $550-$1,695; under 18 free; wkend rates. Crib free. TV; cable (premium), VCR, DVD avail. Restaurants 6:30 am-midnight. Rm serv 24 hrs. Ck-out noon. Valet serv. Meeting rms. Business center. In-rm modem link. Concierge. Gift shop. Exercise equipt. Cr cds: A, D, DS, MC, V.

★★★ **THE ROGER WILLIAMS.** *131 Madison Ave (10016). 212/448-7000; fax 212/448-7007; res 877/847-4444. www.botiquehg.com.* 187 rms, 20 with shower only, 16 story. S, D $195-$400; each addl $20; suites $375; under 12 free. Crib free. Garage parking $17, valet. TV; cable (premium), VCR (movies). Complimentary continental bkfst; afternoon refreshments. Restaurant nearby. Ck-out noon. Business center. In-rm modem link. Concierge. Health club privileges. Bathrm phones. Cr cds: A, C, D, DS, JCB, MC, V.

★★ **ROOSEVELT HOTEL.** *45 E 45th St and Madison Ave (10017). 212/661-9600; fax 212/885-6161; toll-free 888/833-3969. www.theroosevelthotel. com.* 1,013 rms, 100 with shower only, 19 story 30 suites. S $129-$259; D $239-$279; each addl $20; suites $500-$2,500; under 12 free; wkend rates. Crib free. Valet serv. Parking $40. TV; cable, VCR avail. Restaurant 6:30 am-11 pm. Bar noon-2 am. Ck-out noon. Convention facilities. Business center. In-rm modem link. Concierge. Gift shop. Beauty shop.

Exercise equipt. Cr cds: A, C, D, DS, JCB, MC, V.

★★★ **ROYALTON.** *44 W 44th St (10036). 212/869-4400; fax 212/869-8965; toll-free 800/635-9013. www. ianschragerhotels.com.* 169 rms, some with shower only, 16 story. S, D $229-$500; each addl $20; suites $475-$600; under 14 free; wkend rates. Crib free. Pet accepted, some restrictions. Valet parking $45. TV; cable (premium), VCR (movies), CD player. Restaurant 7-1 am. Rm serv 24 hrs. Bar noon-3 am. Ck-out 1 pm. Business servs avail. In-rm modem link. Valet serv. Concierge. Exercise equipt. Bathrm phones, refrigerators, minibars; some fireplaces. Some balconies. Ultramodern rm decor. Cr cds: A, D, DS, JCB, MC, V.

★★★★★ **THE ST. REGIS.** *2 E 55th St (10022). 212/753-4500; fax 212/ 787-3447; toll-free 800/759-7550. www.stregis.com.* Red-carpet treatment awaits at this old-world hotel, just off 5th Avenue. Uniformed doormen and marbled columns greet you; front desk clerks will take you to the room to register. Personal butler service and grand bathrooms are just some of the unique guest room amenities. Don't miss afternoon tea in the lobby accompanied by live harp music or dinner at Lespinasse.

World Famous Times Square

315 rms, 20 story, 92 suites. S, D $400-$940; suites $1,100-$11,500; wkend rates. Crib free. Garage parking, valet, in/out $40. TV; cable (premium), VCR. Restaurant. Afternoon tea in Astor Court 3-5:30 pm; harpist. Rm serv 24 hrs. Bar 11:30-1 am; Fri, Sat to 2 am; Sun noon-midnight. Ck-out noon. Meeting rms. Business center. In-rm modem link. Gift shop. Concierge. Extensive shopping arcade. Barber, beauty shop. Valet serv. Exercise rm; sauna. Massage. Health club privileges. Bathrm phones. Cr cds: A, D, DS, JCB, MC, V.

★★ SALISBURY HOTEL. *123 W 57th St (10019). 212/246-1300; fax 212/977-7752.* 119 rms, 17 story, 85 suites. S $279; D $329; each addl $20; suites $329-$519; each addl $30; under 15 free; wkend rates. Crib free. TV; cable, VCR avail. Complimentary continental bkfst. Ck-out noon. Meeting rms. Business servs avail. In-rm modem link. Concierge. Health club privileges. Many refrigerators, microwaves. Parking $23. Cr cds: A, C, D, JCB, MC, V.

★★ SAN CARLOS HOTEL. *150 E 50th St (10022). 212/755-1800; fax 212/688-9778; toll-free 800/722-2012.* www.sancarloshotel.com. 150 rms, 18 story, 138 kits. S, D $150-$180; each addl $10; suites $200-$350; under 14 free; wkend rates. Crib free. TV, cable (premium). Complimentary continental bkfst. Restaurant 6 am-11 pm. Rm serv. Bar. Ck-out 11 am. Coin lndry. In-rm modem link. Exercise equipt. Barber, beauty shop. Microwaves. Cr cds: A, C, D, JCB, MC, V.

★★★ SHELBURNE MURRAY HILL HOTEL. *303 Lexington Ave (10016). 212/689-5200; fax 212/779-7068; res 800/637-8483.* www.mesuite.com. 264 suites, 16 story. Suites $194-$680; under 12 free; wkend rates. Crib free. Garage parking $27. TV; cable (premium), VCR avail. Restaurant 7 am-10 pm. Rm serv. Bar noon-11 pm. Coffee in rms. Ck-out noon. Coin lndry. Meetings rms. Business servs avail. In-rm modem link. Concierge. Valet serv. Exercise equipt; sauna. Refrigerators, microwaves. Private patios, balconies. Cr cds: A, C, D, DS, JCB, MC, V.

★★★ SHERATON MANHATTAN. *790 7th Ave (10019). 212/581-3300; fax 212/541-9219; res 800/325-3535.* www.sheratonnyc.com. 650 rms, 22 story. S, D $199-$279; each addl $30; suites $650-$750; under 17 free; wkend rates. Crib free. Garage $25. TV; cable (premium), VCR avail. Heated indoor pool; lifeguard. Complimentary continental bkfst, coffee in rms. Restaurant noon-11 pm; Sat, Sun from 4 pm. Rm serv 24 hrs. Bar 11 am-11 pm. Ck-out noon. Business servs avail. In-rm modem link. Concierge. Gift shop. Exercise rm; sauna. Valet serv. Minibars. Refrigerators, microwaves avail. Cr cds: A, C, D, DS, JCB, MC, V.

★★★ SHERATON NEW YORK HOTEL AND TOWERS. *811 7th Ave (10019). 212/581-1000; fax 212/262-4410.* www.sheraton.com. 1,750 rms, 50 story. S, D $259-$269; each addl $30; suites $559-$965; under 17 free; wkend rates. Crib free. Garage $35. TV; cable (premium), VCR avail. Pool privileges. Complimentary coffee in rms. Restaurant 6:30 am-midnight. Bars 11:30-4 am. Ck-out noon. Convention facilities. Business center. In-rm modem link. Gift shop. Exercise rm; sauna. Minibars. Luxury level. Cr cds: A, D, DS, JCB, MC, V.

★★★ SHERATON RUSSELL HOTEL. *45 Park Ave (10016). 212/685-7676; fax 212/889-3193; res 800/325-3535.* www.sheraton.com. 146 rms, 10 story, 26 suites. S $350-$579; D $255-$465; suites $395-$595; under 17 free; wkend rates. Crib $25. Valet, garage parking $35. TV; cable (premium), VCR avail. Complimentary continental bkfst, coffee in rms. Rm serv 24 hrs. Bar from 5 pm. Ck-out noon. Meeting rm. Business center. In-rm modem link. Concierge. Exercise equipt. Health club privileges. Pool privileges. Bathrm phones, minibars; many fireplaces. Cr cds: A, C, D, DS, JCB, MC, V.

★★ SHOREHAM HOTEL. *33 W 55th St (10019). 212/247-6700; fax*

212/765-9741; toll-free 800/553-3347.
92 rms, 11 story, 37 suites. S, D $189;
suites $335; wkend, hol rates. Crib
free. Valet parking $40. TV; cable
(premium), VCR (free movies). Complimentary continental bkfst. Restaurant. Bar. Ck-out noon. Business
servs avail. In-rm modem link.
Concierge. Health club privileges.
Refrigerators. Renovated hotel built
1930. Cr cds: A, D, MC, V.

⊡ ⊠ ⊠ ⟨SC⟩

★★★ **60 THOMPSON.** *60 Thompson
St (10012). 212/431-0400; fax 212/
431 0200. www.60thompson.com.* 100
rms, 8 story. S, D $159-$525; suites
$500-$625. Crib free. TV; cable (premium), VCR avail. Coffee in rms.
Restaurants 7-1 am. Bar 5 pm-2 am.
Ck-out noon. Meeting rms. Business
center. In-rm modem link. Concierge.
Bellhops. Exercise privileges. Cr cds:
A, D, DS, MC, V.

⊡ ⊠ ⊠ ⟨⟩

★★★ **SOFITEL NEW YORK.** *45 W
44th St (10036). 212/354-8844; fax
212/354-2450. www.accor-hotels.com.*

400 rms, 30 story. S, D $25-$450;
suites $756. Pet accepted, some
restrictions. Crib free. TV; cable (premium), VCR avail. Restaurants 6:30
am-midnight. Bar 11-1 am. Rm serv
24hrs. Ck-out noon. Valet serv. Meeting rms. Business servs avail. In-rm
modem link. Concierge. Bellhops.
Gift shop. Exercise equipt. Massage.
Minibars. Cr cds: A, C, D, DS, JCB,
MC, V.

⟨⟩ ⊠ ⊡ ⟨⟩

★★★ **SOHO GRAND HOTEL.** *310
W Broadway (10013). 212/965-3000;
fax 212/965-3200; res 800/965-3000.
www.sohogrand.com.* 364 rms, 17
story. S $259-$369; D $279-$539;
each addl $20; suites $900-$1,799;
under 12 free. Crib free. Pet accepted.
Garage parking $25. TV; cable (pre-
mium), VCR avail. Restaurant 6:30
am-10 pm. Rm serv 24 hrs. Bar
noon-2 am; Sat, Sun from 1 pm. Ck-
out noon. Meeting rms. Business
servs avail. In-rm modem link.
Concierge. Free valet parking. Exercise equipt. Massage. Minibars. Cr
cds: A, D, DS, ER, JCB, MC, V.

⊡ ⟨⟩ ⟨⟩ ⊠ ⟨⟩

★★★ **SOUTHGATE
TOWER SUITE HOTEL.**
*371 7th Ave (10001).
212/563-1800; fax 212/643-
8028; toll-free 800/637-
8483. www.mesuite.com.*
522 kit. suites, 28 story. S,
D $229-$450; under 12
free; each addl $20; suites
$399-$439; wkend, wkly,
monthly rates. Valet parking, $25. Crib free. TV;
cable (premium). Compli-
mentary coffee. Restaurant
7 am-11:30 pm. Bar. Rm
serv 7am-11:30 pm. Ck-out
noon. Coin lndry. Meeting
rms. Business servs avail.
Concierge. Barber. Micro-
waves. Some balconies. Cr
cds: A, C, D, DS, ER, JCB,
MC, V.

⊡ ⊠ ⊠

★ **STANFORD HOTEL.** *43
W 32nd St (10001).
212/563-1500; fax 212/
629-0043; toll-free 800/365-
1114.* 121 rms, 12 story, 30
suites. S $90-$110; D $120-
$150; each addl $20; suites

Grammercy Park, Greenwhich Village

$180-$200. Crib free. TV; cable. Complimentary continental bkfst. Restaurant 7 am-10 pm. Ck-out noon. Business servs avail. In-rm modem link. Refrigerators. Near Madison Square Garden. Cr cds: A, C, D, JCB, MC, V.

D ⟨symbols⟩ **SC**

★ ★ ★ ★ **THE STANHOPE PARK HYATT NEW YORK.** *995 5th Ave at 81st St (10028). 212/774-1234; fax 212/517-0088; toll-free 800/233-1234. www.hyatt.com.* Wonderfully situated directly across from the Metropolitan Museum of Art, this hotel provides an excellent home base for exploring the neighborhood's many museums. It is patterned after luxurious European manor houses, with gold leaf molding and antiques displayed throughout the hotel's intimate public space. 185 units, 17 story, 54 suites. S, D $299-$599; suites $399-$2,000; under 12 free; wkend rates; package plans. Valet parking; $65.Crib free. Pet accepted; $100. TV; cable, VCR, CD players. Restaurant 6:30 am-10 pm. Rm serv 24 hrs. Bar 11 am-1 pm. Ck-out noon. Meeting rms. Business center. Bellhops. Concierge. Valet serv. Exercise rm; sauna. Massage. Minibars. Library. Cr cds: A, C, D, DS, ER, JCB, MC, V.

★ ★ ★ **SURREY HOTEL.** *20 E 76th St (10021). 212/288-3700; fax 212/628-1549; toll-free 800/637-8483. www.mesuite.com.* 133 rms, 16 story. S, D $250-$298; each addl $20; suites $345-$1,500; under 12 free; wkly, monthly rates; wkend rates. Crib avail. TV; cable (premium), VCR (movies). Restaurant 7-10:30 am, noon-2:30 pm, 5:45-11 pm. Bar. Coffee in rms. Ck-out noon. Meeting rm. Business servs avail. In-rm modem link. Valet serv. Bellhops. Concierge. Exercise equipt. Refrigerators, microwaves avail. Cr cds: A, C, D, DS, ER, JCB, MC, V.

★ ★ ★ ★ ★ **TRUMP INTERNATIONAL HOTEL & TOWER.** *1 Central Park W (10023). 212/299-1000; fax 212/299-1150; toll-free 888/448-7867. www.trumpintl.com.* Designed in the flashy businessman spirit of its owner, the rooms of this comfortable hotel are meant to feel like home. Amenities include well-stocked in-room kitchenettes (for a fee a chef from Jean Georges will cook dinner in your room) and tasteful bric-a-brac like antique magnifying glasses and artbooks. 167 kit. units, 52 story. 130 suites. S, D $475; suites $750-$1,500; wkend rates. Crib free. Valet parking $42. TV; cable (premium), VCR (movies). Indoor pool. Complimentary coffee in rms. Restaurant (see also JEAN GEORGES). Rm serv 24 hrs. Bar. Ck-out noon. Business center. In-rm modem link. Concierge. Exercise rm; sauna, steam rm. Massage. Bathrm phones, in-rm jacuzzi tubs, refrigerators, microwaves, minibars. Cr cds: A, C, D, DS, JCB, MC, V.

★ ★ ★ **WALDORF-ASTORIA.** *301 Park Ave (10022). 212/355-3000; fax 212/872-7272; toll-free 800/925-3673. www.hilton.com.* 1,246 rms, 42 story. S, D $179-625; each addl $40; suites $199-$950; children free; wkend rates. Crib free. Garage $45/day. Valet parking. TV; cable (premium), VCR avail. Restaurant 7 am-11:45 pm (see also BULL AND BEAR STEAKHOUSE). Rm serv 24 hrs. Bars 11-3 am; Sun noon-1 am. Ck-out noon. Convention facilities. Business center. In-rm modem link. Concierge. Barber, beauty shop. Shopping arcade. Extensive exercise rm; steam rm. Massage. Refrigerators. Luxury level. Cr cds: A, C, D, DS, ER, JCB, MC, V.

★ ★ **THE WARWICK NEW YORK.** *65 W 54th St (10019). 212/247-2700; fax 212/247-2725; res 800/223-4099. www.warwickhotels.com.* 426 rms, 33 story. S $295-$360; D $325-$380; each addl $25; suites $500-$1,200; under 12 free; wkend rates. Crib free. Garage $26-$40. TV; cable (premium). Restaurant 6:30-12:30 am. Bar 11:30-12:30 am. Ck-out 1 pm. Meeting rms. Business center. Exercise equipt. Health club privileges. Free airport transportation. Many terraces. Cr cds: A, C, D, JCB, MC, V.

★ ★ ★ **W HOTEL - UNION SQUARE.** *201 Park Ave S (10016). 212/253-9119. www.whotels.com.* 270

rms, 25 story. S, D $249-$299; suites $395-$799; under 18 free; wkend rates. Crib free. TV; cable (premium). Restaurant 6:30 am-midnight. Bar 11 am-midnight. Ck-out noon. Valet serv. Meeting rms. Business center. In-rm modem link. Concierge. Exercise equipt. Gametables. Minibars. Cr cds: A, D, DS, MC, V.

★★★ **W NEW YORK.** *541 Lexington Ave (10022). 212/755-1200; fax 212/319-8344. www.whotels.com.* 717 rms, 18 story. S, D $289-$389; 1 bedrm suites $389-$1,600. Crib free. Garage parking $38, valet. Pet accepted. TV; cable (premium), VCR. Restaurant. Rm serv 24 hrs. Ck-out noon. Meeting rms. Business servs avail. In-rm modem link. Concierge. Exercise rm and spa; sauna, steam rm. Valet serv. Minibars. Bar 4 pm-4 am. Cr cds: A, C, D, DS, JCB, MC, V.

★★★ **W NEW YORK COURT.** *130 E 39th St (10016). 212/686-1600; fax 212/779-7822; toll-free 877/946-8357. www.whotels.com.* 199 rms, 17 story. S $185-$285; D $205-$305; each addl $20; suites $400-$850; under 12 free. Crib free. Garage $38. TV; cable (premium). Restaurant 7-10:30 am, noon-2:30 pm, 5 pm-midnight. Rm serv 7 am-11 pm. Bar 5 pm-midnight. Ck-out 1 pm. Business servs avail. Bathrm phones, minibars. Cr cds: A, C, D, DS, JCB, MC, V.

★★ **WYNDHAM HOTEL.** *42 W 58th St (10019). 212/753-3500; fax 212/754-5638; toll-free 800/257-1111.* 212 rms, 16 story. S, D $135-$165; suites $180-$210. Crib free. Pet accepted. TV; cable (premium). Restaurant 7 am-11 pm. Bar noon-11 pm. Ck-out 1 pm. Business servs avail. In-rm modem link. Garage adj. Valet serv. Refrigerator, serv pantry in suites. Cr cds: A, C, D, DS, MC, V.

B&Bs/Small Inns

★ **BROADWAY BED AND BREAK-FAST INN.** *264 W 46th St (10036). 212/997-9200; fax 212/768-2807; toll-free 800/826-6300. www.broadwayinn. com.* 41 rms, 15 with shower only, 3 story. S $105; D $135; each addl $10; suites $195; under 12 free. TV; cable. Complimentary continental bkfst. Restaurant noon-4 am. Rm serv 24 hrs. Ck-out noon, ck-in 3 pm. Luggage handling. Some refrigerators, microwaves. Cr cds: A, D, DS, JCB, MC, V.

★★★ **INN AT IRVING PLACE.** *56 Irving Pl (10003). 212/533-4600; fax 212/533-4611; toll-free 800/685-1447. www.innatirving.com.* 12 rms, 2 with shower only, 3 story. S $295; D $325-$475; each addl $25; suite $375; monthly rates. Children over 12 yrs only. TV; cable (premium), VCR (movies). Complimentary continental bkfst; afternoon refreshments. Dining rm noon-3 pm, 5-10 pm. Bar. Rm serv 24 hrs. Bar. Ck-out noon, ck-in 3 pm. Luggage handling. Business servs avail. In-rm modem link. Health club privileges. Refrigerators, minibars. Elegant country-style inn with all modern conveniences. Cr cds: A, Carte B, D, JCB, MC, V.

All Suites

★★★ **BEEKMAN TOWER SUITE HOTEL.** *3 Mitchell Pl (10017). 212/320-8018; fax 212/753-9366. www.mesuite.com.* 174 kit. suites, 26 story. S, studio suites $260; D $259-$299; each addl $20; 2-bedrm suites $599; under 12 free; wkend rates; lower rates June-Aug. Crib free. Garage $27. TV; cable, VCR avail. Complimentary coffee in rms. Restaurant 7 am-10 pm. Rm serv. Bar 4 pm-1 am; entertainment. Ck-out noon. Coin lndry. Meeting rms. In-rm modem link. Valet serv. Exercise equipt; sauna. Refrigerators, microwaves. Some private patios, balconies. Restored Art Deco landmark completed in 1928. Cr cds: A, D, DS, MC, V.

★★★ **DOUBLETREE GUEST SUITES.** *1568 Broadway (10036). 212/719-1600; fax 212/921-5212; res 800/222-8733. www.doubletree.com.* 460 suites, 43 story. S $189-$350; D $350-$750; each addl $20; under 12 free; wkend rates; higher rates special events. Crib free. Garage; valet parking $35/day. TV; cable (premium) VCR avail. Complimentary coffee in rms. Restaurant 6:30 am-10 pm. Rm serv. Bar from noon. Ck-out noon. Coin lndry. Meeting rms. Business servs avail. In-rm modem link. Concierge. Gift shop. Valet serv. Exercise equipt. Bathrm phones, refrigerators, minibars, wet bars. Cr cds: A, D, DS, MC, V.

D ⚹ ⊠ ♨ SC

★★ **HOTEL DELMONICO.** *502 Park Ave (10022). 212/355-2500; fax 212/ 421-4768; res 800/821-3842. www. hoteldelmonico.com.* 150 kit. suites, 32 story. Suites $315-$635; each addl $30; under 13 free; wkend rates. Pets accepted, $250 deposit. Crib free. Valet parking $36. TV; cable (premium), VCR avail. Bar 5 pm-11 pm. Ck-out noon. Business servs avail. In-rm modem link. Concierge. Exercise rm; sauna. Microwaves. Some balconies. Restored 1929 building. Cr cds: A, D, DS, JCB, MC, V.

⚓ ⚹ ⊠ ♨

Restaurants

★★★★★ **ALAIN DUCASSE.** *155 W 58th St (10019). 212/265-7300. www.alain-ducasse.com.* France's most decorated chef has redefined fine dining in New York. No other experience so closely approximates a meal at the best restaurants of La Republique. From the warm welcome, to the quiet, spacious room, from the doting service, to the seemingly endless parade of courses, each with some neo-Victorian utensil to eat it with, Ducasse has put the haute back into haute cuisine. The everchanging menu and wine list mean there is always something new to enjoy. And the bag of brioche presented on your way out (for breakfast "Monsieur") means the much-talked-about high price tag covers two meals. Specializes in grilled bison loin, filet of striped bass. Hrs: Tues-Sat 7-9 pm; Thurs, Fri noon-2 pm. Closed Sun, Mon. Wine cellar. Res required. Lunch, 3-course $65; dinner prix fixe $160-$280. Entertainment. Cr cds: A, D, DS, JCB, MC, V.

D

★★ **ALVA.** *36 E 22nd St (10010). 212/228-4399.* American contemporary menu. Specialties: grilled pork

rib eye, crispy soft shell crabs. Own desserts. Hrs: noon-3 pm, 5:30-midnight; Sat, Sun from 5:30 pm. Res accepted. Bar. A la carte entrees: lunch $10-$19, dinner $17-$24. Cr cds: A, D, MC, V.

D ⊠

★★★ **AMERICAN PARK AT THE BATTERY.** *State St (10004). 212/809-5508. www.americanpark.com.* Hrs: 11:30 am-10 pm; Sun 11 am-3 pm. Closed hols. Res accepted. Seafood menu. Bar. Wine list. A la carte entrees: lunch $14-$25, dinner $18-$32. Sat, Sun brunch $22.50. Specialties: sesame-crusted yellowfin tuna, roasted peking duck. Valet parking. Outdoor dining. Raw bar. Wraparound vistas of Statue of Liberty, bridges and ferries. Cr cds: A, DS, MC, V.

D

★★★ **AN AMERICAN PLACE.** *565 Lexington Ave (10016). 212/888-5650.* Specializes in seafood and raw bar. Hrs: 11:45 am-9:30 pm, Sat 5:30-10:00 pm. Closed hols. Res accepted. Bar. Wine cellar. A la carte entrees: bkfst $6-$19.50 Sun brunch $12-$24, entrees lunch $18-$26 dinner $26-$34. Menu avail all day. Cr cds: A, D, DS, MC, V.

D ⊠

★★ **ANGELOS AND MAXIE'S STEAKHOUSE.** *233 Park Ave S (10003). 212/220-9200.* Specialties: Angelo and Maxie's 28-oz ribeye steak, Porterhouse steak deluxe for two, grilled veal chop with lemon-parsley butter. Own desserts. Hrs: 11:30 am-4 pm, 5 pm-midnight; Fri to 1 am; Sat 5 pm-1 am; Sun 5-11 pm. Closed Dec 25. Res accepted. Bar. Wine list. A la carte entrees: lunch, dinner $9-$24. Complete meals: lunch $19.99. Bustling steakhouse; murals of cows in back rm. Cr cds: A, D, DS, MC, V.

D ⊠

★★★ **ANNISA.** *13 Barrow St (10014). 212/741-6699.* Contemporary American menu. Specializes in lamb tenderloin, tuna, chicken. Hrs: 5:30-11 pm. Closed Sun. Res accepted. Extensive wine list. Dinner $21-$27. Cr cds: A, MC, V.

★★★ **AQUAGRILL.** *210 Spring St (10012). 212/274-0505.* Specializes in

seafood. Hrs: noon-3 pm, 6-10:45 pm; Fri to 11:45 pm; Sat noon-4 pm, 6-11:45 pm; Sun 6-10:30 pm; Sat, Sun brunch noon-4 pm. Closed Mon; 1st wk July, hols. Res accepted. Wine list. Bar. A la carte entrees: lunch $8.50-$18, dinner $18-$26.50. Sat, Sun brunch $12.50-$20. Outdoor dining. Casual decor. Cr cds: A, D, DS MC, V.
[D]

★★★ **AQUAVIT.** *13 W 54th St (10019). 212/307-7311. www.aquavit. org.* Scandinavian menu. Hrs: noon-3 pm in café, 5:30-10:30 pm; Sun brunch noon-2:30 pm. Closed hols. Res accepted. Bar. Wine cellar. Pre-theater menu. A la carte entrees in café: lunch, dinner $11-$25. Prix fixe: lunch: $20 cafe, $32 dining rm; dinner: $32 cafe, $69 dining rm. Cr cds: A, D, Discover, JCB, MC, V.

★★★ **ARQUA.** *281 Church St (10013). 212/334-1888.* Italian menu. Specializes in homemade pastas, Venetian cuisine, desserts. Hrs: noon-3 pm, 5-10 pm; Fri, Sat to 11:30 pm; Sun from 5 pm. Closed hols; also last 2 wks Aug. Res accepted. Bar. A la carte entrees: lunch, dinner $17-$28. Prix fixe: (Mon-Fri): lunch $19.99, (Sat, Sun) dinner $30. Cr cds: A, D, DS, MC, V.

★★★ **ATLAS.** *40 Central Park S (10019). 212/759-9191. www.atlas restaurant.com.* Contemporary American menu. Specializes in chicken, lamb, oyster soup. Hrs: 5-10 pm; Sat, Sun from noon. Sun brunch 11:30 am-3 pm. Res accepted. Extensive wine list. Lunch $17-$22; dinner $24-$34. Pre-theater $52. Prix fixe $68. Sun brunch $10-$20. Cr cds: A, D, DS, MC, V.

★★★★ **AUREOLE.** *34 E 61st St (10021). 212/319-1660. www.aureole restaurant.com.* Sleek and classy since 1988, this upper East side progressive American spot put now-famous Charlie Palmer on the map. A 1999 overhaul by Adam Tihany gives the dining room a new level of comfort, and the prix fixe menu is as inventive as ever. Contemporary American menu. Specializes in fish, game. Own baking. Hrs: noon-2:30 pm, 5:30-11 pm; Sat 5-11 pm. Closed Sun; hols. Res required. Full-bar. Full wine list. A la carte

entrees: lunch $20-$27. Prix fixe: lunch $35, dinner $69. Tasting menu: dinner $85. Street parking after 7 pm. Jacket. Cr cds: A, C, D, DS, ER, MC, V.

★★★ **BABBO.** *110 Waverly Pl (10011). 212/777-0303. www.babbonyc. com.* Italian cuisine. Specializes in pasta, Northern Italian dishes. Hrs: 5:30-11:30 pm; Sun 5-11 pm. Entrees $15-$25, dinner $35-$50. Bar. Res preferred. Cr cds: A, C, D, ER, MC, V.
[D]

★★★ **BALTHAZAR.** *80 Spring St (10012). 212/965-1414. www.balthazar ny.com.* Hrs: 7:30-11:30 am, noon-2:30 pm, 5:45-11:45 pm; Sat, Sun to 11 am; Sun to 10:45 pm. Sat, Sun brunch 11:30 am-3:30 pm. Res required Sat (dinner). French menu. Bar. Wine cellar. A la carte entrees: bkfst $2.25-$6.50, lunch $11-$20, dinner $16-$32. Sat, Sun brunch $8.50-$19. Specialties: steak frites, chicken Riesling sauteed with mushrooms, skate vigneronne sauteed with vegetables. Street parking. Traditional French brasserie. Raw bar. Cr cds: A, MC, V.
[D]

★★ **BALUCHI'S.** *193 Spring St (10012). 212/226-2828. www.balucis. com.* Indian menu. Specialties: marinated whole leg of lamb, lamb curry in cardamom sauce, vegetable balls in tomato sauce. Hrs: noon-3 pm, 5-11 pm; Sat noon-11:30 pm; Sun noon-11 pm. Res accepted. Bar. Lunch, dinner $10.95-$29.95. Own bread. Indian decor. Totally non-smoking. Cr cds: A, D, MC, V.

★★ **BARAONDA.** *1439 2nd Ave (10021). 212/288-8555.* Hrs: noon-3 pm, 5:30 pm-1 am; Sun noon-midnight; Sun brunch noon-4 pm. Closed Dec 25. Res accepted. Italian menu. Bar. A la carte entrees: lunch $8-$20, dinner $12-$30. Sun brunch $8.50-$12.50. Specializes in pasta, fish, seafood. Street parking. Outdoor dining. Colorful art. Totally non-smoking. Cr cds: A, MC, V.
[D]

★★★ **BARBETTA.** *321 W 46th St (10036). 212/246-9171. www.barbetta restaurant.com.* Italian menu. Hrs: noon-2 pm, 5 pm-midnight. Closed Sun-Mon. Res accepted. A la carte entrees: lunch \$14-\$21, dinner (after 8 pm) \$22-\$29. Complete meal: pre-theater dinner \$41. Cr cds: A, C, D, DS, ER, MC, V.

D

★★ **BAROLO.** *398 W Broadway (10012). 212/226-1102. www.barolo restaurant.com.* Northern Italian menu. Specialties: filet with Barolo wine sauce, trenette with Genovese pesto, risotto with porcini. Antipasto bar. Hrs: noon-midnight; Fri, Sat to 1 am. Res accepted. Bar to 2 am. A la carte entrees: lunch \$11.50-\$23, dinner \$13.50-\$28. Garden dining among cherry trees and fountain. Three levels of dining. Contemporary decor. Cr cds: A, DS, MC, V.

D

★★★ **BAYARD'S.** *1 Hanover Sq (10004). 212/514-9454. www.bayards. com.* Specializes in foie gras, Turbotin, roasted duck breast, rack of lamb. Hrs: 5:30-10:30 pm; Sat to 11:30 pm. Closed Sun. Res accepted. Extensive wine list. Lunch, dinner \$28-\$38. Cr cds: A, MC, V.

★★ **BECCO.** *355 W 46th St (10036). 212/397-7597. www.lidiasitaly.com.* Italian menu. Specialties: grilled rack of lamb, whole spicy free-range chicken, osso buco. Hrs: noon-3 pm, 5 pm-midnight; Sun noon-10 pm. Closed Dec 25. Res accepted; required pre-theater dinner. Bar. A la carte entrees: lunch \$13.95-\$25.95, dinner \$16.95-\$27.95. Pre-theater dinner \$21.95. Three dining rms on two levels. Rustic, Northern Italian atmosphere. Totally nonsmoking. Cr cds: A, C, D, DS, MC, V.

D

★★ **BELLEVIE.** *184 8th Ave (10011). 212/929-4320.* French menu. Specialties: Dover sole, roast duckling with seasonal fruit sauce, filet mignon with pearl onions and wild mushrooms. Hrs: noon-3 pm, 5-11 pm; Fri to midnight; Sat 5 pm-midnight; Sat, Sun brunch 11 am-4 pm. Res accepted. Bar. A la carte entrees: lunch \$6.95-\$12.95, dinner \$14.95-\$21.95. Pre-theater dinner \$21.95. Sat, Sun brunch \$10.95. Duck motif. Contemporary decor. Totally nonsmoking. Cr cds: A, MC, V.

D

★★ **BELLUNO.** *340 Lexington Ave (10016). 212/953-3282. www.newyork. sidewalk.com/bellunoristorante.* Northern Italian menu. Specialties: chicken tenders wrapped in fettucine, pan-seared hangar steak, penne with shrimp and portobello. Hrs: noon-3 pm, 5-10 pm. Closed Sun; hols. Res accepted. Bar to midnight. A la carte entrees: lunch, dinner \$13-\$19. Tri-level; contemporary decor. Totally nonsmoking. Cr cds: A, DS, MC, V.

D

★★ **BEN BENSON'S.** *123 W 52nd St (10019). 212/581-8888.* Hrs: noon-11 pm; Fri to midnight; Sat 5 pm-midnight; Sun 5-10 pm. Closed hols. Res accepted. Steakhouse menu. Bar. A la carte entrees: lunch, dinner \$17.75-\$32.50. Specializes in steak, seafood. Garage parking. Outdoor dining. Cr cds: A, DS, MC, V.

D **≛**

★★ **BICE.** *7 E 54th St (10022). 212/688-1999. www.biceny.com.* Italian menu. Specialties: lobster salad with raspberry vinaigrette, marinated salmon and swordfish with celery root. Own pasta, desserts. Menu changes daily. Hrs: noon-3 pm, 6 pm-midnight. Closed Dec 25. Res accepted. Bar. A la carte entrees: lunch, dinner \$20-\$38. Outdoor dining. Branch of original restaurant in Milan. Cr cds: A, DS, MC, V.

D

★ **BISTRO DU NORD.** *1312 Madison Ave, New York (10028). 212/289-0997.* French menu. Specialties: sauteed calves' liver, 3-peppercorn sirloin steak. Hrs: noon-4 pm, 5-11:30 pm; Sat, Sun brunch noon-4 pm. Closed Dec 25. Res accepted. Bar. Lunch \$10-\$16, dinner \$18-\$25. Complete meal: lunch \$12.95. Pre-theater dinner \$18.45. Sat, Sun brunch \$13.95. French bistro decor. Totally nonsmoking. Cr cds: A, MC, V.

D

★★ **BLUE RIBBON.** *97 Sullivan St (10012). 212/274-0404.* French, Amer menu. Specialties: paella royale, chocolate Bruno. Hrs: 4 pm-4 am. Closed Mon; hols; also last 2 wk in Aug. Bar. A la carte entrees: dinner

$9.50-$28.50. Casual decor. Totally nonsmoking. Cr cds: A, MC, V.

D

★★ **BOATHOUSE CAFE.** *72nd Ave in Central Park (10028).* 212/517-2233. *www.boathouseatcentralpark.com.* Specialties: Maine monkfish, coriander-spiced tuna loin, saddle of rabbit. Hrs: noon-4 pm, 5:30-10 pm; Sat, Sun from 11 am; Sat, Sun brunch to 4 pm. Bar. A la carte entrees: lunch $18-$26, dinner $18-$30. Sat, Sun brunch $11-$20. Child's menu. Outdoor dining overlooking lake. View of Bethesda Fountain. Cr cds: A, DS, MC, V.

D

★★ **BOLO.** *23 E 22nd St (10010).* *212/228-2200.* Spanish menu. Specialties: individual shellfish paella, baby clams in green onion broth. Hrs: noon-2:30 pm, 5:30 pm-midnight; Sat from 5:30 pm; Sun 5:30-11 pm. Closed Dec 25. Res accepted. A la carte entrees: lunch $13-$18, dinner $22-$28. Eclectic decor. Cr cds: A, D, DS, MC, V.

★★ **BOOM.** *152 Spring St (10012).* *212/431-3663.* International menu. Specialties: Vietnamese five-spice grilled quail, pan-seared salmon, Chinese shrimp. Hrs: noon-4 am; Sat, Sun brunch noon-5 pm. Res accepted. Bar. A la carte entrees: lunch $7-$17, dinner $10-$19. Sat, Sun brunch $6-$12. Old World atmosphere; frescoed walls, hanging sculpture. Cr cds: A, D, MC, V.

D

★★★ **BRASSERIE.** *100 E 53rd St (10022).* *212/751-4840. www.restaurant associates.com.* Specializes in mussels, bouillabaisse, pot-au-feu. Hrs: 11:30 am-3 pm, 5:30 pm-1 am; Sun 5:30-10 pm; Sun brunch 11:30 am-3 pm. Res required. Wine, beer. Lunch $11-$19; dinner $15-$28. Entertainment. Cr cds: A, D, MC, V.

D

★★★ **BRASSERIE 8 ½.** *9 W 57th St (10019).* *212/829-0812.* Specializes in ravioli, seafood, chicken. Hrs: 11:30 am-3 pm, 5:30 pm-midnight; Sun to 10 pm. Res accepted. Extensive wine list. Lunch, dinner $24-$35. Cr cds: A, DS, MC, V.

★ **BROOKLYN DINER USA.** *212 W 57th St (10019).* *212/977-1957.* Specialties: chicken pot pie, chicken noodle soup, Chinese chicken salad. Own pastries, desserts. Hrs: 8 am-midnight; Fri, Sat to 1 am; Sun to 11 pm. Bar. A la carte entrees: bkfst $4.50-$12, lunch $9.95-$19.95, dinner $12.95-$19.95. Art Deco style diner. Cr cds: A, DS, MC, V.

D

★ **BRYANT PARK GRILL.** *25 W 40th St (10018).* *212/840-6500.* Contemporary Amer menu. Specialties: confit of duck burritos, Caesar salad with parmesan toast. Hrs: 11:30 am-3:30 pm, 5 pm-1 am. Res accepted. Bar. A la carte entrees: lunch $12.50-$20, dinner $15.50-$23.50. Pre-theater dinner 5-7 pm, $25. Outdoor dining. Windows overlook Bryant Park. Totally nonsmoking. Cr cds: A, DS, MC, V.

D

★★★ **BULL AND BEAR STEAK-HOUSE.** *301 Park Ave (10022).* *212/872-4900.* Specializes in curried lobster, Black Angus prime beef, grilled fish waldorf chicken pot pie. Own baking. Hrs: noon-11:30 pm; Sat, Sun from 5 pm. Res accepted. Bar to midnight. A la carte entrees: lunch $16-$39, dinner $23-$44. Open kitchen. Jazz trio Thurs-Fri. Elegant clublike atmosphere. Jacket. Cr cds: A, D, DS, MC, V.

D

★★★★ **CAFE BOULUD.** *20 E 76th St (10021).* *212/772-2600. www.daniel nyc.com.* Daniel Boulud's second, more casual restaurant has been given a superb culinary life of its own under the direction of chef Andrew Carmellini. Four menus guided by four muses—market, season, garden, and travel—offer an ever-changing selection of expertly prepared food. Service and wine selections match the exciting cuisine. French cuisine. Specialities: butternut squash soup with ricotta dumplings, heirloom tomato risotto, roasted venison with chestnut crest and purée of celery root. Hrs: noon-2:30 pm, 5:45-11 pm; Sun, Mon 5:45-11 pm. A la carte entrees: lunch $20-$32; dinner $26-$38. Prix fixe: lunch:

2-course $28, 3-course $35; dinner $65 and up. Res preferred. Bar. Cr cds: A, MC, V.

D

★ **CAFE DE BRUXELLES.** *118 Greenwich Ave (10011). 212/206-1830.* Belgian, French menu. Specialties: grilled pork chops with apples and mushrooms, seafood casserole, steamed mussels prepared six different ways. Hrs: noon-11:30 pm; Fri, Sat to 12:30 am; Sun noon-10:30 pm; Sun brunch to 3:30 pm. Closed hols. Res accepted. Bar. A la carte entrees: lunch $7.50-$12.50, dinner $13.50-$19.50. Sun brunch $7.50-$12.50. Contemporary decor. Cr cds: A, C, D, ER, MC, V.

D

★★★ **CAFE DES ARTISTES.** *1 W 67th St (10023). 212/877-3500. www.cafedesartistesnyc.com.* Country French menu. Specialties: rack of lamb with basil crust, grilled fillet of tuna, grilled smoked salmon. Hrs: noon-3 pm, 5:30 pm-midnight; Sun 10 am-3 pm, 5:30-11 pm; Sat brunch 11 am-3 pm. Closed Dec 25. Res required. Bar. Wine list. A la carte entrees: lunch $15-$24, dinner $25-$40. Romantic, Old World decor;

Howard Chandler Christy murals. Near Lincoln Center. Jacket (after 5 pm). Cr cds: A, D, MC, V.

D

★★ **CAFE LOUP.** *105 W 13th St (10011). 212/255-4746.* Hrs: noon-3 pm, 5:30 pm-midnight; Mon to 11:30 pm; Sat 5:30 pm-midnight; Sun (brunch) noon-3:30 pm, 5:30-11:30 pm. Res accepted. French bistro menu. Bar. A la carte entrees: lunch $8.50-$14.50, dinner $14.95-$22.50. Sun brunch $8.50-$14.50. Specialties: smoked brook trout, sauteed sweetbreads, crepes au citron. Street parking. French bistro; black and white photographs. Family-owned since 1977. Cr cds: A, C, D, DS, ER, MC, V.

D ➜

★★ **CAFE LUXEMBOURG.** *200 W 70th St (10023). 212/873-7411. www.cafelux.com.* French, American menu. Specialties: country salad, steak frites, fresh fish. Hrs: noon-midnight; Sat brunch noon-3 pm; Sun brunch 11 am-3 pm. Res accepted. Bar. A la carte entrees: lunch $10-$19, dinner $17-$28. Prix fixe: lunch $19.99, dinner $34. Bistro atmosphere; Art Deco

Washington Square Arch in Greenwich Village

decor. Near Lincoln Center. Cr cds: A, D, DS, ER, MC, V.
D

★★ **CAFE NOSIDAM.** *768 Madison Ave (10021). 212/717-5633. www. sidewalk.com.* Italian, American menu. Specializes in pasta, fish, lamb. Hrs: 11:30 am-midnight; Sun to 11 pm; Sun brunch to 3 pm. Res accepted. Bar. A la carte entrees: lunch, dinner $13.95-$28. Complete meals: lunch, dinner $19.95. Sun brunch $19.95. Outdoor dining. Contemporary decor; original art. Cr cds: A, D, MC, V.
D

★★ **CAFE TREVI.** *1570 1st Ave (10028). 212/249-0040.* Northern Italian menu. Specializes in veal, pasta, chicken. Hrs: 5:30 pm-midnight. Closed Sun. Res accepted. Bar. A la carte entrees: dinner $15.50-$24.75. Child's menu. Trattoria atmosphere. Cr cds: A, D, MC, V.
D

★★ **CAFFE BONDI.** *7 W 20th St (10011). 212/691-8136. www.bondi-ny.com.* Sicilian menu. Specialties: pasta con sarde, wild game, seafood. Hrs: 11:30 am-11:30 pm; Sat, Sun brunch noon-5 pm. Bar. A la carte entrees: lunch $12-$21, dinner $14-$24. Complete meals: lunch $19.99, dinner $29. Sat, Sun brunch $6.95-$15. Outdoor dining. Tapestries and changing photographic exhibits add to the casual elegance of this restaurant. Cr cds: A, MC, V.
D

★★ **CAL'S.** *55 W 21st St (10010). 212/929-0740. www.calsrestaurant.com.* Mediterranean menu. Specializes in seafood, duck, steak. Hrs: 11:30 am-midnight; Sat from 5 pm; Sun 5-10:30 pm. Closed Jan 1, July 4, Dec 25. Res accepted. Bar. A la carte entrees: lunch $12.50-$18, dinner $12.50-$24. Outdoor dining. Former warehouse; casual decor. Cr cds: A, DS, MC, V.
D

★★ **CAMPAGNA.** *24 E 21st St (10010). 212/460-0900.* Italian menu. Specialties: scallopine al telefono, ravioli primavera, Florentine ribeye steak. Hrs: noon-2:30 pm, 6-11:45 pm; Sat from 6 pm; Sun 5:30-10:45

pm. Closed hols. Res required. Bar. Wine cellar. A la carte entrees: lunch $13-$18.50, dinner $16-$29.50. Child's meals. Warm, comfortable atmosphere. Cr cds: A, D, MC, V.

★★ **CAPSOUTO FRERES.** *451 Washington St (10013). 212/966-4900. www.capsoutofreres.com.* Contemporary French menu. Specialties: poached salmon, roast duckling, filet of beef with Madeira sauce. Own baking. Hrs: noon-3:30 pm, 6-11 pm; Mon from 6 pm; Fri to midnight; Sat 6-11 pm; Sat, Sun brunch noon-3:30 pm. Res accepted. Bar to midnight. Wine cellar. A la carte entrees: lunch $9-$22, dinner $14-$24. Prix fixe: lunch $19.99. Sat, Sun brunch $8.50-$20. Outdoor dining. In converted neo-Flemish, landmark warehouse (1891). Cr cds: A, D, MC, V.

★ **CARMINE'S.** *2450 Broadway (10024). 212/362-2200. www.carminesnyc.com.* Southern Italian menu. Specialties: country-style rigatoni with sausage, cannellini beans and broccoli; Porterhouse steak for four; chicken scarpariello. Hrs: 11:30 am-11 pm; Fri, Sat to midnight; Sun 2-10 pm. Bar. A la carte entrees: lunch $5.50-$12.50, dinner $16-$46. Complete meals (Mon-Fri): dinner $10.95 5-6:30 pm. Single entrees served family-style for 2-4 people. Outdoor dining. Dining rm, originally a hotel ballroom, is re-creation of 1940s neighborhood Italian restaurant. Cr cds: A, MC, V.
D SC

★★ **CASTELLANO.** *138 W 55th St (10019). 212/664-1975.* Tuscan, Italian menu. Specialties: grilled calamari, fegato Castellano, risotto. Hrs: noon-11 pm; Sat, Sun from 5:30 pm. Closed hols. Res accepted. Bar. A la carte entrees: lunch, dinner $17-$29. Outdoor terrace dining. 3 dining areas on 2 levels. Tuscan decor. Cr cds: A, DS, MC, V.

★★★ **CHANTERELLE FRENCH RESTAURANT.** *2 Harrison St (10013). 212/966-6960. chanterelle.citysearch.com.* French menu. Specialty: grilled seafood sausage. Hrs: noon-2:30 pm, 5:30-11:30 pm; Mon from 5:30 pm. Closed Sun; hols; also 2 wks July. Res

required. Bar. Wine cellar. A la carte
entrees: lunch $18.50-$25. Prix fixe:
lunch $35, dinner $75 and $89.
Chef-owned. Cr cds: A, DS, MC, V.
D

★★ **CHELSEA BISTRO AND BAR.**
*358 W 23rd St (10011). 212/727-
2026. www.nytoday.com/chelseabistro.*
French bistro menu. Specialties:
roasted Atlantic salmon, hangar
steak, roast duck. Hrs: 5:30-11 pm;
Fri, Sat to midnight; Sun 5-10:30 pm.
Res accepted. Bar. Wine list. A la
carte entrees: dinner $17.50-$22.
Glass-enclosed terrace. Cr cds: A,
MC, V.
D

★★ **CHEZ MICHALLET.** *90 Bedford
St (10014). 212/242-8309.* French
menu. Specialties: steak au poivre,
poulet grille a la Marocaine. Hrs:
5:30-11 pm; Sun to 10:30 pm. Closed
Jan 1, Dec 25. Res accepted. Wine,
beer. A la carte entrees: dinner $17.50-
$23.95. Pre-theater dinner 5:30-6:30
pm, $19.95. Bistro decor. Totally
nonsmoking. Cr cds: A, MC, V.

★★ **CHEZ NAPOLEON.** *365 W
50th St (10019). 212/265-6980.*
French menu. Specialties: bouillabaisse, steak au poivre, duck a l'orange. Hrs: noon-2:30 pm, 5-10 pm;
Fri to 11 pm; Sat 5-11 pm. Closed
Sun; hols. Res accepted. Bar. A la
carte entrees: lunch $8-$15, dinner
$13-$20.50. Pre-theater dinner 5-6:30
pm, $19.75. Small French bistro.
Family-owned. Cr cds: A, DS, MC, V.

★★★ **CHICAMA.** *35 E 18th St
(10003). 212/505-2233.* Specializes in
roast suckling pig, hen stew, rum
panela Chilean cured salmon. Hrs:
noon-3 pm, 6 pm-midnight. Res
accepted. Wine, beer. Lunch, dinner
$18-$39. Entertainment. Open
kitchen; wood burning eucalyptus
rotisserie. Cr cds: A, MC, V.
D

★★★ **CHRISTER'S.** *145 W 55th St
(10019). 212/974-7224. www.christers
ny.com.* Scandinavian, Amer menu.
Specialties: gravlax with mustard
sauce, smoked serrano salmon, baked
salmon on oak board. Hrs: noon-2:30
pm, 5:30-11 pm; Sat from 5:30 pm.
Closed Sun; hols. Res accepted. Bar.
A la carte entrees: lunch $24-$26,
dinner $24-$30. Complete meals:

lunch: $19.99. Pre-theater menu $25-
$36. Rustic fishing camp atmosphere
with colorful decor. Cr cds: A, D,
JCB, MC, V.
D

★★ **CHURRASCARIA
PLATAFORMA.** *316 W 49th St
(10019). 212/245-0505. www.
churrascariaplataforma.com.* Hrs:
noon-midnight. Closed Thanksgiving, Dec 25. Res accepted. Brazilian
menu. Bar. Complete meal: lunch
$25, dinner $29. Specializes in serving Brazilian rodizio-style. Brazilian
music Wed-Sat (night). Street parking. Elegant dining. Totally nonsmoking. Cr cds: A, D, MC, V.
D

★★★ **CIBO.** *767 2nd Ave (10017).
212/681-1616. www.citysearch.com/
nyc/cibo.* Contemporary American
menu. Specializes in wild game,
seafood, pasta. Own baking, pasta.
Hrs: 11:30 am-3 pm, 5:30-10 pm; Fri,
Sat to 11 pm; Sat, Sun brunch to
3:30 pm. Closed hols. Res accepted.
Bar. Wine list. Lunch $13-$29, dinner $19-$29. Complete meals:
dinner $24.95. Sat, Sun brunch $7-$19.98.
Outdoor dining. In landmark Daily
News building; contemporary pastel
decor. Cr cds: A, DS, MC, V.
D

★★ **CITE.** *120 W 51st St (10020).
212/956-7100. www.citerestaurant.com.*
French, American menu. Specialties:
spit-roasted chicken, swordfish,
steak au poivre. Own baking. Hrs:
11:30 am-midnight. Closed hols. Res
accepted. Bar. Wine list. A la carte
entrees: lunch, dinner $19.50-
$29.50. Prix fixe: dinner $39.50 and
$59.50. Zinc-covered bar. One-rm
informal bistro. Cr cds: A, C, D, DS,
ER, MC, V.
D

★★ **COCO PAZZO.** *23 E 74th St
(10021). 212/794-0205. www.coco
pazzo.com.* Italian menu. Specializes
in Tuscan cuisine. Hrs: noon-3 pm, 6
pm-midnight; Sun 5:30-11:30 pm;
Sun brunch 11:30 am-3 pm. Closed
hols. Res required. Bar. Wine cellar. A
la carte entrees: lunch $12.50-$18,
dinner $21-$28.50; Sun brunch
$12.50-$18. Decor features large still-

life frescoes in the Morandi style. Jacket. Cr cds: A, DS, MC, V.

[D] [⊐]

★ **COMFORT DINER.** *214 E 45th St (10017). 212/867-4555.* Specialties: Mom's meatloaf, wild mushroom potato pancakes, Cobb salad sandwich. Own desserts. Hrs: 7:30 am-10 pm; Sat, Sun from 9 am. Closed Dec 25. Bkfst $1.99-$9.95, lunch $5.75-$10.95, dinner $5.75-$11.95. Child's menu. 1950s-style diner. Totally nonsmoking. Cr cds: A, C, D, DS, ER, MC, V.

★★★ **CRAFT.** *43 E 19th St (10003). 212/780-0880.* Contemporary American menu. Specializes in arugula and salmon, oysters and lemons, scallops and artichokes. Hrs: 5:30-10 pm. Closed Mon. Res accepted. Wine list. Dinner $32-$45. Cr cds: A, D, DS, MC, V.

★★★ **CUB ROOM.** *131 Sullivan St (10012). 212/677-4100. www.cubroom. com.* New American menu. Specialties: lobster strudel, châteaubriand with wild mushrooms, yellowfin tuna on bed of Asian greens. Hrs: noon-midnight. Sun brunch Closed Sun, Dec 25. Res accepted. Bar to 2 am. Wine list. A la carte entree: lunch, dinner $21-$28. Contemporary decor. Totally nonsmoking. Cr cds: A, D, MC, V.

★★★★★ **DANIEL.** *60 E 65th St (10021). 212/288-0033. www.daniel nyc.com.* Superstar chef Daniel Boulud has built a gastronomic temple for the rich and powerful who like to eat as well as they live. The bilevel dining room is decorated in a mixture of styles that includes ancient-looking mosaics and modern upholstered furniture. The food is contemporary French, with worldly flourishes and a few nods to tradition, and the wine list is long and varied (not to mention very expensive). For a slightly more casual experience you can eat in the lounge. French cuisine. Specialties: ravioli with goat cheese, roasted Alaskan King salmon. Hrs: noon-2 pm Tues-Sat; dinner seatings 5:45-6:45 pm and 9-11 pm Mon-Sat. Closed Sun. Bar to midnight. Prix fixe: dinner 3-course

$72, 6-course $105. Cr cds: A, D, MC, V.

[D]

★★★★ **DANUBE.** *30 Hudson St (10013). 212/791-3771. www.bouley. net.* This beautiful 70-seat dining room, modeled on Hapsburg and awhirl in gold and faux Klimts, serves as the perfect backdrop for chef David Bouley's upscale Austrian-inspired fare. Though the Viennese accents are soft, the basically French cooking is hearty and delicious, and the selection of Austrian-style breads and wines impressive. Austrian, German menu. Hrs: 11:30 am-3 pm, 5:30-11:30 pm. Res required. Wine list. Lunch $22-$32. Tasting menu: 5-courses $35; dinner $22-$32. Tasting menu: 5-courses $85. Entertainment. Jacket. Cr cds: A, C, D, DS, MC, V.

[D]

★★★ **DA SILVANO.** *260 6th Ave (10014). 212/982-2343.* Italian menu. Specialties: boneless quails al radicchio, seasonal Florentine dishes, stewed tripe. Hrs: noon-11:30 pm; Fri, Sat to midnight; Sun 2-11 pm. Res accepted. Serv bar. A la carte entrees: lunch, dinner $12.50-$36. Outdoor dining. Cr cds: A, MC, V.

[D]

★★ **DA UMBERTO.** *107 W 17th St (10011). 212/989-0303.* Northern Italian menu. Specializes in antipasto buffet, wild game, pasta. Hrs: noon-3 pm, 5-11 pm; Sat from 5:30 pm. Closed Sun; Jan 1, Dec 25; also wk of July 4. Res accepted. Bar. A la carte entrees: lunch $15-$26, dinner $18-$32. Complete meal: lunch $19 and $22. Florentine decor. Cr cds: A.

[D]

★★ **DAWAT.** *210 E 58th St (10022). 212/355-7555.* Indian menu. Specialties: curried shrimp, salmon in coriander chutney. Hrs: 11:30 am-3 pm, 5:30-11 pm; Fri, Sat to 11:15 pm; Sun from 5:30 pm. Res required. Bar. A la carte entrees: lunch, dinner $12.95-$22.95. Complete meals: lunch $13.95 and $14.95, dinner $23.95. Parking (dinner). Contemporary East Indian decor. Cr cds: A, C, D, DS, MC, V.

[D]

★★★ **DB BISTRO MODERNE.** *55 W 44th St (10036).* 212/391-2400. Contemporary American menu. Specializes in salmon, lobster, steak. Hrs: 5:30-11 pm. Closed Sun. Res accepted. Extensive wine list. Dinner $23-$29.

★★ **DELEGATES DINING ROOM.** *U.N. General Assembly Bldg (10017).* 212/963-7625. International menu. Specializes in ethnic food festivals, seasonal salads, fresh seafood. Hrs: 11:30 am-2:30 pm. Closed Sat, Sun; hols. Res required. Serv bar. A la carte entrees: lunch $17.50-$25. Buffet: lunch $20.50. Panoramic view of East River. Open to public; identification with photograph required. Jacket. Cr cds: A, MC, V.
D ⬛

★★★ **DUANE PARK CAFE.** *157 Duane St (10013).* 212/732-5555. www.duaneparkcafe.com. Italian, Amer menu. Specialties: seared tuna with savoy cabbage, crispy skate with ponzu, grilled miso-marinated duck salad. Hrs: noon-2:30 pm, 5:30-10 pm; Fri to 10:30 pm; Sat 5:30-10:30 pm. Closed Sun; hols; also first wk July. Bar. A la carte entrees: lunch $14-$16, dinner $18-$26. Prix fixe: lunch $19.99. Intimate atmosphere with Italian accents. Cr cds: A, D, DS, MC, V.

★★★ **ELEVEN MADISON PARK.** *11 Madison Ave (10010).* 212/889-0905. Hrs: 11:30 am-2 pm, 5:30-10:30 pm; Fri 11:30 am-2 pm, 5:30-11 pm; Sat noon-2 pm, 5:30-11 pm; Sun 5:30-11 pm. Closed Labor Day, Dec 24-25, 31 and Jan 1. Price: lunch avg $35, dinner avg $65. Res recommended. Grand setting in historical landmark building. Cr cds: A, DS, MC, V.
D

★★ **EL TEDDY'S.** *219 W Broadway (10013).* 212/941-7070. Contemporary Mexican menu. Specializes in grilled seafood. Hrs: noon-3 pm, 6-11:30 pm; Thurs, Fri to 1 am; Sat 6 pm-1 am; Sun 6-11 pm. Closed Jan 1, Dec 25. Res accepted. Bar. A la carte entrees: lunch $7-$13, dinner $14-$19. Outdoor dining. Wild, eccentric decor spans styles from 1920s to the present. Located in white building with replica of Statue of Liberty's spiked crown on roof. Cr cds: A, D, MC, V.
D

★★★ **ESTIATORIO MILOS.** *125 W 55th St (10019).* 212/245-7400. Hrs: noon-3 pm, 5:30 pm-midnight; Sat 5:30 pm-midnight; Sun 5-10 pm. Closed Jan 1, Dec 25. Res required (dinner). Mediterranean Greek menu. Bar. Wine list. A la carte entrees: lunch, dinner $27-$35. Complete meal: lunch $32.95. Specializes in fresh line-caught fish from around the world. Street parking. Cr cds: A, D, DS, JCB, MC, V.
D

★★★ **FELIDIA.** *243 E 58th St (10022).* 212/758-1479. www.lidias italy.com. Italian menu. Specializes in homemade pasta, veal, seafood. Own baking. Menu changes daily. Hrs: noon-3 pm, 5-11 pm; Sat 5-11:30 pm. Closed Sun; hols. Res accepted. Bar. Wine cellar. A la carte entrees: lunch $20-$29, dinner $21-$25. Complete meals: lunch $28.50. Hanging tapestries, plants throughout different dining rms. Family-owned. Jacket. Cr cds: A, DS, MC, V.
D

★★★ **FIFTY SEVEN FIFTY SEVEN.** *57 E 57th St (10022).* 212/758-5757. www.fshr.com. Specialties: lobster Caesar salad, Maryland crab cakes, thyme-seared Atlantic salmon, prime rib of lamb. Hrs: 7 am-2 pm, 6-10:30 pm. Bar to 1 am; Fri, Sat to 2 am; Sun to midnight. A la carte entrees: bkfst $11-$18.50, lunch $24-$32, dinner $26-$39. Complete meals: lunch $45, dinner $75. Sun brunch $18-$29. Pianist Mon-Sat to 11 pm. Valet parking. Jacket. Cr cds: A, Diners, JCB, DS, MC, V.
D

★★ **FIORELLO'S ROMAN CAFE.** *1900 Broadway (10023).* 212/595-5330. Italian menu. Specialties: mixed antipasto, vitello alla parmigiana, grilled filet of tuna. Own pastries. Hrs: 11:30 am-11:30 pm; Fri 11-12:30 am; Sun 11 am-10:30 pm; Sat, Sun brunch 11 am-3 pm. Closed Dec 25. Res accepted. Bar. A la carte entrees: lunch $14.95-$25.75, dinner $15.75-$28.95. Sat, Sun brunch $13.75-$28.95. Outdoor dining.

Chinatown

Glass-front Italian trattoria with contemporary art; antipasto bar. Family-owned. Totally nonsmoking. Cr cds: A, C, D, DS, ER, MC, V.

[D]

★ ★ ★ **FIREBIRD.** *365 W 46th St (10036). 212/586-0244. www.firebird restaurant.com.* Pre-revolution Russia menu. Specialties: caviar with sour cream and blini, grilled marinated lamb loin, chicken Kiev. Own baking/pastry chef in house. Hrs: 11:45 am-2:30 pm, 5-11 pm; Sun, Mon from 5 pm; Fri, Sat to 11:30 pm. Closed Mon, hols. Res accepted. Bar. Wine cellar. Offers homemade honey vodka. Lunch $17, dinner $32. Entertainment Wed-Sat. Cr cds: A, Diners, JCB, DS, MC, V.

[D]

★ ★ **FIRST.** *87 1st Ave (10003). 212/674-3823.* Specialties: Tokyo roast, paella, roast suckling pig. Hrs: 6 pm-2 am; Fri, Sat to 3 am; Sun 4 pm-1 am; Sun brunch 11 am-3 pm. Closed Dec 25. Res accepted. Bar. A la carte entrees: dinner $13-$21. 5-course tasting $34. Sun brunch $12.95. Stylish industrial decor. Cr cds: A, MC, V.

★ ★ ★ **FLEUR DE SEL.** *5 E 20th St (10004). 212/460-9100.* French menu. Specializes in licorice-beet sauce with venison, honey-sherry gastrique scallops. Hrs: 5:30-10 pm; Fri, Sat to 11:30 pm. Closed Sun. Res accepted. Extensive wine list. Dinner $34-$45. Cr cds: A, MC, V.

★ ★ ★ ★ **THE FOUR SEASONS RESTAURANT.** *99 E 52nd St (10022). 212/754-9494.* Since opening its doors in 1959, this restaurant has served power lunches and celebration dinners. Designed by Mies van der Rohe and Philip Johnson, the bicameral dining room, 1950s modern at its finest, has become the stage on which people announce their arrival into the New York world. The food—Dover sole, steak tartare, roasted duck—and the service—formal and fawning—are pretty good, too. Menu changes seasonally. Own baking. Hrs: Pool Dining Room: noon-2:30 pm, 5-9:30 pm; Sat to 11:15 pm; Grill Room: noon-2 pm, 5-9:30 pm; Sat 5-10 pm. Closed Sun; hols. Res accepted. Bar. Wine cellar. A la carte entrees: Pool Dining Room: lunch $60-$80, dinner $80-$100; Grill Room: prix fixe dinner $59. Jacket required; ties optional. Cr cds: A, D, DS, MC, V, JCB.

[D]

★ ★ ★ **GABRIEL'S.** *11 W 60th St (10023). 212/956-4600. www.gabriels barandrest.com.* Italian menu. Specialties: wood pan-roasted snapper in white wine, baby chicken marinated in buttermilk and rosemary, wood-grilled sturgeon. Hrs: noon-3 om, 5:30-11 pm; Fri to midnight; Sat 5:30 pm-midnight. Closed Sun; hols. Res required. Bar. Wine list. A la carte entrees: lunch $14-$20, dinner $16-$27. Mahogany bar; original art. Cr cds: A, C, Diners, DS, ER, MC, V.

D

★★★ **GALLAGHER'S.** *228 W 52nd St (10019). 212/245-5336. www. gallaghersnysteakhouse.com.* Specializes in prime beef, sirloin steak, seafood. Hrs: noon-midnight. Closed major hols. Res accepted. Bar. A la carte entrees: lunch $12.75-$46.75, dinner $16.95-$46.75. Prix fixe: lunch $20.02. Street parking. Open kitchen. Photographs of sports and theater personalities. Cr cds: A, D, CB, MC, V.

⊒

★★ **GASCOGNE.** *158 8th Ave (10011). 212/675-6564. www.gascogne. citysearch.com.* French menu. Specialties: roasted quail with fresh spicy peaches, cassoulet bean stew with duck confit and sausages, warm fresh foie gras with seasonal fruit. Hrs: noon-3 pm, 6-10:30 pm; Fri, Sat to 11 pm; Sun noon-3 pm, 5-10 pm. Closed hols. Res accepted. Bar. A la carte entrees: lunch $8.75-$18, dinner $21-$23. Sun brunch $8.75-$18. Pre-theatre dinner $27. Garden dining. French country-style decor; farmhouse ambiance. Cr cds: A, MC, V.

★★ **GIGINO TRATTORIA.** *323 Greenwich St (10013). 212/431-1112. www.giginony.com.* Southern Italian menu. Specialties: thin pizza, linguini alla Vongole, spaghetti Padrino. Hrs: 11:30 am-11 pm; Fri to midnight; Sat 4 pm-midnight; Sun from 4 pm. Closed Jan 1, Memorial Day, Dec 25. Res accepted. Bar. A la carte entrees: lunch $10-$18, dinner $12-$21. Outdoor dining. Country farmhouse atmosphere. Cr cds: A, D, MC, V.

D

★★★★ **GOTHAM BAR AND GRILL.** *12 E 12th St (10003). 212/ 620-4020.* Chef/owner Alfred Portale's dedication to this temple of creative American cooking shows. One of the first practitioners of tall food presentations, he remains one of the best because the height doesn't come at the expense of flavor, technique, or creativity. Service is professional and frendly—a true New York dining experience. Specializes in game, seafood, lamb. Own pastries. Menu changes seasonally. Hrs: noon-2 pm, 5:30-10 pm; Fri to 11 pm; Sat 5:30-11 pm; Sun 5:30-10 pm. Closed hols. Res recommended. Bar. A la carte entrees: lunch $15.50-$19, dinner $26-$34. Prix fixe: lunch $19.99. Cr cds: A, D, MC, V.

⊒

★★★★ **GRAMERCY TAVERN.** *42 E 20th St (10003). 212/477-0777. www. gramercytavern.com.* Danny Meyer's haute American restaurant is actually two restaurants in one: the more formal dining rooms in the back offer a multicourse prix-fixe taste of chef Tom Colicchio's seasonal cooking. The tavern in the front serves simpler fare straight through from lunch to late-nite. In either area, don't miss pastry chef Claudia Fleming's superb desserts. American cuisine. Hrs: Mon-Sat noon-2 pm, Sun-Thur 5:30-10 pm, Fri-Sat 5:30-11 pm. Lunch avg $47, dinner avg $56. Res required 1 wk in advance. Bar. Totally nonsmoking. Cr cds: A, DS, MC, V.

D

★★ **HARBOUR LIGHTS.** *Fulton Pier 17 (10038). 212/227-2800. www. harbourlts.com.* Continental, American menu. Specializes in seafood, steak. Hrs: 11-1 am; Sun brunch to 3:30 pm. Closed Dec 25. Res accepted. Bar. A la carte entrees: lunch $15-$29, dinner $24-$34. Parking. Outdoor dining. Glass greenhouse-style building; large wraparound outdoor terrace. Overlooks East River; view of Brooklyn Bridge. Cr cds: A, DS, MC, V.

D ⊒

★★ **HARMONY PALACE.** *98 Mott St (10013). 212/226-6603.* Chinese menu. Specializes in Cantonese banquet dishes. Hrs: 8 am-10:30 pm. Res accepted. A la carte entrees: dim sum $1.95-$6.50, lunch, dinner from $8.50. Original Asian art and objets d'art. Cr cds: A, DS, MC, V.

D

★★ **HARRY CIPRIRANI'S.** *781 5th Ave, New York (10022).* 212/753-5566. Italian menu. Specialties: risotto alla primavera, calf's liver Veneziana, baked green noodles with ham. Hrs: 7-10:30 am, noon-3 pm, 6-10:45 pm. Res accepted. Bar. Wine cellar. A la carte entrees: bkfst $15-$25, lunch $23.95-$37.95, dinner $23.95-$46.95. Complete meals: lunch $25.95-$42.95, dinner $51.95-$64.95. Understated decor; display of photos, posters, and lithographs, reminiscent of Hemingway in Harry's Bar in Venice. Family-owned since 1931. Jacket. Cr cds: A, D, DS, MC, V.
D

★★ **HASAKI.** *210 E 9th St (10003).* 212/473-3327. Japanese menu. Specialties: sushi, sashimi. Sushi bar. Hrs: 5-11:30 pm. Closed Jan 1, July 4, Dec 25. Wine, beer. A la carte entrees: dinner $15-$27. Complete meals: dinner: $17. Rock wall entrance with wooden benches. Totally nonsmoking. Cr cds: A, DS, MC, V.

★★ **HELENA'S.** *432 Lafayette St (10003).* 212/677-5151. *www.helenastapas.com.* Hrs: noon-midnight; Fri, Sat to 1 am; Sat, Sun brunch noon-4 pm. Closed Dec 25. Spanish menu. Bar. A la carte entrees: lunch, dinner $6.95-$12.95. Complete meal: dinner $13-$25. Sat, Sun brunch $6.50-$8.50. Specialties: tapas, paella, parrilladas. Salsa Mon, Wed, Thurs. Street parking. Outdoor dining. Colorful decor; garden. Cr cds: A, MC, V.
D

★★ **HOME.** *20 Cornelia St (10014).* 212/243-9579. Specialties: blue cheese fondue, roasted chicken, sauteed greens with ketchup. Hrs: 9 am-3 pm, 6-11 pm; Sun 5:30-10 pm; Sat, Sun brunch 11 am-4 pm. Closed 2 wks in Jan, July. Res accepted. Wine, beer. A la carte entrees: bkfst $2-$6, lunch $6-$9, dinner $13-$17. Sat, Sun brunch $5-$10. Outdoor dining. Contemporary decor. Totally nonsmoking. Cr cds: A.

★★★ **HONMURA AN.** *170 Mercer St (10012).* 212/334-5253. Japanese menu. Specializes in prawn tempura, soba gnocchi, udon noodles with prawns, chicken, fish cakes and veg-

etables. Hrs: 11 am-2:30 pm, 5:30-10 pm; Fri, Sat to 11:30 pm. Closed Mon. Res accepted. Wine list. Lunch, dinner $12-$20. Cr cds: A, D, MC, V.

★★ **IL CORTILE.** *125 Mulberry St (10013).* 212/226-6060. *www.menusonline.com.* Italian menu. Specialties: capellini piselli e prosciutto, rack of veal sauteed in wine sauce, shrimp and seppioline grilled with garlic. Own pasta. Hrs: noon-midnight; Fri, Sat to 1 am. Closed Thanksgiving, Dec 24, 25. Res accepted. Bar. A la carte entrees: lunch, dinner $12.50-$26. Dining in skylighted garden rm. Cr cds: A, DS, MC, V.
D

★★★ **IL NIDO.** *251 E 53rd St (10022).* 212/753-8450. *www.citysearch.com/nyc/ilnido.* Northern Italian menu. Specializes in seasonal dishes. Own pastries. Hrs: noon-3 pm, 5:30-11 pm. Closed Sun; hols. Res required. Bar. Wine cellar. A la carte entrees: lunch $23-$40, dinner $21-$38. Cr cds: A, C, D, DS, MC, V.
D

★ **I TRE MERLI.** *463 W Broadway (10012).* 212/254-8699. Northern Italian menu. Specialties: herb ravioli with walnut sauce, focaccia sandwiches, sea bass with artichokes. Hrs: noon-1 am; Fri, Sat to 2 am. Res required Fri-Sun dinner. Bar to 4 am. Wine cellar. A la carte entrees: lunch $10-$23, dinner $12-$25. Outdoor dining. Over 1,000 wine bottles line exposed brick walls in converted warehouse building. Cr cds: A, C, D, DS, ER, MC, V.
D

★ **JAPONICA.** *100 University Pl (10003).* 212/243-7752. Japanese menu. Specialties: sushi, tataki, vegetable dumplings. Hrs: noon-10:30 pm; Fri, Sat to 11 pm; summer hrs vary. Closed Jan 1, Dec 25. Wine, beer. A la carte entrees: lunch $9-$26, dinner $14-$33. Japanese decor. Cr cds: A.
D

★★★★★ **JEAN GEORGES.** *1 Central Park W (10023).* 212/299-3900. *www.trumpintl.com.* Sleek, urban, contemporary--these are all words that have been used to describe Jean Georges Vongerichten's elegant dining room in the Trump International Hotel. The restaurant is as polished and professional as any in town, and the food, like the dining room, is serene and sublime. Light but intensely flavored reductions and unusual wild ingredients combine to produce a personalized modern French cuisine that is both stunning to look at and delicious to eat. A fine wine list with selections in all price categories and excellent service complete the experience. Innovative French cuisine. Hrs: Mon-Fri noon-3 pm; Mon-Thurs 5:30-11 pm, Fri-Sat 5:30-11:30 pm. Closed Sun. Prix fixe: $85; tasting menu $115. Bar. Valet. Res recommended. Cr cds: A, MC, V.

D

★★ **JOE ALLEN.** *326 W 46th St (10036). 212/581-6464. www.joeallenprso.com.* Specialties: Caesar salad, sauteed calf's liver, meatloaf with mashed potatoes. Hrs: noon-11:45 pm; Sun, Wed, Sat from 11:30 am; Sun brunch to 4 pm. Closed Thanksgiving, Dec 25. Res accepted; required dinner. Bar. A la carte entrees: lunch $9-$19.50, dinner $12.50-$19.50. Sun brunch $9-$19.50. Casual, American pub atmosphere; posters of failed Broadway shows line walls. Family-owned. Cr cds: MC, V.

D 🔳

★★★ **JO JO.** *160 E 64th St (10021). 212/223-5656.* Contemporary American menu. Specialties: codfish sauteed, roasted duck breast, chicken roasted in ginger, olive and coriander. Hrs: noon-2:30 pm, 6-11 pm; Sat 5:30-11:30 pm. Closed Sun; Jan 1, July 4, Dec 25. Res required. Serv bar. A la carte entrees: lunch, dinner $19-$32. Complete meals: lunch $20, dinner $45-$65. 2-story townhouse; casual French bistro atmosphere. One dining area on main floor, 2 dining rms on 2nd floor. Cr cds: A, DS, MC, V.

★★ **JUBILEE.** *347 E 54th St (10022). 212/888-3569. www.jubileenyc.com.* French bistro menu. Specialties: snails with garlic and parsley butter, mussels prepared five different ways, grilled shell steak with green peppercorn sauce. Own pastries. Hrs: noon-3 pm, 5:30-11 pm; Sat from 5:30 pm; Sun 5:30-10:30 pm. Closed Sun in summer; Jan 1, Dec 24, 25. Res accepted; required dinner. Bar. A la carte entrees: lunch $13-$16.50, dinner $14.50-$23.50. Complete meal: lunch $18. Jazz Thurs. Intimate French country bistro in townhouse bldg. Cr cds: A, D, MC, V.

★★★ **JUDSON GRILL.** *152 W 52nd St (10019). 212/582-5252. www.citysearch.com/nyc/judsongrill.* Specialties: peekytoe crab cocktail, Jamison farm's organic loin of lamb, spring vegetable plate. Hrs: noon-2:30 pm, 5:30-11 pm; Fri to 11:30 pm; Sat 5:00-11:30 pm. Closed Sun. Closed hols. Res accepted. Bar. A la carte entrees: lunch $17-$24.50, dinner $19.50-$36.50. Prix fixe dinner $56. Cr cds: A, C, D, DS, JCB, MC, V.

D

★★ **KEEN'S STEAKHOUSE.** *72 W 36th St (10018). 212/947-3636. www.keenssteakhouse.com.* Specialties: aged Porterhouse steak for 2 or 3, mutton chops. Hrs: 11:45 am-3 pm, 5:30-10 pm; Sat from 5 pm. Closed Sun; hols; also Sat, Sun in summer. Res accepted. Bar. A la carte entrees: lunch $13.50-$20, dinner $16.50-$32.50. Historic restaurant, established 1885; dark oak paneling, leaded-glass windows, famous clay pipe collection on ceiling. Famous patrons have included Teddy Roosevelt, Albert Einstein, and Lillie Langtry, who sued to enter the once all-male premises. Cr cds: A, C, D, DS, MC, V.

★★ **KINGS' CARRIAGE HOUSE.** *251 E 82nd St (10028). 212/734-5490.* Irish, English menu. Specialties: grilled loin of lamb, pan-seared wild salmon, grilled filet mignon. Own pastries. Hrs: noon-3 pm, 6-10:30 pm; Sun 2-9 pm; high tea Mon-Fri 3-4 pm. Closed Dec 25. Res required high tea and Fri, Sat dinner. Bar. Prix fixe: lunch $12.95, dinner $39. High tea $14. Turn-of-the-century carriage house; romantic, intimate atmosphere. Totally nonsmoking. Cr cds: A, D, MC, V.

D 🔳

★ **KIRAN.** *94 Chambers (10007). 212/732-5011.* Indian menu. Specialties: chicken tikka Masala, Tandoori mixed grill. Hrs: 11 am-11 pm; Sat, Sun from noon. Res accepted. Bar. A

la carte entrees: lunch, dinner $7.95-$21.95. Buffet (Mon-Fri): lunch $8.75. Casual decor. Cr cds: A, MC, V.
D

★ ★ ★ ★ **KURUMA ZUSHI.** *7 E 47th St, 2nd floor (10017).* 212/317-2802. The finest, freshest sushi (and nothing but) is served in this small, hard-to-find, second-story restaurant. The decor isn't much, but you can't take your eyes off the team of chefs behind the bar preparing the exquisite bite-sized treats. Service is superb. Prices are on par with Tokyo. Japanese cuisine. Specializes in sushi. Hrs: Mon-Sat 11:30 am-2 pm; dinner 5:30-10pm. Closed Sun. Lunch $20-$100; dinner $42-$120. Bar. Totally nonsmoking. Cr cds: A, MC, V.
D

★ **LA BONNE SOUPE.** *48 W 55th St (10019).* 212/586-7650. *www.labonne soupe.com.* French menu. Seasonal specialties. Hrs: 11:30 am-midnight; Sun to 11 pm; Sun brunch 11:30 am-3 pm. Closed hols. Bar. A la carte entrees: lunch, dinner $8.75-$18.95. Complete meals: lunch, dinner $18.95. Sun brunch $12.75. Child's menu. Limited outdoor balcony dining. Open kitchen. French bistro decor. Cr cds: A, D, MC, V.

★ ★ ★ ★ **LA CARAVELLE.** *33 W 55th St (10019).* 212/586-4252. *www. lacaravelle.org.* The elegant decor of this New York landmark sets the mood for a truly wonderful dining experience in classic and contemporary French cuisine. The menu presents a perfect balance of signature dishes and interpretive seasonal cuisine. Classic and contemporary French menu. Specialties: truffeled pike quenelles in lobster sauce, crispy duck with cranberries, souffles. Own baking. Hrs: noon-2:30 pm, 5:30-10:30 pm. Closed Sun, hols, also 1 wk prior to Labor Day. Res required. Bar. Wine cellar. Lunch $32-$38, dinner from $48-68. Prix fixe: 3-course lunch $38, 3-course dinner $68, 5-course tasting menu $90. 7-course dinner $110. Child's menu. Cr cds: A, D, MC, V.
D

★ ★ ★ ★ **LA COTE BASQUE.** *60 W 55th St (10019).* 212/688-6525. Although the food tends toward the old-fashioned, the overall experience at this formal, elegant, decades-old restaurant is first-rate. The crowded tables don't seem to affect the service. And chef/owner Jean-Jacques Rachou's traditional specialties like cassoulet satisfy beyond measure. French cuisine. Own pastries. Hrs: noon-2:30 pm, 5:30-10:30 pm; Fri to 11:30 pm; Sat 5:30-11:30 pm; Sun 5-10 pm. Closed hols. Res required. Wine list. Bar. Prix fixe: lunch $36, dinner $68. Chef-owned. Jacket. Cr cds: A, D, MC, V.
D

★ ★ ★ ★ **LA GRENOUILLE.** *3 E 52nd St (10022).* 212/752-1495. Like much of the clientele, this grand dame has had a facelift: new menus, new chef, better attitude, and more attention paid to the guests in the dining room and the food in the kitchen. The result is that it may be the best time capsule of a French restaurant still in operation. From the impressive flower arrangements to the doting servers (each with a thicker French accent than the next), to the whole roasts of meat, to the ethereal soufflés, La Grenouille is once again the epitome of classic French dining, at least as it is practiced in New York. French cuisine. Hrs: Tues-Sat noon-2:30 pm, 5:30-11:15 pm. Prix fixe: lunch $45, dinner $80. Res required. Cr cds: A, D, MC, V.

★ ★ **LA MANGEOIRE.** *1008 2nd Ave (10022).* 212/759-7086. *www. lamangeoire.com.* Southern French menu. Specialties: Mediterranean-style fish soup, roasted rack of lamb, lavender-scented creme br°lee. Hrs: noon-2:30 pm, 5:30-10:30 pm; Fri to 11 pm; Sat 5:30-11 pm; Sun brunch 11:30 am-3 pm. Closed hols. Res accepted. Serv bar. A la carte entrees: lunch $7.95-$21, dinner $14.95-$26. Prix fixe: lunch $19.76, dinner 5:30-6:45 pm $19.76-$25. Sun brunch $13.95. Street parking. French country inn atmosphere. Cr cds: A, D, MC, V.
D

★ ★ **LA METAIRIE.** *189 W 10th St (10014).* 212/989-0343. *www.la metairie.com.* French menu. Specialties: filet mignon, rack of lamb. Hrs:

noon-3 pm, 5-11 pm; Fri, Sat to midnight; Sun to 10 pm; Sat, Sun brunch noon-3 pm. Res required. A la carte entrees: lunch $12-$19, dinner $18-$29. Sat, Sun brunch $12-$19. French country atmosphere. Cr cds: A, D, DS, MC, V.

D

★★ **LA TRAVIATA.** *461 W 23rd St (10011). 212/243-5497.* Italian menu. Specialties: veal medallions with prosciutto, filet of red snapper, penne with spicy tomato sauce. Hrs: 11:30 am-10:30 pm; Fri to 11 pm; Sat 4:30-11 pm; Sun brunch 1-9 pm. Closed Sun (Memorial Day-Labor Day); July 4. Res accepted. Bar. Lunch, dinner $11.50-$23.95. Sun brunch $11.50-$23.95. Entertainment Wed-Sat. Northern Italian decor. Cr cds: A, MC, V.

★★★ **LAYLA.** *211 W Broadway (10013). 212/431-0700. www.myriad restaurantgroup.com.* Mediterranean menu. Specialties: grilled chicken tagine, Moroccan-spiced monkfish kebob, grilled salmon wrapped in grape leaves. Hrs: 5:30-10:45 pm; Fri noon-2:30 pm, 5:30-11:30 pm; Sat to 11:30 pm; Sun to 9:45 pm. Closed hols. Res accepted. Bar to midnight. A la carte entrees: lunch $12-$18, dinner $20-$27. Prix fixe: lunch $19.99. Outdoor dining. Arabian Nights decor. Totally nonsmoking. Cr cds: A, D, DS, MC, V.

★★★★ **LE BERNARDIN.** *155 W 51st St (10019). 212/489-1515. www. le-bernardin.com.* Never has the marriage of haute French cuisine and creatures from the sea been as successful as at this elegant midtown restaurant. Under the direction of owner Maguy LeCoze and chef/owner Eric Ripert, Le Bernardin continues to teach Americans how to best enjoy seafood—ever so undercooked or even raw to maximize both flavor and texture. The effect is startlingly creative and delicious. A superb wine list offers many interesting pairings. French, seafood menu. Specialties: monkfish with cabbage, thyme and pepper rare-seared yellowfin tuna, crispy Chinese-spiced red snapper. Own pastries. Hrs: noon-2:30 pm, 5:30-10:30 pm; Fri, Sat to 11 pm. Closed Sun; hols. Res accepted. Bar. Prix fixe: lunch $46, dinner $79.

Street parking. Jacket. Cr cds: A, D, DS, MC, V.

D

★★ **LE BOEUF A LA MODE.** *539 E 81st St (10028). 212/249-1473.* French menu. Specialties: fresh grilled salmon, châteaubriand with sauce, roasted duck. Hrs: 5:30-11 pm. Closed hols; also Sun in July, Aug. Res accepted. Bar. A la carte entrees: dinner $19-$30. Prix fixe: dinner $34. Outdoor dining. Intimate dining rm with colorful murals. Cr cds: A, D, MC, V.

D

★★★★ **LE CIRQUE 2000.** *455 Madison Ave (10022). 212/303-7788. www.lecirque.com.* The celebrity circus is always in town at this legendary eatery, where billionaires and movie stars dine among serious food lovers. Adam Tihany's whimsical decor set within the ornate turn-of-the-century Villard mansion creates the effect of a big top in a European square. The contemporary French food rises to the occasion, with tableside flourishes and creative presentations. French cuisine. Specialties: risotto with lobster, foie gras ravioli with black truffles, striped bass, duck Magret, rack of lamb. Hrs: Mon-Sat 11:45 am-2:30 pm, 5:30-10:30 pm; Sun 5:30-10 pm. Lunch: 3-course $42, a la carte $12-$39; dinner: 5-course $90, a la carte $29-$39. Jacket required (dinner). Cr cds: A, D, MC, V.

D

★★ **LE COLONIAL.** *149 E 57th St (10022). 212/752-0808. www.lecolonial. com.* Vietnamese menu. Specialties: whole red snapper with spicy sour sauce, roast duck with tamarind sauce, sauteed jumbo shrimp with curried coconut sauce. Hrs: noon-2:15 pm, 5:30-10:30 pm; Fri to midnight; Sat 5:30-11 pm; Sun from 5:30 pm. Closed July 4, Thanksgiving, Dec 25. Res accepted. Bar 4:30 pm-1 am. A la carte entrees: lunch $12.50-$19.50, dinner $14.50-$29.50. Multilevel dining. Bamboo furniture, birdcages. Cr cds: A, D, MC, V.

★★ **LE MADELEINE.** *403 W 43rd St (10036). 212/246-2993. www.newyork. sidewalk.com.* Hrs: noon-3 pm, 5-11 pm; Fri, Sat to 11:30 pm. Closed Dec 25. Res accepted. French menu. Bar. A la carte entrees: lunch $8-$22, dinner $16-$23. Child's menu. Specialties: grilled slices of Maine salmon, roasted organic duck with sun-dried cranberries, grilled leg of lamb. Street parking. Outdoor dining. Casual bistro; enclosed garden. Family-owned since 1979. Totally nonsmoking. Cr cds: A, DS, V.

D

★★★ **LE MADRI.** *168 W 18th St (10011). 212/727-8022.* Italian menu. Specializes in regional Italian cuisine, seasonal dishes. Hrs: noon-3 pm, 5:30-11:30 pm; Sun to 10:30 pm; Sun brunch 11:30 am-3:30 pm. Closed hols. Res accepted. Bar. A la carte entrees: lunch $12-$18, dinner $19-$28.50. Sun brunch $21.50. Valet parking. Outdoor dining. Vaulted ceiling supported by columns; colorfully tiled wood-burning pizza oven. Jacket. Cr cds: A, MC, V.

★★ **LEMON.** *230 Park Ave S (10003). 212/614-1200.* Specialties: crispy duck spring rolls, five-spice Chilean sea bass. Hrs: 11:30 am-3:30 pm, 5:30 pm-midnight; Thurs-Sat to 2 am; Sun brunch 11:30 am-4 pm. Closed Jan 1, Dec 25. Res accepted. Bar to 3 am. Lunch $7-$15, dinner $11-$22. Sun brunch $7-$15. Bistro decor. Cr cds: A, D, MC, V.

D

★★★ **LENOX ROOM.** *1278 3rd Ave (10021). 212/772-0404. www.lenox room.com.* Specializes in progressive American cuisine, fresh seafood. Hrs: noon-2:30 pm, 5:30-10:30 pm. Sun brunch noon-2:30 pm. Closed major hols. Res accepted. Bar. A la carte entrees: lunch $12-$17, dinner $19-$28, Sun brunch $9-$15. Complete meals: lunch $20.02. Raw bar. Several intimate dining areas. Cr cds: A, D, DS, JCB, MC, V.

D

★★★ **LE PERIGORD.** *405 E 52nd St (10022). 212/755-6244. www.leperigord. com.* Modern French cuisine. Specialties: confit of duck, grilled Dover sole, boneless quail stuffed with vegetables. Own desserts. Hrs: noon-3 pm, 5:15-10:30 pm; Sat, Sun 5:15-10:30 pm. Closed July. Res accepted. Bar. Wine cellar. A la carte

entrees: lunch $18-$30, dinner $22-$38. Prix fixe: lunch $32, dinner $62. Street parking. Family-owned. Jacket. Cr cds: A, C, D, DS, JCB, MC, V.

★★★ **LE REFUGE.** *166 E 82nd St (10021). 212/861-4505.* French menu. Specialties: roast duck with fresh fruit sauce; grilled salmon with red wine vinaigrette, garlic and olive oil; loin of lamb stuffed with spinach. Own baking. Hrs: noon-3 pm, 5-11 pm; Sun noon-4 pm, 5-9:30 pm; Sat brunch to 3 pm; Sun brunch to 4 pm. Closed hols. Res accepted. Serv Bar. A la carte entrees: lunch $12.50-$15.50, dinner $17.50-$24.50. Sat, Sun brunch $17.50. Garden terrace dining (summer). French country inn decor. Cr cds: MC, V.

★★★★★ **LESPINASSE.** *2 E 55th St (10022). 212/339-6719. www.stregis. com.* Serving formal French food in a room that would make Louis XVI feel at home, Lespinasse is a gastronomic temple in the St. Regis Hotel under the direction of chef Christian Delouvrier. Stunning tableside displays of whole roasted meats and other indulgent presentations make a meal here a truly festive occasion. Doting service, an exceptional wine list, and impressive floral arrangements round out the expensive-but-worth-it experience. French menu. Specialties: poached chicken with black truffles, confit of baby pig, pan-roasted lobster a l'Américain. Hrs: 7-10:30 am, noon-1:45 pm, 5:30-9:45 pm; Fri, Sat to 10:15 pm; Sun 7-11:30 am. Res required. Bar 11:30-1 am; Fri, Sat to 2 am; Sun noon-midnight. Extensive wine list. A la carte entrees: bkfst $14.50-$21, dinner $32-$38. Complete meals: lunch $36 and $45, dinner $78-$130. Valet parking. Jacket. Cr cds: A, D, DS, MC, V.

D

★★ **LOBSTER CLUB.** *24 E 80th St (10021). 212/249-6500.* Eclectic Amer menu. Specialties: matzo brei with wild lilies, Mom's meatloaf, almond-crusted banana split with malted milk balls. Hrs: 11:30 am-3 pm, 5:30-10:30 pm; Fri, Sat to 11 pm; Sun to 10 pm. Closed hols. Res accepted. Bar. A la carte entrees:

lunch $15-$24.50, dinner $16.50-$29. Bilevel dining rm with fireplace. Totally nonsmoking. Cr cds: A, D, MC, V.

★★ **LOLA.** *30 W 22nd St (10010). 212/675-6700. www.lolany.com.* Contemporary American menu. Specialties: Lola-fried chicken with Cuban black beans, pineapple-glazed salmon with noodle cake, corn and rock shrimp. Own pastries. Hrs: noon-3 pm, 6 pm-12:30 am; Sat from 6 pm; Sun brunch sittings 9:30 am, 11:30 am and 1:45 pm. Closed hols. Res accepted. Bar noon-1 am. Wine list. A la carte entrees: lunch $15-$20.50, dinner $22-$32.50. Sun brunch $29.75. Entertainment. Elegant decor; French doors; black and white prints of city. Cr cds: A, MC, V.
D ⬛

★★ **LULIVO FOCACCERIA.** *184 Spring St (10012). 212/343-1445.* Hrs: noon-3:30 pm, 5 pm-midnight; Sat, Sun noon-midnight. Closed Dec 25. Res accepted. Italian menu. Bar. A la carte entrees: lunch $6-$12, dinner $8-$14. Child's menu. Specializes in wood-burning oven pizzas, pasta, salads. Street parking. Outdoor dining. Contemporary Italian decor. Totally nonsmoking.
D

★★ **LUPA.** *170 Thompson St (10012). 212/982-5089.* Specializes in pasta. Hrs: noon-2:45 pm, 5:30-11:30 pm. Res accepted. Wine list. Lunch $8-$10; dinner $12-$17. Entertainment. Cr cds: A, MC, V.
D ⬛

★★ **LUSARDI'S.** *1494 2nd Ave (10021). 212/249-2020.* Northern Italian menu. Specialties: risotto with truffles or wild mushrooms. Hrs: noon-3 pm, 5 pm-midnight. Closed hols. Res accepted. Bar. A la carte entrees: lunch, dinner $14-$26. Italian-style trattoria. Seasonal menu. Totally nonsmoking. Cr cds: A, D, DS, MC, V.

★★★★ **LUTECE.** *249 E 50th St (10022). 212/752-2225. www. arkrestaurants.com.* Chef David Feau has taken this world-famous symbol of French refinement and made it his own. Although some of Andre Soltner's signature dishes remain, Feau's heart is understandably in the more creative, more contemporary portion of the menu. A long wine list evidences the restaurant's illustrious past. Haute French cuisine. Specialties: snails and wild mushrooms in phyllo, sauteed turbot in tarragon broth, roast rack of lamb with mustard honey glaze. Hrs: 11:30 am-2 pm, 5:30-11 pm; Mon, Sat from 5:30 pm. Closed Sun. Res required. Bar. Wine cellar. Table d'hôte: lunch $38. Prix fixe: dinner $65. Cr cds: A, D, MC, V.

★★★ **MALONEY AND PORCELLI.** *37 E 50th St (10022). 212/750-2233. www.maloneyandporcelli.com.* Specialties: angry lobster, crackling pork shank, drunken donuts. Own desserts. Hrs: noon-11:30 pm; Sat, Sun brunch to 3 pm. Closed Jan 1, Dec 25. Res accepted. Bar. Wine list. A la carte entrees: lunch $19.50-$29.75, dinner $22.50-$34.75. Sat, Sun brunch $12.50-$19.50. Two-story restaurant with grand staircase, skylights. Cr cds: A, D, DS, JCB, MC, V.
D ⬛

★ **MANHATTAN BISTRO.** *129 Spring St (10012). 212/966-3459.* Specialties: steak frites, cassoulet, black Angus steak au poivre. Hrs: 11:30 am-midnight; Fri, Sat to 2 am; Sat, Sun brunch 11:30 am-4:30 pm. Closed Memorial Day, Dec 25. Res accepted. Bar from 11:30 am. A la carte entrees: lunch $8.50-$15, dinner $13-$24.95. Complete meals: lunch $13.95, dinner $21.95. Sat, Sun brunch $8.50-$15. Intimate storefront bistro in area of studios, art galleries. Family-owned. Cr cds: A, MC, V.
⬛

★★★ **MANHATTAN GRILLE.** *1161 1st Ave (10021). 212/888-6556. www. manhattangrille.com.* Specializes in steak, lobster. Hrs: noon-11 pm; Sun brunch 11:30 am-3:30 pm. Closed Thanksgiving, Dec 25. Res accepted. Bar from 4 pm. Prix fixe: lunch, pretheater dinner $17.95-$28.95. A la carte entrees: lunch $8.50-$19, dinner $18.75-$35.75. Sun brunch $17.95. Clublike atmosphere; paneling, Oriental rugs, 1920s period lighting. Cr cds: A, C, D, DS, MC, V.
D ⬛

★ ★ ★ **MANHATTAN OCEAN CLUB.** *57 W 58th St (10019). 212/371-7777. www.manhattanocean club.com.* Specialties: red snapper with a leek crust, roasted blackfish, mahi-mahi marinated in Moroccan spices. Own pastries. Hrs: noon-11:30 pm; Sat, Sun from 5 pm. Closed Jan 1, Thanksgiving, Dec 25. Res required. Bar. Wine list. A la carte entrees: lunch, dinner $21-$23. Prix fixe lunch $20.02. Atmosphere of luxury ocean liner; broad sweeping staircase connects 2 floors. Cr cds: A, D, DS, MC, V.
🖃

★ ★ ★ ★ **MARCH.** *405 E 58th St (10022). 212/754-6272.* The newly renovated and expanded home of this elegant, romantic restaurant means it's only slightly easier to get a table. Chef/co-owner Wayne Nish looks to Asia for his inspiration, and the prix-fixe menu reflects his precise technique and creativity. Co-owner Joe Scalice's wine list is one of the most interesting in town. Specialties: confit de foie gras de canard, rack of Colorado lamb, seared rare bluefin tuna. Hrs: 6-10:30 pm. Closed hols. Res required. Bar. Tasting menu: 4-course dinner $68, 7-course dinner $90. Outdoor dining. Jacket. Extensive wine list. Cr cds: A, MC, V.
D

★ ★ **MARLOWE.** *328 W 46th St (10036). 212/765-3815.* Specialties: spiced seared yellowfin tuna, black Angus sirloin with caramelized shallot confit, grilled leg of lamb with ragout of woodland mushrooms. Hrs: noon-3 pm, 5 pm-midnight; Sun brunch noon-3 pm. Closed Dec 25. Res accepted. Bar. A la carte entrees: lunch $6-$13, dinner $9-$24. Complete meals: lunch $10, dinner $19. Sun brunch $4.95-$12.95. Outdoor dining. French country inn atmosphere. Totally nonsmoking. Cr cds: A, D, DS, MC, V.

★ ★ **MAYA.** *1191 1st Ave (10021). 212/585-1818.* Hrs: 5:30-11 pm; Fri, Sat to midnight; Sun brunch 11 am-2 pm. Closed Jan 1, Dec 25. Res accepted. Mexican menu. Bar. A la carte entrees: dinner $16.95-$23.50. Sun brunch $34.95. Specialties: pan-seared red snapper with achiote

paste, grilled butterflied filet mignon, chile relleno. Own tortillas. Street parking. Adobe-style decor; art, sculptures. Totally nonsmoking. Cr cds: A, C, D, DS, MC, V.
D

★ **MED GRILL BISTRO AND CAFE.** *725 5th Ave (10022). 212/751-3276. www.bice.com.* Continental, Italian menu. Specializes in salad, pasta, risotto. Hrs: Cafe 8:30 am-6:30 pm, Bistro 11:30 am-4 pm. Closed hols. Res accepted. Bar 11:30 am-4 pm. A la carte entrees: lunch $9.95-$21.23. Contemporary decor with prints and oils on display; overlooks wall with cascading water. Cr cds: A, C, D, DS, ER, MC, V.
D

★ **MELI MELO.** *110 Madison Ave (10016). 212/686-5551.* Hrs: 11 am-11 pm. Closed Sun; hols. Res accepted. Eclectic menu. Bar. A la carte entrees: lunch $10.95-$13.95, dinner $12.95-$18.95. Specialties: roasted duck with barley risotto and mango sauce, sauteed monkfish with sweet corn salsa, South Mouth marinated double pork chop with corn haystack. Complete meal: dinner $28.50. Street parking. Outdoor dining. Contemporary decor; Mediterranean mural, exotic floral arrangements. Cr cds: A, C, D, MC, V.
D 🖃

★ ★ ★ **MERCER KITCHEN.** *99 Prince St (10012). 212/966-5454.* Hrs: 11 am-11 pm. Closed hols. Res accepted. Eclectic menu. Bar. A la carte entrees: lunch $12-$30, dinner $18-$30. Specialties: roasted duck with barley risotto and mango sauce, sauteed monkfish with sweet corn salsa, South Mouth marinated double pork chop with corn haystack.Prix fixe: lunch $20, dinner $28.50. Street parking. Outdoor dining. Contemporary decor; Mediterranean mural, exotic floral arrangements. Cr cds: A, MC, V.
D

★ ★ ★ **MESA GRILL.** *102 5th Ave (10011). 212/807-7400. www.mesagrill. com.* Contemporary Southwestern menu. Specialties: shrimp and roasted garlic corn tamale, blue corn tortilla-crusted red snapper, black Angus steak. Hrs: noon-2:30 pm,

5:30-10:30 pm; Fri to 11 pm; Sat 5:30-11 pm; Sun 5:30-10:30 pm; Sat, Sun brunch 11:30 am-3 pm. Closed hols. Res accepted. Bar. A la carte entrees: lunch $12-$17, dinner $18-$28. Industrial designed loft. Cr cds: A, D, DS, MC, V.

D

★ **MEZZALUNA.** *1295 3rd Ave (10021).* 212/535-9600. Italian menu. Specializes in wood-burning oven pizza. Own pasta. Hrs: noon-3:30 pm, 6 pm-12:30 am. Closed Dec 25. Wine, beer. A la carte entrees: lunch $13.50-$21, dinner $15-$30. Outdoor dining. Trattoria atmosphere. Antique marble-top tables and bar. Cr cds: A.

★★ **MEZZOGIORNO.** *195 Spring St (10012).* 212/334-2112. *www. mezzogiorno.com.* Northern Italian menu. Specializes in brick-oven pizza. Hrs: noon-3:30 pm, 6 pm-1 am; Sat, Sun noon-1 am. Closed Dec 25. Res accepted. Bar. A la carte entrees: lunch, dinner $13-$16. Outdoor dining. Cr cds: A.

D

★★ **MICHAEL JORDAN'S.** *23 Vanderbilt Ave (10017).* 212/655-2300. Hrs: 11:30 am-midnight. Res accepted. Steakhouse menu. Bar. A la carte entrees: lunch, dinner $11-$31. Specializes in chicken, seafood, steak. Street parking. Train decor. Cr cds: A, MC, V.

★★★ **MICHAEL'S.** *24 W 55th St (10019).* 212/767-0555. Specialties: Florida red snapper with mango and Vidalia sweets, Atlantic swordfish with tomato-basil vinaigrette, Canadian salmon with grilled peppers and onions. Own baking. Hrs: 7:30-9:30 am, noon-3 pm, 5:30-10:30 pm; Sat from 5:30 pm. Closed Sun; hols. Res accepted. Bar. Wine cellar. A la carte entrees: bkfst $13.50-$20, lunch, dinner $26-$37. Pre-theatre: $38. Serv charge 15%. Original artwork throughout. Cr cds: A, D, JCB, MC, V.

★ **MICKEY MANTLE'S.** *42 Central Park S (10019).* 212/688-7777. *www. mickeymantles.com.* Specializes in chicken-fried steak, seafood, hickory-smoked ribs. Hrs: noon-11 pm; Sat to midnight. Res accepted. Bar to 12:30 am; Sun to midnight. A la carte entrees: lunch, dinner $10.95-$22.95. Child's menu. Outdoor dining. Rotating collection of baseball memorabilia; original sports art. Cr cds: A, D, DS, MC, V.

D

★★ **MI COCINA.** *57 Jane St (10014).* 212/627-8273. Mexican menu. Specialties: pechuga con rajas, camarones enchipotlados, enchiladas de mole poblano. Hrs: 5:30-10:45 pm; Fri, Sat to 11:30 pm; Sun 4:30-10:15 pm; Sun brunch 11:30 am-2:45 pm. Closed Dec 24, 25; also 2 wks Aug. Res accepted. Bar. A la carte entrees: dinner $9.95-$17.95. Sun brunch $7.95-$13.95. Child's menu. Modern Mexican atmosphere; colorful decor with yellow stucco walls, red tile floors. Outdoor dining. Cr cds: A, C, D, DS, MC, V.

D

★★ **MONKEY BAR.** *60 E 54th St (10022).* 212/838-2600. Specialties: salmon with asparagus, East Coast halibut, Colorado rack of lamb. Hrs: noon-2:30 pm, 6-11 pm; Fri to 11:30 pm; Sat 5:30-11:30 pm; Sun 6-10 pm. Closed Dec 25. Res accepted. Bar to 2 am; Fri, Sat to 3 am. A la carte entrees: lunch $19-$24, dinner $23-$34. 5-course tasting menu: dinner $65. Pianist. Monkeys hang from lighting; murals of monkeys decorate the bar. Jacket. Cr cds: A, D, DS, MC, V.

D

★★★ **MONTRACHET.** *239 W Broadway (10013).* 212/219-2777. *www.myriadrestaurantgroup.com.* French menu. Specialties: farfalle with escargot, turbot with porcini and asparagus. Own pastries. Hrs: 5:30-11 pm; Fri also noon-2 pm. Closed Sun; hols. Res required. Bar. Wine list. A la carte entrees: lunch $16-$24, dinner $23-$33. Prix fixe: lunch $19.99, dinner $34, $42, tasting $75. Cr cds: A, D, MC, V.

★★ **MORTON'S OF CHICAGO.** *551 5th Ave (10017).* 212/972-3315. *www. mortons.com.* Specializes in steak, lobster. Hrs: 11:30 am-2:30 pm, 5 pm-midnight; Sat from 5 pm; Sun 5-11 pm. Closed hols. Res accepted. Bar. A la carte entrees: lunch, dinner $19.95-$31.95. Counterpart of famous Chicago steakhouse. Cr cds: A, D, DS, MC, V.

D

★★ **MR. K'S.** *570 Lexington Ave (10022). 212/583-1668. www.mrksny. com.* Hrs: 11:30 am-11 pm; Sat, Sun from midnight. Res accepted. Chinese menu. Bar. Wine list. Lunch $16.95-$32.95, dinner $17.95-$37.97. Complete meal: lunch $25, dinner $45. Specialties: chicken supreme, firecracker fish, seared beef medallion with scallion and oyster sauce. Street parking. Art Deco Chinese decor; elegant furnishings. Jacket. Totally nonsmoking. Cr cds: A, D, MC, V.

D

★★★ **NADAMAN HAKUBAI.** *66 Park Ave (10016). 212/885-7111. www.kitano.com.* Japanese menu. Specializes in traditional Kaiseki dishes. Hrs: 11:45 am-2:30 pm, 6-10 pm. Res accepted. Bar. A la carte entrees: lunch, dinner $12-$25. Complete meals: lunch $32, dinner $60-$150. Elegant Japanese decor. Totally nonsmoking. Cr cds: A, D, DS, MC, V.

D

★★★★ **NOBU.** *105 Hudson St (10013). 212/219-0500.* Architect David Rockwell's post-modern Japanese design for Nobu Matsuhisa and Drew Nieporent's first collaboration includes conceptualized trees, a wall made of small stones, and polished wood tables. Somehow Matsuhisa's modern sushi and other specialties, not to mention the hip, downtown crowd, feel at home. Don't miss black cod with miso or the Peruvian tiradito sashimi. Specify your price for the omikasse (chef's tasting) and leave the difficult decision-making process to the kitchen. Japanese menu. Sushi bar. Hrs: 11:45 am-2:15 pm, 5:45-10:15 pm; Sat, Sun from 5:45 pm. Closed hols. Res accepted. Serv bar. A la carte entrees: lunch $12-$30, dinner $18-$30. Complete meals: lunch $19.99. Tasting menu: dinner $70. Cr cds: A, D, MC, V.

D ⊣

★★★ **NOVITA.** *102 E 22nd St (10010). 212/677-2222.* Italian menu. Specialties: porcini ravioli in black truffle sauce, roasted duck with barolo sauce, tuna carpaccio with capers. Hrs: noon-3 pm, 6-11 pm; Fri, Sat 6 pm-midnight; Sun 5-10 pm. Closed hols. Res accepted. Bar. A la carte entrees: lunch $12-$20, dinner $13-$21. Complete meals: lunch $19.99. Outdoor dining. Casual decor. Totally nonsmoking. Cr cds: A, D, MC, V.

★★★ **OAK ROOM.** *768 5th Ave (10019). 212/759-3000. www.fairmont. com.* Traditional European, American menu. Specialties: Black Angus beef, roasted rack of lamb, surf and turf. Seasonal menu. Own baking. Hrs: 11:30 am-3 pm, 5:30-11:30 pm; Sun 5:30-10:30 pm. Pre theatre 5:30-7:30 pm. Res accepted. Bar to 1:30 am; Sun to 12:30 am. Wine list. A la carte entrees: lunch $14-$26, dinner $24-$34. Pre-theater dinner $44, incl free transportation to theaters. Pianist. Valet parking. Historic grand dining rm (1907) with hand-painted murals and 25-ft ceilings. Jacket. Cr cds: A, DS, MC, V.

D

★★★★ **OCEANA.** *55 E 54th St (10022). 212/759-5941. www.oceana restaurant.com.* The first-floor dining room of this multilevel restaurant has the feel of an elegant ocean liner. Rick Moonen's creative prix-fixe menu sets sail for seafood highlights that include various tartares, pan-seared fillets, and other treasures from the sea, all splendidly prepared. The upstairs bar affords a quiet, elegant spot for a drink. Hrs: noon-2:30 pm, 5:30-10:30 pm; Sat from 5:30 pm. Closed Sun; hols. Res suggested. Wine cellar. Complete meals: lunch $42, dinner $65. Located in 2-story townhouse; spacious, bilevel dining rm. Elegant decor. Jacket requested; no jeans. Cr cds: A, D, DS, MC, V.

★★ **ODEON.** *145 W Broadway (10013). 212/233-0507.* French, Amer menu. Specializes in seafood, grilled dishes. Hrs: noon-2 am; Fri, Sat to 3 am; Sun brunch 11:30 am-4 pm. Res accepted. Bar to 4 am. Complete meals: lunch $17. A la carte entrees: lunch $8.50-$21.50, dinner $14-$23. Sun brunch $8.50-$21.50. Child's menu. Outdoor dining. Brasserie in 1930s, cafeteria-style Art Deco. Cr cds: A, D, DS, MC, V.

D

New York's bustling nightlife

★★★ **OLIVES.** *201 Park Ave S (10003). 212/353-8345. www.whotels. com.* Mediterranean menu. Specializes in veal agnolotti al plin, pear-wrapped rack of venison. Hrs: 11 am-2:30 pm, 5:30-10 pm; Fri, Sat to 11:30 pm. Res accepted. Wine list. Lunch $17-$25; dinner $25-$32. Cr cds: A, D, DS, MC, V.

★★ **ONE 51.** *151 E 50th St (10022). 212/753-1144. www.one51.com.* Specialties: pan-seared red snapper, rack of lamb, seared filet mignon. Hrs: noon-3 pm, 5:30-10:30 pm; Sat from 5:30 pm. Closed Sun; hols. Res required. Bar. A la carte entrees: lunch $15-$22, dinner $17-$29. Entertainment Tues-Sat. Terrace dining. Old theater setting; former nightclub from the 1940s. Jacket. Cr cds: A, D, MC, V.
D

★★★ **ONE IF BY LAND, TWO IF BY SEA.** *17 Barrow St (10014). 212/228-0822. www.oneifbyland.com.* French, American menu. Specialties: open-faced Maine crab ravioli, citrus-marinated halibut, tenderloin of veal. Own pastries. Hrs: 5:30 pm-midnight. Closed hols. Res required. Bar 4 pm-2 am. Wine cellar. A la carte entrees: dinner $22-$39. Prix

fixe dinner $62. Pianist; vocalist Fri-Sat. In restored 18th-century carriage house once owned by Aaron Burr; many framed historical documents; dining rm overlooks courtyard garden. Jacket. Cr cds: A, C, D, MC, V.
D

★★ **ORSO.** *322 W 46th St (10036). 212/489-7212. www.orsorestaurant.com.* Regional Italian menu. Hrs: noon-11:45 pm; Wed, Sat from 11:30 am. Res required (1 wk in advance). Bar. A la carte entrees: lunch, dinner $12.50-$22. Italian-style trattoria with skylit, vaulted ceiling; celebrity photo collection. Cr cds: MC, V.

★★ **OSTERIA AL DOGE.** *142 W 44th St (10036). 212/944-3643.* Italian menu. Specializes in Venetian dishes, seafood, pizza. Hrs: noon-11:30 pm; Fri, Sat to midnight; Sun 4:30-10:30 pm. Closed Jan 1, Dec 25. Res accepted. Bar. A la carte entrees: lunch $12.50-$19.50, dinner $13.50-$25. Cr cds: A, D, DS, MC, V.
D

★★★ **OSTERIO DEL CIRCO.** *120 W 55th St (10019). 212/265-3636. www.osteriodelcirco.com.* Italian menu. Specialties: Tuscan fish soup, homemade pastas. Hrs: 11:30 am-2:30 pm, 5:30-11 pm; Fri, Sat to 11:30 pm; Sun

5-10:30 pm; Sat brunch 11:30 am-2 pm. Closed hols. Res accepted. Bar. A la carte entrees: lunch, dinner $14-$34. Prix fixe $20.02. Sat brunch $25. Outdoor dining. Pseudo-circus tent made of red and yellow fabric panels. Cr cds: A, D, Discover, JCB, MC, V.

[D] [⊷]

★★ **OTABE.** *68 E 56th St (10022). 212/223-7575.* Japanese menu. Specialties: swordfish teriyaki, eel teriyaki, traditional Kaiseki tasting menu including sashimi and tempura. Hrs: Teppan Grill: noon-2:30 pm, 5:30-10:30 pm; Sat, Sun from 5:30 pm. Japanese dining room: noon-10:30 pm; Sat, Sun from 5:30 pm. Res accepted. A la carte entrees: lunch, dinner $15-$26. Complete meal: dinner $50-$70. Cr cds: A, D, MC, V.

[D]

★ **OUR PLACE.** *1444 3rd Ave (10028). 212/288-4888.* Chinese menu. Specialties: tangerine beef, Peking duck, Grand Marnier prawns. Hrs: noon-10:30 pm; Fri, Sat to 11 pm. Mon-Sat early-bird dinner 5-7 pm. Closed Thanksgiving. Res accepted. Bar. A la carte entrees: lunch $6.95-$8.95, dinner $11.95-$33. Interior designed by protege of I.M. Pei. Cr cds: A, D, MC, V.

[D]

★★ **OYSTER BAR.** *Grand Central Terminal, Lower Level (10017). 212/490-6650. www.oysterbarny.com.* Specializes in fish, shellfish, smoked salmon. Hrs: 11:30 am-9:30 pm. Closed Sat, Sun; hols. Res accepted. Bars. Wine list. A la carte entrees: lunch, dinner $8.95-$25.95. In landmark RR station; Gustivino-tiled vaulted ceilings, mahogany paneling. Cr cds: A, C, D, MC, V.

[D] [⊷]

★★ **PALM COURT.** *5th Ave at Central Park Sq (10019). 212/759-3000. www.fairmont.com.* Specialties: fresh raspberry Napoleon, scones with Devonshire cream, Brazilian cake. Own baking. Hrs: 6:30 am-midnight; Sun brunch 10 am-2 pm. Res required Sun brunch. Serv bar. A la carte entrees: bkfst $12-$17, lunch, dinner $20-$26. Complete meals: bkfst $19.50-$24. Sun brunch $55.

Pianist, violinist; harpist. Valet parking. Edwardian, columned court off lobby; a New York tradition. Cr cds: A, D, DS, MC, V.

[D]

★★ **PAOLA'S.** *245 E 84th St (10028). 212/794-1890.* Hrs: 5-11 pm. Closed most major hols. Res accepted. Italian menu. Bar. A la carte entrees: dinner $14.95-$28.95. Specialties: pan-seared baby artichokes, veal stuffed with spinach and prosciutto, ravioli stuffed with spinach. Street parking. Outdoor dining. Intimate dining; romantic atmosphere. Totally nonsmoking. Cr cds: A, MC, V.

[D]

★★★ **PARK AVENUE CAFE.** *100 E 63rd St (10021). 212/644-1900. www. parkavenuecafe.com.* Specialties: tuna and salmon tartare with caviar, swordfish chop, Mrs. Ascher's steamed vegetable torte. Hrs: 11:30 am-2:30 pm, 5:30-11 pm; Fri to midnight; Sat 5:30 pm-midnight; Sun 5:30-10:30 pm; Sat, Sun brunch 11 am-2:30 pm. Closed Jan 1, Dec 25. Res accepted. Bar. A la carte entrees: lunch $19.50-$26, dinner $24.50-$33.50. Complete meals: dinner $58-$67. Authentic American antiques, folk art, mix and match plates. Cr cds: A, D, DS, MC, V.

★★ **PARK BISTRO.** *414 Park Ave S (10016). 212/689-1360.* French Provençal menu. Specialties: warm potato salad with goat cheese and herbs, fresh codfish with mashed potato and fried leeks in onion sauce, braised lamb shank with dry fruit sauce. Hrs: noon-3 pm, 5:30-11 pm; Sat, Sun from 5:30 pm. Closed hols. Res accepted. Bar. A la carte entrees: lunch $17-$22.50, dinner $22-$28.50. Casual dining; Parisian bistro decor and atmosphere. Cr cds: A, D, MC, V.

[D] [⊷]

★★★ **PATRIA.** *250 Park Ave S (10003). 212/777-6211. www.patria nyc.com.* Latin American menu. Specialties: Ecuadoran ceviche, Nicaraguan skirt steak, sugarcane tuna with malanga puree, chocolate-filled cigar with edible matches. Hrs: noon-2:45 pm, 6-11 pm; Fri to midnight; Sat 5:30 pm-midnight; Sun 5:30-10:30 pm. Closed Thanksgiving,

Dec 25. Res accepted. Bar to 1 am. A
la carte entrees: lunch $10-$21.
Complete meals: lunch $25, dinner
$52. Painted in striking earth tones
and decorated with colorful mosaics
and Latin American art. Cr cds: A, D,
DS, MC, V.

D

★★★ **PATROON.** 160 E 46th St
(10017). 212/883-7373. Specialties:
lobster and cod cake with snow pea
shoots, wood-grilled Porterhouse
steak for two, spit-fired roast chicken
for two. Own pastries. Hrs: noon-
2:30 pm, 5:30-11 pm; Mon, Tues to
10 pm; Sat from 5:30 pm. Closed
Sun; hols; also Sat in July, Aug. Res
accepted. Bar noon-11:30 pm. Wine
cellar. A la carte entrees: lunch $19-
$36, dinner $26-$40. Prix fixe: lunch
$20. Three-level dining rm with
rooftop garden; Jacket suggested. Cr
cds: A, D, DS, JCB, MC, V.

D **SC**

★★ **PAYARD PATISSERIE AND
BISTRO.** 1032 Lexington Ave (10021).
212/717-5252. www.payard.com. Hrs:
noon-2:30 pm, 6-10:30 pm. Closed
hols. Res accepted. French menu. Bar
11 am-midnight. A la carte entrees:
lunch $19-$22, dinner $19-$25. Specialties: bouillabaisse, New York steak
with homemade french fries, braised
shortribs in red wine. Street parking.
French bistro decor; soaring ceilings,
framed mirrors. Totally nonsmoking.
Cr cds: A, D, MC, V.

D **SC**

★ **PENANG MALAYSIAN.** 109
Spring St (10012). 212/274-8883.
Malaysian menu. Specialties: roti
canai, sotong goreng, udang halia.
Hrs: noon-midnight; Fri, Sat to 1 am.
Bar. A la carte entrees: lunch $5.95-
$19, dinner $7.95-$19. Exotic plants
and a waterfall add to the rainforest
atmosphere of this restaurant. Cr cds:
A, D, MC, V.

SC

★★ **PERIYALI.** 35 W 20th St
(10011). 212/463-7890. Nouvelle
Greek menu. Specializes in charcoal-
grilled fish, octopus, lamb chops.
Own pastries. Hrs: noon-3 pm, 5:30-
11 pm; Sat 5:30-11:30 pm. Closed
Sun. Res required. Bar. A la carte
entrees: lunch $15-$22, dinner $17-
$25. Dining in glass-enclosed garden

courtyard. Greek taverna decor. Cr
cds: A, D, MC, V.

★★★ **PETROSSIAN.** 182 W 58th St
(10019). 212/245-2214. Continental
menu. Specialties: caviar, smoked
salmon, foie gras. Own pastries.
Menu changes 6 times a yr. Hrs:
11:30 am-3 pm, 5:30-11:30 pm; Sat,
Sun brunch 11:30 am-3 pm., Sunday
dinner 5:30pm - 10:30pm Res
accepted. Bar 11:30-1 am. A la carte
entrees: lunch $19, dinner $26-$34.
Prix fixe: lunch $22-$39, dinner $35.
Sat, Sun brunch $12-$25. Jacket. Cr
cds: A, D, MC, V.

★★★★ **PICHOLINE.** 35 W 64th St
(10023). 212/724-8585. Chef-owner
Terrance Brennan continues to
refine his contemporary French
cooking at this restaurant near Lincoln Center. The atmosphere is part
drawing room, part gastronomic
temple. Save room for the extraordinary cheese course, with some 30
selections from around the world.
French, Mediterranean menu. Specialties: grilled octopus salad,
carpaccio of tuna, sautéed sweetbreads, wild mushroom and duck
risotto, tournedos of salmon, daube
of beef shortribs, Moroccan-spiced
loin of lamb. Hrs: 11:45 am-2 pm,
5:30-11:45 pm; Mon 5:30-11:45 pm;
Sun 5-10 pm. Closed hols. Res
accepted. Bar. Wine cellar. A la carte
entrees: lunch $17-$21, dinner $26-
$36. Complete meal: 3-course $60.
Tasting menu: 4-course $70, 7-
course $90. Dining area totally non-
smoking. Two private dining
facilities: wine rm and private party
rm. Cr cds: A, D, MC, V.

D

★★ **PIERRE AU TUNNEL.** 250 W
47th St (10036). 212/575-1220.
French menu. Hrs: noon-3 pm, 5:30-
11:30 pm; Wed, Sat noon-2:30 pm,
4:30-11:30 pm. Closed Mon; hols.
Res accepted. Bar. A la carte entrees:
lunch $10-$20. Complete meals: dinner $32. French country dining rm
decor; fireplace. Family-owned. Cr
cds: A, MC, V.

D

★ **PIG HEAVEN.** 1540 2nd Ave
(10028). 212/744-4887. Chinese
menu. Specializes in pork dishes,
seafood, poultry. Hrs: noon-midnight; Sat, Sun brunch to 4:30 pm.

Res required. Bar. A la carte entrees: lunch $4.95-$6.25, dinner $10.95-$19.95. Cr cds: A, D, DS, MC, V.

D ⌐

★★ **PO.** *31 Cornelia St (10014). 212/645-2189.* Italian menu. Specialties: goat cheese truffle, marinated quail. Hrs: 11:30 am-2:30 pm, 5:30-11 pm; Fri, Sat to 11:30 pm; Sun 11:30 am-2:30 pm, 5-10 pm. Closed Mon; hols; also 2 wks in Feb and Sept. Res accepted. Bar. A la carte entrees: lunch $8-$10, dinner $10-$15. Prix fixe: lunch $21, dinner $35. Outdoor dining. Italian decor. Totally nonsmoking. Cr cds: A.

D

★★★ **POST HOUSE.** *28 E 63rd St (10021). 212/935-2888. www.thepost house.com.* Hrs: noon-11 pm; Fri to midnight; Sat 5:30 pm-midnight; Sun 5:30-11 pm. Closed Jan 1, Thanksgiving, Dec 25. Specializes in steaks, chops, seafood. Res accepted. Bar. Wine list. A la carte entrees: lunch $18.50-$28.50, dinner $22-$46. Own pastries. Club atmosphere. Cr cds: A, D, DS, ER, JCB, MC, V.

★★★ **PRIMAVERA.** *1578 1st Ave (10028). 212/861-8608.* Northern Italian menu. Specialties: baby goat, primavera pasta, risotto ai porcini. Hrs: 5:30 pm-midnight; Sun from 5 pm. Closed hols. Res required. Bar. Wine cellar. A la carte entrees: dinner $19.75-$32.50. Tuscan decor. Jacket. Cr cds: A, D, MC, V.

D ⌐

★★ **PROVENCE.** *38 MacDougal St (10012). 212/475-7500. www.citysearch. com/nycprovence.* Southern French menu. Specializes in seafood, bouillabaisse. Hrs: noon-3 pm, 6-11:30 pm; Fri, Sat to midnight; Sun 5:30-11 pm. Closed hols. Res required. Bar. A la carte entrees: lunch $10-$18, dinner $15.50-$19.50. Sat brunch $10-$18. Cr cds: A.

D SC ⌐

★★ **RAIN.** *100 W 82nd St (10024). 212/501-0776.* Thai menu. Specialties: green curry chicken, crispy whole fish, Thai-style duck fajitas. Hrs: noon-3 pm, 6-11 pm; Fri to midnight; Sat noon-4 pm, 5 pm-midnight; Sun noon-4 pm, 5-10 pm. Closed Dec 25. Res accepted. Bar. A la carte entrees: lunch $6-$14, dinner $11-$22. Thai decor. Cr cds: A, D, DS, MC, V.

D ⌐

★★ **RAOUL'S.** *180 Prince St (10012). 212/966-3518. www.raoulsrestaurant. com.* French menu. Specialty: steak au poivre. Own desserts. Hrs: 5:30 pm-2 am. Res accepted. Bar. Wine list. Dinner $16-$30. Casual French bistro; original artwork, objets d'art. Cr cds: D, MC, V.

⌐

★★★ **THE RED CAT.** *227 Tenth St (10011). 212/242-1122. www.theredcat. com.* Contemporary American menu. Specializes wild striped bass, chargrilled pork chop, mustard-crusted trout. Hrs: noon-3 pm, 5:30-11:30 pm; Fri, Sat to midnight; Sun 5-10 pm. Res accepted. Extensive wine list. Lunch, dinner $17-$28. Cr cds: A, DS, MC, V.

★★ **REDEYE GRILL.** *890 7th Ave (10019). 212/541-9000.* Contemporary Amer menu. Specialties: twelve dancing shrimp, clay pot red Gulf snapper, ribeye steak frites with redeye potatoes. Hrs: 11:30-1 am; Fri, Sat to 2 am; Sun, Mon to 11:30 pm; Sat, Sun brunch to 3 pm. Res accepted. Bar. Wine cellar. A la carte entrees: lunch $13.50-$26.75, dinner $13.50-$36.95. Jazz Tues-Sat, Sun brunch. Outdoor dining. Copper shrimp statues pirouette over raw seafood bar; colorful murals, toy airplanes decorate two separate dining rms. Cr cds: A, D, DS, MC, V.

★★★ **REMI.** *145 W 53rd St (10019). 212/581-4242.* Venetian menu. Specialties: rack of lamb with pistachio-herb crust, seared rare tuna with spinach and shallot sauce, calf's liver in black truffle butter. Hrs: noon-2:30 pm, 5:30-11:30 pm; Sat from 5 pm; Sun 5:30-10 pm. Closed hols. Res required. Bar. A la carte entrees: lunch $14-$22, dinner $16-$28. Outdoor dining. Venetian-style trattoria with high, vaulted ceiling, Gothic detailing and rm-length, fantasy mural of Venice. Cr cds: A, D, JCB, MC, V.

D

★★ **RENE PUJOL.** *321 W 51st St (10019). 212/246-3023.* French menu. Specialties: onion tart, roasted rack of lamb with herb crust, roasted Atlantic salmon with green lentils. Own pastries. Hrs: noon-3 pm, 5-10:30 pm; Fri, Sat to 11:30 pm. Closed Sun; hols. Res accepted. Bar. Wine cellar. A la carte entrees: lunch $17-$27, dinner $20-$35. Complete meals: lunch $26, dinner $38. Infor-

can menu. Hrs: 7:30 am-11 pm; Fri to midnight; Sat 8:30 am-midnight; Sun 8:30 am-10 pm; Sat, Sun brunch 11 am-3 pm (Nov-Apr). Res accepted. Bar noon-11 pm. A la carte entrees: bkfst $6.95-$12.95, lunch, dinner $14-$28; Sat, Sun brunch $19.98. Prix fixe: dinner $23.95, $26.95. Sea-

Central Park

mal country-French atmosphere. Cr cds: A, D, DS, MC, V.

★★★ **RESTAURANT 222.** *222 W 79th St (10024). 212/799-0400. www. restauranttwotwotwo.com.* American, Italian menu. Specialties: steak. Hrs: 5-11 pm. Res accepted. Bar. Wine list. A la carte entrees: dinner $25-$49. Complete meal: pre-theater lunch $20, dinner $29.95.
D

★★★ **RHONE.** *63 Ganesvoort St (10014). 212/367-8440.* Contemporary American menu. Specializes in free range chicken, Colorado lamb, skate, monk fish. Hrs: 5:30 pm-midnight. Res accepted. Extensive wine list. Dinner $24-$29. Cr cds: A, MC, V.

★★ **ROCK CENTER CAFE.** *20 W 50th St (10020). 212/332-7620. www. restaurantassoc.com.* Regional Ameri-

sonal dishes. Parking (after 5 pm; wkends after 11 am). Outdoor dining (May-Oct). Overlooks Rockefeller Center's famous Prometheus fountain and sunken pool (summer), skating rink (winter). Cr cds: A, DS, MC, V.
D

★★★ **ROSA MEXICANO.** *1063 1st Ave, New York (10022). 212/753-7407.* Mexican menu. Specializes in cold avocado soup, sea bass with oranges, enchiladas de mole poblano. Hrs: 5-11:30 pm. Res accepted. Wine list. Dinner $16-$26. Cr cds: A, D, DS, MC, V.
D

★★★ **ROSA MEXICANO.** *61 Columbus Ave (10023). 212/977-7700.* Mexican menu. Specializes in cold avocado soup, sea bass with oranges, enchiladas de mole poblano. Hrs: 5-

10 pm. Res accepted. Wine list. Dinner $25-$38. Cr cds: A, D, DS, MC, V.

★★★ **RUTH'S CHRIS STEAK HOUSE.** *148 W 51st St (10019). 212/245-9600. www.ruthschris.com.* Specializes in steak, lobster. Hrs: noon-midnight; Sat from 4 pm; Sun 4-10 pm. Closed Jan 1, Dec 25. Res accepted. Bar. A la carte entrees: lunch, dinner $19-$35. Men's club decor. Cr cds: A, D, DS, JCB, MC, V.
⊟ D

★★ **SALAAM BOMBAY.** *317 Greenwich St (10013). 212/226-9400.* Indian menu. Specialties: rack of lamb marinated with ginger and lemon, chicken cooked with roasted coconut and spices, undhiyu. Hrs: noon-3 pm, 5:30-11 pm. Res accepted. Bar. A la carte entrees: dinner $9.95-$22.95. Buffet: lunch $10.95. Sitar music wkends. Colorful Indian canopy in middle of room. Totally nonsmoking. Cr cds: A, D, DS, MC, V.
D ⊟

★★ **SAL ANTHONY'S S.P.Q.R..** *133 Mulberry St (10013). 212/925-3120.* Italian menu. Specialties: linguini with fresh clams, whole boneless trout, calamari. Hrs: noon-11 pm; Fri, Sat to midnight. Res accepted. Bar. Complete meals: lunch $9.95, dinner (until 6:30 pm) $18.95. A la carte entrees: dinner $14.75-$21. Parking. Outdoor dining. Spacious, elegant dining area. Cr cds: A, D, DS, MC, V.
D

★★★ **SAN DOMENICO.** *240 Central Park S (10019). 212/265-5959. www.sandomenicony.com.* Italian menu. Specialties: soft egg yolk-filled ravioli with truffle butter, Alaskan prawns with cannellini beans, roasted veal loin with bacon cream sauce. Hrs: noon-2:30 pm, 5:30-11 pm; Sat 5:30-11:30pm; Sun 5:30-10 pm. Pre-theater dinner 5:30-7 pm. Closed Jan 1, Thanksgiving, Dec 25. Res accepted. Bar. Wine cellar. A la carte entrees: lunch $15.50-$32, dinner $16.50-$42.50. Tasting menu: dinner $65. Pre-theater dinner $32. Prix fixe: $19.99. Jacket. Cr cds: A, D, MC, V.
D ⊟

★★ **SAN MARTIN'S.** *143 E 49th St (10017). 212/832-9270. www.sanmartin restibaweb.com.* Continental menu. Specialties: rack of baby lamb, paella Valenciana, roast suckling pig. Hrs: noon-midnight. Res accepted. Bar. A la carte entrees: lunch, dinner $9-$26. Complete meals: lunch $16, dinner $21. Outdoor dining. Family-owned. Cr cds: A, D, DS, MC, V.
D

★★★ **SAN PIETRO.** *18 E 54th St (10022). 212/753-9015. www.sanpietro. net.* Southern Italian menu. Specializes in fish, pasta. Hrs: noon-midnight. Closed Sun; hols. Res accepted. Wine list. Bar. A la carte entrees: lunch, dinner $11-$38. Outdoor dining. Two large dining areas; massive ceramic scene of Amalfi coast. Jacket. Cr cds: A, D, DS, MC, V.
D

★★ **SARABETH'S.** *423 Amsterdam Ave (10024). 212/496-6280. www. sarabeths.com.* Specialties: pumpkin waffles, farmer's omelette, warm berry bread pudding. Hrs: 8 am-3:30 pm, 5:30-10:30 pm; Fri to 11 pm; Sat 5:30-11 pm; Sun 5:30-9:30 pm; Sat, Sun brunch 9 am-4 pm. Closed Dec 25. Res accepted (dinner). Serv bar. A la carte entrees: bkfst $6-$10, lunch $8.50-$14, dinner $10-$19. Sat, Sun brunch $8-$15. New England atmosphere. Totally nonsmoking. Cr cds: A, D, MC, V.
D

★ **SARDI'S.** *234 W 44th St (10036). 212/221-8440. www.sardis.com.* Specialties: shrimp a la Sardi, cannelloni, chicken a la Sardi. Hrs: 11:30-12:30 am; Fri, Sat to 1 am. Res accepted. Bar. A la carte entrees: lunch $11-$28, dinner $20-$32. Prix fixe: lunch $29.50, dinner $41.50. Established 1921. Famous gathering place of theatrical personalities, columnists, publishers, agents; popular for before- and after-theater dinner or drinks. Family-owned. Cr cds: A, C, D, DS, MC, V.
D

★★ **SAVORE.** *200 Spring St (10012). 212/431-1212.* Italian menu. Specialties: corn mousse with wild boar sauce; salad of beets, zucchini, carrots and potatoes marinated in Balsamic vinegar. Own baking, pasta. Hrs: noon-3 pm, 5:30 pm-midnight; Sat, Sun noon-midnight. Closed Dec 25. Res accepted. Bar. Wine cellar. A la carte entrees: dinner $12-$26. Complete meals: lunch $19.99. Outdoor dining. Elegant decor with polished wood, antique furniture, alabaster chandeliers. Totally nonsmoking. Cr cds: A, MC, V.

D

★★ **SAVOY.** *70 Prince St (10012). 212/219-8570.* French, Mediterranean menu. Specializes in seafood, duck, chicken. Hrs: noon-3 pm, 6-10:30 pm; Fri, Sat to 11 pm; Sun to 10 pm. Closed hols. Res accepted. Bar. A la carte entrees: lunch $8-$12, dinner $18-$29. Contemporary decor. Cr cds: A, MC, V.

D

★★ **SCOPA RESTAURANT.** *79 Madison Ave (10016). 212/686-8787.* Hrs: 11:30 am-3 pm, 5:30-10:45 pm. Closed Sun. Res accepted. Wine, beer. Lunch, dinner $24-$29. Entertainment. Cr cds: A, D, DS, MC, V.

D ⌐

★★ **SCREENING ROOM.** *54 Varick St (10013). 212/334-2100. www.the screeningroom.com.* Specialties: panfried artichokes, macaroni with spinach, cedar-planked salmon. Own pastries. Hrs: noon-3 pm, 6-11 pm; Sun, Mon from 6 pm; Fri to 11:30 pm; Sat 6-11:30 pm; Sun brunch 11:30 am-3 pm. Res accepted. Bar. A la carte entrees: lunch $9-$22, dinner $17-$24. Complete meal: dinner $30. Sun brunch $6-$17. Casual decor with movie theater. Cr cds: A, D, DS, MC, V.

D ⌐

★★★ **SEAGRILL.** *19 W 49th St (10020). 212/332-7610. www.restaurant associates.com.* Specialties: Maryland crab cakes with stone-ground mustard, roasted Chilean sea bass, roasted cod with cous cous. Own pastries. Hrs: noon-3 pm, 5-10 pm; Sat from 5 pm. Closed Sun, major hols. Res required. Bar. Wine cellar. A la carte entrees: lunch $19-$28, dinner $21-$32. Prix fixe: dinner $32-$39. Outdoor dining. Floral, garden displays. Overlooks Prometheus fountain and pool (summer); ice skating rink (winter). Jacket (dinner). Cr cds: A, D, DS, MC, V.

D

★★★ **SHAAN.** *57 W 48th St (10020). 212/977-8400.* Indian menu. Specialties: chicken makhani, prawns Bengali, paneer pasanda. Hrs: noon-3 pm, 5:30-11 pm. Res accepted. Bar. A la carte entrees: lunch, dinner $12-$30. Complete meals: lunch $15.95-$18.95, dinner $30- $40. Buffet: lunch $13.95. Entertainment Fri, Sat. Framed Indian tapestries on walls. Totally nonsmoking. Cr cds: A, D, DS, MC, V.

D ⌐

★ **SHABU-TATSU.** *1414 York Ave (10021). 212/472-3322.* Japanese menu. Specialties: shabu-shabu (tabletop cooking), sukiyaki (hot pot with sauce), yakiniku (Japanese barbecue). Hrs: noon-2:30 pm, 5-10:30 pm; Fri to 11:30 pm; Sat noon-11:30 pm; Sun noon-10:30 pm; Sat, Sun brunch to 5 pm. Closed hols. Res accepted. Bar. A la carte entrees: lunch $5.95-$11.95, dinner $8-$17. Complete meals: dinner $28-$38. Sat, Sun brunch $7-$12. Cook your own meal; each table surrounds a stovetop. Totally nonsmoking. Cr cds: A, D, DS, MC, V.

D

★ **SHANG HAI CUISINE.** *89-91 Bayard St (10013). 212/732-8988.* Shanghai menu. Specialties: crispy duck, steamed tiny buns, yellow fish in sweet and sour sauce. Hrs: 10:30 am-10:30 pm. Res accepted. Bar. A la carte entrees: lunch, dinner $4.95-$19.95.

D

★ **SHARK BAR.** *307 Amsterdam Ave (10023). 212/874-8500. www.sharkbar. com.* Regional American menu. Specialties: Louisiana deep-fried crab cakes, Georgia bank farm-bred catfish, honey-dipped Southern fried chicken. Own baking. Hrs: noon-3 pm, 5-11:30 pm; Mon, Tues from 5 pm; Wed to midnight; Thurs to 12:30 am; Fri to 1:30 am; Sat 11:30 am-3 pm (brunch), 5 pm-1:30 am; Sun 11:30 am-3 pm (brunch), 5-11:30 pm. Closed Dec 25. Res accepted. Bar. A la carte entrees: lunch, dinner $10.95-$17.95. Sat, Sun brunch $15.95. Harlem Renaissance-era decor; red velvet, extensive woodwork; multilevel dining. Totally nonsmoking. Cr cds: A, D, MC, V.

★★ **SHUN LEE.** *43 W 65th St (10023).* 212/595-8895. Chinese menu. Specialties: jumbo prawns with broccoli in curry sauce, Peking duck, Norwegian salmon (Szechwan or Mandarin style). Hrs: noon-midnight; Sat from 11:30 am; Sun to 10:30 pm. Closed Thanksgiving. Bar. A la carte entrees: lunch $11.50-$22.95, dinner $15.95-$36. Contemporary decor. Jacket. Cr cds: A, D, MC, V.
D

★★★ **SHUN LEE PALACE.** *155 E 55th St (10022).* 212/371-8844. Chinese menu. Specializes in Cantonese, Hunan and Szechwan dishes. Hrs: noon-11:30 pm; Sun to 11 pm. Closed Thanksgiving. Res required. Bar. Wine cellar. A la carte entrees: lunch $16.50-$24.95, dinner $18.95-$37.95. Complete meals (Mon-Fri): lunch $19.99. Cr cds: A, D, MC, V.
D

★ **SIAM GRILL.** *586 9th Ave (10036).* 212/307-1363. Thai menu. Specialties: sauteed chicken with cashew nuts and chili paste sauce, homemade red and green Thai curry, garlic duck. Hrs: 11:30 am-10:30 pm; Fri to 11 pm; Sat 1-11 pm; Sun 4-10:30 pm. Closed hols. Res accepted. Serv bar. A la carte entrees: lunch, dinner $7.95-$13.95. Complete meals: dinner $8.95. Cr cds: A, MC, V.

★★★ **SMITH & WOLLENSKY.** *797 3rd Ave (10022).* 212/753-1530. *www. smithandwollensky.com.* Specializes in steak, seafood. Hrs: 11:30-2 am. Closed Jan 1, Thanksgiving, Dec 25. Res accepted. Bar. Wine cellar. A la carte entrees: lunch $15-$28, dinner $19-$34. Built 1897; turn-of-the-century decor; old New York steakhouse atmosphere. Outdoor dining. Cr cds: A, D, DS, MC, V.
D

★★ **SOBA-YA.** *229 E 9th St (10003).* 212/533-6966. Hrs: noon-11 pm; early-bird dinner 5-6:30 pm (Tues-Fri). Closed Mon; hols. Res accepted. Japanese menu. Wine, beer. A la carte entrees: lunch, dinner $6.50-$14. Specializes in cold and hot noodle entrees. Street parking. Small fountain at entrance. Totally nonsmoking. Cr cds: A, C, D, DS, ER, MC, V.
D

★ **SOHO STEAK.** *90 Thompson St (10012).* 212/226-0602. Hrs: 6:30-11 pm; Fri, Sat to midnight; Sun 6-10:30 pm; Sat, Sun brunch noon-4 pm. Closed major hols. Continental, Amer menu. Bar. A la carte entrees: dinner $14-$16. Sat, Sun brunch $4.50-$12. Specialties: braised oxtail raviolo, grilled hangar steak, double-cut pork chop with organic barley. Street parking. Bistro atmosphere. Cr cds: A, MC, V.
D

★★★ **SPARKS STEAK HOUSE.** *210 E 46th St (10017).* 212/687-4855. Specializes in steak, lobster, seafood. Hrs: noon-3 pm, 5-11 pm; Fri to 11:30 pm; Sat 5-11:30 pm. Closed Sun; major hols. Res required. Bar. Wine list. A la carte entrees: lunch, dinner $25-$33. Early American decor; etched glass, wood paneling. Jacket. Cr cds: A, D, DS, MC, V.
D

★★ **STEAK FRITES.** *9 E 16th St (10003).* 212/463-7101. French menu. Specializes in black Angus steak. Hrs: noon-11:30 pm; Fri-Sat to 12:30 pm; Sun to 10 pm; Sun brunch noon-4 pm. Closed Jan 1, Dec 25. Res accepted. Bar. A la carte entrees: lunch $8.50-$17.50, dinner $12.50-$19. Sun brunch $7-$17.50. Outdoor dining. French bistro-style atmosphere; murals of Paris scenes. Cr cds: A, DS, MC, V.
D

★★★ **STRIP HOUSE.** *13 E 12th St (10003).* 212/328-0000. Specializes in steak, bone-in rib chops, pork chops. Hrs: 5:30-11 pm. Closed Mon. Res accepted. Extensive wine list. Dinner $41-$50.

★★★★ **SUGIYAMA.** *251 W 55th St (10019).* 212/956-0670. This tiny restaurant specializes in the highly traditional and ritualized Japanese cuisine known as kaiseki. The chef, Nao Sugiyama, is a master, and if you put yourself in his hands by ordering the omikasse, you will not be disappointed. The meal will include delicate cold hors d'oeuvres such as wild Japanese mountain plums suspended in cubes of sweet jelly and fresh soy beans and move to sushi, sashimi, gurgling pots of blowfish, food you cook yourself on hot rocks, broiled black cod with miso sauce, and other fabulous Japanese specialities. The service couldn't be any more attentive or friendly. Specializes in ankimo tofu, monkfish liver tofu pate. Hrs: 5:45-10:30 pm. Closed Sun, Mon. Res accepted. Wine, beer. Dinner prix fixe: 5-course $45-$125. Entertainment. Cr cds: A, D, MC, V.

D

★★ **SUSHI OF GARI.** *402 E 78th St (10021). 212/517-5340.* Specializes in sushi moakase. Hrs: 5-10:45 pm; Sun to 9:45 pm. Closed 2nd Sun of month. Res accepted. Wine, beer. Dinner $15-$100. Entertainment. Cr cds: A, MC, V.

D

★★★ **SUSHISAY.** *38 E 51st St (10022). 212/755-1780. www.sushisay. com.* Japanese menu. Specialties: sushi, bento. Hrs: noon-2:15 pm, 5:30-10 pm; Sat 5-9 pm. Closed Sun; hols. Res required. Bar. A la carte entrees: lunch $18-$33, dinner $19.50-$33. Traditional and serene Japanese decor. Totally nonsmoking. Cr cds: A, D, MC, V.

★★★ **SUSHI YASUDA.** *204 E 43rd St (10017). 212/972-1001.* Specializes

in sushi, shashimi. Hrs: noon-2:15 pm, 6-10:15 pm; Sat from 6 pm. Closed Sun. Res accepted. Extensive wine list. Lunch, dinner $41-$65. Cr cds: A, DS, MC, V.

★★ **SWEET AND TART.** *20 Mott St (10013). 212/964-0380. www.sweet andtart.com.* Chinese menu. Specialties: dim sum, baked conch with curry sauce, filet mignon with black pepper sauce. Hrs: 9 am-11 pm; Sat, Sun from 8:30 am. A la carte entrees: dim sum from $1.90, lunch, dinner $7.95-$20. Fish tank.

★★★ **TABLA.** *11 Madison Ave (10012). 212/889-0667.* Fine American cuisine with Indian influence. Hrs: Mon-Sat noon-2 pm; 5:30-10:30 pm; Sun 5:30-10 pm. Prix fixe: 3-course dinner $52. Res required. Bar. Cr cds: A, DS, MC, V.

D

★★ **TABLE D'HOTE.** *44 E 92nd St (10128). 212/348-8125.* French menu. Specialties: seared tuna with Japanese rice cake, rack of lamb shank with spring pea risotto, bistro-style hangar steak. Hrs: noon-3 pm, 5:30-10:30 pm; Sat 11 am-4 pm; Sun 10:30 am-4 pm. Closed Dec 25. Res accepted. Wine, beer. A la carte entrees: lunch $8.75-$15, dinner $14.50-$26. Sun brunch $8.50-$15. Small, intimate bistro-style dining

New York all abuzz

rm. Totally nonsmoking. Cr cds: A, DS, MC, V.

D SC

★★ **TAORMINA.** *147 Mulberry St (10013). 212/219-1007.* Italian menu. Specializes in seafood, pasta. Hrs: 11 am-11:30 pm; Sat to 1 am; Sun to 11 pm. Closed Thanksgiving, Dec 25, 31. Res required. Bar. A la carte entrees: lunch, dinner $9.90-$19. Valet parking. Modern Italian decor. Cr cds: A, C, D, ER, MC, V.

D

★★ **TAVERN ON THE GREEN.** *Central Park at W 67th St (10023). 212/873-3200. www.tavernonthegreen.com.* Contemporary American menu. Own baking. Specialties: sauteed jumbo lump crabcakes, braised breast of veal, crab-crusted Maine halibut. Hrs: noon-3:30 pm; 5:30-10:45 pm; Fri, Sat to 11:30 pm; Sat, Sun brunch 10 am-3 pm. Res accepted. Bar. A la carte entrees: lunch $14.25-$28.50, dinner $22-$33. Table d'hôte: lunch $19.98-$27.75. Sat, Sun brunch $17.50-$28.75. Entertainment (Tues-Sun) in Chestnut Room. Valet parking. Garden terrace. Gift shop. Elaborate decor; in 1874 building within Central Park. Cr cds: A, DS, MC, V.

D

★★★ **TOCQUEVILLE.** *15 E 15th St (10003). 212/647-1515. www.marcopolo cafe.com.* French menu. Specializes in caramelized scallop, wasabi-crusted salmon, osso buco, lamb rillettes. Hrs: noon-2 pm, 6-10:30 pm. Res accepted. Extensive wine list. Lunch, dinner $22-$33. Cr cds: A, D, DS, MC, V.

★★★ **THE TONIC RESTAURANT & BAR.** *108 W 18th St (10022). 212/929-9755. www.thetonic.com.* American cuisine with French influence. Hrs: Mon-Sat noon-3 pm; 5-11 pm; Sat brunch 11:30 am-3 pm. Closed Sun, hols. A la carte: dinner $25-$32. Bar. Res required. Cr cds: A, C, D, DS, ER, MC, V.

D

★★★ **TOWN.** *15 W 56th St (10019). 212/582-4445.* Contemporary American menu. Specializes in chilled pea soup with prosciutto, escargots in truffled risotto, carpaccio with blood oranges and mint. Hrs: 8 am-2 pm,

5:30-10:30 pm. Res accepted. Extensive wine list. Bkfst $14-$20, lunch $25-$32; dinner $38-$45. Cr cds: A, MC, V.

★★ **TRATTORIA DELL'ARTE.** *900 7th Ave (10019). 212/245-9800.* Italian menu. Specializes in pizza, veal chops, seafood. Own pastas. Hrs: 11:45 am-2:45 pm, 5-11:30 pm; Fri, Sat to 12:30 am; Sun to 10:30 pm; Sat, Sun brunch 11 am-3 pm. Closed Thanksgiving, Dec 25. Res accepted. Bar. A la carte entrees: lunch, dinner $17-$37.50. Sat, Sun brunch $13.75-$24. Authentic Italian antipasto bar. Modern Italian atmosphere. Opp Carnegie Hall; frequented by celebrities. Cr cds: A, DS, MC, V.

D

★★★ **TRIBECA GRILL.** *375 Greenwich St (10013). 212/941-3900. www. interactivegourmetsite.cuisine.com.* Specialties: rare-seared tuna, crab-crusted seabass, rack of lamb. Hrs: 11:30 am-3 pm, 5:30-11 pm; Fri to 11:30 pm; Sat 5:30-11:30 pm; Sun 5-10 pm; Sun brunch 11:30 am-3 pm. Res accepted. Bar. A la carte entrees: lunch $12-$20, dinner $19-$29. Prix fixe: lunch $19.99. Casual dining in converted warehouse. Cr cds: A, DS, MC, V.

D

★★★ **TRIOMPHE.** *49 W 44th St (10019). 212/453-4233. www. triomphe-newyork.com.* French menu. Specializes in roast lamb, lobster, foie gras. Hrs: noon-2:30 pm, 5:45-11 pm. Res accepted. Wine list. Lunch, dinner $25-$32 Cr cds: A, MC, V.

★★★ **TUSCAN SQUARE.** *16 W 51st St (10020). 212/977-7777. www.tuscansquare.com.* Hrs: 11:30 am-11 pm; Sat, Sun to 10:30 pm; Sat, Sun 11:30 am-3:30 pm. Closed hols; also Sun brunch in summer. Res accepted. Italian menu. Bar. A la carte entrees: lunch, dinner $13-$20. Complete meal: 3-course dinner $32.50. Sat, Sun brunch $13-$20. Specialties: ricotta and spinach gnocchi with wild boar sauce, slow-roasted veal marinated in lemon and sage, assorted antipasto. Street parking. Tuscan villa decor. Totally nonsmoking. Cr cds: A, DS, MC, V.

D

★★★ **21 CLUB.** *21 W 52nd St (10019). 212/582-7200. www.21club.*

com. Specialties: steak tartare, 21 burger. Own pastries. Hrs: noon-2:30 pm, 5:30-10 pm; Fri, Sat to 11:30 pm. Closed Sun; hols; also Sat (July 4-Labor Day). Res accepted. Bar. Wine cellar. A la carte entrees: lunch $21-$39, dinner $29-$43. Prix fixe: lunch $32, dinner $36. Jacket. Cr cds: A, D, JCB, DS, MC, V.

D

★ **TYPHOON BREWERY.** *22 E 54th St (10022). 212/754-9006.* Thai menu. Specialties: crispy duck with sweet-and-sour five-spice sauce, grilled rare tuna, pan-seared monkfish. Own baking. Hrs: noon-2:30 pm, 5:30-10:30 pm; Fri to 11:30 pm; Sat in summer 5:30-11:30 pm. Closed Sun; hols. Res accepted. Bar. Wine list. Lunch $12-$18, dinner $13.75-$21. Industrial decor with metal tabletops, brick walls; large beer vats at entrance. Totally nonsmoking. Cr cds: A, DS, MC, V.

D

★★★ **UNION PACIFIC.** *111 E 22nd St (10010). 212/995-8500. www.unionpacificrestaurant.com.* Chef/owner Rocco DiSpirito never stops innovating in his use of exotic seasoning and ingredients from Asia and elsewhere to create his personalized, modern French cuisine. Surprises might include individual fondues or the occasional pile of truffles. The service and decor match the food in creativity and attention to detail. Contemporary American menu with Asian accents. Specialties: Taylor Bay scallops, sea bass with endive and tarragon, salmon in salt crust. Hrs: Mon-Thurs noon-2 pm, 5:30-10:30 pm; Fri, Sat 5:30-11 pm. Closed Sun. Res accepted. Bar. Wine list. Complete meal: lunch $23-$29, prix fixe dinner $65. Street parking. Arched bridge leads to dining room with a small pond and waterfall. Totally nonsmoking. Cr cds: A, D, MC, V.

D

★★★ **UNION SQUARE CAFE.** *21 E 16th St (10003). 212/243-4020.* Italian, American menu. Specialties: grilled marinated filet of tuna, fried calamari with spicy anchovy mayonnaise. Own pastries. Hrs: noon-2:15 pm, 6-10:15 pm; Fri, Sat to 11:15 pm; Sun 5:30-9:45 pm. Closed hols.

Res required. Bar. Wine list. A la carte entrees: lunch $16.50-$18.50, dinner $23-$27. Contemporary Amer bistro. Cr cds: A, C, D, DS, ER, MC, V.

SC

★★★★ **VERITAS.** *43 E 20th St (10003). 212/353-3700. www.veritas-nyc.com.* In a neighborhood of fine restaurants, this homage to fine wine maintains a low profile. Don't let it fool you. Chef Scott Bryan's simple, contemporary American cooking is excellent, the dining room is sophisticated but comfortable, and the wine list—comprising the cellars of two of the world's most serious collectors—is superb. New American cuisine. Hrs: Mon-Fri noon-2:30 pm, 6-10:30 pm; Sat, Sun 5:30-10:30 pm. Lunch, dinner: 3-course $62, a la carte $13-$35. Bar. Res preferred. Cr cds: A, C, D, DS, ER, MC, V.

D

★★ **VIEW.** *1535 Broadway (10036). 212/704-8900. www.marriott.com.* Continental menu. Own baking. Hrs: 5:30-11 pm; Fri, Sat 5 pm-midnight; Sun brunch 10:30 am-2 pm. Res required. Bar. Wine cellar. A la carte entrees: dinner $24.95-$33. Prix fixe: pre-theater dinner $39.95, $49.95. Sun brunch $34.95. Valet parking. Revolving rooftop restaurant, lounge and ballroom. Braille menu. Jacket. Cr cds: A, D, DS, MC, V.

D

★★ **VINCE AND EDDIE'S.** *70 W 68th St (10023). 212/721-0068.* Regional American menu. Specialties: Chesapeake crab cakes, fried calamari with lime juice, pan-roasted chicken. Hrs: noon-midnight. Res accepted. Bar. A la carte entrees: lunch $8.95-$14.95, dinner $17.50-$20.95. Outdoor dining. New England country inn decor. Cr cds: A, DS, MC, V.

★ **VIRGIL'S REAL BARBECUE.** *152 W 44th St (10036). 212/921-9494. www.virgilsbbq.com.* Specialties: barbecued Memphis pork ribs, pulled pork sandwiches, grilled catfish filet. Hrs: 11:30 am-midnight; Mon to 11 pm; Sun to 10 pm. Closed Dec 25. Res accepted. Bar. A la carte entrees: lunch, dinner $6.50-$24.95. Child's meals. Multilevel Southern-style restaurant. Walls lined with Ameri-

cana. Totally nonsmoking. Cr cds: A, D, MC, V.
D

★★★ **VONG.** *200 E 54th St (10022). 212/486-9592. www.jeangeorges.com.* Thai, French menu. Specialties: crab spring roll, fresh fish with wok-fried Napa cabbage, lobster with Thai herbs. Hrs: noon-2:30 pm, 6-11 pm; Sat 5:30-11:30 pm; Sun 5:30-10 pm. Closed hols. Res required. Bar. Wine cellar. A la carte entrees: lunch, dinner $19-$36. Prix fixe: lunch $38. Outdoor dining. Exotic decor of Southeast Asia; ceiling and walls covered with gold-leaf collage; Thai-style seating (sunken seating) in one area of dining rm. Cr cds: A, D, DS, JCB MC, V.
D

★★★ **WALLSE.** *344 W 11th St (10014). 212/352-2300.* Austrian menu. Specializes in Tafelspitz (boiled beef), creamed spinach, potatoes and apples horseradish, seafood. Hrs: noon-2:30 pm, 5:30 pm-midnight; Sat, Sun from 5:30 pm. Res accepted. Wine list. Lunch, dinner $22-$32. Cr cds: A, MC, V.

★★ **WALL STREET KITCHEN AND BAR.** *70 Broad St (10004). 212/797-7070. www.citysearch.com/nyc/walls tkitchen.* Specializes in pizza, steak, hamburgers. Hrs: 11:30 am-11:30 pm. Closed Thanksgiving, Dec 25. Bar. A la carte entrees: lunch, dinner $6.75-$19.50. Restored 1908 building has vaulted ceiling, overhanging balcony, tiered seating. Cr cds: A, DS, MC, V.
D

★★★ **WATER CLUB.** *500 E 30th St (10016). 212/683-3333. www.thewater club.com.* Specializes in lobster, oysters, tuna. Hrs: noon-2:30 pm, 5:30-11 pm; Sun 5:45-10 pm; Sun brunch 11 am-3 pm. Res required. Bar. A la carte entrees: lunch $15-$19, dinner $22-$34. Prix fixe: lunch $19.99, dinner $28. Sun brunch $33. Piano bar. Free valet parking. Outdoor dining (Memorial Day-Labor Day). Located on barge in the East River. Jacket. Cr cds: A, C, D, ER, MC, V.
D

★★ **WILLOW.** *1022 Lexington Ave (10021). 212/717-0703.* French menu. Specialties: seared Atlantic

salmon, rack of lamb, warm chocolate cake with Tahitian ice cream. Hrs: noon-4 pm, 5:30-10:30 pm; Sun brunch 11 am-4 pm. Closed Dec 25. Res accepted. Bar. A la carte entrees: lunch $9-$16, dinner $16.50-$28. Sun brunch $9-$14.50. Outdoor dining. French decor. Totally nonsmoking. Cr cds: A, D, MC, V.

★★★ **WOO LAE OAK.** *148 Mercer St (10012). 212/925-8200. www.woolaeoak soho.com.* Specializes in Korean dishes. Hrs: noon-11 pm; Fri, Sat to 11:30 pm. Res accepted. Lunch prix fixe: $35; dinner a la carte entrees: $14-$24. Entertainment. Cr cds: A, D, JCB, MC, V.

★★ **YANKEE CLIPPER.** *170 John St (10038). 212/344-5959.* Specializes in jumbo shrimp, pan-seared tuna, Norwegian salmon. Hrs: 11:30 am-10 pm; Sun noon-9 pm. Closed Thanksgiving, Dec 25. Res accepted. Bar. A la carte entrees: lunch, dinner $11-$24. Prix fixe: lunch, dinner $23. Three dining areas; main dining rm resembles dining salon on a luxury liner; display of ship models and prints of ships. Cr cds: A, C, D, DS, ER, MC, V.
SC

★★ **ZARELA.** *953 2nd Ave (10022). 212/644-6740. www.zarela.com.* Mexican menu. Specialties: roasted duck, snapper hash. Hrs: noon-3 pm, 5-11 pm; Fri to 11:30 pm; Sat 5-11:30 pm; Sun 5-10 pm. Closed hols. Res accepted. Bar. A la carte entrees: lunch $11-$16, dinner $13-$16.95. Entertainment Tues-Sat. Colorful Mexican decor; paper lanterns, masks, toys, piñatas. Cr cds: A, D, MC, V.

★★★ **ZOE.** *90 Prince St (10012). 212/966-6722. www.zoerest.com.* Contemporary American menu. Hrs: noon-3 pm, 6-10:30 pm; Mon from 6 pm; Fri to 11 pm; Sat 5:30-11:30 pm; Sun 5:30-10 pm; Sat brunch noon-3 pm, Sun 11:30 am-3 pm. Closed July 4, Dec 25. Res accepted. Bar. Wine list. A la carte entrees: lunch $9.50-$14, dinner $16-$25. Sat, Sun brunch $9.50-$14. Eclectic decor. Totally nonsmoking. Cr cds: A, C, D, DS, MC, V.
D

Unrated Dining Spots

2ND AVENUE DELI. *156 2nd Ave (10003).* 212/677-0606. *www. 2ndavedeli.com.* Kosher menu. Specialties: pastrami, corned beef, chopped liver. Hrs: 8 am-midnight; Fri, Sat to 2 am. Closed Jewish hols. Bkfst, lunch, dinner $7.95-$15. Complete meals: dinner $13.40-$20.45. Kosher deli; full menu served all day. Family-owned. Cr cds: A, C, D, DS, MC, V.
D

CARNEGIE DELI. *854 7th Ave (10019).* 212/757-2245. *www.carnegie deli.com.* Kosher deli menu. Specializes in sandwiches, corned beef, cheesecake. Hrs: 6:30-3:45 am. Bkfst $5-$7, lunch $7-$12, dinner $8-$15. Traditional Jewish-style New York deli.
D

CUCINA & CO. *30 Rockefeller Center - Concourse Level (10112).* 212/332-7630. *www.restaurantassociates.com.* Specializes in hot and cold pasta, desserts. Hrs: 7 am-6 pm. Closed Sun May-Nov. Wine, beer. A la carte entrees: bkfst $2.50-$3.95, lunch $5-$13. Outdoor garden dining. Afternoon tea after 3 pm. Bistro atmosphere. Cr cds: A, C, MC, V.
D

ELEPHANT AND CASTLE. *68 Greenwich Ave (10011).* 212/243-1400. Specializes in salads, hamburgers, Indian puddings. Daily specials. Hrs: 8:30 am-midnight; Sat, Sun from 10 am. Wine, beer, setups. A la carte entrees: bkfst $2.75-$7, lunch, dinner $2.75-$11.50. Totally nonsmoking. Cr cds: A, D, MC, V.

EMPIRE DINER. *210 10th Ave (10011).* 212/243-2736. Specializes in sandwiches, omelettes, meatloaf. Own muffins, scones. Open 24 hrs; Sun brunch noon-4 pm. Bar. A la carte entrees: bkfst $1.50-$8.50, lunch, dinner $4.25-$14.95. Sun brunch $9.50. Pianist. Outdoor dining. Authentic chrome and stainless steel Art Deco diner. Cr cds: A, DS, MC, V.
D

FLORENT. *69 Gansevoort St (10014).* 212/989-5779. *www.restaurantflorent. com.* French, American menu. Specialties: mussels, own french fries,
fresh fish. Open 24 hrs. Closed Dec 25. Res accepted. Bar. A la carte entrees: bkfst $3.95-$10.50, lunch $3.95-$13.95, dinner $9.50-$17.95. Chrome- and aluminum-trimmed diner attached to meat market in warehouse area of the Village.
D

HARLEY-DAVIDSON CAFE. *1370 Ave of the Americas (10019).* 212/245-6000. *www.harley-davidsoncafe.com.* Specializes in seafood, barbecue chicken, Harley Hog sandwiches. Hrs: 11:30 am-midnight; Fri, Sat to 1 am. Lunch, dinner $7.50-$19.95. Child's menu. Outdoor dining on wrap-around terrace. Extensive Harley-Davidson motorcycle memorabilia; multimedia displays. Cr cds: A, DS, MC, V.
D

JACKSON HOLE. *1611 2nd Ave (10028).* 212/737-8788. Specializes in sandwiches, hamburgers. Hrs: 10-1 am; Fri, Sat to 4 am; Sat, Sun brunch 10:30 am-3 pm. Closed Thanksgiving, Dec 25. Bar. A la carte entrees: bkfst $4-$6, lunch, dinner $6-$10. Outdoor dining. Chrome and stainless steel Art Deco diner; jukebox. Cr cds: A, MC, V.
D

PANEVINO. *132 W 65th St (10023).* 212/874-7000. Italian menu at Panevino Ristorante; Viennese dessert and coffee menu at Café Vienna. Hrs: Panevino Ristorante 11:30 am-8 pm; Café Vienna 11:30 am-11 pm. Bar. A la carte entrees at Panevino: lunch $10-$14, dinner $13-$21. A la carte desserts at Café Vienna: $5-$7. Outdoor dining. Café is authentic Viennese coffee house. Both establishments overlook Lincoln Center plaza. Cr cds: A, D, DS, MC, V.
D SC

REPUBLIC. *37 Union Sq W (10003).* 212/627-7172. Asian menu. Specialties: salmon sashimi salad, fried wontons. Hrs: noon-midnight. Closed Memorial Day, Dec 25. Bar. Lunch, dinner $6-$9. Former warehouse converted to noodle shop. Totally nonsmoking. Cr cds: A, D, DS, MC, V.
D

THE ROTUNDA. *2 E 61st St (10021). 212/940-8195. www.fourseasons.com.* Hrs: 8 am-midnight, tea 3-5:30 pm. A la carte entrees: bkfst, lunch $6.50-$32. Prix fixe: tea $26. Beaux Arts architecture with marble columns and pilasters. Murals by Edward Melcarth. Cr cds: A, C, MC, V.

SERENDIPITY 3. *225 E 60th St (10022). 212/838-3531. www. serendipity3.com.* Specializes in burgers. Hrs: 11:30-12:30 am; Fri to 1 am; Sat to 2 am; Sun to midnight. Closed Dec 25. Res accepted. A la carte entrees: lunch, dinner $4.50-$15. Art Nouveau decor; Tiffany lamps; marbletop tables. Famous for ice cream specialties, pies, chocolate blackout cake. Enter restaurant through gift shop. Favorite of celebrities. Family-owned. Cr cds: A, D, DS, MC, V.

STAGE DELI. *834 7th Ave (10019). 212/245-7850. www.stagedeli.com.* Kosher deli menu. Specialties: corned beef, pastrami, brisket. Hrs: 6-2 am. Bar. A la carte entrees: bkfst $2.95-$7.50, lunch $4.50-$13.95, dinner $5.50-$20. Deli counter. Well-known New York deli; pickles own meats. Enclosed sidewalk dining. Celebrity photos. Cr cds: A, MC, V.

Bronx (X-0)

Area code 718
Information Chamber of Commerce, 2885 Schley Ave, 10465; 718/829-4111

Jonas Bronck, a Swedish settler, bought 500 acres of land from the Dutch in 1639, lending his name to the future borough. Locally it is always referred to as "the Bronx," never simply "Bronx." It is the only borough in New York City on the North American continent (the others are all on islands).

What to See and Do

Bronx Museum of the Arts. Changing exhibits with a focus on contemporary art and current cultural subjects pertaining to the Bronx. Concerts, family workshops, and special events. (Wed-Fri, also Sat and Sun afternoons) Free admission Wed. 1040 Grand Concourse, at 165th St. Phone 718/681-6000. ¢¢

Bronx Zoo. The largest metropolitan wildlife park in the US. Collection incl rare and exotic animals living in simulated naturalistic habitats. "JungleWorld" re-creates a Southeast Asian rain forest, mangrove swamp, and scrub forest on a grand scale. "Wild Asia," a 40-acre habitat for Asian animals, offers a new concept in zoo land use. "Bengali Express" monorail carries visitors on a 20-min trip to view Siberian tigers, elephants, and other Asian wildlife. "Zoo Center" provides yr-round home for Asian elephants and Malayan tapirs. "Himalayan Highlands" features remote Asian mountaintops with snow leopards, red pandas, and other native animals. "World of Darkness" is the home of nocturnal animals. "World of Birds" exhibits many species in varied natural habitats; walk-through aviary. "Big Birds" features ostriches, emus, and cassowaries. South American Sea Bird Colony. Baboon Reserve with Ethiopian mountain range. Children's Zoo (Apr-Oct, daily) allows active participation. Zoo shuttle train starts near Zoo Center (Apr-Oct, daily). Aerial Skyfari ride (Apr-Oct, daily). Bengali Express (May-Oct, daily). Picnic tables, restaurants. (Daily) Fordham Rd and Bronx River Pkwy. Phone 718/367-1010. ¢¢¢

City Island. Referred to as "a bit of New England in the city," City Island is devoted to shipping and ship building. Seafood restaurants; City Island Historical Nautical Museum (Sun). E of Hutchinson River Pkwy, through Pelham Bay Park, via City Island Bridge. Phone 718/829-4111. and

> **North Wind Undersea Museum.** (Daily) 610 City Island Ave. Phone 718/885-0701.

Edgar Allan Poe Cottage. (1812) Poe wrote "Annabel Lee," "The Bells," and "Ulalume" while living here (1846-1849). Period furniture; exhibits about the poet and his wife.

Films, tours (Sat and Sun). Located at Grand Concourse and E Kingsbridge Rd. Phone 718/881-8900. ¢¢

Fordham University. (1841) 15,000 students. All four original Gothic structures of the Rose Hill campus are designated landmarks: University Chapel (St. John's Church), St. John's Residence Hall, Administration Building, and Alumni House. A second campus is at 60th and Columbus Ave, across from the Lincoln Center for the Performing Arts (see MANHATTAN). Fordham Rd, in North Bronx. Phone 718/817-4000.

The Hall of Fame for Great Americans. A 630-ft, open-air colonnade provides framework for bronze busts of great Americans; exhibits. Hall of Fame Terrace, on campus of Bronx Community College, W 181st St between Sedgewick and University aves. Phone 718/289-5161. **FREE**

Museum of Bronx History. Valentine-Varian House (1758), site of Revolutionary War activities; exhibits on Bronx history. (Sat and Sun) 3266 Bainbridge Ave, at E 208th St. Phone 718/881-8900. ¢¢

The New York Botanical Garden. One of the largest and oldest in the country, this botanical garden consists of 250 acres of natural terrain, 48 gardens. Garden also has the last 40 acres of the forest that once covered New York City. Enid A. Haupt Conservatory has 11 distinct plant environments with changing exhibits and permanent displays incl the Fern Forest, Palm Court, and Desert Houses. Tours. Education courses. (Tues-Sun) Bronx Park, entrance on Southern Blvd, S of Moshulu Pkwy. Phone 718/817-8700. Parking ¢¢ Grounds ¢¢ Conservatory ¢¢

Pelham Bay Park. The city's largest park (2,764 acres) has Orchard Beach, 13 mi of shoreline, fishing; two golf courses (18-hole), wildlife refuge, environmental center, nature trail, visitor center, tennis courts, ball fields, running track, riding stables and bridle paths, picnicking, Hutchinson River and Hutchinson River Pkwy (W); the city's northern limits; Pelham Pkwy, Burr Ave, Bruckner Expy and Watt Ave (S); and Eastchester Bay and Long Island Sound (E) at NE corner of Bronx. Phone 718/430-1832. Also here near southern boundary is

> **Bartow-Pell Mansion Museum and Gardens.** Greek Revival stone mansion (ca 1840) furnished in the Empire period; gardens (Tues-Sun, seasonal) carriage house. (Wed, Sat, and Sun afternoons) Guided tours

Bronx Zoo

Yankee Stadium

and luncheon tours (by appt). 895 Shore Rd N, in Pelham Bay Park. Phone 718/885-1461. ¢¢

Van Cortlandt House Museum. (1748) Georgian house is furnished in 18th-century Dutch-English manner. (Tues-Sun) In Van Cortlandt Park, Broadway at 246th St. Phone 718/543-3344. ¢¢

Wave Hill. Hudson River estate that was, at various times, home to such notables as Mark Twain and Arturo Toscanini; now a public garden and cultural center featuring Wave Hill House (1843), gardens, four greenhouses, nature trails, woods, and meadows; grounds consist of 28 acres overlooking the Hudson. Special events incl concerts, dance programs, art exhibits, and education and nature workshops. (Tues-Sun; closed Jan 1, Dec 25) Free admission Tues, also Sat mornings. 249th St and Independence Ave. Phone 718/549-3200. ¢¢

Yankee Stadium. Home of the New York Yankees. 161st St and River Ave. Phone 718/293-4300.

Motel/Motor Lodge

★★ **LE REFUGE INN.** *620 City Island Ave (10464). 718/885-2478; fax 718/885-1519.* 8 rms, 4 share baths, 3 story, 2 suites, 1 cottage. Rm phones in suites, cottage. S $65; D $85; each addl $15; suites $140; cottage $175. TV; cable. Playground. Complimentary continental bkfst; afternoon refreshments. Dining rm 6-9 pm. Ck-out, ck-in by arrangement. Luggage handling. Picnic tables. Victorian house (1880) with individually decorated rms featuring many antiques. On Long Island Sound with views of Manhattan. Totally nonsmoking. Cr cds: A.

Restaurants

★★ **EMILIA'S.** *2331 Arthur Ave (10458). 718/367-5915. www. arthurave.com.* Italian menu. Specialties: fettuccine marinara, eggplant parmigiana, chicken Daniella with mushrooms. Hrs: noon-10 pm. Closed Mon, Tues; Thanksgiving, Dec 25. Res accepted. Bar. Lunch $9.95-$16.95, dinner $9.95-$25. Family-style restaurant. Cr cds: A, D, DS, MC, V.

★★ **LOBSTER BOX.** *34 City Island Ave (10464). 718/885-1952.* Specializes in lobster, shrimp, fresh fish. Hrs: noon-11 pm; Fri, Sat to 1 am. Closed Jan, Feb. Bar. Lunch $9.95-$15.95, dinner $14.95-$30.95. Valet parking. Terrace dining overlooks L.I. Sound. Family-owned. Cr cds: A, D, DS, MC, V.

★★ **MARIO'S.** *2342 Arthur Ave (10458).* *718/584-1188.* Italian menu. Specializes in pasta, veal, seafood. Hrs: noon-11 pm; Fri, Sat to 11:30 pm. Closed Mon; Dec 25; also first wk Jan, last 2 wks Aug, first wk Sept. Res accepted. Lunch, dinner $13-$28. Valet parking. Family-owned. Cr cds: A, C, D, DS, MC, V.

★★ **SEA SHORE.** *591 City Island Ave (10464).* *718/885-0300.* Specializes in fresh seafood, jumbo lobster. Hrs: 11 am-midnight; Fri, Sat to 2 am. Res accepted. Bar. A la carte entrees: lunch $9.95-$18.95, dinner $16.95-$38.95. Child's menu. Valet parking. Outdoor dining. Greenhouse dining rm and dock area overlooking L.I. Sound; marina. Family-owned. Cr cds: A, C, D, DS, MC, V.

Brooklyn

Area code 718

Information Brooklyn Historical Society, 128 Pierrepont St, 11201, phone 718/254-9830; or the NYC Convention & Visitors Bureau

Many of the novels, plays, films, and television shows about New York City—ranging from *Death of a Salesman* to *The Honeymooners*—are set in Brooklyn rather than Manhattan, perhaps because of widely differing characters of these two boroughs. While Manhattan is world-class in sophistication and influence, Brooklyn, famous for such things as the hot dogs on Coney Island, is and always has been quintessentially American.

Yet there is much more to Brooklyn than the popular stereotype. Manhattanites flock to performances at the renowned Brooklyn Academy of Music, and the Egyptology collection at the Brooklyn Museum com-

pares with those in London and Cairo. Brooklyn's beautiful Prospect Park was designed by Olmsted and Vaux, who considered it more beautiful than another park they designed—Central Park in Manhattan.

The most heavily populated borough, Brooklyn handles about 40 percent of New York City's vast shipping. Brooklyn was pieced together from 25 independent villages and fought valiantly before allowing itself to be taken into New York City in 1898.

What to See and Do

Brooklyn Academy of Music. (1907) Founded in 1859, BAM is the oldest performing arts center in America, presenting original productions in contemporary performing arts in the Next Wave Festival each fall, noted national and international theater, dance, and opera companies, and classical and contemporary music programs. 30 Lafayette Ave, Fort Greene/Clinton Hill.

Brooklyn Children's Museum. Founded in 1899, this is the world's oldest children's museum. Interactive exhibits, workshops, and special events. "The Mystery of Things" teaches children about cultural and scientific objects. "Music Mix" welcomes young virtuosos. Many other hands-on exhibits. (Wed-Fri afternoons; also school hols) 145 Brooklyn Ave, at St. Marks Ave. Phone 718/735-4400. ¢¢

Brooklyn Heights. This 50-blk historic district where Brooklyn started has a wealth of Victorian architecture and beautiful streets. Henry Ward Beecher preached at the **Plymouth Church of the Pilgrims** (Orange St between Hicks and Henry sts), a stop on the Underground Railroad during the Civil War. The **Esplanade** along the East River offers spectacular views of the Brooklyn Bridge, lower Manhattan, and the Statue of Liberty. Centering around Borough Hall, Cadman Plaza.

Brooklyn's History Museum. Headquarters of the Brooklyn Historical Society since 1881. Permanent and changing exhibits deal with Brooklyn history. Displays cover Coney Island, Brooklyn Dodgers, Brooklyn Bridge, Brooklyn Navy Yard; original set of "The Honeymooners" TV show; baseball cards; wax figures. Two-tiered library. (Tues-Sat; closed hols) 128 Pierrepont St. Phone 718/624-0890. ¢¢

Coney Island. Originally a quiet resort community for wealthy New Yorkers, Coney Island was at one time so uncrowded that its dunes were used to represent the Sahara in Valentino's *The Sheik*. Now this three-mi sand bar on the Atlantic Ocean is probably the best-known beach, boardwalk, and amusement park in the country, with four roller coasters, a Wonder Wheel, and many other amusements (fee for each). It is known for its amusement park food, especially the hot dogs at Nathan's Famous (Surf and Stillwell). Coney Island is easily reached from any part of the city by any of four subway lines. Swimming is good, but very crowded on pleasant days. (Easter Sun-second wkend Sept, daily) Surf Ave from Ocean Pkwy to 37th St. Phone 718/266-1234. **FREE** Also in the area are

Astroland Amusement Park. Theme park featuring such rides as Astrotower, Water Flume, and the famous Cyclone roller coaster; has

been in operation since 1927. (Mid-June-Labor Day, daily; Easter-mid-June, wkends) General admission free. Individual ride tickets avail. 1000 Surf Ave, at W 10th St, Coney Island. Phone 718/265-2100. Major ride ticket ¢¢¢¢

New York Aquarium. "Sea Cliffs" exhibit; also varied collection of marine life incl seals, sharks, beluga whales, invertebrates, penguins, sea otters, walrus; dolphin feedings (Apr-Oct, outdoors). Restaurant. (Daily) Parking (fee). Boardwalk and W 8th St, Coney Island. ¢¢

Sheepshead Bay. This area has all the requisites of an ocean fishing community: seafood restaurants, clam bars, tackle shops, fishing boats, and some lovely views. Just E and slightly N of Coney Island via Ocean Pkwy or Shore Pkwy. Phone 718/627-6611.

Gateway National Recreation Area. One of the nation's first two urban national parks. A barrier peninsula across Rockaway Inlet from Coney Island via Flatbush Ave and the Marine Pkwy Bridge. This sprawling, urban recreation area consists of

Coney Island

BROOKLYN HEIGHTS

Brooklyn Heights and Atlantic Avenue provide a wonderful combination of historic Brooklyn (dating to when it was an independent city), fantastic Manhattan skyline views, and some of New York City's best ethnic food and shops.

The best start is to walk from Manhattan over the Brooklyn Bridge—about a 20-minute journey. Started in 1869 and completed in 1883, it was (at that time) the longest suspension bridge in the world (1,600 feet). It is now the oldest existing suspension bridge in America.

Coming off the bridge, follow the right-hand sidewalks onto Adams Street and Cadman Plaza. Walk the length of the Plaza onto Court Street to Brooklyn Borough Hall, a remarkable beaux arts building circa 1848. Free tours are offered on Tuesdays at 1 pm. Leave Borough Hall, walking back the way you came, and turn left onto Montague Street. This neighborhood was Manhattan's first "suburb." Montague is the neighborhood's main street, and it holds a potpourri of restaurants, businesses, and shops. At Clinton Street stands St. Ann's Church. The building contains 60 stained-glass windows, the first ever produced in the United States. Follow Clinton one block to Pierrepont Street, turn left, and stop in at the Brooklyn Historical Society (28 Pierrepont). This landmark building houses exhibits on the borough's past, as well as venues for performances and art exhibits.

At the end of Montague walk up onto the Promenade, the tour's highlight. It stretches north for about six blocks and offers fabulous Manhattan views. Exit the Promenade at Pineapple Street. Turn left onto Columbia Heights and walk to Fulton Landing at its end, once a ferry terminal and now the site of Barge Music, classical concerts staged on a barge moored in the river. Turn right onto Old Fulton Street. At 19 Fulton Street, right under the Brooklyn Bridge, is Patsy Grimaldi's, a.k.a. Patsy's Pizza, a family operation that serves what many have called the city's best pizza.

Continue on Old Fulton, which becomes Cadman Plaza West, and turn right on Henry Street. At this point, feel free to wander among the grid of streets—Clinton, Henry, Hicks, Willow, Cranberry, Orange, and Pineapple—to take in the townhouses and wood-framed buildings. More than half of Brooklyn Heights' structures predate the Civil War. On Henry Street, note the St. George Hotel (100 Henry Street), a landmark built in 1884. Henry runs some 11 bocks before it intersects Atlantic Avenue. Turn left on Atlantic and enter a frenetic and fascinating world of Middle Eastern stores and restaurants. Be sure to visit: Sahadi (187 Atlantic) for a huge choice of fruits, nuts, candies, olives, feta cheese, and grains by the pound; La Bouillabaisse (145 Atlantic) for great seafood; the Moroccan Star (205 Atlantic) for fine Middle Eastern fare; the Waterfront Ale House (155 Atlantic) for microbrew; and, for desert, either the Damascus Bakery (195 Atlantic)—fantastic pita bread and spinach pies and baklava—or Pete's Ice Cream (185 Atlantic), a shop with superb homemade ice cream and baked goods. For one last place to visit, turn left on Boerum Place and walk two blocks to Schermerhorn Street to the Transit Museum, which explores the city's subway and mass-transit system.

approximately 26,000 acres of land and water in two states—New York and New Jersey: Floyd Bennett Field in Brooklyn (Jamaica Bay in Brooklyn and Queens), Breezy Point on the Rockaway Peninsula in Queens, Miller Field, and Great Kills Park on southeastern Staten Island and the Sandy Hook Unit in New Jersey (see). Jamaica Bay Wildlife Refuge in Broad Channel, Queens (9,000 acres) offers wildlife observation and hiking trails. Floyd Bennett Field has nature observation opportunities. Jacob Riis Park in Queens, with a mi-long boardwalk, offers beach and waterfront activities. Fort Tilden in Queens offers exhibits, nature walks, guided and self-guided tours of old defense batteries, sporting events, and fish-

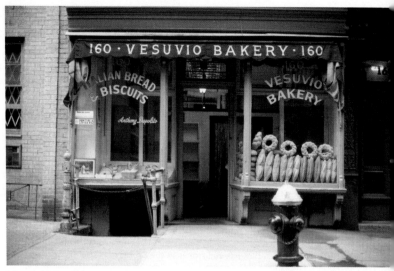

Mangia! Mangia!

ing. Canarsie Pier in Brooklyn offers free wkend summer concerts and restaurants. The Staten Island Unit offers hiking trails, organized athletic programs, and recreational activities. Concession services at some units. Contact Public Affairs Office, Floyd Bennett Field, Building 69, Brooklyn 11234. Phone 718/338-3338.

New York Transit Museum. Exhibits on the history of the New York City transit system displayed within a 1930s subway station. Subway cars on display, incl a 1903 "El" car. Photographs, maps, antique turnstiles. (Tues-Sun; closed hols) Boerum Pl and Schermerhorn St. Phone 718/243-8601. ¢¢

Prospect Park. Planned by Olmsted and Vaux, designers of Central Park, its 526 acres incl the impressive Grand Army Plaza with Memorial Arch (N end of park), the 90-acre Long Meadow, and a 60-acre lake. Boathouse Visitor Center has information on park history and design; art shows (Apr-Nov). Ball fields, boating, ice rink, bridle paths, tennis courts, bandshell, historic carousel, and the Lefferts Homestead, a 1783 Dutch Colonial farmhouse. Bounded by Parkside Ave, Ocean Ave, Flatbush Ave, and Prospect Park W and SW. Phone 718/438-0100 or 718/965-8951. Directly across Flatbush Ave is

Brooklyn Botanic Garden. More than 50 acres with a conservatory complex; fragrance garden for the visually impaired; Japanese Hill and Pond Garden (Tues-Sun); Cranford Rose Garden. One-hr guided tour (Sat and Sun, one departure each day; no tours hols). Steinhardt Conservatory with tropical, temperate, and desert pavilions and the C. V. Star Bonsai Museum. (Tues-Sun; also hols) Children under 16 admitted only with adult. Free admission Tues. Eastern Pkwy, Washington and Flatbush aves, opp Prospect Park. Phone 718/623-7200. ¢¢ Nearby is

Brooklyn Museum of Art. Outstanding collection of art from Egypt; Pacific Islands; North, South, and Central America; the Orient; and Middle East; painting, sculpture, prints, drawings; American and European decorative arts and furnished period rms; costumes, textiles; changing exhibits. Sculpture garden with architectural ornaments from buildings demolished in New York City area. Concerts, gallery talks, lectures, films. Cafeteria; gift shops. (Wed-Sun; closed Jan 1, Thanksgiving, Dec 25) 200 Eastern Pkwy. Phone 718/638-5000. ¢¢¢

Sightseeing tour. Discovery Tour of Brooklyn. Bus tour (six hrs) to many of Brooklyn's sites and neighborhoods. (May-Oct, Thurs and Sat) Departs from Gray Line Bus Terminal in Manhattan. Phone 212/397-2600. ¢¢¢¢

Hotel

★★★ **MARRIOTT BROOKLYN NEW YORK.** *333 Adams St (11201). 718/565-8900. www.marriott.com.* 376 rms, 7 story. S, D $275-$325; suites $275-$450; under 18 free; wkend rates. Crib free. TV; cable (premium), VCR avail. Coffee in rms. Restaurants 6:30 am-midnight. Bar 11 am-midnight. Ck-out noon. Valet serv. Meeting rms. Business center. In-rm modem link. Concierge. Gift shop. Exercise equipt. Refrigerators avail. Cr cds: A, D, DS, MC, V.

Restaurants

★★ **CUCINA.** *254 5th Ave (11215). 718/230-0711. www.cucinarestaurant. com.* Italian menu. Specialties: roast rack of lamb, osso buco and pappardelle. Antipasto bar. Hrs: 5:30-10:30 pm; Fri, Sat to 11 pm; Sun 5-10 pm. Closed Mon, Thanksgiving, Dec 25. Res accepted. Bar. A la carte entrees: dinner $10-$25. Child's menu. Two dining rms; goldleaf wall montage by New York artist. Cr cds: A, D, DS, MC, V.

[D]

★★ **EMBERS.** *9519 3rd Ave (11209). 718/745-3700.* Specializes in pasta, T-bone steak. Hrs: noon-2:45 pm, 5-10:30 pm; Fri to 11:30 pm; Sat noon-1:45 pm, 4:30-11:30 pm; Sun 2-9:30 pm. Closed Thanksgiving, Dec 24, 25. Bar. A la carte entrees: lunch $4.50-$7.95, dinner $10.95-$16.95. Adj to meat market. Cr cds: MC, V.

[D]

★★ **GIANDO ON THE WATER.** *400 Kent Ave (11211). 718/387-7000.* Italian menu. Specializes in seafood, fish. Hrs: noon-11 pm; Sat from 4 pm; Sun 3-9 pm; early-bird dinner 5-7 pm, Sat 4-6 pm, Sun 3-6 pm. Res accepted. Bar. Prix fixe: lunch $19.95, dinner $29.95. A la carte entrees: dinner $12-$27. Pianist Fri, Sat. Valet parking. On East River overlooking Williamsburg and Brooklyn bridges, Manhattan skyline from Empire State

Park Slopes, Brooklyn

Unisphere at Flushing Meadows-Corona Park

Bldg to Statue of Liberty. Cr cds: A, C, D, MC, V.

D

★★ **GREENHOUSE CAFE.** *7717 3rd Ave (11209). 718/833-8200. www. greenhousecafe.com.* Specialties: roast Long Island duckling, seafood festival platter. Hrs: 11:30 am-11 pm; Fri, Sat to midnight; Sun 4-10 pm; Sun brunch noon-3 pm. Closed Dec 25. Res accepted. Bar. A la carte entrees: lunch $5.25-$13. Dinner $10.95-$17.95. Child's menu. Garden atrium. Cr cds: A, DS, MC, V.

D

★★★ **PETER LUGER STEAK HOUSE.** *178 Broadway (11211). 718/387-7400. www.peterluger.com.* Specializes in steak, lamb chops. Hrs: 11:30 am-9:45 pm; Fri, Sat to 10:45 pm; Sun 1-9:45 pm. Res accepted. Bar. Lunch $12.95. A la carte entrees: dinner $28.95-$60.

★★ **PONTE VECCHIO.** *8810 4th Ave (11209). 718/238-6449.* Italian menu. Specializes in pasta, veal, seafood. Hrs: noon-10:30 pm; Fri, Sat to 11:30 pm. Closed July 4, Thanksgiving, Dec 25. Res accepted. Serv bar. A la carte entrees: lunch $14-$22, dinner $27-$32. Valet parking. Cr cds: A, D, MC, V.

★★★ **RIVER CAFE.** *1 Water St (11201). 718/522-5200. www.rivercafe.*

com. Specializes in lamb. Own chocolate desserts. Own baking. Hrs: noon-2:30 pm, 6-11:30 pm; Sun brunch 11:30 am-2:30 pm. Res required. A la carte entrees: lunch $20-$26. Prix fixe: dinner $68, tasting menu $85. Sun brunch $13-$26. Pianist. Valet parking. Jacket. Cr cds: A, D, MC, V.

D

★★ **TOMMASO.** *1464 86th St (11228). 718/236-9883. tommasosrest@ aol.com.* Italian menu. Specializes in regional Italian dishes. Hrs: 4-11 pm; Sat to midnight; Sun 1-10 pm. Closed Dec 25. Res accepted. Bar. A la carte entrees: dinner $8-$20. Opera Thurs-Sun eves. Family-owned. Cr cds: A, C, D, DS, MC, V.

D

Queens (La Guardia & JFK International Airport Areas)

Area code 718

By far the largest borough geographically, Queens occupies 121 square miles of Long Island. Like Brooklyn, it was assembled from a number of small towns, and each of these neighborhoods has retained a strong sense of identity. Parts of the borough are less densely settled than Brooklyn, and the majority of Queens's population are homeowners. Many manufacturing plants, warehouses, and shipping facilities are in the portion called Long Island City, near the East River. Forest Hills, with its West Side Tennis Club, at Tennis Place and Burns Street, is a world-famous center for tennis. Flushing Meadows Corona Park has been the site of two world's fairs; many facilities still stand.

Services and Information

Information. *At La Guardia:* information 718/476-5000; lost and found 718/533-3988; cash machines, upper level Main Terminal, Finger 4, Delta Terminal. At Kennedy: information 718/656-4444; lost and found 718/244-4225.

Airlines. *At La Guardia:* Air Canada, America West, American, Canadian Arlns International, Carnival Arlns, Colgan Air, Continental, Delta, Midway Arlns, Midwest Express, Northwest, TWA, United, USAir. At Kennedy International: Aer Lingus, Aeroflot, Aerolineas Argentinas, Aeromexico, Aeroperu, Air Afrique, Air China, Air Europa, Air France, Air India, Air Jamaica, Air South, Air Ukraine, Alitalia, All Nipon, America West, American, Asiana Arlns, Austrian, Avianca, Balkan-Bulgarian, Biman Bangladesh, British Airways, BWIA, Canadian Arlns Intl, Carnival, Cathay Pacific, China Arlns, Delta, Ecuatoriana, Egyptair, El Al, Eva Airways, Finnair, Ghana Airways, Gulf Air, Guyana Airways, Iberia, Icelandair, Japan Arlns, KLM, Korean Air, Kuwait Airways, LASCA, LAN Chile, Lufthansa, Malev, Northwest, Olympic, Pan Am Air Bridge, Qantas, Royal Air Maroc, Royal Jordanian, Servivensa, Singapore Arlns, South African Airways, Swissair, Air Portugal, Tarom, Transbrasil, Turkish Arlns, TWA, United, USAir, Uzbekistan Arlns, Varig, VASP, Virgin Atlantic.

Transportation

Car Rental Agencies. See IMPORTANT TOLL-FREE NUMBERS.

Public Transportation. Subway and elevated trains, buses (New York Transit Authority), phone 718/330-3322 or 718/330-1234.

Rail Passenger Service. Amtrak 800/872-7245.

What to See and Do

American Museum of the Moving Image. On site of historic Astoria Studios, where many classic early movies were filmed. Museum devoted to art and history of film, television, and video and their effects on American culture. Permanent and changing exhibitions; two theaters with film and video series (screenings wkends). (Tues-Sun; closed hols). 35th Ave at 36th St, in Astoria. Phone 718/784-0077. ¢¢¢

Bowne House. (1661) One of the oldest houses in New York City was built by John Bowne, a Quaker who led a historic struggle for religious freedom under Dutch rule; 17th-19th-century furnishings. (Tues, Sat, and Sun afternoons; closed Easter and mid-Dec-mid-Jan) Under 12 admitted only with adult. 37-01 Bowne St. Phone 718/359-0528. ¢

Flushing Meadow Corona Park. Originally a marsh, this 1,255-acre area became the site of two world's fairs (1939-1940 and 1964-1965). It is now the home of the United States Tennis Association National Tennis Center, where the US Open is held annually. (Phone 718/760-6200). The park is also the site of some of the largest cultural and ethnic festivals in the city. Facilities incl an indoor ice rink, carousel, 87-acre Meadow Lake, and the Playground for All Children, designed for disabled and able-bodied children. Grand Central Pkwy to Van Wyck Expy and Union Tpke to Northern Blvd. Park rangers conduct occasional wkend tours. Phone 718/217-6034. Also on the grounds are

New York Hall of Science. Exhibition hall with hands-on science and technology exhibits. (Daily) Free admission Thurs and Fri afternoons. 111th St and 48th Ave. Phone 718/699-0005. ¢¢¢

The Queens Museum of Art. Interdisciplinary fine arts presentations, major traveling exhibitions; permanent collection incl 9,000-square-ft panorama of New York City, the world's largest three-dimensional architectural model. (Tues-Fri, also Sat and Sun afternoons; closed Jan 1, Thanksgiving, Dec 25) New York City Building. Phone 718/592-9700. ¢¢

Shea Stadium. Home of the New York Mets. 126th St and Roosevelt Ave. Phone 718/507-6387. ¢¢¢¢

Isamu Naguchi Sculpture Museum. Former studio space of Japanese sculptor Isamu Naguchi now holds 12 galleries filled with his stonework and stage set designs. A small but evocative sculpture garden adjoins the museum. (Apr-Oct, Wed-Sun) 32-37 Vernon Blvd, entrance on 33rd Rd. Phone 718/721-1932.

John F. Kennedy International Airport. The airport's 4,930 acres cover an area roughly one-third the size of Manhattan. Much of the air traffic going overseas is handled through here. (See AIRPORT INFORMATION) Van Wyck Expy, S of Southern Pkwy.

La Guardia Airport. Located at Grand Central Pkwy and 94th St. (See AIRPORT INFORMATION) Phone 718/565-5100.

Queens Botanical Garden. Collections incl large rose, herb, Victorian wedding, bee, woodland, and bird gardens; arboretum. (Tues-Sun) 43-50 Main St. Phone 718/886-3800.

Donation

Thoroughbred horse racing. Near Cross Bay Blvd just off Belt Pkwy. IND Subway, Rockaway Beach train.

   Aqueduct. Thoroughbred racing. Equestris dining complex (proper dress required; children admitted only with parent or guardian). Phone 718/641-4700. Jan-May and Oct-Dec. Near Cross Bay Blvd just off Belt Pkwy. IND Subway, Rockaway Beach train.

   Belmont Park. Thoroughbred racing. Home of the Belmont Stakes, the third leg of racing's Triple Crown. Reserved seats. Terrace dining complex (proper dress required); children admitted only with parent or guardian. Phone

516/488-6000. Mid-May-late July. Just outside of Queens in Nassau County, on Cross Island Pkwy via Hempstead Tpke and Plainfield Ave, in Elmont, L.I. Phone 888/285-5961.

Special Event

US Open Tennis. Box office phone 718/760-6200. Late Aug-early Sept.

Motels/Motor Lodges

★★ **BEST WESTERN CARLTON HOUSE JFK AIRPORT.** *138-10 135th Ave, Jamaica (11436).* 718/322-8700 ; *fax 718/529-0749; res 800/528-1234. www.bestwestern.com.* 333 rms, 9 story. S $179-$240; D $189-$250; each addl $25; suites $289-$650; under 18 free. Crib free. TV; cable (premium), VCR avail. Restaurant 6 am-11:30 pm. Bar noon-2 am. Ck-out noon. Convention facilities. Business servs avail. In-rm modem link. Free airport transportation. Exercise equipt. Luxury level. Cr cds: A, DS, MC, V.

★★★ **CROWNE PLAZA LAGUARDIA.** *104-04 Ditmars Blvd, East Elmhurst (11369).* 718/457-6300; *fax 718/899-9768; toll-free 800/692-5429. www.holiday-inn.com.* 358 rms, 200 with shower only, 7 story. S $175-$195; D $195-$205; each addl $20; suites $199-$600; under 19 free; wkly, wkend and hol rates. Crib free. Garage parking $5. TV; cable (premium), VCR (movies avail). Indoor pool; whirlpool, poolside serv. Complimentary coffee in rms. Restaurant 6 am-midnight. Bar 4 pm-2 am. Ck-out noon. Coin lndry. Convention facilities. Business center. In-rm modem link. Concierge. Gift shop. Free airport transportation. Tennis privileges. Exercise rm; sauna. Many refrigerators. Luxury level. Cr cds: A, C, D, DS, JCB, MC, V.

★★ **HOLIDAY INN JFK AIRPORT.** *14402 135th Ave, Jamaica (11436).* 718/659-0200 ; *fax 718/322-2533; toll-free 800/692-5359. www.holiday-inn.com.* 360 rms, 12 story. S, D $169-$189; each addl $15; suites from $239; under 18 free. Crib free.

TV; cable, VCR avail (movies). Indoor/outdoor pool; whirlpool, lifeguard. Restaurant 6 am-10 pm. Bar 11:30-1 am. Ck-out noon. Convention facilities. Business servs avail. Free airport transportation. Exercise equipt; sauna. Cr cds: A, C, D, DS, JCB, MC, V.

Hotels

★★★ **MARRIOTT LAGUARDIA.** *10205 Ditmars Blvd, East Elmhurst (11369). 718/565-8900; fax 718/898-4955; toll-free 800/882-1043. www. marriot.com.* 436 rms, 9 story. S $150; D $170; suites $350-$650; under 18 free; wkly rates; wkend plans. Crib free. Pet accepted. Covered parking $5. TV; cable (premium), VCR avail. Indoor pool; whirlpool, lifeguard. Restaurants 6:30 am-11 pm. Bar 11-1 am. Ck-out 1 pm. Convention facilities. Business center. In-rm modem link. Gift shop. Free airport transportation. Exercise equipt; sauna. Microwaves avail. Luxury level. Cr cds: A, C, D, DS, ER, JCB, MC, V.

★★★ **SHERATON JFK AIRPORT.** *151-20 Baisley Blvd (11434). 718/489-1000.* 184 rms, 12 story. S, D $275-$325; suites $350-$550; under 18 free; wkend rates. Crib free. TV; cable (premium), VCR avail. Coffee in rms. Restaurants 6:30 am-midnight. Bar 11 am-midnight. Ck-out noon. Valet serv. Meeting rms. Business center. In-rm modem link. Concierge. Exercise equipt. Refrigerators avail. Cr cds: A, D, DS, MC, V.

★★★ **SHERATON LAGUARDIA.** *135-20 39th Ave (11354). 718/460-6666.* 173 rms, 12 story. S, D $250-$350; suites $400-$475; under 18 free; wkend rates. Crib free. TV; cable (premium), VCR avail. Coffee in rms. Restaurants 6:30 am-midnight. Bar 11 am-midnight. Ck-out noon. Valet serv. Meeting rms. Business center. In-rm modem link. Concierge. Gift shop. Exercise equipt. Refrigerators avail. Cr cds: A, D, DS, MC, V.

Restaurants

★★ **IL TOSCANO.** *42-05 235th St, Douglaston (11363). 718/631-0300.* Italian menu. Specialties: sweetbreads sauteed with fresh thyme, green peppercorn and sherry; grilled brook trout with raspberry lemon. Hrs: 5-10 pm. Closed Sun. Res required. Bar. A la carte entrees: dinner $14-$24. Casual, trattoria atmosphere. Cr cds: A, DS, MC, V.

★★ **MANDUCATIS.** *13-27 Jackson Ave, Manhattan (11101). 718/729-4602.* Italian menu. Specialties: pappardelle Casertana, eggplant Napoletana. Hrs: noon-3 pm, 5-10 pm; Sat 5-11 pm; Sun 2-8 pm. Closed Sun July-Aug; last 2 wks in Aug; hols. Res accepted. Bar. A la carte entrees: lunch $5-$18, dinner $7-$18.50. Attractive, comfortable neighborhood restaurant. Cr cds: A, D, DS, MC, V.

★★ **MARBELLA.** *220-33 Northern Blvd (11361). 718/423-0100. www. marbella.com.* Spanish, continental menu. Specialties: paella, rack of lamb, duckling Valenciana. Hrs: noon-midnight; Sat to 1 am. Res accepted. Bar. A la carte entrees: lunch $6.95-$10.95, dinner $8.95-$17.95. Harpist Fri-Sun. Parking. Spanish artifacts. Family-owned. Cr cds: A, D, MC, V.

★★ **PARK SIDE.** *107-01 Corona Ave (11368). 718/271-9274.* Italian menu. Specializes in pasta, veal, fish. Hrs: noon-11:30 pm. Res accepted. Bar. A la carte entrees: lunch $10-$18, dinner $10-$21. Valet parking. The five dining areas incl a glass-enclosed garden rm. Cr cds: A, C, D, MC, V.

★ **PICCOLA VENEZIA.** *42-01 28th Ave (11103). 718/721-8470. www. piccola-venezia.com.* Northern Italian menu. Specializes in seafood, rack of lamb, pasta. Hrs: noon-11 pm; Sat 4:30-11:30 pm; Sun 2-10:30 pm. Closed Tues; Jan 1, Dec 25, also July 24-Aug 24. Res accepted. A la carte entrees: lunch $15-$35, dinner $15-$40. Complete meals: dinner $38.95-$46.95. Valet parking. Attractive restaurant with exposed brick walls and etched mirrors. Family-owned. Cr cds: A, C, DS, MC, V.

D ⌐↴

★★★ **PING'S SEAFOOD.** *8302 Queens Blvd (11373). 718/396-1238.* Chinese menu. Specializes in sushi, shashimi, red snapper, Dover sole. Hrs: 6-10:30 pm. Closed Sun. Res accepted. Extensive wine list. Dinner $15-$30. Chinese decor. Cr cds: A, D, DS, MC, V.

★★ **WATER'S EDGE.** *44th Dr at the East River, Long Island City (11101). 718/482-0033. www.watersedgenyc.com.* Specializes in seafood, lobster. Own baking. Hrs: noon-3 pm, 5-11 pm; Fri, Sat 5:30-11:30 pm. Closed Sun. Res required. Bar. Wine cellar. A la carte entrees: lunch $10-$16, dinner $22-$31. Pianist. Valet parking. Complimentary riverboat transportation to and from Manhattan. Outdoor dining. European decor. On riverfront opp United Nations complex; views of New York City midtown skyline. Cr cds: A, D, DS, MC, V.

D

Verrazano-Narrows Bridge

Staten Island

Area code 718

Information Staten Island Chamber of Commerce, 130 Bay St, 10301; 718/727-1900; or the NYC Convention & Visitors Bureau

Staten Island, twice the size of Manhattan with only one twenty-fourth the population, is the most removed, in distance and character, from the other boroughs. At one time, sightseers on the famous Staten Island Ferry rarely disembarked to explore the almost rural character of the island. The completion of the Verrazano Bridge to Brooklyn, however, brought growth and the beginning of a struggle between developers and those who would preserve the island's uncrowded appeal.

What to See and Do

Conference House. Built in the mid-1680s by an English sea captain, this was the site of an unproductive meeting on Sept 11, 1776, between British Admiral Lord Howe, Benjamin Franklin, John Adams, and Edward Rutledge to discuss terms of peace to end the Revolutionary War. The meeting helped to produce the phrase the "United States of America." Rose, herb gardens; open-hearth cooking; spinning and weaving demonstrations. (Apr-Nov, Fri-Sun). 7455 Hylan Blvd, in Tottenville. Phone 718/984-6046. ¢

The Greenbelt/High Rock. An 85-acre nature preserve in a 2,500-acre park. Visitor center, trails. Environmental programs, workshops. Self-guided tours. Urban park ranger-guided tours (by appt). (Daily) No picnicking or camping. 200 Nevada Ave in Egbertville, 7 mi from Verrazano Bridge via Richmond Rd. Phone 718/667-2165. **FREE**

Historic Richmond Town. Outdoor museum complex depicts three centuries of history and culture of Staten Island and surrounding region. Daily life and work of a rural community shown in trade demonstrations and tours of shops and buildings. Among the restoration's 27 historic structures are the Historic Museum; Voorlezer's House (ca 1695), the oldest surviving elementary school in the US; general store; trademen's shops. Special events and demonstrations. (Wed-Sun afternoons; extended hrs July-Aug; closed Jan 1, Thanksgiving, Dec 25) 441 Clarke Ave, Richmond and Arthur Kill rds. Phone 718/351-1611. ¢¢

Jacques Marchais Museum of Tibetan Art. Collection of Tibetan and Asian art in setting resembling Himalayan mountain temple. Terraced sculpture gardens, koi pond. (Apr-Nov, Wed-Sun afternoons; rest of yr by appt) 338 Lighthouse Ave, between New Dorp and Richmondtown. Phone 718/987-3500. ¢¢

Snug Harbor Cultural Center. Founded in 1833 as a seamen's retirement home, Snug Harbor is now a performing and visual arts center with 28 historic buildings featuring Greek Revival and Victorian architecture; art galleries (Wed-Sun, fee); children's museum (Tues-Sun afternoons); botanical garden, sculpture, 83 acres of parkland. (Daily; closed Thanksgiving, Dec 25) 1000 Richmond Terr. Phone 718/448-2500. Grounds **FREE**

Staten Island Zoo. Maintained by the Staten Island Zoological Society. Large collection of native and exotic reptiles, varied species of rattlesnakes, amphibians, marine reef fishes, mammals, birds. Children's center incl a miniature farm. (Daily; closed Jan 1, Thanksgiving, Dec 25) Free admission on Wed afternoon, inquire for hrs. Barrett Park, between Broadway and Clove Rd in W New Brighton. Phone 718/442-3100. ¢¢

NEW JERSEY

Tree-shaded 18th-century towns and historic grounds, on which Revolutionary battles were fought, make this state one of dignified beauty and democratic tradition. More than 800 lakes and ponds, 100 rivers and streams, and 1,400 miles of freshly stocked trout streams are scattered throughout its wooded, scenic northwest corner. The swampy meadows west of the New Jersey Turnpike have been reclaimed and transformed into commercial and industrial areas. The Meadowlands, a multimillion-dollar sports complex, offers horse racing, the NY Giants and the NY Jets NFL football teams, the NJ Devils NHL hockey team, and the NJ Nets NBA basketball team. The coastline, stretching 127 miles from Sandy Hook to Cape May, offers excellent swimming and ocean fishing.

Population: 8,143,412
Area: 7,504 square miles
Elevation: 0-1,803 feet
Peak: High Point Mountain (Sussex County)
Entered Union: Third of original 13 states (December 18, 1787)
Capital: Trenton
Motto: Liberty and prosperity
Nickname: Garden State
Flower: Purple Violet
Bird: Eastern Goldfinch
Tree: Red Oak
Time Zone: Eastern
Website: www.state.nj.us/travel

George Washington spent a quarter of his time here as commander-in-chief of the Revolutionary Army. On Christmas night in 1776, he crossed the Delaware and surprised the Hessians at Trenton. A few days later, he marched to Princeton and defeated three British regiments. He then spent the winter in Morristown, where the memories of his campaign are preserved in a national historical park.

New Jersey often is associated only with its factories, oil refineries, research laboratories, and industrial towns. But history buffs, hunters, anglers, scenery lovers, and amateur beachcombers need only to wander a short distance from its industrial areas to find whatever they like best.

When to Go/Climate

Moderate temperatures in spring and fall make these the best times to visit New Jersey. Summers can be hot and humid; winters can be bitterly cold, particularly in the inland mountain areas. Beaches are lovely, and coastal temperatures are often 5°F lower in summer and higher in winter than inland areas.

AVERAGE HIGH/LOW TEMPERATURES (°F)

ATLANTIC CITY

Jan 40/27	May 66/54	Sept 74/62
Feb 42/29	June 74/62	Oct 64/51
Mar 49/36	July 80/68	Nov 55/42
Apr 57/44	Aug 80/68	Dec 46/33

NEWARK

Jan 38/23	May 72/53	Sept 78/60
Feb 41/25	June 82/63	Oct 67/48
Mar 51/33	July 87/69	Nov 55/39
Apr 62/43	Aug 85/67	Dec 43/29

CALENDAR HIGHLIGHTS

APRIL

Tulip Festival (Cape May). Celebrate Dutch heritage with ethnic foods and dancing, craft show, street fair, garden and house tours. Phone 609/884-5508.

JUNE

IBM/USET Festival of Champions (Somerville). Hamilton Farm. Competition of three Olympic equestrian disciplines. Phone 908/234-0555.

JULY

Night in Venice (Ocean City). Decorated boat parade. Phone 800/BEACH-NJ.

OCTOBER

Atlantic City Marathon (Atlantic City). Phone 609/601-1RUN.

DECEMBER

Reenactment of Crossing of the Delaware (Trenton). Washington Crossing State Park. Departs PA side on the afternoon of Dec 25.

Parks and Recreation Finder

Directions to and information about the parks and recreation areas below are given under their respective town/city sections. Please refer to those sections for details.

NATIONAL PARK AND RECREATION AREAS

Key to abbreviations. I.H.S. = International Historic Site; I.P.M. = International Peace Memorial; N.B. = National Battlefield; N.B.P. = National Battlefield Park; N.B.C. = National Battlefield and Cemetery; N.C.A. = National Conservation Area; N.E.M. = National Expansion Memorial; N.F. = National Forest; N.G. = National Grassland; N.H.P. = National Historical Park; N.H.C. = National Heritage Corridor; N.H.S. = National Historic Site; N.L. = National Lakeshore; N.M. = National Monument; N.M.P. = National Military Park; N.Mem. = National Memorial; N.P. = National Park; N.Pres. = National Preserve; N.R.A. = National Recreational Area; N.R.R. = National Recreational River; N.Riv. = National River; N.S. = National Seashore; N.S.R. = National Scenic Riverway; N.S.T. = National Scenic Trail; N.Sc. = National Scientific Reserve; N.V.M. = National Volcanic Monument.

Place Name	Listed Under
Edison N.H.S.	WEST ORANGE
Gateway N.R.A. (Sandy Hook Unit)	same
Morristown N.H.P.	same

STATE PARK AND RECREATION AREAS

Key to abbreviations. I.P. = Interstate Park; S.A.P. = State Archaeological Park; S.B. = State Beach; S.C.A. = State Conservation Area; S.C.P. = State Conservation Park; S.Cp. = State Campground; S.F. = State Forest; S.G. = State Garden; S.H.A. = State Historic Area; S.H.P. = State Historic Park; S.H.S. = State Historic Site; S.M.P. = State Marine Park; S.N.A. = State Natural Area; S.P. = State Park; S.P.C. = State Public Campground; S.R. = State Reserve; S.R.A. = State Recreation Area; S.Res. = State Reservoir; S.Res.P. = State Resort Park; S.R.P. = State Rustic Park.

Place Name	Listed Under
Allaire S.P.	same
Allamuchy Mountain S.P. (Stephens Section)	HACKETTSTOWN
Barnegat Lighthouse S.P.	LONG BEACH ISLAND
Batsto S.H.S.	BATSTO
Boxwood Hall S.H.S.	ELIZABETH
Cheesequake S.P.	MATAWAN
Ferry House S.H.S.	TRENTON
Fort Mott S.P.	SALEM
Grover Cleveland Birthplace S.H.S.	CALDWELL
High Point S.P.	same
Hopatcong S.P.	LAKE HOPATCONG
Indian King Tavern Museum S.H.S.	HADDONFIELD
Island Beach S.P.	SEASIDE PARK
Liberty S.P.	JERSEY CITY
Old Dutch Parsonage S.H.S.	SOMERVILLE
Parvin S.P.	BRIDGETON
Ringwood S.P.	same
Rockingham S.H.S.	PRINCETON
Round Valley S.P.	CLINTON
Spruce Run S.R.A.	CLINTON
Stokes S.F.	BRANCHVILLE
Steuben House S.H.S.	HACKENSACK
Swartswood S.P.	BRANCHVILLE
Wallace House S.H.S.	SOMERVILLE
Walt Whitman House S.H.S.	CAMDEN
Washington Crossing S.P.	TRENTON
Wharton S.F.	BATSTO

Water-related activities, hiking, riding, various sports, picnicking, camping, and visitor centers are available in many of these areas. There is a $1/person walk-in/bicycle fee in some areas; there is a parking fee ($2-$7) in many areas. In most areas, fees are collected Memorial Day weekend-Labor Day weekend; fees collected year-round at Island Beach (see SEASIDE PARK). No pets in bathing areas, camping areas, or buildings; in other day-use areas, pets must be attended and kept on a six-foot leash.

Bathing at inland beaches, Memorial Day-Labor Day; at ocean beaches from mid-June; cabins ($20-$100); campsites ($10-$12), lean-tos ($15); reservations accepted ($7, nonrefundable). Most areas are wildlife sanctuaries. In addition, 1,700 acres of Palisades Interstate Parks (see) on the Hudson are in New Jersey. There are also more than 20 state-owned historic sites (clearly marked); some with museums and guides. For detailed information contact Division of Parks and Forestry, PO Box 404, Trenton 08625, phone 609/984-0370 or 800/843-6420.

SKI AREAS

Place Name	Listed Under
Campgaw Mountain Ski Area	RAMSEY
Mountain Creek Ski Resort	VERNON

FISHING AND HUNTING

Fishing opportunities abound in New Jersey's fresh and salt waters. No license is required for deep-sea or surf fishing along the 127-mile coastline; *however,* a license is required for taking shellfish. Nonresident clam license: $20; under age 16, $2. A license is required for freshwater fishing for everyone over 16 years of age. Nonresident fishing license: $34; nonresident trout stamp: $20; seven-day nonresident vacation fishing license: $19.50.

Hunting licenses are required for everyone over ten years of age. Firearm or bow and arrow: nonresident, $135.50 each; small game only: nonresident, two-day, $36.50; pheasant and quail stamp: $40 (for wildlife management areas only). Hunter Education Course or resident license from previous year required to purchase license. For information contact Department of Environmental Protection, Division of Fish, Game, and Wildlife, PO Box 400, Trenton 08625-0400, phone 609/292-2965.

Driving Information

Safety belts are mandatory for all persons in front seat of vehicle. Children under five years must be in an approved passenger restraint anywhere in vehicle: ages 18 months-five years may use a regulation safety belt in back seat; however, in front seat, children must use an approved safety seat; children under 18 months must use an approved safety seat anywhere in vehicle. For further information phone 609/633-9300.

INTERSTATE HIGHWAY SYSTEM

The following alphabetical listing of New Jersey towns in *Mobil Travel Guide* shows that these cities are within ten miles of the indicated Interstate highways. A highway map should be checked, however, for the nearest exit.

Highway Number	Cities/Towns within ten miles
Interstate 78	Clinton, Plainfield, Scotch Plains, Somerville, Union.
Interstate 80	Fort Lee, Hackensack, Hackettstown, Paramus, Parsippany, Rockaway, Saddle Brook, Wayne.
Interstate 95	Elizabeth, Fort Lee, Newark, Trenton, Woodbridge.

Additional Visitor Information

The State Division of Travel and Tourism, PO Box 820, Trenton 08625-0820, phone 609/292-2470 or 800/JERSEY-7, publishes a variety of materials for travelers. There are also two periodicals: *New Jersey Monthly* (write Subscription Department, Box 936, Farmingdale, NY 11737, phone 888/419-0419); *New Jersey Outdoors* (write Department of Environmental Protection & Energy, CN-402, Trenton 08625).

There are eight tourist welcome centers and numerous information centers in New Jersey. At these centers visitors will find information racks with brochures to help plan trips to points of interest. For a publication with the locations of the centers, contact the State Division of Travel and Tourism.

New Jersey Driving Tours

The Amusements of the Jersey Shore

Pennsylvania Route 40 leads to the Jersey Shore, where you'll find some of the best-known New Jersey resort towns: Atlantic City, Ocean City, and historic Cape May. People of all ages are sure to find something fun to do in Atlantic City. Children will be delighted by Lucy the Margate Elephant, a six-story elephant-shaped building. If you climb Lucy's legs to the observation area on her back, your children can add "riding an elephant" to the things they've done on their summer vacation—and they'll have a great story to share with their classmates when vacation is over! Story Land, which includes more than 50 storybook buildings, rides, animals, and a playground, will also be a hit with the little ones. A trip to the fantastic world of the Ripley's Believe It or Not! Museum may be of more interest to older children. Adults will enjoy the guided tour of Renault Winery, a visit to the Noyes Museum, and the specialty shops and restaurants of Historic Smithville. Still at a loss for entertainment? A visit to one of the recreation areas along the coast is a sure-fire way to please any family member, young or old. Or spend some time at one of the amusement piers where shopping and food provide distraction for even the hardest to please. Other noteworthy attractions include the Marine Mammal Stranding Center & Museum, which also offers dolphin- and whale-watching tours, and Edwin B. Forsythe National Wildlife Refuge. Looking for the wilder side of Atlantic City? Test your luck at one of a dozen casinos where the action never stops and fortunes are won and lost in an instant. It might be safest to stick to the slot machines....

Head south from Atlantic City to Ocean City, a popular family resort where you can enjoy swimming, fishing, and boating on eight miles of beaches. A walk on the boardwalk bordering the Jersey Shore is an absolute must. Take a ride to the top of the 140-foot-tall Ferris wheel for breathtaking views that stretch for miles. Video arcades, roller coasters, and water slides will keep the kids entertained. In fact, at Li'l Buc's Bay, adults are only admitted if they are accompanied by children—your kids are bound to get a kick out of that! Stop for a snack at one of the outdoor cafes or fill up on sweet goodies like cotton candy and ice cream. After all, you're on vacation!

Cape May, the nation's oldest seashore resort, is at the southernmost tip of New Jersey. History enthusiasts will enjoy exploring Historic Cold Spring Village, a restored 1870 South Jersey farm village with craft shops and demonstrations. Take the ferry across Delaware Bay, or explore on foot with a guided walking tour of the Historic District or a one-hour Ocean Walk tour of area beaches and marine life. As in Atlantic City and Ocean City, there are plenty of opportunities for swimming, boating, and fishing in the Atlantic or in Delaware Bay. (**Approx 125 mi**)

A NORTHERN NEW JERSEY LOOP

Begin in Fort Lee, just south of the George Washington Bridge at Fort Lee Historic Park, part of Palisades Interstate Park, off of County Route 505 (Hudson Terrace/Main Street). The park's Visitor Center and Museum focuses on the role of Fort Lee in the American Revolution. See a reconstructed 18th-century soldier hut and campsite, reconstructed gun batteries, and beautiful Manhattan views. Turn left, leaving the Historic Park. Go one block and turn left at the stop sign (Main Street). In about 50 yards, an unmarked parking lot appears on the left. Turn into it and follow the narrow roadway, Henry Hudson Drive, down toward the river. Follow this tree-covered, 25-mph lane to its end (about 25 minutes), admiring the river views. Stops can be made at one of the two marinas along the way, where walking trails can be accessed. Henry Hudson Drive ends at exit 2 of the Palisades Parkway. Take the parkway north. At exit 3, State Line Lookout is set on the highest point on the Palisades Cliffs, commanding views of the Hudson River, Westchester County, and beyond. There's hiking, a snack bar, information center, and gift shop.

Follow the Parkway into New York State and turn onto I-87/287 (NY Thruway) north. At Suffern, follow I-287 south back into New Jersey. At exit 57 (Oakland), follow Skyline Drive, which travels over Ramapo Mountain and offers some fun-to-drive, twisting mountain roads. At the end, turn right onto Country Road 511 north. Expansive, picturesque Wanaque Reservoir is on the left. County 511 leads to Ringwood State Park, site of the historic homes Ringwood Manor and Skylands Manor, and the New Jersey State Botanical Garden. Leaving the park, return to County 511 and follow it into Greenwood Lake. Continue straight onto Warwick Turnpike, through Upper Greenwood Lake, skirting Waywayanda State Park (a good place for hiking, mountain biking, or swimming), and up into New York State again. At Route 94, turn south (left), driving back into New Jersey and through the town of Vernon. You'll pass Mountain Creek Resort, a major ski center in winter and water/adventure sports park in summer, a great place to stop with the kids. Continue on Route 94 to Route 23, turn right (north) and go into the town of Sussex. In summertime, Sussex is the site of the annual Sussex Air Show, one of the best small-airport shows of its kind, and the Sussex Horse & Farm Show/New Jersey State Fair.

If kids are on the ride, detour to Space Farms Zoo & Museum by following County Route 628 west out of Sussex, turning left onto County Route 519. A private attraction, Space Farms offers a fascinating collection of animals, as well as antique cars and farm equipment. Return to (or continue north from Sussex on) Route 23 into High Point State Park, site of the state's highest elevation. Stop here for a picnic, climb the obelisk that marks the state's zenith, swim, or camp. Continue on Route 23 north into Port Jervis, New York, and take US 209 south, which follows the upper Delaware River on the Pennsylvania side. In Milford, PA, take US 206 south. At Tuttles Corner, turn right onto County Route 580, then left onto County Route 615 to Peters Valley, an arts and crafts center where artists can be watched as they work. The annual crafts fair here is one of the state's finest and biggest. Return to US 206 at Tuttles Corner; this is the heart of Stokes State Forest, which holds a variety of hiking opportunities. Follow US 206 south into Augusta. In the summer, the New Jersey Cardinals minor-league baseball team plays here. At Ross Corner, leave US 206 for Route 15 south, traveling into Lafayette, known for its large number of antique emporia.

Out of Lafayette, follow Route 94 south back to US 206 south, into Stanhope. Here, Waterloo Village offers a living-history look at an iron works and Morris Canal town (circa 1831), a re-created Lenape Indian Village (circa 1625), and a summer-long series of music concerts. Follow County Route 602 into Hopatcong State Park. Lake Hopatcong is the state's largest lake and offers excellent boating and swimming. Follow the local roads around the lake into the village of Hopatcong for some good lakeside dining. From here, take I-80 east back to Fort Lee/New York City.
(**APPROX 110 MI**)

A SOUTHERN NEW JERSEY LOOP

From Philadelphia, follow Route 70 east through the suburbs to the junction of Route 72, and turn right onto 72 east. In a few miles, you'll see the entrance to Lebanon State Forest on the left. Stop at the Visitors Center and pick up a park map, and drive north through the park to Whitesbog Village. This is the heart of the famous Jersey Pinelands. Stroll among the old buildings and talk to the folks who are trying to preserve the place—their office is at the main crossroad. Also in Lebanon State Forest is access to the Batona Trail, south Jersey's longest hiking trail, and a variety of places to hike and swim. Return to Route 72, turn right, and then quickly left onto County 563, a local, two-lane, tree-lined road that meanders south past forest and meadows into Wharton State Forest. Passing through the tiny hamlets of Jenkins and Maxwell, turn right onto County Route 542 westbound at Green Bank. Route 542 parallels the picturesque Mullica River. Follow it to Batsto, and stop for a visit to Historic Batsto Village.

Batsto was an ironworks (supplying munitions for the Revolutionary War and the War of 1812) and a glassmaking center. The restored village includes a mansion and several workers' houses, some of which are occupied today by artisans who are happy to show their work. There's a small nature center, as well as picnic grounds, a nature trail, and plenty of hiking, mountain biking (on some 500 miles of unpaved roads), and canoeing.

Leave Batsto, heading south on County 623, then turn left onto County 643, following the other side of the Mullica River through Sweetwater. At County 612 (Elwood Weekstown Road), turn right on County 563. Turn right at Alternate 511 (Mill Road), and visit the Renault Winery. Renault is a bit "touristy," but their glass collection and very good restaurant (especially for Sunday brunch) make this stop worthwhile. Return to County 563 and turn left. In Egg Harbor City County 563 will become NJ 50. Continue south to Tuckahoe, then turn right onto NJ 49 west into Millville, home to Wheaton Village. Wheaton Village pays homage to Millville's storied glassmaking heritage with the Museum of American Glass, one of the world's finest collections. The Village also holds the T. J. Wheaton Glass Factory and Crafts & Traders' Row, where glass- and craft-making demonstrations are staged, the Down Jersey Folklife Center, many stores, a miniature train ride, and a long list of special events. A nice motel is on-site.

After Millville, consider a detour to Bivalve. (If not, continue on Route 49 west to Bridgeton.) The local roads pass through bucolic fields producing fruits, vegetables, and ornamentals, as well as dairy, poultry, and swine farms. Follow County 555 south out of Millville to County 553 east (left turn) at the tiny hamlet of Dividing Creek. In slightly less than four miles, turn right onto Shell Road, which becomes Lighthouse Road into Bivalve. This tiny spot was once the capital of the oyster industry, and it displays a series of industrial buildings (some half-ruined, some fully-functioning) that create a compelling atmosphere. Return to County 553, turn right into Port Norris, and visit the restored *A. J. Meerwald,* New Jersey's official "tall ship" and an archetype for the heyday of oystering. This is a great chance to explore this little-known facet of New Jersey's heritage.

Follow County 553 back to the west until it reunites with NJ 49. Turn left. Three miles before Bridgeton is Berry's Farm Market (739 Shiloh Pike/NJ 49), one of several terrific farm markets in the area. In town, follow the signs to the Bridgeton Historical District on East Broad Street. This is New Jersey's largest historical district, holding some 2,200 Colonial, Victorian, and Federalist buildings. Downtown has paved-brick walkways, and a scenic promenade fronts the river. A 1,100-acre city park has four museums, a zoo, canoe rentals, swimming, and picnicking. A handful of small restaurants and nice shops can be found here, too. Leave Bridgeton on NJ 49, passing through Salem to Fort Mott State Park, a small park that is noteworthy because of its fortifications (built in 1896), good walking trails, and picnic grounds. Return to NJ 49, accessing I-295 back to Philadelphia. **(APPROX 180 MI)**

PHILADELPHIA AND WESTERN NEW JERSEY

This drive meanders up New Jersey's western border, following the scenic Delaware River from the greater Philadelphia area through the timberlands of Delaware Water Gap National Recreation Area.

From Philadelphia, follow Route 130 to Route 73 north. Turn left, and make a right onto County Route 543. From here, the drive becomes leisurely, following local roads for quite a distance. The scenic Delaware River is on your left, and the road passes through the small towns of Palmyra, Riverton, and Riverside. It merges with Route 130, a major thoroughfare just south of Burlington. In Burlington, go left onto High Street, the main intersection, and into the Historic District, which dates back to 1677. (Ben Franklin learned the printing trade here.) Walking tours are offered by the Burlington Center (phone 609/387-8300), and the Burlington County Historical Society is at 457 High Street. Tours are also offered of the James Fenimore Cooper house. Several fine restaurants are found here, including the Café Gallery, which overlooks the river at 219 High Street.

Leave Burlington northbound on County Route 656, which loops alongside the river and comes back to Route 130. Take Route 130 north into Trenton, the state capital. Among the worthwhile stops in Trenton are the Old Barracks Museum, an original French and Indian War Barracks; the State House, seat of NJ government; the Contemporary Victorian Museum; the War Memorial Theater; and the New Jersey State Museum and Planetarium. For a good meal and jazz, try Joe's Mill Hill Saloon. Leave Trenton on NJ 29 north. Near the junction of I-95 stands the New Jersey State Police Museum and, soon after in Titusville, Washington Crossing State Park. Here, each Christmas Day, Washington's crossing of the Delaware is reenacted. The park also contains nice walking paths, river views, picnic areas, and historical information. Also in Titusville is the Howell Living History Farm (101 Hunter Road, just off NJ 29), a circa 1900 horse-powered farm where visitors join in field, barn, and craft programs on weekends.

Continue on NJ 29 northbound into Lambertville. An exceptionally well-maintained historic town with many Federal-style and Victorian buildings, Lambertville is a treasure trove of antiques shopping, fine dining, bed-and-breakfast lodging, and access to the Delaware & Raritan Canal State Park, where walking, boating, canoeing, biking, fishing, cross-country skiing, and picnicking are possible. NJ 29 continues north along the river. In Stockton, the Stockton Inn on Main Street offers pleasant accommodations. The Prallsville Mills at Delaware & Raritan Canal State Park consist of nine structures dating from 1796 and historical exhibits. The Bull's Island Recreation Area offers 30 miles of hiking trails and superb bird-watching. In Frenchtown, Hunterdon House and The Guesthouse at Frenchtown Brown's Old Homestead are two excellent bed-and-breakfast inns, and Poor Richard's Winery offers tours and tastings.

In Frenchtown, jog left on Ridge Street, then right on Harrison Street, which becomes Milford-Frenchtown Road and eventually Frenchtown Road, leading into Milford, site of The Ship Inn, New Jersey's first brew pub and an excellent spot to stop and dine. Follow County Route 627 out of Milford. In Holland Township, the Vollendam Windmill Museum shows its operational gristmill and replica windmills on summer weekends. In Mount Joy, Route 627 veers inland. Follow it to a merge with Route 173, bearing right, then to the junction of I-78 (exit 6). Take I-78 westbound to exit 4, and follow County Route 687 toward Lower Harmony, switching to County Route 519 northbound in Harmony. Follow Route 519 to Belvidere and visit Four Sisters Winery at Matarazzo Farms, which not only produces some surprisingly nice wines, but has an excellent bakery and stages many special events. Also in town is the Pequest River Book Company, which stocks historic local books, and has an art gallery and café.

Continue on Route 519 north until it meets US 46/I-80 at Columbia. Follow I-80 westbound to exit 1, stopping for a visit to the Delaware Water Gap National Recreation Area, a magnificent outdoor wonderland with swimming, fishing, canoeing, tubing, hiking, camping, biking, cross-country skiing, and all manner of other outdoor activities. The Kittatinny Ranger Station offers information, an audio-visual program, and displays, and rangers present impromptu "Terrace Talks" on weekends. Make the trip to Millbrook Village, located about twelve miles north of I-80 along Old Mine Road (the park's main north-south route), a 19th-century settlement in an ongoing process of restoration. **(APPROX 115 MI)**

NORTHERN SHORE TO ATLANTIC CITY

New Jersey has some 130 miles of coastline. This tour covers the shore from Atlantic Highlands to Atlantic City. While many local roads are noted, the main north/south route is the Garden State Parkway (a toll road). At any given time, the local roads can be abandoned for a quick run down the Parkway to the next desired shore point.

Coming out of the New York metro area, access the Parkway south. Leave the Parkway at exit 117, and follow Route 36 into Atlantic Highlands. Just as the highway crosses the bridge into Highlands, you'll see Gateway National Recreation Area on the left. There's a swimming beach here, but the highlights are Sandy Hook Lighthouse, Fort Hancock (including World War II fortification remnants), and the Visitor Center, which sponsors nature and maritime history programs.

Route 36 continues south through the beach towns of Sea Bright, Monmouth Beach, and Long Branch, then turns inland. Turn right on Route 35. In about 7½ miles, turn right onto Route 33 and head to Ocean Grove. First founded as a religious retreat, Ocean Grove holds a great collection of Victorian architecture. It's also home to the Ocean Grove Auditorium, an extraordinary wooden structure with one of the world's great organs. Stop in for a bite eat—or stay the night—at the Manchester Inn & Secret Garden Restaurant. Follow Route 35 south to County 71 and turn right on Jersey Avenue to get to the heart of Spring Lake, which can also be accessed from the Garden State Parkway via exit 98, once known as the Irish Riviera, now known for its extensive collection of fine bed-and-breakfast inns. This is a great place to spend the night.

The next stop is Point Pleasant Beach, a must for those traveling with small children. It's reached by returning to Route 35 south. Turn right on Route 88, then left on Ocean Avenue. Here Jenkinson's Pavilion Boardwalk & Amusement Park is a shore-side heaven for little ones. It has a terrific small aquarium, and its beach, boardwalk, rides, fun house, arcades, restaurants, shops, and miniature golf are all family-oriented.

Moving south, Ocean Avenue becomes Route 35 and travels through a number of shore towns, most of which attract second-home owners or summer-home renters. In about seven miles, the highway becomes Central Avenue, the main street in Seaside Heights/Seaside Park, a mecca for teens and young adults, filled with amusements, a long boardwalk, and much noise and action. (MTV set up its summer beach house here a few years back.) To the south, Central Avenue becomes the entryway to Island Beach State Park, one of the state's most pristine environments, ideal for those who want the beach without the amusements. The park also has nature trails and hosts excellent nature programs.

Returning north out of the park and into Seaside Heights, turn left onto Route 37 and enter the Garden State Parkway at exit 82. At exit 63, leave the Parkway onto

Route 72 east, which leads to Long Beach Island, a collection of small towns that are very popular with vacationers. Turn right onto Route 9 southbound and in about five miles, after passing through several towns, enter Tuckerton, site of the Barnegat Bay Decoy and Baymen's Museum, an excellent small museum that preserves maritime history, heritage, and the lifestyle of the Jersey shore and its baymen. Drive south on Route 9 for ten miles or so into Oceanville. Following the signs, turn left on East Great Creek Road and right onto Lily Lake Road to reach The Noyes Museum of Art, a surprisingly fine facility set almost literally in the middle of nowhere. From the museum, return to East Great Creek Road, turn right, and follow the signs to the Forsythe Wildlife Refuge, a 42,000-acre tract with a beautiful eight-mile wildlife auto trail that reveals magnificent wetlands and ocean views, and has terrific bird-watching.

Return to Route 9 south. At the junction of Route 30 turn left (east) to go into Atlantic City. Famous for its casinos, "AC" is not everyone's cup of tea, but it does offer an excellent race track, a good (albeit small) historical museum, minor-league baseball, the Ocean Life Center for Marine Education, the world's most famous boardwalk, and two of the region's best golf courses—Blue Heron Pines Golf Club and the Seaview Marriott Resort. **(APPROX 160 MI)**

Allaire State Park

See also Asbury Park, Freehold

(On County 524 in Howell and Wall Townships)

Allaire State Park has more than 3,000 acres and offers a fishing pond for children under 14; multi-use trails, picnic facilities, playground, camping (dump station, summer), and the opportunity to visit a historic 19th-century village (see below). Park (daily). Standard fees when village buildings are open. Contact PO Box 220, Farmingdale 07727; 732/938-2371. Parking fee (Memorial Day-Labor Day, wkends) ¢¢

What to See and Do

Historic Allaire Village. In 1822, James Allaire bought this site as a source of bog ore for his iron-works. The furnace also produced cast-iron items such as hollow-ware pots and kettles, stoves, sadirons, and pipes for New York City's waterworks. Today, visitors can explore the bakery, general store, blacksmith and carpentry shops, worker's houses, the community church, and other buildings still much as they were in 1836. Village grounds and Center (all yr); village buildings (Memorial Day-Labor Day, Wed-Sun); special events (Feb-Dec). Phone 732/938-2253. **FREE**

  Train Rides. Narrow-gauge steam and diesel locomotive rides (Jul-Aug, daily; Mid-Apr-June, Sept-Oct, daily). Phone 732/938-5524. ¢¢

Asbury Park (E-4)

Settled 1871 **Pop** 16,930 **Elev** 21 ft
Area code 732 **Zip** 07712
Information Greater Asbury Park Chamber of Commerce, 308 Main St, PO Box 649; 732/775-7676
Web www.asburyparkchamber.com

This popular shore resort was bought in 1871 by New York brush manufac-turer James A. Bradley and named for Francis Asbury, first American Bishop of the Methodist Episcopal Church. Bradley established a town for temperance advocates and good neighbors. The beach and the three lakes proved so attractive that, by 1874, Asbury Park had grown into a borough, and by 1897, a city. It is the home of the famous boardwalk, Convention Hall, and Paramount Theatre. In September 1934, the SS *Morro Castle* was grounded off this beach and burned with a loss of 122 lives. Asbury Park became the birthplace of a favorite sweet when a local confectioner introduced "saltwater taffy" and watched the sales curve rise with the tide. Today, this is a popular resort area for swimming and fishing.

What to See and Do

Stephen Crane House. Early home of the author of *The Red Badge of Courage* contains photos, drawings, and other artifacts. Tours (by appt). 508 4th Ave. Phone 732/988-2260. **FREE**

The Stone Pony. Legendary nightclub known for unexpected visits from rock musician Bruce Springsteen and others. Incl the Asbury Park Gallery, with a collection of photographs and other memorabilia from the resort town's glory days. (Daily) 913 Ocean Ave. Phone 732/502-0600.

Special Events

Horse racing. Monmouth Park. Oceanport Ave in Oceanport via NJ 35 N to NJ 36; or via Garden State Pkwy exit 105, then E on NJ 36. Thoroughbred racing. Phone 732/222-5100. Wed-Sun, Memorial Day-Labor Day.

Jazz Fest. Phone 732/775-7676 or 732/502-5728. July.

Metro Lyric Opera Series. At the Paramount Theater on the Boardwalk. Sat evenings, July-Aug.

Concerts at the Great Auditorium. Pipe organ recitals. 54 Pitman Ave, Ocean Grove. Phone 732/988-0645. Saturdays, June-Sept.

Ocean Grove House Tour. Tour of Victorian cottages. 50 Pitman Ave, Ocean Grove. Phone 732/774-1869. July.

Restaurant

★ ★ **MOONSTRUCK.** *57 Main Ave, Ocean Grove (07756). 732/988-0123.* Hrs: 5-10 pm; Sat to 10:30 pm; Sun to 9:30 pm. Closed Mon, Tues; hols; also Jan-mid-Feb. Italian, Mediterranean menu. A la carte entrees: dinner $10.95-$22.95. Specialties: Mediterranean antipasto, grilled Asian shrimp, raspberry chicken. Own pastries. Outdoor dining. Two-level dining in casual café atmosphere. Cr cds: MC, V.
D

Atlantic City

(D-7) *See also Ocean City*

Settled 1854 **Pop** 40,517 **Elev** 8 ft
Area code 609
Information Atlantic City Convention & Visitors Authority, 2314 Pacific Ave, 08401; 609/449-7147, 888/ACVISIT, or 800/BOARDWALK
Web www.atlanticcitynj.com

Honeymooners, conventioneers, Miss America, and some 37 million annual visitors have made Atlantic City the best-known New Jersey beach resort. Built on Absecon Island, the curve of the coast shields it from battering northeastern storms while the nearby Gulf Stream warms its waters, helping to make it a year-round resort. A 60-foot-wide boardwalk extends along five miles of beaches. Hand-pushed wicker rolling chairs take visitors up and down the Boardwalk. Absecon Lighthouse ("Old Ab"), a well-known landmark, was first lit in 1857 and now stands in an uptown city park. The game of Monopoly uses Atlantic City street names.

What to See and Do

Absecon Lighthouse. Climb the 228 steps to the top of this 1857 lighthouse, designed by Civil War general George Gordon Meade. Tallest lighthouse in New Jersey, third-tallest in US. (July-Aug, daily; Sept-June,

Thurs-Mon; closed hols) Phone 609/449-1360. ¢¢
Amusement piers.

Garden Pier. Atlantic City Art Center and Atlantic City Historical Museum are located here. (Daily) Boardwalk and New Jersey Ave. Phone 609/347-5837. **FREE**

The Shops on Ocean One. A 900-ft, three-deck shopping pier houses shops, food court, and restaurants. (Daily) Boardwalk at Arkansas Ave. Phone 609/347-8082. **FREE**

Atlantic City Boardwalk Hall. Seats 13,800; special events, concerts, boxing, ice shows, sports events; site of the annual Miss America Pageant. Phone 609/348-7000.

Edwin B. Forsythe National Wildlife Refuge, Brigantine Division. Wildlife drive; interpretive nature trails (daily). Over the years, more than 200 species of birds have been observed at this 45,000-acre refuge. Public-use area has an eight-mi wildlife drive through diversified wetlands and uplands habitat; most popular in the spring and fall, during the course of the waterbird migration, and at sunset, when the birds roost for the evening. Refuge headquarters (Mon-Fri). 9 mi N on US 9. Contact PO Box 72, Great Creek Rd, Oceanville 08231. Phone 609/652-1665. ¢¢

Fishing. Surf and deep-sea fishing. License may be required, check locally. Charter boats (Mar-Nov). Many tournaments are scheduled. Contact Atlantic City Party and Charter Boat Association.

Historic Gardner's Basin. An eight-acre, sea-oriented park featuring the working lobstermen; Ocean Life Center, eight tanks totalling 29,800 gallons of aquariums, exhibiting more than 100 varieties of fish and marine animals, ten exhibits featuring themes on the marine and maritime environment. Picnicking. (Daily; closed Jan 1, Thanksgiving, Dec 25) 800 New Hampshire Ave, at N end of city. Phone 609/348-2880.

Historic Town of Smithville and the Village Greene at Smithville. (1787) Restored 18th-century village with specialty shops and restaurants. Also carousel, train ride, and paddle boats. Village (daily). Special events throughout the yr. 7 mi W on US 30 to Absecon, then 6 mi N on US 9, at Moss Mill Rd. Phone 609/652-7777.

Lucy, the Margate Elephant. Only elephant in the world you can walk through and come out alive. Guided tour and exhibit inside this six-story elephant-shaped building. Built 1881; spiral stairs in Lucy's legs lead to main hall and observation area on her back. Gift shop. (Mid-June-Labor Day, daily; Apr-mid-June and Sept-Oct, Sat and Sun only) S via Atlantic Ave in Margate. Phone 609/823-6473. ¢¢

Marine Mammal Stranding Center & Museum. One of few marine mammal rescue and rehabilitation centers in US. Injured dolphins, turtles, and other marine animals are brought to center for treatment. Museum offers exhibits on mammal species; recuperating animals can be viewed at center. Dolphin and whale-watch trips avail (fee; res required). (Mid-June-Labor Day, Tues-Sun, Labor Day-Dec 25, wkends; Dec 25-May, call for schedule) Over bridge and 2 mi N, at 3625 Atlantic-Brigantine Blvd. Phone 609/266-0538. **Donation**

Noyes Museum. Rotating and permanent exhibits of American art; collection of working bird decoys. (Tues-Sun; closed hols). 12 mi NW via US 9, on Lily Lake Rd in Oceanville. Phone 609/652-8848. ¢¢

Recreation areas. Beach (Memorial Day-mid-Sept; free), surfing at special areas (daily); boating; bicycling and rolling chairs on Boardwalk (daily), golf, tennis.

Renault Winery. Guided tour (approx 45 min) incl wine-aging cellars; press room; antique wine-making equipt; free wine tasting (daily). Restaurants. 16 mi W on US 30 in Egg Harbor City. Phone 609/965-2111. ¢

Storybook Land. More than 50 storybook buildings and displays depicting children's stories; live animals; rides; picnic area, concession. (May-mid-Sept, daily; Mar-Apr and mid-Sept-Thanksgiving, Sat and Sun only) Christmas Fantasy with Lights and visiting with Mr. and Mrs. Santa (Thanksgiving-Dec 30, nightly). Admission incl attractions and unlimited rides. 10 mi W via US 40, 322. Phone 609/641-7847. ¢¢¢

Special Events

LPGA Atlantic City Classic. Phone 609/927-7888. Late June.

Miss America Pageant. Atlantic City Boardwalk Hall. Usually first or second wkend after Labor Day.

Atlantic City Marathon. Phone 609/601-1RUN. Mid-Oct.

Motels/Motor Lodges

★★ **CLARION.** *8029 Black Horse Pike, West Atlantic City (08232). 609/641-3546; fax 609/641-9740; toll-free 800/999-9466. www.clarionhotel. com.* 110 rms, 2 story. July-mid-Sept: S, D $85-$125; each addl $10; under 17 free. Lower rates rest of yr. TV; cable (premium), VCR avail. Pool; wading pool. Supervised children's activities (June-Aug) ages 8-15. Restaurant 7 am-10 pm. Serv bar. Ck-out 11 am. Coin lndry. Meeting rms. Business servs avail. Airport transportation. Indoor and outdoor tennis, pro. Exercise rm; sauna. On bay. Cr cds: A, D, DS, MC, V.

🄳 ⬧ 🄵 🗺 🄺 🖾 🛇

★★ **COMFORT INN.** *539 E Absecon Blvd, Absecon (08201). 609/641-7272; fax 609/646-3286; res 800/228-5150. www.comfortinn.com.* 205 rms, 7 story. S, D $79-$145; each addl $10; under 18 free. Crib avail. TV; cable (premium). Complimentary continental bkfst. Ck-out noon. Meeting rms. Business servs avail. Cr cds: A, C, D, DS, MC, V.

🄳 🗺 🛇

★ **DAYS INN AT PLEASANTVILLE.** *6708 Tilton Rd, Egg Harbor City (08234). 609/641-4500; fax 609/645-8295; res 800/329-7466. www.daysinn. com.* 117 rms, 5 story. July-mid-Sept: S, D $69-$169; each addl $5; suites $89-$189; kit. unit $99-$200; under 13 free; family rates; package plans; hols (2-day min); higher rates special events; lower rates rest of yr. Crib free. TV; cable (premium), VCR avail. Complimentary continental bkfst. Restaurant adj 7 am-midnight. Ck-out 11 am. Meeting rms. Business servs avail. In-rm modem link. Coin lndry. Exercise equipt. Pool; lifeguard. Playground. Game rm. Some refrigerators, microwaves. Picnic tables. Cr cds: A, C, D, DS, JCB, MC, V.

[D] [☂] [⅄] [♨]

★★ **FAIRFIELD INN ATLANTIC CITY NORTH.** *405 E Absecon Blvd, Absecon (08201). 609/646-5000; fax 609/383-8744; toll-free 800/228-2800. www.marriott.com.* 200 rms, 6 story. S $50-$70; D $110-$150; each addl $10; suites $75-$199; under 18 free. Crib free. TV; cable (premium). Pool. Complimentary continental bkfst. Restaurant nearby. Ck-out 11 am. Meeting rms. Business servs avail. In-rm modem link. Cr cds: A, C, D, DS, ER, JCB, MC, V.

[D] [⊶] [⅄] [♨]

★★ **HAMPTON INN ABSECON.** *240 E White Horse Pike, Absecon (08201). 609/652-2500; fax 609/652-2212; toll-free 800/426-7866. www. hamptoninn.com.* 129 rms, 4 story. Memorial Day-Labor Day: S, D $65-$109; suites $92-$146; under 18 free; higher rates hols; lower rates rest of yr. Crib free. TV; cable (premium), VCR avail. Pool; whirlpool, lifeguard. Complimentary continental bkfst. Restaurant adj open 24 hrs. Ck-out 11 am. Coin lndry. Meeting rms. Business servs avail. In-rm modem link. Free airport transportation. Cr cds: A, C, D, DS, MC, V.

[D] [♨] [⊶] [⅄] [♨]

★★ **HAMPTON INN BAYSIDE.** *7079 Black Horse Pike, West Atlantic City (08232). 609/484-1900; fax 609/383-0731; res 800/426-7866. www.hamptoninn.com.* 143 rms, 6 story. June-Sept: S, D $99; family rates; higher rates: hols (2-day min). Crib free. TV; cable (premium). Complimentary continental bkfst. Coffee in rms. Ck-out 11 am. Meeting rm. Business servs avail. Cr cds: A, C, D, DS, MC, V.

[D] [♨] [⅄] [♨] [SC]

★★ **HOLIDAY INN BOARDWALK.** *111 S Chelsea Ave (08401). 609/348-2200; fax 609/345-5110; toll-free 800/548-3030. www.holidayinnac.com.* 220 rms, 21 story. Mid-June-Labor Day: S, D $98-$179; each addl $15; under 19 free; lower rates rest of yr. Crib avail. TV; cable (premium). Pool; poolside serv. Restaurant 7 am-10 pm. Bar 11:30-2 am. Ck-out 11 am. Meeting rms. Business servs

avail. In-rm modem link. Health club privileges. On ocean. Cr cds: A, C, D, DS, MC, V.

[⅄] [♨] [⊶]

★ **SUPER 8.** *229 E US 30; 633 White Horse Pike, Absecon (08201). 609/652-2477; fax 609/748-0666; res 800/800-8000. www.super8.com.* 58 rms, 2 story. July 4-Aug: S, D $55-$125; suites $80-$150; under 12 free; lower rates rest of yr. TV; cable (premium). Complimentary coffee in lobby. Restaurant opp open 24 hrs. Ck-out noon. Business servs avail. Refrigerators avail. Cr cds: A, C, D, DS, MC, V.

[D] [⅄] [♨]

Hotels

★★★ **SHERATON ATLANTIC CITY CONVENTION.** *2 Miss America Way (08401). 609/344-3535.* 502 rms, 12 story. S, D $159-$199; suites $250-$450; under 17 free; wkend rates. Crib free. TV; cable (premium), VCR avail. Indoor pool; whirlpool. Coffee in rms. Restaurants 6:30 am-midnight. Bar 11 am-midnight. Ck-out noon. Lndry serv. Meeting rms. Business center. In-rm modem link. Concierge. Gift shop. Exercise equipt. Refrigerators avail. Casino. Cr cds: A, D, DS, MC, V.

[⊶] [☂] [♨] [☂]

Resorts

★★★ **MARRIOTT RESORT SEA-VIEW.** *401 S New York Rd, Absecon (08201). 609/652-1800; fax 609/652-2307; res 800/228-9290. www. marriott.com.* 297 rms; 3 story. May-Nov: S, D $199-$275; suites $250-$700; under 18 free; golf, package plans; lower rates rest of yr. Crib free. TV; cable (premium), VCR avail (free movies). 2 pools, 1 indoor; whirlpool, poolside serv, lifeguard. Dining rm 6:30 am-10 pm. Box lunches. Snack bar. Bar noon-2 am. Ck-out 12:30 pm, ck-in 4 pm. Coin lndry. Convention facilities. Business center. In-rm modem link. Gift shop. Sports dir. 8 tennis courts, 4 lighted, pro. 36-hole golf, pro, 9-hole putting green; golf school. Rec rm. Game rm. Exercise equipt; sauna. Basketball. Volleyball. Minibars; refrigerator, fireplace in suites. Driving ranges.

Atlantic City at night

Located on 670-acre estate. Cr cds: A, C, D, DS, JCB, MC, V.

★★★ **RESORTS ATLANTIC CITY.**
1133 Boardwalk (08401). 609/344-6000; fax 609/340-7684; toll-free 800/336-6378. www.resortsac.com. 662 rms, 15 story. July-Labor Day: S, D $70-$225; each addl $10; lower rates rest of yr. Crib free. TV; cable. Indoor/outdoor pool; whirlpool. Restaurants open 24 hrs. Bars open 24 hrs. Ck-out noon. Convention facilities. Business servs avail. In-rm modem link. Concierge. Shopping arcade. Valet parking. Airport transportation. Exercise equipt; steam rm, sauna. Game rm. Bathrm phones. Some balconies. First casino in Atlantic City. Cr cds: A, C, D, DS, MC, V.

Casinos

★★★ **BALLY'S PARK PLACE.** *Park and Boardwalk places (08401). 609/340-2000; fax 609/340-4713; res 888/537-0007. www.ballysac.com.* 1,268 rms, 49 story. Mid-June-Sept: S $79-$245; D $95-$289; each addl $15; under 18 free; lower rates rest of yr. Crib free. TV; cable (premium). 2 pools, 1 indoor; whirlpool, poolside serv, lifeguard. Restaurants open 24 hrs. Bars. Ck-out noon. Conven-

tion facilities. Business servs avail. In-rm modem link. Barber, beauty shop. Valet parking; self-park garage. Exercise rm; sauna, steam rm. Massage. Bathrm phones; refrigerators avail. On beach. Cr cds: A, C, D, DS, MC, V.

★★★ **CAESARS ATLANTIC CITY.**
2100 Pacific and Arkansas aves (08401). 609/348-4411; fax 609/343-2405; toll-free 800/524-2867. www.caesars.com. 1,138 rms, 20 story. June-Labor Day: S, D $130-$375; each addl $15; lower rates rest of yr. Crib avail. TV; cable (premium), VCR avail (movies). Pool; whirlpool, lifeguard. Restaurants open 24 hrs. Bars open 24 hrs. Ck-out noon. Convention facilities. Business servs avail. Shopping arcade. Barber, beauty shop. Airport transportation. Tennis. Exercise equipt; steam rm, sauna. Massage. Microwaves avail. On ocean. Cr cds: A, C, D, DS, MC, V.

★★ **CLARIDGE CASINO & HOTEL.**
Boardwalk and Park places (08401). 609/340-3400; fax 609/340-3875; toll-free 800/257-8585. www.claridge.com. 504 rms, 24 story. July-early Sept: S, D $80-$205; each addl $10; under 12 free; lower rates rest of yr. TV; cable (premium). Indoor pool; whirlpool, lifeguard. Restaurant open 24 hrs.

Rm serv 24 hrs. Bar open 24 hrs. Ck-out noon. Meeting rms. Business servs avail. Concierge. Beauty shop. Exercise rm; sauna, steam rm. Refrigerators. On ocean. Cr cds: A, C, D, DS, MC, V.

◻◻◻◻◻◻

★ ★ ★ HILTON CASINO RESORT.
Boston and the Boardwalk (08401). 609/347-7111; fax 609/340-4858; toll-free 877/432-7139. www.hiltonac.com. 803 rms, 22 story. Late June-Sept: S, D $199-$325; each addl $20; suites $210-$400; under 12 free; lower rates rest of yr. Crib free. TV; cable (premium), VCR avail. Indoor pool; whirlpool, poolside serv, lifeguard. Free supervised children's activities (June-Aug). Restaurant, bar noon-2 am. Entertainment. Ck-out noon. Convention facilities. Business servs avail. Concierge. Barber, beauty shop. Valet parking. Exercise rm; sauna. Game rm. Bathrm phones. On beach. Cr cds: A, C, D, DS, MC, V.

◻◻◻◻◻ SC

★ ★ SANDS CASINO HOTEL.
Indiana and Brighton Park (08401). 609/441-4000; fax 609/441-4630; res 609/441-4936. www.acsands.com. 534 rms, 21 story. July-Sept: S, D $50-$105; each addl $15; under 18 free; package plans; lower rates rest of yr. Crib free. TV; cable (premium), VCR avail. Restaurants (see also BRIGHTON STEAKHOUSE). Bar open 24 hrs; entertainment. Ck-out noon. Convention facilities. Business servs avail. Concierge. Beauty shop. Valet, garage parking. Airport transportation. Exercise equipt; sauna. On ocean. Cr cds: A, C, D, DS, ER, JCB, MC, V.

◻◻◻◻

★ ★ SHOWBOAT CASINO & HOTEL.
801 Boardwalk (08401). 609/343-4000; fax 609/343-4057; toll-free 800/621-0200. www.harrahs.com. 755 rms, 25 story. July-mid-Sept: S, D $120-$180; each addl $15; suites $200-$472; under 12 free; lower rates rest of yr. Crib free. TV; cable (premium), VCR avail. Pool; whirlpool, lifeguard. Supervised children's activities. Restaurant open 24 hrs. Bar open 24 hrs; entertainment. Ck-out noon. Convention facilities. Business servs avail. Beauty shop. Airport transportation. Bowling center. Game

rm. Exercise rm; sauna. Bathrm phones. Some refrigerators. Some balconies. On ocean; ocean view from most rms. Cr cds: A, C, D, DS, MC, V.

◻◻◻◻◻◻

★ ★ ★ TROPICANA CASINO & RESORT.
Brighton Ave and the Boardwalk (08401). 609/340-4000; fax 609/343-5211; toll-free 800/843-8767. www.tropicana.net. 1,624 rms, 23 story. Mid-June-Sept: S, D $105-$300; under 18 free; lower rates rest of yr. TV; cable (premium), VCR avail. 2 pools, 1 indoor; whirlpool, poolside serv, lifeguard. Restaurants open 24 hrs. Bars open 24 hrs. Ck-out noon. Business center. In-rm modem link. Shopping arcade. Barber, beauty shop. Valet, garage parking. Lighted tennis. Exercise rm; sauna. Some bathrm phones. On ocean. Cr cds: A, D, DS, MC, V.

◻◻◻◻◻◻

★ ★ ★ TRUMP MARINA HOTEL & CASINO.
Huron Ave & Brigantine Blvd (08401). 609/441-2000; fax 609/345-7604; toll-free 800/777-1177. www.trumpmarina.com. 728 rms, 27 story. July-mid-Sept: S, D $150-$225; each addl $15; suites $175-$275; under 12 free; package plans; lower rates rest of yr. Crib free. TV; cable (premium), VCR avail. Pool; wading pool, whirlpool, poolside serv, lifeguard. Restaurants open 24 hrs. Bars; entertainment. Ck-out noon. Convention facilities. Business servs avail. In-rm modem link. Shopping arcade. Barber, beauty shop. Garage parking. Lighted tennis. Exercise rm; sauna, steam rm. Massage. Health club privileges. Basketball. Lawn games. Game rm. On ocean inlet. Cr cds: A, D, MC, V.

◻◻◻◻◻◻

★ ★ ★ TRUMP PLAZA HOTEL & CASINO.
The Boardwalk and Mississippi Ave (08401). 609/441-6000; fax 609/441-7881; res 800/444-7676. www.trumpplaza.com. 904 rms, 38 story. June-Sept: S, D $200-$245; each addl $10; under 16 free; lower rates rest of yr. Crib avail. TV; cable (premium), VCR avail. Indoor pool; whirlpool, lifeguard. Restaurants open 24 hrs. Bar; entertainment. Ck-out noon. Business servs avail. In-rm modem link. Concierge. Shopping

arcade. Beauty shop. Garage parking. Tennis. Golf privileges. Exercise rm; sauna, steam rm. Massage. Game rm. Bathrm phones. On ocean. Cr cds: A, D, DS, MC, V.

★★★ **TRUMP TAJ MAHAL CASINO RESORT.** *1000 Boardwalk (08401). 609/449-1000; fax 609/449-6818; toll-free 800/825-8888. www. trumptaj.com.* 1,250 rms, 52 story, 246 suites. July-Labor Day: S, D $195-$295; each addl $25; suites $325-$650; lower rates rest of yr. Crib free. TV; cable (premium). Indoor pool; whirlpool, poolside serv, lifeguard. Restaurant open 24 hrs. Bar; entertainment. Ck-out noon. Convention facilities. Business center. Concierge. Shopping arcade. Barber, beauty shop. Valet parking. Exercise rm; sauna, steam rm. Massage. Spa. Casino. Game rm. Bicycles avail. Refrigerators avail. Cr cds: A, C, D, DS, ER, MC, V.

Restaurants

★★★ **BRIGHTON STEAKHOUSE.** *Indiana Ave at Brighton Park (08401). 609/441-4300. www.acsands.com.* Hrs: 5:30-10 pm. Closed Tues, Wed. Res required. American menu. Bar noon-3:30 am. Wine list. A la carte entrees: dinner $20-$60. Specialties:

chateaubriand, pepper-seared tuna, Brighton seafood harvest. Tropical decor. Cr cds: A, D, DS, MC, V.

★ **CAPTAIN YOUNG'S SEAFOOD EMPORIUM.** *1 Atlantic Ocean (08401). 609/344-2001.* Hrs: 11:30 am-9 pm; Sat to 10 pm. Closed Thanksgiving, Dec 25. Bar. Lunch $6.25-$9.95, dinner $13.95-$19.95. Specializes in fresh fish, fresh lobster, crab legs. Overlooks beach and Boardwalk. Cr cds: A, C, D, DS, MC, V.

★★ **CHEF VOLA'S.** *111 S Albion Place (08401). 609/345-2022.* Hrs: 6-11 pm. Closed Mon; Thanksgiving, Dec 24, 25. Res required. Italian menu. A la carte entrees: dinner $13.95-$30. Specializes in steak, veal. Italian decor. Photographs of celebrities.

★★ **DOCK'S OYSTER HOUSE.** *2405 Atlantic Ave (08401). 609/345-0092. www.shorecast.com.* Hrs: 5-10:30 pm. Closed Mon; also Jan, Dec. Res accepted. Bar. Dinner $13.95-$29. Child's menu. Specialties: imperial crab, oyster stew. Pianist Thurs-Sat. Parking. Casual atmosphere in family-owned restaurant since 1897. Cr cds: A, D, MC, V.

Taj Mahal Casino

★ **GRABELS RESTAURANT LOUNGE.** 3901 Atlantic Ave (08401). 609/344-9263. www.grabels.com. Hrs: 3 pm-7 am. Closed Dec 24. Res accepted. Continental menu. Bar. Dinner $4.95-$21.95. Child's menu. Specialties: veal rollintine, Black Angus New York strip, crab cakes. Pianist Wed-Sun. Modern decor; casual dining. Family-owned. Cr cds: A, MC, V.

D ⟶

★ **HARLEY DAWN DINER.** 1402 Black Horse Pike, Folsom (08037). 609/567-6084. Hrs: 6 am-10 pm. Closed Dec 25. Bkfst $1.75-$7.95, lunch $2.25-$5.95, dinner $6.95-$12.95. Child's menu. Specialties: chicken and broccoli Harley Dawn-style, broiled crab cakes, eggs Benedict. Own breads. Authentic diner atmosphere. Cr cds: A, D, DS, MC, V.

D SC ⟶

★★ **OLD WATERWAY INN.** 1660 W Riverside Dr (08401). 609/347-1793. www.oldwaterwayinn.com. Hrs: 5-11 pm. Closed Mon, Tues Oct-Apr. Res accepted. Bar. Dinner $15-$24. Child's menu. Specializes in fresh seafood and Cajun specialities. Own pasta. Outdoor dining. Nautical decor. On waterfront; view of skyline. Cr cds: A, D, MC, V.

D ⟶

★★★ **RAM'S HEAD INN.** 9 W White Horse Pike, Absecon (08201). 609/652-1700. www.ramsheadinn.com. Hrs: noon-3 pm, 5-9:30 pm; Sat 5-10 pm; Sun 1:30-7:30 pm; hrs vary by season. Res accepted. Closed Mon; Labor Day, Dec 24. Continental menu. Bar. Lunch $7.25-$12.95, dinner $16.95-$25.95. Child's menu. Specializes in Colonial American dishes, fresh southern New Jersey seafood. Menu changes seasonally. Own baking. Pianist. Valet parking. Outdoor dining. Colonial decor; gallery with paintings, plants. Jacket (dinner). Cr cds: A, D, DS, MC, V.

D ⟶

★★★ **RENAULT WINERY.** 72 N Bremen Ave, Egg Harbor City (08215). 609/965-2111. www.renaultwinery.com. Hrs: 5-9 pm; Sun brunch 10 am-2 pm. Closed Mon-Thurs; Dec 25. Res required. Wine list. Complete meals: dinner $27.95-$31.95. Sun brunch $14.95. Specializes in fresh seafood, poultry, beef. Menu changes wkly. Pianist/guitarist. Parking. Elegant dining in eclectic Methode Champenoise rm of winery founded in 1864. Cr cds: A, D, DS, MC, V.

D

★★ **SCANNICCHIO'S.** 119 S California Ave (08401). 609/348-6378. Hrs: 4 pm-midnight. Closed hols. Res required wkends. Italian menu. Bar. A la carte entrees: dinner $10.95-$19.95. Specializes in veal, fresh seafood. Intimate ambiance. Cr cds: A, D, DS, MC, V.

D SC

★★ **STEVE AND COOKIE'S BY THE BAY.** 9700 Amherst Ave, Margate (08402). 609/823-1163. www.steveand cookies.com. Hrs: 5-10 pm; Sat to 11 pm; Sat, Sun 10 am-3 pm. Closed Dec 24, Dec 25. Res accepted. Contemporary American menu. Bar 3 pm-1 am. A la carte entrees: dinner $12-$27. Sat, Sun brunch $4-$10. Child's menu. Specialties: crab cakes, char-grilled filet mignon, steamed whole Maine lobster. Jazz. Parking. View of bay and marina. Fireplaces. Casual dining. Cr cds: A, D, DS, MC, V.

D ⟶

Unrated Dining Spot

IRISH PUB AND INN. St James Pl and Boardwalk (08401). 609/344-9063. www.theirishpub.com. Open 24 hrs. Irish, American menu. Bar. A la carte entrees: lunch $1.95-$3.95, dinner $2.95-$6.25. Complete meals: dinner $5.50. Specialty: Dublin beef stew. Irish balladeer Thurs-Sun (summer). Patio dining. Informal, Irish pub atmosphere.

D ⟶

Batsto

(D-7) See also Atlantic City

(Approx 10 mi E of Hammonton)
Area code 609 **Zip** 08037

The Batsto Iron Works, established in 1766, made munitions for the Revolutionary Army from the bog iron ore found nearby. Its furnaces shut down for the last time in 1848. Eighteen years later, Joseph Wharton, whose immense estate totaled nearly 100,000 acres, bought the land. In 1954, the state of New Jersey bought nearly 150 square miles of land in this area, including the entire Wharton tract, for a state forest.

What to See and Do

Batsto State Historic Site. Restored early 19th-century iron and glass-making community. General store, gristmill, blacksmith shop, wheel-wright shop, sawmill, workers' houses, and visitor center are open seasonally to the public. Guided tours of the mansion (fee). Parking fee (Memorial Day-Labor Day, wkends and hols). Phone 609/561-3262. ¢¢

Wharton State Forest. Crossed by NJ 542, 563. Streams wind through 110,000 acres of wilderness. Swimming, fishing, canoeing; limited picnicking, tent and trailer sites, cabins. Standard fees. Along US 206 near Atsion. Phone 609/561-3262. Also here is

> **Atsion Recreation Area.** Swimming, canoeing; picnicking, camping. Standard fees. Phone 609/268-0444.

Beach Haven

(see Long Beach Island)

Bernardsville

(D-3) *See also Morristown*

Pop 7,345 **Elev** 400 ft **Area code** 908
Zip 07924

What to See and Do

Great Swamp National Wildlife Refuge. Nature trails, boardwalk. Observation blind; wilderness area. More than 200 species of birds, fish, reptiles, frogs, ducks, geese, and fox may be seen in this 7,300-acre refuge. Headquarters (Mon-Fri; closed hols). Trails and information booth (daily, dawn-dusk). 1 mi N on US 202, W on N Maple Ave, 2 mi E on Madisonville Rd, 1½ mi NE on Lee's Hill Rd, then right on Long Hill Rd. Phone 973/425-1222. **FREE**

Morristown National Historical Park. (see) Approx 5 mi N on US 2.

Hotel

★ ★ ★ **SOMERSET HILLS HOTEL.** *200 Liberty Corner Rd, Warren (07059). 908/647-6700; fax 908/647-8053; res 800/688-0700. www.shh.com.* 111 units, 4 story. S $170; D $180; each addl $10; suites $250-$310; kits. $145-$185. Crib free. Pet accepted. TV; cable (premium). Pool; poolside serv. Restaurant 6:30 am-11 pm. Bar 11:30-2 am. Ck-out noon. Meeting rms. Business center. In-rm modem link. Concierge. Gift shop. Tennis privileges. 18-hole golf privileges, pro, putting green, driving range. Exercise equipt. Microwaves avail. Nestled in the Watchung Mountains near the crossroads of historical Liberty Corner. Cr cds: A, C, D, MC, V.

B&B/Small Inn

★ ★ ★ **BERNARDS INN.** *27 Mine Brook Rd (07924). 908/766-0002; fax 908/766-4604; toll-free 888/766-0002. www.bernardsinn.com.* 20 rms, 5 story, 4 suites. S, D $180; suites $190-$215. Crib $10. TV; cable (premium). Complimentary continental bkfst. Restaurant (see also THE BERNARDS INN). Bar. Ck-out 11 am, ck-in 4 pm. Business servs avail. In-rm modem link. Luggage handling. Concierge serv. Massage. Health club privileges. Cr cds: A, C, D, MC, V.

Restaurants

★ ★ ★ **THE BERNARDS INN.** *27 Mine Brook Rd (07924). 908/766-0002. www.bernardsinn.com.* Hrs: 11:30 am-3 pm, 5:30-10 pm; Fri, Sat to 11 pm. Closed Sun; hols. Res accepted, required Fri, Sat. Bar. Wine list. A la carte entrees: lunch $9-$13, dinner $21-$32. Specializes in rack of lamb, veal medallion, crème brûlée. Pianist Tues-Sat. Outdoor dining. Elegant dining, turn-of-the-century ambiance. Jacket (dinner). Cr cds: A, D, MC, V.

[D] [≡]

★★★ **LE PETITE CHATEAU.** *121 Claremont Rd (07924). 908/766-4544.* Hrs: 11:30 am-10:30 pm; Sat 5 pm-midnight; Sun 4-9:30 pm. Closed Mon; Dec 25. Res accepted. French menu. Bar. Wine cellar. A la carte entrees: lunch $10.95-$14.95, dinner $18.95-$29.95. Specialties: duck confit, shrimp with portabello and asparagus. Harpist Sat. Parking. Private wine cellar dining rm. Jacket. Cr cds: A, D, MC, V.

[D]

Bordentown

See also Trenton

Settled 1682 **Pop** 3,969 **Elev** 72 ft **Area code** 609 **Zip** 08505
Information Historical Society Visitors Center, Old City Hall, 13 Crosswicks St, PO Box 182; 609/298-1740

A long and honorable history has left an indelible stamp on this town. Bordentown was once a busy shipping center and a key stop on the Delaware and Raritan Canal. In January 1778, Bordentown citizens filled numerous kegs with gunpowder and sent them down the Delaware River to Philadelphia hoping to blow up the British fleet stationed there. But the plan was discovered, and British troops intercepted the kegs and discharged them. In 1816, Joseph Bonaparte, exiled king of Spain and brother of Napoleon, bought 1,500 acres and settled here.

What to See and Do

Clara Barton Schoolhouse. Building was in use as a school in Revolutionary days. In 1851, Clara Barton, founder of the American Red Cross, established one of the first free public schools in the country in this building. (By appt) 142 Crosswicks St. Phone 609/298-0676. **FREE**

Motel/Motor Lodge

★ **DAYS INN.** *1073 Rte 206 (08505). 609/298-6100; fax 609/298-7509; res 800/329-7466. www.daysinn.com.* 131 rms, 2 story. S, D $95-$105; each addl $10; under 12 free. Crib free. Pet accepted. TV; cable. Pool; lifeguard. Restaurant 6:30-10 am, 5-9 pm. Bar 5 pm-1:30 am. Ck-out 11 am. Coin lndry. Meeting rms. Business servs avail. Sundries. Cr cds: A, C, D, DS, JCB, MC, V.

[➔] [D] [≈] [⋈] [♨]

Branchville

(B-3)*See also Vernon*

Pop 845 **Elev** 529 ft **Area code** 201 **Zip** 07826
Information Sussex County Chamber of Commerce, 120 Hampton House Rd, Newton 07860; 201/579-1811
Web www.sussexcountychamber.org

This town in Sussex County is near many attractions in New Jersey's scenic northwest corner.

What to See and Do

Peters Valley. Historic buildings in the Delaware Water Gap National Recreation Area (see DELAWARE WATER GAP, PA) serve as residences and studios for professional craftspeople and summer crafts workshops in blacksmithing, ceramics, fine metals, photography, fibers, and woodworking. Contemporary craft store (Seasonal hrs). Studios (June-Aug, Sat-Sun afternoons). 8 mi NW via US 206, County 560, then S on County 615. Phone 973/948-5200. **FREE**

Space Farms Zoo & Museum. Collection of more than 500 wild animals; early American museum in main building, addl museums on grounds; picnic area, concession; gift shop. Zoo and museum (Apr-Oct). 6 mi N on County 519, in Beamerville. Phone 973/875-5800. ¢¢¢

Stokes State Forest. Located on the Kittatinny Ridge, this 15,482-acre forest incl some of the finest mountain country in New Jersey. Swimming, fishing; hunting, picnicking, camping. Scenic views from Sunrise Mtn; Tillman Ravine, a natural gorge, is in the southern corner of the park. Standard fees. 4 mi N on US 206. Phone 973/948-3820.

Swartswood State Park. A 1,470-acre park on Swartswood Lake. Swimming (Memorial Day-Labor Day), bathhouse, fishing, boating (rentals, Memorial Day-Labor Day); hunting, picnicking, concession, camping. Standard fees. 2 mi S on County 519, then continue 2 mi on County 627, left 3 mi on County 521 to Swartswood, left 1 mi on County 622, right on County 619, ½ mi to park entrance. Phone 973/383-5230.

Special Event

Peters Valley Craft Fair. Peters Valley. More than 150 juried exhibitors; demonstrations, music, food. Last wkend Sept.

Clara Barton Schoolhouse

Bridgeton

(B-7) *See also Millville*

Settled 1686 **Pop** 22,771 **Elev** 40 ft
Area code 856 **Zip** 08302
Information Bridgeton-Cumberland Tourist Association, 50 E Broad St; 856/451-4802 or 800/319-3379

The city of Bridgeton has been recognized as New Jersey's largest historic district, with more than 2,200 registered historical landmarks. There are many styles of architecture here, some of which date back nearly 300 years.

What to See and Do

City Park. A 1,100-acre wooded area with swimming (protected beaches, Memorial Day-Labor Day), fishing, boating (floating dock), canoeing.

Picnic grounds, recreation center; zoo. (Daily) W Commerce St and Mayor Aitken Dr off NJ 49. Phone 856/451-9208. Also here is

New Sweden Farmstead Museum. Reconstruction of first permanent European settlement in Delaware Valley. Seven log buildings incl smokehouse/sauna; horse barn, cow and goat barn, threshing barn; storage house; blacksmith shop; family residence with period furnishings. Costumed guides. (May-Labor Day, Wed-Sat, also Sun afternoons) Phone 856/455-3230. ¢¢

George J. Woodruff Museum of Indian Artifacts. Approx 20,000 local Native American artifacts, some up to 10,000 yrs old; clay pots, pipes, implements. (Mon-Fri afternoons; also by appt; closed hols) Bridgeton Free Public Library, 150 E Commerce St. Phone 856/451-2620. **FREE**

Gibbon House. (1730) Site of New Jersey's only 18th-century tea burning party; genealogical research library (Mar-Dec, Wed and Sun). Events scheduled throughout yr. Gibbon House (early Apr-late Nov, Tues-

Sat; closed Sun in July, Aug); tours (wkdays). 7 mi SW in Greenwich, on Ye Greate St. Phone 856/455-4055. **Donation**

Old Broad Street Church. (1792) Outstanding example of Georgian architecture, with Palladian window, high-backed wooden pews, wine glass pulpit, brick-paved aisles, and brass lamps that once held whale oil. W Broad St and West Ave.

Parvin State Park. This 1,125-acre park offers swimming, bathhouse, fishing, boating, canoeing (rentals); picnicking, concessions, playgrounds, camping (dump station), cabins. Standard fees. 7 mi NE off NJ 77, near Centerton. Phone 856/358-8616.

Special Event

Concerts. Riverfront. Performances by ragtime, military, country and western bands, and others. Sun nights. Phone 856/451-9208. Nine wks July-Aug.

Burlington

(C-5) *See also Bordentown, Mount Holly*

Settled 1677 **Pop** 9,736 **Elev** 13 ft **Area code** 609, 856 **Zip** 08016
Information Burlington County Chamber of Commerce, 900 Briggs Rd, Mt Laurel, 08054; 856/439-2520

In 1774 Burlington, along with New York, Philadelphia, and Boston, was a thriving port. A Quaker settlement, it was one of the first to provide public education. A 1682 Act of Assembly gave Matinicunk (now Burlington) Island in the Delaware River to the town with the stipulation that the revenue it generated would be used for public schools; that act is still upheld. Burlington was the capital of West Jersey; the legislature met here, and in the East Jersey capital of Perth Amboy, from 1681 until after the Revolution. In 1776, the Provincial Congress adopted the state constitution here.

What to See and Do

Burlington County Historical Society. The society maintains **D. B. Pugh Library**, in the Corson-Poley Center, genealogical and historical holdings; Revolutionary War exhibit; **James Fenimore Cooper House** (ca 1780), birthplace of the famous author; **Bard-How House** (ca 1740) with period furnishings; **Captain James Lawrence House**, birthplace of the commander of the *Chesapeake* during the War of 1812 and speaker of the immortal words "Don't give up the ship," contains 1812 objects and costume display. Tour of historic houses (Tues-Sun). 457 High St. Phone 609/386-4773. ¢¢

Friends Meeting House. (1784) (By appt) High St in 300 blk. Phone 609/387-3875. ¢¢

Historic tours. Guided walking tours of 33 historic sites (1685-1829), eight of which are open to the public. (Daily; no tours Easter, Dec 25) Leave foot of High St. Phone 609/386-3993. ¢¢

Old St. Mary's Church. (1703) The oldest Episcopal Church building in the state. (By appt) W Broad and Wood sts. Phone 609/386-0902.

Thomas Revell House. (1685) The oldest building in Burlington County. Incl in Burlington County Historical Society home tour (see). (By appt and during Wood St Fair; see SPECIAL EVENT) 213 Wood St. Phone 609/386-3993. **FREE**

Special Event

Wood Street Fair. Re-creation of colonial fair; crafts, antique exhibits; food; entertainment. First Sat after Labor Day.

Restaurant

★★★ **CAFE GALLERY.** *219 High St (08016). 609/386-6150.* Hrs: 11:30 am-10 pm; Fri, Sat to 11 pm; Sun brunch 11:30 am-3 pm. Closed most major hols. Res accepted. Continental menu. Bar. Lunch $5.75-$9.75, dinner $14.50-$23.50. Sun brunch $9.75-$18.75. Child's menu. Specializes in fresh seafood. Outdoor dining. Restored Colonial building overlooking Delaware River. Cr cds: A, C, D, MC, V.

Caldwell

See also Newark, Newark International Airport Area

Pop 7,584 **Elev** 411 ft **Area code** 973 **Zip** 07006

What to See and Do

Grover Cleveland Birthplace State Historic Site. Built in 1832, this building served as the parsonage of the First Presbyterian Church. It is the birthplace of President Grover Cleveland, the only president born in New Jersey. He lived here from 1837-1841. (Wed-Sun afternoons; closed Jan 1, Thanksgiving, Dec 25, state hols; res recommended) 207 Bloomfield Ave. Phone 973/226-0001. **FREE**

Camden

(B-5) *See also Cherry Hill*

Settled 1681 **Pop** 79,904 **Elev** 23 ft **Area code** 856

Camden's growth as the leading industrial, marketing, and transportation center of southern New Jersey dates from post-Civil War days. Its location across the Delaware River from Philadelphia prompted large companies such as Campbell Soup (national headquarters) to establish plants here. Walt Whitman spent the last 20 years of his life in Camden.

What to See and Do

Camden County Historical Society-Pomona Hall. (1726/1788) Brick Georgian house that belonged to descendants of William Cooper, an early Camden settler; period furnishings. Museum exhibits focus on regional history and incl antique glass, lamps, toys, and early hand tools; fire-fighting equipt; Victor

Talking Machines. Library (fee) has more than 20,000 books, as well as maps (17th century-present), newspapers (18th-20th century), oral history tapes, photographs, and genealogical material. (Tues-Thurs, Sun; closed hols, also Aug) Park Blvd at Euclid Ave. Phone 856/964-3333. Museum ¢

New Jersey State Aquarium. Features one of the largest "open ocean" tanks in the country. Other highlights incl an underwater research station, aquatic nursery, and the opportunity to touch sharks, rays, and starfish in special tanks and pools. Gift shop. Cafeteria. (Daily; closed hols) 1 Riverside Dr, I-676 exit Mickle Blvd. Phone 856/365-3300. ¢¢¢¢

Tomb of Walt Whitman. The vault of the "good gray poet," designed by the poet himself, is of rough-cut stone with a grillwork door. Harleigh Cemetery, Haddon Ave and Vesper Blvd.

Walt Whitman Arts Center. Poetry readings, concerts, and gallery exhibits (Oct-May). Children's theater (late June-Aug, Fri). Art gallery; statuary. Center (Mon-Fri). 2nd and Cooper sts. Phone 856/964-8300.

☒ **Walt Whitman House State Historic Site.** The last residence of the poet and the only house he ever owned; he lived here from 1884 until his death on Mar 26, 1892. Contains original furnishings, books, and mementos. (Wed-Sat, also Sun afternoons) 330 Mickle Blvd. Phone 856/964-5383. **FREE**

Cape May

(C-8) *See also Wildwood and Wildwood Crest*

Settled 1631 **Pop** 4,034 **Elev** 14 ft **Area code** 609 **Zip** 08204

Information Chamber of Commerce, PO Box 556; 609/884-5508. Welcome Center, 405 Lafayette St; 609/884-9562

Web www.capemaychamber.com

Cape May, the nation's oldest seashore resort, is located on the

Cape May

southernmost tip of the state surrounded by the Atlantic Ocean and Delaware Bay. Popular with Philadelphia and New York society since 1766, Cape May has been host to Presidents Lincoln, Grant, Pierce, Buchanan, and Harrison, as well as notables such as John Wanamaker and Horace Greeley. The entire town has been proclaimed a National Historic Landmark because it has more than 600 Victorian homes and buildings, many of which have been restored. The downtown Washington Street Victorian Mall features three blocks of shops and restaurants. Four miles of beaches and a 1¼-mile paved promenade offer vacationers varied entertainment. "Cape May diamonds," often found on the shores of Delaware Bay by visitors, are actually pure quartz, rounded by the waves.

What to See and Do

Cape May-Lewes (DE) Ferry. Sole connection between southern terminus of Garden State Pkwy and US 13 (Ocean Hwy) on the Delmarva Peninsula. 16-mi, 70-min trip across Delaware Bay. (Daily) Phone 609/889-7200. ¢¢¢¢

Emlen Physick Estate. (1879) Authentically restored 18-rm Victorian mansion designed by Frank Fur-

ness. Mansion is also headquarters for the Mid-Atlantic Center for the Arts. (Daily) 1048 Washington St. Phone 609/884-5404. ¢¢

Historic Cold Spring Village. Restored early 1800s South Jersey farm village; 25 restored historic buildings on 22 acres. Craft shops; spinning, blacksmithing, weaving, pottery, broom making, ship modeling demonstrations; folk art; bakery and food shops; restaurant.(June-Sept, daily) 3 mi N via US 109. Phone 609/898-2300. ¢¢

Swimming, fishing, boating. Beaches with lifeguards (fee). Fishing is very good at the confluence of the Atlantic and Delaware Bay. A large harbor holds boats of all sizes; excellent for sailboating and other small-boat activity.

Tours. The Mid-Atlantic Center for the Arts offers the following tours. Contact PO Box 340; Cape May, 08204. Phone 609/884-5404.

Cape May INNteriors Tour & Tea. Features a different group of houses each week, visiting five or more bed-and-breakfast inns and guesthouses. Innkeepers greet guests and describe experiences. (Summer, Mon; rest of yr, Sat; no tours Dec-Jan) Phone 809/884-5404. ¢¢¢¢

Walt Whitman Tomb

Combination Tours. Approx two hrs; incl trolley tour and guided tour of Physick Estate. (June-Oct, daily; rest of yr, Sat and Sun) Begin at Emlen Physick Estate (see). Phone for schedule. ¢¢¢

Mansions by Gaslight. Three-hr tour begins at Emlen Physick Estate. Visits four Victorian landmarks: Emlen Physick House (see), the Abbey (1869), Mainstay Inn (1872), and Humphrey Hughes House (1903); shuttle bus between houses. (Mid-June-Sept, Wed evenings; rest of yr, hol and special tours) ¢¢¢¢

Ocean Walk Tours. A 1½-hr guided tour of Cape May's beaches. Guide discusses marine life and history of the beaches, incl legends of buried treasure. (May-Sept, Tues-Sat) Begins at Promenade and Beach Dr. ¢¢

Trolleys. Half-hr tours on enclosed trolley bus or open-air carriage; three routes beginning at Ocean St opp the Washington St Mall. (June-Oct, daily; reduced schedule rest of yr; no tours Thanksgiving) ¢¢

Walking Tours of the Historic District. Begin at Information Booth on Washington St Mall at Ocean St. Three 90-min guided tours give historical insight into the customs and traditions of the Victorians and their ornate architecture. (June-Sept, daily; reduced schedule rest of yr) ¢¢

Special Events

Tulip Festival. Celebrate Dutch heritage with ethnic foods and dancing, craft show, street fair, garden and house tours. Apr. Phone 609/884-5508.

Sea & Sky Festival. Sample Cape May's variety of seafood while colorful kites and blues music fill the air. June. Phone 609/884-5508.

Promenade Art Exhibit. July.

Victorian Week. Tours, antiques, crafts, period fashion shows. Mid-Oct.

Motels/Motor Lodges

★★ **COACHMAN'S MOTOR INN.** *205 Beach Ave (08204). 609/884-8463; fax 609/884-2643; toll-free 800/357-5828. www.coachmans motorinn.com.* 65 rms, 3 story, 45 kits. No elvtr. Late June-Labor Day (3-day min hols): S $70-$160; D $140-$185; each addl $15-20; kit. units $145-$185; lower rates rest of yr. Crib free. TV. Pool; wading pool. Restaurant 7:30 am-10 pm. Bar; entertainment. Ck-out 11 am. Coin lndry. Tennis. Lawn games. Basketball. Sun deck. On ocean. Cr cds: A, MC, V.

★★ **LA MER MOTOR INN.** *1317 Beach Ave (08204). 609/884-9000; fax 609/884-5004. www.lamermotorinn. com.* 93 rms, 4 story, 14 kits. July-Labor Day: S $118-$136; D $136-$195; each addl $15; kit. units to 5, $160-$170; lower rates May-June, after Labor Day-mid-Oct. Closed rest of yr. TV; VCR avail (movies). Pool; wading pool. Restaurant 5-10 pm. Ck-out 11 am. Coin lndry. Business servs avail. Miniature golf. Some microwaves. Bicycles. Picnic tables, grill. On ocean. Cr cds: A, C, D, DS, MC, V.

★★★ **MAINSTAY INN.** *635 Columbia Ave (08204). 609/884-8690. www. mainstayinn.com.* 9 rms, 3 story, 7 suites. Mar-Dec (2-3-day min): S, D $95-$255; each addl $35. Complimentary full bkfst; afternoon refreshments. Ck-out 11 am, ck-in 2 pm. Lawn games. Some balconies. Beach passes. Built in 1872 as a gentlemen's gambling house. Victorian decor; antiques; 14-ft ceilings. Veranda. Totally nonsmoking.

★★ **MONTREAL INN.** *1019 Beach Dr (08204). 609/884-7011; fax 609/884-4559; toll-free 800/525-7011. www.capemayfun.com.* 70 units, 4 story, 42 kits. Mid-June-mid-Sept: S, D, suites $52-$149; each addl $6-$9; kit. units $140-$165; lower rates Mar-mid-June, mid-Sept-Dec. Closed rest of yr. Crib free. TV; cable (premium). Heated pool; wading pool, whirlpool, poolside serv, lifeguard. Restaurant 8 am-11 pm. Bar from 11 am. Ck-out 11 am. Coin lndry. Business servs avail. In-rm modem link. Valet serv. Free airport transportation. Putting green, miniature golf. Exercise equipt; sauna. Game rm. Refrigerators; many microwaves. Balconies. Picnic tables, grills. On ocean. Cr cds: A, DS, MC, V.

★★ **MOUNT VERNON MOTEL.** *300 Beach Ave, at 1st Ave (08204). 609/884-4665. www.mountvernon motel.com.* 25 units, 2 story, 12 kits. July-Labor Day: S, D $145; each addl $12-$15; kit. units $148; lower rates Apr-June, after Labor Day-Oct. Closed rest of yr. Crib avail. TV; cable (premium). Pool; wading pool. Restaurant adj 8 am-midnight. Ck-out 11 am. Refrigerators; some microwaves. Sun deck. Opp ocean. Cr cds: A, MC, V.

★★ **PERIWINKLE INN.** *1039 Beach Ave (08204). 609/884-9200. www. periwinkleinn.com.* 50 rms, 3 story, 14 kits. July-Aug: S, D $130-$152; each addl $15; suites, kit. units $161-$205; lower rates mid-Apr-June, Sept-mid-Oct. Closed rest of yr. Crib free. TV; cable (premium). Pool; wading pool. Restaurant adj 7 am-10 pm. Ck-out 11 am. Refrigerators; some microwaves. Balconies. Grills. On ocean. Cr cds: A, MC, V.

Hotels

★★ **AVONDALE BY THE SEA.** *Beach and Gurney aves (08204). 609/884-2332; fax 609/884-2073; toll-free 800/676-7030. www.avondalebythe sea.com.* 46 rms, 3 story, 18 suites. Late July-early Sept: S, D $180; each addl $15; suites $164-$192; kit. units $184-$200; package plans; wkends 2-day min; lower rates rest of yr. Crib free. TV; cable. Complimentary continental bkfst. Restaurant adj 8 am-9 pm. Ck-out 11 am. Concierge. Pool. Refrigerators avail. Balconies. Opp ocean. Cr cds: A, DS, MC, V.

★★ **QUEEN'S HOTEL.** *601 Columbia Ave (08204). 609/884-1613. www. queenshotel.com.* 11 rms, 3 story, 2 suites. No elvtr. Mid-June-mid-Sept: S $110-$210; D $75-$220; each addl $25; suites $155-$250; wkend, wkly rates; wkends, hols (3-day min); lower rates rest of yr. Crib free. TV; cable, VCR avail. Complimentary coffee in rms. Restaurant nearby. Ck-out 11 am; ck-in 3 pm. Meeting rms. Concierge serv. Bicycles. Refrigerators; some microwaves. Some balconies. 1 blk to ocean. Totally nonsmoking. Cr cds: A, MC, V.

★★★ **VIRGINIA HOTEL.** *25 Jackson St (08204). 609/884-5700; fax 609/884-1236; toll-free 800/732-4236. www.virginiahotel.com.* 24 rms, 3 story. No elvtr. Memorial Day-Labor Day: S, D $80-$275; each addl $20; under 5 free; wkly rates; lower rates rest of yr. Crib free. TV; VCR (movies $2). Complimentary continental bkfst. Dining rm (see also EBBITT ROOM). Bar 5 pm-midnight; Sat, Sun from noon. Ck-out noon, ck-in 3 pm. Meeting rms. Business servs avail. In-rm modem link. Luggage handling. Concierge serv. Health club privileges. In-rm whirlpools. Balconies. Built 1879; restored. Antique and modern furnishing; amenities. Ocean view from veranda. Cr cds: A, C, D, DS, MC, V.

Historic homes in Cape May

Resorts

★★ **CARROLL VILLA HOTEL.** *19 Jackson St (08204). 609/884-9619; fax 609/884-0264. www.madbatter.com.* 22 rms, 3 story. Memorial Day-mid-Sept: S, D $110-$185; each addl $20; under 2 free; wkly rates; hols, wkends (2-3-day min); lower rates rest of yr. Crib avail. TV in parlor. Complimentary full bkfst. Restaurant (see MAD BATTER). Ck-out 11 am, ck-in 2 pm. Business servs avail. Victorian inn (1882); antiques. Cr cds: A, DS, MC, V.

★★ **GRAND HOTEL.** *1045 Beach Ave (08204). 609/884-5611; fax 609/898-0341; toll-free 800/257-8550. www.grandhotelcapemay.com.* 160 rms, 5 story, 30 suites, 40 kit. units. Late July-Aug: S, D $61-$133; each addl $10; suites $164-$267; kit. units $151-$267; family rates; package plans; lower rates rest of yr. Crib $9. TV; cable. Restaurant 8 am-10 pm. Bar noon-1 am; entertainment Fri, Sat. Ck-out 11 am. Meeting rms. Business servs avail. Sundries. Gift shop. Beauty shop. Coin lndry. Sauna. Indoor/outdoor pool; wading pool, whirlpool, poolside serv, lifeguard. Game rm. Refrigerators; many microwaves. Balconies. Picnic tables, grills. Cr cds: A, DS, MC, V.

★★ **MARQUIS DE LAFAYETTE HOTEL.** *501 Beach Ave (08204). 609/884-3500; fax 609/884-0669; toll-free 800/257-0432. www.marquis capemay.com.* 73 units, 6 story, 43 kits. July-Labor Day: S $99-$249; $129-$279; each addl $18; kit. units $259-$339; under 8 free; wkend rates; lower rates rest of yr. Crib avail. Pet accepted, some restrictions; $20/day. TV. Pool; poolside serv. Complimentary full bkfst. Restaurant. Bar; entertainment. Ck-out 1 pm. Coin lndry. Meeting rms. Business servs avail. Bellhops. Valet serv. Balconies. On ocean. Cr cds: A, D, DS, MC, V.

B&Bs/Small Inns

★★★ **THE ABBEY BED & BREAKFAST.** *34 Gurney St, at Columbia Ave (08204). 609/884-4506; fax 609/884-2379. www.abbeybedandbreakfast.com.* 14 rms in 2 buildings, 3 story. No rm phones. Apr-Dec: S, D $100-$295. Closed rest of yr. Children over 12 yrs only. Complimentary full bkfst; afternoon refreshments. Ck-out 11 am, ck-in after 2 pm. Lawn games. Picnic table. Beach passes, chairs, towels. Refrigerators. Gothic-style inn with 60-ft tower; main house built 1869; cottage built 1873. Stenciled and ruby glass arched windows; library, antiques. Cr cds: DS, MC, V.

★ **ABIGAIL ADAMS BED AND BREAKFAST.** *12 Jackson St (08204). 609/884-1371; fax 609/884-7116; res 888/827-4354. www.abigailadamsinn. com.* 5 rms, 3 with A/C, 2 air-cooled, 2 share bath, 3 story. No elvtr. No rm phones. Apr-Oct: S, D $125-$185; each addl $25; wkends, hols (3-4 day min); lower rates rest of yr. Children over 12 yrs only. TV in some rms; cable. Complimentary full bkfst; afternoon refreshments. Restaurant opp 8 am-10 pm. Ck-out 11 am, ck-

in 2 pm. Luggage handling. Street parking. 100 ft from beach. Built in 1892. Victorian inn; antiques. Totally nonsmoking. Cr cds: A, MC, V.

★ ★ ★ **ANGEL OF THE SEA.** *5 Trenton Ave (08204). 609/884-3369; fax 609/884-3331; res 800/848-3369. www.angelofthesea.com.* 27 rms, 3 story. A/C July, Aug only. No elvtr. No rm phones. June-Oct: S, D $135-$285; each addl $50; lower rates rest of yr. Children over 8 yrs only. TV; cable (premium), VCR avail. Complimentary full bkfst; afternoon refreshments. Ck-out 11 am, ck-in 2 pm.

CAPE MAY: AN ARCHITECTURAL BOUNTY

The Center for the Arts, located at the historic Emlen Physic Estate at 1048 Washington Street (phone 609/884-5404), is a good place to begin a walking tour that explores some of the many (more than 600!) Victorian-era buildings in Cape May. Enjoy the 45-minute house tour, which imparts an excellent, concise history of Cape May. Leaving the estate, turn left, go right onto Madison and, having arrived at the corner of Virginia Street, turn left and walk amid the grid created by Madison, Philadelphia, and Reading Streets as they intersect Virginia, Ohio, Cape May Idaho, Maryland, New York, and New Jersey Streets. The entire neighborhood is rich in antique homes.

Having completed as much neighborhood viewing as you want, return to Madison. Turn left onto Sewell, then right onto Franklin. At the corner of Columbia Avenue, note The Clivedon Inn (709 Columbia) on the right. Turn left on Columbia. Here stand the Henry Sawyer Inn (722 Columbia) with its magnificent garden; the Dormer House (800 Columbia), a Colonial Revivalist home; The Inn at Journey's End (710 Columbia); and The Mainstay Inn (635 Columbia), once a gentlemen's gambling house.

Walk toward the ocean on Howard Street. At Beach Drive stands the Hotel Macomber (727 Beach Drive), built in the Shingle style. Turn right, walk three blocks to Ocean Street, turn right and look for the Queen Anne-style Columbia House (26 Ocean Street) and Twin Gables (731 Ocean Street), with its pair of Gothic gables. Go left on Hughes to Decatur, turn right and in three short blocks enter the downtown shopping district. Here, along the Washington Street Mall, Lyle Lane, Jackson Street, and Perry Street are dozens of shops, restaurants, and inns. Stop at the corner of the Washington Street Mall and Perry to look at Congress Hall, a gargantuan hotel. At 9 Perry, near Beach Drive, stands the King's Cottage, built in the Mansard style with Stick-style detailing. Another excellent Queen Anne-style building, The Inn at 22 Jackson, is found on Jackson Street parallel to Perry. Nearby, the Virginia Hotel (25 Jackson) serves five-star meals in their upscale dining room. You could also take a meal at the Mad Batter (19 Jackson), a Victorian bed-and-breakfast inn, where breakfast on the veranda is a long-standing Cape May tradition.

For a classic Jersey shore finish, return to the beach (at Jackson and Beach Drive) and stroll along the water's edge, or shop and snack along the Promenade. On a summer's eve, another option is to take in a play performed by the professional Cape May Stage. To reach them, stroll back up Jackson (away form the ocean), past the Washington Street Mall to Lafayette Street. Turn right—the theater is in the Visitor Center.

Business servs avail. Concierge serv. Gift shop. Free airport transportation. Some balconies. Picnic tables. Authentic Victorian house (1850). Located opp ocean, swimming beach. Totally nonsmoking. Cr cds: A, DS, MC, V.

★★ **COLVMNS BY THE SEA BED & BREAKFAST.** *1513 Beach Dr (08204). 609/884-2228; fax 609/884-4789. www.colvmns.com.* 11 air-cooled rms, 3 story. No rm phones. July-Aug: S $150-$260; D $160-$275; each addl $40; wkly rates; lower rates rest of yr. Children over 7 yrs only. TV; cable. Complimentary full bkfst; afternoon refreshments. Restaurant nearby. Ck-out 11:30 am, ck-in 2 pm. Bicycles. Library. Refrigerators. Victorian furnishings; antiques. On beach. Totally nonsmoking. Cr cds: MC, V.

★ **INN OF CAPE MAY.** *7 Ocean St, at Beach Dr (08204). 609/884-5555; fax 609/884-3871; toll-free 800/582-5933. www.innofcapemay.com.* 69 rms, 5 story. No rm phones. July-Aug: S, D $98-$275; each addl $20; MAP avail; package plans; lower rates mid-May-June, Sept-mid-Nov. Closed rest of yr. Crib avail. TV; cable. Pool; poolside serv. Restaurant (see also ALEATHEA'S). No rm serv. Bar 11-1 am. Ck-out 1 pm. Meeting rms. Business servs avail. On ocean. Opened 1894; antiques. Cr cds: A, D, DS, MC, V.

★★★ **THE QUEEN VICTORIA B & B INN.** *102 Ocean St (08204). 609/884-8702. www.queenvictoria.com.* 17 rms, 3 story, 6 suites. June-Sept: S $80-$220; D $90-$230; each addl $25; suites $245-$280; lower rates rest of yr. TV; VCR avail. Complimentary full bkfst; afternoon refreshments. Ck-out 11 am; ck-in 3 pm. Bicycles, beach passes. Whirlpool in suites. Restored Victorian villas; rms individually decorated with Victorian antiques. Cr cds: A, MC, V.

★★★ **THE SOUTHERN MANSION.** *720 Washington St (08204). 609/884-7171; fax 609/898-0492; res 609/884-7171. www.thesouthern mansion.com.* 24 rms, 3 story. July-Dec: S, D $140-$350; each addl $35;

suite $175-$350; family rates; lower rates rest of yr. Children over 8 yrs only. TV; cable, VCR avail. Complimentary full bkfst. Ck-out 11 am, ck-in 3 pm. Business servs avail. In-rm modem link. Luggage handling. Concierge serv. Massage. Lawn games. Picnic tables. Built in 1863; 5,000 square ft of verandahs, terraces and solariums; mid-19th century antiques. Totally nonsmoking. Cr cds: A, MC, V.

★★ **VICTORIAN LACE INN.** *901 Stockton Ave (08204). 609/884-1772; fax 609/884-0983. www.victorianlace inn.com.* 5 rms, 2 with shower only, 3 story. July-Aug: S, D $100-$195; each addl $10-15; lower rates Mar-June, Sept-Dec. Closed early Jan-mid-Feb. TV; cable, VCR. Complimentary full bkfst. Restaurant nearby. Ck-out 10 am, ck-in 2 pm. Refrigerators, microwaves, fireplaces. Built in 1869; antiques. Totally nonsmoking. Cr cds: A, MC, V.

Restaurants

★ **ALEATHEA'S.** *7 Ocean Dr (08204). 609/884-5555. www.aleatheas.com.* Hrs: 8 am-noon, 5-10 pm; early-bird dinner 5-6 pm (seasonal). Closed hols; also Sept-mid-May. Res accepted. Bar to 11 pm. Bkfst $3-$15, dinner $14-$32. Child's menu. Specialties: grilled filet mignon, grilled swordfish, baked salmon. Parking. Property built in 1894; view of ocean. Cr cds: A, D, DS, MC, V.

★★ **ALEXANDER'S INN.** *653 Washington St (08204). 609/884-2555. www.alexandersinn.com.* Hrs: 6-10 pm; Sun brunch 10 am-1 pm. Closed Mon, Tues; Jan 1, Thanksgiving, Dec 25. Res accepted. French menu. Setups. Dinner $27.95-$39.95. Complete meals: dinner $39.95-$57.95. Specializes in rack of lamb, rabbit, Angus beef. Own ice cream. Victorian decor; antiques. Cr cds: A, C, D, DS, MC, V.

★★★ **EBBITT ROOM.** *25 Jackson St (08204). 609/884-5700. www.virginia hotel.com.* Amer cuisine with Asian influences. Specialties: pan-seared yellowfin tuna in sesame crust with crisp rice paper, grilled rack of lamb with white bean cassoulet and peach chutney, oven-roasted lobster monkfish wrapped in won ton with dual Tabasco butter sauces. Hrs: 5:30-9:30 pm; Fri, Sat to 10 pm. Res accepted. Valet Parking. Bar. A la carte: dinner $24-$28. Child's menu. Extensive wine list. Pianist; nightly in season, weekends off-season. Intimate Victorian dining rm. Totally nonsmoking. Cr cds: A, C, D, DS, MC, V.

⊠

★ ★ **410 BANK STREET.** *410 Bank St (08204). 609/884-2127. www.410bank street.com.* Hrs: 5-10:30 pm. Closed Nov-Apr. Res accepted. Louisiana French menu. Setups. A la carte entrees: dinner $22-$28. Child's menu. Specializes in grilled fish steaks and prime meats. Porch and garden dining. Restored 1840 Cape May residence. Island atmosphere. Cr cds: A, C, D, DS, MC, V.

★ ★ **FRESCOS.** *412 Bank St (08204). 609/884-0366. www.beachcomber.com.* Hrs: 5-10:30 pm. Closed Nov-Apr. Res accepted. Italian menu. A la carte entrees: dinner $15-$23.95. Child's menu. Specializes in fresh seafood, pasta, veal. Outdoor dining. Three dining areas in restored Victorian summer cottage. Cr cds: A, C, D, DS, MC, V.

⊡

★ ★ **LOBSTER HOUSE.** *Fisherman's Wharf (08204). 609/884-3405. www. thelobsterhouse.com.* Hrs: 11:30 am-3 pm, 4:30-10 pm; Sun from 4 pm; winter hrs vary. Closed Thanksgiving, Dec 24-25. Bar. Lunch $5.75-$12.50, dinner $15.95-$38.95. Child's menu. Specializes in fresh fish, lobster, crab meat. Parking. Outdoor dining. On wharf; nautical decor. Fireplace. Raw seafood bars in main bar and dock. Cr cds: A, D, DS, MC, V.

Ⓓ ⊡

★ ★ **MAD BATTER.** *19 Jackson St (08204). 609/884-9619. www.mad batter.com.* Hrs: 8 am-2:30 pm, 5:30-10 pm; Fri, Sat to 10:30 pm. Closed Jan. Res accepted dinner. Contemporary Amer menu. Setups. A la carte entrees: bkfst, lunch $5-$11, dinner $15-$25. Child's menu. Specializes in fresh seafood, desserts. Outdoor din-

ing. Victorian inn (1882). Cr cds: A, D, DS, MC, V.

Ⓓ

★ ★ **MERION INN.** *106 Decatur St (08204). 609/884-8363. www.merion inn.com.* Hrs: noon-2:30 pm, 5-10 pm, early-bird dinner 5-6 pm. Closed Jan-Mar; also Mon-Thurs Apr-May and mid-Oct-Dec. Res accepted. Bar. Lunch $5.95-$15.95, dinner $14.95-$32.95. Child's menu. Specializes in stuffed lobster tail, fresh grilled fish, steak. Own desserts. Outdoor dining. Turn-of-the-century Victorian decor. Built 1885. Family-owned. Cr cds: A, D, DS, MC, V.

★ ★ **PEACHES AT SUNSET.** *1 W Sunset Blvd (08204). 609/898-0100. www.peachesatsunset.com.* Hrs: 4:30-10 pm. Closed Dec 25; also Mon-Thurs Oct-May. Res accepted. Pacific Rim cuisine. Dinner $17.95-$27.95. Child's menu. Specialties: sea bass with mango salsa, rack of lamb. Free parking. Outdoor dining. Local artwork displayed. Totally nonsmoking. Cr cds: A, D, DS, MC, V.

Ⓓ ⊠

★ ★ **PELICAN CLUB.** *501 Beach Ave (08204). 609/884-3500. www.pelican clubcapemay.com.* Hrs: 5-10 pm. Closed Dec 24, 25. Res accepted. Bar. Complete meals: dinner $12.95-$43. Child's menu. Specializes in lobster, beef tenderloin. Pianist. Valet parking in season. Victorian setting with view of Atlantic Ocean. Cr cds: A, D, DS, MC, V.

Ⓓ

★ **RUSTY NAIL.** *205 Beach Dr (08204). 609/884-0220. www. coachmansmotorinn.com.* Hrs: 7:30-1 am. Closed Nov-mid-Apr. Bar. Complete meals: bkfst $5-$8.50, lunch $6.50-$10. Dinner $9.25-$22. Child's menu. Specializes in crab cakes, prime rib, lemon chicken. Beach decor. Cr cds: A, MC, V.

Ⓓ ⊡

★ ★ ★ **WASHINGTON INN.** *801 Washington St (08204). 609/884-5697. www.washingtoninn.com.* Hrs: 5-10 pm; hrs may vary wkends and off season. Closed Thanksgiving, Dec 24-25. Res accepted; required Sat. Continental menu. Bar. Wine cellar. Dinner $17.95-$25.95. Child's menu. Specializes in steak, veal, fresh seafood. Own baking. Patio dining. Former plantation house (1848). Fireside dining. Cr cds: A, D, DS, MC, V. D

★★ **WATER'S EDGE.** *Beach and Pittsburgh aves (08204). 609/884-1717. www.watersedgerestaurant.com.* Hrs: 5-11 pm; hrs vary off season. Closed Thanksgiving, Dec 25. Res accepted. Bar. A la carte entrees: dinner $19-$28. Child's menu. Specializes in fresh local seafood, free-range veal, Angus steak. Contemporary decor. Patio dining, ocean view. Cr cds: A, D, DS, MC, V. D

Cape May Court House

(C-8) *See also Cape May, Stone Harbor, Wildwood and Wildwood Crest*

Pop 4,704 **Elev** 18 ft **Area code** 609 **Zip** 08210
Information Cape May County Chamber of Commerce, PO Box 74; 609/465-7181
Web www.cmccofc.com

To be accurately named, this county seat would have to be called Cape May Court Houses, for there are two of them—one is a white, 19th-century building now used as a meeting hall.

What to See and Do

Cape May County Historical Museum. Period dining rm (predating 1820), 18th-century kitchen, doctor's rm, military rm with Merrimac flag, Cape May diamonds. Barn exhibits; whaling implements; Indian artifacts; pioneer tools; lens from Cape May Point Lighthouse. Genealogical library. (Mid-Apr-Nov, Tues-Sat; rest of yr, Sat only) Shore Rd, 1 mi N on US 9. Phone 609/465-3535. ¢

Cape May County Park. Zoo has over 100 types of animals. Jogging path, bike trail, tennis courts, picnicking, playground. (Daily) On US 9 at Crest Haven Rd. Phone 609/465-5271.
Donation

Leaming's Run Gardens. Amid 20 acres of lawns, ponds, and ferneries are 25 gardens, each with a separate theme. Eighteenth-century colonial farm grows tobacco and cotton; farm animals. (Mid-May-mid-Oct, daily) Approx 4 mi N on US 9, between Pkwy exits 13 and 17 in Swainton. Phone 609/465-5871. ¢¢¢

Victorian houses. Over 600 fine examples of 19th-century architecture located in the area. Information can be obtained at the Chamber of Commerce Information Center, Crest Haven Rd and Garden State Pkwy, milepost 11 (Easter mid Oct, daily; rest of yr, Mon-Fri; closed hols).

Motel/Motor Lodge

★ **HY-LAND MOTOR INN.** *38 E Mechanic St, Cape May (08210). 609/465-7305; fax 609/465-8776. www.hylandmotorinn.com.* 34 rms, 24 with shower only, 2 story. Mid-June-Sept: S $50-$85; D $55-$89; each addl $10; suite $100-$125; kits $90-$125; under 10 free; lower rates rest of yr. Crib $5. TV; cable. Pool. Restaurant nearby. Ck-out 11 am. Business servs avail. Picnic tables, grill. Cr cds: A, DS, MC, V. D

B&B/Small Inn

★★★ **THE DOCTORS INN.** *2 N Main St (08210). 609/463-9330; fax 609/463-9194. www.doctorsinn.com.* 6 rms, 3 story. June-Oct: D, suites $135-$170; lower rates rest of yr. TV; cable. Complimentary full bkfst. Ck-out 11 am, ck-in 2 pm. Some refrigerators. Built in 1854; pays tribute to physicians and teachers who ministered to the community. Totally nonsmoking. Cr cds: A, DS, MC, V.

Chatham (D-3)

Pop 10,686 **Elev** 244 ft **Area code** 973 **Zip** 07928
Information Township of Chatham, 58 Meyersville Rd; 973/635-4600
Web www.chathamtownship.org

What to See and Do

Great Swamp National Wildlife Refuge. SW of city (see BERNARDSVILLE). Phone 973/425-1222.

Restaurant

★ ★ ★ ★ **RESTAURANT SERE-NADE.** *6 Roosevelt Ave (07928). 973/701-0303. www.restaurantserenade. com.* Located in a converted house in a residential part of town, this bustling restaurant is known for its wine list and the creative cooking of chef James Laird. The restaurant is about 45 minutes from Manhattan. Specializes in contemporary French cuisine. Hrs: noon-2 pm, 6-9:30 pm; Sat 5:30-10 pm. Closed Sun; hols. Res accepted, required Sat. Bar. Wine list. A la carte entrees: lunch $8-$15, dinner $17-$28. Jacket. Cr cds: A, C, D, DS, MC, V.

Cherry Hill

(B-5) *See also Camden, Haddonfield*

Pop 69,965 **Elev** 30 ft **Area code** 856
Information Chamber of Commerce, 1060 Kings Hwy N, Suite 200, 08034; 609/667-1600
Web www.cherryhillnj.com

What to See and Do

Barclay Farmstead. One of the earliest properties settled in what is now Cherry Hill; origins traced to 1684. The township-owned site consists of 32 acres of open space; restored Federal-style farmhouse; operating forge barn; corn crib; Victorian spring house. Grounds (all yr); house tours (Tues-Fri, first Sun each month; and by appt). 209 Barclay Ln. Phone 856/795-6225. ¢

Motels/Motor Lodges

★ ★ **CLARION HOTEL.** *1450 Rte 70 E (08034). 609/428-2300; fax 609/354-7662. www.clarionhotel.com.* 213 rms, 4 story. S $98-$139; D $108-$159;

each addl $10; under 18 free; wkend rates. Crib free. TV; cable (premium), VCR avail. Pool. Coffee in rms. Restaurant. Bar 11-2 am. Ck-out noon. Meeting rms. Business center. In-rm modem link. Gift shop. Airport transportation. Tennis. Exercise equipt. Health club privileges. Microwaves avail. Cr cds: A, C, D, DS, ER, MC, V.

★ **DAYS INN.** *550 Fellowship Rd, Mt Laurel (08054). 609/235-7400; fax 609/778-9729; res 800/228-5151. www.daysinn.com/mtlaurel.* 150 rms, 2 story. S, D $52-$99; each addl $10; under 12 free. Crib free. TV; cable (premium). Pool. Restaurant 7 am-11 pm. Rm serv. Bar 11-2 am. Ck-out noon. Coin lndry. Meeting rms. Business servs avail. In-rm modem link. Valet serv. Exercise equipt. Health club privileges. Refrigerators, microwaves avail. Cr cds: A, C, D, DS, MC, V.

★ ★ **HAMPTON INN.** *121 Laurel Oak Rd, Voorhees (08043). 856/346-4500; fax 856/346-2402. www. hamptoninn.com.* 122 rms, 50 with shower only, 4 story. S, D $88-$95; under 18 free. Crib avail. Pet accepted. TV; cable (premium), VCR avail. Pool. Complimentary continental bkfst. Restaurant adj 11 am-11 pm. Ck-out noon. Business servs avail. In-rm modem link. Health club privileges. Refrigerators, microwaves avail. Cr cds: A, D, DS, MC, V.

★ ★ **HOLIDAY INN.** *Rte 70 and Sayer Ave (08034). 856/663-5300; fax 856/662-2913; toll-free 800/465-4329. www.holiday-inn.com.* 186 rms, 6 story. S, D $99-$109; each addl $8; under 19 free; wkend rates. Crib free. Pet accepted. TV; cable (premium), VCR avail. 2 pools, 1 indoor; wading pool. Restaurant (see also RED HOT & BLUE). Bar 11 am-11 pm. Ck-out noon. Coin lndry. Meeting rms. Business center. In-rm modem link. Valet serv. Exercise equipt; sauna. Microwaves avail. Cr cds: A, C, D, DS, ER, JCB, MC, V.

★ **MCINTOSH INN.** *1132 NJ 73 and Church Rd, Mt Laurel (08054).*

856/234-7194; fax 856/231-8516; res 800/444-2775. 91 rms, 2 story. S, D $50.95-$65.95. Crib free. TV; cable (premium). Complimentary continental bkfst. Restaurant adj open 24 hrs. Ck-out 11 am. Business servs avail. Refrigerators, microwaves avail. Cr cds: A, D, MC, V.

Hotels

★ ★ ★ **HILTON HOTEL.** *2349 W Marlton Pike (08002). 609/665-6666; fax 609/662-3676. www.hilton.com.* 408 rms, 14 story. S $119-$209; D $129-$219; each addl $10; suites $350-$650; under 14 free. Crib free. Pet accepted. TV; cable (premium), VCR avail. Pool; wading pool. Coffee in rms. Restaurant 6 am-11 pm. Bar 11-1 am. Ck-out noon. Convention facilities. Business center. In-rm modem link. Valet serv. Exercise equipt. Some refrigerators; microwaves avail. Cr cds: A, C, D, DS, JCB, MC, V.

Barclay Farmstead, Cherry Hill

★ ★ ★ **RADISSON.** *915 NJ 73N, Mt Laurel (08054). 856/234-7300; fax 856/802-3912; res 800/333-3333. www.radisson.com.* 283 rms, 10 story. S, D $99-$109; suites $250-$350; under 17 free. Crib free. TV; cable (premium). Pool; poolside serv, lifeguard. Restaurant 6:30 am-10 pm; Sat, Sun from 7 am. Bar. Ck-out noon. Coin lndry. Convention facilities. Business servs avail. In-rm modem link. Gift shop. Lighted tennis. Golf privileges. Exercise equipt. Health club privileges. Game rm. Some in-rm whirlpools, refrigerators; microwaves avail. Picnic tables. Some private patios, balconies. Luxury level. Cr cds: A, C, D, DS, ER, JCB, MC, V.

Restaurants

★ **BROOKLAWN DINER.** *NJ 130, Gloucester City (08030). 856/742-0035.* Hrs: open 24 hrs. Closed Dec 25. Res accepted. Greek, American menu. Bar 11 am-10 pm; Sun from 1 pm. Bkfst $1.90-$5.20, lunch $4.50-$5.50, dinner $5.95-$13.50. Buffet: bkfst $5.65. Child's menu. Specialties: prime rib, Greek-style lamb stew, lunch soup and salad special. Parking. American diner; chrome exterior. Totally nonsmoking. Cr cds: A, DS, MC, V.

★ ★ **CAFFE LA BELLA.** *61 E Main St, Morristown (08057). 856/234-7755.* Hrs: 10:30 am-2:30 pm, 4:30-9 pm; Fri, Sat to 9:30 pm; Mon 10:30 am-2:30 pm; Sun 8:30 am-2 pm, 4:30-8:30 pm; Sun brunch 9 am-2 pm. Closed hols. Res required Fri, Sat (dinner). Italian menu. Lunch $4.25-$13.95, dinner $13.95-$22.95. Sun brunch $10.95. Child's menu. Specialties: cioppino, chicken continental, veal romano. Harpist Tues, Sun. Parking. Casual, intimate dining. Totally nonsmoking. Cr cds: MC, V.

★ **GOLDEN EAGLE DINER.** *NJ 73S at I-295,*

Maple Shade (08052). 856/235-8550.
Hrs: 6 am-midnight; Fri, Sat to 4 am.
Res accepted. Bar from 11 am. Bkfst
$1.99-$6, lunch $5.25-$6.95, dinner
$7.95-$13.95. Child's menu. Specializes in prime rib, seafood. Salad bar.
Parking. Cr cds: A, D, DS, MC, V.

★ ★ ★ **LA CAMPAGNE.** *312 Kresson
Rd (08034). 856/429-7647. www.
lacampagne.com.* Hrs: 11:30 am-2:30
pm, 5-10 pm; Sun brunch 10 am-2
pm. Closed Mon. Res accepted.
French menu. Lunch $7.50-$15, dinner $25-$29.50. Sun brunch $10.95-
$19.95. Child's menu. Specializes in
rack of lamb, seafood, duck. Outdoor
dining. Country French decor. Cr
cds: A, D, MC, V.

★ ★ **LOS AMIGOS MEXICAN
RESTAURANT.** *461 NJ 73, West
Berlin (08091). 856/767-5247. www.
losamigosrest.com.* Hrs: 5-11 pm; Fri
to 11 pm; Sat 3-11 pm; Sun 3-10 pm.
Closed Mon; hols. Southwestern
menu. Bar. A la carte entrees: dinner
$9.95-$20.95. Child's menu. Specialties: Southwestern crab cakes,
Tabasco tequila shrimp. Outdoor dining. Fiesta atmosphere; Mexican cantina decor. Family-owned. Cr cds: A,
D, MC, V.

★ ★ **MELANGE CAFE.** *1601 Chapel
Ave (08002). 856/663-7339. www.
melangecafe.com.* Hrs: 11 am-10 pm;
Fri to 11 pm; Sat 4-11 pm; Sun 2-10
pm. Closed Mon; also July 4, Thanksgiving, Dec 25. Res accepted. Italian,
Louisiana menu. A la carte entrees:
lunch $9-$12, dinner $16-$24.
Child's menu. Specialties: pan-
smoked tomato crab bisque, jambal-
aya, seafood étouffé. Parking.
Outdoor dining. Upscale casual dining. Totally nonsmoking. Cr cds: A,
D, DS, MC, V.

★ **RED HOT & BLUE.** *Rte 70 and
Sayer Ave (08034). 856/665-7427.
www.redhotandblue.com.* Hrs: 11 am-
10 pm; Fri to 11 pm; Sat to midnight; Sun from noon. Closed Easter,
Thanksgiving, Dec 25. Res accepted
(dinner). Bar; Fri, Sat to 2 am. Lunch,
dinner $5.50-$13. Child's menu. Specialties: pulled pork, barbecue pork

ribs, beef brisket. Blues Fri, Sat.
Casual, Memphis-style barbecue. Cr
cds: A, D, DS, MC, V.

★ ★ **SIRI'S THAI FRENCH CUISINE.**
*2117 Rte 70W (08002). 856/663-
6781.* Hrs: 11:30 am-10 pm; Fri, Sat
to 11 pm. Closed hols. Res accepted.
Thai, French menu. A la carte
entrees: lunch $9-$15, dinner $12-
$24.95. Specialties: seafood medley,
rack of lamb, crispy duck. Parking.
Thai decor. Totally nonsmoking. Cr
cds: A, D, MC, V.

Clifton (E-2)

Pop 78,682 **Elev** 70 ft **Area code** 973
Information North Jersey Regional
Chamber of Commerce, 1033 US 46
E, PO Box 110, 07011; 973/470-9300
Web www.njrcc.org

What to See and Do

Hamilton House Museum. Early
19th-century sandstone farmhouse
with period furniture; country store;
exhibits. Open-hearth cooking
demonstrations by costumed guides.
(Mar-Dec, First Sun each month,
Tues-Thurs afternoons; closed hol
wkends) 971 Valley Rd. Phone
973/744-5707. **FREE**

Motels/Motor Lodges

★ **HOWARD JOHNSON INN.** *680
Rte 3W (07014). 973/471-3800; fax
973/471-2128; res 800/466-4656.
www.hojo.com.* 116 rms, 4 story. S
$84-$114, D $94-$124; each addl
$10; under 18 free; wkend rates. Crib
free. Pet accepted, some restrictions.
TV; cable (premium). Pool; lifeguard.
Restaurant 7 am-11 pm. Bar 4 pm-2
am. Ck-out noon. Meeting rm. Business servs avail. In-rm modem link.
Sundries. Refrigerators, microwaves
avail. Private patios, balconies. Cr
cds: A, D, DS, MC, V.

★★ **RAMADA INN-CLIFTON.** *265 Rte 3E (07014). 973/778-6500; fax 973/778-8724. www.ramada.com.* 183 rms, 4 story. S, D $89-$139; each addl $10; suites $200; kit units $150; under 12 free; wkend rates. Crib free. Pet accepted. TV; cable (premium). Indoor pool. Restaurant 6:30 am-10 pm; wkends from 7 am. Bar; entertainment. Ck-out noon. Meeting rms. Business servs avail. Sundries. Gift shop. Exercise equipt; sauna. Some refrigerators; microwaves avail. Cr cds: A, C, D, DS, MC, V.

Clinton

(C-3) *See also Flemington*

Pop 2,632 **Elev** 195 ft **Area code** 908 **Zip** 08809

What to See and Do

Red Mill Museum Village. Four-story gristmill (ca 1810). Ten-acre park houses education center, quarry and lime kilns, blacksmith shop, general store, one-rm schoolhouse, log cabin, machinery sheds, herb garden. Also home of Clinton's landmark red mill. Gift shop. (Apr-Oct, Tues-Sun) Outdoor concerts some Sat eves in summer (fee). 56 Main St, off I-78. Phone 908/735-4101. ¢¢

Round Valley State Park. A 4,003-acre park. Swimming, fishing, boating; picnicking, concession (Memorial Day-Labor Day), wilderness camping (access to campsites via hiking or boating only). Standard fees. Off US 22, E of jct I-78; follow signs. Phone 908/236-6355.

Spruce Run State Recreation Area. A 1,290 acres water, 600 acres park. Swimming, fishing, boating (launch, rentals); picnicking, concession, camping (dump station) (Apr-Oct). Standard fees. 3 mi NW off NJ 31. Phone 908/638-8572.

Motel/Motor Lodge

★★ **HOLIDAY INN SELECT OF CLINTON.** *111 Rte 173 (08809). 908/735-5111; fax 908/730-9768; res 888/452-5770. www.holiday-inn.com.* 142 units, 5 story. S $125-$145; D $133-$153; each addl $8; suites $145-$160; under 18 free; wkend rates. Crib free. TV; cable (premium). Indoor pool. Coffee in rms. Restaurant 6:30 am-11 pm. Bar 3 pm-midnight; entertainment Tues-Sat. Ck-out noon. Meeting rms. Business center. In-rm modem link. Sundries. Exercise equipt. Microwaves avail. Some balconies. Cr cds: A, C, D, DS, MC, V.

B&B/Small Inn

★★ **STEWART INN.** *708 S Main St, Stewartsvllle (08886). 908/479-6060; fax 908/479-4211. www.bbianj.com/stewartinn.* 7 rms, 2 story. S, D $95-$135; suite $125-$135. Children over 12 yrs only. TV; VCR avail. Pool. Complimentary full bkfst. Restaurant nearby. Ck-out 11 am, ck-in 3 pm. Business servs avail. Picnic tables, grills. Stone manor house built in 1770s, set amidst 16 acres of lawns, gardens, woods, stream, and pasture. Trout stream, barns and outbuildings with farm animals. Totally nonsmoking. Cr cds: A, DS, MC, V.

Restaurant

★★ **CLINTON HOUSE.** *2 W Main St (08809). 908/730-9300. www.the clintonhouse.com.* Hrs: 11:30 am-2:30 pm, 5-9:30 pm. Closed Dec 25. Res accepted. Bar to midnight. Lunch $6.95-$21.95, dinner $16.95-$26. Child's menu. Specializes in beef, seafood. Built 1743; former stagecoach stop. Family-owned. Cr cds: A, MC, V.

Eatontown

(E-4) *See also Red Bank*

Pop 14,008 **Elev** 46 ft **Area code** 732 **Zip** 07724

Motels/Motor Lodges

★★ **HOLIDAY INN.** *700 Hope Rd, Tinton Falls (07724). 732/544-9300; fax 732/544-0570; toll-free 800/465-*

4329. www.holiday-inn.com. 171 rms, 5 story. S, D $99-$159; each addl $10; suites $115-$225; wkend rates. Crib free. TV; cable (premium). Pool; poolside serv. Restaurant 6:30 am-11 pm. Bar 11:30-2 am. Ck-out noon. Lndry facilities. Meeting rms. Business servs avail. In-rm modem link. Bellhops. Valet serv. Gift shop. Exercise equipt; sauna. Refrigerators, microwaves avail. Cr cds: A, C, D, DS, ER, JCB, MC, V.

★ **RED ROOF INN.** *11 Centre Plaza, Tinton Falls (07724). 732/389-4646; fax 732/389-4509; toll-free 800/843-7663.* www.redroof.com. 119 rms, 3 story. May-Labor Day: S, D $85-$89; each addl $7; under 18 free; lower rates rest of yr. Crib free. Pet accepted, some restrictions. TV; cable (premium). Restaurant nearby. Ck-out noon. Cr cds: A, C, D, DS, MC, V.

Hotels

★★★ **OCEAN PLACE CONFERENCE RESORT.** *1 Ocean Blvd, Long Branch (07740). 732/571-4000; fax 732/571-3314; toll-free 800/411-7321.* www.oceanplace.com. 254 rms, 12 story. Memorial Day-Labor Day: S $170-$205; D $190-$225; each addl $20; suites $350-$1,000; family, wkend rates; lower rates rest of yr. Crib free. TV; cable (premium). VCR avail. 2 pools, 1 indoor; whirlpools, poolside serv, lifeguard. Supervised children's activities (mid-May-early Sept), ages 3-12. Restaurants 6:30 am-10 pm; Sat, Sun from 7 am. Bar 11-2 am; entertainment. Ck-out noon. Convention facilities. Business center. In-rm modem link. Concierge. Shopping arcade. Barber, beauty shop. Free garage parking. RR station transportation. Lighted tennis. Exercise rm; sauna, steam rm. Massage. Balconies. On ocean. Cr cds: A, C, D, DS, ER, MC, V.

★★★ **SHERATON EATONTOWN HOTEL & CONFERENCE CENTER.** *Rte 35, at Industrial Way E (07724). 732/542-6500; fax 732/542-6607; toll-free 800/544-5064.* www.sheraton.com. 208 rms, 6 story. May-Sept: S $154-$164; D $164-$174; each addl

$15; suites $364; wkend rates; lower rates rest of yr. Crib free. TV; cable (premium). Indoor/outdoor pool; whirlpool. Restaurant 6:30 am-11 pm. Bar. Ck-out noon. Meeting rms. Business center. In-rm modem link. Gift shop. Coin lndry. Exercise equipt. Health club privileges. Refrigerators, microwaves avail. Cr cds: A, C, D, DS, MC, V.

Extended Stay

★★ **RESIDENCE INN BY MARRIOTT TINTON FALLS.** *90 Park Rd, Tinton Falls (07724). 732/389-8100; fax 732/389-1573; res 800/331-3131.* www.residenceinn.com. 96 kit. suites. S, D $119-$159. Crib free. Pet accepted. TV; cable (premium), VCR avail. Pool; whirlpool. Complimentary continental bkfst. Restaurant nearby. Ck-out noon. Coin lndry. Meeting rms. Business servs avail. In-rm modem link. Valet serv. Health club privileges. Microwaves. Balconies. Picnic tables, grills. Cr cds: A, C, D, DS, ER, JCB, MC, V.

Restaurant

★★ **JOE & MAGGIE'S BISTRO.** *591 Broadway, Long Branch (07740). 732/571-8848.* Hrs: 11:30 am-2:30 pm, 4-10 pm; Fri, Sat to 11 pm; Sun to 9 pm; early-bird dinner 4-6 pm (Mon-Thurs). Closed Thanksgiving, Dec 25; also day after Labor Day, Super Bowl Sun. Res required Sat (dinner). Contemporary American menu. Bar. A la carte entrees: lunch $5.95-$10.95, dinner $15-$25. Specialties: grilled lamb chops, filet mignon. Street parking. Casual dining; bistro atmosphere. Cr cds: A, D, MC, V.

Edison

(D-3) *See also Woodbridge*

Pop 97,687 **Elev** 95 ft **Area code** 732
Information Chamber of Commerce, 100 Menlo Park, 3rd Fl, PO

Box 2103, 08818-2103; 732/494-0300

Web www.edisonchamber.com

Although Thomas A. Edison's house here has been destroyed, Menlo Park and the Edison Memorial Tower stand in tribute to the great American inventor. Here, on December 6, 1877, the 30-year-old Edison invented the phonograph. Two years later, he perfected the first practical incandescent light, designing and constructing various kinds of electrical equipment we now take for granted. His workshop has been moved to the Ford Museum in Dearborn, Michigan. Edison also built the first electric railway locomotive here in 1880; it ran 1½ miles over the fields of Pumptown.

What to See and Do

Edison Memorial Tower and Menlo Park Museum. A 131-ft tower topped by a 13½-ft-high electric light bulb stands at the birthplace of recorded sound. Museum contains some of Edison's inventions, incl phonographs and lightbulbs (Wed-Sun). 37 Christie St, ½ mi SW of Garden State Pkwy exit 131 off NJ 27 in Menlo Park. Phone 732/549-3299. **FREE**

Hotels

★★ **CLARION HOTEL & TOWERS.** *2055 Lincoln Hwy (08817). 732/287-3500; fax 732/287-8190. www.clarionhotel.com.* 169 rms, 5 story. S, D $119-$149; each addl $10; under 18 free; wkend rates. Crib free. TV; cable (premium). Complimentary continental bkfst. Coffee in rms. Restaurant 7 am-10:30 pm; Fri, Sat to 11 pm. Bar 11-1 am. Ck-out noon. Meeting rms. Business center. In-rm modem link. Bellhops. Gift shop. Exercise equipt. Refrigerators; microwaves avail. Luxury level. Cr cds: A, D, DS, MC, V.

★★★ **SHERATON EDISON HOTEL.** *125 Raritan Center Pkwy (08837). 732/225-8300; fax 732/225-0037. www.sheraton.com.* 274 rms, 12 story. S, D $150-$175; suites $325; under 12 free; wkend rates. Crib free. Pet accepted; fee. TV; cable (premium). Indoor pool; whirlpool. Complimentary coffee in rms. Restaurant 6 am-2 pm, 5-10 pm. Bar. Ck-out noon. Coin lndry. Convention facilities. Business servs avail. In-rm modem link. Concierge. Gift shop. Exercise equipt; sauna. Game rm. Cr cds: A, C, D, DS, JCB, MC, V.

Restaurants

★★ **CHARLIE BROWN'S.** *222 Plainfield Rd (08820). 732/494-6135. www.charliebrowns.com.* Hrs: 11:30 am-10 pm; Fri, Sat to 10:30 pm; Sun to 9 pm. Closed Dec 25. Bar to 2 am. Lunch $4.95-$8.45, dinner $9.75-$16.99. Child's menu. Specialties: prime rib, filet mignon, grilled salmon. Outdoor dining. Rustic American decor; stained glass windows; casual setting. Cr cds: A, D, DS, MC, V.

★★ **MOGHUL.** *1665-195 Oaktree Center (08820). 732/549-5050. www.moghul.com.* Hrs: noon-3 pm, 5:30-10:30 pm; Fri, Sat to 11 pm; brunch

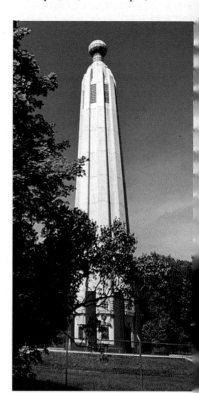

Edison Memorial Tower

noon-3 pm. Closed Mon. Res accepted. North Indian menu. Setups. A la carte entrees: lunch, dinner $8.95-$15.95. Brunch: wkdays $7.95, wkends $9.95. Specializes in chicken, lamb, shrimp. Parking. Elegant decor; Indian artifacts. Cr cds: A, D, DS, MC, V.

D

Elizabeth

(D-3) See also Jersey City, Newark, Newark International Airport Area

Settled 1664 **Pop** 120,568 **Elev** 36 ft **Area code** 908
Information Union County Chamber of Commerce, 135 Jefferson Ave, PO Box 300, 07207; 908/352-0900

More than 1,200 manufacturing industries are located in Elizabeth and Union County. Long before the Revolution, Elizabeth was not only the capital of New Jersey, but also a thriving industrial town. The first Colonial Assembly met here from 1669-1692. Princeton University began in Elizabeth in 1746 as the College of New Jersey. More than 20 pre-Revolutionary buildings still stand. Many noteworthy people were citizens of Elizabeth: William Livingston, first governor of New Jersey; Elias Boudinot, first president of the Continental Congress; Alexander Hamilton; Aaron Burr; General Winfield Scott; John Philip Holland, builder of the first successful submarine; and Admiral William J. Halsey. The Elizabeth-Port Authority Marine Terminal is the largest container port in the United States.

What to See and Do

Boxwood Hall State Historic Site. Home of Elias Boudinot, lawyer, diplomat, president (1783) of the Continental Congress and director of the US Mint. Boudinot entertained George Washington here on April 23, 1789, when Washington was on his way to his inauguration. (Mon-Sat; closed Jan 1, Thanksgiving, Dec 25)

1073 E Jersey St, 1½ blks W of US 1. Phone 973/648-4540.

First Presbyterian Church and Graveyard. The first General Assembly of New Jersey convened in an earlier building in 1668. The burned-out church was rebuilt in 1785-1787, and again in 1949. The Reverend James Caldwell was an early pastor. Alexander Hamilton and Aaron Burr attended an academy where the parish house now stands. Broad St and Caldwell Pl. Phone 908/353-1518.

Warinanco Park. One of the largest Union County parks. Fishing, boating (rentals June-Sept, daily); running track, parcourse fitness circuit, tennis (late Apr-early Oct), handball, horseshoes, indoor ice-skating (early Oct-early Apr, daily). Henry S. Chatfield Memorial Garden features tulip blooms each spring; azaleas and Japanese cherry trees; summer and fall flower displays. Some fees. St. Georges, border of Elizabeth and Roselle. Phone 908/527-4900. **FREE**

Flemington

(C-4) See also Clinton, Somerville

Settled 1738 **Pop** 4,200 **Elev** 160 ft **Area code** 908 **Zip** 08822
Information Hunterdon County Chamber of Commerce, 2200 Rte 31, Suite 15, Lebanon 08833; 908/735-5955
Web www.hunterdon-chamber.org

Originally a farming community, Flemington became a center for the production of pottery and cut glass at the turn of the century.

What to See and Do

Black River & Western Railroad. Excursion ride on old steam train, 11-mi round trip to Ringoes. Picnic area; museum. (July-Aug, Thurs-Sun; Apr-June and Sept-Dec, Sat, Sun and hols) Center Shopping Area. Phone 908/782-9600. ¢¢¢
County Courthouse. (1828) For 46 days in 1935, world attention was

focused on this Greek Revival building where Bruno Hauptmann was tried for the kidnapping and murder of the Lindbergh baby. Main St.

Fleming Castle. (1756) Typical two-story Colonial house built as a residence and inn by Samuel Fleming, for whom the town is named. DAR headquarters. (By appt) 5 Bonnell St. Phone 908/782-8840. **Donation**

Kase Cemetery. John Philip Kase, Flemington's first settler, purchased a tract from William Penn. His family's crumbling gravestones date from 1774 to 1856. Kase's Native American friend, Chief Tuccamirgan, is also memorialized here. Bonnell St, W of Fleming Castle.

Special Events

Stock-car racing. Flemington Fair Speedway. Sat, Apr-Nov.

Flemington Agricultural Fair. Phone 908/782-2413. Late Aug-early Sept.

Motel/Motor Lodge

★★ **RAMADA INN.** *250 Rte 202, at NJ 31 (08822). 908/782-7472; fax 908/782-1975; res 888/298-2054. www.ramada.com.* 104 rms, 2 story, 24 kits. S $95, D $103; each addl $10; suites $125; kit. units $114. Crib avail. Pet accepted. TV; cable (premium). Pool. Complimentary coffee in lobby. Restaurant 6:30 am-10 pm. Bar. Ck-out noon. Valet serv. Coin lndry. Meeting rms. In-rm modem link. Microwaves avail. Cr cds: A, C, D, DS, MC, V.

Restaurants

★★★ **HARVEST MOON INN.** *1039 Old York Rd, Ringoes (08551). 908/ 806-6020. www.harvestmooninn.com.* Hrs: 11:30 am-2:30 pm, 5-9:30 pm; Fri to 10 pm; Sat 5-10 pm; Sun 1-8 pm; early-bird dinner Tues-Fri 5-6 pm. Closed Mon; hols. Res accepted. Bar. Lunch $5.95-$12.95, dinner $16-$26. Complete meal: dinner $19.97. Specialty: pan-seared tuna. Own baking. Piano bar Fri, Sat. Stone building (ca 1811) with two fireplaces. Cr cds: A, D, DS, MC, V.

★★ **UNION HOTEL.** *76 Main St (08822). 908/788-7474.* Hrs: 11 am-

10 pm; Sun noon-8 pm. Closed some major hols. Res accepted. Bar to midnight. Lunch $6-$9.50, dinner $13-$17.50. Child's menu. Specializes in fresh fish, steak. In ornate Victorian hotel (1878) opp historical county courthouse. Cr cds: A, MC, V.

Forked River

(E-6) *See also Toms River*

Pop 4,914 **Elev** 19 ft **Area code** 609
Zip 08731

Restaurant

★★ **CAPTAIN'S INN.** *E Lacey Rd (08731). 609/693-3351.* Hrs: 11:45 am-10 pm. Closed Dec 25. Continental menu. Bar. Lunch from $3.95, dinner $10.95-$19.95. Child's menu. Specialties: crab imperial, steak au poivre, lobster. Entertainment Fri-Sun eves. Docking. Built in 1831. Overlooks river. Cr cds: A, D, MC, V.

Fort Lee

See also Hackensack

Pop 35,461 **Elev** 314 ft **Area code** 201
Zip 07024

Information Greater Fort Lee Chamber of Commerce, 2357 Lemoine Ave; 201/944-7575

North and south of the George Washington Bridge, Fort Lee is named for General Charles Lee, who served in the Revolutionary Army under George Washington. Its rocky bluff achieved fame as the cliff from which Pearl White hung in the early movie serial "The Adventures of Pearl White." From 1907-1916, 21 companies and seven studios produced motion pictures in Fort Lee. Stars such as Mary Pickford, Mabel Normand, Theda Bara, and Clara Kimball Young made movies here.

What to See and Do

Fort Lee Historic Park. (See PAL-
ISADES INTERSTATE PARKS) Phone
201/461-3956.

Motel/Motor Lodge

★ ★ **HOLIDAY INN.** *2339 Rte 4E
(07024). 201/944-5000; fax 201/944-
0623; res 800/465-4329. www.
holiday-inn.com.* 175 rms, 6 story. S
$71-$100; D $81-$100; each addl
$10; under 18 free. Crib free. TV;
cable. Pool. Restaurant 7 am-1 pm.
Bar 5 pm-midnight; closed Sun. Ck-
out noon. Meeting rms. Business
servs avail. Exercise equiptSundries.
Cr cds: A, D, DS, MC, V.

Hotels

★ ★ ★ **HILTON FORT LEE.** *2117 Rte
4 (07024). 201/461-9000; fax
201/585-9807; res 800/345-6565.
www.hilton.com.* 235 rms, 15 story. S,
D $139-$189; under 12 free. Crib
free. TV; cable (premium), VCR avail.
Indoor pool; whirlpool. Coffee in
rms. Restaurant 6:30 am-10:30 pm.
Bars 11-1 am. Ck-out noon. Meeting
rms. Business center. In-rm modem
link. Bellhops. Valet serv. Concierge.
Gift shop. Covered parking. Exercise
equipt; sauna. Cr cds: A, C, D, ER,
JCB, MC.

★ ★ ★ **RADISSON HOTEL ENGLE-
WOOD.** *401 S Van Brunt St, Englewood (07631). 201/871-2020; fax
201/871-6904; res 800/333-3333.
www.radisson.com.* 192 rms, 9 story.
Late Nov-mid Dec: S, D $145-$165;
suites $185-$275; wkend rates; lower
rates rest of yr. Crib free. Pet
accepted, some restrictions. TV; cable
(premium), VCR avail. Coffee in rms.
Restaurant 6:30 am-10 pm. Bar
11:30-1 am. Ck-out noon. Meeting
rms. Business center. Concierge. Coin
lndry. Exercise equipt. Indoor pool.
Some bathrm phones; refrigerators,
microwaves avail. Luxury level. Cr
cds: A, C, D, DS, ER, JCB, MC, V.

Freehold

*(D-4) See also Eatontown, Hightstown,
Lakewood*

Founded 1715 **Pop** 10,976 **Elev** 154 ft
Area code 732 **Zip** 07728
Information Western Monmouth
Chamber of Commerce, 17 Broad St;
732/462-3030
Web www.wmchamber.com

George Washington and the Revolutionary Army defeated the British
under General Sir Henry Clinton at
the Battle of Monmouth near here
on June 28, 1778. Molly Hays carried
water to artillerymen in a pitcher
and from that day on she has been
known as "Molly Pitcher." Formerly
known as Monmouth Courthouse,
Freehold is the seat of Monmouth
County.

What to See and Do

Covenhoven House. (1756) House
with period furnishings; once occupied by General Sir Henry Clinton
prior to the Battle of Monmouth in
1778. (May-Sept, Tues, Thurs, Sat,
and Sun afternoons) 150 W Main St.
Phone 732/462-1466. ¢

**Monmouth County Historical
Museum and Library.** Headquarters
of Monmouth County Historical
Association. Changing exhibits centering on aspects of life in Monmouth county; collections of silver,
ceramics, paintings; exhibits on Battle of Monmouth. Museum (Tues-Sat,
also Sun afternoons); library (Wed-
Sat; both closed hols). 70 Court St.
Phone 732/462-1466. ¢

Turkey Swamp Park. An 1,004-acre
park with fishing, boating (rentals);
hiking trails, ice-skating, picnicking
(shelter), playfields, camping (Mar-
Nov; fee; electric and water
hookups). Special events. 2 mi SW
off I-195, exit 22, County 524 to
Georgia Rd. Phone 732/462-7286.
FREE

Special Event

Harness racing. Freehold Raceway, jct US 9, NJ 33. Phone 732/462-3800. Tues-Sat, mid-Aug-May.

Motel/Motor Lodge

★ **COLTS NECK INN HOTEL.** *6 Rte 537 W, Colts Neck (07722). 732/409-1200; fax 732/431-6640.* 49 rms, 2 story. S $65; D $85; each addl $10; suites $150; under 12 free. TV; cable (premium), VCR avail. Complimentary continental bkfst. Restaurant adj 11:30 am-10 pm. Bar. Ck-out 11 am. Meeting rms. Business servs avail. Refrigerators, microwaves avail. Cr cds: A, C, MC, V.

D ⊠ 🐾 SC

Hotel

★★ **FREEHOLD GARDENS HOTEL.** *50 Gibson Pl (07728). 732/780-3870; fax 732/780-8725; res 800/448-8355. www.freeholdgardens. com.* 114 rms, 5 story. S, D $69-$90; each addl $10; under 13 free; higher rates late May-early Sept. Crib free. Pet accepted, some restrictions. TV; cable. Pool. Complimentary continental bkfst. Restaurant 5-11 pm. Entertainment Fri, Sat. Ck-out noon. Meeting rms. Business servs avail. Health club privileges. Refrigerators avail. Cr cds: A, C, D, JCB, MC, V.

D 🐾 ⊠ ⊠ 🐾

Restaurant

★ **GOLDEN BELL DINER.** *3320 US 9 (07728). 732/462-7259.* Hrs: 6-1 am; Fri, Sat open 24 hrs. Italian, American menu. Lunch $4.95-$8.25, dinner $7-$23. Child's menu. Specialties: Golden Bell fisherman's platter, tropical waffle, chicken salad in pita bread. Greenhouse atrium. Cr cds: A, D, DS, MC, V.

D SC ⊠

Gateway National Recreation Area (Sandy Hook Unit)

(E-3) *See also Red Bank*

(5 mi E of Atlantic Highlands on NJ 36)

Sandy Hook is a barrier peninsula that was first sighted by the crew of Henry Hudson's *Half Moon* (1609). It once was owned (1692) by Richard Hartshorne, an English Quaker, but has been government property since the 18th century. Fort Hancock (1895) was an important harbor defense from the Spanish-American War through the cold war era. Among Sandy Hook's most significant features are the Sandy Hook Lighthouse (1764), the oldest operating lighthouse in the United States, and the US Army Proving Ground (1874-1919), the army's first new-weapons testing site.

The park offers swimming (lifeguards in summer), fishing; guided and self-guided walks, picnicking, and a concession. Visitors are advised to obtain literature at the Visitor Center (daily). There is no charge for entrance and activities scheduled by the National Park Service. Parking fee, Memorial Day wkend-Labor Day. (Daily, sunrise-sunset; some facilities closed in winter) Contact Superintendant, PO Box 530, Fort Hancock 07732; 732/872-5970.

What to See and Do

Twin Lights State Historic Site. (1862) A lighthouse built to guide ships into New York harbor; now a marine museum operated by the State Park Service. (May-Oct, daily; rest of yr, Wed-Sun) Light House Rd, in Highlands. Phone 732/872-1814. **Donation**

Restaurants

★★ **BAHR'S RESTAURANT & MARINA.** *2 Bay Ave, Highlands (07732). 732/872-1245. www.bahrs. com.* Hrs: 11:30 am-9:30 pm; Fri, Sat to 10:30 pm; Sun to 9 pm; Sun brunch 11 am-2:30 pm. Closed Dec 25. Bar. A la carte entrees: lunch, dinner $12.95-$25.95. Sun brunch $5-$9.95. Child's menu. Specializes in fresh seafood. On waterfront; scenic view of the channel. Family-owned. Cr cds: A, DS, MC, V.

★★ **DORIS & ED'S.** *348 Shore Dr, Highlands (07732). 732/872-1565. www.doris-and-eds.com.* Hrs: 5-10 pm; Sat to 11 pm; Sun 3-10 pm. Closed Mon, Tues; also Jan-Feb. Res accepted. Dinner $21-$29. Child's menu. Specialties: grilled tuna with wasabi mayonnaise, sauteed red snapper with fresh rock shrimp. View of Sandy Hook Bay. Cr cds: A, C, D, ER, MC, V.

Gibbstown

Pop 3,758 **Elev** 15 ft **Area code** 856 **Zip** 08027

Information Township of Greenwich, 420 Washington St; 856/423-1038 or 856/423-4913

What to See and Do

Hunter-Lawrence-Jessup House. (1765) Headquarters of Gloucester County Historical Society. Museum contains 16 rms of furnishings and memorabilia from 17th- to 19th-century New Jersey. (Mon, Wed, Fri, last Sat-Sun of each month; closed hols) Approx 7 mi NW via NJ 45, County 534 in Woodbury at 58 N Broad St. Phone 856/848-8531. ¢

Nothnagle Home. (1638-1643) America's oldest log house. (By appt) 406 Swedesboro Rd. Phone 856/423-0916. **FREE**

Motel/Motor Lodge

★★ **HOLIDAY INN SELECT BRIDGEPORT.** *1 Pureland Dr, Swedesboro (08085). 856/467-3322; fax 856/467-3031; res 800/465-4329. www.holiday-inn.com.* 149 rms, 4 story. S, D $79-$129; each addl $10;

suites $149-$189; under 18 free. Crib free. TV; cable (premium), VCR avail. Indoor pool; whirlpool, poolside serv. Coffee in rms. Restaurant 6:30 am-10 pm. Bar 11 am-midnight; entertainment Mon-Fri. Ck-out noon. Coin lndry. Meeting rms. Business servs avail. In-rm modem link. Bellhops. Valet serv. Sundries. Exercise equipt. Game rm. Some refrigerators. Some balconies. Cr cds: A, D, DS, JCB, MC, V.

Hackensack

(E-2) *See also Fort Lee, Paterson*

Settled 1647 **Pop** 42,677 **Elev** 20 ft **Area code** 201

Information Chamber of Commerce, 190 Main St, 07601; 201/489-3700

Hackensack was officially known as New Barbados until 1921 when it received its charter under its present name, thought to be derived from the Native American word *Hacquinsacq.* The influence of the original Dutch settlers who established a trading post here remained strong even after British conquest. A strategic point during the Revolutionary War, the city contains a number of historical sites from that era. Hackensack is the hub for industry, business, and government in Bergen County. Edward Williams College is located here.

What to See and Do

The Church on the Green. Organized in 1686, the original building was built in 1696 (13 monogrammed stones preserved in east wall), and rebuilt in 1791 in Stone Dutch architectural style. It is the oldest church building in Bergen County. Museum contains pictures, books, and colonial items. Enoch Poor, a Revolutionary War general, is buried in the cemetery. Tours (wkdays on request). 42 Court St, NE corner of the Green, S end of Main St, opp County Court House. Phone 201/845-0957. **FREE**

Steuben House State Historic Site.
(1713) Museum of the Bergen
County Historical Society. Enlarged
in 1752 as home of Jan and Annetie
Zabriskie. The house was confiscated
during the Revolutionary War
because the Zabriskies were Loyalists;
it was given to Baron von Steuben,
by the state of New Jersey, as a
reward for his military services. The
baron later sold it back to the original owners. Colonial furniture, glass-
ware, china; Native American
artifacts. (Wed-Sat and Sun afternoons; closed Jan 1, Thanksgiving,
Dec 25) Approx ¼ mi N of NJ 4, at
1209 Main St in River Edge, overlooking river. Phone 201/487-1739.

USS *Ling* Submarine. Restored WWII
fleet submarine; New Jersey Naval
Museum. (Sat-Sun afternoons; closed
hols) Docked at Court and River sts.
Phone 201/342-3268.

Motel/Motor Lodge

★★ **BEST WESTERN ORITANI
HOTEL.** *414 Hackensack Ave (07601).
201/488-8900; fax 201/488-5456; res
800/528-1234. www.bestwestern.com/
oritani.* 99 units, 4 story. S, D $105-
$140. Crib $8. TV; cable (premium).
Pool; sauna. Complimentary continental bkfst. Restaurant noon-2:30
pm, 5:30-10 pm. Bar noon-2:30 pm,
5:30-10:30 pm. Ck-out noon. Meeting rms. Business servs avail. Valet
serv. Sundries. Exercise equipt. Cr
cds: A, C, D, DS, MC, V.
⌘ 🏋 ⛵ 🔥 SC D

Hotels

★★★ **HILTON.** *650 Terrace Ave, Hasbrouck Heights (07604). 201/288-6100;
fax 201/288-6698. www.hilton.com.*
355 rms, 12 story. S, D $159-$199;
each addl $20; suites $220-$500;
under 17 free; wkend rates. Crib free.
Pet accepted. TV; cable (premium),
VCR avail. Heated pool; poolside
serv. Restaurant 6:30 am-11 pm. Bars
11-1:30 am, Sat to 2:30 am. Ck-out 1
pm. Convention facilities. Business
center. In-rm modem link. Gift shop.
Exercise equipt; sauna. Luxury level.
Cr cds: A, C, D, DS, ER, MC, V.
D 🔄 ⌘ 🏋 ✈ ⛵ 🔥 🚶

★★★ **MARRIOTT AT GLEN-
POINTETEANECK.** *100 Frank W.
Burr Blvd, Teaneck (07666). 201/836-*
0600; fax 201/836-0638; res 800/228-
9290. www.marriott.com.* 341 rms, 15
story. S, D $160-$190; suites $300-
$650; wkend rates. Crib free. TV;
cable (premium), VCR avail. Indoor
pool; whirlpool. Coffee in rms.
Restaurant 6:30 am-10 pm. Bar 11-1
am. Ck-out noon. Business center.
In-rm modem link. Concierge. Exercise rm; sauna. Bathrm phones,
refrigerators. Cr cds: A, C, D, DS,
JCB, MC, V.
D ⌘ 🏋 ⛵ 🔥 🚶

Restaurant

★★★ **STONY HILL INN.** *231 Polifly
Rd (07601). 201/342-4085. www.stony
hillinn.com.* Hrs: 11:30 am-3 pm,
5:30-10:30 pm; Sat from 5:30 pm;
Sun 2-9 pm. Closed Dec 25. Continental menu. Bar to midnight. Wine
cellar. A la carte entrees: lunch
$12.95-$21, dinner $15.95-$29.95.
Specializes in continental cusine.
Own pastries. Entertainment Fri, Sat.
Landmark house (1818); period furnishings. Jacket. Cr cds: A, D, MC, V.
D

Hackettstown

(C-2)

Settled ca 1760 **Pop** 10,403 **Elev** 571
ft **Area code** 908 **Zip** 07840
Information Town Hall, 215 Stiger St;
908/852-3130

First called Helm's Mills and then
Musconetcong, citizens renamed the
town for Samuel Hackett, the largest
local landowner. His popularity
increased when he provided unlimited free drinks at the christening of
a new hotel. Hackettstown is located
in the Musconetcong Valley between
Schooleys and Upper Pohatcong
mountains.

What to See and Do

**Allamuchy Mountain State Park,
Stephens Section.** Allamuchy Mountain State Park (7,263 acres) is
divided into three sections. The
Stephens Section (482 acres) is devel-

tion. Tennis. Library. Colonial gristmill (1769). Rms individually decorated with Colonial-style furniture and period reproductions. Cr cds: A, C, D, DS, MC, V.

Haddonfield

See also Camden, Cherry Hill

Settled ca 1713 **Pop** 11,659
Elev 95 ft **Area code** 856
Zip 08033
Information Visitor/Information Center, 114 Kings Hwy E; 856/216-7253

Named for Elizabeth Haddon, a Quaker girl of 20 whose father sent her here from England in 1701 to develop 400 acres of land. This assertive young woman built a house, started a colony, and proposed to a Quaker missionary who promptly married her. The "Theologian's Tale" in Longfellow's *Tales of a Wayside Inn* celebrates Elizabeth Haddon's romance with the missionary.

What to See and Do

Greenfield Hall. Haddonfield's Historical Society headquarters in old Gill House (1747-1841) contains personal items of Elizabeth Haddon; furniture; costumes; doll collection. Boxwood garden; library on local history. On grounds is a house (ca 1735) once owned by Elizabeth Haddon. (Library, Tue, Thurs mornings; museum, Wed-Fri afternoons, other days by appt; closed Aug) 343 King's Hwy E (NJ 41). Phone 856/429-7375. ¢

Indian King Tavern Museum State Historic Site. Built as an inn; state legislatures met here frequently, passing a bill (1777) substituting "State" for "Colony" in all state papers. Colonial furnishings. Guided tours. (Wed-Sun; closed Jan 1, Thanksgiving, Dec 25; also Wed if following Mon or Tues hol) 233 King's Hwy E. Phone 856/429-6792. **Donation**

The Site of the Elizabeth Haddon House. Isaac Wood built this house

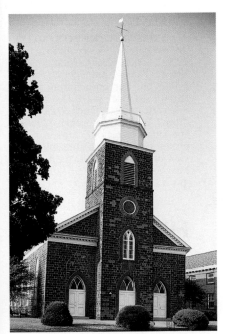
The Church on the Green, Hackensack

oped; the rest (Allamuchy) is natural. Fishing in Musconetcong River; hunting, hiking, picnicking, playground, camping. Standard fees. Willow Grove St, 1½ mi N of US 46. Phone 908/852-3790.

Land of Make Believe. Amusement park at foot of Jenny Jump Mtn incl the Tornado; Old McDonald's Farm; the Red Baron airplane; Santa Claus at the North Pole; a Civil War train; a maze; water park; hayrides; picnic grove; fudge factory. (Mid-June-Labor Day, daily; Memorial Day wkend-mid-June, wkends; Sept, wkend after Labor Day) I-80 exit 12, on County 611, in Hope. Phone 908/459-9000. ¢¢¢¢

Motel/Motor Lodge

★★ **THE INN AT MILLRACE POND.** 313 Johnsonberg Rd, Rte 519 N, Hope (07844). 908/459-4884; fax 908/459-5276; toll-free 800/746-6467. *www.innatmillracepond.com.* 17 rms, 2 story, 4 buildings. S, D $95-$165; each addl $20. TV in some rms; cable. Complimentary bkfst. Restaurant 5-9 pm; Sun 4-7:30 pm. Ck-out noon, ck-in 3 pm. Meeting rms. Business servs avail. Airport transporta-

in 1842, on the foundation of Elizabeth Haddon's 1713 brick mansion, immediately after it was destroyed by fire. The original brew house Elizabeth built (1713) and the English yew trees she brought over in 1712 are in the yard. Private residence; not open to the public. Wood Ln and Merion Ave.

High Point State Park (C-1)

(7 mi NW of Sussex on NJ 23)

High Point's elevation (1,803 ft), the highest point in New Jersey, gave this 15,000-acre park its name. The spot is marked by a 220-foot stone war memorial. The view is magnificent, overlooking Tri-State—the point where New Jersey, New York, and Pennsylvania meet—with the Catskill Mountains to the north, the Pocono Mountains to the west, and hills, valleys, and lakes all around. Elsewhere in the forests of this Kittatinny Mountain park are facilities for swimming, fishing, boating; nature center, picnicking, tent camping (no trailers). Standard fees. Phone 973/875-4800.

Hightstown (D-4))

Pop 5,216 **Elev** 84 ft **Area code** 609
Zip 08520

Motel/Motor Lodge

★★ **RAMADA INN-EAST WINDSOR.** *399 Monmouth St, East Windsor (08520). 609/448-7000; fax 609/443-6227; res 888/298-2054. www.ramada. com.* 200 rms, 4 story. Mid-June-Aug: S, D $79-$129; each addl $10; suite $139-$199; under 12 free; lower rates rest of yr. Crib free. TV; cable (premium). Pool. Restaurant opp 7 am-10 pm. Bar 5 pm-1 am. Ck-out noon. Meeting rms. Business servs avail. Coin lndry. Exercise equipt; sauna. Cr cds: A, C, D, DS, JCB, MC, V.

Restaurant

★★ **FORSGATE COUNTRY CLUB.** *375 Forsgate Dr, Monroe (08831). 732/521-0070. www.forsgatecc.com.* Hrs: 11:30 am-2 pm, 5-9 pm; Sat from 6 pm; Sun brunch from 10:30 am. Closed Mon; Jan 1, Dec 25. Bar. A la carte entrees: lunch $7.50-$18, dinner $8-$27. Sun brunch $22.95. Specializes in regional American dishes. Country club atmosphere; view of golf course. Cr cds: A, D, MC, V.

Hillsdale

See also Montvale, Paramus

Pop 10,087 **Elev** 83 ft **Area code** 201
Zip 07642

Hotel

★★★ **HILTON WOODCLIFF LAKE.** *200 Tice Blvd, Woodcliff Lake (07675). 201/391-3600; fax 201/391-4572; toll-free 800/445-8667. www.hilton woodclifflake.com.* 334 rms, 4 story. S, D $109-$189; each addl $15; suites $325-$450; under 18 free; wknd, wkly, hol rates. Crib free. TV; cable (premium). Complimentary coffee in rms. Restaurant 6:30 am-11 pm. Bar 11:30-12:30 am. Ck-out noon. Convention facilities. Business center. In-rm modem link. Bellhops. Concierge. Sundries. Gift shop. Coin lndry. Airport, RR station transportation. Tennis. Exercise equipt; sauna. Massage. 2 pools, 1 indoor/outdoor; pool, whirlpool, poolside serv, lifeguard. Refrigerators, microwaves avail. Cr cds: A, C, D, DS, MC, V.

Hoboken

See also Jersey City, Secaucus

Settled 1640 **Pop** 38,577 **Elev** 5 ft
Area code 201 **Zip** 07030
Information Hoboken Community Development, 94 Washington St; 201/420-2013

In the early 19th century, beer gardens and other amusement centers dotted the Hoboken shore, enticing New Yorkers across the Hudson. John Jacob Astor, Washington Irving, William Cullen Bryant, and Martin Van Buren were among the fashionable visitors. By the second half of the century, industries and shipping began to encroach on the fun. In 1928-1929, Christopher Morley and Cleon Throckmorton presented revivals of *After Dark* and *The Black Crook* to enchanted New Yorkers. Hoboken is connected to Manhattan by the PATH rapid-transit system.

What to See and Do

Stevens Institute of Technology. (1870) 3,600 students. A leading college of engineering, science, computer science management, and the humanities; also a center for research. Campus tours. Castle Point, E of Hudson St between 5th and 9th sts. Phone 201/216-5105. On campus are

 Davidson Laboratory. One of the largest privately owned hydrodynamic labs of its kind in the world. Testing site for models of ships, hydrofoils, the America's Cup participants, and the Apollo command capsule. (Limited public access) W end of campus. Phone 201/216-5290.

 Samuel C. Williams Library. (1969) Special collections incl set of facsimiles of every drawing by Leonardo da Vinci; library of 3,000 volumes by and about da Vinci; Alexander Calder mobile; the Frederick Winslow Taylor Collection of Scientific Management. (Academic yr) Phone 201/216-5198.

 Stevens Center. (1962) The 14-story hub of campus. Excellent view of Manhattan from George Washington Bridge to the Verrazano Bridge.

Restaurants

★ ★ **BAJA MEXICAN CUISINE.** *104 14th St (07030). 201/653-0610.* Hrs: 5-10:30 pm; Fri, Sat noon-11:30 pm; Sun noon-10 pm. Closed Jan 1, Thanksgiving, Dec 25. Res accepted. Mexican menu. Bar. Lunch, dinner $3.95-$17.95. Specialties: parrillada a la Baja, alambre veracruz, enchiladas a la parrilla. Southwestern decor. Cr cds: A, D, DS, MC, V.

★ **CAFE MICHELINA.** *423 Bloomfield St (07030). 201/659-3663.* Hrs: 11 am-10 pm; Fri to midnight; Sat 3-11 pm; Sun 3-9:30 pm. Closed Mon; hols. Italian menu. A la carte entrees: lunch, dinner $7.95-$13.95. Specialties: chicken portobello with marcella sauce, lobster ravioli, chicken Michelina. Italian decor. Cr cds: MC, V.

★ **GRIMALDI'S.** *133 Clinton St (07030). 201/792-0800. www.grimaldis. com.* Hrs: noon-11 pm; Sat, Sun from 2 pm; Tues, Wed from 5 pm. Closed Mon; Easter, Thanksgiving, Dec 25. Italian menu. A la carte entrees: lunch, dinner $11-$16. Specialties: roasted sweet red peppers, sausage pizza, mushroom pizza. Outdoor dining. Cozy, Italian atmosphere; brick oven; two-level dining area. Cr cds: A, C, MC, V.

★ **MARGHERITAS'.** *740 Washington St (07030). 201/222-2400.* Hrs: 11:30 am-10:30 pm; Fri, Sat to 11:30 pm; Sun 1-9:30 pm. Closed Mon; Easter, Thanksgiving, Dec 25. Italian menu. A la carte entrees: lunch $4.95-$7.95. Dinner $9.95-$15.95. Specialties: ravioli mondella, chicken Carol, shrimp fra diavolo. Own desserts. Italian decor. Cr cds: MC, V.

★ **ODD FELLOWS.** *80 River St (07030). 201/656-9009. www.odd fellowsrest.com.* Hrs: 11:30 am-10:30 pm; Thurs-Sat to 11 pm; Sun to 4 pm (brunch). Closed Thanksgiving, Dec 25. Creole/Cajun menu. Bar. Lunch $7.95-$11.95, dinner $7.95-$16.95. Sun brunch $9. Specialties: catfish, jambalaya, crawfish étouffé. Blues Thurs, Sun. Outdoor dining. Authentic French Quarter decor; exposed brick walls, tiled tabletops. Cr cds: A, MC, V.

Ho-Ho-Kus

See also Paramus

Pop 4,060 **Elev** 111 ft **Area code** 201
Zip 07423
Information Borough of Ho-Ho-Kus,
333 Warren Ave; 201/652-4400

In colonial times, Ho-Ho-Kus was
known as Hoppertown. Its present
name is derived from the Chihohok-
ies, who also had a settlement on
this spot.

What to See and Do

The Hermitage. Stone Victorian
house of Gothic Revival architecture
superimposed on original 18th-
century house. Its span of history
incl ownership by the Rosencrantz
family for more than 150 yrs.
Grounds consist of five wooded
acres, incl a second stone Victorian
house. Docents conduct tours of site
and the Hermitage. Changing
exhibits. Special events held
throughout the yr. Tours. Phone
201/445-8311. ¢¢

Jackson

See also Lakewood, Toms River

Pop 42,816 **Elev** 138 ft **Area code** 732
Zip 08527
Information Chamber of Commerce,
1080 N County Line Rd, PO Box A-C;
732/363-1080

What to See and Do

**Six Flags Great Adventure Theme
Park/Six Flags Wild Safari Animal
Park.** A family entertainment center,
incl 350-acre drive-through safari
park with more than 1,200 free-
roaming animals from six continents; 125-acre theme park featuring
more than 100 rides, shows and
attractions. (Late Mar-late Oct; schedule varies). On NJ 537, 1 mi S of I-
195. Phone 732/928-1821. ¢¢¢¢

Jersey City

*(E-3) See also Newark, Newark Interna-
tional Airport Area*

Settled 1629 **Pop** 240,055 **Elev** 11 ft
Area code 201
Information Jersey City Cultural
Affairs, 1 Chapel Ave, 07305;
201/547-5522

Jersey City's location on the Hudson
River, due west of the southern end
of Manhattan Island, has aided its
growth to such a degree that it is
now the second-largest city in New
Jersey. New Yorkers across the bay
tell time by the Colgate-Palmolive
Clock at 105 Hudson Street; the dial
is 50 feet across, and the minute
hand, weighing 2,200 pounds,
moves 23 inches each minute. Jersey
City's major links with New York are
the 8,557-foot Holland Tunnel,
which is 72 feet below water level;
the Port Authority Trans-Hudson
(PATH) rapid-transit system; and
New York Waterways Ferries, which
run between Exchange Place, the
city's Financial District, and the
World Financial Center in lower
Manhattan.

What to See and Do

Liberty State Park. Offers breathtaking view of New York City skyline;
flag display incl state, historic, and
US flags; boat launch; fitness course,
picnic area. Historic railroad terminal
has been partially restored. The Interpretive Center houses an exhibit
area; adj to the Center is a 60-acre
natural area consisting mostly of salt
marsh. Nature trails and observation
points complement this wildlife
habitat. (Daily) Off NJ Tpke, exit
14B; on the New York Harbor, less
than 2,000 ft from the Statue of Liberty. Boat tours and ferry service to
Ellis Island and Statue of Liberty are
avail. Phone 201/915-3400. Also in
park is

    ⭐ **Liberty Science Center.** Four-
    story structure encompasses Envi-
    ronment, Health, and Invention
    exhibit areas that feature more
    than 250 hands-on exhibits. Geo-

desic dome houses IMAX Theater with a six-story screen. (Daily; closed Thanksgiving, Dec 25) 251 Phillip St. Phone 201/200-1000. Exhibits and IMAX Theater combined passes ¢¢¢¢

Lake Hopatcong (C-2)

(Approx 15 mi N and W of Dover via NJ 15 and unnumbered road)

The largest lake in New Jersey, Hopatcong's popularity as a resort is second only to the seacoast spots. It covers 2,443 acres and has a hilly shoreline of approximately 40 miles. The area offers swimming, stocked fishing, and boating.

What to See and Do

Hopatcong State Park. A 113-acre park with swimming, bathhouse, fishing; picnicking, playground, concession. Historic museum (Sun afternoons). Standard fees. Southwestern shore of lake, in Landing. Phone 973/398-7010.

Motels/Motor Lodges

★ **DAYS INN.** *1691 Rte 46, Ledgewood (07852). 973/347-5100; fax 973/347-6356; res 800/329-7466. www.daysinn.com.* 100 rms, 2 story. S, D $85; each addl $10; under 15 free. Crib free. TV. Pool; lifeguard. Complimentary continental bkfst. Restaurant 11:30 am-9:30 pm; Sun 8 am-1 pm. Bar 4 pm-2 am; entertainment Fri, Sat. Ck-out 11 am. Coin lndry. Meeting rms. Business servs avail. Sundries. 2 tennis courts. Refrigerators, microwaves avail. Cr cds: A, DS, MC, V.

★★ **FOUR POINTS BY SHERATON.** *15 Howard Blvd, Mt Arlington (07856). 973/770-2000; fax 973/770-1287; res 800/325-3535. www.sheraton.com.* 124 rms, 5 story. S, D $130-$140; each addl $10; suites $140-$160; under 18 free; wkend rates. Crib free. Pet accepted. TV; cable (premium). Indoor pool. Coffee in

rms. Restaurant 6:30 am-10 pm. Bar 11-2 am; entertainment Wed, Sat. Ck-out noon. Meeting rms. Business servs avail. Valet serv. Exercise equipt. Refrigerators, microwaves avail. Cr cds: A, D, MC, V.

Lakewood

(D-5) See also Toms River

Settled 1800 **Pop** 36,065 **Elev** 67 ft
Area code 732 **Zip** 08701
Information Chamber of Commerce, 395 Rt 70 W, Suite 125; 732/363-0012

A well-known winter resort in the 1890s, many socially prominent New Yorkers such as the Astors, the Goulds, the Rhinelanders, the Rockefellers, and the Vanderbilts maintained large homes on the shores of Lake Carasaljo.

What to See and Do

Ocean County Park #1. The 325-acre former Rockefeller estate. Lake swimming, children's fishing lake; tennis, platform tennis, picnicking (grills), playground, athletic fields. (Daily) Entrance fee (July-Aug, wkends). 659 Ocean Ave, 1 mi E on NJ 88. Phone 732/370-7380. ¢

Motel/Motor Lodge

★★ **BEST WESTERN LEISURE INN.** *1600 Hwy 70 (08701). 732/367-0900; fax 732/370-4928; res 800/780-7234. www.bestwestern.com.* 105 rms, 2 story. Memorial Day-Sept: S, D $75-$115; each addl $10; lower rates rest of yr. Crib free. TV; cable (premium). Pool. Restaurant 7 am-10 pm. Bar 6-11 pm. Ck-out 11 am. Coin lndry. Meeting rm. Business servs avail. In-rm modem link. Refrigerators avail. Cr cds: A, D, DS, MC, V.

LAMBERTVILLE'S UNIQUE SHOPPING

This tour can cover anywhere from about 1½ miles to many miles, depending on whether you stay within the town proper or extend the walk along the Delaware & Raritan Canal, or even cross the Delaware River into New Hope, Pennsylvania. Lambertville is rich in history, antique shops, fine restaurants, and historic homes. The town has long been the state's shad fishing center, and still celebrates the annual Shad Festival. It was also the country's hairpin-making capital during the early 20th century. Today, Lambertville is a fine antiques and art center. The streets are set out in a grid, with Union and Main Streets running north and south, parallel to the river, and a series of short cross-streets passing between them. A variety of historic homes in the Federalist and Victorian styles can be found here.

Start at the historic Marshall House at 62 Bridge Street. A classic Federalist building, this is the home of the Lambertville Historical Society, which leads one-hour guided walking tours from late June through September, presents a 30-minute film on Lambertville's history, and can supply you with a guide to the town's historic buildings. After visiting the Marshall House, proceed west to Union Street, and head north into the heart of the shopping district. Along this street you'll encounter Phoenix Books (49 North Union), a treasure trove of rare and out-of-print volumes; the Five and Dime (40 North Union), which houses an equally fascinating collection of antique toys; and, all along the street, a number of high-quality antique shops and galleries, from The People's Store at the corner of Union and Church streets and Broadmoor Antiques at 6 North Union to the Best of France at 204 North Union, with many others between. At the north end of Union (ten blocks north), turn right onto Cherry Street. Follow Cherry to North Main, turn right, and begin weaving among the cross streets between North Union and North Main back to Bridge Street. Along North Main, A Mano Gallery specializes in American crafts, jewelry, and glass, while Almirah focuses on colonial-era Indian antique furniture and gifts. Shopping, window shopping, or gallery hopping are best done on Perry, York, Coryell, Church Bridge, and Ferry streets. More shops can be found on Kline's Court (one block on the left from Bridge Street) and Lambert Lane (just across the canal on the right). From Lambert Lane, cross the footbridge onto Lewis Island, home of Fred Lewis, the state's only commercially licensed freshwater shad fisherman.

Back on Bridge Street, take a break at Lambertville Station, which serves New American cuisine, or return to town for other dining options, including The Fish House (2 Canal Street) for local catches of the day, Anton's at the Swan (43 South Main Street) for upscale dining in an historical building, or the Church Street Bistro (11 Church Street) for intimate dinning.

For those with stamina, add one of the two extended walk options. To get in touch with nature, follow the walking/biking path along the Delaware & Raritan Canal, which travels south for many miles, presenting a bucolic view of the canal and the Delaware River. Another option is to cross the Delaware on the Bridge Street bridge and enter New Hope, Pennsylvania, a treasure trove of antique shops and restaurants.

Lambertville

(C-4) See also Trenton

Settled 1705 **Pop** 3,868 **Elev** 76 ft
Area code 609 **Zip** 08530

Information Lambertville Area Chamber of Commerce, 239 N Union St; 609/397-0055
Web www.lambertville.org

What to See and Do

John Holcombe House. Washington stayed here just before crossing the Delaware. Privately owned residence. 260 N Main St.

Marshall House. (1816) James Marshall, who first discovered gold at

Sutter's Mill in California in 1848, lived here until 1834. Period furnishings; memorabilia of Lambertville; small museum collection. (May-mid-Oct, wkends or by appt) 62 Bridge St. Phone 609/397-0770. **FREE**

Motel/Motor Lodge

★ ★ **WOOLVERTON INN.** *6 Woolverton Rd, Stockton (08559). 609/397-0802; fax 609/397-0987; toll-free 888/264-6648. www.woolverton inn.com.* 10 rms, 3 with shower only, 2 story, 2 suites. May-Sept: S, D $90-$140; each addl $35; suites $120-$190; wkends, hols (2-3 day min). Complimentary full bkfst; afternoon refreshments. Restaurant nearby. Ck-out 11 am, ck-in 3-8 pm. Meeting rms. In-rm whirlpool in suites. Totally nonsmoking. Cr cds: A, MC, V.
D ♨ 🗲 🖂 🔥

Hotel

★ ★ ★ **INN AT LAMBERTVILLE STATION.** *11 Bridge St (08530). 609/397-4400; fax 609/397-9744; toll-free 800/524-1091. www.lambertville station.com.* 45 units, 3 story. S, D $85-$95; each addl $15; suites $135. Crib avail. TV; cable (premium). Complimentary continental bkfst. Dining rm 11:30 am-10 pm. Ck-out noon. Meeting rms. Business servs avail. Health club privileges. Fireplace in suites. View of Delaware River. Victorian antiques. Cr cds: A, D, MC, V.
D 🖂 🔥 SC

B&B/Small Inn

★ ★ **CHIMNEY HILL FARM ESTATE.** *207 Goat Hill Rd (08530). 609/397-1516; fax 609/397-9353; toll-free 800/211-4667. www.bbianj.com/ chimneyhill.* 8 rms, 3 story. S, D $135-$325; wkly rates; some lower rates mid-wk. Children over 12 yrs only. Complimentary full bkfst; afternoon refreshments. Ck-out 11 am, ck-in 3 pm. Business servs avail. Downhill ski ½ mi. Picnic tables. Elegant stone and frame manor house built in 1820; furnishings are antiques and period reproductions. Cr cds: A, MC, V.
🖂 🖂 🖂 🔥 SC

Restaurants

★ ★ **ANTON'S AT THE SWAN.** *43 S Main St (08530). 609/397-1960. www. antonsattheswan.com.* Hrs: 6-10 pm; Mon to 9 pm; Sun 4:30-8 pm. Closed Mon; also Jan 1, Dec 25. Res accepted. Contemporary American menu. Bar 4 pm-1 am; Sun 2-11 pm. A la carte entrees: dinner $23-$29. Menu changes monthly. Parking. Local artists display work. Cr cds: A, D, MC, V.

★ ★ **LAMBERTVILLE STATION.** *11 Bridge St (08530). 609/397-8300. www.lambertvillestation.com.* Hrs: 11:30 am-3 pm, 4-10 pm; Fri, Sat to 11 pm; early-bird dinner Mon-Thurs 4-6:30 pm, Fri to 6 pm; Sun brunch 10:30 am-3 pm. Res accepted. Bar. Lunch $6.95-$12.50, dinner $13.50-$22.50. Sun brunch $7.25-$11.50. Child's menu. Specializes in rack of lamb, elk. Jazz Sat, Sun. Renovated RR station with 3 dining areas; 1 dining rm is an old station platform. Victorian-style decor. Cr cds: A, D, MC, V.
D 🖂

Livingston (D-2)

Pop 27,391 **Elev** 307 ft **Area code** 973 **Zip** 07039

This suburban community in southwestern Essex County is named for William Livingston, the first governor of New Jersey.

Restaurant

★ ★ **AFTON.** *2 Hanover Rd, Florham Park (07932). 973/377-1871. www. afton.baweb.com.* Hrs: 11:30 am-2:30 pm, 5-9 pm; Sun noon-8 pm; Sun brunch 11 am-2 pm. Closed Mon; Dec 25. Bar to 11 pm. Complete meals: lunch $7.95-$12.95, dinner $13.50-$18.50. Sun brunch $12.95. Specializes in prime rib, seafood. Family-owned. Cr cds: A, D, MC, V.
D SC

Long Beach Island (F-3)

Six miles out to sea, this island is separated from the New Jersey mainland by Barnegat and Little Egg Harbor bays. NJ 72, going east from Manahawkin on the mainland, enters the island at Ship Bottom. The island is no more than three blocks wide in some places, and extends 18 miles from historic Barnegat Lighthouse to the north. It includes towns such as Loveladies, Harvey Cedars, Surf City, Ship Bottom, Brant Beach, and the Beach Havens at the southern tip. The island is a popular family resort with excellent fishing, boating, and other water sports. For swimming, the bay is calm, while the ocean offers a vigorous surf.

Tales are told of pirate coins buried on the island, and, over the years, silver and gold pieces occasionally have turned up. Whether they are part of pirate treasure or the refuse of shipwrecks remains a mystery.

What to See and Do

Barnegat Lighthouse State Park. Barnegat Lighthouse, a 167-ft red and white tower, was engineered by General George G. Meade and completed in 1858; 217-step spiral staircase leading to lookout offering spectacular view. Fishing; picnicking. Park (daily); lighthouse (Memorial Day-Labor Day, daily; May and Labor Day-Oct, wkends only). Standard fees. At northern end of island. Phone 609/494-2016.

Fantasy Island Amusement Park. Family-oriented amusement park featuring rides and games; family casino arcade. (June-Aug, daily; May and Sept, wkends; schedule varies) Phone 609/492-4000.

Special Event

Surflight Theatre. Engleside and Beach aves, Beach Haven. Broadway musicals nightly. Children's theater, Wed-Sat. May-mid-Oct. Phone 609/492-9477.

Motels/Motor Lodges

★ ★ ★ **THE ENGLESIDE INN.** *30 E Engleside Ave, Beach Haven (08008). 609/492-1251; fax 609/492-9175; toll-free 800/762-2214. www.engleside.com.* 72 units, 3 story, 37 kits. No elvtr. July-Labor Day: S, D $150-$225; each addl $12; suites $290-$375; kit. units $165-$225; lower rates rest of yr. Crib avail. Pet accepted, some restrictions. TV; cable, VCR (movies $2). Pool; poolside serv (in season), lifeguard. Restaurant. Bar. Ck-out 11 am. Meeting rms. Business scrvs avail. Sundries. Exercise equipt. Refrigerators. Private patios, balconies. On beach. Cr cds: A, C, D, DS, MC, V.
🅳 🛎 🌊 🔀 🔥 🐾 🏃

★ **SANDPIPER MOTEL.** *10th St and LBI Blvd, Ship Bottom (08008). 609/494-6909; fax 609/361-2246.* 20 rms, shower only. July-Aug: S, D $110-$140; each addl $5; higher rates wkends and hols (3-day min); lower rates May-June and Sept-Oct. Closed rest of yr. TV; cable. Pool. Restaurant adj 4-10 pm. Ck-out 11 am. Refrigerators. Ocean 1 blk. Cr cds: MC, V.
🌊 🔥 🔀

Resort

★ **SPRAY BEACH INN.** *Ocean and 24th sts, Spray Beach (08008). 609/492-1501; fax 609/492-0504. www.lbiinns.com.* 88 rms, 3 story, 10 kits. Late June-Labor Day: S, D $166-$235; each addl $10; kit. units $155-$195; lower rates rest of yr. Closed Jan. Crib $7. TV; cable, VCR avail. Heated pool; lifeguard. Restaurant 8 am-2:30 pm, 5-10 pm. Bar 10:30-2 am; entertainment wkends, hols in season. Ck-out noon. Business servs avail. Sundries. Refrigerators. On beach. Cr cds: A, MC, V.
🌊 🔥

B&B/Small Inn

★ ★ ★ **AMBER STREET INN BED & BREAKFAST.** *118 Amber St, Beach Haven (08008). 609/492-1611; fax 609/492-9165. www.amberstreetinn. com.* 6 rms, 3 story. Mid-May-mid-Sept: S $110-$165; D $115-$200; each addl $10; suites $125-$165; lower rates rest of yr. Children over 10 yrs only. TV in parlor. Complimentary full bkfst. Restaurant adj 7 am-10 pm. Ck-out 11 am, ck-in 3 pm. Built in 1885; antiques. Totally nonsmoking. Cr cds: MC, V.

Restaurants

★★ **BUCKALEW'S.** *101 N Bay Ave, Beach Haven (08008).* 609/492-1065. *www.buckalews.com.* Hrs: 11:30-1:30 am. Closed Dec 25. Res accepted. Continental menu. Bar. Bkfst $3.95-$8.95, lunch $3.95-$7.95, dinner $13.95-$19.95. Child's menu. Specialties: crab cakes, black and blue tuna, portobello mushroom sandwich. Bands Tues-Sat. Parking. Cr cds: A, DS, MC, V.

★★ **LEEWARD ROOM.** *30 Engleside Ave, Beach Haven (08008).* 609/492-5116. *www.engleside.com.* Hrs: 8 am-noon, 5-10 pm; Sun brunch 8 am-1:30 pm. Closed Dec 25. Res accepted. Japanese menu. Bar 5 pm-1 am. A la carte entrees: bkfst $2.25-$9.50, lunch $2-$10. Dinner $10-$26. Sun brunch $13.95. Child's menu. Specialties: lobster roll, salmon Oscar, prime rib. Parking. Nautical decor. Sushi bar. Cr cds: A, D, DS, MC, V.

★★ **TUCKER'S.** *Engleside Ave & West St (08008).* 609/492-2300. Hrs: 11:30-2 am; early-bird dinner (seasonal) 5-6 pm. Closed Dec 25. Bar. A la carte entrees: lunch $5.95-$11.95, dinner $5.95-$19.95. Child's menu. Specialties: prime rib, crab penne, chicken and biscuits. Entertainment wkends. Parking. Outdoor dining. Cr cds: A, D, DS, MC, V.

Madison

(D-3) *See also Chatham, Morristown*

Settled ca 1685 **Pop** 16,530 **Elev** 261 ft **Area code** 973 **Zip** 07940
Information Chamber of Commerce, 155 Main St, PO Box 152; 973/377-7830

For many years, the quiet suburban town of Madison was called the "Rose City" because of the thousands of bouquets produced in its many greenhouses.

What to See and Do

Drew University. (1867) 2,100 students. A 186-acre wooded campus west of town. College of Liberal Arts, Theological School, and Graduate School. On campus are a Neoclassical administration building (1833), the United Methodist Archives and History Center, and the Rose Memorial Library containing Nestorian Cross collection, government and UN documents and manuscripts, and memorabilia of early Methodism. Tours. Madison Ave, NJ 24. Phone 973/408-3000.

Fairleigh Dickinson University-Florham-Madison Campus. (1958) 3,889 students. (One of three campuses) On site of Twombly Estate (1895); many original buildings still in use. Friendship Library houses numerous special collections incl Harry A. Chesler collection of comic art, and collections devoted to printing and the graphic arts. (Academic yr, Mon-Fri; closed school hols) Tours of campus by appt. 285 Madison Ave, NJ 124. Phone 973/443-8661.

Museum of Early Trades and Crafts. Hands-on look at 18th- and 19th-century artisans. Special events incl Bottle Hill Craft Festival (Oct). Tours. (Tues-Sat, also Sun afternoons; closed hols) Main St (NJ 124) at Green Village Rd. Phone 973/377-2982. ¢¢

Special Event

New Jersey Shakespeare Festival. In residence at Drew University. Professional theater company. Incl Shakespearean, classic, and modern plays; special guest attractions and classic films. (Mid-May-Dec). Phone 973/408-5600 or 973/408-3278.

Matawan

(D-4) *See also Freehold*

Pop 8,910 **Elev** 55 ft **Area code** 732 **Zip** 07747

Information Matawan-Aberdeen Chamber of Commerce, PO Box 522; 732/290-1125

What to See and Do

Cheesequake State Park. This 1,300-acre park offers swimming, bathhouse, fishing; nature tours, picnicking, playground, concession, camping (fee; dump station). Standard fees. Garden State Pkwy, exit 120, right at first traffic light and right at next traffic light onto Gordon Rd, ¼ mi to entrance. Phone 732/566-2161.

Special Event

Concerts. PNC Bank Arts Center, at Telegraph Hill Park on the Garden State Pkwy, exit 116. A 5,302-seat amphitheater; lawn area seats 4,500-5,500. Contemporary, classical, pop, and rock concerts. Phone 732/442-9200. Mid-June-Sept.

Motel/Motor Lodge

★★ **WELLESLEY INN.** *3215 NJ 35, Hazlet (07730). 732/888-2800; fax 732/888-2902; res 800/444-8888. www.wellesleyinnandsuites.com.* 89 rms, 3 story. S $63-$129; D $65-$129; each addl $5; under 18 free. Crib free. Pet accepted, some restrictions; $5. TV; cable (premium). Complimentary continental bkfst. Restaurant nearby. Ck-out 11 am. Business servs avail. Health club privileges. Refrigerators, microwaves avail. Cr cds: A, D, DS, JCB, MC, V.

⬛ 🐾 ➘ 🐾 SC

Hotel

★ **HAZLET HOTEL.** *2870 NJ 35, Hazlet (07730). 732/264-2400; fax 732/739-9735.* 120 rms, 2 story. S, D $72-$99; each addl $5. Crib free. TV; cable (premium). Pool; lifeguard. Restaurant 6:30 am-10 pm. Ck-out noon. Meeting rms. Business servs avail. Health club privileges. Refrigerators avail. Cr cds: A, D, DS, MC, V.

⬛ ➘ ➘ 🐾

Restaurant

★★ **BUTTONWOOD MANOR.** *845 NJ 34 (07747). 732/566-6220. www.buttonwoodmanor.com.* Hrs: 11:30 am-10 pm; Sat to 11 pm; Sun noon-9 pm. Res accepted. Bar. Lunch $5.25-$9.95, dinner $11.95-$24.95. Child's menu. Specializes in duckling, steak, fresh seafood. Entertainment Fri, Sat. Lakeside dining. Cr cds: A, D, MC, V.

⬛ ➘

Metuchen

(see Woodbridge)

Millburn

See also Newark, Newark International Airport Area, Union

Settled 1720s **Pop** 19,765 **Elev** 140 ft **Area code** 973 **Zip** 07041

Information Chamber of Commerce, 343 Millburn Ave, PO Box 651; 973/379-1198

Web www.millburn.com

Once bristling with paper mills and hat factories, Millburn today boasts a thriving downtown with a regional theater, a quiet residential area, and direct access to New York City.

What to See and Do

Cora Hartshorn Arboretum and Bird Sanctuary. A 17-acre sanctuary with nature trails; guided walks. Stone House Museum with nature exhibits (late Sept-mid-June, Tues, Thurs, and Sat). Grounds (daily). 2 mi W on Forest Dr in Short Hills. Phone 973/376-3587. **FREE**

Paper Mill Playhouse. State Theater of New Jersey. A variety of plays, musicals, and children's theater (Wed-Sun); matinees (Thurs, Sat, and Sun). Brookside Dr. Phone 973/376-4343.

Hotel

★★★ HILTON SHORT HILLS HOTEL & SPA. *41 John F. Kennedy Pkwy, Short Hills (07078). 973/379-0100; fax 973/379-6870; toll-free 800/445-8667. www.hilton.com.* 301 rms, 7 story, 37 suites. S $160-$280; D $160-$295; each addl $30; suites $310-$775; family, wkend rates. Crib free. TV; cable (premium), VCR avail. 2 pools, 1 indoor; whirlpool, lifeguard. Restaurant 6:30 am-10:30 pm (see also THE DINING ROOM). Rm serv 24 hrs. Bar 11:30-1:30 am; entertainment. Ck-out 1 pm. Convention facilities. Business center. In-rm modem link. Concierge. Gift shop. Beauty shop. Valet parking. Tennis privileges. Exercise rm; sauna, steam rm. Massage. Spa. Refrigerator in suites. Microwaves avail. Luxury level. Cr cds: A, D, DS, MC, V.

Restaurant

★★★ THE DINING ROOM. *41 John F. Kennedy Pkwy, Short Hills (07078). 973/379-0100. www.hilton.com.* Hrs: 6-10:30 pm. Closed Sun. Bar. Complete meals: 3-course dinner $62, 4-course dinner $72. Specializes in seafood, game, veal. Seasonal menu. Own pastries. Harpist. Valet parking. English drawing room atmosphere. Jacket. Cr cds: A, D, DS, MC, V.

Millville

(B-7) *See also Bridgeton*

Pop 26,847 **Elev** 37 ft **Area code** 856 **Zip** 08332

Information Chamber of Commerce, 25 E Main St, 100 N High St, PO Box 831; 856/825-2600

Web www.millville-nj.com

What to See and Do

Wheaton Village. Buildings incl Museum of American Glass, which houses an extensive glass collection; working factory where demonstrations of glassmaking are given; general store; restored train station; 1876 one-rm schoolhouse. Crafts demonstrations, arcade, shops. Restaurant, hotel. Self-guided tours. (Jan-Feb, Fri-Sun; Mar, Wed-Sun; Apr-Dec, daily; closed hols) 2 mi NE via County 552. Phone 856/825-6800. ¢¢¢

Motel/Motor Lodge

★★ COUNTRY INN - WHEATON VILLAGE. *1125 Village Dr (08332). 856/825-3100; fax 856/825-1317; toll-free 800/456-4000. www.countryinns. com.* 100 rms, 2 story. S, D $75; each addl $5; suites $125-$130; under 18 free. Crib free. TV; cable (premium). Heated pool. Restaurant 7 am-9 pm; Fri, Sat to 10 pm. Bar 11-1 am. Meeting rms. Business servs avail. Health club privileges. Game rm. Some refrigerators. Cr cds: A, C, D, DS, MC, V.

Montclair

See also Newark, Newark International Airport Area

Settled 1666 **Pop** 38,977 **Elev** 337 ft **Area code** 973

Information Chamber of Commerce, 26 Park St, Suite 2025, 07042; 973/226-5500

Web www.montclairchamber.org

Originally a part of Newark, the area that includes Montclair was purchased from Native Americans in 1678 for "two guns, three coats, and thirteen cans of rum." The first settlers were English farmers from Connecticut who came here to form a Puritan church of their own. Shortly after, Dutch from Hackensack arrived, and two communities were created: Cranetown and Speertown. The two communities later were absorbed into West Bloomfield.

During the Revolutionary War, First Mountain served as a lookout point and as a barrier, preventing the British from crossing into the Upper Passaic valley. In the early 1800s, manufacturing began, new roads opened and the area grew. In 1856-1857, a rail controversy arose: West Bloomfield citizens wanted a rail connection with New York City; Bloomfield residents saw no need for it. In 1868, the two towns separated and West Bloomfield became Montclair. This railroad helped to make Montclair the suburban, residential town it is today. One of the town's schools is named for painter George Inness, who once lived here.

What to See and Do

Eagle Rock Reservation. ½ mi W on Bloomfield Ave, then S on Prospect Ave to Eagle Rock Ave in West Orange (see).

Israel Crane House. (1796) Federal mansion with period rms; working 18th-century kitchen; school rm; special exhibits during the year. Country Store and Post Office have authentic items; old-time crafts demonstrations. Research library. (June-Aug, Thurs-Sat; Sept-May, Sun afternoons; other times by appt) 110 Orange Rd. Phone 973/744-1796. ¢¢

The Montclair Art Museum. American art; Native American gallery; changing exhibits. (Tues-Sun; closed hols) Gallery lectures (Sun). Concerts; jazz; film series. 3 S Mountain Ave at Bloomfield Ave. Phone 973/746-5555. ¢¢

Presby Iris Gardens. Height of bloom in mid-May or early June. In Mountainside Park, on Upper Mountain Ave in Upper Montclair. Phone 973/783-5974.

Montvale

Pop 7,034 **Elev** 187 ft **Area code** 201
Zip 07645

Motel/Motor Lodge

★★ **HOLIDAY INN MONTVALE.** *100 Chestnut Ridge Rd (07645). 201/391-7700; fax 201/391-6648; toll-free 888/507-3344. www.holiday-inn. com.* 190 rms, 3 story. S, D $99-$145; each addl $10; under 18 free; wkend rates. Crib free. TV; cable (premium). Pool; poolside serv. Restaurant 6:30 am-10 pm; Sat from 5:30 pm. Bar 11:30-2 am; entertainment. Ck-out noon. Meeting rms. Business servs avail. In-rm modem link. Bellhops. Valet serv. Exercise equipt. Microwaves avail. Cr cds: A, C, D, DS, JCB, MC, V.
D ⌨ 🏋 🔥 SC

Hotel

★★★ **MARRIOTT PARK RIDGE.** *300 Brae Blvd, Park Ridge (07656). 201/307-0800; fax 201/307-0859; toll-free 800/228-9290. www.marriott.com.* 289 units, 4 story. S, D $79-$175; suites $275; under 18 free; wkly, wkend rates. Crib avail. Pet accepted, some restrictions. TV; cable (premium), VCR avail. Indoor/outdoor pool; whirlpool, poolside serv. Restaurant 6:30 am-10 pm. Bars 4:30 pm-2 am. Ck-out noon. Meeting rms. Business center. In-rm modem link. Concierge. Gift shop. Exercise equipt; sauna. Refrigerators avail. Many private patios, balconies. Luxury level. Cr cds: A, C, D, DS, JCB, MC, V.
D 🔫 ⌨ 🏋 🏊 🔥 SC 🏃

Restaurant

★★ **VALENTINO'S.** *103 Spring Valley Rd, Park Ridge (07645). 201/391-2230.* Hrs: 11:30 am-2:30 pm, 5-10 pm; Fri to 11 pm, Sat 5-11 pm. Closed Sun; hols. Res accepted. Italian menu. Bar. A la carte entrees: lunch $8.95-$15.95, dinner $14.95-

$25.95. Specializes in veal, pasta, fish. Cr cds: A, D, DS, MC, V.

Moorestown (C-5)

(see Camden)

Morristown

(D-2) *See also Madison*

Settled ca 1710 **Pop** 18,554 **Elev** 327 ft **Area code** 973
Information Historic Morris Visitors Center, 6 Court St, 07960; 973/631-5151
Web www.morristourism.org

Today, Morristown is primarily residential, but the iron industry, so desperately needed during the Revolutionary War, was responsible for the development of the town and the surrounding county. George Washington and his army spent two winters here, operating throughout the area until the fall of 1781. The first successful experiments with the telegraph were made in Morristown by Samuel F. B. Morse and Stephen Vail. Cartoonist Thomas Nast, writers Bret Harte and Frank Stockton, and millionaire Otto Kahn all lived here. Morristown rises to a 597-foot peak at Fort Nonsense; the Whippany River runs through the town.

What to See and Do

Acorn Hall. (1853) Victorian Italianate house; original furnishings; reference library; restored garden. (Mon, Thurs, Sun; group tours by appt; closed hols) 68 Morris Ave. Phone 973/267-3465. ¢¢

Fosterfields Living Historical Farm. Turn-of-the-century living history farm (200 acres). Self-guided trail; displays; audiovisual presentations; workshops, farming demonstrations; restored Gothic Revival house. Visitor Center. (Apr-Oct, Wed-Sun) 73 Kahdena Rd, off County Rte 510. Phone 973/326-7645. ¢¢

Frelinghuysen Arboretum. Features 127 acres of forest and open fields; natural and formal gardens; spring and fall bulb displays; labeled collections of trees and shrubs; Braille trail; gift shop. Grounds (daily). 1½ mi NE via Morris Ave, Whippany Rd;

Schuyler-Hamilton House, Morristown

entrance from E Hanover Ave. Phone 973/326-7600. **FREE**

Historic Speedwell. Home and factory of Stephen Vail, iron master, who in 1818 manufactured the engine for the SS *Savannah*, first steamship to cross the Atlantic. In 1838, Alfred Vail (Stephen's son) and Samuel F. B. Morse perfected the telegraph and first publicly demonstrated it here in the factory. Displays incl period furnishings in the mansion, exhibit on Speedwell Iron Works, exhibits on history of the telegraph; water wheel, carriage house, and granary. Gift shop. Picnic area. (May-Sept, Sun, Thurs; closed July 4) 333 Speedwell Ave. Phone 973/540-0211. ¢¢

Macculloch Hall Historical Museum. Restored 1810 house and garden; home of George P. Macculloch, initiator of the Morris Canal, and his descendants for more than 140 yrs. American, European decorative arts from the 18th and 19th centuries. Illustrations by Thomas Nast. Garden. (Wed, Thurs, and Sun afternoons; closed hols) 45 Macculloch Ave. Phone 973/538-2404. ¢¢

Morris Museum. Art, science, and history exhibits; permanent and changing. Musical, theatrical events; lectures and films. (Tues-Sun; closed hols) Free admission Thurs afternoons. 6 Normandy Heights Rd. Phone 973/971-3700. ¢¢¢

Morristown National Historical Park. (see) Approx 3 mi S on US 202.

Schuyler-Hamilton House. (1760) Former home of Dr. Jabez Campfield. Alexander Hamilton courted Betsy Schuyler here. Period furniture; colonial garden. (Sun afternoons; other times by appt; closed Easter, Dec 25) 5 Olyphant Pl. Phone 973/267-4039. ¢¢

Motel/Motor Lodge

★★ **BEST WESTERN.** *270 South St (07960).* 973/540-1700; fax 973/267-0241; res 800/688-4646. www.best western.com. 60 rms, 3 story, 14 kits. S $99-$119; D $109-$129; each addl $10; kit. units $110-$120; under 12 free; wkend rates. Crib $10. TV; cable (premium), VCR avail (movies). Ck-out noon. Coin lndry. In-rm modem link. Airport transportation. Exercise

equipt; sauna. Colonial decor. Cr cds: A, C, D, DS, MC, V.

🄳 🕅 �’ 🐾 **SC**

Hotels

★★★ **HEADQUARTERS PLAZA HOTEL.** *3 Headquarters Plaza (07960).* 973/898-9100; fax 973/898-0726; res 800/225-1942. www.hqplaza hotel.com. 256 rms, 16 story. S, D $170-$190; each addl $20; under 12 free; wkend rates. Crib free. TV; cable (premium). Indoor pool privileges. Restaurant 6:30 am-10 pm. Bar 3 pm-1 am. Ck-out noon. Meeting rms. Business center. In-rm modem link. Shopping arcade. Health club privileges. Microwaves avail. Luxury level. Cr cds: A, C, D, MC, V.

🄳 ➥ �’ 🐾 🕅

★★★ **MADISON HOTEL.** *One Convent Rd (07960).* 973/285-1800; fax 973/540-8566; toll-free 800/526-0729. www.themadisonhotel.com. 192 rms, 4 story. S $160-$200; D $180-$200; under 18 free; wkend rates. Crib avail. TV; cable (premium). Indoor pool; whirlpool, poolside serv. Complimentary continental bkfst. Coffee in rms. Restaurants 6:30 am-11 pm. Bar 11-2 am; entertainment. Ck-out noon. Meeting rms. Business center. In-rm modem link. Concierge. Airport transportation. Tennis privileges. Golf privileges. Exercise equipt. Some bathrm phones; microwaves avail. Cr cds: A, C, D, DS, MC, V.

🕅 🄳 🖙 ➥ 🕅 �’ 🐾 **SC** 🕅

★★★ **MARRIOTT HANOVER.** *1401 Rte 10 E, Whippany (07981).* 973/538-8811; fax 973/538-0291; toll-free 800/228-9290. www.marriott.com. 353 rms, 8 story. S, D $150-$199; suites $250-$450; under 17 free; wkend rates. Crib free. TV; cable (premium), VCR avail. Indoor pool; whirlpool. Coffee in rms. Restaurants 6:30 am-midnight. Bar 11 am-midnight. Ck-out noon. Lndry serv. Meeting rms. Business center. In-rm modem link. Concierge. Gift shop. Exercise equipt. Refrigerators avail. Cr cds: A, D, DS, MC, V.

➥ 🕅 🐾 🕅 🄳

★★★ **WESTIN.** *2 Whippany Rd (07960).* 973/539-7300; fax 973/984-1036; toll-free 800/937-8461. 199 rms, 5 story. S, D $175-$225; suites $250-$450; under 17 free; wkend rates.

Crib free. TV; cable (premium), VCR avail. Pool; whirlpool. Coffee in rms. Restaurants 6:30 am-midnight. Bar 11 am-midnight. Ck-out noon. Lndry serv. Meeting rms. Business center. In-rm modem link. Concierge. Gift shop. Exercise equipt. Refrigerators avail. Cr cds: A, D, DS, MC, V.

Conference Center

★★★ **HAMILTON PARK CONFERENCE CENTER.** *175 Park Ave, Florham Park (07932).* 973/377-2424; fax 973/377-9560; toll-free 800/321-6000. www.dolce.com. 219 rms, 5 story. S, D $185; family, wkend, hol rates. Crib avail. TV; cable (premium), VCR avail. Indoor/outdoor pool; whirlpool, poolside serv, lifeguard. Restaurant 6:45 am-10 pm. Bar; entertainment Thurs-Sat. Ck-out noon. Convention facilities. Business center. In-rm modem link. Bellhops. Concierge. Sundries. Lighted tennis. Exercise rm; sauna. Massage. Racquetball. Basketball. Lawn games. Cr cds: A, D, DS, MC, V.

Restaurant

★★ **ROD'S 1890S RESTAURANT.** *NJ 124, Convent Station (07961).* 973/539-6666. www.themadisonhotel. com. Hrs: 11:30 am-11 pm; early-bird dinner 4:30-6 pm; Sun brunch 11 am-3 pm. Closed Dec 25. Bar. Lunch $7.95-$15.95, dinner $15.95-$29.95. Sun brunch $10.50-$15.95. Child's menu. Specializes in prime beef, seafood. Entertainment Wed-Sat. Valet parking. Display of authentic Victorian antiques. Family-owned. Cr cds: A, D, DS, MC, V.

Morristown National Historical Park

(D-2) *See also Bernardsville, Morristown*

(Approx 3 mi S of Morristown on US 202)

This national historical park, the first to be established and maintained by the federal government, was created by an Act of Congress in 1933. Its three units cover more than 1,600 acres, all but Jockey Hollow and the New Jersey Brigade Area being within Morristown's limits. The main body of the Continental Army stayed here in the winter of 1779-1780.

Headquarters and museum (daily); Jockey Hollow buildings (summer, daily; rest of yr schedule varies, phone ahead; closed Jan 1, Thanksgiving, Dec 25). Contact Chief of Interpretation, Washington Pl, Morristown 07960; 973/539-2085.

What to See and Do

Fort Nonsense. Its name came long after residents had forgotten the real reason for earthworks constructed here in 1777. Overlook commemorates fortifications which were built at Washington's order to defend military supplies stored in the village. Ann St.

Jockey Hollow. The site of the Continental Army's winter quarters in 1779-1780 and the 1781 mutiny of the Pennsylvania Line. Signs indicate locations of various brigades. There are typical log huts and an officer's hut among other landmarks. Demonstrations of military and colonial farm life (summer). Visitor center has exhibits and audiovisual programs. 5 mi SW of Morristown. Phone 973/539-2085.

Morristown National Historic Park. Contains Washington memorabilia; period weapons and 18th-century artifacts; audiovisual programs. Washington Pl, directly to the rear of Ford Mansion. Phone 973/539-2085. ¢¢ Admission incl

Ford Mansion. One of the finest early houses in Morristown was built in 1772-1774 by Colonel Jacob Ford, Jr., who produced gunpowder for American troops during the Revolutionary War. His widow rented the house to the army for General and Mrs. Washington when the Continental Army spent the winter of 1779-1780 here. Phone 973/539-2085.

Wick House. Farmer Henry Wick lived here with his wife and daughter. Used as quarters by Major General Arthur St. Clair in 1779-1780. Restored with period furnishings. Jockey Hollow.

Mount Holly

(C-5) *See also Burlington*

Settled 1676 **Pop** 10,728 **Elev** 52 ft **Area code** 609 **Zip** 08060

The mountain that gives this old Quaker town its name is only 183 feet high. For two months in 1779, Mount Holly was the capital of the state; today, it is the seat of Burlington County.

What to See and Do

John Woolman Memorial. (1783) John Woolman, the noted Quaker abolitionist whose *Journal* is still appreciated today, owned the property on which this small, three-story red brick house was built; garden. Picnicking. (Wed-Fri; also by appt) 99 Branch St. Phone 609/267-3226. **Donation**

Mansion at Smithville. (1840) Victorian mansion and village of inventor/entrepreneur Hezekiah B. Smith; home of the "Star" hi-wheel bicycle. Guided tours (May-Oct, Wed and Sun). Victorian Christmas tours (Dec; fee). 801 Smithville Rd. Phone 609/265-5068. ¢¢

Mount Holly Library. Chartered in 1765 by King George III, the library is currently housed in Georgian mansion built in 1830. Historic Lyceum contains original crystal chandeliers, blue marble fireplaces, boxwood gardens; archives date to original 1765 collection. (July-Aug, Tues-Thurs; rest

of yr, Mon-Sat, limited hrs) 307 High St. Phone 609/267-7111. **FREE**

Motels/Motor Lodges

★ **HOWARD JOHNSON INN.** *NJ 541 at NJ Tpke Exit 5 (08060). 609/267-6550; fax 609/267-2575. www.hojo.com.* 90 rms, 2 story. S $58-$95; D $60-$102; each addl $7; under 12 free. Pet accepted. TV; cable (premium), VCR avail. Pool; lifeguard, sauna. Playground. Coffee in rms. Restaurant 6 am-11 pm. Bar 5-11 pm. Ck-out noon. Meeting rms. Cr cds: A, D, DS, MC, V.

★★ **QUALITY INN MCGUIRE AFB.** *21 Wrightstown/Cookstown Rd, Cookstown (08511). 609/723-6500; fax 609/723-7895; res 800/228-5151. www.qualityinn.com.* 100 rms, 2 story. May-Sept: S, D $79-$115; each addl $10; suites $125-$175; under 16 free; higher rates hols; lower rates rest of yr. Crib free. TV; cable. Pool. Complimentary full bkfst. Restaurant 11 am-10 pm. Ck-out 11 am. Business servs avail. Refrigerators avail. Cr cds: A, C, D, DS, ER, JCB, MC, V.

B&B/Small Inn

★★ **ISSAC HILLARD HOUSE B&B.** *31 Hanover St, Pemberton (08068). 609/894-0756; fax 609/894-7899; res 800/371-0756.* 4 rms, 2 story, 1 suite. S $75-$90; D $110-$120; each addl $20; suite $120-$140. TV; cable. Pool. Complimentary full bkfst. Restaurant nearby. Ck-out 11 am, ck-in 3 pm. Victorian house built in mid-18th century. Totally nonsmoking. Cr cds: A, DS, MC, V.

Restaurants

★★★ **BEAU RIVAGE.** *128 Taunton Blvd, Medford (08055). 856/983-1999. www.beau-rivage.com.* Hrs: 11:30 am-2:30 pm, 5:30-9:30 pm; Sat from 5:30 pm; Sun 4-8 pm. Closed Mon; hols; also 2 wks before Labor Day. Res accepted. French menu. Serv bar. Wine cellar. A la carte entrees: lunch $12.50-$15, dinner $20-$25. Specialties: beef Wellington, wild game, souffles. Own pastries. 2 dining areas, 1 upstairs. Parking; valet wkends. Jacket (dinner). Cr cds: A, D, MC, V.

D

★★★ **BRADDOCK'S TAVERN.** *39 S Main St, Medford Village (08055). 609/654-1604. www.braddocks.com.* Hrs: 11:30 am-2:30 pm, 5-10 pm; Sun 11 am-2:30 pm, 4-9 pm. Closed Jan 1, Dec 25. Res accepted. Bar to 2 am. Lunch $5.75-$8.95, dinner $16.95-$26.95. Sun brunch $15.95. Child's menu. Specializes in fresh seafood, beef, veal. Own baking. Cr cds: A, D, DS, MC, V.

D

★★ **CHARLEY'S OTHER BROTHER.** *1383 Monmouth Rd (08060). 609/261-1555. www.charlies otherbrother.com.* Hrs: 11:30 am-2:30 pm, 5-9:30 pm; Fri, Sat to 10:30 pm; Sun 4-9 pm. Closed Dec 25. Res accepted. Bar. Lunch $5.95-$7.95, dinner $15.95-$33. Child's menu. Specializes in fresh seafood, steak, prime rib. Country setting; Tiffany lamps. Cr cds: A, D, DS, MC, V.

D SC ⊟

Newark

(E-3) *See also Elizabeth, Jersey City*

Settled 1666 **Pop** 273,546 **Elev** 146 ft
Area code 973
Web www.state.nj.us/travel

Once a strict Puritan settlement, Newark has grown to become the largest city in the state and one of the country's leading manufacturing cities. Major insurance firms and banks have large offices in Newark, dominating the city's financial life. Newark was the birthplace of Stephen Crane (1871-1900), author of *The Red Badge of Courage,* and Mary Mapes Dodge (1838-1905), author of the children's book *Hans Brinker, or the Silver Skates.* Newark is also an educational center with Newark College of Rutgers University, College of Medicine and Dentistry of New Jersey, New Jersey Institute of Technology, Seton Hall

Law School, and Essex County College.

Transportation

Airport. See NEWARK INTERNATIONAL AIRPORT AREA.
Car Rental Agencies. See IMPORTANT TOLL-FREE NUMBERS.
Public Transportation. Trains, buses (NJ Transit), phone 973/491-9400.
Rail Passenger Service. Amtrak 800/872-7245.

Airport Information

Newark International Airport. For additional accommodations, see NEWARK INTERNATIONAL AIRPORT AREA, which follows NEWARK.

What to See and Do

Minor Basilica of the Sacred Heart. French Gothic in design, it resembles the cathedral at Rheims. Hand-carved reredos. (Daily) 89 Ridge St, at Clifton and 6th aves. **Donation**

The Newark Museum. Museum of art and science, with changing exhibitions. American paintings and sculpture; American and European decorative arts; classical art; the arts of Asia, the Americas, and the Pacific; numismatics and the natural sciences. Also here are the Junior Museum, Mini Zoo, Dreyfuss Planetarium, Garden, with its 1784 schoolhouse, and the Newark Fire Museum. Special programs, lectures, concerts; cafe (lunch). (Wed-Sun, afternoons) 49 Washington St. Phone 973/596-6550.

New Jersey Historical Society. Museum with collections of paintings, prints, furniture, decorative arts; period rm; special exhibitions. Reference and research library of state and local history; manuscripts, documents, maps. (Tues-Sat) 52 Park Pl. Phone 973/596-8500. **FREE**

New Jersey Performing Arts Center. Home of the New Jersey Symphony Orchestra and host to many other performances. 1 Center St. Phone 888/GO-NJPAC.

Old Plume House. Now the rectory of the adjoining House of Prayer Episcopal Church, it is thought to have been standing as early as 1710, which would make it the oldest

IRONBOUND NEWARK

Newark, once moribund, is in renaissance, and the city offers a combination of fascinating history, modern facilities, and some of the finest Spanish-Portugese dining anywhere. This walk first covers the historic Ironbound section, named for the surrounding railroads, the settling site for immigrant groups since the 1830s, now home to about 40 ethnic groups. It continues into the resurgent Four Corners/Military Park section.

Start at Pennsylvania Station, built in 1933 and beautifully decorated with Art Deco wall reliefs and ceiling sculptures. Walk east on Market Street, passing diminutive Mother Cabrini Park, site of a bust of Jose Marti, liberator of Cuba. Turn right onto Union Street. In one block, at Ferry Street, Our Lady of Mount Carmel Roman Catholic Church stands opposite at McWhorter Street. Originally opened in 1848, this building is now home to the Ironbound Educational and Cultural Center. Turn left onto Ferry Street. This is the commercial heart of the Ironbound, and is filled with shops and restaurants. Among the eateries of note are Fornos of Spain (47 Ferry Street) Iberia Peninsula Restaurant (63-69 Ferry Street), Iberia Restaurant (82-89 Ferry Street), and Brasilia Restaurant (132 Ferry Street).

Turn right onto Prospect Street. In ½-block at Number 76 is the Gothic Revival-style Christ Episcopal Church, completed in 1850. Destroyed by vandalism and fire, it was restored in 1978, and now serves as the Chancery Professional Center. At the corner of Lafayette Street stands St. Joseph's Roman Catholic Church, circa 1858, now called Immaculate Heart of Mary. In the basement are hidden catacombs that are replicas of those found in Rome, complete with crypts featuring wax likenesses of Spanish saints. Turn left on Lafayette and walk six blocks to Van Duren. Turn right two blocks to Independence Park. Covering 12½ acres, this was one of the city's first neighborhood parks (circa 1896). Turn left on New York Avenue, go one block and turn right on Pulaski Street. Pass East Side High School, and come to St. Casimir's Roman Catholic Church, built in 1919 in the Italian Renaissance style. Continue to Chestnut Street and turn right. Five blocks down the road stand the remains of the Murphy Varnish Company, once comprised of six major structures; note the carving of a Roman chariot carrying a can of Murphy Varnish on the west side of the building.

Follow Chestnut under the railroad and across McCarter Highway to Broad Street. Turn right and walk through the business district to the Prudential Building at the heart of the Four Corners Historic District. Among the many historic buildings: the National Newark Building, (744 Broad Street), a 34-story neoclassical structure completed in 1930, and 1180 Raymond Boulevard, another Depression-era skyscraper. In two more blocks, Military Park appears. Walk on the left side of the park to the New Jersey Historical Society (52 Park Place), which has an on-site museum and is next door to the historic Robert Treat Hotel. At the end of the park on Center Street stands the architecturally stunning New Jersey Performing Arts Center. Opened in 1997, it has become a world-renowned performance space. Return on Center Street towards Military Park, turn left on Central Street, and go two blocks to the Newark Museum (49 Washington Street), site of the largest collection of Tibetan art outside Tibet, the Dreyfus Planetarium, and the historic 1885 Ballantine House.

building in Newark. 407 Broad St. Phone 973/483-8202.

Symphony Hall. (1925) A 2,811-seat auditorium; home of New Jersey State Opera and the New Jersey Symphony Orchestra; also here is the famous Terrace Ballroom. 1020 Broad St. Phone 973/643-4550.

The Wars of America. Sculptured bronze group by Gutzon Borglum features 42 human figures representing soldiers in the major conflicts in US history. Military Park, bounded by Broad St, Park Pl, Rector St, Raymond Blvd. Other works by Borglum are

Bridge Memorial. This sculpture of a Native American and a Puritan stands on the site of a colonial marketplace. N of Washington Park (Broad St, Washington Pl, and Washington St).

Statue of Abraham Lincoln. Essex County Courthouse, Springfield Ave, and Market St.

Hotel

★ ★ ★ **HILTON NEWARK GATE-WAY.** *One Gateway Center - Raymond Blvd (07102). 973/622-5000; fax 973/824-2188; toll-free 800/932-3322. www.hilton.com.* 253 rms, 10 story. S $199-$229; D $219-$251; each addl $10; suites $239-$350; under 18 free; wkend rates. TV; cable (premium), VCR avail. Pool; lifeguard. Restaurant 6:30 am-10 pm; Sat, Sun 7 am-10 pm. Bar 11:30 am-midnight; Fri, Sat to 1 am. Ck-out noon. Meeting rms. Business center. Bellhops. Valet serv. Shopping arcade. Garage parking; $8. Free airport transportation. Exercise equipt. Luxury level. Cr cds: A, C, D, DS, MC, V.

⬛ 🏊 🏋 ✈ 🍽 ♿ SC 🏋

Newark International Airport Area

See also Newark

Services and Information

Information. 201/961-6000 or 800/247-7433.

Lost and Found. 201/961-6230.

Airlines. Aeroperu, Air Aruba, Air Canada, Air France, Air Jamaica, Alitalia, America West, American, Avianca, British Airways, Carnival, Colgan Air, Continental, Czech Arlns, Delta, El Al, Eva Airways, Kiwi International, Korean Air, Lot, Lufthansa, Mexicana, Midway Arlns, Midwest Express, Northwest, Philippine Arlns, SAS, Swissair, Tap Air Portugal, TWA, United, USAir, Virgin Atlantic, Western Pacific Arlns.

Motels/Motor Lodges

★ ★ **COURTYARD BY MARRIOTT.** *600 US Rte 1 and 9 S, Newark (07114). 973/643-8500; fax 973/648-0662; res 800/321-2211. www.marriott.com.* 146 rms, 3 story. S, D $149-$169; suites $179-$189; children free; package plans. Crib free. TV; cable (premium), VCR avail. Indoor pool; whirlpool. Complimentary coffee in rms. Restaurant 6 am-10 pm. Bar 5-11 pm. Ck-out noon. Coin lndry. Meeting rms. Business servs avail. Valet serv. Sundries. Free airport transportation. Exercise equipt. Health club privileges. Microwave, refrigerator in suites. Some balconies. Cr cds: A, C, D, DS, MC, V.

⬛ 🏊 🏋 ✈ 🍽 ♿ SC

★ **DAYS INN AIRPORT.** *450 US Rte 1 S, Newark (07114). 973/242-0900; fax 973/242-8480; toll-free 800/432-9755. www.daysinn.com.* 191 rms, 8 story. S, D $98.95-$109.95; each addl $5; suites $99-$175; wkend rates. TV; cable (premium). Restaurant 6:30 am-midnight. Bar. Ck-out noon. Coin lndry. Meeting rms. Business servs avail. Free airport transportation. Exercise equipt. Microwaves avail. Cr cds: A, C, D, DS, MC, V.

⬛ 🏋 ✈ 🍽 ♿ SC

★ ★ **HOLIDAY INN NORTH.** *160 Frontage Rd, Newark (07114). 973/589-1000; fax 973/589-2799; res 800/465-4329. www.holiday-inn.com.* 234 rms, 10 story. S, D $139-$229; under 18 free; wkend rates by res. Crib free. TV; cable (premium). Pool; lifeguard. Restaurant 6 am-midnight. Bar 11-2 am. Ck-out noon. Meeting rms. Business servs avail. In-rm modem link. Bellhops. Sundries. Gift shop. Free airport transportation. Exercise equipt. Cr cds: A, D, DS, MC, V.

🏊 ⬛ 🏋 ✈ 🍽 ♿

★ **HOWARD JOHNSON.** *50 Port St, Newark (07114). 973/344-1500; fax 973/344-3311; toll-free 800/446-4656. www.hojo.com.* 171 rms, 3 story. S, D $59.95-$99.99; under 12 free. Crib free. TV; cable (premium). Coffee in rms. Restaurant open 24 hrs; Fri, Sat 6-1 am. Ck-out noon. Coin lndry. Meeting rms. Business servs avail. In-rm modem link. Gift shop. Free airport transportation. Cr cds: A, C, D, DS, MC, V.

★ **ROBERT TREAT HOTEL.** *50 Park Pl, Newark (20036). 973/622-1000; fax 973/622-6410; res 800/578-7878.* 169 rms, 12 story. S $90; D $110; suites $275-$375; under 16 free; wkend rates. Crib avail. TV; cable (premium), VCR avail. Complimentary coffee in rms. Restaurant 7 am-11 pm. No rm serv. Bar 4 pm-midnight; entertainment Thurs. Ck-out noon. Meeting rms. Business servs avail. In-rm modem link. Gift shop. Coin lndry. Free airport, RR station transportation. Exercise equipt. In-rm whirlpool, refrigerator, minibar in suites. Cr cds: A, C, D, DS, JCB, MC, V.

Hotels

★ ★ ★ **HILTON NEWARK AIRPORT.** *1170 Spring St, Elizabeth (07201). 908/351-3900; fax 908/351-9556; res 800/774-1500. www.hilton.com.* 378 rms, 12 story. S, D $142-$209; each addl $10; suites $295-$650; under 18 free; wkend rates. Crib free. TV; cable (premium), VCR avail. Indoor pool; whirlpool. Coffee in rms. Restaurant 6:30 am-11 pm. Rm serv 24 hrs. Bar 4 pm-2 am. Ck-out noon. Convention facilities. Business center. In-rm modem link. Gift shop. Free airport, RR station transportation. Valet parking. Exercise equipt; sauna. Cr cds: A, D, DS, MC, V.

★ ★ ★ **MARRIOTT NEWARK AIRPORT.** *Newark International Airport, Newark (07114). 973/623-0006; fax 973/623-7618; toll-free 800/882-1037. www.marriott.com.* 591 rms, 10 story. S, D $199-$229; suites $450-$550; under 18 free; wkend rates. Crib free. TV; cable (premium), VCR avail. Indoor/outdoor pool; whirlpool, poolside serv. Restaurants 6 am-11 pm. Rm serv 24 hrs. Bars 11:30-1:30 am. Ck-out noon. Convention facilities. Business center. Concierge. Free airport transportation. Exercise equipt; sauna. Some refrigerators. Luxury level. Cr cds: A, C, D, DS, MC, V.

★ ★ ★ **SHERATON NEWARK AIRPORT.** *128 Frontage Rd (07114).*

973/690-5500. 504 rms, 12 story. S, D $85-$249; suites $250-$450; under 17 free; wkend rates. Crib free. TV; cable (premium), VCR avail. Indoor pool; whirlpool. Coffee in rms. Restaurants 6:30 am-midnight. Bar 11 am-midnight. Ck-out noon. Lndry serv. Meeting rms. Business center. In-rm modem link. Concierge. Gift shop. Exercise equipt. Refrigerators avail. Cr cds: A, D, DS, MC, V.

New Brunswick

(D-3)

Settled 1681 **Pop** 48,573 **Elev** 42 ft **Area code** 732

Information Middlesex County Regional Chamber of Commerce, One Distribution Way, Suite 101, Monmouth Junction 08852; 732/821-1700

New Brunswick, the seat of Middlesex County, is on the south bank of the Raritan River. It is both a college town and a diversified commercial and retail city. Rutgers University, the eighth-oldest institution of higher learning in the country and the only state university with a colonial charter, was founded in 1766 as Queens College, and opened in 1771 with a faculty of one—aged 18. Livingston College, Cook College, and Douglass College (for women), all part of the university, are also located here. One of New Brunswick's most important industries is Johnson and Johnson; its company headquarters are located downtown. Joyce Kilmer, the poet, was born in New Brunswick; his house, at 17 Joyce Kilmer Avenue, is open to visitors.

What to See and Do

Buccleuch Mansion. Built in 1739 by Anthony White, son-in-law of Lewis Morris, a colonial governor of New Jersey. Period rms. (June-Oct, Sun afternoons; closed hols) Under ten only with adult. George St and Easton Ave, in 78-acre Buccleuch Park. Phone 732/745-5094. **FREE**

Crossroads Theatre. Professional African-American theater company offering plays, musicals, touring programs, and workshops. (Oct-May, Wed-Sun) 7 Livingston Ave. Phone 732/729-9559.

George Street Playhouse. Regional theater; six-show season of plays and musicals; touring Outreach program for students. A 379-seat house. Stage II Theater; cafe; cabaret. (Tues-Sun) 9 Livingston Ave. Phone 732/246-7717.

Hungarian Heritage Center. Museum of changing exhibits that focus on Hungarian folk life, fine and folk art; library, archives. (Tues-Sun; closed hols) 300 Somerset St. Phone 732/846-5777. **Donation**

New Jersey Museum of Agriculture. Large collection of farm implements; covers three centuries of farming history. Interactive science and history exhibits. (Tues-Sun) 103 College Farm Rd. Phone 732/249-2077. ¢¢

The Rutgers Gardens. Features extensive display of American holly. (Daily) Ryder's Ln (US 1). Phone 732/932-8451. **FREE**

Rutgers-The State University of New Jersey. (1766) 50,000 students. Multiple campuses incl 30 colleges serving students at all levels through post-doctoral studies; main campus on College Ave. Phone 732/932-1766. On campus are

Geology Museum. Displays of New Jersey minerals; dinosaur; mammals, incl a mastodon; Egyptian exhibit with mummy. (Mon-Fri; call for wkend/summer hrs; closed hols) Phone 732/932-7243. **FREE**

Jane Voorhees Zimmerli Art Museum. Paintings from early 16th century through the present; changing exhibits. (Tues-Fri, also Sat and Sun afternoons; closed hols) George and Hamilton sts. Phone 732/932-7237. ¢¢

Special Event

Middlesex County Fair. Cranbury-South River Rd, in East Brunswick. Aug. Phone 732/356-7400.

Motels/Motor Lodges

★★ **HOLIDAY INN SOMERSET.** *195 Davidson Ave, Somerset (08873). 732/356-1700; fax 732/356-0939. www.holiday-inn.com.* 284 rms, 6 story. S, D $135-$159; under 12 free; wkend rates. Crib free. Pet accepted. TV; cable (premium). Pool; poolside serv, lifeguard. Coffee in rms. Restaurant 6:30 am-2 pm, 5-10:30 pm. Bar 11:30-1 am. Ck-out noon. Convention facilities. Business center. In-rm modem link. Bellhops. Valet serv. Sundries. Gift shop. Exercise equipt. Health club privileges. Microwaves avail. Cr cds: A, C, D, DS, MC, V.

⬛ 🐾 🌊 🏃 ⛖ 🗑 🎿

★★★ **HYATT REGENCY.** *2 Albany St (08901). 732/873-1234; fax 732/873-1382; toll-free 800/233-1234. www.hyatt.com.* 286 rms, 6 story. S $180; D $240; suites $270-$700; under 18 free; wkend rates. Crib free. TV; cable (premium). Indoor pool; whirlpool. Coffee in rms. Restaurant (see also 2 ALBANY). Bar 11-1 am; pianist Thurs-Sat. Ck-out noon. Convention facilities. Business center. In-rm modem link. Gift shop. Garage. Tennis. Exercise equipt; sauna. Refrigerators avail. Some balconies. Cr cds: A, C, D, DS, MC, V.

⬛ 🐾 🌊 🏃 🗑 🔥 SC 🎿

★★ **MADISON SUITES HOTEL.** *11 Cedar Grove Ln, Somerset (08873). 732/563-1000; fax 732/563-0352; toll-free 800/372-9099. www.madison suites.com.* 83 suites, 2 story. Suites $130-$158; under 18 free; wkend rates. TV; cable (premium). Complimentary continental bkfst. Ck-out noon. Meeting rms. Business servs avail. In-rm modem link. Valet serv. Coin lndry. Health club privileges. Refrigerators, microwaves. Cr cds: A, C, D, DS, MC, V.

⬛ 🗑 🔥 SC

★★ **MCINTOSH INN OF EAST BRUNSWICK.** *764 Rte 18, East Brunswick (08816). 732/238-4900; fax 732/257-2023; toll-free 800/444-2775. www.mcintoshinn.com.* 107 rms, 2 story. S $54.95-$61.95; D $60.95-$67.95; each addl $3. TV; cable (premium). Complimentary continental bkfst. Restaurant adj open 24 hrs.

Ck-out 11 am. Business servs avail. Cr cds: A, C, D, MC, V.

D

★★ **RAMADA INN.** *195 SR 18 S, East Brunswick (08816).* *732/828-6900; fax 732/937-4838; toll-free 888/298-2054. www.ramada.com.* 137 rms, 4 story. S, D $75-$155; each addl $10; under 18 free. Crib free. TV; cable (premium). Pool. Coffee in rms. Restaurant 6:30 am-10:30 pm. Bar 11:30 am-midnight; entertainment Fri, Sat. Ck-out noon. Meeting rms. Business center. Valet serv. Exercise equipt. Health club privileges. Microwaves avail. Cr cds: A, C, D, DS, MC, V.

D SC

Hotels

★★★ **DOUBLETREE SOMERSET EXECUTIVE MEETING CENTER.** *200 Atrium Dr, Somerset (08873).* *732/469-2600; fax 732/469-4617; res 800/222-8733. ww.doubletree.com.* 360 rms, 6 story. S, D $112-$164; each addl $10; suites $175-$375; family, wkend rates. Crib free. TV; cable (premium), VCR avail. 2 pools, 1 indoor; whirlpool, poolside serv, lifeguard. Restaurant 6:30 am-2 pm; dining rm 5:30-10 pm. Bar 2 pm-1:30 am; entertainment. Ck-out noon. Business center. In-rm modem link. Gift shop. Tennis. Exercise equipt. Refrigerator in suites; microwaves avail. Private patios. Cr cds: A, D, DS, MC, V.

D

★★★ **HILTON AND TOWERS EAST BRUNSWICK.** *3 Tower Center Blvd, East Brunswick (08816).* *732/828-2000; fax 732/828-6958; toll-free 800/445-8667. www.hilton.com.* 405 rms, 15 story. S $99-$205; D $120-$225; each addl $20; suites $430-$620; under 18 free; wkend rates. Crib free. TV; cable (premium), VCR avail. Indoor pool; whirlpool. Coffee in rms. Restaurant 6:30 am-10:30 pm. Rm serv 24 hrs. Bar 11 am-midnight; wkends to 2 am. Ck-out noon. Convention facilities. Business center. In-rm modem link. Concierge. Gift shop. Airport transportation. Exercise equipt; sauna. Some bathrm phones, minibars; refrigerators, microwaves avail. Lux-

ury level. Cr cds: A, C, D, DS, ER, MC, V.

D SC

★★★ **MARRIOTT SOMERSET.** *110 Davidson Ave, Somerset (08873).* *732/560-0500; fax 732/560-3669; res 800/228-9290. www.marriott.com.* 440 rms, 11 story. S, D $179-$204; each addl $15; under 18 free; wkend rates. Crib free. TV; cable (premium), VCR avail. Indoor/outdoor pool; whirlpool, poolside serv (summer). Restaurant 6:30 am-10 pm. Bar 11:30 am-midnight; Fri, Sat to 2 am. Ck-out 11 am. Meeting rms. Business center. In-rm modem link. Concierge. Gift shop. Tennis. Exercise rm; sauna. Refrigerators, microwaves avail. Some balconies. Cr cds: A, D, DS, MC, V.

D

All Suite

★★★ **EMBASSY SUITES HOTEL.** *121 Centennial Ave, Piscataway (08854).* *732/980-0500; fax 732/980-9473; toll-free 800/362-2779. www. embassysuites.com.* 224 suites, 5 story. Suites $185; each addl $20; under 18 free; wkend rates. Crib free. TV; cable (premium). Indoor pool; whirlpool. Complimentary full bkfst. Coffee in rms. Restaurant 11:30 am-2 pm, 5-10 pm. Bar to midnight. Ck-out noon. Coin lndry. Meeting rms. Business servs avail. In-rm modem link. Gift shop. Exercise equipt; sauna. Health club privileges. Game rm. Lawn games. Refrigerators, microwaves. Atrium. Cr cds: A, C, D, DS, MC, V.

D

Restaurants

★★ **ANTONIA'S.** *40 Livingston Ave (08901). 732/828-7080.* Hrs: 11 am-2 pm, 5-9 pm; Mon 11 am-2 pm. Closed Sat, Sun; also major hols. Res accepted. Italian menu. Bar. A la carte entrees: lunch $6.75-$7.95, dinner $8.25-$9.75. Child's menu. Specializes in pasta, eggplant. Parking. Patriotic decor; turn-of-the-century pictures. Cr cds: A, D, DS, MC, V.

D

★★ **DELTA'S.** *19 Dennis St (08901). 732/249-1551. www.deltasrestaurant. com.* Hrs: 11:30-1 am; Fri to 2 am; Sat 5 pm-2 am; Sun 3:30-7:30 pm.

Closed Jan 1, July 4, Dec 25. Res accepted. Entrees: lunch $7-$12, dinner $14.95-$25.95. Piano, guitar Fri, Sat. Street parking. Antiques. Cr cds: A, D, DS, MC, V.

D ⊐

★★★ **THE FROG AND THE PEACH.** *29 Dennis St (08901). 732/846-3216. www.frogandpeach. com.* Hrs: 11:30 am-2:30 pm, 5:30-10:30 pm; Sat from 5:30 pm; Sun 4:30-9:30 pm. Closed hols. Res accepted. Bar to midnight. Wine list. A la carte entrees: lunch $9-$18.95, dinner $19.50-$37. Child's menu. Specialties: pastrami-cured smoked salmon, proscuitto-wrapped tuna. Own baking. Outdoor dining. In renovated industrial building with antique bar, stained glass. Cr cds: A, D, DS, MC, V.

D

★★★ **LA FONTANA.** *120 Albany St (08901). 732/249-7500. www.lafontana ristorante.com.* Hrs: 11:30 am-2:30 pm, 5-10 pm; Fri to 11 pm; Sat 5-11 pm. Closed Sun. Res accepted. Italian menu. Bar. Wine cellar. A la carte entrees: lunch $15, dinner $22-$28. Child's menu. Specializes in aristocratic-style Italian cuisine. Valet parking. 1920s Old World elegance. Jacket. Cr cds: A, D, MC, V.

D ⊐

★★ **MAKEDA ETHIOPIAN RESTAURANT.** *338 George St (08901). 732/545-5115. www.makedas.com.* Hrs: 11:30 am-10:30 pm; Fri, Sat to midnight; Sun 1-10 pm. Closed Jan 1, Thanksgiving, Dec 25. Res accepted. Ethiopian menu. Bar 11:30-2 am. A la carte entrees: lunch $4-$25, dinner $6-$36. Specializes in Ethiopian cuisine. Music Thurs-Sun. Elegant atmosphere with authentic Ethiopian-style seating. Cr cds: A, D, DS, MC, V.

D SC ⊐

★ **MARITA'S CANTINA.** *1 Penn Plz (08901). 732/247-3840.* Hrs: 11:30-2 am; Sun 3-11:30 pm. Closed Easter, Thanksgiving, Dec 25. Res accepted. Mexican menu. Bar to 2 am. Lunch, dinner $4.95-$11.95. Child's menu. Specializes in Mexican cuisine. Own desserts. Entertainment Thurs. Outdoor dining. Cr cds: A, D, MC, V.

D ⊐

★★ **THE OLD BAY.** *61-63 Church St (08901). 732/246-3111. www.oldbay. com.* Hrs: 11:30 am-9:30 pm; Sun 5-9 pm; early-bird dinner 4-6 pm (seasonal). Closed hols. Res accepted. French Creole menu. Bar to 2 am. Lunch $5.45-$10.95, dinner $16.95-$25.95. Specializes in seafood, steaks. Entertainment Thurs-Sat. Street parking. Outdoor dining. Cr cds: A, MC, V.

D

★ **RUSTY NAIL.** *US 130S (08902). 732/821-4141.* Hrs: 11:30 am-10 pm; Sun from noon pm. Res accepted. Bar to 2 am. Lunch $4.25-$7.25, dinner $9.95-$16.95. Child's menu. Specializes in prime roast beef. Cr cds: A, D, MC, V.

D ⊐

★★★ **STAGE LEFT: AN AMERICAN CAFE.** *5 Livingston Ave (08901). 732/828-4444. www.stageleft.com.* Hrs: 5-11 pm; Fri 11:30 am-2 pm, 5-11 pm; early-bird dinner 5:30-7 pm. Closed Mon; also Jan 1, Memorial Day, Dec 25. Res accepted. Bar to 2 am. Wine cellar. A la carte entrees: lunch $9.95-$15.95, dinner $18.95-$26.95. Complete meal: dinner $29. Specializes in chicken, beef, seafood. Valet parking. Outdoor dining. Romantic atmosphere; unique art. Mahogany Art Deco bar. Cr cds: A, MC, V.

D ⊐

★★ **SZECHWAN GOURMET.** *3 Livingston Ave (08901). 732/846-7878.* Hrs: 11:30-2 am; summer hrs to 11:30 pm. Closed Thanksgiving. Chinese menu. Setups. Lunch $4.50-$6.50, dinner $4.50-$13.95. Specialty: General Tso's two treasures of jumbo shrimp and chicken. Street parking. Cr cds: A, DS, MC, V.

⊐

★★ **TERESA'S.** *48 Easton Ave (08901). 732/545-3737.* Hrs: 11 am-11 pm; Fri to midnight; Sun 4-10 pm. Closed Easter, Thanksgiving, Dec 25. Res accepted. Italian menu. Bar to 2 am. A la carte entrees: lunch $7-$11, dinner $11-$21. Child's menu. Specializes in seafood, pasta. Street parking. Outdoor dining. Cr cds: A, MC, V.

D ⊐

★★ **2 ALBANY.** *2 Albany St (08901). 732/873-1234. www.hyatt.com.* Hrs: 6:30 am-10 pm; Sun brunch 10:30 am-2 pm; early-bird dinner 4:30-6:30 pm (seasonal, Thurs-Sat). Res accepted. Mediterranean, Amer menu. Bkfst $4.95-$8.95, lunch $4.95-$11.95, dinner $16.95-$21.95. Bkfst buffet $9.95. Sun brunch $23.95. Child's menu. Specializes in beef, chicken. Piano Thurs-Sat. Parking. Cr cds: A, D, DS, MC, V.

Newfoundland

(D-2) *See also Paterson, Wayne*

Pop 900 **Elev** 756 ft **Area code** 973 **Zip** 07435

Ocean City (D-7)

Pop 15,378 **Elev** 4 ft **Area code** 609 **Zip** 08226

Information Public Relations Department, City of Ocean City, 9th and Asbury aves; 609/525-9300

Families from all over the country come to this popular resort year after year, as do conventions and religious conferences. In accordance with its founder's instructions, liquor cannot be sold here. Ocean City is an island that lies between the Atlantic Ocean and Great Egg Harbor. It has eight miles of beaches, more than two miles of boardwalk, an enclosed entertainment auditorium on the boardwalk, and excellent swimming, fishing, boating, golf, and tennis.

What to See and Do

Historic House. Furnishings and fashions circa 1920-1930. Tours. (Apr-Dec, Mon-Sat) 1139 Wesley Ave. Phone 609/399-1801. **Donation**

Ocean City Historical Museum. Victorian furnishings and fashions; doll exhibit; local shipwreck; historical tours; research library; gift shop.

(Mon-Sat) 1735 Simpson Ave, at 17th St. Phone 609/399-1801. **Donation**

Special Events

Flower Show. Music Pier. June.

Concerts. Music Pier. Pops orchestra and dance band. Mon-Wed, Sun. Late June-Sept. Phone 732/316-1095.

Night in Venice. Decorated boat parade. Mid-July.

Boardwalk Art Show. International and regional artists. Aug.

Hermit Crab Race, Miss Crustacean Contest. 12th St Beach. Crab beauty pageant, races. Phone 609/525-9300 or 800/BEACH-NJ. Early Aug.

Motels/Motor Lodges

★ **DAYS INN OCEAN CITY.** *7th St and Boardwalk (08226). 609/398-2200; fax 609/391-2050; res 800/329-7466. www.daysinn.com.* 80 rms, 4 story, 39 kit. suites. June-Aug: S $60-$160; D $70-$185; each addl $15; kit. suites $70-$215; wkly rates; higher rates sporting events; lower rates Apr-May and Sept-Oct. Closed rest of yr. Crib free. TV; cable, VCR avail (movies). Heated pool; lifeguard. Restaurant nearby. Ck-out 11 am. Coin lndry. Business servs avail. Bellhops. Balconies. Cr cds: A, C, D, DS, MC, V.

★★ **FORUM MOTOR INN.** *800 Atlantic Ave (08226). 609/399-8700; fax 609/399-8704. www.theforuminnoc. homestead.com.* 61 rms, 2-3 story. July-Aug (3-day min): S $64-$164; D $64-$204; each addl $8; some wknd rates; lower rates Apr-May, Sept-Oct. Closed rest of yr. Crib avail, $3. TV; cable (premium). Heated pool; wading pool, lifeguard. Ck-out noon. Coin lndry. Business servs avail. Game rm. Rec rm. Refrigerators. Picnic tables. Sun deck. Cr cds: MC, V.

★ **HARRIS HOUSE.** *1201 Ocean Ave and 12th St (08226). 609/399-7800; fax 609/398-8082. www.harrishouse. net.* 74 rms, 2 story. Late June-Aug: S, D $160; each addl $10; under 12 free; wkly rates; higher rates hols (3-day min); lower rates late Aug-late Oct and Apr-late June; closed rest of yr. Crib free. TV; cable. Heated pool; lifeguard. Complimentary coffee in lobby. Restaurant adj 6 am-9 pm. Ck-out 11 am. Business servs avail. Refrigerators, microwaves avail. On beach. Cr cds: A, DS, MC, V.

⊡ ⇌ ⊠ ⚒

★★ **IMPALA ISLAND INN.** *1001 Ocean Ave (08226). 609/399-7500; fax 609/398-4379. www.ochotels.com.* 109 units in 2 buildings, 2 story. July-Aug; S, D $105-$194; kit. units $1,300-$1,800/wk; lower rates rest of yr. Crib free. TV; cable. 2 pools, 1 heated; wading pool, lifeguard. Restaurant 7 am-9 pm. Ck-out 11 am. Meeting rms. Business servs avail. Refrigerators. Sun deck. Cr cds: A, MC, V.

⊡ ⚏ ⚎ ⚐ ⇌ ⚐ ⊠ ⚒

★ **PAVILION MOTOR LODGE.** *801 Atlantic Ave (08226). 609/399-8080; fax 609/814-0456; res 800/523-2552. www.pavilionmotorlodge.com.* 80 rms, 3 story. Early July-early Sept (3-day min wkends): S, D $80-$160; kit. units $150; lower rates Mar-June and early Sept-Nov; closed rest of yr. Crib avail. TV; cable (premium), VCR avail (movies). Heated pool; wading pool, poolside serv, lifeguard. Restaurant 7:30 am-9 pm. Ck-out 11 am. Coin lndry. Business servs avail. Refrigerators. On beach. Cr cds: A, DS, MC, V.

⇌ ⊠ ⚒ **SC**

Hotels

★★★ **BEACH CLUB HOTEL.** *1280 Boardwalk (08226). 609/399-8555. www.ochotels.com.* 82 rms, 3 story. Mid-June-Labor Day: S, D $158-$305; each addl $10; higher rates wkends, May-mid-June, Labor Day-Nov. Closed rest of yr. Crib free. TV; cable (premium). Pool; wading pool, lifeguard. Restaurant 7 am-9 pm. Ck-out 11 am. Coin lndry. Business servs avail. Bellhops. Golf privileges. Health club privileges. Refrigerators. Balconies. Sun deck. On beach. Cr cds: A, MC, V.

⚏ ⇌ ⚐ ⚒

★★ **PIER 4 HOTEL.** *Broadway Ave and The Bay, Somers Point (08244). 609/927-9141; fax 609/653-2752; toll-free 888/927-9141. www.pier4hotel. com.* 70 rms, 4 story, 8 suites. Apr-Dec: S, D $59-$169; each addl $15; suites $89-$225; under 14 free; wkly rates; wkends, hols (2-day min);

higher rates special events; lower rates rest of yr. Crib free. TV; cable. Complimentary continental bkfst, coffee in rms. Restaurant adj 11-1 am. Ck-out 11 am. Meeting rms. Business servs avail. Coin lndry. Golf privileges. Exercise equipt. Health club privileges. Heated pool; poolside serv. Rec rm. Refrigerators, microwaves. On bay. Cr cds: A, C, D, DS, MC, V.

⊡ ⚏ ⚎ ⇌ ⚐ ⊠ ⚒

Resort

★★ **PORT-O-CALL HOTEL.** *1510 Boardwalk (08226). 609/399-8812; fax 609/399-0387; toll-free 800/334-4546. www.portocallhotel.com.* 99 rms, 9 story. June-Sept: S, D $115-$295; each addl $15; penthouse apt $325-$650; under 18 free; lower rates rest of yr. Crib free. TV; cable (premium). Pool; lifeguard. Free supervised children's activities (June-Aug). Coffee in rms. Restaurant 7 am-2 pm, 5-8 pm; Sun 9:30 am-1:30 pm, 5-8 pm. Ck-out 11 am. Coin lndry. Meeting rms. Business servs avail. In-rm modem link. Bellhops. Sundries. Airport transportation. Golf privileges. Exercise rm; sauna. Refrigerators. Balconies, grills. On ocean. Cr cds: A, C, D, DS, MC, V.

⊡ ⚏ ⚐ ⇌ ⚐ ⊠ ⚒

B&B/Small Inn

★★★ **SERENDIPITY BED & BREAKFAST.** *712 E 9th St (08226). 609/399-1554; fax 609/399-1527; toll-free 800/842-8544. www.serendipitynj. com.* 6 rms, 2 share bath, 3 story. No rm phones. July 4-Labor Day: S $95-$129; D $98-$159; higher rates hols (3-day min); lower rates rest of yr. Children over 10 yrs only. TV; cable. Complimentary full bkfst. Restaurant opp 7 am-9 pm. Ck-out 11 am, ck-in 2 pm. Luggage handling. Picnic tables. Renovated inn built 1912. Totally nonsmoking. Cr cds: A, DS, MC, V.

⚏ ⊠ ⚒

All Suite

★★ **WILD DUNES INN.** *801 E 10th St (08226). 609/399-2910; fax 609/398-4379. www.ochotels.com.* 28

suites, 2 story. S, D $95-$250; wkends, hols (3-day min). Crib free. TV; cable. Restaurant nearby. Ck-out 10 am. Coin lndry. Heated pool; wading pool, lifeguard. Refrigerators, microwaves. Cr cds: A, MC, V.

Extended Stay

★ ★ **RESIDENCE INN BY MAR-RIOTT.** *900 Mays Landing Rd, Somers Point (08244). 609/927-6400; fax 609/926-0145; res 800/331-3131. www.residenceinn.com.* 120 kit. suites, 2 story. Memorial Day-Labor Day: S, D $89-$169; each addl $10; under 12 free; wkly rates; lower rates rest of yr. Pet accepted. TV; cable, VCR avail (movies). Heated pool; lifeguard. Complimentary continental bkfst. Complimentary in-rm coffee. Ck-out 11 am. Coin lndry. Meeting rms. Business servs avail. In-rm modem link. Valet serv. Golf privileges. Health club privileges. Rec rm. Microwaves. Some private patios, balconies. Picnic tables, grills. Cr cds: A, C, D, DS, MC, V.

Restaurants

★ ★ **CRAB TRAP.** *2 Broadway, Somers Point (08226). 609/927-7377.* Hrs: 11-2 am. Closed Dec 24, 25. Bar. Lunch $5.75-$8.95, dinner $11.25-$27.95. Child's menu. Specialties: stuffed lobster tail, prime rib. Entertainment. Nautical decor. On the bay. Family-owned. Cr cds: A, D, DS, MC, V.

★ ★ **DEAUVILLE INN.** *201 Willard Rd, Strathmore (08248). 609/263-2080. www.deauvilleinn.com.* Hrs: 11 am-midnight; summer hrs vary; early-bird dinner 4-6 pm. Closed Dec 25, 26. Bar. Lunch $3.95-$12.50, dinner $8.50-$40. Child's menu. Specializes in fresh seafood, steak, veal. Valet parking. Outdoor dining overlooking bay. Cr cds: A, MC, V.

★ **GREGORY'S.** *900 Shore Rd, Somers Point (08244). 609/927-6665. www. gregorysbar.net.* Hrs: 11-2 am; early-bird dinner 4-6 pm (Mon-Fri). Res accepted. Continental menu. Bar. Lunch $4.50-$9, dinner $6.95-$21.50. Child's menu. Specialties:

steamed lobster, Jersey crab cakes, pan-seared salmon. Parking. Family-owned since 1946. Cr cds: A, D, DS, MC, V.

★ ★ **MAC'S.** *908 Shore Rd, Somers Point (08244). 609/927-4360; fax 609/927-0033.* Hrs: 3:30-11 pm. Closed Dec 25. Res accepted. Italian, American menu. Bar. Dinner $9.95-$30.95. Child's menu. Specializes in seafood, steak. Family-owned. Cr cds: A, DS, MC, V.

Palisades Interstate Parks

See also Fort Lee, Hackensack

(Reached via Palisades Interstate Pkwy, starting at New Jersey end of George Washington Bridge; US 9 W, NJ/NY 17, Dewey Thrwy exit 13)

This 81,067-acre system of conservation and recreation areas extends along the west side of the Hudson River from the George Washington Bridge at Fort Lee, NJ (see), to Saugerties, NY. Its main unit is the 51,679-acre tract of Bear Mountain and Harriman (NY) state parks; the two are contiguous.

Bear Mountain (5,066 acres) extends westward from the Hudson River opposite Peekskill. Only 45 miles from New York City via the Palisades Interstate Parkway, this is one of the most popular recreation areas, with year-round facilities, mostly for one-day visits. Area includes swimming pool (Memorial Day-Labor Day; fee), bathhouse, fishing, boating on Hessian Lake; game fields, nature trails, ice-skating (late Oct-mid-Mar; fee), square dances in July and August. Cafeteria, inn.

Perkins Memorial Drive leads to the top of Bear Mountain, where there is a picnic area and a sightseeing tower. Near the site of Fort Clinton, just west of Bear Mountain Bridge, is the Trailside Museum, with exhibits of local flora, fauna, geology, and history (daily; fee).

Harriman (46,613 acres), southwest of Bear Mountain, includes much wilder country with several lakes. Swimming beaches (Lakes Tiorati, Welch, and Sebago), fishing, boating; hiking, biking, picnicking, miles of scenic drives, tent camping (Lake Welch), cabins (Lake Sebago).

Many smaller parks are located in the New Jersey section of the park system.

Alpine Area (12 acres). This area has fishing, boat basin; hiking, picnicking, concession (seasonal). Outdoor concerts in summer. (Daily, weather permitting) Off Henry Hudson Drive, east of Alpine.

Englewood-Bloomers Area (13 acres). This area offers fishing, boat basin; hiking, picnicking, concession (seasonal). (Daily, weather permitting) Off Henry Hudson Drive, east of junction Palisades Interstate Parkway and NJ 505 in Englewood Cliffs.

Ross Dock (14 acres). Near the southern end of the park system, this area has fishing, boat-launching ramp; hiking, picnicking, playgrounds. (April-mid-November, daily, weather permitting) Off Henry Hudson Drive, north of George Washington Bridge.

Fort Lee Historic Park. This 33-acre facility presents the story of Washington's retreat from Fort Lee in 1776. Visitor's Center/Museum (March-December, Wednesday-Sunday) offers two floors of exhibits; audiovisual displays; a short film; general information; special events. On grounds (daily, daylight hours) are 18th-century soldiers' hut, reconstructed gun batteries, a rifle parapet; overlooks with scenic views of the George Washington Bridge, the Palisades, the Hudson River, and the New York skyline. Gift shop. Parking fee (May-September, daily; April and October-mid-November, weekends and holidays). No pets, bicycles, or fires. Hudson Terrace. Phone 201/461-1776. ¢¢

There are fees for parking and special events. For further information on the New Jersey section contact Palisades Interstate Park Commission, PO Box 155, Alpine 07620; 201/768-1360. Further information on the New York section can be obtained from Palisades Interstate Park Commission, Administration Building, Bear Mountain, NY 10911; 914/786-2701.

Paramus (E-2)

Settled 1660 **Pop** 25,737 **Elev** 58 ft
Area code 201 **Zip** 07652
Information Chamber of Commerce, 58 E Midland Ave, PO Box 325; 201/261-3344
Web www.paramuschamber.com

This old Dutch farm community was an important hub of transportation as long ago as the Revolutionary War; western Paramus became headquarters for the Continental Army as a result. Paramus has grown as a residential community from 4,000 inhabitants in 1946 to its present size.

What to See and Do

New Jersey Children's Museum. Interactive displays in 30 rms. Incl aviation, firefighting, TV studio, hospital. Gift shop. (Daily; closed hols) 599 Valley Health Plaza. Phone 201/262-5151. ¢¢¢

Schoolhouse Museum. Exhibits in 1873 schoolhouse depict life from colonial times through 19th century, with emphasis on local history. Native American relics; early maps; Dutch genealogies; farm implements; doll and toy displays; clothing. Tours (by appt). (May-late Oct, Sun afternoons; closed hols) 650 E Glen Ave, at NJ 17, in Ridgewood. Phone 201/652-4584. **FREE**

Van Saun County Park. Fishing lake; bike trail, tennis (fee), horseshoes, shuffleboard, ice-skating, sledding, picnicking, concession, playgrounds, ball fields (permit). Zoo; train, pony rides (fees). Garden surrounding historic Washington Spring; farmyard. Park (daily). 216 Forest Ave, 1½ mi N of NJ 4. Phone 201/262-2627. **FREE**

Hotel

★★★ **RADISSON INN PARAMUS.**
*601 From Rd (07652). 201/262-6900;
fax 201/262-4955; res 800/333-3333.
www.radisson.com.* 120 rms, 2 story. S,
D $79-$145; each addl $10; wkend
rates. Crib free. Pet accepted, some
restrictions. TV; cable (premium).
Pool. Complimentary coffee in rms.
Restaurant 6:30 am-10 pm; Sat, Sun
from 7 am. Bar. Ck-out noon. Coin
lndry. Meeting rms. Business servs
avail. In-rm modem link. Health club
privileges. Refrigerators. Cr cds: A, D,
DS, MC, V.

Parsippany

Pop 50,649 **Elev** 282 ft **Area code** 973
Zip 07054

Motels/Motor Lodges

★★ **HAMPTON INN.** *3535 Rte 46 E
(07054). 973/263-0095; fax 973/263-
6133. www.hamptoninn.com.* 109 rms,
4 story, 18 kits. S, D $59-$134; kit.
units $135-$179; under 18 free;
wkend rates. Crib free. TV; cable
(premium). Complimentary continental bkfst. Ck-out noon. Business
center. Valet serv (exc wkends). Exercise equipt; sauna. Refrigerators,
microwaves avail. Cr cds: A, C, D,
DS, MC, V.

★ **HOWARD JOHNSON EXPRESS
INN.** *625 Rte 46 E (07054). 973/882-
8600; fax 973/882-3493; res 800/406-
1411. www.hojo.com.* 118 rms, 3
story. S $60; D $64.95-$75.95; under
18 free; wkly rates. Crib free. TV;
cable (premium). Complimentary
continental bkfst. Restaurant nearby.
Ck-out noon. Coin lndry. Meeting
rm. Business servs avail. Refrigerators, microwaves avail. Cr cds: A, C,
D, DS, MC, V.

★ **WELLESLEY INN.** *1255 NJ Rte 10,
Whippany (07981). 973/539-8350; fax
973/539-9338. www.welleslyinnand
suites.com.* 109 rms, 2 story. S $69-
$109; D $69-$119; each addl $10;
under 18 free; family, wkend, wkly,
hol rates. Crib free. Pet accepted,
some restrictions. TV; cable (premium). Complimentary continental
bkfst. Restaurant 11 am-10 pm. Ck-
out noon. Meeting rms. Business
servs avail. Valet serv. Coin lndry.
Pool. Refrigerators, microwaves avail.
Cr cds: A, C, D, DS, MC, V.

★★ **PARSIPPANY HOLIDAY INN
HOTEL & SUITES.** *707 Rte 46 E
(07054). 973/263-2000; fax 973/299-
9029; toll-free 800/465-4329. www.
parsippanyholidayinn.com.* 183 rms, 4
story. S, D $129; suites $119-$159;
under 18 free; lower rates wkends.
Crib free. TV; cable (premium). Pool.
Restaurant 7 am-11 pm. Ck-out
noon. Coin lndry. Meeting rms.
Business servs avail. Sundries. Exercise equipt. Health club privileges.
Microwaves avail. Cr cds: A, C, D,
DS, MC, V.

Hotels

★★★ **HILTON PARSIPPANY.** *1
Hilton Ct (07054). 973/267-7373; fax
973/984-6853; toll-free 800/774-1500.
www.hilton.com.* 510 rms, 6 story. S
$165-$195; D $175-$205; each addl
$20; suites $350-$675; family, wkend
rates. Crib free. Pet accepted, some
restrictions. TV; cable (premium),
VCR avail. Indoor/outdoor pool;
whirlpool. Playground. Coffee in
rms. Restaurants 6:30 am-11 pm;
wkends from 7 am. Rm serv Mon-
Thurs 6:30-2 am. Bar 11-2 am; entertainment. Ck-out noon. Convention
facilities. Business center. In-rm
modem link. Airport transportation.
Tennis. Exercise equipt. Basketball
court. Some bathrm phones; wet bar,
refrigerator in suites. Cr cds: A, D,
DS, MC, V.

★★★ **SHERATON.** *199 Smith Rd
(07054). 973/515-2000. www.sheraton.
com.* 370 rms, 8 story. S, D $159-
$225; suites $250-$450; under 17
free; wkend rates. Crib free. TV; cable
(premium), VCR avail. Pool; whirlpool. Coffee in rms. Restaurants 6:30
am-midnight. Bar 11 am-midnight.
Ck-out noon. Lndry serv. Meeting
rms. Business center. In-rm modem
link. Concierge. Gift shop. Exercise

equipt. Refrigerators avail. Cr cds: A, D, DS, MC, V.

Paterson

(E-2) *See also Clifton, Wayne*

Settled 1711 **Pop** 149,222 **Elev** 100 ft
Area code 973

Information Great Falls Visitor Center, 65 McBride Ave, across from the Great Falls, 07501-1715; 973/279-9587. Special Events Office, 72 McBride Ave, 07501; 973/523-9201

Named after Governor William Paterson, this city owes its present and historic eminence as an industrial city to Alexander Hamilton. He was the first man to realize the possibility of harnessing the Great Falls of the Passaic River for industrial purposes. As secretary of the Treasury, he helped form the Society for Establishing Useful Manufactures in 1791 and, a year later, was instrumental in choosing Paterson as the site of its initial ventures. Paterson was the country's major silk-producing town in the late 1800s. Today, it is a diversified industrial center. The area surrounding the Great Falls is now being restored and preserved as a historic district. Paterson is the seat of Passaic County.

What to See and Do

American Labor Museum-Botto House National Landmark. The history of the working class is presented through restored period rms, changing exhibits, and ethnic gardens. Tours, seminars, and workshops are offered. (Wed-Sat afternoons; closed hols) 83 Norwood St in Haledon. Phone 973/595-7953. ¢

Garret Mountain Reservation. A 575-acre woodland park on a 502-ft-high plateau. Fishing pond (stocked with trout), boat dock, rowboats, paddleboats; trails, stables, picnic groves. Rifle Camp Rd and Mountain Ave. Phone 973/881-4994. **FREE**

✪ **Great Falls Historic District Cultural Center.** Incl 77-ft-high falls, park and picnic area, renovated raceway system, restored 19th-century buildings. 65 McBride. Phone 973/279-9587. **Donation** Also here is

Paterson Museum. Contains shell of original 14-ft submarine invented by John P. Holland in 1878; also his second submarine (31 ft), built in 1881. Paterson-Colt gun collection (1836-1840); mineral display; exhibits on Paterson history, incl the silk and locomotive industries; two locomotives; Curtiss-Wright airplane engines; changing art exhibits. (Tues-Sun; closed hols) Thomas Rogers Building, 2 Market St. Phone 973/881-3874. **Donation**

Lambert Castle. Built by an immigrant who rose to wealth as a silk manufacturer. The 1893 castle of brownstone and granite houses a local-history museum; restored period rms; art-history gallery; changing exhibits; library (Wed, Fri, Sun; closed hols). 3 Valley Rd. Phone 973/247-0085. ¢¢

Rifle Camp Park. This 158-acre park is 584 ft above sea level. Incl nature and geology trails, nature center with astronomical observatory; walking paths, fitness course. Picnic areas. Rifle Camp Rd in West Paterson. Phone 973/881-4832. **FREE**

Plainfield (D-3)

Settled 1685 **Pop** 47,829 **Elev** 118 ft
Area code 908

Information Central Jersey Chamber of Commerce, 120 W 7th St, #217, 07060; 908/754-7250

Web www.erols.com/cjcc

Plainfield, directly south of the Watchung Mountains, is actually the center of a group of associated towns: Scotch Plains (see), Watchung, North and South Plainfield, Fanwood, Green Brook, Warren Township, Dunellen, Middlesex, and Piscataway, all of which are mainly residential. Plainfield is also home to a number of industries.

Princeton University

What to See and Do

Drake House Museum. (1746) General Washington's headquarters in 1777; now the Historical Society of Plainfield headquarters. Period furnishings; diorama depicts Battle of Shorthills. (Sun afternoons) 602 W Front St. Phone 908/755-5831. ¢¢

Littell-Lord Farmhouse Museum. Museum incl a pre-Revolutionary farmstead, 1878 Victorian House, spring house, 1914 pump house, summer kitchen, spring house, corn crib. (Third Sun of month or by appt) **Donation**

Motel/Motor Lodge

★★ **HOLIDAY INN SOUTH PLAINFIELD.** *4701 Stelton Rd, South Plainfield (07080). 908/753-5500; fax 908/753-5500; toll-free 877/214-6161. www.holiday-inn.com.* 173 rms, 4 story. S, D $149; under 12 free; wkend rates. Crib free. Pet accepted, some restrictions. TV; cable (premium). Indoor pool; whirlpool; lifeguard. Coffee in rms. Restaurant 6:30 am-midnight. Bar. Ck-out 1 pm. Coin lndry. Meeting rms. Business servs avail. In-rm modem link. Valet serv. Exercise equipt; sauna. Refrigerators; microwaves avail. Cr cds: A, D.

Princeton

(C-4) *See also Trenton*

Settled 1685 **Pop** 14,203 **Elev** 215 ft **Area code** 609

Information Chamber of Commerce, 216 Rockingham Row, PO Box 431, 08540; 609/520-1776

Web www.princetonchamber.org

In 1776, the first State Legislature of New Jersey met in Princeton University's Nassau Hall. Washington and his troops surprised and defeated a superior British Army in the 1777 Battle of Princeton. From June to November 1783, Princeton was the new nation's capital. Around the same time, Washington was staying at Rockingham in nearby Rocky Hill, where he wrote and delivered his famous "Farewell Orders to the Armies."

Princeton's life is greatly influenced by the university, which opened here in 1756; at that time it was known as the College of New Jersey. In 1896, on the 150th anniversary of its charter, the institution became Princeton University. Woodrow Wilson, the first president of the university who was not a clergyman, held the office from 1902-10. Princeton is also the home of the Institute for Advanced Study, where Albert Einstein spent the last years of his life.

What to See and Do

Bainbridge House. (ca 1766) Birthplace of commander of the USS *Constitution* during War of 1812. Changing exhibits on Princeton history; research library (Tues, Sat; fee), photo archives. Museum shops. Also offers walking tours of historic district (Sun; fee). 158 Nassau St. Phone 609/921-6748. **FREE**

Kuser Farm Mansion and Park. Farm and 1890s summer mansion of Fred Kuser; more than 20 rms open; many original furnishings. Grounds consist of 22 acres with original buildings incl coachman's house, chicken house; tennis pavilion; clay tennis court. Park with picnic areas; quoit courts, lawn bowling, walking trails; formal garden, gazebo. Tours (May-Nov, Thurs-Sun; Feb-Apr, Sat and Sun; limited hrs, call for schedule and hol closings); self-guided tour maps of grounds. Special programs, lectures, and video eves throughout the yr. 10 mi SE via US 206, I-295 to Olden Ave in Hamilton, then ½ mi W to Newkirk Ave. Phone 609/890-3630. **FREE**

Morven. (ca 1750) House of Richard Stockton, signer of the Declaration of Independence. Ransacked during Revolutionary War; was frequently visited by General Washington and other colonial leaders. (Apr-Oct, Wed-Fri, Sun). 55 Stockton St. Phone 609/683-4495.

Princeton Battle Monument. The work of Frederick W. MacMonnies, this 50-ft block of Indiana limestone commemorates the famous 1777 battle when George Washington's troops defeated the British. On Monument Dr, off Stockton St, near Morven.

Princeton Cemetery. Buried in the Presidents' Plot are 11 university presidents, incl Aaron Burr, Sr., Jonathan Edwards, and John Witherspoon. Monument to Grover Cleveland and grave of Paul Tulane, in whose honor Tulane University was named. Witherspoon and Wiggins sts. Phone 609/924-1369.

Princeton University. (1746) 4,500 undergraduate students, 1,650 graduate students. An Ivy League college that has been coeducational since 1969. A campus guide service shows the visitor points of interest on the main campus. Phone 609/258-3603. On campus are

McCarter Theatre. Professional repertory company performs classical and modern drama; concerts; ballet; other special programs yr-round.

Nassau Hall. (1756) Provided all college facilities, classrooms, dormitories, library, and prayer hall for about 50 yrs. New Jersey's first legislature met here in 1776, and the Continental Congress met here in 1783, when Princeton was the capital. During the Revolution, it served as a barracks and hospital for Continental and British troops. Phone 609/258-3000.

The Putnam Sculptures. One of the largest modern outdoor sculpture showcases in the country, with 19 sculptures on display throughout the campus, incl pieces by Picasso, Moore, Noguchi, Calder, and Lipchitz.

Woodrow Wilson School of Public and International Affairs. Designed by Minoru Yamasaki; reflecting pool and "Fountain of Freedom" by James Fitzgerald. Phone 609/258-4831.

Rockingham State Historic Site. On this five-acre site are three buildings: a kitchen, a wash house, and the main building. This was Washington's headquarters Aug 23-Nov 10, 1783, where he wrote his "Farewell Orders to the Armies"; ten rms with period furnishings. (Wed-Sat, also Sun afternoons; closed hols) 4 mi N on US 206, then 2 mi E on County 518 in Rocky Hill. Phone 609/921-8835. **FREE**

The Putnam Sculptures, Princeton

Motels/Motor Lodges

★ **DAYS INN.** *4191 US 1, Monmouth Junction (08852). 732/329-4555; fax 732/329-1041; toll-free 800/329-7466. www.daysinn.com.* 73 rms, 2 story, 7 suites. S $44.95-$59.95; D $59.95-$99.95; each addl $10; suites $150.95; under 12 free. Crib free. TV; cable, VCR avail (movies). Restaurant 6:30-10:30 am. Ck-out 11 am. Business servs avail. Refrigerators, microwaves avail. Cr cds: A, C, D, DS, JCB, MC, V.

★★ **HOLIDAY INN PRINCETON.** *4355 US Hwy 1 S (08540). 609/452-2400; fax 609/452-2494. www. princetonol.com/holidayinn.* 242 rms, 6 story. S, D $99-$179; each addl $10; suites from $225; under 18 free; wkend rates. Crib free. Pet accepted. TV; cable (premium). Indoor pool. Restaurant 6:30 am-10 pm. Bar 11-1 am. Ck-out noon. Meeting rms. Business servs avail. Gift shop. Exercise equipt. Health club privileges. Refrigerators, microwaves avail. Cr cds: A, C, D, DS, MC, V.

Hotels

★★★ **THE FORRESTAL AT PRINCETON HOTEL.** *100 College Rd E (08540). 609/452-7800; fax 609/452-7883; toll-free 800/222-1131. www.forrestal.com.* 290 rms, 3-4 story. S, D $125-$185; each addl $10; suites $275-$650; under 18 free; wkend rates. Crib free. TV; cable (premium), VCR avail. Indoor pool; whirlpool. Restaurant 7 am-10 pm. Bars 11-1 am. Ck-out noon. Convention facilities. Business center. In-rm modem link. Gift shop. Free valet parking. Airport transportation. Lighted tennis. Exercise equipt; sauna. Lawn games. Minibars. Contemporary design and furnishings. On 25 wooded acres. Luxury level. Cr cds: A, C, D, DS, MC, V.

★★★ **HYATT REGENCY PRINCETON.** *102 Carnegie Center (08540). 609/987-1234; fax 609/987-2584; res 800/233-1234. www.hyatt.com.* 348 rms, 4 story. S $89-$179; D $89-$204; suites $200-$575; under 18 free; wkend rates. Crib free. TV; cable (premium), VCR avail. Indoor/outdoor pool; whirlpool, poolside serv. Restaurant 6:30 am-10:30 pm. Bar 11-2 am; entertainment Fri-Sun. Ck-out noon. Business center. In-rm modem link. Gift shop. Airport transportation. Tennis. Exercise equipt; sauna. Health club privileges. Some bathrm phones; microwaves avail. Cr cds: A, C, D, DS, ER, JCB, MC, V.

★★★ **MARRIOTT PRINCETON FORRESTAL VILLAGE.** *201 Village Blvd (08540). 609/452-7900; fax 609/452-1223. www.marriott.com.* 294 units, 6 story. S, D $164-$184; under 18 free; some wkend rates. Crib free. TV; cable (premium), VCR avail. Indoor/outdoor pool; whirlpool, poolside serv, lifeguard. Coffee in rms. Restaurant 6:30 am-11 pm. Bar noon-2 am; entertainment. Ck-out 11 am. Coin lndry. Meeting rms. Business center. In-rm modem link.

Concierge. Gift shop. Tennis. Exercise equipt. Health club privileges. Refrigerators avail. Some private patios, balconies. Shopping center adj. Cr cds: A, C, D, DS, MC, V.

★★★ **NASSAU INN.** *10 Palmer Sq (08542). 609/921-7500; fax 609/921-9385; toll-free 800/862-7728. www. nassauinn.com.* 216 rms, 5 story. S $139-$189; D $159-$209; each addl $20; suites $325-$780; under 13 free. Crib free. Pet accepted. TV; cable (premium). Restaurant 7 am-10 pm. Bar 4 pm-1 am; entertainment Fri, Sat. Ck-out noon. Business center. In-rm modem link. Exercise equipt. Refrigerators avail. Colonial atmosphere, beamed ceilings, fireplaces in public rms. Cr cds: A, D, MC, V.

★★ **NOVOTEL.** *100 Independence Way (08540). 609/520-1200; fax 609/520-0594; res 800/221-4542. www.novotel.com.* 180 rms, 4 story. S $109; D $119; suites $169; under 16 free; wkend rates. Crib free. Pet accepted, some restrictions. TV; cable (premium), VCR avail. Pool; whirlpool. Restaurant 6 am-10:30 pm. Bar. Ck-out 1 pm. Coin lndry. Meeting rms. Business servs avail. In-rm modem link. Valet serv. Free RR station transportation. Exercise equipt. Microwaves avail. Cr cds: A, C, D, DS, JCB, MC, V.

B&B/Small Inn

★★ **PEACOCK INN.** *20 Bayard Ln (08540). 609/924-1707; fax 609/924-0788. www.peacockinn.com.* 17 rms, some share bath, 3 story. S, D $115-$150; higher rates: graduations, reunions. Pet accepted. TV in some rms, lobby; cable (premium). Complimentary bkfst buffet. Dining rm 11:45 am-2:30 pm, 5:30-9:30 pm. Ck-out noon, ck-in 2 pm. Business servs avail. Historic late Georgian Colonial house, built in 1775 and relocated from Nassau St to its present site. Antique furnishings; rms individually decorated. 2 blks from Princeton University campus. Cr cds: A, MC, V.

Extended Stay

★★ **RESIDENCE INN PRINCETON.** *4225 Rte 1 (08543). 732/329-9600; fax 732/329-8422; res 800/331-3131. www.residenceinn.com.* 208 kit. suites, 2 story. S, D $109-$199; under 18 free; wkly, wkend rates. Crib free. Pet accepted, some restrictions; $10. TV; cable (premium). Heated pool; whirlpool. Complimentary continental bkfst. Ck-out noon. Coin lndry. Meeting rm. Business servs avail. Valet serv. Health club privileges. Microwaves; many fireplaces. Balconies. Picnic tables, grills. Cr cds: A, D, DS, V.

Restaurants

★★ **ALCHEMIST AND BARRISTER.** *28 Witherspoon (08540). 609/924-5555. www.alchemistandbarrister.com.* Hrs: 11:30 am-2:30 pm, 5:30-10 pm; Fri, Sat to 10:30 pm; Sun 11:30 am-3 pm (brunch), 5:30-10 pm. Closed Jan 1, July 4, Dec 25. Res accepted. Bar to 2 am. Lunch $8, dinner $18-$33. Sun brunch $7.95-$13. Specializes in seafood, steak. Outdoor dining. Colonial decor. Cr cds: A, D, DS, MC, V.

★ **ANNEX.** *128-1/2 Nassau St (08542). 609/921-7555. www.annex restaurant.com.* Hrs: 11 am-10 pm; early-bird dinner Mon-Thurs 3:30-5:30 pm. Closed Sun; hols. Continental menu. Bar to 1 am. Lunch $4.50-$23, dinner $6.25-$23. Child's menu. Specialties: steak Diane, chicken a la cacciatori, baked stuffed sole with crabmeat. Casual atmosphere. Family-owned. Cr cds: A, D, MC, V.

★★ **GOOD TIME CHARLEY'S.** *40 Main St, Kingston (08528). 609/924-7400. www.gtcharleys.com.* Hrs: 11:30-1 am. Closed Dec 25; also lunch hols. Res accepted. Bar to 2 am. Lunch $5.95-$9.95, dinner $11.95-$25.95. Specializes in prime rib, fresh seafood. Musicians Fri, Sat. Victorian decor. Tiffany lamps; posters. Cr cds: A, C, D, DS, MC, V.

★★ **RUSTY SCUPPER.** *378 Alexander Rd (08540). 609/921-3276. www. rustyscupperrestaurant.baweb.com.* Hrs:

11:30 am-2:30 pm, 5-10 pm; Fri, Sat to 11 pm; Sun 1-9 pm. Closed Dec 25. Res accepted. Bar 11:30-1 am; Sat, Sun from 1:30 pm. Lunch $8-$16.95, dinner $8-$35. Child's menu. Specializes in seafood, prime rib, steak. Salad bar. Outdoor dining. Cr cds: A, MC, V.

Ramsey (E-1)

Pop 14,351 **Elev** 373 ft **Area code** 201 **Zip** 7446

What to See and Do

James A. McFaul Environmental Center. An 81-acre wildlife sanctuary incl museum with natural history displays, lectures, film programs; woodland trail; waterfowl pond; picnic area. Arboretum and perennial gardens. (Daily; closed morning wkends and hols) 3 mi NW off NJ 208 on Crescent Ave in Wyckoff. Phone 201/891-5571.

Skiing. Campgaw Mountain Ski Area. Two double chairlifts, T-bar, two rope tows; patrol, school, rentals; snowmaking; cafeteria. Eight runs, longest run 600 ft; vertical drop 275 ft. (Early Dec-mid-Mar, daily) Lighted x-country trails; half-pipe; x-country and snowboard rentals; night skiing (Mon-Sat); snow tubing. NJ 17 N, exit NJ 202 Suffern, 1.6 mi S on NJ 202, left on Darlington Ave 1 blk, stay to right, 1 mi on Campgaw Rd in Mahwah. Phone 201/327-7800. ¢¢¢¢

Motel/Motor Lodge

★★ **RAMADA INN.** *180 Rte 17 S, Mahwah (07430). 201/529-5880; fax 201/529-4767; toll-free 888/298-2054. www.ramada.com.* 128 rms, 4 story. S, D $79-$121; each addl $10; suites $120-$212; under 16 free. Crib free. TV; cable (premium). Indoor pool. Restaurant 6:30 am-11 pm. Bar. Ck-out noon. Coin lndry. Meeting rms. Business servs avail. In-rm modem link. Valet serv. Sundries. Exercise equipt. Microwaves avail. Cr cds: A, C, D, DS, MC, V.

Hotels

★★★ **SHERATON CROSSROADS HOTEL.** *One International Blvd, Rte 17 N, Mahwah (07495). 201/529-1660; fax 201/529-4709; res 800/325-3535. www.sheraton.com.* 228 units, 14-22 story. S, D $124-$199; each addl $10; suites $260-$750; under 18 free; wkend rates. Crib free. Pet accepted, some restrictions. TV; cable (premium). Indoor pool. Restaurant 6:30 am-11 pm. Bar noon-2 am; entertainment exc Sun. Ck-out noon. Convention facilities. Business center. Concierge. Shopping arcade. Covered parking. Tennis. Exercise equipt; sauna. Refrigerators, microwaves avail. Luxury level. Cr cds: A, C, D, DS, MC, V.

★★ **WELLESLEY INN.** *946 NJ 17N (07446). 201/934-9250; fax 201/934-9719; toll-free 800/444-8888. www.wellesleyinnandsuites.com.* 89 rms, 3 story. S $69-$89; D $85-$94; each addl $5; wkend, monthly rates. Crib free. Pet accepted, some restrictions; $3. TV; cable (premium). Complimentary continental bkfst, coffee in rms. Restaurant adj open 24 hrs. Ck-out 11 am. Business servs avail. Health club privileges. Refrigerators, microwaves avail. Cr cds: A, C, D, DS, MC, V.

Restaurant

★★★ **CAFE PANACHE.** *130 E Main St (07446). 201/934-0030.* Hrs: noon-2 pm, 5-9 pm; Mon to 8 pm; Fri to 10 pm; Sat 5:30-10 pm. Closed Sun; also Easter, Dec 24, 25. Res accepted. French, northern Italian menu. Setups. Lunch $10-$16, dinner $22-$30. Own baking. Guitar, classical music Wed-Thurs. Parking. Totally nonsmoking. Cr cds: A, MC, V.

Red Bank (E-4)

Pop 11,844 **Elev** 35 ft **Area code** 732
Zip 07701

Red Bank, an historic community on the shores of the Navesink River, includes a central business area with shops, restaurants, brokerage firms, and an antique center.

What to See and Do

Allen House. (ca 1750) Lower floor restored as tavern of the Revolutionary period; traveler's bedrooms upstairs. (Days same as Holmes House) 2 mi S on NJ 35, at jct Sycamore Ave in Shrewsbury. Phone 732/462-1466. ¢

Holmes-Hendrickson House. (ca 1750) A 14-rm Dutch Colonial farmhouse with period furnishings. (May-Sept, Tues, Thurs, Sat-Sun; closed hols) Longstreet Rd in Holmdel, W on NJ 520. Phone 732/462-1466. ¢

Monmouth Museum. Changing exhibits of art, science, nature, and cultural history; children's hands-on wing. (Tues-Sun; closed hols) 5 mi W on Newman Springs Rd; on campus of Brookdale Community College in Lincroft. Phone 732/747-2266. ¢¢¢

Motel/Motor Lodge

★★ **COURTYARD BY MARRIOTT.** *245 Half Mile Rd (07701). 732/530-5552; fax 732/530-5756; toll-free 800/321-2211. www.courtyard.com.* 146 rms, 3 story. S $119-$129; D $145-$155; wkend rates. Crib free. TV; cable (premium). Indoor pool; whirlpool. Complimentary coffee in rms. Restaurant 6:30-10 am, 6-10 pm. Bar 6-11 pm. Ck-out noon. Coin lndry. Meeting rms. Business servs avail. In-rm modem link. Valet serv. Exercise equipt. Some refrigerators; microwaves avail. Balconies. Cr cds: A, C, D, DS, MC, V.

D ⌨ 👁 ⚞ ♨ SC

Restaurants

★★★ **FROMAGERIE.** *26 Ridge Rd, Rumson (07760). 732/842-8088. www.fromagerierestaurant.com.* Hrs: 11:30 am-2:30 pm, 5-10 pm; Fri to 11 pm; Sat 5-11 pm; Sun from 4 pm. Closed Dec 25. Res accepted. French menu. Bar. Wine cellar. Lunch $9.95-$13.95, dinner $24.50-$39.50. Specialties: smoked duck with baked lentils, grilled swordfish with roasted red pepper coulis, rack of lamb. Own

Allen House, Red Bank

baking. Valet parking. Family-owned. Jacket. Cr cds: A, D, MC, V.
SC ⟶

★ ★ ★ **MOLLY PITCHER INN.** *88 Riverside Ave (07701). 732/747-2500; toll-free 800/221-1372. www.molly pitcher-oysterpoint.com.* Hrs: 6:30-10:30 am, 11:30 am-3 pm, 5-9 pm; Sat 8-10:30 am, 11:30 am-3 pm, 5-10 pm; Sun 8-10 am, 11 am-2:30 pm (brunch), 5-9 pm. Res accepted. Bar 11:30-2 am. Wine list. A la carte entrees: bkfst $2.95-$12.95, lunch $4.95-$12.95. Dinner $6-$30. Sun brunch $23.95. Child's menu. Specialties: Molly Pitcher chicken pot pie, crab cakes, coriander tuna. Pianist Fri-Sun. Elegant European decor with panoramic views of Navesink River. Jacket (dinner). Cr cds: A, D, MC, V.
D ⟶

★ ★ ★ **THE RAVEN & THE PEACH.** *740 River Rd, Fair Haven (07704). 732/747-4666.* Hrs: 11:30 am-2:30 pm, 5:30-10 pm; Fri, Sat to 11 pm. Closed Dec 25. Res accepted. Contemporary French menu. Bar. Wine cellar. A la carte entrees: lunch $8.50-$15.50, dinner $22.50-$31.50. Child's menu. Specialties: sesame-roasted rack of lamb, black-peppered seared sushi, tuna. Piano Wed-Sun. Valet parking. Outdoor dining. Modern French atmosphere. Cr cds: A, MC, V.
D ⟶

★ ★ ★ **SHADOWBROOK.** *Rte 35, Shrewsbury (07702). 732/747-0200; toll-free 800/634-0078. www. shadowbrook.com.* Hrs: 5:30-9 pm; Sat to 10 pm; Sun 3-9 pm. Closed Mon; Dec 24. Res accepted. Bar. Dinner $20-$33. Child's menu. Specialties: seafood fra diavolo, rack of lamb, veal Française. Valet parking. Fireplace; in Georgian mansion; Victorian antiques. Formal gardens. Family-owned. Jacket. Cr cds: DS, MC, V.
D ⟶

Ringwood State Park

(D-1) *See also Wayne*

(On the New Jersey, New York border)

Ringwood State Park lies in upper Passaic County, near the town of Ringwood, within the heart of the Ramapo Mountains. Consisting of 6,196 acres, the park is reached by routes 23 and 511 from the west and Route 17 and Sloatsburg Road from the east.

Ringwood Manor Section This section features a 51-room mansion containing a collection of Americana; relics of iron-making days (1740); formal gardens. Interpretive tours. Fishing in Ringwood River. Picnic facilities nearby. Tours (Wed-Sun).

Shepherd Lake Section A 541-acre wooded area has trap and skeet shooting all year (fee). The 74-acre Shepherd Lake provides a swimming beach and bathhouse, fishing, boating (ramp). Also available is picnicking (tables and grills).

Skylands Section Located here is a 44-room mansion modeled after an English baronial house (open to the public on select days). The gardens (90 acres) surrounding the manor house comprise the only botanical garden in the state park system (guided tours upon request; phone 973/962-7527). This 1,119-acre section also offers fishing; hunting, hiking, mountain biking.

Standard fees are charged for each section Memorial Day-Labor Day. Phone 973/962-7031.

Rockaway (D-2)

Pop 6,473 **Elev** 534 ft **Area code** 973 **Zip** 7866

Motels/Motor Lodges

★ **HOWARD JOHNSON INN.** *14 Green Pond Rd (07866). 973/625-1200; fax 973/625-1686. www.hojo.com.* 64

rms, 2 story. S, D $79-$99; each addl $10. Crib free. TV; cable (premium). Pool; wading pool. Complimentary continental bkfst (Mon-Fri). Restaurant 6:30-2 am. Bar. Ck-out noon. Business servs avail. Some refrigerators; microwaves avail. Balconies. Cr cds: A, C, D, DS, MC, V.

★ **MOUNTAIN INN OF ROCK-AWAY.** *156 US Hwy 46 (07866). 973/627-8310; fax 973/627-0556; toll-free 800/537-3732.* 86 rms, 2 story, 16 kits. (no ovens). S, D $50-$85; each addl $5; kit. units $85; under 12 free; wkend rates. Crib free. TV. Pool. Complimentary continental bkfst. Restaurant 5-11 pm. Bar. Ck-out 11 am. Coin lndry. Meeting rms. Business servs avail. Valet serv. Cr cds: A, C, D, DS, MC, V.

Rutherford

Pop 18,110 **Elev** 100 ft **Area code** 201

What to See and Do

Fairleigh Dickinson University-Rutherford Campus. (1942) 2,300 students. On campus is the Kingsland House (1670), in which George Washington stayed in August 1783; and the Castle, an 1888 copy of Chateau d'Amboise in France. W Passaic and Montross aves. Phone 201/692-7032.

Professional sports.

New Jersey Devils (NHL). Continental Airlines Arena, 50 NJ 120N. East Rutherford. Phone 800/NJ-DEVIL.

New Jersey Nets (NBA). Continental Airlines Arena, 50 NJ 120 in East Rutherford. Phone 201/935-8888.

Motels/Motor Lodges

★★ **FAIRFIELD INN MEADOW-LANDS.** *850 Rte 120, East Rutherford (07073). 201/507-5222; fax 201/507-0744; res 800/228-2800. www.fairfield inn.com.* 141 rms, 5 story. S, D $89-

$110. Crib avail. TV; cable (premium). Ck-out noon. Meeting rm. Business servs avail. In-rm modem link. Exercise equipt. Refrigerators avail. Cr cds: A, D, DS, MC, V.

★★ **QUALITY INN MEADOW-LANDS.** *10 Polito Ave, Lyndhurst (07071). 201/933-9800; fax 201/933-0658; res 800/228-5151. www.quality inn.com.* 150 rms, 2 story. S $59-$99; D $65-$99; each addl $6; under 18 free; wkend rates. Crib free. TV; cable (premium), VCR (movies). Pool; lifeguard. Restaurant 6:30 am-10 pm. Bar 11-2 am. Ck-out noon. Coin lndry. Meeting rms. Business servs avail. In-rm modem link. Sundries. Airport transportation. Exercise equipt. Health club privileges. Microwaves avail. Stadium, racetrack opp. Cr cds: A, C, D, DS, MC, V.

Hotels

★★ **COURTYARD MEADOW-LANDS.** *1 Polito Ave, Lyndhurst (07071). 201/896-6666; fax 201/896-1309. www.novotel.com.* 227 rms, 6 story. S, D $99-$179; each addl $10; under 18 free; family, wkend, hol rates. Crib free. TV; cable (premium). Complimentary coffee in lobby. Restaurant 6:30 am-midnight. Bar 5 pm-1 am. Ck-out noon. Meeting rms. Business center. In-rm modem link. Coin lndry. Exercise rm; sauna. Health club privileges. Indoor pool; whirlpool. Refrigerators, microwaves avail. Cr cds: A, C, D, DS, MC, V.

★★★ **RENAISSANCE MEADOW-LANDS HOTEL.** *801 Rutherford Ave (07073). 201/231-3100; fax 201/231-3111; toll-free 800/468-3571. www. renaissancehotels.com.* 163 rms, 9 story. S, D $199-$250; suites $275-$450; under 17 free; wkend rates. Crib free. TV; cable (premium), VCR avail. Indoor pool; whirlpool. Coffee in rms. Restaurants 6:30 am-midnight. Bar 11 am-midnight. Ck-out noon. Meeting rms. Business center. In-rm modem link. Concierge. Gift shop. Exercise equipt. Refrigerators avail. Cr cds: A, D, DS, MC, V.

SKYLANDS AT RINGWOOD STATE PARK

Skylands is the official state garden of New Jersey. The walking here is largely on marked dirt paths, with some paved drives and paths. Skylands Manor House is the park's centerpiece. A circa 1922 Tudor-style manor house, it holds, among other items of note, an outstanding collection of antique stained-glass medallions set in leaded windows. Guided house tours are offered one Sunday a month from March through December (phone 973/962-9534). In all, the botanical garden covers 96 acres.

Start at the Visitors Center/Carriage House and pick up a self-guiding tour brochure. Walk first to the right (in the general direction of Parking Lot A), skirting the manor house counter-clockwise. The Winter Garden contains New Jersey's largest Jeffery pine, a century-old upright beech, and an elegant weeping beech. The Japanese umbrella pine is distinctive for its dark-green needles. Also on display here are Atlas cedars and an Algerian fir, a tree that produces seven-inch-tall, purple standing cones.

Walk around the house along the lawn to the Terrace Garden. This garden is comprised of five terraces, each with its own particular ambience. The first centers on an octagonal pool with a swan fountain. Its rock garden is filled with a variety of dwarf plants, including a not-so-dwarf-like 20-foot-tall Dwarf Alberta Spruce. Continue past a pair of Sweet Bay Magnolias, especially beautiful during June, to the third level. Here the centerpiece is a rectangular reflecting pool that, in summer, displays water lilies and tropical fish. Surrounding it are a large collection of azaleas and rhododendrons that bloom in many colors. Next comes the Summer Garden, home to annuals and day lilies, followed by the final terrace level, the Peony Garden.

Walk to the left into the Lilac Garden, which peaks in mid-May. Step onto Maple Avenue, the paved lane, and walk back toward the house. On the right, you'll see the Perennial Garden. A constant flow of color is maintained here from March until November. Just beyond that stands the Annual Garden, a frequently-changing formal garden centered on a 16th-century Italian marble well. Move from there to the right, turn around and walk along Crab Apple Vista, a 1,600-foot grassy allee (or corridor) of 166 Carmine crab apple trees that erupts into full bloom in early- to mid-May. At the end of the Vista stands a series of sculptures known as the Four Continents Statues and, to the left, a collection of horsechestnut trees.

Turn left at the horsechestnut trees, and another world appears, revealing woodland paths that travel past Swan Ponds and through a bog. Following the interlaced and meandering dirt paths here, you'll see a wetland in which duck families, as well as the occasional frog, can be spotted. The paths also travel through a cactus collection, a wildflower garden, and a heather garden, and end at a colorful and flashy, yet formal, Rhododendron Display Garden. From here, follow East Cottage Road as it winds its way back to the Carriage House.

★★★ **SHERATON MEADOW-LANDS HOTEL & CONFERENCE CENTER.** *2 Meadowlands Plaza, East Rutherford (07073). 201/896-0500; fax 201/896-9696; res 800/325-3535. www.sheraton.com.* 425 units, 21 story. S, D $170-$295; each addl $20; suites $250-$600; under 18 free; wkend rates. Crib free. Pet accepted, some restrictions. TV; cable (premium), VCR avail. Indoor pool; whirlpool; poolside serv. Restaurant 6:30 am-11 pm. Bars noon-2 am. Ckout 1 pm. Convention facilities. Business center. In-rm modem link. Concierge. Gift shop. Exercise equipt; sauna. Bathrm phone, wet bar in suites. Cr cds: A, MC, V.

Restaurant

★★★ **SONOMA GRILL.** *64 Hoboken Rd, East Rutherford (07073). 201/507-8989. www.sonomagrill.com.* Hrs: 11:30 am-2:30 pm, 5-10 pm; Fri to 11 pm; Sat 5-11 pm. Closed Sun; hols. Res accepted. Bar. Wine cellar. A la carte entrees: lunch $7.95-$15.95, dinner $8.95-$29.95. Specialties: grilled fresh tuna with black olives, grilled marinated pork chop on Chinese noodles, grilled certified Angus T-bone. Jazz Fri eve. Cr cds: A, D, MC, V.

Saddle Brook

Pop 13,155 **Elev** 90 ft **Area code** 201 **Zip** 07663

Motels/Motor Lodges

★★ **HOLIDAY INN.** *50 Kenney Pl (07663). 201/843-0600; fax 201/843-2822; toll-free 888/446-1106. www. holiday-inn.com.* 147 rms, 12 story. S, D $99-$159; each addl $10; under 18 free; wkend rates. Crib free. TV; cable (premium). Pool. Coffee in rms. Restaurant 6:30 am-10 pm, wkends from 7 am. Bar 11 am-midnight. Ck-out noon. Meeting rms. Business servs avail. In-rm modem link. Exercise equipt. Cr cds: A, D, DS, MC, V.

★★ **RAMADA INN.** *375 W Passaic St, Rochelle Park (07662). 201/845-3400; fax 201/845-0412; toll-free 888/298-2054. www.ramada.com.* 173 rms, 5 story. S $95-$152; D $105-$169; each addl $10; suites $150; wkend rates. Crib free. TV; cable. Indoor pool. Restaurant 6:30 am-11 pm; wkends from 7 am. Bar 11-2 am; entertainment Thurs-Sat. Ck-out noon. Coin lndry. Meeting rms. Business servs avail. Valet serv. Sundries. Exercise equipt. Cr cds: A, C, D, DS, MC, V.

Hotel

★★★ **MARRIOTT SADDLE BROOK.** *Garden State Pkwy and I-80 (07663). 201/843-9500; fax 201/843-7760; toll-free 800/228-9290. www. marriott.com.* 221 rms, 12 story. S, D $89-$209; suites $300-$450; wkend rates. Crib free. TV; cable (premium). 2 pools, 1 indoor; whirlpool, poolside serv, lifeguard. Restaurant 6:30 am-10 pm; Fri, Sat to 11 pm; Sun 7 am-10 pm. Bar 11:30-1 am. Ck-out noon. Meeting rms. Business center. Free parking. Exercise equipt; sauna. Refrigerators avail. Cr cds: A, C, D, DS, ER, JCB, MC, V.

Salem (A-6)

Founded ca 1675 **Pop** 5,857 **Elev** 19 ft **Area code** 856 **Zip** 08079
Information Salem County Chamber of Commerce, 91A S Virginia Ave, Carneys Point, 08069; 856/299-6699
Web www.salemnjchamber.com

Salem is said to be the oldest English settlement on the Delaware River. The town and its surrounding area have more than sixty 18th-century houses and buildings, as well as many points of historical interest. In the Friends Burying Ground on Broadway is the 600-year-old Salem Oak, under which John Fenwick, the town's founder, signed a treaty with the Lenni-Lenape tribe.

What to See and Do

Alexander Grant House. (1721) Headquarters of Salem County Historical Society. Twenty rms with period furniture; Wistarburg glass; Native American relics; dolls; paintings; genealogy library; stone barn. (Tues-Fri afternoons; also open second Sat afternoon of each month) 79-83 Market St. Phone 856/935-5004. ¢¢

Fort Mott State Park. A 104-acre park at Finns Point; established in 1837 as a defense of the port of Philadelphia. North of the park is Finns Point National Cemetery, where more than 2,500 Union and Confederate soldiers are buried. Fishing, ferry ride, picnicking, playground; overlook. 454 Fort Mott Rd. Phone 856/935-3218.

Special Event

Cowtown Rodeo. 12 mi NE on NJ 45, then 3 mi W on US 40, near Woodstown. PRCA sanctioned. Phone

Alexander Grant House, Salem

609/769-3200. Sat evenings, Memorial Day-late Sept.

Sandy Hook

(see Gateway National Recreation Area)

Scotch Plains

(C-4) *See also Plainfield*

Settled 1684 **Pop** 22,732 **Elev** 119 ft
Area code 908 **Zip** 07076

What to See and Do

Watchung Reservation. A 2,000-wooded-acre reservation in the Watchung Mtns incl the 25-acre Surprise Lake. Nature and bridle trails, ice-skating, picnic areas, playground. Ten-acre nursery and rhododendron display garden. 1 mi NE. Phone 908/527-4900. Also here is

Trailside Nature and Science Center. Nature exhibits; special programs; planetarium shows (Sun;

fee). Museum (late Mar-mid-Nov, daily; rest of yr, wkends only; closed some hols). Visitor Center with live reptile exhibit (daily, afternoons). Gift shop. Grounds (daily). 452 New Providence Rd in Mountainside. Phone 908/789-3670. **FREE**

Motel/Motor Lodge

★★ **BEST WESTERN WESTFIELD INN.** *435 North Ave W, Westfield (07090).* 908/654-5600; fax 908/654-6483; res 800/780-7234. *www.best western.com.* 40 rms, 3 story, 15 kits. S $98-$143; D $108-$143; each addl $10; kit. units $112-$153; under 18 free. Crib free. TV; cable (premium). Complimentary continental bkfst. Restaurant noon-10 pm. Ck-out 11 am. Coin lndry. Meeting rm. Valet serv. Health club privileges. Cr cds: A, D, DS, MC, V.
🄳 ⬛ ⬛

Restaurant

★★★ **STAGE HOUSE INN.** *366 Park Ave (07076).* 908/322-4224. *www.stagehouseinn.com.* Hrs: 11:30 am-2 pm, 5:30-9 pm; Fri-Sat til 10 pm; Sun 4-8 pm. Closed Mon; Dec 25. Bar. A la carte entrees: lunch $8-$18, dinner $21-$29. Specialties:

charlotte of Maine crab, pan-roasted cod with crispy potatoes, peas, and black truffle sauce. Outdoor dining. Jacket required. Cr cds: A, DS, MC, V.

Seaside Park

Pop 2,263 **Elev** 6 ft **Area code** 732 **Zip** 08752

What to See and Do

Island Beach State Park. This strip of land (3,002 acres) is across the water, north of Long Beach Island (see), and faces Barnegat Lighthouse. There are two natural areas (Northern Area and Southern Area) and a recreational zone in the center. Excellent swimming and fishing in Atlantic Ocean (seasonal). Nature tours. Picnicking. (Daily) Standard fees. S on Central Ave. Phone 732/793-0506.

Motel/Motor Lodge

★★ **WINDJAMMER MOTOR INN.** *1st and Central aves (08752).* 732/830-2555; fax 732/830-2555. 39 rms, 3 story, 24 kits. June-Sept: S, D $100-$135; each addl $10; kit. units $130; lower rates rest of yr. Crib $5. TV; cable. Heated pool; poolside serv. Restaurant 8 am-7 pm. Bar from 11 am. Ck-out 11 am. Coin lndry. Beach privileges. Cr cds: A, MC, V.

Secaucus

Pop 15,931 **Elev** 12 ft **Area code** 201

Motel/Motor Lodge

★★ **HOLIDAY INN-SECAU-CUS MEADOWLANDS.** *300 Plaza Dr (07094).* 201/348-2000; fax 201/348-6035; res 800/222-2676. www.holiday-inn.com. 161 rms, 8 story. S, D $115-$170; each addl $10; suites $175-$225; under 18 free; wkend, monthly rates. Crib free. TV; cable (premium). Valet parking $3. Restaurant 7 am-11 pm. Bar. Ck-out noon. Coin lndry. Meeting rms. In-rm modem link. Bellhops. Gift shop. Exercise equipt. Refrigerators. Health club privileges. Luxury level. Cr cds: A, C, D, DS, MC, V.

Hotels

★★★ **CROWNE PLAZA.** *2 Harmon Plz (07094).* 201/348-6900; fax 201/864-0963; toll-free 800/227-6963. www.crowneplaza.com. 301 rms, 14 story. S, D $109-$169; each addl $10; suites $190-$350; family, wkend rates. Crib free. TV; cable (premium). Pool; whirlpool, poolside serv. Coffee in rms. Restaurant 6:30 am-11 pm; Sat, Sun from 7 am. Bars 11-2 am. Ck-out noon. Convention facilities.

Island Beach State Park

Business servs avail. In-rm modem link. Concierge. Gift shop. Valet parking avail. Exercise equipt; sauna. Some refrigerators; microwaves avail. Cr cds: A, C, D, DS, MC, V.

D ⌨ 🏃 🗆 🔥 SC

★★★ **RADISSON SUITES-MEAD-OWLANDS.** *350 Rte 3 W Mill Creek Dr (07094). 201/863-8700; fax 201/863-6209; res 800/333-3333. www.radisson.com.* 151 suites, 9 story. S $179-$239; D $189-$249; each addl $20; under 12 free; wkend, monthly rates. Crib avail. Pet accepted, some restrictions. TV; cable (premium), VCR avail. Complimentary coffee in rms. Restaurant 7 am-10 pm. Bar noon-midnight. Ck-out noon. Meeting rms. Business servs avail. In-rm modem link. Coin lndry. Airport, RR station transportation. Exercise equipt. Health club privileges. Indoor pool. Refrigerators, wet bars; microwaves avail. Cr cds: A, C, D, DS, MC, V.

D 🤚 ⌨ 🏃 🗆 🔥 🖐

★★★ **SHERATON SUITES ON THE HUDSON.** *500 Harbor Blvd, Weehawken (07087). 201/617-5600; fax 201/617-5627; toll-free 800/625-5144. www.sheraton.com.* 244 suites, 10 story. Mar-Dec: S $189-$279; D $209-$269; each addl $20; under 18 free; family rates; package plans; lower rates rest of yr. Crib free. Pet accepted. TV; cable (premium), VCR avail. Complimentary continental bkfst, coffee in rms. Restaurant 11:30 am-10 pm. Rm serv from 7 am. Bar from noon. Ck-out noon. Meeting rms. Business center. In-rm modem link. Concierge. Gift shop. Exercise equipt. Indoor pool. Refrigerators, microwaves, wet bars. On river. Cr cds: A, C, D, DS, MC, V.

D ⌨ 🏃 🗆 🔥 🖐

All Suite

★★★ **EMBASSY SUITES SECAU-CUS-MEADOWLANDS.** *455 Plaza Dr (07094). 201/864-7300; fax 201/223-0088; res 800/362-2779. www.embassysuites.com.* 261 suites, 9 story. S, D $199-$259; each addl $25; under 12 free; wkend rates. Crib free. TV; cable (premium), VCR avail. Indoor pool; whirlpool. Complimentary full bkfst. Restaurant 11:30 am-10 pm. Bar noon-midnight. Ck-out noon. Coin lndry. Meeting rms. Busi-

ness center. In-rm modem link. Gift shop. Airport transportation. Exercise equipt; sauna. Health club privileges. Refrigerators, microwaves. Cr cds: A, C, D, DS, MC, V.

D ⌨ 🏃 🗆 🔥 🖐

Ship Bottom

(see Long Beach Island)

Somerset

(see New Brunswick)

Somerville

(C-3) *See also New Brunswick*

Pop 12,423 **Elev** 54 ft **Area code** 908 **Zip** 08876

Information Somerset County Chamber of Commerce, 64 W End Ave, PO Box 833; 908/725-1552

Web www.somersetcountychamber. org

What to See and Do

Duke Gardens. Features 11 gardens under glass, incl colonial, desert, Italian, Asian, English, and tropical (closed Jan 1, Thanksgiving, Dec 25); 45-min guided tour (Oct-May, daily). No high heels, no cameras. On US 206, about 1¼ mi S of Somerville Cir. Res required; contact Duke Gardens Foundation (Mon-Fri). Phone 908/722-3700.

Golf House—USGA Museum and Library. Georgian colonial mansion originally designed as private residence by John Russel Pope, now houses exhibits tracing the evolution of golf. Equipt and artifacts donated by golf's greatest champions, incl Bobby Jones, Byron Nelson, Jack Nicklaus, and Arnold Palmer. Interac-

Wallace House State Historic Site, Somerville

tive displays. Library with more than 13,000 volumes on golf; USGA Research and Test Center. (Daily; closed hols) US 287 to NJ 512, in Far Hills. Phone 800/223-0041.

Old Dutch Parsonage State Historic Site. (1751) Moved from its original location, this brick building was the home of the Reverend Jacob Hardenbergh from 1758 to 1781. He founded Queens College, now Rutgers University, while residing in this building. Some furnishings and memorabilia on display. (Wed-Sun; closed hols; hrs may vary) Phone 908/725-1015.

Wallace House State Historic Site. General and Mrs. Washington made their headquarters here immediately after the house was built in 1778, while the army was stationed at Camp Middlebrook. Period furnishings. (Wed-Sun; closed hols; hrs may vary) Phone 908/725-1015.

Special Event

IMB/USET Festival of Champions. Competition of three Olympic equestrian disciplines. Hamilton Fram, 10 mi N on US 206 in Bedminster. Phone 908/234-0555. Mid- or late June.

Motel/Motor Lodge

★ **DAYS INN.** *118 Rte 206 S, Hillsborough (08844). 908/685-9000; fax 908/685-0601; toll-free 800/329-7466. www.daysinn.com.* 100 rms, 2 story. S, D $100-$150; each addl $5; suites $125-$175; under 17 free. Crib free. TV; cable. Complimentary continental bkfst. Ck-out 11 am. In-rm modem link. Valet serv. Pool. Exercise equipt. Some refrigerators; microwaves avail. Cr cds: A, C, D, DS, MC, V.

Restaurant

★★★ **THE RYLAND INN.** *US 22W, Whitehouse (08888). 908/534-4011. www.therylandinn.com.* Contemporary French menu. Specialties: veal chop with asparagus and morels, warm lobster tart, grilled foie gras with banyuls sauce. Hrs: 11 am-2 pm, 5-9 pm; Fri to 10 pm; Sat 5-10 pm; Sun 5-9 pm. Closed Mon; also 1st wk in Jan. Res accepted. Bar. Wine cellar. A la carte entrees: lunch $13-$16, dinner $26-$36. Eight-course tasting menu: dinner $85. Valet parking. Cigar rm. Organic garden. Jacket. Cr cds: A, D, DS, MC, V.

Spring Lake

See also Asbury Park

Pop 3,567 **Elev** 25 ft **Area code** 732
Zip 07762

Motels/Motor Lodges

★ **BELMAR MOTOR LODGE.** *910 NJ 35 10th Ave, Belmar (07719). 732/681-6600; fax 732/681-6604.* 55 rms, 2 story. Memorial Day-Labor Day: S, D $88-$115; each addl $10; under 14 free; higher rates hols (3-day min); lower rates rest of yr. Crib $3. TV; cable (premium). Pool. Restaurant adj open 24 hrs. Ck-out 11 am. Coin lndry. Opp Belmar Marine Basin. Cr cds: A, C, D, MC, V.

★★ **COMFORT INN.** *1909 SR 35 (07719). 732/449-6146; fax 732/449-6556; res 800/228-5150. www.comfort inn.com.* 70 rms, 2 story. Mid-June-Labor Day: S, D $125-$190; each addl $10; suites from $150; lower rates rest of yr. Crib $5. TV. Pool; lifeguard. Complimentary continental bkfst. Ck-out 11 am. Meeting rm. Business servs avail. In-rm modem link. Exercise equipt. Refrigerator, microwave in suites. Cr cds: A, D, DS, MC, V.

★ **DOOLAN'S.** *700 NJ 71, Spring Lake Heights (07762). 732/449-3666; fax 732/449-2601. www.doolans.com.* 60 rms, 3 story. Memorial Day-Labor Day: S $50-$175; D $55-$275; each addl $10; lower rates rest of yr. Crib $5. TV; cable (premium). Pool; lifeguard. Complimentary continental bkfst. Restaurant 8-10 am, noon-3 pm, 4:30-10 pm; closed for lunch Sat. Bar; entertainment Wed-Sun. Ck-out 11 am. Meeting rms. Cr cds: A, C, D, DS, MC, V.

★ **MARINERS COVE MOTOR INN.** *50 Broadway, Point Pleasant (08742). 732/899-0060; fax 732/701-0260.* 28 rms, 2 story. Memorial Day-Labor Day: S, D $139-$210; under 16 free; family rates; package plans; wkends, hols (2-3 day min). TV; cable. Restaurant adj 6 am-9 pm. Ck-out 11 am, ck-in 2 pm. Heated pool. Refrigerators. Cr cds: A, DS, MC, V.

★ **POINT BEACH MOTEL.** *Ocean and Trenton aves, Point Pleasant Beach (08742). 732/892-5100.* 25 rms, 2 story. Memorial Day-Labor Day: S, D $142-$172; each addl $10; under 8 free; higher rates hols; lower rates rest of yr. Closed Oct-Apr. Crib $10. TV; cable. Heated pool; wading pool. Ck-out 11 am. Refrigerators; microwaves avail. Opp Atlantic Ocean. Cr cds: DS, MC, V.

★ **TRAVELODGE.** *1916 Hwy 35, Wall (07719). 732/974-8400; fax 732/974-8401; toll-free 888/515-6375. www.travelodge.com.* 52 rms, 2 with shower only. S $44-$124; D $54-$159; each addl $5-$10; under 16 free; higher rates some hol wknds. Crib free. TV; cable (premium). Pool. Complimentary continental bkfst, coffee in rms. Ck-out 11 am. Business servs avail. Refrigerators. Cr cds: A, D, DS, MC, V.

★★ **WHITE LILAC INN.** *414 Central Ave (07762). 732/449-0211; fax 732/974-0568. www.whitelilac.com.* 10 rms, 2 share bath, 2½ story. No rm phones. S, D $125-$325; wkly rates; wkends (2-day min); hols (3-day min). Closed Jan. Children over 14 yrs only. TV in some rms; cable (premium). Complimentary full bkfst. Ck-out 11 am, ck-in 2 pm. Free RR station transportation. Some fireplaces. Southern accent; built in 1880. Cr cds: A, DS, MC, V.

Hotels

★★ **BREAKERS HOTEL.** *1507 Ocean Ave (07762). 732/449-7700; fax 732/449-0161. www.breakershotel.com.* 67 units. Mid-June-Labor Day (hol wkends 5-day min): S, D $180-$390; each addl $30; lower rates rest of yr. Crib free. TV. Pool; whirlpool, poolside serv, lifeguard. Restaurant 8 am-4 pm, 4:30-10 pm. Ck-out noon. Meeting rms. Business servs avail. Refrigerators. Restored Victorian oceanfront hotel. Cr cds: A, C, D, MC, V.

★★★ HEWITT WELLINGTON

HOTEL. *200 Monmouth Ave (07762). 732/974-1212; fax 732/974-2338. www.hewittwellington.com.* 29 rms, 3 story, 17 suites. Late June-Labor Day: S, D $150-$220; each addl $40; suites $225-$290; wkly rates; higher rates: wkends (2-day min), hols (3-day min); lower rates rest of yr. Children over 12 yrs only. TV; cable. Heated pool. Coffee in rms. Restaurant 5:30-11 pm. Ck-out 11 am. Meeting rm. Business servs avail. In-rm modem link. Refrigerators. Some balconies. On lake. Renovated Victorian hotel (1880). Cr cds: A, D, DS, MC, V.

B&Bs/Small Inns

★★ ASHLING COTTAGE. *106 Sussex Ave (07762). 732/449-3553; fax 732/449-9067; toll-free 888/274-5464. www.ashlingcottage.com.* 10 rms, 2 share bath, 3 story. No rm phones. Mid-June-mid-Sept (2-day min): S $98-$169; D $199-$275; hols (3-night min); lower rates Apr-mid-June and mid-Sept-Dec; closed rest of yr. TV in lobby. VCR avail (movies). Complimentary full bkfst. Restaurant nearby. Ck-out 11 am, ck-in 1 pm. Business servs avail. Concierge serv. Free RR station, bus depot transportation. Bicycles. Picnic tables. Victorian-style frame house (1877). Antiques. Totally nonsmoking. Cr cds: A, DS, MC, V.

★★★ BAY HEAD GABLES. *200 Main Ave, Bay Head (08742). 732/892-9844; fax 732/295-2196; toll-free 800/984-9536. www.bayheadgables. com.* 11 rms, 3 story. June-Labor Day: S, D $150-$225; wkly rates; higher rates wkends (2-3-day min); open wkends only Apr-June and Labor Day-Dec. Closed rest of yr. TV in sitting rm; cable. Complimentary full bkfst. Restaurant nearby. Ck-out 11 am, ck-in 1 pm. Designed by Stanford White in 1914. Totally nonsmoking. Cr cds: A, DS, MC, V.

★★★ CHATEAU INN. *500 Warren Avenue (07762). 732/974-2000; fax 732/974-0007; toll-free 877/974-5253. www.chateauinn.com.* 38 rms, 2 story. Late June-Labor Day: S $159-$209; D $179-$259; each addl $15; suites $219-$299; lower rates rest of yr. TV; cable (premium), VCR (movies). Beach, pool privileges. Meeting rm. Business servs avail. Health club privileges. Bicycles. Refrigerators; some fireplaces; microwaves avail. Private patios. Renovated Victorian hotel (1888). Overlooks parks, lake. Cr cds: A, D, DS, MC, V.

★★ THE INN AT THE SHORE. *301 4th Ave, Belmar (07719). 732/681-3762; fax 732/280-1914. www.theinn attheshore.com.* 10 rms, 6 share baths. S, D $115-$199; each addl $20; under 12 free. Crib free. Complimentary full bkfst. Restaurant nearby. Ck-out noon, ck-in 2 pm. Business servs avail. In-rm modem link. Luggage handling. Refrigerator, microwave avail. Victorian-style ambience in house built in 1888; many antiques. Cr cds: A, MC, V.

★★ NORMANDY INN. *21 Tuttle Ave (07762). 732/449-7172; fax 732/449-1070; toll-free 800/449-1888. www. normandyinn.com.* 19 rms, 3 story. June-Sept: S $95-$198; D $179-$346; each addl $20; lower rates rest of yr. Crib avail. TV avail; VCR avail. Complimentary full bkfst. Business servs avail. Bicycles. Some fireplaces. Porches. Built as private residence in 1888; 19th-century antiques. Cr cds: A, C, D, DS, MC, V.

★★ THE SANDPIPER INN. *7 Atlantic Ave (07762). 732/449-6060; fax 732/528-3390; toll-free 800/824-2779. www.sandpiperinn.com.* 15 rms, 8 with shower only, 4 story. Mid-June-early Sept: S $199-$279; D $150-$210; each addl $50; lower rates rest of yr. Children over 16 yrs only. TV; cable. Indoor pool. Complimentary continental bkfst; afternoon refreshments. Dining rm (see also THE SANDPIPER). Ck-out noon, ck-in 3 pm. Business servs avail. Refrigerators. Opp beach. Victorian inn built 1888; casual atmosphere in elegant surroundings. Cr cds: DS, MC, V.

Restaurants

★ **FAMILY TREE TAVERN.** *2420 NJ 35, Manasquan (08736).* 732/528-5950. Hrs: 11:30 am-11 pm. Continental menu. Bar to 2 am. Lunch $5.95-$7.95, dinner $8.95-$19.95. Child's menu. Specialties: coconut shrimp, chicken Elizabeth, tournedos Diane. Pianist Thurs-Sat eves. Casual, family atmosphere. Cr cds: A, D, DS, MC, V.
D ⊸

★★ **HEAT WAVE CAFE.** *513 Main St, Bay Head (08742).* 732/714-8881. *www.heatwavecafe.com.* Hrs: 5-10 pm. Closed Mon; Jan 1, Thanksgiving, Dec 25. Res accepted. A la carte entrees: dinner $18.95-$25.95. Street parking. Outdoor dining. Totally nonsmoking. Cr cds: A, DS, MC, V.
D

★★ **MARLINS CAFE.** *1901 Ocean Ave, Point Pleasant Beach (08742).* 732/714-8035. Hrs: noon-2 am; early-bird dinner 4-7 pm (Mon-Fri). Continental, American menu. Bar. Lunch $4.95-$19.95, dinner $7.95-$19.95. Specialty: Chilean sea bass. Own baking. Child's menu. Parking. Cr cds: A, MC, V.
D ⊸

★★★ **OLD MILL INN.** *Old Mill Rd, Spring Lake Heights (07762).* 732/449-1800. *www.oldmillinn.com.* Hrs: 11:30 am-10 pm; Fri, Sat to 11 pm; Sun to 9 pm; early-bird dinner Mon-Fri 2:30-6 pm; Sun brunch 11 am-3 pm. Closed Dec 24; Mon (Sept-May). Res accepted. Bar. Lunch $6.95-$14.95, dinner $18.95-$35.95. Sun brunch $9.95-$19.95. Child's menu. Specializes in seafood, steak. Own baking. Entertainment Fri, Sat. Valet parking. Outdoor dining. Lakeside view. Cr cds: A, D, MC, V.
D ⊸

★★ **THE SANDPIPER.** *7 Atlantic Ave (07762).* 732/449-4700. *www.sandpiperinn.com.* Hrs: 11:30 am-3 pm, 5-11 pm; early-bird dinner to 6:30 pm; Sun brunch 11 am-2 pm. Res accepted. Contemporary American menu. Setups. Lunch $6.50-$9.50, dinner $13.95-$22.95. Complete meals: lunch $6.50-$11.95, dinner $13.95-$21.95. Sun brunch $14.95. Child's menu. Specialties: pistachio-encrusted halibut, chicken

and shrimp forestiere. Own baking. Pianist Sat. Candlelit dining in Victorian setting. Cr cds: D, MC, V.
D ⊸

★★ **TESAURO'S.** *401 Broadway, Point Pleasant Beach (08742).* 732/892-2090. Hrs: 4:30-10 pm. Closed Mon; also Thanksgiving, Dec 25. Res accepted. Italian, American menu. Bar. A la carte entrees: dinner $12.95-$21.95. Specialties: veal saltimbocca, chicken and sausage, lobster and shrimp fra'diavolo. Valet parking. Family-owned since 1967. Festive atmosphere. Fireplace. Cr cds: A, D, MC, V.
D ⊸

Stanhope

See also Lake Hopatcong, Rockaway

Pop 3,584 **Elev** 882 ft **Area code** 973 **Zip** 07874

What to See and Do

Waterloo Village Restoration. Known as the Andover Forge during the Revolutionary War, it was once a busy town on the Morris Canal. The 18th-century buildings incl Stagecoach Inn, houses, craft barns, gristmill, apothecary shop, general store. Music festival during summer (fee). (Mid-Apr-mid-Nov, Wed-Sun; closed Thanksgiving, Dec 25) I-80 exit 25; follow signs. Phone 973/347-0900. ¢¢¢

Motel/Motor Lodge

★★ **CROSSED KEYS INN.** *289 Pequest Rd, Andover (07821).* 973/786-6661; fax 973/829-1689. *www.crossed keys.com.* 5 rms, 2 share bath, 2 story, 1 cottage. S, D $125-$185; each addl $25; cottage $175; wkends, hols (2-day min). TV; cable. Complimentary full bkfst. Ck-out 11 am, ck-in after 2 pm. Game rm. Lawn games. Some fireplaces. Totally nonsmoking. Cr cds: A, MC, V.
⊠ 🐾

B&B/Small Inn

★★★ **THE WOODEN DUCK B & B.** *140 Goodale Rd, Newton (07860). 973/300-0395; fax 973/300-0395. www.woodenduckinn.com.* 7 rms, 2 story, 1 guest house. S, D $100-$175; hols (2-day min). Children over 12 yrs only. TV; cable, VCR (movies). Complimentary full bkfst. Ck-out 11 am, ck-in 2 pm. Business servs avail. In-rm modem link. Luggage handling. Gift shop. Downhill ski 20 mi; x-country ski on site. Pool. Game rm. Lawn games. Picnic tables. On 17 acres. Totally nonsmoking. Cr cds: A, DS, MC, V.

⬛🛉🏊🏖🎿🔥

Restaurant

★★ **THE BLACK FOREST INN.** *249 US 206N (07874). 973/347-3344. www.blackforestinn.com.* Hrs: 11:30 am-2 pm, 5-10 pm; Sun 1-8 pm. Closed Tues; Jan 1, Dec 24, 25. Res accepted. German, continental menu. Bar. A la carte entrees: lunch $8.75-$15.50, dinner $16.75-$22.50. Specializes in veal, seafood. Classic European elegance. Cr cds: A, D, MC, V.

🅳 ⬛

Stone Harbor

(C-8)

Pop 1,128 **Elev** 5 ft **Area code** 609 **Zip** 08247

Information Stone Harbor Chamber of Commerce, 212 96th St, PO Box 422; 609/368-6101. Cape May County Chamber of Commerce, PO Box 74, Cape May Court House 08210; 609/465-7181

What to See and Do

Wetlands Institute. Environmental center focusing on coastal ecology. Also incl observation tower; marsh trail; aquarium; films and guided walks (July and Aug, daily). Bookstore. (Mid-May-mid-Oct, daily; rest of yr, Tues-Sat; closed Easter, July 4, Thanksgiving; also two wks late Dec-early Jan) 3 mi E off Garden State

Pkwy exit 10, on Stone Harbor Blvd. Phone 609/368-1211. ¢¢

Special Events

Sail into Summer Boat Show. Pleasure boating, family entertainment, musicians, food. Phone 609/368-6101. First wkend May.

Wings 'n Water Festival. Arts and crafts, decoys; entertainment; seafood. Phone 609/368-1211. Third full wkend Sept.

Motel/Motor Lodge

★★ **DESERT SAND RESORT COMPLEX.** *7888 Dune Dr, Avalon (08202). 609/368-5133; fax 609/368-1849; toll-free 800/458-6008. www.desertsand. com.* 90 units, 3 story, 15 suites, 31 kits. July-Aug: S $72-123; D $80-$163; each addl $10; suites $163-$205; kits. $170-$357; wkly rates; higher rates hols; lower rates mid-Apr-June, Sept-Oct. Closed rest of yr. Crib avail. TV; cable. 2 pools, 1 indoor; whirlpool, lifeguard. Restaurant (see also MIRAGE) 8:30 am-10 pm. Bar noon-midnight. Ck-out 11 am. Coin lndry. Meeting rms. Business servs avail. Exercise equipt. Refrigerators; microwaves avail. Cr cds: MC, V.

🅳🏖🏃🏊🔥🛀

Resort

★★★ **AVALON GOLDEN INN HOTEL & COFERENCE CENTER.** *7849 Dune Dr, Avalon (08202). 609/368-5155; fax 609/368-6112; res 609/368-5155. www.goldeninn.com.* 154 rms, 3 story, 76 kits. June-Labor Day: S, D $70-$275; each addl $15; suites $245-$345; kit. units $214-$275; under 12 free; lower rates rest of yr. Crib avail. TV; cable (premium), VCR (movies). Heated pool; wading pool, poolside serv, lifeguard. Supervised children's activities (mid-June-late Sept). Restaurant 8 am-11 pm. Bar 11-2 am; entertainment wkends. Ck-out 11 am. Meeting rms. Business servs avail. In-rm modem link. Bellhops. Tennis privileges. Golf privileges. Health club privileges. Refrigerators. Balconies. Picnic tables. On beach. Cr cds: MC, V.

🅳⬛🛉🏃🏖🔥🛀🎾

Restaurant

★ ★ **MIRAGE.** *7888 Dune Dr, Avalon (08202). 609/368-1919. www.desert sand.com.* Hrs: 8 am-1 pm, 5-9:30 pm. Closed Nov-Mar. Res accepted (dinner). Continental menu. Bar. A la carte entrees: bkfst $3.95-$8.95, dinner $7.95-$25.95. Child's menu. Specialties: mixed grill, veal Bianca. Own pastries. Pianist Fri-Sun. Casual, contemporary decor. Cr cds: MC, V.
D

Toms River (E-5)

Pop 7,524 **Elev** 40 ft **Area code** 732
Information Toms River-Ocean County Chamber of Commerce, 1200 Hooper Ave, 08753; 732/349-0220

What to See and Do

Cooper Environmental Center. A 530-acre facility with three-mi bay front. Boat tours (summer; free); seven miles of marked trails, picnicking (grills), playground. Nature center. (Daily) 1170 Cattus Island Blvd, E on NJ 37 to Fischer Blvd, follow signs. Phone 732/270-6960. **FREE**

Motels/Motor Lodges

★ ★ **HOLIDAY INN.** *290 Rte 37 E (08753). 732/244-4052; fax 732/244-4000; res 800/465-4329. www.holidayinn.com.* 122 rms, 4 story. Memorial Day-Labor Day: S, D $109-$149; each addl $10; higher rates wkends; lower rates rest of yr. Crib free. TV; cable (premium). Indoor pool; whirlpool, poolside serv. Restaurant 6:30 am-10 pm. Bar 11-2 am; entertainment. Ck-out noon. Coin lndry. Valet serv. Meeting rms. Business servs avail. Sauna. Game rm. Refrigerators. Cr cds: A, C, D, DS, MC, V.
D 🌊 📶 🐾 **SC**

★ **HOWARD JOHNSON HOTEL.** *955 Hooper Ave (08753). 732/244-1000; fax 732/505-3194; res 800/654-2000. www.tomsriverhojos.com.* 96 rms, 2 story. S $60-$199; D $70-$229; each addl $10; under 18 free; higher rates some hols. Crib free. Pet accepted, some restrictions; $10. TV; cable, VCR avail (movies). Indoor/outdoor pool. Restaurant 11 am-9 pm. Bar. Ck-out noon. Meeting rms. Business servs avail. In-rm modem link. Cr cds: A, C, D, DS, MC, V.
D 🐾 🌊 📶 🐾 **SC**

★ ★ **QUALITY INN.** *815 W Rte 37 (08755). 732/341-2400; fax 732/341-6469; res 800/228-5151. www.quality inntr.com.* 100 rms, 2 story. Memorial Day-Labor Day: S, D $75-$195; each addl $10; suites $129-$229; under 18 free; lower rates rest of yr. Crib free. TV; cable. Pool; poolside serv, lifeguard. Playground. Complimentary continental bkfst. Coffee in rms. Restaurant noon-8 pm. Bar; entertainment. Ck-out 11 am. Meeting rms. Business servs avail. In-rm modem link. Valet serv. Sundries. Airport transportation. Exercise equipt; sauna. Refrigerators avail. Cr cds: A, DS, ER, JCB, MC, V.
D 🌊 🏋 ✈ 📶 🐾 **SC**

★ ★ **RAMADA INN AND SUITES.** *2373 Rte 9 (08755). 732/905-2626; fax 732/905-8735; res 888/298-2054. www.ramada.com.* 154 rms, 3 story, 48 kits. Memorial Day-Labor Day: S $72-$139; D $79-$132; each addl $10; suites $119-$159; under 12 free; lower rates rest of yr. Crib free. TV; cable (premium). Pool; whirlpool, lifeguard. Complimentary continental bkfst. Restaurant 7 am-10 pm. Bar. Ck-out noon. Coin lndry. Meeting rms. Business servs avail. In-rm modem link. Sundries. Tennis. Exercise equipt. Game rm. Refrigerators avail. Cr cds: A, C, D, DS, MC, V.
D 🏊 🌊 🏋 📶 🐾

Restaurant

★ **THE OLD TIME TAVERN.** *Dover Mall Rte 166 (08753). 732/349-2387; fax 732/505-5976. www.theoldtime tavern.com.* Hrs: 11:30-1 am; Sun to midnight. Closed Dec 25. Bar. Complete meals: lunch $3.95-$9.95. A la carte entrees: dinner $5.95-$14.95. Child's menu. Specializes in steak, seafood, selected Italian dishes. Cr cds: A, C, D, MC, V.
D 📶

Trenton

(C-4) *See also Princeton*

Settled 1679 **Pop** 85,403 **Elev** 50 ft
Area code 609

Information Mercer County Chamber of Commerce, 214 W State St, 08608-1002; 609/393-4143

Web www.mercerchamber.org

The capital of New Jersey since 1790, Trenton is one of the fastest growing business and industrial areas in the country and a leading rubber-manufacturing center since colonial times. After crossing the Delaware on December 26, 1776, George Washington attacked the British-held town eight miles to the northwest.

What to See and Do

College of New Jersey. (1855) 6,150 students. A 250-acre wooded campus with two lakes. Tours of campus. 4 mi N on NJ 31. Phone 609/771-1855. On campus is the

College Art Gallery. (Feb-May and Sept-Dec, Mon-Fri, Sun; closed hols) Phone 609/771-2652. **FREE**

New Jersey State Museum. (Tues-Sun; closed hols). 205 W State St, adj to Capitol. Phone 609/292-6464. **FREE** Incl

Auditorium. Lectures; films; music; children's theater. Some fees.

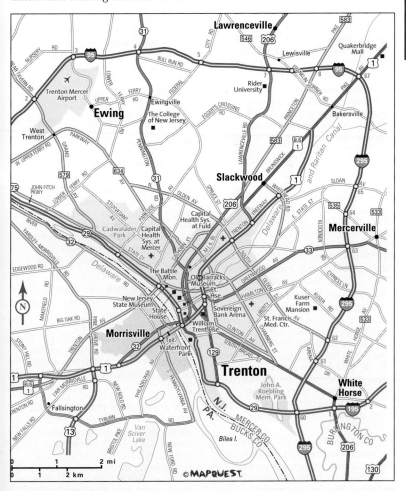

Main Building. Fine art, cultural history, archaeology and natural science exhibits. (Tues-Sun; closed state hols) **FREE**

Planetarium. One of few Intermediate Space Transit planetaria (duplicates motions of space vehicles) in the world. Programs (wkends; July-Aug, Tues-Sun). Over four yrs only exc children's programs. Tickets 30 min in advance. Phone 609/292-6303. ¢¢

The Old Barracks Museum. One of the finest examples of colonial barracks in the US. Built in 1758-1759, it housed British, Hessian, and Continental troops during the Revolutionary War. Museum contains restored soldiers' squad rm; antique furniture; ceramics; firearms; dioramas. Guides in period costumes. (Daily; closed hols) Barrack St, opp W Front St. Phone 609/396-1776. ¢¢¢

Sesame Place. A family play park featuring characters from *Sesame Street*. Rte 1 S to Oxford Valley exit. Phone 215/752-7070. ¢¢¢¢

☒ Washington Crossing State Park. This 996-acre park commemorates the famous crossing on Christmas night, 1776, by the Continental Army, under the command of General George Washington. Continental Lane, at the park, is the road over which Washington's army began its march to Trenton, Dec 25, 1776. Natureal trails. Picnicking, playground. Visitor center and nature center (Wed-Sun); open-air summer theater (fee). Standard fees. (See SPECIAL EVENTS) 8 mi NW on NJ 29, at 355 Washington Crossing-Pennington Rd, in Titusville. Phone 609/737-0623. Also in park is

Ferry House State Historic Site. Building sheltered Washington and some of his men on Dec 25, 1776, after they had crossed the Delaware from the Pennsylvania side. It is believed that the strategy to be used for the attack on Trenton was discussed here. Restored as a living history colonial farmhouse; special programs throughout the yr. (Wed-Sun) Phone 609/737-2515.

William Trent House. (1719) Trenton's oldest house is an example of Georgian architecture. It was the home of Chief Justice William Trent, for whom the city was named. Colonial garden. (Daily, afternoons; closed hols) 15 Market St. Phone 609/989-3027. ¢¢

Special Events

Trenton Kennel Club Dog Show. Mercer County Central Park. Early May.

Heritage Days. First wkend June.

Reenactment of Crossing of the Delaware. Washington Crossing State Park. Departs PA side on the afternoon of Dec 25.

Motel/Motor Lodge

★ **HOWARD JOHNSON LODGE.** *Rte 1 S, Lawrenceville (08648). 609/896-1100; fax 609/895-1325; res 800/446-4656. www.hojo.com.* 104 rms, 2 story. S $62.50-$88; D $68.50-$110; each addl $10; under 18 free; higher rates special events. Crib free. Pet accepted. TV; cable (premium). Pool. Complimentary continental bkfst. Restaurant open 24 hrs. Ck-out noon. Meeting rm. Business servs avail. In-rm modem link. Valet serv. Sundries. Private patios, balconies. Cr cds: A, C, D, DS, MC, V.

[D] [🐾] [≈] [≋] [👤] [SC]

Restaurants

★★ **DIAMONDS.** *132 Kent (08611). 609/393-1000. www.diamonds restaurant.com.* Hrs: 11:30 am-2:30 pm, 4:30 pm-midnight; Sat from 4:30 pm; Sun from 3:30 pm. Closed hols. Res accepted. Italian menu. Bar 11-2 am. Lunch $7-$15, dinner $16-$33. Specializes in seafood, steak, veal. Valet parking. Italian decor. Cr cds: A, C, D, DS, MC, V.

★★ **MARSILIO'S.** *541 Roebling Ave (08611). 609/695-2986.* Hrs: 11:30 am-2 pm, 5-10 pm; Fri, Sat to 11 pm. Closed Sun; hols. Res accepted. Italian menu. Bar. Lunch $6.45-$19.95, dinner $12.95-$26. Child's menu. Specializes in veal, chicken. Italian decor. Cr cds: A, MC, V.

[D] [⬛]

★★ **MERLINO'S WATERFRONT.** *1140 River Rd (08628). 609/882-0303. www.merlinoswaterfront.webatonce. com.* Hrs: 11:30 am-9 pm; Sat 4-11 pm. Closed Dec 25. Res accepted. Continental menu. Bar. Lunch $4.95-$7.95, dinner $11.95-$18.95. Specializes in veal, beef, seafood. Outdoor dining. Paneled dining rms, fire-places. Spacious grounds. Cr cds: A, D, DS, MC, V.

Wayne (D-2)

Pop 54,069 **Elev** 200 ft **Area code** 973 **Zip** 07470

Information Tri-County Chamber of Commerce, 2055 Hamburg Tpke; 973/831-7788

Web www.tricounty.org

Wayne is the home of William Paterson University of New Jersey (1855).

Vernon (D-1)

Pop 1,737 **Elev** 564 ft **Area code** 973 **Zip** 7462

Information Vernon Township Municipal Building, 21 Church St; 973/764-4055

What to See and Do

Action Park. Theme park incl 75 self-operative rides, shows and attractions. Action Park has more than 40 water rides, incl river rides and Tidal Wave Pool; also Grand Prix race cars, bungee jumping, miniature golf, children's park; food, picnic area. Three daily shows, wkend festival series. (Mid-June-Labor Day, daily; late May-mid-June, Thurs-Sun) NJ 94. Phone 973/827-2000. ¢¢¢¢ Also here is

Skiing. Mountain Creek Ski Resort. Gondola; four quad, triple, double chairlifts; three surface lifts, rope tow; school, rentals; snowmaking; cafeterias, restaurants, bars, night club; nursery. Forty-three runs; vertical drop 1,040 ft. (Dec-Mar, daily) Night skiing. Health spa, country club (daily). NJ 94. Phone 973/827-2000. ¢¢¢¢

B&B/Small Inn

★★ **APPLE VALLEY INN.** *967 Rte 517, PO Box 302, Glenwood (07418). 973/764-3735; fax 973/764-1050; res 973/764-3735. www.applevalleyinn. com.* 7 rms, 5 share bath, 3 story. No elvtr. S, D $110-$150; each addl $25. Premium cable TV in common rm; VCR avail (movies). Complimentary full bkfst. Ck-out 11 am, ck-in before 9 pm. Pool. Built in 1831; antiques. Cr cds: A, DS, MC, V.

What to See and Do

Dey Mansion. (ca 1740) Restoration of Washington's headquarters (1780); period furnishings. Guided tours. Picnic tables. (Wed-Sun; closed hols) 199 Totowa Rd. Phone 973/696-1776. ¢

Terhune Memorial Park (Sunnybank). Estate of the late Albert Payson Terhune, author of *Lad, a Dog* and many other books about his collies. Scenic garden; picnic area. (Daily) 2½ mi N on US 202N. Phone 973/694-1800. **FREE**

Van Riper-Hopper (Wayne) Museum. (ca 1786) Dutch Colonial farmhouse with 18th- and 19th-century furnishings; local historical objects; herb garden; bird sanctuary. 533 Berdan Ave. Phone 973/694-7192. Also here is

Mead Van Duyne House. Restored Dutch farmhouse. Phone 973/694-7192.

Motels/Motor Lodges

★★ **BEST WESTERN FAIRFIELD EXECUTIVE INN.** *216-234 Rte 46E, Fairfield (07004). 973/575-7700; fax 973/575-4653. www.bwfei.com.* 171 rms, 4 story. S $88; D $101; each addl $13; suites $114-$166; under 16 free; family, wkend, wkly, hol rates. Crib free. TV; cable (premium), VCR avail (movies). Complimentary full bkfst, coffee in rms. Restaurant 6 am-11 pm. Bar 11-1:30 am; entertainment Thurs-Sun. Ck-out noon. Meeting rms. Business center. In-rm modem link. Bellhops. Valet serv. Sundries. Coin lndry. Exercise equipt; sauna. Health club privileges. Indoor pool; whirlpool, poolside serv. Game rm. Rec rm. Refrigerators; some in-rm whirlpools; wet bar in suites; microwaves avail. Cr cds: A, C, D, DS, MC, V.

★★ **HOLIDAY INN.** *334 Rte 46 E Service Rd (07470). 973/256-7000; fax 973/890-5406; res 800/465-4329. www.holiday-inn.com.* 139 rms, 2 story. S $105; D $115; under 18 free. Crib free. TV; cable (premium). Pool; poolside serv, lifeguard. Restaurant 6:30 am-2 pm, 5-10 pm. Bar 11-2 am; 5 pm-12:30 am; entertainment. Ck-out noon. Meeting rms. In-rm modem link. Valet serv. Sundries. Health club privileges. Miniature golf. Microwaves avail. Cr cds: A, C, D, DS, MC, V.

★★ **HOLIDAY INN TOTOWA.** *1 US 46W, Totowa (07512). 973/785-9000; fax 973/785-3031; res 800/465-4329. www.holiday-inn.com.* 155 rms, 5 story. S, D $99-$149; each addl $6; under 18 free. Crib free. TV; cable (premium), VCR avail. Pool. Complimentary bkfst. Coffee in rms. Restaurant 6:30 am-11 pm Mon-Fri. Ck-out noon. Meeting rms. Business servs avail. In-rm modem link. Bellhops. Valet serv. Sundries. Exercise equipt. Indoor parking. Refrigerators. Cr cds: A, C, D, DS, MC, V.

★ **WELLESLEY INN.** *1850 NJ 23 and Ratzer Rd (07470). 973/696-8050; fax 973/696-8050; toll-free 800/446-4656.* 149 rms, 2 story. S $109-$118; D $119-$128; each addl $10; under 16 free. Crib free. Pet accepted, some restrictions. TV; cable (premium). Pool. Complimentary continental bkfst. Ck-out noon. Coin lndry. Business servs avail. In-rm modem link. Valet serv. Some refrigerators; microwaves avail. Private patios, balconies. Cr cds: A, C, D, DS, MC, V.

Hotel

★★★ **RADISSON HOTEL & SUITES.** *690 Rte 46 E, Fairfield (07004). 973/227-9200; fax 973/227-4308; res 800/333-3333. www. radisson.com.* 204 rms, 5 story, 61 suites. S $185-$195; D $195-$215; each addl $10; suites $195-$425; under 18 free. Crib $10. TV; cable (premium), VCR avail. Indoor pool. Restaurant 6:30 am-10 pm. Bar 11-1:30 am; entertainment Thurs-Sat. Ck-out noon. Meeting rms. Business center. In-rm modem link. Bellhops. Gift shop. Exercise equipt; sauna. Bathrm phones, in-rm whirlpools; some refrigerators; microwaves avail. Cr cds: A, D, DS, ER, MC, V.

West Orange

(D-2) *See also Newark, Newark International Airport Area*

Pop 44,943 **Elev** 368 ft **Area code** 973 **Zip** 07052

Information West Orange Chamber of Commerce, PO Box 83; 973/731-0360

Web www.westorange.com

What to See and Do

Eagle Rock Reservation. A 644-ft elevation in the Orange Mtns; visitors see a heavily populated area that stretches from the Passaic River Valley east to New York City. Hiking trails, picnicking, bridle paths. Restaurant. (Daily) NW via Main St and Eagle Rock Ave. Phone 973/268-3500.

☒ Edison National Historic Site. Main St and Lakeside Ave. Phone 973/736-5050.

Edison Laboratory. Built by Edison in 1887, it was his laboratory for 44 years. During that time, he was granted more than half of his 1,093 patents (an all-time record). Here he perfected the phonograph, motion picture camera, and electric storage battery. One-hr lab tour (no video cameras, strollers) incl the chemistry lab and library; demonstrations of early phonographs. Visitor center has exhibits; films (daily; closed Jan 1, Thanksgiving, Dec 25). Phone 973/736-5050. ¢

Turtle Back Zoo. This 20-acre park features animals in natural surroundings; sea lion pool; miniature train ride (one mi). Picnicking, concessions. Gift shop (hrs vary). (Daily; closed Thanksgiving, Dec 25; limited schedule Dec-Mar) 560 Northfield Ave, 3 mi W on I-280, exit 10, in South Mountain Reservation. Phone 973/731-5800. ¢¢¢ Adj is

South Mountain Arena. Indoor ice rink. Hockey games, special events. Phone 973/731-3828.

Restaurants

★ ★ ★ **HIGHLAWN PAVILION.** *Eagle Rock Reservation (07052). 973/731-3463. www.highlawn.com/ home.html.* Hrs: noon-3 pm, 5:30-10 pm; Fri to 11:30 pm; Sat 5-11:30 pm; Sun 5-9 pm. Closed Dec 24. Res accepted. Bar to midnight. A la carte entrees: lunch $8-$16.50, dinner $15.95-$28.75. Specializes in veal chop, steak, fresh seafood. Oyster bar. Pianist Thurs-Sat. Valet parking. Outdoor dining. Located in county park on top of mountain; view of NY skyline. Food preparation visible from dining rm. Jacket. Cr cds: A, C, D, DS, MC, V.
D

★ ★ ★ **THE MANOR.** *111 Prospect Ave (07052). 973/731-2360. www.the manorrestaurant.com/home.html.* Hrs: noon-2:30 pm, 6-10 pm; Sat 6 pm-midnight; Sun to 8:30 pm. Closed Mon; Dec 24. Continental menu. Bar to 2 am. Wine cellar. A la carte entrees: lunch $9.50-$15, dinner $23-$30. Lobster buffet Tues-Fri $36.95; Sat $39.95. Buffet: Wed (lunch) $19.95; Sun $31.95. Specialties: rack of lamb, Dover sole, beef Wellington. Own baking. Pianist Tue-Sun; band, vocalist Fri, Sat. Jacket. View of formal gardens. Cr cds: A, D, DS, MC, V.
D

Wildwood and Wildwood Crest

(C-8) *See also Cape May*

Pop 5,463 **Elev** 8 ft **Area code** 609 **Zip** 08260
Information Greater Wildwood Chamber of Commerce, 3306 Pacific Ave, PO Box 823; 609/729-4000
Web www.gwcoc.com

Wildwood's busy boardwalk extends for approximately two miles along the five miles of protected sandy beach it shares with North Wildwood and Wildwood Crest, two neighboring resorts. The area offers swimming, waterskiing, ocean and bay fishing, boating, sailing; bicycling, golf, tennis, and shuffleboard.

What to See and Do

Boat trips. Sightseeing and whale-watching cruises aboard *Big Flamingo.* (July-Nov, daily) Capt Sinn's Dock, 6006 Park Blvd in Wildwood Crest. Phone 609/522-3934.

Motels/Motor Lodges

★ ★ **ADVENTURE MOTOR INN.** *5401 Ocean Ave, Wildwood Crest (08260). 609/729-1200; fax 609/523-1485. www.adventurerinn.com.* 104 rms, 6 story. July-early Sept: S, D $140-$330; each addl $12; under 3 free; higher rates wkends (3-day min); lower rates early-Sept-Oct and mid-Apr-June. Closed rest of yr. Crib $8. TV; cable. Heated pool; wading pool, lifeguard. Restaurant 7 am-8 pm. Ck-out 11 am. Coin lndry. Meeting rms. Business servs avail. Sundries. Gift shop. Game rm. Refrigerators; microwaves avail. On beach. Cr cds: A, D, DS, MC, V.
D

★ **AQUARIUS MOTOR INN.** *4712 Ocean Ave, Wildwood (08260). 609/729-0054; toll-free 800/982-1831. www.aquariusmotorinn.com.* 28 rms, 4 story. S, D $110-$159; under 18 free; wkly, wkend rates; lower rates Apr-June and Sept-Oct. Closed rest of yr.

Crib free. TV; cable (premium). Heated pool; wading pool. Complimentary coffee in lobby. Restaurant opp 7 am-11 pm. Ck-out 10 am. Coin lndry. Business servs avail. Refrigerators, microwaves. Balconies. Picnic tables. Opp beach. Cr cds: A, DS, MC, V.

⛱ 🏊 SC

★★ **ARMADA BY THE SEA.** *6503 Ocean Ave, Wildwood Crest (08260). 609/729-3000; fax 609/729-7472; toll-free 800/399-3001. www.armada motel.com.* 56 rms, 5 story, 40 kits. Mid-July-Aug: up to 4 persons $166-$189; each addl $10; kit. units up to 4 persons $163-$290; some lower rates rest of yr. Closed Oct-mid-Apr. Crib $5. TV; VCR avail (movies). Heated pool; wading pool. Restaurant nearby. Ck-out 11 am. Coin lndry. Meeting rms. Business servs avail. Sundries. Game rm. Refrigerators, microwaves. Balconies. Picnic tables, grill. Sun decks. Cr cds: A, DS, MC, V.

D ⛱ 🏊

★★ **ASTRONAUT MOTEL.** *511 E Stockton Rd, Wildwood (08260). 609/522-6981; fax 609/523-1927. www.beachcomber.com.* 33 kit. units, 3 story. No elvtr. July-early Sept: up to 6 persons $134-$180; lower rates Apr-June, early Sept-mid-Oct. Closed rest of yr. Crib avail. TV. Pool; wading pool. Restaurant nearby. Ck-out 11 am. Coin lndry. Sundries. Shuffleboard. Refrigerators, microwaves. Sun decks. Picnic tables, grills. Cr cds: DS, MC, V.

⛱ 🏊

★★ **ATTACHE.** *5707 Ocean Ave, Wildwood Crest (08260). 609/522-0241; fax 609/523-8379. www.attache-motel.com.* 42 rms, 3 story, 26 kits. Mid-July-late Aug: up to 4 persons $130-$175; each addl $10; kit. units for 4 persons $130-$215; family rates; lower rates mid-Apr-mid-July, late Aug-mid-Oct. Closed rest of yr. Crib avail. TV; cable, VCR avail. Heated pool; wading pool. Restaurant nearby. Ck-out 11 am. Guest lndry. Business servs avail. Refrigerators, microwaves. Some balconies. Picnic tables, grills. Cr cds: A, MC, V.

🛄 ⛱ 🏊

★★ **CAPE COD INN MOTEL.** *6109 Atlantic Ave, Wildwood Crest (08260).* *609/522-1177; fax 609/729-2353. www.capecodinnmotel.com.* 50 units, 3 story, 27 kits. Mid-July-mid-Aug: S, D $110; each addl $10; kits. $120; family rates; higher rates wkends, hols (3-day min); lower rates May-June, mid-Aug-Sept. Closed rest of yr. TV; cable (premium). Pool; wading pool. Restaurant nearby. Ck-out 10 am. Coin lndry. Meeting rm. Business servs avail. Sundries. Game rm. Miniature golf. Refrigerators, microwaves. Picnic tables. Cr cds: A, DS, MC, V.

D ⛱ 🏊 🏊

★★ **CARIBBEAN MOTEL.** *5600 Ocean Ave, Wildwood Crest (08260). 609/522-8292; fax 609/729-3212; toll-free 800/457-7040.* 30 rms, 2 story, 9 kits. July-Labor Day: up to 4 persons $119; kit. units for 4 persons $128; lower rates May-June, after Labor Day-Sept. Closed rest of yr. TV; cable. Heated pool; wading pool. Complimentary coffee in rms. Restaurant opp 7 am-10 pm. Ck-out 11 am. Coin lndry. Game rm. Lawn games. Refrigerators; some microwaves. Sun deck. Picnic tables, grills. Cr cds: MC, V.

⛱ 🏊

★★ **FLEUR DE LIS.** *6105 Ocean Ave, Wildwood Crest (08260). 609/522-0123; fax 609/523-0893. www.fleur delismotel.com.* 44 rms, 3 story, 32 kits. Mid-July-late Aug: S $51-$103; D $55-$123; each addl $10; kits. $140-$184; higher rates wkends (3-day min); lower rates mid-Apr-mid-July and Sept-mid-Oct. Closed rest of yr. Crib $5. TV; cable. Pool; wading pool. Restaurant adj 7 am-9 pm. Ck-out 11 am. Coin lndry. Business servs avail. Game rm. Refrigerators, microwaves. On beach. Cr cds: MC, V.

🛄 ⛱ 🏊 🏊

★★ **IMPERIAL 500 MOTEL.** *6601 Atlantic Ave, Wildwood Crest (08260). 609/522-6063; fax 609/522-7643; toll-free 800/522-1255. www.imperial500. com.* 45 rms, 3 story, 26 kits. July-Labor Day: S, D for 4, $100-$135; each addl $10; kit. units $135; lower rates May-June, after Labor Day-Sept. Closed rest of yr. Crib avail. TV; cable. Heated pool; wading pool. Restaurant nearby. Ck-out 11 am. Coin lndry. Meeting rm. Business servs avail. Sundries. Shuffleboard. Rec rm. Lawn games. Refrigerators, microwaves. Sun deck. Picnic tables, grills. Cr cds: DS, MC, V.

★ **IVANHOE MOTEL.** *430 E 21st Ave, North Wildwood (08260). 609/522-5874; fax 609/523-2323. www.ivanhoemotel.com.* 40 rms, 2 story. July-Aug: S $98; D $165; each addl $10-$15; family, wkly rates; lower rates rest of yr. Crib $8. TV; cable (premium). Heated pools; wading pool. Coffee in rms. Restaurant nearby. Ck-out 10 am. Coin lndry. Meeting rms. Business servs avail. Refrigerators, microwaves. Some balconies. Opp beach. Cr cds: A, C, D, DS, MC, V.

★★ **JOLLY ROGER MOTEL.** *6805 Atlantic Ave, Wildwood Crest (08260). 609/522-6915; fax 609/522-3767; toll-free 800/337-5232. www.jollyroger motel.com.* 74 rms, 3 story. Mid-July-mid-Aug: S, D $102-$121; each addl $7; kits. $112-$158; under 5 free; wkends, hols (3-day min); lower rates mid-May, late Aug-late Sept. Closed rest of yr. Crib $10. TV; cable. Pool; wading pool, lifeguard. Supervised children's activities (July-Aug), ages 4-16. Restaurant nearby. Ck-out 11 am. Coin lndry. Meeting rms. Tennis. Game rm. Refrigerators; some microwaves. Balconies, grills. Picnic tables. Cr cds: MC, V.

★★ **LEVOYAGEUR MOTEL.** *232 E Andrew Ave, Wildwood (08260). 609/522-6407; fax 609/523-1834; toll-free 800/348-0846. www.levoyageur motel.com.* 33 rms, 3 story, 14 kits. July-Aug: S $40-$89; D $89-$118; each addl $10; suites $112; kits. $123; under 5 free; wkly, hol rates; lower rates Apr-June, Sept-Oct. Closed rest of yr. Crib $9. TV; cable. Heated pool; wading pool. Restaurant nearby. Ck-out 10:30 am. Coin lndry. Meeting rm. Game rm. Refrigerators; many microwaves. Balconies. Picnic tables. Cr cds: A, DS, MC, V.

★ **MADRID OCEAN RESORT.** *427 E Miami Ave, Wildwood Crest (08260). 609/729-1600; fax 609/729-8483. www.beachcomber.com.* 54 rms, 5 story, 24 kits. July-Labor Day: S, D $140-$185; each addl $10; suites

$160; kit. units up to 4 persons $175; higher rates wkends; lower rates mid-May-June, after Labor Day-Sept. Closed rest of yr. Crib avail. TV. Heated pool; wading pool. Restaurant 7:30 am-9 pm. Ck-out 11 am. Coin lndry. Business servs avail. Sundries. Rec rm. Sun deck. Refrigerators; microwaves avail. All oceanfront rms. Cr cds: A, MC, V.

★ **NEW COMPASS MOTEL.** *6501 Atlantic Ave, Wildwood Crest (08260). 609/522-6948; fax 609/729-9363. www.compassmotel.com.* 50 rms, 3 story, 25 kits. July-Aug: S, D $98-$122; each addl $10; family rates; wkly, wkend rates; higher rates hols (3-day min); lower rates May-June, Sept-Oct. Closed rest of yr. Crib $10. TV; cable. Heated pool; wading pool. Complimentary coffee in rms. Restaurant nearby. Ck-out 11 am. Meeting rms. Business servs avail. Refrigerators; microwaves. Cr cds: DS, MC, V.

★★ **OCEAN HOLIDAY MOTOR INN.** *6501 Ocean Ave, Wildwood Crest (08260). 609/729-2900; fax 609/523-1024; toll-free 800/321-6232. www. oceanholiday.com.* 56 rms, 5 story, 51 kits. July-Aug: S, D $70-$170; each addl $10; kit. units (up to 4 persons) $100-$255; hol wkends (3-day min); lower rates Apr-June, Sept-Oct. Closed rest of yr. Crib $5. TV; cable (premium), VCR avail. Pool; wading pool. Restaurant nearby. Ck-out 11 am. Coin lndry. Meeting rms. Business servs avail. Sundries. Game rm. Refrigerators, microwaves. Some private patios, balconies. Picnic tables, grills. Cr cds: A, MC, V.

★ **OCEANVIEW.** *7201 Ocean Ave, Wildwood Crest (08260). 609/522-6656; fax 609/522-6793; toll-free 800/647-6656. www.oceanviewmotel. net.* 110 rms, 4 story, 36 suites, 61 kit. units. July-Aug: S $105-$145; D $150; each addl $10; suites $130-$150; kit. units $130-$160; family rates; package plans; lower rates May-June, Sept-Oct. Closed rest of yr. Crib $9. TV; cable (premium). Restaurant opp 7 am-9 pm. Ck-out 11 am. Business servs avail. Coin lndry. Heated pool; wading pool, lifeguard. Miniature golf. Playground. Supervised children's activities (late June-early Sept). Game rm. Refrigerators. Picnic tables, grills. On beach. Cr cds: DS, MC, V.

★ **PANORAMIC MOTEL AND APTS.** 2101 Surf Ave, N Wildwood (08260). 609/522-1181; fax 609/523-2323. www.panoramicmotel.com. 25 rms, 2 story. July-Sept: S $65-$98; D $98-$150; each addl $10-$15; family, wkly rates; lower rates rest of yr. Crib $8. TV; cable (premium). Heated pool; wading pool. Complimentary coffee in rms. Restaurant nearby. Ck-out 10 am. Coin lndry. Meeting rms. Business servs avail. Refrigerators, microwaves. Some balconies. On beach. Cr cds: A, C, D, DS, MC, V.

Hotels

★★★ **PAN AMERICAN HOTEL.** 5901 Ocean Ave, Wildwood Crest (08260). 609/522-6936; fax 609/522-6937. www.panamericanhotel.com. 78 rms, 4 story, 39 kits. Early July-early Sept $165-$175; each addl $12; suites $195-$200; kit. units $175-$185; lower rates mid-May-early June, early Sept-mid-Oct. Closed rest of yr. Crib free. TV; VCR avail. Heated pool; wading pool, lifeguard. Sauna. Free supervised children's activities (mid-June-Labor Day); ages 4-10. Restaurant 7:30 am-8 pm. Ck-out 11 am. Meeting rm. Coin lndry. Business servs avail. Sundries. Rec rm. Refrigerators; some microwaves. Sun deck. Balconies. Cr cds: MC, V.

★★★ **PORT ROYAL HOTEL.** 6801 Ocean Ave, Wildwood Crest (08260). 609/729-2000; fax 609/729-2051; res 609/729-2000. www.portroyalhotel.com. 100 rms, 6 story, 50 kits. Late June-Labor Day: S $81-$170; D $160-$176; each addl $12; kit. units for 4 persons $190-$205; lower rates May-late June, after Labor Day-mid-Oct. Closed rest of yr. Crib avail. TV; VCR avail. Heated pool; wading pool, sauna. Free supervised children's activities (mid-June-Labor Day); ages 3-10. Restaurant 7:30 am-8 pm in season. Ck-out 11 am. Coin lndry. Meeting rm (off-season). Business servs avail. Sundries. Rec rm, game

rm in season. Some microwaves. Balconies. Cr cds: MC, V.

Resorts

★★ **BRISTOL PLAZA RESORT.** 6407 Ocean Ave, Wildwood Crest (08260). 609/729-1234; fax 609/729-9363; toll-free 800/433-9731. www.bristolplazamotel.com. 55 rms, 5 story, 41 kits. Mid-July-late Aug: S, D (up to 4) $158-$205; family rates; wkly, wkend, hol rates; lower rates May-mid-July and late Aug-Oct. Closed rest of yr. Crib $10. TV; cable. Heated pool; wading pool. Sauna. Complimentary coffee in rms. Restaurant nearby. Ck-out 11 am. Coin lndry. Business servs avail. Refrigerators; many microwaves. Balconies. Picnic tables. Opp ocean. Cr cds: DS, MC, V.

★★ **CRUSADER OCEAN FRONT RESORT.** 6101 Ocean Ave, Wildwood Crest (08260). 609/522-6991; fax 609/522-2280; toll-free 800/462-3260. www.crusaderresort.com. 61 units, 3 story, 54 suites, 37 kits. July-Aug: S, D $160-$168; each addl $12; kit. units $166-$245; lower rates Apr-June and Sept-Oct. Closed Nov-Mar. Crib avail. TV; cable (premium), VCR avail. Heated pool; wading pool, lifeguard. Sauna. Restaurant 7 am-8 pm. Ck-out 11 am. Coin lndry. Meeting rms. Business servs avail. Sundries. Gift shop. Game rm. Refrigerators, microwaves. Some balconies. Picnic tables. Ocean beach; boardwalk. Cr cds: A, MC, V.

★★★ **EL CORONADO MOTOR INN.** 8501 Atlantic Ave, Wildwood Crest (08260). 609/729-1000; fax 609/729-6557; toll-free 800/227-5302. www.elcoronado.com. 113 rms, 6 story, 63 kit. suites. July-Aug: S, D $130-$174; each addl $10; kit. suites $180-$272; under 12 free; wkly, wkend (3-night min), hol rates; lower rates May-June and Sept-Oct. Closed rest of yr. Crib avail. TV; cable (premium). Pool; wading pool, whirlpool, poolside serv, lifeguard. Sauna. Supervised children's activities (July-Aug). Restaurant 7 am-4 pm. Ck-out 11 am. Coin lndry. Meeting rms. Business servs avail. In-rm modem link. Gift shop. Game rm. Refrigerators, microwaves. Balconies. Cr cds: DS, MC, V.

★★ **NASSAU INN.** *6201 Ocean Ave, Wildwood Crest (08260). 609/729-9077; fax 609/729-2208; toll-free 800/336-9077. www.nassauinnmotel. com.* 56 rms, 5 story. July-early Sept: S, D $115-$125; each addl $10; kits. $170-$180; family rates; package plans; lower rates early Sept-mid-Oct and May-June. Closed rest of yr. Crib $9. TV; cable. Heated pool; wading pool. Restaurant adj 7 am-9 pm. Ck-out 11 am. Coin lndry. Business servs avail. Game rm. Refrigerators; many microwaves. On beach. Cr cds: DS, MC, V.

★ **ROYAL HAWAIIAN BEACH-FRONT RESORT.** *500 E Orchid Rd, Wildwood Crest (08260). 609/522-3414; fax 609/522-1316. www.royal hawaiianresort.com.* 88 rms, 5 story, 56 kits. Mid-July-Aug: S, D $103; suites, kit. units for 4 $129-$229; each addl $10; lower rates mid-May-mid-July, Sept-Oct. Closed rest of yr. Crib avail. TV; cable (premium). Pool; wading pool, lifeguard. Playground. Ck-out 11 am. Coin lndry. Business servs avail. Valet serv. Rec rm. Exercise equipt; sauna. Refrigerators, microwaves. Balconies. Sun deck. Grills. On ocean. Cr cds: A, DS, MC, V.

B&B/Small Inn

★★★ **CANDLELIGHT INN.** *2310 Central Ave, North Wildwood (08260). 609/522-6200; fax 609/522-6125; toll-free 800/992-2632. www.candlelight-inn.com.* 10 rms, 8 with A/C, 4 story. No rm phones. May-Oct: S, D $135-$170; lower rates rest of yr. Adults only. Complimentary full bkfst; afternoon refreshments. Ck-out 11 am, ck-in 1 pm. Business servs avail. Whirlpool, sun deck. Lawn games. Health club privileges. Some in-rm whirlpools, microwaves, fireplaces. Grills. Queen Anne/Victorian-style house (ca 1905); restored. Antique furnishings. Large porch with swing and hammocks. Totally nonsmoking. Cr cds: A, DS, MC, V.

Restaurants

★★ **CAPTAIN'S TABLE.** *8701 Atlantic Ave, Wildwood Crest (08260).* 609/522-2939. Hrs: 8 am-noon, 4:30-10 pm. Closed mid-Oct-Mother's Day. Buffet: bkfst $3.95-$8.50. Dinner $9.95-$23.95. Child's menu. Specializes in Maine lobster, steak. Nautical decor; ocean view. Family-owned. Cr cds: A, D, DS, MC, V.

★★ **GARFIELD'S GIARDINO RISTORANTE.** *3800 Pacific Ave, Wildwood (08260).* 609/729-0120. *www.garfieldsnj.com.* Hrs: 11:30-3 am; July, Aug 4-11 pm; winter hrs vary. Res accepted. Italian, seafood menu. Bar. Complete meals: dinner $6.95-$19.95. Child's menu. Specializes in fresh seafood, veal, poultry. Entertainment July, Aug. Two dining areas in garden setting. Cr cds: A, D, DS, MC, V.

★ **MENZ RESTAURANT AND BAR.** *985 NJ 47S, Rio Grande (08242).* 609/886-5691. Hrs: 4-9 pm; Sun from 2 pm. Closed winter months. Res accepted. A la carte entrees: dinner $14.95-$31.95. Child's menu. Specializes in seafood. Antique decor; music boxes, clocks, stained glass. Totally nonsmoking. Cr cds: MC, V.

Woodbridge

Settled 1664 **Pop** 97,203 **Elev** 21 ft
Area code 732 **Zip** 07095
Information Chamber of Commerce Visitor Center, 52 Main St; 732/636-4040

Here, where the first cloverleaf interchange in the United States was constructed in 1929, cross two of the country's busiest roads—the Garden State Parkway and the New Jersey Turnpike. Also in Woodbridge are seaway and river port areas visited by thousands of vessels annually.

What to See and Do

Barron Arts Center. Built in 1877 in Romanesque Revival style. Originally

the first free public library in Middlesex County, now an arts and cultural
center with art exhibits; workshops;
lectures; poetry sessions; concerts;
special events. Gallery (Sun-Fri;
closed hols). 582 Rahway Ave. Phone
732/634-0413. **FREE**

Hotels

★ ★ ★ **HILTON WOODBRIDGE.** *120
Wood Ave S, Iselin (08830). 732/494-
6200; fax 732/603-7777; res 800/774-
1500. www.hilton.com.* 200 rms, 7-11
story. S $125-$177; D $135-$193;
each addl $15; under 18 free; wkend
rates. Crib free. TV; cable (premium),
VCR. Indoor pool; whirlpool, lifeguard. Restaurant 6 am-midnight;
dining rms 11 am-10 pm. Bar noon-1
am; entertainment. Meeting rms.
Business center. In-rm modem link.
Gift shop. Exercise rm. Bathrm
phones. Cr cds: A, C, D, DS, MC, V.
🄳 ⇌ 🕇 ⇲ 🖍 **SC** 🕴

★ ★ ★ **SHERATON AT WOOD-
BRIDGE PLACE.** *515 Rte 1 S, Iselin
(08830). 732/634-3600; fax 732/634-
0258; res 800/325-3535. www.
sheraton.com.* 253 rms, 7 story. S, D
$190-$209; each addl $10; suites
$265; under 12 free; wkend rates.
Crib free. TV; cable (premium). 2
pools, 1 indoor; whirlpool, poolside
serv. Restaurants 6:30-11 pm. Bar 11-
1 am. Ck-out noon. Convention
facilities. Business center. In-rm
modem link. Gift shop. RR station
transportation. Exercise equipt.
Health club privileges. Game rm.
Microwaves avail. 40-ft atrium lobby,
marble fountain. Luxury level. Cr
cds: A, C, D, DS, MC, V.
🄳 ⇌ 🕇 ⇲ 🖍 🕴

ATTRACTION LIST

Attraction names are listed in alphabetical order followed by a symbol identifying their classification and then city. The symbols for classification are: [S] for Special Events and [W] for What to See and Do

1890 House Museum [W] *Cortland, NY*

Absecon Lighthouse [W] *Atlantic City, NJ*

Acorn Hall [W] *Morristown, NJ*

Action Park [W] *Vernon, NJ*

Activities [W] *Ausable Chasm, NY*

Adirondack Artisans Festival [S] *North Creek, NY*

Adirondack Canoe Classic [S] *Saranac Lake, NY*

Adirondack Lakes Center for the Arts [W] *Blue Mountain Lake, NY*

Adirondack Museum [W] *Blue Mountain Lake, NY*

Adirondack Park [W] *Blue Mountain Lake, NY*

Adirondack Park [W] *North Creek, NY*

Adirondack Park [W] *Old Forge, NY*

Adirondack Park [W] *Plattsburgh, NY*

Adirondack Park [W] *Potsdam, NY*

Adirondack Park [W] *Wilmington, NY*

Adventure on a Shoestring [W] *Manhattan, NY*

African-American Museum [W] *Hempstead (L.I.), NY*

Akwesasne Museum [W] *Massena, NY*

Albany Institute of History and Art [W] *Albany, NY*

Albright-Knox Art Gallery [W] *Buffalo, NY*

Alexander Grant House [W] *Salem, NJ*

Alice T. Miner Colonial Collection [W] *Plattsburgh, NY*

Allamuchy Mountain State Park, Stephens Section [W] *Hackettstown, NJ*

Allan H. Treman State Marine Park [W] *Ithaca, NY*

Allegany State Park [W] *Jamestown, NY*

Allegany State Park [W] *Olean, NY*

Allen House [W] *Red Bank, NJ*

Allentown [W] *Buffalo, NY*

Alling Coverlet Museum [W] *Palmyra, NY*

Almond Dam Recreation Area [W] *Hornell, NY*

Americade [S] *Lake George Village, NY*

American Bible Society Gallery/Library [W] *Manhattan, NY*

American Craft Museum [W] *Manhattan, NY*

American Labor Museum-Botto House National Landmark [W] *Paterson, NJ*

American Maple Museum [W] *Watertown, NY*

American Museum of Fire Fighting [W] *Hudson, NY*

American Museum of Natural History [W] *Manhattan, NY*

American Museum of the Moving Image [W] *Queens (La Guardia & JFK International Airport Areas), NY*

American Numismatic Society [W] *Manhattan, NY*

Amusement piers [W] *Atlantic City, NJ*

Antique Boat Museum, The [W] *Clayton (Thousand Islands), NY*

Antique Boat Show [S] *Clayton (Thousand Islands), NY*

Antique Car Parade [S] *Garden City (L.I.), NY*

Antiques on the Hudson [W] *Nyack, NY*

Apple Festival [S] *New Paltz, NY*

Apple Harvest Festival [S] *Ithaca, NY*

Aquarium of Niagara Falls, NY [W] *Niagara Falls, NY*

Aqueduct [W] *Manhattan, NY*

Aqueduct [W] *Queens (La Guardia & JFK International Airport Areas), NY*

Arcade and Attica Railroad [W] *Arcade, NY*

Architecture in Buffalo [W] *Buffalo, NY*

Arnot Art Museum [W] *Elmira, NY*

Artpark [W] *Niagara Falls, NY*

Arts & Crafts Festival [S] *Warrensburg, NY*

Asia Society Galleries, The [W] *Manhattan, NY*

Astroland Amusement Park [W] *Brooklyn, NY*

Astro Minerals Gallery of Gems [W] *Manhattan, NY*

Atlantic City Boardwalk Hall [W] *Atlantic City, NJ*

Atlantic City Marathon [S] *Atlantic City, NJ*

Atsion Recreation Area [W] *Batsto, NJ*

Auditorium [W] *Trenton, NJ*

Autumn Harvest Festival [S] *Cooperstown, NY*

Bainbridge House [W] *Princeton, NJ*

Balloon Festival [S] *Syracuse, NY*

Balloon Rally [S] *Binghamton, NY*

Barclay Farmstead [W] *Cherry Hill, NJ*

Bardavon Opera House [W] *Poughkeepsie, NY*

Barnegat Lighthouse State Park [W] *Long Beach Island, NJ*

Barron Arts Center [W] *Woodbridge, NJ*

Bartow-Pell Mansion Museum and Gardens [W] *Bronx, NY*

Baseball [S] *Elmira, NY*

Batavia Downs Race Track [W] *Batavia, NY*

Batsto State Historic Site [W] *Batsto, NJ*

Battlefield [W] *Saratoga National Historical Park, NY*

Battle Island State Park [W] *Fulton, NY*

Battle Monument [W] *West Point (US Military Academy), NY*

Bayard Cutting Arboretum [W] *Bay Shore (L.I.), NY*

B.C. Open PGA Golf Tournament [S] *Binghamton, NY*

Beaver Lake Nature Center [W] *Syracuse, NY*

Belmont Park [W] *Manhattan, NY*

Belmont Park [W] *Queens (La Guardia & JFK International Airport Areas), NY*

Benjamin Patterson Inn Museum Complex [W] *Corning, NY*

Bennington Battlefield State Historic Site [W] *Greenwich, NY*

Bethpage State Park [W] *Bethpage (L.I.), NY*

Bill of Rights Museum [W] *Yonkers, NY*

Binghamton University, State University of New York [W] *Binghamton, NY*

Black River & Western Railroad [W] *Flemington, NJ*

Bloomingdale's [W] *Manhattan, NY*

Blue Mountain [W] *Blue Mountain Lake, NY*

Boardwalk Art Show [S] *Ocean City, NJ*

Boat cruise. *Chautauqua Belle* [W] *Chautauqua, NY*

Boat excursion. M/V *Juniper* [W] *Plattsburgh, NY*

Boating [W] *Dunkirk, NY*

Boating [W] *Ticonderoga (Lake George Area), NY*

Boating [W] *Tupper Lake, NY*

Boat ride [W] *Niagara Falls, NY*

Boat Trips [W] *Alexandria Bay (Thousand Islands), NY*

Boat trips [W] *Buffalo, NY*

Boat trips [W] *Skaneateles, NY*

Boat trips [W] *Wildwood and Wildwood Crest, NJ*

Boldt Castle [W] *Alexandria Bay (Thousand Islands), NY*

Book of Mormon Historic Publication Site [W] *Palmyra, NY*

Bow Bridge [W] *Lake Luzerne, NY*

Bowling Green [W] *Manhattan, NY*

Bowman Lake State Park [W] *Norwich, NY*

Bowne House [W] *Queens (La Guardia & JFK International Airport Areas), NY*

Boxwood Hall State Historic Site [W] *Elizabeth, NJ*

Bridge Memorial [W] *Newark, NJ*

Bronck Museum [W] *Coxsackie, NY*

Bronx Museum of the Arts [W] *Bronx, NY*

Bronx Zoo [W] *Bronx, NY*

Brookhaven National Laboratory [W] *Riverhead (L.I.), NY*

Brooklyn Academy of Music [W] *Brooklyn, NY*

Brooklyn Botanic Garden [W] *Brooklyn, NY*

Brooklyn Bridge [W] *Manhattan, NY*

Brooklyn Children's Museum [W] *Brooklyn, NY*

Brooklyn Heights [W] *Brooklyn, NY*

Brooklyn Museum of Art [W] *Brooklyn, NY*

Brooklyn's History Museum [W] *Brooklyn, NY*

Broome County Performing Arts Theater, the Forum [S] *Binghamton, NY*

Broome County Veterans Memorial Arena & Convention Center [S] *Binghamton, NY*

Brotherhood Winery [W] *Goshen, NY*

Buccleuch Mansion [W] *New Brunswick, NJ*

Buffalo & Erie County Botanical Gardens [W] *Buffalo, NY*

Buffalo & Erie County Historical Society [W] *Buffalo, NY*

Buffalo & Erie County Naval & Military Park [W] *Buffalo, NY*

Buffalo Bills (NFL) [W] *Buffalo, NY*

Buffalo Museum of Science [W] *Buffalo, NY*

Buffalo Philharmonic Orchestra [S] *Buffalo, NY*

Buffalo Raceway [W] *Buffalo, NY*

Buffalo Sabres (NHL) [W] *Buffalo, NY*

Buffalo State College [W] *Buffalo, NY*

Buffalo Zoological Gardens [W] *Buffalo, NY*

Burlington County Historical Society [W] *Burlington, NJ*

Burnham Point State Park [W] *Clayton (Thousand Islands), NY*

Buttermilk Falls [W] *Ithaca, NY*

Cadet Chapel [W] *West Point (US Military Academy), NY*

Camden County Historical Society-Pomona Hall [W] *Camden, NJ*

Campgaw Mountain Ski Area [W] *Ramsey, NJ*

Camping. Fish Creek Pond State Public Campground [W] *Tupper Lake, NY*

Canal Bridge [W] *Lockport, NY*

Canandaigua Lady [W] *Canandaigua, NY*

Canastota Canal Town Museum [W] *Canastota, NY*

Candlelight Tours [S] *Tarrytown, NY*

Canoeing [W] *Old Forge, NY*

Cape May County Historical Museum [W] *Cape May Court House, NJ*

Cape May County Park [W] *Cape May Court House, NJ*

Cape May INNteriors Tour & Tea [W] *Cape May, NJ*

Cape May-Lewes (DE) Ferry [W] *Cape May, NJ*

Captain Bill's Seneca Lake Cruises [W] *Watkins Glen, NY*

Caramoor Center for Music and the Arts [W] *Mt Kisco, NY*

Carnegie Hall [W] *Manhattan, NY*

Castellani Art Museum [W] *Niagara Falls, NY*

Castle Clinton National Monument [W] *Manhattan, NY*

Cathedral Church of St. John the Divine [W] *Manhattan, NY*

Catskill Fly Fishing Center & Museum [W] *Roscoe, NY*

Catskill Game Farm [W] *Catskill, NY*

Catskill Park [W] *Shandaken, NY*

Cave of the Winds Trip [W] *Niagara Falls, NY*

Cayuga Lake State Park [W] *Seneca Falls, NY*

Cayuga Museum/Case Research Lab Museum [W] *Auburn, NY*

Cayuga Museum Iroquois Center [W] *Auburn, NY*

Cedar Point State Park [W] *Clayton (Thousand Islands), NY*

CEK Mees Observatory [W] *Rochester, NY*

Central New York Maple Festival [S] *Cortland, NY*

Central Park [W] *Manhattan, NY*

Central Park Concerts [S] *Manhattan, NY*

Champlain Monument [W] *Plattsburgh, NY*

Chapman Historical Museum, The [W] *Glens Falls, NY*

Chautauqua Amphitheater [W] *Chautauqua, NY*

Chautauqua County Fair [S] *Dunkirk, NY*

Chautauqua Institution, The [W] *Chautauqua, NY*

Cheesequake State Park [W] *Matawan, NJ*

Chemung County Fair [S] *Elmira, NY*

Chemung Valley History Museum [W] *Elmira, NY*

Chenango County Fair [S] *Norwich, NY*

Chenango Valley State Park [W] *Binghamton, NY*

Children's Museum [W] *Utica, NY*

Children's Museum of Manhattan [W] *Manhattan, NY*

Chinatown [W] *Manhattan, NY*

Chinese New Year [S] *Manhattan, NY*

Chittenango Falls State Park [W] *Cazenovia, NY*

Christmas season [S] *Manhattan, NY*

Christmas Star Show [S] *Manhattan, NY*

Chrysler Building [W] *Manhattan, NY*

Church of the Ascension [W] *Manhattan, NY*

Church on the Green, The [W] *Hackensack, NJ*

Circle Line Sightseeing Yachts [W] *Manhattan, NY*

City Center [W] *Manhattan, NY*

City College of New York [W] *Manhattan, NY*

City Hall/Observation Tower [W] *Buffalo, NY*

City Hall Park [W] *Manhattan, NY*

City Island [W] *Bronx, NY*

City Park [W] *Bridgeton, NJ*

Clara Barton Schoolhouse [W] *Bordentown, NJ*

Clark Botanic Garden [W] *Westbury (L.I.), NY*

Clermont State Historic Site [W] *Hudson, NY*

Cloisters, The [W] *Manhattan, NY*

Clothesline Festival [S] *Rochester, NY*

Coe Hall [W] *Oyster Bay (L.I.), NY*

Cold Spring Harbor Whaling Museum [W] *Huntington (L.I.), NY*

Coles Creek State Park [W] *Massena, NY*

Colgate University [W] *Hamilton, NY*

College Art Gallery [W] *Trenton, NJ*

College of New Jersey [W] *Trenton, NJ*

Colonel William Bond House [W] *Lockport, NY*

Columbia University [W] *Manhattan, NY*

Columbus Day Parade [S] *Manhattan, NY*

Combination Tours [W] *Cape May, NJ*

Comedies, dramas, and musicals [S] *Rochester, NY*

Concerts [S] *Bridgeton, NJ*

Concerts [S] *Matawan, NJ*

Concerts [S] *Ocean City, NJ*

Concerts at the Great Auditorium [S] *Asbury Park, NJ*

Coney Island [W] *Brooklyn, NY*

Conference House [W] *Staten Island, NY*

Constable Hall [W] *Boonville, NY*

Convention Days Celebration [S] *Seneca Falls, NY*

Cooper Environmental Center [W] *Toms River, NJ*

Cooper-Hewitt National Design Museum [W] *Manhattan, NY*

Cooperstown Concert Series [S] *Cooperstown, NY*

Cooper Union [W] *Manhattan, NY*

Cora Hartshorn Arboretum and Bird Sanctuary [W] *Millburn, NJ*

Cornell University [W] *Ithaca, NY*

Corn Hill Arts Festival [S] *Rochester, NY*

Corning Museum of Glass, The [W] *Corning, NY*

Cortland Repertory Theatre [S] *Cortland, NY*

Country Music Park [W] *Cortland, NY*

County Courthouse [W] *Flemington, NJ*

Covenhoven House [W] *Freehold, NJ*

Cowtown Rodeo [S] *Salem, NJ*

Craft Days [S] *Oneida, NY*

Crailo State Historic Site [W] *Albany, NY*

Cross-country skiing [W] *Glens Falls, NY*

Crossroads Theatre [W] *New Brunswick, NJ*

Crown Point Reservation State Campground [W] *Crown Point, NY*

Crown Point State Historic Site [W] *Crown Point, NY*

Cumming Nature Center of the Rochester Museum & Science Center [W] *Naples, NY*

Custom House [W] *Sag Harbor (L.I.), NY*

Dairy, The [W] *Manhattan, NY*

David Conklin Farmhouse [W] *Huntington (L.I.), NY*

Davidson Laboratory [W] *Hoboken, NJ*

"Day of a Playwright." [W] *Binghamton, NY*

Delaware & Hudson Canal Museum [W] *Kingston, NY*

Delta Lake State Park [W] *Rome, NY*

Devil's Hole State Park [W] *Niagara Falls, NY*

DeWitt Historical Society & Museum [W] *Ithaca, NY*

Dey Mansion [W] *Wayne, NJ*

Discovery Center of the Southern Tier [W] *Binghamton, NY*

Dodge-Pratt-Northam Art and Community Center [W] *Boonville, NY*

Drake House Museum [W] *Plainfield, NJ*

Drew University [W] *Madison, NJ*

Duck, Decoy, and Wildlife Art Show [S] *Clayton (Thousand Islands), NY*

Duke Gardens [W] *Somerville, NJ*

Dunkirk Lighthouse [W] *Dunkirk, NY*

Durham Center Museum [W] *Cairo, NY*

Dutch Apple Cruises Inc [W] *Albany, NY*

Dutchess County Fair [S] *Rhinebeck, NY*

Dyckman House Park and Museum [W] *Manhattan, NY*

Eagle Point [W] *Schroon Lake, NY*

Eagle Rock Reservation [W] *Montclair, NJ*

Eagle Rock Reservation [W] *West Orange, NJ*

Eastman School of Music of the University of Rochester [W] *Rochester, NY*

Eaton's Neck Lighthouse [W] *Northport (L.I.), NY*

Edgar Allan Poe Cottage [W] *Bronx, NY*

Edison Laboratory [W] *West Orange, NJ*

Edison Memorial Tower and Menlo Park Museum [W] *Edison, NJ*

Edison National Historic Site [W] *West Orange, NJ*

Edwin B. Forsythe National Wildlife Refuge, Brigantine Division [W] *Atlantic City, NJ*

Eisenhower Lock [W] *Massena, NY*

Elbert Hubbard Museum, The [W] *East Aurora, NY*

Eleanor Roosevelt National Historic Site at Val-Kill [W] *Hyde Park, NY*

Elizabeth Cady Stanton House [W] *Seneca Falls, NY*

Ellis Island Immigration Museum [W] *Manhattan, NY*

Elmira College [W] *Elmira, NY*

El Museo del Barrio [W] *Manhattan, NY*

Emerson Park [W] *Auburn, NY*

Emlen Physick Estate [W] *Cape May, NJ*

Empire State Building [W] *Manhattan, NY*

Empire State Plaza [W] *Albany, NY*

Enchanted Forest/Water Safari [W] *Old Forge, NY*

Erie Canal [W] *Amsterdam, NY*

Erie Canal Museum [W] *Syracuse, NY*

Erie Canal Village [W] *Rome, NY*

Erie County Fair [S] *Buffalo, NY*

Erwin Park [W] *Boonville, NY*

Evangola State Park [W] *Dunkirk, NY*

Everson Museum of Art [W] *Syracuse, NY*

Fair Haven Beach State Park [W] *Oswego, NY*

Fairleigh Dickinson University-Florham-Madison Campus [W] *Madison, NJ*

Fairleigh Dickinson University-Rutherford Campus [W] *Rutherford, NJ*

Fall Arts Fest [S] *Boonville, NY*

Family Festival [S] *Lake George Village, NY*

Fantasy Island [W] *Niagara Falls, NY*

Fantasy Island Amusement Park [W] *Long Beach Island, NJ*

Farmers' Museum and Village Crossroads, The [W] *Cooperstown, NY*

Federal Hall National Memorial [W] *Manhattan, NY*

Federal Reserve Bank of New York [W] *Manhattan, NY*

Fenimore Art Museum [W] *Cooperstown, NY*

Fenton Historical Center [W] *Jamestown, NY*

Fern Park [W] *Old Forge, NY*

Ferry House State Historic Site [W] *Trenton, NJ*

Ferry to Bridgeport, CT [W] *Port Jefferson (L.I.), NY*

Festival of Nations [S] *Schenectady, NY*

Fillmore Glen State Park [W] *Cortland, NY*

Finger Lakes Antique Show [S] *Ithaca, NY*

Finger Lakes Race Track [W] *Canandaigua, NY*

First Night [S] *Albany, NY*

First Presbyterian Church and Graveyard [W] *Elizabeth, NJ*

Fishing [W] *Atlantic City, NJ*

Fishing [W] *Saranac Lake, NY*

Flatwater Weekend [S] *Tupper Lake, NY*

Fleming Castle [W] *Flemington, NJ*

Flemington Agricultural Fair [S] *Flemington, NJ*

Flower Show [S] *Ocean City, NJ*

Flushing Meadow Corona Park [W] *Queens (La Guardia & JFK International Airport Areas), NY*

Folklife Festival [S] *Massena, NY*

Forbes Magazine Galleries [W] *Manhattan, NY*

Fordham University [W] *Bronx, NY*

Fordham University [W] *Manhattan, NY*

Ford Mansion [W] *Morristown National Historical Park, NJ*

Forest Industries Exhibit Hall [W] *Old Forge, NY*

Fort Delaware Museum of Colonial History [W] *Barryville, NY*

Fort Hill Cemetery [W] *Auburn, NY*

Fort Klock [W] *Canajoharie, NY*

Fort Lee Historic Park [W] *Fort Lee, NJ*

Fort Lennox [W] *Rouses Point, NY*

Fort Mott State Park [W] *Salem, NJ*

Fort Niagara State Park [W] *Niagara Falls, NY*

Fort Nonsense [W] *Morristown National Historical Park, NJ*

Fort Ontario State Historic Site [W] *Oswego, NY*

Fort Plain Museum [W] *Canajoharie, NY*

Fort Rickey Children's Discovery Zoo [W] *Rome, NY*

Fort Stanwix National Monument [W] *Rome, NY*

Fort Ticonderoga [W] *Ticonderoga (Lake George Area), NY*

Fort Ticonderoga Ferry [W] *Ticonderoga (Lake George Area), NY*

Fort Wellington National Historic Site [W] *Ogdensburg (Thousand Islands), NY*

Fort William Henry Museum [W] *Lake George Village, NY*

Fosterfields Living Historical Farm [W] *Morristown, NJ*

Foundry School Museum [W] *Garrison, NY*

Four Mile Creek State Park Campground [W] *Niagara Falls, NY*

Franklin County Fair [S] *Malone, NY*

Franklin County Historical & Museum Society [W] *Malone, NY*

Franklin D. Roosevelt Presidential Library and Museum [W] *Hyde Park, NY*

Frank Lloyd Wright houses [W] *Buffalo, NY*

Fraunces Tavern Museum [W] *Manhattan, NY*

Frederic Remington Art Museum [W] *Ogdensburg (Thousand Islands), NY*

Frelinghuysen Arboretum [W] *Morristown, NJ*

Frick Collection, The [W] *Manhattan, NY*

Friedsam Memorial Library [W] *Olean, NY*

Friends Meeting House [W] *Burlington, NJ*

Fullager Farms Family Farm & Petting Zoo [W] *Penn Yan, NY*

F.X. Matt Brewing Company [W] *Utica, NY*

Garden Pier [W] *Atlantic City, NJ*

Garment District, The [W] *Manhattan, NY*

Garnet Hill Lodge , Cross-Country Ski Center, and Mountain Bike Center [W] *North Creek, NY*

Garret Mountain Reservation [W] *Paterson, NJ*

Garvies Point Museum and Preserve [W] *Glen Cove (L.I.), NY*

Gateway National Recreation Area [W] *Brooklyn, NY*

General Clinton Canoe Regatta [S] *Bainbridge, NY*

General Clinton Canoe Regatta [S] *Norwich, NY*

General Grant National Memorial [W] *Manhattan, NY*

General Philip Schuyler House [W] *Saratoga National Historical Park, NY*

Genesee Country Village and Museum [W] *Avon, NY*

Genesee Country Village & Museum [W] *Rochester, NY*

Genesee County Agricultural Fair [S] *Batavia, NY*

Geneva Historical Society Museum [W] *Geneva, NY*

Geology Museum [W] *New Brunswick, NJ*

George Eastman House [W] *Rochester, NY*

George Gustav Heye Center of the National Museum of the American Indian, The [W] *Manhattan, NY*

George J. Woodruff Museum of Indian Artifacts [W] *Bridgeton, NJ*

George Street Playhouse [W] *New Brunswick, NJ*

Gibbon House [W] *Bridgeton, NJ*

Gilbert Lake State Park [W] *Oneonta, NY*

Gillander Glass Factory Tours and Store [W] *Port Jervis, NY*

Glenn H. Curtiss Museum [W] *Hammondsport, NY*

Glenora Wine Cellar [W] *Watkins Glen, NY*

Glimmerglass Opera [S] *Cooperstown, NY*

Glimmerglass State Park [W] *Cooperstown, NY*

Goat Island [W] *Niagara Falls, NY*

Golden Harvest Festival [S] *Syracuse, NY*

Golf House—USGA Museum and Library [W] *Somerville, NJ*

Gore Mountain Mineral Shop [W] *North Creek, NY*

Goshen Historic Track [W] *Goshen, NY*

Grand Central Station [W] *Manhattan, NY*

Granger Homestead [W] *Canandaigua, NY*

Grass Point State Park [W] *Clayton (Thousand Islands), NY*

Grassroots Festival [S] *Ithaca, NY*

Grave of Samuel Wilson [W] *Troy, NY*

Gray Line [W] *Manhattan, NY*

Gray Line bus tours [W] *Buffalo, NY*

Great American Weekend [S] *Goshen, NY*

Great Escape and Splashwater Kingdom Fun Park, The [W] *Lake George Village, NY*

Great Falls Historic District Cultural Center [W] *Paterson, NJ*

Great Swamp National Wildlife Refuge [W] *Bernardsville, NJ*

Great Swamp National Wildlife Refuge [W] *Chatham, NJ*

Greek Peak [W] *Cortland, NY*

Greenbelt/High Rock, The [W] *Staten Island, NY*

Greenbelt Riverfront Park [W] *Ogdensburg (Thousand Islands), NY*

Greenfield Hall [W] *Haddonfield, NJ*

Green Lakes State Park [W] *Syracuse, NY*

Greenport Maritime Festival [S] *Greenport (L.I.), NY*

Greenwich Village [W] *Manhattan, NY*

Grover Cleveland Birthplace State Historic Site [W] *Caldwell, NJ*

Guggenheim Museum SoHo [W] *Manhattan, NY*

Guild Hall Museum [W] *East Hampton (L.I.), NY*

Guy Park State Historic Site [W] *Amsterdam, NY*

Hall of Fame for Great Americans, The [W] *Bronx, NY*

Hamilton Grange National Memorial [W] *Manhattan, NY*

Hamilton House Museum [W] *Clifton, NJ*

Hamlin Beach State Park [W] *Rochester, NY*

Hampton Classic Horse Show [S] *Southampton (L.I.), NY*

Hanford Mills Museum [W] *Oneonta, NY*

Hangar Theatre [S] *Ithaca, NY*

Harbor Festival [S] *Manhattan, NY*

Harlem [W] *Manhattan, NY*

Harness racing [S] *Freehold, NJ*

Harness Racing Museum and Hall of Fame [W] *Goshen, NY*

Harriet Tubman Home [W] *Auburn, NY*

Hartwick College [W] *Oneonta, NY*

Heckscher Museum of Art [W] *Huntington (L.I.), NY*

Heritage & Crafts Weekend [S] *Tarrytown, NY*

Heritage Days [S] *Trenton, NJ*

Heritage Festival [S] *Massena, NY*

Heritage Museum [W] *Ticonderoga (Lake George Area), NY*

Herkimer County Historical Society [W] *Herkimer, NY*

Herkimer Home State Historic Site [W] *Herkimer, NY*

Hermitage, The [W] *Ho-Ho-Kus, NJ*

Hermit Crab Race, Miss Crustacean Contest [S] *Ocean City, NJ*

Hickory Ski Center [W] *Warrensburg, NY*

High Falls Gorge [W] *Wilmington, NY*

High Falls in the Brown's Race Historic District [W] *Rochester, NY*

High Rock Spring [W] *Saratoga Springs, NY*

Hill Cumorah [W] *Palmyra, NY*

Hill Cumorah Pageant, The [S] *Palmyra, NY*

Hispanic Day Parade [S] *Manhattan, NY*

Hispanic Society of America [W] *Manhattan, NY*

Historic Allaire Village [W] *Allaire State Park, NJ*

Historical Museum of the Darwin R. Barker Library [W] *Dunkirk, NY*

Historical Society of Rockland County [W] *Spring Valley, NY*

Historical Society Serving Sleepy Hollow and Tarrytown, The [W] *Tarrytown, NY*

Historic Beth Joseph Synagogue [W] *Tupper Lake, NY*

Historic Cherry Hill [W] *Albany, NY*

Historic Clinton Academy [W] *East Hampton (L.I.), NY*

Historic Cold Spring Village [W] *Cape May, NJ*

Historic Congress Park [W] *Saratoga Springs, NY*

Historic Gardner's Basin [W] *Atlantic City, NJ*

Historic House [W] *Ocean City, NJ*

Historic Mulford Farm [W] *East Hampton (L.I.), NY*

Historic Richmond Town [W] *Staten Island, NY*

Historic Speedwell [W] *Morristown, NJ*

Historic Stockade Area, The [W] *Schenectady, NY*

Historic tours [W] *Burlington, NJ*

Historic Town of Smithville and the Village Greene at Smithville [W] *Atlantic City, NJ*

Hither Hills State Park [W] *Montauk (L.I.), NY*

H. Lee White Marine Museum [W] *Oswego, NY*

Hofstra University [W] *Hempstead (L.I.), NY*

Holland Land Office Museum [W] *Batavia, NY*

Holmes-Hendrickson House [W] *Red Bank, NJ*

Home of Franklin D. Roosevelt National Historic Site [W] *Hyde Park, NY*

"Home Sweet Home" House [W] *East Hampton (L.I.), NY*

Hook Mill [W] *East Hampton (L.I.), NY*

Hoopes Park Flower Gardens [W] *Auburn, NY*

Hopatcong State Park [W] *Lake Hopatcong, NJ*

Horse racing [W] *Manhattan, NY*

Horse racing. Monmouth Park [S] *Asbury Park, NJ*

Horton Point Lighthouse & Nautical Museum [W] *Southold (L.I.), NY*

Howe Caverns [W] *Howes Cave, NY*

Hudson River Maritime Museum [W] *Kingston, NY*

Hudson River Museum of Westchester, The [W] *Yonkers, NY*

Hudson River National Estuarine Research Reserve [W] *Rhinebeck, NY*

Hudson Valley Children's Museum [W] *Nyack, NY*

Huguenot Street Old Stone Houses [W] *New Paltz, NY*

Hungarian Heritage Center [W] *New Brunswick, NJ*

Hunter-Lawrence-Jessup House [W] *Gibbstown, NJ*

Huntington Summer Arts Festival [S] *Huntington (L.I.), NY*

Huntington Trade School [W] *Huntington (L.I.), NY*

Hyde Collection [W] *Glens Falls, NY*

ICP/Midtown [W] *Manhattan, NY*

IMB/USET Festival of Champions [S] *Somerville, NJ*

Indian King Tavern Museum State Historic Site [W] *Haddonfield, NJ*

International Center of Photography [W] *Manhattan, NY*

International Seaway Festival [S] *Ogdensburg (Thousand Islands), NY*

Intrepid Sea-Air Space Museum [W] *Manhattan, NY*

Iroquois National Wildlife Refuge [W] *Batavia, NY*

Isamu Naguchi Sculpture Museum [W] *Queens (La Guardia & JFK International Airport Areas), NY*

Island Beach State Park [W] *Seaside Park, NJ*

Israel Crane House [W] *Montclair, NJ*

Ithaca College [W] *Ithaca, NY*

Ithaca Festival [S] *Ithaca, NY*

Jacob K. Javits Convention Center [W] *Manhattan, NY*

Jacques Cartier State Park [W] *Ogdensburg (Thousand Islands), NY*

Jacques Marchais Museum of Tibetan Art [W] *Staten Island, NY*

James A. McFaul Environmental Center [W] *Ramsey, NJ*

James Baird State Park [W] *Poughkeepsie, NY*

James Vanderpoel House [W] *Hudson, NY*

Jane Voorhees Zimmerli Art Museum [W] *New Brunswick, NJ*

Jazz Fest [S] *Asbury Park, NJ*

Jazz Festival [S] *Lake George Village, NY*

Jefferson County Fair [S] *Watertown, NY*

Jefferson County Historical Society Museum [W] *Watertown, NY*

Jewish Museum [W] *Manhattan, NY*

Jewish Theological Seminary of America [W] *Manhattan, NY*

Jockey Hollow [W] *Morristown National Historical Park, NJ*

John Brown Farm Historic Site [W] *Lake Placid, NY*

John Drew Theater at Guild Hall [W] *East Hampton (L.I.), NY*

John F. Kennedy International Airport [W] *Queens (La Guardia & JFK International Airport Areas), NY*

John Holcombe House [W] *Lambertville, NJ*

John Jay Homestead State Historic Site [W] *Mt Kisco, NY*

John Neilson House [W] *Saratoga National Historical Park, NY*

Johnson Hall State Historic Site [W] *Johnstown, NY*

John Woolman Memorial [W] *Mount Holly, NJ*

Jones Beach Theatre [S] *Jones Beach State Park, NY*

Joseph Lloyd Manor House [W] *Huntington (L.I.), NY*

Joseph Papp Public Theater [W] *Manhattan, NY*

Joseph Smith Home [W] *Palmyra, NY*

Junior Museum [W] *Troy, NY*

JVC Jazz Festival-New York [S] *Manhattan, NY*

Kase Cemetery [W] *Flemington, NJ*

Kenan Center [W] *Lockport, NY*

Kent-Delord House Museum [W] *Plattsburgh, NY*

Keuka Lake State Park [W] *Penn Yan, NY*

Kissam House [W] *Huntington (L.I.), NY*

Kring Point State Park [W] *Alexandria Bay (Thousand Islands), NY*

Kuser Farm Mansion and Park [W] *Princeton, NJ*

Kykuit, The Rockefeller Estate [W] *Tarrytown, NY*

Laboratory for Laser Energetics [W] *Rochester, NY*

Labrador Mountain [W] *Cortland, NY*

La Guardia Airport [W] *Queens (La Guardia & JFK International Airport Areas), NY*

Lake Erie State Park [W] *Dunkirk, NY*

Lake excursions [W] *Lake George Village, NY*

Lake George Battlefield Picnic Area [W] *Lake George Village, NY*

Lake Placid Center For the Arts [W] *Lake Placid, NY*

Lake Placid Marina [W] *Lake Placid, NY*

Lakeside Festival [S] *Lake George Village, NY*

Lake Taghkanic State Park [W] *Hudson, NY*

Lambert Castle [W] *Paterson, NJ*

Lander's Delaware River Trips [W] *Barryville, NY*

Landmark Center (Campbell-Whittlesey House Museum), The [W] *Rochester, NY*

Landmark Theatre [W] *Syracuse, NY*

Land of Make Believe [W] *Hackettstown, NJ*

Lansing Manor [W] *Stamford, NY*

Lauder Museum [W] *Amityville (L.I.), NY*

Leaming's Run Gardens [W] *Cape May Court House, NJ*

Le Roy House [W] *Batavia, NY*

Letchworth State Park [W] *Geneseo, NY*

Liberty Helicopters [W] *Manhattan, NY*

Liberty Science Center [W] *Jersey City, NJ*

Liberty State Park [W] *Jersey City, NJ*

Library and Art Gallery [W] *Canajoharie, NY*

Lilac Festival [S] *Rochester, NY*

Lincoln and Roosevelt Baths [W] *Saratoga Springs, NY*

Lincoln Center for the Performing Arts [W] *Manhattan, NY*

Lincoln Center Guided Tours [W] *Manhattan, NY*

Littell-Lord Farmhouse Museum [W] *Plainfield, NJ*

Live TV shows [S] *Manhattan, NY*

Livingston County Historical Museum [W] *Geneseo, NY*

Locust Grove [W] *Poughkeepsie, NY*

Locust Lawn [W] *New Paltz, NY*

Long Island Fall Festival at Huntington [S] *Huntington (L.I.), NY*

Long Island Maritime Museum [W] *Sayville (L.I.), NY*

Long Point on Lake Chautauqua State Park [W] *Bemus Point, NY*

Long Point State Park [W] *Watertown, NY*

Lorenzo State Historic Site [W] *Cazenovia, NY*

Lowe Art Gallery [W] *Syracuse, NY*

Lower East Side Tenement Museum [W] *Manhattan, NY*

LPGA Atlantic City Classic [S] *Atlantic City, NJ*

Lucy-Desi Museum [W] *Jamestown, NY*

Lucy, the Margate Elephant [W] *Atlantic City, NJ*

Luykas Van Alen House [W] *Hudson, NY*

Lyndhurst [W] *Tarrytown, NY*

Macculloch Hall Historical Museum [W] *Morristown, NJ*

Macdonough Monument [W] *Plattsburgh, NY*

Macy's Herald Square [W] *Manhattan, NY*

Madam Brett Homestead [W] *Fishkill, NY*

Madison County Historical Society, Cottage Lawn Museum [W] *Oneida, NY*

Madison County Hop Fest [S] *Oneida, NY*

Madison Square Garden [W] *Manhattan, NY*

Mahopac Farm and Museum [W] *Mahopac, NY*

Main Building [W] *Trenton, NJ*

Mansion at Smithville [W] *Mount Holly, NJ*

Mansion House, The [W] *Oneida, NY*

Mansions by Gaslight [W] *Cape May, NJ*

Marine Mammal Stranding Center & Museum [W] *Atlantic City, NJ*

Marshall House [W] *Lambertville, NJ*

Martin Van Buren National Historic Site [W] *Hudson, NY*

Marymount College [W] *Tarrytown, NY*

Massena Car Show [S] *Massena, NY*

Maverick Concerts [S] *Woodstock, NY*

McCarter Theatre [W] *Princeton, NJ*

McClintock House [W] *Waterloo, NY*

Meadowbrook State Public Campground [W] *Saranac Lake, NY*

Meadowlands Sports Complex [W] *Manhattan, NY*

Mead Van Duyne House [W] *Wayne, NJ*

Memorial Art Gallery (University of Rochester) [W] *Rochester, NY*

Metro Lyric Opera Series [S] *Asbury Park, NJ*

Metropolitan Museum of Art [W] *Manhattan, NY*

MetroStars (MLS) [W] *Manhattan, NY*

Michie Stadium [W] *West Point (US Military Academy), NY*

Middlesex County Fair [S] *New Brunswick, NJ*

Mid-Hudson Children's Museum [W] *Poughkeepsie, NY*

Millard Fillmore Museum [W] *East Aurora, NY*

Miller Bell Tower [W] *Chautauqua, NY*

Miller Hill Restoration [W] *White Plains, NY*

Mills Mansion State Historic Site [W] *Hyde Park, NY*

Mills-Norrie State Park [W] *Hyde Park, NY*

Mine Kill State Park [W] *Stamford, NY*

Minor Basilica of the Sacred Heart [W] *Newark, NJ*

Miss Amelia's Cottage Museum [W] *Amagansett, NY*

Miss America Pageant [S] *Atlantic City, NY*

Model Train Show [S] *Clayton (Thousand Islands), NY*

Monmouth County Historical Museum and Library [W] *Freehold, NJ*

Monmouth Museum [W] *Red Bank, NJ*

Monroe County Fair [S] *Rochester, NY*

Montauk Point State Park [W] *Montauk (L.I.), NY*

Montclair Art Museum, The [W] *Montclair, NJ*

Montezuma National Wildlife Refuge [W] *Seneca Falls, NY*

Montgomery Place [W] *Rhinebeck, NY*

Monticello Raceway [W] *Monticello, NY*

Montour Falls [W] *Watkins Glen, NY*

Monument [W] *White Plains, NY*

Mormon Historic Sites and Bureau of Information [W] *Palmyra, NY*

Morris-Jumel Mansion [W] *Manhattan, NY*

Morris Museum [W] *Morristown, NJ*

Morristown National Historical Park [W] *Bernardsville, NJ*

Morristown National Historical Park [W] *Morristown, NJ*

Morristown National Historic Park [W] *Morristown National Historical Park, NJ*

Morton National Wildlife Refuge [W] *Sag Harbor (L.I.), NY*

Morven [W] *Princeton, NJ*

Mountain Creek Ski Resort [W] *Vernon, NJ*

Mount Gulian Historic Site [W] *Fishkill, NY*

Mount Holly Library [W] *Mount Holly, NJ*

Mount Pisgah Veterans Memorial Ski Center [W] *Saranac Lake, NY*

Munson-Williams-Proctor Institute [W] *Utica, NY*

Muscoot Farm [W] *Pound Ridge, NY*

Museum of American Folk Art [W] *Manhattan, NY*

Museum of Bronx History [W] *Bronx, NY*

Museum of Early Trades and Crafts [W] *Madison, NJ*

Museum of Jewish Heritage [W] *Manhattan, NY*

Museum of Modern Art (MOMA), The [W] *Manhattan, NY*

Museum of Television & Radio, The [W] *Manhattan, NY*

Museum of the City of New York [W] *Manhattan, NY*

Museums at Stony Brook, The [W] *Stony Brook (L.I.), NY*

Museum Village [W] *Monroe, NY*

Music Hall Theater [W] *Tarrytown, NY*

NASCAR Race Day [S] *Elmira, NY*

Nassau Hall [W] *Princeton, NJ*

Nassau Veterans Memorial Coliseum [W] *Hempstead (L.I.), NY*

National Baseball Hall of Fame and Museum [W] *Cooperstown, NY*

National Bottle Museum [W] *Saratoga Springs, NY*

National Museum of Dance [W] *Saratoga Springs, NY*

National Museum of Racing and Hall of Fame [W] *Saratoga Springs, NY*

National Shrine of the North American Martyrs [W] *Amsterdam, NY*

National Soaring Museum and Harris Hill Soaring Site [W] *Elmira, NY*

National Soccer Hall of Fame [W] *Oneonta, NY*

National Trout Derby [S] *Geneva, NY*

National Warplane Museum [W] *Elmira, NY*

National Women's Hall of Fame [W] *Seneca Falls, NY*

Natural Stone Bridge and Caves [W] *Schroon Lake, NY*

Newark Museum, The [W] *Newark, NJ*

New Jersey Children's Museum [W] *Paramus, NJ*

New Jersey Devils (NHL) [W] *Rutherford, NJ*

New Jersey Historical Society [W] *Newark, NJ*

New Jersey Museum of Agriculture [W] *New Brunswick, NJ*

New Jersey Nets (NBA) [W] *Rutherford, NJ*

New Jersey Performing Arts Center [W] *Newark, NJ*

New Jersey Shakespeare Festival [S] *Madison, NJ*

New Jersey State Aquarium [W] *Camden, NJ*

New Jersey State Museum [W] *Trenton, NJ*

New Sweden Farmstead Museum [W] *Bridgeton, NJ*

New Windsor Cantonment State Historic Site [W] *Newburgh, NY*

New York Aquarium [W] *Brooklyn, NY*

New York Botanical Garden, The [W] *Bronx, NY*

New York City Post Office [W] *Manhattan, NY*

New York Giants (NFL) [W] *Manhattan, NY*

New York Hall of Science [W] *Queens (La Guardia & JFK International Airport Areas), NY*

New York Historical Society, The [W] *Manhattan, NY*

New York Islanders (NHL) [W] *Manhattan, NY*

New York Jets (NFL) [W] *Manhattan, NY*

New York Knicks (NBA) [W] *Manhattan, NY*

New York Liberty (WNBA) [W] *Manhattan, NY*

New York Mets (MLB) [W] *Manhattan, NY*

New York Public Library for the Performing Arts [W] *Manhattan, NY*

New York Public Library [W] *Manhattan, NY*

New York Rangers (NHL) [W] *Manhattan, NY*

New York Shakespeare Festival & Shakespeare in the Park [S] *Manhattan, NY*

New York State Canal Cruises [W] *Syracuse, NY*

New York State Museum [W] *Albany, NY*

New York Stock Exchange [W] *Manhattan, NY*

New York Transit Museum [W] *Brooklyn, NY*

New York University [W] *Manhattan, NY*

New York Yankees (MLB) [W] *Manhattan, NY*

Niagara County Historical Center [W] *Lockport, NY*

Niagara Falls Convention & Civic Center [W] *Niagara Falls, NY*

Niagara Power Project Visitor Center [W] *Niagara Falls, NY*

Niagara Reservation State Park [W] *Niagara Falls, NY*

Niagara Scenic Trolley [W] *Niagara Falls, NY*

Niagara's Wax Museum of History [W] *Niagara Falls, NY*

Night in Venice [S] *Ocean City, NJ*

Ninth Avenue International Food Festival [S] *Manhattan, NY*

Northeast Classic Car Museum [W] *Norwich, NY*

Northern Westchester Center for the Arts [W] *Mt Kisco, NY*

Northport Historical Museum [W] *Northport (L.I.), NY*

North Wind Undersea Museum [W] *Bronx, NY*

Norton Memorial Hall [W] *Chautauqua, NY*

Nothnagle Home [W] *Gibbstown, NJ*

Noyes Museum [W] *Atlantic City, NJ*

NYC Marathon [S] *Manhattan, NY*

NY State Catskill Fish Hatchery [W] *Liberty, NY*

NY State Fair [S] *Syracuse, NY*

NY State Woodsmen's Field Days [S] *Boonville, NY*

Ocean City Historical Museum [W] *Ocean City, NJ*

Ocean County Park #1 [W] *Lakewood, NJ*

Ocean Grove House Tour [S] *Asbury Park, NJ*

Ocean Walk Tours [W] *Cape May, NJ*

Ogdensburg, NY-Johnstown, Ontario International Bridge [W] *Ogdensburg (Thousand Islands), NY*

Olana State Historic Site [W] *Hudson, NY*

Old Barracks Museum, The [W] *Trenton, NJ*

Old Bethpage Village Restoration [W] *Bethpage (L.I.), NY*

Old Borden Farm [W] *Mahopac, NY*

Old Broad Street Church [W] *Bridgeton, NJ*

Old Dutch Church [W] *Kingston, NY*

Old Dutch Church of Sleepy Hollow [W] *Tarrytown, NY*

Old Dutch Parsonage State Historic Site [W] *Somerville, NJ*

Old Forge Lake Cruise [W] *Old Forge, NY*

Old Fort Niagara [W] *Niagara Falls, NY*

Old Halsey House [W] *Southampton (L.I.), NY*

Old House, The [W] *Southold (L.I.), NY*

Old Plume House [W] *Newark, NJ*

Old Rhinebeck Aerodrome [W] *Rhinebeck, NY*

Old St. Mary's Church [W] *Burlington, NJ*

Old Stone Fort Museum Complex [W] *Howes Cave, NY*

Old Westbury Gardens [W] *Westbury (L.I.), NY*

Oliver House Museum [W] *Penn Yan, NY*

Olympic Arena and Convention Center [W] *Lake Placid, NY*

Olympic Sports Complex (Mount Van Hoevenberg Recreation Area) [W] *Lake Placid, NY*

Oneida County Fair [S] *Boonville, NY*

Oneida County Historical Society [W] *Utica, NY*

Onondaga Historical Association Museum [W] *Syracuse, NY*

Onondaga Lake Park [W] *Syracuse, NY*

Ontario County Fair [S] *Canandaigua, NY*

Ontario County Historical Society [W] *Canandaigua, NY*

Open-air concerts [S] *Syracuse, NY*

Opus 40 & Quarryman's Museum [W] *Saugerties, NY*

Orange County Fair [S] *Middletown, NY*

Orient Point, NY-New London, CT, Ferry [W] *Greenport (L.I.), NY*

Oswego County Historical Society [W] *Oswego, NY*

Oswego Speedway [S] *Oswego, NY*

Outlet Trail, The [W] *Penn Yan, NY*

Owego Strawberry Festival [S] *Owego, NY*

Oyster Festival [S] *Oyster Bay (L.I.), NY*

Pageant of Steam [S] *Canandaigua, NY*

Palestine Park [W] *Chautauqua, NY*

Palmyra Historical Museum [W] *Palmyra, NY*

Panama Rocks Folk Fair [S] *Jamestown, NY*

Panama Rocks Park [W] *Jamestown, NY*

Paper Mill Playhouse [W] *Millburn, NJ*

Parades [W] *West Point (US Military Academy), NY*

Paradox Lake [W] *Schroon Lake, NY*

Parrish Art Museum [W] *Southampton (L.I.), NY*

Parvin State Park [W] *Bridgeton, NJ*

Paterson Museum [W] *Paterson, NJ*

Pelham Bay Park [W] *Bronx, NY*

Penfield Homestead Museum [W] *Crown Point, NY*

Peters Valley [W] *Branchville, NJ*

Peters Valley Craft Fair [S] *Branchville, NJ*

Peter Whitmer Farm [W] *Waterloo, NY*

Petrified Sea Gardens [W] *Saratoga Springs, NY*

Phelps General Store Museum [W] *Palmyra, NY*

Philipsburg Manor [W] *Tarrytown, NY*

Pierpont Morgan Library [W] *Manhattan, NY*

Pixley Falls State Park [W] *Boonville, NY*

Planetarium [W] *Trenton, NJ*

Planting Fields Arboretum [W] *Oyster Bay (L.I.), NY*

Police Museum [W] *Manhattan, NY*

Pollock-Krasner House and Study Center [W] *East Hampton (L.I.), NY*

Polo Matches [S] *Skaneateles, NY*

Polo. Saratoga Polo Association [S] *Saratoga Springs, NY*

Potsdam College of the State University of New York [W] *Potsdam, NY*

Potsdam Public Museum [W] *Potsdam, NY*

Powwow [S] *Southampton (L.I.), NY*

Pratt Rocks [W] *Stamford, NY*

Presby Iris Gardens [W] *Montclair, NJ*

Princeton Battle Monument [W] *Princeton, NJ*

Princeton Cemetery [W] *Princeton, NJ*

Princeton University [W] *Princeton, NJ*

Proctor's Theatre [W] *Schenectady, NY*

Professional sports [W] *Buffalo, NY*

Professional Sports [W] *Manhattan, NY*

Professional sports [W] *Rutherford, NJ*

Promenade Art Exhibit [S] *Cape May, NJ*

Prospect Mountain State Parkway [W] *Lake George Village, NY*

Prospect Park [W] *Brooklyn, NY*

Prospect Park Visitor Center [W] *Niagara Falls, NY*

Prospect Point Observation Tower [W] *Niagara Falls, NY*

Prudential Building [W] *Buffalo, NY*

P.S. 1 Contemporary Art Center [W] *Long Island, NY*

Public beach [W] *Old Forge, NY*

Public campgrounds [W] *Schroon Lake, NY*

Putnam Pond State Public Campground [W] *Ticonderoga (Lake George Area), NY*

Putnam Sculptures, The [W] *Princeton, NJ*

Q-R-S Music Rolls [W] *Buffalo, NY*

Queens Botanical Garden [W] *Queens (La Guardia & JFK International Airport Areas), NY*

Queens Museum of Art, The [W] *Queens (La Guardia & JFK International Airport Areas), NY*

Racing [S] *Goshen, NY*

Rafting [W] *North Creek, NY*

Raquette River Outfitters [W] *Tupper Lake, NY*

Raynham Hall Museum [W] *Oyster Bay (L.I.), NY*

Recreation [W] *Chautauqua, NY*

Recreation areas [W] *Atlantic City, NJ*

Recreation areas. Stewart Park [W] *Ithaca, NY*

Recreation Center [W] *Saratoga Springs, NY*

Recreation. Veterans Memorial Park [W] *Bolton Landing (Lake George Area), NY*

Red Mill Museum Village [W] *Clinton, NJ*

Reenactment of Crossing of the Delaware [S] *Trenton, NJ*

Renault Winery [W] *Atlantic City, NJ*

Rensselaer County Historical Society [W] *Troy, NY*

Rensselaer Polytechnic Institute [W] *Troy, NY*

Rensselaerville [W] *Albany, NY*

Replica of Hancock House [W] *Ticonderoga (Lake George Area), NY*

Replica Trolley Tours [W] *Elmira, NY*

Reservoir State Park [W] *Niagara Falls, NY*

Rifle Camp Park [W] *Paterson, NJ*

Ring of Fire [S] *Canandaigua, NY*

Riverhead Country Fair [S] *Riverhead (L.I.), NY*

Riverspark Visitor Center [W] *Troy, NY*

Roberson Museum and Science Center [W] *Binghamton, NY*

Robert H. Treman [W] *Ithaca, NY*

Robert Louis Stevenson Memorial Cottage [W] *Saranac Lake, NY*

Robert Moses State Park [W] *Bay Shore (L.I.), NY*

Robert Moses State Park [W] *Massena, NY*

Robert Moses State Park [W] *Massena, NY*

Rochester Historical Society [W] *Rochester, NY*

Rochester Institute of Technology [W] *Rochester, NY*

Rochester Museum & Science Center [W] *Rochester, NY*

Rochester Philharmonic Orchestra [S] *Rochester, NY*

Rockefeller Center [W] *Manhattan, NY*

Rock Hall Museum [W] *Rockville Centre (L.I.), NY*

Rockingham State Historic Site [W] *Princeton, NJ*

Rockport Boat Lines [W] *Alexandria Bay (Thousand Islands), NY*

Rockwell Falls & Chasm [W] *Lake Luzerne, NY*

Rockwell Museum, The [W] *Corning, NY*

Rogers Environmental Education Center [W] *Hamilton, NY*

Rogers Rock State Public Campground [W] *Hague, NY*

Roosevelt-Vanderbilt National Historic Sites [W] *Hyde Park, NY*

Rosamond Gifford Zoo at Burnet Park [W] *Syracuse, NY*

Rose Center for Earth and Space [W] *Manhattan, NY*

Rose Hill Mansion [W] *Geneva, NY*

Ross Park Zoo [W] *Binghamton, NY*

Roswell P. Flower Memorial Library [W] *Watertown, NY*

Round Valley State Park [W] *Clinton, NJ*

Roycroft Summer Festival of Arts & Crafts [S] *East Aurora, NY*

Rush Rhees Library [W] *Rochester, NY*

Russell Sage College [W] *Troy, NY*

Rutgers Gardens, The [W] *New Brunswick, NJ*

Rutgers-The State University of New Jersey [W] *New Brunswick, NJ*

Sackets Harbor Battlefield State Historic Site [W] *Sackets Harbor, NY*

Sagamore Hill National Historic Site [W] *Oyster Bay (L.I.), NY*

Sagan Planetwalk [W] *Ithaca, NY*

Sag Harbor Whaling and Historical Museum [W] *Sag Harbor (L.I.), NY*

Sagtikos Manor [W] *Bay Shore (L.I.), NY*

Sail into Summer Boat Show [S] *Stone Harbor, NJ*

St. Lawrence Seaway, The [W] *Massena, NY*

St. Lawrence University [W] *Canton, NY*

Ste. Marie Among the Iroquois [W] *Syracuse, NY*

St. Patrick's Cathedral [W] *Manhattan, NY*

St. Patrick's Day Parade [S] *Manhattan, NY*

St. Paul's Chapel [W] *Manhattan, NY*

St. Paul's Church National Historic Site [W] *Yonkers, NY*

Salt Museum [W] *Syracuse, NY*

Sampson State Park [W] *Geneva, NY*

Samuel C. Williams Library [W] *Hoboken, NJ*

San Gennaro Festival [S] *Manhattan, NY*

Santa's Home Workshop [W] *Wilmington, NY*

Saratoga Equine Sports Center [W] *Saratoga Springs, NY*

Saratoga Lake [W] *Saratoga Springs, NY*

Saratoga Monument [W] *Saratoga National Historical Park, NY*

Saratoga National Historical Park [W] *Saratoga Springs, NY*

Saratoga Performing Arts Center [W] *Saratoga Springs, NY*

Saratoga Performing Arts Center [S] *Saratoga Springs, NY*

Saratoga Race Course [S] *Saratoga Springs, NY*

Saratoga Spa State Park [W] *Saratoga Springs, NY*

Schenectady Museum & Planetarium and Schenectady Heritage Area, The [W] *Schenectady, NY*

Schoellkopf Geological Museum [W] *Niagara Falls, NY*

Schoharie Crossing State Historic Site and Visitors Center [W] *Amsterdam, NY*

Schomburg Center for Research in Black Culture [W] *Manhattan, NY*

Schoolhouse Museum [W] *Paramus, NJ*

Schuyler-Hamilton House [W] *Morristown, NJ*

Schuyler Mansion State Historic Site [W] *Albany, NY*

Schweinfurth Memorial Art Center [W] *Auburn, NY*

Sciencenter [W] *Ithaca, NY*

Sci-Tech Center [W] *Watertown, NY*

Scottish Games [S] *Syracuse, NY*

Sea & Sky Festival [S] *Cape May, NJ*

Secret Caverns [W] *Howes Cave, NY*

Self-guided walking tour [W] *Ausable Chasm, NY*

Selkirk Shores State Park [W] *Oswego, NY*

Senate House State Historic Site [W] *Kingston, NY*

Seneca Falls Historical Society Museum [W] *Seneca Falls, NY*

Seneca Lake State Park [W] *Geneva, NY*

Seneca Lake Whale Watch [S] *Geneva, NY*

Seneca Park Zoo [W] *Rochester, NY*

Sesame Place [W] *Trenton, NJ*

Seward House [W] *Auburn, NY*

Shaker Heritage Society [W] *Albany, NY*

Shaker Museum and Library [W] *Hudson, NY*

Shea's Performing Arts Center [W] *Buffalo, NY*

Shea Stadium [W] *Queens (La Guardia & JFK International Airport Areas), NY*

Sheepshead Bay [W] *Brooklyn, NY*

Shopping [W] *Manhattan, NY*

Shops on Ocean One, The [W] *Atlantic City, NJ*

Sightseeing tour. Discovery Tour of Brooklyn [W] *Brooklyn, NY*

Sightseeing Tours [W] *Manhattan, NY*

Silas Wright House and Museum [W] *Canton, NY*

Site of the Elizabeth Haddon House, The [W] *Haddonfield, NJ*

Six Flags Darien Lake [W] *Batavia, NY*

Six Flags Great Adventure Theme Park/Six Flags Wild Safari Animal Park [W] *Jackson, NJ*

Six Mile Creek Vineyard [W] *Ithaca, NY*

Six Nations Indian Museum [W] *Saranac Lake, NY*

Skiing [W] *Cortland, NY*

Skiing [W] *North Creek, NY*

Skiing. Belleayre Mountain [W] *Shandaken, NY*

Skiing. Bristol Mountain Ski & Snowboard Resort [W] *Canandaigua, NY*

Skiing. Catamount Ski Area [W] *Hillsdale, NY*

Skiing. Gore Mountain [W] *North Creek, NY*

Skiing. Holiday Mountain Ski Area [W] *Monticello, NY*

Skiing. Hunter Mountain Ski Resort [W] *Hunter, NY*

Skiing. Kissing Bridge Ski Area [W] *East Aurora, NY*

Skiing. McCauley Mountain [W] *Old Forge, NY*

Skiing. Ski Windham [W] *Windham, NY*

Skiing. Swain Ski Center [W] *Hornell, NY*

Skiing. Titus Mountain Ski Area [W] *Malone, NY*

Skiing. Toggenburg Ski Center [W] *Cazenovia, NY*

Skiing. West Mountain Ski Resort [W] *Glens Falls, NY*

Skiing. Whiteface Mountain Ski Center [W] *Wilmington, NY*

Sleepy Hollow Cemetery [W] *Tarrytown, NY*

Smith Opera House for the Performing Arts [W] *Geneva, NY*

Snow Ridge Ski Area [W] *Boonville, NY*

Snug Harbor Cultural Center [W] *Staten Island, NY*

SoHo [W] *Manhattan, NY*

Solomon R. Guggenheim Museum [W] *Manhattan, NY*

Song Mountain [W] *Cortland, NY*

Sonnenberg Gardens [W] *Canandaigua, NY*

Southampton College of Long Island University [W] *Southampton (L.I.), NY*

Southampton Historical Museum [W] *Southampton (L.I.), NY*

Southeast Museum [W] *Brewster, NY*

South Mountain Arena [W] *West Orange, NJ*

South Street Seaport [W] *Manhattan, NY*

South Street Seaport Events [W] *Manhattan, NY*

South Street Seaport Museum [W] *Manhattan, NY*

South Street Seaport Neighborhood [W] *Manhattan, NY*

Space Farms Zoo & Museum [W] *Branchville, NJ*

Spruce Run State Recreation Area [W] *Clinton, NJ*

Staller Center for the Arts [W] *Stony Brook (L.I.), NY*

Stars and Stripes Riverfront Festival [S] *Troy, NY*

State Barge Canal Locks #2 and #3 [W] *Seneca Falls, NY*

State Capitol [W] *Albany, NY*

Staten Island Ferry [W] *Manhattan, NY*

Staten Island Zoo [W] *Staten Island, NY*

State parks [W] *Ithaca, NY*

State University of New York College at New Paltz [W] *New Paltz, NY*

State University of New York [W] *Oswego, NY*

State University of New York College at Plattsburgh [W] *Plattsburgh, NY*

State University of New York at Stony Brook [W] *Stony Brook (L.I.), NY*

State University of NY at Buffalo [W] *Buffalo, NY*

Statue of Abraham Lincoln [W] *Newark, NJ*

Statue of Liberty Exhibit [W] *Manhattan, NY*

Statue of Liberty National Monument [W] *Manhattan, NY*

Stephen Crane House [W] *Asbury Park, NJ*

Steuben House State Historic Site [W] *Hackensack, NJ*

Stevens Center [W] *Hoboken, NJ*

Stevens Institute of Technology [W] *Hoboken, NJ*

Stock-car racing [S] *Flemington, NJ*

Stokes State Forest [W] *Branchville, NJ*

Stone House Day [S] *Kingston, NY*

Stone Pony, The [W] *Asbury Park, NJ*

Stone-Tolan House [W] *Rochester, NY*

Stony Brook State Park [W] *Hornell, NY*

Stony Point Battlefield State Historic Site [W] *Stony Point, NY*

Storm King Art Center [W] *Newburgh, NY*

Storybook Land [W] *Atlantic City, NJ*

Storytelling in the Park [W] *Manhattan, NY*

Strasenburgh Planetarium of the Rochester Museum and Science Center [W] *Rochester, NY*

Strong Museum [W] *Rochester, NY*

Studio Arena Theatre [W] *Buffalo, NY*

Studio Museum in Harlem, The [W] *Manhattan, NY*

Suffolk County Historical Society [W] *Riverhead (L.I.), NY*

Suffolk County Vanderbilt Museum [W] *Northport (L.I.), NY*

Suggett House Museum and Kellogg Memorial Research Library [W] *Cortland, NY*

SummerMusic [S] *Canandaigua, NY*

Sunken Meadow State Park [W] *Huntington (L.I.), NY*

Sunnyside [W] *Tarrytown, NY*

Sunset Serenades [S] *Tarrytown, NY*

SUNY College Summer Repertory Theatre [S] *New Paltz, NY*

Surflight Theatre [S] *Long Beach Island, NJ*

Susan B. Anthony House [W] *Rochester, NY*

Swartswood State Park [W] *Branchville, NJ*

Swimming [W] *Dunkirk, NY*

Swimming [W] *Lake George Village, NY*

Swimming Beaches. Municipal Beach [W] *Ogdensburg (Thousand Islands), NY*

Swimming, boating, fishing [W] *Lake Luzerne, NY*

Swimming, fishing, boating [W] *Cape May, NJ*

Swimming. Municipal Beach [W] *Plattsburgh, NY*

Symphony Hall [W] *Newark, NJ*

Syracuse Heritage Area Visitor Center [W] *Syracuse, NY*

Syracuse Stage [S] *Syracuse, NY*

Syracuse University [W] *Syracuse, NY*

Tackapausha Museum & Preserve [W] *Massapequa Park (L.I.), NY*

Taconic State Park [W] *Hillsdale, NY*

Target Rock National Wildlife Refuge [W] *Huntington (L.I.), NY*

Taste of Buffalo [S] *Buffalo, NY*

Taughannock Falls [W] *Ithaca, NY*

Teddy Roosevelt Celebration [S] *North Creek, NY*

Temple Emanu-El [W] *Manhattan, NY*

Ten Broeck Mansion [W] *Albany, NY*

Terhune Memorial Park (Sunnybank) [W] *Wayne, NJ*

Terwilliger Museum [W] *Waterloo, NY*

Thanksgiving Day Parade [S] *Manhattan, NY*

Theodore Roosevelt Birthplace National Historic Site [W] *Manhattan, NY*

Theodore Roosevelt Inaugural National Historic Site [W] *Buffalo, NY*

Theodore Roosevelt Sanctuary & Audubon Center [W] *Oyster Bay (L.I.), NY*

Thomas Paine Cottage [W] *New Rochelle, NY*

Thomas Paine National Historical Association [W] *New Rochelle, NY*

Thomas Revell House [W] *Burlington, NJ*

Thompson House [W] *Port Jefferson (L.I.), NY*

Thoroughbred horse racing [W] *Queens (La Guardia & JFK International Airport Areas), NY*

Thousand Islands Museum [W] *Clayton (Thousand Islands), NY*

Thousand Islands Skydeck [W] *Alexandria Bay (Thousand Islands), NY*

Thunder Ridge Ski Area [W] *Brewster, NY*

Timespell [W] *Watkins Glen, NY*

Times Square and the Theater District [W] *Manhattan, NY*

Tinman Triathlon [S] *Tupper Lake, NY*

Tioga County Fair [S] *Owego, NY*

Tioga County Historical Society Museum [W] *Owego, NY*

Tioga Gardens [W] *Owego, NY*

Tioga Scenic Railroad [W] *Owego, NY*

Tomb of the Unknown Soldier of the American Revolution [W] *Rome, NY*

Tomb of Walt Whitman [W] *Camden, NJ*

Tour road [W] *Saratoga National Historical Park, NY*

Tours [W] *Cape May, NJ*

Town Marine Museum [W] *Amagansett, NY*

Toy Festival [S] *East Aurora, NY*

Trailside Nature and Science Center [W] *Scotch Plains, NJ*

Train Rides [W] *Allaire State Park, NJ*

Trenton Kennel Club Dog Show [S] *Trenton, NJ*

Trinity Church [W] *Manhattan, NY*

Trolleys [W] *Cape May, NJ*

Troy Savings Bank Music Hall [W] *Troy, NY*

Tulip Festival [S] *Albany, NY*

Tulip Festival [S] *Cape May, NJ*

Turkey Swamp Park [W] *Freehold, NJ*

Turtle Back Zoo [W] *West Orange, NJ*

Twin Lights State Historic Site [W] *Gateway National Recreation Area (Sandy Hook Unit), NJ*

Uihlein Sugar Maple Research-Extension Field Station [W] *Lake Placid, NY*

Ukrainian Museum [W] *Manhattan, NY*

Ulster County Fair [S] *New Paltz, NY*

Ulster Performing Arts Center [W] *Kingston, NY*

Uncle Sam Boat Tours [W] *Alexandria Bay (Thousand Islands), NY*

Uncle Sam Boat Tours [W] *Clayton (Thousand Islands), NY*

Union College [W] *Schenectady, NY*

United Nations [W] *Manhattan, NY*

University at Albany, State University of New York [W] *Albany, NY*

University of Rochester [W] *Rochester, NY*

US Merchant Marine Academy [W] *Great Neck (L.I.), NY*

US Open Tennis [S] *Queens (La Guardia & JFK International Airport Areas), NY*

USS *Ling* Submarine [W] *Hackensack, NJ*

Utica College of Syracuse University [W] *Utica, NY*

Utica Zoo [W] *Utica, NY*

Valentown Museum [W] *Victor, NY*

Van Cortlandt House Museum [W] *Bronx, NY*

Van Cortlandt Manor [W] *Tarrytown, NY*

Vanderbilt Mansion National Historic Site [W] *Hyde Park, NY*

Vanderbilt Museum Planetarium [W] *Northport (L.I.), NY*

Van Riper-Hopper (Wayne) Museum [W] *Wayne, NJ*

Van Saun County Park [W] *Paramus, NJ*

Van Wyck Homestead Museum [W] *Fishkill, NY*

Vassar College [W] *Poughkeepsie, NY*

Vernon Downs [W] *Oneida, NY*

Verona Beach State Park [W] *Oneida, NY*

Victorian Doll Museum [W] *Rochester, NY*

Victorian houses [W] *Cape May Court House, NJ*

Victorian Week [S] *Cape May, NJ*

Visitor Center and Museum [W] *Saratoga National Historical Park, NY*

Visitors Center [W] *Stamford, NY*

Visitors Center [W] *West Point (US Military Academy), NY*

Walkabout [S] *Schenectady, NY*

Walking Tours of the Historic District [W] *Cape May, NJ*

Walk through downtown Manhattan [W] *Manhattan, NY*

Wallace House State Historic Site [W] *Somerville, NJ*

Wall Street [W] *Manhattan, NY*

Walter Elwood Museum [W] *Amsterdam, NY*

Walt Whitman Arts Center [W] *Camden, NJ*

Walt Whitman Birthplace State Historic Site [W] *Huntington (L.I.), NY*

Walt Whitman House State Historic Site [W] *Camden, NJ*

Ward Pound Ridge Reservation [W] *Pound Ridge, NY*

Warinanco Park [W] *Elizabeth, NJ*

War of 1812 Battlefield Walking Tour [W] *Ogdensburg (Thousand Islands), NY*

Warrensburg Museum of Local History [W] *Warrensburg, NY*

Wars of America, The [W] *Newark, NJ*

Washington Crossing State Park [W] *Trenton, NJ*

Washington Heights Museum Group [W] *Manhattan, NY*

Washington's Headquarters State Historic Site [W] *Newburgh, NY*

Washington's Headquarters [W] *White Plains, NY*

Washington Square [W] *Manhattan, NY*

Washington Square Art Show [S] *Manhattan, NY*

Watchung Reservation [W] *Scotch Plains, NJ*

Waterloo Memorial Day Museum [W] *Waterloo, NY*

Waterloo Village Restoration [W] *Stanhope, NJ*

Water Mill Museum [W] *Southampton (L.I.), NY*

Water Slide World [W] *Lake George Village, NY*

Watkins Glen International [S] *Watkins Glen, NY*

Watkins Glen State Park [W] *Watkins Glen, NY*

Wave Hill [W] *Bronx, NY*

Wellesley Island [W] *Alexandria Bay (Thousand Islands), NY*

Wertheim National Wildlife Refuge [W] *Westhampton Beach, NY*

Westbury Music Fair [W] *Westbury (L.I.), NY*

Westcott Beach State Park [W] *Sackets Harbor, NY*

West Point Museum [W] *West Point (US Military Academy), NY*

Wetlands Institute [W] *Stone Harbor, NJ*

Wharton State Forest [W] *Batsto, NJ*

Wheaton Village [W] *Millville, NJ*

Whirlpool State Park [W] *Niagara Falls, NY*

White Birches Campsite [W] *Windham, NY*

Whiteface Mountain Memorial Highway [W] *Wilmington, NY*

White Water Derby [S] *North Creek, NY*

White water rafting [W] *Lake Luzerne, NY*

Whitney Museum of American Art at Philip Morris [W] *Manhattan, NY*

Whitney Museum of American Art [W] *Manhattan, NY*

Wick House [W] *Morristown National Historical Park, NJ*

Widmer's Wine Cellars [W] *Naples, NY*

Willard Hanmer Guideboat, Canoe, and War Canoe Races [S] *Saranac Lake, NY*

Willard Memorial Chapel & Welch Memorial Building [W] *Auburn, NY*

Willard Mountain Ski Area [W] *Greenwich, NY*

William Trent House [W] *Trenton, NJ*

Windsor Vineyards [W] *Poughkeepsie, NY*

Wine & Grape Museum of Greyton H. Taylor [W] *Hammondsport, NY*

Winery tours [W] *Watkins Glen, NY*

Wing Ding Weekend [S] *Batavia, NY*

Wings 'n Water Festival [S] *Stone Harbor, NJ*

Winter Carnival [S] *Lake George Village, NY*

Winter Carnival [S] *Saranac Lake, NY*

Wintergarden [W] *Niagara Falls, NY*

Women's Rights National Historical Park [W] *Seneca Falls, NY*

Woodlawn Cemetery [W] *Elmira, NY*

Woodlawn National Cemetery [W] *Elmira, NY*

Woodrow Wilson School of Public and International Affairs [W] *Princeton, NJ*

Woodsmen's Days [S] *Tupper Lake, NY*

Woodstock Artists Association Gallery [W] *Woodstock, NY*

Woodstock Music Festival Monument [W] *Monticello, NY*

Wood Street Fair [S] *Burlington, NJ*

Woods Valley Ski Area [W] *Rome, NY*

Woolworth Building [W] *Manhattan, NY*

World Financial Center [W] *Manhattan, NY*

World Series of Bocce [S] *Rome, NY*

World's Largest Garage Sale and Foliage Festival [S] *Warrensburg, NY*

Yaddo Gardens [W] *Saratoga Springs, NY*

Yankee Stadium [W] *Bronx, NY*

Yeshiva University [W] *Manhattan, NY*

Yeshiva University Museum [W] *Manhattan, NY*

Yonkers Raceway [W] *Manhattan, NY*

Yonkers Raceway [W] *Yonkers, NY*

Zaddock Pratt Museum [W] *Stamford, NY*

Zane Grey Museum [W] *Barryville, NY*

Zoom Flume Waterpark [W] *Cairo, NY*

Zoom Flume Waterpark [W] *Catskill, NY*

LODGING LIST

Establishment names are listed in alphabetical order followed by a symbol identifying their classification and then city and state. The symbols for classification are: [AS] for All Suites, [BB] for B&Bs/Small Inns, [CAS] for Casinos, [CC] for Cottage Colonies, [CON] for Villas/Condos, [CONF] for Conference Centers, [EX] for Extended Stays, [HOT] for Hotels, [MOT] for Motels/Motor Lodges, [RAN] for Guest Ranches, and [RST] for Resorts

1770 HOUSE, THE [BB] *East Hampton (L.I.), NY*
19TH GREEN [HOT] *Old Forge, NY*
60 THOMPSON [HOT] *Manhattan, NY*
A B & B AT DARTMOUTH HOUSE [BB] *Rochester, NY*
ABBEY BED & BREAKFAST, THE [BB] *Cape May, NJ*
ABIGAIL ADAMS BED AND BREAKFAST [BB] *Cape May, NJ*
ACORN INN B & B [BB] *Canandaigua, NY*
ADAM'S MARK [HOT] *Buffalo, NY*
ADELPHI HOTEL [HOT] *Saratoga Springs, NY*
ADIRONDACK INN BY THE LAKE [HOT] *Lake Placid, NY*
ADIRONDACK MOTEL [MOT] *Saranac Lake, NY*
ADVENTURE MOTOR INN [MOT] *Wildwood and Wildwood Crest, NJ*
ALBERGO ALLEGRIA [BB] *Windham, NY*
ALEXANDER HAMILTON HOUSE [BB] *Tarrytown, NY*
ALGONQUIN HOTEL [HOT] *Manhattan, NY*
ALPENHAUS [MOT] *Glens Falls, NY*
ALPINE AIR MOTEL [MOT] *Lake Placid, NY*
ALPINE MOTOR INN [MOT] *Lake Placid, NY*
ALPINE VILLAGE RESORT [CC] *Lake George Village, NY*
AMBER STREET INN BED & BREAKFAST [BB] *Long Beach Island, NJ*
AMERITANIA HOTEL [HOT] *Manhattan, NY*
AMSTERDAM COURT [HOT] *Manhattan, NY*
ANGEL OF THE SEA [BB] *Cape May, NJ*
APPLE VALLEY INN [BB] *Vernon, NJ*

AQUARIUS MOTOR INN [MOT] *Wildwood and Wildwood Crest, NJ*
ARMADA BY THE SEA [MOT] *Wildwood and Wildwood Crest, NJ*
ART DEVLINS OLYMPIC MOTOR INN [MOT] *Lake Placid, NY*
ASA RANSOM HOUSE [BB] *Buffalo, NY*
ASHLING COTTAGE [BB] *Spring Lake, NJ*
ASTRONAUT MOTEL [MOT] *Wildwood and Wildwood Crest, NJ*
ATHENAEUM HOTEL [HOT] *Chautauqua, NY*
ATTACHE [MOT] *Wildwood and Wildwood Crest, NJ*
AVALON GOLDEN INN HOTEL & COFERENCE CENTER [RST] *Stone Harbor, NJ*
AVALON HOTEL, THE [HOT] *Manhattan, NY*
AVONDALE BY THE SEA [HOT] *Cape May, NJ*
AVON INN [MOT] *Avon, NY*
BALLY'S PARK PLACE [CAS] *Atlantic City, NJ*
BARK EATER INN, THE [MOT] *Lake Placid, NY*
BAYFRONT COTTAGES [BB] *Lake George Village, NY*
BAY HEAD GABLES [BB] *Spring Lake, NJ*
BAYSIDE INN & MARINA [MOT] *Cooperstown, NY*
BEACH CLUB HOTEL [HOT] *Ocean City, NJ*
BEACHCOMBER RESORT [RST] *Montauk (L.I.), NY*
BEAR MOUNTAIN INN [HOT] *Palisades Interstate Parks, NY*
BEEKMAN ARMS [HOT] *Rhinebeck, NY*

BEEKMAN TOWER SUITE HOTEL
[AS] *Manhattan, NY*
BELHURST CASTLE [BB] *Geneva, NY*
BELLEVUE [HOT] *Watkins Glen, NY*
BELMAR MOTOR LODGE [MOT]
Spring Lake, NJ
BEN CONGER INN [BB] *Cortland, NY*
BENJAMIN, THE [HOT] *Manhattan,
NY*
BERNARDS INN [BB] *Bernardsville, NJ*
BERTRAND'S MOTEL [MOT] *Clayton
(Thousand Islands), NY*
BEST INN [MOT] *Poughkeepsie, NY*
BEST WESTERN [MOT] *Amsterdam,
NY*
BEST WESTERN [MOT] *Dunkirk, NY*
BEST WESTERN [MOT] *Herkimer, NY*
BEST WESTERN [MOT] *Morristown, NJ*
BEST WESTERN [MOT] *Old Forge, NY*
BEST WESTERN AIRPORT [MOT]
Albany, NY
BEST WESTERN BATAVIA INN [MOT]
Batavia, NY
BEST WESTERN BINGHAMTON
REGENCY HOTEL &
CONFERENCE CENTER [MOT]
Binghamton, NY
BEST WESTERN CAPTAIN'S
QUARTERS HOTEL [MOT]
Oswego, NY
BEST WESTERN CARLTON HOUSE
JFK AIRPORT [MOT] *Queens (La
Guardia & JFK International
Airport Areas), NY*
BEST WESTERN CARRIAGE HOUSE
[MOT] *Watertown, NY*
BEST WESTERN GATEWAY INN
[MOT] *Utica, NY*
BEST WESTERN GOLDEN ARROW
[MOT] *Lake Placid, NY*
BEST WESTERN HOTEL [MOT]
Sayville (L.I.), NY
BEST WESTERN INN [MOT]
Manhattan, NY
BEST WESTERN INN & SUITES [MOT]
Cooperstown, NY
BEST WESTERN INN AT SMITHVILLE
[MOT] *Plattsburgh, NY*
BEST WESTERN INN OF COBLESKILL
[MOT] *Howes Cave, NY*
BEST WESTERN INN-ON THE AVE
[MOT] *Buffalo, NY*
BEST WESTERN INN ON THE RIVER
[MOT] *Niagara Falls, NY*
BEST WESTERN LEISURE INN [MOT]
Lakewood, NJ
BEST WESTERN MARSHALL MANOR
[MOT] *Elmira, NY*
BEST WESTERN MARSHALL MANOR
[MOT] *Syracuse, NY*
BEST WESTERN NYACK ON
HUDSON [MOT] *Nyack, NY*

BEST WESTERN OF LAKE GEORGE
[MOT] *Lake George Village, NY*
BEST WESTERN ORITANI HOTEL
[MOT] *Hackensack, NJ*
BEST WESTERN SEAPORT INN
[MOT] *Manhattan, NY*
BEST WESTERN SOVEREIGN HOTEL-
ALBANY [MOT] *Albany, NY*
BEST WESTERN SUMMIT INN [MOT]
Niagara Falls, NY
BEST WESTERN UNIVERSITY INN
[MOT] *Canton, NY*
BEST WESTERN UNIVERSITY INN
[MOT] *Ithaca, NY*
BEST WESTERN WESTFIELD INN
[MOT] *Scotch Plains, NJ*
BEST WESTERN WOODWARD [MOT]
Manhattan, NY
BIRCH CREEK INN [BB] *Shandaken,
NY*
BIRD & BOTTLE, THE [BB] *Garrison,
NY*
BIRD'S NEST, THE [MOT] *Skaneateles,
NY*
BLACK MOUNTAIN SKI LODGE &
MOTEL [MOT] *North Creek, NY*
BLUSHING ROSE BED & BREAKFAST
[BB] *Hammondsport, NY*
BONNIE CASTLE HOTEL & RESORT
[RST] *Alexandria Bay (Thousand
Islands), NY*
BONNIE VIEW RESORT [RST] *Bolton
Landing (Lake George Area), NY*
BOX TREE [HOT] *Manhattan, NY*
BRAE LOCH INN [BB] *Cazenovia, NY*
BREAKERS HOTEL [HOT] *Spring Lake,
NJ*
BREWSTER INN [MOT] *Cazenovia, NY*
BRISTOL PLAZA RESORT [RST]
*Wildwood and Wildwood Crest,
NJ*
BROADWAY BED AND BREAKFAST
INN [BB] *Manhattan, NY*
BROMAN'S GENESEE FALLS INN [BB]
Letchworth State Park, NY
BROOKWOOD INN [HOT] *Rochester,
NY*
BROWN'S WELCOME INN HOTEL
[HOT] *Glens Falls, NY*
BRYANT PARK [HOT] *Manhattan, NY*
BUCCANEER MOTEL [MOT] *Clayton
(Thousand Islands), NY*
BUDGET HOST INN [MOT] *Riverhead
(L.I.), NY*
BURCLIFFE BY THE SEA [MOT]
Montauk (L.I.), NY
CABOOSE MOTEL [MOT] *Bath, NY*
CAESARS ATLANTIC CITY [CAS]
Atlantic City, NJ
CANANDAIGUA INN ON THE LAKE
[BB] *Canandaigua, NY*

CANDLELIGHT INN [BB] *Wildwood and Wildwood Crest, NJ*

CANOE ISLAND LODGE [RST] *Diamond Point, NY*

CAPE COD INN MOTEL [MOT] *Wildwood and Wildwood Crest, NJ*

CAPTAIN THOMSON'S RESORT ALEXANDRIA [MOT] *Alexandria Bay (Thousand Islands), NY*

CARIBBEAN MOTEL [MOT] *Wildwood and Wildwood Crest, NJ*

CARL'S RIP VAN WINKLE [MOT] *Catskill, NY*

CARLYLE, THE [HOT] *Manhattan, NY*

CARROLL VILLA HOTEL [RST] *Cape May, NJ*

CASABLANCA HOTEL [HOT] *Manhattan, NY*

CASTLE AT TARRYTOWN, THE [HOT] *Tarrytown, NY*

CASTLE INN [MOT] *Olean, NY*

CATHEDRAL FARMS COUNTRY INN [BB] *Oneonta, NY*

CATSKILL MOUNTAIN LODGE [MOT] *Catskill, NY*

CENTENNIAL HOUSE [HOT] *East Hampton (L.I.), NY*

CENTURY HOUSE HOTEL, THE [HOT] *Albany, NY*

CHAMBERS [HOT] *Manhattan, NY*

CHATEAU INN [BB] *Spring Lake, NJ*

CHATEAU MOTOR LODGE [MOT] *Niagara Falls, NY*

CHESTNUT INN AT OQUAGA LAKE [BB] *Deposit, NY*

CHIMNEY HILL FARM ESTATE [BB] *Lambertville, NJ*

CIRCLE COURT [MOT] *Ticonderoga (Lake George Area), NY*

CLARIDGE CASINO & HOTEL [CAS] *Atlantic City, NJ*

CLARION [MOT] *Atlantic City, NJ*

CLARION [MOT] *Cherry Hill, NJ*

CLARION HOTEL & TOWERS [HOT] *Edison, NJ*

CLARION HOTEL FIFTH AVENUE [HOT] *Manhattan, NY*

CLARION UNIVERSITY HOTEL & CONFERENCE CENTER [HOT] *Ithaca, NY*

CLARKSON INN, THE [HOT] *Potsdam, NY*

CLEARVIEW MOTEL & RESTAURANT [MOT] *Canton, NY*

COACHMAN MOTOR LODGE [MOT] *Elmira, NY*

COACHMAN'S MOTOR INN [MOT] *Cape May, NJ*

COLGATE INN [MOT] *Hamilton, NY*

COLONEL WILLIAMS MOTOR INN [MOT] *Lake George Village, NY*

COLONIAL MANOR [MOT] *Lake George Village, NY*

COLONIAL MOTEL [MOT] *Stamford, NY*

COLTS NECK INN HOTEL [MOT] *Freehold, NJ*

COLVMNS BY THE SEA BED & BREAKFAST [BB] *Cape May, NJ*

COMFORT INN [MOT] *Atlantic City, NJ*

COMFORT INN [MOT] *Binghamton, NY*

COMFORT INN [MOT] *Corning, NY*

COMFORT INN [MOT] *Cortland, NY*

COMFORT INN [MOT] *Hornell, NY*

COMFORT INN [MOT] *Jamestown, NY*

COMFORT INN [MOT] *Newburgh, NY*

COMFORT INN [MOT] *Saugerties, NY*

COMFORT INN [MOT] *Spring Lake, NJ*

COMFORT INN AND SUITES [MOT] *Albany, NY*

COMFORT INN FAIRGROUNDS [MOT] *Syracuse, NY*

COMFORT INN MANHATTAN [MOT] *Manhattan, NY*

COMFORT INN THE POINTE [MOT] *Niagara Falls, NY*

COMFORT INN WEST [MOT] *Rochester, NY*

COMFORT SUITES [MOT] *Buffalo, NY*

COMFORT SUITES [MOT] *Oneida, NY*

COOPERHOOD INN & SPA, THE [HOT] *Shandaken, NY*

CORNING DAYS INN [MOT] *Corning, NY*

COUNTRY CLUB MOTEL [MOT] *Old Forge, NY*

COUNTRY INN - WHEATON VILLAGE [MOT] *Millville, NJ*

COUNTRY MOTEL [MOT] *Utica, NY*

COURTYARD BY MARRIOTT [MOT] *Newark International Airport Area, NJ*

COURTYARD BY MARRIOTT [MOT] *Poughkeepsie, NY*

COURTYARD BY MARRIOTT [MOT] *Red Bank, NJ*

COURTYARD BY MARRIOTT [MOT] *Rochester, NY*

COURTYARD BY MARRIOTT [MOT] *Syracuse, NY*

COURTYARD BY MARRIOTT [MOT] *Tarrytown, NY*

COURTYARD BY MARRIOTT ALBANY AIRPORT [MOT] *Albany, NY*

COVEWOOD LODGE [CC] *Old Forge, NY*

CRESTHAVEN RESORT MOTEL LAKE GEORGE [RST] *Lake George Village, NY*

CROMWELL MANOR INN [BB] *West Point (US Military Academy), NY*

CROSSED KEYS INN [MOT] *Stanhope, NJ*

CROSSROADS RESTAURANT HOTEL [HOT] *Malone, NY*

CROWNE PLAZA [HOT] *Manhattan, NY*

CROWNE PLAZA [HOT] *Secaucus, NJ*

CROWNE PLAZA [HOT] *White Plains, NY*

CROWNE PLAZA AT THE UNITED NATIONS [HOT] *Manhattan, NY*

CROWNE PLAZA HOTEL [HOT] *Albany, NY*

CROWNE PLAZA LAGUARDIA [MOT] *Queens (La Guardia & JFK International Airport Areas), NY*

CROWNE PLAZA ROCHESTER [HOT] *Rochester, NY*

CROWN POINT BED & BREAKFAST [BB] *Crown Point, NY*

CRUSADER OCEAN FRONT RESORT [RST] *Wildwood and Wildwood Crest, NJ*

DANFORDS INN [BB] *Port Jefferson (L.I.), NY*

DAVIDSON'S MOTEL [MOT] *Watertown, NY*

DAVIS MOTEL AND COTTAGE [MOT] *Schroon Lake, NY*

DAYS HOTEL NEW YORK CITY [MOT] *Manhattan, NY*

DAYS INN [MOT] *Auburn, NY*

DAYS INN [MOT] *Batavia, NY*

DAYS INN [MOT] *Binghamton, NY*

DAYS INN [MOT] *Bordentown, NJ*

DAYS INN [MOT] *Cherry Hill, NJ*

DAYS INN [MOT] *Cherry Hill, NJ*

DAYS INN [MOT] *Geneseo, NY*

DAYS INN [MOT] *Lake Hopatcong, NJ*

DAYS INN [MOT] *Liberty, NY*

DAYS INN [MOT] *New Paltz, NY*

DAYS INN [MOT] *Oswego, NY*

DAYS INN [MOT] *Princeton, NJ*

DAYS INN [MOT] *Rochester, NY*

DAYS INN [MOT] *Schenectady, NY*

DAYS INN [MOT] *Somerville, NJ*

DAYS INN [MOT] *Watertown, NY*

DAYS INN AIRPORT [MOT] *Newark International Airport Area, NJ*

DAYS INN AT PLEASANTVILLE [MOT] *Atlantic City, NJ*

DAYS INN AT THE FALLS [MOT] *Niagara Falls, NY*

DAYS INN BATH [MOT] *Bath, NY*

DAYS INN BUFFALO AIRPORT [MOT] *Buffalo, NY*

DAYS INN DUNKIRK FREDONIA [MOT] *Dunkirk, NY*

DAYS INN LAKE GEORGE [MOT] *Lake George Village, NY*

DAYS INN OCEAN CITY [MOT] *Ocean City, NJ*

DAYS INN - PLATTSBURGH [MOT] *Plattsburgh, NY*

DERING HARBOR INN [MOT] *Shelter Island, NY*

DESERT SAND RESORT COMPLEX [MOT] *Stone Harbor, NJ*

DESMOND HOTEL & CONFERENCE CENTER [CONF] *Albany, NY*

DICKENSON HOUSE ON JAMES [BB] *Syracuse, NY*

DOCTORS INN, THE [BB] *Cape May Court House, NJ*

DOLCE TARRYTOWN HOUSE [HOT] *Tarrytown, NY*

DOOLAN'S [MOT] *Spring Lake, NJ*

DORAL ARROWWOOD CONFERENCE RESORT [CONF] *White Plains, NY*

DOUBLETREE GUEST SUITES [AS] *Manhattan, NY*

DOUBLETREE SOMERSET EXECUTIVE MEETING CENTER [HOT] *New Brunswick, NJ*

DOWNES MOTEL [MOT] *Cortland, NY*

DRAKE-SWISSOTEL, THE [HOT] *Manhattan, NY*

DRIFTWOOD [MOT] *Niagara Falls, NY*

DRIFTWOOD MOTEL & COTTAGES [MOT] *Montauk (L.I.), NY*

DUMONT PLAZA HOTEL [HOT] *Manhattan, NY*

DUNHAMS BAY LODGE [RST] *Lake George Village, NY*

DUTCHESS MOTEL [MOT] *Lake George Village, NY*

DYLAN [HOT] *Manhattan, NY*

EASTGATE TOWER [HOT] *Manhattan, NY*

EAST HAMPTON HOUSE [MOT] *East Hampton (L.I.), NY*

EAST NORWICH INN [MOT] *Oyster Bay (L.I.), NY*

EASTSIDE INN [MOT] *Manhattan, NY*

ECONO LODGE [MOT] *Albany, NY*

ECONO LODGE [MOT] *Elmira, NY*

ECONO LODGE [MOT] *Ithaca, NY*

ECONO LODGE [MOT] *Lake George Village, NY*

ECONO LODGE [MOT] *Lake Placid, NY*

ECONO LODGE [MOT] *Malone, NY*

ECONO LODGE [MOT] *Massena, NY*

ECONO LODGE [MOT] *Poughkeepsie, NY*

ECONO LODGE [MOT] *Rochester, NY*

ECONO LODGE [MOT] *Smithtown (L.I.), NY*

ECONO LODGE [MOT] *Syracuse, NY*

ECONO LODGE CANANDAIGUA [MOT] *Canandaigua, NY*

ECONO LODGE NIAGARA FALLS [MOT] *Niagara Falls, NY*

ECONO LODGE ROCHESTER [MOT] *Rochester, NY*

EDGEWOOD RESORT [RST] *Alexandria Bay (Thousand Islands), NY*

EGGERY COUNTRY INN [BB] *Hunter, NY*

EL CORONADO MOTOR INN [RST] *Wildwood and Wildwood Crest, NJ*

EMBASSY SUITES [AS] *Syracuse, NY*

EMBASSY SUITES HOTEL [AS] *New Brunswick, NJ*

EMBASSY SUITES SECAUCUS-MEADOWLANDS [AS] *Secaucus, NJ*

EMERSON INN AND SPA [BB] *Saugerties, NY*

EMPIRE [HOT] *Manhattan, NY*

ENGLESIDE INN, THE [MOT] *Long Beach Island, NJ*

ESSEX HOUSE - A WESTIN HOTEL [HOT] *Manhattan, NY*

EXECUTIVE INN [MOT] *Endicott, NY*

EXIT 45 [MOT] *Victor, NY*

FAIRFIELD INN [MOT] *Atlantic City, NJ*

FAIRFIELD INN [MOT] *Syracuse, NY*

FAIRFIELD INN [MOT] *Wayne, NJ*

FAIRFIELD INN MEADOWLANDS [MOT] *Rutherford, NJ*

FAIR WIND LODGE [RST] *Clayton (Thousand Islands), NY*

FITZPATRICK MANHATTAN HOTEL [HOT] *Manhattan, NY*

FLEUR DE LIS [MOT] *Wildwood and Wildwood Crest, NJ*

FLORAL PARK MOTOR LODGE [MOT] *Floral Park (L.I.), NY*

FORRESTAL AT PRINCETON HOTEL, THE [HOT] *Princeton, NJ*

FORT WILLIAM HENRY RESORT [RST] *Lake George Village, NY*

FORUM MOTOR INN [MOT] *Ocean City, NJ*

FOUNTAIN VIEW MOTEL [MOT] *Richfield Springs, NY*

FOUR POINTS BY SHERATON [MOT] *Dunkirk, NY*

FOUR POINTS BY SHERATON [MOT] *Lake Hopatcong, NJ*

FOUR POINTS BY SHERATON [MOT] *Niagara Falls, NY*

FOUR POINTS BY SHERATON [MOT] *Rochester, NY*

FOUR SEASONS HOTEL NEW YORK [HOT] *Manhattan, NY*

FOUR SEASONS MOTEL [MOT] *Malone, NY*

FOX INN [MOT] *Penn Yan, NY*

FRANKLIN [HOT] *Manhattan, NY*

FREEHOLD GARDENS HOTEL [HOT] *Freehold, NJ*

FRIAR TUCK RESORT AND CONVENTION CENTER [RST] *Catskill, NY*

FRIENDS LAKE INN [BB] *Warrensburg, NY*

GARDEN CITY HOTEL [HOT] *Garden City (L.I.), NY*

GARNET HILL LODGE [BB] *North Creek, NY*

GATE HOUSE MOTEL [MOT] *Corning, NY*

GAVIN'S GOLDEN HILL RESORT [RST] *Cairo, NY*

GENESEE COUNTRY INN [BB] *Rochester, NY*

GENESSEE INN EXECUTIVE QUARTERS [MOT] *Syracuse, NY*

GENEVA ON THE LAKE [HOT] *Geneva, NY*

GEORGIAN MOTEL [MOT] *Lake George Village, NY*

GERSHWIN [HOT] *Manhattan, NY*

GIDEON PUTNAM HOTEL, THE [HOT] *Saratoga Springs, NY*

GLEN IRIS INN [BB] *Letchworth State Park, NY*

GLEN SANDERS MANSION INN [BB] *Schenectady, NY*

GORHAM [HOT] *Manhattan, NY*

GRAND HOTEL [RST] *Cape May, NJ*

GRAND HYATT [HOT] *Manhattan, NY*

GRAND UNION MOTEL [MOT] *Saratoga Springs, NY*

GRAYCOURT MOTEL [MOT] *Glens Falls, NY*

GREEN GLEN BED & BREAKFAST [BB] *East Aurora, NY*

GREENVILLE ARMS 1889 INN [BB] *Cairo, NY*

GREENWOODS BED & BREAKFAST [BB] *Canandaigua, NY*

GREGORY HOUSE COUNTRY INN [MOT] *Albany, NY*

GUEST HOUSE, THE [BB] *Roscoe, NY*

GURNEY'S INN RESORT AND SPA [RST] *Montauk (L.I.), NY*

HAMILTON PARK CONFERENCE CENTER [CONF] *Morristown, NJ*

HAMMONDSPORT MOTEL [MOT] *Hammondsport, NY*
HAMPTON INN [MOT] *Buffalo, NY*
HAMPTON INN [MOT] *Cherry Hill, NJ*
HAMPTON INN [MOT] *Parsippany, NJ*
HAMPTON INN [MOT] *Smithtown (L.I.), NY*
HAMPTON INN ABSECON [MOT] *Atlantic City, NJ*
HAMPTON INN ALBANY-WOLF ROAD [MOT] *Albany, NY*
HAMPTON INN & SUITES [MOT] *Victor, NY*
HAMPTON INN BAYSIDE [MOT] *Atlantic City, NJ*
HAMPTON INN CARRIER CIRCLE [MOT] *Syracuse, NY*
HAMPTON INN LONG ISLAND [MOT] *Bay Shore (L.I.), NY*
HAMPTON INN ROCHESTER NORTH [MOT] *Rochester, NY*
HAMPTON INN SOUTH [MOT] *Rochester, NY*
HARRIS HOUSE [MOT] *Ocean City, NJ*
HAZLET HOTEL [HOT] *Matawan, NJ*
HEADQUARTERS PLAZA HOTEL [HOT] *Morristown, NJ*
HEADWATERS MOTOR LODGE [MOT] *Boonville, NY*
HEDGES INN [BB] *East Hampton (L.I.), NY*
HELMSLEY MIDDLETOWNE [HOT] *Manhattan, NY*
HELMSLEY PARK LANE HOTEL, THE [HOT] *Manhattan, NY*
HELMSLEY WINDSOR [HOT] *Manhattan, NY*
HEMLOCK HALL HOTEL [MOT] *Blue Mountain Lake, NY*
HERALD SQUARE [HOT] *Manhattan, NY*
HERITAGE OF LAKE GEORGE, THE [MOT] *Lake George Village, NY*
HERKIMER MOTEL [MOT] *Herkimer, NY*
HEWITT WELLINGTON HOTEL [HOT] *Spring Lake, NJ*
HICKORY GROVE MOTOR INN [MOT] *Cooperstown, NY*
HILTON [HOT] *Hackensack, NJ*
HILTON [HOT] *White Plains, NY*
HILTON AND TOWERS EAST BRUNSWICK [HOT] *New Brunswick, NJ*
HILTON CASINO RESORT [CAS] *Atlantic City, NJ*
HILTON FORT LEE [HOT] *Fort Lee, NJ*
HILTON HOTEL [HOT] *Cherry Hill, NJ*
HILTON HOTEL [HOT] *Huntington (L.I.), NY*
HILTON LAKE PLACID RESORT [RST] *Lake Placid, NY*

HILTON NEWARK AIRPORT [HOT] *Newark International Airport Area, NJ*
HILTON NEWARK GATEWAY [HOT] *Newark, NJ*
HILTON NEW YORK [HOT] *Manhattan, NY*
HILTON PARSIPPANY [HOT] *Parsippany, NJ*
HILTON PEARL RIVER [HOT] *Spring Valley, NY*
HILTON SHORT HILLS HOTEL & SPA [HOT] *Millburn, NJ*
HILTON TARRYTOWN [HOT] *Tarrytown, NY*
HILTON WOODBRIDGE [HOT] *Woodbridge, NJ*
HILTON WOODCLIFF LAKE [HOT] *Hillsdale, NJ*
HISTORIC GRAND ROYALE, THE [HOT] *Binghamton, NY*
HOBBIT HOLLOW BED & BREAKFAST [BB] *Skaneateles, NY*
HOLIDAY INN [MOT] *Auburn, NY*
HOLIDAY INN [MOT] *Binghamton, NY*
HOLIDAY INN [MOT] *Buffalo, NY*
HOLIDAY INN [MOT] *Cherry Hill, NJ*
HOLIDAY INN [MOT] *Eatontown, NJ*
HOLIDAY INN [MOT] *Fort Lee, NJ*
HOLIDAY INN [MOT] *Ithaca, NY*
HOLIDAY INN [MOT] *Jamestown, NY*
HOLIDAY INN [MOT] *Johnstown, NY*
HOLIDAY INN [MOT] *Kingston, NY*
HOLIDAY INN [MOT] *Newburgh, NY*
HOLIDAY INN [MOT] *Oneonta, NY*
HOLIDAY INN [MOT] *Plattsburgh, NY*
HOLIDAY INN [MOT] *Rochester, NY*
HOLIDAY INN [MOT] *Saddle Brook, NJ*
HOLIDAY INN [MOT] *Sayville (L.I.), NY*
HOLIDAY INN [MOT] *Schenectady, NY*
HOLIDAY INN [MOT] *Spring Valley, NY*
HOLIDAY INN [MOT] *Syracuse, NY*
HOLIDAY INN [MOT] *Toms River, NJ*
HOLIDAY INN [MOT] *Utica, NY*
HOLIDAY INN [MOT] *Waterloo, NY*
HOLIDAY INN [MOT] *Wayne, NJ*
HOLIDAY INN [MOT] *Yonkers, NY*
HOLIDAY INN ALBANY-TURFON WOLF ROAD [MOT] *Albany, NY*
HOLIDAY INN BOARDWALK [MOT] *Atlantic City, NJ*
HOLIDAY INN DOWNTOWN [MOT] *Manhattan, NY*
HOLIDAY INN ELMIRA RIVERVIEW [MOT] *Elmira, NY*

HOLIDAY INN EXPRESS [MOT]
  Poughkeepsie, NY
HOLIDAY INN GRAND ISLAND
  [MOT] *Niagara Falls, NY*
HOLIDAY INN JFK AIRPORT [MOT]
  *Queens (La Guardia & JFK
  International Airport Areas), NY*
HOLIDAY INN MONTVALE [MOT]
  Montvale, NJ
HOLIDAY INN MOUNT KISCO
  [MOT] *Mt Kisco, NY*
HOLIDAY INN NORTH [MOT]
  *Newark International Airport
  Area, NJ*
HOLIDAY INN PRINCETON [MOT]
  Princeton, NJ
HOLIDAY INN-SARATOGA SPRINGS
  [MOT] *Saratoga Springs, NY*
HOLIDAY INN-SECAUCUS
  MEADOWLANDS [MOT]
  Secaucus, NJ
HOLIDAY INN SELECT [MOT]
  Niagara Falls, NY
HOLIDAY INN SELECT BRIDGEPORT
  [MOT] *Gibbstown, NJ*
HOLIDAY INN SELECT OF CLINTON
  [MOT] *Clinton, NJ*
HOLIDAY INN SOMERSET [MOT]
  New Brunswick, NJ
HOLIDAY INN SOUTH PLAINFIELD
  [MOT] *Plainfield, NJ*
HOLIDAY INN
  SYRACUSE/LIVERPOOL [MOT]
  Syracuse, NY
HOLIDAY INN TOTOWA [MOT]
  Wayne, NJ
HOLIDAY INN TURF [RST] *Lake
  George Village, NY*
HOLLAND AMERICAN COUNTRY
  INN [MOT] *Bath, NY*
HORNELL ECONO LODGE [MOT]
  Hornell, NY
HOTEL BEACON [HOT] *Manhattan,
  NY*
HOTEL BEDFORD [HOT] *Manhattan,
  NY*
HOTEL BENTLEY 500 [HOT]
  Manhattan, NY
HOTEL DELMONICO [AS]
  Manhattan, NY
HOTEL EDISON [HOT] *Manhattan,
  NY*
HOTEL ELYSEE [HOT] *Manhattan, NY*
HOTEL GIRAFFE [HOT] *Manhattan,
  NY*
HOTEL PLAZA ATHENEE [HOT]
  Manhattan, NY
HOTEL SARANAC OF PAUL SMITH'S
  COLLEGE [HOT] *Saranac Lake,
  NY*

HOTEL THAYER [HOT] *West Point (US
  Military Academy), NY*
HOTEL VIENNA [MOT] *Windham, NY*
HOTEL WALES [HOT] *Manhattan, NY*
HOWARD JOHNSON [MOT] *Albany,
  NY*
HOWARD JOHNSON [MOT] *Newark
  International Airport Area, NJ*
HOWARD JOHNSON [MOT] *Wayne,
  NJ*
HOWARD JOHNSON EXPRESS INN
  [MOT] *Binghamton, NY*
HOWARD JOHNSON EXPRESS INN
  [MOT] *Parsippany, NJ*
HOWARD JOHNSON HOTEL [MOT]
  Niagara Falls, NY
HOWARD JOHNSON HOTEL [MOT]
  Norwich, NY
HOWARD JOHNSON HOTEL [MOT]
  Toms River, NJ
HOWARD JOHNSON INN [MOT]
  Clifton, NJ
HOWARD JOHNSON INN [MOT]
  Elmira, NY
HOWARD JOHNSON INN [MOT]
  Mount Holly, NJ
HOWARD JOHNSON INN [MOT]
  Newburgh, NY
HOWARD JOHNSON INN [MOT]
  Parsippany, NJ
HOWARD JOHNSON INN [MOT]
  Rockaway, NJ
HOWARD JOHNSON LODGE [MOT]
  Trenton, NJ
HOWARD JOHNSON PLAZA [MOT]
  Manhattan, NY
HOWARD JOHNSON RESORT HOTEL
  [RST] *Lake George Village, NY*
HOWARD JOHNSON RESORT INN
  [RST] *Lake Placid, NY*
HOWE CAVERNS MOTEL [MOT]
  Howes Cave, NY
HUDSON [HOT] *Manhattan, NY*
HUDSON HOUSE RIVER INN [BB]
  Garrison, NY
HUDSON VALLEY RESORT [RST]
  Ellenville, NY
HUNGRY TROUT MOTOR INN
  [HOT] *Wilmington, NY*
HUNTER INN [HOT] *Hunter, NY*
HUNTING INN [BB] *East Hampton
  (L.I.), NY*
HUNTINGTON COUNTRY INN
  HOTEL [HOT] *Huntington (L.I.),
  NY*
HYATT REGENCY [MOT] *New
  Brunswick, NJ*
HYATT REGENCY BUFFALO [HOT]
  Buffalo, NY
HYATT REGENCY PRINCETON
  [HOT] *Princeton, NJ*

HYATT REGENCY ROCHESTER [HOT] *Rochester, NY*

HY-LAND MOTOR INN [MOT] *Cape May Court House, NJ*

IMPALA ISLAND INN [MOT] *Ocean City, NJ*

IMPERIAL 500 MOTEL [MOT] *Wildwood and Wildwood Crest, NJ*

INN, THE [MOT] *Watertown, NY*

INN AT COOPERSTOWN [BB] *Cooperstown, NY*

INN AT GREAT NECK [HOT] *Great Neck (L.I.), NY*

INN AT HOUGHTON CREEK, THE [BB] *Arcade, NY*

INN AT IRVING PLACE [BB] *Manhattan, NY*

INN AT LAMBERTVILLE STATION [HOT] *Lambertville, NJ*

INN AT MEDFORD [MOT] *Sayville (L.I.), NY*

INN AT MILLRACE POND, THE [MOT] *Hackettstown, NJ*

INN AT SARATOGA [HOT] *Saratoga Springs, NY*

INN AT SILVER MAPLE FARM [BB] *Canaan, NY*

INN AT THE BEECHES [MOT] *Rome, NY*

INN AT THE FALLS [BB] *Poughkeepsie, NY*

INN AT THE SHORE [BB] *Spring Lake, NJ*

INN AT TURNING STONE [BB] *Oneida, NY*

INN OF CAPE MAY [BB] *Cape May, NJ*

INTER-CONTINENTAL CENTRAL PARK SOUTH NEW YORK [HOT] *Manhattan, NY*

INTER-CONTINENTAL THE BARCLAY NEW YORK [HOT] *Manhattan, NY*

INTERLAKEN LODGE & RESTAURANT [BB] *Lake Placid, NY*

IROQUOIS, THE [HOT] *Manhattan, NY*

ISLAND VIEW MOTEL [MOT] *Lake Luzerne, NY*

ISSAC HILLARD HOUSE B&B [BB] *Mount Holly, NJ*

IVANHOE MOTEL [MOT] *Wildwood and Wildwood Crest, NJ*

J. HARPER POOR COTTAGE [BB] *East Hampton (L.I.), NY*

JOHN MILTON INN [BB] *Syracuse, NY*

JOLLY HOTEL MADISON TOWERS [HOT] *Manhattan, NY*

JOLLY ROGER MOTEL [MOT] *Wildwood and Wildwood Crest, NJ*

JULIANA MOTEL [RST] *Diamond Point, NY*

JUST A PLANE BED & BREAKFAST [BB] *Letchworth State Park, NY*

KIMBERLY HOTEL [HOT] *Manhattan, NY*

KINGS INN [MOT] *Endicott, NY*

KITANO HOTEL, THE [HOT] *Manhattan, NY*

KNIGHTS INN [MOT] *Corning, NY*

KNIGHTS INN [MOT] *Fulton, NY*

KNIGHTS INN [MOT] *Syracuse, NY*

KNOTT'S MOTEL ON THE LAKE [MOT] *Oneonta, NY*

LA DUCHESSE ANNE [BB] *Woodstock, NY*

LAKE CREST MOTEL [MOT] *Lake George Village, NY*

LAKE FLOWER INN [MOT] *Saranac Lake, NY*

LAKE FRONT MOTEL & RESTAURANT [MOT] *Cooperstown, NY*

LAKE 'N PINES MOTEL [MOT] *Cooperstown, NY*

LAKE PLACID LODGE [HOT] *Lake Placid, NY*

LAKE PLACID RESORT HOLIDAY INN [RST] *Lake Placid, NY*

LAKE SIDE MOTEL [MOT] *Saranac Lake, NY*

LAKE VIEW MOTEL AND COTTAGES [MOT] *Cooperstown, NY*

LA MER MOTOR INN [MOT] *Cape May, NJ*

LAMPLIGHT INN BED & BREAKFAST [BB] *Lake Luzerne, NY*

LANDMARK MOTOR INN [MOT] *Glens Falls, NY*

LANZA'S COUNTRY INN [MOT] *Liberty, NY*

LA TOURELLE COUNTY INN [BB] *Ithaca, NY*

L'AUBERGE DES 4 SAISONS [MOT] *Shandaken, NY*

LEDGE ROCK AT WHITEFACE [MOT] *Wilmington, NY*

LEDGES RESORT MOTEL ALEXANDRIA BAY [MOT] *Alexandria Bay (Thousand Islands), NY*

LENHART HOTEL [HOT] *Bemus Point, NY*

LENOX HOTEL & SUITES [HOT] *Buffalo, NY*

LE PARKER MERIDIEN [HOT] *Manhattan, NY*

LE REFUGE INN [MOT] *Bronx, NY*

LEVOYAGEUR MOTEL [MOT] *Wildwood and Wildwood Crest, NJ*

LIBRARY [HOT] *Manhattan, NY*

LINCKLAEN HOUSE [MOT]
 Cazenovia, NY
LINDEN VALLEY [BB] Hillsdale, NY
LOCKPORT MOTEL [MOT] Lockport,
 NY
LOMBARDY, THE [HOT] Manhattan,
 NY
LONG LAKE MOTEL [MOT] Long
 Lake, NY
LORD AMHERST MOTOR HOTEL
 [HOT] Buffalo, NY
LOWELL, THE [HOT] Manhattan, NY
LUCERNE HOTEL, THE [HOT]
 Manhattan, NY
LYDEN GARDENS [HOT] Manhattan,
 NY
MADISON HOTEL [HOT] Morristown,
 NJ
MADISON SUITES HOTEL [MOT]
 New Brunswick, NJ
MADRID OCEAN RESORT [MOT]
 Wildwood and Wildwood Crest,
 NJ
MAIDSTONE ARMS [MOT] East
 Hampton (L.I.), NY
MAINSTAY [BB] Southampton (L.I.),
 NY
MAINSTAY INN [MOT] Cape May, NJ
MANSFIELD [HOT] Manhattan, NY
MANSION HILL INN [BB] Albany, NY
MARGARETVILLE MOUNTAIN INN
 BED & BREAKFAST [BB]
 Shandaken, NY
MARINERS COVE MOTOR INN
 [MOT] Spring Lake, NJ
MARK, NEW YORK, THE [HOT]
 Manhattan, NY
MARQUIS DE LAFAYETTE HOTEL
 [RST] Cape May, NJ
MARRIOTT ALBANY [HOT] Albany,
 NY
MARRIOTT AT
 GLENPOINTETEANECK [HOT]
 Hackensack, NJ
MARRIOTT BROOKLYN NEW YORK
 [HOT] Brooklyn, NY
MARRIOTT BUFFALO NIAGARA
 [HOT] Buffalo, NY
MARRIOTT EAST SIDE [HOT]
 Manhattan, NY
MARRIOTT HANOVER [HOT]
 Morristown, NJ
MARRIOTT HOTEL & CONFERENCE
 CENTER LONG ISLAND
 [HOT] Garden City (L.I.), NY
MARRIOTT ISLANDIA [HOT]
 Smithtown (L.I.), NY
MARRIOTT LAGUARDIA [HOT]
 Queens (La Guardia & JFK
 International Airport Areas), NY

MARRIOTT LONG ISLAND
 MELVILLE [HOT] Plainview
 (L.I.), NY
MARRIOTT NEWARK AIRPORT
 [HOT] Newark International
 Airport Area, NJ
MARRIOTT PARK RIDGE [HOT]
 Montvale, NJ
MARRIOTT PRINCETON FORRESTAL
 VILLAGE [HOT] Princeton, NJ
MARRIOTT RESORT SEAVIEW [RST]
 Atlantic City, NJ
MARRIOTT ROCHESTER AIRPORT
 [HOT] Rochester, NY
MARRIOTT SADDLE BROOK [HOT]
 Saddle Brook, NJ
MARRIOTT SOMERSET [HOT] New
 Brunswick, NJ
MARRIOTT WESTCHESTER [HOT]
 Tarrytown, NY
MAYFLOWER HOTEL ON THE PARK
 [HOT] Manhattan, NY
MCINTOSH INN [MOT] Cherry Hill,
 NJ
MCINTOSH INN OF EAST
 BRUNSWICK [MOT] New
 Brunswick, NJ
MELODY MANOR RESORT [RST]
 Bolton Landing (Lake George
 Area), NY
MERCER HOTEL [HOT] Manhattan,
 NY
METROPOLITAN HOTEL [HOT]
 Manhattan, NY
MICHELANGELO HOTEL, THE
 [HOT] Manhattan, NY
MICROTEL [MOT] Buffalo, NY
MICROTEL INN [MOT] Albany, NY
MILBURN [HOT] Manhattan, NY
MILFORD PLAZA [MOT] Manhattan,
 NY
MILLENIUM HOTEL NEW YORK
 BROADWAY [HOT] Manhattan,
 NY
MILLENNIUM NEW YORK UN
 PLAZA [HOT] Manhattan, NY
MILL GARTH COUNTRY INN [BB]
 Amagansett, NY
MILLHOUSE INN [BB] Canaan, NY
MIRBEAU INN & SPA [HOT]
 Skaneateles, NY
MIRROR LAKE INN RESORT AND
 SPA [RST] Lake Placid, NY
MOHAWK MOTEL AND COTTAGE
 [MOT] Lake George Village, NY
MOHICAN MOTEL [MOT] Lake
 George Village, NY
MOHONK MOUNTAIN HOUSE [RST]
 New Paltz, NY

MONTAUK YACHT CLUB RESORT AND MARINA [RST] *Montauk (L.I.), NY*

MONTREAL INN [MOT] *Cape May, NJ*

MORGANS [HOT] *Manhattan, NY*

MORGAN SAMUELS INN [BB] *Canandaigua, NY*

MOUNTAIN INN OF ROCKAWAY [MOT] *Rockaway, NJ*

MOUNTAIN VIEW [MOT] *Lake Placid, NY*

MOUNT VERNON MOTEL [MOT] *Cape May, NJ*

MUSE, THE [HOT] *Manhattan, NY*

NASSAU INN [HOT] *Princeton, NJ*

NASSAU INN [RST] *Wildwood and Wildwood Crest, NJ*

NEVELE GRANDE RESORT [RST] *Ellenville, NY*

NEW COMPASS MOTEL [MOT] *Wildwood and Wildwood Crest, NJ*

NEW PARROT MOTEL [MOT] *Watertown, NY*

NEW YORK HELMSLEY HOTEL [HOT] *Manhattan, NY*

NEW YORK MARRIOTT MARQUIS [HOT] *Manhattan, NY*

NEW YORK PALACE [HOT] *Manhattan, NY*

NEW YORK'S HOTEL PENNSYLVANIA [HOT] *Manhattan, NY*

NORDICK'S MOTEL [MOT] *Lake George Village, NY*

NORMANDY INN [BB] *Spring Lake, NJ*

NORTH STAR RESORT [RST] *Alexandria Bay (Thousand Islands), NY*

NORTHWARD HOTEL RESORT [RST] *Bolton Landing (Lake George Area), NY*

NORTHWAY MOTEL [MOT] *Lake Placid, NY*

NOVOTEL [HOT] *Princeton, NJ*

NOVOTEL MEADOWLANDS [HOT] *Rutherford, NJ*

NOVOTEL NEW YORK [HOT] *Manhattan, NY*

OCEAN HOLIDAY MOTOR INN [MOT] *Wildwood and Wildwood Crest, NJ*

OCEAN PLACE CONFERENCE RESORT [HOT] *Eatontown, NJ*

OCEANVIEW [MOT] *Wildwood and Wildwood Crest, NJ*

O'CONNOR'S RESORT COTTAGES [CC] *Lake George Village, NY*

OLD DROVERS INN [BB] *Poughkeepsie, NY*

OLD LIBRARY B & B [BB] *Olean, NY*

OLIVER LOUD'S INN [BB] *Rochester, NY*

OMNI BERKSHIRE PLACE [HOT] *Manhattan, NY*

ONTARIO PLACE HOTEL [HOT] *Sackets Harbor, NY*

ON THE AVE HOTEL [HOT] *Manhattan, NY*

OSWEGO [HOT] *Oswego, NY*

OWEGO TREADWAY INN [HOT] *Owego, NY*

PAN AMERICAN HOTEL [HOT] *Wildwood and Wildwood Crest, NJ*

PANORAMIC MOTEL AND APTS [MOT] *Wildwood and Wildwood Crest, NJ*

PANORAMIC VIEW [HOT] *Montauk (L.I.), NY*

PARAMOUNT [HOT] *Manhattan, NY*

PARK OAK MOTEL [HOT] *Batavia, NY*

PARKWAY MOTEL OF VESTAL [MOT] *Binghamton, NY*

PARSIPPANY HOLIDAY INN HOTEL & SUITES [MOT] *Parsippany, NJ*

PAVILION MOTOR LODGE [MOT] *Ocean City, NJ*

PEACOCK INN [BB] *Princeton, NJ*

PEEKSKILL INN [HOT] *Peekskill, NY*

PENINSULA, THE [HOT] *Manhattan, NY*

PERIWINKLE INN [MOT] *Cape May, NJ*

PICKWICK LODGE [MOT] *Cairo, NY*

PIER 4 HOTEL [HOT] *Ocean City, NJ*

PIERRE NEW YORK, THE [HOT] *Manhattan, NY*

PINE POINT COTTAGES & MOTEL [CC] *Lake Luzerne, NY*

PINE TERRACE MOTEL & RESORT [CC] *Tupper Lake, NY*

PINE TREE POINT RESORT [RST] *Alexandria Bay (Thousand Islands), NY*

PLACID BAY INN ON LAKE PLACID [BB] *Lake Placid, NY*

PLAZA, THE [HOT] *Manhattan, NY*

PLAZA FIFTY [HOT] *Manhattan, NY*

POINT, THE [BB] *Saranac Lake, NY*

POINT BEACH [MOT] *Spring Lake, NJ*

PORTAGE HOUSE [MOT] *Niagara Falls, NY*

PORT-O-CALL HOTEL [RST] *Ocean City, NJ*

PORT ROYAL HOTEL [HOT] *Wildwood and Wildwood Crest, NJ*

PRIDWIN HOTEL AND COTTAGES SHELTER ISLAND [MOT] *Shelter Island, NY*

QUALITY INN [MOT] *Rome, NY*

QUALITY INN [MOT] *Toms River, NJ*

QUALITY INN GRAN VIEW [MOT] *Ogdensburg (Thousand Islands), NY*
QUALITY INN JERSEY CITY [MOT] *Jersey City, NJ*
QUALITY INN MCGUIRE AFB [MOT] *Mount Holly, NJ*
QUALITY INN MEADOWLANDS [MOT] *Rutherford, NJ*
QUALITY INN NEWARK [MOT] *Palmyra, NY*
QUEENSBURY HOTEL [HOT] *Glens Falls, NY*
QUEEN'S HOTEL [HOT] *Cape May, NJ*
QUEEN VICTORIA B & B INN, THE [BB] *Cape May, NJ*
RADISSON [HOT] *Cherry Hill, NJ*
RADISSON [HOT] *Manhattan, NY*
RADISSON HOTEL [HOT] *Corning, NY*
RADISSON HOTEL [HOT] *Newark International Airport Area, NJ*
RADISSON HOTEL [HOT] *Utica, NY*
RADISSON HOTEL & SUITES-AIRPORT [HOT] *Buffalo, NY*
RADISSON HOTEL & SUITES [HOT] *Wayne, NJ*
RADISSON HOTEL ENGLEWOOD [HOT] *Fort Lee, NJ*
RADISSON HOTEL ROCHESTER [HOT] *Rochester, NY*
RADISSON INN PARAMUS [HOT] *Paramus, NJ*
RADISSON SUITES [HOT] *Buffalo, NY*
RADISSON SUITES-MEADOWLANDS [HOT] *Secaucus, NJ*
RAMADA EAST END [MOT] *Riverhead (L.I.), NY*
RAMADA INN [MOT] *Flemington, NJ*
RAMADA INN [MOT] *Kingston, NY*
RAMADA INN [MOT] *Lake Placid, NY*
RAMADA INN [MOT] *New Brunswick, NJ*
RAMADA INN [MOT] *Newburgh, NY*
RAMADA INN [MOT] *Ramsey, NJ*
RAMADA INN [MOT] *Saddle Brook, NJ*
RAMADA INN [MOT] *Syracuse, NY*
RAMADA INN [MOT] *Tarrytown, NY*
RAMADA INN [MOT] *Utica, NY*
RAMADA INN [MOT] *Watertown, NY*
RAMADA INN [MOT] *White Plains, NY*
RAMADA INN AIRPORT & CONFERENCE CENTER [MOT] *Ithaca, NY*
RAMADA INN & CONVENTION CENTER [MOT] *Schenectady, NY*
RAMADA INN AND SUITES [MOT] *Toms River, NJ*

RAMADA INN AT THE FALLS [MOT] *Niagara Falls, NY*
RAMADA INN BY THE FALLS [MOT] *Niagara Falls, NY*
RAMADA INN-CLIFTON [MOT] *Clifton, NJ*
RAMADA INN-EAST WINDSOR [MOT] *Hightstown, NJ*
RAMADA INN GLENS FALLS [MOT] *Glens Falls, NY*
RAMADA INN RIVER RESORT [MOT] *Ogdensburg (Thousand Islands), NY*
RAMADA INN ROCHESTER [MOT] *Rochester, NY*
RAMADA LIMITED [MOT] *Albany, NY*
RAMADA PLAZA HOTEL [MOT] *New Rochelle, NY*
RAM'S HEAD INN [BB] *Shelter Island, NY*
RED COACH INN, THE [BB] *Niagara Falls, NY*
RED RANCH [MOT] *Catskill, NY*
RED ROOF INN [MOT] *Buffalo, NY*
RED ROOF INN [MOT] *Eatontown, NJ*
RED ROOF INN [MOT] *Rochester, NY*
RED ROOF INN [MOT] *Syracuse, NY*
RED ROOF INN [MOT] *Utica, NY*
REDWOOD MOTOR LODGE [MOT] *Watertown, NY*
REGENCY HOTEL, THE [HOT] *Manhattan, NY*
REGENT WALL STREET, THE [HOT] *Manhattan, NY*
RENAISSANCE MEADOWLANDS HOTEL [HOT] *Rutherford, NJ*
RENAISSANCE NEW YORK TIMES SQUARE [HOT] *Manhattan, NY*
RENAISSANCE WESTCHESTER [HOT] *White Plains, NY*
RESIDENCE INN BY MARRIOTT [EX] *Buffalo, NY*
RESIDENCE INN BY MARRIOTT TINTON FALLS [EX] *Eatontown, NJ*
RESIDENCE INN BY MARRIOTT [EX] *Fishkill, NY*
RESIDENCE INN BY MARRIOTT [EX] *Ocean City, NJ*
RESIDENCE INN BY MARRIOTT [EX] *Rochester, NY*
RESIDENCE INN BY MARRIOTT [EX] *Syracuse, NY*
RESIDENCE INN PRINCETON [EX] *Princeton, NJ*
RESORTS ATLANTIC CITY [RST] *Atlantic City, NJ*
RIHGA ROYAL, JW MARRIOTT [HOT] *Manhattan, NY*
RITZ-CARLONT, BATTERY PARK, THE [HOT] *Manhattan, NY*

RITZ-CARLTON, NEW YORK, THE
[HOT] *Manhattan, NY*
RIVEREDGE RESORT HOTEL [RST]
*Alexandria Bay (Thousand
Islands), NY*
ROARING BROOK RANCH & TENNIS
RESORT [MOT] *Lake George
Village, NY*
ROCKING HORSE RANCH RESORT
[RST] *New Paltz, NY*
ROCK LEDGE MOTEL, COTTAGES &
EFFICIENCY [MOT] *Alexandria
Bay (Thousand Islands), NY*
RODEWAY INN [MOT] *Canajoharie,
NY*
ROGER WILLIAMS , THE [HOT]
Manhattan, NY
ROOSEVELT HOTEL [HOT]
Manhattan, NY
ROOSEVELT INN [MOT] *Hyde Park,
NY*
ROOSEVELT INN & SUITES [RST]
Saratoga Springs, NY
ROSCOE MOTEL [MOT] *Roscoe, NY*
ROSE INN [BB] *Ithaca, NY*
ROSEWOOD INN [BB] *Corning, NY*
ROSLYN CLAREMONT HOTEL [HOT]
Roslyn (L.I.), NY
ROYAL ATLANTIC BEACH RESORT
[MOT] *Montauk (L.I.), NY*
ROYAL HAWAIIAN BEACHFRONT
RESORT [RST] *Wildwood and
Wildwood Crest, NJ*
ROYALTON [HOT] *Manhattan, NY*
ROYCROFT INN [HOT] *East Aurora,
NY*
SAGAMORE, THE [RST] *Bolton
Landing (Lake George Area), NY*
ST. CHARLES [HOT] *Hudson, NY*
ST. ELMO ACCOMMODATIONS
[MOT] *Chautauqua, NY*
ST. REGIS, THE [HOT] *Manhattan, NY*
SALISBURY HOTEL [HOT] *Manhattan,
NY*
SAN CARLOS HOTEL [HOT]
Manhattan, NY
SANDPIPER INN, THE [BB] *Spring
Lake, NJ*
SANDPIPER MOTEL [MOT] *Long
Beach Island, NJ*
SANDS CASINO HOTEL [CAS]
Atlantic City, NJ
SANDS MOTEL [MOT] *Montauk (L.I.),
NY*
SANDY POINT [MOT] *Long Lake, NY*
SANTORINI'S BEACHCOMBER
RESORT MOTEL [MOT]
Southold (L.I.), NY
SARANAC INN GOLF & COUNTRY
CLUB [RST] *Saranac Lake, NY*
SARA PLACID MOTOR INN [MOT]
Saranac Lake, NY

SARATOGA ROSE [MOT] *Lake
Luzerne, NY*
SAXON INN [MOT] *Hornell, NY*
SCHULTE'S HOTEL [MOT] *Lake
Placid, NY*
SCOTT'S OQUAGA LAKE HOUSE
[RST] *Deposit, NY*
SCRIBNER HOLLOW LODGE [RST]
Hunter, NY
SEA CREST ON THE OCEAN [MOT]
Amagansett, NY
SERENDIPITY BED & BREAKFAST
[BB] *Ocean City, NJ*
SHAHEEN'S [MOT] *Tupper Lake, NY*
SHAMROCK [MOT] *Long Lake, NY*
SHELBURNE MURRAY HILL HOTEL
[HOT] *Manhattan, NY*
SHERATON [HOT] *Parsippany, NJ*
SHERATON ATLANTIC CITY
CONVENTION [HOT] *Atlantic
City, NJ*
SHERATON ATLANTIC CITY WEST
[HOT] *Atlantic City, NJ*
SHERATON AT WOODBRIDGE
PLACE [HOT] *Woodbridge, NJ*
SHERATON CIVIC CENTER [HOT]
Poughkeepsie, NY
SHERATON CROSSROADS HOTEL
[HOT] *Ramsey, NJ*
SHERATON EATONTOWN HOTEL &
CONFERENCE CENTER [HOT]
Eatontown, NJ
SHERATON EDISON HOTEL [HOT]
Edison, NJ
SHERATON JFK AIRPORT [HOT]
*Queens (La Guardia & JFK
International Airport Areas), NY*
SHERATON LAGUARDIA [HOT]
*Queens (La Guardia & JFK
International Airport Areas), NY*
SHERATON MANHATTAN [HOT]
Manhattan, NY
SHERATON MEADOWLANDS HOTEL
& CONFERENCE CENTER
[HOT] *Rutherford, NJ*
SHERATON NEWARK AIRPORT
[HOT] *Newark International
Airport Area, NJ*
SHERATON NEW YORK HOTEL AND
TOWERS [HOT] *Manhattan, NY*
SHERATON RUSSELL HOTEL [HOT]
Manhattan, NY
SHERATON SARATOGA SPRINGS
[HOT] *Saratoga Springs, NY*
SHERATON SMITHTOWN HOTEL
[HOT] *Smithtown (L.I.), NY*
SHERATON SUITES AT LINCOLN
HARBOR [HOT] *Secaucus, NJ*
SHERATON SYRACUSE UNIVERSITY
HOTEL & CONFERENCE
CENTER [HOT] *Syracuse, NY*

SHERWOOD INN [HOT] *Skaneateles, NY*

SHOREHAM HOTEL [HOT] *Manhattan, NY*

SHOWBOAT CASINO & HOTEL [CAS] *Atlantic City, NJ*

SIDNEY SUPER 8 MOTEL [MOT] *Bainbridge, NY*

SILVER SANDS MOTEL [MOT] *Greenport (L.I.), NY*

SIMMON'S WAY VILLAGE INN [BB] *Hillsdale, NY*

SMALLING MOTEL [MOT] *Potsdam, NY*

SOFITEL NEW YORK [HOT] *Manhattan, NY*

SOHO GRAND HOTEL [HOT] *Manhattan, NY*

SOMERSET HILLS HOTEL [HOT] *Bernardsville, NJ*

SOUND VIEW INN [MOT] *Greenport (L.I.), NY*

SOUTHAMPTON INN [MOT] *Southampton (L.I.), NY*

SOUTHERN MANSION, THE [BB] *Cape May, NJ*

SOUTHGATE TOWER SUITE HOTEL [HOT] *Manhattan, NY*

SOUTHSHORE MOTOR LODGE [MOT] *Dunkirk, NY*

SPRAY BEACH INN [RST] *Long Beach Island, NJ*

SPRINGSIDE INN [MOT] *Auburn, NY*

SPRINGS MOTEL [MOT] *Saratoga Springs, NY*

STANFORD HOTEL [HOT] *Manhattan, NY*

STANHOPE PARK HYATT HOTEL, THE [HOT] *Manhattan, NY*

STATLER HOTEL, THE [HOT] *Ithaca, NY*

STEWART HOUSE [BB] *Catskill, NY*

STEWART INN [BB] *Clinton, NJ*

STILES MOTEL [MOT] *Corning, NY*

STILLBAY RESORT [RST] *Lake George Village, NY*

STONEFENCE LODGING INC [RST] *Ogdensburg (Thousand Islands), NY*

STONEHELM LODGE [MOT] *Plattsburgh, NY*

STRATHALLAN HOTEL [AS] *Rochester, NY*

SUGARBUSH BED & BREAKFAST [BB] *Utica, NY*

SUN CASTLE MOTEL AND VILLAS [MOT] *Lake George Village, NY*

SUNRISE HILL INN [HOT] *Victor, NY*

SUNRISE MOTEL [MOT] *Owego, NY*

SUNSET BEACH [MOT] *Shelter Island, NY*

SUNSET MOTEL [MOT] *Greenport (L.I.), NY*

SUNSET PARK [MOT] *Tupper Lake, NY*

SUPER 8 [MOT] *Atlantic City, NJ*

SUPER 8 [MOT] *Buffalo, NY*

SUPER 8 [MOT] *Massena, NY*

SUPER 8 [MOT] *Norwich, NY*

SUPER 8 [MOT] *Oneonta, NY*

SUPER 8 [MOT] *Syracuse, NY*

SUPER 8 MOTEL [MOT] *Amsterdam, NY*

SUPER 8 MOTEL [MOT] *Auburn, NY*

SUPER 8 MOTEL [MOT] *Bath, NY*

SUPER 8 MOTEL [MOT] *Glens Falls, NY*

SUPER 8 MOTEL [MOT] *Hyde Park, NY*

SUPER 8 MOTEL [MOT] *Ithaca, NY*

SUPER 8 MOTEL [MOT] *Kingston, NY*

SUPER 8 MOTEL [MOT] *Middletown, NY*

SUPER 8 MOTEL [MOT] *Newburgh, NY*

SUPER 8 MOTEL [MOT] *Nyack, NY*

SUPER 8 MOTEL [MOT] *Oneida, NY*

SURREY HOTEL [HOT] *Manhattan, NY*

SUSSE CHALET INN [MOT] *Spring Valley, NY*

SUSSE CHALET INN [MOT] *Troy, NY*

SUTHERLAND HOUSE BED & BREAKFAST [BB] *Canandaigua, NY*

SWISS HUTTE [RST] *Hillsdale, NY*

TALL PINES MOTEL [MOT] *Lake George Village, NY*

THREE VILLAGE INN [MOT] *Stony Brook (L.I.), NY*

THRIFTLODGE AMERICANA [MOT] *Niagara Falls, NY*

TOWN & COUNTRY MOTOR INN [MOT] *Lake Placid, NY*

TRAVELODGE [MOT] *Newark International Airport Area, NJ*

TRAVELODGE [MOT] *Spring Lake, NJ*

TRAVELODGE FALLS VIEW [MOT] *Niagara Falls, NY*

TREASURE COVE RESORT MOTEL [MOT] *Diamond Point, NY*

TRIBECA GRAND [HOT] *Manhattan, NY*

TROPICANA CASINO & RESORT [CAS] *Atlantic City, NJ*

TROUTBECK INN [BB] *Poughkeepsie, NY*

TROUT HOUSE VILLAGE RESORT [RST] *Hague, NY*

TRUMP INTERNATIONAL HOTEL & TOWER [HOT] *Manhattan, NY*

TRUMP MARINA HOTEL & CASINO [CAS] *Atlantic City, NJ*

TRUMP PLAZA HOTEL & CASINO [CAS] *Atlantic City, NJ*

TRUMP TAJ MAHAL CASINO RESORT [CAS] *Atlantic City, NJ*

TUPPER LAKE MOTEL [MOT] *Tupper Lake, NY*

TWIN GABLES OF WOODSTOCK [BB] *Woodstock, NY*

VAGABOND INN, THE [MOT] *Naples, NY*

VICTORIAN B&B, THE [BB] *Rochester, NY*

VICTORIAN LACE INN [BB] *Cape May, NJ*

VICTORIAN MANOR HOTEL, THE [MOT] *Buffalo, NY*

VICTORIAN VILLAGE RESORT MOTEL [MOT] *Bolton Landing (Lake George Area), NY*

VIKING RESORT [RST] *Penn Yan, NY*

VILLAGE HAVEN MOTEL [BB] *Buffalo, NY*

VILLAGE INN OF RHINEBECK [MOT] *Rhinebeck, NY*

VILLAGE MOTEL [MOT] *Richfield Springs, NY*

VIRGINIA HOTEL [HOT] *Cape May, NJ*

WADING RIVER [MOT] *Riverhead (L.I.), NY*

WALDORF-ASTORIA [HOT] *Manhattan, NY*

WARWICK NEW YORK, THE [HOT] *Manhattan, NY*

WATERTOWN ECONO LODGE [MOT] *Watertown, NY*

WAVE CREST RESORT [MOT] *Montauk (L.I.), NY*

WAYNE VILLA MOTEL [MOT] *Palmyra, NY*

WEBBS YEAR ROUND LAKE RESORT [RST] *Chautauqua, NY*

WEDGEWOOD INN [MOT] *Potsdam, NY*

WELLESLEY INN [MOT] *Matawan, NJ*

WELLESLEY INN [HOT] *Ramsey, NJ*

WELLESLEY INN [HOT] *Rochester, NY*

WELLESLEY INN [HOT] *Rochester, NY*

WELLESLEY INN [HOT] *Spring Valley, NY*

WELLSLEY INN [HOT] *Fishkill, NY*

WESTCHESTER HOUSE BED & BREAKFAST [BB] *Saratoga Springs, NY*

WESTIN [HOT] *Morristown, NJ*

WEST WINDS MOTEL & COTTAGES [MOT] *Clayton (Thousand Islands), NY*

WHITEFACE CHALET [BB] *Wilmington, NY*

WHITE INN [BB] *Dunkirk, NY*

WHITE LILAC INN [MOT] *Spring Lake, NJ*

W HOTEL - UNION SQUARE [HOT] *Manhattan, NY*

WILD DUNES INN [AS] *Ocean City, NJ*

WILDWOOD ON THE LAKE [MOT] *Lake Placid, NY*

WILLIAM SEWARD INN [MOT] *Chautauqua, NY*

WINDHAM ARMS HOTEL [HOT] *Windham, NY*

WINDJAMMER MOTEL [MOT] *Ogdensburg (Thousand Islands), NY*

WINDJAMMER MOTOR INN [MOT] *Seaside Park, NJ*

WINTER CLOVE INN ROUND TOP [MOT] *Cairo, NY*

W NEW YORK [HOT] *Manhattan, NY*

W NEW YORK COURT [HOT] *Manhattan, NY*

WOLFFIS MAPLE BREEZE RESORT [RST] *Catskill, NY*

WOODEN DUCK B & B, THE [BB] *Stanhope, NJ*

WOOLVERTON INN [MOT] *Lambertville, NJ*

WYNDHAM HOTEL [HOT] *Manhattan, NY*

WYNDHAM SYRACUSE [HOT] *Syracuse, NY*

RESTAURANT LIST

Establishment names are listed in alphabetical order followed by a symbol identifying their classification and then city and state. The symbols for classification are: [RES] for Restaurants and [URD] for Unrated Dining Spots.

21 CLUB [RES] *Manhattan, NY*
25 EAST AMERICAN BISTRO [RES] *Port Jefferson (L.I.), NY*
2 ALBANY [RES] *New Brunswick, NJ*
2ND AVENUE DELI [URD] *Manhattan, NY*
410 BANK STREET [RES] *Cape May, NJ*
540 PARK [RES] *Manhattan, NY*
56TH FIGHTER GROUP [RES] *Bethpage (L.I.), NY*
95 SCHOOL STREET [RES] *Southampton (L.I.), NY*
ABEL CONKLIN'S [RES] *Huntington (L.I.), NY*
ABIS JAPANESE RESTAURANT [RES] *Mamaroneck, NY*
ADMIRALS' INN [RES] *Alexandria Bay (Thousand Islands), NY*
AFTON [RES] *Livingston, NJ*
AKBAR [RES] *Garden City (L.I.), NY*
ALAIN DUCASSE [RES] *Manhattan, NY*
ALCHEMIST AND BARRISTER [RES] *Princeton, NJ*
ALEATHEA'S [RES] *Cape May, NJ*
ALEXANDER'S INN [RES] *Cape May, NJ*
ALLYN'S [RES] *Poughkeepsie, NY*
ALPS CHALET [RES] *Niagara Falls, NY*
ALVA [RES] *Manhattan, NY*
AMATO'S [RES] *Amityville (L.I.), NY*
AMBASSADOR GRILL [RES] *Manhattan, NY*
AMERICAN BOUNTY [URD] *Hyde Park, NY*
AMERICAN HOTEL [RES] *Sag Harbor (L.I.), NY*
AMERICAN PARK AT THE BATTERY [RES] *Manhattan, NY*
AN AMERICAN PLACE [RES] *Manhattan, NY*
ANGELINA CENTINI'S [RES] *Ithaca, NY*
ANGELOS AND MAXIE'S STEAKHOUSE [RES] *Manhattan, NY*
ANNEX [RES] *Princeton, NJ*
ANNISA [RES] *Manhattan, NY*
ANTHONY'S [RES] *Plattsburgh, NY*

ANTONIA'S [RES] *New Brunswick, NJ*
ANTON'S AT THE SWAN [RES] *Lambertville, NJ*
A.P. SMITH [RES] *Saranac Lake, NY*
AQUAGRILL [RES] *Manhattan, NY*
AQUAVIT [RES] *Manhattan, NY*
ARCH [RES] *Brewster, NY*
ARGO [RES] *Binghamton, NY*
ARQUA [RES] *Manhattan, NY*
ARTOS [RES] *Manhattan, NY*
ARTUROS ITALIAN RESTAURANT [RES] *Floral Park (L.I.), NY*
ASA RANSOM HOUSE [RES] *Buffalo, NY*
ATHENAEUM [RES] *Chautauqua, NY*
ATLAS [RES] *Manhattan, NY*
AUBERGE ARGENTEUIL [RES] *Hartsdale, NY*
AUBERGE MAXIME [RES] *Brewster, NY*
AUBERGINE [RES] *Hillsdale, NY*
AUREOLE [RES] *Manhattan, NY*
AVERIL CONWELL DINING ROOM [RES] *Lake Placid, NY*
BABBO [RES] *Manhattan, NY*
BAHR'S RESTAURANT & MARINA [RES] *Gateway National Recreation Area (Sandy Hook Unit), NJ*
BAJA MEXICAN CUISINE [RES] *Hoboken, NJ*
BALTHAZAR [RES] *Manhattan, NY*
BALUCHI'S [RES] *Manhattan, NY*
BANGKOK [RES] *Rochester, NY*
BANTA'S STEAK & STEIN [RES] *Newburgh, NY*
BANTA'S STEAK & STEIN [RES] *Poughkeepsie, NY*
BARAONDA [RES] *Manhattan, NY*
BARBETTA [RES] *Manhattan, NY*
BARNEY'S RESTAURANT [RES] *Glen Cove (L.I.), NY*
BAROLO [RES] *Manhattan, NY*
BASILICO [RES] *Southampton (L.I.), NY*
BAYARD'S [RES] *Manhattan, NY*
BEAR CAFE [RES] *Woodstock, NY*
BEAU RIVAGE [RES] *Mount Holly, NJ*
BECCO [RES] *Manhattan, NY*

BEECHES, THE [RES] *Rome, NY*
BEEF 'N BARREL [RES] *Olean, NY*
BEEKMAN 1766 TAVERN [RES] *Rhinebeck, NY*
BELHURST CASTLE [RES] *Geneva, NY*
BELLEVIE [RES] *Manhattan, NY*
BELLPORT [RES] *Sayville (L.I.), NY*
BELLPORT CHOWDER HOUSE [RES] *Sayville (L.I.), NY*
BELLUNO [RES] *Manhattan, NY*
BEN BENSON'S [RES] *Manhattan, NY*
BEN CONGER INN [RES] *Cortland, NY*
BENNY'S [RES] *Westbury (L.I.), NY*
BENNY'S STEAK HOUSE [RES] *Watertown, NY*
BERNARDS INN, THE [RES] *Bernardsville, NJ*
BEVANDA RISTORANTE [RES] *Great Neck (L.I.), NY*
BICE [RES] *Manhattan, NY*
BIRD & BOTTLE INN [RES] *Garrison, NY*
BISTRO DU NORD [RES] *Manhattan, NY*
BLACK FOREST INN, THE [RES] *Stanhope, NJ*
BLUE RIBBON [RES] *Manhattan, NY*
BOATHOUSE CAFE [RES] *Manhattan, NY*
BOB & RUTH'S VINEYARD [RES] *Naples, NY*
BOBBY VAN'S [RES] *Southampton (L.I.), NY*
BOLO [RES] *Manhattan, NY*
BONGIORNO'S [RES] *Albany, NY*
BONNIE CASTLE MANOR [RES] *Alexandria Bay (Thousand Islands), NY*
BONWIT INN [RES] *Smithtown (L.I.), NY*
BOOM [RES] *Manhattan, NY*
BOOMERS [RES] *Corning, NY*
BOX TREE [RES] *Manhattan, NY*
BRADDOCK'S TAVERN [RES] *Mount Holly, NJ*
BRAE LOCH INN [RES] *Cazenovia, NY*
BRASSERIE [RES] *Manhattan, NY*
BRASSERIE 8 ½ [RES] *Manhattan, NY*
BREWSTER INN [RES] *Cazenovia, NY*
BRIGHTON STEAKHOUSE [RES] *Atlantic City, NJ*
BROMAN'S GENESEE FALLS INN [RES] *Letchworth State Park, NY*
BROOKLAWN DINER [RES] *Cherry Hill, NJ*
BROOKLYN DINER USA [RES] *Manhattan, NY*
BROOKLYN PICKLE [URD] *Syracuse, NY*
BRUZELL'S [RES] *Great Neck (L.I.), NY*
BRYANT & COOPER STEAK HOUSE [RES] *Roslyn (L.I.), NY*

BRYANT PARK GRILL [RES] *Manhattan, NY*
BUCKALEW'S [RES] *Long Beach Island, NJ*
BULL AND BEAR STEAKHOUSE [RES] *Manhattan, NY*
BULLS HEAD INN [RES] *Howes Cave, NY*
BUON GIORNO [RES] *Rockville Centre (L.I.), NY*
BUTTONWOOD MANOR [RES] *Matawan, NJ*
CAFE BACI [RES] *Westbury (L.I.), NY*
CAFE BOULUD [RES] *Manhattan, NY*
CAFE DE BRUXELLES [RES] *Manhattan, NY*
CAFE DES ARTISTES [RES] *Manhattan, NY*
CAFE GALLERY [RES] *Burlington, NJ*
CAFE GIRASOLE [RES] *Oyster Bay (L.I.), NY*
CAFE LOUP [RES] *Manhattan, NY*
CAFE LUXEMBOURG [RES] *Manhattan, NY*
CAFE MICHELINA [RES] *Hoboken, NJ*
CAFE NOSIDAM [RES] *Manhattan, NY*
CAFE PANACHE [RES] *Ramsey, NJ*
CAFE SPASSO [RES] *Westbury (L.I.), NY*
CAFE TAMAYO [RES] *Saugerties, NY*
CAFE TREVI [RES] *Manhattan, NY*
CAFFE BONDI [RES] *Manhattan, NY*
CAFFE LA BELLA [RES] *Cherry Hill, NJ*
CAL'S [RES] *Manhattan, NY*
CAMPAGNA [RES] *Manhattan, NY*
CANAL SIDE INN [RES] *Herkimer, NY*
CANTERBURY ALES OYSTER BAR & GRILL [RES] *Oyster Bay (L.I.), NY*
CANTERBURY BROOK INN [RES] *West Point (US Military Academy), NY*
CAPE HOUSE [RES] *Troy, NY*
CAPRICCIO [RES] *Jericho (L.I.), NY*
CAPSOUTO FRERES [RES] *Manhattan, NY*
CAPTAIN'S INN [RES] *Forked River, NJ*
CAPTAIN'S TABLE [RES] *Wildwood and Wildwood Crest, NJ*
CAPTAIN YOUNG'S SEAFOOD EMPORIUM [RES] *Atlantic City, NJ*
CARAVELA [RES] *Tarrytown, NY*
CARMINE'S [RES] *Manhattan, NY*
CARNEGIE DELI [URD] *Manhattan, NY*
CARTWRIGHT INN [RES] *Rochester, NY*
CASA BASSO [RES] *Westhampton Beach, NY*
CASA MIA [RES] *Middletown, NY*

CASTEL GRISCH [RES] *Watkins Glen, NY*
CASTELLANO [RES] *Manhattan, NY*
CATAMOUNT CAFE [RES] *Shandaken, NY*
CATHEDRAL FARMS RESTAURANT [RES] *Oneonta, NY*
CATSKILL ROSE [RES] *Woodstock, NY*
CAVALLARIO'S STEAK & SEAFOOD HOUSE [RES] *Alexandria Bay (Thousand Islands), NY*
CELLO [RES] *Manhattan, NY*
CHANTERELLE FRENCH RESTAURANT [RES] *Manhattan, NY*
CHARLEY'S OTHER BROTHER [RES] *Mount Holly, NJ*
CHARLIE BROWN'S [RES] *Edison, NJ*
CHATEAU BELLEVIEW [RES] *Hunter, NY*
CHEF ANTONIO [RES] *Mamaroneck, NY*
CHEF VOLA'S [RES] *Atlantic City, NJ*
CHELSEA BISTRO AND BAR [RES] *Manhattan, NY*
CHEQUIT INN [RES] *Shelter Island, NY*
CHEZ MICHALLET [RES] *Manhattan, NY*
CHEZ NAPOLEON [RES] *Manhattan, NY*
CHEZ PIERRE [RES] *Saratoga Springs, NY*
CHICAMA [RES] *Manhattan, NY*
CHOWDER POT PUB [RES] *Greenport (L.I.), NY*
CHRISTER'S [RES] *Manhattan, NY*
CHRISTOPHER'S [RES] *Oneonta, NY*
CHRISTOS [RES] *Poughkeepsie, NY*
CHURRASCARIA PLATAFORMA [RES] *Manhattan, NY*
CHURRASQUEIRA BAIRRADA [RES] *Hempstead (L.I.), NY*
CIBO [RES] *Manhattan, NY*
CIRO'S [RES] *Lake Luzerne, NY*
CITE [RES] *Manhattan, NY*
CLARKSON HOUSE [RES] *Niagara Falls, NY*
CLASSICO [RES] *Roslyn (L.I.), NY*
CLAUDIO'S [RES] *Greenport (L.I.), NY*
CLINTON HOUSE [RES] *Clinton, NJ*
CLIPPER INN [RES] *Clayton (Thousand Islands), NY*
COAST GRILL [RES] *Southampton (L.I.), NY*
COCO PAZZO [RES] *Manhattan, NY*
COLEMAN'S [RES] *Syracuse, NY*
COMFORT DINER [RES] *Manhattan, NY*
COMO [RES] *Niagara Falls, NY*
CORNUCOPIA [RES] *Port Jervis, NY*

COSIMO'S ON UNION [RES] *Newburgh, NY*
COUNTRY HOUSE [RES] *Stony Brook (L.I.), NY*
COYOTE GRILL [RES] *Rockville Centre (L.I.), NY*
CRAB TRAP [RES] *Ocean City, NJ*
CRABTREE'S [RES] *Floral Park (L.I.), NY*
CRABTREE'S KITTLE HOUSE [RES] *Mt Kisco, NY*
CRAFT [RES] *Manhattan, NY*
CRANBERRY BOG [RES] *Albany, NY*
CRYSTAL BAY [RES] *Peekskill, NY*
CUB ROOM [RES] *Manhattan, NY*
CUCINA [RES] *Brooklyn, NY*
CUCINA & CO. [URD] *Manhattan, NY*
DAFFODIL'S [RES] *Buffalo, NY*
DAKOTAS [RES] *Albany, NY*
DANIEL [RES] *Manhattan, NY*
DANO'S ON CAYUGA [RES] *Ithaca, NY*
DANUBE [RES] *Manhattan, NY*
DA SILVANO [RES] *Manhattan, NY*
DA UMBERTO [RES] *Manhattan, NY*
DAVE'S GRILL [RES] *Montauk (L.I.), NY*
DAWAT [RES] *Manhattan, NY*
DAWAT [RES] *White Plains, NY*
DB BISTRO MODERNE [RES] *Manhattan, NY*
DEAUVILLE INN [RES] *Ocean City, NJ*
DE FINO'S HERITAGE INN [RES] *Lake Luzerne, NY*
DELEGATES DINING ROOM [RES] *Manhattan, NY*
DELTA'S [RES] *New Brunswick, NJ*
DIAMONDS [RES] *Trenton, NJ*
DINING ROOM, THE [RES] *Millburn, NJ*
DINING ROOM, THE [RES] *Skaneateles, NY*
DINOSAUR BAR-B-QUE [RES] *Rochester, NY*
DIWAN [RES] *Port Washington (L.I.), NY*
DOCKSIDE [RES] *Port Jefferson (L.I.), NY*
DOCK'S OYSTER HOUSE [RES] *Atlantic City, NJ*
DORA'S [RES] *Westhampton Beach, NY*
DORIS & ED'S [RES] *Gateway National Recreation Area (Sandy Hook Unit), NJ*
DOUG'S FISH FRY [RES] *Skaneateles, NY*
DUANE PARK CAFE [RES] *Manhattan, NY*
EAST HAMPTON POINT [RES] *East Hampton (L.I.), NY*

EASY STREET CAFE [RES] *Hyde Park, NY*
EBBITT ROOM [RES] *Cape May, NJ*
ELEPHANT AND CASTLE [URD] *Manhattan, NY*
ELEVEN MADISON PARK [RES] *Manhattan, NY*
EL TEDDY'S [RES] *Manhattan, NY*
EMBERS [RES] *Brooklyn, NY*
EMILE'S [RES] *Geneva, NY*
EMILIA'S [RES] *Bronx, NY*
EMPIRE DINER [URD] *Manhattan, NY*
EQUUS [RES] *Tarrytown, NY*
ESCOFFIER, THE [URD] *Hyde Park, NY*
ESTIATORIO MILOS [RES] *Manhattan, NY*
FAMILY TREE TAVERN [RES] *Spring Lake, NJ*
FARMHOUSE [RES] *Oneonta, NY*
FELIDIA [RES] *Manhattan, NY*
FERNWOOD [RES] *Catskill, NY*
FIFTY SEVEN FIFTY SEVEN [RES] *Manhattan, NY*
FIORELLO'S ROMAN CAFE [RES] *Manhattan, NY*
FIREBIRD [RES] *Manhattan, NY*
FIRST [RES] *Manhattan, NY*
FLEUR DE SEL [RES] *Manhattan, NY*
FLO-JEAN [RES] *Port Jervis, NY*
FLORENT [URD] *Manhattan, NY*
FORSGATE COUNTRY CLUB [RES] *Hightstown, NJ*
FOUR SEASONS RESTAURANT, THE [RES] *Manhattan, NY*
FOX HOLLOW [RES] *Huntington (L.I.), NY*
FRANKLIN STREET GRILLE [RES] *Watkins Glen, NY*
FRANK'S STEAKS [RES] *Jericho (L.I.), NY*
FREDERICK'S [RES] *Huntington (L.I.), NY*
FRESCOS [RES] *Cape May, NJ*
FRIENDS LAKE INN [RES] *Warrensburg, NY*
FROG AND THE PEACH, THE [RES] *New Brunswick, NJ*
FROMAGERIE [RES] *Red Bank, NJ*
GABRIELLA'S ON THE SQUARE [RES] *Cooperstown, NY*
GABRIEL'S [RES] *Manhattan, NY*
GALLAGHER'S [RES] *Manhattan, NY*
GARFIELD'S GIARDINO RISTORANTE [RES] *Wildwood and Wildwood Crest, NJ*
GARLOCK'S [RES] *Lockport, NY*
GASCOGNE [RES] *Manhattan, NY*
GASHO OF JAPAN [RES] *Hawthorne, NY*
GAULIN'S [RES] *Tarrytown, NY*

GEORGE MARTIN [RES] *Rockville Centre (L.I.), NY*
GEORGE WASHINGTON MANOR [RES] *Roslyn (L.I.), NY*
GIANDO ON THE WATER [RES] *Brooklyn, NY*
GIGINO TRATTORIA [RES] *Manhattan, NY*
GIRAFE [RES] *Bernardsville, NJ*
GIULIO CESARE [RES] *Westbury (L.I.), NY*
GLEN IRIS INN [RES] *Letchworth State Park, NY*
GLEN LOCH MILL [RES] *Syracuse, NY*
GLEN SANDERS MANSION [RES] *Schenectady, NY*
GOLDEN BELL DINER [RES] *Freehold, NJ*
GOLDEN EAGLE DINER [RES] *Cherry Hill, NJ*
GOLDEN PEAR [URD] *Southampton (L.I.), NY*
GOOD TIME CHARLEY'S [RES] *Princeton, NJ*
GORDON'S [RES] *Amagansett, NY*
GOSMAN'S [RES] *Montauk (L.I.), NY*
GOTHAM BAR AND GRILL [RES] *Manhattan, NY*
GRABELS RESTAURANT LOUNGE [RES] *Atlantic City, NJ*
GRAMERCY TAVERN [RES] *Manhattan, NY*
GREENHOUSE CAFE [RES] *Brooklyn, NY*
GREGORY HOUSE [RES] *Albany, NY*
GREGORY'S [RES] *Ocean City, NJ*
GRILL AT STRATHALLAN, THE [RES] *Rochester, NY*
GRIMALDI'S [RES] *Hoboken, NJ*
HANDS INN [RES] *Norwich, NY*
HARBOUR LIGHTS [RES] *Manhattan, NY*
HARLEY-DAVIDSON CAFE [URD] *Manhattan, NY*
HARLEY DAWN DINER [RES] *Atlantic City, NJ*
HARMONY PALACE [RES] *Manhattan, NY*
HARRALDS [RES] *Fishkill, NY*
HARRY CIPRIRANI'S [RES] *Manhattan, NY*
HARVEST [RES] *Montauk (L.I.), NY*
HARVEST MOON INN [RES] *Flemington, NJ*
HASAKI [RES] *Manhattan, NY*
HEAT WAVE CAFE [RES] *Spring Lake, NJ*
HEIDI'S BRAUHAUS [RES] *Mahopac, NY*
HELENA'S [RES] *Manhattan, NY*
HIGHLAWN PAVILION [RES] *West Orange, NJ*

HILL TOP INN [RES] *Elmira, NY*
HOLLOWAY HOUSE [RES]
    Canandaigua, NY
HOME [RES] *Manhattan, NY*
HONMURA AN [RES] *Manhattan, NY*
HOOK, LINE & SINKER [RES] *Utica,
    NY*
HORNED DORSET [RES] *Utica, NY*
HOT BISCUIT DINER [RES]
    *Ticonderoga (Lake George Area),
    NY*
HOUSE OF PETILLO [RES] *Jamestown,
    NY*
HUDSON HOUSE [RES] *Garrison, NY*
HUDSON'S RIBS & FISH [RES] *Fishkill,
    NY*
HULBERT HOUSE [RES] *Boonville, NY*
ICHI RIKI [RES] *Nyack, NY*
ICHI RIKI [RES] *Tarrytown, NY*
IL CAPPUCINO [RES] *Sag Harbor
    (L.I.), NY*
IL CORTILE [RES] *Manhattan, NY*
IL NIDO [RES] *Manhattan, NY*
IL TOSCANO [RES] *Queens (La
    Guardia & JFK International
    Airport Areas), NY*
INN AT OSBORNE HILL [RES] *Fishkill,
    NY*
INN AT POUND RIDGE [RES] *Pound
    Ridge, NY*
INN BETWEEN [RES] *Syracuse, NY*
INN ON THE HARBOR [RES]
    Huntington (L.I.), NY
IRISH PUB AND INN [URD] *Atlantic
    City, NJ*
IRONSTONE [RES] *Jamestown, NY*
I TRE MERLI [RES] *Manhattan, NY*
JACKSON HOLE [URD] *Manhattan,
    NY*
JACK'S OYSTER HOUSE [RES] *Albany,
    NY*
JACQUES CARTIER [RES] *Alexandria
    Bay (Thousand Islands), NY*
JAMES LANE CAFE AT THE HEDGES
    [RES] *East Hampton (L.I.), NY*
JAPONICA [RES] *Manhattan, NY*
JEAN GEORGES [RES] *Manhattan, NY*
JENNY'S ICE CREAM [URD] *Buffalo,
    NY*
JERICHO TAVERN [RES] *Bainbridge,
    NY*
J.J. MANNION'S [RES] *Yonkers, NY*
JOE ALLEN [RES] *Manhattan, NY*
JOE & MAGGIE'S BISTRO [RES]
    Eatontown, NJ
JOHN DUCK JR [RES] *Southampton
    (L.I.), NY*
JOHN'S FLAMING HEARTH [RES]
    Niagara Falls, NY
JOHN THOMAS STEAK HOUSE [RES]
    Ithaca, NY

JO JO [RES] *Manhattan, NY*
JOLLY FISHERMAN & STEAK HOUSE
    [RES] *Roslyn (L.I.), NY*
JOSHUA'S [RES] *Woodstock, NY*
JUBILEE [RES] *Manhattan, NY*
JUDSON GRILL [RES] *Manhattan, NY*
JUSTIN'S GRILL [RES] *Syracuse, NY*
KEEN'S STEAKHOUSE [RES]
    Manhattan, NY
KELLOGG'S PAN-TREE INN [RES]
    Canandaigua, NY
KING & I [RES] *Nyack, NY*
KINGS' CARRIAGE HOUSE [RES]
    Manhattan, NY
KIRAN [RES] *Manhattan, NY*
KITLAS [RES] *Utica, NY*
KREBS, THE [RES] *Skaneateles, NY*
KURUMA ZUSHI [RES] *Manhattan, NY*
LA BONNE SOUPE [RES] *Manhattan,
    NY*
LA BUSSOLA [RES] *Glen Cove (L.I.),
    NY*
LA CAMELIA [RES] *Mt Kisco, NY*
LA CAMPAGNE [RES] *Cherry Hill, NJ*
LA CARAVELLE [RES] *Manhattan, NY*
LA COQUILLE [RES] *Roslyn (L.I.), NY*
LA COTE BASQUE [RES] *Manhattan,
    NY*
LA FONTANA [RES] *New Brunswick,
    NJ*
LA GRENOUILLE [RES] *Manhattan,
    NY*
LAKE PLACID LODGE [RES] *Lake
    Placid, NY*
LA MANGEOIRE [RES] *Manhattan, NY*
LA MARMITE [RES] *Roslyn (L.I.), NY*
LA MASCOTTE [RES] *Smithtown (L.I.),
    NY*
LAMBERTVILLE STATION [RES]
    Lambertville, NJ
LA METAIRIE [RES] *Manhattan, NY*
LA PACE [RES] *Glen Cove (L.I.), NY*
LA PANETIERE [RES] *White Plains, NY*
LA PARMA ITALIAN [RES] *Roslyn
    (L.I.), NY*
LASCA'S [RES] *Auburn, NY*
LA SERRE [RES] *Albany, NY*
LA TRAVIATA [RES] *Manhattan, NY*
L'AUBERGE DES 4 SAISONS [RES]
    Shandaken, NY
LAUNDRY [RES] *East Hampton (L.I.),
    NY*
LAYLA [RES] *Manhattan, NY*
LE BERNARDIN [RES] *Manhattan, NY*
LE BISTRO LALIBERTE [RES] *Lake
    Placid, NY*
LE BOEUF A LA MODE [RES]
    Manhattan, NY
LE CANARD ECHAINE [RES] *Kingston,
    NY*
LE CHEF [RES] *Southampton (L.I.), NY*

LE CIRQUE 2000 [RES] *Manhattan, NY*

L'ECOLE ENCORE [RES] *Albany, NY*

LE COLONIAL [RES] *Manhattan, NY*

LEEWARD ROOM [RES] *Long Beach Island, NJ*

LE MADELEINE [RES] *Manhattan, NY*

LE MADRI [RES] *Manhattan, NY*

LEMON [RES] *Manhattan, NY*

L'ENDROIT [RES] *Roslyn (L.I.), NY*

LENOX ROOM [RES] *Manhattan, NY*

LE PAVILLON [RES] *Poughkeepsie, NY*

LE PERIGORD [RES] *Manhattan, NY*

LE PETITE CHATEAU [RES] *Bernardsville, NJ*

LE PROVENCAL [RES] *Mamaroneck, NY*

LE REFUGE [RES] *Manhattan, NY*

LE SOIR [RES] *Sayville (L.I.), NY*

LESPINASSE [RES] *Manhattan, NY*

L'EUROPE [RES] *Pound Ridge, NY*

LINCOLN HILL INN [RES] *Canandaigua, NY*

LOBSTER BOX [RES] *Bronx, NY*

LOBSTER CLUB [RES] *Manhattan, NY*

LOBSTER HOUSE [RES] *Cape May, NJ*

LOBSTER INN [RES] *Southampton (L.I.), NY*

LOBSTER ROLL [RES] *Amagansett, NY*

LOCK III [RES] *Fulton, NY*

LOCUST TREE [RES] *New Paltz, NY*

LOG JAM, THE [RES] *Lake George Village, NY*

LOLA [RES] *Manhattan, NY*

LONDON UNDERGROUND CAFE [RES] *Corning, NY*

LOS AMIGOS MEXICAN RESTAURANT [RES] *Cherry Hill, NJ*

LOTUS EAST [RES] *Smithtown (L.I.), NY*

LULIVO FOCACCERIA [RES] *Manhattan, NY*

LUPA [RES] *Manhattan, NY*

LUSARDI'S [RES] *Manhattan, NY*

LUTECE [RES] *Manhattan, NY*

MACDUFF'S [RES] *Jamestown, NY*

MAC'S [RES] *Ocean City, NJ*

MAD BATTER [RES] *Cape May, NJ*

MAIDSTONE ARMS [RES] *East Hampton (L.I.), NY*

MAIER'S BRICK CAFE [RES] *Rockville Centre (L.I.), NY*

MAINE MAID INN [RES] *Jericho (L.I.), NY*

MAISON LAFITTE [RES] *Tarrytown, NY*

MAKEDA ETHIOPIAN RESTAURANT [RES] *New Brunswick, NJ*

MALONEY AND PORCELLI [RES] *Manhattan, NY*

MANDUCATIS [RES] *Queens (La Guardia & JFK International Airport Areas), NY*

MANETTI'S [RES] *Canandaigua, NY*

MANHATTAN BISTRO [RES] *Manhattan, NY*

MANHATTAN GRILLE [RES] *Manhattan, NY*

MANHATTAN OCEAN CLUB [RES] *Manhattan, NY*

MANOR, THE [RES] *West Orange, NJ*

MANSION HILL [RES] *Albany, NY*

MARBELLA [RES] *Queens (La Guardia & JFK International Airport Areas), NY*

MARCH [RES] *Manhattan, NY*

MARGHERITAS' [RES] *Hoboken, NJ*

MARINER, THE [RES] *Nyack, NY*

MARIO'S [RES] *Bronx, NY*

MARIO'S VIA ABRUZZI [RES] *Rochester, NY*

MARITA'S CANTINA [RES] *New Brunswick, NJ*

MARLINS CAFE [RES] *Spring Lake, NJ*

MARLOWE [RES] *Manhattan, NY*

MARSILIO'S [RES] *Trenton, NJ*

MARYJANE'S IL MONASTERO [RES] *East Hampton (L.I.), NY*

MAYA [RES] *Manhattan, NY*

MCCARTHY'S [RES] *Canton, NY*

MED GRILL BISTRO AND CAFE [RES] *Manhattan, NY*

MEETING HOUSE CREEK INN [RES] *Riverhead (L.I.), NY*

MELANGE CAFE [RES] *Cherry Hill, NJ*

MELI MELO [RES] *Manhattan, NY*

MENZ SEAFOOD [RES] *Wildwood and Wildwood Crest, NJ*

MERCER KITCHEN [RES] *Manhattan, NY*

MERION INN [RES] *Cape May, NJ*

MERLINO'S WATERFRONT [RES] *Trenton, NJ*

MERRILL MAGEE HOUSE [RES] *Warrensburg, NY*

MESA GRILL [RES] *Manhattan, NY*

MEZZALUNA [RES] *Manhattan, NY*

MEZZOGIORNO [RES] *Manhattan, NY*

MICHAEL JORDAN'S [RES] *Manhattan, NY*

MICHAEL'S [RES] *East Hampton (L.I.), NY*

MICHAEL'S [RES] *Manhattan, NY*

MICHELANGELO [RES] *White Plains, NY*

MICKEY MANTLE'S [RES] *Manhattan, NY*

MI COCINA [RES] *Manhattan, NY*

MILLERRIDGE INN [RES] *Jericho (L.I.), NY*

MILLIE'S PLACE [RES] *Great Neck (L.I.), NY*

MILL RIVER INN [RES] *Oyster Bay (L.I.), NY*
MIRABELLE [RES] *Smithtown (L.I.), NY*
MIRAGE [RES] *Stone Harbor, NJ*
MIRKO'S [RES] *Southampton (L.I.), NY*
MOGHUL [RES] *Edison, NJ*
MOHAWK STATION [RES] *Ilion, NY*
MOLLY PITCHER INN [RES] *Red Bank, NJ*
MONKEY BAR [RES] *Manhattan, NY*
MONTCALM SOUTH [RES] *Lake George Village, NY*
MONTEVERDE RESTAURANT AT OLDSTONE [RES] *Peekskill, NY*
MONTRACHET [RES] *Manhattan, NY*
MOONSTRUCK [RES] *Asbury Park, NJ*
MOOSEWOOD [RES] *Ithaca, NY*
MORTON'S OF CHICAGO [RES] *Manhattan, NY*
MOUNTAIN BROOK [RES] *Hunter, NY*
MOUNTAINVIEW [RES] *Bay Shore (L.I.), NY*
MR. K'S [RES] *Manhattan, NY*
NADAMAN HAKUBAI [RES] *Manhattan, NY*
NAPLES HOTEL [RES] *Naples, NY*
NICK & TONI'S [RES] *East Hampton (L.I.), NY*
NINO'S [RES] *Manhattan, NY*
NOBU [RES] *Manhattan, NY*
NO MATCH SOUTHERN COOKIN' [URD] *Olean, NY*
NOVITA [RES] *Manhattan, NY*
NUMBER FIVE [RES] *Binghamton, NY*
OAK ROOM [RES] *Manhattan, NY*
OCEANA [RES] *Manhattan, NY*
ODD FELLOWS [RES] *Hoboken, NJ*
ODEON [RES] *Manhattan, NY*
OGDEN'S [RES] *Albany, NY*
OLD BAY, THE [RES] *New Brunswick, NJ*
OLD DROVERS INN [RES] *Poughkeepsie, NY*
OLDE BRYAN INN [RES] *Saratoga Springs, NY*
OLD HEIDELBERG [RES] *Letchworth State Park, NY*
OLD LIBRARY [RES] *Olean, NY*
OLD MAN RIVER [URD] *Buffalo, NY*
OLD MILL [RES] *Old Forge, NY*
OLD MILL INN [RES] *Spring Lake, NJ*
OLD ORCHARD INN [RES] *East Aurora, NY*
OLD RED MILL INN [RES] *Buffalo, NY*
OLD TIME TAVERN, THE [RES] *Toms River, NJ*
OLD WATERWAY INN [RES] *Atlantic City, NJ*
OLIVES [RES] *Manhattan, NY*
OLIVE TREE [RES] *Rochester, NY*
ONE 51 [RES] *Manhattan, NY*

ONE IF BY LAND, TWO IF BY SEA [RES] *Manhattan, NY*
ORCHID [RES] *Garden City (L.I.), NY*
ORSO [RES] *Manhattan, NY*
OSTERIA AL DOGE [RES] *Manhattan, NY*
OSTERIO DEL CIRCO [RES] *Manhattan, NY*
OTABE [RES] *Manhattan, NY*
OUR PLACE [RES] *Manhattan, NY*
OYSTER BAR [RES] *Manhattan, NY*
PAINTER'S [RES] *West Point (US Military Academy), NY*
PALM [RES] *East Hampton (L.I.), NY*
PALM [RES] *Manhattan, NY*
PALM COURT [RES] *Manhattan, NY*
PANEVINO [URD] *Manhattan, NY*
PAOLA'S [RES] *Manhattan, NY*
PARK AVENUE CAFE [RES] *Manhattan, NY*
PARK BISTRO [RES] *Manhattan, NY*
PARK SIDE [RES] *Queens (La Guardia & JFK International Airport Areas), NY*
PARTRIDGE BERRY INN [RES] *Watertown, NY*
PASCALE [RES] *Syracuse, NY*
PASTABILITIES [URD] *Syracuse, NY*
PATIO [RES] *Westhampton Beach, NY*
PATRIA [RES] *Manhattan, NY*
PATROON [RES] *Manhattan, NY*
PAYARD PATISSERIE AND BISTRO [RES] *Manhattan, NY*
PAYNE STREET CORNER [RES] *Hamilton, NY*
PEACHES AT SUNSET [RES] *Cape May, NJ*
PELICAN CLUB [RES] *Cape May, NJ*
PENANG MALAYSIAN [RES] *Manhattan, NY*
PEPPER MILL [RES] *Cooperstown, NY*
PERIYALI [RES] *Manhattan, NY*
PETER LUGER STEAK HOUSE [RES] *Brooklyn, NY*
PETITE ON MAIN [RES] *Huntington (L.I.), NY*
PETROSSIAN [RES] *Manhattan, NY*
PHOEBE'S GARDEN CAFE [RES] *Syracuse, NY*
PICCOLA VENEZIA [RES] *Queens (La Guardia & JFK International Airport Areas), NY*
PICHOLINE [RES] *Manhattan, NY*
PIERRE AU TUNNEL [RES] *Manhattan, NY*
PIG HEAVEN [RES] *Manhattan, NY*
PING'S SEAFOOD [RES] *Queens (La Guardia & JFK International Airport Areas), NY*
P.J. MCGLYNN'S [RES] *Rhinebeck, NY*

PLAINVILLE FARMS [RES] *Syracuse, NY*
PLUMBUSH INN [RES] *Garrison, NY*
PO [RES] *Manhattan, NY*
PONTE VECCHIO [RES] *Brooklyn, NY*
PORK'S & GLENN'S SEAFOOD HOUSE [RES] *Bay Shore (L.I.), NY*
POST HOUSE [RES] *Manhattan, NY*
PRIMA PIZZA PASTA [URD] *Buffalo, NY*
PRIMAVERA [RES] *Manhattan, NY*
PROSPECT, THE [RES] *Hunter, NY*
PROVENCE [RES] *Manhattan, NY*
RAAY-NOR'S CABIN [RES] *Rockville Centre (L.I.), NY*
RAIN [RES] *Manhattan, NY*
RAINDANCER STEAK PARLOUR [RES] *Amsterdam, NY*
RAJ MAHAL [RES] *Rochester, NY*
RAMAPOUGH INN [RES] *Spring Valley, NY*
RAM'S HEAD INN [RES] *Atlantic City, NJ*
RAM'S HEAD INN [RES] *Shelter Island, NY*
RAOUL'S [RES] *Manhattan, NY*
RAVEN & THE PEACH, THE [RES] *Red Bank, NJ*
REBECCA'S [RES] *Hudson, NY*
RED CAT, THE [RES] *New York City, NY*
RED COACH INN [RES] *Niagara Falls, NY*
REDEYE GRILL [RES] *Manhattan, NY*
RED HOOK INN [RES] *Rhinebeck, NY*
RED HOT & BLUE [RES] *Cherry Hill, NJ*
REDS [RES] *Coxsackie, NY*
REDWOOD [RES] *Naples, NY*
REKA'S [RES] *White Plains, NY*
REMI [RES] *Manhattan, NY*
RENAULT WINERY [RES] *Atlantic City, NJ*
RENE PUJOL [RES] *Manhattan, NY*
REPUBLIC [URD] *Manhattan, NY*
RESTAURANT 222 [RES] *Manhattan, NY*
RESTAURANT SERENADE [RES] *Chatham, NJ*
RESTAURANT X AND BULLY BOY BAR [RES] *Nyack, NY*
RHONE [RES] *New York City, NY*
RIALTO [RES] *Westbury (L.I.), NY*
RICHARDSON'S CANAL HOUSE [RES] *Rochester, NY*
RIVER CAFE [RES] *Brooklyn, NY*
RIVER CLUB [RES] *Bainbridge, NY*
RIVER CLUB [RES] *Nyack, NY*
RIVERSIDE INN [RES] *Niagara Falls, NY*

RIVER STATION STEAK & SEAFOOD [RES] *Poughkeepsie, NY*
RIVERVIEW [RES] *Sayville (L.I.), NY*
ROCCI'S [RES] *Cortland, NY*
ROCK CENTER CAFE [RES] *Manhattan, NY*
ROD'S 1890S RESTAURANT [RES] *Morristown, NJ*
ROONEYS [RES] *Rochester, NY*
ROSA MEXICANO [RES] *Manhattan, NY*
ROSA MEXICANO [RES] *Manhattan, NY*
ROTUNDA, THE [URD] *Manhattan, NY*
ROYAL SAVAGE INN [RES] *Plattsburgh, NY*
ROYCROFT INN [RES] *East Aurora, NY*
RUDY'S BEAU RIVAGE [RES] *Tarrytown, NY*
RUSCHMEYER'S [RES] *Montauk (L.I.), NY*
RUSTY NAIL [RES] *Cape May, NJ*
RUSTY NAIL [RES] *Cortland, NY*
RUSTY NAIL [RES] *Middletown, NY*
RUSTY NAIL [RES] *New Brunswick, NJ*
RUSTY SCUPPER [RES] *Princeton, NJ*
RUTH'S CHRIS STEAK HOUSE [RES] *Manhattan, NY*
RYLAND INN, THE [RES] *Somerville, NJ*
SABATINI'S LITTLE ITALY [RES] *Oneonta, NY*
SADIE J'S CAFE [RES] *Chautauqua, NY*
ST. ANDREW'S CAFE [RES] *Hyde Park, NY*
SALAAM BOMBAY [RES] *Manhattan, NY*
SAL ANTHONY'S S.P.Q.R. [RES] *Manhattan, NY*
SALVATORE'S ITALIAN GARDENS [RES] *Buffalo, NY*
SAN DOMENICO [RES] *Manhattan, NY*
SANDPIPER, THE [RES] *Spring Lake, NJ*
SAN MARTIN'S [RES] *Manhattan, NY*
SAN PIETRO [RES] *Manhattan, NY*
SANTA FE [RES] *Tarrytown, NY*
SARABETH'S [RES] *Manhattan, NY*
SARDI'S [RES] *Manhattan, NY*
SAVORE [RES] *Manhattan, NY*
SAVOY [RES] *Manhattan, NY*
SAVOY [RES] *Rome, NY*
SCANNICCHIO'S [RES] *Atlantic City, NJ*
SCHLESINGER'S STEAK HOUSE [RES] *Newburgh, NY*
SCHOONER [RES] *Rockville Centre (L.I.), NY*

SCOPA RESTAURANT [RES]
    Manhattan, NY
SCOTCH 'N SIRLOIN [RES] Rochester,
    NY
SCREENING ROOM [RES] Manhattan,
    NY
SCRIMSHAW [RES] Albany, NY
SEAFOOD BARGE [RES] Southold
    (L.I.), NY
SEAGRILL [RES] Manhattan, NY
SEA SHORE [RES] Bronx, NY
SEASONS [RES] Watkins Glen, NY
SERENDIPITY 3 [URD] Manhattan, NY
SHAAN [RES] Manhattan, NY
SHABU-TATSU [RES] Manhattan, NY
SHADOWBROOK [RES] Red Bank, NJ
SHAGWONG RESTAURANT [RES]
    Montauk (L.I.), NY
SHANG HAI CUISINE [RES]
    Manhattan, NY
SHARK BAR [RES] Manhattan, NY
SHIPYARD [RES] Albany, NY
SHOLETTE'S STEAK & ALE [RES]
    Ogdensburg (Thousand Islands),
    NY
SHUN LEE [RES] Manhattan, NY
SHUN LEE PALACE [RES] Manhattan,
    NY
SIAM GRILL [RES] Manhattan, NY
SIENA [RES] Buffalo, NY
SILO [RES] Bainbridge, NY
SIMMON'S WAY [RES] Hillsdale, NY
SIRI'S THAI FRENCH CUISINE [RES]
    Cherry Hill, NJ
SIR THETFORD'S SIRLOIN ROOM
    [RES] Windham, NY
SMITH & WOLLENSKY [RES]
    Manhattan, NY
SNAPPER INN [RES] Sayville (L.I.), NY
SOBA-YA [RES] Manhattan, NY
SOHO STEAK [RES] Manhattan, NY
SONOMA GRILL [RES] Rutherford, NJ
SPARKS STEAK HOUSE [RES]
    Manhattan, NY
SPENCER'S [RES] Corning, NY
SPINNAKER'S [RES] Sag Harbor (L.I.),
    NY
SPOT [RES] Binghamton, NY
SPRINSIDE INN [RES] Auburn, NY
STAGE DELI [URD] Manhattan, NY
STAGE HOUSE INN [RES] Scotch
    Plains, NJ
STAGE LEFT: AN AMERICAN CAFE
    [RES] New Brunswick, NJ
STARR BOGGS' [RES] Westhampton
    Beach, NY
STATION [RES] Ithaca, NY
STATION ROAD [RES] Southampton
    (L.I.), NY
STEAK FRITES [RES] Manhattan, NY

STELLA RISTORANTE [RES] Floral
    Park (L.I.), NY
STEVE AND COOKIE'S BY THE BAY
    [RES] Atlantic City, NJ
STEVE'S PIER I [RES] Oyster Bay (L.I.),
    NY
STEWART HOUSE [RES] Catskill, NY
STONY HILL INN [RES] Hackensack,
    NJ
STRIP HOUSE [RES] Manhattan, NY
SUGIYAMA [RES] Manhattan, NY
SUNNY'S [RES] Batavia, NY
SUSAN'S [RES] Peekskill, NY
SUSHI OF GARI [RES] Manhattan, NY
SUSHISAY [RES] Manhattan, NY
SUSHI YASUDA [RES] Manhattan, NY
SWEET AND TART [RES] Manhattan,
    NY
SWISS HUTTE [RES] Hillsdale, NY
SZECHWAN GOURMET [RES] New
    Brunswick, NJ
TABLA [RES] Manhattan, NY
TABLE D'HOTE [RES] Manhattan, NY
TAORMINA [RES] Manhattan, NY
TARDELLI'S [RES] Potsdam, NY
TAVERN AT STERUP SQUARE [RES]
    Troy, NY
TAVERN ON THE GREEN [RES]
    Manhattan, NY
TERESA'S [RES] New Brunswick, NJ
TESAURO'S [RES] Spring Lake, NJ
THOUSAND ISLANDS INN [RES]
    Clayton (Thousand Islands), NY
THREE VILLAGE INN [RES] Stony
    Brook (L.I.), NY
TOCQUEVILLE [RES] Manhattan, NY
TOKYO JAPANESE [RES] Rochester, NY
TOMMASO [RES] Brooklyn, NY
TONIC RESTAURANT & BAR, THE
    [RES] Manhattan, NY
TOWN [RES] Manhattan, NY
TRATTORIA DELL'ARTE [RES]
    Manhattan, NY
TRAVELER'S REST [RES] Mt Kisco, NY
TRIBECA GRILL [RES] Manhattan, NY
TRILLIUM [RES] Bolton Landing (Lake
    George Area), NY
TRIOMPHE [RES] Manhattan, NY
TUCKER'S [RES] Long Beach Island, NJ
TUSCAN SQUARE [RES] Manhattan,
    NY
TWIN TREES [URD] Syracuse, NY
TYPHOON BREWERY [RES]
    Manhattan, NY
UNADILLA HOUSE [RES] Bainbridge,
    NY
UNION HALL INN [RES] Johnstown,
    NY
UNION HOTEL [RES] Flemington, NJ
UNION PACIFIC [RES] Manhattan, NY

UNION SQUARE CAFE [RES] *Manhattan, NY*
VALENTINO'S [RES] *Montvale, NJ*
VAN RENSSELAER ROOM [RES] *Troy, NY*
VEEDER'S [RES] *Albany, NY*
VERANDA [RES] *Glen Cove (L.I.), NY*
VERITAS [RES] *Manhattan, NY*
VESUVIO [RES] *Hunter, NY*
VICTOR GRILLING COMPANY [RES] *Victor, NY*
VICTOR KOENIG'S [RES] *Floral Park (L.I.), NY*
VIEW [RES] *Manhattan, NY*
VILLA COFFEE HOUSE [RES] *Niagara Falls, NY*
VILLAGE COAL TOWER [RES] *Rochester, NY*
VILLAGE INN [RES] *Massena, NY*
VILLAGE SQUARE CAFE [RES] *Liberty, NY*
VILLAGE WAY [RES] *Port Jefferson (L.I.), NY*
VILLA PAUL [RES] *Hampton Bays (L.I.), NY*
VINCE AND EDDIE'S [RES] *Manhattan, NY*
VIRGIL'S REAL BARBECUE [RES] *Manhattan, NY*
VONA'S [RES] *Oswego, NY*
VONG [RES] *Manhattan, NY*
WALLIE'S OF GREENWICH [RES] *Greenwich, NY*
WALLSE [RES] *Manhattan, NY*
WALL STREET KITCHEN AND BAR [RES] *Manhattan, NY*
WASHINGTON INN [RES] *Cape May, NJ*
WATER CLUB [RES] *Manhattan, NY*
WATERHOUSE [RES] *Lake Luzerne, NY*
WATER'S EDGE [RES] *Cape May, NJ*
WATER'S EDGE [RES] *Queens (La Guardia & JFK International Airport Areas), NY*
WEBB'S-THE CAPTAIN'S TABLE [RES] *Chautauqua, NY*
WESTBURY MANOR [RES] *Westbury (L.I.), NY*
WHITE INN, THE [RES] *Dunkirk, NY*
WILDERNESS INN #2 [RES] *Wilmington, NY*
WILDFLOWER CAFE [RES] *Watkins Glen, NY*
WILLOW [RES] *Manhattan, NY*
WOO LAE OAK [RES] *Manhattan, NY*
WYLANDS COUNTRY KITCHEN [URD] *Huntington (L.I.), NY*
XAVIAR'S RESTAURANT [RES] *Garrison, NY*
YAMAGUCHI [RES] *Port Washington (L.I.), NY*

YANKEE CLIPPER [RES] *Manhattan, NY*
YE HARE N' HOUNDS INN [RES] *Bemus Point, NY*
YOBO [RES] *Newburgh, NY*
YONO'S [RES] *Albany, NY*
ZARELA [RES] *Manhattan, NY*
ZOE [RES] *Manhattan, NY*

CITY INDEX

Notes

Notes

Notes

Mobil Travel Guides

Please check the guides you would like to order:

☐ 0-7627-2619-9
California
$18.95

☐ 0-7627-2618-0
Florida
$18.95

☐ 0-7627-2612-1
Great Lakes
Illinois, Indiana, Michigan,
Ohio, Wisconsin
$18.95

☐ 0-7627-2610-5
Great Plains
Iowa, Kansas, Minnesota,
Missouri, Nebraska, North
Dakota, Oklahoma, South
Dakota
$18.95

☐ 0-7627-2613-X
Mid-Atlantic
Delaware, Maryland,
Pennsylvania, Virginia,
Washington D.C., West
Virginia
$18.95

☐ 0-7627-2614-8
**New England and Eastern
Canada**
Connecticut, Maine, Massachu-
setts, New Hampshire, Rhode
Island, Vermont, Canada
$18.95

☐ 0-7627-2616-4
New York/New Jersey
$18.95

☐ 0-7627-2611-3
Northwest
Idaho, Montana, Oregon, Wash-
ington, Wyoming, Canada
$18.95

☐ 0-7627-2615-6
Southeast
Alabama, Arkansas, Georgia, Ken-
tucky, Louisiana, Mississippi,
North Carolina, South Carolina,
Tennessee
$18.95

☐ 0-7627-2617-2
Southwest
Arizona, Colorado, Nevada, New
Mexico, Texas, Utah
$18.95

Please ship the books above to:

Name: _____

Address: _____

City: _____ State _____ Zip _____

Total Cost of Book(s)	$_____	☐ Please charge my credit card.
Shipping & Handling	$_____	☐ Discover ☐ Visa
(Please add $3.00 for first book $1.50 for each additional book)		☐ MasterCard ☐ American Express
Add 8.75% sales tax	$_____	Card #_____
Total Amount	$_____	Expiration _____
☐ My Check is enclosed.		Signature _____

Please mail this form to: **Mobil Travel Guides
1460 Renaissance Drive, Suite 401
Park Ridge, IL 60068**

Mobil
Travel Guide®

New England
Eastern Canada
Connecticut
Maine
Massachusetts
New Hampshire
Rhode Island
Vermont
New Brunswick
Nova Scotia
Ontario
Prince Edward
  Island
Quebec

Northwest
Idaho
Montana
Oregon
Washington
Wyoming
Alberta
British Columbia
Manitoba

Great Plains
Iowa
Kansas
Minnesota
Missouri
Nebraska
North Dakota
Oklahoma
South Dakota

Great Lakes
Illinois
Indiana
Michigan
Ohio
Wisconsin

California

New York
New Jersey

Southwest
Arizona
Colorado
Nevada
New Mexico
Texas
Utah

Southeast
Alabama
Arkansas
Georgia
Kentucky
Louisiana
Mississippi
North Carolina
South Carolina
Tennessee

Florida

Mid-Atlantic
Delaware
Maryland
Pennsylvania
Virginia
Washington, D.C.
West Virginia

Add your opinion!

Help make the Guides even more useful. Tell us about your experiences with the hotels and restaurants listed in the Guides (or ones that should be added).

Find us on the Internet at www.mobiltravelguide.com/feedback

Or copy the form below and mail to Mobil Travel Guides, 1460 Renaissance Drive, Suite 401, Park Ridge, IL 60068. All information will be kept confidential.

Your name _____   Were children with you on trip? ☐ Yes ☐ No

Street _____   Number of people in your party _____

City/State/Zip _____   Your occupation _____

Establishment name _____

☐ Hotel ☐ Resort ☐ Restaurant
☐ Motel ☐ Inn ☐ Other

Street _____   City _____   State _____

Do you agree with our description? ☐ Yes ☐ No   If not, give reason _____

Please give us your opinion of the following:

Decor	Cleanliness	Service	Food
☐ Excellent	☐ Spotless	☐ Excellent	☐ Excellent
☐ Good	☐ Clean	☐ Good	☐ Good
☐ Fair	☐ Unclean	☐ Fair	☐ Fair
☐ Poor	☐ Dirty	☐ Poor	☐ Poor

2003 Guide rating _____ ★
Check your suggested rating
☐ ★
☐ ★★
☐ ★★★
☐ ★★★★
☐ ★★★★★
☐ ✓ unusually good value

Date of visit _____   First visit? ☐ Yes ☐ No

Comments _____

_____

Establishment name _____

☐ Hotel ☐ Resort ☐ Restaurant
☐ Motel ☐ Inn ☐ Other

Street _____   City _____   State _____

Do you agree with our description? ☐ Yes ☐ No   If not, give reason _____

Please give us your opinion of the following:

Decor	Cleanliness	Service	Food
☐ Excellent	☐ Spotless	☐ Excellent	☐ Excellent
☐ Good	☐ Clean	☐ Good	☐ Good
☐ Fair	☐ Unclean	☐ Fair	☐ Fair
☐ Poor	☐ Dirty	☐ Poor	☐ Poor

2003 Guide rating _____ ★
Check your suggested rating
☐ ★
☐ ★★
☐ ★★★
☐ ★★★★
☐ ★★★★★
☐ ✓ unusually good value

Date of visit _____   First visit? ☐ Yes ☐ No

Comments _____

_____

Notes